Diatessarica
PART X, SECTION V

THE FOURFOLD GOSPEL
THE FOUNDING
OF THE NEW KINGDOM
OR
LIFE REACHED THROUGH DEATH

THE FOURFOLD GOSPEL

SECTION V
THE FOUNDING OF THE NEW KINGDOM
OR
LIFE REACHED THROUGH DEATH

BY

EDWIN A. ABBOTT

Honorary Fellow of St John's College, Cambridge
Fellow of the British Academy

"*Since God made man so good—here stands my creed—
God's good indeed.*"   W. M. LETTS

WIPF & STOCK · Eugene, Oregon

Wipf and Stock Publishers
199 W 8th Ave, Suite 3
Eugene, OR 97401

The Fourfold Gospel; Section V
The Founding of the New Kingdom or Life Reached Through Death
By Abbott, Edwin A.
Softcover ISBN-13: 978-1-6667-0102-9
Hardcover ISBN-13: 978-1-6667-0103-6
eBook ISBN-13: 978-1-6667-0104-3
Publication date 2/9/2021
Previously published by Cambridge University Press, 1917

This edition is a scanned facsimile of the original edition published in 1917.

PREFACE

(1) *Diatessarica and The Fourfold Gospel as a whole*

THIS is the last of many works, published in a series entitled *Diatessarica*, all of which deal directly or indirectly with the Fourfold Gospel. It will be convenient to prefix to the special remarks introducing the present volume a general statement of the method of investigation, and the principal assumptions, underlying the whole series of which this volume, *The Founding of the New Kingdom*, constitutes the conclusion.

1. It is assumed that there is a continuity between the thoughts of Jesus and the thoughts of the Hebrew Scriptures, especially such Scriptures as He habitually quoted—sometimes appealing to them as "the Law and the Prophets."

2. Whenever the Gospels introduce a doctrine of Jesus on any subject, the first question to be asked by those who wish to study it closely will be "What do the Hebrew Scriptures say about it generally, and, more especially, in the particular passage where they mention it for the first time?"

For example, if we wish to study Christ's thoughts about the Temple, which is nowhere mentioned in the Law, we must go back to what is written in the Law concerning the "Tabernacle," or "Tent of Meeting," which was the origin of the Temple subsequently mentioned by the Prophets.

PREFACE

3. The second question to be asked is, "How was the Hebrew rendered by the LXX, and by the other early translators, in Greek, and how was it likely to be rendered in Aramaic, so far as we can judge from the Aramaic Targums in the second and later centuries?"

Take for example "Tent of Meeting"—the above-quoted name given to the Tabernacle Instead of "Meeting," the LXX habitually has "Testimony," and our Authorised Version has "Congregation." But the second-century Targumist Onkelos has the Aramaic equivalent of the Hebrew "Meeting." It is important to add that this does not mean a chance meeting It is a "meeting by appointment" or "assignation" The second-century translator Aquila, as will be shewn hereafter, renders it "appointment."

4. The third question to be asked is, "Has the Hebrew word any associations which, if not comprehended, would prevent our comprehension of its full meaning?"

For example, the first two instances of the above-mentioned "*appointment*"—apart from the "appointed-times," or "seasons," marked out by the heavenly bodies in the first chapter of Genesis—refer to God's promises to Abraham concerning the birth of Isaac "at this *appointed-time*," and again, "At the *appointed-time* I will return to thee." The word is also regularly used to mean an "*appointed-feast*" in which Israel went up to meet the Lord in Jerusalem. Habakkuk connects it with "waiting," thus, "The vision is yet for the *appointed-time*...wait for it." In New Hebrew it is applied to the "*appointing*" or "*designating*" of a bride This single word, then, might suggest to Jews (1) a wedding "feast," (2) "waiting"—possibly for the home-coming of a bride or of a bridegroom or master of the house, (3) a "meeting" between bridegroom and bride. And it connects all these thoughts with

PREFACE

the Tabernacle or Temple to which Israel, the Wife, was wont to go up to meet Jehovah her Husband, according to the words of Isaiah "Thy Maker is thine husband, the Lord of hosts is his name."

This connection is missed by the LXX, and must have been difficult for early Gentile Christians to realise. But it illustrates many parables in the Gospels, and some precepts, which, apart from this metaphor, are hardly capable of being fully understood

5   Having answered the three above-mentioned questions to the best of our ability, we proceed to apply the answers to the Gospels   We begin with the Three Synoptists. The first place is given to Mark, because Mark (so far as concerns the threefold Synoptic tradition) contains the earliest extant original from which Matthew and Luke borrowed.

After noting what Matthew and Luke borrow from the parallel Mark, we examine with special attention 1st, what they altogether fail to borrow, that is to say, what they reject ; and 2nd, what they partially borrow, that is to say, borrow but alter.   Then we endeavour, in each case, to find a reason for the rejection or alteration.

For example, Mark says that false witnesses accused Jesus of saying "I will destroy this temple that is made with hands, and, after an interval of three days, will build another not made with hands."   The parallel Matthew has "I am able to destroy the temple of God, and, after an interval of three days, to build it."   This, Matthew says, is the charge brought by "two"—presumably false witnesses—after "many false witnesses" have accused Jesus ineffectively.   Luke omits the whole.   We have to ask "Why did Matthew alter Mark's words and Luke omit them altogether?"

6   In order to answer this and similar questions we

may begin by arguing from internal evidence—as, for example, that Matthew regarded the Marcan report of the accusation as erroneous, while Luke regarded the accusation as negligible because false, besides being obscure and perhaps erroneously reported But we must not neglect external evidence, if there is any. And such evidence may be reasonably expected from the Fourth Evangelist, who is universally recognised as later than the Three Synoptists, and who would feel bound (we may suppose) to take cognisance of any authoritative Gospels that preceded his own, and to do his best to remedy any evil likely to accrue to the Churches from their discrepancies, as well as from their deficiencies. "How does John act," we must ask, "where the Synoptists differ? Does he remain silent, or does he intervene? And, if he intervenes, does he intervene for or against Mark, the earliest of the Evangelists?"

For example, bearing on the charge of "destroying the temple" we find the following Johannine tradition· "Jesus said unto them [*i e.* to the Jews] '*Destroy this temple and in three days I will raise it up*'...but he spake of *the temple of his body*" That is to say, John in the first place regards Jesus as *having really connected the word "destroy" with the word "temple*," but in such a context as to shew that He Himself made no threat of destroying it. In the second place he regards Jesus as having used the word "temple" to mean not (as is written in Mark) "a temple made with hands," but a temple *not* made with hands, a Person, apparently meaning the "body" of the Son of Man, regarded as the Tabernacle of Meeting between God and Man. Such a thought might be unintelligible to Christ's accusers, but Isaiah had prepared the way for it in the words "Thus saith the high and lofty One that inhabiteth eternity, whose name is Holy: I dwell in the

PREFACE

high and holy place, with him also that is of a contrite and humble spirit, to revive the spirit of the humble, and to revive the heart of the contrite ones"

Jerome, commenting on this connection in Isaiah between "the high and lofty One" and "the contrite and humble spirit," appropriately quotes from the Fourth Gospel "No man hath ascended into heaven but he that descended out of heaven, even the Son of man, who is in heaven" And John has prepared the way for such a conception of an ascending and descending Person, who is a Mediator, or Tent of Meeting, or Tabernacle, between God and Man, by saying in his Prologue that the Word "became flesh" and "*tabernacled* among us"

These facts appear to explain Matthew's alteration of Mark and Luke's omission. Mark had given no indication of the fact that Jesus had actually spoken about destroying the "temple," but in a sense, and in a context, quite different from that which was supplied by the Marcan accusers. Matthew had made the accusation a little less harsh but not more consistent with fact. Luke omitted the whole as hopelessly obscure. John intervenes, partly to correct Mark, and partly to explain him, but still more to set forth a fundamental doctrine of Jesus, namely, that the Son of Man was God's Tabernacle, Tent of Meeting, or Temple This, then, we feel justified in calling an instance of "Johannine Intervention."

7. Passing to other divergences of Luke from Mark, we try to examine them impartially, prepared to find two classes of them—John intervening sometimes for Luke against Mark as well as for Mark against Luke. But we find very few indeed of the former class The latter on the other hand are found, on a first examination, to be numerous, and, on further examination, to be very numerous indeed

PREFACE

Take, for example, the apparently insignificant detail, peculiar to Mark, in the casting of lots for Christ's garments at the Crucifixion, where Mark alone inserts *"what each should take"* (literally *"who should take what"*). Here John tells us that Mark is not strictly correct. About the "garments," he says, "they made four parts, to every soldier a part." But about the "coat" which was "without seam," they said "'Let us not rend it, but cast lots for it, whose it shall be,' that the scripture might be fulfilled which saith, 'They parted my garments among them, and upon my vesture did they cast lots.'" In this case, Johannine Intervention appears to be based on the poetry of the Psalms regarded as prophecy

8   Intervention may be based not upon prophecy but upon mere allusion

For example, Mark, Matthew, and John, in a narrative about the anointing of Jesus by a woman, represent Him as uttering an extremely obscure saying about His "embalming"—mistranslated "burial" or "burying." Luke omits the whole narrative but has another in which the woman is described as "a sinner" and no "embalming" is mentioned. "Embalming" is nowhere mentioned by the Prophets, and it was not a Jewish custom. But it is mentioned in Genesis as practised for Jacob and Joseph, who, though they died in Egypt, were "embalmed" and buried—Jacob at once, but Joseph not till the lapse of many years—in the Land of Promise

Any allusion on the part of Jesus to such a detail—archaic and in modern eyes insignificant—must seem at first sight far-fetched and wildly improbable. But the hypothesis is at all events not contrary to fact and truth—as is the rendering "burying" for "embalming." And it is mentioned here as being one of many instances where John does certainly intervene for Mark against Luke, but where

PREFACE

the reason and the exact meaning of his intervention are uncertain. It will be found discussed in its place.

To omit this and other such instances would have very greatly shortened this laborious work and would have avoided some natural accusations of fancifulness and "ingenuity." But it would not have been fair to the reader. The author is conscious of many faults—especially defects in arrangement, and condensation; but he has desired to keep his conscience clear from at least one defect that he regards as unpardonable—the purchase of a clear, brief, and forcible persuasiveness at the cost of fairness to the reader and allegiance to truth.

9. It remains to add that the primary object of *Diatessarica* and *The Fourfold Gospel* has been, not to elicit, in each instance, an immediate answer to the question "What is the historical fact?" but to prepare the way for others who may hereafter elicit it, by shewing them how much help they may derive from the Fourth Gospel and from Jewish poetic literature, and how inadequate must be their appreciation of the spiritual depth and height of Christ's conceptions until they learn to familiarise themselves with His realisation of a Personal Tabernacle or Tent of Meeting mediating between man and God, between the children and the Father—between "him that is of a contrite spirit" and "the high and lofty One that inhabiteth eternity."

(ii) *The present volume*

Three preceding volumes of *The Fourfold Gospel* have treated of the Beginning, the Proclamation, and the Law, of what Christians may briefly call "the New Kingdom." The present volume treats of what may be called its "founding" —not its establishment, for it is as yet far from being established, but the means and manner by which it was founded. We shall have to study in what sense the Kingdom was a kingdom of life, and by what means Christ, the Founder, taught us to recognise that the life was to be reached through death, and victory through defeat

The four volumes deal very largely with words, critically considered as words, Hebrew, Aramaic, Greek, and sometimes Latin and Syriac—not to speak of the variations in our own Authorised and Revised Versions And at the conclusion of this laborious task the author may naturally ask himself with some searchings of heart: "Is it thus that I can hope to draw nearer to the Most High God? Can Lexicons, Concordances. Indices, and ancient commentaries on still more ancient writings, technically called 'scriptures,' be the appointed and foreordained avenues to the highest spiritual truth, and to such apprehension as is possible for mortals of the immortal and incomprehensible Creator?"

I should be disposed to substitute, instead of any defence of my own, an imaginary defence, such as the Fourth Evangelist might be supposed to make—and indeed does make, by implication—in his Gospel. It will save space, and avoid a tedious repetition of "he may have thought," if I may be allowed, instead of such a clause, to substitute inverted commas and to represent him, thinking aloud, as follows.

"The religion of Israel is based indeed on the writings that they call scriptures, and the Lord Jesus Christ continually quoted them. Writings consist of words It may therefore be said by some that He 'founded His religion on words.' But it would not be true. He founded it on Himself as being the eternal Word, the Logos, the foundation, and fulfilment of those 'words.' The Pharisees forgot

PREFACE

the creative Word that lay beneath the words of the Law. The brethren in the Christian Churches are also in danger of forgetting the creative Word that lay beneath the words of the Gospel of Jesus Christ as set forth in the books of Mark, Matthew, and Luke. In this book, therefore, I will endeavour to draw forth the Word from beneath those words, and to help the reader to perceive something of the glory of the grace and the truth which shone forth from Him so as to make His teaching something above and beyond a Law (like the Law of Moses) but rather like a living and helpful Friend.

"For example, Mark's introduction speaks of 'the beginning of the Gospel,' and of 'preaching' or 'proclaiming,' and of 'baptism,' and of 'repentance' and of 'remission of sins.' Now the brethren have begun to use these words in their schools and churches in a formal way, as physicians, lawyers, and others, use the terms peculiar to their several occupations, and as the Scribes use their scribal words in their schools and synagogues—speaking for example of 'the Gospel' as the Pharisees speak of 'the Law,' as though it had a being of its own apart from the Spirit of Jesus. I will therefore not use these expressions. Instead of mentioning the word 'Gospel,' I will shew, as in a drama, what the Gospel was. Instead of using the word 'proclaim'—as though Jesus were a herald crying aloud the precise proclamation and the exact words that the king has appointed for him to cry—I will relate what Jesus taught, in its spiritual effect, as the Son speaking freely in the name of the Father. Lastly, instead of mentioning the Greek 'repentance,' which means merely 'a change of mind,' I will bring Jesus before the reader, as it were on the stage of the theatre of this world, calling on mankind to turn from darkness to the Light.

"As for 'the beginning of the Gospel,' which Mark

PREFACE

seems to declare to have been 'John'—that is to say, the preaching of John the Baptist—I will go back to the 'beginning' indeed, namely, to the one eternal Word that was the origin of all these temporary words, so that the first sentence of my book shall be, 'In the beginning was the [one] Word.' And the next shall shew that this was no ordinary word, for 'the Word was toward the [one] God.' And the next after that shall shew that the Word was indeed Himself a Person, and divine: 'And the Word was God.'"

If this imaginary soliloquy represents at all adequately the attitude of the Fourth Evangelist to the Three, then, in reply to the question "What have you gained from all this study of words?" I should feel emboldened to reply that I have made two gains, one negative, the other positive. The negative gain has been that I have been freed (partially at all events, no man is fully free) from the domination of words. The positive gain has been some increase of reverent recognition of the blended beauty and awfulness of the mysterious ways of the Eternal Word through whom is revealed the Eternal Thought "whose service is perfect freedom."

To the possibility of negative gain almost every page in this work will testify, shewing that, whatever Jesus said or did, He said or did in special circumstances or with special metaphor, paradox, or hyperbole, that have been often variously regarded by His biographers. These special circumstances often indicate that He did not lay down, and did not wish to lay down, precedents that we might exactly follow independently of our own circumstances at the present day. The Three Gospels imply, and the Fourth asserts, that Christ's Spirit, not the words uttered by Him before His Spirit was given, is, in the ultimate resort, to dictate and control our action.

PREFACE

The positive gain has been described above as "reverent recognition." This phrase has been chosen to indicate something different from a merely intellectual insight into causes and effects. Yet it does imply insight—a spiritual insight into the Sacrifice of Christ on the Cross as being no isolated event, nor arbitrarily foreordained mystery, but the natural centre round which there revolves the universal sphere of visible and invisible existence, so far as we mortals can rightly conceive of it.

The Synoptists do not indicate this fundamental truth with any clearness. When they represent Jesus as predicting His sufferings, death, and resurrection, they reproduce, and make more definite, a few of His definite words (especially those about "rising again" in "three days" or on "the third day") probably borrowed from one or two of the prophets. But they do not clearly reveal Christ's underlying sense that He, in thus fulfilling the Father's will, was to win a victory. He was to endure a humiliation that would end in exaltation, and to experience a suffering of pain, or even of death, that would become the way to the joy of eternal life. The Fourth Gospel, we must not say ignores all the Synoptic definite phrases, but should rather say, assumes them all. It tells us what they all meant, and what was Christ's feeling at the bottom of them. Consequently it represents Him as speaking about His future death as a "lifting up" or "glorifying," never as a "killing" or as a "crucifying."

These considerations, though they have by no means led us to prefer the Fourth Gospel in all cases to the Three, have led us to regard it as a supplement to them, and in many cases as a necessary supplement. This we have found to hold good more especially about Mark's Gospel. Mark sometimes barely and inadequately reports deep sayings of Jesus with such brevity and obscurity that they are omitted by Luke and occasionally by Matthew also. In such cases we have often found that John steps in, not to repeat in amended Marcan language what Jesus actually said, but to teach us in Johannine language what Jesus actually meant.

In such cases, the meaning has been often found to go back to poetry—ancient poetry in the Hebrew Scriptures interpreted by later poetry in Jewish traditions. And here it should be added that the Fourth Gospel, though largely indebted to Philo, is also much more than is generally supposed akin to Jewish poetic or Haggadic thought, such as is found in the Midrash or ancient Jewish commentaries on Scripture.

These, though compiled after the Talmuds, often point back to a period earlier than that of many traditions in the Talmuds. We lose a great deal of light on the Gospels if we assume that Jewish literature in the first century was mainly Talmudic or legal. Much of it, especially before the fall of Jerusalem, would be Haggadic, that is, poetic.

Now the poets and prophets of Scripture, and the poets of the Haggada, even the saddest of them, while pouring forth sorrow for the past and the present, are almost always in some sense optimists as to the future. To this rule John—who in one of his aspects is certainly a Jewish poet—affords no exception. This may seem to discredit his Gospel. Optimists in these days (1917) are silent or speak in subdued tones. Men's minds are busy thinking rather about diabolical evil and how to crush it, than about the goodness of God and how to exalt it. Yet those Christians who believe that the Spirit of Christ has seldom had fair play in Christian Churches will not allow themselves to be laughed out of a reasonable optimism based on experience This wonderful mixture of good and evil called "the world" does seem to be on the whole, or in many respects, "going onward"—sceptics may say "halting onward" or even "muddling onward"—toward some far-off goal of goodness

Take for example the Christian belief that all human beings may approach God, with a reasonable hopefulness, calling Him "our Father." It came to us from the Jews. But when, and whence, did it come to the Jews? Apparently not till very late. Not till long after the period when God was regarded by them as the Father of Israel. Indeed the Lexicon tells us that the word is not thus used in the Hebrew Scriptures except in a phrase of one of the later Psalms where God is called "Father of the fatherless." May we not take comfort from the thought that so beautiful a title sprang from so sad a source? And is not this often God's way—or, if agnostics shake their heads, at all events *the* way? Does not the want usefully, or sometimes necessarily, precede the gift? "If I go not away," said Jesus to His disciples, "the Spirit will not come unto you."

So in these present days God may be constraining us to feel the want of His Fatherhood by allowing us—nations and churches and classes and individuals—to feed ourselves first with the unsatisfying substitutes afforded by pleasure and wealth and power, and physical or mental excitements. There is at present, and rightly, a growing feeling at least in this country against the accumulation of excessive wealth by individuals And popular contempt and aversion may sometimes be useful in discouraging it. But they can never be a substitute for a truly Christian conscience, for the voice that should speak in a man's heart, saying, "Shall I live in luxury and give my workpeople a starving wage?" The time will come, we may reasonably hope, when a Christian will say "I had sooner be a scavenger before the gates of Sion than a multimillionaire in the City of Mammon." And this, the selfish accumulation of wealth, is but one form of that "greediness" which is the source of all sin. A similar feeling of abhorrence—if we are to be Christians indeed—must extend to other provinces of selfishness, including the sins of the flesh· "Shall I destroy the Man within me and serve the Beast?"

Is this an optimistic dream? It is at all events more reasonable than the supposition that by any appeal to mere self-interest, and by any merely mechanical organizations of conferences and councils, war should be abolished and the reign of perpetual peace insured. The machinery is not to be despised or ignored but it cannot be worked by itself without the Spirit. We need the Peace-Giver Himself in the universe, in every nation, in every social community, in every family, in every human heart. It is a very hard task for man to make himself, and to keep himself, one with the Son of God, and consequently one with the City of the Universe. Yet Marcus Aurelius aimed at nothing less, declaring that every good man ought to say, "That which does not hurt the City does not hurt me."

How much more ought Christians to aspire to such a triumph over their own selfishness, over the lower self that rebels against the higher! And how desirable it is that in attempting to achieve such a victory we should put aside everything that comes in between us and the Lord Jesus Christ, in whom and through whom we are to "overcome the world"—that "world" of God's gifts which we are apt to convert into a world of the devil's temptations.

It is quite right to study the words of the Gospels with all possible care, honesty, and diligence, but the student's object should always be to reach the Word through the words. Small indeed would then seem many of the differences that divide Churches and theologians. They would be swallowed up in our apprehension of "the love

PREFACE

of God which is in Christ Jesus our Lord," and "the peace of God which passeth all understanding." Not for nothing does Jesus in the Fourth Gospel emphasize this peace. "Peace I bequeath unto you, *the peace that is my own I give you*," and again "These things I have spoken unto you that in me ye may have *peace*. In the world ye must have tribulation: but be of good cheer, I have overcome the world."

There are many forms in which men may patch up a peace—individual with individual, class with class, nation with nation—a peace of self-interest and convenience But there is only one kind of peace that is permanent, that which is based—whether in individuals, or in classes, or in nations—on the acceptance of the Spirit of the Son of Man, that is to say, of that ideal Humanity to which all human beings owe allegiance, and which we Christians identify with Jesus Christ. The Spirit of the Son of Man we have found to be the Spirit of self-sacrifice, a sacrifice of self for the sake of others. In accordance with the Law of self-sacrifice the Son of Man passed through apparent defeat on the Cross to the real victory of the Resurrection, through the death of "the grain of wheat" to the life that "beareth much fruit." We are to do the same

This is the lesson of the Gospels. But in too many cases "self-sacrifice" has been confused with "sacrifice for oneself, sacrifice for one's own salvation." That is a very different thing As though a soldier should suppose that in fighting for his country he is fighting to save his own life! Too often, corrupted thus, the Gospel has failed. But there is all the more hope that, if we take its lesson to heart in the future, it will no longer so greatly fail

PREFACE

My thanks are due to my old friend and schoolfellow Mr W. S. Aldis, M A , formerly Principal of the Durham College of Science, for most valuable corrections· and suggestions, made in revising the proofs of this volume—as also those of preceding volumes of this series, from the beginning (1900). I have also to thank the Rev. J. Hunter Smith, M.A , formerly my colleague as Assistant Master at King Edward's School, Birmingham, for copious illustrations, from modern sources, bearing on many points of difficulty.

From a third friend (of more than sixty years' standing) Mr H. Candler, formerly Mathematical Master at Uppingham, I had confidently hoped to receive a frank and trenchant criticism like that which I have gratefully acknowledged in many previous volumes, and though he has been removed by death I desire to testify here to the inspiring memory of his uncompromising honesty.

To my daughter I owe not only the Indices at the end of the volumes, but also a close and searching recension of the whole work, which has detected innumerable faults, and has gone far to remedy the author's increasing infirmities of memory and defects in exact and accurate expression.

Lastly, to the Cambridge University Press, my thanks, paid on many previous occasions, must be reiterated and emphasized, not only for the accuracy of their printing, but also for their skill in dealing with the complicated arrangement of the footnotes—never so complicated as in this, the concluding volume of the series.

EDWIN A. ABBOTT.

Wellside, Well Walk,
   Hampstead, N W 3

   3 *Apr.* 1917

CONTENTS

	PAGE
REFERENCES AND ABBREVIATIONS .	XXIX

CHAPTER I
THE TRANSFIGURATION AND ITS SEQUEL
[Mark ix 2—13]

		PAGE
§ 1	"Glory," in the Three Gospels and in the Fourth	1
§ 2	"Went up into the mountain to pray," in Luke	6
§ 3	"After six days" or "about eight days" . .	8
§ 4	The Johannine equivalent of "praying on the mountain"	10
§ 5	"His garments...so as no fuller on earth can whiten," in Mark . .	13
§ 6	"Beloved" in Mark and Matthew, "Chosen" in Luke	20
§ 7	"While they were coming down from the mountain he charged them," in Mark .	24
§ 8	"How is it written?" in Mark	32

CHAPTER II
"THE KINGDOM OF GOD" AND "LITTLE CHILDREN"
[Mark ix 14—50]

§ 1	"Little children" . . .	38
§ 2	"Little children," in the Fourth Gospel .	44
§ 3	The "little child" with the "dumb and deaf spirit," in Mark	48
§ 4	"All things are possible to him that believeth," in Mark	53
§ 5	"This kind can come out by nothing save by prayer," in Mark	55
§ 6	The first Synoptic passage mentioning the "delivering up" of "the Son of man"	62
§ 7	"He would not that any man should know [it]," in Mark	64
§ 8	The question who is "the greatest" . . .	70

CONTENTS

			PAGE
§ 9	"Taking a little child in his arms," in Mark		75
§ 10	"In my name," and "because ye are Christ's," in Mark		79
§ 11	"If thine eye offend thee," in Mark and Matthew		86
§ 12	"The unquenchable fire," in Mark		90
§ 13	The undying "worm," in Mark		96
§ 14	"For every one shall be salted with fire," in Mark		98
§ 15	"Have salt in yourselves, and be at peace one with another," in Mark		101
§ 16	Johannine doctrine on fire		103
§ 17	How John expresses "salting with fire"		105
§ 18	"Tribulation"		108

CHAPTER III
MARRIAGE AND CHILDREN
[Mark x 1—16]

§ 1	Divorce, the discussion of, how originated		112
§ 2	"And he blessed them," in Mark		116

CHAPTER IV
HOW TO ENTER INTO THE KINGDOM
[Mark x. 17—52]

§ 1	"And Jesus looking upon him loved him," in Mark		123
§ 2	"Children, how hard it is," in Mark		127
§ 3	"He shall receive a hundredfold...with persecutions," in Mark		133
§ 4	"But many that are first shall be last," in Mark and Matthew		141
§ 5	"First Simon" in Matthew, and "first" in John		147
§ 6	"And Jesus was going before them, and they were amazed," in Mark		151
§ 7	"With the baptism that I am baptized withal shall ye be baptized," in Mark		155
§ 8	"Not mine to give but for those for whom it hath been prepared," in Mark and Matthew		160
§ 9	"They that are accounted to rule," in Mark		161
§ 10	"To give his life a ransom for many," in Mark and Matthew		164
§ 11	"The son of Timaeus, Bartimaeus," in Mark		165
§ 12	"In the way," in Mark		169

CONTENTS

CHAPTER V

JESUS VISITS THE TEMPLE
[Mark xi 1—25 (26)]

			PAGE
§ 1	"A colt tied at the door without in the open street," in Mark		171
§ 2	The origin of Mark's tradition		174
§ 3	The ass and the foal of the Messiah in Genesis		175
§ 4	John on the "finding" of the ass		176
§ 5	(R V) "Branches (*marg* layers of leaves)," in Mark		180
§ 6	"Hosanna," in Mark, Matthew, and John		182
§ 7	"The coming kingdom of our father David," in Mark		190
§ 8	"He looked round about upon all things," in Mark		193
§ 9	John on Christ's visits to the Temple		196
§ 10	The symbolism of the fig-tree, misunderstood by Luke		205
§ 11	Does John intervene?		209
§ 12	"Carrying a vessel through the temple," in Mark		212
§ 13	"For all the nations," in Mark		215
§ 14	"A scourge of cords," in John		217
§ 15	"Doves," "tables," and "money-changers," in all but Luke		218
§ 16	What followed after the purification of the Temple		220
§ 17	"Have faith in God," in Mark		227
§ 18	"Believe that what he saith is coming to pass," and "Believe that ye [have] received," in Mark		230
§ 19	Johannine Intervention		234
§ 20	"Whensoever ye stand praying," in Mark		236

CHAPTER VI

JESUS "WALKING" IN THE TEMPLE
[Mark xi 27—xii 44]

§ 1	John on the "walking" of Jesus		242
§ 2	The parable of the murderous husbandmen		249
§ 3	The payment of tribute		255
§ 4	The resurrection of the dead		260
§ 5	"What commandment is the first?" in Mark		266
§ 6	"Scribes" and "the Son of David"		273
§ 7	"Scribes" and a poor widow, in Mark and Luke		278

CONTENTS

CHAPTER VII
THE LAST DAYS
[Mark xiii 1—37]

			PAGE
§ 1	The casting down of the Temple		284
§ 2	"When shall these things be?"		286
§ 3	"Wars.. the beginning of travail," in Mark and Matthew		289
§ 4	Persecutions		294
§ 5	"The Abomination of Desolation" and its sequel, in Mark and Matthew		305
§ 6	The "shortening" of "the days," in Mark and Matthew		313
§ 7	The "gathering" of "the elect," in Mark and Matthew		320
§ 8	"The fig-tree"		324
§ 9	"About that day...knoweth no one...not even the Son, save only the Father," in Mark and Matthew		326
§ 10	"The porter," in Mark and John		331
§ 11	The "faithful servant (*or*, steward)," in Matthew and Luke		334
§ 12	The disciple that "follows," and the disciple that "waits," in John		336

CHAPTER VIII
THE ANOINTING AT BETHANY
[Mark xiv 1—11]

§ 1	"After two days," in Mark and Matthew		339
§ 2	Clement of Alexandria on the Anointing		347
§ 3	Origen and others on the Anointing		352
§ 4	Words and phrases common to Mark and John		355
§ 5	Words and phrases common to Luke and John		360
§ 6	The single phrase common to all the Synoptists		363
§ 7	"Bethany," in Mark, Matthew, and John		365
§ 8	(R V) "Burying," or "burial," in Mark, Matthew, and John		374
§ 9	"Verily...for a memorial of her," in Mark and Matthew		382
§ 10	Mark's narrative as a whole		384
§ 11	A review of the evidence		386

CONTENTS

CHAPTER IX

THE LAST SUPPER
[Mark xiv 12—25]

			PAGE
§	1	Judas Iscariot's agreement with the chief priests	390
§	2	The "man bearing a pitcher," in Mark and Luke	392
§	3	The designation of Judas as the betrayer	397
§	4	Christ's last words about, or to, Judas	407
§	5	The Institution of the Eucharist	413

CHAPTER X

THE INTERVAL BEFORE THE ARREST
[Mark xiv. 26—42]

§	1	The going forth to the Mount of Olives	431
§	2	"Stumbling," and "being scattered," in Mark and Matthew	435
§	3	"I will go-before you to Galilee," in Mark and Matthew	438
§	4	"Before the cock crow twice," in Mark	440
§	5	The beginning of the Passion	444
§	6	"He began...to be sore troubled," in Mark and Matthew	450
§	7	"My soul is exceeding-sorrowful even unto death," in Mark and Matthew	454
§	8	"All things are possible unto thee," in Mark	458
§	9	"The hour" in Mark and John, and "the cup" in all the Gospels	459
§	10	"The spirit indeed is willing, but the flesh is weak," in Mark and Matthew	467
§	11	The last words of Jesus to the disciples	469

CHAPTER XI

THE ARREST OF JESUS
[Mark xiv. 43—52]

§	1	The Synoptic "multitude" or Johannine "cohort"	477
§	2	The words and acts of Jesus during the arrest	488
§	3	"They all left him," in Mark	496
§	4	"A certain young man," in Mark	500

CONTENTS

CHAPTER XII
THE TRIAL BEFORE THE HIGH PRIEST
[Mark xiv. 53—72]

			PAGE
§ 1	"To the high priest," in Mark		504
§ 2	"Peter warming himself," in Mark and John		510
§ 3	"False witnesses" about "the temple," in Mark and Matthew		513
§ 4	The questioning of Jesus by the High Priest, in Mark and Matthew		519
§ 5	The smiting of Jesus		525
§ 6	"Thou also wast with Jesus," in Mark and Matthew		528
§ 7	"He began to anathematize," in Mark and Matthew		532

CHAPTER XIII
THE TRIAL BEFORE PILATE
[Mark xv 1—15]

§ 1	The Praetorium	540
§ 2	The charge of claiming to be a king	545
§ 3	Christ's silence before His judges	548
§ 4	The Custom of Release	552
§ 5	Barabbas	554
§ 6	The scourging of Jesus	559

CHAPTER XIV
THE MOCKING AND THE CRUCIFIXION
[Mark xv 16—37]

§ 1	The "purple" or "scarlet," and the "crown"	563
§ 2	The carrying of the Cross	570
§ 3	"Wine mingled-with-myrrh," in Mark	575
§ 4	"Casting lots" for Christ's garments	576
§ 5	"It was the third hour," in Mark	579
§ 6	The Superscription on the Cross	583
§ 7	The mocking of Christ on the Cross	589
§ 8	"Crucified-with," in Mark, Matthew, and John	591
§ 9	"My God," in Mark and Matthew	595
§ 10	"Why hast thou forsaken me?" in Mark and Matthew	598
§ 11	"Elijah," in Mark and Matthew	602

CONTENTS

			PAGE
§ 12	"Reed," or "hyssop," in Mark, Matthew, and John		603
§ 13	Christ's last utterance		607
§ 14	Christ's death	. . .	611

CHAPTER XV

THE BURIAL
[Mark xv 38—47]

§ 1	The "rending" of "the veil"	616
§ 2	"From afar" . . .	626
§ 3	Joseph of Arimathaea	633
§ 4	The entombing .	639

CHAPTER XVI

THE ANNOUNCEMENT OF CHRIST'S RESURRECTION
[Mark xv 47—xvi 8]

§ 1	What the women did before, and immediately after, the sabbath	645
§ 2	What the names of the women were	652
§ 3	"When the sun was risen," in Mark . . .	660
§ 4	Mark's peculiar tradition about "the stone"	663
§ 5	"Rolled up in a place by itself," in John . . .	670
§ 6	"A young man," in Mark	673
§ 7	"The Nazarene," in Mark .	681
§ 8	"He is not here" .	683
§ 9	"See [thou], [here is] the place," in Mark	687
§ 10	"And to Peter," in Mark	691
§ 11	"Goeth before you into Galilee," in Mark and Matthew	693
§ 12	"For they feared," in Mark .	699

CHAPTER XVII

THE RESURRECTION
[Mark-Appendix xvi 9—20]

§ 1	The general character of the Mark-Appendix	704
§ 2	The Mark-Appendix, Luke, and John	707
§ 3	The Mark-Appendix on Christ's last words .	714
§ 4	The Mark-Appendix and the Lucan Discourse to the Seventy .	722

CONTENTS

		PAGE
§ 5	The Ascension in the Mark-Appendix	727
§ 6	"And sat down at the right hand of God," in the Mark-Appendix	733
§ 7	"The accompanying signs," in the Mark-Appendix	735

INDICES

I	Scriptural Passages	743
II	English	766
III	Greek	793

REFERENCES AND ABBREVIATIONS

REFERENCES

(i) *a*. References to the first nine Parts of Diatessarica (as to which see pp 797—8) are by paragraphs in black Arabic numbers —

    1— 272 = *Clue*
    273— 552 = *Corrections of Mark.*
    553—1149 = *From Letter to Spirit.*
    1150—1435 = *Paradosis.*
    1438—1885 = *Johannine Vocabulary.*
    1886—2799 = *Johannine Grammar*
    2800—2999 = *Notes on New Testament Criticism*
    3000—3635 = *The Son of Man*
    3636—3999 = *Light on the Gospel from an ancient Poet*

(i) *b* References to the Sections of the Tenth Part of Diatessarica, entitled *The Fourfold Gospel*, are by pages The five Sections of the complete work are —

    (Section 1) *Introduction*
    (Section 2) *The Beginning*
    (Section 3) *The Proclamation of the New Kingdom*
    (Section 4) *The Law of the New Kingdom*
    (Section 5) *The Founding of the New Kingdom*

(ii) The Books of Scripture are referred to by the ordinary abbreviations, except where specified below But when it is said that Samuel, Isaiah, Matthew, or any other writer, wrote this or that, it is to be understood as meaning *the writer, whoever he may be, of the words in question*, and not as meaning that the actual writer was Samuel, Isaiah, or Matthew

(iii) The principal Greek MSS are denoted by ℵ, A, B, etc , the Latin versions by *a*, *b*, etc , as usual The Syriac version discovered by Mrs Lewis on Mount Sinai is referred to as SS, *i e* "Sinaitic Syrian " It is always quoted from Prof Burkitt's translation I regret that in the first three vols of Diatessarica Mrs Lewis's name was omitted in connection with this version

(iv) The text of the Greek Old Testament adopted is that of B, edited by Prof Swete, of the New, that of Westcott and Hort

(v) Modern works are referred to by the name of the work, or author, vol , and page, *e g* Levy iii 343 *a*, *i e* vol iii p 343, col. 1.

REFERENCES AND ABBREVIATIONS

ABBREVIATIONS

Aq = Aquila's version of O T
Brederek = Brederek's *Konkordanz zum Targum Onkelos*, Giessen, 1906
Burk = Prof F C Burkitt's *Evangelion Da-mepharreshe*, Cambridge University Press, 1904
Chr = *Chronicles*
Clem Alex 42 = Clement of Alexandria in Potter's page 42
Dalman, *Words* = *Words of Jesus*, Eng Transl 1902, *Aram G* = *Grammatik des Judisch-Palastinischen Aramaisch*, 1894
En = Enoch ed Charles, Clarendon Press, 1893
Ency = *Encyclopaedia Biblica*, A & C Black, 1899
Ephrem = Ephraemus Syrus, ed Moesinger
Etheridge = Etheridge's translations of the Targums on the Pentateuch
Euseb = the Ecclesiastical History of Eusebius
Field = Origenis Hexaplorum quae supersunt, Oxford, 1875, also Otium Norvicense, 1881
Gesen = the Oxford edition of Gesenius
Goldschm = *Der Babylonische Talmud*, 1897—1912, ed Goldschmidt
Goodspeed = Goodspeed's *Indices*, (1) *Patristicus*, Leipzig, 1907, (ii) *Apologeticus*, Leipzig, 1912
Hastings = Dictionary of the Bible, ed Hastings (5 vols)
Hor Heb = *Horae Hebraicae*, by John Lightfoot, 1658—74, ed Gandell, Oxf 1859
Iren = the treatise of Irenaeus against Heresies
Jer Targ or Targ Jer (abbrev for Jerusalem Targum), or Jon Targ (i e Targum of Jonathan, abbrev for the Targum of Pseudo-Jonathan) = the Targum of Pseudo-Jonathan on the Pentateuch, of which there are two recensions—both quoted (*Notes on N T Criticism*, Pref p viii) by ancient authorities under the name "Jerusalem Targum" The two recensions are severally denoted by Jer I and Jer II On other books, the Targum is referred to as simply "Targ"
Jon Targ , see Jer. Targ
Justin = Justin Martyr (*Apol* = his First Apology, *Tryph* = the Dialogue with Trypho)
K = *Kings*
Krauss = Krauss's *Griechische und Lateinische Lehnworter* etc , Part ii, Berlin, 1899

REFERENCES AND ABBREVIATIONS

Levy = Levy's *Neuhebraisches und Chaldaisches Worterbuch*, 4 vols, Leipzig, 1889, Levy Ch = *Chaldäisches Worterbuch*, 2 vols, 1881

L S = Liddell and Scott's Greek Lexicon

Mechilta, see Wu(nsche)

Onk = the Targum of Onkelos on the Pentateuch

Origen is referred to variously, e g *Hom Exod* 11 25 = lib 11 ch 25 of Hom Exod, but Orig on Exod 11 25 = the commentary *ad loc*, Lomm 111 24 = vol 111 p 24 of Lommatzsch's edition.

Oxf Conc = *The Oxford Concordance to the Septuagint*

Pec = peculiar to the writer mentioned in the context

Pesikta, see Wu(nsche)

Philo is referred to by Mangey's volume and page, *e g* Philo 11 234, or, as to Latin treatises, by the Scripture text or Aucher's pages (P A)

Pistis = *Pistis Sophia*, ed Petermann (marginal pages).

Ps Sol = *Psalms of Solomon*, ed Ryle and James, Cambr 1891

R, after Gen, Exod, Lev etc means *Rabboth*, and refers to Wunsche's edition of the Midrash on the Pentateuch, e g *Gen r* (on Gen xII 2, Wu p 177)

Rashi, sometimes quoted from Breithaupt's translation, 1714

S = *Samuel*, s = "see"

Schottg = Schottgen's *Horae Hebraicae*, Dresden and Leipzig, 1733

Sir = the work of Ben Sira, *i e* the son of Sira   It is commonly called Ecclesiasticus (see *Clue* **20** *a*)   The original Hebrew used in this work is that which has been edited, in part, by Cowley and Neubauer, Oxf 1897, in part, by Schechter and Taylor, Cambr 1899, in part, by G Margoliouth, *Jewish Quart Rev*, Oct 1899 (also printed in *About Hebrew Manuscripts* (Frowde, 1905) by Mr E N Adler, who discovered the missing chapters)

SS, see (111) above

Steph Thes = Stephani *Thesaurus Graecae Linguae* (Didot)

Sym = Symmachus's version of O T

Targ (by itself) is used where only one Targum is extant on the passage quoted

Targ Jer, Targ Jon, and Targ Onk, see Jer Targ, Jon Targ, and Onk, above

Tehillim = Midrash on Psalms, ed Wunsche (2 vols)

Test xII Patr = Testaments of the Twelve Patriarchs ed Charles, 1908 (Gk, Clarendon Press, Eng, A & C Black)

Theod = Theodotion's version of O T

Thes Syr = Payne Smith's *Thesaurus Syriacus*, Oxf. 1901.

Tromm = Trommius' *Concordance to the Septuagint*

Tryph = the Dialogue between Justin Martyr and Trypho the Jew

REFERENCES AND ABBREVIATIONS

Walton = *Biblia Sacra Polyglotta*, 1657.
Wetst = Wetstein's *Comm on the New Testament*, Amsterdam, 1751
W H = Westcott and Hort's New Testament.
Wu = Wunsche's translation of *Rabboth* etc , 1880—1909 (including *Mechilta, Pesikta Rab Kahana, Tehillim* etc).

(a) A bracketed Arabic number, following Mk, Mt , etc indicates the number of instances in which a word occurs in Mark, Matthew, etc , e g ἀγάπη Mk (0), Mt (1), Lk (1), Jn (7)

(b) Where verses in Hebrew, Greek, and Revised Version, are numbered differently, the number of R V is given alone

(c) In transliterating a Hebrew, Aramaic, or Syriac word, preference has often, but not invariably, been given to that form which best reveals the connection between the word in question and forms of it familiar to English readers Where a word is not transliterated, it is often indicated (for the sake of experts) by a reference to Gesen , *Thes Syr* , Levy, or Levy *Ch*

CHAPTER I

THE TRANSFIGURATION AND ITS SEQUEL
[Mark ix. 2—13]

§ 1. *"Glory," in the Three Gospels and in the Fourth*[1]

THE Transfiguration is expressly described by Luke as a

---

[1] Mk ix 2—8
(R V)
(2) And after six days Jesus taketh with him Peter, and James, and John, and bringeth them up into a high mountain apart by themselves and he was transfigured before them
(3) And his garments became glistering, exceeding white, so as no fuller on earth can whiten them
(4) And there appeared unto them Elijah with Moses and they were talking with Jesus

Mt xvii 1—8
(R V)
(1) And after six days Jesus taketh with him Peter, and James, and John his brother, and bringeth them up into a high mountain apart
(2) And he was transfigured before them and his face did shine as the sun, and his garments became white as the light
(3) And behold, there appeared unto them Moses and Elijah talking with him

Lk. ix 28—36
(R.V)
(28) And it came to pass about eight days after these sayings, he took with him Peter and John and James, and went up into the mountain to pray
(29) And as he was praying, the fashion of his countenance was altered, and his raiment [be came] white [and] dazzling
(30) And behold, there talked with him two men, which were Moses and Elijah,
(31) Who appeared in glory, and spake of his decease (*or*, departure) which he was about to accomplish at Jerusalem
(32) Now Peter and they that were with him were heavy with sleep but when they were fully awake (*or*, having remained awake), they saw his glory, and the two men that stood with him

A. F.   1 (Mark ix. 2—8)   1

THE TRANSFIGURATION AND ITS SEQUEL

manifestation of "glory[1]." Mark and Matthew do not use the word in this narrative, but both of them have used the word in the preceding context in such a way as to prepare the reader to accept Luke's description[2]. Mark also, and Mark alone, represents the sons of Zebedee as asking Jesus soon afterwards

Mk ix. 2—8 (R.V.) *contd*	Mt xvii. 1—8 (R.V.) *contd.*	Lk ix. 28—36 (R.V.) *contd*
(5) And Peter answereth and saith to Jesus, Rabbi, it is good for us to be here and let us make three tabernacles, one for thee, and one for Moses, and one for Elijah (6) For he wist not what to answer, for they became sore afraid (7) And there came a cloud overshadowing them and there came a voice out of the cloud, This is my beloved Son: hear ye him	(4) And Peter answered, and said unto Jesus, Lord, it is good for us to be here if thou wilt, I will make here three tabernacles; one for thee, and one for Moses, and one for Elijah (5) While he was yet speaking, behold, a bright cloud overshadowed them and behold, a voice out of the cloud, saying, This is my beloved Son, in whom I am well pleased; hear ye him (6) And when the disciples heard it, they fell on their face, and were sore afraid (7) And Jesus came and touched them and said, Arise, and be not afraid.	(33) And it came to pass, as they were parting from him, Peter said unto Jesus, Master, it is good for us to be here. and let us make three tabernacles, one for thee, and one for Moses, and one for Elijah not knowing what he said. (34) And while he said these things, there came a cloud, and overshadowed them and they feared as they entered into the cloud (35) And a voice came out of the cloud, saying, This is my Son, my chosen (*many anc. auth* my beloved Son) hear ye him.
(8) And suddenly looking round about, they saw no one any more, save Jesus only with themselves.	(8) And lifting up their eyes, they saw no one, save Jesus only	(36) And when the voice came (*or*, was past), Jesus was found alone. And they held their peace, and told no man in those days any of the things which they had seen

[1] Lk ix 31—2 οἱ ὀφθέντες ἐν δόξῃ...εἶδαν τὴν δόξαν αὐτοῦ.
[2] Mk viii 38, Mt xvi 27 "in the glory of his Father," Lk. ix. 26 "in his own glory and the Father's," on which see *Son* 3492 *l.*

THE TRANSFIGURATION AND ITS SEQUEL

that they may sit on either side of Him in His "glory[1]." Clearly they did not understand what His "glory" meant Here, then, we may conveniently consider what it did mean

In all the Marcan passages that refer to glory there appears to be some reference to the "thrones" mentioned by Daniel predicting the divine judgment "I beheld till thrones were placed, and one that was ancient of days did sit[2]" But in the Synoptic passages now before us, a reference to Daniel is made peculiarly probable because they all mention garments of an exceeding or dazzling whiteness, and Daniel says about the Person who "sat" enthroned "His raiment was white as snow" Such descriptions of the exceeding whiteness of "raiment" occur nowhere else in the Bible except here and in two of the accounts of the angelic manifestations at Christ's resurrection[3].

In the Fourth Gospel the glory of Kingdom is subordinated to that of Fatherhood, and the glory of judging to that of saving John appears never to use the word "glorify" without some thought of the Deliverance that is celebrated in the Song of Moses and the Lamb, accomplished by a Redeemer whose glory it was to die that others might live[4].

The first Johannine mention of "glory" is in the Prologue, "*and we beheld his glory* [i e *the glory of the Word*], glory as of the only begotten from the Father[5]." This can hardly refer (or at least cannot primarily refer) to any manifestation of visible glory, such as might be supposed to have been seen at the Transfiguration Yet it may allude to the tradition peculiar to Luke's narrative, "Now Peter and they that were with him were heavy with sleep but when they were fully awake (*or*, having remained awake), *they saw his glory*, and the

---

[1] Mk x 37 "in thy glory," Mt xx 21 "in thy kingdom" Lk omits the narrative The only other Marcan mention of glory is Mk xiii 26 μετὰ δυνάμεως πολλῆς καὶ δόξης, but Mt xxiv 30, Lk xxi 27 μετὰ δυνάμεως καὶ δόξης πολλῆς
[2] Dan vii 9
[3] Mk ix 3, Mt xvii 2, Lk ix 29, comp. Mk xvi 5 "white," but Mt xxviii 3 "white as snow," Lk xxiv 4 "dazzling"
[4] See *Son* **3463** foll., **3565** foll
[5] Jn i 14

two men that stood with him[1]." Luke, who alone mentions "glory" in the narrative of the Transfiguration, takes it here as a visible, not a spiritual splendour, not one seen in a dream or vision, since the disciples were fully "awake[2]." John, at the outset of his Gospel, connects with "glory" a mention of "grace and truth." He also says "*we beheld it*"—an expression that would naturally include all the disciples and not merely "Peter and those that were with him[3]." And whereas Luke says that Moses and Elijah, along with Jesus, "appeared in glory," John implies that a distinction must be drawn between different kinds of glory. For glory in the highest sense, if it included "grace and truth," did not belong to Moses "The Law was given through Moses; the [gift of] grace and the [gift

---

[1] Lk ix 32, which follows "There talked with him two men, that were Moses and Elijah, who appeared *in glory*." Lk. ix 32 is taken by Cyril (see Cramer) as implying previous sleep βραχύ πως ἀπονυστάζουσιν.

[2] See *Acts of John* §§ 3—6 for several manifestations followed by § 7 "another *glory* (δόξαν) will I tell you, brethren." Comp 2 Pet 1. 16—18 "For we did not follow cunningly devised fables, when we made known unto you the power and coming of our Lord Jesus Christ, but we were eyewitnesses of his majesty For he received from God the Father honour and glory, when there came such a voice to him from the excellent *glory*, This is my beloved Son, in whom I am well pleased and this voice *we* [*ourselves*] (ἡμεῖς) heard come out of heaven, when we were with him in the holy mount." The mention of "cunningly devised fables" explains Luke's anxiety to emphasize the fact that the witnesses of the glory "were fully awake" Contrast the emphatic "*we*," ἡμεῖς, in 2 Pet., with its absence in Jn i 14 ἐθεασάμεθα.

[3] The contexts in *Acts of John* § 5 "Peter and James were wroth because I spake with the Lord," and § 6 "I heard Him say 'John, go thou to sleep,' and thereupon I feigned to be asleep," indicate early heresies that claimed for special apostles special revelations of material glory But the following tradition includes all the Twelve *Petr. Apoc* §§ 2—3 "And further (προσθείς) the Lord said, 'Let us go (ἄγωμεν) to the mountain (εἰς τὸ ὄρος) and pray (εὐξώμεθα).. and while we were praying there suddenly appear two men standing before the Lord (εὐχομένων ἡμῶν ἄ[φνω φαίν]ονται δύο ἄνδρες ἑστῶτες ἔμπροσθεν τοῦ Κυρίου)."

THE TRANSFIGURATION AND ITS SEQUEL

of] truth [that were to be developed out of the Law] came [into being] through Jesus Christ[1]."

It is very seldom indeed that Luke introduces a tradition about *fact* of any importance, peculiar to himself, in the midst of a Synoptic narrative. But he introduces more than one here. For besides mentioning the wakefulness, or awaking, of Peter and his companions, he says that Jesus "went up into the mountain *to pray*," and that the subject of the conversation between Jesus and Moses and Elijah was the "departure" that Jesus "was about to accomplish at Jerusalem." There is no contextual tradition peculiar to Mark[2], except a clause about a "fuller" in connection with Christ's "garments" ("exceeding white, such as no fuller on earth is able to whiten"). This will be discussed after the "praying" mentioned by Luke alone at this point

---

[1] Jn 1 17

[2] In Mk ix. 6 οὐ γὰρ ᾔδει τί ἀποκριθῇ, the text varies SS has "what he was saying" Origen first (*Comm. Matth* xii 40) quotes it as (Lomm iii 194) ἀπεκρίθη, but afterwards (*ib* 41, Lomm iii 200) as ἐλάλει D has λαλήσει but *d* "loquebatur"

Perhaps τί ἀποκριθῇ may have arisen (1) from a recollection of a tradition pec to Mk xiv 40 οὐκ ᾔδεισαν τί ἀποκριθῶσιν αὐτῷ, or (2) from a reluctance to admit that Peter was, for the moment, not in possession of his faculties, or (3) from both these causes The parall Lk ix 33 μὴ εἰδὼς ὃ λέγει seems intended as a correction of Mark The sense is improved by it For the words in Mark are not an "answer" to any question expressed or implied, and this is not an occasion where a superfluous "answer" might be used to mean (Gesen 773) "speak in view of circumstances" For these reasons Mk ix 6 is not discussed above as a tradition peculiar to Mark

Mechilt, on Exod xv 9 "The enemy said, *I will follow*," adds "*And he knew not what he said*" That is, Pharaoh "followed," to his own destruction, not to the destruction of Israel

See *From Letter* **885—90** for Patristic comments on Mk ix 6 etc There was perhaps some common Semitic original of Mk ix 6, and Mt xvii 5 ἔτι αὐτοῦ λαλοῦντος, capable of being interpreted "*He had not finished* to speak" (comp Levy iii 570 *a* לא הספיק לומר, of Akiba's martyrdom) or "*He did not know* while speaking" This is more probable than the conjectures in *Corrections* **422—3**

THE TRANSFIGURATION AND ITS SEQUEL

§ 2. *"Went up into the mountain to pray," in Luke*[1]

In commenting on the baptism of Jesus it was pointed out that Luke alone describes Jesus as "praying" where the parallel Mark and Matthew mention "ascending"; and the Odes of Solomon and the Syriac Version of the Psalms were quoted to shew how the phrase "Jesus lifted up his soul," *i.e.* in prayer, might be taken to mean "lifted himself up," or *vice versa*[2]. In the Psalms, the Targumist thrice supplies *"in prayer,"* where the Psalmist mentions simply the *"lifting up" of "the soul*[3]*"* to God. Luke may have done the same thing here. What Luke adds about the subject of Christ's conversation with Moses and Elijah is consistent with the view that, in this "praying," Jesus was raised into a region of revelation and vision (like "the third heaven" to which Paul was "caught up") —into which His three disciples also received an insight with a power of hearing celestial utterances, not audible to those who were not to some extent similarly lifted up. The condition of the disciples, "weighed down with sleep," oscillating between dream and vision, might be regarded by some as similar to that of the same three disciples at Gethsemane; but Luke dissents from that view by saying that on that occasion Jesus "found them *slumbering for sorrow*[4]"

According to this view, *"the mountain"* in Luke is not the

---

[1] Lk ix 28

[2] *Beginning* pp 110—1.

[3] Ps xxv 1, lxxxvi 4, cxliii. 8

[4] Lk ix 32 βεβαρημένοι ὕπνῳ resembles Mk xiv 40 οἱ ὀφθαλμοὶ καταβαρυνόμενοι (Mt βεβαρημένοι), where parall. Lk. xxii. 45 has κοιμωμένους ἀπὸ τῆς λύπης In canon. LXX, βαρεῖσθαι occurs only in Exod vii 14 (of Pharaoh), and βαρέως (apart from Gen xxxi 35 μὴ βαρέως φέρε) only in Is vi 10 τοῖς ὠσὶν αὐτῶν βαρέως ἤκουσαν In NT βαρέως occurs only in Mt xiii 15, Acts xxviii 27 (both quoting Isaiah) Steph. *Thes.* quotes no instance of διαγρηγορεῖν earlier than Herodian There is no reason for explaining it (*Corrections* **424**) by Hebr confusion, for Luke's motive in inserting this detail might well be to shew that what the disciples saw was no dream or vision What they saw was seen "when they were fully awake" (perhaps **a** better **rendering** than "having remained awake")

6 (Mark ix 2—8)

THE TRANSFIGURATION AND ITS SEQUEL

same thing as "a high mountain" in Mark and Matthew, and may be closer to the original tradition, which contemplated a spiritual mountain[1]. The Marcan "high mountain" has been supposed in ancient times to mean Tabor, or the Mount of Olives, which are not "high[2]", but in modern times, Hermon, which is high, but open to objection, as being out of the way, and hardly likely to be called *"the holy mountain"* in the second Petrine Epistle[3]. "The holy mountain," in the Psalms and Prophets, meant Mount Zion[4]. But when this, under the title of "the mountain of the Lord's house," is spoken of as being "established in the top of the mountains" and as the resort of "all nations[5]," it is obviously a metaphorical region, a spiritual "House of Prayer." It is quite conceivable that this thought, and even this phrase, was in use among pious Essenes, who did not go up to the Temple in Jerusalem. Perhaps it was in use among the disciples of John the Baptist—who is not described as going up with Jesus to the Temple, when Jesus went up to purify it at the Passover, or as going up on any occasion.

Thus we could explain *"the mountain"* in Luke here, and *"the holy mountain"* in the Petrine Epistle, and also such expressions as that in the *Acts of John* "He taketh me and James and Peter into *the mountain where His custom was to pray*[6]." Thus, too, we can explain the sudden mention of *"the mountain"* (not "a mountain") at the conclusion of Matthew's Gospel as being *"the mountain* where Jesus [had] appointed to them [to meet Him][7]." This does not oblige us to deny that in a literal sense there may have been places, such as that for example on the Mount of Olives, and others on mountains of Galilee, to which Jesus "oft-times resorted with his disciples[8]." But it helps us to recognise that, in a spiritual sense, Jesus laid stress on the need of our "ascending

---

[1] Mk-Mt ὄρος ὑψηλόν, Lk τὸ ὄρος
[2] See *From Letter* 867 a   [3] 2 Pet 1 18
[4] See *Son* 3468 c—g on "The Holy Mountain"
[5] Is 11 2, comp Mic iv 1
[6] *Acts of John* § 3.   [7] Mt xxviii 16
[8] Jn xviii 2

THE TRANSFIGURATION AND ITS SEQUEL

in heart and mind" into the Mountain of the Lord's House of Prayer in heaven, when we offer up prayer in any place, high or low, upon earth

§ 3. *"After six days" or "about eight days"*[1]

Jerome's only comment on this clause in Matthew is that Matthew mentions the "intermediate" days, Luke "adds the first and the last"; but he does not explain why Luke does this[2] Nothing occurs during this interval. Then why is any interval mentioned by all the Synoptists? Having been mentioned by Mark and Matthew as "six days," why is it altered—perhaps inaccurately and certainly unnecessarily—to "eight days"?

Origen mentions, but does not comment on, Luke's divergence[3]. He regards the "six days" as those of "creation," followed by "the new sabbath[4]" But how "*new*"? Is not the day that follows the "six" rather to be called "the *old* sabbath"? Might it not be said that "the *new* sabbath" is a title to be given rather to "the eighth day," being the first day of the New Creation, the day of Christ's Resurrection? Some thought of this kind may explain Luke's alteration For the superiority of the eighth day to the seventh is a prominent subject in the earliest Christian writers, among whom Justin Martyr regards the eighth day as the emblem of the true Circumcision as well as of the Resurrection[5].

---

[1] Mk ix. 2, Mt xvii. 1 καὶ μετὰ (Mt μεθ') ἡμέρας ἕξ, Lk ix 28 ἐγένετο δὲ μετὰ τοὺς λόγους τούτους ὡσεὶ ἡμέραι ὀκτώ

[2] Jerome adds "Non enim dicitur 'Post dies octo...' sed 'die octavo'"—apparently reading Lk as ἡμέρᾳ ὀγδόῃ

[3] Origen on Mt xvi 28, Lomm iii 179

[4] Origen, Lomm iii 189—91

[5] Barn xv 8—9, Justin M *Tryph* §§ 24, 41 "a type of the true circumcision, by which we are circumcised from deceit and iniquity through Him who rose from the dead τῇ μιᾷ τῶν σαββάτων ἡμέρᾳ, [namely through] our Lord Jesus Christ " Comp. *ib* § 138 "a symbol of the eighth day, wherein Christ appeared when He rose from the dead, [the day] for ever the first in power" So Clem Alex freq 636—7, 712—3, 811 Among those who rest in "God's holy hill" (Ps xv 1) some (*ib* 794) are promoted from the seventh to the eighth grade See also Philo *Quaest Gen* on Gen xvii 12

8 (Mark ix. 2—8)

THE TRANSFIGURATION AND ITS SEQUEL

Some may explain Mark's "after six days" by saying that, although such interval-clauses are rare in the Gospels, they are occasionally used where the interval is emphasized, and that this is the case here: "Precisely six days after the Lord's prophecy *'There are some here of those standing* [*by*]...' the prophecy was fulfilled." But would Mark have inserted it if it had happened to be "*four* days," or "*five* days"? It is very unlikely. Luke might have done so in the Acts, but probably not in his Gospel. The Bible does not often mention intervals of days except for special reasons or in allusions[1]

Not improbably, therefore, the Marcan tradition "after six days" is to be explained allusively If so, it would seem to allude to the ancient description of the ascent of Moses to Mount Sinai, where it is said "The cloud covered it *six days, and on the seventh day* he called unto Moses out of the midst of the cloud...and Moses was in the mount forty days and forty nights[2]." The Transfiguration was regarded as the occasion of the giving of the New Law, attested by Moses and Elijah the representatives of the Old Law and the Prophets, and given on a New Mountain of God. According to the precedents of Moses and Elijah there were intervals of "six days," or "forty days[3]," before ascending In Mark, an interval of "forty days" has been already assigned to the Temptation. Here the interval mentioned is "six days", and it was probably mentioned originally, not as an exact measure of the time, but as the type of the interval between the proclamation of the Gospel and the Coming of the Kingdom of God

The period of "*six days*" is frequently mentioned in the Old Testament antithetically to "the seventh day," or in connection with the labour that is to precede the sabbath, but

---

[1] Strong's Concordance gives (*a*) "four days" only once in O T (Judg. xi. 40, about the dead), and in N T only in Jn xi 17, 39 (about the dead) and Acts x 30, (*b*) "five days" only once in O T (Numb. xi. 19, see context), and in N T only in Acts xx. 6, xxiv 1

[2] Exod xxiv 16—18 See *Synoptic Gospels* 1 213 (by C G Montefiore) to which I am indebted for this suggestion

[3] I K xix 8

THE TRANSFIGURATION AND ITS SEQUEL

is otherwise very rare[1]. It is therefore worth noting that it occurs only once elsewhere (apart from sabbatarian antithesis) in the New Testament. There, it is connected with the coming of Jesus to Bethany "*six days* before the Passover[2]." A common Jewish view of the "six days" during which Moses was waiting to ascend the mountain was that they were spent in purifying him for the presence of God[3]; and John immediately proceeds to describe the anointing of Jesus in connection with "embalming," as a preparation for the Crucifixion, which, in the Fourth Gospel, is regarded as a "lifting up" to the throne of God. The Johannine Gospel begins with one implied hexaemeron[4]. The Johannine "six days" may be the expression of another. But this would not preclude the Evangelist from including an allusion to the gift of the New Law through Jesus Christ, the Son, as distinguished from the gift of the Old Law through Moses, the Servant.

§ 4 *The Johannine equivalent of "praying on the mountain"*

The above-mentioned coincidence of a single phrase ("six days")—apparently an insignificant one—between the earlier Synoptists and John, leads us to reflect on the much more striking difference as to the term "mountain" so common in all the Synoptists and so rare in the Fourth Gospel. The only instance of it there in Christ's words is where He says "*Neither*

---

[1] Josh vi 3—14 is hardly an exception
[2] Jn xii 1 There is sabbatarian antithesis in Lk xiii 14
[3] Comp Jer *Joma* i 1 (Schwab p 157), *Aboth* R Nathan (*init*) "Moses was sanctified in the cloud and received the Torah from Sinai as it is written (Exod xxiv 16) 'And the Glory of the Lord abode upon Mount *Sinai*,' which means on Moses,... to purify him So says R Jose the Galilaean" R Akiba differed. But others supported R Jose, see *Numb r* on Numb vii. 1 (Wu p 296) Jer *Joma* and *Numb r* mention "seven days" as the period of sanctification, whereas Scripture and *Aboth* R Nathan mention "six days" Comp Jn xi 55—xii 1 "to *purify* (ἁγνίσωσιν) themselves . *six days* before the Passover"—an instance (*Joh Gr* **2646**) of Johannine irony to which Origen *ad loc.* calls attention
[4] See *Proclam* p 15, *Joh Gr* **2624**, *Son* **3583** (ix) *b*, (xii) *c* foll

THE TRANSFIGURATION AND ITS SEQUEL

in Jerusalem nor in this mountain shall ye worship the Father[1]." The essence of worship, Jesus adds, is to pray not on a mountain but "in spirit and in truth."

Not only is "praying on a mountain" excluded from the Fourth Gospel but even all direct mention of Christ's "praying" on any occasion. Yet John does represent Jesus in fact as praying to the Father twice during the week before the last Passover. The second prayer is the very long one uttered just before His arrest. The first is a brief and passionate one, when Jesus exclaims, "Now is my soul troubled. And what shall I say? 'Father, save me from this hour'? But for this cause came I, unto this hour *Father, glorify thy name*[2]."

The preceding Johannine context describes Jesus as proclaiming "The hour is come that the Son of man *should be glorified*[3]." The reason for the proclamation seems slight, being merely a petition to Philip, "Sir, we would see Jesus," uttered by "certain Greeks among those that went up to worship at the feast." But Jesus sees in this petition a verification of the Law of the Harvest, and a revelation of the Father's will that the Son, who is the Seed, shall "die" that it may "bear much fruit." This seems to correspond to the more definite and less poetic Lucan tradition that Jesus was to "accomplish his departure (*or*, decease) in Jerusalem." The scene of this petition of the Greeks is what Jews called the Mountain of the Lord's House in Jerusalem to which they had "come up" to worship[4]. Jesus welcomed them as worshippers in no mere material mountain but in spirit and in truth

---

[1] Jn iv 21 In Jn, ὄρος occurs only in iv 20, 21, vi 3, 15 (and the interpolated viii 1).

[2] Jn xii 27—8 On the punctuation see *Joh Gr* 2057, 2389 *a*, 2512 *b—c* No prayer is uttered before, even at the raising of Lazarus There it is implied that Jesus has quietly prayed (Jn xi 41 "Father, I thank thee that thou heardest me") But no prayer is recorded.

[3] Jn xii. 23

[4] On "*the Mountain of the House*," see *From Letter* 981 *b*. "Going up" to the feast is mentioned in Jn xii 20 about the Greeks, but not about Jesus. See, however, *Joh Gr* 2264—5 on Jesus as "going up" to a feast in a mystical sense

11 (Mark ix 2—8)

THE TRANSFIGURATION AND ITS SEQUEL

Then the Son offers Himself to the Father, a willing sacrifice, in the prayer "Father, glorify thy name." The answer, "I have both glorified it and will glorify it again," does not include the word "Son," but it is felt to be implied, or rather, taken for granted, so that "Thou art my Son" would, in this context, rather weaken than strengthen the meaning. An inexpressible mystery of "glorifying" the divine Name is suggested, as if the Father is sacrificing His own Son, while the Son is sacrificing Himself to His own Father, and divine Love identifies the Sacrificer with the Sacrificed. This answer is uttered by a "voice from heaven"—not "from a cloud" as in the Synoptic account of the Transfiguration—and the multitude took it for mere "thunder," while others said "an angel hath spoken to him."

These variations in popular apprehension seem to illustrate the Evangelist's doctrine that mere external signs and wonders are of no avail in themselves, apart from the preparation of the mind that is to receive them. The "multitude" was not prepared. "Others" were only partially prepared. But there was at least some one present who, if not fully at the moment, at all events afterwards, was able to discern that the revelation beneath this voice was a revelation of victory through defeat and life through death. The Evangelist hears the words "Now shall the prince of this world be cast out," and reflects "Yes, but the prince was destined at first to prevail." He hears "I, if I be lifted up from the earth, will draw all men unto myself"—and adds "Yes, but He was first to die." And hence, long afterwards, he wrote down his reflection. "This he said, signifying by what manner of death he should die[1]."

---

[1] Jn xii 31—3. On "voices" in O.T., meaning "thunders," see *From Letter* 728. Origen, on the Transfiguration (*Comm Matth* xii 32, Lomm iii 182) seems to assume that the "voice" is a voice of thunder, when he speaks of (Mt. xvi 28) "'*some of those standing by*' Jesus (ἑστηκότων παρὰ τῷ Ἰησοῦ), when they are enabled to follow Him as He draws them onward and as He goes up into the '*high mountain*' (ib xvii 1) of His manifestation. Of which 'some of those *standing by Jesus* (τινες τῶν ἑστώτων παρὰ (?) Ἰησοῦν) are deemed worthy, if they be either a Peter whom '*the gates of Hades*

12 (Mark ix 2—8)

THE TRANSFIGURATION AND ITS SEQUEL

§ 5. *"His garments...so as no fuller on earth can whiten,"* in Mark[1]

This curious Marcan tradition about "no fuller" may have a bearing on the most important Lucan addition to the older account of the Transfiguration. Mark and Matthew tell us merely that Moses and Elijah conversed with Jesus. But

have no power against,' or '*the sons of thunder*' and [those who are to be] begotten (οἱ τῆς βροντῆς υἱοὶ καὶ γεννώμενοι) from the mighty-voicedness (ἀπὸ τῆς μεγαλοφωνίας) of God [when He is] thundering and calling aloud with a great voice from heaven (βροντῶντος καὶ μεγάλα οὐρανόθεν βοῶντος) to them that have ears and are wise Such as these 'do not taste of death.'"

The ancient commentary on Mark attributed to Jerome extends this explanation of "sons of thunder" (Boanerges) so as to include Peter. "Jesus named them Boanerges, that is, Sons of Thunder, since the exalted merit of *these three* deserves to hear, on the Mountain, the thunder of the Father, thundering through the cloud, 'This is my beloved Son'" See *Proclamation* p 411 and *Son* **3468** b

[1] Mk ix 3 καὶ τὰ ἱμάτια αὐτοῦ ἐγένετο στίλβοντα λευκὰ λίαν οἷα γναφεὺς ἐπὶ τῆς γῆς οὐ δύναται οὕτως λευκᾶναι Many authorities omit the clause about a "fuller"—perhaps as being a homely illustration—and insert "snow" or "light": SS "He was transfigured before them and he became gleaming and his clothing became whitened as the snow," D στιλβοντα λευκα λια ως χιων ως ου δυναται τις λευκαναι επι της γης, d "splendida candida nimis qualia non potest quis candida facere super terrā" *Diatess* has "And while they were praying, Jesus changed, and became after the fashion of another person, and his face shone like the sun, and his raiment was very white like the snow, and as the light of lightning, so that nothing on earth can whiten like it"—a very interesting illustration of the way in which an early distasteful tradition ("fuller") can be smothered under a heap of later picturesque paraphrases Codex *a* has "fulgentia, candida valde, tanquam nix," *b* "splendida, velut nix, qualia quis non potest facere super terram"

Origen (*Comm. Matth* xii 39, Lomm iii 194) says τότε δὲ κατὰ τὸν Μάρκον γίνονται τὰ ἱμάτια αὐτοῦ λευκὰ καὶ στίλβοντα ὡς τὸ φῶς, οἷα γναφεὺς ἐπὶ τῆς γῆς οὐ δύναται οὕτως λευκᾶναι καὶ τάχα οἱ μὲν ἐπὶ τῆς γῆς γναφεῖς οἱ ἐπιμελούμενοί εἰσι σοφοὶ τοῦ αἰῶνος τούτου λέξεως etc, indicating that "the fullers on earth" are contrasted with "the Fuller in heaven" The same Heb that means "*fuller*" means also "*wash*," as in Ps li 7 "*wash* me and I shall be whiter than snow"

THE TRANSFIGURATION AND ITS SEQUEL

Luke adds what they conversed about. It was the "exodus" or "departure" that Jesus was "destined" to "fulfil" in Jerusalem. Did Luke supply these words because he felt that this *must* have been the subject of their conversation, or because he found them in some early record outside Mark? Or is there in Mark any expression out of which Luke (or others whom Luke followed) may have inferred that the Vision predicted some "departure" corresponding to the mysterious "burial" of Moses[1], or to the miraculous "ascent" of Elijah?

It will be observed that Matthew and Luke add severally that the "face" or "countenance" of Christ "shone," or "was altered." And this is natural. For it seems strange, at first, that so much stress should be laid by Mark on "garments" alone, and this in a change so complete that it is called in effect "metamorphosis[2]." But it seems less strange when we reflect that "white raiment" is mentioned in Daniel—perhaps uniquely in Hebrew Scripture, and at all events with singularly solemn emphasis—as follows "I beheld till thrones were placed, and one that was ancient of days did sit, *his raiment was white as snow*[3]." Rashi explains "white" as meaning "*that He may whiten the sins of His people*," and this is the view of Jewish tradition generally[4]; it signifies the fulfilment of the promise in Isaiah "Though your sins be as scarlet they shall be *as white as snow*[5]." How could the followers of Christ gain the fulfilment of this

---

[1] Deut xxxiv. 6 R V txt "he buried him," marg "he was buried," see *Law* p 382

[2] Mk ix. 2, Mt xvii. 2 μετεμορφώθη, a word avoided by Lk ix 29.

[3] Dan vii 9 Jerome *ad loc* calls attention to the "white garments" in the Transfiguration

[4] See *From Letter* **864** *b* (quoting passages from Schottgen) and *Chag* 14 *a*, *Pesikt* Wu p 213 "when He forgives the sins of the Israelites, He is clothed in white, as it is said (Dan vii 9) 'and his clothing is white as snow'" See also *Deut r* Wu p 41, *Pesikt.* Wu p 209, and *Tehill.* Wu ii p 84, on the various garments of the Lord In Eccles ix 8 "let thy garments be always white" is explained in *Sabb* 153 *a* (for edification rather than in accurate interpretation) as meaning that we are to be always in a state of penitence and good works

[5] Is 1 18

THE TRANSFIGURATION AND ITS SEQUEL

promise? The answer is given in Revelation, where one of the elders asks "These that are arrayed in the white robes, who are they, and whence came they?" and the answer is "These are they that come out of the great tribulation, and they washed their robes, and *made them white in the blood of the Lamb*[1]."

The Hebrew "fuller" occurs only in Malachi and Isaiah, and in a passage of Kings parallel to Isaiah[2]. Isaiah twice mentions "the fuller's field," first as the auspicious meeting-place of Ahaz with the prophet who brought him a message of redemption, and then as the place where the enemies of Hezekiah boasted on the eve of their own destruction. The other instance is in the context of a prophecy of Malachi quoted by all the Synoptists, "Behold, I send my messenger and he shall prepare the way before me." Malachi, after saying that the Lord "will suddenly come to his temple," adds that "the messenger of the covenant" is "like a refiner's fire and like the soap of *the fuller*, and he shall sit as a refiner and he shall purify the sons of Levi[3]." This, and its context, might be applied to the coming of Christ to the Temple in a literal sense, and to His attempt to purify it from the abuses that made it a house of traffic. But there are reasons for thinking that in a more general sense the term "fuller" might be applied by Jewish Christians in the earliest decades of the Church to Jesus as being at once the Purifier and the Lamb of God[4]. Such an application must seem fanciful to us, of course, like multitudes of plays on

---

[1] Rev. vii 14

[2] Is vii 3, xxxvi 2 (also 2 K. xviii 17) Rashi (on Is vii 3) says that the Rabbis explained "fuller" as *more than a mere name*, see *b Sanhedr* 104 a, *j Sanhedr* x 1, *Lev r*. (on Lev. xxvi 42) Wu p 255 Jerome (on Is vii. 3) calls attention to the identity of the place with that mentioned in Is xxxvi 2, and says that Isaiah was bidden to "go forth to the impious king...in the field of *the fuller*, *where defilements and stains [of sin] were purged away*," not so much for the king's sake as for the people's

[3] Mal iii 1—3.

[4] Gesen 460—1 gives כבם "(tread), wash," particip "fuller," כבש "lamb," כבש Heb "subdue," Aram. "tread down"

15 (Mark ix 2—8)

THE TRANSFIGURATION AND ITS SEQUEL

words in the Jewish Haggada. But would it be much more fanciful than the play of words in "Siloam, which is, by interpretation, Sent[1]"?

In one celebrated instance, where the Sanhedrin desire to send a message to a newly-elected Patriarch asking him to resign his office, it is said that the messenger was "a fuller" and it is added "but many say that he was R Akiba[2]." The word used in the Babylonian Talmud is very similar to the word signifying "lamb," used in Scripture about the lamb offered day by day, morning and evening, in the Temple[3]. Now concerning the passage ordaining this sacrifice, Jewish traditions tell us that Hillel and Shammai differed; Shammai said that the "lamb" meant "the treading down," or "crushing"

---

[1] Jn ix 7

[2] Gratz (Engl Transl ii. 348) assumes that it was Akiba "Akiba, who was ever ready to be of service, undertook the delicate commission" j Berach iv 7^d says that it was "a fuller (קצר), and many call him R Akiba," b Berach 28 a does not mention Akiba, but when the Sanhedrin asked "Who will go?" it says that "(?) a fuller (ההוא כובס)" said "I will go" Goldschmidt says in a note that כובסין "fullers" are often mentioned in the Talmud, but refers only to Baba Bathra 134 a "parables of fullers" mentioned along with "astronomy" and "geometry" and other sciences with which R Jochanan was conversant Goldschmidt suggests that it means "wahrsch. eine Secte od. Klasse," but alleges no passages that support such a conjecture

Berliner on Berach 28 a says "Dieser Ausdruck kommt oft vor, und im jerusalemischen Talmud steht dafur fast immer קצראיקצר, Abschneider, Verkurzer Nach genauer Erwagung aller hierher gehorenden Stellen (vergl Succah 28, 1, Kethuboth 103, 2, Baba Bathra 134, 1) glauben wir uns berechtigt, annehmen zu durfen, dass dies eine besondere sehr gering geachtete Sekte war, deren Ursprung schon zur Zeit des Bestehens des Tempels, ja noch weiter hinaus zu suchen sei"

It is worth noting that in Baba Bathra 134 a "parables of fullers" are connected with what Goldschmidt interprets as "Fuchsfabeln," משלות שועלים, and that the latter term occurs again (apparently meaning "subtle disputations") in Sanhedr 38 b, where "(?) a certain fuller (ההוא כובס)" comes forward and solves a problem put forth by an unbeliever.

[3] Numb xxviii 3—4, lamb כבש, see p 15, n. 4

16 (Mark ix. 2—8)

THE TRANSFIGURATION AND ITS SEQUEL

of sin, but Hillel said that it meant "the washing away" of sin[1]. These two great Rabbis flourished just before the birth of Christ. We may therefore suppose that, during the period of Christ's preaching, the memory of such a controversy would make the metaphorical meaning of "a *fuller*" well known among a large circle of Jews, and that many would connect it with the thought of the "lamb" of the daily offering To some of these, in the recording of a vision of the Messiah in white garments, it would be natural, not only to write that His garments were (as in Daniel) "white as snow," but also to feel and say that they were of such a whiteness as no mere earthly "fuller" could produce[2]

Such a thought would go some way toward making easy the very difficult Johannine tradition that the Baptist said concerning Jesus, before the latter had a single disciple, "Behold the Lamb of God, which taketh away the sin of the world![3]" If explained as poetic or prophetic hyperbole, it is, though intelligible, very difficult. But if "lamb" and "fuller" were interchangeable terms in certain prominent discussions of the time, and if "fuller" was also a name that could be given to a Rabbi whose teaching was of a pure and illuminating nature, then much of the difficulty disappears. It will still remain a startling saying, but not so startling, if it sprang from an austere prophet suddenly recognising as his successor one who had a nature to which he could lay no claim—the nature of the Lamb, the nature of the pure and heavenly Fuller, who could wash sins away with a stream of purity not derived from earthly baptism of the body, but flowing from

---

[1] See Levy ii 288 *b* quoting *Jelamdenu*, and add *Pesikt* Wu pp 21, and 75—6

[2] The quaint and (to us perhaps) almost irreverent conception of God as "a fuller" may be illustrated from Siphra in Jalk. Sim i fol 166 *b*, ii fol 58 *a* quoted in Schottgen ii 555 "God took all the sins of Jacob and Esau and poured them on His own garments, whence they became red as scarlet, as it is said 'Wherefore are thy *garments red?*' (comp Is lxiii. 2) Then He sat down and washed them *white*, as it is said (Dan vii 9) 'His *garment* was *white as snow*'"

[3] Jn i 29, on which see *Son* **3519—20**

THE TRANSFIGURATION AND ITS SEQUEL

heaven into the inmost soul. According to this view, the Marcan mention of "a fuller" would be very far from being an otiose detail and a sign of homely diffuseness It would be part of the original vision It had been mentioned by Peter, perhaps—not very long before fragments of a Petrine Gospel were committed to writing by Mark—in some account of a vision of martyrdom, embodied in a manifestation of Moses, Elijah, and the Lord Jesus Christ, in which Peter had been prepared to "taste of death," and follow his Master in glory. The Lord had appeared in "white garments," white with no earthly cleansing but with such a sacrificial stream of purification as could issue from none but the Cleanser in heaven. By such a vision Peter had been taught that he, too, must "whiten his garments in the blood of the Lamb[1]."

At the time when Matthew wrote, the metaphor of "the fuller" might well have become obsolete. The followers of Hillel and Shammai would understand it, but it would be hardly suitable for a Gospel that contemplated the fulfilment of the command "Make disciples of all the nations[2]." Hence the now obscure Marcan allusion was paraphrased by Matthew into a mere description of splendour suffusing the Messiah's countenance and garments. Luke followed Matthew in dispensing with the word "fuller." But, having some sense of a doctrine latent under the word, Luke added in the context a clause (about a *"departure in Jerusalem"*) that might refer to a martyrdom such as Luke mentions elsewhere in the tradition that "it cannot be that a prophet should perish out of Jerusalem[3]."

Passing to the Fourth Gospel we of course recognise that the author has not intervened in favour of Mark in any conscious and definite allusion to the word under consideration. But if we say to ourselves "'*Fuller*' means '*Washer*.' Does John describe Jesus as '*washing*'?" we shall have to reply that he certainly does this. Setting aside the doctrine of regeneration through water and the Spirit, and the flow of blood and water

---

[1] Rev vii. 14   [2] Mt xxviii 19   [3] Lk. xiii 33.

THE TRANSFIGURATION AND ITS SEQUEL

from Christ on the Cross, we have a whole scene devoted to the washing of the feet of the disciples by their Master.

But this scene, though prominent and picturesque, represents only a minor kind of purification. A deeper revelation of the purifying glory of God reveals Him as the Father continually sacrificing, or receiving as a sacrifice, His own Son—the fulfilment of the rudimentary dispensation wherein Jehovah, in the Temple, besides the annual Passover, received day by day the sacrifice of the Lamb. With this tradition in his mind, John would know that the Voice on the Mount of Transfiguration, where Jesus stood between Moses and Elijah, meant, in effect: "Look on Him who stands between these two as His two Witnesses. The Law was given through Moses Wonder-working Prophecy, in its most wonderful form, was given through Elijah[1]. But the grace and the truth that were to come through the Law and the Prophets, redeeming men from sin as well as judging them for sin—these were given through Him, my Son, my Witness or Martyr, my Lamb of Sacrifice, whose blood will take away the sins of the world, giving unto the sons of men white garments wherein they may stand arrayed before my throne."

Here we should note that in the scene of the Johannine Voice from heaven John says nothing that directly suggests the thought of the Fuller. What he says there, in the person of Jesus, commenting on the redeeming efficacy of the Messiah's death, is "And I, if I be lifted up from the earth, will draw all men unto myself[2]." There is no metaphor there, of the

---

[1] Why should Elijah, who made no recorded prophecies about the Day of the Lord, be accepted as the type of "the prophets"? Perhaps partly because it was the Prophet's business to bear witness to Jehovah, when Israel went astray from Him; and Elijah did this preeminently when he stood up for the Lord against the king of Israel and his four hundred and fifty "prophets of Baal" in the presence of the oscillating people It was not the main duty of a Hebrew prophet to predict the future with accuracy. See below, p 36, n 1

[2] Jn xii 32 But, indirectly, "draw all men unto myself" implies "draw unto the light," and hence "enlighten," "clothe in light," "make (ib 36) sons of light" Comp Targ on Zech ix

THE TRANSFIGURATION AND ITS SEQUEL

purifying stream that is to "whiten" the garments of the faithful.

This truth comes later on, related as a fact and no metaphor, "One of the soldiers with a spear pierced his side, and straightway there came out blood and water[1]." The spiritual significance of the fact, however, as being one that needs to be "seen" and "believed" by those who are spiritually prepared to "see" and "believe," is at once suggested: "And he that hath seen hath borne witness, and his witness is true; and he [*i.e.* the Lord Jesus] knoweth that he saith true, that ye also may believe[2]" The importance of this spiritual fact is not seen till near the conclusion of the Johannine Epistle: "This is he that came by water and blood, Jesus Christ; not with the water only, but with the water and with the blood[3]."

§ 6   *"Beloved" in Mark and Matthew, "Chosen" in Luke*[4]

In discussing the Synoptic accounts of the Voice from heaven at Christ's baptism, it has appeared that there was a connection between Jewish thoughts about the Messiah as being (1) the

---

11—15 "ye with whom a covenant has been made *with blood*...they shall be *shining* (זהר) like blood that *shines* (זהר) on the side of the altar"

[1] Jn xix 34
[2] Jn xix 35   See *Joh Gr* 2383—4 on "*he* (ἐκεῖνος) knoweth"
[3] 1 Jn v 6   The Epistle proceeds, *ib* 7—8 "*And it is the Spirit* that beareth witness because the Spirit is the truth   For there are three that bear witness, *the Spirit*, and the water, and the blood"   In the Gospel there is a mention of "spirit" a little before the "water" and the "blood," thus, Jn xix 30 "He rested his head (*Joh Voc* 1451—8, *Joh Gr* 2644 (1), 2713) [on the Father's bosom] and delivered over *his spirit* [to the Father]"

The whole scene is so imbued with allusive mystery that it does not seem to me fanciful to suppose that John regards the Law and the Prophets as, so to speak, standing by the Cross, and attesting the Sacrifice, when he quotes (*ib* 36—7) from the Law "A bone of him shall not be broken," and from the Prophets, "They shall look on him whom they pierced"

[4] Mk ix 7, Mt xvii 5 ὁ υἱός μου ὁ ἀγαπητός, Lk ix 35 ὁ υἱός μου ὁ ἐκλελεγμένος

THE TRANSFIGURATION AND ITS SEQUEL

Son of God, (2) the Elect or Pure One of God, (3) the Purifier[1] Now, in the Transfiguration, there is again brought before us the thought of the Purifier in the term "fuller." This leads us to ask anew whether Jewish tradition recognises any connection between "son" and the notion of purifying

There is no such connection in respect of the Hebrew *ben*, "son," but there is in respect of the Aramaic *bar*, "son" *Bar*, "son," occurs in two passages of the Hebrew Scriptures. Concerning the expression in Proverbs "What, *my son?*" the Midrash says "It is not said 'What, *my son* [*in Hebrew*] (*ben*)?' but 'What, *my son* [*in Aramaic*] (*bar*)?' That means '*the precepts and warnings of the Law*,' which is called *bar* [i e. *pure or bright*]—as in the Psalm 'Kiss the *Pure* [*bar*] lest he be angry'—because all its words are *pure*[2]." Rashi's comment on Proverbs says that the mother desires her son to be "*whitened* (dealbatus)," and this word occurs (in Hebrew) in a Talmudic comment on the passage in Proverbs[3].

These traditions confirm the view that in the original the Voice from heaven mentioned neither "beloved" nor "chosen," but resembled the opening of the Epistle to the Hebrews, which contrasts God's speaking in old days through the "Prophets" with His present speaking through "a Son," or "his Son[4]." Peter desires to make three tabernacles for Jesus and the two witnesses, as if the three were on a level. There comes a corrective Voice saying, in effect, "This is [no prophet, but] *my Son*. Hearken unto Him [above all prophets]." It was desirable to shew that "*my Son*" here did not mean "one of my sons" in any sense, either angelic or human[5] This could

---

[1] See *Beginning* pp 124—7

[2] *Numb r* Wu p 214 on Prov xxxi 2, quoting Ps ii 12 as "Kusset den *Lauteren*," rep in *Lev r* Wu p 83, with "Kusset den *Auserwählten*" This shews that *bar* might be rendered "chosen" or "pure," as in Cant vi 9, 10 (see R V txt and marg).

[3] *Sanhedr* 70 b מלובן, Goldschm "hubschen," Levy ii 467 b "wohlgestalteten (*eig* weissen)"

[4] Heb 1 1—2

[5] Gesen 120 a, בן, referring to "sons" in Gen vi 2, 4, Job i 6, ii. 1, xxxviii. 7 etc On Dan iii 25 (בר) A V "the form of the fourth

21 (Mark ix 2—8)

THE TRANSFIGURATION AND ITS SEQUEL

be suggested by adding the Greek "beloved," which, in LXX, repeatedly represents the Hebrew "only," with or without "son," so as to mean "*only son*[1]." Mark, followed by Matthew, has done this. Luke has perhaps been influenced by the twofold meanings of *bar* in Hebrew and Aramaic severally. In Hebrew it is twice rendered "elect" by LXX, when applied to the "pure" or "chosen" Bride in the Song of Songs[2]. Luke has combined this with "son" ("this is my *Son, my Chosen*")

John nowhere describes a Voice from heaven as calling Jesus either "beloved Son," or "Son," or "Chosen." He would have been compelled to do this, or else to contradict the Synoptists, if he had related the baptism of Jesus by the Baptist. But he has not related it He refers to it by implication, however, in these words uttered by the Baptist, "He that sent me to baptize with water, he said unto me, Upon whomsoever thou shalt see the Spirit descending and abiding upon him, the same is *he that baptizeth in the Holy Spirit.*" Then follows a disputable passage given by R.V. thus, "And I have seen, and have borne witness that *this is the Son of God,*" where recent evidence indicates that the true reading is "*this is the Elect of God*[3]" With either reading, however, the passage seems inconsistent with what precedes[4]. Whereas we should have expected the Baptist to exclaim "I have seen *him that 'baptizeth in the Holy Spirit,*'" he exclaims, in effect, "I have seen *the Son* (or, *the Elect*) *of God*"

A reasonable explanation is that John had in view a tradition based on the Aramaic word for "son," with its suggestion of

is like *the Son of God* (בר אלהין)," the Midrash says that God sent Satan to smite Nebuchadnezzar for saying this and made him correct "his *son* (בריה)" into "his *angel*" (*Exod r* Wu p 159, sim on Cant vii. 8, Wu. p. 175). R V has "like *a son of the gods*"

[1] In Gen xxii 2, 12, 16 etc יחיד=ἀγαπητός In Judg xi 34 יחידה=μονογενής, (A) μονογενὴς ἀγαπητή

[2] Cant vi 9, 10 בר R V. "The *choice* one.. *clear* as the sun" but marg. "*pure*" in both cases.

[3] Jn i 33—4 See *Oxyr Pap* ii 7, No 208, 3rd cent, where space and facts suggest the reading ἐκλεκτός, which is also in SS. Blass gives the evidence fully and places ὁ ἐκλεκτὸς τοῦ θεοῦ in his text

[4] See *Beginning* p 124

22 (Mark ix 2—8)

THE TRANSFIGURATION AND ITS SEQUEL

the meanings "chosen," "pure," and "purifying," and that the "purifying" included the thought of "baptism."

The Fourth Evangelist does not deny that a Voice announcing the advent of a "Son" actually and objectively came from heaven, but he suggests to us that the Baptist, subjectively, did not hear it in that form. To the Baptist it came as an announcement of the "Elect of God." And the sense in which the Baptist understood this the Baptist himself expresses by "the Lamb of God," that is, the purifying daily sacrifice. This was only one aspect of the Word, but it was a baptismal aspect and characteristically emphasized by John the Baptizer. By confining himself to this subjective announcement, the Fourth Evangelist avoids arbitrating between the different versions of the objective Voice from heaven given by the Synoptists.

When a Johannine Voice from heaven, the only one in the Fourth Gospel, at last comes before us, it contains no mention of the word "Son." The word "Son" is indeed once mentioned just before it, but only in the title "Son of man"—"the hour is come that the *Son of man* should be glorified[1]." The whole of the context takes it for granted that Jesus is the Son of God, and that it is needless for a Voice from heaven, at this stage, to proclaim that truth. The truth that needed to be proclaimed was that the Father in heaven had glorified, and would glorify, His name of Father in one who was wont to call Himself Son of Man while making His disciples feel that He was Son of God. As for the uniqueness of this Sonship it is expressed at the outset of the Gospel in the Johannine term *Monogenēs*[2], which suggests, without mentioning, the Synoptic "beloved[3]." The preceding context also mentions "glory" for the first time, and suggests that the "glory" of the Father consists in giving Himself to those who are willing to "receive" Him, and that the "glory" of the Son consists in making us desirous to receive

---

[1] Jn xii 23
[2] Jn i 18, comp *ib.* 14   On *Monogenēs*, in Jn and Plato, see *Beginning* pp 28—31
[3] See p 22, n 1, above, quoting Judg xi 34 (LXX) μονογενής, (A) μονογενὴς ἀγαπητή, where "Ἄλλος" has ποθητή

THE TRANSFIGURATION AND ITS SEQUEL

this Gift, with which the Son identifies Himself; it also connects this glory of the Son and Heir with a "grace" and a "truth" that cannot be conveyed through any "law[1]"

§ 7. "*While they were coming down from the mountain he charged them,*" *in Mark*[2]

Luke omits everything that may have happened "*while they were coming down,*" and passes on at once to the time "*when they had come down*[3]." The precept to "*tell no one*" is omitted by Luke. It should be noted that Luke alone adds "*on the next

---

[1] Jn i 14—17
[2] Mk ix 9—10 (R V)

(9) And as they were coming down from the mountain, he charged them that they should tell no man what things they had seen, save when the Son of man should have risen again from the dead
(10) And they kept the saying, questioning among themselves what the rising again from the dead should mean

Mt xvii 9 (R V.)

(9) And as they were coming down from the mountain, Jesus commanded them, saying, Tell the vision to no man, until the Son of man be risen from the dead.

Lk ix 36 b—37 (R V)

(36) ...And they held their peace, and told no man in those days any of the things which they had seen
(37) And it came to pass, on the next day, when they were come down from the mountain.

[3] The interval between the Transfiguration and Christ's rejoining the nine disciples would seem to have been regarded by Mark as a short one. But if, as modern commentators suggest, the mountain was Hermon and the nine disciples remained in or near Caesarea, the rejoining would take some time Prof Swete (on Mk) says that Hermon "overlooked Caesarea," and "offered a perfect solitude," and that "one of its southern spurs became the ὄρος ἅγιον of the Gospel (2 Pet i 18)", but Dr McNeile says (on Mt xvii 3) "If the high mountain (ὄρος ἅγιον 2 Pet) was near Caesarea, it was probably Mt Hermon, some 14 miles to the north " "Fourteen miles" was a long way to go, if the sole object of going was to obtain "a perfect solitude," and the downward return, though quicker, would take several hours The hypothesis of "one of its southern spurs" diminishes the difficulty raised by "fourteen miles," but at the cost of introducing a touch of tameness into our interpretation of Mk-Mt "bringeth them *up into a high mountain*"

THE TRANSFIGURATION AND ITS SEQUEL

day" in connection with *"from the mountain."* In *Clue* it was pointed out that Luke might be explained from the Vision of Elijah where the Hebrew has "Go forth and stand *on the mountain,"* but the LXX has "Go forth *on the morrow* and stand... *on the mountain,"* apparently confusing הַר *"mountain"* with חָר part of the word for *"to-morrow,"* and combining the two renderings[1]. This can now be confirmed by a similar combination in a variation from LXX where the Hebrew has מָחָר *"to-morrow,"* but a Translator has confused this with מַהֵר *"hasten,"* and has combined the correct and the incorrect rendering (*"Hasten,* Saul, *to-morrow*... ")[2]. If this is a correct explanation, Luke may have been in some measure led to differ from Mark and Matthew by inferences arising from the clause interpreted by him as meaning "on the next day[3]"

But other questions also arise, apart from the supposition that Luke is here drawing from Hebrew sources. Luke deviates from Mark's order by placing his mention of the silence about the Vision before his mention of the descent from the mountain[4]. Such deviations would occur when an Evangelist, industriously collecting detached traditions, differed from the Evangelists that preceded him as to the order in which they were to be placed One has occurred already in the Healing of Jairus' Daughter where Luke places a precept about silence after, and Mark before, a command to give the girl food There, as here, Mark used the word "charge" This leads us to inquire into other uses of the word "charge" in Mark and their parallels, and into its use in LXX and its equivalent in Hebrew

The Marcan instances of "charge," given below with their

---

[1] *Clue* **144** *a*, quoting 1 K xix 11.

[2] 1 S xxviii 19 מָחָר, "cras," where Field gives, as the reading of "Ἄλλος," τάχυνον δέ, Σαούλ αὔριον, and adds "ni fallor, duplex versio est vocis וּמָחָר, pictae וּמַהֵר" Origen *ad loc* quotes τάχυνον αὔριον

[3] That Luke here followed a Hebrew original is indicated also by his use of ἐν τῷ with infin on which see *Son* **3333** *e—g*, *Proclam*. p 153 etc

[4] Not that Luke is inconsistent with Mark, but Luke passes over what happened *"while they were going down* (καταβαινόντων),*"* and relates what happened *"when they had come down* (κατελθόντων) *"*

25 (Mark ix 9—10)

THE TRANSFIGURATION AND ITS SEQUEL

parallels[1], reveal the following facts. With the exception of one doubtful passage in Matthew, where the disciples are said to have been "rebuked" by Jesus that they should not tell people

---

[1] Διαστέλλομαι, in W. H txt of the Gospels, occurs only in Mark, as follows —

(1) Mk v 43   Mt. om   Lk viii 55—6
(Jairus' daughter)

καὶ <u>διεστείλατο</u> αὐτοῖς πολλὰ ἵνα μηδεὶς γνοῖ τοῦτο, καὶ εἶπεν δοθῆναι αὐτῇ φαγεῖν.

καὶ διέταξεν αὐτῇ δοθῆναι φαγεῖν...ὁ δὲ παρήγγειλεν αὐτοῖς μηδενὶ εἰπεῖν τὸ γεγονός.

Here αὐτοῖς means the parents. The order of Mark is reversed in Luke.

(2) Mk vii. 36   Mt om   Lk om
(The Stammerer)

καὶ <u>διεστείλατο</u> αὐτοῖς ἵνα μηδενὶ λέγωσιν ὅσον δὲ αὐτοῖς <u>διεστέλλετο</u>, αὐτοὶ μᾶλλον περισσότερον ἐκήρυσσον

Here αὐτοῖς refers to no defined persons, but probably to "they," meaning friends of the Stammerer, implied in vii 32 "they-bring (φέρουσιν)"

(3) Mk viii 15   Mt xvi 6   Lk xii 1

καὶ <u>διεστέλλετο</u> αὐτοῖς λέγων Ὁρᾶτε, βλέπετε ἀπὸ τῆς ζύμης...

Ὁ δὲ Ἰησοῦς εἶπεν αὐτοῖς, Ὁρᾶτε καὶ προσέχετε ἀπὸ τῆς ζύμης .

Ἐν οἷς ἐπισυναχθεισῶν τῶν μυριάδων. . ἤρξατο λέγειν πρὸς τοὺς μαθητὰς αὐτοῦ πρῶτον, Προσέχετε ἑαυτοῖς ἀπὸ τῆς ζύμης....

In Mark, αὐτοῖς refers to a vague "they" implied in viii 14 "they-forgot (ἐπελάθοντο)," where parall Mt xvi 5 supplies μαθηταί.

(4) Mk ix 9—10   Mt xvii 9   Lk ix 36 b—7

(9) καὶ καταβαινόντων αὐτῶν ἐκ (marg ἀπό) τοῦ ὄρους διεστείλατο αὐτοῖς ἵνα μηδενὶ ἃ εἶδον διηγήσωνται, εἰ μὴ ὅταν ὁ υἱὸς τοῦ ἀνθρώπου ἐκ νεκρῶν ἀναστῇ.

(10) καὶ τὸν λόγον ἐκράτησαν πρὸς ἑαυτοὺς συνζητοῦντες τί ἐστιν τὸ ἐκ νεκρῶν ἀναστῆναι.

καὶ καταβαινόντων αὐτῶν ἐκ τοῦ ὄρους ἐνετείλατο αὐτοῖς ὁ Ἰησοῦς λέγων Μηδενὶ εἴπητε τὸ ὅραμα ἕως οὗ ὁ υἱὸς τοῦ ἀνθρώπου ἐκ νεκρῶν ἐγερθῇ (marg. ἀναστῇ).

(36) ...καὶ αὐτοὶ ἐσίγησαν καὶ οὐδενὶ ἀπήγγειλαν ἐν ἐκείναις ταῖς ἡμέραις οὐδὲν ὧν ἑώρακαν

(37) ἐγένετο δὲ τῇ ἑξῆς ἡμέρᾳ κατελθόντων αὐτῶν ἀπὸ τοῦ ὄρους ...

The order of Mark is again, as in (1), reversed by Luke

that He was the Christ (but some authorities in Matthew have "charged"), the word is confined, in the Gospels, to Mark. Mark uses "charge" four times (out of five) to mean an injunction of secrecy. In the first instance, "he charged them much that *no man should know this*"—i.e. the restoration to life of Jairus' daughter—it seems impossible to take the words literally since the crowd outside "knew" that the girl was dead[1]. Matthew omits the "charge" and the context. Luke has "gave command to them not to tell anyone that which had been done"—which might be strained to mean "not to talk about the details of the healing."

In the second passage (containing two instances), the Healing of the Stammerer—a miracle peculiar to Mark—the precept "that they should speak to no one [about it]" does not present the same difficulty.

In the third passage, the "charge" does not refer to keeping anything secret. It is to "beware of the leaven of the Pharisees." And the word "*charged*"—for which "warned" might be substituted—is superfluous except for emphasis, and is omitted by Matthew and by Luke[2]. In Mark and Matthew, the command to "beware of leaven" is followed by a dialogue shewing that "leaven" is metaphorically used for "doctrine." This is wholly omitted by Luke.

Διαστέλλομαι occurs in W H marg once, in Matthew, as follows, after the Confession of Peter:—

Mk viii. 30	Mt xvi 20	Lk ix 21
καὶ ἐπετίμησεν αὐτοῖς ἵνα μηδενὶ λέγωσιν περὶ αὐτοῦ.	τότε ἐπετίμησεν (W. H. marg. and Tisch. διεστείλατο) τοῖς μαθηταῖς ἵνα μηδενὶ εἴπωσιν ὅτι Αὐτός ἐστιν ὁ Χριστός.	ὁ δὲ ἐπιτιμήσας αὐτοῖς παρήγγειλεν μηδενὶ λέγειν τοῦτο

[1] Lk viii. 53 "knowing that she was dead"
[2] Mk viii 15 "charged them saying 'See, beware...'" is merely an emphatic form of "said 'Beware..'" Comp "told and warned," and Aquila's use of the Marcan διαστέλλομαι to render the Hiph. of זהר, in 2 K vi. 10 "And the king of Israel sent to the place which the man of God *told him of* and *warned* him (והזהירה)," where LXX has merely εἶπεν αὐτῷ, but Aq adds καὶ διεστείλατο αὐτῷ 2 K vi 9 contains the warning "Beware that thou pass not such a place."

(Mark ix. 9—10)

THE TRANSFIGURATION AND ITS SEQUEL

In the fourth passage, the one that follows the Transfiguration, Matthew substitutes for "charged" the word "commanded," but both describe a command of Jesus to the three disciples to tell no one what they had seen. Luke omits the command to be silent, saying merely "And they were silent, and told no man in those days[1]." Luke also omits the following verses of Mark-Matthew describing a conversation between Jesus and the disciples (during the descent from the mountain) about "rising from the dead" and about Elijah, as well as one verse peculiar to Matthew "Then the disciples understood that he spake unto them concerning John the Baptist."

Turning to Greek outside the New Testament, we find that in literary Greek, Mark's word mostly signifies separation, in the way of "distinctive" expression, "specific instructions" etc.[2] In LXX it represents several Hebrew words; but, when used in the middle as Mark uses it, it corresponds mostly to a Hebrew word that means in Daniel "shine" or "shining," but in Ezekiel and elsewhere "warn," "instruct[3]." In Exodus Jethro says to Moses "Thou shalt *expressly-teach* them[4] the statutes and the laws, and shalt shew them the way wherein they must walk, and the work that they must do." There is no suggestion of "warning" here Nor is there in the Targums, which repeat the Hebrew word (perhaps in the sense of "enlighten"); the Jerusalem Targum also amplifies the

---

[1] "*In those days*" appears to mean "When I say, '*they were silent,*' I do not mean '*always silent.*' Else, of course, the Transfiguration would not have been recorded " It would be sometimes easy to confuse the Heb *vaw* meaning "in order that" with *vaw* meaning "and," in such a sentence as "And he spake unto them *and* [accordingly] they were silent " See Gesen 254 *a*

[2] See Steph *Thes* II. 1324–5 διαστέλλω

[3] See Gesen pp 263—4 on (I) זהר "shine," quoting Dan. xii 3 "and they that make [others] wise shall *shine* as the *shining* of the firmament"; (II) זהר "warn," of which the only instance in the Pentateuch is Exod. xviii 20 But it occurs freq in Ezekiel iii 17, 18 etc , meaning "warn " Aquila renders it by διαστέλλομαι both in Exod xviii. 20 and elsewhere

[4] Exod xviii 20 זהר, LXX "testify (διαμαρτυρῇ) to them," Aq. διαστελῇ.

28 (Mark ix. 9—10)

THE TRANSFIGURATION AND ITS SEQUEL

passage so as to shew what is taught. "*Expressly-teach* (or, *enlighten*) them about the statutes and laws, make them to understand the prayer that they are to offer in the house of congregation, the manner of visiting the sick, of burying the dead, of being fruitful in doing good, and in the work and process of justice, and how to conduct themselves among the wicked[1]"

In all this, there is no suggestion of "warning" but only of the *distinctive* precepts suggested by the Hebrew word, or of the illumination suggested by its Aramaic associations. But in Ezekiel the notion of "warning" is conveyed as soon as the prophet receives the injunction to break off his dumbness of "seven days," and to begin his prophecy.—"Son of man, I have made thee a watchman unto the house of Israel, therefore hear the word at my mouth, and *warn* them from me[2]" The word is then repeated several times, and the LXX, after first rendering it "threaten," settles down to the Marcan word under consideration (which is also Aquila's rendering). The prominence thus given by LXX to this Greek word for "*charge*," in connection with the prophecies of Ezekiel whom God habitually addressed as "*son of man*," might naturally induce some early Evangelists to use it about certain utterances of Jesus the Son of Man either in the Hebrew sense of "warn" or in the later Hebrew and Aramaic sense of "illuminate"

---

[1] Levy *Ch* 1 212 *b* shews that זהר, in Aramaic, mostly implies "light" or "enlightening" The middle, "Be thou enlightened!" means "Take warning." *Mechilt* on Exod xviii 27 represents Jethro as saying to Moses, "Thou art the sun, and Aaron, thy brother, is the moon What need of the lamp with you?" This favours the view that Jews would connect *zohar* in Exodus with "enlightening" rather than with "warning" Could *zohar* be used about Christ's occasional esoteric instruction to the disciples as to healing etc.—meaning "enlighten," but seeming to Mark to mean "warn"?

[2] Ezek. iii. 17 LXX $\delta\iota\alpha\pi\epsilon\iota\lambda\eta\sigma\eta$, Aq $\delta\iota\alpha\sigma\tau\epsilon\lambda\hat{\eta}$, Sym $\pi\rho o\phi\upsilon\lambda\acute{a}\xi\epsilon\iota\varsigma$, but in *ib* 18, 20, 21 etc LXX has $\delta\iota\alpha\sigma\tau\acute{\epsilon}\lambda\lambda o\mu\alpha\iota$ In *ib* 21, "*he took warning*" נזהר is rendered by LXX "*thou didst warn him*" This suggests that Mk "*he warned them [to be silent]*" might be taken by Luke as "*they were warned,* or, *took warning [to be silent],*" that is, "*they were silent*"

The word *zohar* is popularly connected with Jewish cabbalistic doctrine that was once supposed by Christians to go back to the first or second century. It is now believed to be a production of the thirteenth century. Nevertheless the selection of such a title, meaning "splendour" or "shining," when combined with the Biblical application of the word to Moses as the Instructor or Illuminator in connection with the old Law, indicates that even the earliest of our Evangelists might be influenced by the associations of the word in those cases where he records some injunctions of secrecy or some illuminating doctrine not generally known.

In the present instance, for example, it is inconsistent with reasonable views of Luke's honesty and industry as a historian to suppose that he would altogether omit the dialogue during the descent from the mountain without good grounds for suspecting that it was not historical in detail, but was an expansion of some brief and obscure or ambiguous statement. For example, it might have been "And when they had come down from the mountain *he instructed them*, or *he warned them*, or *they took warning*, concerning the things that they had seen." What was this "instruction" or "warning"? Luke has previously given us a hint in the words "They spake concerning his departure which he was to accomplish in Jerusalem[1]." Even Matthew, though he has not inserted these words, has inserted, a little before, in the first prediction of resurrection on the third day, the words "He must depart to Jerusalem[2]."

Mark has had neither of these insertions[3]; but if we suppose him to be conflating[4] an obscure original so as to make it include a reference to the latent "departure," he must be regarded as taking "warned" in a double sense, and as combining two interpretations. One is, "Be ye warned that this vision signifies that I shall depart from you, and that I shall pass, as I said before, through three days of death to resurrection." The other interpretation assumes that Jesus "warned" the disciples

---

[1] Lk ix 31   [2] Mt xvi 21   [3] Mk viii 31
[4] On the Marcan habit of "conflation," see *Son* **3107** *k*, **3265**, **3353** (1) *a*

THE TRANSFIGURATION AND ITS SEQUEL

to "keep silence" till the fulfilment of the prediction. And here Mark inserts that the disciples "kept the saying [in mind] questioning among themselves what was the [meaning of the words] 'rise from the dead[1].'" Matthew and Luke omit this, perhaps because it might be taken to mean that the disciples questioned what was the meaning of the phrase "rising from the dead" in general. But the Marcan context shews that Mark meant "They questioned among themselves *what was the meaning of the phrase 'rise from the dead' applied to Jesus*, since they could not at that time believe that His prediction referred to His own literal death."

John intervenes twice to explain how the disciples might be said to "keep in mind" predictions of this kind and also to "question among themselves" as to their meaning. First, he represents Jesus as saying near the beginning of the Gospel "Destroy this temple and in three days I will raise it up," adding "But he spake of the temple of his body. When therefore he was raised from the dead, his disciples *remembered that he spake this*"—that is to say, they did not understand it at first, but they "kept it in mind" and understood it finally[2] Secondly, near the close of the Gospel, he represents Jesus as saying to the disciples, concerning His death and resurrection, "A little while and ye behold me no more, and again a little while and ye shall see me," whereupon "some of his disciples said to one another, What is this that he saith unto us[3]?" The very words of the questioning are here given, and Christ's subsequent explanation, namely, that He was on the point of departure. "I came forth from the Father and have come into the world. Again I leave the world and go to the Father[4]."

This is also the Johannine version of that "departure" which Luke mentions in his account of the Transfiguration as destined to be accomplished by Jesus. John therefore may

---

[1] Mk ix 10 .

[2] Jn ii 19—22 John here mentions "three days"—a phrase connected by Mark (viii 31) and Matthew (xii 40) with Christ's resurrection (comp Mk xiv 58, Mt xxvi 61 etc), but by Luke only (ii 46) with the finding of the Child Jesus in the Temple.

[3] Jn xvi 17.   [4] Jn xvi. 28

THE TRANSFIGURATION AND ITS SEQUEL

be said to intervene in order to explain Luke as well as to explain Mark. But Luke writes in his own person; Mark records, very obscurely, words that he believed to have been uttered by Christ Himself. Luke omits them. It is a fact of history that Christ's language about His resurrection was not understood by His disciples. It is an inevitable inference that they must have questioned among themselves about it. Mark says that they did this. John dramatically brings them before us in the act of doing it.

§ 8. *"How is it written?"* in Mark[1]

Two questions arise at this point. First, did Jesus use the clause "how is it written?" attributed to Him by Mark but not by the parallel Matthew? Secondly, why is the whole of

---

[1] Mk ix 11—13
(R V)
(11) And they asked him, saying, The scribes say that Elijah must first come (Or, [How is it] that the scribes say...come?)
(12) And he said unto them, Elijah indeed cometh first, and restoreth all things and how is it written of the Son of man, that he should suffer many things and be set at nought?
(13) But I say unto you, that Elijah is come, and they have also done unto him whatsoever they listed, even as it is written of him

Mt xvii 10—13
(R V.)
(10) And his disciples asked him, saying, Why then say the scribes that Elijah must first come?

(11) And he answered and said, Elijah indeed cometh, and shall restore all things:

(12) But I say unto you, that Elijah is come already, and they knew him not but did unto him whatsoever they listed Even so shall the Son of man also suffer of them
(13) Then understood the disciples that he spake unto them of John the Baptist

Lk. om
Compare Lk i 17 (R V.) And he shall go before his face in the spirit and power of Elijah. ..

32 (Mark ix. 11—13)

the context, about John the Baptist, which is inserted by Matthew, omitted by Luke and John?

There is an antecedent probability that Jesus, after the martyrdom of John the Baptist, would prepare His disciples to anticipate a similar martyrdom for Himself. Mark has recently described Jesus as proclaiming to the disciples the new Law, the Law of Life through Death, and Victory through Defeat, as foreshadowed in the prophecies of Isaiah and Hosea about "suffering many things" and being "raised up after three days"—which Jesus applied to the Son of Man[1]. If Jesus regarded John the Baptist as a Messenger of God, working in the spirit and power of Elijah, and as passing through martyrdom to glory, then the recent vision of Elijah on the mountain might lead Him to say, in reply to the question[2] whether Elijah must not first come, "For us, Elijah has 'come.' John the Baptist is our Elijah. You think he has not 'come' because he has died as a martyr. But is it not written concerning the Son of Man that he, too, should 'suffer many things' as a martyr? Elijah has 'come' and 'suffered many things' as a martyr in the same way, even as it is written *about him* [*the Son of Man*][3]." This, if taken by readers to mean "as it is written *about him* [*namely, Elijah*]," might naturally present difficulty[4]. It has been at all events altered by Matthew. But the difficulty itself, and the confused condition of the context, make it probable that Mark is recording a very early

---

[1] Mk viii 31. See *Son* 3184—5.

[2] "The question." It is a question put modestly in the form of a statement. "The scribes say [do they not?] that Elijah must first come. [What must we reply to them?]"

[3] See *Son* 3246 foll. and 3246 *d—i*, on "The 'coming' of Elijah," where it is maintained that the phrase peculiar to Mark, "as it is written of him," refers, not to John the Baptist, but to the Son of Man, like the preceding clause (also peculiar to Mark) "written of the Son of Man."

[4] Some have suggested that "written about *him*" refers to Elijah and to a quasi-martyrdom, which he endured at the hands of Jezebel. But this does not seem probable in view of the fact that he escaped from her hands and, in due course, was taken up to heaven.

THE TRANSFIGURATION AND ITS SEQUEL

tradition about some actual utterance of Jesus in which He testified to the Law of Martyrdom as applying to Himself as well as to the Baptist.

The omission of this passage by Luke and John accords with the general rule of these Evangelists to omit or alter passages that give what in their days seemed a disproportionate prominence to John the Baptist[1]. But Luke and John follow this rule in different ways, as regards the early identification of John the Baptist with Elijah Luke explains, in his account of the Baptist's birth (through the Song of Zachariah), that he is to "go before" the Messiah "in the spirit and power of Elijah," which amounts to saying "not that he *will be* Elijah, but he *will be in the character of* Elijah[2]." John introduces a direct negative uttered by the Baptist himself in reply to emissaries of the Pharisees "And they asked him, What then? Art thou Elijah? And he saith, I am not[3]."

This is a remarkable instance of Johannine freedom from conventionality. John probably knew that there were current in the first century a great number of beliefs about Elijah, and also beliefs (such as Origen argues against when dealing with the words "Elijah is come[4]") in some doctrine of *metempsychosis*, so that the words of Jesus recorded here by Mark might be taken as implying the latter doctrine. He certainly knew—if Mark's and Matthew's Gospels were important enough to attract his attention—that Jesus was reported by Mark to have said "Elijah is come," and that Matthew emphasized this ("is come *already*") and added "Then understood the disciples that he spake unto them of John the Baptist." And yet, in spite of these very ancient traditions, he does not hesitate to represent the Baptist as being expressly asked by the priests and Levites sent from Jerusalem "Art thou Elijah?" and as replying "I am not[5]." Perhaps we may suppose that

---

[1] See *Beginning* p 71, *Law* p 219
[2] Lk 1 17   [3] Jn 1 21
[4] Origen on Mt xvii. 10 foll , see also Jerome on Mt xi 14 "if ye will receive it...," which he interprets as indicating "mysticum (sermonem) "
[5] Jn 1 21

THE TRANSFIGURATION AND ITS SEQUEL

the Fourth Evangelist argued to this effect: "I know that Jesus called John 'Elijah.' And so he was, to the *Jews*. But now, to the Gentile Churches he is not 'Elijah'—who is to Gentiles merely an ancient wonderworking prophet—but a 'witness' to the Light of the World And the Baptist himself spoke of himself in this subordinate character, calling himself 'a voice[1].'"

Some further comment is demanded by the Lucan tradition about Christ's conversation with Moses and Elijah They converse about Christ's "exodus (departure)[2]." The mention of His "exodus" is followed, at no great interval, by a mention of His "*analēmpsis* (receiving up)[3]." "Exodus" is very rare, and "analēmpsis" is unique, in the New Testament. The former is appropriate to the Leader of the Exodus, Moses; the latter to the only Israelite "received up" into heaven, Elijah. These Lucan peculiarities perhaps represent Luke's rebellion against the view (adopted by Origen and Jerome)[4] that Elijah represented "the prophets"—Elijah, who could hardly be said to have uttered a word of prophecy about the Messiah or the Messianic Kingdom! It might seem to Luke that Elijah was the type of Christ's Ascension, as Moses, the deliverer of Israel from Egypt, was the type of Christ's

---

[1] This Johannine scene testifies indirectly to the historical character of the Marcan tradition about "the scribes" and the "coming" of Elijah See *Hor. Heb* on Mt. xvii 10 "It would be an infinite task to produce all the passages out of the Jewish writings concerning the expected coming of Elias"

[2] Lk. ix. 31 τὴν ἔξοδον αὐτοῦ ἣν ἤμελλεν πληροῦν ἐν Ἰερουσαλήμ It recurs only in Heb. xi. 22 τῆς ἐξόδου τῶν υἱῶν Ἰσραήλ, 2 Pet. 1 15 μετὰ τὴν ἐμὴν ἔξοδον.

[3] Lk ix. 51 ἐν τῷ συμπληροῦσθαι τὰς ἡμέρας τῆς ἀναλήμψεως αὐτοῦ Ἀνάλημψις does not occur in LXX. But Luke's language recalls 2 K ii 1 "when the Lord would take up Elijah," ἐν τῷ ἀνάγειν. Note the Hebraic ἐν τῷ in both passages (*Proclamation* p. 153)

[4] Origen *Fragm* on Lk., Lomm. v. 244 Μωυσῆς ὁ νόμος καὶ Ἠλίας ὁ προφητικὸς λόγος, Jerome *Epist*. (transl. Fremantle, p 399) *Contr Jovin* ii 15 "Although Moses and Elias were properly types of the Law and the Prophets, as is clearly witnessed by the Gospel" (Lk ix. 31).

THE TRANSFIGURATION AND ITS SEQUEL

deliverance of mankind out of darkness through His death and resurrection.

Probably, however, Moses and Elijah were associated in the vision of the Transfiguration, simply (or mainly) because they were associated in the spiritual expectations of all pious Jews, owing to the prophecy of Malachi—who is the only prophet that mentions Elijah, and who mentions him along with Moses[1]. The prominence thus afforded (or at least suggested) by Luke to Elijah, as the type of the ascending Saviour, would not be likely to commend itself to John, who frequently speaks of Jesus as "lifted up" on the Cross, and seems to prefer to think of Him thus, rather than as received up in the Chariot.

One more point remains to be mentioned. There can be hardly any doubt that "Hear ye him" in the Transfiguration is a repetition, and fulfilment, of the Deuteronomic "*Unto him shall ye hearken*," in the words of Moses: "The Lord thy God will raise up unto thee a prophet from the midst of thee, of thy brethren, like unto me; *unto him ye shall hearken*[2]" Tertullian points this out[3]. But he is not followed by Origen, Jerome, or Chrysostom in their several commentaries on the Transfiguration[4]. Those, however, who miss this allusion miss the

---

[1] Mal. iv. 4—5. *Hor Heb* on Lk ix 30 quotes *Deut r* (on Deut. x 1, Wu p 55) where God says to Moses "You two [*i e* you and Elijah] shall come together," and *Pesikt* 93 a "Moses did not die [for the just die not] but went up into the highest, to minister before God" These are late traditions, but the text of Deut xxxiv 6 "He [*i e.* God] buried him" favoured such traditions at an early date R Ismael (Rashi) declared that Moses "buried himself."

The first "prophet" mentioned in Scripture is (Gen xx. 7) Abraham And the Hebrew word does not mean primarily "one who *predicts*," but "one who *interprets*" (Gesen 611 b "spokesman...") that is to say, interprets the will of God to men.

[2] Deut xviii 15.

[3] Tertull *Adv Marc* on Lk ix 35

[4] Chrys. actually explains "Hearken unto Him" as meaning "Even if He desire to be crucified do not oppose ($\mu\grave{\eta}$ $\dot{a}\nu\tau\iota\pi\acute{\epsilon}\sigma\eta s$)," where the sing "oppose [thou]" is curiously incompatible with "hearken [ye]"

THE TRANSFIGURATION AND ITS SEQUEL

meaning of the presence of Moses, who in this vision abdicates in favour of his successor, as if saying "Thou art He concerning whom I said to Israel, *Unto Him shall ye hearken*, a prophet, 'like unto me' in bringing a Law, but surpassing me in bringing a greater Law, the Prophet above prophets, the Son proclaiming the Law of Sonship."

All this John—and John alone of the Evangelists—makes abundantly clear. His pregnant references to Moses contrast curiously with his barren references to Elijah. The latter is not mentioned except interrogatively or negatively[1]. The former is mentioned repeatedly as testifying to the Son either by express testimony or by symbolical action[2]

---

[1] Jn 1. 21 "Art thou Elijah?" *ib* 25 "if thou art neither the Christ, nor Elijah, nor yet the Prophet" This passage is introducing to the reader the technical term "the Prophet," meaning, "the Prophet of whom Moses spoke as a successor to himself."

[2] Moses is mentioned, either by the Evangelist or by Christ, as follows· Jn 1. 17 "The Law was given through *Moses*...the [gift of] grace and the [gift of] truth (*or*, the grace and the truth [that are conveyed by the Law]) came into being through *Jesus Christ*", iii 14 "Even as *Moses* lifted up the serpent in the wilderness, so... *the Son of Man*", v 45—6 "Think not that *I* shall accuse you... he that accuseth you is *Moses*...for if ye were believers in *Moses*, ye would be believers in *me, for he wrote concerning me*"; vii 19 "Did not *Moses* give (οὐ M. ἔδωκεν) *you the Law*, and [yet] none of you doeth the Law?" vii 22—3 "For this cause *hath Moses given you circumcision*—not that it is [in truth] from Moses but from the fathers—and ye.. that the Law of Moses may not be broken" This is Christ's last mention of Moses

But I have purposely deferred the difficult instance in vi 32 οὐ M ἔδωκεν ὑμῖν τὸν ἄρτον It is usual to render this (differently from vii. 19) negatively But the Johannine view of Moses is generally positive, that he does things typically, preparing the way for their realisation in Christ Perhaps, then, the meaning is "Was it not Moses who gave you the '*bread from heaven*' [*of which ye spake* (Jn vi 31)]? Yes, but my Father gives you true bread from heaven [not the rudimentary bread given by Moses]" The Jews had been just quoting complacently Ps lxxviii 24—5 "He gave them bread from heaven to eat", Jesus says, in effect, "Was it not Moses, the rudimentary shepherd of Israel, who gave you that rudimentary bread? But my Father gives you more than that"

37 (Mark ix 11—13)

CHAPTER II

"THE KINGDOM OF GOD" AND "LITTLE CHILDREN"
[Mark ix. 14—50]

§ 1   *"Little children*[1]*"*

WE are now approaching the time when Jesus will be found proclaiming to His disciples a doctrine of "receiving"—either receiving Jesus Himself or receiving the Kingdom of God. Both proclamations mention "little-children," thus:—"Whosoever receiveth one of such *little-children* in my name receiveth me," and "Whosoever shall not receive the kingdom of God as *a little-child*, he shall in no wise enter therein[2]."

These utterances will come before us in their order. But there intervenes the Healing of the Lunatic Child. And here the question arises—perhaps of small importance but worth noting—why Matthew and Luke substitute "*child* (or, *boy*)," *pais*, for the term "*little-child*," *paidion*, used by Mark[3]. A reasonable reply is that Mark himself tells us that the boy had been subject to fits "from the-time-when-he-was-*a-little-child*[4]" He had been a *paidion*, now he was a *pais*. But this only shifts the question from Matthew-Luke to Mark:—"Why did Mark use *paidion* when he ought to have used *pais*?" Turning over Mark's short Gospel we note that it uses *paidion* twice as often as Luke does (apart from Luke's Introduction)[5].

---

[1] In this section "little-child" will be used invariably to represent παιδίον.

[2] Mk ix 37, x 15

[3] Mk ix 24, Mt xvii 18, Lk ix 42

[4] Mk ix 21 ἐκ παιδιόθεν

[5] Mk (12), Lk 1 59—ii 40, about the child John and the child Jesus (7), later on (6)

"THE KINGDOM OF GOD"

This leads us to ask whether Luke had any special reason for avoiding the word as far as possible and Mark for using it.

Luke's reason for avoiding it may have been that *paidion* conveyed to him the same notion of simple ignorance that Paul intended to convey to the Corinthians when he wrote, "Brethren, be not *little-children* in your minds[1]," which is also the notion that it conveyed to Philo, who dilates on the application of the term to Ishmael[2] This, too, characterizes the Epictetian use of the term[3] It is perhaps significant that Hermas never uses the word. Instead of *paidion* Luke uses, on one occasion, the word "babe[4]"

It is more difficult to say why Mark uses *paidion* so freely in his descriptions of healing, before he comes to Christ's doctrine of "little-children[5]" But the following facts may help us to a reasonable hypothesis. In LXX, *paidion* is for the most part loosely used for Hebrew "son," "infant," and "lad"—nearly ninety times But it is once used, in Isaiah's prophecy of the Suffering Servant, to represent a Hebrew word forms of which mean, with about equal frequency, "*sucking-child*" or "*sucker [of a tree]*"·—"He grew up before him as a *tender plant*," where Aquila and Theodotion have "*suckling*," a term often applied in later Hebrew to "pupils" at school and applicable to Jesus at first as the "pupil" of John the Baptist[6]

---

[1] 1 Cor xiv 20, followed by "On the other hand (ἀλλὰ) in malice be infants (νηπιάζετε) But in [your] minds (ταῖς δὲ φρεσὶν, i e in effect "brains") become full-grown [men] (τέλειοι γίνεσθε)" This is the only mention of παιδίον in the Pauline Epistles

[2] Philo 1 393—4

[3] In Epictetus, children are to be kindly treated and occasionally humoured (1 29 31), though not to be spoiled and pampered. But I have not found an instance where a child is taken as the type of simple truthfulness, or of some virtue to be imitated.

[4] Lk. xviii 15 βρέφη, parall Mk x 13, Mt. xix 13 παιδία

[5] Mk v 39, 40 (*bis*), 41, vii 28 "from the crumbs of the little-children (τῶν παιδίων)" (Mt xv 27 "from the crumbs that fall from the table of their masters (τῶν κυρίων αὐτῶν))," vii 30 (Mt xv 28 ἡ θυγάτηρ αὐτῆς), ix 24 (Mt xvii 18, Lk ix 42 παῖς)

[6] Is liii 2, on which see *Son* **3519** *e* and *Notes* **2998** (xlix *a*)

"THE KINGDOM OF GOD"

In the Apostolic Fathers, almost the only instance of *paidion* in the singular is in Clement of Rome, quoting from this prophecy of Isaiah[1]. Barnabas uses the word once in the singular, but thrice in the plural First, he connects it with the land of "milk and honey," and with a "reshaping" of man Perhaps this "reshaping" implies regenerating as a babe at the breast, but he does not mention the word "*suckling*[2]." Later on, he connects *paidia* (pl.) with those who "sprinkle for remission of sins[3]." These are all the instances of *paidion* in the Apostolic Fathers.

In the early Apologists, *paidion* is practically confined to Justin Martyr[4] He uses it nearly thirty times, but almost

---

[1] Clem Rom § 16 quoting Is liii 2 ἀνηγγείλαμεν ἐναντίον αὐτοῦ ὡς παιδίον, ὡς ῥίζα ἐν γῇ διψώσῃ This when unpunctuated would mean "We made announcement before him as a *little-child* as a root in the dry ground …" Justin Martyr (*Tryph* § 42) takes this as meaning "We, *i e* the Church of Christ, like a [weak or simple] *child* made announcement . ." And Origen (*Comm Rom* viii 5, Lomm vii 219) seems to take it similarly "Annuntiavimus *sicut puer* ante ipsum, sicut radix in terra sitienti," as though the Apostles complained of the failure of their "announcement" Jerome says "LXX transtulerunt ἠγγείλαμεν ὡς παιδίον ἐναντίον αὐτοῦ, *i e* Annuntiavimus sicut *parvulum* (not, *parvulus*) coram eo," without explanation

[2] Barn vi 8—9 "The land of milk and honey" appears to represent Jesus To enter into that land is to be "reshaped (ἀναπλάσσεσθαι)," by faith in Jesus *ib* 11 "Since therefore, having renewed (ἀνακαινίσας) (? ἀνεκαίνισεν) us by the remission of our sins, He made us [to be] a new type, so as to have the soul of *little-children* (παιδίων) inasmuch as He reshapes us (ἀναπλάσσοντος αὐτοῦ ἡμᾶς)" Later on, it is said (vi 17) "Why, then, the milk and the honey? Because at first the *little-child* is kept alive (ζωοποιεῖται) by honey [and] then by milk" In Numb xiv 3—31 the men of Israel reject the land of milk and honey, and God says "your *little ones* (παιδία), which ye said would be a prey, them will I bring in" But there the Heb is טף

[3] In Barn viii 1, where Jesus is described as typified by the Red Heifer, "the men in whom sins are full-grown (τοὺς ἄνδρας ἐν οἷς εἰσὶν ἁμαρτίαι τέλειαι)" who slay the heifer, are contrasted with "the little-children (τὰ παιδία (*bis*))" who collect the ashes for the purpose of purifying the people

[4] The only exception is Tatian §§ 33—4 (*bis*) about some mythological birth

40 (Mark ix. 14—29)

AND "LITTLE CHILDREN"

always in quoting or alluding to quotation[1]. He regards it as a name of the Messiah. But he does not deduce this from Isaiah's prophecy about the Suffering Servant There, being misled by LXX, he regards *the Church as being "as a little-child"* in its "announcement" of the Gospel[2]. The Messianic name he deduces from the prophecy (LXX) "Unto us a *little-child is born*," where the LXX and Aquila have *paidion*[3] Justin quotes this in his Apology[4] In his Dialogue, he does not quote this phrase, but alludes to it when he says that the Messiah is "King, and Priest, and God, and Lord, and Angel, and Man, and Captain, and Stone, and a *Little-Child being born*[5]"

These facts, while shewing the variety of forms in which Christ's Doctrine of Little Children might pass from Jewish into Greek vocabulary, leave it still an open question what word or words Jesus used when He spoke of them But there is an

---

[1] The instances in § 42 and § 84 allude to prophecy Justin refers mostly to Isaiah, or to the Introduction in Matthew Perhaps the only use of παιδίον in his own name is *Tryph* § 103 "the Herod that killed the *little-children* (παιδία) in Bethlehem" (Mt 11 16 τοὺς παῖδας τοὺς ἐν B) With three exceptions it is singular.

[2] His comment on "as a little-child" is of a Pauline character: *Tryph* § 42 'It signifies that the wicked became subject to Him .. and that all have become as one little-child Such a thing as you may witness in the body although the members are enumerated as many, all are called *one*, and are a *body* For, indeed, a commonwealth and a church, though many individuals in number, are in fact as one creation (ὡς ἐν πρᾶγμα) .. "

[3] Is ix. 6 "Unto us a child is born, unto us a son is given " The repetition of ילד as noun and verb could not be expressed except by γέννημα ἐγεννήθη LXX and Aq have παιδίον ἐγεννήθη, Sym νεανίας ἐγεννήθη

[4] *Apol* § 35 παιδίον ἐγεννήθη ἡμῖν καὶ νεανίσκος (Heb "son," LXX υἱός) ἡμῖν ἀπεδόθη. He takes "the government shall be on his shoulders (*sic*)" as referring to the Cross Justin seems to combine LXX παιδίον with another reading like that of Sym , νεανίας, and to omit υἱός

[5] *Tryph* § 34 "a little-child being born (παιδίον γεννώμενον)," perhaps "one that is born as a little-child " He does not quote Is ix 6 exc in § 76 "Isaiah calls Him the angel of mighty counsel '

"THE KINGDOM OF GOD"

antecedent probability that He would sometimes use a word that suggested the dependence of the child on the mother for its food. This we might gather from the prayer: "I thank thee, O Father, Lord of heaven and earth, that thou hast hidden these things from the wise and prudent and hast revealed them unto *babes*," when taken along with Christ's quotation from the eighth Psalm "Out of the mouth of *babes* and sucklings hast thou perfected praise[1]" This Hebrew word for "babe"—besides that it closely resembles, and is derived by many from, a rare Hebrew word meaning "suck[2]"—is also often connected (as in the eighth Psalm) with the comparatively frequent Hebrew word that regularly means "suck [at the breast][3]."

This latter Hebrew word, *yânak*, is more common in Aramaic than in Hebrew[4]. And in Aramaic and late Hebrew it frequently has a metaphorical meaning as in the Targum on Solomon's Song "And in that day King Messiah shall be revealed to the congregation of Israel, and the sons of Israel shall say unto Him, 'Come, be thou our Brother, and let us go up to Jerusalem and we will *suck* with thee the ordinances of the Law even as *a suckling sucks* the breasts of its mother[5].'" The thought goes back to what is almost the only mention of

---

[1] Mt xi 25, Lk x 21, Mt xxi 16, quoting Ps viii 2

[2] Strong's Concordance derives עוֹלֵל, or עֹלֵל, "babe," from עוּל, a rare word meaning "give suck," and "sucking child," but Gesen 760 *b* prefers a different derivation (comp *ib* 732 *a*) Rashi (on Ps viii 2) takes it as meaning "educati in inquinamento" See Taylor's *Aboth* p 97 on "The Ages of Man," where a cynical view is taken of the descent of man from "king" to "ape" But there is a reservation "A son of Torah, like David, is a king, though old" See Wagenseil's *Sota* p. 76

[3] See Gesen 413, יָנַק, comp *ib* 760 *b*

[4] In Gen xxxiii 13, 14 Onk twice renders יֶלֶד—"infant" or "newly born child"—by יָנַק In Is lxv 20 עוּל "suckling," and in Job xix 18 עֲוִילִים "boys," Targ. has יָנַק. See also Levy *Ch.* i 338 quoting, *inter alia*, 1 K iii 7 "ego *puer* (נַעַר) parvus (קָטֹן)," Targ. "ego *lactens* (יָנִיק) parvus (זְעֵיר)," where Walton rightly substitutes "puer" for "lactens" since the literal rendering would not express the meaning.

[5] See Targum on Cant viii 1

42 (Mark ix. 14—29)

the "*sucking-child*" in the Law[1], where Moses disclaims the power of acting as the mother or nurse of Israel: "Have I brought them forth that thou shouldest say unto me, Carry them in thy bosom as the nursing-father carrieth the *sucking-child*[2]?"—a thought repeated in Isaiah, where God says to the remnant of Israel "Hearken unto me, O house of Jacob, and all the remnant of the house of Israel, which have been borne [by me] from the belly, which have been carried from the womb[3]."

No other word for "child" conveys, so clearly as this, the notion of constant dependence on the parents. There is perhaps something slightly repellent in the fact that it seems to give to the Father the part of the Mother. But the conception of God as having attributes of a mother[4] is elsewhere implied in Hebrew Scriptures. And this conception—of the child on the mother's breast or freshly weaned from it—accords with the saying of the Psalmist, which could hardly fail to be in our Lord's mind when He connected His doctrine of Childhood with precepts of humility: "Lord, my heart is not haughty ...I have stilled and quieted my soul like a weaned child with his mother. My soul is with me like a weaned child. O Israel, hope in the Lord[5]...." Such a spontaneous and clinging dependence on the Mother or Father for spiritual food and spiritual hope is at the opposite pole from a "voluntary humility[6]" that makes a man abase himself before God, as before a Master, in order to secure immunity from the punishment due for the infraction of rules.

In view of this collective evidence as to the Jewish traditions about "the sucking-child," it would be unwise to emphasize

---

[1] The only other, in the Law, is Deut xxxii 25 "*The suckling* with the man of gray hairs (Gesen 413 *a*)"

[2] Numb xi 12   [3] Is xlvi 3

[4] See *Son* **3426, 3502**, comp **3506**

[5] Ps cxxxi 1—3. One of the comments in *Tehillim* ad loc represents God as saying to David, "Thou hast made thyself like the *sucking child*. By thy life! As there is no sin in the *sucking child*, so is there also no sin in thee"

[6] Col ii 18

"THE KINGDOM OF GOD"

as being unique, and yet still more unwise to neglect, Isaiah's use of the term in the prophecy of the Suffering Servant as accepted by Aquila and Theodotion, "He shall go up before him as a *sucking-child*" The word may here mean one that sucks truth; but it may also mean the scion of a royal house that has been cut down like a felled tree[1]. The only other instance of the participial noun formed from *yânak* in Isaiah closely follows the prediction "There shall come forth *a shoot out of the stock* of Jesse, and a *branch out of his roots* shall bear fruit"; it is in a passage predicting a universal peace when "*The sucking-child* shall play on the hole of the asp, and the weaned child shall put his hand on the basilisk's den[2]"

§ 2. "*Little children*," *in the Fourth Gospel*

This conception of "a little child" as a "*suckling*" must be distinguished from that which is indicated in contrasts between "the great [child]" and "the little [child]" in such phrases as "the great [child] shall serve the little [child]," meaning "the *elder* shall serve the *younger*." Such a contrast plays a part, and verbally rather a large part, in the doctrine of the Synoptic Gospels, where Christ's doctrine deprecates ambition and pride of place. But the Fourth Gospel cautions us against being misled by these negative deprecations into supposing that the way to become like God is to refuse to be "great." Though it scarcely mentions the word "little-child," and nowhere mentions "sucking-child," yet it represents the Father as being "declared" to us by "the only begotten Son, who is *in the bosom of the Father*," and it represents "the disciple that beareth witness" to the Son by writing the Gospel as being

---

[1] On Is liii 2, Ibn Ezra says (*The Jewish Interpreters of Isaiah* liii p 43) "R Sa'adyah interprets the whole Parashah of Jeremiah... he 'came up before him *like a sucker*,' for when he began to prophesy *he was a youth*," ib p 64 (Jacob ben Reuben) "*came up like a sucker before him to suck in his knowledge*" The Servant may be regarded (1) as a sucker springing from the root of a felled tree, the House of David (or from captive Israel) and also (2) as a Disciple of Truth

[2] Is xi 1—8   Gesen 413 gives יוֹנֵק as "suckling" in Is xi 8 and often, but as "sapling (*sucker*)" uniquely in Is liii 2

AND "LITTLE CHILDREN"

the same that "reclined in *the bosom of Jesus*[1]." Indirectly, it expresses the constant dependence of the Son on the Father, and that of the disciples on the Son, far more forcibly than we find it expressed by the Synoptists.

In this Gospel Jesus mentions "little-child" only twice. On the first occasion, the term is typical, as in the Prophets, of the promise and joy of a home, as coming through sorrow: "The woman, when she is bringing forth, hath sorrow because her hour is come, but when she hath given birth to *the little-child*, she remembereth no more the anguish, because of the joy that a human being is born into the world[2]." Epictetus, typically, bids us beware of imitating the Beast that is in us so as to destroy "the Human Being" that is in us[3]. The Johannine passage, typically, speaks of "the little-child," and of its being "born" (within us) somewhat as Justin mentions "*the little-child being born*," along with King, and Stone, and

---

[1] Jn 1 18, xiii 23, referred to in xxi 20 "the disciple whom Jesus loved.. who also leaned back on his breast at the supper"
See *Light* 3814 *l—o* on "The Holy Milk," and 3817 *a* foll "Clement of Alexandria on 'the Babe,'" where it is said (3817 *c*) "The Odes of Solomon shew no trace of caution in using the most exuberant language about 'babes' and 'milk' and the 'breasts' of God as the Nursing Father Clement on the contrary passes (108—9) into a long defence of the term 'babes,' in order to shew that it does not imply a preference for folly, and that it is not inconsistent with the Pauline doctrine of 'the full-grown man'" John, in the opening of his Gospel, suggests the thought of Prov viii 30 (R V. "master-workman," Aq $\tau\iota\theta\eta\nu o\nu\mu\acute{\epsilon}\nu\eta$) which the Midrash on Gen 1 1 (Wu p 1), in one of its traditions, connects with Numb xi 12 "nursing-father" Instead of "milk" the Fourth Gospel substitutes the "blood" of the Son, which is typified by the wine at Cana (comp Is lv 1 "buy wine and milk without money")

[2] Cramer (on Jn xvi 21, p 364) prints as from Ammonius $\tau\alpha\acute{\upsilon}\tau\eta$ $\delta\grave{\epsilon}$ $\tau\hat{\eta}$ $\pi\alpha\rho\alpha\beta o\lambda\hat{\eta}$ $\kappa\alpha\grave{\iota}$ $o\acute{\iota}$ $\pi\rho o\phi\hat{\eta}\tau\alpha\iota$ $\kappa\acute{\epsilon}\chi\rho\eta\nu\tau\alpha\iota$ $\sigma\upsilon\nu\epsilon\chi\hat{\omega}s$ $\tau\hat{\eta}$ $\upsilon\pi\epsilon\rho\beta o\lambda\hat{\eta}$ $\tau\hat{\omega}\nu$ $\dot{\omega}\delta\acute{\iota}\nu\omega\nu$ $\tau\grave{\eta}\nu$ $\dot{\alpha}\theta\upsilon\mu\acute{\iota}\alpha\nu$ $\pi\alpha\rho\alpha\beta\acute{\alpha}\lambda\lambda o\nu\tau\epsilon s$. On $\dot{\omega}\delta\hat{\iota}\nu\epsilon s$ in the Synoptists see Mk xiii 8, Mt xxiv 8

[3] Epict ii 9 3 ὁ ἄνθρωπος, as the type of humanity In Jn xvi 21 there is very probably an allusion to the birth (*Son* 3414 (ii) *d*) of Isaac, i e "Laughter" But that does not exclude the thought of Man in general

45 (Mark ix, 14—29)

other titles of the Messiah[1]. On the second occasion, Jesus addresses the disciples as "little-children" in very peculiar circumstances. He has been already raised from the dead and already recognised by them. Yet now, after this recognition, He stands unrecognised for the moment on the shore of Tiberias. They have been toiling all night in their fishing-boat, but to no purpose, and Jesus, who knows this, says to them "Little-children, you have [I think] caught nothing to eat[2]?" This is the passage placed by Clement of Alexandria at the very beginning of his long discourse on the *paidia* and *paides* (the "little-children" and the "children") of Scripture[3] He draws attention to the fact that Jesus calls them "children" although they are "already in the position of recognised disciples[4]." Then he goes on to quote passages from the New and the Old Testament, and from the latter (almost immediately) he quotes the words of Isaiah "Behold, I, and the little-children that God hath given to me[5]."

But these last words are also quoted in the Epistle to the Hebrews and applied, not to the Mother, the Church of Spiritual Israel, but to Jesus, who speaks of the redeemed whom He has "sanctified," first, as His "brethren," but secondly, as His

---

[1] *Tryph* § 34, see above, p 41 The only previous Johannine mention of παιδίον is in Jn iv. 49, where, in reply to Christ's words "Except ye see signs and wonders ye will in no wise believe," the nobleman simply says "Sir, come down ere my *little-child* die." Jesus, presumably taking this as a proof of belief, says at once "Go thy way, thy son liveth."

[2] Jn xxi. 5 παιδία, μή τι προσφάγιον ἔχετε, See *Joh Gr* **2703** (2) "The Lord does not ask for information. He *knew that the disciples had caught no fish and that it was not possible for them to have caught fish* because they had been toiling without Him in the 'night' of spiritual darkness and had not cast the net on the 'right side' of the ship "

[3] Clem. Alex. 104 foll, on which see *Light* **3817** *a—i*.

[4] Τοὺς ἤδη ἐν ἕξει τῶν γνωρίμων παῖδας προσειπών. On γνωρίμων see *Introd*. p 17 n

[5] The passages are quoted in this order (104—5) Jn xxi 4—5, Mt. xix. 14, xviii. 3, xxi. 9, xxi 16, comp. Ps. viii 2, Jn xiii 33 (τεκνία, Clem Alex reads παιδία), Mt xi 16, 17, Ps cxiii. 1, Is. viii 18 (quoted in Heb. ii. 13).

AND "LITTLE CHILDREN"

"little-children" The reason is, that "both he that sanctifieth and they that are sanctified are all from one [Father]." Hence Jesus is described as saying, not only "I will declare thy name unto my brethren" but also "Behold, I and *the little-children* that God hath given to me[1]." The Epistle—though it does not expressly say it as Clement does—assumes that Jesus is the *Paidion* or "Little-Child," and that He is speaking of the other *paidia* or "little-children," as being God's "gift" to Him. This gives us a clue to the meaning of the very common Johannine phrase, denoting the redeemed, or the Church—"*all that thou hast given me*" or "*all that thou hast given him*" —repeatedly uttered by the Son to the Father[2]. It is uttered by the *Paidion*, or "little-child" of prophecy, speaking about the *paidia*, or "little-children" of prophecy, who are at once His "brethren" and His "little-children"

All these Greek details, in which the Jewish *word* "sucking-child" finds little or no place, must not prevent us from recognising the original Jewish *thought* as being the centre round which Synoptic and Johannine traditions alike revolve, and as having been in our Lord's mind persistently, not only when He spoke of "babes" or of "babes and sucklings," but also when He spoke of "the pure in heart" and the little ones that "behold the face of the Father in heaven[3]."

---

[1] Heb ii 11—13
[2] See *Joh Gr* 2422, 2740—4.
[3] In the Johannine Epistle παιδία occurs twice certainly 1 Jn ii 13, 18, and once doubtfully iii 7 τεκνία (marg παιδία) μηδεὶς πλανάτω ὑμᾶς Probably the writer is at first distinguishing "beginners in the faith," παιδία, from "fathers" and "young men" But perhaps he may also include the suggestion that all those whom he addresses may be regarded in these three aspects

The Acts of John (§ 1) begins with a statement of the perplexity caused by the assertion of Drusiana, "To me the Lord like (ὡς) John [? 'as also to John,' the MS has ἰωάννη] appeared in the tomb (ἐν τῷ μνήματι), and like (ὡς) a young man (νεανίσκος)." John replies that the Lord did actually appear in various forms (§ 2) *e.g.* to James as a παιδίον, but to John simultaneously as an ἀνήρ, and soon afterwards to John as an elderly man, but to James as a freshly-bearded young man (νεανίσκος) On νεανίσκος see Justin M *Apol* § 35

"THE KINGDOM OF GOD"

§ 3. *The "little-child" with the "dumb and deaf spirit," in Mark¹*

Almost all the traditions peculiar to Mark in this exorcistic narrative are omitted by John. The omissions are in accordance

---

quoted above, p 41, n. 4. All these legends may have arisen from attempts to reconcile the LXX prophecies about Jesus as the παιδίον with the feeling that He was the Perfect Man, the Bridegroom of the Church.

¹ In the following passage R V. renders παιδίον by "child" in Mk ix. 24. But in Mk ix. 36, 37 its rendering is "little child."

Mk ix 14—29 (R.V)	Mt. xvii 14—21 (R.V)	Lk. ix 37—43, xvii 6 (R.V.)
(14) And when they came to the disciples, they saw a great multitude about them, and scribes questioning with them.	(14) And when they were come to the multitude,	(ix. 37) And it came to pass, on the next day, when they were come down from the mountain, a great multitude met him
(15) And straightway all the multitude, when they saw him, were greatly amazed, and running to him saluted him.		
(16) And he asked them, What question ye with them?	there came to him a man, kneeling to him, and saying,	(38) And behold, a man from the multitude cried, saying, Master (*or*, Teacher), I beseech thee to look upon my son, for he is mine only child:
(17) And one of the multitude answered him, Master (*or*, Teacher), I brought unto thee my son, which hath a dumb spirit,	(15) Lord, have mercy on my son for he is epileptic, and suffereth grievously· for oft-times he falleth into the fire, and oft-times into the water	
(18) And wheresoever it taketh him, it dasheth him down (*or*, rendeth him) and he foameth, and grindeth his teeth, and pineth away and I spake to thy disciples that they should cast it out; and they were not able		(39) And behold, a spirit taketh him, and he suddenly crieth out, and it teareth (*or*, convulseth) him that he foameth, and it hardly departeth from him, bruising him sorely
	(16) And I brought him to thy disciples, and they could not cure him.	(40) And I besought thy disciples to cast it out, and they could not

AND "LITTLE CHILDREN"

with what may be called the regular exceptions to the Rule of Johannine Intervention. John never describes an exorcism

Mk ix. 14—29 (R V) *contd*	Mt. xvii. 14—21 (R.V) *contd*.	Lk. ix 37—43, xvii 6 (R.V) *contd*.
(19) And he answereth them and saith, O faithless generation, how long shall I be with you? how long shall I bear with you? bring him unto me	(17) And Jesus answered and said, O faithless and perverse generation, how long shall I be with you? how long shall I bear with you? bring him hither to me	(41) And Jesus answered and said, O faithless and perverse generation, how long shall I be with you, and bear with you? bring hither thy son
(20) And they brought him unto him and when he saw him, straightway the spirit tare (*or*, convulsed) him grievously, and he fell on the ground, and wallowed foaming		(42) And as he was yet a coming, the devil dashed him down (*or*, rent him), and tare (*or*, convulsed) [him] grievously.
(21) And he asked his father, How long time is it since this hath come unto him? And he said, From a child		
(22) And ofttimes it hath cast him both into the fire and into the waters, to destroy him but if thou canst do anything, have compassion on us, and help us	(15) ...for ofttimes he falleth into the fire and oft-times into the water	
(23) And Jesus said unto him, If thou canst! All things are possible to him that believeth.		
(24) Straightway the father of the child cried out, and said (*many anc auth. add* with tears), I believe, help thou mine unbelief		
(25) And when Jesus saw that a multitude came running		

"THE KINGDOM OF GOD"

or refers to one   Also he never mentions the words "dumb" and "deaf"—both of which are here inserted by Mark but omitted by Matthew and Luke   If therefore the reader asks what is the object of printing the passages below in full, the answer is that it is partly in order that he may perceive the

Mk ix. 14—29 (R.V) *contd.*	Mt xvii 14—21 (R V) *contd*	Lk ix 37—43, xvii 6 (R.V) *contd.*
together, he rebuked the unclean spirit, saying unto him, Thou dumb and deaf spirit, I command thee, come out of him, and enter no more into him	(18) And Jesus rebuked him, and the devil went out from him and the boy was cured from that hour	But Jesus rebuked the unclean spirit, and healed the boy, and gave him back to his father
(26) And having cried out, and torn (*or,* convulsed) him much, he came out and [the child] became as one dead, insomuch that the more part said, He is dead		
(27) But Jesus took him by the hand, and raised him up, and he arose		(43) And they were all astonished at the majesty of God ...
(28) And when he was come into the house, his disciples asked him privately, [saying], We could not cast it out (*or,* [How is it] that we could not cast it out?)	(19) Then came the disciples to Jesus apart, and said, Why could not we cast it out?	
(29) And he said unto them, This kind can come out by nothing, save by prayer (*many anc. auth add* and fasting)	(20) And he saith unto them, Because of your little faith for verily I say unto you, If ye have faith as a grain of mustard-seed, ye shall say unto this mountain, Remove hence to yonder place, and it shall remove, and nothing shall be impossible unto you	(xvii 6) And the Lord said, If ye have faith as a grain of mustard-seed, ye would say unto this sycamine-tree, Be thou rooted up, and be thou planted in the sea, and it would have obeyed you
	(21) [*Many authorities, some ancient, insert* But this kind goeth not out save by prayer and fasting]	

AND "LITTLE CHILDREN"

kind of Marcan tradition that John regularly refrains from inserting in any form, even when Luke omits it

But a second object is to avoid the appearance of suppressing any Marcan traditions that may seem to break the Johannine Rule For example, there is the statement that the multitude, when they saw Jesus descending from the mountain, "were greatly amazed, and running to him, saluted him[1]." There are also some words of Jesus about the power of belief ("all things are possible to him that believeth") and of prayer ("this kind can come out by nothing save by prayer[2]").

The words of Jesus are more important than the narrative of events and will receive separate consideration, but the Marcan clause about "amazement" may be dealt with at once On a previous occasion Mark, followed by Luke, emphasized the astonishment produced by Jesus on the multitude by His exorcistic power[3]. Here and later on, in order to express the feeling produced by His personal presence or utterances, he employs forms of a word used by Plutarch to mean something almost amounting to dementia[4] After the descent from the Mount of Transfiguration it is conceivable that Jesus was regarded by Mark as retaining traces of a divine brightness that caused "amazement" amounting to terror But this might seem to some inconsistent with their "running to him and saluting him " Victor distinguishes between the scribes to whom Jesus said "What question ye?" and who could not have seen His glory, and the multitude who did see it and were attracted by it. But such a distinction only shews that he found Mark's text difficult and that Matthew and Luke may have condensed it because of its difficulty.

---

[1] Mk ix 15 [2] Mk ix 23, 29
[3] Mk i 26 ἐθαμβήθησαν, Lk iv 36 θάμβος
[4] Mk ix 15 ἐξεθαμβήθησαν, x 32 ἐθαμβοῦντο Mk x 24 ἐθαμβοῦντο refers to "amazement" at Christ's words about "a rich man "
See Steph *Thes* quoting Plut *Vit* 273 C θαμβοῦντι with παραπεπληγμένῳ τὸν λογισμόν and *Vit* 729 E—F βλαπτομένῳ τὴν γνώμην ἐοικὼς [ἢ διὰ θείας ἥττης τεθαμβημένος]. In LXX, θαμβέω expresses alarm, panic, terror, but not reverent fear Goodspeed gives only ἔκθαμβος in Herm *Vis* iii 1 5, of awe inspired by a vision Θαμβέω and θάμβος are not in Epictetus

"THE KINGDOM OF GOD"

Not improbably the original account has been confused and distorted by conflation[1]. But we cannot thus explain the words peculiar to Mark later on, where, after the phrase "they were going up to Jerusalem"—common to the Three —Mark alone has "And Jesus was going before them, and *they were amazed*, and they that followed were afraid[2]" The context of these words indicates that Mark again regards Christ's visible form as suffused with the glory of the impending sacrifice in Jerusalem in such a way that even the multitudes outside the circle of His disciples were "afraid," while the disciples themselves were "amazed." Such a notion—or at all events the emphasizing of such a notion—appears to be deprecated by John all through his Gospel. Not only does he habitually associate the "glorifying" of Jesus with the Crucifixion, but also, when he says in his Prologue "we beheld his glory," he separates the conception from that of a glory that "amazes" by adding "glory as of the only begotten from the Father, full of grace and truth."

Probably John is to be regarded, not as intervening with reference to this Marcan passage in particular, but as having in view all Mark's traditions about the "amazement" caused by Christ's personal presence, and all the Synoptic narratives of the Transfiguration, and the general views of Christians in

---

[1] This is suggested by the Marcan repetition of "*running together*," when compared with Matthew's account. The prominence given by Matthew to "*a man*," and the fact that Mark calls him "*one of the multitude*," and adds (what Matthew does not add) "*a great multitude*," and "*all the multitude*," might be explained by the Hebrew phrase "*the multitude as one man*," thus "And behold, when he *approached, the multitude as one man* ran to him" "As one man" meant "*all*" or "*altogether*" Mark took it so here (comp. also Mk ix 25 "a *multitude* came running *together*") But Matthew has mistaken this as meaning "*When he approached the multitude, one man,* i e *a certain man,* ran to him." Mark seems to have conflated it as two statements. Heb כאחד, "as one [man]" = ὁμοῦ (A) Ezr ii 64, ἐπὶ τὸ αὐτό Eccles xi 6, ἅμα Is lxv 25, ἕως εἰς Ezr vi 20, and is left untranslated in Ezr iii 9

[2] Mk x. 32, parall. Mt. xx 17 and comp Lk xviii 31 (and perhaps Lk. xix 28).

(Mark ix. 14—29)

the first century concerning the nature of the awe or reverence —in Scripture commonly called "fear"—that man should feel toward God. John subordinates, almost to excess, this necessary and not ignoble "fear" which the Hebrew Scriptures emphasize and which some Jewish traditions over-emphasize. Perhaps he assumes its existence in the feelings of awe and reverent admiration with which—as is suggested in the above-quoted Prologue —we are to behold the "glory" of the Only-begotten "full of grace and truth[1]." In his Epistle John goes so far as to say "Perfect love casteth out fear;...he that feareth hath not [yet] been made perfect in love[2]" Only once in his Gospel does he represent Jesus as using the word, and that is when the disciples, in the storm on the sea, think their approaching Saviour to be a phantom Then Jesus says, "It is I, *fear not*[3]." Probably "It is I" meant more in Greek than it seems to mean in English Its literal meaning is I AM, and all pious readers of the Scriptures, in Hebrew or Greek, knew what that meant, or rather, how much more it meant than they could hope at present to apprehend For them it meant "I am the Eternal"; for the Fourth Evangelist it meant "I am the Eternal Love."

§ 4   "*All things are possible to him that believeth,*" *in Mark*[4]

The omission of these words by Matthew and Luke must be classified with the omission of somewhat similar words by Luke alone in a later passage, the Withering of the Fig-tree, where Matthew follows Mark Those will be discussed in detail, more conveniently, there But we may briefly state here reasons for thinking that John intervenes

The Synoptists differ as to things "possible" Mark is not alone in having, later on, "*All things are possible* with God[5],"

---

[1] Jn i 14   [2] 1 Jn iv 18   [3] Jn vi 20   [4] Mk ix 23
[5] Mk x 27 πάντα γὰρ δυνατὰ παρὰ [τῷ] θεῷ W H print this as a quotation and refer in their notes to Gen xviii 14 μὴ ἀδυνατεῖ (פלא ni) παρὰ τῷ θεῷ ῥῆμα, Job xlii 2 ἀδυνατεῖ (בצר) δέ σοι οὐδέν, Zech viii 6 (*bis*) ἀδυνατήσει (פלא) It is parall. to Mt xix 26 παρὰ δὲ θεῷ πάντα δυνατά, Lk xviii 27 δυνατὰ παρὰ τῷ θεῷ ἐστίν (which follows τὰ ἀδύνατα παρὰ ἀνθρώποις)

"THE KINGDOM OF GOD"

but he alone has, at Gethsemane, "Abba, Father, *all things are possible* to thee¹." He also places just before the last of these utterances the statement that Jesus prayed that "*if it is [indeed] possible*²" the cup might pass from Him. Instead of this if-clause—which might be criticized as inconsistent with "all things are possible to thee"—Luke has "if thou dost [so] will and purpose." Luke omits all the Marcan statements that "all things are possible" Matthew omits all of them except "All things are possible with God"

So much for Synoptic utterances and silences about things "possible" and "impossible." In LXX, the first (and perhaps only) instance of "*not possible*" is one where the Hebrew has "*not right*," literally "*not appointed*³." In the time of Epictetus the controversy among Greek philosophers about "possibilities" was so threadbare and seemed to him so unprofitable that he disclaims any knowledge about the subject⁴, but he represents Zeus as saying to the Philosopher, "*If it had been practicable*, I would have done so-and-so for you⁵." That it is always "possible" to do right is almost the only aspect in which Epictetus condescends to look at "possibilities"

It has been shewn in the Introduction, and other Parts of this work, that John intervenes repeatedly on this subject In particular whereas Mark says that Jesus "was not able" to do many mighty works, John emphasizes the inability of the Son to do anything that He did not see the Father doing⁶ Practically John's view is that what the Father wills is both right and possible, and what He does not will is (as the Greeks would say) "not *Themis*," *i.e.* not fit, or just, or possible, for the Son.

---

¹ Mk xiv 36 πάντα δυνατά σοι, om. in Mt xxvi 39, Lk xxii. 42
² Mk xiv 35, Mt xxvi. 39 εἰ δυνατόν ἐστιν. The parall L! . xxii 42 has εἰ βούλει, "if thou dost [so] *will and purpose* "
³ Exod viii 26 "it is not *meet* (כון ni.) (δυνατόν)" כון (regularly rendered by some form of ἕτοιμον) = sometimes ἀληθής, εὐθύς, and σαφῶς, but nowhere else δυνατόν But ἀδυνατεῖν "to be impossible" occurs in Gen. xviii. 14 μὴ ἀδυνατεῖ παρὰ τῷ θεῷ ῥῆμα, lit " surpassing (פלא) more-than Jehovah," R V " too hard (*marg* wonderful) for the Lord "
⁴ Epictet ii 19 5—9   ⁵ Epictet i i 10 εἰ οἷόν τε ἦν
⁶. Mk vi 5, on which see *Introd.* pp 4—8, 23, and *Law* p 137 foll

54 (Mark ix. 14—29)

Hence John would ratify the Marcan saying "All things are possible to him that believeth," but only with an interpretation that would seem to some to refine the saying into nothing: "All things that the believer wills are possible to him, because he, having a vision of God's will, wills that which God wills." In fact, however, this saying leaves us still free to believe in the wonder-working power of prayer (as will be seen in the next section) since prayer may be the mysterious means by which we may not only lift up our hearts to the Father in heaven and open our hearts to the vision of His will, but may also send forth heart-influences into the hearts of others and influence them in ways undefinable, and yet spiritually—and sometimes perhaps physically—palpable.

§ 5   "*This kind can come out by nothing save by prayer,*" *in Mark*[1]

It will be seen below that Matthew apparently assumes this to mean "save by the prayer of faith." At all events he paraphrases Christ's answer as meaning "Your failure was through want of faith." But he makes no attempt to explain "this kind." And he drops the word "prayer" altogether. Yet he adds a saying of Jesus which—without mentioning prayer ("ye shall *say to* this mountain," not "*pray concerning* this mountain")—implies that the prayer of a living faith ("faith as a grain of mustard-seed") can move mountains. Luke,

---

[1] Mk ix 28—9
καὶ εἰσελθόντος αὐτοῦ εἰς οἶκον οἱ μαθηταὶ αὐτοῦ κατ' ἰδίαν ἐπηρώτων αὐτόν Ὅτι ἡμεῖς οὐκ ἠδυνήθημεν ἐκβαλεῖν αὐτό, καὶ εἶπεν αὐτοῖς Τοῦτο τὸ γένος ἐν οὐδενὶ δύναται ἐξελθεῖν εἰ μὴ ἐν προσευχῇ.

Mt xvii 19—20
τότε προσελθόντες οἱ μαθηταὶ τῷ Ἰησοῦ κατ' ἰδίαν εἶπαν Διὰ τί ἡμεῖς οὐκ ἠδυνήθημεν ἐκβαλεῖν αὐτό, ὁ δὲ λέγει αὐτοῖς Διὰ τὴν ὀλιγοπιστίαν ὑμῶν· ἀμὴν γὰρ λέγω ὑμῖν, ἐὰν ἔχητε πίστιν ὡς κόκκον σινάπεως, ἐρεῖτε τῷ ὄρει τούτῳ Μετάβα ἔνθεν ἐκεῖ, καὶ μεταβήσεται, καὶ οὐδὲν ἀδυνατήσει ὑμῖν.

[Lk xvii 5—6]
καὶ εἶπαν οἱ ἀπόστολοι τῷ κυρίῳ Πρόσθες ἡμῖν πίστιν εἶπεν δὲ ὁ κύριος Εἰ ἔχετε πίστιν ὡς κόκκον σινάπεως, ἐλέγετε ἂν τῇ συκαμίνῳ [ταύτῃ] Ἐκριζώθητι καὶ φυτεύθητι ἐν τῇ θαλάσσῃ καὶ ὑπήκουσεν ἂν ὑμῖν.

Lk xvii 5—6 is parall to Mk xi 23—4 (and Mt xxi 21—2), see below, pp 220 foll, 227 foll

while here wholly omitting the dialogue between the disciples and Jesus, inserts later on a saying of Jesus ("ye could have said to this sycamine-tree") similar to Matthew's present addition

In Mark, several ancient MSS and Versions insert "*and fasting*" after "*prayer*[1]" Some of the best Latin Versions, while inserting "*fasting(s)*," have also the plural "*prayers*," and one important one has "*prayers*" alone[2]. Also a very ancient writer quoted by Clement of Alexandria refers to this Marcan narrative in such a way as to shew that his text did not contain the regular New Testament word for "prayer," namely, *proseuchè*, but a shorter form, *euchè*, which means "vow" or "votive prayer" or "prayer" of any kind[3]. This word *euchè* in the New Testament—apart from two instances where it means "vow[4]"—occurs only in the Epistle of James "The *prayer* (? or *vow*) of faith shall save the sufferer[5]" As to this,

---

[1] Tertullian *De Jejun* § 8 and Jerome *Contr Jovin* ii 15, assume that fasts as well as prayers are to be "the weapons for overcoming the more direful demons" Mark however has assigned to Jesus previously (ii 20) words implying that Christ's disciples were not taught by Him at that time to fast For "fast" synonymous with "pray" see *Proclam* p 320, and comp *Son* 3407 (iv) *a*, 3550 *a—d*

[2] Mk ix 29, *b* and *Vindebon* "orationibus et jejuniis (*or* -io)," *k* "orationibus" alone

[3] Clem Alex 993 (*Decerpt Theodot* § 15) τῆς πίστεως τὴν εὐχὴν ἰσχυροτέραν ἀπέφηνεν ὁ σωτὴρ τοῖς πιστοῖς ἀποστόλοις—ἐπί τινος δαιμονιῶντος ὃν οὐκ ἴσχυσαν καθαρίσαι—εἰπὼν "Τὰ τοιαῦτα εὐχῇ κατορθοῦται " The text continues, Ὁ μὲν πιστεύσας ἄφεσιν ἁμαρτημάτων ἔλαβεν παρὰ τοῦ Κυρίου, ὁ δ' ἐν γνώσει γενόμενος, ἅτε μηκέτι ἁμαρτάνων, παρ' ἑαυτοῦ τὴν ἄφεσιν τῶν λοιπῶν κομίζεται This seems to be a Gnostic utterance magnifying *gnōsis* above faith If that is the meaning of what precedes, we must render it, "The Saviour shewed forth to the faithful apostles—in the case of a certain demoniac whom they were not strong enough to purify—*prayer* (τὴν εὐχήν) [as being] stronger than faith (τῆς πίστεως ..ἰσχυροτέραν), saying, 'Such things are set right by *prayer* (εὐχῇ) '" But ἰσχυροτέραν might mean "stronger than usual," or "of special strength " Then the meaning would be "shewed forth the *prayer of faith* [as being] specially strong "

[4] Acts xviii 18, xxi 23   [5] Jas v 15

AND "LITTLE CHILDREN"

Lightfoot says "the idea of a vow may possibly be present, though it is certainly not prominent[1]." Comparing this passage with the one quoted by Clement we find that the Gnostic writer, though referring to Mark, may possibly be using the same phrase as that in James, meaning "*The prayer* (or *vow*) *of faith* is more powerful than any other" But the Gnostic writes ambiguously He might mean "Prayer, *euchè*, is more powerful *than faith.*"

These facts lead us to inquire into the general distinction between *euchè* and *proseuchè* Inquiry shews that *proseuchè* is non-existent in literary Greek before the first century[2] When it did make its appearance there, it meant a Jewish "*praying-place*" or "*proseucha*," and in that sense it is used abundantly by Philo and Josephus[3]. It must have penetrated into Latin in the first century since Juvenal makes a man contemptuously ask "In what *proseucha* shall I look for you[4]?" But Paul brought it into vogue in his Epistles by using it not only in the singular to mean the public prayer of the Church to which

---

[1] See Lightf on Clem Rom § 41 εὐχῶν He adds "The v l προσευχῶν has parallels in James v 15, 16, Ign *Ephes* 10, *Rom* 9 It is explained by the tendency to substitute a common word for a less common"

[2] See Steph *Thes.* vi. 1915 It is perhaps a consequence of this that προσευχή does not occur in the correct text of Clem Rom. nor in the Index to Clem Alex, but it is freq in Ignatius

[3] See Wetstein on Lk vi 12 ἐν τῇ προσευχῇ τοῦ θεοῦ, quoting fully from the Halicarnassian Decree made in the time of Julius Caesar, Joseph *Ant* XIV 10 23 τὰς προσευχὰς ποιεῖσθαι (the right of making their *proseuchae*) πρὸς τῇ θαλάσσῃ κατὰ τὸ πάτριον ἔθος, and *Vit* §§ 53—57 where, after several mentions of ἡ προσευχή as the "*house of prayer*," the prayers themselves are called *euchai*, § 57 ἤδη δὲ ἡμῶν.. εἰς εὐχὰς τραπομένων. Sim Philo ii 565, 567, 568 etc No doubt Luke must have meant "in the act of prayer to God," but he must have known that to educated Greeks it would also convey a mystical allusion to "God's [heavenly] house of prayer" To Greeks and Romans a temple was the house of the deity whose image it contained "Ventum erat ad *Vestae*" means "We had come to [*the house*] *of Vesta*" A Jewish *proseucha* contained no image It was "*a* [*house of*] *prayer*"

[4] Juvenal I. iii 296

he was writing[1], but also in the plural to mean private prayers, especially those of intercession[2]. Luke twice uses the singular to mean the act of praying[3], and James says that Elijah "prayed *with a [special] prayer* that it might not rain[4]" Matthew also represents Jesus as saying "Whatsoever things ye shall ask *in your prayer (proseuchè)*"; but the parallel Mark has "whatsoever things ye *pray for* and ask[5]." The only place where the Synoptists agree in using the singular "prayer" is in the quotation of Jesus from Isaiah "My house shall be called a house of *prayer*[6]." Apart from that, the only place where Mark uses *proseuchè* is the one now under consideration, and this, as we have seen, is doubtful, since there is an ancient quotation of it using *euchè*, and the latter would be more in accordance with early Christian Greek

Here we might stop and say "Not improbably the Greek original had *euchè*. There are several instances where the old word *euchè* has been corrupted into the newer *proseuchè* brought into vogue by Paul, and by Luke in the Acts. But this conclusion is not of much use. It does not help us to understand why Jesus laid stress on mere 'prayer' whereas He seems to have meant 'the prayer of faith,' nor what He meant by '*this*

---

[1] Rom xii. 12, 1 Cor vii 5, Phil iv 6, Col iv 2 τῇ προσευχῇ mostly of public prayer.

[2] Rom i 10, Eph i 16, 1 Thess i 2, Philem 4, "my prayers" or "our prayers," for those to whom the letter is addressed

[3] Lk vi. 12 (see above, p 57, n 3) and xxii 45 (not in Mk xiv. 37, Mt. xxvi 40) ἀναστὰς ἀπὸ τῆς προσευχῆς Perhaps Luke desired to habituate his readers to the LXX and Pauline use of the word in order to rescue it from the contemptuous sense attached to it by such writers as Juvenal. He uses it nine times in the Acts; in two of these (Acts xvi 13, 16) R.V gives "place of prayer"

[4] Jas v 17 προσευχῇ προσηύξατο, "prayed with a prayer," is perhaps not an ordinary instance of Hebraic reduplication It may be in imitation of the special and frequent "vowed a vow" Gen xxviii 20, xxxi 13, Numb xxi 2 etc

[5] Mk xi 24 πάντα ὅσα προσεύχεσθε καὶ αἰτεῖσθε, Mt xxi 22 πάντα ὅσα ἂν αἰτήσητε ἐν τῇ προσευχῇ. The latter appears to define the prayer as that of the Congregation or Church.

[6] Mk xi 17, Mt xxi 13, Lk xix 46 from Is lvi 7

AND "LITTLE CHILDREN"

kind' Surely He could not have meant that any other 'kind' of devil could have been driven out without 'prayer'?"

This indicates that something remains to be explained as to the "kind" of devil. Putting mere verbal distinctions aside, and looking to the facts, we perceive that the "kind" of possession from which the deaf and dumb lunatic was suffering precluded the boy from being impressed for any good purpose by all but the most familiar influences. Attempts of well-meaning strangers to act directly on the sufferer by shouting and gesticulating might even make matters worse The disciples, it would seem, had made matters worse At all events they had failed. It is quite intelligible that some special preparation was needful before Jesus could undo the mischief and utter with effect the words "Thou dumb and deaf spirit, I charge thee, come out of him." Between Himself and the boy the father stood as interpreter. But the interpreter had no faith. The father was perturbed by the failure of the disciples and could not at once believe in their Master. The child, so far as his nature could take in impressions from without, was infected by the father's unbelief. Nothing could be done without the father's prayer, a real and genuine prayer, not expressing a mere desire but having some spark of passionate conviction that, in some form, the prayer would be granted

In this way Jesus led the Syrophoenician woman on to pour forth to Him a mother's prayers till the time came for Him to say "O woman, great is thy faith[1]" In some such way also He put a kind of reproach on the nobleman of Capernaum, as if he shared the unbelief of his neighbours, until He elicited the father's prayer "Sir, come down" and replied "Go thy way, thy son liveth[2]." And perhaps we may add the events preceding the raising of Lazarus—including the delay of Christ's arrival, the sorrow of the sisters, and the tears of Mary. These indicate a desire of the Fourth Evangelist to claim for domestic affection, and for the prayer that is inspired by it, some of that influence which we are too often disposed to assign

---

[1] Mt xv 28, comp. Mk vii 29   [2] Jn iv 49—50

"THE KINGDOM OF GOD"

exclusively to such prayer as that of Elijah. The prayer of love, too, "availeth much[1]."

This being the case it is worth noting—not as a complete explanation of Mark's text, but as a partial explanation of Luke's omission of the whole and Matthew's alteration of a part—that there may have been some confusion, in Greek MSS, arising out of the syllable *pros*, which might be the first syllable of *proseuchè*. When *proseuchè* came into fashion in Christian circles and drove out *euchè*, *pros euchè* would naturally be taken as *proseuchè*, especially as words are not divided in ancient Greek MSS. But $\overline{pros}$, with a line above it, is also an abbreviation of "*father's*," so that $\overline{proseuchè}$ might mean "*father's prayer*[2]." It is conceivable that Mark's Gospel, which abounds in details about exorcism, here described Jesus—who sent His disciples to cast out devils—as giving them instructions how to deal with special "kinds" and, in particular, with this kind (the "deaf and dumb") as needing parental cooperation. This will certainly seem to modern readers very strange and (as it were) too businesslike. Probably it would seem rather strange to the later Evangelists, and hence they would omit it. But if we place ourselves in the position of the disciples whose "business" it was, *inter alia*, to cast out devils, it will seem less strange. At all events it removes the difficulty of supposing that Mark regarded Jesus as saying "Some exorcisms do not require prayer, but the exorcism of a deaf and dumb spirit does require it[3]."

---

[1] Jas v 16. Comp Mk v 36 (Lk viii. 50) μὴ φοβοῦ, μόνον πίστευε —where Luke adds καὶ σωθήσεται—as if the issue for the child depended on the father's faith. Matthew omits this.

[2] See Scrivener, Codex D, *Introd* p xviii, quoting $\overline{πρὸς}$ in Jn vi 65 and $\overline{πρς}$ elsewhere. Also see 2 Chr vi 4 "unto David," πρὸς Δ., where A has $\overline{πρς}$ (a mere scribal error).

[3] Not improbably Hebrew corruption may be a partial cause of Mark's extant text. For the context requires some mention of "faith." It is therefore worth noting that in "this *kind*," המין הזה, there may be found a close resemblance between המין "*kind*" and הימין (Levy Ch 1 198) "*believe*." The latter may have dropped out from contiguity with the former.

AND "LITTLE CHILDREN"

We pass to the Fourth Gospel. John never mentions either "prayer" or the act of "praying." But of course he implies prayer. Only his view is that the Son is in so close a communion with the Father that the word "pray" is less suitable than "request"—with an implied addition perhaps of "inquiring" the Father's will—as when Jesus says to the disciples "I will request the Father on your behalf" and reiterates the word in similar contexts[1]. These instances, it is true, are in the Last Discourse and refer to the future action of the Son. But prayer, silent prayer, is implied before, when Jesus says, near the grave of Lazarus, "Father, I thank thee that *thou didst hear me*, and I [for my part] knew that *thou dost at all times hear me*. But for the sake of the multitude that standeth round I [have] said [this] that they may believe that thou didst send me[2]." This implies that "at all times" when Jesus wrought a sign, the Son "requested" or "inquired" and the Father "heard," and that this is to be taken for granted.

As regards prayers not proceeding from Jesus, John distinguishes—and once at all events in a very subtle and perplexing manner—between (1) "asking [to know]" and (2) "asking [to receive][3]." In the Gospel, after Jesus "perceived" that the disciples "were desirous to *ask* him," that is, "to *ask* [*to know*]" the meaning of a saying of His that had troubled them, and after He had reassured them about His return to

---

[1] Ἐρωτάω, of the Son "asking" the Father, occurs in Jn xiv 16, xvi 26, xvii 9, 15, 20. See *Joh Gr* **2630** *c—i*

[2] Origen, on Jn xi 41—2, assumes that Jesus prayed for Lazarus, as also for the daughter of Jairus

[3] "Ask [to know]," ἐρωτάω, "ask [to receive]," αἰτέω or αἰτοῦμαι. The two occur in 1 Jn v 14—16, where—after repeatedly encouraging his readers to "ask [to receive]" (αἰτώμεθα (*bis*), αἰτήματα, ᾐτήκαμεν, αἰτήσει)—the writer goes on to say that there is "a sin unto death," and οὐ περὶ ἐκείνης λέγω ἵνα ἐρωτήσῃ. This appears to mean that we must not pray, even with an interrogatory "if it be thy will," where our consciences tell us that at present it cannot be God's will. It may be illustrated by Exod xxxii 32 "if thou dost purpose to forgive —[it shall be well]," where both a question and a prayer are implied (see below, p. 463)

them, He adds "In that day ye shall not *ask me any* [*question*]...
if ye shall *ask* [*to receive*] anything of the Father, he will give it
you in my name. Hitherto ye have not *asked* [*to receive*]
anything in my name *Ask* [*to receive*] and ye shall receive[1]"
These last words place no direct restriction on prayer. Verbally
they might mean "Ask what you like." But the reader is
made to feel that "in my name" pervades both the precept to
pray and the promise that the prayer shall be fulfilled.

John altogether avoids the words "pray" and "prayer"
(both in his Gospel and in his Epistle)—whether in narrative
or in precept. Perhaps he felt that the importance attached
in some quarters to public prayer, prayer in the *proseucha*, had
led to an underrating of the value of private prayer, uttered
or unuttered—best described without technicalities as "*asking*,"
but with the constant addition of the "name" of the Son, so
as to remind the Christian, whenever he "asked," that he, too,
was a son, and must "ask" as from a father.

There is no reason to suppose that John, who avoids all
narratives of Christ's exorcisms, intervened in order to explain
a Marcan misunderstanding in one of them, but he certainly
does emphasize the influence of personal affection on Jesus in
two important narratives of healing or restoring to life[2].

§ 6. *The first Synoptic passage mentioning the*
"*delivering up*" *of* "*the Son of man*"

We now come to the first of several Synoptic passages in
which Jesus predicts that the Son of Man will be "*delivered up*,"
either "*into the hands of men* (or, *of sinful men*)," or "*to the chief
priests and the scribes*," or "*to the Gentiles*," or "*into the hands of*

---

[1] Jn xvi 17—23. This agrees with 1 Jn v 14—16 "Asking
to *receive*" is limited by what one's conscience "*knows*" (implied in
"asking to *know*") concerning the will of God

[2] Jn iv 46—54, xi. 3 foll As to the former, compare the healing
in Mt viii 6 foll, Lk vii 2 foll But in Mt the sufferer is called
ambiguously throughout "*my boy*" and "*the boy*", in Lk., "*servant*"
(repeatedly) and "*my boy*" In Jn, it is "*the son*," "*his son*," "*my
little-child*," "*thy son*," "*his boy*," "*thy son*"—variations perhaps
pointing to early doubts (which Jn clears up) about the meaning
of "*boy*"

AND "LITTLE CHILDREN"

the sinful." Mark and Matthew connect this, the first of the series, with a mention of "Galilee." Luke does not. But later on, Luke describes the angels at Christ's tomb as referring to a similar prediction uttered "in Galilee," as shewn below[1]

In a previous discussion of these passages the conclusion was arrived at that they are all based on an original prediction that the Son of Man would be "delivered up for transgressors[2]" Referring the reader to that discussion we need do no more here than ask what is the Johannine attitude toward the prediction about the "delivering up" of the Messiah in general, and also toward that part of it which is omitted by Luke here (though not later on) and which mentions "three days" (or "the third day").

As to the "delivering up"—which, when used passively by the Synoptists, might sometimes mean either "delivered up by God" or "delivered up by Judas Iscariot"—John avoids ambiguity by almost always avoiding the passive and by connecting the word repeatedly with Iscariot[3]. He also

Mk ix 30—32 (R V)	Mt xvii 22—3 (R V)	Lk ix 43 b—45 (R V)	Lk xxiv 6—7 (R V)
(30) And they nt forth from ence, and passed ough Galilee, and would not that y man should ow it (31) For he ight his disciples, d said unto them, e Son of man is ivered up into the nds of men, and ey shall kill him, d when he is led, after three ys he shall rise un (32) But they derstood not the ring, and were aid to ask him	(22) And while they abode (*some anc auth* were gathering themselves together) in Galilee, Jesus said unto them, The Son of man shall be delivered up into the hands of men, (23) And they shall kill him, and the third day he shall be raised up And they were exceeding sorry	(43b) But while all were marvelling at all the things which he did, he said unto his disciples, (44) Let these words sink into your ears for the Son of man shall be delivered up into the hands of men (45) But they understood not this saying, and it was concealed from them, that they should not perceive it. and they were afraid to ask him about this saying	(6) He is not here, but is risen (*om by some anc auth*) remember how he spake unto you when he was yet in Galilee, (7) Saying that the Son of man must be delivered up into the hands of sinful men, and be crucified, and the third day rise again

[2] See *Son* **3253—61**

[3] See Jn vi 64 τίς ἐστιν ὁ παραδώσων, and vi 71, xii 4, xiii 2 etc. where it is connected with Iscariot The only instance of the passive is xviii 36 ἵνα μὴ παραδοθῶ τοῖς Ἰουδαίοις.

expresses the divine "delivering up" by using the uncompounded verb "deliver" (literally "give") thus: "God so loved the world that he *gave* his only begotten Son that everyone that believeth in him might not perish but might have life eternal[1]." Paul similarly uses both "gave" and "gave-up" (or "delivered-up") in his Epistles concerning the Father "giving" His Son to die for sinners[2].

As regards the "three days," John mentions the phrase once for all at the outset of his Gospel in the saying of Jesus "Destroy this temple, and in three days I will raise it up[3]." This appears to be a case of Johannine Intervention. For Mark connects "three days" with the "raising up" of the "temple" much later on, in an accusation brought against Jesus by "false witnesses[4]." Luke omits it. John inserts it, but implies that it was not exactly "false," but metaphor misunderstood at the time as literally true[5].

§ 7. "*He would not that any man should know* [*it*]," *in Mark*[6]

While considering this first Synoptic prediction of Jesus about the "delivering up" of the Son of Man we must not

---

[1] Jn iii 16

[2] Gal. 1 4 "Jesus Christ who *gave* himself for our sins," ii 20 "the Son of God, who loved me and *gave himself up* ($\pi\alpha\rho\alpha\delta\acute{o}\nu\tau o s$) for me," comp. Rom viii 32 "God.. *gave him up* ($\pi\alpha\rho\acute{\epsilon}\delta\omega\kappa\epsilon\nu$) for us all," Eph. v. 2 "Christ . *gave himself up*" See *Son* **3536**

[3] Jn ii 19.

[4] Mk xiv 58, Mt xxvi 61, Lk om

[5] Of course it was open to Christians to believe, and they probably did believe—and were intended by John to believe—that the words "Destroy this temple" were also literally fulfilled by the action of the Jewish people resulting in the destruction of the Temple by the Romans

[6] Mk ix 30 καὶ οὐκ ἤθελεν ἵνα τις γνοῖ, Latt. codd "quenquam scire," but SS "should be aware *of him*," and Walton sim for the Arab , Pers , and Aethiop "him" ("de se" or "eum") Comp Mk vii 24 οὐδένα ἤθελεν γνῶναι, Latt codd "neminem voluit scire," but SS "should know *of him*," and Walton sim for Arab and Aethiop

In Mk v 43 διεστείλατο αὐτοῖς πολλὰ ἵνα μηδεὶς γνοῖ τοῦτο, "this"

AND "LITTLE CHILDREN"

pass over the words that Mark alone prefixes to it   What motive led Jesus to desire that no man "should know" as He passed through Galilee?   Celsus implies twice that it was cowardice, first, in the person of a hostile Jew, saying "You run this way and that way, along with your disciples, away from [enemies]", secondly, in his own person, bringing a charge of "hiding" and most shameful flight[1]   In the present passage, Mark's context professes to give a reason ("for he taught"), as if saying, "He did not desire to be recognised, *for* He predicted that He would soon die"   But this seems a *non sequitur*, and it is not surprising that Matthew and Luke omit the clause[2]. It becomes intelligible, however, if the tradition is regarded as having meant something to this effect   "Jesus now knew and began to teach that His hour was at hand and that *He was to die in Jerusalem   For this reason He passed rapidly through Galilee* avoiding attempts to arrest Him *in that region*[3]."

---

is inserted (parall Lk viii 56 παρήγγειλεν αὐτοῖς μηδενὶ εἰπεῖν τὸ γεγονός)
 Compare the ambiguity in —

Mk vi 33	Mt xiv 13	Lk ix 11
καὶ εἶδαν αὐτοὺς ὑπάγοντας καὶ ἔγνωσαν πολλοί	ἀκούσαντες οἱ ὄχλοι ἠκολούθησαν αὐτῷ	οἱ δὲ ὄχλοι γνόντες ἠκολούθησαν αὐτῷ
R V	R V	R V
"and [the people] saw them going, and many knew [them]"	"when the multitudes heard [thereof] they followed him"	"but the multitudes perceiving [it] followed him."
A V	A V	A V
"and the people saw them departing, and many knew [him]"	"when the people had heard [thereof] they followed him."	"and the people when they knew [it] followed him."

 In view of Marcan usage as a whole, it is probable that Mk vi 33 ἔγνωσαν means "recognised *the fact*" (as R V in parall Lk "perceiving *it*")

[1] Origen *Cels* i 65, ii 10
[2] The difficult "*for*" is omitted by codex *k* and is altered into "*and*" by SS, and into "*but*" by *b* and *Brix*.
[3] Comp Lk xiii 33 "It cannot be that *a prophet perish out of Jerusalem*"   How could this be said after the recent death of the Baptist "out of Jerusalem"?   If "*a prophet*" could be regarded as an error (*Joh Gr* **2492** *a*) for "*the prophet*"—referring to the Suffering

"THE KINGDOM OF GOD"

This passage invites us to consider what Matthew calls a fulfilment of prophecy parallel to another Marcan passage about "not making known" —

Mk ııı 12	Mt xıı. 16—17	Lk vı 19 foll. om
And he charged them much that they should not make him known.	And he charged them that they should not make him known that it might be fulfilled	

About the prophecy of Isaiah that Matthew proceeds to quote—one seldom noticed in the Talmud and Midrash—Ibn Ezra says "Most of the commentators refer this expression ('my servant') to the pious Israelites, the Gaon to Cyrus, I to the prophet[1]" Justin Martyr and other early Christian writers lay stress on the mention of "the Gentiles" made by Isaiah here, but they do not explain the deviation of Matthew's text from Isaiah's, as given below, and the precise meaning of either[2] Matthew's context leaves it open to suppose that a period of quiet and unobtrusive action on the part of the Messiah—during

---

Servant in Isaiah—that would remove the difficulty Origen (*Comm Matth* xıı 20, Lomm ııı 165, and Lomm ıv 241) allegorizes the passage

But Wetstein *ad loc* affords a satisfactory explanation by shewing that οὐκ ἐνδέχεται, "it is *not* [humanly] *possible*," is probably used, in bitter and ironical condemnation of the Sanhedrin, for "it is *not* [legally] *possible*," referring to the enactment in *Sanhedr* 2 a "a false prophet *cannot be judged* except by the Council of the Seventy-one" (comp *ıb* 89 *a*)

[1] Is xlıı 1 foll "Behold, my servant. .he shall bring forth judgment to the Gentiles He shall not cry, nor lift up, nor cause his voice to be heard in the street A bruised reed shall he not break, and the smoking flax shall he not quench he shall bring forth judgment in truth He shall not fail nor be discouraged till he have set judgment in the earth, and the isles shall wait for his law," Mt xıı 18 foll "Behold, my servant .he shall declare judgment to the Gentiles He shall not strive, nor cry aloud, neither shall any one hear his voice in the streets A bruised reed shall he not break, and smoking flax shall he not quench, till he send forth judgment unto victory And in his name shall the Gentiles hope"

[2] Justin M *Tryph* §§ 123, 135

(Mark ıx 30—32)

which He *would not* "cry aloud"—might be followed by a period when He would "bring forth judgment" to all the world, including "the Gentiles" and when (presumably) He *would* "cry aloud[1]"

The Marcan traditions that Jesus desired "not to be known" were liable to accusation such as that of Celsus, who alleged that Jesus "ran away" disgracefully from danger. John avows that Jesus "departed from Judaea" or "would not walk in Judaea[2]," because of the hostility of the Jews, but he implies that there was also a destiny, or "hour," that regulated His movements, by saying "*his hour* was not yet come"—a phrase practically confined to the Fourth Gospel[3] On one occasion, the Feast of Tabernacles, Jesus goes up to Jerusalem "as it were in secret[4]," and there, while accusing the Jews of wishing to kill Him, He predicts His own death in the words "I go unto him that sent me; ye shall seek me and shall not find me," upon which the Jews say "Will he go unto the Dispersion among (*lit* of) the Greeks and teach the Greeks[5]?"

Why does John write "teach *the Greeks*," if he means, and might have written, "teach *the Dispersion*," or "teach *them*," i e *the Dispersion of the Jews among the Greeks*? It is probably an instance of Johannine irony. The men of Jerusalem speak contemptuously of their dispersed brethren as "Greeks," quasi-foreigners, heretical by nature and suitable proselytes for an heretical Messiah. But they unconsciously predict that which literally came to pass Christ, through His apostles, began by "going unto the Dispersion among the Greeks," but very soon proceeded to "teach the Greeks" themselves

As soon as the Jews have finished speaking, John says "Now on the last day, the great [day] of the feast, Jesus stood and *cried* [*aloud*][6]." This is the second of three instances

---

[1] This is the view apparently taken in Origen's *De rect Fid* § 1, Lomm xvi 287, where Is xlii 1—2 is contrasted with 1 Thess iv 16—17 and Dan vii. 13

[2] Jn iv 3, vii 1, comp xi 7—8

[3] See Jn ii 4 "my hour," vii 30, viii 20, xiii 1 "his hour," comp Jn vii 6—8 (bis) "*mv appointed time* (καιρός)"

[4] Jn vii. 10.   [5] Jn vii 33—5   [6] Jn vii 37

where the Fourth Gospel represents Jesus as "crying aloud" And the utterance here bears witness to the Spirit ("he spake concerning the Spirit[1]"). The first utterance was during the same Feast, a little earlier, when the Jews spoke contemptuously about "knowing" whence Jesus came: "We know this [man] whence he is. But when the Christ comes no one understands whence he is," in reply to which "Jesus *cried aloud* in the temple, teaching and saying, Ye both know me, and know whence I am[2]." This bears witness to the Father

The third instance bears witness to the Son, as will be perceived from the context. It is a "cry" uttered shortly after the arrival of "certain Greeks" who "desire to see Jesus" The context should be noted. Jesus has welcomed this coming of the "Greeks" as a token of the advent of the day of God's glory, and He has warned the multitude to "believe in the light," that they may become children of light. Then the Evangelist has passed into comment, saying in effect, "And now Jesus departed and 'was hidden' from the Jews. For, in spite of His signs, they could not 'believe in the Light,' since, as Isaiah said, God had blinded their eyes, and even those rulers who believed did not confess, for they loved the glory of men rather than the glory of God."

It is immediately after this that John places Christ's last public utterance, and the third and last "cry" as part of it: "But Jesus *cried aloud* and said, He that believeth on me, believeth not on me, but on him that sent me...I am come a light into the world, that whosoever believeth on me may not abide in the darkness[3]"

In *Johannine Grammar* it was shewn that these three acts of "crying aloud" represent mystically a threefold testimony to the Father, the Son, and the Holy Spirit[4]. But it might have been added that they seem also to contain an allusion to the prophecy of Isaiah, as interpreted by Matthew—about "*not* crying," at first, and about "bringing judgment to the Gentiles"

---

[1] Jn vii 39   [2] Jn vii. 27—8
[3] Jn xii 44—6   [4] *Joh Gr* **2618**

AND "LITTLE CHILDREN"

Perhaps, too, John regarded the threefold "crying aloud" of Jesus as a kind of threefold farewell utterance corresponding to that in the *Nunc Dimittis*, where Simeon thanks God for having seen God's salvation, "a light for revelation to the Gentiles and the glory of thy people Israel[1]" But there is this great difference, that whereas Simeon's vision is of spiritual parallelism between the new-born Gentile world and faithful Israel, the thought in the Fourth Gospel is one of spiritual contrast between the simple faith and insight of the Gentiles and the self-seeking blindness of Israel after the flesh.

Our conclusion is that the Fourth Evangelist desires to make us see the unvarying principle on which Christ based His varying practice. Sometimes He "would not that any man should know" His movements, but sometimes He desired them to be known As a rule He was not given to "crying aloud," but He did "cry aloud" on three notable occasions The Son acts according to the Father's bidding If He leaves Judaea to avoid death, He also goes back to Judaea to save life[2]. When His brethren wish Him to go up to Jerusalem, go up publicly He will not, but He goes "as it were in secret" to the Feast of Tabernacles because His "time" is "not yet come[3]." Yet, soon afterwards, He "went up into the temple and taught" with such freedom that some of the citizens of Jerusalem say "Is not this he whom they seek to kill? And lo, he speaketh openly[4]" On two occasions we are told, perhaps ambiguously, that He "was hidden" from the Jews in the Temple[5]. On

---

[1] Lk ii 32 Note the reiterations in Isaiah (xlii 1—6) "bring forth *judgment to the Gentiles* shall bring forth *judgment in truth*. . *judgment in the earth* . the isles shall wait for his law (Mt in his name shall the Gentiles hope). for a covenant of the people, for a *light of the Gentiles*" Comp Jn vii 35 "the dispersion of *the Greeks*. *the Greeks*" (with context), xii 20 "*certain Greeks*," followed by (*ib.* 28) "a voice from heaven" and (*ib* 31) "now is *the judgment of this world*," with repeated mentions of (*ib* 35) "*light*," concluding with the mention of (*ib* 46—8) "*light*" and "*judging*"—all of which (*ib* 49—50) proceed from the Father through the Son

[2] Jn x 39—40, xi 8   [3] Jn vii 3—10   [4] Jn vii 25—6

[5] Jn viii 59, xii 36 Comp *Joh Gr.* **2543** Probably John plays on the twofold meaning "was hidden" and "hid himself" He (Mark ix 30—32)

"THE KINGDOM OF GOD"

one of these they had attempted to stone Him. Some might suggest, perhaps, that a circle of His disciples "hid" their Master in a literal sense, but the Evangelist desires to suggest a different kind of "hiding," as may be seen from his context "These things spake Jesus and departed and *was hidden* from them. But though he had done so many signs before them they would not believe in him...because Isaiah said...*He hath blinded their eyes*[1]"

§ 8. *The question who is "the greatest*[2]*"*

Mark relates, first, a coming of the disciples to Capernaum, secondly, a questioning of the disciples by Jesus "in the house"

suggests that the "hiding" was literal and miraculous but also that it was typical of a spiritual blinding whereby Christ "was hidden" from those who rejected Him

[1] Jn xii 36—40. John quotes a passage of Isaiah (vi 10) also quoted by the Synoptists. But in his description of Jesus as being "hidden" from the Jews he has perhaps in view Is xlv 15 "Verily thou art a God that hidest thyself, O God of Israel, the Saviour." His Gospel constantly suggests to us that it is part of the teacher's business to suppress the desire to teach all that he knows, and that God "hides" whenever He "reveals." But the "hiding" is very different in different circumstances, sometimes being a chastisement, sometimes a blessing

[2] Mk ix 33—7 (R.V)	Mt xvii 24—5, xviii 1, xxiii 11, xviii 2—5, x 40 (R V)	Lk ix 46—8, xxii 26 (R V)
(33) And they came to Capernaum and when he was in the house he asked them, What were ye reasoning in the way? (34) But they held their peace for they had disputed one with another in the way, who [was] the greatest (*lit* greater). (35) And he sat down, and called the twelve, and he saith unto them, If any man would be first,	(xvii 24) And when they were come to Capernaum, they that received the half-shekel came to Peter, and said, Doth not your master (*or*, teacher) pay the half-shekel? (25) He saith, Yea And when he came into the house, (xviii 1) In that hour came the disciples unto Jesus, saying, Who then is greatest (*lit* greater) in the kingdom of heaven?	(ix. 46) And there arose a reasoning among them, which of them should be greatest (*lit* greater)

as to their "reasoning in the way", thirdly, the fact that they had been disputing, "in the way," as to "who [was] the greatest" (literally "[the] greater"), fourthly, Christ's settlement of the discussion, fifthly, His confirmation of the settlement by taking a child in His arms and saying that whosoever received such a child in His name received Him Matthew and Luke omit the questioning of the disciples by Jesus. Matthew inserts a questioning of Jesus by the disciples. Luke inserts no questioning of any kind, but implies that Jesus saw, without questioning, "the reasoning of their heart"

But Matthew inserts a questioning of Peter by Jesus in the

Mk ix 33—7 (R V) contd	Mt xvii 24—5, xviii. 1, xxiii 11, xviii 2—5, x 40 (R V) contd	Lk ix. 46—8, xxii. 26 (R V.) contd
he shall be last of all, and minister of all (36) And he took a little child, and set him in the midst of them and taking him in his arms, he said unto them, (37) Whosoever shall receive one of such little children in my name, receiveth me and whosoever receiveth me, receiveth not me, but him that sent me	(xxiii 11) But he that is greatest (lit greater) among you shall be your servant (or, minister) (xviii 2) And he called to him a little child, and set him in the midst of them, (3) And said, Verily I say unto you, Except ye turn, and become as little children, ye shall in no wise enter into the kingdom of heaven (4) Whosoever therefore shall humble himself as this little child, the same is the greatest (lit greater) in the kingdom of heaven (5) And whoso shall receive one such little child in my name receiveth me. (x 40) He that receiveth you receiveth me, and he that receiveth me receiveth him that sent me	(47) But when Jesus saw the reasoning of their heart, he took a little child, and set him by his side, (48) And said unto them, Whosoever shall receive this little child in my name receiveth me and whosoever shall receive me receiveth him that sent me for he that is least (lit lesser) among you all, the same is great (xxii 26) But ye [shall] not [be] so but he that is the greater among you, let him become as the younger; and he that is chief, as he that doth serve

context, as well as a mention of "the house" For immediately after the "coming to Capernaum," Matthew says that men "came to Peter and said, Doth not your master pay the half-shekel?" and that, when Peter "came into the house," Jesus questioned him about "tribute" and *"kings of the earth"* Then follows the narrative of the *Statēr*, ending with the words of Jesus "Give unto them for me and thee." And then, without a break, Matthew proceeds "In that hour came the disciples unto Jesus, saying, Who, then, is *greatest in the kingdom of heaven?*" Here, the addition of "then," and "in the kingdom of heaven," seems to connect the question "Who is the greatest?" with the preceding story about Peter—as though Peter seemed "the greatest," having been specially favoured both by the miracle and by being associated with his Master ("for me and for thee")[1].

Origen asks the meaning of Matthew's phrase "*in that hour*" or "*in that day*," expressly saying that the MSS vary This affords external evidence for the conclusion to which internal evidence also points, that at an early period there was doubt about the date and the occasion of this doctrine on the question "Who is the greatest?" The Diatessaron says that the tax-collectors came "*when Simon went forth without*" But these words occur nowhere in the New Testament except after Peter's denial (in Mark and Matthew)[2]. And Origen regards Jesus in the story of the *Statēr* as symbolically "comforting" Peter and assuring him that he is "free" from sin, and "a son" of God[3] These are indications that Matthew's narrative may be another version of the story of Peter's fishing—or rather taking the lead in fishing—which John places after Christ's resurrection[4]

---

[1] So Clem Alex 947 Πέτρος . ὑπὲρ οὗ μόνου καὶ ἑαυτοῦ τὸν φόρον ὁ σωτὴρ ἐκτελεῖ, and Origen (and Jerome) on Mt xvii. 24—7

[2] Mk xiv 68 ἐξῆλθεν ἔξω, Mt xxvi 75 ἐξελθὼν ἔξω, [Lk xxii. 62] This will be discussed in its order, p. 537 foll.

[3] Origen *Comm Matth* xiii 11, Lomm iii. 232

[4] See *Notes* **2999** (vii)—(xvi) on the story of the Stater If "went forth *without*" meant "*outside the circle* (Heb *house*) of *Christ's disciples*," then Mt xvii 25 "when he came *into the house*" would mean "when he returned *to that house*" In Mark, the repeated

AND "LITTLE CHILDREN"

These Synoptic variations are followed by still more important deviations in Matthew and Luke from the Marcan version of Christ's words "If any one desires to be first he shall be last of all" Their natural meaning is *"He shall be punished by being* last of all." But this punitive meaning is out of place here A better sense would be given by substituting the imperative *"Let him become,* or, *make himself,* last of all," which Luke has elsewhere[1] That would resemble the Synoptic tradition with the imperative, "If any one desires to follow me *let him take up* his cross[2]" There are many instances of such an imperative in the New Testament[3]. There is probably no instance in the New Testament (except in a Mark-Matthew

---

(IX 33—4) *"in the way"* may naturally have been omitted by Mt - Lk as superfluous But the word is frequent in the Acts, and occurs also in Hermas, to mean "the Way of the Lord" in a particular sense, namely, "the Way of the Gospel"—as distinct from "the way of the Law" concerning which Jethro said to Moses (Exod xviii 20) "thou shalt shew them *the way wherein they must walk"* Doubtless Mark took it literally both here and in other passages where he alone inserts it, but it might have meant originally "*in [reasoning concerning] the Way"* When Jesus said (Mk vi 8, Lk ix 3, comp Mt x 10) "Take nothing *for the* (Lk. ins τὴν) *way,"* it is probable that His disciples understood Him as including the meaning "Take nothing *for the Way [of the Lord],"* which perhaps Lk.'s τὴν emphasizes

In Mk x 17 "when he was going forth *to [the] way,"* Matthew and Luke—who omit the clause—perhaps discerned another superfluity But it was the way to Jerusalem, and the way to the Cross And it introduces the story of the rich young man, who did not understand what the Way meant, to which succeeds, after an interval, the story of the blind beggar who (Mk x 52) "followed Jesus *in the way"* There is much to be said for the hypothesis, here and elsewhere, of a twofold meaning in Mark See *Light* **3755** *c—j* on "The Way of the Lord" and "The Way," and *Law* pp 494—5 To these add that (Levy i 163 *a,* 424 *b*) the Aramaic and Hebrew words for "way" may be used to denote "incidental (beilaufig)" teaching

[1] Lk xxii 26 ὁ μείζων γινέσθω ὡς ὁ νεώτερος This is parall to ἔσται (rep) in Mk x 43—4, Mt xx 26—7
[2] Mk viii 34, Mt xvi 24, Lk. ix 23
[3] Comp 1 Cor xiv 35 εἰ δέ τι μανθάνειν θέλουσιν . .ἐπερωτάτωσαν, 2 Thess iii 10 εἴ τις οὐ θέλει ἐργάζεσθαι μηδὲ ἐσθιέτω, etc

73 (Mark ix 33—7)

"THE KINGDOM OF GOD"

repetition of this tradition later on) where "*he shall be*," in such a sentence as Mark's, means "*let him become*[1]." It is not surprising that Matthew and Luke have altered it and that the Diatessaron omits it Origen, it is true, extracts a non-punitive sense out of Mark, but he does it with the preface that the words "are able to be understood as meaning" so-and-so, and in his own words, when paraphrasing Mark, he (like Luke) alters "*he shall be*" into "*let him become*[2]."

It would be rash to say that Origen is wrong For the Hebrew future sometimes represents the imperative[3], and Mark's Greek may be Hebraic, to be interpreted Hebraically. But the point of importance for us is, that Mark has not clearly expressed this doctrine as to "who is the greatest?," that Matthew and Luke have deviated from it, and that we may consequently expect to find Johannine Intervention.

John intervenes as follows in two ways, first, as to the general question (in Mark and Matthew) "*Who is the greatest?*" and secondly, as to the particular question (in Luke) "*which of*

---

[1] Mk x 43—4, Mt xx 26—7, ἔσται ὑμῶν διάκονος.. ἔσται πάντων (Mt ὑμῶν) δοῦλος The future would naturally be used of consequent reward, or consequent punishment (but not of duty) as in 1 Cor iii 12, 14, 15, 17 When the Apostle passes to what *ought* to be done he uses the imperative, *ib* 18 εἴ τις δοκεῖ σοφὸς εἶναι... μωρὸς γενέσθω ἵνα γένηται σοφός

In Mt xxiii 11 there is no "if-clause" (as there is in the parall Mk ix 35) and the future may be the legal future "[The Law is that] the greatest of you *shall be* your servant"

[2] Origen (on Mt xix 30, Lomm iii 383 foll) Οὕτω δὲ δύναται νοεῖσθαι καὶ τό (Mk ix 35) "Εἴ τις θέλει πρῶτος εἶναι ἔσται πάντων ἔσχατος"—ὡς εἰ ἔλεγεν · Ἐπεὶ νῦν τὰ πρωτεῖα λαμβάνουσιν οἱ ἀπὸ τῶν ἐθνῶν . εἴ τις βούλεται τὸ ἀληθινὸν πρῶτον ἀναλαβεῖν, γενέσθω ἐν τοῖς ὑπὸ τοῦ νῦν Ἰσραὴλ ἐσχάτοις εἶναι νενομισμένοις, i e "If anyone wills and purposes to attain the real and ideal FIRST, *let him become* [one] among those who by the Israel of this present world are thought of as last"

Also on Mt xviii 2 foll, Origen, when he comes to Mk ix 35 (Lomm iii 245), quotes with γενέσθαι (εἴ τις θέλει πρῶτος γενέσθαι), and prob (Cod Reg) with ἔστω, having previously said that the first place shall be obtained by τὸν γενόμενον πάντων ἔσχατον

[3] E g Gen i 3 "Let there be light," LXX γενηθήτω, Aq γενέσθω, Sym ἔστω, Exod xxxv 2, 1 K ii 24 "let him die," LXX Exod τελευτάτω, but 1 K θανατωθήσεται

them should be the greatest " In his Gospel, the GREATER is always identified with the Father and Giver in heaven, who is continually giving to the Son and through the Son, and of whom the Son says that He is "*greater* than all," and, later on, "The Father is *greater* than I[1]" This is the general view of greatness Not till the Last Discourse, and after the Washing of Feet, comes the particular warning to the disciples "A servant is not *greater* than his lord nor an apostle *greater* than he that sent him[2]." By that time it has been made clear to them that the greatness they are to aim at consists in divine love and divine giving, or grace[3], and that the Father, though called GREATER by the Son, is *not* "greater" than the Son according to any measurement of this world; for almost in the same sentence in which the Father is called "greater than all," the Son says "I and the Father are one[4]." When Jesus says to Peter—in the only passage where the Fourth Gospel suggests a thought of superiority of one disciple over another—"lovest thou me more than these[5]?" the question is obviously a gentle rebuke and may include the meaning "Dost thou still, as in old days, desire to be foremost and first? If thou dost, there is only one way. He is the greatest whose love is the greatest. And he who loves the shepherd will feed the sheep "

§ 9   "*Taking a little child in his arms,*" *in Mark*

Both here and later on, Matthew and Luke omit the Marcan tradition that Jesus "took a little child in his arms[6]" Also,

---

[1] Jn x 29, xiv 28   [2] Jn xiii 16, xv 20
[3] Comp Jn xv 13 "greater love hath no one than this, that one lay down his life for his friends "
[4] Jn x 29—30   [5] Jn xxi 15
[6] Mk ix 36   Mt xviii 2   Lk ix 47

καὶ λαβὼν παιδίον   καὶ προσκαλεσάμενος   ἐπιλαβόμενος παι‐
ἔστησεν αὐτὸ ἐν μέσῳ   παιδίον ἔστησεν αὐτὸ ἐν   δίον ἔστησεν αὐτὸ παρ
αὐτῶν καὶ ἐναγκαλισά‐   μέσῳ αὐτῶν   ἑαυτῷ
μενος αὐτό..

                                                              Lk xviii 17
Mk x 16   Mt xix 15   foll om
καὶ ἐναγκαλισάμενος   καὶ ἐπιθεὶς τὰς χεῖρας
αὐτὰ κατευλόγει τιθεὶς   αὐτοῖς ..
τὰς χεῖρας ἐπ' αὐτά

See *Son* **3425** *a—f* on the "carrying" of Israel by Jehovah, and

"THE KINGDOM OF GOD"

instead of (Mark and Matthew) "caused [the child] to stand in the midst of them [i e the disciples]," Luke has "caused [the child] to stand by his side." There are other variations, some pointing to early Semitic or Greek corruption[1] But these do not greatly diminish the probability that Mark has preserved the original tradition, and that there were two distinct acts. In the first, Jesus placed the little child within the circle of the disciples, identifying it with them In the second, He took it up in His arms, identifying it with Himself This has been modified by Matthew and Luke, partly perhaps owing to

---

on its paraphrase, or misrepresentation, in LXX Similar causes to those which influenced the translators of Deut i 31 "carried," LXX ἐτροφοφόρησε or ἐτροποφόρησε, Aq ἦρεν, Sym ἐβάστασεν, may have influenced Matthew and Luke here—Mark being alone in preserving Christ's symbolical action

[1] See *Son* **3518** *a* on the Marcan traditions about "raising up," Mk i 31 (not in Lk iv 39), ix 27 "raised up" the demoniac child (not in Mt -Lk) In Mk x 16, ἐναγκαλισάμενος is altered by D into προσκαλεσάμενος which is also in the text of the parall Lk xviii 16 and in Mt xviii 2 (Mt xix 15 om the word) Ἐναγκαλίζομαι, in LXX, occurs only in Prov vi 10 (rep xxiv 33) "*folding* (חבק) the hands," Aq. περιλαμβάνω

In Mk ix 36, SS has "And he had taken (נסב) a *certain* (חד) lad and made him to stand (*or*, raised him up) among them and *looked* (חר) at him" (instead of "*embraced*"), and in Lk ix 47, omitting "*certain* (חד),"SS has "*took hold of* (אחד) a lad" (Curet inserts "*certain*") "and made him to stand (*or*, raised him up) *by them*" (instead of (Curet) "*by him*") Comp Mk ix 27 (the demoniac child) "*took hold of* (אחד) him by the hand and made him to stand (*or*, raised him up) " These facts indicate that there may have been confusion between חר "*looked*" and חד "*a certain*," and also between Heb אחד "*one*," "*a certain*" and Aram אחד "*take hold of*" (Heb אחז) (see *Corrections* **487** (1) (ζ) foll , and Gesen. 28 *a* on Job viii 17).

In 1 K 1 2, Heb "*in the bosom of*" is paraphrased in LXX by μετά, and in 1 K iii. 20, Heb "*from my side* (אצל) . in her *bosom* (חיק)" are both rendered in Targ by forms of לות In Goodspeed, κόλπος occurs only in 2 Clem. § 4 ἐὰν ἦτε μετ' ἐμοῦ συνηγμένοι ἐν τῷ κόλπῳ μου, on which Lightf says that it is perhaps from the Gospel of the Egyptians and that the language is derived from Is xl 11 τῷ βραχίονι... καὶ ἐν τῷ κόλπῳ, where the latter clause, though om in the best MSS of LXX, is in several MSS and Versions, and in the Hebrew.

corruption of the text, partly because they did not perceive the distinct meanings of the two symbolical acts, and, in particular Christ's thought of the Father of Israel, "carrying" His child in "the wilderness" as described in Deuteronomy. It is true that Mark sometimes repeats one and the same tradition in two forms, but in this case the evidence indicates either that he has not done so, or that, if he has done so, the rare word for "embracing" or "taking in the arms" was a part of the original. The action is so emotional and original that we can explain its omission by Matthew and Luke We could not explain its insertion (without authority) by Mark

In the Fourth Gospel the thought of the Child in the "bosom" of the Father is brought before us at first only in a metaphysical form as the Word "*[looking] toward*, or [*in close relation*] *with*, God[1]," but very soon definitely, as "*the only begotten Son*, who is *in* (lit. *to*) the *bosom* of the Father[2]" The word does not occur again till the evening of the Last Supper, where it is connected with the thought of love: "There was at the table reclining in the *bosom* of Jesus one of his disciples, *whom Jesus loved*[3]" The Greek word here—as also above— used for "bosom" means, strictly speaking, the fold of the garment over the breast, not the breast itself. But the Gospel proceeds to use the latter term "He leaning back, as he was, on the *breast* of Jesus[4]" This is repeated later on, after a dialogue about loving, when Peter "seeth the disciple *whom Jesus loved* following—[that same disciple] who also leaned back on his *breast* at the supper[5]." Finally this "disciple" is mentioned in almost the last sentence of the book: "This is the disciple that beareth witness of these things and wrote these things; and we know that his witness is true[6]"

Even if these passages stood alone we might reasonably infer that this Johannine picture of the disciple in Christ's

---

[1] Jn 1 1 πρός
[2] Jn 1 18 εἰς τὸν κόλπον
[3] Jn xiii 23
[4] Jn xiii 25
[5] Jn xxi 20 Jesus has previously asked Peter (xxi 15—17) "Lovest (ἀγαπᾷς) thou me more than these?" and then, twice (but using first ἀγαπᾷς, then φιλεῖς), "Lovest thou me?"
[6] Jn xxi 24

bosom, whom Jesus loved, is intended, not only to describe actual fact (or, actual vision) as regards one disciple, but also to suggest to us the thought of all the disciples whom Jesus loves and carries like little children in His bosom. As the Only begotten Son in the bosom of the Father uniquely declares the Father, so such a bosom disciple (it is suggested) bears witness to, and uniquely declares, the Son. Such a disciple is the representative of Jesus in every region of His love "When Jesus therefore saw his mother and *the disciple* standing by *whom he loved*, he saith unto his mother, Woman, see, *thy son*! Then saith he to the disciple, See, thy mother[1]!" It is from the Word with God, the Only begotten who is, like a Little Child, in the bosom of the Father, that there comes, to those who receive Him, authority to become "[newborn] children of God". "As many as received him, to them he gave authority to become [newborn] children of God, to them that believe in his name, who were begotten, not from...but from God[2]." Thus the doctrine of regeneration goes hand in hand with the doctrine of belief, or faith, in the name of the Son. But it is not to be merely barren belief: "If a man love me *he will keep my word*, and my Father will love him, and we will come unto him and make our abode with him[3]." The Father does not "come" alone, nor the Son alone; nor do they come without the fulfilment of a condition ("if"); they come, united, in the Spirit of Love to those who welcome them in that Spirit

Our conclusion is that John has intervened in favour of Mark, or rather in favour of the Hebrew thought latent in Mark. The Law said to Israel "The Lord thy God *carried* thee as *a man doth carry his son*[4]" Isaiah, in the Hebrew text, predicted that the Shepherd of Israel would not only gather the lambs with His arm but also "*carry them in his bosom*[5]" These metaphors were regarded by Jesus as meaning, in effect, "The idols of the heathen are carried by their worshippers, and the kings of this world are carried in state by the subjects whom

---

[1] Jn xix 26   See *Proclam.* p 473.
[2] Jn i 12—13.   [3] Jn xiv 23
[4] Deut i 31   [5] Is xl 11

AND "LITTLE CHILDREN"

they oppress, but the True God is the Nursing Father who carries His children as babes and sustains them as though He were their nurse." Then followed the inference that the true and real man in the New Kingdom—the man "made in the image and conformed to the likeness" of God—is to be, not a servant or subject, but a child, being born from above and resting as a babe on the bosom of the Father in heaven. Being Himself this ideal Child, Jesus desired passionately to impart to His disciples, as to His fellow-children, the sense of the need of this regeneration, and He imparted it not only by uttered word but also through passionate action which Mark has most faithfully described. John does not describe it but leads us to the thought of what it implies—partly by Christ's doctrine, partly by Johannine comment, partly by Johannine drama, introducing the character of the beloved disciple reclining on the "bosom" of Jesus.

§ 10 *"In my name," and "because ye are Christ's," in Mark*[1]

Luke omits the Marcan tradition "There is no man that shall do a mighty work in my name and be able quickly to

[1] Mk ix 38—41 (R V)	Mt x 42 (R V)	Lk ix 49—50 (R V)
(38) John said unto him, Master (*or,* Teacher), we saw one casting out devils in thy name and we forbade him, because he followed not us		(49) And John answered and said, Master, we saw one casting out devils in thy name, and we forbade him, because he followeth not with us
(39) But Jesus said, Forbid him not for there is no man which shall do a mighty work (*lit* power) in my name, and be able quickly to speak evil of me		(50) But Jesus said unto him, Forbid [him] not for he that is not against you is for you.
(40) For he that is not against us is for us	And whosoever shall give to drink unto one of these little ones a cup of cold water only, in	
(41) For whosoever shall give you a		

"THE KINGDOM OF GOD"

speak evil of me," though he inserts the words of Jesus that precede and follow it. Perhaps Luke had in view the "vagabond Jews" who practised exorcism with adjuration through "*Jesus-whom-Paul-preacheth*"—as though this compound "name" were a name of power in the world of demons[1]. Mark's tradition may have been used by some impostors to justify themselves in the eyes of Christians. "We cast out devils in the name of Jesus; consequently we are Christians." The meaning attached by Mark to "in my name" must be illustrated by the Marcan context, where "*name*" is mentioned in the Greek, though not in the R V. text, "*in [the] name that* [R.V. (text) *because*] ye are Christ's," and also by the parallel Matthew which has "*in* (lit *into*) *the name* of a disciple."

Matthew also substitutes "*one of these little ones*" for the Marcan "*you*" (in "give *you* a cup of water")[2]. And this

Mk ix 38—41 (R V) *contd.*	Mt x 42 (R V) *contd*	Lk ix 49—50 (R V)
cup of water to drink, because (*lit* in name that) ye are Christ's, verily I say unto you, he shall in no wise lose his reward	the name of a disciple, verily I say unto you, he shall in no wise lose his reward	

[1] Acts xix 13 "took upon them to *name* over them...the *name* of the Lord Jesus, saying, I adjure you by *Jesus whom Paul preacheth*"

[2] Clem Alex 579 and 953 (quoting Mt x 42 loosely) and Jerome and Chrys. *ad loc* assume that "these little ones" meant either apostles or disciples of Christ in general, without implying spiritual littleness in the sense of weakness This is more probable than the notion that Jesus meant, by "little ones," those who need *teaching*, as in the Midr. on Gen xiv. 1 (Wu p 191) quoted by Wetstein on Mt x 42—a saying of no authority, put into the mouth of king Ahaz Tertull *Adv Marc* iv 35 quotes Lk xvii 2 "one of these little ones" as meaning "one of His disciples" Christ's tender and affectionate use of the word "little one" may be perhaps illustrated by Is lx 22, but more by Jewish thoughts about "the little one" as exemplified in Benjamin and David (Jacob also, as compared with Esau, is "the little one") See *Proclam.* p 419 referring to *Aboth* iv 26 on the name "Samuel the Little"

Clem Rom § 46 (see Lightf) twice mentions τῶν ἐκλεκτῶν μου, in quoting the Gospels, where Lk xvii. 2 has τῶν μικρῶν τούτων, but

AND "LITTLE CHILDREN"

usefully reminds us that the preceding Marcan context has been speaking of a "little-child" or "one of such little-children" as Christ's representative. Matthew also has spoken of a special "*little-child*" as being placed by Jesus "in the midst of" the disciples, and of Jesus as saying "Whosoever receiveth one such *little-child* in my name receiveth me." This "*little-child*" Jerome prefers to regard, not (1) as the Holy Spirit (which is Origen's view), nor (2) as a "casual (quemlibet) little one" introduced as a type of simple childhood, but (3) as "Jesus Himself[1]." This last view (and by what act or gesture Jesus "placed Himself in their midst") Jerome does not clearly explain But it is useful as reminding us of the language of Jesus about John the Baptist and Himself as "children in the market place[2]," and as suggesting to us that in the Marcan passage under consideration, "in the name *that ye are Christ's*" may have originally been "in the name of *the Little-Child.*" This, being interpreted—and rightly—as meaning "in the name of *the Messiah*," may have caused Mark to render it by the paraphrase in his extant text[3].

If this explanation is correct, the original of Mark's tradition

---

Mk ix 42 adds τῶν πιστευόντων and Mt xviii 6 τῶν πιστευόντων εἰς ἐμέ Here (1) Lk seems to have preserved the original, (2) Mk paraphrased, (3) Mt made the paraphrase clearer, (4) Clem Rom occidentalised the mental "little ones" as "elect" The meaning is retained by Clement, but the homely and spiritual beauty is gone, submerged in technical theology

[1] Jerome on Mt xviii 2 "Vel simpliciter quemlibet parvulum, ut aetatem quaereret et similitudinem innocentiae demonstraret vel certe parvulum statuit in medio eorum *seipsum*, qui non ministrari sed ministrare venerat, ut eis humilitatis tribueret exemplum Alii parvulum interpretantur Spiritum sanctum, quem posuerit in cordibus discipulorum, ut superbiam in humilitatem mutaret" Origen *Comm Matth* xiii 18 (Lomm iii 243) describes the Holy Spirit as being "called by the Saviour, and made to stand in the moral centre of the disciples of Jesus (σταθὲν ἐν μέσῳ τῷ ἡγεμονικῷ τῶν μαθητῶν Ἰησοῦ)," that is, in their heart and conscience

[2] Mt xi 11—19, Lk vii 28—35, see *Son* **3523—5**

[3] See *Son* **3534** *d* where reasons are given for preferring this explanation to the one offered in *Clue* **268—72** (that the original was "in the NAME," *i e.* "in God's name")

might be regarded by the Fourth Evangelist as meaning "When I speak of doing a work '*in my name*' I do not mean 'in the name of Jesus' as a wizard might say 'in the name of Iao'— some supposed Being of which he knew nothing except that this combination of syllables enabled him to work wonders Nor is it like 'in the name of Caesar,' meaning 'in the name of the Power at present on the imperial throne' I mean 'in the name of Jesus the Little One of God,' inseparable from the Father; or 'Jesus the Anointed or Messiah of God,' inseparable from the Anointing Spirit of Regeneration The name of Jesus must not be used as a charm, loosened and detached from the thoughts of Son of God and Anointed of God." Luke gives the impression of not perceiving that Jesus is associating Himself, as the Little One, with the disciples, who are also "little ones" Whereas Mark has "he that is not against *us* is for *us*," Luke has "*you*" instead of "*us*" He has also omitted the Marcan words "There is no man that shall do a mighty work in my name...speak evil of me"; perhaps because he did not perceive that "in my name" meant "in my Spirit," and obviously no one speaking "in the Spirit of Jesus" could "speak evil" of Jesus Himself

Turning to Johannine facts, we find the name "Christ" apparently used by Jesus thus "And this is eternal life, that they should know thee, the only true God, *and* [*him*] *whom thou sentest—Jesus Christ*[1]" This extremely difficult expression may perhaps be best explained, if the text is correct (which is by no means certain), as a paraphrase intended to sum up the doctrine of "eternal life," which is here mentioned for the last time in this Gospel. It was mentioned for the first time in a passage that speaks of "the Son of man" as destined to be "lifted up" on earth, in consequence of the action of God in heaven, who "so loved the world that he gave his only begotten Son that whosoever believeth on him should not perish but have eternal life[2]" Now we are at last told what "eternal life" is. We might have supposed that the definition would stop short

---

[1] Jn xvii 3, on which see *Joh Gr* **1936**
[2] Jn iii 14—16

at "to know thee, the only true God." But the text adds words apparently intended to remind us that when we speak of "*only*," or "*alone*," in connection with God, we must not stop at that word if there is a danger of its being misunderstood as "solitary." We must go on to say that He is not really "alone," since He is, and always was, with the Son—who declares Him[1], and who is here brought before our view as giving His account of the work that He had to do as the Man (Jesus), as the Messiah (Christ), and as the Messenger from heaven to earth ("whom thou hast sent")[2].

Returning to the Marcan traditions "in my name" and "speak evil of me," we are naturally led to illustrate them from the Pauline saying "No man speaking in the Spirit of God saith Jesus *is anathema*[3]"; for Mark's "*speak-evil-of*" is used by him and by Matthew to express "cursing" (as used by LXX in rendering the Mosaic decree "he that *curseth* father or mother let him die the death [4]"). Paul has perhaps in view such public "*speaking-evil-of* (or, *cursing*) the Way [of Christ]" in the synagogue as he himself experienced on the part of Jews in Ephesus[5]. A parallel to this Pauline saying about the anathematizing of Jesus is found in the Johannine Epistle "Prove

---

[1] Jn i. 18 "The only begotten Son that is in the bosom of the Father, he *hath declared* him." "Only begotten (μονογενής) Son" balances, as it were, "*only* (μόνος) true God." Neither epithet implies solitude.

[2] It must be admitted that this explanation of the mention of "Jesus" is not satisfactory. It has been suggested (comp. *Joh. Gr.* **2768**—9) that υἱόν σου, after ὃν ἀπέστειλας, may have been written ΥΝCΟΥ and corrupted into ΙΗCΟΥ *i.e.* Ἰησοῦν, and then Χριστόν added.

[3] 1 Cor. xii. 3.

[4] Mk vii. 10, Mt xv. 4 κακολογέω, quoting Exod. xxi. 17 R.V. "curse" (marg. "revile"). The causative (pi.) of the verb קלל means (Gesen. 886 *b*) "*prop.* make contemptible," but in Exod. xxi. 17 it is parall. to (xxi. 15) "strike" and implies something more serious than bringing into contempt. It occurs in Gen. xii. 3 "I will bless them that bless thee and him that *curseth* thee will I *curse*." The noun קללה is rendered (about 30 times) without exception as "curse," ἀρά, κατάρα etc. Goodspeed gives κακολογέω only in *Didach.* § 2 οὐ κακολογήσεις, "non maledices."

[5] Acts xix. 9 κακολογοῦντες τὴν ὁδόν...

"THE KINGDOM OF GOD"

the spirits, whether they are of God, because many false prophets are gone out into the world...every spirit that *looseth* (or, *confesseth not*) Jesus is not of God; and this is the [spirit] of the *antichrist*...[1]" The two together bring us back to the meaning that appears to be latent under the Marcan tradition· "There is no fear that one who really casts out devils *in my name, that is, in the name of the Little One, the Spirit of Sonship,* will find it possible, a few minutes afterwards, to curse me in the Synagogue For the casting out is in the Spirit of Christ, but the cursing would be in the spirit of the antichrist."

It should be noted that this saying ("Forbid him not") is the only one in the Synoptic Gospels that is recorded—(so far as concerns the first part of it)—as having come from Jesus to the Apostle John[2] In its inclusive spirit it resembles the post-

---

[1] I Jn iv 1—3 RV marg gives no parall. to 1 Cor xii 3 except this An examination of the authorities alleged in Westcott's excursus on I Jn iv 3 W-H txt μὴ ὁμολογεῖ, marg. λύει, should be supplemented by a consideration of Jn ii 19 λύσατε, applied to the Holy Place and also to Christ's "body." The facts, as a whole, suggest as the most probable conclusion that "looseth Jesus," though no longer extant in Greek MSS, was the original reading in the Epistle If so, it may have been used with more than one allusion, (1) "loose the name 'Jesus' from the name 'Christ,'" (2) "loose Jesus, the Son, from the Father and the Spirit," (3) "loose, i e *pull down,* the One Holy PLACE, the divine unity of the Father, the Son, and the Spirit" The Jew that said to an evil spirit (Acts xix 13) "I adjure you by *Jesus whom Paul preacheth*" would be condemned by John as "loosing Jesus," using the name as a mere charm, detached from all those emotions of love and pity and faith with which a disciple of Jesus strove to relieve the sufferings of those whom Jesus loved

[2] Mk ix 38—50 seems continuous The first part is certainly addressed to John Nothing, in Mark's text, indicates whether the whole is, or is not, addressed to John John's appeal is in the plural, "*we* saw" The reply is also in the plural, "Forbid ye not," which continues in what follows. But the parallel columns of Matthew and Luke indicate that the whole is not regarded by them as addressed to one disciple, on a single occasion At Mk ix 41, Luke departs from Mark At Mk ix 42, Matthew (xviii 6) returns to Mark, and Luke (xvii 1—2) has a parallel elsewhere Mk ix 43—8 has a parallel in Matthew (xviii 8—9) but none in Luke Mk ix

AND "LITTLE CHILDREN"

resurrectional utterance to Peter "What God hath cleansed, that make not thou common[1]" If the utterance to John was also post-resurrectional we could understand the introduction of the phrase "*in the name that ye are Christ's*[2]."

49—50 has a parallel elsewhere in Matthew (v 13, Sermon on the Mount) and a parallel elsewhere in Luke (xiv 34—5)

[1] Acts x 15

[2] Perhaps the difference of prepositions in the phrase "in my (or, thy) name" ought not to pass quite unnoticed. Ἐπί in Mk ix 39 ἐπὶ τῷ ὀνόματί μου, and Mk ix 37, Mt xviii 5, Lk ix 48, contrasts curiously with ἐν in Mk ix 38, Lk ix 49 ἐν τῷ ὀνόματί σου "In (ב) the name of the Lord," in Hebrew, would literally be rendered by ἐν But the early books of LXX favour ἐπί, e g Exod v 23, Deut xviii. 5, 19, 20 etc. Note, however, Deut xviii 20 ἐν ὀνόματι θεῶν ἑτέρων and prep ἐν omitted in Deut. xviii 7, 22 In 2 Chr. xiv 11 (Asa speaks) "O Lord, ..we rely on thee, and in (ἐπί) thy name are we come against this multitude," R V marg refers to 1 S xvii. 45 (David speaks to Goliath) "I come unto thee in (ἐν) the name of the Lord," and we might have expected ἐπί in both, to denote reliance "*on*" God. But it is not so In Deut xxi 5 LXX ἐπί, Field assumes that Aq , Sym , and Theod would use ἐν as the literal rendering of the Hebrew The tradition of Mark and Luke about the words of John the son of Zebedee may have preserved the Semitic preposition, while such words of Christ's reply as Mark alone records were handed down in a separate tradition following the LXX in style

The scriptural Hebrew "*in* the name" must be distinguished from the later Hebrew "*to* the name," exemplified in Mt x 41 "he that receiveth a prophet *to the name of a prophet* (εἰς ὄνομα προφήτου)"— on which see Wetstein *ad loc* and Dalman *Words* pp 306, 123, 183— meaning "looking to his character as a prophet" Of this Gesenius (1027—8) gives no instance But see *Oxyr Pap* 37 17 (A D 49) βούλεται ὀνόματι ἐλευθέρου . ἀπενεγκάσθαι, "she wishes to take away the child *on the ground that it was free-born*" This is a legal use apparently borrowed from the Latin "nomen" meaning "account" (also applied to a safe and responsible debtor who is "a good *name*") It is also used of "property standing in the name of," or "to the account of," with ἐξ 247 31, 265 45, 1274 11, with ὑπ(έρ) 1288 22, also ἐπ' ὀνόματος 1102 23, ὀνόματος without prep 1135 2, 1192 4 etc It appears to have passed through Latin and Greek legal usage into later Hebrew where "operam dat legi *in nomen ejus* (לשמה)" means (*Berach* 17 *a*) studying the Law *as being the Law* (Wetstein)

85 (Mark ix. 38—41)

"THE KINGDOM OF GOD"

§ 11. *"If thine eye offend thee," in Mark and Matthew*[1]

There is no very obvious connection between Mark's tradition about the "reward" for "a cup of water" and Mark's next

[1] In Mark, verses 44 and 46 (which are identical with verse 48) are omitted by R V, following "the best ancient authorities"

Mk ix 42—50 (R.V)	Mt xviii 6—9, v. 13 (R V)	Lk xvii 1—2, xiv 34—5 (R V.)
(42) And whosoever shall cause one of these little ones that believe on me (*many anc auth omit* on me) to stumble, it were better for him if a great millstone (*lit* a millstone turned by an ass) were hanged about his neck, and he were cast into the sea	(xviii 6) But whoso shall cause one of these little ones which believe on me to stumble, it is profitable for him that a great millstone (*lit* a millstone turned by an ass) should be hanged about his neck, and [that] he should be sunk in the depth of the sea (7) Woe unto the world because of occasions of stumbling! for it must needs be that the occasions come, but woe to that man through whom the occasion cometh	(xvii. 1) And he said unto his disciples, It is impossible but that occasions of stumbling should come but woe unto him through whom they come! (2) It were well for him if a millstone were hanged about his neck, and he were thrown into the sea, rather than that he should cause one of these little ones to stumble
(43) And if thy hand cause thee to stumble, cut it off it is good for thee to enter into life maimed, rather than having thy two hands to go into hell (*lit* Gehenna), into the unquenchable fire (45) And if thy foot cause thee to stumble, cut it off it is good for thee to enter into life halt, rather than having thy two feet to be cast into hell (*lit* Gehenna). (47) And if thine eye cause thee to	(8) And if thy hand or thy foot causeth thee to stumble, cut it off, and cast it from thee it is good for thee to enter into life maimed or halt, rather than having two hands or two feet to be cast into the eternal fire (9) And if thine eye causeth thee to stumble, pluck it out, and cast it from thee it is good for thee to enter into life with one eye, rather than having two eyes to be cast into the	

AND "LITTLE CHILDREN"

words, which may be rendered for brevity's sake "whosoever shall *offend* one of these little ones[1]." Moreover Mark has combined the warning against "offending little ones" with a

Mk ix 42—50 (R V) *contd*	Mt xviii 6—9, v 13 (R V) *contd*.	Lk xvii 1—2, xiv 34—5 (R V) *contd*.
stumble, cast it out it is good for thee to enter into the kingdom of God with one eye, rather than having two eyes to be cast into hell (*lit* Gehenna), (48) Where their worm dieth not, and the fire is not quenched	hell (*lit* Gehenna) of fire	
(49) For every one shall be salted with fire [*many anc auth add* and every sacrifice shall be salted with salt]	(v 13) Ye are the salt of the earth but if the salt have lost its savour, wherewith shall it be salted? it is thenceforth good for nothing, but to be cast out, and trodden under foot of men	(xiv 34) Salt therefore is good but if even the salt have lost its savour, wherewith shall it be seasoned?
(50) Salt is good but if the salt have lost its saltness, wherewith will ye season it? Have salt in yourselves, and be at peace one with another		(35) It is fit neither for the land nor for the dung-hill [men] cast it out...

[1] Lk. xvii 1 "It is impossible that offences should not come" follows (xvi 1—13) a warning to use wealth with a view to salvation in the next world, and then (*ib* 14—18) a passing allusion to the avarice of the Pharisees, and to John the Baptist and the law of divorce (as to which the Pharisees had not supported the Baptist in his protest against Herod Antipas), and then (*ib* 19—31) the parable of Dives and Lazarus.

Hence, in the Synopticon, it will be found that Lk. xvii. 1 "It is impossible.." comes just after the passage where, in the parallel Mark, Jesus speaks about the "reward" for giving "*a cup of water*," and where, in Luke, Dives cries "Father Abraham...send Lazarus that he may *dip the tip of his finger in water and cool my tongue*" Perhaps this was not thought an accidental coincidence by the author of *Joseph the Carpenter* who says (§ 1) "A single *cup of water*, if a man shall find it *in the world to come, is greater and better than all the wealth of this whole world*"

"THE KINGDOM OF GOD"

warning against allowing one's own members to "offend" oneself. The two sins appear at first sight so distinct that the combination is somewhat perplexing—apparently suitable to a verbal index rather than to a record of doctrine. Luke has omitted the whole of the warning against what may be called "self-offending." Clement of Rome quotes the Synoptists freely to warn the Corinthians against "offending," not "little ones," but "the elect," by schism and discord[1]. Justin Martyr on the other hand (in his Apology) quotes Matthew on "self-offending" as a specimen of Christ's inculcation of purity[2].

The doctrine of "offences," as set forth in the Three Gospels and in the Fourth, has been previously discussed[3]. But an answer is due here to the special question "What, if anything, does John teach, as equivalent to the Marcan doctrine about 'the eye' and other bodily members as causes of 'offence'?" The answer is that John goes to the spiritual root of all Mark's precepts by substituting for all these members the single word "flesh." Luke omits the only Synoptic tradition about the antithesis between the flesh and the spirit[4]. John emphasizes it. First, he himself introduces a suggestion of it in the Prologue to his Gospel[5]. Then he represents Jesus as intro-

---

[1] Clem. Rom. *Cor.* § 46 Ἵνα τί διέλκομεν καὶ διασπῶμεν τὰ μέλη τοῦ Χριστοῦ... εἶπεν γάρ, Οὐαὶ τῷ ἀνθρώπῳ ἐκείνῳ· καλὸν ἦν αὐτῷ εἰ οὐκ ἐγεννήθη ἢ ἕνα τῶν ἐκλεκτῶν μου σκανδαλίσαι· κρεῖττον ἦν αὐτῷ περιτεθῆναι μύλον καὶ καταποντισθῆναι εἰς τὴν θάλασσαν ἢ ἕνα τῶν ἐκλεκτῶν μου διαστρέψαι. Clement is here giving the first place to a late utterance placed by Mark (xiv. 21) and Matthew (xxvi. 24) (comp. Lk. xxii. 22) at the Lord's Supper; he gives the second place to a version of the earlier utterance in Mk. ix. 42, Mt. xviii. 6, Lk. xvii. 2 in which he substitutes "*elect*" for "*little ones.*" Clement of Alexandria 561 follows the Roman Clement. The passage placed first by Clement (Mk. xiv. 21 etc.) refers, in effect, to the "offence" that was on the point of being caused to Christ's disciples by Judas Iscariot (Gal. v. 11 "the *offence of the cross*").

[2] Justin Martyr *Apol.* § 15 περὶ μὲν οὖν σωφροσύνης τοσοῦτον εἶπεν Ὃς ἂν ἐμβλέψῃ .. followed by εἰ ὁ ὀφθαλμός σου (Mt. xviii. 9).

[3] See *Law* chap. v §§ 9—10.

[4] Mk. xiv. 38, Mt. xxvi. 41.

[5] Jn. i. 13 οὐδὲ ἐκ θελήματος σαρκός...ἀλλ' ἐκ θεοῦ is bolder than οὐκ ἐκ σαρκὸς ἀλλ' ἐκ πνεύματος.

88 (Mark ix. 42—50)

AND "LITTLE CHILDREN"

ducing more than a suggestion of it in the dialogue with Nicodemus about Regeneration[1] Jesus also repeats it in the doctrine about giving His own flesh and blood for the life of the world; and in this last instance there occurs the first of the two Johannine mentions of "offending," thus, "Doth this *offend* you?...It is *the spirit* that quickeneth, *the flesh* profiteth nothing[2]."

What is the outcome of all this? It is—as elsewhere in the Fourth Gospel—that we are not to rest in negatives but to pass upward to affirmatives We are not to cut off and cast away the flesh of the body of man, we are to take into ourselves the flesh and blood of the body of the Son of Man. It was in order that we might be "begotten," not "from the will of the flesh" but "from God," that "the Word became flesh" It is written that, after the first Genesis, "*all flesh* corrupted God's way upon the earth," and Philo's comment is "Above all things, the name of 'flesh' is given to man when devoted to self-love[3]" This is what John assumes all through his Gospel And the remedy for this "self-love," John teaches us, is, not to destroy self, or the love of self, but to take into ourselves another love and another self, the love of the Father brought into our hearts by the Son—in whose Spirit we are to receive another self, being born again from above[4].

---

[1] Jn iii 6 "That which is born of the flesh is flesh, and that which is born of the Spirit is spirit"

[2] Jn vi 61—3

[3] Gen vi. 12, on which Philo says "Ante omnia hominem amori sui deditum carnem dixit" When Jesus says (Jn viii 15) "Ye judge according to *the flesh*," the meaning is "according to *the fleshly eye*," which sees only that which suits one's own love of self That is the "eye" which, according to Mark, we are to "cast out" Such a person is "*alone*" when he judges Jesus says (*ib* viii 16) "If I judge, my judgment is true, for I am *not alone*, but I and the Father that sent me"

[4] As all the Synoptists mention the doom pronounced on the man that should "offend" one of the "little ones," there is no reason why John should intervene about it Yet it is worth noting that John's first instance of "offending" is followed by a mention of the falling away of many disciples, and then by a mention of "one of the

(Mark ix. 42—50)

"THE KINGDOM OF GOD"

§ 12. *"The unquenchable fire," in Mark*

"The *unquenchable* fire," in Mark, here corresponds to "the *eternal* fire" in the parallel Matthew[1]. Yet Matthew and Luke have "*unquenchable*" in their records of John the Baptist's teaching, "But the chaff he will burn up in *unquenchable* fire[2]," following "fire," without "unquenchable," in both Gospels, "Every tree that bringeth not forth good fruit is cut out [of the ground[3]] and cast into *fire*[4]."

What are the Hebrew and Greek associations with the word "unquenchable"? In the doctrine of the Baptist, is there any reason why the tree should be cast only into "fire," but the chaff be burnt up in "unquenchable fire"? In the doctrine of Jesus, is there any connection between Matthew's alteration of "unquenchable" into "eternal," and Matthew's subsequent omission of the Marcan words "Where their worm dieth not and the fire is not quenched[5]"? On these last words, as found in Isaiah, what has Jewish tradition to say, and is there any evidence to shew how they were regarded by Jesus? These are the questions now before us

---

Twelve" who is described (vi 70) as "a devil" The context seems to me to indicate that Judas is regarded as in some degree causing this "offence"

[1] Mk ix 43 ἀπελθεῖν εἰς τὴν γέενναν εἰς τὸ πῦρ τὸ ἄσβεστον, Mt xviii 8 βληθῆναι εἰς τὸ πῦρ τὸ αἰώνιον

[2] Mt iii 12, Lk. iii 17 τὸ δὲ ἄχυρον κατακαύσει πυρὶ ἀσβέστῳ.

[3] Mt iii 10, Lk. iii 9 ἐκκόπτεται καὶ εἰς πῦρ βάλλεται In Dan iv 14, ἐκκόπτειν=Aram "cut *down* [a tree]" גדד (but "the stump" is to be left) This is an exceptional meaning for ἐκκόπτω It might=כרת, "eradicate," or (as Aq in Deut xix 5) "cut *out* [branches for firewood]," חטב . In Rom xi 22, 24 it is used of "cutting *out* [a branch from one tree to graft on another]"

[4] "Into *fire*," not "into *the fire*" Comp 1 Pet 1 7 "tried by *fire*" The insertion or omission of "the" in the phrase "in [the] fire" may depend not only on Greek context but also on precedents in Hebrew—where "in *the* fire" is almost universal (Mandelk 156 gives Ezek xxiv 12 "her rust goeth not forth [even] *in fire*" as almost the only exception) See below, p 103, n 1

[5] Mk ix 48 ὅπου ὁ σκώληξ αὐτῶν οὐ τελευτᾷ καὶ τὸ πῦρ οὐ σβέννυται (comp Is lxvi 24)

AND "LITTLE CHILDREN"

In LXX, the adjective "unquenchable," *asbestos*, occurs only in Job (most MSS) "A fire *not blown [by man]* shall devour him," where the Targum has "the fire *of Gehenna which is not blown [by man]*[1]" Elsewhere, Biblical Hebrew and Greek use the verb *"quench,"* occurring for the first time in the Law of the whole burnt offering enacting that the fire "shall be kept burning," and "shall not be quenched[2]." This is also used of quenching metaphorically a destructive flame or one kindled by the wrath of God[3] In particular, Isaiah, after he has said to Israel about the Gentiles "They shall bring all your brethren out of all the nations for an offering unto the Lord...as the children of Israel bring their offering in a clean vessel into the house of the Lord,..." concludes his prophecy with a mention of fire that shall not be quenched· "And they shall go forth [from Jerusalem] and shall look upon the carcases of the men that *have rebelled*[4] *against me ; for their worm shall not die, and their fire shall not be quenched*; and they shall be an abhorring unto all flesh[5]." This accords with words near the commencement

---

[1] Job xx. 26, לא נפח, B א[2] ἄκαυστον, L S "unburnt," "incombustible," but used in B to mean "not kindled [by man]"

[2] Lev vi 9 "The burnt offering shall be on the place of burning (מוקדה) upon the altar all night unto the morning, and the fire of the altar shall be burning (תוקד) thereon (*lit* in it, as A V , בו)— LXX adds "it shall not be quenched"—" (12) the fire upon the altar shall be burning (תוקד) in it, it *shall not be quenched* (לא תכבה) . (13) fire continually (תמיד) shall be burning (תוקד) on the altar, it *shall not be quenched* (לא תכבה) "

Rashi's remark "He that quenches the fire on the altar *transgresses two negative precepts,"* is worth noting in view of the fact that the LXX interpolates *"it shall not be quenched"* so as to make *three* (not "two"), and that many MSS of Mk ix 43—50 have interpolated two repetitions of Mk ix 48 ("where their worm dieth not and the fire is not quenched")

[3] Gesen 459 (including references to Is lxvi. 24 "bodies of renegade Israelites," Is. 1. 31 "people and idols" etc)

[4] Is lxvi 24 "rebelled," R V has "transgressed against me" (as also LXX παραβαίνω) But the same phrase פשע בי is rendered by R V "rebelled against me" in Is 1 2 ; and "transgressed" does not so well express "renegades" or "treaty-breakers " See *Son* **3499** (11) *b*

[5] Is lxvi 20—24. *Tehill.* (on Ps iv 8, Wu 1 48) defends Isaiah

"THE KINGDOM OF GOD"

of the book of Isaiah· "I have...brought up children and they have *rebelled*[1] *against me*...I will...thoroughly *purge away thy dross and will take away all thy tin*...Zion shall be redeemed with judgment...But the destruction of the *rebellious and the sinners* shall be together, and they that forsake the Lord shall be consumed...and the strong shall be as tow, and his work as a spark; and they shall both burn together, and *none shall quench them*[2]"

So far, there is nothing to shew why Matthew and Luke, in the doctrine of the Baptist, insert the Greek *asbestos*, "unquenchable," to describe the fire when burning up the chaff, but not to describe it when burning the tree. But the impression left by the distinction is, that the simple "fire" is used about burning an unfruitful "tree," of no use for fruit, yet good for fuel as long as it lasts, but "unquenchable fire" is used about "fire that will not be quenched till it has completely done its purifying work." It is a paradox. "Chaff" could be consumed in a momentary flame, a tree could not. But if "chaff" means "every particle, however small, of impurity," then we can understand the paradoxical insertion. This explanation accords with the style of the Mark-Matthew tradition, which is Hellenic not Hebraic. English Biblical words ending in *-able* and beginning with *in-* or *un-*, generally point to a Greek origin[3]. They are foreign to Hebrew, which prefers to say "there is no quenching." *Asbestos* is inappropriate in Mark's tradition, where the context speaks of *Gehenna*. But it is appropriate in the

---

against the charge of ending his prophecy in gloom by saying "He is treating of the Gentiles." But the context indicates that they are (as Gesen. 459) "renegade Israelites."

[1] Is. i. 2 "rebelled," ἠθέτησαν, i.e. broken the unwritten compact of family affection (ἀθετέω freq. = "set aside a treaty," "break a compact.") Heb. פשע (Tromm.) = ἀθετέω 11 times and παραβαίνω nowhere except Is. lxvi. 24.

[2] Is. i. 2—31. Ibn Ezra says "They that rebel (פושעים)" are worse than "sinners (חטאים)." The former might naturally mean apostates.

[3] Exceptional words in O.T., e.g. "unsearchable" and "incurable," are represented in Hebrew by "there is not (*or*, was not)" and nouns

AND "LITTLE CHILDREN"

Matthew-Luke tradition if the intention is to imply—as to "quenched"—not only "*it is not*" but also "*it cannot be*."

In Greek literature, asbestos is applied to anything that is "irrepressible" (including "laughter[1]"). But it is also used literally by Philo and Plutarch, who severally apply it to the sacred flame in the Tabernacle of Israel, and in the Temple at Delphi[2]. The various uses of *asbestos* in early Greek, and the absence of the word from the LXX, may explain why, in recording the doctrine of Jesus, Matthew prefers some other word or phrase[3], why Luke prefers no epithet at all[4], and why *asbestos* is rarely used by early Fathers and Apologists[5].

---

[1] See Steph *Thes* on ἄσβεστος, to which add Euseb vi 41 16—18, ἀσβέστῳ πυρί...κατεκάησαν, of martyrs burned with "unslaked lime," quoted from a description of the Decian persecutions by Dionysius. Such a use of the term, if common among early Christians, might prevent its application to the fire of Gehenna.

[2] Philo i 378, and Plutarch *Vit.* 66 B, quoted by Wetstein on Mt iii 12. To these add Philo ii 254 quoting Lev vi 9 as πῦρ ἐπὶ τοῦ θυσιαστηρίου καυθήσεται διὰ παντὸς ἄσβεστον.

[3] Mt xviii 8, xxv 41 τὸ πῦρ τὸ αἰώνιον: elsewhere v. 22, xviii 9 τὴν γέενναν τοῦ πυρός, xiii 42, 50 τὴν κάμινον τοῦ πυρός.

[4] Lk xii 49.

[5] Ἄσβεστος, in the Early Fathers (apart from Hermas *Sim* ix. 10 1 "unslaked lime"), occurs (Goodspeed) twice. Ignatius *Eph.* § 16 ὁ τοιοῦτος, ῥυπαρὸς γενόμενος, εἰς τὸ πῦρ τὸ ἄσβεστον χωρήσει is in a passage said by Lightfoot to be "founded on" 1 Cor iii 16 foll, vi 9, 10, 19. The passage implies that the "corrupters" of God's "house" are οἰκοφθόροι (explained by Hesychius as μοιχοί, comp Orig *Cels* vii 63 φθείρειν . οἶκον). But it seems also to be founded on 1 Cor iii 13—15 which connects the "work" of the Christian builder with "fire" thus "The day shall declare it, because it is revealed *in fire*, and *the fire* itself shall prove each man's work of what sort it is . If any man's work shall abide.. he shall receive a reward. If any man's work shall *be burned* he shall suffer loss, but he himself shall be saved, yet so as *through fire*." Then comes the warning (1 Cor iii 17) "If any man *destroyeth* the temple of God, him shall God *destroy*."

The work is supposed to be a building. The builders are to build up Man, or Humanity, to be a temple for God. Paul, playing on the double meaning of φθείρειν "*corrupt*" or "*destroy*," distinguishes "workers [at the building]"—some of whose work is worthless and "will be burned up (κατακαήσεται)" while they themselves will

"THE KINGDOM OF GOD"

To these facts we may add that the heretic Simon Magus, who is represented to have quoted from Deuteronomy and the Gospels in support of his doctrine that "consuming fire" was the divine Original, does not mention the word "unquenchable" in the course of this exposition[1]. We are thus led to the conclusion that the emphatic expressions about an "unquenchable

---

be "punished [as it were with fining] ($\zeta\eta\mu\iota\omega\theta\dot\eta\sigma o\nu\tau\alpha\iota$)"—from "*corrupters* (or, *destroyers*) [of the building]" whom God will "*destroy*"

Ἄσβεστος occurs also in 2 Clem. § 17 which says, after quoting Is lxvi. 24, that the righteous, "when they see how those who have denied Jesus . . . are punished with terrible torments in unquenchable fire, will give glory to their God." (The writer has previously (§ 7) quoted Is lxvi. 24.)

Apart from a quotation from Homer in Tatian § 8 ("*irrepressible* laughter") and from Mt iii. 12, Lk. iii. 17 in *Tryph* § 49, ἄσβεστος occurs only in Justin *Tryph* § 120, which says that Christ will cut the Jewish nation in two (like Isaiah sawn asunder) and raise some to the place of the Patriarchs but send others "to the condemnation of *the unquenchable fire*." Ἄσβεστος does not occur in *Test. XII Patr.*

[1] Hippol. vi. 4 says that Simon based on Deut. iv. 24 the doctrine that fire was the originating principle, and (later on, *ib.*) says that the fruit has been produced for the storehouse but the chaff for the fire (Mt iii. 12, Lk. iii. 17). Later on (vi. 11) Simon seems to blend Jn xii. 24 with Mt iii. 10, Lk. iii. 9 "If a tree *continues alone* it is utterly destroyed. For somewhere near (says [the Gospel]) the axe [is] by the roots of the tree. *Every tree* (says [the Gospel]) that *produces not good fruit is hewn down and cast into fire.*" I have not found a mention of "quenching" or "unquenchableness" in these chapters.

It is hard to make sense out of Simon's apparent perversion of the clear metaphor in Jn xii. 24 "Except a grain of wheat fall into the earth and die it abideth by itself alone, but if it die it beareth much fruit." Is it the result of some question like "What if it does abide alone? What then? What is the punishment?" Perhaps Simon transposes the question from the "grain" to the "tree" and says "If the tree remains without the vivifying principle it is handed over to the destroying principle."

For us, the main value of the Simonian doctrines is that they help us to understand why the Fourth Evangelist passed over the Baptist's teaching—and Christ's teaching—about "fire." It was already too fully and too variously recorded in such a way as to originate superstitions and juggleries.

AND "LITTLE CHILDREN"

fire" attributed to Jesus by Mark, alone among the Evangelists, did not find favour either with heretics or with the orthodox in the early Church, and yet we see for ourselves that the *thought* of an unquenchable fire was prominent in the ancient Scriptures, both in the Law and in the Prophets

In the Fourth Gospel "fire" is mentioned but once, and then in a parable about the fate of the unfruitful branches of "the true vine". "I am the true vine, and my Father is the husbandman Every branch in me that beareth not fruit, he taketh it away, and every [branch] that beareth fruit, he purifieth it [by pruning] that it may bear more fruit " As to the branches that He "taketh away" it is added "Unless a man abide in me, he is [? at once] cast out like the branch [above-mentioned] and is withered up, and THEY gather them together and cast them into the fire and they are burned[1]"

There is a vague suggestion that while the hand that "taketh away" belongs to One, the "gatherers for the fire" are more than one For the rest, there is nothing to satisfy curiosity about the fire It is all done in the way of nature "The fire" is the natural place for that which is useless except as fuel At the same time the reader is made to feel that this "nature" is not dead machinery but a vital order of things in which he himself is to play a part. He may, if he will, "abide" in the Vine, Christ's love. If he will not abide in it, that is, in the Law of brotherhood, "he is cast out and withered " What casts him out? In the main, he himself, but also the hand of the Husbandman. There is a curious interlacing—and there may be some uncertainty in the disentangling—of metaphor (or personification) and literal statement, but there can be no uncertainty at all about the moral and spiritual lesson Man is part of a whole, a living part of a living whole, and the destiny of each part is to help by being helped.

---

[1] Jn xv 1—6 On the aorist $ἐβλήθη$ see *Joh Gr* **2443**c, **2445**, **2754—5** On "THEY" see *Joh Gr* **2426**, *From Letter* **738** a—b etc

"THE KINGDOM OF GOD"

§ 13 *The undying "worm," in Mark*[1]

We have seen above that Isaiah's prediction of the "worm" and the "fire"—here reproduced by Mark—was regarded by some Jews as applying to Gentiles on whose torments the Jews were to "look[2]." It is perhaps not an accidental coincidence that, although Luke does not insert the fire-and-worm tradition, yet, just in the place that would be parallel to it—and following after the Marcan doctrine about the "cup of water"—he inserts a parable describing Abraham, with a faithful Israelite in his bosom, as holding a dialogue with an unfaithful Israelite who is in Hades, suffering torments.

It is probable that many of the Pharisees in Christ's time considered that in the world to come—in the New Jerusalem, or in Abraham's bosom—they would look upon the torments of Gentiles, publicans, and sinners in Gehenna. Luke at all events prefixes to his parable a statement that the Pharisees "who were lovers of money" scoffed at Jesus, who, in the course of a reply, said to them "Ye are they that justify yourselves in the sight of men...that which is exalted among men is an abomination in the sight of God[3]" Then, still apparently addressing the Pharisees, after a rapid reference to John the Baptist, whom they had not supported in his protest against "adultery" in high places, Jesus introduces the picture of the "rich man" in Hades and "in torments."

It seems to contain allusions, not at once obvious, to Jewish prejudices. For example, a Jewish tradition bids us take care to be among those who "*see*" the torment, not among those who "*are seen*[4]." But here it is Dives in torment who "lifted up his eyes and *seeth* Abraham[5]." Moreover, whereas some Jewish traditions, and Christian too[6], imply that those who "see" rejoice over those who suffer, no joy is manifest in

---

[1] Mk ix 48 ὅπου ὁ σκώληξ αὐτῶν οὐ τελευτᾷ
[2] Is lxvi 20—24 "they shall look upon the carcases," see above, p 91, n 5 *ad fin*
[3] Lk. xvi 14 foll.
[4] See Midrash on Eccles. vii 14—15 (Wu p 103)
[5] Lk. xvi 23   [6] See above, p 93, n 5 *ad fin*

Abraham He still calls the sufferer "son." And the sting of brotherly affection forces Dives to pray, even in the midst of his own anguish, that his "five brethren" may not "come into this place of torment." This sting is not mere torture. According to some Jewish traditions, it may be regarded as coming from "the worm[1]."

The total result of Luke's narrative is an impression that either the "Hades" that he mentions here is not the same as the "Gehenna" that he once mentions elsewhere, or else that he regards both Hades and Gehenna as places where those who suffer may still be regarded as sons by Abraham and still be capable of an unselfish affection

Luke's picture of Abraham seeing Dives in torment meets some objections that might be brought against ancient interpretations of Isaiah, and suggests a pathetic—though hardly complete—explanation of the "worm." But it does not illustrate Mark's context—which attacks religious jealousy and exclusiveness and represses "we forbade him" by "forbid him not." Jesus appears to call the man described as "casting out devils" in His "name" one of "His little ones." The attempt of John to "forbid" him He seems to regard as a "causing to stumble," against which His disciples are to be warned. Rather than persist in such action it would be better to perish, for persistence implies entrance into Gehenna, the region of the worm and the fire. When they desire to cast others out from the royal City, the children of the Kingdom are warned that they may be casting themselves out into a place of weeping and gnashing of teeth, the home of remorse and envy

The Fourth Gospel describes such an act of exclusiveness in detail. The man born blind and healed by Jesus is cast out of the synagogue for refusing, in effect, to adopt the language of the rulers who say "Give glory to God. we know that this man is a sinner[2]." But the result is that the outcast sees,

---

[1] See *Son* **3499** (iv) *a* quoting *Berach* 18 *b* about "the worm" as painful to "the dead," where the context speaks of a dead father's knowledge or ignorance of the sorrows of his children

[2] Jn ix 24 In effect, this is a command to the man to "speak-evil-of (κακολογεῖν) Jesus," see above, p. 83

"THE KINGDOM OF GOD"

and the casters out, blind before, become more blind than ever. Such is the "judgment" passed upon them[1]. And this thought recurs at the close of Christ's public career· "They were not able to believe," it is said, "for that Isaiah said again, He hath blinded their eyes and he hardened their heart[2]" Some indeed of the rulers "believed" in Jesus, after a fashion, "but because of the Pharisees they did not confess it lest they should be put out of the synagogue[3]." Thus "the Jews" were shut out or shut themselves out from the City of God, but concerning the man whom they shut out, the excommunicated, it is said, as of no other in this Gospel, that he "worshipped" Jesus[4]

§ 14 *"For every one shall be salted with fire," in Mark*[5]

Matthew and Luke omit these words, and many authorities alter them in Mark—perhaps because they might be interpreted as meaning that every one shall be salted with the fire of Gehenna or Hades. But the Marcan tradition may be explained, both as to its meaning and as to its context, if we suppose Mark to be abridging a doctrine of fire in which this came as a conclusion. "It is not enough to avoid evil; follow after that which is good. Set your thoughts not on the unquenchable fire of Gehenna but rather on the unquenchable fire of the altar of the Lord Aim not at self-mutilation but at self-devotion. Present your bodies as a continual living sacrifice on that altar[6]. But whoso would present such a sacrifice must be

---

[1] Jn ix 39 "For judgment came I into this world, that they which see not may see, and that they which see may become blind"
[2] Jn xii 39—40   [3] Jn xii 42.   [4] Jn ix. 38.
[5] Mk ix 49 πᾶς γὰρ πυρὶ ἁλισθήσεται, with many variations for which see Swete and *Journ Theol. Stud* Oct. 1915, pp 16—7 (Burkitt)
[6] Comp. Rom. xii 1 "Present your bodies a living sacrifice," and the following verses—most of them laying stress on positive precepts, but terminating with the contrast "Be not conquered by the evil but conquer the evil with the good" The context (*ib* 18—20) has the Marcan word, rare in N T, εἰρηνεύειν (*"be at peace"*) and shews how to "heap coals of fire" on the head of an "enemy" A contrast between "peace" and "victory," with a mention of "tribulation" in the context, is found in Jn xvi 33

salted with fire. The Scripture says that every sacrifice on the visible altar shall be salted with salt. So every one that would present himself as a sacrifice on the invisible and spiritual altar must be salted with the fire of the Holy Spirit, the Spirit of love, trust, and peace—peace even under trials and troubles and persecutions."

At the same time, we must not pass over the Hebrew and Jewish practice of "salting" newly born children Ezekiel takes this for granted; Jerome writes of it as an existing custom; and so does the Talmud, which permits it to be performed on the sabbath[1]. It is very probable that Jesus—with whom the thought of "the little ones" was always near at hand —was referring to the doctrine of regeneration In this there is nothing incompatible with the doctrine of sacrifice. Unless a human being is born again he cannot "present his body as a sacrifice" to God. If Jesus referred to the new birth as a "salting," it would seem to be only one of many homely metaphors adapted for Galilaean hearers, women as well as men.

Philo somewhat resembles Mark in the order of some observations about a sacrifice of praise or thanks, and a mention of salt. For he places first the Levitical commandment to keep the fire burning and "unquenched." He tells us that "the sacred flame is the symbol of thanksgiving (*lit*

---

[1] See Ezek xvi 4 "In the day that thou wast born thy navel was not cut, neither wast thou washed in water to cleanse thee, thou wast not salted at all, nor swaddled at all " The Targum accepts all these statements as literal Jerome says *ad loc* "The tender bodies of infants .. *are wont to be salted by midwives* (*solent ab obstetricibus sale contingi*, ut sicciora sint et restringantur) " Then he quotes Mt v 13 ("Ye are the salt of the earth"), Coloss iv 6, and Lev ii 13 ("omne sacrificium vestrum sale salietur"), but not Mark In *Sabb* 129 *b*, the "salting" is allowed on the sabbath Rashi, on Ezek , like Jerome, uses the present tense as of a present custom ("hinc est quod sale *fricent* infantem"). *Enc Bib* ii 1503 describes the "salting" as "still kept up to the present day " Hastings (iv. 632) about "the newborn infant in the East," says that "during the first week salt water is applied daily to the lips and flexures of the body," as "a hardening process "

"THE KINGDOM OF GOD"

of the eucharist)[1]"; and then he adds "*After this*, it [*i.e.* the Law] says 'On every offering ye shall offer salt[2].'" As a fact, the injunction to add "salt" comes much earlier than the law of the burnt offering; but the order followed by Philo is natural where the first thought is about a sacrifice and the second thoughts are about how, and in what spirit, it is to be presented.

Plutarch, supplementing Philo, may help us to understand how the Marcan doctrine of "salt" might be expanded for Greek-speaking Christians in other traditions than those of Matthew and Luke. For Plutarch reminds us that Homer called salt "divine[3]," and that Plato declared "the body of salt" to be "most beloved by the Gods in accordance *with the Law of human nature*[4]." Plutarch adds that men ascribe a divine nature to things that are common and wide-reaching in application to their needs—as, for example, *the water, the light, the seasons*," and that such ascription is specially due to salt, since it has the divine quality of preserving for a long time the bodies of the dead, and since it "arrays itself against death." Salt, he says, does as it were "the work of the soul," keeping together what would otherwise fall to pieces. This praise of salt he concludes by calling attention to the fact—or what is alleged by him as a fact—that lightning has the same power of preserving bodies from putrefaction, and by asking "What wonder, therefore, if *salt, having the same power as the divine fire*, was itself also supposed to be divine by the ancients[5]?"

The Fourth Gospel, though it nowhere mentions "salt," implies a sympathy with the feeling that would ascribe "a

---

[1] Philo ii 254 quoting Lev. vi 9 thus πῦρ...καυθήσεται διὰ παντὸς ἄσβεστον.

[2] Philo ii 255 Μετὰ ταῦτά φησιν (Lev ii 13).

[3] *Iliad* ix 214

[4] Plut *Mor* 684 F Πλάτωνος δὲ τῶν ἁλῶν σῶμα κατὰ νόμον ἀνθρώπων θεοφιλέστατον εἶναι φάσκοντος, from Plato *Tim* 60 D—E ἁλῶν κατὰ λόγον νόμου θεοφιλὲς σῶμα (on κατὰ λόγον νόμου see Archer-Hind)

[5] Plut. *Mor*. 685 B—D. Comp Plato *Symp* 177 B ἐνῆσαν ἄλες ἔπαινον θαυμάσιον ἔχοντες, which suggests that "praises of salt" were not uncommon See Pliny *H N* xxxi 102 on the proverb that for certain diseases "nihil esse utilius sale et sole."

100 (Mark ix 42—50)

AND "LITTLE CHILDREN"

divine nature" to the elemental things that help us. It does not shrink from representing Jesus as saying, in effect, "I am the Light," "I am the Bread," "I am the giver of the Water." In all these cases the epithet "living" is implied if it is not expressed. The Light is "the life of men." The Bread is expressly called "living." Plutarch might tell us that this meant "bread made with salt" as distinguished from the bread of the Egyptian priests[1]. The Fourth Evangelist (we may be sure) would have in view no such literal details as these. But he would not think the epithet "living" a small detail, and he would probably tell us that he included in it what Mark meant by "salt" and "salting." It was a form of expressing the influence of the Holy Spirit, which invigorated life besides being a preservative against death.

§ 15. *"Have salt in yourselves, and be at peace one with another," in Mark*[2]

Matthew and Luke differ from Mark as to the contexts in which they mention "salt." Matthew apparently takes salt to mean a purifying influence exerted by the prophets of the old Dispensation and to be exerted by the preachers of the Gospel. Both the prophets and the preachers he regards as being themselves purified by persecution and preserved from the corruption of sloth and self-will: "Blessed are ye when [men] shall reproach you...for so persecuted they the prophets that were before you *Ye are the salt of the earth*[3]." This is

---

[1] Plut *Mor* 684 F τοὺς Αἰγυπτίους ἱερέας ἁγνοὺς ὄντας ἀπέχεσθαι τὸ πάμπαν ἁλῶν ὥστε καὶ τὸν ἄρτον ἄναλον προσφέρεσθαι

[2] Mk ix 50 ἔχετε ἐν ἑαυτοῖς ἅλα καὶ εἰρηνεύετε ἐν ἀλλήλοις. Elsewhere in NT εἰρηνεύω occurs only in Rom xii 18 εἰ δυνατόν. .μετὰ πάντων ἀνθρώπων εἰρηνεύοντες, and 2 Cor xiii 11 εἰρηνεύετε, 1 Thess v. 13 εἰρηνεύετε ἐν ἑαυτοῖς (prob not meaning "in yourselves," but "among yourselves," though it suggests an inclusion of the former meaning as well) On the strange reading ἐν αὐτοῖς see Lightfoot *ad loc*

[3] Mt v 11—13 Luke is parallel as far as Mt v 12 (Lk vi 23), but breaks off there, and does not mention "salt" till much later, as the moral appended to Lucan parables (the Building of the Tower and the Plan of Campaign) illustrating the Doctrine of Renunciation (Lk xiv 25—35)

in the Sermon on the Mount   The parallel Luke makes no mention of salt. Later on, when multitudes are following Jesus on the way to Jerusalem, Luke represents Him as "turning" to them and teaching them that those who come to Him need special renunciation   They must think before they begin to build the "tower" or wage the "war"· "Whosoever he be of you that renounceth not all that he hath, he cannot be my disciple; *salt therefore is good*· but if even the salt hath lost its savour...[1]?"

This question—as to what is done if the salt loses its savour—is found also here in Mark, and Matthew includes it in the Sermon on the Mount   But Matthew and Luke hardly give a positive answer to the question. They imply that little or nothing can be done. The salt must be thrown away—though perhaps, says Matthew (according to a doubtful modern interpretation), it may help to make a footpath. Apparently they were not satisfied with the answer given by Mark: "Have salt in yourselves, and be at peace one with another." Perhaps they were in doubt as to its meaning. Hermas uses the precept "*be at peace among yourselves*" to forbid those who are in authority in the Church to set a bad example by dissension[2]. With a similar application, Clement of Rome exhorts any member of the Church of Corinth who feels that he is a cause of discord to say "I will depart where ye will—only let the flock of Christ be at peace with the appointed presbyters[3]" If early Christians narrowed down the precept "have salt in yourselves" so as to make it mean simply "avoid discord among yourselves," it is not surprising that Matthew and Luke omitted it as being hardly weighty enough to come at the close of a very solemn warning.

We pass to the examination of Johannine doctrine corresponding to the Marcan metaphors of "salt" and "fire" and to the precept "be at peace one with another." Is John's con-

---

[1] Lk. xiv 33—4
[2] Hermas *Vis* iii 9 2—10
[3] Clem Rom § 54 ἄπειμι οὗ ἐὰν βούλησθε, καὶ ποιῶ τὰ προστασσόμενα ὑπὸ τοῦ πλήθους· μόνον τὸ ποίμνιον τοῦ Χριστοῦ εἰρηνευέτω μετὰ τῶν καθεσταμένων πρεσβυτέρων

ception of "peace" like that of Mark? And whence is that "peace" to be obtained? And has John anything to say that bears on Matthew's apparent axiom, that "persecution" helps to make the preachers of the Gospel "the salt of the earth"?

§ 16. *Johannine doctrine on fire*[1]

The Matthew-Luke tradition of the Baptist's doctrine on fire says, "Every tree that bringeth not forth good fruit is hewn down and cast into (lit.) fire[2]." Taken literally, this would condemn to fire every tree—including cedars and oaks—that does not bear "good fruit." Another difficulty is the insertion of "good" This, at first sight, seems superfluous But it is explicable if the sentence is as it were against hypocritical fruit-trees, trees that profess to bear eatable fruit but in fact produce only that which is uneatable. It is obvious that the Baptist meant "every *fruit-tree*" But, more particularly, he probably had in mind the Vine of Israel, in contrast with the wild vine mentioned in the word of the Lord to Ezekiel,

---

[1] In Jn xv 6 εἰς τὸ πῦρ βάλλουσιν, may we infer anything from John's insertion of the article (τὸ πῦρ) as contrasted with Mk ix. 22 εἰς πῦρ αὐτὸν ἔβαλεν, Mt iii 10 (rep Mt vii 19), Lk. iii 9 εἰς πῦρ βάλλεται? The question is complicated by the fact that the lit Hebrew almost without exception (Mandelk 155—6) says "in (*or*, with) *the fire*" (*when the phrase is used absolutely*) whereas LXX says "in *fire*" Also in Greek, as in English, one may speak of a child "falling into *the fire*" (as in Mt xvii 15, but not in the parall Mk ix 22 "into fire. into waters") meaning "*the fire [on the hearth]*" (comp. Acts xxviii 5 "shaking off (the viper) into *the fire*") It is worth noting that in O T the only instance of Heb "in *fire*," *used absolutely*, is Ezek xxiv 12, where the meaning is "*not [even] in fire* [much less in water]," and the only instance of "in *water*," *used absolutely*, is (Mandelk. 670) Ezek xvi 4 "*not [even] in water* wast thou washed" Perhaps John wished to avoid the suggestion that "into *fire*" here meant "not into water" He preferred to say "into *the fire*"—as being the natural place for the unfruitful vine-branches

[2] Mt. iii. 10, Lk. iii 9 πᾶν οὖν δένδρον μὴ ποιοῦν καρπὸν καλόν, but W H bracket καλόν in Luke, and Origen (*Comm Joann* VI. 14, Lomm 1 219) expressly says that "good" is omitted in Luke, because there the words are addressed to the multitudes, and the meaning is fruit of any kind.

"THE KINGDOM OF GOD"

"Son of man, what is the vine tree more than any tree, the vine branch that is among the trees of the forest[1]?" This means, as Rashi says, "I do not speak unto thee about the vine of the vineyards that beareth fruit, but about the branches of the [wild] vine that groweth in the forest." The context implies that the wild vine is appointed by nature to be burned ("the vine tree, among the trees of the forest, which I have given to the fire for fuel") and is of no other use. But the Baptist is speaking of Israelites as trees appointed to bear fruit, for whom it is a condemnation to degenerate, falling back as it were into the wild vine and out of the cultivated vine—the Vine of the Vineyard of the Lord. Isaiah had accustomed Israelites to this personification or allegory of the degenerate and ungrateful Vine, bound to produce "fruit" worthy of the name, and failing to produce anything but "wild grapes[2]," and this thought perhaps is latent under the Baptist's expression "good fruit."

The Fourth Gospel takes us back to the positive doctrine about the Vine, which, in the Prophets, is more common than the negative doctrine. John makes no mention of the "wild vine" or the "tree that bringeth not forth good fruit." But beginning from the true Vine, he describes the Husbandman, God, as "cleansing" those branches that bear fruit and taking away those that bear none[3]. This is metaphor. But he passes on into allegory when he implies that the "branches" have a power of "abiding" or "not abiding" in the Vine "*The branch* cannot bear fruit of itself except it *abide in the vine*," "I am the vine, ye are the branches. *he that abideth in me*,...the same beareth much fruit," "If a man abide not •in me he is [? at once][4] cast forth outside like *the branch* [above mentioned] and is [at once] withered; and THEY [then][5] gather them, and cast them into the fire, and they are burned[6]."

---

[1] Ezek. xv 2, comp Jerem xxiv 2
[2] Is v 2—4   [3] Jn xv 2
[4] "At once," see above, p 95, n 1
[5] "THEY," see *Joh Gr* **2426**. Nonnus supplies αἰθέριοι δρηστῆρες Comp Rev xiv 18 ἄγγελος. .[ὁ] ἔχων ἐξουσίαν ἐπὶ τοῦ πυρός In Jn xv. 6 "the branch"=τὸ κλῆμα (R V has "a branch")
[6] Jn xv 1—6.

104 (Mark ix. 42—50)

AND "LITTLE CHILDREN"

This is the only mention of the Greek word "fire" in the Fourth Gospel, and it cannot be said that this "fire" purifies. The pruning-knife purifies, the fire destroys It is only in a symbolical form, if at all, that the Evangelist suggests the thought of fire as a purifying influence. He speaks of a "[fire] of coals" on two occasions, first, when Peter denied his Master, and secondly, after Christ's resurrection, when the same Apostle received not only the food that was to prepare him for following Christ but also a special command to "follow " Thus, says Ephrem Syrus, in a fiery trial Peter fell, and by a fiery purification he was uplifted and strengthened[1].

A mystical suggestion of this kind was not likely to add to heretical perversions (such as those mentioned above[2]) of the fire-doctrine of the Synoptists. And the "fire of coals" is well adapted to suggest the stinging of a conscience that does not pain openly and momentarily, but gnaws like a worm that will not cease, or burns like embers that will not expire, until nothing remains to be consumed. For the most part, however, the Fourth Evangelist prefers other ways of expressing what Mark calls the "salting" that the disciples of Christ are to "have in themselves[3]."

§ 17. *How John expresses "salting with fire"*

John's non-use of the metaphor of fire to express purifying influence is probably based on other grounds beside the fear of heretical perversion of fire-doctrine The Fourth Gospel is, in one aspect, the Gospel of Nature Earth and the fruits of the earth including bread and wine; water and especially water that is pure and running, or (as the Greek and Hebrew have it) "living"; wind or spirit or the breath that we breathe— these three elemental metaphors are well suited to express in a homely and natural way that invisible life of the soul which

---

[1] Jn xviii 18, xxi 9 "[fire] of coals," $ἀνθρακιά$, on which see *Son* 3369 *a—e* Modern prosaic sobriety shrinks from discrediting John with such allusions But the Fourth Gospel is not modern and not prosaic

[2] See above, p 94, n 1

[3] Mk ix 50

"THE KINGDOM OF GOD"

corresponds to the visible life of the body. Fire is not so well suited. The other three elements, or their products, represent internal sources of life; fire represents an external influence.

Yet something more is wanted beside food and breath for the development of the body, and similarly something more is needed for the soul. Both want exercise. Both must learn to "endure hardness," and to cast off everything that conduces to sloth and uselessness, preventing fruitful action. Let us consider whether this finds any expression in the Johannine metaphor of the Vine that is to bear fruit, with its accompanying thought of pruning.

"Pruning" is not indeed mentioned And perhaps pruning is not exactly the process implied John may be alluding to the Hebrew Law, which regards a fruit-tree in the Promised Land as having a kind of Hebrew humanity, so that it has to be "circumcised" before it takes its place in the service of the nation. The Law said that for three years after an Israelite had planted a fruit-tree he was to "*treat-as-uncircumcised its uncircumcision* [namely], its fruit " In other words he was to take it away and destroy it. This the LXX paraphrases as "Ye shall *cleanse* [*by taking from*] *around* [*it*] *its uncleanness*[1]." This explains the extraordinary expression in John, who applies the verb "cleanse" (nowhere else used in the New Testament in any sense) to the cleansing of the fruit-bearing branches of the Vine. "Every branch that beareth fruit, he cleanseth it that it may bear more fruit[2]."

Philo quotes the Levitical passage as enjoining complete dependence upon God, the only Planter, and as bidding us "cleanse the uncleanness" of what we suppose we ourselves have planted: "For it bids us cut away self-conceit, and self-conceit is unclean by nature[3]." Elsewhere Philo refers to the

---

[1] Lev xix 23 עָרֵל, LXX περικαθαριεῖτε τὴν ἀκαθαρσίαν αὐτοῦ, followed by ὁ καρπὸς αὐτοῦ... The translators have ἀκροβυστιεῖτε τὴν ἀκροβυστίαν αὐτῶν See Gesen. 790 b Heb. עָרֵל =(Tromm) ἀκρόβυστος (1), ἀπερικάθαρτος (1), ἀπερίτμητος (26)   [2] Jn xv 2 καθαίρει αὐτό ..

[3] Philo 1 53 κελεύει καθαρίσαι τὴν ἀκαθαρσίαν αὐτοῦ—τοῦτο δέ ἐστι, τὸ δοκεῖν φυτεύειν 'Αποτεμεῖν γὰρ οἴησιν ἐπαγγέλλεται, οἴησις δὲ ἀκάθαρτον φύσει

AND "LITTLE CHILDREN"

Law still more fully, with repeated mentions of "cleansing," and "clean," and "cleansing around[1]." No instance is given in the Greek Thesaurus of "cleanse" applied to a tree, either in the sense of pruning, or in the sense of discarding immature fruit in saplings. It may be added that LXX uses "cleansing around" (in two forms) concerning literal "circumcising" and concerning circumcising "the heart[2]." The same Greek word is also applied to the "cleansing" of the sins of Isaiah by fire from the altar, and to the forbidden worship of Moloch by a father "causing" his son "to pass through the fire[3]."

In setting forth this doctrine of "abiding" in the Vine and of being "cleansed" in it in order to bear much fruit, Jesus says "Now are ye *clean* because of the word that I have spoken unto you[4]." This appears to refer to the words "Ye are *clean*, but not all[5]"—uttered previously, after Jesus had washed the feet of the disciples, and had communicated to all but Judas some share in the New Covenant of brotherly love which, He said, was to be the sign of their discipleship. The offscouring[6] from the washing of their feet Jesus had as it were taken upon Himself, when He wiped it upon the napkin with which He had girded Himself, and symbolically admitted them into this New Covenant. In both utterances—in the simile of the Washing and in the simile of the Vine—there is an allusion to the New and cleansing Covenant of the circumcision of the heart, a heart created anew in the Spirit of the new Love that Jesus had brought into the world ("even as I have loved you, that ye also love one another[7]")

It remains to consider whether John expresses in any other form that training and disciplining of the soul which corresponds

---

[1] Philo 1. 344—6 κάθαρσις, ἀκάθαρτος, περικαθαίρεσθαι, ἀπερικάθαρτος.
[2] Josh v 4 περικαθαίρω (מול), Deut xxx 6 περικαθαρίζω (מול).
[3] Is vi 7 περικαθαρίζω (כפר), Deut xviii 10 περικαθαίρω (עבר hi.)
[4] Jn xv 3   [5] Jn xiii. 10—11
[6] This would naturally be called, in the language of 1 Cor iv 13, περικάθαρμα or περίψημα, terms said by Origen (*Comm. Joann* xxviii. 14, Lomm ii 355) to be more applicable to Jesus than to any apostle
[7] Jn xiii. 34.

"THE KINGDOM OF GOD"

to the Marcan "salting with fire" and to the Johannine "cleansing [of the vine]."

§ 18. "*Tribulation*[1]"

We have seen above that Matthew, in the Sermon on the Mount, placed before the words "Ye are *the salt* of the earth" an exhortation to rejoice under persecution. This suggests the thought that persecution had "salted" the Prophets of old and would similarly "salt" the preachers of the Gospel: "Rejoice... for so *persecuted* they the prophets that were before you. Ye are the *salt* of the earth[2]." "The earth" is "the world[3]." It may be fairly replied that the persecuting world can no more "salt" a prophet so as to keep him "the salt of the world," than it can "enlighten" a prophet so as to keep him "the light of the world." Yet still the world's persecution of the prophet may be made by God the instrument for keeping the prophet unworldly.

Luke, later on, says "*Salt therefore is good*," but does not connect the saying with any mention of "persecution" (having, instead, several precepts enjoining self-renunciation)[4]. "Tribulation" is used synonymously with "persecution" for the sake of the Gospel in the explanation of the Parable of the Sower, where Mark and Matthew say "When there cometh to pass *tribulation or persecution* because of the Word"; but Luke has "in time of *temptation*[5]." And in the Discourse on the Last Days, where Mark and Matthew predict "*tribulation*," the parallel Luke predicts "*distress*" (literally "*necessity*" or "*straits*")[6]. Luke never uses the word "tribulation" in his Gospel.

---

[1] "Tribulation" is used as the rendering of $\theta\lambda\hat{\iota}\psi\iota s$ throughout this section

[2] Mt v 12—13. If the two verses are to be regarded as disconnected, then "Ye are the salt" (Chrys.) may be taken as introducing $\hat{\epsilon}\gamma\kappa\acute{\omega}\mu\iota\alpha$ after $\pi\alpha\rho\alpha\acute{\iota}\nu\epsilon\sigma\iota s$. See McNeile, *ad loc* on the paradox in "salt of the earth" in view of Ps cvii 34 "a salt desert."

[3] See *Son* 3442 *c—h* on "The earth" variously interpreted

[4] Lk. xiv 34   [5] Mk iv 17, Mt xiii 21, Lk. viii 13

[6] Mk xiii 19, Mt xxiv 21 $\theta\lambda\hat{\iota}\psi\iota s$, Lk. xxi 23 $\mathring{\alpha}\nu\acute{\alpha}\gamma\kappa\eta$

Yet he uses it several times in the Acts—twice in Stephen's speech, once in his own description of the persecution that followed Stephen's martyrdom, and twice in the Pauline declarations· "Through many *tribulations* we must enter into the kingdom of God," and "Bonds and *tribulations* await me[1]" In none of the Gospels does "tribulation" occur except in utterances of Christ, and Luke may have been influenced by the fact that the word does not appear to have been in literary use before the end of the first century; and, as then used— meaning literally "pressure" or "squeezing"—it may have seemed to him not quite appropriate for a historian recording utterances of Jesus[2] The following parallels seem to shew Luke drawing out from Mark's brief and vernacular "tribulation" (or "pressure") all that seemed to him implied in the original.—

Mk xiii. 24 (R.V.)	Mt. xxiv. 29 (R.V)	Lk. xxi. 25—6 (R.V.)
After that *tribulation* the sun shall be darkened..	After the *tribulation* of those days the sun shall be darkened...	There shall be signs in sun... and upon the earth *distress* of nations, in *perplexity* ... men *fainting* (or, *expiring*) for fear, and for expectation ...[3]

Origen tacitly explains Luke's motive in his comment on the first of the very numerous instances of "tribulation" in the Psalms. "The divine Scripture," he says, "with a meaning of its own...seems to give the name of '*tribulation*' to that which environs and meets the saint for the purpose of training, whereas that which befalls the sinner it calls '*scourge*.' For it

---

[1] Acts vii. 10, 11, xi 19, xiv 22, xx 23
[2] See Steph *Thes* on θλίψις
[3] "Distress"=συνοχή, "perplexity"=ἀπορία In LXX, θλίψις freq =צרה or צר, συνέχω=(1) צור, (1) צרר, συνοχή (a rare word) = (2) מצור, (1) (by error) צד (read as צר), ἀπορία=(1) צרה, ἀπορoῦμαι= (1) צרר

109 (Mark ix. 42—50)

says 'Many are the *tribulations* of the righteous' and 'Many are the *scourges* of the sinner[1].'"

Origen's view agrees with such inferences as would naturally be drawn from Scripture and Jewish tradition. The first Biblical mention of (LXX) "tribulation" is where Jacob says "I will make there an altar unto God, who answered me in the day of my *tribulation* (R.V. *distress*)[2]." The Midrash on an earlier passage in Genesis remarks that the elect Patriarch (Jacob) and the elect Prophet (Moses) were both subjected to fear and anxiety. God had promised to be with them, but "*the righteous must not build upon that in this world*," "*In this world the righteous must have no self-confidence*[3]."

Let us turn to the Fourth Gospel. Above we find it suggesting "tribulation" under the metaphor of "cleansing" the fruitful boughs of the Vine—an act that Philo described as the "cutting away" of "self-conceit." Now looking on a little we find a mention of "persecution" where Jesus says to the disciples "If they *persecuted* me they will also *persecute* you[4]," thus strengthening them that they might not "stumble[5]," and preparing them for a general antagonism with "the world[6]." And at this point, in quite a new metaphor, the naturalness and the ultimate fruitfulness of some kind of suffering and "tribulation" are brought before us in a sentence alluding to the ancient "sorrow" of childbirth predicted for Eve, but describing it as swallowed up in the joy that follows "The woman when she is bringing forth [a child] hath *sorrow* because

---

[1] Origen on Ps iv. 1, quoting Ps xxxiv. 19, xxxii 10. "With a meaning of its own"=ἰδίως.

[2] Gen. xxxv. 3

[3] See *Gen. r.* (Wu. p 373) on Gen. xxxii 7 "Self-confidence (Selbstvertrauen)" appears to mean here what a man of the world might call "confidence in his fortune," while a man calling himself religious, yet feeling the same thing, might disguise it under the phrase "confidence in God."

[4] Jn xv 20.

[5] Jn xvi 1 ἵνα μὴ σκανδαλισθῆτε, comp. Mk iv 17 γενομένης θλίψεως ἢ διωγμοῦ διὰ τὸν λόγον εὐθὺς σκανδαλίζονται (sim Mt xiii 21)

[6] Jn xvi. 20 "Ye shall weep and lament, but the world shall rejoice"

her hour is come, but when she is delivered of the little-child she no longer remembereth the *tribulation* for the joy that a man is born into the world. And ye now therefore have *sorrow*, but I will see you again, and your heart shall rejoice and your joy no man shall take from you[1]."

Soon after this, comes the final mention of "tribulation," at the conclusion of Christ's Last Discourse. It is in a sentence closely resembling the Midrashic comment quoted above on Jacob's *"tribulation"* as being, *"in this world,"* inevitable "These things have I spoken unto you that in me ye may have peace In the world ye have *tribulation* but be of good cheer, I have gained the victory over the world[2]." Thus the final mention of "peace" by Christ before His crucifixion is connected with a mention of "victory" that implies war, and with a "tribulation" through which that victory is to be achieved

All these Johannine words are far removed from the words of Mark But they accord not only with Hebrew and Jewish thought, but also with Mark himself when Mark is interpreted in accordance with the thought that underlies his brief traditions

---

[1] Jn xvi 21—2. W. H. txt ἀρεῖ "shall take" "Bringing forth"=τίκτῃ, "sorrow"=λύπην The first Biblical mention of λύπη is combined with τίκτω in Gen. iii 16 "Multiplying will I multiply thy *sorrows*...in *sorrows shalt thou bring forth children* (ἐν λύπαις τέξῃ τέκνα) "

[2] Jn xvi 33 "Ye have (ἔχετε)" is given by W H without alternative, but naturally it has been altered by many authorities into the future, the meaning being probably "ye have [in store]" SS has "that there may be to you in me peace, *and* [*yet that*] *in the world there may be to you distress*," perhaps meaning "that ye may have peace in me, and this in spite of inevitable tribulation in the world "

CHAPTER III

MARRIAGE AND CHILDREN

[Mark x. 1—16]

§ 1. *Divorce, the discussion of, how originated*[1]

MARK and Matthew say that certain Pharisees questioned Jesus in public on the lawfulness of divorce, and mentioned the

---

[1] Mk x 1—12 (R V)

(1) And he arose from thence, and cometh into the borders of Judaea and beyond Jordan and multitudes come together unto him again, and, as he was wont, he taught them again

(2) And there came unto him Pharisees, and asked him, Is it lawful for a man to put away [his] wife? tempting him.

(3) And he answered and said unto them, What did Moses command you?

(4) And they said, Moses suffered to write a bill of divorcement, and to put her away.

(5) But Jesus said unto them, For your hardness of heart he wrote you this commandment

(6) But from the

Mt xix. 1—10
v. 31—2 (R V)

(xix. 1) And it came to pass when Jesus had finished these words, he departed from Galilee, and came into the borders of Judaea beyond Jordan,

(2) And great multitudes followed him, and he healed them there

(3) And there came unto him (*many auth ins* the) Pharisees, tempting him, and saying, Is it lawful [for a man] to put away his wife for every cause?

(4) And he answered and said, Have ye not read, that he....

(7) They say unto him, Why then did Moses command to give her a bill of divorcement, and to put [her] away?

(8) He saith unto them, Moses for your

Lk. xvii 11, xvi. 18 (R.V.)

(xvii 11) And it came to pass, as they were (*or*, as he was) on the way to Jerusalem, that he was passing through the midst of (*or*, between) Samaria and Galilee

MARRIAGE AND CHILDREN

ordinance of Moses, but do not add any reference to the divorces that had preceded the marriage of Herodias to Herod Antipas.

Mk x 1—12 (R V) contd	Mt xix 1—10, v 31—2 (R V) contd	Lk xvii 11, xvi 18 (R V) contd
beginning of the creation, Male and female made he them. (7) For this cause shall a man leave his father and mother, and shall cleave to his wife (*some anc auth omit* and shall . wife), (8) And the twain shall become one flesh, so that they are no more twain, but one flesh (9) What therefore God hath joined together, let not man put asunder (10) And in the house the disciples asked him again of this matter (11) And he saith unto them, Whosoever shall put away his wife, and marry another, committeth adultery against her (12) And if she herself shall put away her husband, and marry another, she committeth adultery	hardness of heart suffered you to put away your wives but from the beginning it hath not been so (4) And he answered and said, Have ye not read, that he which made (*some anc auth* created) |them¹ from the beginning made them male and female, (5) And said, For this cause shall a man leave his father and mother, and shall cleave to his wife, and the twain shall become one flesh ? (6) So that they are no more twain, but one flesh What therefore God hath joined together, let not man put asunder (9) And I say unto you, Whosoever shall put away his wife, except for fornication, and shall marry another, committeth adultery (*some anc auth* saving for the cause of fornication, maketh her an adulteress, *as in* v 32) and he that marrieth her when she is put away committeth adultery (*some anc auth* omit the last sentence) (10) The disciples say unto him, If the case of the man .	(xvi 18) Every one that putteth away his wife, and marrieth another, committeth adultery and he that marrieth one that is put away from a husband committeth adultery.

A. F.

MARRIAGE AND CHILDREN

In Mark the Pharisees ask "Is it lawful for a man to *put away his wife?*" but Matthew has "*put away his wife for every cause.*" Luke omits the question altogether

Afterwards Mark (and Mark alone) tells us that in private "the disciples asked him again of this matter " And now Jesus modifies the phrase in such a way as to suggest a reference to Herod —"Whosoever shall put away his wife *and marry another*, committeth adultery." Matthew also has—not as in private, but as part of the public doctrine—"put away his wife...*and marry another.*" And this same combination is given by Luke, but in quite a different context. Luke represents Jesus as saying consecutively, in an attack on the covetousness of the Pharisees, (1) "The law and the prophets [were] until John," (2) "It is easier for heaven and earth to pass away than for one tittle of the law to fall," (3) "Every one that putteth away his wife and marrieth another, committeth adultery, and he that marrieth one that is put away from a husband committeth adultery[1]."

This indicates that the Pharisees described by Mark and Matthew as questioning Jesus are to be regarded as putting a dilemma before Him Either He must dissent from John the Baptist's condemnation of Herod (which they knew He would not do) or else He would come into collision with Herod

Mk. x 1—12 (R V.)	Mt xix 1—10, v 31—2 (R V) *contd*	Lk xvii 11, xvi. 18 (R.V)
	(v 31) It was said also, Whosoever shall put away his wife, let him give her a writing of divorcement.	
	(32) But I say unto you, that every one that putteth away his wife, saving for the cause of fornication, maketh her an adulteress and whosoever shall marry her when she is put away committeth adultery	

[1] Lk xvi. 14—18

MARRIAGE AND CHILDREN

and probably share the Baptist's fate[1]. This also explains Mark's brief language, which assumes that "put away his wife," in the lips of the Pharisees, meant in general "put away his wife at his own pleasure," and was meant to include the particular question, "Was it lawful for Herod Antipas to put away his wife [*as he did*] *and* [i e *in order to*] marry another?" Further, it explains Matthew's amplification of the first part of Mark's text (adding "for every cause[2]") and his alteration of the second part ("if she herself put away her husband"), if the latter referred to the divorce of a husband by Herodias—an act assumed by Mark to be referred to, but quite exceptional, and not contemplated by Jewish Law.

A tacit allusion to John the Baptist in Mark and Matthew (corresponding to the one expressed in Luke) is not incompatible with Christ's general condemnation of the Rabbinical laxity in allowing divorce, and also with His condemning a continued adherence to the letter of the ancient Law itself[3] Luke, when he says that "not a tittle of *the Law* shall fall," seems to mean, not the Law permitting divorce, but the Law

---

[1] Some motive, not quite clear, seems to underlie the variations in Mk x 1, Mt xix 1 "into the borders of Judaea and (Mt. *om* and) beyond Jordan" (Mt. has "*from Galilee and came* into the borders...," comp. Lk. xvii. 11 "between (διὰ μέσον) (?) Samaria and Galilee"). The text may have originally meant that Jesus was on the point of passing out of the jurisdiction of Herod Antipas, and that the Pharisees desired to bring down on Him the hostility of Antipas before He entered Judaea See *Corrections* **438** (1)—(v) John may perhaps be said to intervene as to "beyond Jordan" which Luke never uses (*Joh Voc* **1714** *b*, **1813** *b*) But the question is complicated by the possibility of allusion, see below, pp 152—5

[2] Origen, on Mt xix 3 (Lomm. iii. 303), says that Mark has τὸ ἰσοδυναμοῦν Probably he regarded Mark as using ἔξεστιν to mean "there is absolute power," which Matthew expressed by adding "for every cause," i e. any cause that might seem sufficient to the husband

[3] Deut xxiv. 1 "If she find no favour in his eyes because he hath found some unseemly thing in her (ὅτι εὗρεν ἐν αὐτῇ ἄσχημον πρᾶγμα)" on which *Hor. Heb* (on Mt xix 3) says (*J Sotah* fol 16. 2) "The school of Shammai permitted not divorces but only in the case of adultery"

MARRIAGE AND CHILDREN

forbidding adultery, which Law he regards as having been broken by Herod Antipas and Herodias.

There are good reasons why John would not intervene here. First, there is the non-logical nature of the argument from Genesis, and the very different "precept of Moses," and the Jewish interpretations of that "precept", secondly, there is the fact that some of the utterances of Jesus on this subject were bound up with the special case of Herod Antipas, a name not mentioned in his Gospel, thirdly, some of these utterances referred to the connivance of the Pharisees at Herod's conduct contrasted with the Baptist's condemnation of it—a condemnation mentioned by all the Synoptists but not by John[1].

Incidentally, it would be true to say that (1) in this passage Mark, followed by Matthew, represents Jesus as appealing from the Law of Moses to that which was "from the beginning"; and (2) somewhat similarly, as to healing on the sabbath, John represents Jesus as going back, in thought at least though not in word, to "the beginning," by saying "My Father worketh hitherto and I work[2]" There is no such argument anywhere in Luke But as regards the main subject, divorce, Johannine intervention was not to be expected and does not exist

§ 2 *"And he blessed them," in Mark*[3]

This is the only instance in which Jesus is described by Mark as "blessing" persons Matthew does not retain (nor

---

[1] Mk vi 18, Mt xiv. 4, Lk. iii 19
[2] See *Son* **3583** (1) quoting Mk x 6, Mt xix 4, Jn v 17
[3]

Mk x. 13—16 (R V)	Mt xix 13—14, xviii 1—3, xix 15 (R V)	Lk xviii 15—17 (R.V.)
(13) And they brought unto him little children, that he should touch them, and the disciples rebuked them (14) But when Jesus saw it, he was moved with indignation, and said unto them, Suffer the little	(xix. 13) Then were there brought unto him little children, that he should lay his hands on them and pray and the disciples rebuked them (14) But Jesus said, Suffer the little children, and forbid	(15) And they brought unto him also their babes, that he should touch them but when the disciples saw it, they rebuked them (16) But Jesus called them unto him, saying, Suffer the little children to come

116 (Mark x. 13—16)

MARRIAGE AND CHILDREN

does he describe elsewhere) the act of "blessing" persons, though he retains here the "laying on" of "hands[1]" Luke retains neither, and does not describe Jesus as "blessing" persons till after His resurrection[2]. Here Luke also alters "children" into "babes." He introduces the incident, after a contrast between a proud Pharisee and a humble Publican, abruptly, thus · "But he that humbleth himself shall be exalted And they brought unto him even their (*lit.* the) babes that he might touch them[3]" "Touching" (which is

Mk x 13—16 (R V) *contd*	Mt xix 13—14, xviii 1—3, xix 15 (R V) *contd*	Lk xviii 15—17 (R V) *contd*
children to come unto me, forbid them not for of such is the kingdom of God (15) Verily I say unto you, Whosoever shall not receive the kingdom of God as a little child, he shall in no wise enter therein (16) And he took them in his arms, and blessed them, laying his hands upon them.	them not, to come unto me for of such is the kingdom of heaven (xviii 1) In that hour Who then is greatest (*lit* greater) in the kingdom of heaven? (2) And he called to him a little child, and set him in the midst of them, (3) And said, Verily I say unto you, Except ye turn, and become as little children, ye shall in no wise enter into the kingdom of heaven (xix 15) And he laid his hands on them, and departed thence	unto me, and forbid them not for of such is the kingdom of God (17) Verily I say unto you, Whosoever shall not receive the kingdom of God as a little child, he shall in no wise enter therein

Mt xviii 1—5 is also parallel to Mk ix 34 foll. See above, p 70 foll

[1] Mk x 16 καὶ ἐναγκαλισάμενος αὐτὰ κατευλόγει τιθεὶς τὰς χεῖρας ἐπ' αὐτά, D προσκαλεσάμενος, SS "and he called them," *b* "convitans," *c, d, f, ff, q, r* (Swete) "convocans," see above, chap ii § 9 The parall Mt xix 15 καὶ ἐπιθεὶς τὰς χεῖρας αὐτοῖς ἐπορεύθη ἐκεῖθεν includes a parall to Mk x 17 καὶ ἐκπορευομένου αὐτοῦ Luke omits this, but has προσεκαλέσατο in Lk xviii 16.

[2] Lk xxiv 50, 51

[3] Lk xviii 15 προσέφερον δὲ αὐτῷ καὶ τὰ βρέφη ἵνα αὐτῶν ἅπτηται

MARRIAGE AND CHILDREN

also Mark's word) might seem to Luke different from Matthew's parallel phrase, "laying on hands," and a less formal act. Hence Luke might omit Mark's "blessed" as being also too formal Matthew's omission of "blessing" may be explained in the same way At the beginning of his narrative he has "that he might lay his hands on them and *pray* " "Praying for" is different from, and less formal than, "bestowing a blessing on," and does not imply any conscious act, or even conscious receptiveness, in the person for whom the prayer is offered.

But all these divergences from Mark excite a reasonable suspicion that Mark is diverged from because difficult, and that here, as often, the difficult version is the right one. This is confirmed by Mark's very rare and very strong word, inadequately rendered "blessed " It is very hard to say why Mark uses it. It does not occur in the New Testament elsewhere, nor even in LXX except in Tobit[1]. Goodspeed does not give it as occurring in any Apologist or early Father. The Thesaurus gives no instance of it outside Tobit and Plutarch[2]. In Plutarch it is used thrice, and always of exaggerated eulogy ("*pour-out-praise*"). One of these instances occurs in a discussion where some one, depreciating marriage, declares that legislators, because citizens are needful for the state, "*pour out praise*" on marriage. The defender of marriage has previously exclaimed "Marriage and the coming together of husband and wife, than which there neither is nor ever has been a holier yoke—dost thou call this shameful[3]?" Now in

---

(Mk ἄψηται, and παιδία without τά)   R V renders τὰ βρέφη, as Greek idiom necessitates, "their babes "   Who "they" are is not stated. But probably they are the mothers of babes in the "multitudes" mentioned in Mk x 1 as being taught by Jesus

[1] Tob. xi 1, 17
[2] L S "Plut. 2 66 A, LXX, etc " is misleading   The "etc " should have come after "A" to shew that there are two other instances in Plutarch, viz *Mor* 750 C, 1069 C (or E)
[3] Plut *Mor* 750 C Καὶ ὁ Δαφναῖος, Αἴσχιστον δὲ καλεῖς, ἔφη, γάμον καὶ σύνοδον ἀνδρὸς καὶ γυναικὸς, ἧς οὐ γέγονεν οὐδ' ἔστιν ἱερωτέρα κατάζευξις, Ἀλλὰ ταῦτα μὲν, εἶπεν ὁ Πρωτογένης, ἀναγκαῖα πρὸς γένεσιν ὄντα, σεμνύνουσιν οὐ φαύλως οἱ νομοθέται καὶ κατευλογοῦσι πρὸς τοὺς πολλούς

MARRIAGE AND CHILDREN

the Synoptic passage under consideration, this blessing of children is preceded almost immediately in Matthew by an argument of the disciples that "it is not expedient to marry" and by Christ's reply[1] This suggests that the blessing of children described by Mark was part of a series of Christ's acts and sayings bearing on marriage and the birth of children, and that Mark has omitted some argument against marriage that called forth an emphatic protest from Jesus.

This suggestion is favoured by the fact that the first two Biblical instances where God is introduced as "blessing" are connected with the propagation of animal life; and the second of these connects "blessing" and "multiplying" with a creation of man in the image of God, expressly mentioning "male" and "female[2]" This passage Mark (followed by Matthew) has in the previous context represented Jesus as quoting[3], in reply to the Pharisees, and apparently in the presence of the multitudes whom He had been teaching[4] Now it would seem that some of the mothers in the crowd—after hearing Christ's maintenance of the divine ordinance of matrimony—press forward that He may "touch" their little ones The disciples, engaged in discussing the divorce question, obstruct the parents. Jesus, resenting the interference of the obstructing disciples, does more than "touch" the children. He "*blesses*" them, or "*pours forth blessing*" on them Thus not only does He sanction the inference that the faith of parents can avail for their infant children, but He appears indirectly to teach the disciples and the multitudes an object lesson, saying, in effect,

---

[1] Mt. xix 10—12

[2] Gen 1 22, 28. Neither of these verses about "blessing" occurs in the Index to Philo (ed Richter)

[3] Mk x 6 ἀπὸ δὲ ἀρχῆς κτίσεως (quoting Gen 1 27) ἄρσεν καὶ θῆλυ ἐποίησεν ⌈αὐτούς⌉, Mt xix 4 οὐκ ἀνέγνωτε ὅτι ὁ κτίσας ἀπ' ἀρχῆς ἄρσεν καὶ θῆλυ ἐποίησεν αὐτούς, Mark favours the view that "male and female" were so created "from the beginning" (and not the male before the female) Matthew's arrangement of the words does not favour it Rashi says "Est autem *expositio mystica* quod creaverit illum *duas facies habentem* ab initio sed postea *illum separaverit*"

[4] Mk x 1

(Mark x 13—16)

MARRIAGE AND CHILDREN

what the Epistle to the Hebrews says, that "marriage" is to be "had in honour[1]"

The First Epistle to Timothy speaks of certain Christians as "forbidding to marry[2]" Paul himself, under the pressure of a missionary life, and with an overhanging uncertainty as to the day of the Coming of the Lord, is dubious as to the general propriety of marriage for Christians[3]. Luke, in his version of the Parable of the Refusal of the King's Invitation, inserts as one excuse "I have married a wife and therefore I cannot come[4]" From these facts, and from Matthew's peculiar tradition about "eunuchs for the kingdom of heaven's sake" (which seems out of place or erroneously reported) we may infer that some readers would not easily understand the strong language in which Mark describes Christ as "pouring-out-blessing" on children—if it meant that He blessed them not only for their own sakes, but also as being the representatives of the concord and affection of family life.

In the previous context of both Mark and Luke, the typical meaning of "little children" is expressed in an ambiguous

---

[1] Heb xiii 4 τίμιος ὁ γάμος ἐν πᾶσιν, on which see Westcott
[2] 1 Tim. iv 3
[3] Comp Epictet iii 22 67 foll praising marriage as an institution in an ideal city (σοφῶν πόλιν), but regarding it as perhaps unfit for the Cynic in the present battle of good against evil if he is to be "without distraction (ἀπερίσπαστον)" (comp 1 Cor vii 35) and "wholly given to the service of God "
[4] Lk xiv 20, not in Mt xxii 5 The tradition peculiar to Matthew (xix 12) about "eunuchs for the kingdom of heaven's sake" is perhaps out of place, and separated from context that would make it intelligible Apart from historical passages in Jeremiah (xxix 2 etc) the only mention of "eunuchs" in the Prophets is in Is lvi 3—4 "neither let the eunuch say, Behold, I am a dry tree For thus saith the Lord of the eunuchs that keep my sabbaths... " In the Pauline Epistles, the question about marriage is raised, not by Paul himself, but by the Corinthians (1 Cor. vii 1 "the things whereof ye wrote") consulting Paul If it were raised by Jewish missionaries of Christ, after Christ's resurrection, the answer would naturally be in a tone of consolation, as in Isaiah, regarding the eunuch's condition as an evil, but an evil that might be overruled to good See McNeile's note on Mt xix 12

MARRIAGE AND CHILDREN

sentence "Whosoever shall not receive the kingdom of God as a little child[1]." "Child" might be, but is not, the object Matthew clears away the ambiguity, but narrows the interpretation, thus, "Except ye turn and become as little children," and then adds, as explanation, "Whosoever shall humble himself as this little child, the same is the greatest in the kingdom of the heavens[2]" But in truth it is not a conscious "self-humbling," or "making oneself little," that is contemplated by Jesus It is the affectionate clinging of the little one to the parents, or to the mother's breast, as is indicated by an ancient comment on Mark[3].

Turning to the Fourth Gospel, we see that so far as the first part of Mark's tradition about "receiving the kingdom of God as a little child," John is not bound to intervene by the rule of Johannine Intervention For Luke follows Mark *verbatim* But the whole of the Fourth Gospel, from the Prologue onwards, is permeated with the thought of the Word, or Son, above, "in the bosom of the Father," and with the thought of men, below, as receiving the Son from above, and thereby receiving authority to become "God's children[4]"

As regards the second part of Mark's tradition, which represents Jesus as "pouring out blessing" on the little children brought to Him, the question is whether we accept the suggestion

---

[1] Mk x 15, Lk xviii 17 See Origen *Comm Matth* xiii 19 (Lomm iii 247) ἀμφίβολος ἡ λέξις and *Comm Matth* xv 9 (Lomm iii 345) σχεδὸν δὲ ταῖς αὐταῖς λέξεσι καὶ ὁ Μάρκος, μάλιστα τὰ τελευταῖα, ὡσαύτως ἐξέθετο Neither in these passages, nor elsewhere, does he quote Mk x 16 "blessed."

[2] Mt xviii 3—4. This is also parall to Mk ix 36

[3] See Cramer on Mk x 13 containing Victor's collection of traditions about the typical child: "When it is whipped by the mother the child still seeks her, and honours her above all things, and even though you shew him a crowned queen he does not prefer her to his mother in rags" It adds "And it is well said 'He took them in His arms and poured blessing on them' For [by that act] there is brought back again as it were into the arms of the Creator His handiwork, which had been separated from Him in the beginning and had fallen away from [His arms, or bosom] (χωρισθὲν αὐτοῦ κατ' ἀρχὴν καὶ ἐκπεπτωκός)"

[4] Jn i 1, 12, 18 etc

MARRIAGE AND CHILDREN

that the "blessing" indirectly upholds the sanctity of marriage, about which Jesus has previously quoted from Genesis the words describing the creation of mankind as male and female. If we do, Johannine intervention may be asserted, not indeed of a verbal, but (as often) of a dramatic kind. For John is the only Evangelist that describes Jesus as present at "a marriage[1]." The marriage takes place at the conclusion of the Johannine Hexaemeron that corresponds to the six days of Creation in Genesis[2] Jesus does not indeed pronounce a verbal blessing on the marriage, but, at the request of His mother, He bestows a practical and typical blessing on the wedded pair by supplying them with "the good wine[3]"

---

[1] Jn ii 1
[2] On "the new Hexaemeron" see *Joh Gr.* **2624**.
[3] Jn ii 10   "Wine" is connected with the thought of "blessing" in many passages of Scripture   Gesen 139 *b* under "blessing" refers to "new wine" implied in Is lxv. 8   See also Levy 1 268 *a* and *b* "*the cup of blessing,*" a term used both in Heb and Aramaic, to mean *a cup of wine over which a blessing was spoken,* and used by Paul (1 Cor x 16) in connection with the Christian Eucharist as a term with which his readers would be familiar

CHAPTER IV

HOW TO ENTER INTO THE KINGDOM

[Mark x. 17—52]

§ 1. *"And Jesus looking upon him loved him," in Mark*[1]

In the narratives printed below[2], describing how a rich man failed to enter the Kingdom, there are several striking differences,

---

[1] Mk x 21.
[2] Mk x. 17—22 (R.V)

Mk x. 17—22 (R.V)	Mt xix 16—22 (R V)	Lk xviii 18—23 (R V)
(17) And as he was going forth into the way (*or*, on his way), there ran one to him, and kneeled to him, and asked him, Good Master (*or*, Teacher), what shall I do that I may inherit eternal life? (18) And Jesus said unto him, Why callest thou me good? none is good save one, [even] God (19) Thou knowest the commandments, Do not kill, Do not commit adultery, Do not steal, Do not bear false witness, Do not defraud, Honour thy father and mother (20) And he said unto him, Master (*or*, Teacher), all these things have I ob-	(16) And behold, one came to him and said, Master (*or*, Teacher *some anc auth prefix* Good), what good thing shall I do, that I may have eternal life? (17) And he said unto him, Why askest thou me concerning that which is good? One there is who is good (*some anc auth* Why callest thou me good? None is good save one, [even] God) but if thou wouldest enter into life, keep the commandments (18) He saith unto him, Which? And Jesus said, Thou shalt not kill, Thou shalt not commit adultery, Thou shalt not steal, Thou shalt	(18) And a certain ruler asked him, saying, Good Master (*or*, Teacher), what shall I do to inherit eternal life? (19) And Jesus said unto him, Why callest thou me good? none is good, save one, [even] God (20) Thou knowest the commandments, Do not commit adultery, Do not kill, Do not steal, Do not bear false witness, Honour thy father and mother (21) And he said, All these things have I observed from my youth up (22) And when Jesus heard it, he said unto him, One thing thou lackest yet· sell all that

123 (Mark x 17—22)

HOW TO ENTER INTO THE KINGDOM

some of which imply verbal transpositions (1) Where Mark and Luke have "*Good Master*, what shall I do?" Matthew has "Master, what *good thing* shall I do?" with a corresponding difference in Christ's reply[1] (2) Mark and Luke represent Jesus as saying "*One thing is lacking* (Luke, *wanting*) to thee," but Matthew's only mention of "lacking" is "*What lack* I yet?" and Matthew represents Jesus as adding "If thou wouldest be perfect[2]" (3) In Mark and Luke, Jesus mentions several of the Commandments, but Matthew alone inserts "Thou shalt

Mk x 17—22 (R V) *contd*	Mt xix 16—22 (R V) *contd*	Lk. xviii 18—23 (R V) *contd*
served from my youth (21) And Jesus looking upon him loved him, and said unto him, One thing thou lackest go, sell whatsoever thou hast, and give to the poor, and thou shalt have treasure in heaven and come, follow me (22) But his countenance fell at the saying, and he went away sorrowful for he was one that had great possessions	not bear false witness, (19) Honour thy father and thy mother and, Thou shalt love thy neighbour as thyself (20) The young man saith unto him, All these things have I observed what lack I yet? (21) Jesus said unto him, If thou wouldest be perfect, go, sell that thou hast, and give to the poor, and thou shalt have treasure in heaven and come, follow me (22) But when the young man heard the saying, he went away sorrowful for he was one that had great possessions.	thou hast, and distribute unto the poor, and thou shalt have treasure in heaven and come, follow me (23) But when he heard these things, he became exceeding sorrowful, for he was very rich

[1] Mk x. 17, Lk xviii 18 διδάσκαλε ἀγαθέ, τί ποιήσω (Lk. ποιήσας); Mt xix 16 διδάσκαλε, τί ἀγαθὸν ποιήσω, It would be easy to confuse ΑΓΑΘΕ with ΑΓΑΘΟ (*i e* ἀγαθόν) But we should still have to suppose that Matthew (or Mark and Luke) altered Christ's reply (as well as the order of the words in the question)

[2] Mk x 21 ἕν σε ὑστερεῖ, Lk xviii 22 ἔτι ἕν σοι λείπει, Mt xix 20 τί ἔτι ὑστερῶ, Confusion would be easy between ετι (*i e* ἕν τι) and ετι Mt xix 21 εἰ θέλεις τέλειος εἶναι implies, but does not assert, that something is "lacking"

HOW TO ENTER INTO THE KINGDOM

love thy neighbour as thyself[1]." (4) Mark alone inserts "Do not defraud[2]"

Besides these variations, all of which concern words of Jesus, there is a statement, peculiar to Mark, which imputes a motive to Jesus, "And Jesus, looking stedfastly upon him, loved him[3]." "Looking stedfastly" appears to imply Christ's insight into the mind of the man whom He was intending to test. The man professed to have kept all the Commandments from his youth, including (according to Matthew) the Commandment to love one's neighbour as oneself[4]. Can it be denied that if the man was honest, he thought too well of himself and deceived himself[5]? He was rich, and Mark himself elsewhere speaks of "the deceitfulness of riches[6]." It has been therefore suggested in a previous part of this work that Mark has erroneously substituted "loved" for the very similar word

---

[1] Mk x 19, Lk xviii 20, Mt xix 18—19

[2] Mk x 19 Μὴ ἀποστερήσῃς, Del פשע Comp Lev. xix 13 "Thou shalt not (A V.) *defraud* (R V *oppress*) thy neighbour, nor rob him; the wages of a hired servant shall not abide with thee all night" (where Rashi explains פשע as "defraudat mercenarium mercede"), and Deut xxiv 14 פשע, A ἀποστερήσεις, B ἀπαδικήσεις, of a hireling's pay The word is also Aram. and Syr SS and many authorities omit the clause in Mk x 19, probably because it seemed wrong to add to "the Ten Commandments" Josephus, however (*Ant* iii. 5. 4), says that it was "not lawful" for him to set down their exact words, but only their "import." In Mk, the word seems appropriate to "their import" The rich man would not be tempted to "steal," but he might be tempted to "keep back" what was morally "due" to neighbours or dependants

[3] Mk x 21 ὁ δὲ Ἰησοῦς ἐμβλέψας αὐτῷ ἠγάπησεν αὐτόν. Comp Mk x 27 ἐμβλέψας αὐτοῖς ὁ Ἰησοῦς, where Jesus is regarded as not only "looking stedfastly" at the disciples but also having insight into their feelings

[4] Origen (on Mt xix 22, Lomm iii 367) uses ἠγάπα, but in a different context, ἔχων κτήματα πολλὰ ἅπερ ἠγάπα

[5] Comp Gal vi 3 "if any man seemeth [to himself] to be something when he is nothing he *deceiveth* (φρεναπατᾷ) himself," and Jas i. 26 "*deceiving* (ἀπατῶν) his own heart "

[6] Mk iv 19 (Mt xiii 22) ἡ ἀπάτη τοῦ πλούτου—the only mention of ἀπάτη in the Gospels

HOW TO ENTER INTO THE KINGDOM

(in Greek) "deceived," and that the original stated that Jesus looked stedfastly at the man and saw that "*he deceived* himself[1]."

How does John deal with this Marcan tradition about a would-be disciple whom "Jesus loved"? Only indirectly perhaps, but still effectively Some would say that he intervenes directly, since he is the only other Evangelist that describes Jesus as "loving", and he mentions an actual, not a would-be, "disciple whom Jesus loved[2]" But putting that aside as a mere verbal coincidence, we may regard the Johannine Nicodemus as in some respects a parallel to the Synoptic questioner. Luke describes the latter as "a ruler"; all the Synoptists say that he was rich, and they all agree that he came to Jesus saluting Him as "teacher," and asking to be taught the way to eternal life John says of Nicodemus that he was "a ruler of the Jews", that he came to Jesus saluting Him as "rabbi" and "a teacher come from God," and receiving from Jesus instruction as to the way of entering into the kingdom of God[3], and later on, John, agreeing with Jewish tradition, leads us to infer that he was rich since he joined with Joseph of Arimathaea in giving to the body of Jesus a costly burial[4]

But John represents Jesus as giving to Nicodemus a very different reply from that which the Synoptists describe as given to their "rich man." Instead of the Synoptic "one thing is lacking to thee," or "if thou wouldest be perfect," the Johannine reply is, in effect, "The one thing needful for thee is that love of God and man which belongs to those who are

---

[1] See *Beginning* pp. 263—4 where this is given among several explanations It is also suggested that the original of Mk x 21 may have meant "*one thing* is lacking to thee" in a different sense from that which is commonly attached to the words, so that Jesus meant "Thou lackest *the one thing needful*" (comp Lk. x 41—2)

[2] Jn xi 5, xiii. 23 etc. If John knew of the Marcan tradition as now extant and regarded it as erroneous he might see an additional reason for emphasizing the reticence of "the disciple" whom Jesus really "loved " The Marcan young man is by no means reticent Strong's Concordance has "*loved*" Mt. (0), Mk (1), Lk. (1), Jn (22).

[3] Jn iii 1—2 foll.

[4] Jn xix 38—9 On the wealth of Nicodemus, see *Corrections* **519**.

HOW TO ENTER INTO THE KINGDOM

born from above." And the end corresponds to the beginning. Nicodemus is described at the end as joining with Joseph of Arimathaea in burying Jesus, but there is a distinction; Joseph is called "a disciple of Jesus" (though "secretly for fear of the Jews") Nicodemus, even with such a qualification of secrecy, is not so called[1] On the whole it may be said that the Fourth Evangelist, whether consciously alluding or not alluding to the Marcan peculiar tradition, makes it more difficult for us than before to suppose that Jesus regarded with special "love" the rich man here mentioned by the Synoptists[2]

§ 2. *"Children, how hard it is," in Mark*[3]

The word here translated "hard" means etymologically "squeamish," and hence "crossgrained" about persons, and

---

[1] Jn xix. 38—41 It may be argued that the stand-point of Nicodemus has been already described But has it? Do his words (Jn vii 51) "Doth our law judge the man [accused] except it first hear from himself. .?" describe any definite "stand-point"? Do they not rather suggest an oscillation, or an attempt to be just and coldly impartial, putting aside the previously uttered conviction (iii 2) "we know that thou art a teacher come from God"?

[2] It must be admitted·that in one very important respect the rich young ruler differs from the rich Nicodemus The former came to Jesus openly, not "by night", and his combination of a love of righteousness with a love of wealth, and of complacency with self-distrust, may have drawn forth from Jesus a special compassion and pitying love But against this view is the hard fact that Matthew and Luke omit the words "Jesus, looking upon him, loved him"

[3]

Mk x 23—7 (R V)	Mt xix 23—6 (R V)	Lk xviii 24—7 (R V)
(23) And Jesus looked round about, and saith unto his disciples, How hardly shall they that have riches enter into the kingdom of God! (24) And the disciples were amazed at his words But Jesus answereth again, and saith unto them, Children, how	(23) And Jesus said unto his disciples, Verily I say unto you, It is hard for a rich man to enter into the kingdom of heaven	(24) And Jesus seeing him said, How hardly shall they that have riches enter into the kingdom of God!

(Mark x 17—22)

HOW TO ENTER INTO THE KINGDOM

"awkward" or "difficult" about things[1]. It is frequent in literary Greek, but from Old Testament Greek it cannot be illustrated

Mk x. 23—7 (R.V.) contd	Mt xix 23—6 (R V.) contd.	Lk xviii 24—7 (R V) contd
hard is it for them that trust in riches (some anc auth omit for.. riches) to enter into the kingdom of God!		
(25) It is easier for a camel to go through a needle's eye, than for a rich man to enter into the kingdom of God	(24) And again I say unto you, It is easier for a camel to go through a needle's eye, than for a rich man to enter into the kingdom of God	(25) For it is easier for a camel to enter in through a needle's eye, than for a rich man to enter into the kingdom of God
(26) And they were astonished exceedingly, saying unto him (many anc auth saying among themselves), Then who can be saved?	(25) And when the disciples heard it, they were astonished exceedingly, saying, Who then can be saved?	(26) And they that heard it said, Then who can be saved?
(27) Jesus looking upon them saith, With men it is impossible, but not with God for all things are possible with God.	(26) And Jesus looking upon [them] said to them, With men this is impossible, but with God all things are possible .	(27) But he said, The things which are impossible with men are possible with God

The *Diatessaron*, besides inserting "those that rely on their possessions," transposes the text as follows (as also D transposes Mk x 24 and 25)

"And when Jesus saw his sadness, he looked towards his disciples, and said unto them, How hard it is for them that have possessions to enter the kingdom of God!

"Verily I say unto you, it is difficult for a rich man to enter the kingdom of heaven And I say unto you also, that it is easier for a camel to enter the eye of a needle, than for a rich man to enter the kingdom of God. And the disciples were wondering at these sayings. And Jesus answered and said unto them again, My children, How hard it is for those that rely on their possessions to enter the kingdom of God! And those that were listening wondered more, and said amongst themselves, being agitated, Who, thinkest thou, can be saved? And Jesus looked at them intently, and said unto them, With men this is not possible, but with God [it is]. it is possible for God to do everything "

[1] Mk x 24 τέκνα, πῶς δύσκολόν ἐστιν εἰς τὴν βασιλείαν τοῦ θεοῦ εἰσελθεῖν

HOW TO ENTER INTO THE KINGDOM

except from a translation of the saying of Elijah to Elisha "Thou hast asked *a hard thing*," i e. a thing *against nature*[1]. In the present passage the entrance into the Kingdom of God is described as being, not indeed impracticable, but effected "*with difficulty*," or "*awkwardly*," or "as it were *against nature*." It is not Hebraic Greek, but vernacular, and almost confined to Hermas among early Christian writers[2].

This fact bears on the interpretation of the phrase rendered by R.V. "*they that have riches*" The parallel Matthew has "*a rich* [*man*]," and this would lead the English reader to infer that the three Synoptists had, in effect, the same word ("*rich*," "*riches*"). But the Marcan word (used also by Luke) does not mean "riches." From LXX we can learn little about it[3]. But in literary and vernacular Greek it means "*money*," often in a bad sense[4] When used elsewhere in the New Testament, where it is confined to the Acts, it means "*price*" (once) in the singular, and a bribe of "*money*" (thrice) in the plural (concerning "*money*" offered by Simon Magus to Peter and hoped for by Felix from Paul)[5] It is found in Greek proverbs corresponding to

---

[1] 2 K 11 10 LXX ἐσκλήρυνας τοῦ αἰτήσασθαι, but Ἄλλος has δύσκολον ᾔτησω The only other instance is Jerem xlix 8, where LXX renders אִיד "calamity" by δύσκολα

[2] Δύσκολον (adj and adv) occurs (Goodspeed) in Ign *Rom* § 1 and *Smyrn* § 4 "if haply they may repent—which [indeed] is difficult, but [still] the Lord Jesus Christ hath power to effect this," elsewhere only in Hermas (about 10 times) (mostly δυσκόλως)

[3] In canon LXX, χρήματα (plur) occurs about ten times and = four different Heb words In Dan xi 13, 24, 28 רְכוּשׁ, LXX has χρήματα, Theod ὕπαρξις It does not occur in the Pentateuch, nor in the Prophets outside Daniel

[4] Steph *Thes* quotes Aristot *Eth* iv 1 χρήματα λέγομεν πάντα ὅσων ἡ ἀξία νομίσματι μετρεῖται, and Pind *Isthm* ii 17 (also Alcae 50, L S) χρήματα, χρήματ' ἀνήρ Thuc ii 60 κρείσσων χρημάτων and χρήμασιν νικᾶσθαι, and Eurip *Hec* 865 χρημάτων δοῦλος illustrate the freq unfavourable use of the word Comp Epictet Mosch 5 οὐ τὰ χρήματα φίλοι ἀλλ' ὁ φίλος χρήματα *Ib* Stob. 33 (Schweig 10) τὸν μὲν τοῦ σώματος δεσμὸν λύει ..κακία διὰ χρημάτων seems to mean "releases by means of bribes "

[5] Acts iv 37 τὸ χρῆμα, "the price"; viii 18, 20, xxiv 26 χρήματα, "money "

such English ones as "*money* makes the man" Perhaps Mark intends to accentuate the unfavourable sense he attaches to it by a previous use of a less unfavourable phrase, "great possessions." Now perhaps he represents Jesus as pronouncing a warning to "the monied class[1]."

Side by side with this vernacular Greek form of Christ's utterance is a Hebraic one, in all the Synoptists, about a "rich man" and a "camel." Mark alone has placed between the two a third utterance in which Jesus says to the disciples, "Children, how hard it is [for them that trust in riches] to enter into the kingdom of God[2]!" Many authorities omit the bracketed words. For their insertion, we may argue "Jesus must have meant '*them that trust in riches*,' not '*the rich*,' for

---

[1] Delitzsch gives as the rendering of "*them that have* money," "*the masters of* (בעלי) money" Comp Eccles vii 12 "Wisdom is a defence [even as] money is a defence, but wisdom preserveth the life of *its master* (בעליה)," v r τὸν ἔχοντα αὐτήν (A B א τὸν παρ' αὐτῆς mistaking the noun for the prepositions ב and על) R V "the life of *him that hath it*" The Heb בעל, *baal*, is rendered by ἔχω in Eccles x 20 ὁ ἔχων (B ὁ τὰς) πτέρυγας, "*that which hath* wings," lit "*a master of* wings" (where Aq has ὁ κυριεύων πτέρυγος, Sym τὸ πτερωτόν, Theod ὁ ἔχων πτέρυγας) So in Dan viii 6, 20 LXX and Theod have "the ram. .that had the horns," where Heb has "*that was master of the horns*" It will be perceived that "the master of" means, not "the possessor of" anything whatever, but "the possessor of" *some characteristic*, so that "the masters of money" might mean those who are notable for their money and for nothing else

Ἔχω, in LXX, represents 59 different Heb words or idioms. It seems prob. that Mark had some reason for not using πλούσιος here, which the parallel Mt adopts, and which Mark himself has in the context. "*Masters*, or *lords*, *of* money" might be interpreted as "*proud of* their money," "*trusting in* money" (Cramer, p 381 ἀντεχο-μένοις χρημάτων) Thus the Marcan variations might be explained

On the Marcan peculiarity (x 23) περιβλεψάμενος see *Beginning* p. 263, *Proclam* p 361, and especially *Introd* p 93 When it represents a mere gesture, it would not be likely to be reproduced in the Fourth Gospel, but its use in Mk xi 11 is different and will be discussed in its place

[2] See W H *Notes on Select Readings* p 26 But add that SS has twice (Mk x 23, 24) "them that trust in their wealth"

HOW TO ENTER INTO THE KINGDOM

Abraham was '*rich*.'" Against their insertion, we may argue "If Jesus had meant '*them that trust in riches*,' He would have said that their entrance into the Kingdom was '*impossible*,' not '*difficult*.'" And would not such an explanation have banished all "astonishment" from the disciples? It will be seen above that the Diatessaron, which adopts the doubtful explanatory clause, alters the order so as to make it the climax of Christ's utterances But the result is a *non sequitur* "Those that were listening *wondered more*" They ought to have "*wondered less*" And they ought to have said—not "Who then can be saved?"—but "Now the Lord's lesson is clear If we are rich we must not trust in our riches"

It seems certain that Jesus must have uttered something much stronger than a condemnation of "them that trust in riches," some warning against "money" in itself as being a dangerous temptation to the soul that does not constantly turn to God as the Giver, and hear His voice, as Abraham heard it, promising Himself as man's "reward[1]" Though we may be uncertain of the exact nature and order of Christ's words, we can hardly be wrong in assuming that the rich self-righteous young ruler, who was confident that he had performed all the commandments, would be regarded by Jesus as being on the level of Ephraim, whom Hosea represents as saying "Surely I am become rich, I have found me wealth, in all my labours they shall find in me no iniquity...[2]" Measuring spiritual things by "money," the young man thought himself really rich—rich in goodness—and able to "do" some "good thing" at will. He was willing perhaps to give alms to the amount of several hundred denarii—to "inherit eternal life"

This implied offer to do some "good thing" was, in effect, of the nature of a bribe, an offer of "money" to Jesus for the poor in order to secure from Him a verdict that would ratify

---

[1] Gen xv. 1 "I am thy exceeding great reward."
[2] Hos xii 8 Comp Zech xi 5 "they that sell them (*i e* the flock) say, Blessed be the Lord, for I am rich," and Rev iii 17 "Because thou sayest, I am rich ..and knowest not that thou art the wretched one and miserable and poor..."

HOW TO ENTER INTO THE KINGDOM

the man's good opinion of himself; and Jesus, knowing that the man would fail to pass His test, and that he would gain by failure, tests him so that he fails. It is in the light of the failure of this rich young man that we must interpret the following words of Jesus, "Children, how hard it is," and the rest. The man was a type of *"them that have money."* It is true that Abraham (or rather Abram) might also be said to have "had money." In the first Biblical passage that uses the word "rich," we find that "Abram was very *rich in cattle, in silver, and in gold*[1]" But Abraham was *not of the class of "them that have money."* He was of *the class of them that have righteousness and faith.* He was not the typical "rich man" but the typical "friend of God[2]." Before he became "rich" Scripture says that he had obeyed the voice of God bidding him become an exile[3].

Our conclusion is that Jesus, beginning from the occasion of the failure of the rich young man, goes on to impress on His disciples the hardness of entering into the Kingdom, *for all, not only for the rich,* as amounting to an "impossibility[4]" unless they receive the Spirit of God. Those who lightheartedly asked to "enter" were in a position resembling that of Elisha when he "asked" from Elijah "a hard thing," a thing "against nature" in some sense, and not to be accomplished except with supernatural help. This it is that makes the disciples exclaim "Then who can be saved?"—because their Master had declared that it was "hard"—"hard," not for the rich, but "hard" absolutely—to enter into the Kingdom.

All this, from a different point of view and with some difference of language, John sets forth in the Dialogue with Nicodemus, where the Synoptic "hard" is latent under the Johannine "not possible" (literally "not able"). Jesus begins by saying "Except a man be born from above, it is *not possible*

---

[1] Gen xiii 2

[2] Is xli 8, Jas ii 23

[3] Gen xii 1 It was also an early Jewish belief that he had been thrown into a furnace by Nimrod for refusal to worship false gods, see *Son* **3501** *g, Light* **3822**

[4] Mk x 27 "With men it is impossible, but not with God"

HOW TO ENTER INTO THE KINGDOM

for him to see the kingdom of God," and the last saying of Nicodemus is "How is it *possible* that these things should be[1]?"

§ 3   "*He shall receive a hundredfold...with persecutions,*" in Mark[2]

The noun rendered "*persecutions*" occurs nowhere else in the Gospels except in the Mark-Matthew phrase "when tribulation or *persecution* ariseth," where Luke has "in time of

---

[1] Jn iii 2—9   Note the reiterations   (2) οὐδεὶς γὰρ δύναται. , (3) οὐ δύναται.., (4) πῶς δύναται , μὴ δύναται. , (5) οὐ δύναται.. , (9) πῶς δύναται , Nicodemus recognises that it is "impossible" for any man to work such "signs" as Jesus worked without the aid of God, but he does not recognise that it is "impossible" to enter the "Kingdom of God" without the action of God in a still more wonderful way, not externally aiding but internally regenerating. This is differently expressed in Mt. vii 13 εἰσέλθατε διὰ τῆς στενῆς πύλης, Lk xiii 24 ἀγωνίζεσθε εἰσελθεῖν διὰ τῆς στενῆς θύρας, where Luke's ἀγωνίζομαι emphasizes the need of human co-operation   John emphasizes the need of divine operation

[2]
Mk x 28—31 (R V)	Mt xix 27—30 (R V)	Lk xviii 28—30, xiii 30 (R.V)
(28) Peter began to say unto him, Lo, we have left all, and have followed thee (29) Jesus said, Verily I say unto you,	(27) Then answered Peter and said unto him, Lo, we have left all, and followed thee, what then shall we have? (28) And Jesus said unto them, Verily I say unto you, that ye which have followed me, in the regeneration when the Son of man shall sit on the throne of his glory, ye also shall sit upon twelve thrones, judging the twelve tribes of Israel (29) And every one that hath left houses, or brethren, or sisters, or father, or mother (*many anc auth. add* or wife), or children, or lands, for my name's sake, shall	(xviii. 28) And Peter said, Lo, we have left our own (*or*, our own [homes]), and followed thee (29) And he said unto them, Verily I say unto you,
There is no man that hath left house, or brethren, or sisters, or mother, or father, or children, or lands, for my sake, and for the gospel's sake, (30) But he shall receive a hundredfold now in this time, houses, and brethren, and sisters, and		There is no man that hath left house, or wife, or brethren, or parents, or children, for the kingdom of God's sake, (30) Who shall not receive manifold more in this time, and in the world (*or*, age) to come eternal life

133   (Mark x. 28—31)

HOW TO ENTER INTO THE KINGDOM

temptation[1]" In literary Greek the noun means "pursuing" or "chasing." Plutarch uses it when describing Antiochus as separated from his friends "while following the hounds *and [engaged] in [the] chase*[2]." In LXX, it occurs once as a rendering of "*he that pursueth* evil[3]" In Goodspeed, the noun occurs

Mk x 28—31 (R V) *contd*	Mt xix 27—30 (R V) *contd*	Lk xviii 28—30 xiii 30 (R V) *contd*
mothers, and children, and lands, with persecutions, and in the world (*or*, age) to come eternal life (31) But many [that are] first shall be last, and the last first	receive a hundredfold (*some anc. auth* manifold), and shall inherit eternal life (30) But many shall be last [that are] first, and first [that are] last	(xiii 30) And behold, there are last which shall be first, and there are first which shall be last

The phrase peculiar to Mark (x 30) "*with persecutions*" is commented on at great length by Clem Alex (who appears to have had a different reading from our present text, see below, p 140, n 8) but not by Origen (as far as Lommatzsch's Index shews) nor by Tertullian (as far as Rigaud's Index shews) nor in Jerome's commentary on the parall Matthew. Origen's only reference (in Lomm) to Mk x. 30 is in a statement that Jesus did *not* include "wife" (as the parall. Lk xviii 29 does), *Exhort ad Mart* § 16 (Lomm xx 254) οὐ γὰρ εἴρηται· Πᾶς ὅστις ἀφῆκεν ἀδελφούς, ἢ ἀδελφὰς, ἢ γονεῖς, ἢ τέκνα, ἢ ἀγρούς, ἢ οἰκίας, ἢ γυναῖκα, ἕνεκεν τοῦ ὀνόματός μου, πολλαπλασίονα λήψεται ἐν γὰρ τῇ ἀναστάσει τῶν νεκρῶν οὔτε γαμοῦσιν... (Mt xxii. 30, Mk xii 25)

Victor, on Mark, has preserved a tradition that justifies "renouncing the *wife*" in some circumstances, as also Jesus bade disciples "lose, or destroy, their life (ἀπολέσας τὴν ψυχήν)" It explains "persecutions" as a word "darkly hinting (αἰνίττεσθαι)" at distractions and temptations placed in the way of believers by their families Δοκεῖ δέ μοι καὶ τοὺς διωγμοὺς ἐνταῦθα αἰνίττεσθαι ἐπειδὴ γὰρ πολλοὶ ἦσαν, καὶ πατέρες εἰς ἀσέβειαν ἕλκοντες παῖδας, καὶ γυναῖκες ἄνδρας, ὅταν ταῦτα κελεύσωσι, φησί, μήτε γυναῖκες ἔστωσαν, μήτε πατέρες· ὅπερ οὖν καὶ ὁ Παῦλος ἔλεγεν, "εἰ δὲ καὶ ὁ ἄπιστος χωρίζεται, χωριζέσθω."

Victor's use of αἰνίττεσθαι suggests Origen's comment on "persecutors" in Ps cxix 157 (see below, p 140, n 8, *ad fin*) ἐχθροὺς ὁρατοὺς καὶ ἀοράτους αἰνίττεται.

[1] Mk iv 17, Mt xiii 21, parall Lk viii 13
[2] Plutarch *Mor* 184 F ἔν τινι κυνηγεσίῳ καὶ διωγμῷ
[3] Prov xi 19 מרדף LXX has διωγμὸς δὲ ἀσεβοῦς, "the pursuit, i e the aim, of the impious man" In Lam iii 19, διωγμός is a

HOW TO ENTER INTO THE KINGDOM

only twice. In the Epistle of Clement of Rome to the Corinthians, it apparently refers not to external, but to internal "persecution¹."

The verb "persecute" is never used by Mark. Matthew attributes it four times to Jesus in the Sermon on the Mount, but Luke, in at least three of these four instances, has some different word². Where however Matthew has, later on, "ye [*i.e* Jews] *shall pursue* [*them*] *from city to city*," the parallel Luke has "*shall pursue*" without any modifying clause, apparently taking "pursue" as having a local meaning³. In the Discourse on the Last Days, Mark and Matthew represent Jesus as saying "If any man saith unto you 'See, here is the Christ,' or 'See there,' do not believe", but a passage in Luke (not in that Discourse) has "Do not go away nor *pursue*," i.e. "do not *follow them*"—the only instance in the New Testament where "pursue" is applied to a personal object in a friendly sense⁴. On the other hand, in the same Discourse, where Mark and

---

misrendering of מרודי (*leg* as מרדף, which perhaps occurs (Gesen 923 *a*) in Is xiv 6, but Targ *leg.* מרדת).

¹ Clem Rom *Cor* § 3. The preceding context describes the degeneracy of the Church. "All glory was given unto you, and that was fulfilled which is written (Deut xxxii 15, very freely quoted) '*My beloved ate and kicked*' Hence jealousy and envy, [and] strife and sedition, *persecution* and tumult, war and captivity"—that is, a repetition of the history of rebellious Israel. In *Mart Polyc* § 1 it refers to external persecution of Christians

² Mt v 10 οἱ δεδιωγμένοι ἔνεκεν δικαιοσύνης, Lk om , Mt v 11 ὅταν ὀνειδίσωσιν ὑμᾶς καὶ διώξωσιν, Lk vi 22 ὅταν μισήσωσιν ὑμᾶς. . καὶ ὅταν ἀφορίσωσιν ὑμᾶς καὶ ὀνειδίσωσιν; Mt v 12 οὕτως γὰρ ἐδίωξαν τοὺς προφήτας, Lk vi 23 κατὰ τὰ αὐτὰ γὰρ ἐποίουν τοῖς προφήταις, Mt v 44 τῶν διωκόντων ὑμᾶς, Lk vi 27 τοῖς μισοῦσιν ὑμᾶς

³   Mt xxiii 34   Lk xi 49
ἐξ αὐτῶν ἀποκτενεῖτε καὶ σταυ-   ἐξ αὐτῶν ἀποκτενοῦσιν καὶ διώ-
ρώσετε, καὶ ἐξ αὐτῶν μαστιγώσετε ἐν   ξουσιν (AD ἐκδιώξουσιν)
ταῖς συναγωγαῖς ὑμῶν καὶ διώξετε
ἀπὸ πόλεως εἰς πόλιν

⁴ Mk xiii 21, Mt xxiv 23, Lk xvii 23. Luke places the saying, as one addressed to the disciples, after a similar one addressed to Pharisees "Men shall not say, 'See here' or '[See] there.'"

135 (Mark x 28—31)

HOW TO ENTER INTO THE KINGDOM

Matthew do not mention "persecution," Luke alone represents Jesus as expressly predicting it[1].

These facts, indicating that Luke differs from Matthew in his use of the verb "persecute," make it probable that he does not take the same view of the noun "persecution" as was taken in Mark's Original—both in the Parable of the Sower, and here in the statement that a Christian's reward is to be "with persecutions." Mark appears to assume "persecution" as a condition of reward. So does the Sermon on the Mount[2] Paul says to the Galatians, "We, brethren, as Isaac was, are children of promise But as then he that was born after the flesh *persecuted* him [that was born] after the Spirit, even so it is now[3]" This appeal to precedent implies something like a rule or law. "Persecution" is not mentioned in the literary Greek of the Wisdom of Solomon, but the author assumes that the righteous man will be "grievous" to the unrighteous, who will treat him despitefully and "condemn him with a shameful death[4]."

The Pauline assumption of a kind of Law of Persecution may be illustrated from a passage of Ecclesiastes, as rendered

---

[1] Mk xiii 9

παραδώσουσιν ὑμᾶς
εἰς συνέδρια καὶ εἰς συναγωγὰς δαρήσεσθε...

Mt xxiv. 9

παραδώσουσιν ὑμᾶς
εἰς θλίψιν καὶ ἀποκτεν-
οῦσιν ὑμᾶς...

Lk xxi. 12

ἐπιβαλοῦσιν ἐφ'
ὑμᾶς τὰς χεῖρας αὐτῶν
καὶ διώξουσιν παραδι-
δόντες εἰς τὰς συνα-
γωγὰς καὶ φυλακάς...

Comp Dan iv 25 "that *thou shalt be driven* (טרד) from men," Theod καὶ σὲ ἐκδιώξουσιν ἀπὸ τῶν ἀνθρώπων, LXX (see context) "his angels run down against thee and shall lead thee away into prison (εἰς φυλακὴν ἀπάξουσί σε) and send thee into a desolate place," *ib* 32 Theod ἀπὸ τῶν ἀνθρώπων σε ἐκδιώκουσιν, LXX οἱ ἄγγελοι διώξονταί σε

In Mark and Luke, but not in Matthew, the context proceeds to say that the disciples shall be brought before kings (Mk σταθήσεσθε, Lk ἀπαγομένους—which is used by LXX alone)

[2] Mt v. 12 "for so persecuted they the prophets," see above, p 101

[3] Gal iv 28—9 Comp 2 Tim iii 12 "All that would live godly in Christ Jesus shall *be persecuted*"

[4] Wisd ii 12—20. Διώκω in Wisd means (1) "chase away," as the mists chased by the sun, (2) "chase" as criminals, runaway slaves etc

HOW TO ENTER INTO THE KINGDOM

by the Targum and Jewish Midrash, as well as by LXX, "God shall seek after *him that is persecuted*[1]" The Midrash exemplifies God's action from the instances of Abel, Noah, Abraham, Isaac, Jacob, Joseph, Moses, and Israel, and adds that similarly God accepts as offerings only those beasts that are "chased" (*or* "persecuted"), but not those that "chase" (the "persecutors"), thus playing on the meaning of *râdaph*, "*pursue*" or "*chase*[2]"

Modern readers may be pardoned if they fail to perceive how Abraham and Isaac are types of the "*persecuted*" But all Jews believed that Abraham was persecuted by Nimrod[3] Paul also, as we have seen, assumes (strangely, but unmistakeably) the "persecution" of Isaac by Ishmael[4]. And Genesis describes Isaac as badly treated by the Philistines until they recognised that God was with him[5]

Here we must note a verbal similarity between Genesis and Mark. Mark alone says that the reward shall be "a hundredfold" Genesis says about Isaac that he "sowed in that land and found in the same year *an hundredfold*, and the Lord blessed him[6]." This is not only the first, but also, with one exception, the only Old Testament instance of "a hundredfold[7]" In the other instance it is used of divine increase. It is appropriately used by Mark in describing the Christian's reward as corresponding to that of Isaac whom God "blessed" But Luke, and perhaps Matthew, have substituted "manifold"

---

[1] Eccles iii 15 R V "God seeketh again *that which is passed away*," marg "Heb *driven away*" (nif of רדף "chase," "pursue"), Gesen 923 *a*, "seeketh *the pursued* (i e *what has disappeared, is past*, but dub)." Rashi interprets it as "*the persecuted*"

[2] See *Pesikt* (Wu pp 96—7) and *Lev r* (Wu pp 186—7) on Lev xxii 27 "a bullock or a sheep"

[3] See *Son*, **3501** *g*, *Light* **3822**

[4] See Gen xxi. 9 and Rashi's numerous explanations of Ishmael's "mocking"

[5] Gen xxvi 1—33 *Pesikt* recognises Isaac's persecution as coming from the Philistines (and does not mention persecution by Ishmael) [6] Gen xxvi 12

[7] The other is 2 S. xxiv 3 "Now the Lord thy God add unto the people .*an hundredfold*"

HOW TO ENTER INTO THE KINGDOM

These apparently petty verbal details are not petty if they are used as adjuncts to the consideration of the similarity between the picture of Peter, and the picture of Abraham (with Isaac in the background), both in the attitude of expectants of reward. In Mark, it is true, Peter does not mention "reward." He merely says to Jesus "Behold we have left all things and have followed thee." But Mark implies, and Matthew adds, "What then shall we have?" In Genesis, Abraham says merely "O Lord God, what wilt thou give me[1]?" but he implies a reference to what has preceded, as if saying, "Thou hast said unto me, 'Get thee out of thy country, and from thy kindred, and from thy father's house[2],' and I have renounced all these things at thy word." Commenting on this utterance of the Patriarch, Philo represents him as saying to God, "Thou, Lord, art my country and my kinsfolk and my father's hearth[3]", and this thought would naturally be connected with the thought of their forefather by pious Jews, who would see in the lives of Abraham and Isaac, and in the whole history of faithful Israel, God's divine recompense, "a hundredfold," for all the earthly blessings that Abraham renounced[4].

Regarded in this light—as an allusion to the "persecution" of all the saints, from Abel downward, and to the "reward" promised for the first time to Abraham and in part fulfilled by the birth of Isaac—the Marcan tradition "along with persecutions" is seen to give us the only Marcan glimpse of a doctrine that actually played a large part in Christ's teaching

---

[1] Gen xv 2   [2] Gen xii 1
[3] Philo i 477
[4] Philo connects the mystical use of "a hundred" with Abraham's "planting" as well as with Isaac's "sowing" thus (i 607) 'Αλλὰ καὶ "'Αβραὰμ ἄρουραν φυτεύει" (Gen xxi 33 LXX) χώματος, ἑκατοστῷ λόγῳ πρὸς ἀναμέτρησιν τοῦ χωρίου, καὶ 'Ισαὰκ "ἑκατοστεύουσαν εὑρίσκει κριθήν" (Gen xxvi 12 LXX), and he comments elsewhere (i 619) on Gen xxvi 12 "Isaac *found in the same year*"—not "reaped" but "found"—"a hundredfold." In the context, he contrasts αἰών with χρόνος apparently taking "the same year" to mean the latter. Philo's distinction between αἰών and χρόνος corresponds to Mark's distinction between αἰών and καιρός. I have not found any explanation of "a hundredfold" in connection with Abraham's planting.

HOW TO ENTER INTO THE KINGDOM

Jesus recognised for Himself, and endeavoured to impress on His disciples, that the Teacher of the truths of heaven and eternity and the spirit must come into collision with the children of the earth and the hour and the flesh, and that, on earth, and during the hour, and in the flesh, the latter must gain a temporary victory. But Mark's brief phrase was likely to be ignored amid the great differences in the Synoptic contexts[1], and also because it contradicted the views of those who regarded Christ's words as promising a Millennium on earth ("in this time") in which there would be no room for "persecutions[2]."

In the Fourth Gospel,* though "persecution" is never mentioned, and "persecute" only twice, the Law of Persecution is clearly recognised, and accepted as it were by Jesus for Himself and His disciples in the words "If the world hateth you, ye know that it hath hated me before [it hated] you....If they persecuted me, they will also persecute you[3]." The

---

[1] On these, see *Corrections* **446—7** But the verbal facts there collected must of course be supplemented by others, such as the influence exerted by Jewish traditions about persecution, and about the renunciations of Abraham, and about the "hundredfold" that Isaac "found" Questions might also arise as to the renunciation of "wife," mentioned by Luke (xviii 29) alone

[2] Origen, on Gen xxvi 12, besides commenting at great length on "barley" and its allegorical meaning in the Gospels, has a brief comment on a "hundredfold" "Isaac, the word of the Law [as distinct from the word of the Gospel], sows barley and yet even in the [inferior produce of] barley itself finds a hundredfold return For even in the Law you find *martyrs, whose [privilege] is the hundredfold return*" This assumes an allegorical connection between "a hundredfold" and "persecutions"

That Origen is alluding to the "hundredfold" in Mark is made probable by the fact that in *Comm Rom* 1 4 he calls attention to the fact that "Mark seems to make a distinction between Christ and the Gospel" in Mk x 29 "propter me vel propter Evangelium" Elsewhere he says (*Exhort ad Mart* § 14) "that I may receive *manifold* (Mt xix 29 v r) or, *as Mark says* (x 30), *a hundredfold*" Subsequently he alternates between the two words, saying once (*ib*) "*manifold*, or, to speak definitely, *a hundredfold*"

[3] Jn xv 18—20

HOW TO ENTER INTO THE KINGDOM

reason alleged for the beginning of this persecution is Christ's act of healing on the sabbath, "For this cause the Jews *began-to-persecute* Jesus because he was doing these things on the sabbath", and the deadly nature of their "persecution" is indicated in what follows about their "seeking to kill him[1]" Christ's prediction of "persecution" is preceded by a promise of the Paraclete[2] and of present peace ("my peace I give unto you")[3], and by a suggestion that it is of the nature of a "cleansing," or pruning, of the fruitful branches of the Vine that they may "bear more fruit[4]", and by a bestowal of the title of "friends," appointed to "bear fruit[5]"; and then, after a frank preparation of the disciples for an internecine conflict with the hostile religious "world" ("whosoever killeth you shall think that he offereth service unto God[6]") the Discourse terminates with the assurance, "These things have I spoken unto you that in me ye may have peace In the world ye [must] have tribulation but be of good cheer; I have gained the victory over the world[7]."

Indirectly these last words give the Johannine answer to the question of the disciples, expressed or implied by the Synoptists, "What shall we have?" The answer is "peace" But it is not peace of an ordinary kind It is peace in the Son ("in me ye may have peace"); and it implies such unity with the Father that the Son says to them "If ye shall ask anything of the Father, he will give it you in my name...Ask and ye shall receive, that your joy may be fulfilled[8]"

---

[1] Jn v 16, 18   [2] Jn xiv 16   [3] Jn xiv 27
[4] Jn xv 1—2.   [5] Jn xv 15—16
[6] Jn xvi 2   [7] Jn xvi 33
[8] Jn xvi 23—4 Space does not allow a discussion of the comment made by Clement of Alexandria on μετὰ διωγμῶν He twice quotes Mk x 30 with ἔχειν thus (949) Ταύτης δὲ ὁμοίως ἔχεται τῆς γνώμης καὶ τὸ ἑπόμενον "Νῦν ἐν τῷ καιρῷ τούτῳ ἀγροὺς καὶ χρήματα καὶ οἰκίας καὶ ἀδελφοὺς ἔχειν μετὰ διωγμῶν" Then, after saying that Jesus did not call on His disciples to give up their "brethren" etc literally, he adds Τὸ δὲ μετὰ διωγμῶν ταῦτα ἕκαστα ἔχειν ἀποδοκιμάζει, apparently meaning "But He disapproves of our retaining these things '*along with persecutions*'" [Perhaps a negative has dropped out, "*not along with persecutions*" Clark's rendering is "And the expression

HOW TO ENTER INTO THE KINGDOM

§ 4. *"But many that are first shall be last," in Mark and Matthew*[1]

This sentence is ambiguous because "first" and "last" may be used either in respect of time, or in respect of metaphorical place, that is to say, rank, or dignity. In Mark, the context does not indicate what the meaning is. It may be (1) "Many that are *first in the time of coming to me* shall be *last in the time of receiving their reward*," or (2) "Many that are *first in the time of coming to me* shall be *last in rank and dignity in the Kingdom of God*," or (3) "Many that are *first in rank and dignity now*, i.e. *in the Kingdom of this World*, shall be *last in rank in the Kingdom of God*[2]." The conjunction *"but,"* used by Mark and Matthew, is not adversative. It might differ little from *"and."* SS reads *"for"* instead of *"but."*

'with persecutions' rejects the possessing of each of those things"] Then he proceeds to define two kinds of persecution, (1) one proceeding from enemies, (2) but another, and far worse, from one's own soul and its passions (ὁ δὲ χαλεπώτατος ἔνδοθέν ἐστι διωγμὸς ἐξ αὐτῆς ἑκάστῳ τῆς ψυχῆς προπεμπόμενος).

The comment—whatever may be its precise meaning—indicates that in very early days the Marcan tradition must have caused difficulty, and that it would be likely to elicit Johannine intervention. Origen, on Ps cxix 157 "many are my persecutors," says τὸ πλῆθος ἐχθροὺς ὁρατοὺς καὶ ἀοράτους αἰνίττεται.

[1] Mk x 31, Mt xix 30 πολλοὶ δὲ ἔσονται πρῶτοι ἔσχατοι καὶ [οἱ] (Mt om οἱ) ἔσχατοι πρῶτοι, SS *"for"* instead of *"but"*, and in Mt, *a, b*, Corb have "sunt," Corb "enim", Lk xiii 30 καὶ ἰδοὺ εἰσὶν ἔσχατοι οἳ ἔσονται πρῶτοι, καὶ εἰσὶν πρῶτοι οἳ ἔσονται ἔσχατοι.

[2] Mark's omission of οἱ at first, and (bracketed) insertion of it subsequently, suggest that his exact meaning may have been "Many shall be, [though now] first [in the kingdom of this world], last [in the Kingdom of God], and *the last* [i e last in the kingdom of this world], [shall be] first [in the Kingdom of God]" This would agree with Lk xvi 15 "that which is exalted among men," [namely wealth greedily grasped and giving power to the graspers], "is an abomination in the sight of God." If that is the meaning, δέ, in Mark, differs little from καί. It may be rendered "now" or "and indeed" (like the parall Lk "and behold") SS "for" (in that case) gives the meaning at all events better than "but"

141 (Mark x. 28—31)

HOW TO ENTER INTO THE KINGDOM

Matthew, who follows Mark in placing this saying at the conclusion of Christ's doctrine about the Reward in the Kingdom, indicates his way of interpreting it by immediately adding "For the kingdom of heaven is like unto a man that is a householder," and by relating how this man, after hiring labourers at different hours of the day, paid them all the same wage and paid the last first ("pay them their hire, beginning from the last unto the first") Those who were hired first complain, but without success Then it is added "So the last shall be first, and the first last[1]" Here, "first" and "last" refer to time (but with a suggestion also that those who are paid last are treated as last in merit though they were the first to work)

Luke does not follow Mark in connecting this saying with the doctrine about the Reward in the Kingdom. He places it after a saying of Jesus about the exclusion of certain persons from the feast of Abraham amid the faithful of Israel "Ye shall see...yourselves cast forth without. And they shall come from the east and west and from the north and south...And behold, there are last that shall be first, and there are first that shall be last[2]" Now the first part of these words is in Matthew also, very similarly But Matthew, besides having "*the children of the kingdom,*" where Luke has "*ye,*" places the saying after the expression of Christ's wonder at the faith of the Centurion whom he apparently regards as a type of the Gentile converts to the Church[3]

These facts throw light on Luke's interpretation of the ambiguous word "*last*" and of its application to the history of the Church. He appears to use it as it is used in the Odyssey ("last [men]" and "last of men[4]") to mean *men coming from the extreme boundaries of the earth*, as mentioned in such prophecies of Isaiah as "Lo, these shall come *from far, and these from the north and from the west, and these from the land of Sinim*[5]." But he considered that it ought to be placed, not

---

[1] Mt. xx 1—16   [2] Lk xiii 28—30
[3] Mt. viii 10—12   [4] *Odyss* 1 23, vi 205
[5] Is. xlix 12, comp Is viii 9—10 "all ye of far countries," and xlix. 6 "I will also give thee for a light to the Gentiles that thou

HOW TO ENTER INTO THE KINGDOM

in connection with the doctrine of Reward (as in Mark), nor in connection with the Centurion's faith (as in Matthew), but in connection with a warning and reproach uttered by Jesus, while on His way to Jerusalem, and as denoting the Gentiles under the term *"last,"* contrasted with the Pharisees who were *"first*[1]*"*

Passing to early Christian writers for their interpretation of Mark's saying about "first" and "last," we find Clement of Alexandria, in a detailed exposition of the whole Marcan narrative, quoting the words and saying that they are "full as a flood both as to meaning and as to [need of] explanation," but that they do not come within his scope because he is dealing with the question of a rich man's salvation, and these words go beyond that question and are of general application[2]. Irenaeus, in an argument about the Incarnation, after contrasting Eve and the Virgin Mary—and speaking (very ob-

---

mayest be my salvation *as far as the utmost part* (קצה) *of the earth* (ἕως ἐσχάτου τῆς γῆς)" Ἔσχατος, about "the *utmost* (ἐσχάτου) [part] of the earth," occurs in N T only in Acts 1 8 "ye shall be my witnesses...*as far as the utmost [part] of the earth*," and xiii 47 (Paul and Barnabas quoting Is xlix 6 "*as far as the utmost [part] of the earth*")

[1] The thought of Israel as a Missionary, or at all events as an instrument for the recognition of God as (1) a chastising Judge, or (2) a Saviour, may be illustrated from the expression "*ends of the earth*" (Gesen 67 a אפסי ארץ) (1) in Deut xxxiii 17, 1 S ii 10 etc, and (2) in Mic v 4 "great unto the ends of the earth," Jerem xvi 19 "unto thee shall the nations come from the ends of the earth," Is xlv 22 "look unto me, and be ye saved, all the ends of the earth," *ib* lii 10 "all the ends of the earth shall see the salvation of our God" The Heb אפס (pl) is found only in this phrase It is variously rendered by forms of ἔσχατος (2), ἄκρος (5) πέρας (6), but in almost every case it refers to the spread of God's glory In one instance, Gk ἔσχατος represents Heb "far off," Is viii 9 "all ye of far countries" (there in hostile sense, but illustrative of Eph. ii 13 "ye [Gentiles] that were far off," in friendly sense)

[2] Clem. Alex 950 ἔσονται οἱ πρῶτοι ἔσχατοι πρῶτοι [*sic* Klotz, but Hinrichs, Leipzig 1909 ἔσονται οἱ πρῶτοι ἔ καὶ οἱ ἔ π] τοῦτο πολύχουν μέν ἐστι κατὰ τὴν ὑπόνοιαν καὶ τὸν σαφισμόν, οὐ μὴν ἕν γε τῷ παρόντι τὴν ζήτησιν ἀπαιτεῖ, οὐ γὰρ μόνον ῥέπει πρὸς τοὺς πολυκτήμονας, ἀλλ' ἁπλῶς πρὸς ἅπαντας ἀνθρώπους τοὺς πίστει καθάπαξ ἑαυτοὺς ἐπιδιδόντας

HOW TO ENTER INTO THE KINGDOM

scurely) about a "first compact" as "loosing" from a "second tie," and of a "second tie" as taking the place of the "first," which has been cancelled—says "For this reason did the Lord declare that *the first indeed should be last and the last first*. And the Prophet too signifies this same thing, saying, Instead of thy fathers there are born unto thee children. For the Lord being born [as] *first begotten of the dead* and receiving into His bosom the fathers of old time [before the flood] regenerated them into the life of God, becoming Himself the beginning of the living since Adam had become the beginning of the dying[1]." All this is justly described by editors of Irenaeus as fanciful and obscure, but it has a historical value. It shews us that in the days of Irenaeus the Marcan tradition actually called forth what Clement calls "a flood," in the form of explanatory comment; and it suggests that, already in the days of Matthew and Luke, the "flood" had begun in Matthew's parable of the Workmen and the Denarius which Luke does not insert. It was perhaps an Apostolic Targumistic exposition of Christ's brief words, which words it repeated at its close.

Origen, on Matthew, begins by saying that the words about "first" and "last" make some kind of sense when taken as referring to time, according to their simple meaning, namely, that those who are called early to Christ's service must be diligent not to fail in their course so as to fall behind others whose call comes later[2]. Then he proceeds to apply the "first" and "last" to the Jews and the Gentiles. After this, he discusses the question whether the "first" may not mean "angels," many of whom "were [originally] first with respect to men [yet] become last with respect to some men[3]." It is remarkable that Jerome, in his commentary on Matthew, says nothing about the meaning of "first" and "last." He leaves us in doubt whether he thought that the "flood" of comment

---

[1] Iren. III. 22. 4, on which see Grabe. Clark's transl quotes Massuet's opinion that the writer's remarks are "paulo subtiliora."

[2] Origen on Mt xix 30, *Comm. Matth.* xv. 26.

[3] Origen *Comm Matth* xv 27 πολλοὶ μὲν ἀγγέλων οἱ πρῶτοι ἦσαν ἀνθρώπων γίνονταί τινων ἀνθρώπων ἔσχατοι On πρῶτος thus used with gen see *Joh Gr* **2665**—7.

HOW TO ENTER INTO THE KINGDOM

mentioned by Clement might now profitably be left without further addition, or whether he thought it already superabundant and fanciful[1]

We now pass to the question whether Biblical precedent and Jewish interpretation throw any light on the antithesis between "the first" and "the last." It resembles the antithesis between "*the great*" and "*the little*," which has previously come before us in a passage where all the Synoptists agree that the disciples had been discussing who was to be "*greater [than the rest]*," but Mark alone adds that Jesus (apparently assuming "*greater*" to be synonymous with "*first*") said to them "If any one desireth to be *first* he shall be last of all and servant of all[2]."

Now this points back to the ancient story of the birth of Rebecca's children, and to the prophecy (quoted by Paul) "The *elder* shall serve the *younger*," rendered by LXX "The *greater* shall serve the *less*[3]." The context in Genesis proceeds to describe Esau as being born "*the first*" of the two "*The first came forth*" This is the exact and literal rendering; for the Hebrew word regularly means "first," "former," etc and never "firstborn." But the LXX renders it here uniquely "the firstborn son[4]."

---

[1] See Jerome's *Letters* xlvi 10 where, after saying that Jerusalem is the Christian Athens, he adds, "We ourselves are among *the last*, not *the first*, yet we have come hither to see the *first* of all nations." Then after describing the concourse of many nations, he says "Yet amid this great concourse. all strive after humility, that greatest of Christian virtues Whosoever is *last* is here regarded as *first*"

[2] Mk ix 35 Mt xxiii 11 is similar, but comes in a different context See the parallels above, p 70 foll

[3] Gen xxv 23 where R.V marg refers to Obad 18—21, as well as to the quotation in Rom ix 12. Hos xii 3 ("took his brother by the heel") refers to the narrative LXX has ὁ μείζων δουλεύσει τῷ ἐλάσσονι See *Son* 3521 foll on the various meanings of 'greater" and "less" in Hebrew and Greek

[4] Gen xxv 25 ἐξῆλθεν δὲ ὁ υἱὸς ὁ πρωτότοκος πυρράκης ὅλος ὡσεὶ δορὰ δασύς Πρωτότοκος = בכור more than a hundred times, but here ὁ υἱὸς ὁ π = הראשון, "*the first*," or "*the former*' This (Gesen 911 b) is given as the first Biblical instance of ראשון "*former*

HOW TO ENTER INTO THE KINGDOM

The LXX here commits what Jews would regard as a fatal error, for the Jews would regard Esau as "first" indeed in this world, but *not* "first" in God's sight, and not really "firstborn." The Talmud appears rarely to refer to Esau's being "first," but the Midrash repeatedly mentions it in a bad sense, contrasting it with "first" in a good sense applied to God, or the Temple, or the Messiah Thus Pesikta represents God as saying to Israel in effect, "If ye begin the Feast of Tabernacles for me on the *first* day, I will appear to you as 'the FIRST' (*i e.* God), and avenge you on '*the first*' (i e. Esau), and will build for you 'the first' (*i e.* the Temple) and will bring unto you 'the First' (*i.e.* the Messiah)[1]."

In contrast with Esau, who is regarded as firstborn only in a literal and earthly sense, Scripture presents David as "the little one" in his father's house, but one whom the Psalmist describes as "*made firstborn*" (a unique combination of words) "by God[2]." In Hebrew poetry and Jewish tradition there were probably frequent contrasts between the false firstborn (Esau) and the true firstborn (David) Some of these might extenuate the fancifulness of Origen, who detects a contrast of meaning in the identical epithet "red" or "ruddy"—applied to the two, but implying murderous hatred in Esau while it implies beauty and goodness in David[3] At all events this epithet "red" is

---

[*in time*]" Tromm. gives ראשון as = πρῶτος more than a hundred times, also πρότερος (15), but πρωτότοκος only here

[1] *Pesikt* § 28 *ad fin*, quoting Lev xxiii 40, Is. xli 4, Gen xxv 25, Jerem xvii. 12, Is xli 27 *Pesach* 5 *a* is to the same effect So are *Gen. r.* on Gen xxv 24—5 and on Gen xxxii 2, of which the latter implies that everything about Edom (*i e* Esau) was "red," and alludes to Is lxiii 2 "red in thine apparel," as predicting the vengeance to be exacted from Edom Sim *Exod r* (on Exod xii 2), *Lev r.* (on Lev xxiii 40)

[2] 1 S. xvi. 11 (see *Son* **3522** *b*) Heb "the little one," Ps lxxxix 27 "I also will make him *firstborn* (בכור)" Gesen 114 *a* gives a few other instances of the figurative use of "*firstborn*" but none of "*firstborn*" with "*make*"

[3] Origen on 1 S xvi. 12 (Lomm xi 286) Elsewhere, on Ps xxii 9 "thou art he that took me out of the womb," he contrasts this phrase, implying God's election, as follows, τῶν ἄλλων ἀνθρώπων οὐκ

HOW TO ENTER INTO THE KINGDOM

applied in Scripture to none but Esau and David[1] And the Midrash on Genesis contains a tradition of R Abba bar Kahana about the alarm of Samuel, before anointing David to be king, when he saw the youth for the first time. "Why was Esau 'red'? Because it was as if he would be a shedder of blood When Samuel found David 'red,' he feared and said 'Is this man also a shedder of blood like Esau?' But God said to him, 'He is beautiful in the eyes[2].'"

These facts suffice to shew that Christ's doctrine about the "first" and the "last" goes back to Hebrew Scripture and probably to Jewish tradition, and that its exposition in the Synoptic Gospels varied in such a way that we might naturally expect some further exposition in the Fourth Gospel

§ 5. "First Simon" in Matthew[3], and "first" in John

I have found no early comment of importance on the epithet "first," assigned by Matthew alone to Simon, except that of Jerome "The order of the Apostles, and the merit of each one, was for Him to distribute who searches the secrets of the heart" That Matthew did not mean merely first in order of calling (that is, by the sea of Galilee) or first in order of naming (that is, "naming as an apostle," or naming by a new name, "Peter") but "first in rank," appears from several considerations.

Matthew alone represents Jesus as saying to Peter "I will give unto thee the keys of the kingdom of heaven[4]." "*First*" would be superfluous if attached to a name placed first in a list and meaning merely "first in the list" In Chronicles, when

---

ἐκσπασμένων (sic) ἀλλ' ἐξερχομένων, "ἐξῆλθε γάρ, φησὶν, ὁ 'Ησαῦ (Gen xxv 25)"

[1] Gesen 10 b אדמוני, Gen xxv 25, 1 S xvi. 12, xvii 42 (again applied to David).

[2] *Gen r* on Gen xxv 25 referring to 1 S xvi 12. "A good eye," or "a beautiful eye," implied kindliness (the opposite of "an evil eye," which implied envy)

[3] Mt x 2 Τῶν δὲ δώδεκα ἀποστόλων τὰ ὀνόματά ἐστιν ταῦτα· πρῶτος Σίμων ὁ λεγόμενος Πέτρος...

[4] Mt xvi 19

HOW TO ENTER INTO THE KINGDOM

"*first*" (A.V.) is attached to a name in a list of names it corresponds to the Hebrew "*head*," "*chief*," "*ruler*," and is rendered "*chief*" by R.V. and "*ruler*" by LXX[1]. In other passages the LXX "first" corresponds to the Hebrew "head" or "chief" applied to persons[2]. The word was also applied by Jews to the president of a course of priests that happened to be serving, or of a court of justice, or of a synagogue[3]. There can be little doubt that Luke, who uses the Greek "first" to mean "chief" or "principal" rather freely in the Acts[4], would understand Matthew's "first" as claiming some priority of rank for Peter Luke does not insert it in his apostolic list. As Mark also does not insert it, the word does not belong technically to the province marked out by the rule of Johannine Intervention; but while inquiring into Johannine doctrine generally about "*the first*," we shall find it profitable to inquire whether John has anything to say about the word in connection with the calling, or naming, of Peter.

John does not use the word "first" in the sayings of Christ, and (apart from "the last day") he does not use the word "last" at all. But he uses "first" in the sayings of the Baptist in such an antithetical way as to suggest "later," or "last," giving it a peculiar and spiritual significance in connection with the nature of Christ: "This was he [of] whom I said, He that cometh *behind me* is become *before me*, because he was *my First*," "This is [indeed] he in whose behalf I [myself] said, *Behind me* cometh a man (*vir*) who is become *before me*, because he was *my*

---

[1] 1 Chr xii 9 This happens to be not only the first of several instances but also one in which the number is "eleven" (unique in such lists, Gesen 911 *a*). This might remind early Christian Hebraistic Evangelists of the number of Christ's apostles, reckoned without Judas Iscariot For "*first*" A V. = "*chief*" R V, see 1 Chr xxiii 19, 20, xxiv 21

[2] 1 Chr xi 11 LXX "*first* (πρῶτος) of the thirty," Heb ראש, R V. "*chief*," Nehem xii 46 πρῶτος τῶν ἀδόντων, also 2 K xxv 18, 2 Chr xxvi 20 etc. "*chief* priest"

[3] See Schurer II 1 184, 221, 257, II 11 64

[4] Acts xiii 50, xxv 2, xxviii 17, comp xvi 12, xvii 4, xxviii 7 Πρῶτος pl. means "*chief*" in Mk vi 21, Lk xix 47 (comp. Lk xv 22 στολὴν τὴν πρώτην) In Mk x. 44, Mt xx 27, "*chief(est)* A.V. = "*first*" R.V.

148 (Mark x 28—31)

First[1]." These sayings distinguish "first" from prior in mere time and from prior in mere place, and give it the meaning of priority in nature. Also, by using the word as a quasi-noun, the Evangelist suggests to the reader the thought of "the First" as thrice used by Isaiah in the title "*the First and* (or, *and with*) *the Last*[2]" Thus the opening utterance in the drama of the Fourth Gospel—for no one has spoken hitherto—coming immediately after the Prologue, suggests to any reader familiar with the language of prophecy a conception of "first" as *being not opposed but preparatory to "last,"* and of both as being included in the divine Nature, which is threefold:—"first" and "midst" and "last," or "was" and "is" and "will be[3]"

Incidentally, the Fourth Gospel discourages those who regarded Simon Peter as being called to be an apostle, or called by the name Peter, with some kind of priority implied in Matthew's title of "*first*" A compromise might have been suggested, namely, that Simon was called, along with his brother Andrew, first in order of time, just before the calling of the sons of Zebedee. But this suggestion John puts aside by saying that Andrew and an unnamed companion came to Jesus before any other disciples, and that "Andrew *first found his own brother Simon*," and "brought him unto Jesus," saying to him "we have found the Messiah[4]" He adds that Jesus

---

[1] Jn i 15 (for various readings see *Joh Gr* Index) λέγων—οὗτος ἦν ὁ εἰπών—'Ο ὀπίσω μου ἐρχόμενος ἔμπροσθέν μου γέγονεν, ὅτι πρῶτός μου ἦν, i 30 οὗτός ἐστιν ὑπὲρ οὗ ἐγὼ εἶπον Ὀπίσω μου ἔρχεται ἀνὴρ ὃς ἔμπροσθέν μου γέγονεν, ὅτι πρῶτός μου ἦν

[2] Is xli 4, xliv 6, xlviii 12 (Gesen 911 b) The LXX has severally (xli. 4) ἐγὼ θεὸς πρῶτος, καὶ εἰς τὰ ἐπερχόμενα ἐγώ εἰμι, (xliv 6) (θεὸς σαβαώθ) Ἐγὼ πρῶτος καὶ ἐγὼ μετὰ ταῦτα, πλὴν ἐμοῦ οὐκ ἔστιν θεός, (xlviii 12) ἐγώ εἰμι πρῶτος, καὶ ἐγώ εἰμι εἰς τὸν αἰῶνα

[3] Revelation thrice uses ἔσχατος in this phrase i 17, ii 8, xxii 13 supplementing it severally thus (1) καὶ ὁ ζῶν, (2) ὃς ἐγένετο νεκρὸς καὶ ἔζησεν, (3) ἐγὼ τὸ Ἄλφα καὶ τὸ Ὦ, [ὁ] πρῶτος καὶ [ὁ] ἔσχατος, ἡ ἀρχὴ καὶ τὸ τέλος. It also has xxi 6 ἐγὼ τὸ Ἄλφα καὶ τὸ Ὦ, ἡ ἀρχὴ καὶ τὸ τέλος, and iii 14 τάδε λέγει ὁ Ἀμήν...ἡ ἀρχὴ τῆς κτίσεως τοῦ θεοῦ.

[4] Jn i 41 "he *first* findeth his own brother," see *Joh Gr* **1901** b, **1985** W H read πρῶτον But whatever be the reading, the text implies that Andrew, after becoming a convert, brought Simon to

HOW TO ENTER INTO THE KINGDOM

did not exactly name Simon "Peter" ("thou *art Peter*") but said "Thou art Simon, the son of John, thou *shalt be called Cephas* (or, *Peter*)[1]," and that, later on, He momentarily withdrew the title, saying "*Simon, son of John,* lovest thou me[2]?" Also, he represents Peter as making a confession of faith to Jesus, not in his own name singly, but in that of all the disciples[3]. And immediately after Christ's resurrection, the disciple that first "believed" is not Peter, but Peter's unnamed companion[4], of whom it is twice[5] said that he "came *first*" to the sepulchre after "outrunning" Peter. In all this there is a desire, not to disparage Simon, the apostle of impulse and utterance and action, but to distinguish him from the unnamed apostle of insight and reticence, and to exhibit the two, at the close of the Gospel, as serving Jesus in their several ways, one "following," the other "tarrying[6]."

But all this incidental doctrine about Andrew and the unnamed disciple, as being the "first" to do this or that, is altogether subordinate to the thought of Christ as being our FIRST, in whom we are to be all one. This FIRST is also COMING; "Abraham," says Jesus, "exulted in order that he might see my day"; yet He says also "Before Abraham was I AM[7]." As for the way in which the FIRST is to become

---

Jesus before the latter had become a convert and before he was named Peter "In some sense, if priority could be claimed by the first disciple to bring another disciple to Jesus, it could be claimed by Andrew"—such is the impression produced on the reader Comp *Introd* pp 143—4

- [1] Jn i 42   [2] Jn xxi 15—17
[3] Jn vi 68—9 "Lord, to whom shall we go?...Thou hast the words of eternal life, and we perfectly (*Joh Voc* **1629**, *Joh Gr* **2475**) believe and know that thou art the Holy One of God"
[4] Jn xx 8 "and he saw and believed" Of Peter it is said (*ib* 6) "he beholdeth," but not "he believed"
[5] Jn xx 4, 8.   [6] Jn xxi 22—3
[7] Jn viii. 56, 58. On Jn i 9 ἐρχόμενον, prob to be taken with φῶς, "the light...[continually] coming," see *Joh Gr* **2277, 2508.** Its technical sense of "coming from God" or "coming as the Deliverer" may in part explain the omission of πρὸ ἐμοῦ by many authorities in Jn x 8 πάντες ὅσοι ἦλθον πρὸ ἐμοῦ The meaning "came [professing

(Mark x 28—31)

HOW TO ENTER INTO THE KINGDOM

LAST, it is set before us in the Washing of Feet, not as a penalty or degradation, but as an act of divine service wherein the Son represents to us the Father in heaven, and shews us how we are to conform ourselves to His image as His children on earth[1] If we do this, there can be no first or last in the worldly sense among those about whom Jesus says to the Father "I in them and thou in me, that they may be perfected into one[2]"

§ 6. *"And Jesus was going before them, and they were amazed," in Mark*[3]

This passage has been discussed above with other Marcan

to be the Deliverer]" may have seemed deducible from ἦλθον—without πρὸ ἐμοῦ, which some heretics might interpret as definitely condemning all the ancient heroes of Israel

[1] Jn xiii. 4—17 [2] Jn xvii 23
[3] Mk x 32—4 (R.V.)

Mk x 32—4 (R.V.)	Mt. xx 17—19 (R V)	Lk xix 28, xviii 31—3 (R V.)
(32) And they were in the way, going up to Jerusalem; and Jesus was going before them and they were amazed; and they that followed (*or*, but some as they followed) were afraid And he took again the twelve, and began to tell them the things that were to happen unto him, [saying],	(17) And as Jesus was going up to Jerusalem, he took the twelve disciples apart, and in the way he said unto them,	(xix. 28) And when he had thus spoken, he went on before, going up to Jerusalem (xviii 31) And he took unto him the twelve, and said unto them,
(33) Behold, we go up to Jerusalem; and the Son of man shall be delivered unto the chief priests and the scribes, and they shall condemn him to death, and shall deliver him unto the Gentiles.	(18) Behold, we go up to Jerusalem; and the Son of man shall be delivered unto the chief priests and scribes, and they shall condemn him to death, (19) and shall deliver him unto the Gentiles to mock, and to scourge, and to crucify and the	Behold, we go up to Jerusalem, and all the things that are written by (*or*, through) the prophets shall be accomplished unto the Son of man. (32) For he shall be delivered up unto the Gentiles, and shall be mocked, and shamefully en-
(34) And they shall mock him, and shall spit upon him,		

HOW TO ENTER INTO THE KINGDOM

passages of the same kind[1], and it has been shewn that John prefers to describe the wonder inspired in the disciples by their Master as a feeling caused by His "grace and truth," rather to be called "reverence" than amazement or "fear" as here ("they that followed were afraid"). But it is worth noting that on this occasion the amazement and "fear" recorded by Mark might have a correspondence with a particular passage in the Book of Joshua, where it is said about the first Jesus when he led Israel across the Jordan (LXX) "The Lord magnified Jesus before the face of all Israel and they *feared him*, as they *feared Moses*...[2]" This passage appears to be almost unique in Scripture. Nowhere else does Scripture speak thus of "*fearing*" *persons*—in the sense of honouring or reverencing them—except in the Levitical precept "Ye shall *fear* every man his mother and his father[3]" Scripture describes Israel as fearing to "come nigh" Moses when they saw that "the skin of his face shone[4]," but not as "fearing him."

The long account of Israel's crossing the Jordan under Joshua begins thus: "This day will I begin to magnify thee in the sight of all Israel, that they may know that, as I was with Moses, so I will be with thee[5]" Origen, describing John the

Mk x 32—4 (R V) *contd*	Mt xx 17—19 (R V) *contd*	Lk xix 28, xviii 31—3 (R V) *contd*
and shall scourge him, and shall kill him, and after three days he shall rise again	third day he shall be raised up	treated, and spit upon. (33) And they shall scourge and kill him and the third day he shall rise again

[1] Mk x 32, on which see above, Chap. II. § 3
[2] Josh iv 14 LXX ἐφοβοῦντο αὐτὸν ὥσπερ [AF + ἐφοβοῖντο] Μωυσῆν
[3] Lev xix 3. Gesen 431 b gives under this heading only these instances of "fear" with accus of person. In 1 K iii 28 ἐφοβήθησαν ἀπὸ προσώπου τοῦ β, the LXX correctly renders the Heb which has not the accusative
[4] Exod xxxiv. 30.
[5] Josh iii 7 Mk x 1 "cometh.. *and beyond Jordan* (ἔρχεται εἰς τὰ ὅρια τῆς Ἰουδαίας καὶ πέραν τοῦ Ἰορδάνου)," though obscured by the insertion of "and," leaves no doubt, when it is combined with Mk x 46 "and they come *to Jericho*" that Jesus had been "beyond,

HOW TO ENTER INTO THE KINGDOM

Baptist as baptizing "beyond Jordan," breaks off to devote a long section to Israel crossing Jordan under "Jesus," *i.e* Joshua, as being typical of Christian baptism[1]; and this, for Christians, would be a natural application[2]. The Baptist, "in the Wilderness," would represent the Law; Jesus, in the Jordan, being baptized in it, and also the first of those baptized by the Holy Spirit, would represent the Gospel. When Jesus passed "over the Jordan" at any time He might be regarded as passing to the conquest of the Promised Land But on the occasion we are now considering He had recently passed over it for the last time, going up to the glorious victory of the Cross in Jerusalem. Moreover, like a spiritual Joshua, immediately after crossing the Jordan, He might be said to take Jericho in a spiritual capture, bestowing sight on the blind, and leading the multitude onward in His train, rejoicing in His triumph Might not all this recall to the earliest disciples in their Christian hymnal worship the first crossing of the Jordan by the Leader whom the Lord "magnified" in the sight of Israel so that they "feared him as they feared Moses"?

In the Fourth Gospel, apart from descriptions of the acts of John the Baptist, the phrase "across Jordan" occurs only once, "And he went away again *beyond Jordan* into the place where John was at first baptizing[3]." Christ's first "crossing

---

i e eastward of, Jordan" just before He "came to Jericho" which was westward of Jordan If so, He had crossed the Jordan just before He "came to Jericho"

The parall Mt xix 1 omits "and" ($\mathring{\eta}\lambda\theta\epsilon\nu$ $\epsilon\mathring{\iota}s$ $\tau\grave{\alpha}$ $\mathring{o}$ $\tau\hat{\eta}s$ $\mathring{I}$ $\pi\acute{\epsilon}\rho\alpha\nu$ $\tau o\hat{v}$ $\mathring{I}o\rho\delta\acute{\alpha}\nu o v$). This might mean "He came to ..*passing-over* the Jordan," as in Jn x 40 $\mathring{a}\pi\hat{\eta}\lambda\theta\epsilon\nu$ $\pi\acute{a}\lambda\iota\nu$ $\pi\acute{\epsilon}\rho\alpha\nu$ $\tau o\hat{v}$ $\mathring{I}o\rho\delta\acute{\alpha}\nu o v$ Comp $\pi\acute{\epsilon}\rho\alpha\nu$ with verb of motion in Jn vi 17 and especially xviii 1 "went forth *passing-over* Cedron " Here, Westc says, "probably with a significant reference" to David crossing the Kidron. It is not improbable that also in Mk-Mt. here—a unique Synoptic use of "over" or "passing across" in connection with Christ's movements—there is a "significant reference" to Joshua, the first "Jesus," crossing Jordan to Jericho

[1] Origen *Comm Joann* vi 26
[2] See [Tertull *Reply to Marcion* iii 80—90 (Clark iii 346—7)]
[3] Jn x. 40.

HOW TO ENTER INTO THE KINGDOM

of the Jordan" from this place is implied but not expressed[1]. It is at this place ("Bethany beyond Jordan") that Jesus receives the news of the sickness of Lazarus and says "Let us go into Judaea again." This would involve a second "crossing of the Jordan." The disciples remonstrate and Thomas says "Let us also go that we may die with him[2]." If this journey "into Judaea" had ended in Jerusalem, a case might be made out for supposing that the Johannine journey ("across Jordan") coincided with that under discussion in Mark, and that the alarm expressed by the disciples and Thomas in John, corresponded to the amazement and fear of Christ's disciples and followers in Mark. But the feelings ascribed to Thomas and his companions differ too much from those described in Mark to allow, in this instance, the inference of any Johannine allusion or intervention of this particular kind. It would be nearer the truth to say that in the Fourth Gospel the disciples are never represented as "fearing" except when they have been separated from their Master and fail to recognise Him as He approaches them[3].

It is otherwise as to the general use of the phrase "beyond Jordan." Here John probably intervenes for Mark against Luke who never uses it. Luke, as a historian, might object to it because of its geographical ambiguity[4]. But John would not be likely on that account to sacrifice a phrase replete with Scriptural poetic associations, and capable of being freed from ambiguity by a careful arrangement of the context[5]. It was from beyond Jordan that Jesus, like Joshua advancing to victory over the kings of Canaan, Himself advanced to victory over

---

[1] The first "crossing of the Jordan" would take place when Jesus (Jn 1 43) ἠθέλησεν ἐξελθεῖν εἰς τὴν Γαλιλαίαν. This was (*Beginning* p 213), according to Origen, "to find the lost, namely, Philip."

[2] Jn xi 16   [3] Jn vi 19—20

[4] See *Joh Voc.* 1714 b, 1813 b. John also supports Mk-Mt against Luke in the phrase "*sea* of Galilee" (*Joh Voc* 1811 d), not "*lake*" as Luke.

[5] Jn i 28 "Bethany beyond Jordan" clearly means "Bethany E. of Jordan" contrasted with Bethany W of Jordan, near Jerusalem, and iii 26, x 40 clearly refer to the former.

death, as typified in the raising of Lazarus. At the same time John is careful to fortify his readers against the objection "In departing from 'beyond Jordan,' that is, Peraea, Jesus was fleeing from Herod Antipas, who ruled over it[1]." John tells us, in effect, that this was not so. The great danger was from the Jews, as the disciples implied, when in answer to their Master's words, "Let us go into Judaea again," they replied "Rabbi, the Jews were but now seeking to stone thee; and goest thou thither again[2]?"

§ 7. *"With the baptism that I am baptized withal shall ye be baptized," in Mark*[3]

It will be seen, in the texts printed below, that Matthew omits mention of baptism, not only here in Christ's promise to

---

[1] Comp. Lk. xiii 31, where "certain Pharisees" say to Jesus "Get thee out, and go hence; for Herod would fain kill thee."
[2] Jn xi 7—8 See above, p. 65.
[3] Mk x 35—40   Mt xx 20—23   Lk om.
    (R V)   (R V)

Mk x 35—40 (R V)	Mt xx 20—23 (R V)	Lk om.
(35) And there come near unto him James and John, the sons of Zebedee, saying unto him, Master (*or*, Teacher), we would that thou shouldest do for us whatsoever we shall ask of thee	(20) Then came to him the mother of the sons of Zebedee with her sons, worshipping [him], and asking a certain thing of him.	
(36) And he said unto them, What would ye that I should do for you?	(21) And he said unto her, What wouldest thou? She saith unto him, Command that these my two sons may sit, one on thy right hand, and one on thy left hand, in thy kingdom.	
(37) And they said unto him, Grant unto us that we may sit, one on thy right hand, and one on [thy] left hand, in thy glory		
(38) But Jesus said unto them, Ye know not what ye ask Are ye able to drink the cup that I drink? or to be	(22) But Jesus answered and said, Ye know not what ye ask Are ye able to drink the cup that I am about to drink?	Comp Lk xii 50 (R.V.) But I have a baptism to be baptized

HOW TO ENTER INTO THE KINGDOM

the sons of Zebedee, but also before in His question to them (Mark) "Are ye able to drink the cup that I drink, or to be baptized...?" where Matthew stops short at "drink[1]." Luke omits the whole narrative This is therefore a case where we might expect some kind of Johannine intervention as to the sons of Zebedee, and, more particularly, as to the "baptism" wherewith they were to be "baptized."

Why should Matthew omit the mention of baptism? One reason may be that he found the Marcan tradition already used —as it was before the days of Irenaeus—by heretics who introduced new rites of "redemption." These might affirm not only that the Lord said "I have another baptism to be baptized with," but also that He "appointed *as an addition this redemption* to the sons of Zebedee...saying, 'Can ye be baptized with the baptism which I shall be baptized with[2]?'" Another reason may be that Christians in the first century found it hard, as Origen appears to have done[3], to define the

Mk x 35—40 (R.V.) *contd*.	Mt xx 20—23 (R.V.) *contd*	Lk om.
baptized with the baptism that I am baptized with? (39) And they said unto him, We are able And Jesus said unto them, The cup that I drink ye shall drink, and with the baptism that I am baptized withal shall ye be baptized (40) But to sit on my right hand or on [my] left hand is not mine to give but [it is for them] for whom it hath been prepared ·	They say unto him, We are able (23) He saith unto them, My cup indeed ye shall drink but to sit on my right hand, and on [my] left hand, is not mine to give, but [it is for them] for whom it hath been prepared of my Father	with and how am I straitened till it be accomplished!

[1] Mk x 38—9, Mt xx 22—3
[2] Iren 1 21 2, quoting Lk xii 50 and Mk x. 38
[3] Origen on Mt xx 22 (Lomm iv 15 foll and 1 266) In the latter passage (*Comm Joann* vi 37) the words ἵνα γὰρ τολμηρότερον βασανίζων τὸν λόγον στῶ πρὸς τὰ ὑπὸ τῶν πλείστων ὑπονοούμενα indicate his dissent from the prevalent interpretation

156 (Mark x 35—40)

HOW TO ENTER INTO THE KINGDOM

difference between the cup and the baptism, and the way in which the sons of Zebedee actually drank the cup and were baptized with the baptism. James the son of Zebedee died as a martyr and might be said to have fulfilled Christ's prediction, but how was it fulfilled by John the son of Zebedee, who was believed to have lived to a great age and to have died a natural death?

In attempting to explain Matthew's omission we must start from ancient facts and not import into them modern notions. The Greek word *baptizein*, rendered by us "baptize," means literally "immerse," and metaphorically implies for the most part immersion *in evil of some kind*[1]. In canonical LXX it occurs only once literally and once corresponding to Heb "frighten[2]"; but Aquila uses it metaphorically in Job[3] "Yet wilt thou *immerse* me in the ditch," where the word rendered "*ditch*" means "[*the*] *pit* [*of Sheol*]" and recurs in the Psalms (R V txt) "Thou wilt not leave my soul to Sheol; neither wilt thou suffer thy holy one to see *corruption* (marg *the pit*)[4]" The word therefore, when used metaphorically and paradoxically with "fire," might be connected with something bordering on Sheol, something suggestive of extreme and depressing humiliation, as well as fiery trial.

In attempting to define Christ's meaning more closely we are hampered by the want of evidence in the New Testament. For Matthew nowhere represents Jesus as using the word "baptize"—or "baptism" except about "John's baptism[5]"—till after the Resurrection, and then in a tradition that he alone

---

[1] See Steph *Thes* ii 109, which shews that it means "*plunged*" in debt, sleep, drinking, perplexity etc

[2] 2 K. v 14 "dipped [himself]," Is xxi 4 "hath affrighted "

[3] Job ix 31 "immerse," טבל, "pit" שחת (see Gesen 1001) Heb. שחת = (Tromm) βόθρος, βόθυνος (4), φθορά, διαφθορά etc (12), θάνατος (5). Βαπτίζω occurs also in Jerem xxxviii 22 (Sym) ἐβάπτισαν εἰς τέλμα τοὺς πόδας σου, Heb "thy feet *are sunk* in the mire," Aq κατέδυσαν (hif of טבע), LXX καταλύσουσιν (prob error for κατακλύσουσιν). See also Ps lxix 2 (Sym).

[4] Ps xvi 10 (LXX διαφθοράν) is quoted about Christ in Acts ii 27, xiii 35

[5] Mt xxi. 25 "the baptism of John"

157 (Mark x. 35—40)

HOW TO ENTER INTO THE KINGDOM

has recorded[1]. Luke omits the whole of the Marcan story under consideration. But he represents Jesus elsewhere as saying on the only occasion when He mentions baptism (except about "John's baptism"), "I came to cast fire on the earth... But I have a baptism to be baptized with; and how am I straitened till it be accomplished[2]!" This, so far as it goes, indicates that Jesus used the term metaphorically, in the sense of a fiery trial. It points to the conclusion that, in Mark also, "baptism" should be interpreted as something approaching to temporary "immersion in the pit," that is, in Sheol, or as the Psalmist says, in "the dust of death[3]."

Now turning to the preceding context in Mark we see that it predicts for the Messiah not only death but also painful humiliation and "mocking" before death, and this is what is predicted at great length in the Psalm just quoted[4] It would therefore be quite consistent that Mark should represent Jesus as first predicting, in language that was clear to Himself though not to the disciples, the cup of humiliation and the immersion in Sheol, and then as saying immediately afterwards to the sons of Zebedee "Are you prepared to drink my cup and to undergo my immersion?"—not meaning a baptismal purification like that introduced by John the Baptist, nor like the familiar immersion of hands or feet on certain occasions, but meaning a "plunging in the pit" or a "bringing down to the dust of death." A trace of this thought, in the use of the word "buried," may be found in the Pauline Epistles, "All we who were baptized into Christ Jesus were baptized into his

---

[1] Mt xxviii 19 "baptizing them into the name of the Father and of the Son and of the Holy Ghost"   [2] Lk. xii 49—50

[3] Ps xxii. 15 "My strength is dried up...*and thou hast brought me into the dust of death* For dogs..." What Justin Martyr calls "the whole Psalm," almost verse by verse, is applied by him to Christ, *Tryph* §§ 98—106 (§ 99 "I will demonstrate to you that the whole Psalm refers thus to Christ"). Origen's frequent expositions of the italicised words (*ad loc* and *Comm Joann* xx 31 etc) indicate that he regarded them as referring to the Fall of Man as well as to Christ's death, and Jerome refers them to the Incarnation as well as to the Descent into Sheol

[4] Mk x. 34, Ps xxii 7—18

HOW TO ENTER INTO THE KINGDOM

death; we were buried therefore with him through baptism into death," and "Having been buried with him in baptism[1]." But it is not surprising that the dark aspect of the word *"baptize"* was at once subordinated, and soon ignored, in early Christian literature, imbued as it was with the conception of baptism as an "enlightening" of the soul[2].

In the Fourth Gospel baptism is practically not mentioned except in connection with the Baptist or with a statement that the Baptist's practice was carried on by Christ's disciples, as to which it is noteworthy that the Evangelist first describes Jesus as "baptizing," and then, instead of cancelling it as an error, adds a correction, "Howbeit Jesus himself baptized not, but his disciples [did][3]."

But as regards the applicability of "baptism" (in the sense of martyrdom) to John the son of Zebedee, the Gospel may possibly imply something of the kind—if at least we may regard him as identical with "the disciple whom Jesus loved"—in the comparison tacitly drawn between this disciple and Peter at the close of the Gospel. Peter is bidden to "follow" Christ in a special way after Jesus has predicted "by what manner of death he should glorify God," namely, by crucifixion. The beloved disciple, though not bidden to follow, is seen "following"; and about him Jesus says to Peter "If I will that he tarry while I am coming, what is that to thee? Follow thou me[4]" Hence, says the Gospel, "this saying went forth among the brethren, that that disciple should not die" The best interpretation of this obscure passage appears to be that the unnamed disciple lived to a great age and did not "follow" Christ by a martyr's death, but that he "followed" Him in a different way while "tarrying," by living a martyr's life[5]

---

[1] Rom vi 3—4, Col ii 12
[2] See *Joh Gr* 2532 c on φωτίζω and *Son* 3407 (vii) *a* quoting Justin Martyr *Apol* § 61 "this washing is called *enlightening* (φωτισμός)"
[3] Jn. iv. 1—2   [4] Jn xxi 19—23, see p. 302, n. 2
[5] See Jerome's comment on Mt xx. 23 indicating early doubt as to the applicability of the "cup" to John, because, in his case, "the persecutor did not shed blood" The Fourth Gospel appears tacitly to protest against such technical distinction

HOW TO ENTER INTO THE KINGDOM

§ 8 *"Not mine to give but for those for whom it hath been prepared," in Mark and Matthew*[1]

Matthew, after "prepared," adds "by my Father," and Origen discusses "what things are given by the Saviour [and] what things by the Father[2]." Also the best Latin MSS, and the Syro-Sinaitic, have rendered ΑΛΛΟΙϹ, in Mark, as "for others" (which would be its usual meaning)[3]. Jerome, on Matthew, takes "prepared by my Father" as referring to the worthy· "Whoever shall have so conducted himself as to be worthy of the Kingdom of Heaven." It is "prepared," he says, "not for a person but for a life." He strenuously dissents from unnamed critics who thought that the reference was to "Moses and Elias whom they [*i.e.* the sons of Zebedee] had recently seen speaking with Him on the mountain."

John appears to intervene in the only passage in which he uses the word "prepare." There Jesus says "In my Father's house are many abiding-places" and then (in an obscure context) twice uses the phrase "go to (*or*, go and) prepare a place for you[4]." Whatever may be the exact interpretation of the sentence, the context indicates a perfect unity between the Father and the Son, so that what the Son speaks of "preparing," the Father Himself might be said to be "preparing," or to have already "prepared[5]." And here we may note that Jews would see a sacred meaning, not obvious to Gentiles, in this thought of a "prepared place." For the verbal noun *mâcoun*, derived from *coun* "prepare," while meaning etymologically "prepared place," means regularly "the fixed place of Jehovah's abode

---

[1] Mk x 40 οὐκ ἔστιν ἐμὸν δοῦναι, ἀλλ' οἷς ἡτοίμασται, Mt. xx. 23 + ὑπὸ τοῦ πατρός μου.

[2] Origen on Mt xx 23 (Lomm. iv 14)

[3] That is to say, ἄλλοις would occur in Greek literature much more frequently than ἀλλ' οἷς For confusion between ἄλλα and ἀλλά in Jn vi 23 see *Law* p 60 foll

[4] Jn xiv 2—3, on which see *Joh Gr.* **2080—6**

[5] Jn xiv 9 "He that hath seen me hath seen the Father," *ib* 13 "Whatsoever ye shall ask in my name, that will I do, that the Father may be glorified in the Son"

HOW TO ENTER INTO THE KINGDOM

on earth," the Temple[1]. To be in that "prepared place" was to be in a region that excluded all favouritism—all thought of what Jerome called "preparation for a person" as distinct from "preparation for a life."

Thus the Fourth Gospel indirectly meets all such personal claims as those of the sons of Zebedee, and all misunderstandings arising from the narrative about them. It suggests a unity in which are merged all thoughts of equality, inequality, and rivalry. It admits, at the outset, that the abiding-places in the Father's House are "many"; but it adds simultaneously that the essential object is to be not at the right hand or at the left, but where Christ is ("that *where I am* there ye also may be") and, later on, it declares that the Father and the Son will come and take up their abode in the believer's heart[2].

§ 9. *"They that are accounted to rule," in Mark*[3]

For Mark's *"they that are accounted to rule"* Matthew substitutes *"rulers,"* and. Luke *"kings"*; but there is abundant

---

[1] Gesen 467 *b* gives, as the first instance, Exod xv 17 "the mountain of thy inheritance, the *prepared* [*place*] (מכון) for thy abiding...thy hands *prepared*," LXX ἕτοιμον, Aq. and Sym ἔδρασμα, ...LXX ἡτοίμασαν, Aq. ἥδρασαν.

[2] Jn xiv 2, 3, 23

[3]
Mk x 41—5 (R V)	Mt xx 24—8 (R V.)	Lk xxii 24—7 (R V.)
(41) And when the ten heard it, they began to be moved with indignation concerning James and John	(24) And when the ten heard it, they were moved with indignation concerning the two brethren	(24) And there arose also a contention among them, which of them is accounted to be greatest (*lit* greater).
(42) And Jesus called them to him, and saith unto them, Ye know that they which are accounted to rule over the Gentiles lord it over them, and their great ones exercise authority over them.	(25) But Jesus called them unto him, and said, Ye know that the rulers of the Gentiles lord it over them, and their great ones exercise authority over them.	(25) And he said unto them, The kings of the Gentiles have lordship over them; and they that have authority over them are called Benefactors.
(43) But it is not so among you but whosoever would be-	(26) Not so shall it be among you but whosoever would	(26) But ye [shall] not [be] so· but he that is the greater

HOW TO ENTER INTO THE KINGDOM

evidence to shew that the Greek phrase meaning literally "those seeming to be rulers" means in effect "those commonly called rulers," or "those reputed to be rulers," with a tacit implication that they are unworthy of the name[1] Luke has also altered Mark's significant words "abuse-their-lordship" and "abuse-their-power" by dropping that part of the verbs which signifies abuse[2] Thus Luke has taken the sting out of the Marcan tradition and converted it into a statement, perhaps mildly ironical, that "rulers," simply because they are rulers, are called by their flatterers "benefactors[3]"

John, though he nowhere uses the phrase "*those seeming to be rulers*" to mean "those whom the world calls rulers," goes

Mk x 41—5 (R.V.) *contd*	Mt xx 24—8 (R.V.) *contd*	Lk xxii. 24—7 (R V) *contd*
come great among you, shall be your minister (*or*, servant)	become great among you shall be your minister (*or*, servant)	among you, let him become as the younger; and he that is chief, as he that doth serve.
(44) And whosoever would be first among you, shall be servant (*lit* bondservant) of all	(27) And whosoever would be first among you shall be your servant (*lit* bondservant)	(27) For whether is greater, he that sitteth-at-meat (*lit* reclineth), or he that serveth ? is not he that sitteth-at-meat (*lit* reclineth) ? but I am in the midst of you as he that serveth
(45) For verily the Son of man came not to be ministered unto, but to minister, and to give his life a ransom for many	(28) Even as the Son of man came not to be ministered unto, but to minister, and to give his life a ransom for many	

[1] Mk x 42 οἱ δοκοῦντες ἄρχειν, Mt xx 25 οἱ ἄρχοντες, Lk xxii 25 οἱ βασιλεῖς SS, in Mk, has briefly "Ye know that the chiefs of the peoples are their lords Not so ." See Wetstein on Mk, quoting Epict *Ench* 51 (error for 33) τῶν ἐν ὑπεροχῇ δοκούντων and Plutarch *Vit.* 1047 C τὸν καιρόν, ᾧ δουλεύουσιν οἱ δοκοῦντες ἄρχειν, besides Gal. ii 9, *Susann.* 16 etc.

[2] Mk-Mt κατακυριεύουσιν, κατεξουσιάζουσιν, Lk. κυριεύουσιν, ἐξουσιάζοντες Comp Origen on Mt (Lomm iv 22) οὐκ ἀρκούμενοι τῷ κυριεύειν ...κατακυριεύουσιν αὐτῶν

[3] On εὐεργέτης, as a title or surname, see Steph *Thes* iii 2248. Epictetus uses it twice, (1) ironically, of Chrysippus whom he regards as a pretender (1 4 29) "O, [joy] for [our] great good-fortune! O, [joy] for [our] great *benefactor*, who points the path out [for us]!" (2) seriously, of our God and Father, whom (1 6 42) we fail to recognise as our "*benefactor.*"

HOW TO ENTER INTO THE KINGDOM

to the root of the Marcan thought by introducing (alone among the Evangelists) "the ruler of this world", whom he regards as the source of all misrule, the ruler for a time, *de facto* but not *de jure*, already "judged," and destined to be speedily "cast out[1]"

There is a preparation for this, in the parable of the Good Shepherd, where John assumes that all his readers knew—the Jews from the Psalms and the Gentiles from Homer—that kings were called shepherds of their peoples. There, after Jesus has said "I am the door of the sheep," He adds immediately "All that came before me are thieves and robbers[2]." The text is disputed[3]. Some authorities omit "before me", some omit "all". And the Greek for "*before me*" is, in itself, ambiguous. With most verbs it would naturally mean "before my time." But with some verbs—such as "come," "speak," "do"—the Greek "before me," from Homer downwards, might mean "*in my behalf,*" or "*representing me*[4]."

That is probably the meaning of the Evangelist in any case. Jesus is regarded as the incarnate Logos, the Shepherd of Humanity, teaching men that all rulers of the type of Nimrod—who claimed for themselves, as a cover for their arrogant self-seeking, that they came in His behalf and stood in His place—were thieves and robbers, false shepherds, rulers sent by "the ruler of this world," not by Him. Mark expressed this by saying that such rulers only "*seem*" to rule, and that they "*abuse their lordship*" and their "*authority*". Luke omitted the words indicating the "*seeming*" and the "*abuse*". But they appear necessary for the full understanding of Christ's

---

[1] Jn xii 31, xiv 30, xvi. 11 [2] Jn x 7—8
[3] See Blass, who prints πάντες ὅσοι ἦλθον κλέπται ἦσαν καὶ λῃσταί, SS has "and all those that have come are the thieves and the robbers."
[4] Steph *Thes* is not so full on this point as L S. But both shew that πρὸ ἐμοῦ with a personal object, apart from the phrase οἱ πρὸ ἐμοῦ [γενόμενοι], would naturally mean in many contexts "for my sake," or "as my representative." Comp. *Iliad* x 286 πρὸ Ἀχαιῶν ἄγγελος ἤει, xxiv. 734 ἀθλεύων πρὸ ἄνακτος, Xen *Cyrop*. IV 5. 44 ἐγὼ... πράττων πρὸ ὑμῶν, Soph *Oed T* 10 πρὸ τῶνδε φωνεῖν, Epictet 1. 24. 6 πρὸ σοῦ κατάσκοπος ἀποσταλεὶς Διογένης.

HOW TO ENTER INTO THE KINGDOM

doctrine, and John, essentially though indirectly, inculcates the truth that Mark had (perhaps too briefly) implied.

§ 10. *"To give his life a ransom for many," in Mark and Matthew*[1]

These words, and their context in Mark and Matthew, and the parallels in Luke, have been discussed in a previous volume[2]. The conclusion arrived at was that John's attitude toward Luke's version is that of one partly accepting, but partly correcting and supplementing, as though saying, "Jesus did not merely talk about being a minister at the table to the disciples as Luke relates; He also made Himself their minister in fact; He assumed the clothing, as well as the office, of one of the lowest class of those waiting at table[3]"

Beside this, it has been shewn[4] in *Diatessarica* that John indirectly answers a question arising out of the difficult word "ransom," which Luke omits, "To whom was the ransom paid?" There was no "ransom" paid to Satan. Our Redeemer laid down His life for us, contending against "the wolf." Ransoms as a rule are paid by the conquered. But our ransom was paid by our Conqueror[5], conquering and ransoming us by conquering the evil in us.

As a minor point it was shewn that whereas Luke both here and elsewhere avoids speaking about Christ's *"soul,"* John represents Jesus as thrice using the expression "my *soul* (or, *life*)[6]." This is a case of Johannine verbal Intervention in a definite matter, more easy to prove than the indirect and non-verbal Intervention as to "ransom." The proof of the latter will depend in part on many other instances where John appears to intervene as to old Synoptic doctrine with new Johannine metaphor. If we consider these cumulatively we may reasonably say, not only that the Synoptic "ransom"

---

[1] Mk x 45, Mt xx 28
[2] *Son* 3267—78
[3] *Son* 3276
[4] *Son* 3438—43
[5] Christ might be described as conquering us by conquering the evil in us, and at the same time "ransoming" us from our sinful selves (*Son* **3438**)
[6] *Son* **3434**

HOW TO ENTER INTO THE KINGDOM

is illustrated by the Johannine Shepherd laying down life in conflict against "the wolf," but also that the illustration is intentional.

§ 11. *"The son of Timaeus, Bartimaeus," in Mark*[1]

The omission of this name in the parallel Matthew and Luke, the substitution of two blind men for one in Matthew—

[1] Mk x 46—52 (R V.)

Mt xx 29—34 (R V)

Lk xviii 35—43 (R V.)

Mk x 46—52 (R V.)	Mt xx 29—34 (R V)	Lk xviii 35—43 (R V.)
(46) And they come to Jericho and as he went out from Jericho, with his disciples and a great multitude, the son of Timaeus, Bartimaeus, a blind beggar, was sitting by the way side (47) And when he heard that it was Jesus of Nazareth, he began to cry out, and say, Jesus, thou son of David, have mercy on me (48) And many rebuked him, that he should hold his peace but he cried out the more a great deal, Thou son of David, have mercy on me (49) And Jesus stood still, and said, Call ye him And they call the blind man, saying unto him, Be of good cheer rise, he calleth thee (50) And he, casting away his garment, sprang up, and came to Jesus (51) And Jesus answered him, and said, What wilt thou that I should do unto	(29) And as they went out from Jericho, a great multitude followed him (30) And behold, two blind men sitting by the way side, when they heard that Jesus was passing by, cried out, saying, Lord, have mercy on us, thou son of David (31) And the multitude rebuked them, that they should hold their peace but they cried out the more, saying, Lord, have mercy on us, thou son of David. (32) And Jesus stood still, and called them, and said, What will ye that I should do unto you ? (33) They say unto him, Lord, that our eyes may be opened (34) And Jesus, being moved with compassion, touched their eyes and straightway they received their sight, and followed him	(35) And it came to pass, as he drew nigh unto Jericho, a certain blind man sat by the way side begging (36) And hearing a multitude going by, he inquired what this meant. (37) And they told him, that Jesus of Nazareth passeth by (38) And he cried, saying, Jesus, thou son of David, have mercy on me (39) And they that went before rebuked him, that he should hold his peace : but he cried out the more a great deal, Thou son of David, have mercy on me (40) And Jesus stood, and commanded him to be brought unto him and when he was come near, he asked him, (41) What wilt thou that I should do unto thee ? And he said, Lord, that I may receive my sight. (42) And Jesus said unto him, Receive thy sight thy

HOW TO ENTER INTO THE KINGDOM

together with the mention of two more blind men described by Matthew elsewhere as simultaneously healed—and the Syriac reading "Timaeus, Bar Timaeus" (that is, "Timaeus, son of Timaeus"), indicate early obscurity. Victor has preserved the following explanation of Matthew's substitution: "It is possible that Mark and Luke have made mention of the more illustrious of the two, as also Mark has made clear by the name, saying the son of Timaeus, Bartimaeus, a blind man, as being illustrious at that time[1]." This assumes (as Origen does) that Timaeus is derived from the Greek *tīmios*, "honourable[2]." But this explanation is

Mk x 46—52 (R V) *contd.*	Mt xx 29—34 (R.V)	Lk xviii 35—43 (R V) *contd.*
thee? And the blind man said unto him, Rabboni, that I may receive my sight (52) And Jesus said unto him, Go thy way, thy faith hath made thee whole (*or*, saved thee). And straightway he received his sight, and followed him in the way.		faith hath made thee whole (*or*, saved thee) (43) And immediately he received his sight, and followed him, glorifying God and all the people, when they saw it, gave praise unto God

Comp. Mt. ix 27—31 (after the healing of Jairus' daughter) (27) And as Jesus passed by from thence, two blind men followed him, crying out, and saying, Have mercy on us, thou son of David (28) And when he was come into the house, the blind men came to him and Jesus saith unto them, Believe ye that I am able to do this? They say unto him, Yea, Lord (29) Then touched he their eyes, saying, According to your faith be it done unto you (30) And their eyes were opened And Jesus strictly (*or*, sternly) charged them, saying, See that no man know it (31) But they went forth, and spread abroad his fame in all that land

[1] Cramer on Mk x. 51 ἐνδέχεται γὰρ τοῦ ἐπιφανεστέρου μνήμην Μάρκον τε καὶ Λουκᾶν πεποιῆσθαι, ὥσπερ καὶ ὀνόματι δεδήλωκεν ὁ Μάρκος εἰπών, τὸν υἱὸν Τιμαίου Βαρτίμαιον τυφλόν, ὡς ἐπιφανῆ τότε ὄντα.

[2] Origen *Comm Matth* xvi 12 (Lomm iv. 38) τὸν τῆς τιμῆς ἐπώνυμον Τιμαῖον καὶ τὸν υἱὸν αὐτοῦ Βαρτίμαιον, ὅπερ ἐστὶν υἱὸν Τιμαίου. Μήποτε δὲ διὰ τὸ τίμιον τοῦ πατριάρχου Ἰακώβ...τροπικῶς ἐκεῖνός ἐστιν ὁ Τιμαῖος....

HOW TO ENTER INTO THE KINGDOM

antecedently improbable, and is not mentioned by Jerome[1]. It is also unusual that a Jew should be called by the same name as his father except in special circumstances[2].

We have therefore to consider other possibilities, and one is, that the enemies of Jesus might stigmatize this beggar—a conspicuous instance of His miraculous powers—as being under the curse of God, not only because he was a beggar[3], but also because he "was *unclean (Tâmè)* and the son of the *unclean (Bar-Tâmè)*[4]." The Evangelists might reply, playing on this word and on the Greek *Tīmè*[5], which is also adopted into late

---

[1] Jerome, on Mt xx 29 foll., allegorizes at great length, but does not mention the Marcan Bartimaeus In *Onomastica* p. 66 he says "*Barsemia* filius caecus, quod et ipsum corrupte quidam Bartimaeum legunt" He apparently derives it from Aram. סמיא "blind" (Levy Ch ii 170 a). *Hor Heb.*, on Mk, says (*inter alia*) "What if תימיא, *Thima (sic)*, be the same with סימיא *Simai, blind...*?"

[2] *Hor. Heb* (on Lk 1. 59) says that in the case of a deceased husband whose wife bore a son to the husband's brother, the husband's name might perhaps be given to the son: "Otherwise, indeed, it was very seldom that the son bore the name of the father" See *Corrections* **448** d

[3] See Ps xxxvii 25 "I have not seen the righteous forsaken nor his seed *begging* (בקש) *[their] bread*" Comp. Ps. cix. 10 "Let his children . *beg* (שאל) " LXX "*let them be beggars,*" ἐπαιτησάτωσαν. This is the only instance of ἐπαιτεῖν in canon. LXX But it occurs in Sir. xl 28 "it is better to die than *to beg* (ἐπαιτεῖν) (Heb hithp of בלל, besiege with entreaties)" Luke, if we may judge from Lk xvi 3 ἐπαιτεῖν αἰσχύνομαι, appears to use it to mean systematic or importunate beggary. Προσαιτεῖν occurs in LXX only in Job xxvii 14 "If his children be multiplied, it is for the sword, *and his offspring shall not be satisfied with bread (ἐὰν δὲ καὶ ἀνδρωθῶσιν προσαιτήσουσιν)*" Steph *Thes* vi 1851 quotes Plutarch and Lucian as using προσαίτης, and Suidas as saying that it = ἐπαίτης, but does not enable us to distinguish exactly between them Προσαίτης is non-occurrent in LXX It occurs in N T only here (Mk x 46) and Jn ix 8 (of the man born blind)

[4] See Gesen 379—80 shewing the frequency of טמא and its derivatives Levy ii. 153 b quotes *Sabb* 67 a "Son of clay, son of (בר) *uncleanness* (טמא)" as names of a demon in an incantation

[5] See *Hor Heb.* which quotes Esth iii 8 Targ "no *profit (Timai)*" from Gk τιμή, on which see Krauss p 264

HOW TO ENTER INTO THE KINGDOM

Hebrew, "Not so, but *Timaeus*, i.e honourable, and the son of Timaeus" Horae Hebraicae leaves us free to believe this by saying "Perhaps there was a Timaeus of some more noted name in that age, either for some good report or some bad"

We turn to the Johannine account of Christ's healing a blind man There the disciples seem to assume that either the man had sinned or his parents, saying to Jesus "Who did sin, this man, or his parents, that he should be born blind?" Jesus replies "Neither did this man sin nor his parents, but that the works of God should be made manifest in him." But John represents the Pharisees as apparently assuming afterwards, in spite of the miracle, that the man *had* sinned, or his parents, or both, so that he was "altogether born in sins[1]." This would be equivalent to saying that he was "Unclean and the son of the Unclean, or *Tâmè* and *Bartâmè*." This, judged by the ordinary standard of transliteration from Hebrew to Greek, is not far from "Timaeus and Bartimaeus."

According to the Synoptists, Jesus healed blindness on several occasions, and the scene and details of one such healing may have been confused with the scene and details of another. This might cause early confusion[2].

---

[1] Jn ix. 2—3, 34

[2] *The Gospel according to St Matthew*, ed A H. McNeile, p 128, contains the following interesting remarks on Mt ix 27—31.

"Mk twice relates the cure of a blind man (viii 22—26, x 46—52); Mt. twice relates the cure of two blind men (here, xx 29—34). The second instances in Mk and Mt are parallels, but the present passage is widely different from Mk viii. 22—26, and cannot be derived from it, although both of Mt's narratives appear to contain a reminiscence of Mk viii 22—26 in the touching of the eyes Mt may have derived it from an unknown source, but more probably it is compiled by a later hand from xx 29—34 and Mk x 46—52, with 1. 43—45. Notice the following points of similarity to ch xx. (1) δύο τυφλοί (2) ἐλέησον ἡμᾶς υἱὲ Δαυείδ The title occurs also in Mk x., where it is not, as in Mt , a characteristic of the evangelist (3) The Lord asked them a question as a spur to their faith (note ποιῆσαι and ποιήσω) (4) He touched their eyes (5) He spoke of their faith (Mk, not Mt in ch xx) (6) 'Their eyes were opened'..., xx 33 'that our eyes may be opened' Thus all the essential points in the two accounts are the same But the remainder of the narrative

HOW TO ENTER INTO THE KINGDOM

We cannot say that John intervenes as to these Synoptic narratives of the healing of blindness, but we may fairly say that he makes suggestions that bear on them. He suggests that the Marcan names were not really names but appellations; that they were applied not to two blind men but to one[1]; that the man was really a beggar; that, because he was born blind, he was supposed by the Pharisees to be, but was not, born in sin; and that he was a conspicuous instance of the way in which Jesus, the Light of the World, revealed the light to those that sat in darkness, and combined spiritual with physical healing.

§ 12   *"In the way," in Mark*[2]

The parallel Matthew omits "in the way"; naturally, for it seems superfluous, if not bathos. Luke substitutes "glorifying God." He also adds that "all the people seeing [it] gave praise to God" This reads like an addition made by Luke in order to obtain an appropriate end to the story. But in early Christian tradition, "the Way" meant "the way of the Christian faith." Hence "he followed Jesus in the Way" might mean "he became a convert." When this poetic play on the phrase failed to be understood the phrase would be dropped (as by Matthew) or altered (as by Luke)[3].

There are several minor reasons for thinking that John, in spite of many differences, wrote with some view to Mark's story In Mark, there is probably an implied contrast between a poor blind man, who had nothing but a cloak to encumber him on his way to Jesus, and a previously mentioned rich ruler, who

---

seems to be due to Mk 1 43—45, note the uncommon words ἐμβριμᾶσθαι and διαφημίζειν, and the fact that the Lord's injunction was disobeyed, which are the very points that Mt omits in viii 2—4 "

In addition to these points, note also Mt ix 29 ἥψατο τῶν ὀφθαλμῶν αὐτῶν, contrasted with xx 34 ἥψατο τῶν ὀμμάτων αὐτῶν On ὄμμα—in N T elsewhere only in Mk viii 23—see *Law* p 485

[1] Matthew's duplication (*Law* pp. 70, 74) may have arisen from a version of Mk υἱὸς Τιμαίου ὁ καὶ Βαρτίμαιος, by the omission of ὁ. Mk's txt υἱὸς Τιμαίου Βαρτίμαιος is a very unusual order of words

[2] Mk x 52, Mt xx 34, Lk xviii 43.

[3] See *Light* **3755** *g—h* on "The Way"

HOW TO ENTER INTO THE KINGDOM

had great possessions[1]. In John, there is a contrast between a poor blind man, assumed by everybody to be "born in sin" because he was born blind, and Pharisees who say "we see," and who bid the poor man stigmatize as a "sinner" the Healer who has given him sight.

Both narratives are full of passion. "Rabboni," for example, is an appellation that occurs nowhere in the New Testament except in the exclamation of the blind man, in Mark, praying for light, and of Mary Magdalene, in John, when it flashes upon her that she sees the risen Saviour[2] And if the blind man in the Gospel of Mark is represented to have followed Jesus "in the way," meaning, in the Way of Life and Light, this finds a parallel in the Gospel of John, which tells us that the blind man not only "believed" but also "worshipped" Jesus[3].

---

[1] Mk x. 50—52 (R V) "casting away his garment" (not in the parall Mt -Lk) "...followed him in the way." Contrast Mk x 21—2 "Come, follow me. But his countenance fell...for he was one that had great possessions "

[2] Mk x 51, Jn xx 16   [3] Jn ix. 38.

CHAPTER V

JESUS VISITS THE TEMPLE

[Mark xi. 1—25 (26)]

1. *"A colt tied at the door without in the open street,"*
   in Mark[1]

IN the following investigation we shall have to study, in detail, evidence bearing on the Greek word *amphodon*, unique

---

[1] Mk xi 1—7 a (R V)

(1) And when they draw nigh unto Jerusalem, unto Bethphage and Bethany, at the mount of Olives, he sendeth two of his disciples,
(2) And saith unto them, Go your way into the village that is over against you, and straightway as ye enter into it, ye shall find a colt (πῶλον) tied, whereon no man ever yet sat; loose him, and bring him.
(3) And if any one say unto you, Why do ye this? say ye, The Lord hath need of him, ￼and straightway he will send (*lit* sendeth) him back (*or* again) hither.

Mt. xxi 1—7 a (R.V.)

(1) And when they drew nigh unto Jerusalem, and came unto Bethphage, unto the mount of Olives, then Jesus sent two disciples,
(2) Saying unto them, Go into the village that is over against you, and straightway ye shall find an ass (ὄνον) tied, and a colt (πῶλον) with her. loose [them], and bring [them] unto me.
(3) And if any one say aught unto you, ye shall say, The Lord hath need of them, and straightway he will send them.
(4) Now this is come to pass, that it might be fulfilled which was spoken by (*or*, through) the prophet, saying,
(5) Tell ye the

Lk xix. 28 b—35 a (R.V.)

(28) ...going up to Jerusalem
(29) And it came to pass, when he drew nigh unto Bethphage and Bethany, at the mount that is called [the mount] of Olives, he sent two of the disciples,
(30) Saying, Go your way into the village over against [you], in the which as ye enter ye shall find a colt (πῶλον) tied, whereon no man ever yet sat loose him, and bring him.
(31) And if any one ask you, Why do ye loose him? thus shall' ye say, The Lord hath need of him.

JESUS VISITS THE TEMPLE

in the New Testament, rendered by R V. "open street[1]." It is probably a relic of poetry. But that, in itself, is not incom-

Mk xi 1—7 a (R.V) *contd*	Mt. xxi 1—7 a (R.V) *contd*	Lk xix 28 b—35 a (R.V) *contd*
(4) And they went away, and found a colt (πῶλον) tied at the door without in the open street, and they loose him	daughter of Zion, Behold, thy King cometh unto thee, Meek (πραΰς), and riding upon an ass (ὄνον), And upon a colt the foal of an ass (πῶλον υἱὸν ὑποζυγίου).	(32) And they that were sent went away, and found even as he had said unto them
(5) And certain of them that stood there said unto them, What do ye, loosing the colt (πῶλον) ?	(6) And the disciples went, and did even as Jesus appointed them,	(33) And as they were loosing the colt (πῶλον), the owners thereof said unto them, Why loose ye the colt (πῶλον) ?
(6) And they said unto them even as Jesus had said and they let them go	(7) And brought the ass (ὄνον) and the colt (πῶλον) ...	(34) And they said, The Lord hath need of him
(7) And they bring the colt (πῶλον) unto Jesus....		(35) And they brought him to Jesus ...

For all this detail John substitutes xii. 14—15 "And Jesus, having found a young ass (ὀνάριον), sat thereon; as it is written, Fear not, daughter of Zion behold, thy King cometh, sitting on an ass's colt (πῶλον ὄνου)."

[1] Mk xi. 4 καὶ ἀπῆλθον καὶ εὗρον πῶλον δεδεμένον πρὸς θύραν ἔξω ἐπὶ τοῦ ἀμφόδου For ἀμφόδου, the Latin versions have *platea, transitu*, and *bivio*, SS and Syr. (Walton) *platea* Mk xi. 2, Lk xix 30 "as ye enter," imply that the animal will be found at the entrance, not of the house, but of the village Mt. xxi 2 omits "as ye enter"

Ἄμφοδον is used by LXX only in Jerem xvii 27, xlix. 27 to mean "palace," ארמון, but by Sym repeatedly to mean "street" or "outside place," Heb חוץ See *Oxf Conc*. In Amos v. 16, Sym ἀμφόδοις = Heb רחבות, LXX πλατείαις The Egyptian Papyri shew that it regularly means a "quarter" of a city. Wetstein, on Mk, quotes Epiphanius as testifying to the Alexandrian use of the word in the sense of a "square" or "block" of houses But the usage of Sym indicates that he took it to mean a "*square*" *in the sense of an open space* And it is so used in Acts xix 28—9 (D) δραμόντες εἰς τὸ ἄμφοδον, (d) "*currentes in campo*"—i.e. the open space at the entrance into the theatre—followed by ὥρμησαν...εἰς τὸ θέατρον Steph *Thes* quotes Polyb *Exc. Vat* xl 7 οὐ θύρᾳ, τὸ δὴ λεγόμενον, ἀλλ' ἀμφόδῳ, where it seems to be used proverbially to imply publicity These differences of usage throw light on Justin Martyr's apparent allusion to Mark's word, mentioned below, p. 174, n. 3.

On the reasons for rejecting the suggestion that ἄμφοδον was a

JESUS VISITS THE TEMPLE

patible with the historical truth of the context. Historical fact, related in, and modified by, the language of ancient poetry or prophecy, is not to be confused with non-historical narrative derived entirely from ancient poetry or prophecy and having no basis of fact. Mark's narrative may belong to the former class, and may be influenced, in expression, by that prophecy of Jacob about the Messiah in Genesis which speaks of the "tying" of a "foal[1]." It will be shewn that the context in Genesis was variously interpreted by the Jews themselves in ancient times so as to introduce some suggestion of such a phrase as Mark's "at the door without in the *amphodon*."

But the historical action of Jesus was probably influenced, not by Jacob's prophecy, but by some words of Zechariah, predicting that the Messiah will come "riding upon an ass, even upon a colt, the foal of an ass[2]," where the ass appears to be the symbol of "peace[3]." Matthew, influenced by this prophecy, has rejected the Marcan tradition about "the door" (and "the open street"). He has also quoted in full the prophecy of Zechariah. But, quoting it in Greek, which renders the Hebrew "*even*" (the ambiguous *vaw*) by "*and*," he represents the Prophet as mentioning—and Jesus as riding upon—"an ass *and* a colt the foal of an ass." Luke adheres to Mark in mentioning one animal alone, namely, "a colt." But he, like

---

translation of "Bethphage," as if the latter were "a place of the parting of ways," בית פגעא, see Dalman, *Words* p 68.

[1] Gen xlix. 10—11 (R V txt) "The sceptre shall not depart from Judah, nor the ruler's staff from between his feet, until Shiloh come, and unto him shall the obedience of the peoples be. Binding his foal unto the vine, and his ass's colt unto the choice vine; he hath washed his garments in wine, and his vesture in the blood of grapes"

[2] Zech. ix. 9 (Heb) "Rejoice greatly, O daughter of Zion, shout, O daughter of Jerusalem behold, thy king cometh unto thee. he is just, and having salvation (*or*, victory) (Heb. *lit.* saved), lowly, and riding upon an ass, even (*lit.* and) upon a colt the foal of an ass"

[3] There appears to be a suggestion of "peace," and of contrast between the "ass" and the "[war] horse," in Zech. ix. 10 "I will cut off the chariot from Ephraim, and the *horse* from Jerusalem, and the battle bow shall be cut off, and he shall speak *peace* unto the nations"

JESUS VISITS THE TEMPLE

Matthew, rejects the Marcan tradition about "the door without in the *amphodon*"

§ 2 *The origin of Mark's tradition*

In tracing Mark's tradition we are at a disadvantage because his text is so seldom quoted by ancient authorities The Diatessaron omits the Marcan phrase together with its context[1]. But Justin Martyr (though it is not certain that he elsewhere quotes a single phrase of Mark[2]) seems to have preserved an allusion to Mark's meaning here when, in his Apology and in his Dialogue, he says, severally, "the foal of an ass stood bound to a vine at *a certain entrance* of a village," and "a certain ass in [very] truth, along with its foal, bound to [a wall] in *a certain entrance* of a village called Bethphage[3]"

In the Apology, Justin has previously quoted the prophecy of Jacob about the foal and the vine, and he ventures to represent Christ's foal as fastened to "a vine"—not mentioned in any Gospel, he also, like Mark, mentions only one animal. In the Dialogue, although he quotes Jacob's prophecy ("binding to the vine"), he omits "vine" in describing the fulfilment of it; and, like Matthew, he mentions two animals. Moreover, like Matthew, the Dialogue proceeds to quote Zechariah about the King "riding upon an ass and the foal of an ass." In effect, Justin seems to give us two traditions, one, for Gentiles, based on Genesis and agreeing rather with Mark than with Matthew; the other, for Jews, based on Zechariah, and agreeing rather with Matthew than with Mark. But the latter, as well as the former, contains a curious mention of "*a certain entrance*," which we will now examine.

---

[1] *Diatess.* omits the whole of Mk xi 4

[2] Justin's alleged references to Mk ii 17 and Mk xii. 25, 30 might refer to Luke and Matthew.

[3] *Apol.* § 32 Πῶλος γάρ τις ὄνου εἱστήκει ἔν τινι εἰσόδῳ κώμης πρὸς ἄμπελον δεδεμένος, *Tryph.* § 53 ὄνον δέ τινα ἀληθῶς σὺν πώλῳ αὐτῆς προσδεδεμένην ἔν τινι εἰσόδῳ κώμης Βεθφαγῆς λεγομένης.

Clark renders ἔν τινι εἰσόδῳ severally "at *the* entrance" and "in *an* entrance," but τις does not mean "the," and means (here) more than "an" In *Tryph* , it has been proposed to emend προσδεδεμένην into πρὸς ἄμπελον δεδεμένην

JESUS VISITS THE TEMPLE

§ 3. *The ass and the foal of the Messiah in Genesis*

In Genesis the Hebrew for *"foal"* is confusable with the Hebrew for *"city"*, and the Hebrew for *"ass"* is confusable with a word in Ezekiel meaning *"entrance."* And that these words were actually confused in very early times, earlier than most traditions of the Talmud, we learn from the Targum of Onkelos, who—according to Rashi[1], combining these two confusions, and taking the vine to be Israel—gives the following paraphrase.—"Israel shall dwell around his [*i.e.* Israel's] city, the peoples shall build his temple, and the righteous shall be round about him, and the doers of the law [shall be abiding] in his doctrine[2]."

Turning to Ezekiel for the context of the word meaning "entrance," we find that it occurs nowhere else in the whole of the Bible, and that it denotes the "entrance" to the "house" of God, and Rashi declares it to be Aramaic, so called because it "afforded entrance and exit to all that came into the Court[3]."

---

[1] Rashi on Gen xlix. 11. "Onkelos [*locum istum*] interpretatus est de rege Messia (videlicet hoc modo) vitis sunt Israelitae; pullus est (urbs) Hierosolyma, palmes sunt Israelitae (veluti scriptum est) et ego plantavi te palmitem, pullum asinae suae (interpretatus est Onkelos) aedificabunt templum ejus (respexit autem Onkelos quoad explicationem dictionis אֲתוֹנִי ad locum illum) porta הָאֵיתוֹן *i. e.* introitus, in libro Ezechielis (xl 15)." Jerome mentions the possibility of the former confusion (*Quaest Gen.* ad loc) "Pro *pullo* in Hebraeo possit legi *urbem suam*" Both might be represented by עִיר Also Ezek xl. 15 "*entrance,*" אֵיתוֹן, or יָאתוֹן, resembles אָתוֹן "*she-ass*"; and a play on '*entrance*" and "*she-ass*" might possibly (but not very probably) bear on the interpretation (*Gen r* ad loc) that in the Messiah's days the majority of Israel will be in their own land

[2] Jer Targ I and II have paraphrases quite different from that of Onkelos They retain the Hebrew "*binding,*" but in an entirely different context —Jer. I (Etheridge) "He hath *girded his loins* and descended and arrayed the battle...," Jer II (Etheridge) "*Binding his loins*, and going forth to war against them that hate him... "

[3] Ezek. xl. 15, Rashi, "Dicitur autem porta introitus, quoniam illa introitum et exitum praebebat omnibus, qui veniebant ad atrium, (vocis Hebraeae) בִּיאָה id est, introitus, Chaldaica interpretatio est אֵיתוֹן."

JESUS VISITS THE TEMPLE

This enables us to understand the phrase in Onkelos "*the peoples shall build his temple,*" if the Gentiles are regarded as being bound to the "entrance" of the Temple. The notion of "entrance" would also be connected in the minds of Jerusalemites of the first century with the very name of Bethphage; since it is described in the Talmud as a kind of border line or partywall, called sometimes "within the walls of the city and reckoned as Jerusalem itself" and sometimes "the outmost place in Jerusalem[1]."

All this indicates that Mark's accumulation of words signifying externality had a symbolic meaning in early times. Onkelos interpreted and allegorized Genesis from the point of view of a Jew. Early Christians allegorized Christ's action as Christians. For them, the "foal" meant the Gentiles, never subjected to the yoke of the Law, and standing, "bound," outside the gate of the House, or City, of God[2]. As a rule, an ass or foal, thus "bound" or "tied up," would be under shelter. But this is "outside" Origen says "Who is it that is 'outside'? It is the [proselytes] from the Gentiles, who were strangers to the covenants and aliens from the promise of God, [standing] in the open way [*amphodon*] and not resting (*or,* feeding) under shed or roof, bound by their own sins...[3]."

§ 4 *John on the "finding" of the ass*

Chrysostom, in his comment on the Johannine Finding of the Ass, asks "How is it that the other [evangelists] say that

---

[1] *Hor. Heb.* 1 p 81 "outmost (חיצין)" In Prov. 1 20 "Wisdom crieth *in the street* (בחוץ)," A.V. "*without,*" LXX ἐν ἐξόδοις [Sym ἐν ἀμφόδοις, s Field], Targ. has בשוקא, which occurs in Mk xi 4, SS, Burk. "in the street"

[2] Comp Clem Alex 106—7 "*And he bound* (the Scripture says) *the colt to the vine,* having bound this simple and childlike people to the Word, whom it figuratively represents as a Vine." Sim. Origen *Hom Genes.* xvii. 7 "Ipse enim alligavit ad vitem pullum suum qui dixit, *Ego sum vitis vera* (Jn xv. 1)"

[3] Origen *Comm Joann.* x. 18, Lomm. 1. 333, where there appears to be a contrast between ἐπὶ τοῦ ἀμφόδου and ὑπὸ στέγην ἢ οἰκίαν ἀναπαυομένοι, indicating that the former implies "left out in the cold (*or,* uncared for)."

JESUS VISITS THE TEMPLE

Jesus sent disciples and said, '*Loose ye the ass and the colt,*' but this [evangelist] says nothing of that kind, but [merely] that, '*having found a young ass, He sat thereon*'?" His answer is "Because it was likely that both these things came to pass, and that, after the loosing of the ass, while the disciples were bringing [it], *He* [*Himself*], *having found* [*it*], *sat thereon*[1]." This, as it stands, is hardly intelligible. But it suggests that Chrysostom has condensed, and obscurely expressed, some early tradition using "found" in a mystical sense and saying that the real Finder was Christ. Origen says something of this kind when he points out the same difference between John and the Three, and says that the language is "somewhat figurative[2]."

No doubt, if "finding" must always imply some ignorance in the finder, John would not have transferred the act from the disciples to Jesus. But in Scripture Jehovah is repeatedly described—either Himself or through an angel—as "finding" a wandering soul. The angel of the Lord "found" Hagar "in the wilderness[3]." The Lord Himself "found" Israel "in a desert land and in the waste howling wilderness[4]", and Hosea

---

[1] Ὅτι ἀμφότερα γενέσθαι εἰκὸς ἦν, καὶ μετὰ τὸ λυθῆναι τὴν ὄνον ἀγόντων τῶν μαθητῶν, εὑρόντα αὐτὸν ἐπικαθίσαι. Here αὐτόν is prob. emphatic, as in the passage quoted from Origen in the next note.

[2] Origen *Comm. Joann.* x. 18, Lomm. 1 335 Πλὴν οὗτος ὑπ' αὐτοῦ φησι τοῦ Ἰησοῦ εὑρίσκεσθαι τὸ ὀνάριον ἐφ' ᾧ καθέζεται ὁ Χριστός, πλέον τι περὶ τούτου (v. r. τοῦτο) τροπικώτερον δηλουμένου ὀναρίου παριστάς, μείζονα εὐεργεσίαν χωρήσαντος τὴν (Gal. 1 1) "οὐκ ἀπ' ἀνθρώπων, οὐδὲ δι' ἀνθρώπων, ἀλλὰ διὰ Ἰησοῦ Χριστοῦ." He means that as Paul, the Apostle of the Gentiles, so also the Gentile world itself, the formerly untrained "colt," was pressed into the service of Christ.

[3] Gen. xvi. 7, on which see Philo *Quaest. Gen.* ad loc.

[4] Deut. xxxii. 10. On this, see *Numb. r* (on Numb. 11. 2, Wu p. 14) "A great *finding* hath God wrought over Israel, as it is said (Hos ix 10) '*Like grapes* in the wilderness did I find Israel.'" It adds "The world was a '*wilderness*' before the Israelites came forth from Egypt," perhaps implying that Jehovah had also "found" Israel before the Exodus. [In theory, Hos xii 4 "he found him in Bethel," might refer to the Lord as "finding" Jacob, when he went forth as a homeless wanderer, but the Targum and Rashi take Jacob as the person "finding"] Jesus (Jn 1 43) "*findeth* Philip"—to whom (*Son*

JESUS VISITS THE TEMPLE

represents the Lord as saying "*I found* Israel like grapes in the wilderness." Such a "finding" is almost equivalent to "saving," and Philo explains it thus when allegorizing the story of Hagar.

John seems here to put aside the finding of the ass by the disciples, on the same principle as that on which, in the Feeding of the Five Thousand, he puts aside the distribution of the bread by the disciples[1]. There Jesus was the real Distributer. Here Jesus is the real Finder. The minute distinctions between "ass," and "colt," and the Semitic "son of a beast of burden" (R.V. "foal of an ass")—these, too, John puts on one side, substituting one word *onarion* ("little-ass"). This word was known to disciples of Epictetus as representing the name given by that philosopher to the fleshly body, the drudge of the mind or spirit[2].

We have seen that Onkelos wholly paraphrased the Binding of the Ass by the Messiah in Genesis as a Building up of the Judaean City or Church. Justin Martyr and Clement of Alexandria regard the "foal" or "colt" in the Gospels as a type of the Gentiles, or the new childlike people (not yet subjected to the yoke of the Law)[3]. It was not unnatural that Christians, even in the first century, should connect the Riding of their Messiah into Jerusalem with such thoughts as these. As Onkelos introduced a mention of the peoples or Gentiles, so might Christian Evangelists, from the Christian point of view,

---

3377 *a*) according to tradition, He said "Let the dead bury their dead"—and also (Jn v. 14) "*findeth* in the temple" one to whom He says "Sin no more, lest a worse thing befall thee."

[1] See *Law* pp 332, 355—6.

[2] Epict. iv 1. 79—80 (where ὀνάριον occurs five times) ὅλον τὸ σῶμα οὕτως ἔχειν σε δεῖ ὡς ὀνάριον ἐπισεσαγμένον. The context bids us recognise that our "body," "hand" etc are not our real selves but merely tools. Ὀνάριον occurs also in *ib* ii 24. 18 literally, ih a remark about the impracticability of playing with an ass, we gambol with little children, but who gambols with an ass? "For even though it be a little-thing (μικρόν) it is still a little-ass (ὅμως ὀνάριόν ἐστιν)." Steph. *Thes* gives no instance of it (as distinct from ὀνίδιον) except from a comic poet (circ. A.C. 280). It is not in Goodspeed.

[3] Justin Martyr *Tryph.* § 53, Clem Alex 106—7

JESUS VISITS THE TEMPLE

regarding the Gentiles as corresponding to the "foal" or "colt," and as subjecting themselves to Jesus

In the Fourth Gospel, immediately after the mention of Christ's literal riding on the ass, when the Pharisees have exclaimed "Lo, the world hath gone after him," "certain Greeks" come to Philip saying, "Sir, we would see Jesus[1]." It is a mere hint Nothing is said of any definite conversion. Nothing of any kind is added about the Greeks But Jesus replies to their request—conveyed through Philip and Andrew—"The hour is come that the Son of Man should be glorified." These words certainly imply much more than is written They point to a not distant time when the gate of the House of God shall be thrown open to the Gentile world which is regarded as, at present, "standing bound, at the door, without, in the open street"

But as to the actual riding on the ass, what are we to conclude? Did Jesus deliberately ride thus, in the conviction that He was riding to some mysterious consummation of His career, and endeavouring, in dumb show, to inculcate on the vast multitude that the consummation would be brought about, not through war symbolized by the war-horse, but through peace —it might be, even after His death—symbolized by the ass? That is in accordance with His antecedent predictions about "the third day" after His death (derived from Hosea), and it accords also with the prophecy of Zechariah, which does not speak of the "ass" without a suggestion that it symbolized "peace," and without an antithetical mention of the "chariot" and the "horse": "I will cut off *the chariot* from Ephraim, and *the horse* from Jerusalem, and the battle bow shall be cut off, and he shall speak *peace* unto the nations[2]."

---

[1] Jn xii 20 foll
[2] Zech ix 10, quoted by Origen on Jn xii 15 and on Mt. xxi 5

JESUS VISITS THE TEMPLE

§ 5. (R.V.) "*Branches* (marg. *layers of leaves*)," *in Mark*[1]
No instance has been alleged where "branches" or "layers of leaves" is the correct rendering of Mark's word[2]. Wherever

[1] Mk xi. 7—10 (R.V.)	Mt xxi 7—9 (R.V.)	Lk xix 35—8 (R.V.)
(7) And they bring the colt unto Jesus, and cast on him their garments, and he sat upon him	(7) And brought the ass and the colt, and put on them their garments, and he sat thereon	(35) And they brought him to Jesus · and they threw their garments upon the colt, and set Jesus thereon
(8) And many spread their garments upon the way, and others branches (*lit* layers of leaves), which they had cut from the fields.	(8) And the most part of the multitude spread their garments in the way, and others cut branches from the trees, and spread them in the way	(36) And as he went, they spread their garments in the way.
(9) And they that went before, and they that followed, cried, Hosanna, Blessed [is] he that cometh in the name of the Lord	(9) And the multitudes that went before him, and that followed, cried, saying, Hosanna to the son of David Blessed [is] he that cometh in the name of the Lord, Hosanna in the highest	(37) And as he was now drawing nigh, [even] at the descent of the mount of Olives, the whole multitude of the disciples began to rejoice and praise God with a loud voice for all the mighty works (*lit* powers) which they had seen,
(10) Blessed [is] the kingdom that cometh, [the kingdom] of our father David Hosanna in the highest.		(38) Saying, Blessed [is] the King that cometh in the name of the Lord peace in heaven, and glory in the highest

Jn xii 12—15 (R V.) (12) On the morrow a great multitude (*some anc auth* the common people) that had come to the feast, when they heard that Jesus was coming to Jerusalem, (13) took the branches of the palm-trees, and went forth to meet him, and cried out, Hosanna: Blessed [is] he that cometh in the name of the Lord, even the King of Israel (14) And Jesus, having found a young ass, sat thereon, as it is written, (15) Fear not, daughter of Zion behold, thy King cometh, sitting on an ass's colt

[2] Mk xi. 8
καὶ πολλοὶ τὰ ἱμάτια αὐτῶν (marg ἑαυτῶν) ἔστρωσαν εἰς τὴν ὁδόν, ἄλλοι δὲ στιβάδας κόψαντες ἐκ τῶν ἀγρῶν

Mt xxi 8
ὁ δὲ πλεῖστος ὄχλος ἔστρωσαν ἑαυτῶν τὰ ἱμάτια ἐν τῇ ὁδῷ, ἄλλοι δὲ ἔκοπτον κλάδους ἀπὸ τῶν δένδρων καὶ ἐστρώννυον ἐν τῇ ὁδῷ

Lk. xix. 36
πορευομένου δὲ αὐτοῦ ὑπεστρώννυον τὰ ἱμάτια ἑαυτῶν ἐν τῇ ὁδῷ

Jn xii. 12—13 ὄχλος πολὺς ὁ ἐλθὼν εἰς τὴν ἑορτήν...ἔλαβον τὰ βαΐα τῶν φοινίκων καὶ ἐξῆλθον εἰς ὑπάντησιν αὐτῷ

JESUS VISITS THE TEMPLE

it is used absolutely, its natural meaning is bedding, mattress, or rug to recline on. Epictetus uses Mark's word thus in a warning to a host, entertaining a few guests "It is absurd that many souls should wait on a few *stuffed-couches*"—meaning that the waiters, who stand, ought not to be in excess of the guests, who recline[1] This is the regular Greek use. The meaning is illustrated by Juvenal's line about "the *cophinus* and furniture of straw[2]" of the Jews, that is, their basket and bedding. In Mark, the pilgrims that came up to the Passover would seem to have taken some of the leaves and rushes that they carried in their "*cophini*," and to have scattered them on the ground before Jesus as an extemporised act of homage. That, at least, was probably the original meaning of the tradition in Mark.

But Mark himself may be suspected of not knowing this meaning. For he adds "*having cut them from the fields*," as though the "cutting" were simultaneous with the scattering Matthew departs still further from it, for he alters "bedding" into "boughs," and "fields" into "trees" Luke omits both "bedding" and "boughs" These alterations or omissions of Mark's text constitute a case for Johannine Intervention

That John does intervene can hardly be doubted although the correctness of his intervention is uncertain Without contradicting either Mark or Matthew as to the action of the pilgrims accompanying Jesus *into* Jerusalem, John describes the action of those who came forth to meet Jesus *from* Jerusalem. These, he says, "took *the branches of the palm-trees*" and went out to meet Him

John's word for "branches"—which, by itself, means palm-branches—has been the subject of much comment[3] And

---

[1] Epict *Fragm* 23 (Schw. 33, Schenkel p 468) Μελέτω σοι ἐν τοῖς σιτίοις ὅπως σοι οἱ ὑπουργοῦντες μὴ πλείους τῶν ὑπουργουμένων ὑπάρχωσιν ἄτοπον γὰρ ὀλίγαις στιβάσι πολλὰς δουλεύειν ψυχάς, see also Steph *Thes* Etymologically it means "pressed [leaves, rushes, straw etc]," but in practice it means "bedding"

[2] Juvenal *Sat.* iii 14, vi 542, "cophinus foenumque supellex"

[3] See the very full discussion in Steph. *Thes* ii. 47—8 on βαΐς, βαΐον, quoting 1 Macc. xiii 51 μετὰ αἰνέσεως καὶ βαΐων, and Chaeremon

181 (Mark xi. 7—10)

JESUS VISITS THE TEMPLE

no one has satisfactorily explained why the Book of Maccabees speaks of a procession "with thanksgiving and *branches* (of palm-trees)" without the article, while John here calls them "*the branches* of the palm-trees" The forms of the Greek word vary and one of them might be confused with the Marcan word for "bedding[1]." It is not safe to say that John has correctly explained Mark's original but it is safe to say that he has attempted to explain it[2]

§ 6. "*Hosanna*," *in Mark, Matthew, and John*[3]

It will be seen, in the parallel columns printed above, that Luke omits Hosanna but inserts in its place several words

---

Stoicus ap Porphyr De abst 4, 7 about Egyptian priests, Κοίτη δ' αὐτοῖς ἐκ τῶν σπαδίκων τοῦ φοίνικος, ἃς καλοῦσι βαῖς, ἐπέπλεκτο. This connects the word with bedding It occurs as a rendering (for κάλλυνθρα) in Lev · xxiii 40 כפת "branches [of palms]."

[1] If John had before him a tradition about "their bedding and their garments," τὰς στιβάδας καὶ τὰ ἱμάτια, the difficulty and uniqueness of τὰς στιβάδας might lead him to read it as τάς τε βαΐδας (comp his use of τε in Jn 11 15 τά τε πρόβατα καὶ τοὺς βόας). When he altered this into βαΐα, he might still retain the article, in spite of its difficulty, explaining it as "the palm-branches usual in processions of honour"

[2] See 2 Macc x 3—7 on the re-dedication, or "cleansing (καθαρισμός)," of the Temple by Judas Maccabaeus θύρσους, καὶ κλάδους ὡραίους, ἔτι δὲ καὶ φοίνικας ἔχοντες, ηὐχαρίστουν τῷ εὐοδώσαντι καθαρίσαι τὸν ἑαυτοῦ τόπον. This is said to have been in imitation of the thanksgiving in the Feast of Tabernacles "They kept eight days *after the manner of* [*the Feast of*] *Tabernacles* (σκηνωμάτων τρόπον)." These "*thursoi*," or "bunches of twigs and branches," appear to correspond to 1 Macc xiii 51 βαΐων carried in the (*ib* 50) "cleansing" of the "Tower" of Jerusalem by Simon who (*ib* 52) "ordained that that day should be kept every year [with gladness]"

[3] For the parallel texts, see above, p 180.
This section was written before I had read Prof. F. C Burkitt's note on Mk xi 9 (*Journ Theol Studies*, Jan. 1916), in which he says (p 142) —
"The conclusions to which these ritual facts seem to point are these —
(1) 'Hosanna' had come to be a cry for good luck to God at the Feast of Tabernacles, from quite ancient times, before the minor details of the Feast were finally stereotyped.

JESUS VISITS THE TEMPLE

suggesting that he regarded it as a doxology, ascribing praise, and might, and glory, to God: "They began to *praise* God with a loud voice for all *the mighty works* that they were seeing, saying.. in heaven [may there be] *peace* and *glory*...[1]." This agrees with the earliest Christian use of the word, outside the Gospels, "*Hosanna* to the God of David," in the *Didachè*, near the conclusion of the Eucharistic Service[2] It agrees also with the earliest Patristic explanation of the word confidently set forth by Clement of Alexandria It is, he says, "*light, and glory, and praise, along with supplication to the Lord*—for this is the meaning of the [word] *Hosanna*, when interpreted in Greek[3]"

The explanation of this long paraphrase is to be found in Luke's rare verb "praise," *ainein*, combined with Matthew's noun "praise," *ainos*, in the parallel context The chief priests blame Jesus for not checking "the children that were crying in the temple and saying *Hosanna* to the Son of David." Jesus

---

(ii) The fact that the name for the thyrsi is *Hosanna*, not *Hosianna* (הוֹשַׁעְנָא not הוֹשִׁיעָה נָא), suggests that the Gospels are correct in giving this shortened form as a popular exclamation.

(iii) Psalm cxviii, composed for the Dedication of the Temple by Judas Maccabaeus, gives us a hint of the ritual procession to the Temple then made, it confirms 2 Macc x 6 in representing this procession as modelled upon the ancient procession at the Feast of Tabernacles

(iv) Psalm cxviii 25 is not the ultimate source of the cry *Hosanna*, but *Hosanna* finds a place in the Psalm because the ancient cry of *Hosanna* was used at that Dedication

(v) It is a fair deduction to suppose that the behaviour of the Galilean crowd at our Lord's Entry into Jerusalem was based on what was appropriate for *Hanukka*, for the Feast of the Dedication, rather than by what was appropriate for Tabernacles"

[1] Lk xix 37—8 ἤρξαντο...αἰνεῖν τὸν θεὸν φωνῇ μεγάλῃ περὶ πασῶν ὧν εἶδον δυνάμεων, λέγοντες...ἐν οὐρανῷ εἰρήνη καὶ δόξα ἐν ὑψίστοις.

[2] *Didach* x 6 τῷ θεῷ Δαβίδ (so the MS) The Lat has "*filio David*" The context is as follows —"For thine is (ἐστὶν) the power and the glory for ever, let grace come and this world pass away. *Hosanna* to the God of David. If any one is holy, let him come, if any one is not, let him repent Maran atha. Amen."

[3] Clem Alex. 104—5 φῶς καὶ δόξα καὶ αἶνος μεθ᾿ ἱκετηρίας τῷ κυρίῳ τουτὶ γὰρ ἐμφαίνει ἑρμηνευόμενον Ἑλλάδι φωνῇ τὸ ὡσαννά.

JESUS VISITS THE TEMPLE

replies "Did ye never read, 'Out of the mouth of babes and sucklings thou hast perfected *praise*¹'?" This, at least, is how the words of the Psalm, quoted by Jesus according to Matthew, read in Greek. But the Hebrew has, not '*praise*," but "*strength*²."

The Hebrew "give *strength*" is elsewhere used in ascriptions³. But Greeks might well say "How can men 'give *strength* to God'? It is better to write 'give *praise*'" Hence the Hebrew *strength*, in the Psalm just quoted, is rendered by LXX "praise," *ainos*, and sometimes elsewhere "honour" (as well as "power" and "might⁴") Clement might well be unable to find in Greek one word that would suffice by itself to render the Hebrew⁵. The phrase really meant "Thine is the kingdom, that is to say, the kingdom of light and glory and divine majesty⁶."

Now the Aramaic word corresponding to the Hebrew "*strength*" used in ascriptions closely resembles *Osanna*⁷ And *Ossanna* (or *Osanna*) (not *Hosanna*) is the form found in the early Latin versions before Jerome⁸ This similarity may throw light on the reply of Jesus to the chief priests above quoted. It indicates that, in Aramaic, Jesus might say something like "Out of the mouth of babes...thou hast perfected *Osanna*"— as a reply to the complaint that the children were "saying

---

¹ Mt xxi. 16 κατηρτίσω αἶνον.

² Ps viii. 2 עֹז, R V "*strength*," LXX αἶνον, Aq and Sym κράτος

³ See Gesen. 739, instancing Ps. xxix 1, xcvi 7 etc

⁴ Tromm. (which omits αἶνος (1) by error) gives עֹז as =δόξα (3), δύναμις (23), ἰσχύς (29), κράτος (6), τιμή (3).

⁵ Cramer, on Mk xi 9, prints Τὸ γὰρ "ὡσαννά" ὕμνος ἑρμηνεύεται This is quite inadequate

⁶ For a doxological mention of light see *Acts of John* on the Eucharist § 11 "We praise thee, O Father, we give thanks to thee, O Light, wherein dwelleth not darkness Amen"

⁷ Ps viii 2 Targ עֻשְׁנָא, i e *us(h)na*, freq in Psalms, Levy Ch ii 248 *b*

⁸ As the earliest Greek MSS never use the aspirate, they afford no guidance on this point Jerome, as will be seen below, by his theory of the derivation of the word from Hebrew (not Aramaic) committed himself to the insertion of the Latin aspirate "Hosanna"

JESUS VISITS THE TEMPLE

Hosanna." The meaning, in both cases, would be an ascription of praise and glory. This also throws light on Luke's omission of "Hosanna," and his parallel addition of words signifying "praise," "mighty works," and "glory." Apparently he is not omitting, but substituting[1]. So, too, Clement of Alexandria is substantially justified in his paraphrase of Osanna, provided that we regard it as Aramaic, not Hebrew

Against this view of derivation from Aramaic we have the opinion of Origen—expressed in his commentary on Matthew—that Hosanna is derived from the Hebrew, transliterated as *Osienna*, of words in the 118th Psalm "I beseech, O Lord, *save now* (*osienna*), I beseech, O Lord, prosper [us] now; blessed [be] he that cometh in the name of the Lord[2]" But Origen makes no mention of this in his earlier work (the commentary on John) where he quotes passages mentioning Hosanna and their contexts[3] In his commentary on Matthew he puts forth his suggestion as a novelty ("it seems to me") from which others might differ, and explains that he was led to it by the similarity of *hosanna* to the Hebrew *hosienna(n)*, which comes in the Psalm above quoted just before the words "Blessed is he that cometh in the name of the Lord[4]"

---

[1] Lk xix 38 ἐν οὐρανῷ εἰρήνη, καὶ δόξα, substituted for Mk-Mt ὡσαννά, before ἐν τοῖς [Lk om τοῖς] ὑψίστοις, may be illustrated, not only by Lk ii 14 "glory to God *in the highest*, and on earth peace to men of his good pleasure," but also by *Jewish Prayer Book* (comp ed Singer, p 76) "He that maketh peace *in His high places* (במרומיו) may He make peace upon us (עלינו) and upon all Israel, and say ye, Amen"

[2] Ps cxviii 25

[3] *Comm. Joann* x 15 (Lomm. 1 316) καὶ ἔκραζον Ὡσαννὰ, εὐλογημένος ἐν ὀνόματι κυρίου ὁ βασιλεὺς τοῦ Ἰσραήλ (omitting ὁ ἐρχόμενος), x 18 (Lomm 1 335) κεκραγότα Εὐλογημένος ὁ ἐρχόμενος ἐν ὀνόματι κυρίου καὶ Ὁ βασιλεὺς τοῦ Ἰσραήλ (omitting Ὡσαννά)

[4] Origen *Comm Matth* xvi 19 (Lomm iv 58) "It seems to me that the equivalent of the [expression] (τὰ ἀντὶ τοῦ) (Ps cxviii 25) *O Lord, save now* (ὦ κύριε σῶσον δή) placed before the [expression] (*ib* 26) *Blessed* [is] *he that cometh in the name of the Lord*, is set forth Hebraically in the [expression] (Mt xxi 9) *Hosanna to the son of David* And thus also ran the Hebrew phrasing Ἀννὰ (LXX ὦ)

JESUS VISITS THE TEMPLE

This seems a happy conjecture. But we should have to suppose that the crowd of pilgrims that shouted *Hosanna* shouted in Hebrew, for the Aramaic "save now" is quite different from the Hebrew[1]. The alternative would be to suppose that although they shouted in Aramaic, some Gospel written in Hebrew recorded the word in Hebrew Jerome adopts this supposition[2]. But he does not explain why Matthew should have transliterated the Hebrew word instead of translating it "*Save now!*"—the obvious translation, given by LXX, Aquila, Symmachus, and Theodotion.

The question is complicated by the fact that the Hebrew phrase "*Save now*" was connected in the Talmud with the Feast of Tabernacles, and with a procession of branch-bearers

---

ἀδωναϊ (LXX κύριε) *hosiennan* (LXX σῶσον δή).... Then it seems to me that the Gospels being written continuously"—*i e.* (?) so as to blend *hosie* "save" with *na* "now"—"by persons not knowing the [Hebrew] language have been confused in those expressions of the text which contain these [syllables] from the above-mentioned psalm (ἐν τοῖς κατὰ τὸν τόπον ἔχουσι ταῦτα ἀπὸ τοῦ προειρημένου ψαλμοῦ). But if you would learn the exact [meaning] of the phrasing, hear Aquila.. .And now let this be added, that, on this point, the foregoing remarks represent our view (καὶ εἰς ταῦτα δὲ ἡμεῖς μὲν τοσαῦτα εἴδομεν), but if anyone differs from us, let him look further into it and teach [us] But in one of the sections on the Gospel according to John I partially investigated this point as well [as others] when my object was to expound Jn xii 12 *On the morrow....*"

[1] "Save" Heb ישע is regularly rendered by Onk. פרק And in Ps cxviii 25, the Syr has פרק for ישע The Targ omits "*save*" while retaining "prosper us." The Targumist supposes the verse to be uttered by the parents of David as part of a dialogue between them and David's brethren and David and "the builders," and it paraphrases thus · "*We beseech thee, O Lord, now*, said the builders, *we beseech thee, O Lord, to prosper [us] now*, said Jesse and his wife." The Midrash on Ps. cxviii 25 retains "save," and assigns the words differently as follows "The men of Jerusalem say from the inside, *O, Eternal, save now*, and the men of Judah say from the outside, *O, Eternal, prosper us.*"

[2] See Jerome's letter on *Hosanna* (*Epist* xx), written to Damasus in reply to a request for an explanation of the word. Neither in the summary of his letter, nor in his *Matth Comment.* where he gives the letter's substance, is Origen's name mentioned.

JESUS VISITS THE TEMPLE

usual during that Feast. In this the above-quoted words of the Psalm (*"save now"*) were habitually recited, so that the Hebrew *"save-now"* became a title given both to the Feast, and to the day of the procession, and to the prayer for salvation, and even to the "bundle" of branches carried in it[1]. The carrying of palm-branches was also practised at the Feast of Dedication "as in the feast of tabernacles," and might be extemporised on any public rejoicing[2] In Revelation, the bearers of palm-branches, instead of crying "Save, O Lord,", cry "*Salvation* [belongeth] unto our God." This seems to be an ascription, like other following clauses · "Blessing and glory ...and power and might...[belong] unto our God for ever and ever. Amen[3]."

John does not attempt to paraphrase "Hosanna" as Luke does He accepts it without attempt at explanation, but in such a context as to suggest that the cry did not come from *all* the multitude Luke might lead hasty readers to the conclusion that it did, since he mentions the "praise " as uttered by "*the whole multitude of the disciples.*" Mark and Matthew say that the cry "Hosanna" came from "those who went before and those who followed " John alone says "A great multitude that had come to the feast...*went forth to meet him,* and cried out Hosanna, blessed is he that cometh in the name of the Lord[4]." It is implied (no doubt) that this crowd, after having met Jesus, turned round and preceded Him into the City John adds, "the multitude therefore that was with him when

---

[1] See Lev xxiii 40, and Wetstein's note on Mt. xxi. 9 "Then also they recited Ps. cxviii 24—5. And in separate prayers, which they use to this day, they make mention of *Saving* (*Salutis*), whence both the branch-bundle (fasciculo) and the prayers, and the feast itself, have been named by them *Hosanna* from *Saving* (a *Salute*)." Levy 1. 461 *a* gives instances.

[2] See 2 Macc x. 6 (comp. 1 Macc. xiii 51—2).

[3] Rev. vii 10, 12 On God's "salvation," as implying that in saving others God, as it were, saves the honour of His own Name, see *Exod. r* on Exod. xxii 1 (Wu p 233) quoting the lit. Heb of Zech ix 9 "*saved* (נושע)," not "*having salvation*," which would have been מושיע.

[4] Jn xii. 12—13.

JESUS VISITS THE TEMPLE

he called Lazarus out of the tomb...bare witness[1]." Apparently this second "multitude" includes the disciples and others, who had accompanied Jesus from Bethany, and who now followed Him into Jerusalem. These are not said to have cried "Hosanna". Thus John, besides correcting an impression that might have been derived from Luke, appears to be explaining, and correcting, the Marcan "those who *went before* and those who *followed after*." He seems to say, in effect, "It should have been 'those who at first went *out*, and afterwards went *before*[2].'"

---

[1] Jn xii 17

[2] Prof Burkitt says (*Journ. Theol Stud.* Jan. 1916, p 151) "In Lk. xix 37 b.. for ΑΠΑΝ the newly-discovered text W is found to read ΑΠΑΝΤΑΝ. ..Origen also has ΑΠΑΝΤΑΝ," and "quite clearly understands by it ἀπαντᾶν 'to meet,' for the subsequent χαίροντες αἰνεῖν is changed," by Origen, "into χαίροντες καὶ αἰνοῦντες" I may add that ἀπαντᾶν is confirmed by Origen's comment on Lk. (Lomm v 228) "If He had not come to the descent [of the Mount of Olives] the multitude would not have been able to *meet* Him (non ei poterat *occurrere* multitudo)." This is important, for Lommatzsch prints Origen i. 315 ἅπαν τὸ πλῆθος, in spite of the bad syntax—ἤρξατο ἅπαν τὸ πλῆθος τῶν μαθητῶν χαίροντες καὶ αἰνοῦντες.

That Luke would not have written ἀπαντᾶν is suggested by the fact that (*Notes* **2999** (iii) *d*) ἀπαντᾶν is mostly used (by careful writers) of evil that "befalls" or is "met." As parall to Mk xiv. 13 ἀπαντήσει, Lk xxii 10 has συναντήσει, and in Lk. xvii 12 W H marg. ὑπήντησαν is perh. correct (txt ἀπήντησαν) In Hermas *Vis* iv 2. 1—3, first ὑπαντᾶν is used of a virgin, and then ἀπαντᾶν (v r ὑπαντᾶν) of a monster (θηρίον), meeting Hermas In Justin M (apart from a quotation (*Tryph.* § 58) of Gen. xxviii. 11) ἀπαντᾶν is used only *Apol* § 60 of "monsters (θηρία)" (but *Apol*. § 44 uses the middle, ἀπαντήσεσθαι (along with ἀμείψεσθαι) apparently signifying divine visitation for good or ill) In Melito (Euseb *H E.* iv. 26. 8) ἀπαντᾶν is used of persecution "befalling" the Church.

These facts are of some interest as they suggest a question as to John's use of (Jn xii 13) ὑπάντησιν applied to the multitude in a parallel to Lk xix 37. Did John write with allusion to some Greek tradition already current about the "meeting" of the multitude and derived from an interpretation of Lucan sources? The answer is uncertain Hebrew sources might originate confusion owing to (*Notes* **2999** (iii) *g*) "the frequent oscillation (*Corrections* **472** *c*, **474** *a*)

JESUS VISITS THE TEMPLE

To some slight extent this Johannine picture resembles the picture presented by the Midrash (above quoted) on the Processional Psalm, "*The men of Jerusalem say from the inside, O, Eternal, save now,* or *Hosanna.*" Not improbably, John desired to suggest that the word *Hosanna* had a technical Jewish meaning, with which "*the men of Jerusalem*" were familiar, but on which it was unprofitable to dilate for Gentile readers[1]. "*Hosanna*"—like the title in the Johannine context, "King of *Israel*[2]" (where John alone inserts "Israel")—suggests Jewish traditions some of them likely to be used by the multitude in a narrow, restrictive, and transitory sense. Probably John does not take a very favourable view of the acclamations of

---

between 'meet' and 'call'" But here the case for Greek corruption seems strong.

[1] Prof Burkitt says very instructively (*Journ Theol Stud* Jan. 1916, p 140) "We may thus distinguish here two distinct tendencies in Christian documents On the one hand there was a tendency to get rid of *Hosanna* altogether as a 'barbarous' word this is seen in the paraphrase given by Luke, and also in W On the other hand the texts that retain *Hosanna* tend to add an object in the dative.

"This brings us to consider what the meaning of *Hosanna* was Here again there are two traditions, the one *grammatical*, the other *ritual* It is as if we were asking the meaning of the German cry *Hoch!*, and one should say it meant 'high' and another that it meant 'hurrah!' The ultimate derivation of *hosanna* is, no doubt, הושיעה נא, i e. 'save-oh!' No doubt, also, the original use of the word as an exclamation is to be seen in 2 Sam xiv 4, 2 Kings vi 26, where הושיעה is used as the call of a suppliant to the King, like *Haro ! à mon aide !* But the general import of a ritual exclamation is not necessarily exhausted by its grammatical derivation when we shout 'God save the King !' we do not think of the King as in particular need of rescue or salvation "

Though the Heb verb ישע, "save," was superseded in Aram by פרק, yet the technical Heb. noun הושענא, *Hosanna,* "save-now," was adopted into Aramaic as a noun, Levy *Ch* 1 196 *b* "Der Bachweide (auch Myrte) die man mit dem Feststrauss verbindet, Hosiana, Hosana, weil man dabei dieses Gebet sagte (Esth. Targ. II iii. 8) 'sie machen die Hosiana (entlehnt von Ps cxviii 25 הושיעה נא verkurzt (הושע־נא)' "

[2] On "King of Israel," see below, p 191, n 4.

the multitude and their "blessing[1]." Perhaps he mentally contrasts it with the impending arrival of "certain Greeks" and their simple request to Philip "Sir, we would see Jesus[2]"

§ 7. *"The coming kingdom of our father David," in Mark*[3]

The expression "our father David" occurs nowhere else in the Bible According to a Jewish tradition, "the fathers call no one *'our father'* except the three patriarchs[4]" But Peter, in the Acts, speaks of "the patriarch David," apparently meaning that he was the founder of the royal line of the kings of the Chosen People[5]. And Jeremiah (followed by Ezekiel) regards the future royal Deliverer of Israel, not merely as a son of David, but as David himself, so that God says concerning Israel "They shall serve the Lord their God, and *David their king, whom I will raise up unto them*[6]."

Such a phrase as "the kingdom of our father David" might well be familiar to the peasants of Palestine during the period when they looked for the re-establishment of a Davidic reign; but it might become obsolete at the end of the first century, when the hopes of Jewish patriots were modified by the fall of Jerusalem, and those of Jewish Christians by the resurrection of Him whom they had learned to call the Son of God, or the Son of the Father, or still, occasionally, the Son of David, but no longer "the son of our father David."

Accordingly Matthew substitutes the conventional "son of David" placed after "Hosanna," apparently as an ascription, "Hosanna to *the son of David*"; he does not in his own narrative

---

[1] See *Law* p 319 n on εὐλογημένος, nowhere used in Jn except here, and perhaps regarded as the cry of the fickle multitude (as in Philo, who (1. 453) distinguishes it from εὐλογητός)

[2] Jn xii 21.

[3] Mk xi 10. So SS, and W.H , *a* "benedictum regnum patris nostri David," *k* "benedictus qui venit in regnum (*sic*) patri (*sic*) nostri David"

[4] Wetstein on Mk xi. 10, quoting *Massecheth Semachoth* Levy i 2 quotes traditions calling Moses "father of wisdom and father of the prophets" etc but not "our father"

[5] Acts ii. 29.

[6] Jerem. xxx, 9, comp Ezek. xxxiv 23—4

JESUS VISITS THE TEMPLE

mention "*coming kingdom*" or "*kingdom*" at all, but suggests the thought of it in the phrase "*thy King cometh unto thee,*" loosely quoted from Zechariah in the form "Tell ye the daughter of Zion, Behold, *thy King cometh unto thee*[1]."

Luke mentions "*the King*" in his own narrative, as part of the acclamation of the disciples, and appears to mean by it "the ideal, or Messianic, King," perhaps also defining by it "he that cometh," which really means the Deliverer. "Blessed [is] He that Cometh, the King[2]." John prefers to divide "He that Cometh[3]" from "King," and to define the latter as being, not of the secular nation ("the Jews"), but of the nation regarded theologically ("Israel") '—"'*He that Cometh*'... and '*The King of Israel*[4]'"

In addition to these variations in the four Gospels, there are in Matthew and John strange departures from the text of Zechariah, which both of them misquote[5] No explanation of these difficulties is attempted by Jerome[6] But Origen grapples

---

[1] Mt. xxi. 5   [2] Lk xix 38.
[3] On "He that Cometh" see *Son* 3240—1.

[4] Jn xii 13   Comp Jn i 49 "the Son of God...the *King of Israel*" In the Synoptists this title occurs nowhere but in Mk xv 32, Mt xxvii. 42, where Luke, missing the meaning, substitutes (xxiii 37) "*the King of the Jews*" In O T , "*the king of Israel*" (apart from Saul and David) mostly means the king of the ten tribes. But see Is xliv 6 "The Lord, the *King of Israel*" and Zeph iii. 15 "The *King of Israel*, even the Lord " The title might be given to the Messiah as the representative of the One King, or as the second David

[5] Zech ix 9 R V , "Rejoice greatly, O daughter of Zion; shout, O daughter of Jerusalem   behold, thy king cometh unto thee: he is just, and having salvation (*or*, victory) (Heb. saved), lowly, and riding upon an ass, even upon a colt the foal of an ass," LXX Χαῖρε σφόδρα, θύγατερ Σειών· κήρυσσε, θύγατερ Ἱερουσαλήμ ἰδοὺ ὁ βασιλεύς σου ἔρχεταί σοι δίκαιος καὶ σώζων, αὐτὸς πραΰς καὶ ἐπιβεβηκὼς ἐπὶ ὑποζύγιον καὶ πῶλον νέον, quoted in Mt. xxi. 5 Εἴπατε τῇ θυγατρὶ Σιών Ἰδοὺ ὁ βασιλεύς σου ἔρχεταί σοι πραΰς καὶ ἐπιβεβηκὼς ἐπὶ ὄνον καὶ ἐπὶ πῶλον υἱὸν ὑποζυγίου, quoted in Jn xii. 15 Μὴ φοβοῦ, θυγάτηρ Σιών· Ἰδοὺ ὁ βασιλεύς σου ἔρχεται, καθήμενος ἐπὶ πῶλον ὄνου

[6] Jerome on Mt. xxi. 5 merely says that the riding on two animals is impossible and therefore must be allegorized. On Zech. ix. 9 he

191   (Mark xi. 7—10)

JESUS VISITS THE TEMPLE

with them[1]. Origen also frankly asks how the joyful tone of Zechariah's prophecy can be reconciled with the "weeping" of Jesus, which Luke describes as occurring, after the acclamations of the disciples, when He "drew nigh" and "saw the city[2]." In his opinion the Gospel narratives are permeated with allegory, and the quotations from Zechariah are influenced by Christian allusions. Such allusion could explain John's alteration of the prophetic "rejoice greatly," into "fear not." The former might be addressed to Israel of old expecting the revival of the Kingdom of David; the latter to the remnant of Israel, preserved from the destruction which was soon to fall on Jerusalem.

Origen is extremely fanciful in some of his explanations, but at all events he recognises that the Evangelists would not'

again allegorizes the two animals as representing the Jews and the Gentiles.

[1] In *Comm. Joann* x 17 (Lomm. 1 326) Origen says that Matthew has both altered and curtailed Zechariah's text, and adds "the Jews press us with arguments not to be despised" as to the Christian application of the context In *ib* x 18 (Lomm 1 336) he says that the Johannine "Fear not, daughter of Zion"—part of the Johannine quotation—"is not mentioned at all (οὐδ' ὅλως. εἴρηται)" in the prophecy Also, on Mt. xxi. 5 (Lomm iv. 45—6) Origen points out the discrepancies in detail between Zechariah, Matthew, and John, and says of the latter, "Indicating that the discussion of the passage requires *knowledge* (γνώσεως), John introduces the remark (Jn xii 16) *Now these things his disciples knew not* (οὐκ ἔγνωσαν) *at the first* (τὸ πρότερον)."

[2] *Comm. Matth* xvi. 15 (Lomm iv 46—7) "One would naturally inquire how, with any consistency (εὐλόγως), command is given (according to the prophet) that the daughter of Zion should rejoice greatly, and the daughter of Jerusalem make [glad] proclamation because of the Rider on the ass...when, after a short [interval] He (Lk. xix 41) *having seen* it, [namely] Jerusalem, *wept* [saying] '*Thou that killest the prophets*' and so on" (txt perhaps corrupt)

Origen has here connected with the weeping of Jesus—which Luke alone mentions in connection with the City (xix. 41 ἰδὼν τὴν πόλιν ἔκλαυσεν ἐπ' αὐτήν)—words ("thou that killest") placed by Luke (xiii. 34) some time before His coming to Jerusalem, but by Matthew (xxiii. 37) immediately before He leaves the Temple for the last time— a position that seems much more appropriate.

192 (Mark xi. 7—10)

JESUS VISITS THE TEMPLE

have altered the words of Zechariah without some reason, and he calls our attention to the Johannine recognition of some latent mystery in Christ's action not perceived by the disciples at the time: "These things his disciples knew not at the first, but when Jesus was glorified, then they remembered that these things had been written of him and [that] they did these things to him[1]." "Remembered" must not be taken as implying "They forgot at first but remembered later on." It means "They knew at first with their senses, but not with their minds, that is to say not with full recognition of the meaning of what they knew; afterwards their spirits were enlightened and they knew with their minds[2]." This ignorance, which John attributes to the disciples, the parallel Luke attributes, in a more intense form, to Jerusalem as a whole: "If thou hadst known...the things that belong unto peace! But now are they hid from thine eyes[3]." This, in Luke, is consistent with his context, which represents none of the people of Jerusalem, but only Christ's disciples, as acclaiming Christ[4].

§ 8. *"He looked round about upon all things," in Mark*[5]

These words and their Marcan context are omitted by the Diatessaron[6]. They describe a preliminary visit of Jesus to the

---

[1] Jn xii 16 "remembered (ἐμνήσθησαν)"

[2] Comp. ἐμνήσθησαν in Jn ii 17, 22 "*remembered* that it was written," "*remembered* that he had said," meaning "*recalled with recognition of the real meaning*," and ὑπομνήσει in Jn xiv 26 "the Paraclete ..shall *bring to your remembrance* all that I said unto you"

[3] Lk xix 42   [4] Lk xix. 37

[5] Mk xi 11 (R V)	Mt xxi 10—11 (R V)	Lk. om.
And he entered into Jerusalem, into the temple, and when he had looked round about upon all things, it being now eventide, he went out unto Bethany with the twelve	(10) And when he was come into Jerusalem, all the city was stirred, saying, Who is this? (11) And the multitudes said, This is the prophet, Jesus, from Nazareth of Galilee	

[6] After Mk xi. 10 *a* "our father David," *Diatess* has Lk xix. 38

JESUS VISITS THE TEMPLE

Temple in which there is no action but only a *"looking round*[1]*,"* with a view to the action of the morrow when the Temple is to be visited again and purified. Matthew and Luke represent the Temple as being purified at once[2] No writer in the New Testament except Mark (and Luke once, following Mark) uses the word "look-round" Mark applies it five times to Jesus.

The first instance is where Jesus asks "Is it lawful on the sabbath day to do good...?" and those who are asked "held their peace" Then Jesus, *"when he had looked round about on them* with anger, being grieved at the hardness of their heart," healed the man[3] The silence of those whom Jesus questions and on whom He "looks" with indignation, recalls the words of the Lord in Isaiah "And when *I look*, there is *no man...that, when I ask of them, can answer a word*[4]" And the mention of *"no man,"* as a reason for the intervention of the Lord, may be illustrated from other passages in Isaiah[5]. Moreover the rare Greek verb "look round about" occurs in Exodus to describe one of the earliest and most conspicuous instances of intervention

---

"Peace in heaven and praise in the highest," and then Jn xii 12 "And a great multitude . "

[1] Mk xi 11 καὶ εἰσῆλθεν εἰς Ἱεροσόλυμα εἰς τὸ ἱερόν καὶ περιβλεψάμενος πάντα...μετὰ τῶν δώδεκα

[2] Mt xxi. 12—13. Luke, after xix 38 "glory in the highest," inserts (*ib* 39—40) a remonstrance from Pharisees in the crowd, then Christ's weeping at the sight of the city (*ib* 41—4 "And when he drew nigh, he *saw the city* .. thy visitation"), and then xix 45 "And he entered into the temple, and began to cast out them that sold" There is no interval in Luke between "*he saw the city*" and "*he entered into the temple*," such as would enable the reader to suppose the "*seeing*" to refer to a preliminary visit

[3] Mk iii 5. The parall. Lk vi. 10 "And he looked round about on them all, and said unto him," omits Christ's "grief," and also the "silence" of those whom He had questioned

[4] Is xli 28.

[5] Is lix 15—16 "Yea, truth is lacking. and the Lord saw it, and it displeased him that there was no judgment And *he saw that there was no man*, and wondered that there was no intercessor therefore his own arm brought salvation unto him," lxiii 4—5 "The year of my redeemed is come And *I looked and there was none to help*...therefore mine own arm brought salvation unto me."

JESUS VISITS THE TEMPLE

for the oppressed, where it is said of Moses "He saw an Egyptian smiting an Hebrew, one of his brethren. And *he looked round about him* this way and that way, and when he saw that there was *no man*, he smote the Egyptian[1]" "No man" here seems to mean simply "no one to witness the action of Moses", but theoretically it might mean "no one else to help," and it is explained by Philo as meaning that Moses surveyed the whole of human nature and perceived that no human being was fixed and stable, but only the True God[2].

It is highly improbable that Mark himself used this Greek verb in this first instance with any allegorical purpose. Probably he is recording a Petrine reminiscence of the actual gestures of Jesus, a turning round of the whole body such as is ascribed to the Buddha in Buddhist Suttas[3] In connection with the purification of the Temple, the question of the meaning is complicated by the various senses attached to the word in Greek literature, and by the fact that Mark himself applies it to Jesus in various ways, and once to the disciples[4]. But this is certain, that the verse of Mark containing this clause adds a preliminary visit to the Temple not mentioned by Matthew and Luke. On the day after this first visit, Jesus, according to Mark, makes a second, and (on the way) condemns a fig-tree from which He has sought fruit in vain—after which He purifies

---

[1] Exod ii 11—12.

[2] Philo i 94—5 περιβλεψάμενος δὲ τὴν ὅλην ψυχὴν ὧδε καὶ ἐκεῖσε, καὶ μηδένα ἰδὼν ἑστῶτα, ὅτι μὴ τὸν ὄντα θεόν Comp Baruch iv 36, v 5 "*look round* to the east" to behold God's Deliverance

[3] See *Buddhist Suttas*, T. W Rhys Davids, 1881, p 64 It is however limited to the practice of the Buddhas in "looking *backward*" The context describes the Buddha's last view of a familiar place

[4] Περιβλεψάμενος, in Mark, precedes (iii 5) αὐτούς, (iii 34) τοὺς περὶ αὐτὸν κύκλῳ καθημένους, (v 32) ἰδεῖν τὴν τοῦτο ποιήσασαν (where it implies search), and here (xi 11) πάντα In x 23 it is used absolutely In ix 8, περιβλεψάμενοι is applied to the disciples after the vision in the Transfiguration, "looking about them" and "seeing no one"

The active, used of "turning round to look back" in Gen xix. 17, Josh viii 20, might have described Jesus as "turning round" to take a final view of the Temple when leaving it for the last time

JESUS VISITS THE TEMPLE

the Temple. But according to Matthew, the Temple has been already purified before Jesus condemns the fig-tree.

Luke omits the condemnation of the fig-tree, and the omission raises the question of Johannine Intervention. So does the Matthew-Luke omission of Mark's preliminary visit. In the discussion of John's attitude toward the two Marcan traditions it will be convenient to include a Lucan parable about a fig-tree to which the owner has come seeking fruit for three successive years in vain, so that he consequently commands it to be cut down[1].

§ 9. *John on Christ's visits to the Temple*[2]

In the accounts, printed below,. of Christ's visits to the Temple, it will be seen that John differs from the Synoptists

---

[1] Lk xiii. 6—9 It follows traditions peculiar to Luke (xiii. 1—5) about Galilaeans whose blood Pilate had mingled with their sacrifices, and about "those eighteen upon whom the tower of Siloam fell," concluding with the warning "Except ye repent ye shall all likewise perish."

[2] The first visit in Mk (xi. 11) having been discussed above, pp 193—6, we have to start from the second visit in Mk Parts of it are parallel to parts of the first visit in Mt -Lk.

Mk xi 12—19 (R V) [*The second visit in Mk*]	Mt. xxi. 12—19 (R V) [*The second visit in Mt*] Mt xxi. 18—19	Lk xiii. 6—9, xix. 45—8, xxi 37—8 (R V) [?] Lk. xiii. 6—9
(The condemning of the fig-tree)	(The condemning of the fig-tree)	(The parable of the fig-tree)
(12) And on the morrow, when they were come out from Bethany, he hungered. (13) And seeing a fig-tree afar off having leaves, he came, if haply he might find anything thereon and when he came to it, he found nothing but leaves, for it was not the season of figs (14) And he answered and said un-	(18) Now in the morning as he returned to the city, he hungered (19) And seeing a (*or*, a single) fig-tree by the way side, he came to it, and found nothing thereon, but leaves only, and he saith unto it, Let there be no fruit from thee henceforward for ever And immediately the fig-tree withered away.	(6) And he spake this parable, A certain man had a fig-tree planted in his vineyard, and he came seeking fruit thereon, and found none. (7) And he said unto the vinedresser, Behold, these three years I come seeking fruit on this fig-tree, and find none. cut it down, why doth it also cumber the ground?

196 (Mark xi. 12—19)

JESUS VISITS THE TEMPLE

both positively and negatively. Positively, he represents Jesus as going up to the Temple, before the final Passover, on four

Mk xi 12—19 (R V) *contd* [*The second visit in Mk*] *contd*		Lk xiii. 6—9, xix 45—8, xxi 37—8 (R V) *contd* [?] Lk xiii. 6—9
(The condemning of the fig-tree) *contd* to it, No man eat fruit from thee henceforward for ever And his disciples heard it	Mt xxi 12—19 (R V)	(The parable of the fig-tree) *contd* (8) And he answering saith unto him, Lord, let it alone this year also, till I shall dig about it, and dung it (9) And if it bear fruit thenceforth, [well], but if not, thou shalt cut it down
	[*The first visit in Mt*] Mt. xxi. 12—14 (R V)	[*The first visit in Lk.*] Lk xix. 45—8 (R V)
(15) And they come to Jerusalem and he entered into the temple, and began to cast out them that sold and them that bought in the temple, and overthrew the tables of the money-changers, and the seats of them that sold the doves; (16) And he would not suffer that any man should carry a vessel through the temple (17) And he taught, and said unto them, Is it not written,, My house shall be called a house of prayer for all the nations? but ye have made (πεποιήκατε) it a den of robbers (18) And the chief priests and the scribes	(12) And Jesus entered into the temple of God (*many anc auth omit* of God), and cast out all them that sold and bought in the temple, and overthrew the tables of the money-changers, and the seats of them that sold the doves (13) And he saith unto them, It is written, My house shall be called a house of prayer but ye make it a den of robbers (14) And the blind and the lame came to him in the temple and he healed them	(45) And he entered into the temple, and began to cast out them that sold, (46) Saying unto them, It is written, And my house shall be a house of prayer but ye have made (ἐποιήσατε) it a den of robbers (47) And he was teaching daily in the temple But the chief priests and the scribes and the principal men of the people sought to destroy him (48) And they could not find what they might do, for the people all hung upon him, listening

JESUS VISITS THE TEMPLE

occasions[1], not one of which is mentioned by the Synoptists—unless we suppose that the first Johannine visit, including a

Mk xi 12—19 (R V) contd		
[*The second visit in Mk*] contd. heard it, and sought how they might destroy him for they feared him, for all the multitude was astonished at his teaching		
[*The end of the second visit in Mk*] Mk xi 19 (R V) And every evening (*lit.* whenever evening came) he (*some anc auth* they) went forth out of the city.	[*The end of the first visit in Mt.*] Mt xxi 15—17 (R V) (15) But when the chief priests and the scribes saw the wonderful things that he did, and the children that were crying in the temple and saying, Hosanna to the son of David, they were moved with indignation, (16) And said unto him, Hearest thou what these are saying? And Jesus saith unto them, Yea did ye never read, Out of the mouth of babes and sucklings thou hast perfected praise? (17) And he left them, and went forth out of the city to Bethany, and lodged there	[*Daily visits in Lk*] Lk. xxi 37—8 (R V.) (37) And every day he was teaching in the temple, and every night he went out, and lodged in the mount that is called [the mount] of Olives. (38) And all the people came early in the morning to him in the temple, to hear him.

[1] The Johannine mentions of the Temple in narrative, with their contexts (R V), are given below It will be seen that in every case there is a previous reference to one of the Jewish feasts whether the word "feast" be used or not For the sake of completeness, the mention of the Temple in the interpolated passage Jn viii 1—2 is also given

(1) Jn ii 13—21 "And *the passover of the Jews* was at hand, and Jesus went up to Jerusalem. (14) And he found *in the temple* those that sold oxen and sheep and doves, and the changers of money

JESUS VISITS THE TEMPLE

purification of the Temple, which John records as Christ's first public act, is to be identified with the Synoptic visit and

---

sitting (15) And he made a scourge of cords, and cast all *out of the temple*, both the sheep and the oxen, and he poured out the changers' money, and overthrew their tables, (16) and to them that sold the doves he said, Take these things hence, make not my Father's house a house of merchandise. (17) His disciples remembered that it was written, The zeal of thine house shall eat me up (18) The Jews therefore answered and said unto him, What sign shewest thou unto us, seeing that thou doest these things? (19) Jesus answered and said unto them, Destroy this temple (*or*, sanctuary) and in three days I will raise it up (20) The Jews therefore said, Forty and six years was this temple (*or*, sanctuary) in building, and wilt thou raise it up in three days? (21) But he spake of the temple (*or*, sanctuary) of his body."

(2) Jn v 1, 14 "After these things there was *a* (or, *the* [(?) above-mentioned, see Introd.* p 81]) *feast of the Jews.* . Afterward Jesus findeth him *in the temple*. . "

(3 *a*) Jn vii 2, 14, 28 "Now *the feast of the Jews, the feast of tabernacles,* was at hand... But when it was now *the midst of the feast* Jesus went up *into the temple* and taught .. Jesus therefore cried *in the temple* . "

[(Interpolated) Jn viii 1, 2 "But Jesus went unto the mount of Olives And early in the morning he came again *into the temple*, and all the people came unto him, and he sat down and taught them."]

(3 *b*) viii. 20, 59 "These words spake he in the treasury as he taught *in the temple*...But Jesus . went *out of the temple*" The Feast of Tabernacles covers Jn vii 2—viii 59, thus 3 *a* and 3 *b* cover a single "going up" for a "feast"

(4) x. 22, 23, 39 "And it was *the feast of the dedication* at Jerusalem it was winter, and Jesus was walking *in the temple* in Solomon's porch. . They sought again to take him and he went forth out of their hand "

There is no further mention of the Temple, connected with Jesus, in Johannine narrative But there is a mention of people (Jn xi 56) "*standing in the temple*" and wondering whether Jesus will come for the Passover And Jesus says (Jn xviii 20) "I ever taught in synagogues (Gk synagogue) and *in the temple* "

There are good reasons (*Introd* p 81) for placing Jn chap v after chap. vi which says (vi. 1) "Now the passover was near." Hence Jn v 1 (אC etc ἦν ἡ ἑορτή) may mean "The above-mentioned feast had [now] arrived "

JESUS VISITS THE TEMPLE

purification of the Temple, which the Synoptists place as almost Christ's last public act[1].

Negatively, when John comes to speak of the final Passover, where the Synoptists represent Jesus as riding into Jerusalem and purifying the Temple, John, though he too describes the riding, makes no mention at all of the Temple—nor even of Jerusalem, except as it were casually, "when they heard that Jesus was coming to Jerusalem[2]." Mark, on the other hand, multiplies his mentions of "coming to Jerusalem" day by day. For example, where Matthew and Luke say that Jesus "entered into the temple" and cleansed it, Mark says "*And they come to Jerusalem*, and he entered into the temple[3]."

Examining John's mentions of the Temple, and of Christ's words or deeds in the Temple, we find that in every case the mention of the Temple is preceded by some mention of Passover, or Feast, or Feast of Tabernacles, or Feast of Dedication, sometimes at an interval but never so long a one as to obscure the suggestion that the Feast is the cause of Christ's presence in the Temple. This accords with Luke's tradition that the parents of Jesus *used to go year by year to Jerusalem on the occasion of the Passover*, and that when He was twelve years old, they went up "after the custom of the feast[4]." The Law commanded all males of suitable age to go up thrice in the year[5]. Luke's tradition, which says that Christ's mother also

---

[1] The *Diatessaron* does identify the two. Consequently it omits Jn ii 12—13 and places Jn ii 14 a almost immediately after one of Luke's latest parables "(Lk. xix 11—27) And he spake a parable because he was nearing Jerusalem.. slay them before me (Mk xi. 15 a, loosely rendered) And when Jesus entered Jerusalem he went up to (Mt xxi 12 a) the temple of God and (Jn ii 14, loosely rendered) found there oxen and sheep and doves..." Clark's edition of the *Diatessaron* gives Mt. xxi 12 a alone, without Mk xi. 15 a, but wrongly, since Mt. has merely "went into the temple of God," whereas Mk prefixes "*they come to Jerusalem*"

[2] Jn xii 12. This is the last Johannine mention of Jerusalem.

[3] Jerusalem occurs in (*a*) Mk xi. 1, Mt xxi. 1, om. by Lk xix 29, but see Lk. xix. 28; (*b*) Mk xi. 11, Mt xxi. 10, om. Lk.; (*c*) Mk xi 15, om. Mt. xxi. 12, Lk xix 45; (*d*) Mk xi. 27, om Mt. xxi 23, Lk. xx. 1.

[4] Lk. ii. 41—2.   [5] Exod. xxiii. 14 foll.

JESUS VISITS THE TEMPLE

went up (though women's obligation was not included in the Law), leads to the inference that, in the family of Jesus, attendance at the feasts would be regular.

Now Luke himself, according to the best authorities, tells us that Jesus at a very early period in His public life was preaching in the synagogues of Judaea[1]. It is true that the parallel Mark and Matthew mention Galilee. But Luke aims at chronological order And for this and other reasons, given in a previous volume[2], it seems probable that Luke here inserts in its right place a statement of historical doings in Judaea about the nature of which he himself says nothing because he knew nothing and Mark and Matthew recorded nothing There would be a natural tendency to alter Judaea into Galilee, as many authorities have done in the text of Luke itself.

But if, as a fact, Jesus preached in Judaea quite early in His career, it becomes probable that at an early period, and more than once, He went up to Feasts at Jerusalem. In that case, before the publication of any of our extant Gospels, there would be traditions telling how Jesus went up to "a feast" at Jerusalem, or to "the feast"—meaning "the feast" last mentioned in the traditional context—and that He said this or that Such traditions it would be difficult or impossible for Evangelists to arrange chronologically Luke has preserved one of these, relating how Jesus went up for the first time to Jerusalem at the Passover, and had conversations with the teachers, saying afterwards, to His mother, "Knew ye not that I must be in my Father's house (*or*, business)[3]?"

If Jesus went up to the Feasts at Jerusalem on several occasions, saying and doing things unknown to Galilaean evangelists, they might pass over these visits in their chronological order but make some reference to them in their account of the final visit to the Passover in which they regarded Jesus as going up to Jerusalem to seek fruit from Israel as being the

---
[1] Lk iv 44
[2] See *Proclam* pp 240—42 on Mk i 39, Lk iv 44 (R V (Lk) txt "Galilee," but marg "Judaea", and W. H txt "Judaea" without alternative)
[3] Lk. ii. 49.

JESUS VISITS THE TEMPLE

Vineyard of the Lord of hosts, and from Judah as being the Lord's "pleasant plant[1]." One parable of this kind uttered in Jerusalem all the Synoptists have preserved, shewing how the Lord of the Vineyard deals with the refractory vinedressers[2]. Another similar parable Luke has placed earlier, wherein the owner of a fig-tree comes seeking fruit "these three years" and finding none, so that he commands the tree to be cut down[3].

No other Evangelist has this. But Mark, followed by Matthew, has placed in his account of Christ's daily visits to Jerusalem a story about one visit in which Jesus comes seeking fruit in vain, from a fig-tree, on His way to the Temple, and commands the tree to be henceforth barren and dead; and it dies accordingly. This story Mark and Matthew place in different positions among their accounts of Christ's visits (printed above), so that the parallelism between the two is disturbed. The parallel Luke wholly omits it. It seems as though Mark has confused and conflated a literal with a poetical account, so as to make two visits out of one. Matthew, except in respect of order, has followed Mark. But Luke seems to be right both in rejecting the literal version and in substituting a poetical or parabolic one. Further, Luke may be right in placing the parable in a comparatively early position before Jesus came to Jerusalem for the final Passover.

Again, Luke agrees with Mark in describing Jesus as teaching, during one of these daily visits, a doctrine about almsgiving, and about a correct judgment of its merit, placing the widow's mite above the larger offerings of the rich[4]. The parallel Matthew omits this, but inserts a condemnation of the Pharisees for emphasizing outward observances of tradition to the neglect of "judgment[5]", to which Luke has a parallel, mentioning

---

[1] Is v. 7.
[2] Mk xii. 1—12, Mt xxi 33—46, Lk. xx. 9—19
[3] Lk xiii 6—9 The "three" visits to the fig-tree might be perhaps regarded, in accordance with Johannine chronology, as corresponding to three visits to Jerusalem. But I have not found any ancient adoption of this view.
[4] Mk xii. 41—4, Lk. xxi. 1—4.
[5] Mt. xxiii. 23, Lk. xi 42.

JESUS VISITS THE TEMPLE

'judgment," but at an earlier date and not in Jerusalem. Now Mark and Luke say that the teaching about the widow's mite was in the Temple, near "the treasury." "The treasury" is nowhere else mentioned in the New Testament except by John[1], in recording a discourse of Jesus in the Temple, presumably at the conclusion of the Feast of Tabernacles, wherein Jesus says to the Pharisees that they *"judge* after the flesh" and explains why His own judgment is true: "If I judge, my *judgment* is true, for I am not alone, but I and the Father that sent me[2]"

Is there any reason for thinking that in Mark's original, as in the Fourth Gospel, the Treasury was regarded as the appropriate place for a doctrine about "judgment" of a certain kind—that judgment which distinguishes dross from pure metal and false coin from true? In Mark, it is said that Jesus, *"having sat down* over against the treasury, beheld how the multitude cast money into the treasury[3]." *"Having sat down"* is altered by Codex Bezae into "*[while] sitting,*" and by the Syro-Sinaitic Version into "*standing*"—in which latter form Origen twice quotes it[4]. The parallel Luke has "*having looked up* he saw." "*Having sat down*" is the more difficult reading, and might naturally be altered by Luke and modified by editors of Mark. But if it was the original, what was its original force?

A reasonable answer may be supplied from Malachi's account of the Messiah's coming to the Temple. "The Lord .. *shall suddenly come to his temple*...and he shall *sit as a refiner* and purifier of silver, and he shall purify the sons of Levi... and they shall offer unto the Lord offerings in righteousness[5]." Jesus regarded ostentatious offerings of the rich as dross or brass. The Refiner was to "*sit*" in authority and to teach Israel to separate the dross or brass from the silver According to this view, "*sat*" is not superfluous, nor need it be taken as a literal statement rightly rejected by Luke. It implies not only the general authority of a teacher, but also a special

---

[1] Jn viii 20 [2] Jn viii. 15—16. [3] Mk xii. 41.
[4] Origen Lomm. ii 151, 155 [5] Mal. iii. 1, 3.

JESUS VISITS THE TEMPLE

allusion to the authority of the Messiah, teaching men how to distinguish true sacrifice from false and "to offer offerings in righteousness" Not improbably a similar allusion is latent in the Lucan account of the boy Jesus unexpectedly found "in the temple *sitting* in the midst of the teachers, both hearing them and asking them questions[1]." It is perhaps implied that even in this first visit to the Father's house, the Child separates truth from falsehood, pure metal from dross.

In addition to these facts, indicating that Jesus visited Jerusalem on more than one occasion, there is evidence, derived from Mark's mention of "cornfields" and "plucking ears of corn[2]," that the original of the Marcan narrative of Christ's public life must have covered a longer period than that of one year (extending from the sequel of one Passover to the beginning of another) This agrees with the text of John which speaks of

---

[1] Lk ii 46 See the very full comment in *Hor Heb* ad loc on "sitting," and also Schottgen, who begins by saying "It was lawful for no one to *sit* in the temple," and proceeds to quote *Aboth R Nathan* § 39 (*Aboth* VI F) on different kinds of "sitting." During the time of Hillel disciples did not "sit" but stood in the presence of their teachers, not till a later period did they "sit on the ground " Here, however, Jesus is described as not only "sitting," but also "*sitting in the midst of the teachers*" *Hor Heb.* says "It is less wonder if they suffer him to sit amongst them, being but twelve years of age, whenas they promoted R Eleazar Ben Azariah to the presidency itself when he was but sixteen" But the writer fails to add that this Eleazar was (Schurer II 1 372) "a rich and eminent priest, whose genealogy is traced back to Ezra," whose wealth was proverbial, and who was elected in a crisis to fill a gap which he filled only for a time It is futile to compare such a "promotion" of a youth of sixteen with the position assigned to Jesus at the age of twelve in Luke's story *Hor Heb*, however, is of value as shewing the difficulty felt by so learned a writer in attempting to explain the Lucan narrative literally It cannot be thus explained It points back to a poetic story derived from the picture of the Judge or Refiner in Malachi

Cyril of Alexandria substitutes (Cramer *ad loc*) $\mu\epsilon\tau\alpha\xi\acute{\upsilon}$ for $\grave{\epsilon}\nu$ $\mu\acute{\epsilon}\sigma\omega$ so as to make it clear that Jesus is seated "*amidst* the teachers" (and not, as some have supposed, on the floor, with the teachers seated in chairs forming a semi-circle round Him)

[2] *Introd* pp. 89—90, quoting Mk ii 23.

JESUS VISITS THE TEMPLE

two Passovers before the final one. Even John's omission to give us in every case the name of the "feast" that he mentions, regrettable though it is for many reasons, is very instructive if we can assume that he does not want to mystify his readers. For then it proves that he did not himself know in each case the name of the "feast" and that he set down a vague tradition as he found it. That would explain many chronological variations in the Synoptists It might also explain other errors. Sayings uttered in Jerusalem might sometimes be liable to misinterpretation if recorded as being uttered to an audience in Galilee.

§ 10. *The symbolism of the fig-tree, misunderstood by Luke*

That Luke misunderstood the symbolism of the fig-tree in Christ's doctrine appears from his version of the following words of Jesus uttered a little later on:—

Mk xiii. 28	Mt xxiv. 32	Lk. xxi. 29—30
Now from the fig-tree learn her parable· when her branch is now become tender, and putteth forth its leaves, ye know that the summer is nigh.	Now from the fig-tree learn her parable when her branch is now become tender, and putteth forth its leaves, ye know that the summer is nigh.	(29) And he spake to them a parable Behold the fig-tree, and all the trees· (30) When they now shoot forth, ye see it and know of your own selves that the summer is now nigh.

The peculiarity of the fig-tree, as here mentioned, was that its fruit appeared before its leaves, so that, when the leaves themselves appeared, they announced, not the coming, but the ripening, of the fruit—not spring but "*summer.*" Pliny notes this exception to the ordinary rule of fruit-trees[1]. Luke seems

[1] Pliny *Nat Hist.* xvi. 49 (113). Other trees, he says, have the fruit under the leaf, except the fig ("excepta fico") He adds "*et demum serius folium nascitur quam pomum.*" *Hor. Heb* on Mt. xxi. 19 indicates a great variety of Jewish traditions about various kinds of figs. These might naturally vary in the different climates of Galilee and Judaea. But the language of Mark, and the testimony of Pliny, make it clear that the original of the Synoptic tradition referred to the ordinary fig and to its exceptional character among

JESUS VISITS THE TEMPLE

to have missed this allusion to an exceptional characteristic At all events he has added "*and all the trees*[1]"—as if the meaning were "When trees (lit.) push forth, you know that summer is near." This is obscure since "push forth" might have for its object "buds" or "fruit" No instance is alleged of its use thus without an object But Aquila employs it about "ripening," with "green figs" as object[2] Luke seems to use it absolutely in the sense of putting forth leaf and to apply it to trees in general, not fruit-trees alone.

Mark may perhaps be paraphrased as follows. "Seeing afar off leaves on a fig-tree, Jesus came up to it on the chance that[3] it might have fruit [*It ought to have had according to rule But Jesus came only on the chance*]—and when He came to it He found nothing but leaves—for it was not [yet] the season for figs[4]." The fig-tree, so to speak, if it was not deceiving, was bound to have fruit since it had leaves But it was deceiving. It gave the spectators the impression that it had fruit before the time, whereas it had none, and would have none at any time.

The first Biblical mention of the leaves of the fig-tree is

---

fruit-trees Pliny himself says that there were exceptional fig-trees that followed the rule of other fruit-trees, but those are not contemplated by Mark

[1] The *Diatessaron*, immediately after Lk xxi 28 "Your salvation is near," places Mt xxiv. 32 foll "Learn the example of *the fig-tree*" It does not add (from Lk xxi 29) "*and all the trees*," here or anywhere.

[2] Cant ii 13 "The fig-tree *hath ripened* (R.V. *ripeneth*) her greenfigs" LXX ἐξήνεγκεν ὀλύνθους αὐτῆς, Aq προέβαλεν, Sym ἐξέθηλεν

[3] Mk xi. 13 "On the chance that," εἰ ἄρα, only here in the Gospels Comp Acts viii 22 εἰ ἄρα where it is implied that Simon Magus is not forgiven, and 1 Cor. xv. 15 εἴπερ ἄρα οὐκ which introduces as an impossibility the non-raising of the dead In Acts xvii 27 εἰ ἄρα γε, the γε makes a difference.

[4] Ephrem on Mt. xxi. 19 supposes the season to be late, after the fig-gathering, and the owner to be in fault for not leaving (Deut xxiv 19—21) a gleaning. Origen expatiates on the peculiar merit of "fruits of the Spirit" if they are forthcoming when "not in season" (Lomm. iv 79—82) but does not help the reader to understand the action imputed to Jesus.

(Mark xi. 12—19)

JESUS VISITS THE TEMPLE

connected with sin. With such leaves Adam and Eve clothed their nakedness just before they "hid themselves from the presence of the Lord God"; and Philo allegorizes these fig-leaves as indicating the sweetness of pleasures[1]. The context might be applied to the soul of man, fleeing from God into itself and from the service of God into selfishness or self-service[2]. In Mark, the unfruitful but leafy fig-tree may have been intended to signify the splendour of the Temple, which, under the appearance of solemn service to God, was used for the service of men, and, to a large extent, for the gains of monopolising priests and avaricious rulers[3] Thus conducted, the ritual of the Temple might well seem an obstruction rather than a help to religion, a fruitful fig-tree that had become a barren fig-tree, cumbering the ground—a thought that indicates how the Lucan parable, and the Marcan narrative, about a fig-tree, might proceed from one and the same original

According to Luke, Jesus, on His way to Jerusalem—but on an earlier occasion, and not in one of these daily visits from Bethany—used language about "uprooting" a "sycamine-tree" very similar to that placed here in Mark and Matthew —

Mk xi 22—3	Mt xxi 21	Lk. xvii 6
Have faith in God. Verily I say unto you, Whosoever shall say unto this mountain, Be thou taken up and cast into the sea it shall be [done] for him	Verily I say unto you, if ye have faith and . ye shall not only do the [deed] of the fig-tree, but even if ye shall say to this mountain, Be thou taken up and cast into the sea, it shall come to pass	If ye have faith as a grain of mustard-seed ye would say to this sycamine-tree, Be thou rooted up and be thou planted in the sea, and it would have obeyed you

There is abundant evidence to shew that a Jewish teacher would use phrases about rooting up trees or mountains in a metaphorical sense, speaking of obstacles or difficulties in the way of the acceptance of the Law[4]. Such phrases Jesus might

---

[1] Philo *Quaest. Gen* on Gen. iii. 7   [2] Comp. *Law* p. 507
[3] On the monopolies see *Son* **3585** c
[4] See *From Letter* **764** foll. on the Rabbinical title Uprooter of Trees or Mountains, and comp. 1 Cor. xiii. 2

JESUS VISITS THE TEMPLE

apply to spiritual difficulties, the obstacles presented by sin. And it is conceivable, and indeed antecedently probable, that when He stood on the Mount of Olives and looked upon the Temple, which He had attempted to purify, and on the whole of what the Jews called the Mountain of the Lord's House, He would regard that "mountain" as no longer the Lord's, but as an opposing "mountain" to be addressed in the words of Zechariah, "Who art thou, O *great mountain*? Before Zerubbabel [thou shalt become] a plain; and he shall bring forth the head stone with shoutings of Grace, grace, unto it[1]." Such a saying Luke, finding it attributed to Jesus as He was "going to Jerusalem[2]," might assign to an earlier period while Jesus was journeying by slow stages to the City, and before the time when He began a course of daily visits to the Temple. In that case he would have to interpret "*this* sycamine-tree" as meaning literally a casual tree indicated by a gesture of Jesus. But really, in the original saying, it might have meant the visible Temple—"*this* barren tree that I see before me."

As regards the parallelism between "this mountain" in Mark and "this sycamine-tree" in the passage last quoted from Luke, it has been shewn that a similar parallelism is found in Jewish tradition between "*this mountain*" and "*this plane-tree*[3]." Both of them meant Mount Gerizim. In the Fourth Gospel the Samaritan woman speaks of worshipping God "*in this mountain*" (that is, Gerizim), whereas the Jews say that "the place where men ought to worship" is "*in Jerusalem.*" Jesus replies "Neither *in this mountain, nor in Jerusalem*"; the place of worship is to be—"in spirit and truth[4]."

---

[1] Zech. iv. 7

[2] Luke from ix 51 onward ("set his face to go to Jerusalem") is describing Christ's journey to Jerusalem; and the saying about the (xvii. 6) "sycamine-tree," is closely followed by (xvii. 11) "as he was going (ἐν τῷ πορεύεσθαι) to Jerusalem." What Luke regards as one journey in several stages, John may have regarded (and perhaps correctly) as separate journeys in separate years

[3] See *Son* 3364 *l—q*.   [4] Jn iv. 20, 21, 24.

JESUS VISITS THE TEMPLE

§ 11. *Does John intervene?*

The Docetae (according to Hippolytus) declaring "the First God" Himself to be as it were the seed of a fig-tree, blended together the Parable of the Search for fruit from the Fig-Tree in Luke with the Curse of the Fig-Tree in Mark-Matthew, along with strange allusions to the clothing of the nakedness of Adam and Eve[1]. From a different point of view, that of the ordinary Greek reader, we might expect to find in John something that might meet the apparent jibe of Epictetus, "You can only have figs in the regular time of the year; if you long for them in winter, you are a fool[2]."

Nothing, however, of the nature of a definite intervention can be found in John. But Jesus, after calling Nathanael "an Israelite indeed without guile," is represented as saying to him "When thou wast *under the fig-tree* I saw thee[3]." The two sayings perhaps imply that Nathanael, under the stress of the temptations of the flesh and the world, had not clothed himself in falsehood or hypocrisy but remained "without guile." John nowhere again mentions the fig-tree. But this passage leads us to ask how he would express, 1st, the similitude, suggested by Mark, between the misused Temple and a barren fig-tree, 2nd, the lessons inculcated by it concerning the fruit that God sought from Israel, and God's treatment of the fruitful and the unfruitful.

Roughly and briefly we may say that John places before us a positive along with a negative aspect of the Congregation, or Church, or Body, of Israel. First he regards it as the Temple and later on as the Vine. As to the Temple, he represents

---

[1] Hippol viii 1   The seed is described as "refuge of those that fear, covering of the naked, veil of shame, fruit sought after ($\zeta\eta\tau o\acute{u}\mu\epsilon\nu o\varsigma$ $\kappa\alpha\rho\pi\acute{o}\varsigma$), to which came the Seeker (it is said) thrice, and found not, wherefore also (it says) He cursed the fig-tree."

[2] Epict iii 24 86

[3] Jn 1 47—8   See *Son* 3375 *f—k* on "THE FIG-TREE" in Jn, where the conclusion is "the story of Nathanael under the 'fig-tree' is probably to be regarded as a version of the story of Zacchaeus in the 'sycomore'"

JESUS VISITS THE TEMPLE

Jesus as Himself using a phrase "destroy (*lit* loose) this temple," a form of which Mark and Matthew place only in the mouths of false witnesses testifying against Jesus. The Gospels vary as follows:—

Mk xiv. 58	Mt. xxvi. 61	Jn ii. 19
We heard him say, *I will destroy*[1] this temple that is made with hands, and in three days I will build another made without hands.	This man said, *I am able to destroy*[1] the temple of God, and to build it in three days.	Jesus answered and said unto them, *Destroy*[1] this temple, and in three days I will raise it up

John adds "But he spake of the temple of his body[2]"

The variation of imperative and indicative may be illustrated by the following:—

Mk xiv. 27 and Mt. xxvi. 31	Zech xiii. 7 (Heb)
It is written, *I will smite* the shepherd, and the sheep (Mt. + of the flock) shall be scattered abroad.	*Smite* [*thou*] the shepherd, and the sheep shall be scattered

If Jesus said "*Destroy* this temple," the imperative would be quite intelligible as meaning "*Go on in your evil way, if ye are so resolved, and destroy this temple*[3], this body of the faithful of Israel"—followed by a warning, "But know that on the third day it shall be raised up." But some, taking "temple" literally, would read into the words a contrast between "this temple" (of stone) and "another[4]." They would also find in the words a prophecy that Jesus would or could[5] destroy the temple of stone (as it was destroyed through the hand of the Romans) and build it up again as the Church of Christ. Luke

---

[1] "Destroy" is in Mk-Mt. καταλύω, in Jn λύω.
[2] Jn ii 21
[3] For a similar imperative see Mt xxiii. 32 "*Fill ye* then up the measure," where, however, W H marg and SS have "*ye will fill*" (D "*ye filled*") [The parallel Luke differs] There are similar variations in the Gk of some of the imperatives in Is viii 9—10 "*Make an uproar...gird yourselves..take counsel.. speak the word*" (see Field)
[4] Mk xiv. 58 "build *another*."
[5] "Could," Mt xxvi. 61 "*I am able*"

JESUS VISITS THE TEMPLE

omits the whole as a false accusation. John intervenes to shew the truth on which the falsehood was based. He does not deny that Jesus, on some occasion, invoked or predicted destruction on the visible building of the Temple, but at all events he does not record it. He records, instead, a warning addressed to the rulers of the Jews that if they persist in their course they will be destroying—though not ultimately, yet as far as they can—the true and invisible Temple of God[1].

As to the other metaphor, that of a tree, the Fourth Evangelist substitutes "vine" for "fig," and again fixes our thoughts mainly on the positive aspect. He does not—as Isaiah does in his parable of the Vineyard—describe the whole of the Vine as being retributively "trodden down" for failing to bear good fruit[2]. Isaiah's parable is addressed to rebellious Israel. The Johannine parable is addressed not to "the Jews" but to those to whom Jesus says afterwards "I am the vine, ye are the branches," that is, to the disciples. To them He has said "I am the true vine, and my Father is the husbandman. Every branch in me that beareth not fruit, he taketh it away, and every [branch] that beareth fruit, he cleanseth it, that it may bear more fruit[3]." This differs both from the Marcan story of cursing and from the Lucan Parable of condemnation. In both of those, there was "a coming to look" for fruit, as for something external. In John, there is no "coming to look." Everything is internal and personal. The Vine is in fact the Lord Himself; the branches, if they abide in Him, are as it were His limbs. The action of "the husbandman," God, is for the good of the Vine as a whole, through fire and steel—fire for the unfruitful, the pruning-knife for the fruitful branches. In conclusion, we must say that if John intervenes it is rather in favour of Luke than in favour of Mark, in order to shew the justice and impartiality of the Lord of the Vineyard.

---

[1] At the same time the impending destruction of the visible Temple is not left wholly unmentioned. But it is the Jews who mention it, Jn xi 48 "If we let him alone..., *the Romans will come and take away both our place* and our nation." It is an instance of Johannine irony, see *Son* 3106 a.

[2] Is v 5   [3] Jn xv. 1—6

JESUS VISITS THE TEMPLE

§ 12. *"Carrying a vessel through the temple," in Mark*[1]

This is omitted by Matthew and Luke. Wetstein quotes, in illustration of Mark, Josephus against Apion, as saying that no vessel was allowed to be carried "*in templo*[2]." But the Latin gives "*in templum,*" and the context indicates that the meaning is "*into the Holy Place*"; for it adds "there were therein only the altar, the table, the censer, and the candlestick."

This, therefore, does not help us to understand Mark. But John perhaps does by saying that there were "in the temple people selling oxen and sheep[3]" (not mentioned by the Synoptists). The care of these animals might necessitate the "carrying" of "vessels." Along with this Johannine addition must be considered the Johannine substitution of "Make not my Father's house a house of merchandise[4]" for the Synoptic "Ye made it a den of robbers." Origen says that the Synoptic words are "more severe" than the Johannine[5]. Is this so? And what is John's attitude to the Synoptic narratives as a whole?

The first point to be noted is that the exact words in Jeremiah are "Is this house...become a den of robbers in your eyes?" And these words do not refer to any "robbery" *committed inside the Temple*. They refer to sins committed outside. This is indicated by the preceding question "Will ye *steal, murder, and commit adultery, and swear falsely...and come and stand before me in this house...* and say 'We are delivered'; that ye may do all these abominations[6]?" That is to say, the people came into God's House, as robbers might come into their cave, commemorating or condoning their exploits rather than repenting of them, but at all events not continuing them in the House itself.

The Gospels on the other hand refer to a systematic extortion,

---

[1] Mk xi 16 καὶ οὐκ ἤφιεν ἵνα τις διενέγκῃ σκεῦος διὰ τοῦ ἱεροῦ
[2] Joseph *Contr Ap* ii 8
[3] Jn ii 14.   [4] Jn ii 16.
[5] Origen *Comm. Joann* x 17 (Lomm 1 328) τοὺς πάντας...χαλεπώτερα ὅσον ἐπὶ τοῖς λοιποῖς εὐαγγελισταῖς παρὰ τὸν Ἰωάννην ἀκούσαντας
[6] Jerem. vii 9—10

JESUS VISITS THE TEMPLE

practised by the rulers of the Temple, and in the Temple, on the pilgrims who came to offer sacrifice—frauds so open and coercive that they deserved to be called "robberies" rather than thefts[1].

Jerome in his commentary on Matthew explains this at great length. But the length of his explanation indicates that in the first century educated Greeks might not understand the force of the word "robbers" and might think that it savoured of exaggeration In the place of this fervid sentence from Jeremiah—which was probably only one of many sayings of Jesus on the abuses of the Temple—John substitutes another saying that refers to the busy "merchandise," or traffic, implied by Mark's tradition about "carrying vessels." There is in this saying a unique use of the Greek word *emporion*, i e. "emporium" or "place of traffic[2]." John has "Make not my Father's house *a house of emporium*." Why does he not say "*an emporium*"? Probably because he has in view the Synoptic tradition "My Father's house shall be *a house of prayer*," and he wishes to contrast "*house of prayer*" with "*house of merchandise*."

But if he wished to do this, why did he not (instead of *emporium*) use *emporia* which regularly means merchandise in LXX--and in the single instance where it occurs in Matthew[3]— whereas *emporium* never has this meaning? The most probable explanation is, that John had in view a saying based on Isaiah's mention of Tyre (LXX) "she shall be an *emporium to all the kingdoms of the world*" and on Ezekiel (LXX) "Thou shalt say to Tyre,...the *emporium of the peoples*[4]" These are the only instances of *emporium* (sing) in the LXX

But in Isaiah, the Hebrew for "*she shall be an emporium*" is "*she shall play the harlot*," and Ibn Ezra illustrates the expression by a Deuteronomic one, "*the hire of an harlot*[5]" and paraphrases the context of Isaiah as meaning that "all the

---

[1] See *Son* **3585** *c*
[2] Steph *Thes* gives no instance of it
[3] Mt xxii 5 "one to his merchandise (ἐμπορίαν) "
[4] Is xxiii. 17, Ezek. xxvii 3. The only other LXX instance of ἐμπόριον is pl. Deut. xxxiii 19. [5] Deut xxiii. 18

JESUS VISITS THE TEMPLE

kingdoms" will "come to her for *merchandise*." The same connection between "fornication" and "merchandise" is found in Revelation where the writer says that "the kings of the earth committed *fornication*" with "Babylon the great," and then speaks of "the *merchants* of the earth" as mourning over the loss of their "*merchandise*" in her[1].

All this is very unlike Western thought. But when the metaphor is probed it will be found accordant with the thoughts of the prophets of Israel. In the Temple of God, all human thought must go up in sacrifice and God-worship, not gad about in self-pleasing and self-worship. Israel's concentrated worship of the One God is wedded union; Israel's gadding about to the love of false gods is harlotry It would seem, then, that Mark's quaint and obscure tradition about "carrying vessels" points to something much deeper than at first appears—to a consecration of the traffic of greediness resulting in a desecration of the ordinances of pure worship. This "traffic" Jesus could not but condemn. And the form in which John alleges Him to have condemned it accords with the precedents set by two of the greatest prophets of Israel[2].

Possibly a third prophet has also contributed to Mark's tradition. The last words of Zechariah, describing the future holiness of the Temple, say—according to Aquila, whom Jerome follows—"There shall be no more a *trafficker* in the house of the Lord of hosts[3]." This is preceded by a poetic forecast about the "*pots*," or "*vessels*," in the Lord's House, which are all to

---

[1] Rev xviii. 2—3, 9—11.

[2] See *Son* 3370 c, where mention should have been made of John's use of ἐμπόριον. Westcott says (on Jn ii 16) that ἐμπόριον means the place of traffic and not the subject or art of trafficking (ἐμπορία): "comp. Ezek xxvii. 3 (LXX). Thus the 'house' is here regarded as having become a market-house...." I do not understand this. It can hardly be intended to suggest that the genitive is appositional (like "the name of George") "the house of (i e *that is called*) emporium."

[3] Zech xiv 21 R V txt "*Canaanite*," marg "*trafficker*," on which see Jerome The Targ has "*trafficker*," and so has Rashi Comp Hos xii 7 R V. txt "*trafficker*," marg. "*Canaan[ite]*," Targ. "*traffickers*." *Pesach.* 50 a supports "trafficker" in both passages

JESUS VISITS THE TEMPLE

be "holy," destined (as Rashi interprets the passage) to be of gold and silver, sanctified to the Lord's use, made out of the bells of the horses (war-horses being discarded in the days of peace)—so that henceforth (it might be inferred) no ordinary vessel of clay was to be allowed in the sacred precincts[1]. This is remote, in tone, from the bare prose of the Marcan tradition about "carrying a vessel through the temple." But the prophetic simultaneous mention of "vessel" and "traffic" is worth noting, in view of Mark's mention of "vessel," simultaneously with John's mention of "traffic," in the evangelistic accounts of the Purification of the Temple.

§ 13. *"For all the nations," in Mark*[2]

Reasons have been given in *Diatessarica*[3] for believing that the clause "for all the nations," though omitted by Matthew and Luke, was a part of the original tradition. We can see one reason why Matthew and Luke might omit the clause when we examine the context in which Justin Martyr quotes Christ's words from Matthew and Luke. It is in a fierce attack on Jews and on their rejection of Jesus. "He [*i.e.* Jesus] appeared distasteful to you [Jews] when He cried among you, *It is written, My house is a house of prayer, but ye have made it a den of robbers*[4]" Justin makes it appear that Jesus was "distasteful" to the Jews simply because He accused them of making the Temple "a den of robbers," and because they were actually "robbers." But if Jesus said "a house of prayer *for all the nations*," there was somewhat more reason for His being

---

[1] Zech xiv 20—21 "The *pots* in the Lord's house shall be like the bowls before the altar. Yea, every *pot* in Jerusalem and in Judah shall be holy unto the Lord of hosts."

[2] Mk xi 17 quoting fully Is lvi 7 "My house shall be called a house of prayer *for all the nations* (so LXX, but Heb *peoples*)," Codex *k* om "for all the nations." Pseudo-Jerome, on Mk, says "'*House of prayer*' according to Isaiah, '*Den of robbers*' according to Jeremiah," which looks as though he omitted "for all the nations," as introducing a separate thought and weakening the antithesis.

[3] *Son* 3353 (i)—(iv) on "*The inclusiveness of the Gospel*," and 3468 *c* foll. on "*The Holy Mountain*."

[4] Justin M. *Tryph.* § 17

"distasteful" to them. Had the accusation of "robbery" been Christ's uppermost feeling, there would have been much to say for omitting the Marcan mention of "all the nations."

But probably that accusation was not Christ's uppermost feeling. The uppermost feeling was more probably that "zeal" for the Father's "house" which consumed, or "ate," the Son's heart[1], a sympathetic indignation at seeing the outrage done by His professed ministers, the Jewish priests, to His Gentile children, the proselytes, as well as to the poor among their own countrymen, whom they "made to stumble" by their extortions. And if Jesus was purifying that part of the Temple, or Mountain of the House, which was called "the Court of the Nations (*or*, Gentiles)" where beasts were sold for sacrifice, there would be a special force in Isaiah's words "*for all the nations*," as though Jesus said to the chief priests, "How can the Lord make 'strangers[2]' from the nations joyful in His 'holy mountain,' and how can His house be 'called a house of prayer for all the nations,' Gentiles as well as Jews, when you, His priests, fill the Mountain of His House, the Court of the Gentiles, with noise, traffic, and extortion that make prayer impossible[3]?"

John, almost immediately after the Riding into Jerusalem, places a mention of "*certain Greeks* among those that went up to worship at the feast" who say to Philip, "Sir, we would see Jesus[4]" This immediately follows a testimony from the Pharisees themselves to the universal attraction exercised by Jesus "Behold how ye prevail nothing; lo, *the world* is gone after him[5]" Coming together at this point, the two passages remind us that John has himself described the "body" of Jesus as being a "temple[6]," or, in other words, a "house of prayer", and now he seems to bring Him before us as a "house of prayer" not only for "certain Greeks" but also for "all the world"

---

[1] Jn ii 17, quoting Ps lxix 9
[2] Is lvi 6—7 "Also *the strangers* . even them will I bring to *my holy mountain* and make them joyful in *my house of prayer*, and their sacrifices shall be accepted "
[3] Quoted from *Son* **3353** (iii)
[4] Jn xii 20—21   [5] Jn xii 19
[6] Jn ii. 21.

JESUS VISITS THE TEMPLE

§ 14. *"A scourge of cords," in John*[1]

Why does John insert this picturesque detail? Why do the Synoptists omit it? Of what nature were the "cords"? Whence were they obtained? What typical meaning, if any, may be attached to this Johannine insertion? Does it indicate a historical fact omitted by the Three Gospels or a symbolism peculiar to the Fourth?

It has been suggested that the cords were "probably *the rushes* which were littered down for the cattle to lie on[2]" But the Johannine word never means "*rushes*" either in LXX or in Greek literature[3] Etymologists may use the word thus, but other writers do not Moreover "rushes" would seem more suitable to the bank of the Nile than to the neighbourhood of Jerusalem[4].

A different explanation presents itself in the words of the Psalm "Bind the sacrifice *with cords* even to the horns of the altar[5]" Each victim, presumably, would have a cord attached to it for the purpose of leading it, and binding it, to receive the sacrificial stroke. From such "cords" Jesus might construct, and encourage His followers to construct, the "scourge" in question. No doubt, John would see in this a typical action— the true Sacrifice, the Lamb of God, casting out the false sacrifices, the "bullocks" and "lambs" about which the Lord had said "I delight not in their blood[6]." But that does not,

---

[1] Jn ii 15 καὶ ποιήσας φραγέλλιον ἐκ σχοινίων Nonnus calls the whip "counterfeit," νόθην ἱμάσθλην, indicating that he read ὡς after ποιήσας, with the best Latin versions, which have *tanquam*, or *quasi*

[2] So Alford. Westcott says "The 'cords' (σχοινία, properly of twisted rushes) would be at hand" Keim speaks of the whip as made of "rushes"

[3] In LXX, σχοινίον represents Heb. חבל, "cord," more than 20 times, and never represents Heb "bulrush" or "rush" Steph *Thes* vii 1677 and L S give no instance where it means "rush" See Acts xxvii 32 "ropes" (the only other N.T instance).

[4] Exod ii 3, Is xviii 2

[5] Ps cxviii 27, "cords," עבתים, variously interpreted (Gesen 721 b) in ancient and modern times.

[6] Is i. 11.

in a case like the present, afford grounds for rejecting the alleged action as a fiction. It is too original to be treated thus, yet not too original for a great Jewish prophet

But, if historical, why is the "scourge of cords" omitted by the Synoptists? The first answer that suggests itself is "Because in the Synoptic narrative there is no mention of the sheep and oxen that would require them." If we ask why there are no sheep and oxen, the answer might be given "Because, after one or two visits of Jesus to the Temple, He had succeeded in abating the market abuse to such an extent that the sheep and oxen were removed and nothing remained but the doves." If we could believe this, we might explain not only the Synoptic omission of the sheep and oxen in the account of the visit to the final Passover, but also the Johannine omission of all cleansing of the Temple in the final visit. Unquestionably this view presents great difficulties. And in some ways it would be less difficult to believe that Mark had fastened on one abuse—the oppression of the *poor*, who bought doves—to the neglect of other abuses, as to sheep and oxen, which affected only the rich. But in any case the "scourge of cords" does not appear to have been a Johannine invention.

§ 15 *"Doves," "tables," and "money-changers," in all but Luke*[1]

Luke omits these Marcan details, partly perhaps because, at the time when he was writing, the Temple had fallen and details about its service had lost their interest, but partly also because he did not see the force of them. Why this distinction between the "tables" of the money-changers and the "seats[2]" of them that sold doves? Why introduce "money-changers" at all, since selling, not money-changing, was the fault? Why mention "doves" alone, and no other sacrificial victims?

John treats these details as obscure but not out of date. He perhaps regarded them as a useful and enduring protest against the view, not unknown among early Christian teachers,

---

[1] Mk xi 15, Mt xxi. 12, Jn ii 14—16.
[2] SS, in Mk, has "tables...*tables*" for "tables...*seats*"

JESUS VISITS THE TEMPLE

that religion might be made a "way of gain[1]." At all events he intervenes as to each point. As for the "tables" and the "seats" the radical thought was perhaps not about distinctions between tables and stalls or seats but about "sitting." It was unseemly for anyone to "sit" in the Lord's House except by special commission. The true Messiah was to "sit" therein and to purify the sons of Levi[2]. A false Messiah, a representative of Mammon, might also "sit in the temple of God[3]," and claim men's worship. These salesmen and money-changers in their *cathedrai*, as Mark calls their seats, were such representatives. They sat, so to speak, *in cathedra*, exercising the authority of Mammon. John expresses this by the word "sitting," which is to be understood with allusion to the Hebrew sense "sitting [as if with authority][4]."

In the next place, as to the Marcan "money-changers," John explains the meaning by not only using it himself but also adding to it two depreciatory words ("small-change" and "dealers-in-small-change") which suggest that these men made a discreditable gain out of those who came to them to exchange their money for the coin that was exacted by custom for sacrifices in the Temple. The noun, "small-change," is not used in the Greek Bible anywhere but here; but it is frequent in Epictetus in the sense of "pelf" as being the object of the worldly minded, who "refer everything to paltry pelf[5]." Thus John consistently shapes his narrative so as to bring out for Greek readers the base, unspiritual, and God-detested nature of the "merchandise" that Luke was content to term mere "selling." In the Double Tradition of Matthew and Luke Jesus says, "Ye cannot serve God and Mammon[6]." The incompatibility that is conveyed to

---

[1] 1 Tim vi 5 νομιζόντων πορισμὸν εἶναι τὴν εὐσέβειαν.

[2] Mal iii 3

[3] 2 Thess ii. 4 εἰς τὸν ναὸν τοῦ θεοῦ καθίσαι, comp. Ezek. xxviii 2 "I *sit* in the seat of God."

[4] See Exod. xviii 14, Mal. iii. 3 etc.

[5] Epict ii 10 20 εἰ ἐπὶ κερμάτιον πάντα ἀνάγεις Κερμάτιον is very freq. (see iii 2. 8, iii. 5 3 etc), and κέρμα occurs in ii. 10. 14, ii. 10. 19, iv. 3 2, iv. 9. 9.

[6] Mt vi. 24, Lk. xvi 13.

JESUS VISITS THE TEMPLE

Jews in those words is indirectly suggested here in the contrast implied between such sacrifices as ought to be offered to the One God and such sacrifices as were actually offered in the Jewish Temple under the control of the priests, the hierophants of "small change[1]"

§ 16. *What followed after the purification of the Temple*[2]

The Diatessaron describes the departure of Jesus from the Temple, after the purification of it, as follows:—"And when

---

[1] If the κέρματα represent the brass or copper coins of the poor received, and often over-received, by the κολλυβισταί, then the Johannine word (Jn ii. 15) ἐξέχεεν, "poured forth," signifies a retributive "shedding," as it were, of that which the miserly extortioner values as his own blood. It was the blood of the poor and he has to give it back.

[2] Mk xi 18—19 and its parallels are printed above (pp 197—8), but are repeated here for the sake of continuity.

Mk xi 18—25 (R V)	Mt xxi 15—17, 19 b, 20—22, vii 7, vi. 14—15 (R V)	Lk. xix. 47 b—48, xxi 37—8, xvii 5—6, xi 9, 4 (R V)
(18) And the chief priests and the scribes heard it, and sought how they might destroy him, for they feared him, for all the multitude was astonished at his teaching (19) And every evening (*lit.* whenever evening came) he (*some anc auth* they) went forth out of the city. (20) And as they passed by in the morning, they saw the fig-tree withered away from the roots. (21) And Peter calling to remembrance saith unto him, Rabbi, behold, the fig-tree which thou cursedst is withered away (22) And Jesus answering saith un-	(xxi 15) But when the chief priests and the scribes saw the wonderful things that he did, and the children that were crying in the temple and saying, Hosanna to the son of David; they were moved with indignation, (16) And said unto him, Hearest thou what these are saying? And Jesus saith unto them, Yea did ye never read, Out of the mouth of babes and sucklings thou hast perfected praise? (17) And he left them, and went forth out of the city to Bethany, and lodged there (19)..And immediately the fig-tree withered away.	(xix. 47)...But the chief priests and the scribes and the principal men of the people sought to destroy him (48) And they could not find what they might do, for the people all hung upon him, listening. (xxi 37) And every day he was teaching in the temple, and every night he went out, and lodged in the mount that is called [the mount] of Olives. (38) And all the people came early in the morning to him in the temple, to hear him (xvii 5) And the apostles said unto the Lord, Increase our faith.

JESUS VISITS THE TEMPLE

eventide was come, he left all the people, and went outside the city to Bethany, he and his twelve, and he remained there. And all the people, because they knew the place, came to him, and he received them; and them that had need of healing he healed. And on the morning of the next day, when he returned

Mk xi 18—25
(R V) *contd*
to them, Have faith in God
(23) Verily I say unto you, Whosoever shall say unto this mountain, Be thou taken up and cast into the sea; and shall not doubt in his heart, but shall believe that what he saith cometh to pass, he shall have it

(24) Therefore I say unto you, All things whatsoever ye pray and ask for, believe that ye have received them, and ye shall have them
(25) And whensoever ye stand praying, forgive, if ye have aught against any one; that your Father also which is in heaven may forgive you your trespasses [*Many anc auth add ver* 26 But if ye do not forgive, neither will your Father which is in heaven forgive your trespasses.]

Mt xxi 15—17, 19 *b*, 20—22, vii 7, vi 14—15 (R V) *contd*
(20) And when the disciples saw it they marvelled, saying, How did the fig-tree immediately wither away?
(21) And Jesus answered and said unto them, Verily I say unto you, If ye have faith, and doubt not, ye shall not only do what is done to the fig-tree, but even if ye shall say unto this mountain, Be thou taken up and cast into the sea, it shall be done
(22) And all things, whatsoever ye shall ask in prayer, believing, ye shall receive
(vii 7) Ask, and it shall be given you, seek, and ye shall find; knock, and it shall be opened unto you
(vi 14) For if ye forgive men their trespasses, your heavenly Father will also forgive you
(15) But if ye forgive not men their trespasses, neither will your Father forgive your trespasses

Lk xix 47 *b*—48, xxi 37—8, xvii. 5—6, xi. 9, 4 (R V) *contd*
(6) And the Lord said, If ye have faith as a grain of mustard-seed, ye would say unto this sycamine-tree, Be thou rooted up, and be thou planted in the sea, and it would have obeyed you.

(xi. 9) And I say unto you, Ask, and it shall be given you, seek, and ye shall find; knock, and it shall be opened unto you
(4) And forgive us our sins, for we ourselves also forgive every one that is indebted to us...

JESUS VISITS THE TEMPLE

to the city from Bethany, he hungered[1]." It is difficult to trace the sources of these confused traditions about "knowing" the "place" and "receiving." Matthew says, much earlier, that, when Jesus crossed the Lake to Gennesaret, "*the men of that place knew him*"; John, much later, says that Judas "*knew the place*" to which "Jesus oft-times resorted with his disciples", and Luke, describing the concourse of the Five Thousand, says that Jesus "*received them...and them that had need of healing he healed*[2]." The last of these traditions has certainly been utilised by the Diatessaron here And the Diatessaron is instructive as indicating that the accounts of Christ's sojourning near Jerusalem—which the Synoptists confine to days in the last week—may have originally belonged to days in preceding weeks, months, or even years

Mark, after recording the words of Jesus, "Ye have made it [*i.e* the Temple] a den of robbers," says "And the chief priests and the scribes *heard* [*it*][3] and began to seek how they might destroy him." Luke omits "*heard* [*it*]." And it is hardly credible that "the chief priests and the scribes"—to whom Luke adds "the chief [men] of the people"—were all present and all "heard" the words at the moment of utterance More probably they would hear the report about the words, and about Christ's acts in general. Matthew seems to favour this view. At all events he substitutes "seeing" for "hearing" and mentions "the wonderful things that he did," and "the boys crying aloud in the temple" because of them[4].

---

[1] *Diatess* § 32 It arranges the preceding context as follows — 1st, the Purification of the Temple (mostly as Jn), 2nd, the Widow's Mite, 3rd, the Prayers of the Pharisee and the Publican

[2] Mt. xiv. 35, Jn xviii. 2, Lk ix 11

[3] Mk xi 18 ἤκουσαν without an object Lk xix 47 agrees but omits ἤκουσαν

[4] Mt xxi 15—16 Jerome on Hab ii 11 "The stone shall cry out of the wall" (preceded by *ib* 9 "woe unto him that getteth an evil gain for his house") combines Mt xxi 16 and Lk xix 40 as follows "(Mt) Have ye not read that it is written, From the mouths of babes and sucklings thou hast perfected praise? and (Lk) If these should hold their peace the stones will cry out" He adds that "Although most think that this is to be understood as meaning,

JESUS VISITS THE TEMPLE

John does not verbally follow either Mark and Luke in mentioning a purpose to "destroy" Jesus, or Matthew in describing "wonderful things" that draw forth songs of praise, or the Synoptists generally in describing Jesus as going forth from Jerusalem at night. But in fact he suggests all these things. As to the "destroying," Jesus says "Loose, i e destroy, this temple" and it is added "He spake of the temple of his body[1]" It is also added that Nicodemus, "the teacher of Israel," came to Jesus "by night." The reason for choosing night-time we are supposed to guess already, and it is suggested more clearly

'If the Jews hold their peace the Gentiles will confess me,' yet according to a truer interpretation, '.. the stones themselves (lapides ipsi)... will be able to sound forth my greatness.'" Jerome evidently regards the Lucan "stones," in a literal sense, as belonging to the Temple, although Luke regards them as lying on the road, being mentioned by Jesus before He (xix 41) "drew nigh and saw the city." Space does not permit a full comparison of Mt with Lk, but the following conclusions are probable

Matthew has here followed a tradition—followed also by the *Acts of Pilate* (§ 1)—that Hosanna was uttered, not by the Jews, but always by "*the sons*, or *children*, of the Hebrews," meaning the common people or multitude, as distinct from the Pharisees or rulers. This Matthew has misinterpreted as "*little children* of the Hebrews," taking Christ's "babes and sucklings" literally, whereas it meant "simple and illiterate" as distinct from "scribes." Luke followed an earlier tradition that "*the stones*" of the Temple would "cry out" (which, says *Pesach* 57 *a*, they did on four occasions). But he has placed this before Jesus "saw the city," so that he might be regarded as meaning the stones in the road (comp Lk iii 8). It has been suggested (McNeile on Mt xxi 15) that there might be a confusion between Aram "stones" אבניא, and "children" בניא. I have not been able to find an instance of such a confusion nearer than Ps. cxviii. 22 "the *stone* that the builders rejected," Targ "the *youth* . among the sons of Jesse," which appears to be merely paraphrase (*Son* 3594 *c*). But it is antecedently probable that there would be at this point some playing on "*stones*" of the Temple, and the "*stone*" of the corner, and "*builders*" of the people (i e the Sanhedrin) (*Son* 3600 *a*). "Sons of the peoples" (*Joma* 71 *b*) meaning "descendants of Gentiles," might illustrate the interpretation (Jerome above) "the Gentiles will confess me." Comp Mt iii 9 "*stones...children* to Abraham"

[1] Jn ii. 19, 21.

later on, as being "fear of the Jews[1]." Not a single miracle or sign is mentioned as being wrought in or near the Temple. Yet it is said, immediately after the purification of the Temple, "when he was in Jerusalem at the passover, during the feast, many believed on his name, *beholding his signs, which he was [continually] doing*[2]." "His signs" assumes that everyone knew Jesus to be a great worker of signs, although no sign has been hitherto described except the one at Cana. And the same thing is implied by the first words of Nicodemus to Jesus, "Rabbi, we know that thou art a teacher come from God; for no man can do these signs that thou doest except God be with him[3]."

We are not told what these "signs" were, or when or where they were worked, or what impression they produced at the time on those who witnessed them. Why does not John, like Matthew, tell us all this, or something of it? Why does he thus, in his own person, cursorily mention "his signs," leaving it to Nicodemus to emphasize their importance? It is apparently because he himself regards them as of very little importance. Nicodemus, speaking in the plural for "the Pharisees" and "rulers," implies that they are convinced by the signs ("*we know*") that Jesus is "a teacher come from God." But in the Temple the Jews have asked for a special sign ("what sign shewest thou to us?"). And what Nicodemus "knew" did not embolden him to come to Jesus by day. He seems to have meant "We know but dare not confess." Such "knowing" was not an important moral gain.

That this is John's view appears from an expression in the context—unique in the New Testament and very rare in Greek literature—in which he seems to play on the word "*believe*" or "*trust*" so as to disparage the belief or faith of those whose trust in Christ was based on His powers as a wonder-worker and not on His person or character as being that of the Son of

---

[1] Jn iii. 1—2   Comp. xix 38—9 "for fear of the Jews." This applies directly to Joseph alone, but the reader is made to feel that it applies to Nicodemus also

[2] Jn ii. 23.   [3] Jn iii. 2.

(Mark xi. 18—25 (26))

JESUS VISITS THE TEMPLE

God: "Many *trusted in* (lit *into*) *his name,* but Jesus *did not trust himself to them* because he knew all men." Origen discusses the difference between "believing in the name of Jesus" and "believing Jesus," and comes to the conclusion that the former is a rudimentary kind of belief and the latter an advanced one. The former is like that of the two disciples of John the Baptist believing in Christ on the testimony of the Baptist; the latter is of a personal kind due to the direct influence of Christ, like that of Andrew (after he had conversed with Christ) and Peter and Nathanael and Philip[1].

No instance is given in the Thesaurus of the phrase "*I trust myself to you,*" but it might advantageously have given several instances of a kindred phrase of Epictetus, who argues against the notion that a man is bound to reciprocate a "trust" or "confidence" that may be given him by a garrulous fool, or perhaps (in pretence) by an artful informer; because a soldier in disguise "*trusts his own* [*thoughts*] *to you*"—about the Emperor, for example—it does not follow that you are to "*trust your own* [*thoughts*] to him[2]." This antithesis appears, in a homely way, to illustrate John's language and to shew how carefully he distinguishes from one another, at the outset of his Gospel, different kinds of faith, trust, belief, or confidence, although he never actually uses any of these nouns

Mark has on two occasions mentioned scribes from Jerusalem as originating the opposition to Jesus in Galilee. The first of them introduces the scribes as imputing Christ's signs to Beelzebub; the second deals with the importance attached by

---

[1] See *Joh Voc.* **1483**—**7** and Origen *Comm. Joann* x. 28 (Lomm. 1 372) Καὶ τοῦτο δὲ τηρητέον, ὅτι πολλοὶ πιστεύοντες εἰς τὸ ὄνομα αὐτοῦ οὐχ ὡς Ἀνδρέας καὶ Πέτρος καὶ Ναθαναὴλ καὶ Φίλιππος πιστεύουσιν, ἀλλὰ τῇ μαρτυρίᾳ Ἰωάννου πείθονται, λέγοντος Ἰδού, ὁ ἀμνὸς τοῦ θεοῦ ἢ τῷ ὑπ' Ἀνδρέου εὑρεθέντι Χριστῷ, ἢ τῷ εἰπόντι Ἰησοῦ τῷ Φιλίππῳ Ἀκολούθει μοι ἢ τῷ φάσκοντι Φιλίππῳ Ὃν ἔγραψε Μωυσῆς καὶ οἱ προφῆται, εὑρήκαμεν, Ἰησοῦν υἱὸν τοῦ Ἰωσὴφ ἀπὸ Ναζαρέτ. Οὗτοι δὲ ἐπίστευσαν εἰς τὸ ὄνομα αὐτοῦ, θεωροῦντες αὐτοῦ τὰ σημεῖα ἃ ἐποίει· καὶ [?διὰ] σημεῖα πιστεύουσιν, οὐκ εἰς αὐτόν, ἀλλ' εἰς τὸ ὄνομα αὐτοῦ, ὁ Ἰησοῦς οὐκ ἐπίστευσεν ἑαυτὸν αὐτοῖς. The text is obscure and possibly corrupt. Perhaps διά should be inserted before σημεῖα.

[2] Epictet iv 13 6

JESUS VISITS THE TEMPLE

the Pharisees to the washing of hands   Both of these mentions of Jerusalem are omitted by Luke[1]   Yet they give the reader a glimpse into the possibility of an alliance between the influence of the Temple as controlled by the Chief Priests, and the influence of the Law as interpreted by the Pharisees; and the incompatibility between these combined influences and the Spirit of the Son of God   There are advantages in having this set before the reader earlier and more fully

The Fourth Gospel suggests the thought of this incompatibility at the outset by recording a conversation between Jesus and Nicodemus, a Pharisee with good disposition and tendencies, yet with no spiritual conviction, and consequently no courage. He comes to Jesus by night   And he himself represents his fellow-Pharisees as "knowing" that Jesus was "a teacher come from God." Thereby he implies that they are hypocrites in opposing Him.   Neither Nicodemus nor the other Jerusalemites who "believe in the name" of Jesus are regarded as really believing in Him   They trust only in His power to work wonders. Therefore it is said—apparently with a mystical play on the words—that Jesus would not entrust to them that most precious of possessions which is here called "himself[2]"

According to this view, the Dialogue with Nicodemus, like the Dialogue with the Woman of Samaria, even if it does not contain a single sentence that Jesus ever uttered, contains a historical record of His thoughts, and of the conflict between His thoughts and those of the scribes and the chief priests.   The scribes stood for the letter of the Law; Jesus for

---

[1] Mk iii 22 "the scribes that came down from Jerusalem" is parall. to Mt xii 24 "*the Pharisees*" and Lk. xi. 15 "*some of* them," *i e.* of the multitudes   Mk vii. 1—where Matthew also (xv 1) mentions "Jerusalem"—refers to•Christ's journeying in North Palestine which is wholly omitted by Luke.   Comp Jn i 19 "the Jews sent...from Jerusalem priests and Levites," and *ib.* 24 R V. txt "and they had been sent"— R V. marg "and [certain] had been sent"—"from (R V *marg* from among) the Pharisees "

[2] Comp Lk xvi. 12 "Who will entrust to you *your own,*" or "*our own,*" or as Marcion had it (see Tertull Adv. Marc) "*that which is mine?*"   It means the treasure appointed by God for man, the Spirit of Christ, the opposite of the Mammon mentioned in the context

JESUS VISITS THE TEMPLE

the breath of the Spirit of Love. The priests stood for the ritual of the Temple; Jesus stood for Man as being God's true Temple. There was no prospect of peace or truce between these conflicting principles, and John thinks it best to let us know this from the beginning.

§ 17. *"Have faith in God," in Mark*[1]

Mark's meaning appears to be "Have faith, not in man, nor in this visible world and the things of this world, but *in God*." But Matthew omits *"in God"* as superfluous. Luke draws out what he supposes to be its meaning by adding *"as a grain of mustard-seed,"* that is to say, "faith of vital force able to increase what is very small so that it shall become great."

"Have faith (*or,* belief)" expresses in two Greek words what "believe" expresses in one. And the imperative *"believe in God"* occurs in only one passage of the Old Testament, describing a great danger impending on Judah from a hostile league, when Jehoshaphat—encouraged by the prophet who declared that God would fight for them—said "Hear me, O Judah... *believe-firmly in the Lord your God,* so shall ye be firmly-established; *believe his prophets,* so shall ye prosper[2]." An ancient Jewish comment on the words in Exodus that follow the drowning of the Egyptians "They [*i.e.* Israel] *believed in the Lord and in his servant* Moses[3]," quotes these words of Jehoshaphat along with many other texts on "belief" or "faith" but no other instance of the imperative. In the New

---

[1] Mk xi 22 ἔχετε πίστιν θεοῦ, Mt xxi. 21 ἐὰν ἔχητε πίστιν, Lk. xvii 6 εἰ ἔχετε πίστιν ὡς κόκκον σινάπεως. Comp Mt xvii 20 ἐὰν ἔχητε πίστιν ὡς κόκκον σινάπεως after the cure of the demoniac boy (where the parall Mk ix 29 differs, and the parall Lk ix 43 omits all words of Jesus)

[2] 2 Chr xx 20, on which see Gesen 53 *a* comparing Is vii 9 "if ye *believe not firmly* ye will not be *confirmed,*" a play on אמן which in the passive means "confirmed" but in the causative "believe firmly."

[3] Exod xiv 31 (see *Mechilta*) This is immediately followed by the Song of Moses

JESUS VISITS THE TEMPLE

Testament we find one in the Fourth Gospel where Jesus says to His disciples "Let not your heart be troubled. *Believe in God, believe also in me*[1]."

These words of Jesus immediately follow His saying to Peter "The cock shall not crow till thou hast denied me thrice[2]." Mark also (not followed by Matthew) brings in Peter, just before recording the precept "Have faith in God." But Mark represents Peter as speaking about the withered fig-tree. This, if taken literally, leads us quite away from the thought in John. But if it was originally metaphorical it leaves us free to suppose that John is intervening to explain the thought at the bottom of the Marcan original—the thought that induced Luke here to omit the episode of the fig-tree and to connect the uprooting of a sycamine-tree with the forgiveness of sins[3].

Let us assume the fig-tree to represent, in the original tradition underlying Mark, the power of Mammon ruling in the visible Temple, and let us suppose the abuses of the Temple to have been suddenly, though only temporarily, suppressed by Jesus and His followers. It would be quite natural that such a momentary triumph—really one of a startling character as Origen says—should be taken by the more sanguine among Christ's disciples as a pledge of speedy success for all their Master's plans and for the establishment of the Kingdom of God on earth. Against such anticipations Jesus—not being Himself certain of the how and the when—might naturally warn them They were too definite in their belief. They had faith in the present, or in the morrow, or in the near future

---

[1] Jn xiv 1, on which see *Joh Gr* 2236—40 And to the reasons there given for rendering the ambiguous πιστεύετε imperatively add the paraphrase of Nonnus, ἀλλὰ θεῷ καὶ ἐμοὶ πιστεύσατε

[2] Jn xiii 38.

[3] Lk xvii 6 This does not mention Peter Nor does Lk xvii 5 "and *the apostles* said unto the Lord, Increase our faith" But if we go back to Lk xvii 4 about forgiving seven times a day, we find that it is parall to Mt xviii 21 foll "*Peter* said to him...." This indicates that the later Evangelists, as well as Mark, are dealing with Petrine metaphor about the eradication of sin by forgiveness in the narrative (in Mk-Mt) or parable (in Lk) about a fig-tree

JESUS VISITS THE TEMPLE

Perhaps also they had faith in some miraculous intervention, such as saved Israel under Moses at the Red Sea, and Judah under Jehoshaphat in the wilderness of Tekoah. The sub-Marcan tradition perhaps meant "You are not to have faith in any such things, but only in God Himself"

If this was the meaning, it is obscurely expressed. The deviations of Matthew and Luke from it point to a sense of its obscurity. And Mark's context seems to contain an attempt at explanation: "All things soever that ye pray for and ask, believe that ye [have] received them and they shall be [done] for you[1]." But this might well seem to make the text more difficult than ever   For this promise can only be true, and only ought to be true, with the proviso that men pray for that which is according to the will of a righteous God. Without such a caution, and read without attention to the curious past tense ("believe that *ye* [*have*] *received*") the words encourage superstition of the worst kind

Luke omits these words of Mark. This he might do all the more safely because elsewhere, when he represents Jesus as saying "Ask, and it shall be given unto you," it is preceded, at a short interval, by the Lord's Prayer, in which the first things prayed for are the hallowing of God's name and the coming of His Kingdom. This might be thought a sufficient guarantee that importunate prayer was discouraged; yet in the interval Luke gives a parable about a man asking a friend for three loaves in the dead of night to entertain an unexpected guest, and prevailing by mere persistence; and elsewhere another parable about an unjust judge who redresses a wrong done to a widow simply to avoid being wearied by her entreaties[2]

These traditions about importunate prayer, peculiar to Luke, lead us on from the thought of the Marcan "faith, or, belief, in God" to the thought of the Marcan condition for obtaining things prayed for ("believe that ye have received

---

[1] Mk xi. 24

[2] Lk. xi. 9 "Ask, and it shall be given unto you", xi 1—4 contains the Lord's Prayer, xi 5—8 describes the importunate friend. Lk. xviii 1—8 describes the importunate widow

them"). They make us reflect on Origen's observation that there is "no vestige" in Mark of anything like what is meant by the Lord's Prayer[1] When Matthew introduces the Lord's Prayer he prefixes to it a saying of Jesus which, according to our English Versions, forbids "vain repetitions." Why does Luke omit this? Did he believe that it was erroneously expressed? And did he consequently insert his traditions about the importunate friend and the widow to shew that all "repetitions" in prayer were not forbidden by Jesus? It will be convenient to touch on this point in considering the next Marcan phrase "believe that ye [have] received."

§ 18. *"Believe that what he saith is coming to pass," and "Believe that ye [have] received," in Mark*[2]

In Mark, there are two statements of the condition for success in prayer. The first is that a man should "*believe that what he saith is coming to pass.*" The second is "All things whatsoever ye pray for and ask, *believe that ye [have] received* [*them*], and they shall be [done] for you" A form of the second is reproduced in the parallel Matthew, but with a transposition of the "*receiving*" that makes the saying easier and leaves the object of the "believing" doubtful: "Whatsoever ye shall ask in prayer, *believing* [?], *ye shall receive.*" Both of these are omitted by Luke. Luke has nothing of the nature of a promise of the fulfilment of prayer except the unconditional "Ask, and it shall be given you." This Luke has in common with Matthew, and in a parallel to a passage in Matthew's Sermon on the Mount, where Matthew—after a warning against the wrong kind of prayer and a statement of the right kind of prayer—returns abruptly to the subject of "asking" and

---

[1] Orig. *De Orat. Libell.* § 18. Ζητήσαντες δὲ καὶ παρὰ τῷ Μάρκῳ μήποτε λανθάνῃ ἡμᾶς ἡ τοιαύτη ἰσοδυναμοῦσα ἀναγεγραμμένη, οὐδ' ἴχνος ἐγκείμενον προσευχῆς εὕρομεν.

[2] Mk xi. 23—4   Mt. xxi. 22   Lk. om

ὃς ἂν...πιστεύῃ ὅτι   πάντα ὅσα ἂν αἰτή-
ὃ λαλεῖ γίνεται, ἔσται   σητε ἐν τῇ προσευχῇ
αὐτῷ...πάντα   ὅσα   πιστεύοντες λήμψεσθε
προσεύχεσθε   καὶ   αἰ-
τεῖσθε, πιστεύετε ὅτι
ἐλάβετε, καὶ ἔσται ὑμῖν.

JESUS VISITS THE TEMPLE

"receiving" at the close of a collection of miscellaneous precepts, mostly negative, as will be seen below:—

Mt. vi. 5 foll   Lk. om.
[*Against praying and fasting amiss*]

(5) And when ye pray, ye shall not be as the hypocrites...

(7) And in praying use not vain repetitions, as the Gentiles do, for they think that they shall be heard for their much speaking...

Mt vi. 9—13   Lk. xi. 1—4
[*The Lord's Prayer*]

(9) After this manner therefore pray ye, Our Father.
(13) . into temptation, but deliver us from the evil [one].

(1) And it came to pass... teach us to pray, even as John also taught his disciples.
(2) And he said unto them, When ye pray, say Father...
(4) ... into temptation.

Mt. vi 14—15   Lk. om.
[*About the duty of forgiving*]

(14) For if ye forgive[1]..
(15) But if ye forgive not....

Mt. vi. 16—18   Lk. om.
[*About the wrong and the right kind of fasting*]

Mt. vi. 19—34   Lk xii. with passages from xi and xvi.
[*Against avarice, evil desire, and worldly anxiety*]

Mt. vii. 1—5   Lk. vi. 37—8, 41—2
[*Against judging others*]

Mt. vii 6 foll.   Lk xi. 8 foll.
[*About asking*]

(6) Give not that which is holy unto the dogs.. lest they.. turn and rend you.
(7) *Ask, and it shall be given you, seek, and ye shall find.*...

(After the Lord's Prayer and the parable of the importunate borrower of loaves)
(8) . he will arise and give him as many as he needeth.
(9) And I say unto you *Ask, and it shall be given you, seek, and ye shall find* . .

---

[1] Comp Mk xi 25 "Forgive...that also your Father in heaven may forgive you...."

JESUS VISITS THE TEMPLE

This final precept, coming in Matthew after many other precepts addressed to Christ's disciples alone[1], and in Luke after the disciples have received from Him the Lord's Prayer, clearly means "Ask *thus*," "Ask, *as my disciples*," or "Ask, *in the spirit of the prayer that I have given you*." Yet, taken by itself, it might encourage nominal Christians to ask in a spirit of selfishness for whatever they liked; and there was some danger that Luke's peculiar parables about the success of importunate petitioners might have the same effect.

It might be urged that the prohibition in Matthew "*Use not vain repetitions*" would prevent such an abuse of prayer[2].

---

[1] "Alone," that is, not to the "multitudes" below, who do not ascend the mountain—because, as Origen and Jerome concur in saying (on Mt v. 1), "turbae ascendere non valent," (Lomm III 74) εἰς τὸ ὄρος ...ἔνθα οὐχ οἷοί τε ἦσαν οἱ ὄχλοι γενέσθαι

[2] Mt vi 7 προσευχόμενοι δὲ μὴ βατταλογήσητε, D βλαττολογησηται, d "vana loquimini," Latt codd "multum loqui" [but in Lk. xi 2 D has βαττολογειτε, d "multum loqui"] Curet. "be babbling" But SS has "saying *idle* [*things*] *battâlâthâ*" to render βατταλογεῖν. *Battâlâ* or *battâlâthâ* occurs again in Curet and SS of Mt xii. 36 "every *idle* word" to render Gk ἀργόν, and *Thes Syr.* 509 foll gives abundant instances of its use to represent ἀργόν, καταργέω etc

In Greek literature, βατταλογέω can hardly be said to exist. No instance of it is given before Simplicius (in 6th century) (in *Comm Epict Ench* 37, Schweig p 340, where it is spelt βαττολογέω) Origen spells the word βαττολόγεω as if from λέγω, and he says (*De Orat* § 21) that we are guilty of *battologia* when we pray in a hap-hazard and worldly fashion for worldly things This suits neither etymology nor Matthew's context

If it were derived from the Hebrew and Aramaic *bâtal* in the sense of "cease," "intermit," it might mean "slacken," in the sense of slackening one's thoughts in prayer, as the *Aboth* iv 14 warns us against "*slackening*, (or *idling*) from the Law" Also Levy 1 212 a gives forms of *bâtal* as meaning "futile," "futility" etc. According to Steph *Thes* (II 195—6, which perhaps a little exaggerates) Hesych identifies βαττολογεῖν with βατταρίζειν Now βατταρίζειν is used by Cicero (*ad Att* vi 5) to mean "talk incoherently" This suggests that two causes may have been at work in creating and interpreting Matthew's tradition Hebrew or Aramaic influence would suggest the meaning "worthless stuff," Greek influence would suggest "incoherent stammering" Jesus, before giving His disciples a very short prayer, may have warned them against using it, or any

JESUS VISITS THE TEMPLE

But Matthew's peculiar word forbidding the abuse (*battalogein*) is of doubtful meaning according as one emphasizes "*vain*" or "*repetition*." It may forbid (1) prayer that is idle, futile, listless babbling, or (2) prayer that is earnest, intense, reiteration of attempts to "weary" the Supreme ("weary" is the Horatian word)[1] into conformity with our desires. Matthew may have taken one view of the word, Luke another. Luke nowhere inserts a prohibition of *battalogia*. Luke also joins Mark elsewhere in a saying that condemns the scribes for "making long prayers in pretence," where the parallel Matthew omits the sentence that contains this accusation[2]. Possibly therefore Matthew regarded Christ's precept as meaning, by implication, "Pray not with slackness, or intermission," "Pray without intermission."

If this was at the bottom of Christ's precept we may infer that its essential meaning was carried on by Paul in his precept to the Thessalonians "Pray without ceasing," about which Origen frankly confesses that once, when he read it, he asked how it could possibly be fulfilled; and discussing it in several passages, he concludes that a spiritual rather than a temporal "ceasing" is contemplated, and that the whole of the Christian's life, even eating, drinking, and sleeping, may be regarded as a stream of prayer, offered to God's glory[3].

If Paul's precept "pray without *ceasing* (or, *intermission*)" is a vernacular Greek rendering of the Aramaic Greek in Matthew "when ye pray, do not *intermit*, or *remit*, or utter *loose futilities*," this might be expressed positively in literary Greek by a word

---

prayer, as a mere string of incantations, repeated from morning till evening like (1 K xviii 26) "O Baal, hear us!"

[1] Hor *Odes*, I ii 26

[2] Mk xii. 40, Lk xx 47, omitted by Mt after Mt xxiii 7 which is parall to Mk xii 38—9

[3] 1 Thess v 17, Orig *Hom Sam* 1 9 (Lomm xi 304—5), "Ego cum legerem aliquando apud Apostolum quod dixit '*sine intermissione orate*,' quaerebam si praeceptum hoc possibile esset impleri," comp *ib* 381 (on Ps 1 2 "in his law doth he meditate day and night") and *De Orat* § 12, § 22 "Let the whole of our prayerful life say *without ceasing*, 'Our Father that is in heaven'"

JESUS VISITS THE TEMPLE

that signifies "tensely" or "intensely" as opposed to "loosely," applied to prayer by Luke in the Acts and perhaps—but the passage is doubtful—in his Gospel[1]. This last doubtful passage, if it is genuine, corresponds to the context of one in Mark and Matthew where Jesus "prayed saying the same words"; and, if it is not genuine, it leaves a blank in Luke indicating that he did not accept any tradition at all to the effect that Jesus repeated a prayer or uttered a prayer with new intensity. This adds one more to many passages shewing incompleteness in Mark, and divergence between Matthew and Luke, as to Christ's doctrine of prayer We have now to consider how, if at all, John intervenes.

§ 19. *Johannine Intervention*

The Johannine intervention is in part dramatic Jesus Himself thrice addresses the Father in language of prayer or of thanksgiving for answered prayer In the first instance, Jesus says, at the grave of Lazarus, "Father, I thank thee that *thou heardest me*; and I knew that thou hearest me always[2]." This accords with Origen's view that Jesus regards life itself as a stream of unceasing prayer; for He has not prayed aloud, but it is implied that He has prayed and that the Father heard Him Also it accords with the tradition peculiar to Mark "Believe that ye [*have*] *received*." Jesus thanks God for something not future but past, "*thou heardest me*." In the second instance, after Jesus has enunciated the doctrine of the grain of wheat and of life through death, He exclaims, "Now is my soul troubled, and what shall I say? [Shall I say] *Father, save me from this hour?* [Nay], but for this cause came I, unto this hour. Father, glorify thy name[3]." The previous prayer was uttered in silence. This is uttered aloud, in one brief phrase

The next is a very long prayer rivalling in length the Old Testament prayers of Daniel and Nehemiah and justifying the wise saying of R. Eliezer, who said that there was a time for long

---

[1] Acts xii 5 ἐκτενῶς, comp *ib* xxvi. 7 ἐκτενείᾳ, and Lk xxii. 44 [[ἐκτενέστερον]].
[2] Jn xi. 41—2.   [3] Jn xii. 27—8.

JESUS VISITS THE TEMPLE

prayers as well as for short ones[1]. It is a prayer of the Son to the Father that the disciples may be one as the Father and the Son are one, and may be kept from evil and sanctified and perfected in the divine unity. There is no mention of sin, as there is in the Synoptic traditions about prayer, but it is implied in the words "that thou shouldest keep them from the evil [one][2]"

In this long prayer there is no mention of any promise of fulfilment in reply to that asking which Mark connects with prayer ("whatsoever ye pray for and *ask*"). Nor does it occur in the earlier part of the Fourth Gospel, for the promise cannot be given till Judas has gone out from the disciples Then and not till then does Jesus say to them, after predicting His own departure, "By this shall all men know that ye are my disciples if ye have love one to another," and, a little afterwards, "He that believeth on me, the works that I do shall he do also, and greater works than these shall he do, because I go unto the Father. And *whatsoever ye shall ask in my name, that will I do*... If ye shall ask [me] anything in my name I will do it[3]."

The "greater works" are manifestly the works of the Gospel. They imply the saving of souls and the forgiving of sins[4]. Mark connects the forgiving of sins with the moral of the withering of the fig-tree. But it is manifest that "works," in John, do not point to such a material miracle. It is also manifest that whatever the disciples ask in Christ's "name" is supposed to be asked (so to speak) in His voice, or person, as is implied also in the words, "*If ye abide in me and my words abide in you*, ask whatsoever ye will and it shall be done unto you"; and this, in substance, is reiterated later on[5]. These passages clear away the obscurity of the Marcan tradition about "believing" that one

---

[1] See *Mechilt* on Exod xiv 15, and xv 25, Wu pp. 93 and 148—9. The prayers framed by ancient Rabbis for very special occasions are called (*Berach. Mishn* iv 2 and 5) "short."

[2] Jn xvii 15   [3] Jn xiii 35, xiv. 12—14.

[4] Not that works of healing would be excluded, but they would not be characterized as "greater works" in such a context

[5] Jn xv 7, comp. *ib* 16, and xvi 23, 24, 26. The same doctrine is repeated in 1 Jn iii. 22, v. 14 See *Joh. Gr.* 2536 on αἰτοῦμαι, 2630 *a*—*i* on ἐρωτάω

JESUS VISITS THE TEMPLE

"has received." It was Mark's way of expressing an intense belief in a Supreme and Righteous Will, of whom the Jews used to say "He spake and *it was done.*" The disciples of Christ were to pray for such things alone as were in accordance with that Will What they prayed for in that faith would in some way (though not perhaps in any way exactly conceived by them) be ultimately accomplished[1].

§ 20. *"Whensoever ye stand praying,"* in *Mark*[2]

The Greek *stēkein* here used for stand is not alleged in the Thesaurus to occur earlier than this passage of Mark[3]. In LXX it occurs thrice (always with various readings) to represent severally the Hebrew "stand still," "rest firmly," and "stand[4]." Paul uses it in military metaphor as of soldiers on guard "Watch ye, *stand* in the faith, *quit you like men*[5], be strong," adding however "Let all that ye do be done in love," as if to suggest that "love" is the main part of the soldier's panoply. In the Epistle to the Ephesians ("stand therefore") the Greek literary imperative is used[6]. But in the earlier Epistles *stēkein* occurs several times and always probably with a suggestion of standing fast against an enemy and for the cause of Christ[7].

---

[1] It is implied in 2 Cor. xii 8 that prayer also taught the person praying to shape his will to God's will Comp Mk x. 30 "with persecutions" (not in parall. Mt -Lk) and Jn xvi 33 "in the world ye [must] have tribulation," both of which strike at the notion that prayer could secure a reward "after the flesh "

[2] Mk xi. 25 ὅταν στήκετε προσευχόμενοι, ἀφίετε εἴ τι ἔχετε κατά τινος

[3] See, however, H. van Herwerden's *Lexicon Suppletorium* p 759, quoting a pagan inscription ὅς ποτε...ἔστανεν (=ἔστησεν) Ἑρμῆν, νῦν στήκω (=ἕστηκα)

[4] Exod. xiv. 13 A στήκετε (B στῆτε) יצב hithp , Judg. xvi 26 (of a house *resting* (כון ni.) on pillars) B στήκει (A ἐπεστήρικτο), I K viii 11 "the priests were not able to *stand* (עמד) (B στήκειν, A στῆναι) to minister."

[5] 1 Cor xvi 13 "Quit you like men (ἀνδρίζεσθε)," comp 1 S iv 9, 2 S. x 12, encouragement before battle

[6] Eph vi 14 στῆτε οὖν followed by the description of the Christian's armour.

[7] Gal. v. 1 τῇ ἐλευθερίᾳ στήκετε .. implies a conflict, and Phil. 1 27 ὅτι στήκετε ἐν ἑνὶ πνεύματι is followed by a mention of "adver-

JESUS VISITS THE TEMPLE

The Pauline usage points to the conclusion that the Marcan tradition may be based on some early tradition about "standing" not understood by Matthew and Luke. It leads us to seek some Biblical precedent bearing on "standing" during prayer. The earliest is one about Abraham, "But *Abraham stood yet before the Lord*[1]." Here both Onkelos and the Jerusalem Targum paraphrase "stood" as "ministered in prayer," and the context implies intercessional prayer[2] "*Stand and pray*," especially when expressed by a Jew through the Greek *stēkein*, might mean prayers not necessarily uttered for oneself, but often for others—such prayers as Paul and (doubtless) all the Apostles habitually used for those whom they had converted or hoped to convert[3].

A prayer of this kind seems indicated here, by the Marcan context about the Temple as being a den of robbers, and about the withering of the fig-tree and the uprooting of "this mountain" The Apostles are being taught to pray for the Church and for the souls of men. And the words "stand praying" suggest not only the Jewish custom of standing for prayer, but also the precedent of Abraham—not indeed standing at any visible altar, but interceding, with an offering of prayer and praise, between Sodom and "the Judge of all the world" who is not exempt from the necessity that He must "do right[4]."

Matthew and Luke have omitted this ancient allusion.

---

saries", Phil iv 1 στήκετε ἐν κυρίῳ is followed by a warning against discord, and 1 Thess iii 8 ἐὰν ὑμεῖς στήκετε ἐν κυρίῳ is followed at some distance by a metaphor of the Christian's armour (v 8) But 2 Thess ii 15 is of the nature of a mannerism, without any special connection

[1] Gen. xviii 22

[2] Gen xviii 22 Onk "And Abraham yet *ministered in prayer* before the Lord," Jer Targ "And Abraham now besought mercy for Lot and *ministered in prayer* before the Lord "

[3] See *Hor Heb* on Mt vi 5 and Gesen 763 on עמד meaning standing before Jehovah for intercession Gen xix 27, Deut. iv 10, Jerem. xv 1, xviii 20 etc Comp Heb x 11 "every priest... *standeth* day by day.. offering the same sacrifices," Deut x 8 "to *stand* before the Lord to minister unto him " (comp. *ib* xviii 7).

[4] Gen xviii. 25 "shall not the Judge of all the earth do right?"

JESUS VISITS THE TEMPLE

Not that they were ignorant of the technical Jewish use of *'stand,"* but perhaps they wished to avoid it as unintelligible to Gentiles or as implying a Jewish formalism. At all events Matthew elsewhere describes formal Pharisees who love to pray "standing" in the synagogues[1]. Luke, too, describes both a Publican and a Pharisee as going up to the Temple to pray, and both as *"standing"*—though with a difference[2] Neither Matthew nor Luke, however, uses the strong Marcan word[3].

---

[1] Mt. vi 5

[2] Lk xviii. 11 ὁ Φαρισαῖος σταθείς...ib. 13 ὁ δὲ τελώνης μακρόθεν ἑστώς The former participle perhaps implies more formality than the latter. The sinner, who feels himself to be "far off," does not "take up his stand" If so, μακρόθεν emphasizes the distinction

[3] It should be added that Matthew has a tradition that verbally resembles the one in Mark, as follows (v 23—4) "If therefore thou art offering thy gift at the altar, and there rememberest that thy brother *hath aught against thee* (ἔχει τι κατὰ σοῦ), leave (ἄφες) there thy gift before the altar, and go thy way, first be reconciled to thy brother, and then come and offer thy gift" Ἀφίετε in Mark (xi. 25 ἀφίετε εἴ τι ἔχετε κατά τινος) means "leave," "let go," or "remit," and ἔχετέ τι κατά τινος means "*have aught against some one*" It has been shewn (*From Letter* 1066 and *Son* 3353 (iv) *g*) that ἀφίημι is adopted into late Hebrew and ambiguous, so that ἄφες might be used in Aramaic to mean "*let it be,*" or "*give it up,*" in more than one sense

Jerome says about Mt v 23 "Non dixit, Si tu habes aliquid adversus fratrem tuum, sed si frater tuus habet aliquid adversum te—ut durior reconciliationis tibi imponatur necessitas" Prof Burkitt says that Aphraates quotes twice "that *against thy brother thou hast aught of enmity*" This raises the question of the relation between Mt and Mk in their several traditions about ἄφεσις Not improbably Mark's was the earlier, dealing with the question "If thou hast anything against thy brother," Matthew's a later and supplementary one dealing with the question "If thy brother hath anything against thee" Jesus, in His doctrine, was mainly occupied in teaching His disciples how to forgive, not how to be forgiven

Mark may have regarded the precept as meaning "When you are standing and on the point of offering up the sacrifice of prayer, *give up all angry thought* or desire of vengeance against your neighbour." But another Evangelist might add words to explain that the "standing" was as it were before an altar, and that the prayer was of the nature of a "gift" or "offering" on the altar, and that *the offering must be*

JESUS VISITS THE TEMPLE

Possibly John thought that the word ought to have a place in the Christian vocabulary as representing the erect, active, and intercessory attitude of Christian prayer. At all events the word is attributed to John the Baptist testifying about Jesus, "In the midst of you *there standeth* one whom ye know not...the latchet of whose shoe I am not worthy to unloose[1]" Now the next sentence of the Baptist's testimony is "Behold, *the Lamb of God, that taketh away the sin of the world*[2]." The thought is in itself not unnatural, that the Evangelist sees a connection between this strong word for "*standing*" as applied to a priest or intercessor, and the sacrificial "*lamb*." And this

---

"*given up*" (i.e. "desisted from") till the evil thought against one's neighbour was banished. Then Matthew may have paraphrased the latter part as implying a departure from the altar to the neighbour (who is presumed to be the injured party) for the purpose of reconciliation.

Hor Heb. (on Mt v. 24) puts the argument against the literal interpretation thus.—The offended brother might perhaps be absent in the furthest parts of the land of Israel. The argument for it he puts thus.—It was the custom to defer private sacrifices to the feast next following, and "all the Israelites were present at the feasts, and any brother against whom one had sinned was not then far from the altar."

But even if the brother was "not far," he would be busy with his own sacrifices, and hardly at leisure to hear fully and satisfactorily what the offender had to say. And besides, what if the offended brother refused unreasonably to be reconciled? Was the offerer still to "leave there the gift before the altar"?

Wetstein (on Mt.) quotes *Pesach* iii. 7 on the question "What is an Israelite to do, if he suddenly recollects, when on the point of some important business, e.g. the circumcision of his son, that he has not destroyed the leaven in his house?" The answer is, "Let him return and do it, if possible. If not, *let him destroy it in his heart.*" In this spirit, the precept "be reconciled" might inculcate reconciliation, at once in will and intention, and as soon as possible in act and material compensation.

Delitzsch in Mt. v. 23 gives the Heb. as נגד יש "there is against." But Wetst. quotes *Koheleth* iv. 13, *Schir R.* i. 4 על יש and so Heb Clem.) I can find nothing in Levy.

[1] Jn i. 26—7. Two of the best MSS (BL) have στήκει.
[2] Jn i. 29.

JESUS VISITS THE TEMPLE

is confirmed by Revelation, which introduces the Lamb in this attitude: "I saw in the midst of the throne and of the four living creatures, and in the midst of the elders, a *Lamb standing, as though it had been slain*...[1]." Origen, when quoting the Johannine "*there standeth*," habitually uses the ordinary word for "standing," not the Marcan one. He takes the Johannine "standing in the midst" as signifying the divine and stedfast influence of the Word of Life in the midst of the Universe and extending through the whole of it[2]. But the incorrectness of his reading invalidates his interpretation. A fair case appears to be made out for the conclusion that John revived the Marcan and Pauline word, discarded by most early Christian writers[3], in order to represent the intercessory attitude of Jesus, revealed as the Lamb of God to the last of the prophets of Israel[4]

---

[1] Rev. v. 6 "standing (ἑστηκός)." Στήκω could not be expected, as it does not occur in N T. except in Paul, Mark, and John. In Mk iii. 31 ἔξω στήκοντες—where most MSS have στάντες or ἑστηκότες or ἑστῶτες—there is perhaps a suggestion of the meaning "they [*resolutely*] stood outside," as being outside the circle of the disciples (see below, p 629, n 2)

[2] Origen *ad loc.* (Lomm. 1 234) προηγουμένως μὲν οὖν ἕστηκεν ὁ πατήρ...ἕστηκε δὲ καὶ ὁ Λόγος αὐτοῦ ἀεὶ ἐν τῷ σώζειν. He quotes Jn 1 26 very frequently, but I have not found him reading στήκειν except in *Cels.* ii. 9 (*Cels* v 12 has ἕστηκεν)

[3] Goodspeed does not contain στήκω.

[4] It must be admitted, however, that the last part of the Marcan precept passes into the region of congregational prayer ("forgive us our trespasses") as distinct from intercessory prayer ("forgive all sinners their trespasses"). Compare the mixture of traditions at the end of the Way of Light in Barnabas § 19 "Thou shalt utterly hate the evil one. Thou shalt judge justly. Thou shalt not make schism, but shalt make peace (εἰρηνεύσεις) by bringing together contending [parties] (μαχομενους συναγαγών) Thou shalt make confession over (ἐπὶ) thy sins. *Thou shalt not draw near* (προσήξεις) *to prayer with* (ἐν) *an evil conscience*" The *Didachè*, § 4, in the corresponding section on the Way of Life, after some clauses similar to these, ends thus: "*In the Church* (ἐν ἐκκλησίᾳ) shalt thou confess thy transgressions (παραπτώματα), and *thou shalt not approach* (προσελεύσῃ) *to thy prayer with* (ἐν) *an evil conscience*." Later on the *Didachè* has § 14 "On the Lord's Day [the day] of the Lord, being gathered together, break bread and give thanks (εὐχαριστήσατε)

JESUS VISITS THE TEMPLE

having before confessed your sins *that your sacrifice may be pure* · But as for every one that holds to his quarrel (πᾶς δὲ ἔχων τὴν ἀμφιβολίαν) with his neighbour (ἑταίρου) let him not come together with you, until they be reconciled, *that your sacrifice be not made common* (κοινωθῇ). For this [sacrifice] is that which is spoken of by the Lord *In every place and time* (χρόνῳ) *to offer* (προσφέρειν) *to me sacrifice*" (comp Mal 1 11).

These passages shew that at an early period there might be a transference to the Christian Eucharist, and to Christian Prayer, of language derived from the sacrificial altar in the Jewish Temple.

CHAPTER VI

JESUS "WALKING" IN THE TEMPLE

[Mark xi. 27—xii. 44]

§ 1. *John on the "walking" of Jesus*[1]

THE "walking" of Jesus mentioned here by Mark alone is expressed as "teaching" and as "teaching and preaching the

---

[1] Mk xi 27—33 (R V)

Mt xxi 23—7 (R V)

Lk xx 1—8 (R V)

(27) And they come again to Jerusalem and as he was walking in the temple, there come to him the chief priests, and the scribes, and the elders,
(28) And they said unto him, By what authority doest thou these things? or who gave thee his authority to do these things?
(29) And Jesus said unto them, I will ask of you one question (*lit* word), and answer me, and I will tell you by what authority I do these things
(30) The baptism of John, was it from heaven, or from men? answer me
(31) And they reasoned with them-

(23) And when he was come into the temple, the chief priests and the elders of the people came unto him as he was teaching, and said, By what authority doest thou these things? and who gave thee this authority?
(24) And Jesus answered and said unto them, I also will ask you one question (*lit* word), which if ye tell me, I likewise will tell you by what authority I do these things
(25) The baptism of John, whence was it? from heaven or from men? And they reasoned with themselves, saying, If we shall say, From heaven, he will say unto us, Why then

(1) And it came to pass, on one of the days, as he was teaching the people in the temple, and preaching the gospel, there came upon him the chief priests and the scribes with the elders,
(2) And they spake, saying unto him, Tell us By what authority doest thou these things? or who is he that gave thee this authority?
(3) And he answered and said unto them, I also will ask you a question (*lit* word), and tell me.
(4) The baptism of John, was it from heaven, or from men?
(5) And they reasoned with themselves, saying, If we

JESUS "WALKING" IN THE TEMPLE

gospel," severally, by the parallel Matthew and Luke[1]. It has been shewn in *Proclamation* that Luke nowhere describes Jesus as "walking," and that he may have had objections to the word because of its Greek associations, but that John emphasizes what Luke omits and draws out of the word mystical meanings rooted in Hebrew thought[2]. At the same time attention was called to a passage in *Notes*, discussing the Hebrew conception of what may be called, not the "immanence," but the "inambulance," of God[3]. This is based on the Promise in Leviticus "I will set my tabernacle among you...and *I will walk to and fro among you*, and will be your God, and ye shall be my people," where, as a substitute for "walk to and fro," Onkelos has

Mk xi. 27—33 (R.V.) *contd.*	Mt. xxi. 23—7 (R.V.) *contd.*	Lk. xx 1—8 (R V.) *contd.*
selves, saying, If we shall say, From heaven, he will say, Why then did ye not believe him? (32) But should we say, From men— (*or*, But shall we say, From men?) they feared the people for all verily held John to be a prophet (*or*, for all held John to be a prophet indeed) (33) And they answered Jesus and say, We know not And Jesus saith unto them, Neither tell I you by what authority I do these things	did ye not believe him? (26) But if we shall say, From men; we fear the multitude, for all hold John as a prophet (27) And they answered Jesus, and said, We know not He also said unto them, Neither tell I you by what authority I do these things	shall say, From heaven; he will say, Why did ye not believe him? (6) But if we shall say, From men, all the people will stone us for they be persuaded that John was a prophet. (7) And they answered, that they knew not whence [it was] (8) And Jesus said unto them, Neither tell I you by what authority I do these things
[1] Mk xi 27 Καὶ ἔρχονται πάλιν εἰς Ἱεροσόλυμα Καὶ ἐν τῷ ἱερῷ περιπατοῦντος αὐτοῦ ἔρχονται πρὸς αὐτὸν οἱ ἀρχιερεῖς καὶ οἱ γραμματεῖς καὶ οἱ πρεσβύτεροι...	Mt xxi 23 *a* Καὶ ἐλθόντος αὐτοῦ εἰς τὸ ἱερὸν προσῆλθαν αὐτῷ διδάσκοντι οἱ ἀρχιερεῖς καὶ οἱ πρεσβύτεροι τοῦ λαοῦ...	Lk xx 1 Καὶ ἐγένετο ἐν μιᾷ τῶν ἡμερῶν διδάσκοντος αὐτοῦ τὸν λαὸν ἐν τῷ ἱερῷ καὶ εὐαγγελιζομένου ἐπέστησαν οἱ ἀρχιερεῖς καὶ οἱ γραμματεῖς σὺν τοῖς πρεσβυτέροις.

[2] *Proclam.* pp. 13—17.

[3] See Origen *Hom. Genes.* i 13 (Lomm viii. 122) "in hoc non solum inhabitat Deus sed etiam *inambulat.*"

JESUS "WALKING" IN THE TEMPLE

"I will make my Shechinah to dwell" and the Jerusalem Targum "I will make the glory of my Shechinah to dwell[1]" Paul briefly summarizes this promise: "We are a sanctuary of the living God: even as God said, *I will dwell in them and walk in them*, and I will be their God, and they shall be my people[2]" Rashi says that "set my tabernacle" refers to "the House of the Sanctuary," and that "I will walk among you" refers to "walking in Paradise," where Israelites will walk—not fearing and "hiding themselves" from God like Adam and Eve[3]. But in ancient Jewish tradition the Targums indicate that "walking" was paraphrased as little more than a repetition of "dwelling," and the Indices to the Talmuds and Midrash contain few or no references to the Levitical "walking[4]."

The only reference to it that I have found is one in the Midrash on Lamentations which adds the Levitical promise to the long list of divine promises that will *not* be fulfilled if Israel is faithless. Thus the conception of God as ceasing to "walk" in Israel would be parallel to the conception of God's heavenly "tabernacle," or Shechinah, as gradually withdrawing itself from the Temple Of this there were recognised in Jewish tradition ten stages[5].

In John, we find a somewhat different conception. He first describes the Logos as making His "tabernacle" among men[6]. Then He is described thrice as "walking" (besides walking

---

[1] See *Notes* 2998 (xxviii) *f* foll quoting Lev xxvi. 11—12 where LXX has ἐμπεριπατήσω ἐν ὑμῖν, but ἐν μέσῳ ὑμῶν would be a more literal rendering of בתוככם.

[2] 2 Cor. vi 16 "I will dwell in them," ἐνοικήσω ἐν αὐτοῖς LXX has διαθήκην, for σκηνήν (which is read by F)

[3] Gen iii 8

[4] The ref to Lev xxvi 12 in Schwab's Index to Jer Talmud is a misprint. There is no ref to Lev. xxvi 12 in the vols hitherto publ. (1916) of Goldschmidt's Bab Talm Wunsche's vols of Midrash refer only to *Echa* Introd. Wu p 11

[5] See Schottg. ii 470, and Wagenseil's *Sota* p 938 foll —quoting *Sabb* 15 *a* and *Rosch Hasch* 31 *a*—also Rashi on Ezek. ix. 3, and Joseph. *Bell* vi. 5. 3.

[6] Jn i 14 ἐσκήνωσεν, not in N T elsewhere except 4 times in Rev., where see vii. 15, xxi 3

JESUS "WALKING" IN THE TEMPLE

once on the sea) First, beyond Jordan[1], the Baptist "looking-stedfastly on Jesus *walking*, saith, Behold, the Lamb of God[2]." Secondly, He "walks" in Galilee, where the context implies a previous hostility in Judaea· "And after these things Jesus *was walking in Galilee*, for he *would not [any longer] walk* in Judaea because the Jews were seeking to kill him[3]" Thirdly, "Jesus *was walking in the temple in Solomon's porch*"; and the result of this is an attempt of the Jews to stone Him, after which He "went forth out of their hand, and went away again beyond Jordan into the place where John was at the first baptizing[4]." After this, Jesus does not return to Judaea till the time comes for the raising of Lazarus. When this produces no result on the rulers except increased desire to kill Him, the word is used negatively thus: "Jesus therefore *would no longer walk openly among the Jews*, but departed thence into the country near to the wilderness[5]."

Henceforth, there is no mention of Christ's ever coming to the Temple or teaching in it. The Jews, before the last Passover, "as they stood in the temple," ask one another whether He will "come to the feast," and "when they heard that Jesus was coming to Jerusalem" went forth to meet Him as He rode publicly into the city[6]. John describes the riding, and a discourse of Jesus, presumably in the Temple, but does not mention the Temple. There is also an arrival of "certain Greeks," who had "come up to worship at the feast," presumably in the Temple, and a Voice from heaven, and several utterances from Jesus—all presumably in the Temple—and then a final warning and a departure. "Jesus therefore said unto them, *Yet a little while is the light among you Walk while ye have the light... While ye have the light, believe on the light, that ye may become sons of light.* These things spake Jesus and departed and was hidden from them[7]." All this apparently takes place while Jesus is doing what Mark describes as "walking in the

---

[1] Jn i 28   [2] Jn i 36
[3] Jn vii. 1   [4] Jn x 23, 31, 39—40
[5] Jn xi. 54.   [6] Jn xi. 56, xii. 12—13
[7] Jn xii 35—6, where R V has txt "*hid himself*," marg "*was hidden*," see *Joh Gr* **2538—43**.

245   (Mark xi 27—33)

JESUS "WALKING" IN THE TEMPLE

temple." Yet the Temple, throughout this narrative, is not mentioned by John

In the passage last quoted, *"was hidden"* and *"hid himself"* are given as alternatives, and it is not easy to follow the Johannine thought. Concerning the same verb—applied to Adam and Eve, when they *"hid themselves"* (LXX *"were hidden"*) because they "heard the voice of the Lord God *walking"* in paradise—Origen refers to passages in the Pentateuch about the Lord tabernacling or walking in Israel, and declares that the "walking" is of a spiritual nature[1]. Possibly John is alluding to the same Hebrew passages. The Word or Son of the Lord God, the Light of the world, is "walking" as Light before the sons of Adam in the Temple at Jerusalem, exhorting them to walk as children of light, but they will not obey. They constrain Him to hide Himself from them, or they hide Him from themselves—expressed in either way, the spiritual meaning is the same—by their love of darkness. Rejecting the Shechinah, or divine Glory, that constitutes the true Temple, the Jews are virtually fulfilling the words of Jesus "Destroy this temple (or, sanctuary)", and when Jesus "departed and was hidden from them," He takes the last vestige of its holiness with Him. Some feeling of this kind in John may perhaps explain why he omits all mention of the Temple just at that point in Christ's career at which all the Synoptists repeatedly mention it and describe it as the scene of His continuous and final teaching. The reason is that the Fourth Evangelist has by this time given up (so to speak) the Temple of stone and is fixing his gaze on the Temple of the Spirit Hence, where the Synoptists see Jesus leaving the visible Temple of the Jews for the last time, John sees the invisible Temple departing from the nation for ever.

---

[1] Origen *De Orat.* § 23 (Lomm xvii 180). He says that the "hiding" also was of a spiritual nature: "It is not said that really (read ὅτι ὄντως for ὅτι οὕτως) 'they desired to be hidden,' but [that] really (ὄντως) they were hidden" (i e hidden by their sins from the eyes of Him who will not look on iniquity) Origen quotes here as from "Deuteronomy" (xxiii 14) what in *Comm Matth* x 15 he quotes more correctly from "Leviticus" (xxvi 12)

JESUS "WALKING" IN THE TEMPLE

In the Synoptists, the first of the subjects of Christ's final teaching is introduced by the question "*By what authority doest thou these things?*" This corresponds to the Johannine question following the Purification of the Temple—"*What sign shewest thou unto us*, seeing that thou doest these things[1]?" In the Synoptists, Jesus meets this question by another, "The baptism of John, was it from heaven?" This the Synoptists have described as a device for the purpose of silencing the questioners, because they were afraid to say yes or no. But it may also have a deeper meaning: "What do you mean by 'authority'? You would believe in a Messiah on the 'authority' of a sign in heaven, or on the 'authority' of a prophet such as John the Baptist, if you accepted John as 'a prophet as one of the prophets[2]' But it is necessary to believe in a Messiah, if at all, on His own 'authority,' as the result of the influence from His Spirit, a moral more than an intellectual influence, flowing into the heart and not merely convincing the mind against the will."

Two defects appear on the surface of the Synoptic narrative. First, it gives us no definition, or clear suggestion, of the nature of the "authority" of the Messiah. Secondly, it might give some the impression that those who believed in the Messiah on the authority of the Baptist would have had an adequate belief. To remedy these defects is an integral part of the object of the Fourth Gospel At the outset it tells us that John the Baptist was emphatically "a human being" or "man"—that is to say, "man, not God, like the Logos[3]"—not "the light" but sent to testify "concerning the light"; and that the Word, or Life, or Light, gave to those who received Him "authority" to become children of God[4]. Later on, Jesus says that He has testimony greater than that of John, that John was a mere "lamp" preparatory to the dawn[5]. Jesus also appeals to the testimony of the Father and the Son (as being analogous to that of the

---

[1] Mk xi 28, Mt xxi 23, Lk xx. 2, Jn ii 18.
[2] Mk vi 15
[3] See *Joh Gr* 2277 "ἄνθρωπος is contrasted with Λόγος."
[4] Jn i 6—12   [5] Jn v. 33—6

JESUS "WALKING" IN THE TEMPLE

"two human beings" or "men," required in the Law) in such a way as to dispel the notion that a mere sign from heaven, or mere "authority" on earth, could produce the belief that He desires[1]. Toward the end of the Gospel John brings his indirect exposition dramatically to a close in a dialogue where Jesus corrects Pilate for saying "I have *authority* to crucify thee and have *authority* to release thee[2]"

According to this view the transition from the question "By what authority?" to the question "Whence came the baptism of John?" was not a mere counter-device of Jesus to meet the devices of His adversaries It meant that if they did not recognise the moral and spiritual force of John's testimony it followed that they would not recognise the nature of divine testimony or the nature of the divine authority to which the Baptist was sent to testify. The Baptist, like Isaiah, believing in God as the Husbandman of Israel, had said to the rulers of Israel "Bring forth fruit worthy of repentance," and he warned them not to be content to reply, "We have Abraham for our father[3]" But according to the Fourth Gospel some of them did, in effect, make this reply[4]. Those who made it had virtually closed their eyes to spiritual light. How could they see the incarnate Righteousness of God, if they did not know the meaning of that true righteousness which Abraham their ancestor had in view when he said "Shall not the Judge of all the earth do right[5]?"

---

[1] Jn viii 17—18. Comp Deut xvii 6

[2] Jn xix. 10—11 See the Index on "Authority" in *Proclamation*, and especially p 174 foll. on "Authority and the spirit of sonship, in John."

[3] Mt iii 9, Lk iii 8 "We have Abraham as our father"

[4] Jn viii. 33 "We are Abraham's seed," *ib* 39 "Our father is Abraham"

[5] Gen. xviii 25

JESUS "WALKING" IN THE TEMPLE

§ 2. *The parable of the murderous husbandmen*[1]

In the Synoptic narratives printed below there are very few points that call for Johannine intervention. Isaiah, personify-

[1] Mk xii 1—12 (RV)

(1) And he began to speak unto them in parables A man planted a vineyard, and set a hedge about it, and digged a pit for the winepress, and built a tower, and let it out to husbandmen, and went into another country

(2) And at the season he sent to the husbandmen a servant (*lit* bondservant), that he might receive from the husbandmen of the fruits of the vineyard

(3) And they took him, and beat him, and sent him away empty

(4) And again he sent unto them another servant (*lit* bondservant), and him they wounded in the head, and handled shamefully

(5) And he sent another, and him they killed and many others, beating some, and killing some

(6) He had yet one, a beloved son he sent him last unto them, saying, They will reverence my son

(7) But those husbandmen said among

Mt xxi 33—46 (RV)

(33) Hear another parable There was a man that was a householder, which planted a vineyard, and set a hedge about it, and digged a winepress in it, and built a tower, and let it out to husbandmen, and went into another country

(34) And when the season of the fruits drew near, he sent his servants (*lit* bondservants) to the husbandmen, to receive his fruits (*or*, the fruits of it)

(35) And the husbandmen took his servants (*lit* bondservants), and beat one, and killed another, and stoned another

(36) Again, he sent other servants (*lit* bondservants) more than the first and they did unto them in like manner

(37) But afterward he sent unto them his son, saying, They will reverence my son.

(38) But the husbandmen, when they

Lk xx 9—19 (RV)

(9) And he began to speak unto the people this parable A man planted a vineyard, and let it out to husbandmen, and went into another country for a long time

(10) And at the season he sent unto the husbandmen a servant (*lit.* bondservant), that they should give him of the fruit of the vineyard but the husbandmen beat him, and sent him away empty

(11) And he sent yet another servant (*lit* bondservant) and him also they beat, and handled him shamefully, and sent him away empty

(12) And he sent yet a third and him also they wounded, and cast him forth

(13) And the lord of the vineyard said, What shall I do? I will send my beloved son it may be they will reverence him

(14) But when the husbandmen saw him,

249 (Mark xii 1—12)

JESUS "WALKING" IN THE TEMPLE

ing a tree, likened Israel to a tree that had been chosen and planted and carefully cultivated as a good vine, but had (so to

Mk xii 1—12 (R V.) *contd.*	Mt xxi. 33—46 (R.V.) *contd.*	Lk. xx. 9—19 (R.V.) *contd.*
themselves, This is the heir, come let us kill him, and the inheritance shall be ours	saw the son, said among themselves, This is the heir, come, let us kill him, and take his inheritance	they reasoned one with another, saying, This is the heir let us kill him, that the inheritance may be ours
(8) And they took him, and killed him, and cast him forth out of the vineyard. (9) What therefore will the lord of the vineyard do? he will come and destroy the husbandmen, and will give the vineyard unto others	(39) And they took him, and cast him forth out of the vineyard, and killed him. (40) When therefore the lord of the vineyard shall come, what will he do unto those husbandmen? (41) They say unto him, He will miserably destroy those miserable men, and will let out the vineyard unto other husbandmen, which shall render him the fruits in their seasons	(15) And they cast him forth out of the vineyard, and killed him. What therefore will the lord of the vineyard do unto them? (16) He will come and destroy these husbandmen, and will give the vineyard unto others And when they heard it, they said, God forbid (*lit.* Be it not so)
(10) Have ye not read even this scripture; The stone which the builders rejected, The same was made the head of the corner (11) This was from the Lord, And it is marvellous in our eyes?	(42) Jesus saith unto them, Did ye never read in the scriptures, The stone which the builders rejected, The same was made the head of the corner This was from the Lord, And it is marvellous in our eyes? (43) Therefore say I unto you, The kingdom of God shall be taken away from you, and shall be given to a nation bringing forth the fruits thereof (44) And he that falleth on this stone shall be broken to pieces but on whom-	(17) But he looked upon them, and said, What then is this that is written, The stone which the builders rejected, The same was made the head of the corner? (18) Every one that falleth on that stone shall be broken to pieces, but on

speak) rebelled both against nature and against its owner by manifesting itself as a wild vine[1]. The Synoptic Gospels transfer the rebellion from the vine to the vinedressers. In the prophecy, the Vine refuses to bear good fruit; in the Gospels, the husbandmen refuse to give the owner his due share of the fruit, and kill the servants sent to receive it. Isaiah says "The vineyard of the Lord of hosts is the house of Israel... and he looked for judgment, but behold, oppression; for righteousness, but behold, a cry," and for this cause the vineyard was to be "laid waste[2]."

This is poetry. The Evangelists say, in prose, that the owner "will give the vineyard to others." But they differ as to the utterance of this last saying For Mark writes, as words of Jesus, "What will the lord of the vineyard do? He will come and destroy the husbandmen" Matthew expands this as a question of Jesus ("What...?") answered by the Pharisees ("They say, He will wretchedly destroy those wretches..."). Luke sides with Mark, and says that the Pharisees, far from acquiescing in the verdict of destruction, replied "May it not be so!"

If these last words point to the destruction of Jerusalem by the Romans, then we may say that John describes a somewhat similar situation, in language that partakes of irony, where

Mk xii. 1—12 (R.V.) *contd.*	Mt xxi. 33—46 (R.V.) *contd.*	Lk. xx. 9—19 (R.V.) *contd.*
	soever it shall fall, it will scatter him as dust (*some anc auth omit* verse 44).	whomsoever it shall fall, it will scatter him as dust.
(12) And they sought to lay hold on him, and they feared the multitude, for they perceived that he spake the parable against them; and they left him, and went away	(45) And when the chief priests and the Pharisees heard his parables, they perceived that he spake of them (46) And when they sought to lay hold on him, they feared the multitudes, because they took him for a prophet	(19) And the scribes and the chief priests sought to lay hands on him in that very hour, and they feared the people. for they perceived that he spake this parable against them.

[1] Is. v. 1—7. [2] Is. v. 6—7

he represents the Pharisees as saying about Jesus "If we thus let him alone, all will believe in him, and the Romans will come and take away our [holy] place and our nation." The High Priest replies "Ye know nothing at all, nor consider that it is expedient for you that one man should die for the people and not the whole nation perish." This unconscious prophecy of the High Priest John recognises as having been actually fulfilled[1] But he also gives us the impression that half of what the Pharisees said was also fulfilled: they *did not* "let Jesus alone," but the Romans *did* "take away" their "place." In other words the "vineyard" spoken of by Isaiah was "laid waste and trodden down."

Elsewhere, John adds a brief supplementary parable about the Vine, addressed to Christ's disciples as distinct from Christ's enemies—somewhat like the Pauline exhortation to Gentiles, "engrafted" in the olive-tree of Israel, not to be "high-minded[2]." In this, the Vine is Christ Himself; the rebellion (so to speak) is in some of the branches, which refuse to bear fruit and to abide in the Vine; the punishment is to be cast out, withered, and burned[3].

Another point deserves notice, apart from a certain literary and grammatical interest, because the omission of it might seem the omission of an instance of the failure of Johannine Intervention. It concerns the final words of Jesus in replying to the Pharisees. All the Synoptists agree that Jesus quoted from the Psalms up to the words "the head of the corner" But after that, Mark and Matthew continue the quotation "From the Lord *this* (fem.) came to pass and [it] is marvellous (fem.) in our eyes," where Luke has "Every one that falleth on that stone shall be broken to pieces; but on whomsoever it shall fall, it will scatter him to dust[4]."

This has been discussed in *Johannine Grammar*, where attention was called to instances of the Hebrew feminine

---

[1] Jn xi 48—52. [2] Rom. xi. 16—24.
[3] Jn xv. 1—6
[4] Mk xii. 11, Mt xxi 42, Lk xx 18, W. H. bracket Mt. xxi. 44 which is parallel to Lk xx 18

JESUS "WALKING" IN THE TEMPLE

"*this*" interpreted mystically[1] To the facts there stated the following may be added. The Latin versions, almost without exception, take the Greek feminine "this" to mean "this stone[2]." The Greek "stone" is frequently feminine when it means a precious stone[3]. But "precious stone" here seems at first sight impossible because in the preceding sentence ("the stone that the builders rejected") "stone" is masculine. That however may not have been regarded as an insuperable objection since the context might be paraphrased thus: "The stone that the builders rejected [as worthless] was made the head of the corner. *This* [*precious stone*] was from the Lord[4]."

A poetical interpretation of this kind is given in the commentary on Mark attributed to Jerome: "This is the rejected stone of the corner uniting in a pure meal the lamb [of the Passover] with the bread [of the Eucharist], finishing the Old Testament, beginning the New. This bringeth forth wonders (praestat mira) in our eyes, *like the topaz*." The peculiarity of the topaz, according to Strabo, was that it shone brightly in the night but was liable to be overlooked in the day[5] According to the Johannine Prologue, "the light shineth in the darkness and the darkness overcame it not[6]." The "foundations" of the New Jerusalem might be regarded as "looked for[7]" but invisible in the light of this material world, though visible, after death, in the spiritual world, and the same thing might apply to "the head stone" of the spiritual Temple An ancient comment on

---

[1] *Joh Gr* 2396—7, 2622

[2] In Mt xxi 42, *d* has "facta est haec," *Brix* "factum est istud," the rest masc =lapis, in Mk xii 11, all have masc

[3] See Steph *Thes.* v 292

[4] See 1 Pet ii. 4—8 on the double nature of Christ, the Living Stone, "elect and precious" to believers, but to others "a stone of stumbling."

[5] Strabo xvi 6 (770) says ὅσον μεθ' ἡμέραν μὲν οὐ ῥᾴδιον ἰδεῖν ἔστι (ὑπεραυγεῖται γάρ), Diod Sic iii 38 (not 39 as L S. etc) describes it as θαυμαστὴν ἔγχρυσον πρόσοψιν παρεχόμενος, using the LXX word (θαυμαστή)

[6] Jn i 5

[7] Heb xi 10 "he *looked for* the city that hath *the foundations*, whose builder and maker is God."

JESUS "WALKING" IN THE TEMPLE

"the corner stone" in Mark says that this "was *a wonder from the Lord* to men of understanding, when, after death, Christ appeared living, King over things in heaven and things on earth[1]." Also Zechariah, before describing the "bringing forth" of "the head stone" of the Temple, speaks of "the stone" "set before" the High Priest Joshua, and mentions its "seven eyes," and "the graving thereof[2]." And Revelation says that "the luminary" of the New Jerusalem was "like unto a *most precious stone*[3]"

All these passages point to the conclusion that Mark's use of the feminine "this" might be regarded by some, in very early times, as referring to the precious corner stone, and as having a mystical significance. The result tends to lessen the apparent fancifulness of the hypothesis that John intervened, in an allusion to Mark's "*this*," with a threefold repetition of "*these things*[4]."

---

[1] Mk xii 11 (Cramer)   [2] Zech iii 9, iv. 7

[3] Rev xxi 11 φωστήρ In canon LXX, this word occurs only in Gen 1 14, 16, Dan. xii 3 (LXX) But it occurs in Ps lxxiv. 16, Aq and Sym, "luminary," Heb. מאור, Targ. "lunam," Rashi "lumen Legis," see also Prov. xv. 30 "light (מאור) of the eyes," Aq. φωστήρ (Sym. φωτισμός) ὀφθαλμῶν, LXX θεωρῶν ὀφθαλμός It occurs once elsewhere in N T (Philipp ii 15) It is suggestive of a light shining in darkness

[4] Jn xii. 16 "*These things* understood not his disciples...*these things* were written .. they had done *these things* unto him " On this and other instances of threefold repetition, see *Joh. Gr* 2612—23 For the elaboration of the mystical doctrine of זאת (= αὔτη) see Schottgen ii Index "זאת Cabbalistis denotat Messiam 45, 140," where p 140 quotes Dan ii 35, Ps cxviii 22 etc

Mk xii 12 "*and they left him and went their way*," being omitted by the parall Mt -Lk., might seem to demand Johannine Intervention But in fact it is found, only transposed, in Mt xxii 22 "they marvelled, *and left him and went their way*," with a variation in the parall Lk xx 26 "they marvelled *at his answer and held their peace*," where Mk xii. 17 has simply "and they marvelled greatly at him"

See also p 256, n 1, quoting Jn vii 32—46, which relates how "officers," sent by the chief priests and Pharisees to arrest Jesus, did, in effect, 'leave" Him, and "go their way," and "hold their peace," because "they marvelled" at His teaching

JESUS "WALKING" IN THE TEMPLE

§ 3. *The payment of tribute*[1]

In this narrative there is no difference of importance between

[1] Mk xii 13—17 (R V.)

(13) And they send unto him certain of the Pharisees and of the Herodians, that they might catch him in talk

(14) And when they were come, they say unto him, Master (*or*, Teacher), we know that thou art true, and carest not for any one for thou regardest not the person of men, but of a truth teachest the way of God Is it lawful to give tribute unto Caesar, or not? Shall we give, or shall we not give?

(15) But he, knowing· their hypocrisy, said unto them, Why tempt ye me? bring me a penny, that I may see it.

(16) And they brought it And he saith unto them, Whose is this image and superscription? And they said unto him, Caesar's.

(17) And Jesus said unto them, Render unto Caesar the things that are Caesar's, and unto God the things that are God's And they marvelled greatly at him.

Mt. xxii 15—22 (R V)

(15) Then went the Pharisees, and took counsel how they might ensnare him in [his] talk

(16) And they send to him their disciples, with the Herodians, saying, Master (*or*, Teacher), we know that thou art true, and teachest the way of God in truth, and carest not for any one· for thou regardest not the person of men

(17) Tell us therefore, What thinkest thou? Is it lawful to give tribute unto Caesar, or not?

(18) But Jesus perceived their wickedness, and said, Why tempt ye me, ye hypocrites?

(19) Shew me the tribute money And they brought unto him a penny

(20) And he saith unto them, Whose is this image and superscription?

(21) They say unto him, Caesar's. Then saith he unto them, Render therefore unto Caesar the things that are Caesar's, and unto God the things that are God's

(22) And when they heard it, they marvelled, and left him, and went their way.

Lk xx 20—26 (R V)

(20) And they watched him, and sent forth spies, which feigned themselves to be righteous, that they might take hold of his speech, so as to deliver him up to the rule and to the authority of the governor

(21) And they asked him, saying, Master (*or*, Teacher), we know that thou sayest and teachest rightly, and acceptest not the person [of any], but of a truth teachest the way of God

(22) Is it lawful for us to give tribute unto Caesar, or not?

(23) But he perceived their craftiness, and said unto them,

(24) Shew me a penny Whose image and superscription hath it?

And they said, Caesar's

(25) And he said unto them, Then render unto Caesar the things that are Caesar's, and unto God the things that are God's.

(26) And they were not able to take hold of the saying before the people and they marvelled at his answer, and held their peace.

(Mark xii. 13—17)

the Synoptists till the last verse, where Mark says that "they wondered-out-of-measure at him"; this is amplified by Matthew and Luke, both of whom add words indicating that Christ's questioners were disconcerted or silenced, but that they were not filled with the wonder that partakes of admiration[1]. The reader is left by Mark in suspense as to the nature of the "wonder." Luke removes the suspense by saying, in effect, "They were not able to take hold of His saying before the people [to His discredit] and it was this, not Jesus Himself, but the cleverness of His answer, that caused their wonder." This is a very reasonable paraphrase of Mark. It agrees with an ancient comment on Mark preserved by Victor: "So they

---

[1] Mk xii. 17 b
...καὶ ἐξεθαύμαζον ἐπ' αὐτῷ

Mt. xxii. 22
καὶ ἀκούσαντες ἐθαύμασαν, καὶ ἀφέντες αὐτὸν ἀπῆλθαν

Lk. xx 26
καὶ οὐκ ἴσχυσαν ἐπιλαβέσθαι τοῦ ῥήματος ἐναντίον τοῦ λαοῦ, καὶ θαυμάσαντες ἐπὶ τῇ ἀποκρίσει αὐτοῦ ἐσίγησαν.

Possibly Mark's original gave rise to diverse interpretations that influence Matthew and Luke. The Marcan ἐξεθαύμαζον, unique in N T., might express a Hebrew reduplication, "they were astonished with [a great] astonishment" See *Clue* 137 a "For instances of reduplication of cognate noun and verb in Mk alone, see Mk i 26, iii 28, v 42 (comp xiii. 19, 20)" Now (*Law* pp. 98—9, on Mk v 42 "they were *amazed with a great amazement*") "hearing" and "amazement" (שמע and שמם) are confusable in Heb (see *Indices to Diatessarica* p. 33) Matthew may have here rendered the Hebrew "*Having been amazed* they were amazed" as "*Having heard* they were amazed," while adding a clause ("and letting him alone they departed") to indicate that they were foiled in their plot Luke seems to have paraphrased at greater length—taking "they were amazed" as including "struck dumb with amazement," that is, "were silent." It should be noted that in such phrases as Lk. xx. 26 οὐκ ἴσχυσαν ἐπιλαβέσθαι τοῦ ῥήματος (v r αὐτοῦ ῥήματος) and Lk xx 20 ἐπιλάβωνται αὐτοῦ λόγου (v. r τῶν λόγων), parall. Mk xii 13 λόγῳ, Mt xxii 15 ἐν λόγῳ, confusion might easily arise between "not able to *take hold of* [him] *in word*" and "not able to *arrest him*" Also Mt. ἀφέντες αὐτόν might mean that officers "left" Jesus free, though sent to arrest Him John relates that officers *were* thus sent and *did* thus leave Jesus unarrested (vii 32, 44). They said (*ib* 46) "Never man so spake"

JESUS "WALKING" IN THE TEMPLE

departed wondering that His reply had given them nothing to take hold of."

But was this really all that called for admiration in Christ's reply? Was there nothing in it except a verbal dexterity, by which Jesus avoided giving a hold to His enemies? Did the saying substantially mean "Since you use Caesar's coin, you must pay him his due"? If so, the words "and to God the things that are God's" would seem to be a mere appendix Origen, in his commentary on Matthew[1], says, "Since the soul is, by nature, stamped with (*lit.* according to) the image of God, we owe other things [beside the debt to Caesar] to its [*i e.* the soul's] King, namely God, things that agree and correspond to the nature and essence of the soul. And these are [first] the ways that lead toward virtue, and [then] the actions according to virtue." Ignatius, perhaps referring to the Gospel narrative, says that there are "two coinages, the one of God and the other of the world, and each of them has its own stamp engraved upon it, the unbelievers [having] the stamp of this world, but *the believers [that is to say, those who through their belief abide] in love*, [having] the stamp of God the Father through Jesus Christ...[2]"

If Jesus is assuming and teaching doctrine of this kind, then we are to regard Him not as evading but as attacking, not so much parrying a blow aimed at Him through the denarius of the Empire, as attempting to pierce the consciences of His people by a particular allusion to the shekels of the Temple, and to those payments for sacrifices, through which the money-changers in the Temple were allowed by the priests to defraud the poor He had already stigmatized these defrauders as "robbers" converting the Temple into their "den." And now He may be taking advantage of their cunning question about Caesar's denarius to retort on them with a warning to question themselves about God's denarius, that is, divine humanity, "Are you paying Him His tribute, filial love toward Him and brotherly kindness toward His children?"

---

[1] Origen Lomm iv 140 See *Law* p 277 on the Denarius of Fire.

[2] Ign *Magn* § 5, where see Lightf on the conception of the "coinage" of humanity in Greek literature.

JESUS "WALKING" IN THE TEMPLE

How, if at all, does John deal with this subject—that is to say, the admiration or wonder extorted from Christ's enemies by His utterances, combined as it was with an absolute blindness on their part to their spiritual beauty? He represents "the Jews[1]" as marvelling at Christ's teaching in the Temple and saying "*How knoweth this man letters* [i.e., *book-learning*], never having learned?" Here there may be a latent allusion to a well-known passage in prophecy. Isaiah, while describing Israel as blind and as "drawing near" to God "with their mouth" but not with their "heart"—words quoted by Jesus in Mark and Matthew[2]—divides them into two classes, to both of which "all vision is become as the words of a book that is sealed[3]." One class is not "learned in book-learning", the other is "learned in book-learning" but cannot unseal the book[4]. Both classes are content to learn the fear of God by rote, as "a commandment of men that hath been learned by rote[5]."

The phrase "to know book-learning" in Isaiah is unique or rare in the Old Testament[6]. John puts it into the mouth of the opponents of Jesus—largely composed of those "book-learned" people whom we commonly call "scribes"—and they characteristically express, in a superior and perhaps slightly contemptuous tone, their astonishment that their enemy speaks so like a scribe· "How *knoweth this* [*man*] *book-learning*, never having learned?" There is irony in this complacency of the

---

[1] Jn vii. 13—15 "No man spake openly of him for fear of *the Jews*...(14)...Jesus...went up into the temple and taught... (15) *The Jews* therefore marvelled, saying, How knoweth this man letters (γράμματα)...?" "The Jews" are distinguished from (*ib* 12) "the multitudes."

[2] Mk vii 6, Mt xv. 8.   [3] Is xxix 11 foll

[4] Comp Rev. v. 1 foll "a book...sealed with seven seals"

[5] Is xxix 13 "*a commandment of men that hath been taught* [*them*], R.V. marg *learned* [*by rote*]" The opposite of this is Jn vi 45 διδακτοὶ θεοῦ, from Is. liv. 13 "*disciples* of the Lord" lit "*the taught* of the Lord," *i e*. not of men

[6] Gesen 707 *b* gives, under a separate heading, ספר in Is xxix 11—12 (LXX γράμματα), and Dan. 1 4 (LXX and Theod γράμματα), 17 (LXX γραμματική [?τέχνη], Theod γραμματική) as meaning "*book-learning.*" The noun סופר meant a "*scribe*"

JESUS "WALKING" IN THE TEMPLE

blind leaders of the blind   Jesus replies, in effect, that His learning or teaching is from God Himself and not from books, and that it goes to the root of things   Those who judge without kindness according to the letter of the Law are blind to its spirit of kindness and judge according to appearance: "Judge not according to appearance, but judge righteous judgment[1]"

At the same time John gives us a glimpse into the state of mind of some of the "unlearned" Jews, who oscillate between the scribes and Jesus.   He tells us directly—what we might have indirectly but confidently inferred from the Synoptists—that the teaching of Jesus in the Temple was far more personal and less scribal than we might have inferred from the Synoptic texts   Mark selected especially those topics—some of them comparatively superficial—which were not selected by Jesus Himself but by His adversaries with a view to entrap Him. The selection of these might give a false impression of the tenor of Christ's teaching   Yet Jesus, even when dealing with apparent superficialities, went down deep to origins and first principles   The deepest of these was also the highest, the doctrine that we must look up to the Father through the Son in the Spirit of love:—"If any man thirst let him come unto me"   Not that, in this shape, the doctrine could be understood at present:—"This spake he of the Spirit," but "the Spirit was not yet given[2]."   Yet even those who could not understand felt a touch of something like understanding.   The chief priests and the Pharisees had "sent officers" to take Him, but they returned without a prisoner, and to the question "Why did ye not take him?" their reply was, "Never man so spake[3]."

---

[1] Jn vii 24   Comp Is v 7 "He looked for judgment, but behold oppression (*or*, shedding of blood)," and Jn vii 19 "Why seek ye to kill me?"

[2] Jn vii 37—9.   In the context, the words "Let him come unto *me*.   he that believeth on *me*" should perhaps be read as implying that Jesus speaks in the name of the Wisdom, or Holy Spirit, of God, as in Mt xxiii 34 "*I* (*emph*.) *send...*" parall to Lk. xi 49 "*The Wisdom of God said,* 'I will send...' " (see *Son* **3583** (1)).

[3] Jn vii. 32, 46.

JESUS "WALKING" IN THE TEMPLE

§ 4. *The resurrection of the dead*[1]

In the texts printed below, Luke, while adding matter of his own, follows Mark pretty closely except that he omits the

[1]

Mk xii 18—27 (R V)	Mt. xxii 23—33 (R V)	Lk. xx. 27—38 (R V)
(18) And there come unto him Sadducees, which say that there is no resurrection, and they asked him, saying,	(23) On that day there came to him Sadducees, which say (*lit* saying) that there is no resurrection, and they asked him,	(27) And there came to him certain of the Sadducees, they which say that there is no resurrection; and they asked him, saying,
(19) Master (*or*, Teacher), Moses wrote unto us, If a man's brother die, and leave a wife behind him, and leave no child, that his brother should take his wife, and raise up seed unto his brother	(24) Saying, Master (*or*, Teacher), Moses said, If a man die, having no children, his brother shall marry his wife (*lit* shall perform the duty of a husband's brother to his wife) and raise up seed unto his brother	(28) Master (*or*, Teacher), Moses wrote unto us, that if a man's brother die, having a wife, and he be childless, his brother should take the wife, and raise up seed unto his brother
(20) There were seven brethren and the first took a wife, and dying left no seed,	(25) Now there were with us seven brethren; and the first married and deceased, and having no seed left his wife unto his brother,	(29) There were therefore seven brethren and the first took a wife, and died childless,
(21) And the second took her, and died, leaving no seed behind him, and the third likewise	(26) In like manner the second also, and the third, unto the seventh (*lit* seven)	(30) And the second,
(22) And the seven left no seed Last of all the woman also died	(27) And after them all the woman died	(31) And the third took her, and likewise the seven also left no children, and died
		(32) Afterward the woman also died
(23) In the resurrection whose wife shall she be of them? for the seven had her to wife	(28) In the resurrection therefore whose wife shall she be of the seven? for they all had her	(33) In the resurrection therefore whose wife of them shall she be? for the seven had her to wife
(24) Jesus said unto them, Is it not for this cause that ye err, that ye know not the scriptures, nor the power of God?	(29) But Jesus answered and said unto them, Ye do err, not knowing the scriptures, nor the power of God	(34) And Jesus said unto them, The sons of this world (*or*, age) marry, and are given in marriage
(25) For when they shall rise from the dead, they	(30) For in the resurrection they neither marry, nor	(35) But they that are accounted worthy to attain to that world (*or*, age), and

JESUS "WALKING" IN THE TEMPLE

charge brought by Jesus against the Sadducees, "Do ye not err...?...... ye greatly err[1]," and also the reason alleged by Jesus for their error "for this cause, not knowing the scriptures nor the power of God[2]." Luke also limits the scope of Mark's charge Mark has "there come Sadducees, [a class of people] that say there is no resurrection"; Matthew narrows this into "[some] Sadducees, saying there is no resurrection"; Luke narrows it still further: "some of the Sadducees, those of them who [not only do not accept as an article of faith but even aggressively] deny a resurrection[3]"

Mk xii. 18—27 (R V) contd.	Mt. xxii 23—33 (R.V) contd	Lk xx. 27—38 (R.V.) contd.
neither marry, nor are given in marriage, but are as angels in heaven.	are given in marriage, but are as angels (*many anc auth add* of God) in heaven	the resurrection from the dead, neither marry, nor are given in marriage, (36) For neither can they die any more for they are equal unto the angels, and are sons of God, being sons of the resurrection.
(26) But as touching the dead, that they are raised, have ye not read in the book of Moses, in [the place concerning] the Bush, how God spake unto him, saying, I [am] the God of Abraham, and the God of Isaac, and the God of Jacob? (27) He is not the God of the dead, but of the living. ye do greatly err	(31) But as touching the resurrection of the dead, have ye not read that which was spoken unto you by God, saying, (32) I am the God of Abraham, and the God of Isaac, and the God of Jacob? God is not [the God] of the dead, but of the living. (33) And when the multitudes heard it, they were astonished at his teaching.	(37) But that the dead are raised, even Moses shewed, in [the place concerning] the Bush, when he calleth the Lord the God of Abraham, and the God of Isaac, and the God of Jacob (38) Now he is not the God of the dead, but of the living for all live unto him.

[1] Mk xii. 24—7 οὐ διὰ τοῦτο πλανᾶσθε...,..πολὺ πλανᾶσθε

[2] Mk xii. 24 οὐ διὰ τοῦτο πλανᾶσθε μὴ εἰδότες τὰς γραφὰς μηδὲ τὴν δύναμιν τοῦ θεοῦ, the parall Mt. xxii. 29 omits οὐ διὰ τοῦτο

[3] Mk xii. 18   Mt xxii. 23   Lk xx. 27

καὶ ἔρχονται Σαδδουκαῖοι πρὸς αὐτόν, οἵτινες λέγουσιν ἀνάστασιν μὴ εἶναι...   ἐν ἐκείνῃ τῇ ἡμέρᾳ προσῆλθον αὐτῷ Σαδδουκαῖοι, λέγοντες μὴ εἶναι ἀνάστασιν...   προσελθόντες δέ τινες τῶν Σαδδουκαίων, οἱ λέγοντες ἀνάστασιν μὴ εἶναι...

JESUS "WALKING" IN THE TEMPLE

The Sadducees are said to have accepted the Pentateuch but to have rejected or subordinated the rest of the Scriptures, and this statement about them is confirmed by the fact that Jesus, in His controversy with them, appeals to the Pentateuch, and not to the rest of the Scriptures where He could have found much more cogent texts for proving the Resurrection. This being the case, was it right to say that the Sadducees did not "*know*" the Scriptures, instead of saying that they did not "*accept*" a large part of them? Doubtless, Mark's tradition meant that they did not really "*know*" even those Scriptures that they accepted, that is to say, did not know their spirit, and the revelation that they contained of the underlying "power of God." But Luke may well have felt that Mark did not make this meaning clear.

Accordingly Luke first gives a brief description of the changed condition awaiting those who are "accounted worthy to attain that aeon[1]." These, he says, are "*equal-to-angels*"

---

[1] Lk xx. 35 οἱ δὲ καταξιωθέντες τοῦ αἰῶνος ἐκείνου τυχεῖν καὶ τῆς ἀναστάσεως τῆς ἐκ νεκρῶν... (36) οὐδὲ γὰρ ἀποθανεῖν ἔτι δύνανται, ἰσάγγελοι γάρ εἰσιν, καὶ υἱοί εἰσιν θεοῦ τῆς ἀναστάσεως υἱοὶ ὄντες. Wetstein on Lk xx 35, and Dalman *Words* p 119, shew that the phrase "worthy of the life, or world, to come" is frequent in the Talmud, and Wetstein on Lk xvi 8 shews the same about "*sons of the world to come*," as opposed to "*sons of this world.*" It means "worthy of the future life" (as in Heb "son of death," or "of scourging" (Gesen 121 b) may mean "worthy of death, or scourging"). Luke extends these phrases from meaning the elect on earth to mean fruition in heaven He adds "they can no longer die." Perhaps he does this in order to shew that he does not mean "sons of eternal life on earth." John however says the same thing about the life that springs from belief in Christ, apparently without regard to its being on earth or in heaven (xi 25—6), "I am the resurrection and the life. He that believeth on me, though he die [in appearance], yet shall he live [in truth] And whosoever liveth and believeth on me shall never [in truth] die."

Justin Martyr asserts (*Tryph.* § 80) that he and all right-minded Christians are assured that there will be first a resurrection of the dead and a millennium in Jerusalem, which will then be built as the prophets predict, and he concludes a long proof of this, from Isaiah (lxv. 17—25), by saying (*ib* § 81) that John one of the apostles of Christ prophesied this millennium, to be followed by the general

JESUS "WALKING" IN THE TEMPLE

—an expression substituted by him for the Marcan "*as angels in heaven*[1]." Then he says that "*even Moses*"—though his part was rather that of Lawgiver than that of Prophet and Revealer —"*intimated*," or "*indicated*[2]," that the dead are raised, "in [the place about] the Bush" when he calls the Lord "the God of Abraham, and the God of Isaac, and the God of Jacob." This was not "taught" by Moses, or "proclaimed," or "revealed," or even "shewn," but it was "intimated" or "indicated" by

---

and eternal resurrection and judgment of all men, "even as our Lord also said (Lk xx 36) They shall neither marry nor be given in marriage, but shall be equal to the angels, the children of the God of the resurrection (τέκνα τοῦ θεοῦ τῆς ἀναστάσεως ὄντες)."

[1] Ἰσάγγελος is not alleged (Steph *Thes*) from any author before Luke It is analogous to ἰσοδαίμων Luke substitutes "*equal* to angels" for "*like* (ὡς) angels," because men, having experienced temptation, sin and redemption, can never be "like" angels, who have not had these experiences But they may be "equal [in rank]" to angels Yet the word raises difficult questions as to the nature of the equality The Biblical phrase rendered "a little lower than *the angels*" in the LXX and Targum of Ps viii 5, and its adoption in Heb ii 7, should be compared with Philo i 164 "Abraham, having quitted mortality (ἐκλιπὼν τὰ θνητά) is gathered to the people of God (προστίθεται τῷ θεοῦ λαῷ), enjoying the fruit of incorruptibility, having become *equal to angels* (ἴσος ἀγγέλοις γεγονώς) For angels are God's army, bodiless and blessed souls" Origen (*Cels* iv 29) says that angels are only superior to men "on these terms (οὕτως)," namely, that men, when perfected, become "*equal-to-angels*" Elsewhere he says (*De Princip* iv 29, Lomm xxi 466) that Christ is in Gabriel and Michael, as also in Paul and Peter See Mayor's note on Clem Alex 866, shewing that Clem. Alex. freq uses ἰσάγγελος to express the progress of the soul.

[2] Lk xx 37 ἐμήνυσεν, not "shewed (ἐδήλωσε)" or "manifested (ἐφανέρωσε)" Μηνύω, μηνυτής, μήνυτρον, in classical Greek, mostly imply "giving information" (as in Jn xi 57), an "informer," "the price of information", but Steph *Thes* quotes Philo as saying (?ref.) μηνύοντος διὰ συμβόλων τοῦ θεοῦ and it is used thus by Justin Martyr *Apol* §§ 32, 35, 40, and Clem. Alex 667, 849 (parall to ἀλληγορεῖν) etc. to mean "indication through signs or symbols" Such a "sign" would be the burning bush Perhaps, therefore, the indirectness of the "indication" of the Resurrection is regarded by Luke as consisting not only in the words ("I am the God of Abraham") but also in the circumstances ("the bush" not consumed in the fire)

263 (Mark xii 18—27)

the sign of the Bush—burning but not consumed—when studied as the sequel of the promise made to the faithful Abraham and carried on through Isaac and Jacob to their descendants in Egypt

"The God of Abraham" could not have been revealed as a name of God, if Abraham had been a mere creature of days, dying for ever, therefore Abraham and his faithful descendants must rise from the dead That is the line of argument. Luke adds, "For all live unto him [*i e* God]." Apparently by "all," he means "all that *really live*, all that *have spiritual life.*" These, he says, "live to God." That is, they live only in correspondence to Him, as the planets shine only in correspondence to the sun. Origen is probably right in interpreting Luke thus[1] Perhaps Luke adds the words to make the Marcan text clear. But the addition itself is far from clear.

John, though he nowhere mentions Sadducees, teaches, through the acts and sayings of Jesus, a doctrine that bears on the Synoptic narrative of Christ's controversy with them He concentrates himself on the positive and essential meaning of "resurrection" Instead of protesting that it *is not* life in the flesh, he insists that it *is* life in Christ. He represents Jesus

---

[1] Origen *ad loc* (Lomm iv 171) says that "All live to him" is "*no ordinary praise of the Patriarchs*, namely, that such a one as our Saviour testifies to them, not only that they live, but also *that the life that they live they live unto God*" Probably he does not render πάντες "they all"—which would be hardly possible about three He means "All that [really] live"—as the three Patriarchs, for example, did—"live unto God"

Comp 4 Macc vii 19 "those who believe that to God they do not die—for [they are] (ὥσπερ γάρ, but ʾὥσπερ οὐδὲ, with ℵ) [even] as our patriarchs, Abraham, Isaac [and] Jacob—but live to God," xvi 25 "They [the seven martyrs] saw (ἰδόντες) that, for the sake of God having died (διὰ τὸν θεὸν ἀποθανόντες), men (*or*, they) live unto God (ζῶσιν τῷ θεῷ) [even as] Abraham and Isaac and Jacob and all the patriarchs" In the second passage, the meaning may be general, (1) men, having died for God, or particular, (2) they saw that they, the seven brethren, having died for God, *were destined to live*, but the latter is a strained rendering of ζῶσιν These passages indicate that Luke was following some current Jewish doctrine which he utilised to explain Christ's words

JESUS "WALKING" IN THE TEMPLE

as saying to Martha "*I am the resurrection and the life*[1]" We have found Luke omitting the Marcan mention of "*the power of God.*" John nowhere in the whole of his Gospel uses the word "power" But he proceeds dramatically to represent Christ as being God's incarnate power—"Christ the power of God," as Paul says[2]—by raising Lazarus from the dead

Also, whereas Luke as it were apologizes for the way in which Moses indirectly "indicated," rather than inculcated, the doctrine of the Resurrection, John will have no such apology. Only, what the Synoptists say about the Resurrection and the Life, John says about the Messiah who *is* "the resurrection and the life." "*If ye believed Moses,*" Jesus says to the Jews, "ye would believe me, for he wrote of me[3]" In the preceding context He declares that the Jews are blind, and deaf, and insensible to the meaning of the Scriptures[4]. "They search[5]" them, but they find no real meaning in them because they are dead to the spirit and power of them, which is their real meaning This is Mark over again, "*Ye know not the scriptures nor the power of God.*"

We have seen that Luke, besides omitting this, omits also the Marcan condemnation "Ye do greatly err," or literally, "are caused to err." In John, there is a condemnation far weightier and fuller, for it implies that they erred, not through temporary lapse but through permanent moral defects and faults, negative and positive—want of the love of God and God's glory, excess of the love of self and their own glory[6] It is perhaps characteristic of Luke that he regards the Resurrection as proved by something like a logical weighing of evidence, so that to reject it was a logical rather than a moral error That is not the Johannine view.

---

[1] Jn xi 25   [2] 1 Cor 1 24   [3] Jn v 46
[4] Jn v 37—8 "ye have neither *heard*...nor *seen*.. and ye have not *his word abiding in you*" implies defect in (1) hearing, (2) sight, (3) feeling or perception.
[5] Jn v 39 "Ye search," ἐρευνᾶτε, prob. indicative, see *Joh Gr* **2439** (1)—(11)
[6] Jn v 42 "Ye have not the love of God in yourselves," *ib* 44 "how can ye believe—ye who receive glory from one another?"

JESUS "WALKING" IN THE TEMPLE

The addition of Luke ("all live unto him") is quoted by Justin Martyr at the end of a long demonstration of a first resurrection—a Messianic millennium, based on a long prophecy of Isaiah The same prophecy is alleged by Irenaeus to prove the same things. Both writers stigmatize as heretics those who refuse to accept the prophecy in a literal sense, and both of them allege the Revelation of John as supporting their views against dissentients[1]. These allegations, and their controversial contexts, make it probable that at a very early date the nature and circumstances of the Coming of the Lord and of the consequent resurrection of the disciples would be much discussed, and that the Fourth Evangelist would intervene as to the Synoptic narrative under discussion; and the Johannine texts above quoted make it probable that he has actually done so.

§ 5. *"What commandment is the first?" in Mark*[2]

Luke omits the whole of this discussion. The Diatessaron places immediately after it a combination of Mark and Luke

---

[1] Justin (*Tryph* §§ 80—81) quotes Is lxv 17—25 Irenaeus (v. 34 4) quotes Is. lxv. 18—22. Justin quotes "John one of the apostles of Christ" as prophesying this millennium. Irenaeus (v 35 2) says "In the Apocalypse John saw this new Jerusalem" and quotes Is lxv 17—18

[2]
Mk xii 28—34 (R.V)	Mt xxii 34—40, 46 (R V)	Lk xx 39, x 25— 8, xx 40 (R.V.)
(28) And one of the scribes came, and heard them questioning together, and knowing that he had answered them well, asked him, What commandment is the first of all?	(34) But the Pharisees, when they heard that he had put the Sadducees to silence, gathered themselves together	(xx. 39) And certain of the scribes answering said, Master (*or*, Teacher), thou hast well said.
(29) Jesus answered, The first is, Hear, O Israel, The Lord our God, the Lord is one (*or*, The Lord [is] our God, the Lord is one)	(35) And one of them, a lawyer, asked him a question, tempting him, (36) Master (*or*, Teacher), which is the great commandment in the law?	(x 25) And behold, a certain lawyer stood up and tempted him, saying, Master (*or*, Teacher), what shall I do to inherit eternal life? (26) And he said unto him, What is written in the law? how readest thou?
(30) And thou shalt love the Lord thy God with (*ht*	(37) And he said unto him, Thou shalt love the Lord thy	

266 (Mark xii 28—34)

thus: "[Mark] And Jesus saw him [*i e.* the scribe] that he had answered wisely; and he answered and said unto him, 'Thou art not far from the kingdom of God' [Luke] 'Thou hast

Mk xii 28—34 (R V) *contd*.	Mt xxii. 34—40, 46 (R.V.) *contd*	Lk xx 39, x 25—8, xx 40 (R.V.) *contd*
from) all thy heart, and with (*lit* from) all thy soul, and with (*lit* from) all thy mind, and with (*lit* from) all thy strength. (31) The second is this, Thou shalt love thy neighbour as thyself There is none other commandment greater than these (32) And the scribe said unto him, Of a truth, Master (*or*, Teacher), thou hast well said that he is one, and there is none other but he (33) And to love him with all the heart, and with all the understanding, and with all the strength, and to love his neighbour as himself, is much more than all whole burnt offerings and sacrifices (34) And when Jesus saw that he answered discreetly, he said unto him, Thou art not far from the kingdom of God And no man after that durst ask him any question	God with all thy heart, and with all thy soul, and with all thy mind (38) This is the great and first commandment (39) And a second like [unto it] is this (*or*, And a second is like unto it), Thou shalt love thy neighbour as thyself (40) On these two commandments hangeth the whole law, and the prophets. (46) And no one was able to answer him a word, neither durst any man from that day forth ask him any more questions	(27) And he answering said, Thou shalt love the Lord thy God with (*lit.* from) all thy heart, and with all thy soul, and with all thy strength, and with all thy mind, and thy neighbour as thyself (28) And he said unto him, Thou hast answered right this do, and thou shalt live. (xx 40) For they durst not any more ask him any question.

The very ample Marcan traditions about the nature of the commandment to "love," and about its being "first," and "none greater," are summarised in Jn xiii 34—5 "A *new commandment*...if ye have *love* one to another" This implies the preeminence of a New Commandment corresponding to the preeminence of the Old one It is not however regarded as preeminent, or "*first*," or "*greater*," but as having a new significance, and as being essential.

267 (Mark xii. 28—34)

JESUS "WALKING" IN THE TEMPLE

spoken rightly; do this, and thou shalt live.' And he, as his desire was to justify himself, said unto him, 'And who is my neighbour?' Jesus said unto him 'A man went down from Jerusalem' [the Parable of the Good Samaritan]¹" According to this arrangement the scribe is regarded as possibly a mere lip-believer "desiring to justify himself." In *word*, he had "*spoken* rightly" In *word*, he was "not far from the kingdom of God" But was he sincere? Was he one of the "little ones²" who, according to Mark, constituted God's Family or "King-

---

¹ *Diatess.* also combines Mark and Luke at the outset thus (Mk xii 28) "And one of the scribes, of those that knew the law (Lk x. 25 νομικός), when he saw the excellence of his answer to them, desired to try him (Lk. x. 25, comp. Mt. xxii. 35) and said unto him (Lk x. 25) 'What shall I do to inherit eternal life?' and (Mk xii 28, Mt. xxii. 36) 'Which of the commandments is greater and has precedence in the Law?'"

Mark does not represent the scribe as "tempting" or "trying" Jesus Matthew may have inferred it from the context Delitzsch renders νομικός in Mt xxii. 35 by מֵבִין "making wise" (with "in the Law") but in Lk. x. 25 by מְבַעֲלֵי "of the Masters" (with "of the Law"). In Job xxxiv 36, LXX confuses בִּין with בָּחֻן "tempt" (*Corrections* 466 (η)) And confusion may have arisen from attempts to describe the *status* of this particular "scribe" (see Levy i 248—9 on בַּעַל shewing that a scribe might be called Master of Haggada, or of Mikra (Bible text) or of Mishna or of Talmud etc.).

Victor, on Mark, says that he can be reconciled with Matthew thus "The man at first was 'tempting' Jesus, but having been benefited by the reply [of Jesus] he was [afterwards] praised [by Jesus]," implying that the reply reminded the man of the duty of love toward one's neighbour and converted him from his loveless state of jealousy and envy.

Νομικός, "lawyer," used here alone by Matthew but freq. in Luke, has a technical meaning in Epictetus ii 13. 6—8, Strabo xii (p 539), implying a legal adviser indispensable for a man that does not know the laws of the country (and see Plutarch *Quaest Rom* 271 E—F on the names "Caius" etc technically used by νομικοί) Comp Rom ii 19, 1 Cor i 19—20. The use of it in Mt -Lk, and their insertion of πειράζων, make it probable that they regarded Mark as taking too favourable a view of "the scribe" and as not understanding the tacit warning implied in the words "*not far from* the kingdom of God," that is to say, outside it, and perhaps permanently outside, though close to the gate.   ² Mk x. 14.

JESUS "WALKING" IN THE TEMPLE

dom"? *"Those who are far off"* is sometimes a technical term for Gentiles In that sense, *"not far off"* might mean "an orthodox Jew" and, perhaps, one who exulted in his orthodoxy[1]. This possibility must not be forgotten

The word "discreetly," employed by Mark to describe the character of the scribe's reply, must be noted on account of its unusual character, not being used elsewhere in Biblical Greek It mostly means "sensibly," and may be applied to those who have a reasonable sense of changed circumstances and are open to new facts and new arguments[2] But it might be taken to mean "adapting oneself to circumstances," "prudently cautious" In that sense, it might imply insincerity or dishonesty—meaning "wisely" in the sense in which the unjust steward is said to have "done wisely[3]" In the same sense the serpent is said to have been "wiser" than all the other creatures in Paradise; and we are told that Pharaoh proposed to "deal wisely," *i e* cunningly, with the Israelites in Egypt[4] Since

---

[1] Comp Acts ii 39 (a Petrine speech) "to your children and to *all that are afar off*," *ib.* xxii 21 (a Pauline speech) "*far hence unto the Gentiles*," Eph ii 13—17 "*ye that once were far off. . peace to you that were far off*," referring to Is lvii 19 In Luke, the Prodigal Son (who represents the Gentiles) is seen (xv 20) "while he was still *far off*," and the Publican, as contrasted with the Pharisee, (xviii 13) "stood *far off*"

[2] Mk xii 34 νουνεχῶς, *a, k* "sensate," *b, d*, Vulg "sapienter," SS (Burk) "well," Syr (Walton) "sapienter " Νουνεχής does not occur anywhere in the Early Fathers (Goodspeed) but is freq in Justin Martyr, meaning "sensible," "open to conviction," *Apol* §§ 12, 46, 2 *Apol* § 11 In *Tryph* § 87 νουνεχέστατα . ἠρώτησας is said by Justin to his Jewish antagonist, who has protested that he asks for information and not merely to raise a difficulty Wetstein (on Mk) quotes Polyb as frequently using the adv with πραγματικῶς, φρονίμως and ἡμέρως Pseudo-Jerome, on Mk, asks "Quare non est longe qui venit *callide*?" which seems to imply a rendering of νουνεχῶς as "cunningly "

[3] Lk. xvi 8 φρονίμως Delitzsch has a form of ערם "shrewd," but SS חכם "wise "

[4] Gen iii. 1 φρονιμώτατος, Heb ערום, Onk sim. *i e* (R V) "subtil," but v r. (s Brederek) חכים, i e "*wise*," Aq. Theod. πανοῦργος. Comp. Exod i 10 "let us *deal wisely* (חכם)," κατασοφισώμεθα.

JESUS "WALKING" IN THE TEMPLE

the scribe began to speak with the object of "tempting" Jesus it is natural to suppose that, when he was foiled, he made a discreet or artful reply to cover his defeat. Luke himself, in a parallel but different context, represents a phrase of similar approval as being uttered without real approval· "But certain of the scribes answering said, 'Master, thou hast well said'"—not that they really felt this, their real feeling being one of fear—"*for they no longer dared to question him about anything*[1]" And Mark says the same thing after the scribe's "discreet" reply and Christ's answer to it This points to the conclusion that the answer was felt to be a rebuke No one "dared to question Jesus any more[2]" and to bring upon himself a similar rebuke. From this it follows that, among the reasons for Luke's omission of the Marcan narrative, one may have been a doubt as to the application of the phrase "thou hast well said," or, "answered rightly," or, "answered discreetly"—a doubt not only as to the person answering but also as to the motive of the answer[3]

Luke substitutes for the Marcan theoretical question as to what *is* ("What *is* the first commandment?") a practical one as to what must be *done*, "What shall I *do* to inherit eternal life?" followed by another question bearing on the doing, "Who is the 'neighbour' whom I am commanded to love?" No direct answer is given to this by Jesus Indirectly, in the parable of the Good Samaritan—who shewed himself a real "neighbour"—we are taught that our "neighbour" is the man that acts kindly to us But if that is so, "love" becomes an easy affair, much easier than that which is contemplated in the Sermon on the Mount where the command is given "Love your enemies" The moral of the parable is not a definition,

---

[1] Lk. xx. 39—40   [2] Mk xii. 34
[3] A combination of the two great commandments of love to God (Deut vi. 5) and love to our neighbour (Lev xix 18) is found in *Test XII Patr*, Dan § 5 "Love the Lord through all your life, and one another with a true heart" (see Charles's note) It comes there as a climax—after "keep His law," "depart from wrath," "hate lying," "speak truth each one with his neighbour," and after the promise "So...shall ye be in peace, having the God of peace...."

270   (Mark xii 28—34)

JESUS "WALKING" IN THE TEMPLE

but a precept, "Go and do like the Samaritan who made himself a 'neighbour' to a Jewish stranger in distress and thereby made the Jew his neighbour." This is a beautiful moral appended to a beautiful story, but it does not answer the question "Who *is* my neighbour?" It leaves the lawyer able to say "If God meant 'Love *every human being* as thyself' why did He not say so? If He meant 'Love *a limited class of human beings*' why did He not define the limit?"

How does John intervene, if at all, on these subjects, first, as to the nature, duty, and scope of love, and then as to the question whether the first and highest commandment enjoins love? As to the nature and scope of "loving" John says, in his first mention of the word, "God so *loved* the world that he gave his only begotten Son, that whosoever believeth on him should not perish but have eternal life[1]" Yet in the Epistle he says "*Love* not the world neither the things that are in the world[2]" In this contradiction there is no mere play on different meanings of "the world" It is rather a warning about the different meanings of "love" John never tells us to love our enemies or even to love our neighbours. Perhaps he felt that the attempt to love these sometimes ended in hypocrisy[3]. When he says "He that loveth not his brother whom he hath seen, cannot love God whom he hath not seen[4]," he clearly assumes that the "brother" is no enemy, or bestial or diabolic being, but a believer in Christ, lovable for his own sake as well as for Christ's And in Christ's last commandments to the disciples, as recorded by John, we are bidden to love, not enemies, nor strangers, but "one another[5]."

Jesus calls this a new commandment Its newness appears to consist in the new character of the love. They are, He says, to love one another "even as I have loved you" What follows later on implies that kind of love which induces a man to "lay down his life for his friends[6]." This takes us back to the first

---

[1] Jn iii 16 [2] 1 Jn ii 15
[3] Rom xii 9 "*the love* [that is to be the sign of the Church, must be] without hypocrisy"
[4] 1 Jn iv. 20 (so W. H. without altern.)
[5] Jn xiii 34—5 [6] Jn xv 13

(Mark xii. 28—34)

Johannine mention of the word, "God so loved the world"—which shews that the Father made a sacrifice of the Son, and that the Son made a sacrifice of Himself, and all for an unloving or even hostile world, in order that it might, if possible, be brought into the region of love. Thus, although we are not taught in word to love strangers or enemies, we are led by the love of Christ to feel for them something corresponding to the love of the Father—and this was for all "the world."

Thus emphasizing the self-sacrificing love of the Father and the Son—or of the Father through the Son—John emphasizes that unity of God, and that unity of God's commandments (merged as they are in one) which Luke omits. The Marcan proclamation "the Lord our God is one" is nowhere mentioned by Matthew or Luke. But John has "I and the Father are one[1]." And the Marcan prominence given to the "first" Commandment is illustrated by several Johannine passages which imply the Law of Self-sacrifice as exemplified in the Son receiving the love and the commandment of the Father: "Therefore doth the Father love me because I lay down my life ...I have authority to lay it down and I have authority to take it again. This commandment received I from my Father[2]." The last Johannine sentence of Christ's public teaching, though it merely mentions "speaking" and not acting, implies that the one commandment is, in effect, Self-sacrifice, incarnate in the Son of God and identified with eternal life. "I know that his commandment is life eternal[3]." The Unity of God Himself is connected (in the

---

[1] Jn x 30.   [2] Jn x 17—18

[3] Jn xii 50. The Pauline occasional use of ἐντολή in a somewhat depreciative sense (Rom vii 8—13, Eph ii. 15, Tit 1. 14, comp. Heb vii 16—18) may have led to such a contempt for ἐντολαί as Clem Alex condemns in heretics (893) δυσαρεστούμενοι ταῖς θείαις ἐντολαῖς —τουτέστι τῷ ἁγίῳ πνεύματι Hence Clem Alex 834 τὰς ἐντολὰς... ἔδωκεν ..ἐκ μιᾶς ἀρυτόμενος πηγῆς ὁ κύριος traces them all back to their source A similar feeling pervades John, who would have us regard them as a gift, not as a yoke, and as incarnate in Christ Comp. *Maccoth* 24 a on Amos v 4 Moses has 613 commandments, David 11, Isaiah 6, Micah 3, Isaiah "again (wiederum)" 2, Amos 1, "Seek

JESUS "WALKING" IN THE TEMPLE

Fourth Gospel) with the unity of man with man, and of Man collectively with God, through the fulfilment of the One Commandment. To some the Johannine repetition of "one" attributed to Jesus in His Last Prayer may seem to border on superfluity, but it is assuredly deliberate[1].

§ 6 *"Scribes" and "the Son of David"*[2]

Mark implies that the Messianic title, "Son of David," was insisted on by *"the scribes"* in the course of their doctrine

---

ME, and ye shall live." This may be compared with Lk x 28 "Do this and thou shalt live."

[1] Jn xvii 11 "that they may be *one*, even as we [*are one*]," *ib*. 21—3 "that they may all be *one*...that they may be *one*, even as we [are] *one*...that they may be perfected into *one*"

[2]

Mk xii 35—8 (R.V.)	Mt xxii 41—6 (R V)	Lk xx 41—6 (R V)
(35) And Jesus answered and said, as he taught in the temple, How say the scribes that the Christ is the son of David?	(41) Now while the Pharisees were gathered together, Jesus asked them a question, (42) Saying, What think ye of the Christ? whose son is he? They say unto him, [The son] of David. (43) He saith unto them, How then doth David in the Spirit call him Lord, saying,	(41) And he said unto them, How say they that the Christ is David's son?
(36) David himself said in the Holy Spirit, The Lord said unto my Lord, Sit thou on my right hand, till I make thine enemies the footstool of thy feet (*some anc auth* underneath thy feet).	(44) The Lord said unto my Lord, Sit thou on my right hand, till I put thine enemies underneath thy feet?	(42) For David himself saith in the book of Psalms, The Lord said unto my Lord, Sit thou on my right hand, (43) Till I make thine enemies the footstool of thy feet
(37) David himself calleth him Lord, and whence is he his son? And the common people (*or*, the great multitude) heard him gladly (38) And in his teaching he said, Beware of the scribes...	(45) If David then calleth him Lord, how is he his son? (46) And no one was able to answer him a word....	(44) David therefore calleth him Lord, and how is he his son? (45) And in the hearing of all the people he said unto his disciples, (46) Beware of the scribes....

A F   273 (Mark xii. 35—8)   18

JESUS "WALKING" IN THE TEMPLE

generally. But his context ("answered and said") might be taken to mean that Jesus said this in answer to some particular and recent utterance. Accordingly Matthew inserts a statement of the Pharisees that Christ is the Son of David, made in reply to a question of Jesus "What think ye of the Christ? Whose son is he?" Now all the Synoptists have represented this title as being recently applied by a blind beggar, or "two blind men," in the neighbourhood of Jericho to Jesus on His way to Jerusalem[1]. Luke, perhaps for this reason, drops the word "scribes" here, and describes Jesus as now putting to His former questioners—who "durst not ask him any more questions"—a question on His own account, "How say [they]"—*that is, people in general*—"that the Christ is David's son?" This is quite different from the tradition in Mark.

Mark's emphasis on "the scribes" recalls Matthew's account of Herod "gathering together all the chief priests and *scribes of the people*" when "he inquired of them where the Christ should be born; and they said unto him, In Bethlehem of Judaea[2]." It recalls also a Johannine passage where those Jews who on scriptural or scribal grounds dispute the possibility that Jesus could be the Christ, are contrasted with "*[some] of the multitude*" thus. "*[Some] of the multitude* therefore, when they heard these words [of Jesus preaching in the Temple] said, This is of a truth the prophet. *Others [of the multitude]* said, This is the Christ. But *some* said, What, doth the Christ come out of Galilee? Hath not the scripture said that the Christ cometh of the seed of David, and from Bethlehem, the village where David was[3]?"

Here alone does John mention "David," and it is in connection with Bethlehem. But, much earlier, Bethlehem is

---

[1] Mk x. 47—8, Mt xx. 30—31, Lk. xviii 38—9, rep twice.
[2] Mt. ii 4—5.
[3] Jn vii 40—42 οἱ δὲ ἔλεγον, since οἱ μέν does not precede, might mean "but they, *i.e.* the previous speakers, said," that is to say, "Those who had called Jesus 'the prophet' moderated the enthusiasm of those who said that He was 'the Christ'." But no version takes it thus. We must perhaps suppose that ἄλλοι is regarded as equiv to οἱ μέν. This is Jn's only mention of Bethlehem.

JESUS "WALKING" IN THE TEMPLE

probably to be supposed as being in the mind of Nathanael when he raises a scribal objection to Philip's acceptance of Jesus as the Deliverer, on the ground that He *cannot* "come out of Nazareth[1]." No doubt the meaning is " He *must* come out of Bethlehem " In that passage, John makes no attempt to meet this objection of Nathanael's either through words of his own or through words of Jesus. Nathanael overrides his own logical and scriptural argument by sheer illogical faith

Later on, John represents Nicodemus as being apparently silenced by a scribal objection based on locality, "Art thou also of Galilee? Search, and see that out of Galilee ariseth no prophet (*or*, not the prophet)[2]." This follows almost immediately after the utterance in the Temple, above quoted, about David and Bethlehem, and it is in the Council chamber of the Sanhedrin where the chief priests and Pharisees (no doubt including "scribes") are assembled. "Search and see" implies an appeal to those learned in the Scriptures, as "the scribes" specially professed to be, and the passage supports Mark in the view that "the scribes" emphasized some connection between the Messiah and David The speakers in the Fourth Gospel mention " the seed of David " only in connection with the identity of birthplace for Christ and David. Luke, in his own person, emphasizes these details, " Joseph went up from Galilee out of the city of Nazareth, into Judaea, to the city of David, which is called Bethlehem, because he was *of the house and family of David*[3]."

The impression left on us by John is, not that he disbelieved in Christ's birth at Bethlehem and descent from " the house and family of David," but that he regarded the acceptance of these details as not necessary for Christians It was natural for scribes to lay stress on them, but Jesus desired disciples to accept Him for His own sake—apart from " David " and " Bethlehem "—without such scribal conditions. Hence John

---

[1] Jn 1 46
[2] Jn vii. 52. See *Joh. Gr* 2492 "No one has satisfactorily explained the extraordinary statement attributed to the Pharisees 'Out of G ariseth no prophet '" The sense demands the insertion of *o* before προφήτης.   [3] Lk ii 4

JESUS "WALKING" IN THE TEMPLE

represents no enlightenment as being given even to the guileless Nathanael—either when he seemed likely to stumble at the mention of "Nazareth" or on any subsequent occasion. Nathanael, overriding the objection suggested by "Nazareth," hails Jesus as Son of God and King of Israel; and Jesus accepts his homage, and promises a future vision of glory, in which there shall be revealed no Son of David, but a mediating Son of Man, on whom the angels of God ascend and descend[1].

While considering the Johannine attitude toward "scribal" conditions, we should note the fact that the word "scribe," abundantly used by Mark and often, though less often, by Matthew and Luke, is never used by John[2].

Perhaps one reason for this is the technical nature of the Synoptic word. Outside Palestine, *grammateus*, "clerk," or "scribe," might mean "town-clerk," as in the Lucan narrative of the tumult in Ephesus[3]. But of course John could not, and

---

[1] Jn 1. 51 See *Joh. Gr.* 2275, *Son* 3136 foll., 3374 foll.
On the words of Jesus "David ..calleth him Lord" there was no reason why John should intervene, as they are in all the Synoptists and are fairly consonant with what we learn from Justin Martyr (*Tryph* §§ 33, 83) about Jewish tradition concerning the 110th Psalm, namely, that in the second century they referred the Psalm to Hezekiah. This agrees with the hypothesis that in the first century Jews referred it to the Messiah, but in the second (when Christians had referred it to *their* Messiah) to Hezekiah. Later on, the Rabbis referred it (says Rashi) to Abraham. But *Tehill* 1 163, after mentioning Abraham and Moses as instances of God's condescension, quotes R. Judan, in the name of R. Chama, as referring it to the Messiah. The Synoptists clearly assume that the Jews in Christ's time accepted the statement "David calleth him Lord," as applying to the Messiah, so that no one ventured to contradict it.

[2] *Joh Voc* 1692 gives γραμματεύς Mk 22, Mt 19, Lk 14, Jn 0

[3] Acts xix 35. It is not used (Goodspeed) in the early Fathers. Justin, the only Apologist that has it, uses it only in his Dialogue with the Jew, and there almost always with "Pharisees," and mostly in quotations. *Tryph.* § 103 ὑπὸ τῶν Φαρισαίων καὶ γραμματέων κατὰ τὴν διδασκαλίαν ἐκπεμφθέντες if not corrupt, may mean scribes ("[so called] in respect of their teaching [of the Scripture]." But comp. *ib.* § 102 "the Pharisees and scribes, and, in short, the teachers in your nation," which favours the old emendation καὶ τῶν διδασκάλων.

JESUS "WALKING" IN THE TEMPLE

does not, omit the *fact* of "*scribi&m*" Only he dramatizes it. The basis of "*scrib-ism*" (morally as well as etymologically) is "*scrip-ture*"; and among the first dramatic utterances in the Fourth Gospel are those based on some scriptural definition, or name, of a future Saviour, or of His fore-runner, or of His birthplace:—"I am not *the Christ*," "Art thou *Elijah*?" "Art thou *the Prophet*?" "We have found *the Messiah*," "We have found *him of whom Moses in the law, and the prophets, did write*," "Can any (? the) good thing come out of *Nazareth*[1]?" The earlier instances exemplify the inflexible scribism of the "priests and Levites from Jerusalem"; the last of all exemplifies the flexible scribism of the open-minded Nathanael[2] But they are all forms of "scribism" Other forms of it follow in rapid succession throughout the Gospel, and especially where "Jews" or Pharisees are mentioned as distinct from "multitude" Indeed no Synoptic Gospel is so permeated with the thing though the word is nowhere to be found[3]

---

[1] Jn 1 20, 21, 41, 45, 46.

[2] On Jn vii 41—2 Chrys remarks that the objection "Doth the Christ come from Galilee?" uttered by hostile Jews, and "out of Nazareth can any good come?" uttered by Nathanael, do not seem to be regarded in the same way He concludes that Nathanael was "a lover of truth" and was helped accordingly, whereas the Jews merely wished to overthrow the popular belief that Jesus was the Christ "Lover of truth" is probably implied in Jn 1 47 "*truly an Israelite*" (whether Israel means (*Son* 3140 *a*—*b*) "seeing God" or "striving with [the aid of] God") Nathanael was (Mt xiii 52) a "scribe made a disciple to the kingdom of heaven," and consequently he "brought forth things new" as well as "old."

[3] "Scribe" occurs uniquely and significantly in the interpolated Jn viii 3

JESUS "WALKING" IN THE TEMPLE

§ 7. *"Scribes" and a poor widow, in Mark and Luke*[1]

Mark concludes his account of Christ's teaching in the Temple with a condemnation of "scribes" that "devour

---

[1] Mk xii 37 b—44 (R V.)

(37) ...And the common people (*or*, the great multitude) heard him gladly.

(38) And in his teaching he said, Beware of the scribes, which desire to walk in long robes, and [to have] salutations in the marketplaces,

(39) And chief seats in the synagogues, and chief places at feasts

(40) They which devour widows' houses, and for a pretence make (*or*, even while for a pretence they make) long prayers, these shall receive greater condemnation

(41) And he sat down over against the treasury, and beheld how the multitude cast money (*lit.*

Mt xxiii 1—7 (R V)

(1) Then spake Jesus to the multitudes and to his disciples, saying,

(2) The scribes and the Pharisees sit on Moses' seat

(3) All things therefore whatsoever they bid you, [these] do and observe. but do not ye after their works, for they say, and do not.

(4) Yea, they bind heavy burdens and grievous to be borne [*many anc. auth. omit* and grievous to be borne], and lay them on men's shoulders; but they themselves will not move them with their finger

(5) But all their works they do for to be seen of men: for they make broad their phylacteries, and enlarge the borders [of their garments],

(6) And love the chief place at feasts, and the chief seats in the synagogues,

(7) And the salutations in the marketplaces, and to be called of men, Rabbi

Lk. xx 45—xxi 4 (R V)

(45) And in the hearing of all the people he said unto his disciples,

(46) Beware of the scribes, which desire to walk in long robes, and love salutations in the marketplaces, and chief seats in the synagogues, and chief places at feasts,

(47) Which devour widows' houses, and for a pretence make long prayers · these shall receive greater condemnation.

[Comp Lk xi 43 Woe unto you Pharisees! for ye love the chief seats in the synagogues, and the salutations in the marketplaces.]

(xxi. 1) And he looked up, and saw the rich men that were casting their gifts into the trea-

JESUS "WALKING" IN THE TEMPLE

widows' houses" and a story that exalts the almsgiving of "a poor widow" Luke closely follows Mark in both. There is consequently no question here about the rule of Johannine Intervention[1].

Mk xii 37 b—44 (R V.) *contd*.	Lk. xx 45—xxi 4 (R V.) *contd*
brass) into the treasury and many that were rich cast in much.	sury (*or*, and saw them that. .treasury, and they were rich)
(42) And there came a (*lit* one) poor widow, and she cast in two mites, which make a farthing.	(2) And he saw a certain poor widow, casting in thither two mites.
(43) And he called unto him his disciples, and said unto them, Verily I say unto you, This poor widow cast in more than all they which are casting into the treasury	(3) And he said, Of a truth I say unto you, This poor widow cast in more than they all
(44) For they all did cast in of their superfluity, but she of her want did cast in all that she had, [even] all her living	(4) For all these did of their superfluity cast in unto the gifts · but she of her want did cast in all the living that she had.

[1] Mk xii 37 "heard him gladly," omitted by Mt -Lk, can hardly be called an instance of the failure of Johannine Intervention. For it is a variation of Mk xi 18 "was astonished at his teaching," parall Mt om, parall Lk xix. 48 "hung upon him, listening." John dramatizes this in vii 46 "never man so spake," uttered by "the officers," to their rulers, the "chief priests and Pharisees"

But, with reference to Johannine Intervention, some notice is due here to Mk xii 41 καθίσας parallel to Lk xxi 1 ἀναβλέψας. Origen —(on Jn viii 20, Lomm ii 150 foll) commenting on Christ's doctrine in the Treasury about "judging"—quotes Mk and Lk fully (Lomm. ii 155), but substitutes ἑστώς for καθίσας in Mk, and explains ἀναβλέψας as referring to spiritual insight. SS agrees with Origen in substituting "*standing*" for "*sitting*" in Mk This is very natural, since (see above, p 204, n 1) "it was not lawful to *sit* in the Temple" Hence, too, we may explain Lk's substitution of "*looking up*"— perhaps intended to suggest spiritual as well as literal vision Schottgen (on Mk xii 42) quotes *Bab Bathr* 10 b "Non ponat homo λεπτὸν

JESUS "WALKING" IN THE TEMPLE

But Matthew's deviations demand attention. For he altogether omits the story of the widow. He also omits the charge of "devouring widows' houses," and that of "making long prayers for a pretence." The latter, in Mark, may correspond to "make broad their phylacteries and enlarge the fringes [of their garments]" in Matthew[1]. If it does, we are led to ask whether "devour widows' houses," in Mark, may be based on some Jewish metaphorical expression of a phrase in Matthew. And this again leads us to examine the metaphor—in Matthew alone—"They bind heavy burdens and grievous to be borne, and lay them on *men's shoulders*[2]"

"The shoulder-Pharisee" has the first place in both the Talmuds, where seven classes of Pharisees are distinguished. He is (presumably) the worst, for the list ends with the best, the Pharisee of love. The Babylonian Talmud explains "*the shoulder-Pharisee*" as meaning a Pharisee like Shechem ("*shoulder*") who was circumcised for his own advantage and not for the honour of God. But the Jerusalem Talmud says "he carries his precepts *upon his shoulder*," or "he accepts the law as a burden," perhaps meaning (as Levy suggests) that he "stoops *his shoulders*" under the Law so as to make it appear that he is a martyr[3]

[*unum*] in cistam eleemosynarum." One *mite* might be given for alms, but not for temple-alms. Jesus may not have seen a particular widow giving her "two mites," but Mark may have dramatized what He said about the typical "widow" as though He said it about a single person. Comp Sir xxxii (xxxv) 15 "Do not the tears run down *the widow's* cheeks. . ?" Perhaps Jesus said "Behold, *the widow* giveth *her two mites* and this is more than the gifts of the rich." It would be easy to take it as meaning "*this widow*" and to explain "*her two mites*" as meaning "*all that she had*"

It has been shewn above (p 203) that Mark's "sitting" may be explained as an allusion to Mal iii 3 "*He shall sit* as a refiner. . and shall purify the sons of Levi . and they shall *offer unto the Lord offerings in righteousness*" The widow's offering was one of these

[1] Mt xxiii. 5 See *Son* 3635 a—b.
[2] Mt xxiii 4
[3] See *Hor Heb* (on Mt iii 7) quoting *Sota* 22 b "*This* [*Pharisee*] *does as Shechem*" (with the Gloss, "who is circumcised (Gen xxxiv 2—26), but not for the honour of God"). It also quotes *J. Berach.* ix.

JESUS "WALKING" IN THE TEMPLE

Now this explanation, though clear enough to a Jew when the allusion to Shechem is pointed out, is far from clear to Gentiles. And it would be very natural that a translator, writing Greek in the fluent rhetorical style perceptible in Matthew's addition, should take the clause as meaning, not "lade, as it were, burdens on *their own* shoulders," but "lade, as it were, burdens on *other people's* shoulders." This Matthew appears to have done and to have made this the first and foremost charge against the Pharisees. If this explanation is true we can understand why Luke, who often follows Matthew in rhetorical additions of this kind, has not followed him here but has adhered to Mark.

Returning to Mark's narrative we are in the first place confirmed—by its condemnation of scribes—in the view that the scribe who previously questioned Jesus about the one commandment was really "tempting Jesus," as well as "desiring to justify himself", so that in fact he received from Jesus not praise, but latent warning, in the words "thou art not far from the kingdom of God." Mark's narrative, from beginning to end, represents Jesus as waging two wars, one against "the scribe" as a type, and the other for "the widow" as a type. The scribes and their book-learning, supporting extortionate priests, had reduced the Temple to a den of robbers and had given dominance to an ostentatious fulfilment of the letter of the Law and to ostentatious giving of alms by a class

---

5 (7) "*He carrieth his precepts upon his shoulders,*" and adds "that is, as the *Aruch* explains it, 'wood to make a booth [in the feast of Tabernacles] or something of that nature'." This far-fetched explanation in the *Aruch* (1001 A.D.) shews nothing but the difficulty of the allusion. *J. Berach.* itself adds as a further definition of the first (or, Shechem) Pharisee "The first is like unto a man that would *take the Divine commandments upon his shoulders to take them away*," i.e. get rid of them. But the explanation given by Levy (iv 143 *a*) is far more probable, namely, that it is a play on the name of Shechem (Gen xxxiv. 2) and the meaning of Heb. *shechem* "shoulder." Shechem was circumcised "for a pretence," and the Shechem-Pharisee carried on his shoulders the yoke of the Law, for all men to see it, as though it were a crushing burden. In none of these explanations is there a thought of laying burdens on other people's shoulders.

JESUS "WALKING" IN THE TEMPLE

that oppressed the poor With this antithesis Mark ends, 'They all [*i.e* the rich] did cast into [the treasury] from their superfluity, but she from her want did cast in all that she had."

Passing to the Fourth Gospel, and inquiring what conclusion is assigned there to Christ's teaching in the Temple, we find ourselves confronted first with a textual difficulty Christ's teaching appears at first sight to conclude with the words "While ye have the light, believe on the light, that ye may become sons of light," followed by a statement that Jesus departed, "These things spake Jesus and departed and was hidden from them[1]." Then follows the Evangelist's comment, namely, that the Light was hidden from them through their own fault, "for they loved the glory of men more than the glory of God[2]"—words that seem to sum up the Synoptic particularities about "long robes" and "salutations" and "chief seats." But then, when we are ready as it were to pass out of the Temple with Jesus for the last time, the Gospel adds "But Jesus cried aloud and said," introducing a doctrine about Himself as "light" ("I am come, light, into the world") and about a "commandment" given to Him by the Father, and about His knowledge that "His commandment is eternal life[3]"

To what period and place are we to assign this crying aloud? Some authorities have the present or imperfect as the tenses of the verbs "cried" and "said[4]"; and I have found no comment on the place except in Nonnus, who says that it was "inside the Temple[5]." Most readers will feel that it could hardly have been anywhere else[6]. But they will also probably feel that John could not expect us to assume that Jesus, the departing Light, after He had withdrawn from the Temple and had been "hidden" from the Jews, informally returned to it again in a visit unmentioned by the Evangelist, in order to make these few final remarks. The way out of the difficulty is to suppose

---

[1] Jn xii. 36, see *Joh Gr* **2543**.
[2] Jn xii 39—43
[3] Jn xii 44—50, R V. "a light."
[4] Jn xii 44 (Blass)
[5] Ἰησοῦς δ' ἴαχησε θυώδεος ἔνδοθι νηοῦ
[6] The two other instances of κράζω in Jn applied to Jesus are in Jn vii 28, 37, both denoting utterances in the Temple

JESUS "WALKING" IN THE TEMPLE

that the past tense, "cried aloud," is pluperfect, as often in John elsewhere, and that the Evangelist, in accordance with his habit of adding parentheses or appendices, introduces an appendix to shew that the Light did not desert the Jews without full warning, "But Jesus *had cried and said*[1]."

The last sentence in this Johannine appendix to Christ's teaching in the Temple combines the two words introduced by the question of the scribe in Mark, "What is the first *commandment*?" and by the parallel question of the lawyer in Luke, "What shall I do to inherit *eternal life*[2]?" In John, the "commandment" of the Father to the Son is that He should die and rise again for the redemption of mankind; and at the conclusion of the "crying aloud" Jesus says "I know that his *commandment is eternal life*[3]."

---

[1] See *Joh Gr* 2459—62 on Aorist for English Pluperfect, and 2631—5 (ii) on Johannine Parentheses.
[2] Mk xii. 28, Lk. x. 25.
[3] Jn xii. 50.

CHAPTER VII

THE LAST DAYS

[Mark xiii. 1—37]

§ 1 *The casting down of the Temple*[1]

IN the Marcan text ("what manner of stones") there appears to be an allusion to the immense size and careful preparation of the stones employed by Herod in the rebuilding of the Temple, which was in effect the construction of a new building[2] A pious Jew might contrast these with the corner stone mentioned in

---

[1]
Mk xiii 1—2 (R.V.)	Mt. xxiv 1—2 (R.V)	Lk xxi. 5—6 (R.V)
(1) And as he went forth out of the temple, one of his disciples saith unto him, Master (*or*, Teacher), behold, what manner of stones and what manner of buildings!	(1) And Jesus went out from the temple, and was going on his way; and his disciples came to him to shew him the buildings of the temple.	(5) And as some spake of the temple, how it was adorned with goodly stones and offerings, he said,
(2) And Jesus said unto him, Seest thou these great buildings? there shall not be left here one stone upon another, which shall not be thrown down.	(2) But he answered and said unto them, See ye not all these things? verily I say unto you, There shall not be left here one stone upon another, that shall not be thrown down	(6) As for these things which ye behold, the days will come, in which there shall not be left here one stone upon another, that shall not be thrown down

For Mk xiii. 1 "*one*" parall. to Lk xxi. 5 "*some*," comp Mk xii 28 "*one*" perhaps parall. to Lk xx 39 "*some*," on which see *Corrections* 463 In Greek, εἰπόν [ ] ἐκ τῶν μαθητῶν with an ellipsis of τινες, meaning "*some of* the disciples said," might easily be taken as an error for εἰπέν [τις] ἐκ, "*one of* them said."

[2] Joseph *Ant.* xv. 11. 1—7.

THE LAST DAYS

the Psalms and in the prophecy of Zechariah, and a Christian Jew would reflect that this exclamation "what manner of stones!" was addressed to the Messiah at the very moment when He, the rejected Corner Stone, was going forth out of the Temple, leaving it to become a heap of stones, a ruin.

Luke says that the Temple was "adorned with goodly stones and *dedicated-gifts*," using the word "*anathēma*," unique in N T.[1] Josephus, in the passage where he describes Herod's goodly stones, adds that "there were fixed in the circuit of the whole temple barbaric spoils, and all these King Herod *dedicated*, adding all that he had taken from the Arabians[2]." Now a fragment of Epictetus, using the very phrase employed by Luke, "adorn with dedicated-gifts," says "If it be thy purpose to *adorn the city with dedicated-gifts*, *dedicate* first unto thyself that best of *dedicatory-gifts*, mildness, and righteousness, and beneficence[3]." These were just the qualities that Herod did not possess David was forbidden to build the Temple as being a man that had shed much blood[4]. Herod was notoriously a shedder of blood. The Greek word *anathēma*, said by the Grammarian Moeris to be the Attic form of the Hellenic *anathĕma*, occurs in the latter form almost invariably in LXX, and means "something dedicated to Jehovah for the purpose of destruction" In this sense Paul uses *anathĕma*[5]. Luke must have known all this when he inserted (what Mark and Matthew have not inserted) this "adornment with dedicated gifts," and he may have inserted

---

[1] Lk xxi 5, Tisch has ἀναθέμασιν with (Alford) ADXא, but W H ἀναθήμασιν with BQ. *Oxf Conc LXX* gives ἀνάθεμα, ἀνάθημα under one heading, and always = חרם "*dedicated to destruction*"—except in Judith (1), Macc (3) where it means "*dedicated-gift*" Thayer quotes Moeris ἀνάθημα ἀττικῶς, ἀνάθεμα ἑλληνικῶς

[2] *Ant*. xv 11 3 τοῦ δ' ἱεροῦ παντὸς ἦν ἐν κύκλῳ πεπηγμένα σκῦλα βαρβαρικά, καὶ ταῦτα πάντα βασιλεὺς Ἡρώδης ἀνέθηκεν προσθεὶς ὅσα καὶ τῶν Ἀράβων ἔλαβεν. Josephus freq. uses ἀνάθημα and ἀνατίθημι. See Wetst (on Lk xxi 5) quoting *Ant* xii 2 7 and 5. 4, xvii 10 3. On Luke, as imitating Josephus, see *Introd* p 115.

[3] Epict *Fragm*. Stob 59 (Schweig 80) τὴν πόλιν ἀναθήμασι κοσμεῖν, comp. Philo ii 589 ἀναθήμασι κοσμήσας...τὸ ἱερόν

[4] 1 Chr. xxii. 8, xxviii. 3.   [5] Rom. ix. 3, 1 Cor. xii. 3 etc

THE LAST DAYS

it allusively. Habakkuk said that when a man "buildeth" with blood "the stone shall cry out of the wall[1]" against him. Similarly the stones in the Herodian temple, built up into a temple of ostentation by a man of blood, and used as a temple of extortion by priests of Mammon, might be regarded as crying out for dissolution[2].

There is nothing here that calls for Johannine Intervention since Luke does not omit or contradict anything in Mark. In the Johannine narrative of the Cleansing of the Temple attention is fixed on the spiritual corruption that is destroying the Temple ("destroy ye this temple") and on the spiritual nature of the Temple that will take its place. The Jews, not the disciples, emphasize the length of time—"forty and six years"—needed for the construction of the present Temple, as contrasted with the "three days" in which it is to be reconstructed[3]. The language of the Jews represents a literal, that of Jesus a mystical view. The passage appears to have no contact with the Mark-Luke tradition about the admiration of the disciples for the goodly "stones."

§ 2. "*When shall these things be*[4]?"

The original question seems to have been simply "When shall these things be, and what [shall be] the sign?" But this

---

[1] Hab ii 11—12.

[2] On the other hand, Luke (xix 40) describes Jesus, on the way to the City, as speaking of "stones" that would "cry out" in praise of the Messiah if the children of Israel were silent. These "stones" ought consistently to be on the road, outside the Temple, but we have seen (above, p 222, n. 4) that Jerome regards them as belonging to the Temple.

[3] Jn ii. 19—20. See *Son* 3194 b (referring to *Joh. Gr.* 2023—4) as to the "forty-six years," and as to the refusal of pious Jews to regard Herod as the builder (rather than the repairer) of the Temple

[4]
Mk xiii. 3—4 (R V)	Mt xxiv. 3 (R V.)	Lk xxi 7 (R V)
(3) And as he sat on the mount of Olives over against the temple, Peter and James and John and	(3) And as he sat on the mount of Olives, the disciples came unto him privately, saying,	(7) And they asked him, saying, Master (*or*, Teacher), when therefore shall these things be? and

THE LAST DAYS

was felt not to go far enough. It was written in the beginning of the prophecy of Jeremiah. "I have put my words in thy mouth, see, I have set thee...to destroy and to overthrow, to build and to plant[1]." The same words might seem necessarily to apply to Jesus. He had prophesied "destroying and overthrowing" But He would assuredly also "build and plant" When would *all this* take place? "What [shall be] the sign when *all these things* are about to be accomplished?" So writes Mark. Matthew follows Mark but expresses *"all"* in detail, making three questions in effect —(1) When shall the Temple be cast down? (2) What shall be the sign of Christ's Parousia ("thy coming, *lit* presence")? (3) What shall be the sign of "the accomplishment of the aeon[2]?" Luke, on the other hand, here rejects the Marcan addition of *"all,"* confining the subject ("these things") to the mere destruction of the Temple. Later on, he retains *"all"* (with Mark) in a prophecy that "this generation shall not pass away till *all things* (Mark *all these things*) shall have come to pass[3]", but in the present passage, we may say that Luke regards "these things" as limited to the fall of the Temple—included in the fall of Jerusalem which he definitely describes as "compassed with armies."

John, too, has a Discourse on the Last Days. But it has nothing to do with any prophecy about the Temple. It is

Mk xiii 3—4 (R.V.) *contd.*	Mt. xxiv. 3 (R V) *contd.*	Lk xxi. 7 (R V) *contd*
Andrew asked him privately, (4) Tell us, when shall these things be? and what [shall be] the sign when these things are all about to be accomplished?	Tell us, when shall these things be? and what [shall be] the sign of thy coming (*lit.* presence), and of the end of the world (*or*, the consummation of the age)?	what [shall be] the sign when these things are about to come to pass?

[1] Jerem 1 9—10.

[2] Mt xxiv 3. (1) Παρουσία and (ii) συντέλεια occur in no Gospel except Mt (i) xxiv 3, 27, 37, 39, (ii) xiii 39, 40, 49, xxiv. 3, xxviii 20 Συντέλεια occurs elsewhere in N.T only in Heb. ix 26 νυνὶ δὲ ἅπαξ ἐπὶ συντελείᾳ τῶν αἰώνων

[3] See *Son* **3583** *a*, quoting Mk xiii. 30, Mt xxiv. 34, Lk. xxi. 32.

addressed to the disciples, terrified by Christ's predictions of His departure from them, and it is wholly personal. Christ's "presence" indeed is promised, but not an external *parousia*. It is an "abiding" of the Son and the Father in the heart of the believer. Or it is the gift of a *Paraclete*, the Son's second Self, to be "friend in need" to the disciples, representing the Son in their hearts. Whereas the Marcan Discourse is embodied in Christ's answer to questions from Peter, James, John, and Andrew, and no particular questioners are mentioned in the parallel Matthew and Luke, John mentions as questioners Peter, Thomas, Philip, and the "Judas" called "not Iscariot[1]"

Mark and Matthew say that the questions were addressed to Jesus by the disciples as He sat on the Mount of Olives privately. Luke leaves us under the impression that they were uttered in the Temple. John does not contradict this, but implies that such questions as he records were uttered in the chamber of the Last Supper[2], and he nowhere mentions the Mount of Olives. Luke mentions the Mount of Olives at the conclusion of the Discourse on the Last Days as being Christ's lodging-place by night, and (consistently) after the Last Supper[3].

But Luke does not connect the Mount of Olives with any utterance of Jesus about the Last Days except indirectly, and that in the Acts, after the Resurrection: "Then returned they unto Jerusalem from *the mount called Olivet, which is nigh unto Jerusalem, a sabbath day's journey off*[4]." This follows the question "Lord, dost thou at this time restore the kingdom to Israel?" to which Jesus replies "It is not for you to know times or seasons, which the Father hath set within his own authority[5]." At the conclusion of this reply, Jesus "was taken up[6]." But the Ascension, according to Luke's Gospel, took place after Jesus had "led them out until they were *over against Bethany*[7]." It seems to follow that the Ascension is regarded as taking place between Bethany and Jerusalem, somewhere on the Mount of

---

[1] Jn xiii 37, xiv. 5—22. [2] Jn xiv. 31.
[3] Lk xxi. 37, xxii. 39.   [4] Acts i. 12.
[5] Acts i 6—7   [6] Acts i. 9.
[7] Lk. xxiv. 50.

THE LAST DAYS

Olives, and as closely following an utterance of Jesus warning the disciples not to expect to know certain "times and seasons."

These statements of Luke could not fail to turn the minds of Christians to the thought of the precise place where Jesus, after the Resurrection, answered the question of the disciples as to the time of the restoration of the kingdom of Israel and also ascended to heaven. Luke suggests that it was "over against Bethany," and yet only "a sabbath day's journey" (*i e* about six stadia) from Jerusalem. But John tells us that Bethany was about fifteen stadia from Jerusalem[1]. A reader of Luke's Gospel and Acts, ignorant of the topography of Jerusalem and without the help of John, would naturally suppose that the place of the Ascension was quite close to Bethany, and that Bethany was little more than six stadia from Jerusalem. John dissipates that impression.

Mark and the Acts, taken together, indicate that a questioning of Jesus about the Coming of the New Kingdom may have taken place on the Mount of Olives *both before and after Christ's resurrection*[2]. *The accounts of His replies to them on these two occasions may have been intermingled.* This may explain in part the very great deviations of Luke from Mark and Matthew as to Christ's Discourse on the Last Days.

§ 3. "*Wars...the beginning of travail," in Mark and Matthew*[3]

In the prediction of "wars" Luke alone adds that they will be accompanied by "pestilences"—as well as by "earthquakes"

---

[1] Jn xi 18.
[2] See *Pistis Sophia* § 4 "Quum μαθηται sederent apud sese in monte olivarum," following § 1 "Quum Jesus resurgeret e mortuis et transigeret undecim annos loquens cum suis μαθηταις...."

[3]
Mk xiii 5—8 (R V)	Mt. xxiv 4—8 (R V)	Lk xxi 8—12 a (R V)
(5) And Jesus began to say unto them, Take heed that no man lead you astray. (6) Many shall come in my name,	(4) And Jesus answered and said unto them, Take heed that no man lead you astray (5) For many shall come in my	(8) And he said, Take heed that ye be not led astray for many shall come in my name, saying, I am [he], and, The time is at hand. go

THE LAST DAYS

and "famines," which Mark and Matthew also mention. It is probable that Luke, who often closely imitates Thucydides, has borrowed from him an alliterative combination of "*limoi* and *loimoi*," "*famines* and *pestilences*," well known in Greece at the time of the Peloponnesian war, and connected by the historian with a Greek oracle in such a way that the jingle would be familiar to everyone who had even a smattering of Greek literature[1]. By adding also "tumults"—literally "unsettlements"—and "terrifying portents from heaven," Luke gives us the impression that he had in view the unsettled condition within the city of Jerusalem, and the portents in heaven above it, before it was taken by the Romans, which Josephus has recorded[2]. At

Mk xiii 5—8 (R V) *contd*	Mt xxiv 4—8 (R V) *contd*	Lk xxi 8—12 *a* (R V) *contd*
saying, I am [he], and shall lead many astray.	name, saying, I am the Christ, and shall lead many astray	ye not after them
(7) And when ye shall hear of wars and rumours of wars, be not troubled [these things] must needs come to pass, but the end is not yet	(6) And when ye shall hear of wars and rumours of wars see that ye be not troubled for [these things] must needs come to pass, but the end is not yet	(9) And when ye shall hear of wars and tumults, be not terrified for these things must needs come to pass first, but the end is not immediately
(8) For nation shall rise against nation, and kingdom against kingdom there shall be earthquakes in divers places, there shall be famines these things are the beginning of travail	(7) For nation shall rise against nation, and kingdom against kingdom and there shall be famines and earthquakes in divers places (8) But all these things are the beginning of travail	(10) Then said he unto them, Nation shall rise against nation, and kingdom against kingdom (11) And there shall be great earthquakes, and in divers places famines and pestilences, and there shall be terrors and great signs from heaven (12) But before all these things...

[1] See *Introd* pp 114—20, and especially p 119 quoting Thuc ii 54 and adding "The noun λοιμός occurs in canon LXX only in 1 K viii. 37, Ezek. xxxvi 29, as a various reading and error for λιμός. In the MSS of Lk xxi. 11, the order of the two nouns varies."

[2] Joseph *Bell*. vi 5 3 "There stood over the city a star resembling a sword, and a comet that continued a whole year (καὶ παρατείνας ἐπ' ἐνιαυτὸν κομήτης)."

THE LAST DAYS

the same time it must be noted that in the only LXX passage where the Lucan word *"terrifying-portent"* occurs, the Targum renders it by the same word by which it elsewhere renders *"travail-pangs*[1]*."* The "travail-pangs," or "cords," of the Messiah is a recognised phrase in the Talmud—meaning the terrors and miseries that precede the days of the Messiah[2]. Luke appears to be expressing it as a Greek historian by "portents from heaven." Also, in his next sentence, he seems to paraphrase Mark's "beginning" (*"beginning* of travail") as though it meant that the persecution of the disciples would be "before," *i.e.* would be the beginning of, the horrors that would follow (*"Before all these things* they will lay their hands on you[3]").

John, although he does not use the word "travail," expresses the Jewish thought about the "travail-pangs" of the Messiah in Christ's Last Discourse when Jesus says " A woman *when she is in travail* (lit. *is bringing forth*) hath sorrow because her hour

---

[1] Is xix 17 "shall become for *a terror* (חגה) unto Egypt," LXX φοβητρον, Targ דחלא, which Targ also uses to render Is xxi 3 "*pangs* (צירים) have seized me," Targ "*timor* (דחלא) apprehendit eos" Yet on the following Hebrew words, "like the pangs of (ציר) a woman that is bringing forth," the Targ uses the ordinary Aramaic for "travail-pangs" חבלין. The Aramaic דחלא, "fear," represents (Brederek) a great number of Hebrew words and is mostly a religious fear, good or bad, of God, of false gods, of death etc

[2] *Hor Heb* on Mk xiii. 8 quotes *Sanhedr* 98 b about "the travail-pangs of Messiah" as meaning "the terrors and sorrows" that shall accompany His coming, and also *Sabb* 118 a about "three miseries," namely, (1) "the travail-pangs of Messiah," (2) "the judgment of hell," (3) "the war of Gog and Magog"

[3] Mk xiii 8 ἀρχὴ ὠδίνων ταῦτα, if δέ be inserted (as in the parall. Mt) might be taken as meaning "But the beginning of the travail-pangs will be these things"—namely, the things about which I now warn you This might be paraphrased as "But before all these wars shall come the persecutions"

The metaphor of ὠδίν, in N T, occurs only here and Acts ii 24 λύσας τὰς ὠδῖνας τοῦ θανάτου It is used literally (in simile) only in 1 Thess v 3 'Ωδίνω occurs only in Gal. iv 19, 27 (metaph) and Rev xii 2 "A woman arrayed with the sun...crieth out *travailing in birth*" It might be applied to (1) Christ's resurrection, (2) the birth of the Church

is come; but when she is delivered of the child, she remembereth no more the anguish for the joy that a man is born into the world[1]" There the context ("I will see you again") shews that the "man" is the Saviour, loosed from "the cords of death" and born for the "woman," who is the Church[2].

This is an instance shewing how John sometimes intervenes to explain a brief Marcan tradition based on Hebrew prophecy and Jewish interpretation, not readily intelligible to Greeks. Such a tradition might be reduced by the historian Luke to prose, partly because he thought a historian should not (in his own person) write poetry, and partly because an Aramaic version of the original suggested a satisfactory non-metaphorical rendering. John does not use the Synoptic metaphorical word "travail-pangs," but he uses the Synoptic thought and expands the metaphor into a simile that no Greeks could fail to understand.

In the same indirect way, John deals with the word "wars." All the Synoptists use it in a literal sense and connect it with a warning of Jesus not to be alarmed or frightened[3] John never mentions it. Adhering to his general custom he prefers an admixture of a positive to a purely negative doctrine. Instead of saying merely "Be *not* alarmed at the *wars* of the world," Jesus says, in the Fourth Gospel, first, "*Peace* I leave with you, *the peace that is my own* I give unto you," and then He adds "Let not your heart be troubled, neither let it be afraid[4]." And later on, in the last sentence of His Discourse, He again implies war by mentioning "peace" and by adding a mention of conquest. "These things have I spoken unto you that in me ye may have *peace*. In the world ye [must] have tribulation but be of good cheer, *I have conquered* the world[5]."

Some doctrine about "peace" must have been part of the Gospel of our Saviour, as indeed of any Jewish teacher regarded by Jews as the Messiah. For the very name "Jerusalem" includes "peace" Philo tells us that it means "the vision of

---

[1] Jn xvi. 21. [2] Jn xvi 22
[3] Mk xiii. 7, Mt xxiv. 6 μὴ θροεῖσθε, Lk. xxi 9 μὴ πτοηθῆτε.
[4] Jn xiv. 27. [5] Jn xvi 33

peace¹" It would be impossible for any Messiah following on the lines of Hebrew prophecy to fail to recognise that if Jerusalem was to be cast down by war, it must also be built up by peace—the war transient and on earth, the peace permanent and from heaven This was foreshadowed in the person of Melchizedek, the ancient priest of Salim—that is, of "peace"—to whom Abraham paid tithes after the war against the five kings². The Messiah was to be "a priest for ever after the order of Melchizedek" *The Odes of Solomon* says "Peace was prepared for you before ever your war was." That is the view that appears to underlie the Marcan metaphor under consideration, as well as the Talmudic metaphor of "the travail-pangs of the Messiah³." The evil is to be a transient phase preparing the way for the enduring good⁴.

---

¹ Philo 1. 691—² "The city of God is called by Hebrews Jerusalem, which name, being translated, is Vision of Peace Wherefore seek not the City of HIM WHO IS in this or that earthly site.. but in a soul that is free from war ($\psi\upsilon\chi\hat{\eta}$ $\dot{\alpha}\pi o\lambda\acute{\epsilon}\mu\omega$)," that is, free from internal "war" God alone is "peace," corruptible existence is "continuous war"

² See Heb v 6 quoting Ps cx 4, based on Gen xiv 18

³ See *Light* 3809 *b—c* quoting the Midrash on Gen xiv. 1 "Because the empires went to war, Redemption came to Abraham" In Jer. *Berach* ii 4 (3) the future mother of the Messiah is described as saying "On the day of the infant's birth, the Temple of Jerusalem is [destined to be] destroyed" To this a stranger replies "We are certain that if, because of his **a**dvent, the Temple is destroyed, it will also be rebuilt by him."

Hor Heb (on Mk xiii 8) quotes from Jerome (*Contr Judaeos* i 2) the following "R Samuel Bar Nachaman said, Whence prove you that in the day when the destruction of the Temple was, Messias was born? He answered, From Isaiah (lxvi 7) 'Before she travailed she brought forth. .'" Jerome says "It is in the *Great Genesis* [*Bereshith Rabba*] a very ancient book" No such passage occurs in Wunsche's edition of *Beresh R*, which does not quote Is lxvi 7 except to say (Wu p 417, on Gen xxxviii 1) that it means "Before the first Subjugator (Pharaoh) was born the last Deliverer was already born" Is. liii 11 "the *travail* (עָמָל) of his soul," *i e*, troublesome toil, has no connection with child-birth

⁴ The following Synoptic difference occurs after the words, common to all the Synoptists, "I am [he]," or "I am the Christ".—

THE LAST DAYS

§ 4. *Persecutions*[1]

The next section of the Discourse on the Last Days deals

| Mk xiii. 6 | Mt. xxiv 5 | Lk. xxi 8 |
| and shall deceive many | and shall deceive many | and the season has drawn near, go not after them |

—where "deceive" (A V) is retained as the rendering of πλανάω, so as to accord with the rendering of πλάνη "deceit," and πλάνος "deceiver." Luke omits this (as also he omits Mk xiii. 22, Mt xxiv 24 ἀποπλανᾶν, πλανᾶσθαι, later on), having only the passive, and this but once (xxi 8).

It must be admitted that John nowhere indicates, verbally, in his Gospel, what Mark appears to mean, that "many" believers will be "deceived" into unbelief. But all through the Last Discourse John indicates something corresponding to this. The word "*many [people]*" he never assigns to Jesus. But he repeatedly uses "*the world*" as a substitute for it. And "the world" is regarded as incapable of seeing the truth because it is under the rule of (xiv 30) "*the ruler of the world*." It is said that (xvi 11) "*the ruler of this world has been judged*" and that (*ib.* 8—9) "the world" will be "convicted" in respect of "sin." And the Epistle says (1 Jn 1 8) "If we say that we have *no sin we deceive* (πλανῶμεν) ourselves." In the Last Prayer Jesus prays "not for the world," but for those whom the Father has given Him "out of the world" (Jn xvii 6—9), not that He should (*ib* 15) "take them out of the world," but that He should "keep them from the evil [one]." All this implies a vast present predominance of a spirit of "deceit" or "self-deceit."

Intervention of any direct kind, however, is reserved for the Johannine Epistles. Comp 1 Jn 1 8, ii 26, iii 7 (which mention "deceiving," πλανάω), *ib* iv 6 "the spirit of *deceit*," 2 Jn 7 "many *deceivers* (πλάνοι) have gone forth into the world. This is the *Deceiver* and the Antichrist." The "deceivers" are not those who say that in a certain time or place they will work a miraculous deliverance, but those who, while professing to teach Christ's truth, do not teach righteousness, and do not make the love of the brethren the basis of their teaching.

[1] Mk xiii 9—13 (R.V.)	Mt xxiv 9—14 (R V)	Lk xxi. 12—19 (R V)
(9) But take ye heed to yourselves for they shall deliver you up to councils, and in synagogues	(9) Then shall they deliver you up unto tribulation, and shall kill you and ye shall be hated of	(12) But before all these things, they shall lay their hands on you, and shall persecute you, de-

(Mark xiii 9—13)

THE LAST DAYS

with persecutions. The difficulty of discussing it is increased by the fact that Matthew omits here, but places elsewhere (in the Precepts to the Twelve), a great deal that Mark places here For example, the Marcan precept "Be not anxious beforehand what ye shall speak," to which the parallel Luke is similar, has in Matthew nothing similar here, but something closely similar in Matthew's Precepts to the Twelve "Be not anxious how or

Mk xiii 9—13 (R V) contd	Mt xxiv 9—14 (R V) contd	Lk xxi 12—19 (R V) contd
shall ye be beaten, and before governors and kings shall ye stand for my sake, for a testimony unto them (10) And the gospel must first be preached unto all the nations (11) And when they lead you [to judgment], and deliver you up, be not anxious beforehand what ye shall speak but whatsoever shall be given you in that hour, that speak ye for it is not ye that speak, but the Holy Ghost (12) And brother shall deliver up brother to death, and the father his child, and children shall rise up against parents, and cause them to be put to death (*or*, put them to death) (13) And ye shall be hated of all men for my name's sake but he that endureth to the end, the same shall be saved	all the nations for my name's sake (10) And then shall many stumble, and shall deliver up one another, and shall hate one another (11) And many false prophets shall arise, and shall lead many astray (12) And because iniquity shall be multiplied, the love of the many shall wax cold (13) But he that endureth to the end, the same shall be saved (14) And this gospel (*or*, these good tidings) of the kingdom shall be preached in the whole world (*lit* inhabited earth) for a testimony unto all the nations, and then shall the end come	livering you up to the synagogues and prisons, bringing you before kings and governors for my name's sake (13) It shall turn unto you for a testimony (14) Settle it therefore in your hearts, not to meditate beforehand how to answer. (15) For I will give you a mouth and wisdom, which all your adversaries shall not be able to withstand or to gainsay (16) But ye shall be delivered up even by parents, and brethren, and kinsfolk, and friends; and [some] of you shall they cause to be put to death (*or*, shall they put to death) (17) And ye shall be hated of all men for my name's sake. (18) And not a hair of your head shall perish (19) In your patience ye shall win your souls (*or*, lives).

what ye shall speak[1]" It will therefore be convenient to print the persecution-extracts from Matthew's Precepts below and to repeat Mark and Luke along with them in parallel columns[2]. Another version of the precept "Be not anxious"

[1] Mk xiii 11	Mt x 19—20 (Precepts)	Lk xxi 14—15
καὶ ὅταν ἄγωσιν ὑμᾶς παραδιδόντες, μὴ προμεριμνᾶτε τί λαλήσητε, ἀλλ' ὃ ἐὰν δοθῇ ὑμῖν ἐν ἐκείνῃ τῇ ὥρᾳ τοῦτο λαλεῖτε, οὐ γάρ ἐστε ὑμεῖς οἱ λαλοῦντες ἀλλὰ τὸ πνεῦμα τὸ ἅγιον	ὅταν δὲ παραδῶσιν ὑμᾶς, μὴ μεριμνήσητε πῶς ἢ τί λαλήσητε δοθήσεται γὰρ ὑμῖν ἐν ἐκείνῃ τῇ ὥρᾳ τί λαλήσητε οὐ γὰρ ὑμεῖς ἐστε οἱ λαλοῦντες ἀλλὰ τὸ πνεῦμα τοῦ πατρὸς ὑμῶν τὸ λαλοῦν ἐν ὑμῖν	θέτε οὖν ἐν ταῖς καρδίαις ὑμῶν μὴ προμελετᾶν ἀπολογηθῆναι, ἐγὼ γὰρ δώσω ὑμῖν στόμα καὶ σοφίαν ᾗ οὐ δυνήσονται ἀντιστῆναι ἢ ἀντειπεῖν ἅπαντες οἱ ἀντικείμενοι ὑμῖν
[2] Mk xiii 9—13 (R.V.)	Mt x 17—22 (R.V.)	Lk xxi 12—19 (R.V.)
(9) But take ye heed to yourselves: for they shall deliver you up to councils; and in synagogues shall ye be beaten, and before governors and kings shall ye stand for my sake, for a testimony unto them (10) And the gospel must first be preached unto all the nations (11) And when they lead you [to judgment], and deliver you up, be not anxious beforehand what ye shall speak· but whatsoever shall be given you in that hour, that speak ye for it is not ye that speak, but the Holy Ghost (12) And brother shall deliver up brother to death, and the father his child, and children shall rise up against parents, and cause them to be put to death	(17) But beware of men for they will deliver you up to councils, and in their synagogues they will scourge you, (18) Yea and before governors and kings shall ye be brought for my sake, for a testimony to them and to the Gentiles (19) But when they deliver you up, be not anxious how or what ye shall speak for it shall be given you in that hour what ye shall speak (20) For it is not ye that speak, but the Spirit of your Father that speaketh in you (21) And brother shall deliver up brother to death, and the father his child and children shall rise up against parents and cause them to be put to death (or, put them to	(12) But before all these things, they shall lay their hands on you, and shall persecute you, delivering you up to the synagogues and prisons, bringing you before kings and governors for my name's sake (13) It shall turn unto you for a testimony (14) Settle it therefore in your hearts, not to meditate beforehand how to answer (15) For I will give you a mouth and wisdom, which all your adversaries shall not be able to withstand or to gainsay (16) But ye shall be delivered up even by parents, and brethren, and kinsfolk, and friends, and [some] of you shall they cause to be put to death (or, shall they put to death).

is placed by Luke on an earlier occasion and this too is printed below in Greek[1].

It would be linguistically and archaeologically interesting to investigate all the Synoptic variations[2], but space necessitates our limitation to traditions of Mark, or Mark and Matthew, omitted by Luke. These are (1) (Mark) "ye shall be beaten," (2) (Mark-Matthew) a statement that "the gospel" must be "preached" everywhere, (3) (Mark-Matthew) "He that endureth to the end, the same shall be saved." To these it will be convenient to add (4) (Mark) "It is not ye that speak but the Holy Spirit"; for this, though it has parallels in Matthew and Luke elsewhere, has no parallel in Matthew's or Luke's Discourse on the Last Days.

(1) In the parallel to Mark's prediction of "beating[3],"

Mk xiii 9—13 (R V) *contd*	Mt x 17—22 (R V) *contd*	Lk xxi 12—19 (R V) *contd*
(*or*, put them to death) (13) And ye shall be hated of all men for my name's sake but he that endureth to the end, the same shall be saved.	death) (22) And ye shall be hated of all men for my name's sake but he that endureth to the end, the same shall be saved	(17) And ye shall be hated of all men for my name's sake. (18) And not a hair of your head shall perish (19) In your patience ye shall win your souls (*or*, lives)
[1] Mk xiii 11 καὶ ὅταν ἄγωσιν ὑμᾶς παραδιδόντες, μὴ προμεριμνᾶτε τί λαλήσητε, ἀλλ' ὃ ἐὰν δοθῇ ὑμῖν ἐν ἐκείνῃ τῇ ὥρᾳ τοῦτο λαλεῖτε, οὐ γάρ ἐστε ὑμεῖς οἱ λαλοῦντες ἀλλὰ τὸ πνεῦμα τὸ ἅγιον	Mt x. 19—20 ὅταν δὲ παραδῶσιν ὑμᾶς, μὴ μεριμνήσητε πῶς ἢ τί λαλήσητε δοθήσεται γὰρ ὑμῖν ἐν ἐκείνῃ τῇ ὥρᾳ τί λαλήσητε οὐ γὰρ ὑμεῖς ἐστε οἱ λαλοῦντες ἀλλὰ τὸ πνεῦμα τοῦ πατρὸς ὑμῶν τὸ λαλοῦν ἐν ὑμῖν	Lk xii 11—12 Ὅταν δὲ εἰσφέρωσιν ὑμᾶς ἐπὶ τὰς συναγωγὰς καὶ τὰς ἀρχὰς καὶ τὰς ἐξουσίας, μὴ μεριμνήσητε πῶς [ἢ τί] ἀπολογήσησθε ἢ τί εἴπητε τὸ γὰρ ἅγιον πνεῦμα διδάξει ὑμᾶς ἐν αὐτῇ τῇ ὥρᾳ ἃ δεῖ εἰπεῖν

[2] In particular Mt xxiv 9 παραδώσουσιν ὑμᾶς εἰς θλίψιν invites discussion. But it will be more conveniently discussed when we come to Mk xiii 19 θλίψις and to the question why Luke never uses θλίψις

[3] Mk xiii. 9 παραδώσουσιν ὑμᾶς εἰς συνέδρια καὶ εἰς συναγωγὰς δαρήσεσθε The *Diatessaron* omits this and follows Luke (xxi 12) who (like Mt xxiv 9) makes no mention of "beating" or "scourging." Consequently the *Diatessaron* confines Christ's prediction of scourging to the Precepts to the Twelve, Mt x 17 παραδώσουσιν γὰρ ὑμᾶς εἰς συνέδρια καὶ ἐν ταῖς συναγωγαῖς αὐτῶν μαστιγώσουσιν ὑμᾶς Mark's

THE LAST DAYS

Luke mentions "*persecuting*[1]." John represents Jesus, in the Discourse on the Last Days, as saying to the disciples "If they *persecuted* me they will also *persecute* you[2]." This is the only Johannine use of "persecute" in Christ's words[3]. John does not say here that this "persecuting" was to be in "synagogues." But a little later he represents Jesus as saying to the disciples. "These things have I spoken unto you that ye should not be made to stumble.... They shall *put you out of the synagogue*, yea, the hour cometh that whosoever killeth you shall think that he offereth service unto God[4]." John previously mentions

tradition (*lit*) "ye shall be beaten *into* (εἰς) synagogues" might be defended by Mk i 21 (v r) "he [habitually] *taught into* (εἰς) the synagogue," *i e* "he [habitually] went into the synagogue and taught", but it is more difficult, since the "beating" cannot so easily be regarded as habitual In Lk xii 11 εἰσφέρωσιν (or φέρωσιν) ἐπὶ (or εἰς) τὰς συναγωγάς suggests "*carrying* into the synagogues," which might point to a tradition "Ye shall be carried" (comp. αἶρε (αὐτὸν) in Lk xxiii. 18, Jn xix 15, Acts xxi 36, xxii 22). Αρθησεσθε might be a corruption of Mk δαρησεσθε written (Steph. *Thes* ii 1008) δαρθησεσθε It may be suggested that Mk xiii 9 is itself a corruption for καὶ εἰς συναγωγας δ' ἀρθήσεσθε (for καὶ...δὲ see Mt x. 18 etc) But in favour of δαρήσεσθε is (1) the strangeness of the phrase, (2) the fact that Mark might use it as a fulfilment of a prophecy implied in his version of the Parable of the Vineyard where δέρω is twice used (Mk xii 3, 5) Δέρω is used by Luke also there (xx. 10, 11) and in Acts v 40 of the "beating" of the Apostles in the presence of the Sanhedrin This makes it all the more remarkable that Luke nowhere describes Jesus as predicting this kind of persecution for His disciples

[1] Lk xxi 12 πρὸ δὲ τούτων πάντων ἐπιβαλοῦσιν ἐφ' ὑμᾶς τὰς χεῖρας αὐτῶν καὶ διώξουσιν παραδιδόντες εἰς τὰς συναγωγὰς καὶ φυλακας Διώκω, "drive," might be either a general term "persecute," or a particular term "drive [with blows]" (comp ἐργοδιώκτης). See Wetstein (on Mt. x. 17), quoting Epiphan. *Haer Ebionit* I. 10, p. 135, τὸν δὲ ἄνδρα ἁρπάζουσιν σύροντες χαμαὶ καὶ βοῶντες καὶ αἰκίας ἐπιφέροντες οὐ τὰς τυχούσας, ἀπάγουσι μὲν εἰς τὴν συναγωγὴν, καὶ μαστίζουσι τοῦτον, and *Evang. Petr* § 3, MS εὕρωμεν, edd txt σύρωμεν.

[2] Jn xv 20

[3] The only other instance of διώκω in Jn is Jn v. 16 ἐδίωκον τὸν Ἰησοῦν followed by v 18 "sought *the more to kill him*," which implies that διωκω did not refer to small acts of persecution

[4] Jn xvi. 1—2.

THE LAST DAYS

"*putting out of the synagogue*" as a punishment inflicted, or impending, on followers of Jesus[1] The Greek "persecute," meaning "drive," might also mean "drive out" or "drive away"

It is difficult to see how "*drive out from synagogue*" could be confused with "*persecute in synagogue*"—though punishment inflicted *in* a synagogue might often terminate in expulsion *from* the synagogue. But the following facts should be considered together. (1) Here, where Mark connects "synagogues" with beating, Luke connects them with "delivering up" preceded by "persecuting"; (2) Luke, and Luke alone, mentions an instance where Jesus was actually cast out of a synagogue (the one in Nazareth) with the intention of killing Him[2]; (3) John, and John alone, thrice uses the compound adjective "outside-synagogue" (*aposynagōgos*), twice in narrative, and once in Christ's words when He prepared His disciples to expect "casting out from the synagogue" as a punishment. It does not seem unreasonable to suspect some confusion between a literal and a moral "casting out," such as might explain, in part, Luke's extraordinary and improbable story, and also the Synoptic omission of the Johannine prediction—a prediction by no means improbable.

Comparing Mark's tradition about "*beating* (lit) *into synagogues*" following "they shall deliver you up to *councils* (or, *synedria*)" with the version given by Matthew in the Precepts to the Twelve, we see that, in the latter, Matthew has both the Marcan words thus. "They will deliver you up to *synedria*, and in their *synagogues* they will scourge you" This appears to mean "They will deliver you up to the *synedrion*, or *Council of Three*, attached to every synagogue, and then, after being condemned by it, you will be *taken into the synagogue to be beaten*"—thus explaining Mark's "*beaten into the synagogues*[3]"

---

[1] Jn ix 22, xii 42   [2] Lk iv 29
[3] See *Hor Heb* on Mt x 17, which also calls attention to Mt (*ib*) προσέχετε ἀπὸ τῶν ἀνθρώπων "beware *of men*," and asks "Of whom else should they beware?" It suggests that אנשי, "*men of*," might have meant "*men of the great assembly*," "*men of the house of judgment*" etc The Aramaic phrase for "the men of the great

THE LAST DAYS

(2) About the statement of Mark and Matthew that "the Gospel" shall be "preached" everywhere John could not verbally intervene For he abstains, not only as Luke does, from the word *evangelion*, "gospel," but also from the verb *evangelize*, which Luke very often uses, and from the verb "*preach*," which all the Synoptists use Yet the *thought* of "the preaching of the Gospel" underlies the Johannine Discourse, though expressed in different words. In John, the disciples are not to "preach," but to "bear witness." And "the Gospel" to which they bear witness is "the Son" Himself. Or we may describe it as all that is implied by the indwelling of the Son in the hearts of men, uniting them with the Father through the Spirit of truth and love.

Therefore, in the Johannine Last Discourse, instead of saying to the disciples, "Ye shall preach the Gospel," Jesus says to them "When the Paraclete is come...he shall bear witness of me, and ye also bear witness[1]" To what audience are the Apostles to "bear" this "witness" about the Son? It is not stated in detail (as being "kings" or "governors" or "nations") but it is implied that the disciples bear witness to the world at large. The Paraclete, it is said, will "convict *the world*[2]," but the Paraclete cannot do this except through the

---

council" is (Levy *Ch* 1 373 *b*) אנישי כנישתא רבתא Perhaps the similarity of the first two words might cause the second to be dropped

[1] Jn xv 26—7 καὶ ὑμεῖς δὲ μαρτυρεῖτε, *lit* "and, what is more, ye too [are appointed to] bear witness" Comp Is xliii 10, 12, xliv 8, "*ye are my witnesses*," where the context represents the Lord as having proclaimed Himself to be the One Creator and Redeemer, in the presence of Israel, whom He thrice *declares to be His* "*witnesses*," that is, appointed to bear witness to the world concerning this truth It *implies* an imperative ("*become ye* my witnesses") and is once mistranslated as an imperative by LXX xliii 10 γένεσθε But it *is* indicative So it is here, almost certainly, in Jn, though Westcott raises a doubt The indicative is supported by the Johannine use of καὶ...δὲ in vi 51, viii 16, 17, and 1 Jn 1 3 The Spirit, and the Spirit alone, "will be" the primary and originating Witness, but the Apostles "are," for the time, the appointed agents for conveying the witness of the Spirit to the world Chrys καὶ ὑμεῖς δὲ ἔχετε τὸ ἀξιόπιστον, though not perhaps exactly expressing the meaning, accepts the indicative   [2] Jn xvi 7—8

THE LAST DAYS

disciples. Later on, Jesus says that the unity of the disciples among themselves, and with God, is to cause "the world" to believe: "That they may all be one; even as thou, Father, art in me, and I in thee, that they also may be in us, that *the world may believe* that thou didst send me[1]."

(3) The Mark-Matthew tradition "He that *endureth to the end*, the same shall be saved," is parallel to the Lucan "In your *endurance* ye shall win your souls[2]." John nowhere speaks of "enduring." The verb means literally "wait-under," *i.e.* "wait-under stress," and especially "under pressure of attack from an enemy." Hence, in literary Greek, with an accusative, it means "resist an enemy" or anything regarded as an enemy, *e.g.* a temptation. But in LXX it frequently represents a Hebrew word meaning "wait-eagerly-for," and especially for the help of Jehovah[3]. Symmachus frequently corrects the LXX word when thus used, and sometimes he substitutes a word compounded of "*wait*" and "*up*[4]."

John uses the uncompounded verb "*wait*" or "*abide*[5]." He does not however define it by its object as the Psalmists do ("*await the Lord*") but by the element, atmosphere, or region of the waiting, "await *in the Lord*." Nor does he speak of "waiting *till the end*" as Mark and Matthew do. "End" is a word that John never uses except in the sentence "Jesus, having loved his own [disciples] that were in the world, loved them *to the end*[6]." What was that "*end*"? According to the letter it would mean "the end of Christ's earthly life." But John suggests that Christ is Himself in some sense "the end,"

---

[1] Jn xvii. 21 In emphasizing and defining this "witness" of the disciples, John may have been influenced by the occurrence of the Synoptic phrase εἰς μαρτύριον in very different contexts, Mk xiii. 9 εἰς μαρτύριον αὐτοῖς, Mt xxiv 14 εἰς μαρτύριον πᾶσιν τοῖς ἔθνεσιν, Lk xxi 13 ἀποβήσεται ὑμῖν εἰς μαρτύριον

[2] Mk xiii 13, Mt xxiv 13 ὁ δὲ ὑπομείνας εἰς τέλος οὗτος σωθήσεται, Lk. xxi 19 ἐν τῇ ὑπομονῇ ὑμῶν κτήσεσθε τὰς ψυχὰς ὑμῶν.

[3] See Gesen 875 *b*, and *Oxf. Conc LXX* ὑπομένω.

[4] *E g* Ps xxv 5, xxvii. 14, LXX ὑπομένω, Sym. ἀναμένω.

[5] Μενω, in A V of N T, means abide, continue, dwell, endure, be present, remain, stand, tarry [for] (see Strong's Concordance).

[6] Jn xiii. 1. See *Joh. Gr.* 2319—21.

THE LAST DAYS

the spiritual "end," and that He loved His disciples and will love them to an end that is without any end, a timeless perfection.

Hence the Johannine "waiting" is not a resistance of temptation up to some definite point of time. Nor does it imply (as Luke implies) that a man "wins" his own soul, or spiritual life, by such resistance. It would be truer to say that a man retains and develops his spiritual life by "abiding" in Him who is the end as well as the beginning· "*Abide in me, and I in you*.... He that *abideth in me*, and *I in him*, the same beareth much fruit.... If ye *abide in me*, and my words *abide in you*, ask whatsoever ye will and it shall be done unto you[1]." It is also implied at the end of the Gospel that the "awaiting" or "abiding" of the disciple whom Jesus specially "loved" may or may not continue while some "coming" of Jesus is being accomplished There is to be a "coming." But· as to the question whether the disciple will "abide" during its accomplishment Peter is told not to busy himself: "If I will that he *abide while I am coming*, what is that to thee[2]?"

(4) In the Discourse on the Last Days Mark alone mentions "the Holy Spirit" as "speaking"; Matthew says practically the same thing in the Precepts to the Twelve, and Luke something similar elsewhere, but not in the Discourse[3]; Luke, in the Discourse, does not mention the Holy Spirit, but mentions a promise of "a mouth" and "wisdom"—where the Diatessaron, instead of "mouth," substitutes "understanding."

All this calls for Johannine Intervention, and accordingly a large part of the Johannine Final Discourse does intervene. It deals with the doctrine of the Spirit, who is to be what Greeks would call the Paraclete, but Romans the Advocate. The Johannine Paraclete, however, means more than Advocate.

---

[1] Jn xv 4—7, comp *ib*. 10—16

[2] Jn xxi 22 The R V "tarry" has the disadvantage of not expressing the fact that the beloved disciple, whether he lives or dies, will be "abiding" in the Lord. On ἕως ἔρχομαι, "*while* I am coming" (not, as R V. "*till* I come") see *Law* p 525

[3] See the texts on pp 296—7, quoting Mk xiii 11, Mt x 20 Lk. xxi 15, and Lk xii. 12 "the Holy Spirit shall teach you."

THE LAST DAYS

The latter represents Luke's conception. It suggests a barrister, one possessing "a mouth and wisdom," sparing his client the trouble of "practising beforehand" how to "make his *apologia*[1], or, *defence*." But Paraclete, though it includes that, is, in itself, not quite so technical; and John takes pains to make it wholly untechnical, giving it the general meaning of "a friend called in to aid," and, in particular, the Friend, the Other Self, whom the Son calls in from His Father in heaven to help His brethren, whom He is leaving behind Him on earth.

Both Luke and John agree that the Spirit will "teach" the disciples. But in a somewhat different way. Luke writes, in one passage, "The Holy Spirit shall teach you in that very hour"—that is, in the hour when the disciples are on their trial—"what ye ought to say", and in another he mentions the promise of "a mouth and wisdom" that "adversaries shall not be able to withstand or gainsay[2]." This negative aspect, suggested by "adversaries" and "not able," is somewhat too prominent to suit the Johannine conception of the Paraclete "The Paraclete, the Holy Spirit, whom the Father will send in my name, *he shall teach you all things, and bring to your remembrance all that I said unto you. Peace I leave with you, the peace that is my own I give unto you…*[3]"

It may be doubted whether "the Holy Spirit," or the tradition peculiar to Luke in the Discourse, "a mouth and wisdom," better represents the original; and whether John, in setting forth his doctrine of the personality of the Holy Spirit, is departing from Christ's doctrine (accurately expressed by Luke) or returning to and explaining Christ's doctrine—set forth by Mark in the old customary form ("Holy Spirit"), and slightly, but not sufficiently, conformed by Matthew to Christ's new and more emotional teaching ("the Spirit of your Father").

On the one hand the "sin against the Holy Spirit," a doctrine prominent in Mark, accords with the thought of Isaiah about Israel's "grieving" God's Holy Spirit[4]. Also Haggai,

---

[1] Lk xxi 14 ἀπολογηθῆναι rep Lk xii 11, and Acts (6 times)
[2] Lk xii 12, xxi. 15   [3] Jn xiv. 26—7.
[4] Is lxiii 10—11

303 (Mark xiii 9—13)

one of the Prophets of the New Temple—that Temple which spiritually played so large a part in Christ's doctrine—represents God as saying to Israel "*My Spirit* standeth in the midst of you[1]." And Zechariah, another of that band of Prophets, represents Zerubbabel, the builder of the New Temple, as being encouraged with the words "Not by an army, nor by power, but by *my Spirit*, saith the Lord of hosts[2]." But in each of these cases the Targum departs from the original. In Isaiah, for example, the Targum has "They grieved the Prophets concerning His Holy Word"; and Ibn Ezra remarks about the Hebrew text "This is a figurative expression. Some understand by 'the Holy Spirit' the angel of the Lord[3]." Similarly we may suppose that Jesus spoke of the Holy Spirit as a Person, in the language of Isaiah; and that some of His disciples might say—somewhat in the Targumistic tone—"These are figurative expressions." Then they might paraphrase "Holy Spirit," for example, as "mouth and wisdom."

On the other hand, it may be reasonably said in favour of Luke that "mouth and wisdom" is not likely to be a Greek paraphrase. Jesus would probably express His promise of the Spirit in many forms. Luke may have merely selected one of these ("a mouth and wisdom") here and another ("the Holy Spirit shall teach you") elsewhere. In Exodus, where the Lord says to Moses about Aaron "He shall be to thee as a *mouth*," both the Targums have paraphrased "*mouth*" as "*interpreter*." Mark may have paraphrased here, while Luke adhered to the original[4].

---

[1] Hag. ii 5.   [2] Zech. iv. 6.
[3] Ibn Ezra on Is lxiii 10. Comp Targ on Ps li 11 Heb (R V) "thy holy spirit," *lit.* "the spirit of thy holiness," but Targ. "the prophetic spirit of thy holiness."
[4] Comp. *Son* 3622 a—b, 3623 a foll., on Heb. "sword of *two mouths*," i e "two-edged sword," applicable to the Holy Spirit. And see Exod iv 16 "a *mouth*," Onk and Jer. Targ "an *interpreter*." Beneath the Lucan word "mouth" there may be latent an allusion to the Hebrew metaphor of the "mouth" or "edge" of a "sword," which Luke interpreted too negatively Schottgen on Heb iv 12 quotes from R. Nachman "Gladius.. (1) *consumit* et (2) *vitam*

THE LAST DAYS

The conclusion is doubtful   But whatever may have been the original of the passages here considered, it is probable that the personal aspect of the Holy Spirit, sometimes even expressed so as to suggest the thought of a divine Mother, was more prominent in Christ's doctrine than would be inferred from the Synoptic Gospels alone. The language used by Origen and Jerome indicates that it was current in the Gospel according to the Hebrews   The Talmuds never favoured such expressions, and among Christians other views about the birth of Jesus would first overshadow and then discredit a Gospel that described Jesus as saying "My Mother, the Holy Spirit[1]." Nevertheless we shall understand the original history at the bottom of the Gospels all the better for keeping these words before us as possibly representing one phase of Christ's thought and, on rare occasions, of His doctrine and most emotional utterance.

§ 5. *"The Abomination of Desolation" and its sequel, in Mark and Matthew*[2]

This part of the Discourse is probably based on what Eusebius calls " an oracle," given through revelation to those of

---

tribuit" The life-giving aspect of "the sword" might be put on one side by some as being paradoxical

[1] See *Son* 3430 *a—b* quoting Origen and Jerome

[2] Mk xiii 14—19 (R V)	Mt. xxiv 15—21 (R V)	Lk xxi. 20—22, xvii 31, xxi 23—4 (R V)
(14) But when ye see the abomination of desolation standing where he ought not (let him that readeth understand), then let them that are in Judaea flee unto the mountains	(15) When therefore ye see the abomination of desolation, which was spoken of by (*or*, through) Daniel the prophet, standing in the (*or*, a) holy place (let him that readeth understand), (16) Then let them that are in Judaea flee unto the mountains	(xxi 20) But when ye see Jerusalem compassed with armies, then know that her desolation is at hand (21) Then let them that are in Judaea flee unto the mountains, and let them that are in the midst of her depart out; and let not them that are in the

THE LAST DAYS

approved repute in Jerusalem, by which (he says) the Christians "were commanded to remove from the city and to dwell in a certain city of Peraea, [people] call it Pella[1]" If the Christians had had Luke's clear words before them, "When ye see Jerusalem encircled by armies," they would not have needed an "oracle." But a revelation somewhat like that given to Peter at Joppa[2], but much fuller, may have been given to selected disciples (Mark mentions Peter and Andrew and the sons of Zebedee[3])

Mk xiii 14—19 (R V) contd	Mt xxiv 15—21 (R V) contd	Lk xxi 20—22, xvii 31, xxi 23—4 (R V) contd
		country enter therein
		(22) For these are days of vengeance, that all things which are written may be fulfilled
		xvii 31
(15) And let him that is on the housetop not go down nor enter in, to take anything out of his house	(17) Let him that is on the housetop not go down to take out the things that are in his house	(31) In that day, he which shall be on the housetop, and his goods in the house, let him not go down to take them away and let him that is in
(16) And let him that is in the field not return back to take his cloke	(18) And let him that is in the field not return back to take his cloke	the field likewise not return back
		xxi 23—4
(17) But woe unto them that are with child and to them that give suck in those days!	(19) But woe unto them that are with child and to them that give suck in those days!	(23) Woe unto them that are with child and to them that give suck in those days! for there shall be great distress
(18) And pray ye that it be not in the winter	(20) And pray ye that your flight be not in the winter, neither on a sabbath	upon the land (or, earth), and wrath unto this people
(19) For those days shall be tribulation, such as there hath not been the like from the beginning of the creation which God created until now, and never shall be	(21) For then shall be great tribulation, such as hath not been from the beginning of the world until now, no, nor ever shall be	(24) And they shall fall by the edge of the sword, and shall be led captive into all the nations and Jerusalem shall be trodden down of the Gentiles, until the times of the Gentiles be fulfilled.

[1] *Notes* **2837** (iii) *a* quoting Euseb iii 5 3
[2] Acts x. 13 foll
[3] Mk xiii 3

THE LAST DAYS

and may afterwards have been incorporated in Christ's ante-resurrectional utterances. This would explain the extraordinary freedom with which Luke diverges from Mark. There would be for some time a feeling in the Church that the words were of the nature of an "oracle," or dark saying. They required interpretation—"he that readeth let him understand[1]." But "he that readeth" was not a part of the words of Jesus, nor was the context words of Jesus in the ordinary sense.

The Mark-Matthew traditions of importance omitted by Luke at this point are two, 1st, a prediction of an Abomination of Desolation, and 2nd, a precept—if it may be so called—"pray that your flight be not in winter."

(1) In place of "the abomination of desolation" Luke has "Jerusalem surrounded by armies." This is not Luke's invention. It has been shewn elsewhere[2] that Daniel's Hebrew meant "*on the wing* of abominations one that maketh desolate[3]," and that the word "*wing*," besides meaning part of a temple or other building, may be applied to *the "wing" of an invading army*, as it is by the Targum interpreting Isaiah's words about the invasion of Judaea by Sennacherib: "The stretching out of *his wings* shall fill the breadth of thy land, O Immanuel[4]."

There is a great diversity of early Christian opinion as to what this Abomination may have been. Justin Martyr, from whom we might have expected a comment as part of a proof of Christ's prophetic power, makes no comment at all upon it, nor upon the context[5]. Irenaeus, after quoting the second Epistle to the Thessalonians about "the man of sin" destined to be "revealed" as "sitting in the temple of God[6]," proceeds to apply this to the Temple in Jerusalem and to quote Matthew as referring to it in the words "the abomination of desolation...

---

[1] Mk xiii. 14, Mt xxiv 15, om by Luke xxi 20
[2] *Notes* Pref p xvi foll and **2837** (iii).   [3] Dan. ix 27.
[4] Is viii 8, comp Jerem. xlviii 40 "shall fly as an eagle and extend his wings," Targ "as an eagle that flieth, so shall a king go up with his army and encamp."
[5] Clark's Scriptural Index to Justin contains a reference to Mt. xxiv 11, but none to Mt xxiv. 15—21, nor to Mk xiii. 14—19, nor to Lk. xxi. 20—22, xvii 31.   [6] 2 Thess. ii 3—4.

standing in the holy place[1]." This personification of the Abomination is favoured by the best text in Mark, which reads "standing" as masculine in spite of the neuter gender of "abomination[2]."

What course does John take? In Christ's words, he makes no mention of anything that could be called a warning to the disciples to flee from Jerusalem at some distant period. But in Christ's acts, dramatically, he represents Jesus as Himself going forth from the doomed City because the Power of Sin, the Ruler of this world, is at hand, and as saying to the disciples "The prince of the world cometh...Arise, let us go hence[3]." Except in this possibly typical "going hence," John passes by all the detailed precepts that related to the special tribulation of the siege of Jerusalem, and sums them all up in one or two utterances by Jesus of a general nature applicable to all time, such as "In the world ye [must] have *tribulation*; but be of good cheer, I have overcome the world[4]."

The one point in which John perhaps intervenes for Mark is, that he helps us to understand Mark's description of the Abomination as in some sense implying a person[5].

(2) The precept to "pray" that the "flight be not in winter"—to which Matthew adds "neither on a sabbath[6]"—seems at first sight to be (and perhaps is) wholly omitted by Luke. But since we have found Luke's "Jerusalem surrounded by armies" to be, in reality, a parallel to "Abomination of Desolation," it is worth noting that the Hebrew for "winter" is very similar to, and is once actually confused with, the

---

[1] Iren v. 25 1—2 Jerome mentions (1) Antichrist, (2) the image of the Emperor brought into the Holy Place by Pilate, (3) the equestrian statue of Hadrian "quae in ipso Sancto Sanctorum loco usque in praesentem diem stetit"

[2] Mk xiii. 14 ἑστηκότα. Inferior MSS have the neuter, *a* has "stare," Corb. "stantem," *k* "stans"

[3] Jn xiv 30—31 See *Joh Gr* **2428** quoting Joseph. *Bell* vi 5 3 about the Voice in the Temple saying "Let us depart hence."

[4] Jn xvi. 33

[5] Comp. Mk ix. 20, 26 where πνεῦμα is regarded as masc., and also 2 Thess. ii 6—7 τὸ κατέχον οἴδατε followed by μόνον ὁ κατέχων ἄρτι ἕως ἐκ μέσου γένηται. [6] Mk xiii 18, Mt xxiv 20

THE LAST DAYS

Hebrew for "a reproach," that is, "an object of reproach[1]" In this sense, "reproach" is frequently used in prophecy, as in Daniel's expostulation to the Lord "Jerusalem and thy people are become *a reproach* [i.e. object of reproach or contempt] to all that are round about us[2]." Luke in his version of the last Days avoids the name of "Daniel" and substitutes "all things that are written[3]" We ought not therefore to be surprised that Luke does not use Daniel's word for "*reproach.*" But he uses language (not in the parallel Mark) borrowed from Isaiah, to express a warning against *a moral drunkenness that would, in effect, make the disciples to be a reproach.* He says it would cause the day of the Lord to come on men "*as a snare*[4]." There is evidence enough for a *prima facie* hypothesis that there has been some confusion between "*winter*" and "*reproach*"

If however there has been such a confusion, it will appear probable that the error lies with Luke and not with Mark, since the Marcan detail can be found in other traditions of Jewish or Hebrew literature. There are several such traditions, given below, about the kindness of God in arranging the going forth of Israel on various occasions so that it might not befall them in "*winter*" when women and children would suffer[5].

---

[1] *Son* **3367** foll and **3369** *a*, quoting Prov xx. 4
[2] Dan ix. 16   [3] Lk. xxi. 22.
[4] Lk. xxi 34 ὡς παγίς. See *Son* **3368** *c—d* comparing Is v. 30, xxiv 19—20 (LXX and Theod) with Lk. xxi 25, 34, 36, and noting the words in common, namely, forms of κραιπάλη, σάλος, and κατισχύω To these add παγίς in Is xxiv 17
[5] Wetstein (on Mt.) quotes thus "*Tanchuma* 52 2 Clementiam magnam exhibuit Deus Israeli, nam decima mensis Tebet oportuerat eos migrare S D. Ezek xxiv 2 Quid fecit Deus S B Si transmigrent jam, inquit, hieme, morientur omnes tempus ergo iis elongavit, atque eos abduxit aestate. *Eccha R* i 14 Vigilavit Deus S B quomodo immitteret mihi malum illud, dixitque si illos captivos duco in solstitio Tebet, ecce percutientur frigore et morientur sed ecce abducam illos in aequinoctio Thamus, ut, etiamsi dormiant in viis et plateis, nemo ex illis laedatur *Bamidbar R* iii Dixit R. Akiba non eduxit eum ex Aegypto nisi mense commodo ad exeundum, non mense Thamus propter ardorem, nec in Tebet propter frigus, sed in Nisan, qui justus est ad exeundum ad iter, nec frigore nec ardore gravi"   [*Continued*

THE LAST DAYS

Moreover the thought of "winter," if not needful, is at all events helpful in the Mark-Matthew context, "Let him that is in the field not return back to take his cloak[1]." Luke's historical sense perhaps prevents him from accepting this. At all events, in his peculiar tradition about "the days of the Son of man," he omits "cloak," and is content to speak of "his goods in the house[2]" But both "cloak" and "winter" sound like parts of the early "oracle."

In what follows, whereas Mark and Matthew speak of unprecedented "tribulation," *thlīpsis*, the parallel Luke speaks of "necessity," *anankè*[3]. In LXX, both these Greek words are used as renderings of one Hebrew word, but the Marcan word is much more frequent than the Lucan[4]. Writing as a Greek historian, Luke probably disliked *thlīpsis*, "tribulation," because

---

These traditions may be based on the dates given, first for the approach of Nebuchadnezzar's army, and then for the capture of Jerusalem, and then for the carrying away of the people, 2 K xxv 1, 3, 8 (all omitted in parall 2 Chr xxxvi 11 foll) "in the tenth month, in the tenth day of the month," "on the ninth day of the [fourth] month," "in the fifth month, on the seventh day of the month " In *ib* 3, Rashi makes no comment on "the [fourth] month", Syr. has "*fifth* month," Arab "*fourth* month" as also Josephus *Ant* x 8 2 Ezek. xxiv 1—2, after mentioning "*the tenth month*, in the tenth [day] of the month," has "Son of man, write thee the name of the day, [even] of *this selfsame day; the king of Babylon drew close unto Jerusalem this selfsame day*" This would be *in winter* But the city was not taken (Josephus says) till eighteen months afterwards, that is, *in summer*. The emphasis laid by Ezekiel on the date of the "drawing close to Jerusalem" will explain the Jewish traditions about the delay, or respite, from winter to summer

See *Hor Heb* (on Mk xiii 32) quoting Joseph. *Bell.* vi 4 5 about the fatal "tenth day of the month" and *Taanith* ch v where R. Jochanan Ben Zaccai says it was the ninth day, but adds "If I had not lived in that age I had not judged it but to have happened on the tenth day "

[1] Mk xiii 16, Mt. xxiv. 18
[2] Lk xvii 31 "his goods," τὰ σκεύη αὐτοῦ
[3] Mk xiii 19, Mt xxiv 21, Lk xxi 23
[4] Tromm gives צרה = ἀνάγκη (4), θλίψις (55) Ἀνάγκη is good literary Greek and occurs in the Apocrypha more frequently than in the whole of canon LXX.

THE LAST DAYS

it is mostly used (outside LXX) to mean medical "constriction" or "pressure[1]." At all events in the Parable of the Sower where Mark and Matthew use it, Luke uses a substitute[2]. Here, in the Last Days, Mark and Matthew repeat it later on, but Luke again avoids it[3].

Passing to the Fourth Gospel we find that John shews no dislike for the word *thlīpsis*. He does not indeed use it before the Final Discourse. But there, like Mark and Matthew, he uses it twice. It is not however used in exactly the Marcan sense. In Mark, the meaning seems mainly physical, and there is nothing hopeful in the context of the predictions of "tribulation" and of the "woe" pronounced on "those with child." But John represents Jesus as saying "The woman when she is giving birth hath sorrow...but when she hath brought forth the child she no longer remembereth the *tribulation*..."—and then as concluding His discourse with the words "These things have I said unto you that in me ye may have peace. *In the world ye* [*must*] *have tribulation.* But be of good cheer; I have overcome the world[4]."

This is in accordance with Hebrew and Jewish views of "tribulation." The first mention of *thlīpsis* is in Genesis, where Jacob says to his household "Put away the strange gods that are among you, and purify yourselves...and let us...go up to Bethel, and I will make there an altar unto God, who answered me in the day of my *tribulation* and was with me in the way that I went[5]." Resh Lachish, commenting on the

---

[1] Steph *Thes* gives θλίψις as occurring (outside LXX) only in Strabo and Galen. But it is freq in Artemidorus (see Wetst on Rom ii 9). In Luke's time, however, Greek historians would probably avoid it. The noun does not occur in the Indices to Epictetus and Plutarch.

[2] Mk iv 17, Mt xiii 21 γενομένης θλίψεως ἢ διωγμοῦ διὰ τὸν λόγον, Lk viii 13 ἐν καιρῷ πειρασμοῦ

[3] Mk xiii 24 μετὰ τὴν θλίψιν ἐκείνην, Mt. xxiv. 29 μετὰ τὴν θλίψιν τῶν ἡμερῶν ἐκείνων, Lk xxi 25 om

[4] Jn xvi 21, 33

[5] Gen xxxv 2—3. *Deut r* (on Deut iii 24, Wu p 23) says "The idol [i e strange god] is near and far, but God is far and near." The strange gods were "among" the household of Jacob, but not

THE LAST DAYS

saying of David to Israel "The Lord hear thee in the day of tribulation!" likens the utterance to that of women comforting a woman in childbirth with the words "*He who heard thy mother will also hear thee* Even so David said to Israel, *He who heard Jacob will also hear thee*[1]." The Jewish comment on the Psalm uses the same illustration from childbirth It adds that, just as a weary traveller who sees a burial place outside a city's walls knows that the city is not far off, so those who see tribulations must also see, not far away, redemption. And it will come from "the God of Jacob"—not from the God of Abraham or Isaac, but "the God of Jacob," the Wrestler, who knew what trial and tribulation meant[2]. ·

The Synoptists themselves recognise that *after* this tribulation (or, in Luke, "necessity") there will come deliverance; but John's brief tradition means more than this It suggests that joy will come *through* tribulation. This is in accordance with the doctrine in the Acts that "*through many tribulations* we must needs enter into the Kingdom of God[3]." The Marcan addition about the unprecedented nature of the tribulation appears to be from Daniel[4]. The parallel Lucan addition certainly omits, and rather discredits, the notion of unprecedentedness[5]. In these circumstances it would be very natural that early discussion should arise among Christians concerning the *thlīpsis* that their Master was said to have predicted, and concerning the Marcan mention of "women with child" in the context, and the previous Marcan mention of "the beginning of travail-pangs[6]" The Jews were familiar with the prophetic

---

really helpful. They were "near" and "[really] far" God is in heaven, and therefore, locally, "far," but "[really] near"

[1] *Deut r* on Deut iii 24, Wu p 24, quoting Ps xx 1 Heb ענה = "hear and answer," R V "answer"

[2] *Tehill* on Ps xx 1.   [3] Acts xiv 22

[4] Dan xii. 1 "tribulation such as never was since there was a nation," LXX θλίψεως οἵα οὐκ ἐγενήθη ἀφ' οὗ ἐγενήθησαν, Theod. θλίψις οἵα οὐ γέγονεν ἀφ' ἧς γεγένηται ἔθνος ἐν τῇ γῇ, *Vulg* "(tempus) quale non fuit ab eo ex quo gentes esse coeperunt."

[5] Possibly some took LXX ἀφ' οὗ ἐγενήθησαν to mean "since they [i e Israel] came into existence [as a nation]"

[6] Mk xiii 8, Mt xxiv 8 See above, p 291, n 3.

THE LAST DAYS

metaphor (reproduced in Revelation) of the Mother of whom it is said that she "was with child, and she crieth out, travailing in birth," and afterwards "fleeth into the wilderness[1]" It is a national metaphor. But it might be misunderstood by Gentiles as applying to individuals, if for example the "oracle" above mentioned said "Shall there not be affliction and a crying out of woe in those days to the woman that is with child and travailing in birth?"

Mark has perhaps thus misunderstood it. But that must remain doubtful. It is less doubtful that John has intervened in order to connect the Marcan traditions about "tribulation" and "women with child"—as also the previous Marcan tradition about "the beginning of travail-pangs"—in one brief prophecy of a general kind, intelligible to Gentiles, and having for its scope not merely the fall of Jerusalem but the destiny of the Church and mankind as a whole And such a doctrine it is probable that Jesus actually taught

§ 6 *The "shortening" of "the days," in Mark and Matthew*[2]

The word here used for "shorten" means mostly "truncate,"

[1] Rev xii 2, 6
[2]

Mk xiii 20—23 (R V)	Mt xxiv 22—5 (R.V)	Lk xvii 23 (R V)
(20) And except the Lord had shortened the days, no flesh would have been saved but for the elect's sake, whom he chose, he shortened the days	(22) And except those days had been shortened, no flesh would have been saved but for the elect's sake those days shall be shortened	
(21) And then if any man shall say unto you, Lo, here is the Christ, or, Lo, there, believe [it] (*or*, [him]) not	(23) Then if any man shall say unto you, Lo, here is the Christ, or, Here, believe [it] (*or*, [him]) not	(23) And they shall say to you, Lo, there! Lo, here! go not away, nor follow after [them]
(22) For there shall arise false Christs and false prophets, and shall shew signs and wonders, that they may	(24) For there shall arise false Christs, and false prophets, and shall shew great signs and wonders; so as to	

313 (Mark xiii 20—23)

THE LAST DAYS

"mutilate," "chip[1]." Also the Greek *Kūrios*, here used for "Lord" by Mark (but not by Matthew) without the article, to mean "Jehovah," in words assigned to Christ, and not in a quotation from the Old Testament, is unique in the Gospels[2].

Concerning the words in Isaiah "*Except the Lord of hosts had left us a very small remnant,*" Ibn Ezra says "These are the words of the Israelites"; and they are appropriate as a congregational utterance, or as a pious ejaculation of a representative of the congregation, as in the Psalms ("Except it had been the Lord that was on our side—let Israel now say—except it had been the Lord that was on our side[3]"). There are other passages in the Psalms where such a phrase as "unless

Mk xiii 20—23 (R V) contd.	Mt xxiv 22—5 (R.V.) contd
lead astray, if possible, the elect	lead astray, if possible, even the elect.
(23) But take ye heed behold, I have told you all things beforehand.	(25) Behold, I have told you beforehand.

[1] Κολοβόω, once in LXX, 2 S. iv 12, Polyb 1 80 13, Diod 1. 78 is used of cutting off the hand, foot, or nose No instance is alleged in Steph. *Thes* of its being used like σμικρύνω, ὀλιγόω etc. (in Ps lxxxix 45, Prov x 27, comp Ps cii 23) to mean "shortening" of days in the mere sense of diminution It is used as a prefix (e g κολοβόριν Lev xxi 18) to signify physical defect In Hermas (*Sim* ix 8. 5 etc) it is repeatedly used about stones for building, spoiled by being "chipped"

In *Son* **3353** *d* foll it was suggested that Mark and Matthew have been misled by mistaking the Hebrew (see Is. x. 23) for "strictly decide," "decree" (*lit* "cut," "sharpen") as if it meant "cut short" But it was admitted that this "would not justify Mark, whose word κολοβόω means 'curtail,' 'maim,' 'mutilate'" Now therefore I retract that suggestion in favour of one that endeavours to explain κολοβόω as springing, not from a mere blunder of Mark, but from an allusion to an ancient "shortening of days" in the history of Israel

[2] See *Son* **3353** *f*, **3492**

[3] Ps. cxxiv 1—2 In Is 1 9, the prophet has said to the Israelites, in the name of the Lord, 1. 7—8 "Your country is desolate ...as a besieged city" They reply "*Except the Lord of hosts had left us a very small remnant* we should have been as Sodom... " The prophet retorts that the rulers *are* rulers of Sodom (1 10) "Hear the word of the Lord, ye rulers of Sodom...."

THE LAST DAYS

the Lord" occurs in an expression of thanks, and it seems likely to have been in the original, though inappropriate for an utterance of Christ[1].

Matthew, whether objecting or not to Mark's unique use of an active verb with *Kūrios*, at all events substitutes a passive verb without *Kūrios*. But he retains the word "truncate" with its suggestion of something more passionate than a mere diminution, a suggestion that the days are the enemies of Israel. This leads us to ask whether the Old Testament ever represents the Lord as "shortening days" for Israel's sake, and, in particular, as shortening them in order to deliver Israel from an Adversary who might be regarded as using the "days" for the destruction of the people. Such an instance there is, perhaps uniquely, in the life of David where Jehovah is described, both in Samuel and in Chronicles, as cutting short the three days of appointed plague for Israel when there seemed a danger that the whole nation would be destroyed[2].

One of these narratives mentions "the anger of the Lord," the other mentions "Satan" or "an adversary," as bringing this pestilence on Israel; but both relate that the Lord said to the destroying angel "It is enough[3]; now stay thine hand"

---

[1] See Gesen. 530 b, referring to Ps xciv 17, xxvii. 13 And comp. Ps cvi 23 "he said that he would destroy them had not Moses, his elect, stood before him in the breach" This passage, like that in Mk-Mt, contemplates an intervention of the Lord for the sake of "*the elect*," though in a different sense.

[2] 2 S xxiv. 15 "So the Lord sent a pestilence upon Israel *from the morning even to the time appointed*." The parall 1 Chr xxi 14 omits the italicised words They were variously and quaintly interpreted, but in any case as meaning less than one day See Rashi *ad loc* and *Berach* 62 b 1 *Tehill* on Ps xvii 1 Wu p 130 says that there was a danger that the whole of Israel might perish in the three days, since 70,000 perished in one hour. Origen says (*Hom Numb* ix. 8, Lomm x. 90) "intra *sex horas* abbreviatum videtur"

[3] 2 S xxiv 1—16, 1 Chr xxi. 1—15, LXX (1) πολύ (v r ἱκανόν), (2) ἱκανούσθω σοι The Heb רב "abundant!" (Gesen. 913 a) may mean "it is abundant [*for me*]" or "abundant [*for thee*]" In Gen xlv 28 it is taken by Rashi and Targums as implying "it is an unexpected and superabundant joy, or favour, to me," but in 1 K. xix. 4 the

THE LAST DAYS

This recalls the part played by "Satan" in the afflictions of Job, and suggests the thought that the Destroyer might be regarded as taking pleasure in an occasion that caused pain to the Supreme Himself, for it is said that He "repented him of the evil[1]"; and Isaiah says about the Lord that whenever Israel was afflicted "in all their affliction he was afflicted[2]."

The intercession of the sinful David for Israel after the flesh differed manifestly in many respects from the intercession of the sinless Son of David for Israel after the spirit; yet the appointed "three days" for the angel of death, and the "shortening" of them, might well appeal to early Jewish Christians as illustrating the kindness of God in shortening the three days during which the power of darkness was allowed to appear to triumph over the light by hiding Jesus from His disciples. And hence might come the personification, so to speak, of the days during which He was thus hidden. The days might seem to be the agents of the Adversary, stretching out their hands against the faith of the disciples; but the hands were cut off, and the days "maimed," by the mercy of the Lord. Thus we might explain why Mark preferred this strong and personifying word instead of saying in plain prose that the days would be "shortened."

In modern times, those who believe in the Coming of the Son of Man are apt to think of it as only a single event, a coming on the clouds of heaven. But we can hardly deny that to the disciples of Jesus the first fulfilment of any predictions of Coming must have seemed to have taken place when He first came to them after His death. The interval between death

---

Targ has "this suffices to me as the end [of my life]"—a cry of weariness (followed by "usque quo conturbabor?"). When "to thee (*or*, you)" is supplied by the Hebrew, it implies that the person addressed has gone far enough, or too far, Deut iii 26, Ezek. xlv 9 etc. In 1 Chi xxi 15, LXX inserts "*for thee*"—probably with justification, for the impression left by the story is that רב here means "*Thou* hast gone abundantly far" (not that God says to the angel "*My will* is abundantly fulfilled") If so, the expression implies a rebuke

[1] 2 S. xxiv 16, 1 Chr xxi. 15
[2] Is. lxiii. 9, on which see *Son* 3518 *f*.

THE LAST DAYS

and manifestation is predicted by the Gospels in various phrases. Some say "on the third day," some "in three days," or "after three days," or "three days and three nights[1]." But the records of the Resurrection represent it as being little more than two nights and a day. The records when compared with the predictions might well suggest a "shortening" of "the days," and the first Christians might exult in this shortening—or as Mark calls it, "cutting short"—as a sign of God's kindness in protecting His elect from the Adversary, Satan, by lightening the burden laid upon their expectant faith. To such a "shortening" John may be alluding when he represents Jesus as saying to the disciples "A little while and ye behold me no more, and again a little while and ye shall see me[2]." They, in their perplexity, ask one another what is meant by this sentence. But they also ask about another sentence—"and, '*Because I go to the Father*[3].'" Jesus had uttered the second sentence before the first. But He had not connected the two. The disciples, however, do so, and rightly. For the meaning is, as their Master explains, that His departure and His return are of the nature of a travail and of a birth. In a few hours He will go away. In a few more hours He will return, born anew for them, and henceforth never to be separated from them. And the reason for the non-separation is that the Son *goes to the Father*, the source of all spiritual unity. The Father will be in them, as He also, the Son, will be in them, for all eternity.

It may be urged that the Johannine "little while" implies indeed a "short" period but still something different from a "shortening"—different at least from any artificial "shortening" of the nature of curtailment or truncation. That is true, but is it not also John's deliberate purpose to make this difference? It is in accordance with his general practice of basing the Gospel on laws of spiritual Nature. The "shortening" that he implies is a natural one, in accordance with that kind Providence or Word of God which ordains shortness for a mother's travail and duration for a mother's joy

---

[1] See *Son* 3190—7 (iv), 3586 [2] Jn xvi. 16
[3] Jn xvi. 17, comp. xvi 10

(Mark xiii. 20—23)

THE LAST DAYS

According to Mark, the Lord will "cut short" the days "for the sake of the chosen ones whom he hath chosen[1]"; and then Mark adds that false Christs and false prophets will arise and work signs "to lead quite astray, if it were possible, the chosen ones[2]." Luke omits the whole of this. It suggests difficulties about "the chosen ones" (in Greek, "the elect") and leads us to ask how they could possibly be "led quite astray" if it was God who "elected them." John seems to desire to make us give up the attempt to solve this insoluble question. He tells us that Jesus Himself "chose" Judas whom, at an early period, He pronounced "a devil," and yet that He chose disciples out of the world that they might bear fruit[3].

As regards the Marcan "false prophets," we must admit that Luke nowhere inserts a warning against them, nor writes of them as existent except in the past[4]. Nor does he ever use the transitive "lead astray" to denote their activity[5]. John is similarly silent in his Gospel. But this cannot be urged as an exception to the rule of Johannine Intervention without mentioning that the Johannine Epistle supplies both these deficiencies[6]. There "many false prophets" are spoken of as "having gone out into the world," and the popular anticipation of "*Antichrist*" ("ye have heard that *antichrist* cometh") is corrected by saying

---

[1] Mk xiii. 20 διὰ τοὺς ἐκλεκτοὺς οὓς ἐξελέξατο, Mt. xxiv. 22 διὰ δὲ τοὺς ἐκλεκτούς.

[2] Mk xiii. 22 πρὸς τὸ ἀποπλανᾶν, εἰ δυνατόν, τοὺς ἐκλεκτούς, Mt xxiv. 24 ὥστε πλανᾶσθαι, εἰ δυνατόν, καὶ τοὺς ἐκλεκτούς.

[3] See *Law* p 142 "He uses the term 'electing' in different senses—perhaps deliberately—now including, now excluding Judas."

[4] Lk vi. 26 "Woe [unto you], when all men shall speak well of you! For in the same manner did their fathers to the false prophets." This implies a danger that some of Christ's disciples might fall into the sins of the false prophets of old

[5] He uses the verb once passively Lk xxi 8 βλέπετε μὴ πλανηθῆτε

[6] See I Jn iv 1 "many *false-prophets*" and *ib.* ii 26 "these things have I written unto you concerning *those who are leading you astray* (τῶν πλανώντων ὑμᾶς)," iii 7 "let no one *lead you astray*" In Jn, the verb is only used (vii 12 πλανᾷ τὸν ὄχλον, *ib* 47 μὴ καὶ ὑμεῖς πεπλάνησθε,) by the enemies of Jesus

THE LAST DAYS

"even now there have arisen *many antichrists*[1]." This seems intended to warn the readers to beware of an antichristian spirit, instead of merely anticipating a single enemy of Christ, and it may reasonably be supposed to be written with allusion to the Marcan traditions about "false-prophets and false-christs" omitted by Luke

A brief comment must suffice for the Marcan tradition, not in Luke, "But [as for] you, beware. I have told you *all things* beforehand[2]." This, coming at the end of a section, may mean "In what precedes, I have told you of all your perils It is for you to beware of them" But Matthew omits "*all things*" and subjoins to "I have told you beforehand" the words "If therefore they shall say unto you, Behold, he is in the wilderness...do not believe [it][3]." This seems to limit the words to a warning against "false-christs." Luke omits this warning in either form

John represents Jesus, not indeed as predicting "*all things*," but·as predicting much more than Matthew mentions. Jesus says to the disciples on the night of the Last Supper, 1st, about His betrayal by Judas, "I tell you before it come to pass, that, when it is come to pass, ye may believe that I am [he]", 2nd, about His departure, "And now I have told you before it come to pass, that, when it is come to pass, ye may believe"; 3rd, about the persecutions awaiting the disciples themselves, "But these things have I spoken unto you, that, when their hour is come, ye may remember them, how that I told you[4]." Thus John keeps a middle course between Mark and Matthew.

---

[1] 1 Jn ii 18, comp *ib* 22, iv 3
[2] Mk xiii 23   W H. omit R V "behold" (after "beware," R V "take ye heed"), without alternative.
[3] Mt xxiv 25—6.
[4] Jn xiii. 19, xiv. 29, xvi. 4.

THE LAST DAYS

§ 7. *The "gathering" of "the elect," in Mark and Matthew*[1]

In what follows concerning the signs in heaven and the coming of the Son of Man, Luke—while inserting some details of his own in Thucydidean Greek[2]—does not omit anything of

[1] Mk xiii 24—7 (R V)	Mt xxiv 29—31 (R V)	Lk xxi 25—8 (R V)
(24) But in those days, after that tribulation, the sun shall be darkened, and the moon shall not give her light, (25) And the stars shall be falling from heaven, and the powers that are in the heavens shall be shaken	(29) But immediately, after the tribulation of those days, the sun shall be darkened, and the moon shall not give her light, and the stars shall fall from heaven, and the powers of the heavens shall be shaken	(25) And there shall be signs in sun and moon and stars; and upon the earth distress of nations, in perplexity for the roaring of the sea and the billows, (26) Men fainting (*or,* expiring) for fear, and for expectation of the things which are coming on the world (*lit* the inhabited earth) for the powers of the heavens shall be shaken.
(26) And then shall they see the Son of man coming in clouds with great power and glory	(30) And then shall appear the sign of the Son of man in heaven and then shall all the tribes of the earth mourn, and they shall see the Son of man coming on the clouds of heaven with power and great glory	(27) And then shall they see the Son of man coming in a cloud with power and great glory (28) But when these things begin to come to pass, look up, and lift up your heads; because your redemption draweth nigh.
(27) And then shall he send forth the angels, and shall gather together his elect from the four winds, from the uttermost part of the earth to the uttermost part of heaven	(31) And he shall send forth his angels with a great sound of a trumpet (*or,* a trumpet of great sound, *many anc. auth.* with a great trumpet), and they shall gather together his elect from the four winds, from one end of heaven to the other	

[2] See *Introd* p 119 on Lk xxi 25—6 ἀπορία, and ἀποψυχόντων (Mark xiii. 24—7)

THE LAST DAYS

importance in Mark[1] except the account of the "gathering" of "the elect." This omission is not surprising in view of the difficulty of Mark's phrase "to the uttermost part *of heaven*," following "from the uttermost part *of earth*[2]." The Diatessaron omits "*of earth*[3]." Origen takes it fancifully as referring to one of three "abiding-places (conversationes)[4]." Victor offers an obscure geographical explanation, which apparently implies that the boundaries of earth and heaven are identical[5].

Matthew substitutes "*of heaven*" for "*of earth*." He also alters Mark's "*he* will gather" into "*they* will gather," and "*the* angels" into "*his* angels." Thus he emphasizes the fact that the Son of Man, like a king, acts through servants, and that "the angels" are His servants ("*his* angels"). In the same spirit, having in view a king with a great army, he adds that the gathering shall be preceded by the sound of a great "*trumpet.*" Consistently, in the preceding verse, Matthew has added to the Marcan tradition about "*seeing the Son of Man*" another about the "*appearing*" of "*the ensign, or standard, or sign, of the Son of Man.*" All this gives a military aspect to a metaphor that, in Mark, has no touch of militarism.

Luke conveys to the Gentile reader the meaning latent in the Hebrew "gather." To Jews the gathering of Israel meant the gathering of Israelites scattered in various regions as captives, so that it implied release from captivity[6]. This

---

[1] Mk xiii 25 "the stars (ἀστέρες) shall be *falling* from the heaven," altered to Lk xxi 25 "there shall be signs in...stars," can hardly be called an omission of importance. It is a change from poetic hyperbole to prose.

[2] Mk xiii 27 ἀπ' ἄκρου γῆς ἕως ἄκρου οὐρανοῦ.

[3] *Diatess* ("from the end of heaven to its [other] end") makes no attempt (as Origen does) to add Mark's tradition to Matthew's

[4] Origen (on Mt xxiv 31, Lomm iv 319) "multorum coelorum multarum (*or,* multa) conversationum initia."

[5] Victor on Mk xiii 27 (apparently corrupt) τὸ δὲ ἀπ' ἄκρου γῆς ἕως ἄκρου οὐρανοῦ, διδάσκει ἡμᾶς τὰ αὐτὰ εἶναι τῆς γῆς καὶ οὐρανῶν ἄκρα ὥστε Χριστῷ πιστεύειν δεῖ, καὶ μὴ ἀπατᾶσθαι ὡς ἐλαχίστου μορίου τῆς γῆς οὔσης ἐν μέσῳ τοῦ οὐρανοῦ ἀπείροις μεγέθεσιν ὑπερβαλόντος αὐτήν

[6] Gesen. 868 a קבץ (pi.) "usu of Jehovah gathering his dispersed people," in LXX = συνάγω (71), ἐπισυνάγω (3), εἰσδέχομαι (14) etc.

THE LAST DAYS

might naturally be called (as Luke calls it) "redemption" or "ransom[1]" It did not imply a mere gathering into one place, but a gathering into a region or city of freedom, such as is contemplated in the "song" predicted by Isaiah, "We have a strong city....Open ye the gates, that the righteous nation which keepeth truth may enter in[2]." Luke regards the oppressed

---

Comp. Is liv. 7 Heb אקבץ "I will *gather* thee," LXX "I will *pity* (ἐλεήσω) thee," Aq. Sym ἀθροίσω, Theod. συνάξω

[1] Lk xxi 28 ἀπολύτρωσις Comp Justin M *Tryph* § 86 "Moses with a rod was sent to the ransoming (ἀπολύτρωσιν) of the people"—the only instance of ἀπολύτρωσις in Goodspeed.

[2] Is xxvi 1—2 "In that day shall this song be sung in the land of Judah We have a strong city,.. *Open the gates*, that the righteous nation which keepeth truth may enter in." Rashi explains "the righteous nation" as meaning the Israelites returning from captivity, and "keeping truth" as implying a faithful waiting for the proof of the truth of God's promises R V marg refers to Ps cxviii 19—20 "*Open to me the gates of righteousness*" (which is preceded by "the Lord hath chastened me sore, but he hath not given me over unto death") where the context implies redemption Again, R V marg in this Psalm refers to Ps xxiv 7—9 "*Lift up your heads, O ye gates*...."

This and Lk xxi 28 are perhaps the only instances in the Bible of the phrase "*lift up your heads*," and perhaps Luke had in view this Psalm of exultation The LXX takes "heads" as "rulers" ("lift up the gates, O rulers") Origen (*ad loc*) assumes the gates to be those of heaven (ὡς γὰρ.. κλίνας οὐρανούς, οὐκ ἀνοίξας, κατέβη, τὸν αὐτὸν τρόπον ἀναληφθείς..) Jerome (*ad loc*) apparently prefers to take them as the gates of Sheol (*Son* 3615 *b—c*) The *Descensus* (A) § 5 (§ 21) quotes the Psalm (LXX) in describing the shouting that welcomed the approach of Christ to the gates of Sheol Clement of Alexandria (762—3), writing on the Descent, after saying that the Lord "preached the gospel to those also that were in Hades," proceeds "At all events the Scripture says (comp Job xxviii 22) Hades saith to Destruction, We have not seen His form but we have heard His voice," which lends itself to the assumption (see *Descens* §§ 3—8) that these two were the chief "gate-keepers" of Hell Now in Job xxxviii 17 "Hast thou seen the *gates* of the shadow of death?" LXX has "Have the *gate-keepers* of Hell seen and crouched before thee?" The name "*gate-keeper*" is given to Cerberus in Greek literature, and might be given to slaves chained at the gate to keep off intruders (see below, p 331, n 5) The

322 (Mark xiii. 24—7)

THE LAST DAYS

as bowed down under fetters from which the Deliverer calls them to "look up," as Jesus enabled a daughter of Abraham, bowed down by Satan[1]. They had not dared before, but now they will dare, to "lift up their heads" against the enemies that trampled on them[2]. All these details are implied in Mark's saying that the Lord "will gather together toward [himself]" the elect, and Luke draws them out

John puts first a mention of *"gathering into one"* not uttered by Jesus[3]. Here, without actually mentioning the Lucan word *"ransom,"* John introduces the essence of it in the prediction (as commented on by himself) that he assigns to the high priest, Caiaphas: "It is expedient for you that *one man should die for the people,* and that the whole nation perish not[4]" But instead of Mark's technical term "elect," John, in his own person, substitutes "children of God," thus, "He [i e. Caiaphas] prophesied that Jesus should die for the nation; and not for the nation only, but that he might also gather together into one *the children of God that are scattered abroad*[5]." Later on, in the Last Prayer, Jesus repeatedly prays that the disciples may be all *"one"* or *"perfected* into *one"* even as the Father and the Son are *"one*[6]." Thus John retains Mark's *"gather to-*

Heb שער "gate-keeper" =LXX (6) "gate," and Heb "gate" = LXX (3) "gate-keeper" Luke may have followed some early tradition, referring to the Descent, and taking the cry as "Lift up your heads, ye *keepers-of-the-gate,* i e. ye that sit in chains, as slaves, at the entrance of the prison-house"

[1] Lk xxi 28 ἀνακύψατε Philo (ii 433) describes thus the "emergence" of the earth, purified by fire, after being cast down "to Tartarus itself (πρὸς αὐτὸν Τάρταρον)," when ἄρξεταί ποτε διαπνεῖν καὶ ἀνακύπτειν In (genuine) N T, ἀνακύπτω occurs elsewhere only in Lk xiii 11 about the woman who was "not able to look up" because "Satan" had "bound" her

[2] In canon LXX, ἀνακύπτω occurs only in Job x 15 (Heb) "I will not *lift up my head*" The Heb. phrase elsewhere (and prob there, too) implies the "looking up" of one who has been cast down by enemies (see Gesen 670 *a* on Judg viii 28, Zech ii 4 (R V 1 21), Job x. 15, Ps lxxxiii 2)

[3] Jn xi 52 [4] Jn xi. 50, rep xviii 14
[5] Jn xi 52 [6] Jn xvii. 11, 21, 22, 23.

THE LAST DAYS

gether," but explains the region into which the gathering is to tend as being a spiritual one, the unity of the Father and the Son.

§ 8 *"The fig-tree*[1]*"*

What follows describes the advent of a spiritual springtime. The word "spring" does not occur in our Revised Version of the Old Testament[2] But the Song of Songs describes its signs: "Lo, the winter is past...the time of the pruning is come... the fig-tree ripeneth her green figs, and the vines are in blossom[3]." This seems to describe different stages of the spring, and the ripening (or, spicing)[4] of the green figs is placed before the

---

[1] Mk xiii. 28—31 (R.V.)

(28) Now from the fig-tree learn her parable. when her branch is now become tender, and putteth forth its leaves, ye know that the summer is nigh,

(29) Even so ye also, when ye see these things coming to pass, know ye that he (*or*, it) is nigh, [even] at the doors

(30) Verily I say unto you, This generation shall not pass away, until all these things be accomplished

(31) Heaven and earth shall pass away but my words shall not pass away

Mt xxiv 32—5 (R V)

(32) Now from the fig-tree learn her parable when her branch is now become tender, and putteth forth its leaves, ye know that the summer is nigh,

(33) Even so ye also, when ye see all these things, know ye that he (*or*, it) is nigh, [even] at the doors

(34) Verily I say unto you, This generation shall not pass away, till all these things be accomplished

(35) Heaven and earth shall pass away, but my words shall not pass away

Lk. xxi 29—33 (R V)

(29) And he spake to them a parable Behold the fig-tree, and all the trees

(30) When they now shoot forth, ye see it and know of your own selves that the summer is now nigh.

(31) Even so ye also, when ye see these things coming to pass, know ye that the kingdom of God is nigh

(32) Verily I say unto you, This generation shall not pass away, till all things be accomplished

(33) Heaven and earth shall pass away but my words shall not pass away.

[2] When LXX has ἔαρ (Gen viii 22, Ps lxxiv 17, Zech xiv 8) as a rendering of Heb., it is חרף (Gesen. 358 *a*) "harvest-time," "autumn" (or early winter). A V has "spring" once (Ezek xvii 9)

[3] Cant ii 11—13, R.V marg "*the pruning,*" LXX τομῆς, Aq and Sym κλαδεύσεως, and so Gesen (274 *b* זמיר) but Jewish tradition gives "*the singing*" (and so R V txt).

[4] Gesen. 334 *b* חנט.

THE LAST DAYS

flowering of the vine because the fruit of the fig-tree comes before its leaves[1]. Mark does not quite accord with the Song, since he makes the fig-tree put out *"leaves,"* not *"figs"* Luke omits both *"leaves"* and *"figs"*, and he uses the word used by Aquila in his rendering of the Song (*"cast forth"*)—but without *"figs"* or *"leaves*[2]*."* Also Luke, perhaps having in view the fact that the Song mentions the vine as well as the fig-tree, adds *"and all the trees."*

But this does not appear in accordance with the earliest traditions, which point to a contrast like that in Jeremiah between "good figs" and "bad figs[3]" There, the good are the Jews carried away captive to the land of the Chaldeans The bad are those who remain in Jerusalem, or dwell in Egypt. Mark has described in effect the "bad" fig-tree, the corrupt Jerusalem and its Temple, when he described the withering of the barren fig-tree Now he describes the good fig-tree, the future remnant of Israel, the Church of Christ, purified by trials and tribulations. These have been severe for a time, but now the disciples are called on to regard them as signs of growth and development. Like winter, or like the pruning-hook, they are intended to prepare the ransomed believers to bring forth fruit

John intervenes to explain that the spiritual meaning of "summer" does not depend on its being one of four seasons of the year, but on its fruitfulness. The same Hebrew word means both "summer" and "product of summer," whether grain or fruit[4] John's first mention of "fruit" is connected with an invisible "harvest," in which "he that reapeth...gathereth fruit unto life eternal[5]." The next is connected with "death" and a grain of wheat "If it die it beareth much *fruit*[6]" Then follows a group of sayings about "fruit" in connection with

---

[1] See above, p 205 foll
[2] Lk xxi 30 ὅταν προβάλωσιν ἤδη, Cant ii 13 חנטה, LXX ἐξήνεγκεν, Aq προέβαλεν, Sym ἐξέθηλεν
[3] Jerem xxiv. 2, 5, 8
[4] Gesen 884 b קיץ, given by Tromm as = ἀμητός (3), θέρος, -ινός, -ισμός (7), ὀπώρα (3), παλάθη (2)
[5] Jn iv 35—6   [6] Jn xii 24.

THE LAST DAYS

"the true vine," in which "the husbandman," that is the Father, "taketh away every branch that beareth not fruit, and cleanseth every branch that beareth fruit, that it may bear more *fruit*[1]." Here we find a suggestion of that "pruning"—for "cleansing" means "pruning"—which appears to be mentioned in the Song of Solomon as one of the signs of spring This cleansing or pruning is later on expressed by the "tribulation," or travail-pangs, through which the Church must pass to the new birth[2].

§ 9 *"About that day...knoweth no one...not even the Son, save only the Father," in Mark and Matthew*[3]

Luke omits this saying about the "day" here In the Acts he represents Jesus as saying to the disciples, after His resurrec-

---

[1] Jn xv 1—2   [2] Jn xvi. 21, 33

[3] Mk xiii 32—37 (R V) | Mt xxiv 36, xxv 13—15, xxiv. 42—46 (R V) | Lk xxi 34—36, xii 35—43 (R V)

(32) But of that day or that hour knoweth no one, not even the angels in heaven, neither the Son, but the Father

(xxiv 36) But of that day and hour knoweth no one, not even the angels of heaven, neither the Son (*many auth , some anc , omit* neither the Son), but the Father only

(xxi 34) But take heed to yourselves, lest haply your hearts be overcharged with surfeiting, and drunkenness, and cares of this life, and that day come on you suddenly as a snare
(35) For [so] shall it come upon all them that dwell on the face of all the earth

(33) Take ye heed, watch and pray (*some anc auth om* and pray) for ye know not when the time is
(34) [It is] as [when] a man, sojourning in another country, having left his house, and given authority to his servants (*lit* bondservants), to each one his work, command-

(xxv. 13) Watch therefore, for ye know not the day nor the hour.
(14) For [it is] as [when] a man, going into another country, called his own servants (*lit* bondservants), and delivered unto them his goods
(15) And unto one he gave five talents, to another two, to

(36) But watch ye at every season, making supplication, that ye may prevail to escape all these things that shall come to pass, and to stand before the Son of man
(xii 35) Let your loins be girded about, and your lamps burning,
(36) And be ye

326 (Mark xiii 32—7)

THE LAST DAYS

tion, "It is *not for you to know times or seasons* that the Father

Mk xiii 32—37 (R V) *contd*	Mt xxiv. 36, xxv 13—15, xxiv 42—46 (R V) *contd*	Lk. xxi 34—36, xii 35—43 (R V) *contd*
ed also the porter to watch (35) Watch therefore for ye know not when the lord of the house cometh, whether at even, or at midnight, or at cockcrowing, or in the morning, (36) Lest coming suddenly he find you sleeping (37) And what I say unto you I say unto all, Watch	another one, to each according to his several ability, and he went on his journey (xxiv. 42) Watch therefore. for ye know not on what day your Lord cometh (43) But know this (*or*, But this ye know), that if the master of the house had known in what watch the thief was coming, he would have watched, and would not have suffered his house to be broken through (*lit* digged through). (44) Therefore be ye also ready· for in an hour that ye think not the Son of man cometh (45) Who then is the faithful and wise servant (*lit* bondservant), whom his lord hath set over his household, to give them their food in due season? (46) Blessed is that servant (*lit* bondservant), whom his lord when he cometh shall find so doing	yourselves like unto men looking for their lord, when he shall return from the marriage feast, that, when he cometh and knocketh, they may straightway open unto him (37) Blessed are those servants (*lit* bondservants) whom the lord when he cometh shall find watching: verily I say unto you, that he shall gird himself, and make them sit down to meat, and shall come and serve them (38) And if he shall come in the second watch, and if in the third, and find [them] so, blessed are those [servants]. (39) But know this (*or*, But this ye know), that if the master of the house had known in what hour the thief was coming, he would have watched, and not have left his house to be broken through (*lit* digged through). (40) Be ye also ready. for in an hour that ye think not the Son of man cometh. (41) And Peter said, Lord, speakest thou this parable unto us, or even unto all?

THE LAST DAYS

hath set within his own authority[1]." This might imply that the Son, now that He had risen from the dead, "*knew*," or was on the point of "*knowing*," the "*times*," but that He did not think fit to impart this knowledge to the disciples. But it might also imply that the Father still kept this knowledge within "his own authority," so that not even the risen Saviour knew it, or would know it till He had ascended to the Father, if then. Luke's silence in the Gospel, and his obscure statement in the Acts, favour the view that he regarded the Marcan utterance as post-resurrectional and as being—though clear—likely to be misused by being wrongly dated.

John represents Jesus as saying to the disciples, "If ye loved me, ye would have rejoiced because I go unto the Father, for the Father is greater than I[2]." That is to say, the perfect unity between the Father and the Son is consistent with an ampler inclusiveness of the Father in heaven as compared with a narrower inclusiveness of the Son on earth. This epithet "greater" does not appear to be intended to make a comparison between the Father in heaven and the Son in heaven. It has been previously introduced to shew how the Son Himself, after ascending to the Father, will be greater than His previous self in His power to help a believer to do greater works. "The

Lk xxi 34—36, xii 35—43 (R V) *contd*
(42) And the Lord said, Who then is the faithful and wise steward, whom his lord shall set over his household, to give them their portion of food in due season ?
(43) Blessed is that servant (*lit* bondservant) whom his lord when he cometh shall find so doing

---

[1] Acts 1 7   Origen quotes this in his comment on Mt. xxiv 36 (Lomm iv 330—1) and gives a long explanation, after which he adds "alia expositio quae famosior est."

[2] Jn xiv 28.

(Mark xiii. 32—7)

works that I do shall he do also; and *greater* works than these shall he do, because I go unto the Father[1]."

The Synoptic phrase *"that day"* is used thrice in the Johannine Last Discourse. But the Synoptists mean by it a definite day of a visible Coming at some unknown date. John means something very different *"In that day* ye shall know that I am in my Father and ye in me and I in you," *"In that day* ye shall ask me no [question]; verily, verily, I say unto you, If ye shall ask anything of the Father he will give it you in my name," *"In that day* ye shall ask in my name [2]" "That day" does not begin at any particular "hour." It is a permanent spiritual state of union between man's soul and the Father through the Spirit of the Son.

John seems to take a pleasure in detemporising (so to speak), as well as delocalising, the coming of the Lord. When he says "Jesus loved the disciples *to the end*" this is the only occasion where he mentions "the end" as a noun[3]. And when Jesus is said to have "known that *all things had been ended*" and to have cried aloud "*It is ended*[4]," this is the only Johannine occasion where "end" is used as a verb. "End" here implies, in fact, an end that is a beginning—an *omega* that is also an *alpha*. When John desires to speak of the "coming" of the Son in some special form visible to men he generally speaks of it as a manifesting[5]. This is in accordance with the use of the Targumists

---

[1] Jn xiv 12.

[2] Jn xiv 20, xvi 23 (on which see above, pp 61—2), xvi 26

[3] Jn xiii 1

[4] Jn xix 28, 30 τετέλεσται (*bis*). There is an intention in repeating τετέλεσται "He said to Himself... and then He said aloud, '*All is ended*'" Nonnus repeats τετέλεστο thus νοήσας ὅττι θοῶς τετέλεστο τετέλεστο πανυστατίῳ φάτο μύθῳ

[5] "Manifesting," φανερόω, a verb not used by the Synoptists except Mark (iv. 22) on which see *Law* p 28 foll. Mark alone says that "manifestation" is the *object*, Mt -Lk say it is the *invariable sequel*. It is also in Mk-App xvi 12, 14 (of post-resurrectional manifestations). In Jn i 31 ἵνα φανερωθῇ τῷ 'I, it implies that the Messiah is already in Israel but needs to be manifested or revealed, in *ib* xxi. 1 (*bis*), 14, it is used of post-resurrectional manifestations. In 1 Jn i 2 (*bis*) it is used of the Incarnation, but *ib* ii. 28 of the (second) Parousia

THE LAST DAYS

who habitually say "God manifested Himself," or "was manifested,' instead of "God came[1]." "Manifested" is the word that he uses even on the single occasion when he uses (in the Epistle) the technical word *parousia*, denoting what is commonly called the Second Coming of the Lord. "Abide in him, that, *if he shall be manifested*, we...may not shrink in shame from him at his *parousia*[2]." Not that he avoids the word "come" in a spiritual sense. On the contrary he uses it freely, but so freely as to disappoint us if we ask at once "Is He to 'come'? Then when is the 'coming'?" The beginning of the Prologue speaks of the Light as continually "coming into the world[3]", the Last Discourse frequently speaks of the Father and the Son and the Paraclete as "coming" to believers and abiding in them[4]; and Christ's final utterance, addressed to Peter, seems to speak of the "coming" either as a continuous process, or at all events as a matter of which the details are not to affect Peter's conduct or to divert him from following Christ in the path prescribed to him. *If I will that he abide while I am coming*, what is that to thee? Follow thou me[5]."

---

[1] Φανερόω occurs in LXX only in Jerem xxxiii 6 "I will reveal," נגלה "To be revealed" in Targum corresponds to 'come" in Scripture, when the latter is used about God, *Son* 3314 *c*, 3334 *b* etc.

[2] I Jn ii 28. Παρουσία is not used in the Gospels except Mt xxiv. 3, 27, 37, 39.

[3] Jn i 9.

[4] Jn xiv 3, 18, 23, 28, xvi 7, 8, 13, 28.

[5] Jn xxi 22—3, see *Law* pp 525—6. Here it should be noted that "abide while I am coming" is the Johannine equivalent of the Synoptic "watch," or "watch and pray." John never uses the word "watch." Consequently he omits Marcan details connected with "watching" such as Mk xiii 35 "cock-crowing," *ib* 36 "lest coming suddenly he find you sleeping," etc. John emphasizes the more positive precept of "abiding (μένω)"—a word that occurs in the Fourth Gospel more than three times as often as in the Synoptists taken all together.

THE LAST DAYS

§ 10 *"The porter," in Mark and John*[1]

Mark, alone of the Synoptists, specially mentions a "porter," better called "doorkeeper," among the servants of a man who is away from home, and who has assigned to them their several tasks. The task of the "doorkeeper" is to "keep awake," or "watch." The duty of watching is specially emphasized by Mark, and he concludes by emphasizing its universality, "What I say unto you, I say unto all, '*Watch*[2]'"

What they were to "watch" for was the "coming" of "the lord of the house," and the first "coming" was that which followed closely on Christ's resurrection. Then He was variously manifested to various disciples. But Mary, and the seven fishermen, did not at first recognise Him; nor did the two disciples at Emmaus; nor did "some" on the "mountain" mentioned by Matthew[3]. Long afterwards the rich and pleasure-loving Laodiceans are warned that there is a danger of their being deaf to the voice of the Lord at a later coming: "Behold, I stand at the door and knock. If any man hear my voice and open the door, I will come in to him and will sup with him[4]." This implies, though it does not mention, the metaphor of a doorkeeper of souls in the Laodicean Church. This doorkeeper ought to be ready to hear, and quick to open, when the voice of the Lord demands entrance[5].

---

[1] Mk xiii 34
Ὡς ἄνθρωπος ἀπόδημος ἀφεὶς τὴν οἰκίαν αὐτοῦ καὶ δοὺς τοῖς δούλοις αὐτοῦ τὴν ἐξουσίαν, ἑκάστῳ τὸ ἔργον αὐτοῦ, καὶ τῷ θυρωρῷ ἐνετείλατο ἵνα γρηγορῇ (see *Son* 3299 foll.)

Mt xxv 14—15
Ὥσπερ γὰρ ἄνθρωπος ἀποδημῶν ἐκάλεσεν τοὺς ἰδίους δούλους καὶ παρέδωκεν αὐτοῖς τὰ ὑπάρχοντα αὐτοῦ, καὶ ᾧ μὲν ἔδωκεν πέντε τάλαντα (introducing the parable of the talents)

[Lk om., but comp. xix 12]
ἄνθρωπός τις εὐγενὴς ἐπορεύθη (introducing the parable of the pounds)

Comp. Jn x. 3 τούτῳ ὁ θυρωρὸς ἀνοίγει.

[2] "Watch," ἀγρυπνεῖν occurs once, and γρηγορεῖν thrice, in Mk xiii 33—7

[3] Jn xx. 14, 15, xxi. 4, Lk xxiv. 16, Mt xxviii. 17.

[4] Rev. iii. 20

[5] Lucian (*Calumn.* § 30) uses the word "*doorkeeper*" in an illustrative context, bidding us thrust back and shut out bad and

THE LAST DAYS

In the Fourth Gospel Jesus, before His death, is represented as promising His presence after death: "If a man love me, he will keep my word, and my Father will love him, and we will come unto him, and make our abode with him[1]" But no spiritual "doorkeeper" is mentioned there, or anywhere else except in the Parable of the Good Shepherd. "He that entereth in through the door is a [true] shepherd of the sheep. To him *the doorkeeper* openeth, and the sheep hear his voice...[2]."

demoralising talk, and welcome, and let in, its opposite· "A man must set Reason, [like] a strict *doorkeeper*, over all utterances (ἐπιστήσαντα ἀκριβῆ θυρωρὸν τὸν λογισμὸν ἅπασι τοῖς λεγομένοις),. .For it would be ridiculous to appoint *doorkeepers* for our house but to leave our ears and mind (διάνοιαν) open [and unprotected]"

Socrates says to Protagoras (*Phileb* 62 D) "Then do you want me—like some *doorkeeper* pushed and hustled by a mob—to give in, and throw the doors wide open, and let all the sciences stream in, the less defective and the perfect in one flood?"

In Memoriam § 94, speaking of "communion with the dead," implies the need of some doorkeeper, different from "doubt," at the "portal" of the soul that desires to be visited by them·

"But when the heart is full of din
And doubt beside the portal waits,
They can but listen at the gates,
And hear the household jar within."

In the passage quoted above from Lucian, the distracting influences that are to be kept out of the soul by the "doorkeeper" are of the nature of the voices of Sirens, stirring up in the soul a tumult of the passions Comp Lk xxi. 34 "Lest haply your hearts be overcharged with surfeiting and drunkenness, and cares of this life, and that day come on you suddenly as a snare"

Language that might have a very real significance on the eve of our Lord's death preparing the disciples to await His resurrection and first Coming, might come by degrees to have less and less significance when the disciples began to look forward to a second Coming on the clouds of heaven and to apply the old language to a new anticipation

[1] Jn xiv 23
[2] Jn x 2—3 "a [true] shepherd" (R.V. marg "a shepherd," R V. txt "the shepherd") This prepares the way for *ib.* 11 "*the* good shepherd," who is the pattern of every "[true] shepherd." "True" is illustrated by Philo's distinction (1. 306, *Law* pp 254—5) between the "shepherd" and the cattle-feeder.

THE LAST DAYS

Here "the doorkeeper" appears to mean a guardian-conscience, a predisposition to receive good influences and reject evil ones. Such a guardianship may exist in a community as well as in a single soul But the metaphor of a "doorkeeper" is not so natural to apply to a community as to an individual—and Chrysostom's statement that the Evangelist "abode in the metaphor" perhaps covers Chrysostom's difficulty in expanding the metaphor into a simile[1]. It is certain that John has followed Mark in his application of the metaphor of a doorkeeper to the spiritual opening of the heart to the approach of the Lord, but the reason for it is doubtful. Probably, however, one reason for this Johannine intervention is the fact that Matthew and Luke have interpreted the Marcan "doorkeeper" as though it meant a steward or controller of the household, perhaps with special allusion to Peter[2].

---

[1] Chrys on Jn x. 3 "He abode in (ἐπέμεινε) the metaphor so as to make the saying more vivid (ἐμφαντικώτερον) But if you please also to test the parable by literal interpretation, nothing forbids [your] understanding Moses here as 'doorkeeper'" Origen (Introd to *Comm Joann*, Lomm 1 4) says to Gregory "Knock at that which is closed in them [the scriptures] and it shall be opened to thee by *the doorkeeper* of whom Jesus said, 'To him the doorkeeper openeth'" This may mean that every one of Christ's shepherds of the flock must approach the Truth through the door, namely, Christ, and that he will then be admitted by the "doorkeeper," the responsive Spirit (of all Truth, and especially the Truth of divine humanity) which answers to the Voice that demands entrance in the name of the Son But it is obscurely expressed—as also by Clem Alex 698 Both writers seem to blend, or identify, the Johannine tradition with (Mt vii. 7, Lk xi. 9) "Knock, and it shall be opened unto you" (which indeed Origen quotes in his context) [In *Son* 3303 *b* "Also the gospel expressly says (Jn x 3) 'To him'—that is, to the Good Shepherd—'the Porter openeth,'" the word "Good" ought perhaps not to have been inserted]

[2] The metaphor of "opening" is applied in O T to the "ears" and "eyes," but not to the heart or mind, although Wetstein on Lk xxiv 45 quotes "Preces Judaeorum *Aperi cor meum in lege tua* Ipse *aperit cor nostrum* in lege sua (Is 1 5 'the Lord God hath opened mine ear')" Ibn Ezra and Rashi explain Isaiah as referring to the vision in the course of which his ears were opened so that he heard the Lord say (Is vi 8) "Who will go for us?" The metaphor

THE LAST DAYS

§ 11. *The "faithful servant* (or, *steward)," in Matthew and Luke*[1]

In a previous volume[2], it has been shewn that the "doorkeeper" might be regarded as the "gatekeeper," and thus taken as "he that sits in the gate"—according to the Hebrew phrase applied to one in authority—or else as "he that has the keys of the gate," that is, the controller of the king's palace. To the facts there alleged, it should be added that "gatekeepers of the temple," while regularly called "gatekeepers" in Ezra, are called "doorkeepers" in Esdras[3]. And the disgrace of the unfaithful steward in Matthew-Luke[4] has a parallel in Isaiah (also mentioning the power of the "key" in its context), where the Lord says "Get thee unto this *treasurer* (marg *steward*) even unto Shebna, who is over the house"—soon to be replaced by a worthier steward of whom it is said "*The key of the house* of David will I lay upon his shoulder, and he shall open and none shall shut, and he shall shut and none shall open*[5].*"

---

is in 2 Macc 1 4 "*to open your heart* in His law." Luke represents the risen Saviour as being unrecognised by the two disciples at Emmaus till He had (xxiv 45) "*opened their mind* (διήνοιξεν αὐτῶν τὸν νοῦν) that they should *understand the scriptures*," and comp Acts xvi 14 καί τις γυνὴ...σεβομένη τὸν θεὸν ἤκουεν, ἧς ὁ Κύριος διήνοιξε τὴν καρδίαν προσέχειν τοῖς λαλουμένοις ὑπὸ Παύλου, where Chrys. compares Lk xxiv 45, and speaks of "pioneering grace (ἡ προοδοποιοῦσα χάρις)" as the cause of the success of the Apostles. The woman had apparently passed through some preparatory training in the Scriptures. Plutarch says (*Mor.* 36 D) that the reading of poetry "tends to open (προανοίγει) and incline (προσκινεῖ) the mind of the young to the words of philosophy."

[1] For the texts, see above, pp 327—8
[2] See *Son* **3297—305** "The Son of Man coming unexpectedly"
[3] Θυρωρός, in LXX, is almost confined to 1 Esdr. Πυλωρός is freq in Chr., Ezr., and Nehemiah (=שׁוֹעֵר)
[4] Mt xxiv 48 foll, Lk xii 45 foll
[5] Is xxii 15—22 For "to this treasurer (*or* steward)" LXX has εἰς τὸ παστοφόριον. Comp 1 Chr. ix 26 (Heb.) "For in [a position of] trust were they (LXX ἐν πίστει εἰσὶ), the four powerful- [men] (*i e.* chiefs) *of the porters* (נברי השערים, LXX δυνατοὶ τῶν πυλῶν *i e* having power *over the gates*)—they (הם), the Levites—and [they] were over the *chambers* (LXX παστοφόρια) and over the treasuries

334 (Mark xiii 32—7)

THE LAST DAYS

Mark's tradition represents the doorkeeper as on the watch merely to let in the Master of the House. This appears to have been the original, or central, conception, to which others— either interpretative or subsidiary—have been added by later Evangelists. One of these gives a picture of some one watching (or rather failing to watch)—not to let in the Master but to keep out a housebreaker[1]. Another picture, describing the welcome given to the Master on his return from "a wedding," suggests another confused interpretation of "doorkeeper" as meaning, according to Hesychius, "the paranymph, he that keeps shut the door of the wedding-chamber[2]." Matthew's and Luke's parables about the "talents" and "pounds[3]" appear to be expansions of Mark's brief statement that the Master gave to each servant his appointed *exousia*, i.e. "authority," or "province of work," here confused with, or taken as meaning, *ousia*, "resources" or "property[4]." Lastly, Mark's

---

(R V) in the house of God " This passage shews how a chief of porters might be confused with a common porter

Ps lxxxiv 10 הסתופף "*make myself a threshold*," R V marg "*stand at the threshold*," R V txt "*be a doorkeeper*," is unique, and throws no light on the usage of "*doorkeeper*" in general

[1] See *Son* 3300 on the possibility of confusion between the "steward" i e "master of the house[hold]," and "the lord of the house" i e the steward's master

[2] See Hesych Θυρωρός, ὁ παράνυμφος (sic), ὁ τὴν θύραν τοῦ θαλάμου κλείων

[3] See *Son* 3302 *a* on the Heb "*gate*" as meaning also "*estimation*" in Hebrew and nothing but "estimation" in Aramaic It might be taken as referring to the property delivered "according to estimation," ten talents to one, five to another

[4] Ἐξουσία could not be taken as οὐσία (or vice versa) except in a forced interpretation, but οὐσία might be a rendering of Heb "house" (comp Tob xiv 13 οὐσίαν v r οἰκίαν) and see *Son* 3299 *f* for "House of Lysanias" which sometimes seems to mean a tetrarchy Matthew (in the Talents) has (xxv 21) "over *many things* (πολλῶν)" whereas Luke (in the Pounds) has (xix 17) "over *cities* (πόλεων)" The two (*Paradosis* 1397) might be confused in Greek Also Heb "gates" = freq "cities" in LXX. Luke gives us the impression that he knew the parable to refer to ἐξουσία, not to οὐσία, and that he did his best to bring in the correct meaning in some form, "have thou *authority* over ten cities "

THE LAST DAYS

phrase "what I say unto you I say unto all" seems to have raised the question what was meant by "you." "Did it mean 'the apostles'?" Those who asked this question might go on to speak of possible inferences "If so, *perhaps* the Lord said it in answer to one of the apostles, *perhaps* Peter[1], who asked 'Sayest thou this parable to us or also to all?'" This view being adopted—and the word "*perhaps*" being dropped—there may have resulted a tradition that one of the apostles, probably Peter, definitely asked this question[2].

§ 12. *The disciple that "follows," and the disciple that "waits," in John*

We have now to ask whether John has anything to say that bears upon the Matthew-Luke tradition about a special upper

---

In Mark (xiii 34), SS has "his property." The Syr of Walton omits "his," as also do *a*, *k*, and *Corb*, and *Brix* "data servis suis potestate cujusque operis" Perhaps Mark may mean that the Master of the House took an unusual course He did *not* appoint one servant to whom he entrusted control of the household in his absence—like Pharaoh, who made Joseph (Ps cv 21) "lord of his house and ruler of all his substance, to bind his princes at his pleasure." On the contrary, the Master imparted "*the authority*" to all his servants—to each one the authority over the province of work appointed for him, from the highest to the lowest, from the most active, who might be constantly at work, down to "the doorkeeper," whose time might be mainly spent in watching

[1] Lk xii 41 See *Son* 3301 quoting Mk xiii 1 "one of his disciples"

[2] It would be natural, as the years passed on after the first Coming or Resurrection, that the precepts about "watching" should be regarded largely as addressed not to all Christians individually but to the presbyters "watching" for the souls entrusted to their charge Comp Acts xx 31, Heb xiii 17 (referring to elders).

In concluding this study of the Precepts of Watching it is natural to ask for O T precedents None occur (as far as A V Concordance indicates) except in the words of Ezra, during the return from Babylon, delivering to their custodians the holy vessels that were to find a home in the New Temple (Ezr. viii 28—9) "Ye are holy unto the Lord and the vessels are holy...*Watch and keep* [*them*] *until ye weigh them* before the chiefs of the priests...in the chambers of the

THE LAST DAYS

servant in the sense of steward, not a mere doorkeeper, but a keeper of the keys of the House. Reasons will be given for thinking that John does say something on this point, not directly, but indirectly and dramatically, as follows.

In the narrative of Christ's manifestation after the Resurrection for the last time, to the disciples fishing on the sea of Tiberias, the part played by the fishermen is twofold—action and recognition[1]. The action is originated by Peter, "I go a-fishing." They also go with him. They all act, but they do not recognise "The disciples knew not that it was Jesus." After the draught of fishes, there comes recognition. But not to all, and not to Peter, only to an unnamed disciple "That disciple, therefore, whom Jesus loved, saith unto Peter 'It is the Lord.'" It is Peter that first reaches the Lord on the shore, and it is Peter that "went up and drew the net to the land." We may almost say that all the action is Peter's. But the recognition had come from some one without a name, "the disciple whom Jesus loved."

Later on, Jesus deals indirectly with the question of "greater" servants and "less" servants, and with the part to be played by Peter if he claims to be superior to his companions "Lovest thou me more than these?" Peter is responsive to "lovest," but dumb to "more than these." "Thou knowest that I love thee" is all he will now say. He will claim no superiority in loving. And now that he has cast aside the desire to be great as compared with others, Jesus shews him the way to be great in reality, assigning to him, first, the work for his activity,

---

house of the Lord .." LXX ἀγρυπνεῖτε καὶ τηρεῖτε ἕως στῆτε ἐνώπιον... Comp Lk xxi 36 ἀγρυπνεῖτε...ἵνα κατισχύσητε...σταθῆναι ἔμπροσθεν .. Both LXX and Luke agree in connecting "watching" with a future "standing." The "standing" in the LXX is a mere error (στῆτε for στήσητε). Yet in view of the likelihood of a Christian application of Isaiah's Return from Captivity (Is. lii 11 "Be ye clean, ye that bear the vessels of the Lord") it seems by no means improbable that the Lucan tradition is based on Ezr viii. 28—9 (LXX). The Heb. imperative שִׁקְדוּ "watch ye" occurs there alone in O.T. to mean "watch," and also in Lk xxi 36 (Delitzsch and Clementine Heb.).

[1] Jn xxi 3—11.

THE LAST DAYS

"Feed my sheep," and secondly the work for his endurance, which is implied in following Jesus in the way of the Cross, "Follow thou me[1]."

Being commanded to "follow" and seeing the unnamed disciple also "following," without such a command, Peter says, "Lord, what shall this man do?" The question assumes that "this man" will "do" something, and that the Lord, in departing from His disciples, will, as Mark says, "give to each his work." What, then, is to be the "work" of this disciple whom Jesus specially loves? The reply of Jesus indicates that the work of this servant may possibly be best described as abiding or waiting: "If I will that he wait [on earth] while I am coming, what is that to thee[2]?"

The next sentence shews that the disciple does more than wait. "This is the disciple that beareth witness concerning these things, and that wrote these things, and we know that his witness is true[3]." This implies that as Peter by preaching, so the unnamed disciple by writing, acted as a "doorkeeper," opening the gate of the Church for converts to Christ And the preceding context implies that whatever this disciple "wrote" would be inspired by the same Spirit of recognition that moved him to say to Peter "It is the Lord." The waiting Apostle, moved by this Spirit, may be said in some sense to have opened the door for the working Apostle The Lord gave "to each one his work."

---

[1] Jn xxi 15—19.   [2] Jn xxi. 20—23
[3] Jn xxi 24.

CHAPTER VIII

THE ANOINTING AT BETHANY[1]

[Mark xiv. 1—11]

§ 1. *"After two days," in Mark and Matthew*

THE sequence in Mark, "Now *after two days was the passover* ...and while he was in Bethany...there came a woman," gives

[1] Mk xiv. 1—11 (R.V.)

(1) Now after two days was [the feast of] the passover and the unleavened bread: and the chief priests and the scribes sought how they might take him with subtilty, and kill him.

Mt xxvi 1—16 (R V)

(1) And it came to pass, when Jesus had finished all these words, he said unto his disciples,
(2) Ye know that after two days the passover cometh, and the Son of man is delivered up to be crucified
(3) Then were gathered together the chief priests, and the elders of the people, unto the court of the high priest, who was called Caiaphas,
(4) And they took counsel together that they might take Jesus by subtilty, and kill him.

Lk. xxii 1—3 [vii 36—8], xxii 3—6 (R V)

(xxii. 1) Now the feast of unleavened bread drew nigh, which is called the Passover.
(2) And the chief priests and the scribes sought how they might put him to death, for they feared the people
(3) And Satan entered into Judas who was called Iscariot....

(2) For they said, Not during the feast, lest haply there shall be a tumult of the people.

(5) But they said, Not during the feast, lest a tumult arise among the people

THE ANOINTING AT BETHANY

the impression that the anointing by the woman in Bethany took place "two days" before "the passover." But the

Mk xiv 3—9 (R.V.)	Mt xxvi 6—13 (R V)	Lk vii 36—8 (R V)	Jn xii 1—8 (R V)
(3) And while he was in Bethany in the house of Simon the leper, as he sat at meat, there came a woman having an alabaster cruse (*or*, a flask) of ointment of spikenard (*lit* pistic nard) very costly, [and] she brake the cruse, and poured it over his head	(6) Now when Jesus was in Bethany, in the house of Simon the leper, (7) There came unto him a woman having an alabaster cruse (*or*, a flask) of exceeding precious ointment, and she poured it upon his head as he sat at meat	(36) And one of the Pharisees desired him that he would eat with him And he entered into the Pharisee's house, and sat down to meat (37) And behold, a woman which was in the city, a sinner, and when she knew that he was sitting at meat in the Pharisee's house, she brought an alabaster cruse (*or*, a flask) of ointment, (38) And standing behind at his feet, weeping, she began to wet his feet with her tears, and wiped them with the hair of her head, and kissed (*lit.* kissed much) his feet, and anointed them with the ointment	(1) Jesus there fore six days befor the passover cam to Bethany, wher Lazarus was, whon Jesus raised fror the dead (2) So they mad him a suppe there and Marth. served; but Lazaru was one of then that sat at mea with him (3) Mary there fore took a poun(of ointment o spikenard (*lit* pisti nard), very precious and anointed th feet of Jesus, an(wiped his feet witl her hair and th(house was fille(with the odour o the ointment
(4) But there were some that had indignation among themselves, [saying], To what purpose hath this waste of the ointment been made? (5) For this ointment might have been sold for above three hundred pence, and given to the poor And they murmured against her (6) But Jesus said, Let her alone, why trouble ye her? she hath	(8) But when the disciples saw it, they had indignation, saying, To what purpose is this waste? (9) For this [ointment] might have been sold for much, and given to the poor (10) But Jesus perceiving it said unto them, Why trouble ye the woman? for she hath wrought a good work upon	Lk om	(4) But Juda Iscariot, one of hi disciples, whicl should betray him saith, (5) Why was no this ointment sol(for three hundre(pence, and given t(the poor? (6) Now this h said, not because h cared for the poor but because he wa a thief, and havin the bag (*or*, box took away (*or* carried) what wa put therein (7) Jesus there

(Mark xiv. 1—11)

THE ANOINTING AT BETHANY

Diatessaron detaches the Marcan tradition "*after two days* was

Mk xiv. 1—11 (R V) contd	Mt. xxvi 1—16 (R V) contd.	Jn xii. 1—8 (R.V) contd.
wrought a good work on me (7) For ye have the poor always with you, and whensoever ye will ye can do them good but me ye have not always (8) She hath done what she could she hath anointed my body aforehand for the burying (9) And verily I say unto you, Wheresoever the gospel shall be preached throughout the whole world, that also which this woman hath done shall be spoken of for a memorial of her	me (11) For ye have the poor always with you, but me ye have not always (12) For in that she poured (*lit* cast) this ointment upon my body, she did it to prepare me for burial (13) Verily I say unto you, Wheresoever this gospel shall be preached in the whole world, that also which this woman hath done shall be spoken of for a memorial of her	fore said, Suffer her to keep it (*or*, Let her alone [it was] that she might keep it) against the day of my burying (8) For the poor ye have always with you, but me ye have not always.

Mk xiv 10—11 (R V)	Mt xxvi 14—16 (R V)	Lk. xxii 3—6 (R V)
(10) And Judas Iscariot, he that was one (*lit* the one) of the twelve, went away unto the chief priests, that he might deliver him unto them	(14) Then one of the twelve, who was called Judas Iscariot, went unto the chief priests, (15) And said, What are ye willing to give me, and I will deliver him unto you? And they weighed unto him thirty pieces of silver	(3) And Satan entered into Judas who was called Iscariot, being of the number of the twelve, (4) And he went away, and communed with the chief priests and captains, how he might deliver him unto them. (5) And they were glad, and covenanted to give him money.
(11) And they, when they heard it, were glad, and promised to give him money And he sought how he might conveniently deliver him [unto them].	(16) And from that time he sought opportunity to deliver him [unto them].	(6) And he consented, and sought opportunity to deliver him unto them in the absence of the multitude (*or*, without tumult).

the passover," placing it long after the Marcan verses that describe the Anointing[1] These it combines with John's "six days" as follows. "(Jn xii 1 foll) And Jesus, *six days before the passover*, came to Bethany... and they made a feast for him there and Martha was serving, while Lazarus was one of them that sat [at meat] with him (Mk xiv. 3 a) *And at the time of Jesus' being at Bethany in the house of Simon the leper* (Jn xii. 9) great multitudes of the Jews heard that Jesus was there, and they came... that they might look also on Lazarus... (Jn xii. 3 a) And Mary (Mk xiv. 3 b and Mt. xxvi. 7) *took a case of the ointment of fine nard of great price, and opened it and poured it out on the head of Jesus as he was reclining...*" The Diatessaron places this before the Entry into Jerusalem, and it implies, though it does not assert, that the anointing took place shortly after Christ's arrival at Bethany, that is to say, about "*six days*" (not "*two days*") before the Passover Thus John appears to be regarded by the compiler of the Diatessaron as intervening; not, however, on this occasion explaining Mark but correcting him

Luke omits "*after two days*" Luke also omits the Marcan words indicating a resolution of the chief priests *not* to take Jesus during the Feast ("not during the feast") for fear of a tumult of the people. Luke's reason for omitting these clauses may be explained by the fact that he found Mark and Matthew apparently taking different views about their meaning This is indicated by Mark's "for" and Matthew's "but" in the following parallels:—

Mk xiv 2	Mt. xxvi 5
For they said, Not during the feast, lest haply there shall be a tumult of the people.	*But* they said, Not during the feast, lest a tumult arise among the people.

Comp Jn xiii 1—2 (R V) (1) Now before the feast of the passover, Jesus, knowing that his hour was come...loved them [the disciples] unto the end (*or*, to the uttermost) (2) And during supper, the devil having already put into the heart of Judas Iscariot, Simon's [son], to betray him....

[1] Mk xiv 1—2 is placed in *Diatess* § 41, Mk xiv 3 foll in *Diatess* § 39 Mt xxvi 2 "Ye know that *after two days* is the passover" does not occur till *Diatess.* § 44

THE ANOINTING AT BETHANY

These words follow the resolution (in Matthew as well as in Mark) to "take him *with subtilty* and kill him." Mark appears to have meant to emphasize and to explain "with subtilty," as if the rulers said "We must take him *with subtilty, for* we cannot resort to force during the feast, lest there be a tumult. We must dissemble and delay " Matthew, on the other hand, appears to have missed the force of *"with subtilty"*, so he emphasizes the *contrast* between the desire of the rulers to "kill" Jesus, and the fear that compelled them to delay: "We will kill him, *but* we are afraid to do it during the feast " Luke retains the Marcan "for," but in an ambiguous context, saying in effect: "They sought how to kill Jesus [(1) at once, or (2) quietly], *for* they feared [the consequences on] the people [of (1) delay, or (2) public arrest][1] "

If we ask what was Mark's object in inserting the evangelistic statement *"after two days was the passover,"* we may find a partial answer in the parallel Matthew, which transfers the words to Jesus "*Ye know that after two days the passover cometh* and the Son of Man is [to be] delivered up to be crucified " Mark appears to be suggesting—but very obscurely—that the intentions of the chief priests to defer Christ's death till after

---

[1] See Wetstein on Mt xxvi 5 quoting the Mishna of Jer *Sanhedr.* x 4 about the practice of delaying an execution till a feast-day· "Non occiditur neque a judicibus civitatis suae, neque a Synedrio quod est Jafne, sed ad summum Synedrium quod Hierosolymis est deducitur, atque istic in custodia asservatur usque ad festum, et in festo interficitur (Deut xvii 13) Verba R Akibae " (Comp Acts xii 4)

The reason for the delay was (Deut xvii 13) "All the people shall hear, and fear, and do no more presumptuously " The Mishna adds (Schwab) "R Judah said that it was not right to torture the condemned by making him suffer the long suspense of death, but that he should be executed at once " This, however, affords additional evidence of the old rule—to delay execution till a feast-day—observed when Jerusalem was standing Accordingly we may suppose (with Wetstein) that Herod (Acts xii 4) was keeping Peter in custody with a view to his execution during the Feast of Unleavened Bread ("intending after the [first day of the] passover to bring him forth to the people") And we may suppose that Barabbas was a prisoner reserved in the same way to be "brought forth to the people after the [first day of the] passover."

THE ANOINTING AT BETHANY

the Passover were frustrated by providence. This view may be paraphrased as follows: "God had ordained that Christ, the Paschal Lamb, should die during the Feast. The supper at Bethany, and the anointing there, and the consequent rebellion of Judas Iscariot, who went out from the supper to offer to betray his Master, were all ordained that the rulers might take Jesus speedily, so that the sacrifice of Christ, ' our Passover[1],' should happen at the divinely appointed time. This was the Lord's will[2]." Matthew also took this view. But he followed perhaps some version of this view that regarded "the Lord" as meaning "Jesus[3]." At all events he says, in effect, "This was not only the Lord's will, it was also predicted by the Lord Jesus Himself."

Luke omits all this, as also he omits the narrative of the Anointing in Bethany (placing another narrative of anointing at the house of a Pharisee much earlier) The only trace of a suggestion in Luke's text here that he knew anything about the supper at Bethany is contained in the following parallels:—

Mk xiv. 10	Mt. xxvi. 14	Lk xxii 3—4
And Judas Iscariot, (*lit.*) the one of the twelve, went away unto the chief priests....	Then one of the twelve, who was called Judas Iscariot, went unto the chief priests....	And Satan entered into Judas who was called Iscariot, being of the number of the twelve. And he went away and communed with the chief priests....

Here Luke perhaps follows Mark in the use of "*went away*" In Mark, the word suggests that Judas "went away" from the supper at Bethany. It is but a faint suggestion. But it is strengthened by John, who alone names Judas Iscariot at that supper as murmuring at the cost of the anointing, and as being

---

[1] 1 Cor v 7 "our passover . Christ"
[2] Comp Jn xiii 27 "What thou art doing do *more quickly*," on which see *Joh Gr* **1918, 2439** (v) *a*, **2554** *c—e*
[3] Comp Mt xxiii 34 where words said by Luke (xi. 49) to be uttered by the "Wisdom of God" are regarded as uttered by Jesus.

THE ANOINTING AT BETHANY

rebuked by Jesus. There is an appropriateness in the supposition that from the table where he murmured at the waste of three hundred pence Judas "went away" to earn thirty pieces of silver, and that Luke repeated the Marcan expression although he omitted the preceding Marcan context

We have seen above that Luke, at this stage, connects "Judas Iscariot" with "Satan." John does not do this in his account of the supper at Bethany, but in his account of the Last Supper he says "the devil having already put into the heart of Judas Iscariot, Simon's son, to betray him[1]" This "already" may very well refer to the supper at Bethany, and may allude to the "entering of Satan into Judas Iscariot" mentioned by Luke[2]. John himself places that "entering" later on[3]. And perhaps he means the reader to say: "The irrevocable fall of Judas took place not at the supper in Bethany but at the Last Supper."

We may also partially explain the Johannine apparent deviation ("six days") from the Marcan date ("after two days") by the following hypothetical paraphrase of Mark, indicating his method of arranging, or disarranging, events: "The Passover and the Unleavened were now to come *after two days*, and the Jews were still delaying the execution of their purpose to kill Jesus, the Paschal Lamb [*In order to explain how their delay was cut short I must go back a little. A few days previously, some six days before the Passover,*] when Jesus was present at a supper in Bethany, and was anointed with precious ointment, there had been a murmuring of disciples at the costly waste, and Judas Iscariot had gone away in discontent And now, *two days before the Passover*, just when the chief priests were deciding to delay, Judas appeared before them with an offer to betray his Master. This changed their plans. Accordingly, they decided on an immediate arrest by night, and at once began to make preparations for it."

This view agrees with the arrangement of the Diatessaron which combines Matthew and Luke in order to shew how the

---

[1] Jn xiii 2   [2] Lk xxii 3.
[3] Jn xiii 27 "And after the sop, then entered Satan into him"

THE ANOINTING AT BETHANY

prophecy of Jesus "*after two days*...the Son of man is [to be] delivered up to be crucified" came to be fulfilled; and how the plan of the chief priests, "not during the feast," came to be frustrated. It was because "Satan entered into Judas," and Judas promised the chief priests to betray Jesus, and they "were pleased," and Judas "from that moment was seeking opportunity to betray him[1]."

If Matthew transferred the words from evangelistic comment to Christ's own lips it suggests itself that he saw in them an allusion to the prophecy of Hosea—apparently often referred to in the Gospels—the only passage in the Old Testament where "*after two days*" occurs, "*After two days* will he [*i.e.* the Lord] revive us...[2]." There may have seemed to Matthew a noteworthy coincidence between Christ's prediction of His resurrection "*after two days*" and of His redemptive sacrifice on the Cross "*after two days*." But in any case it is probable that he has been misled by Mark, and that John has led his readers in the right direction by rearranging events and substituting "six" days for "two."

Perhaps John has another object besides chronological correctness. He may have desired to turn the minds of his readers away from a literal reckoning of the days and hours implied in the Synoptists about the Eucharist, the Passion, and the Resurrection[3], by suggesting a New Genesis of "six days" —a hexaemeron at the close of his Gospel as also at the beginning[4]. The story of the first hexaemeron included a mention

---

[1] *Diatess* xliv 1—10, combining Mt xxvi 1—5, Lk xxii 2 b—4 a, Mt xxvi 15, Mk xiv 11 a, Lk xxii 6. Jn xiii 27 "do *more quickly*" may perhaps imply that even at the moment of that utterance, there was a danger, so to speak, that the crucifixion might be put off till after the time of the Paschal sacrifice.

[2] Hos vi 2.

[3] According to John, "the Passover" would be Christ Himself (1 Cor v 7) on the Cross, the Paschal Lamb, and not any Paschal meal before the crucifixion. This difference between the Three Synoptists and John on this point might naturally influence the latter in his description of the sequence of events, and in phrases referring to the Passover. See above, p 10, n 3.

[4] See *Introd* p 130, *Proclam.* p 15.

THE ANOINTING AT BETHANY

of "the third day[1]" and described the first building up of Christ's little Church at Cana, but only in the rudimentary form then possible, before the Spirit was given. The story of the second hexaemeron includes a mention of "six days," during which there is a hint of expansion in the mention of "certain Greeks," who are brought near to Jesus[2]. But toward the close of the six days Christ's little Church is to be "scattered[3]." Then comes a "sabbath[4]," a Jewish sabbath, a sabbath of death. Not till "the first day of the week[5]" that follows, will Jesus rise from the dead, and the New Church be born.

§ 2. *Clement of Alexandria on the Anointing*

We now come to an event, or events, as to which the Evangelists themselves appear to differ, and some of the most ancient commentators not only differ from one another but also in some cases appear to have changed their own minds. The discussion of it will be extremely laborious. But to leave it undiscussed would be to pass over one of the most important instances of Christ's mysterious power of calling out passionate devotion, and to make no attempt to realise the revelation that it contains of His divine yet human nature.

Apart from a brief allusion by Ignatius to the Anointing of Christ as resulting in "incorruption for the Church[6]," the earliest

---

[1] Jn ii 1   [2] Jn xii 1, 20   [3] Jn xvi 32
[4] Jn xix 31   [5] Jn xx 1.
[6] Ign *Eph* § 17 (Lightf.) "For this cause the Lord received *ointment* (μύρον) on His head, that He" (? it) "might breathe (πνέῃ) incorruption upon the Church. Be not anointed (ἀλείφεσθε) with the ill odour (δυσωδίαν) of the teaching of the prince of this world, lest he lead you captive..." Lightf says "A reference to the incident in the Gospels, Matt xxvi 7 sq., Mark xiv 3 sq., [Luke vii. 37 sq.], John xii. 3 sq." He is right in including John, who alone says that "the house was filled with the odour of the ointment." But where is there any reference to Luke? There is nothing here peculiar to Luke. And Luke represents Christ's "feet," not His "head," as being anointed. In Ignatius, there is antithesis between "*incorruption* (ἀφθαρσίαν)" and *Eph* § 16 "*corrupters-of-houses* (οἰκοφθόροι)" as to which Lightf quotes Orig. *Cels*. vii 63 φθείρειν τὸν ἄλλου ἀνθρώπου οἶκον, Plutarch *Mor* 12 B γυναικῶν οἰκοφθορίαι

THE ANOINTING AT BETHANY

Christian reference to it is in a chapter of Clement of Alexandria on "The Use of Ointments and Crowns." He deprecates their use, but makes the following admission "I know that the woman [in Luke] having brought an alabaster-cruse of ointment at the Holy Supper anointed the feet of the Lord...." After continuing to quote from Luke as to the woman's action and reception of forgiveness, he proceeds "But this may be a symbol of the Lord's teaching and of His suffering (or, Passion)." The "feet," he says, may be the apostles going forth to preach the Lord's Gospel, the "tears" are repentance. Then, introducing the word "*oil (elaion)*" (which no Gospel mentions as used in either anointing), he plays on its similarity to "*mercy (eleos)*": "'The *oil*,' which is the Lord Himself, whence comes the *mercy* that is [poured] on us[1]"

Then, without any interval, he adds "But the ointment—oil adulterated-with-guile—is Judas, the traitor, wherewith

γαμετῶν, and Hesych οἰκοφθόροι, μοιχοί, to shew that the word may refer to sexual "corruption," as well as to the "corruption" of heresy

A somewhat similar antithesis is found in 2 Cor 11 16 "savour... unto death.. savour...unto life," where it is copiously illustrated by Wetstein from Jewish literature It might also be illustrated by the first and almost unique mention of "nard" in O T Cant 1 12 "my spikenard" On this, the Targum says that, while Moses was on Sinai, the Bride, Israel, corrupted herself, and her odour became worse than that of absinth, and leprosy visited her Rashi says that in "nardus mea edit odorem suum" the word "odor" is put for "foetor," so that the sense is "While the divine Glory was still on Sinai, I defiled myself with the Calf"

The only other mention of μύρον in Goodspeed's two vols, besides that in Ignatius, is in Justin M *Tryph* § 22 μύρα (from Amos v 18 —vi 7), § 86 τῶν ἄλλων τῶν τῆς συνθέσεως τοῦ μύρου χρισμάτων before quoting Ps xlv 7 "the oil of gladness above thy fellows"

[1] Clem Alex 205 Ἀλλὰ καὶ πάθος ἐμφαίνει δεσποτικὸν (μυστικῶς ταύτῃ νοοῦσι) τὸ ἔλαιον, ὃ αὐτός ἐστιν ὁ Κύριος, ἀφ' οὗ τὸ ἔλεος τὸ ἐφ' ἡμᾶς Oxf Conc gives under one heading "ἔλαιον (ἔλεον)" The two are interchanged in the MSS (where Heb = "oil") of Ps xcii 10, cix 24 etc Though "oil" is not mentioned by Luke as being used, it is mentioned in the words he assigns to Jesus, after the anointing, (vii 46) "My head with *oil* (ἐλαίῳ) thou didst *not* anoint, but she hath anointed my feet with ointment (μύρῳ)" See p 350

THE ANOINTING AT BETHANY

[the] Lord was anointed-with-chrism as to His feet—being [thereby] released from His sojourn in the world[1]. For the [bodies of the] dead are anointed-with-perfume[2]. And as for 'tears' [in Luke], it is we, the sinners, [we] that have repented, [we] that have believed in Him, to whom He has 'forgiven sins' [as to the woman in Luke]. And the 'hair' that is dishevelled is sorrowing Jerusalem.... And the Lord Himself teaches us that Judas is adulterated-with-guile, saying 'Whosoever shall dip along with me in the dish, he shall deliver me up[3].' Thou seest the companion-at-table, the man-of-guile And this same Judas betrayed the Teacher with a kiss For [one and] the same man is found a hypocrite and bringing a kiss 'adulterated-with-guile,' imitating another ancient hypocrite...[4]"

---

[1] Clem. Alex. 205 τὸ δὲ μύρον δεδολωμένον ἔλαιόν ἐστιν ὁ Ἰούδας ὁ προδότης ᾧ τοὺς πόδας ἐχρίσθη Κύριος (τῆς ἐν κόσμῳ ἀναστροφῆς ἀπαλλαττόμενος) Μυρίζονται γὰρ οἱ νεκροί. The language is forced and fanciful but probably explicable as an allusion (see p 350) to Ps cxli 5 (LXX) The renderings "anointed-with-chrism" and "anointed-with-perfume" are intended to distinguish χρίω and μυρίζω from "anoint," ἀλείφω

[2] "Anointed-with-perfume (μυρίζονται)" This word does not occur in the Gk Test except in Mk xiv 8 προέλαβεν μυρίσαι (parall to Mt xxvi 12 βαλοῦσα. τὸ μύρον) It is quite different from ἀλείφω and χρίω Artemidorus (1 75), writing Περὶ Μύρων, says Μυρίζεσθαι γυναιξὶ πάσαις ἀγαθὸν πλὴν μοιχευομένων Ἀνδράσι δὲ πρὸς αἰσχύνης ἔσται πλὴν τῶν ἔθος ἐχόντων μυρίζεσθαι This probably means (see editor's note) "It will be a sign of disgrace for men [as distinct from women], except for such effeminate creatures as are men only in name " Artemidorus also recognises μύρα as a sign of death, if a sick man dreams of them ib iv 22 νοσοῦντι δὲ πονηρὰ τὰ μύρα διὰ τὸ συνεισφέρεσθαι νεκρῷ Plutarch Mor 142 A compares a wife that is afraid to smile on her husband, for fear of appearing bold and unchaste, to a woman who, "for fear of seeming to *anoint* her head *with perfume* (ἵνα μὴ δοκῇ μυρίζεσθαι τὴν κεφαλὴν) does not even *anoint herself* (μηδὲ ἀλειφομένης)."

Irenaeus 1 21 3, and 4, twice uses μυρίζουσι about heretical anointing with "balsam," and adds τὸ γὰρ μύρον τοῦτο τύπον τῆς ὑπὲρ τὰ ὅλα εὐωδίας εἶναι λέγουσιν   [3] Mt. xxvi 23

[4] Φίλημα δεδολωμενον ἔχων   Comp Gen xxxiii 4 (Field) "LXX καὶ κατεφίλησεν αὐτόν, Ἑβρ οὐεσσάκη " This calls attention to a peculiar pointing of the Heb "and he [i e Esau] kissed him " Con-

THE ANOINTING AT BETHANY

All this, and there is more, is extremely bewildering, and seems at first sight unlikely to repay examination. But Clement's fancies deserve attention if they point back to earlier fancies of the same kind, and if they were the causes (at least in part) of Origen's (and Jerome's) early view—that the Anointing in the Four Gospels was the act of one woman. It is therefore worth while to try to disentangle some of the knots in this Clementine comment.

First, it appears to be based on Luke's narrative of an anointing by a woman that was a sinner in the house of Simon a Pharisee. There is not a phrase that comes exactly from any other source. But, at the beginning, there is a phrase, "*at the Holy Supper*[1]," quite inconsistent with the early place given by Luke to his narrative. And later on, Clement's comment abruptly introduces "the traitor Judas" in connection with an "anointing" of "feet" and "ointment," and "adulterated oil"—language that seems vaguely to refer to the Anointing in Bethany. Later still, Judas is mentioned as "dipping in the dish," which clearly alludes to Mark's (and Matthew's) account of the Eucharist[2].

Now Luke alone mentions "*oil*" as the gift that is *not* offered by Simon the Pharisee ("my head with *oil* thou didst not anoint[3]"). And in a passage from the Psalms, the LXX not only mentions the "oil (*elaion*)" of a sinner, but also contrasts it (as Clement does) with "mercy (*eleos*)" in the words "The righteous will chasten me with *mercy*...but let not the *oil* of a sinner (*lit.*) fatten my head[4]." Clement does

---

cerning this, Field prints an ancient scholium ("videtur Origenis esse") saying that the Jews pointed the Hebrew thus in order to indicate that the "kiss" was a treacherous one, κατὰ δόλον γὰρ κατεφίλησε τὸν Ἰακώβ. Some Rabbis (Rashi) took this view, but not all. It is probable that Clement is alluding to the kiss of Esau as the "ancient hypocrite."

[1] Clem Alex 205 παρὰ τὸ δεῖπνον τὸ ἅγιον. The Lord's Supper is described in Lk xxii. 14 foll., the Anointing in Lk vii 36—40
[2] Mk xiv 20, Mt xxvi 23   [3] Lk vii 46
[4] Ps cxli 5 R V "Let the righteous smite me, [it shall be] a kindness, and let him reprove me, [it shall be as] oil upon the head" (quoted from LXX by Clem Alex elsewhere (145), but not here)

not here expressly quote this Psalm, but both Origen and Jerome follow the LXX in the phrase "*the oil of a sinner*," and the hypothesis that Clement is alluding to it, and applying it to Judas, makes his words so much clearer that we can hardly doubt that it is true.

It remains to explain the extraordinary fancifulness of the connection between Judas and the "oil adulterated by guile," contrasted with the "oil" of "mercy" "Guile" in the four Gospels, so far as narrative is concerned, is restricted to a passage—immediately before the Anointing in Bethany—where it is said that the rulers of the Jews sought to seize Jesus "by guile"—which "guile" Judas almost immediately supplies[1]. Now "guileless" is a Greek term applied in the Petrine Epistle to "the milk of the word," and applied in Papyri to corn, or wine, or anything that is unadulterated[2]. Clement, who regards the treacherous Judas as anointing the feet of Jesus for the path of death, calls his treachery "adulterated oil" in contrast with the implied guilelessness of the "*oil (elaion)*" that is "*mercy (eleos)*."

As for the "ancient hypocrite" whom Judas "imitated" when he brought "a kiss adulterated with guile," it has been pointed out that it probably refers to the kiss given by Esau to Jacob. On this, a scholium attributable to Origen tells us "In every Hebrew book '*kissed*' is dotted, not that it may be left unread, but to suggest the wickedness of Esau, for he kissed Jacob in guile[3]."

It will be observed that no attempt is made by Clement to explain the differences of scene and circumstance in the Gospel narratives, even those differences as to the "head" or "feet" of Jesus which might affect an allegorizing interpretation He is absorbed in his own motive. And his motive is, first, to protest against a literalistic interpretation, which would justify

---

[1] Mk xiv 1, Mt. xxvi 4 Elsewhere δόλος in Gospels occurs only in Mk vii. 22 (a list of sins), Jn 1 47 "an Israelite in whom is no guile"

[2] 1 Pet ii. 2 ἄδολον See *Berlin Urkunde* 290 13, 586 13, *Oxy. Pap* 101 38 etc

[3] See above, p 349, n 4, quoting Gen xxxiii 4.

THE ANOINTING AT BETHANY

Christians in using expensive ointments; secondly, a desire to draw out the contrast between two invisible anointings, that of the false Israel, the traitor, unto death, that of the true Israel, penitent and forgiven, unto life[1].

§ 3. *Origen and others on the Anointing*

Origen, in a passage of his Johannine Commentary, speaks of "the woman that had done the deeds of evil and repented," as being "enabled by her genuine conversion from her evil deeds to pour down a sweet-odour on Jesus", and then adds that she diffused in "the whole house" the breath of the ointment[2]. The "pouring down" is peculiar to Mark and Matthew[3]. The

---

[1] The passage relating to ointments terminates as follows, 206 "It is not unfitting then that He should indicate (καταμηνύειν) on the one hand oil [pure and simple] as a disciple that has received mercy (ἔλαιον μὲν ὡς μαθητὴν ἠλεημένον), but on the other hand [oil] adulterated-with-guile (*lit* guileful, δολερὸν δέ) as a traitor—oil drugged (ἔλαιον πεφαρμαγμένον) This then, you see, was what was prophesied by the feet [of Jesus] anointed-with-perfume (οἱ μυριζόμενοι πόδες) namely, the treachery of Judas when the Lord took the path [ὁδεύοντος Κύριον, or ? Κύριον, providing the Lord with the path] to His passion. And the Saviour Himself washing-clean (ἀπονίπτων) the feet of the disciples (Jn xiii 5)...signified in a figure (ἠνίξατο) their going forth to be the benefactors of the nation ...And for these the ointment breathed fragrance...for indeed the Passion of the Lord hath filled [all] with fulness—us on the one hand with fulness of sweet savour, but the Hebrews with fulness of sin This the Apostle most clearly shewed when he said (2 Cor ii 14—16) 'Thanks be to God. for we are to God a sweet savour of the Lord. .to the one a savour of death unto death, to the other a savour of life unto life.'"

It is the thought of this antithesis that mainly leads Clement away from the task of a commentator to that of an allegorizer. But it is not likely that Clement was the first Christian writer to allegorize the stories of the Anointing It will be seen below that Jewish traditions about "spikenard (νάρδος)"—which in O T occurs only in Cant i 12, iv 13, 14—contain a similar thought of antithesis between the savour of faithfulness and that of unfaithfulness

"Treachery" is the term used to describe Israel as an unfaithful wife in Jerem iii 20, comp Hos v 7 (Gesen 93 *b*).

[2] Origen *Comm Joann* i 12, Lomm. l. 27

[3] "Pour down," καταχέω, Mk xiv 3, Mt xxvi 7, unique in N.T.

THE ANOINTING AT BETHANY

tradition about "the house" is peculiar to John[1]. The tradition that the woman was "a sinner" is peculiar to Luke[2]. Here, then, Origen assumes that the four Evangelists are speaking of one and the same woman.

Origen's Commentary on Matthew is a later work. But even there, in the earlier portion of it, he confuses the Lucan "Simon the Pharisee" with the Marcan "Simon the leper" in a highly figurative passage likening Israel to a wife that has become adulterous, and the Gentiles to the harlot, Rahab, who has become penitent. The latter he describes as "no longer playing the harlot but coming to the feet of Jesus, and wetting them with the tears of repentance" so that "on account of her He spoke in reproach to Simon the leper, the former people, such things as are written[3]".

But later on in the Commentary on Matthew, when he comes to discuss the Anointing in its place, he compares it, not now poetically but critically, with the other three accounts. He begins by saying "Many think that the four Evangelists have written about one woman"; and he admits that there is "much similarity and a kind of family-likeness (cognatio quaedam)" in the narratives—mentioning in particular the coincidence of name between Simon the Pharisee and Simon the leper. But he asks how it is possible to harmonize the details of anointing the head in some narratives and the feet in others, and to suppose that the woman is regarded in each narrative as a sinner. Some, he says, will infer that there were four different women; but he himself "rather agrees" that there were three,

---

Mk κατεχεεν αὐτοῦ τῆς κεφαλῆς, Mt κατεχεεν ἐπὶ τῆς κεφαλῆς αὐτοῦ ἀνακειμένου. Origen omits "head."

[1] Παντὶ τῷ οἴκῳ τὴν τοῦ μύρου πνοὴν.. ἐμπεποιηκυίας, Jn xii 3 ἡ δὲ οἰκία ἐπληρώθη ἐκ τῆς ὀσμῆς τοῦ μύρου.

[2] Lk. vii 37.

[3] *Comm Matth* xii 4, Lomm iii 136—7. Comp the allegorical outburst in Pseudo-Jerome on Mk xiv 1 with its reference to the "scarlet line (Josh ii 18)" of Rahab. "Now let us sprinkle our book with blood [of the Paschal Lamb] and the thresholds of our houses and let us place the scarlet line of thread round the House of our Prayer..."

(1) the unnamed woman in Mark and Matthew, (2) the sinner in Luke, (3) Mary the sister of Martha in John[1].

Jerome similarly varies. In his treatise against Jovinianus (A.D. 393), he speaks of "a distinction indicated by the two women in the Gospel, the penitent, and the holy woman, one of whom held His feet, the other His head. Some authorities, however, think there was only one woman, and that she who began at His feet gradually advanced to His head[2]." In a later letter (398 A.D.) he says "A harlot washes His feet with her tears and against His burial anoints His body with the ointment of good works." This is followed by a confusion between Simon the Pharisee and Simon the leper. "Simon the leper invites the Master with His disciples": and it is preceded by "Martha and Mary make ready a feast and then welcome the Lord to it"—which probably refers to the Johannine account of Martha "ministering," but might refer to the Lucan account of Martha "cumbered with much serving[3]."

In his Commentary on Matthew, however, Jerome shews that he has decided against the view of "some authorities" above mentioned. "Let no one think that one and the same woman poured ointment on the head and on the feet. For the latter washes [the feet] with her tears and wipes them with her hair, and is manifestly called a harlot. But of the former nothing of this kind is written[4]."

Chrysostom, while giving up as superficial[5] the view that the four Gospels speak of one woman, says "In the Three, there seems to me to be one and the same woman, but in John not [the same], but a different [one], marvellous [in character], the

---

[1] Origen on Mt xxvi 6 foll., Lomm. iv. 392 foll., iv. 394 "ego autem magis consentio tres fuisse." So, too, on Cant. i. 12 "nardus mea" (*Cant. Hom.* ii. 2, Lomm. xiv. 258) Origen says that the woman mentioned by John was distinct from the one mentioned by Luke, but even there he says inaccurately "Maria...effudit super *caput* (instead of *pedes*) Jesu."

[2] *Letters* (*Contr. Jovin.* ii. 29) transl. Fremantle p. 410 a.

[3] Jerome *Letters* lxxi. 2 transl. Fremantle p. 152 b.

[4] Jerome, on Mt xxvi 6 foll.

[5] Chrys on Mt xxvi 6 ἡ γυνὴ αὕτη δοκεῖ μὲν εἶναι μία καὶ ἡ αὐτὴ παρὰ τοῖς εὐαγγελισταῖς ἅπασιν, οὐκ ἔστι δέ.

354 (Mark xiv 1—11)

THE ANOINTING AT BETHANY

sister of Lazarus." Then he proceeds to assume that the woman in Matthew was conscious of "impurity," and says "She did not approach Jesus as a mere man, for otherwise she would not have 'wiped [Him] with her hair'." The "wiping" with the "hair" is nowhere mentioned by Matthew. But Chrysostom adds "That part of the body which was the most precious of all, namely, her *head*, she applied to the *feet* of Christ." The "head" of the woman, and the "feet" of Christ, are mentioned by Luke, but nowhere by Matthew—on whom Chrysostom is nominally writing a commentary.

All this looseness is very regrettable but also very instructive. It shews that Luke's narrative, about the "woman that was a sinner," had taken such hold of Christian thought that early believers were disposed to read sinfulness even into such ancient narratives of Anointing as did not mention it. And this may help us to understand how the story of the woman taken in adultery came to be interpolated in the Fourth Gospel. That Gospel, mentioning Mary the sister of Lazarus by name, made critics like Origen ask "Is it possible that this Mary whom 'Jesus loved[1],' could have been 'a sinner'?" The answer being in the negative, the Fourth Gospel might seem to some to shew a deficiency which the interpolation aimed at supplying. It is in language resembling that of many passages in Luke where the style is Hebraic.

§ 4. *Words and phrases common to Mark and John*

From the facts alleged above it appears that poetic imagery and doctrinal motive have influenced very early writers, even the prosaic Jerome, commenting on the narratives of Anointing. It does not follow that the same two causes influenced the Evangelists themselves; but we ought to be prepared to find traces of such influence—especially in Mark whose Gospel often shews signs of a poetic original. Even if we cannot find our way back to any combination of their details so as to say confidently

---

[1] Jn xi 1—5 "Lazarus of Bethany,...the village of Mary and her sister Martha... Now Jesus loved Martha and her sister, and Lazarus" The reversal of names is curious

THE ANOINTING AT BETHANY

"This represents the historical fact," we may be able to shew in some instances probable causes of ramification, if we begin from Mark, and inquire what Marcan details are omitted by later Synoptists but retained by John.

Mark and John have in common (1) "nard," (2) "pistic," or "spikenard," (3) "three hundred denarii," (4) "let her alone."

(1) "*Nard*[1]" is not a Greek word. It is not alleged as occurring before the first century except as the transliteration in LXX of a Hebrew *nêrd* that occurs in two passages of the Song of Songs. In the first of these, many Rabbinical traditions recognise an obscure reference to the "evil odour" of Israel, the unfaithful Bride of Jehovah[2]. The word is common in first-century Latin. Mark, who has many Latin-Greek words, might retain it without perceiving any allusion to LXX Matthew might reject it as not Greek and not necessary. Luke might reject the word, but retain and greatly amplify the supposed allusion to the unfaithful and adulterous Bride, Israel. John, rejecting Luke's view, and rejecting also the Rabbinical view of the "nard" in the Song of Songs, might go back to Mark's word as one that poetically expressed the offering made by the Church to her Saviour.

(2) "*Pistic*" is transliterated in SS, *d*, and *k*. *Pistacia* is given by Krauss as a Hebrew name—in Pliny, *pistacium*, and similarly in the Greek of the second century—for "pistacium-nut", and the word is sometimes used in Hebrew to mean a measure (like our "barley-corn")—"a nut-size" of any herbal compound[3] Nonnus calls it *pistikè*, making the *i* long, which indicates that he regarded it as distinct from the Greek *pistikè* "faithful" But Artemidorus uses the expression "a *pistic* and home-keeping woman[4]," and repeats it twice as "a *faithful* (*pistè*) and home-keeping woman[5]," to mean a faithful wife[6]

---

[1] Mk xiv 3, Jn xii 3
[2] See above, p 347, n 6 *ad fin*
[3] See Levy iii 450 *a*, iv 82 *a* In Pliny (xiii. 51, xxiii 150) *pistacia* are mentioned merely as an antidote against a serpent's sting
[4] Artemid ii 32 πιστικὴν καὶ οἰκουρόν   [5] *Ib*. ii 66, iii 54
[6] Plutarch *Vit* 281 c φιλικῶς καὶ πιστικῶς (of men) means "on terms of faithful friendship."

THE ANOINTING AT BETHANY

These are sufficient reasons for not being surprised at the insertion of the word in any ancient Gospel that alluded to a contrast between a faithful and an unfaithful woman, expressed in the language of the Song of Songs, with a play on the double meaning—"*pistacia*" in Semitic, "*faithful*" in Greek. Mark might retain this, whether he understood the allusion or did not. Matthew might reject it because he did not understand it. Luke might reject it because he did *not* regard the sinful woman as "*faithful*" at first, but only after the Lord had said "thy *faith* (*pistis*) hath saved thee[1]." John, rejecting Luke's view, might go back to Mark's word, placing it in a new framework of circumstance so as to shew that she was *not* "a sinner."

(3) "*Three hundred denarii*" is altered by Matthew into "much[2]." The words and their context lie outside Luke's version. John may have retained it simply because it was the ancient tradition and more life-like than Matthew's. But in the Feeding of the Five Thousand we have found John retaining a Marcan tradition about "two hundred denarii," omitted by Matthew and Luke[3], and there it seemed probable that John gave the words an allegorical interpretation. Perhaps it may be so here also. It may be one of many instances of Johannine irony. The murmurers may be regarded as unconsciously testifying to the special affection that prompted the gift of the ointment, or to its spiritual value. In the Bible, "three hundred pieces of silver" is used perhaps only once, and there as a mark of special affection, of Joseph's gift to Benjamin[4]. But an allusion to Joseph and Benjamin is very unlikely here. If there is symbolism, it is more probably to be looked for in the very early Christian identification of "three hundred" with T, the sign of the Cross, based on a passage in Genesis mentioning "armed servants of Abram eighteen and three hundred[5]." Rabbinical tradition said that 318 corresponded to the name

---
[1] Lk. vii. 50
[2] Mk. xiv. 5, Jn. xii. 5, comp. Mt. xxvi. 9.
[3] *Law* pp. 274—82
[4] Gen. xlv. 22. Rashi and *Gen. r.* make no comment
[5] Gen. xiv. 14.

THE ANOINTING AT BETHANY

of "Eliezer" ("God is my help"); but first-century Christian tradition said that "300" meant the Cross (T), while "10" and "8" represented the name of "Jesus[1]." Such an allusion would be appropriate to the context which describes Mary on one side, and Judas on the other, as preparing the way for the Crucifixion. "'*This could have been sold for three hundred pence*'—so spake Judas, speaking a truth beyond his knowledge, for her offering of loving faith was so precious that it could buy Salvation, yes, the Salvation of the Cross"

(4) "*Let her alone,*" is addressed, in Mark, to the disciples (plural, *aphete*); in John, to Judas (singular, *aphes*)[2] The Greek Imperative is the same as that used in the Crucifixion ("let alone"), where Mark has the plural and Matthew the singular—resulting in two quite different meanings[3]. It is also peculiar to Mark's version of the story of the Syrophoenician woman, where evidence points to its meaning originally "let alone[4]." Now a form of this same verb occurs in Luke's story of "the woman that was a sinner," a form almost peculiar to Luke and to the Johannine Epistle, meaning "*remit (sins)*[5]." In Greek, "*let her*

---

[1] In ancient Hebrew, as well as in Greek, *tau* might be represented by a cross (T) See Barn. § 9 (on Gen xiv 14) "'I' is 'ten', 'H' is 'eight'; there you have IH[COYN], *i e* Jesus. But because the Cross was destined to find its grace in the 'T,' he says also 'three hundred'" Clem Alex 782 adopts this ("they say") as the first instance of "the mystical meanings of numbers" in his treatise on the subject

[2] Mk xiv 6 R V, Jn xii 7 R V marg

[3] Mk xv 36, Mt xxvii 49 ἄφετε (Mt. ἄφες) ἴδωμεν. The two meanings are quite different See *From Letter* **1056—68**, including remarks on the doubtful tradition peculiar to Lk [xxiii 34] Πάτερ, ἄφες αὐτοῖς

[4] Mk vii 27 See *Son* **3353** (iv) *g* foll

[5] Ἀφέωνται in N T occurs only in Lk v 20, 23 (parall to Mk-Mt ἀφίενται), vii. 47, 48, Jn xx 23 (v r ἀφίονται), 1 Jn ii 12 ἀφέωνται (but Latin "remittuntur" points to ἀφίονται) Lk xi 4 ἀφίομεν uses the form in -ω, whereas the parall Mt vi 12 ἀφήκαμεν uses the form in -ημι

Steph *Thes*. (ἀφίημι 2662—3) quotes Suicer as saying that ἀφέωκα is "Doric" for ἀφεῖκα, and this is repeated by modern commentators But not a single instance has been hitherto alleged of the early existence of the active, ἀφέωκα, nor indeed of the passive

THE ANOINTING AT BETHANY

alone" might be almost identical with *"it is remitted to her,"* that is, *"she is forgiven*[1]*."* That there was some early ambiguity about *"let her alone"* is suggested by the fact that it is supplemented in Mark, and supplanted in Matthew, by *"why trouble ye the woman ?"*—indicating that Mark added an easy paraphrase to a difficult original and that Matthew preferred the paraphrase by itself. It is undeniable that Luke twice alters the form of the Marcan word in the Healing of the Paralytic (" thy sins *are forgiven* "). In the Anointing, Luke may have regarded Mark as

---

outside N T Nor has anyone explained why Luke, and probably John, should prefer a "Doric" form (Blass § 23 7 "Doric and Ionic" Suicer adds "also Ionic"). The words "Thy sins are forgiven thee" must surely have been most familiar and most sacred to all Greek-speaking Christians, before Luke and John wrote their Gospels If so, what motive could induce these two Evangelists to resort to "Doric" or "Doric and Ionic" forms, unknown in LXX, to express forgiving?

Suicer may have been led into error by some MSS that wrote αφεωνται for αφεονται (the substitution of ω for o being quite common in many MSS) The form ἀφέω is found in Exod xxxii 32 ἀφεῖς "thou *forgivest*," and Rev ii 20 ἀφεῖς "thou *sufferest*" The former describes the intercession of Moses that Israel may be "forgiven", the latter describes a rebuke for "suffering," i e tolerating, Jezebel The two passages illustrate the ramifications of the use of ἀφίημι and indicate how various forms of it might be assigned to various phrases It is possible that the Attic perfect ἀφεῖνται and the Attic present ἀφίενται might be felt by some to lay too much emphasis on the past ("have been but are not now") or on the present ("are in the act of being") The vernacular ἀφέονται more correctly ἀφίονται, may therefore have been preferred Sophocl Lex quotes Dorotheus (600 A D.) as twice using forms of ἀφέω

Goodspeed gives no instance of ἀφέωκα active or passive Steph. *Thes* 2662 D gives (from "inscr. Arcad. nuper reperta") imperat ἀφεώσθω, and refers (803 A) to *Tab Heracl* 2, 105 ἀνεῶσθαι, and (804 A) to Herod ii. 165 ἀνέωνται. The Papyri have *Berl Urkund* (39 A D) 1078 ἐπιμελώσθε for ἐπιμελεῖσθε, and *Oxyr.* (127 A D) 496 15 αἱρῶται for αἱρῆται

[1] Αφιεται, or αφειται, being written with -ε for αι, or *vice versa* (as often in MSS, *Joh Gr.* **2658** *e*), and αυτη being taken for αυτην, or *vice versa* (*Corrections* **360** *a*, *Joh Gr.* **2687** *d*), might cause confusion. D has αφεωντε in Mk ii. 5, αφιοντε in Mt. ix 2 and αφαιωνται in Lk. v. 20.

THE ANOINTING AT BETHANY

erroneously taking "*she is forgiven*" as meaning "*let her alone.*" John may be intervening in favour of Mark's interpretation.

§ 5. *Words and phrases common to Luke and John*

Luke and John agree in saying that the woman described in their several narratives "wiped" the "feet" of Jesus with her "hair" (Luke "the hairs of her head")[1]. This Greek word for "wipe" is not used in the canonical LXX. John, however, uses it not only in this narrative but also before, when first mentioning Lazarus and Martha· "There was a certain [man] [lying] sick, Lazarus (*lit*) from Bethany out of the village of Mary and Martha her sister. Now Mary was the [woman] that (*or*, the [Mary] that) anointed the Lord with ointment and *wiped* his feet with her hair, whose brother Lazarus was lying sick[2]"

John uses the word again to describe an act of Jesus. "He began to wash the feet of the disciples and to *wipe* [*them*] with the napkin with which he was girded[3]." This "wiping" of the feet of the disciples after they had been dipped in water presents no difficulty, but it is not so simple in the Johannine narrative of the Anointing. The difficulty is stated thus in Horae Hebraicae: "Did she not wash his feet before she anointed them? I do not ask whether she did not wash them with her *tears*, as before (Luke vii)....but did she not wash his feet *at all*? I ask this because the custom of the country seems to persuade she should do so." The writer supports his objection by an instance where a maid brings first water for washing, and then oil for anointing, and then he adds "Either therefore this

---

[1] Lk vii 38, Jn xii 3

[2] Jn xi 1—2 Contrast the first mention of Martha and Mary in Luke (x 38—9)· "Now as they were going on their way he entered into a certain village And a certain woman, by name Martha, received him into her (*lit* the) house And this [woman] had a sister called Mary, who also, sitting at (παρκαθεσθεῖσα πρὸς) the Lord's feet, was listening to his word" Martha is here placed before Mary There is no indication that the "village" is Bethany Luke has previously mentioned (vii 38, 44) the woman that "wiped (ἐκμάσσω, *bis*)" the feet of Jesus

[3] Jn xiii 5

360 (Mark xiv 1—11)

THE ANOINTING AT BETHANY

word (she *wiped*) must relate to some previous washing of his feet; or, if it ought to refer to the ointment, it scarcely would suppose wiping off the ointment now laid on, but rather, that with the hairs of her head she rubbed and chafed it[1]"

It seems obvious that John must have had some strong reason for twice describing Mary as not only "anointing" but also "wiping." "Anointing" alone suffices for Mark and Matthew, why does it not suffice for John? And if he must add "wiping" why does he add it in such a context as to suggest that the ointment is "wiped" off as soon as it is laid on? In Luke, the "wiping" is intelligible—tears being wiped off the feet, and the ointment being then poured on them—but it is not so in John.

Turning to Hebrew and Jewish literature for some explanation we find that the regular Hebrew for "*wipe*," also used in Aramaic and Syriac, is transliterated, though very rarely, both in Hebrew and Syriac, as the Greek word *moichas*, "adulteress[2]" Not much importance would be attached to this if we did not find that the only mention of *moicheia* in John occurs in a narrative, interpolated in his Gospel, and written in Lucan style, about a woman taken in adultery and pardoned by Jesus[3]. This suggests that John may have emphasized his own interpretation of a doubtful word—regarded by some, but not by him, as meaning "adulteress" or "woman that was a sinner"—by twice repeating that it had quite a different meaning If that is so, John is here intervening, not in favour of Mark who is silent on the point, but against Luke

---

[1] See *Hor Heb* on Jn xii 2 quoting *Menacoth* 85 b By "previous washing" the writer seems to suggest a pluperf rendering of ἐξέμαξεν "Now she *had previously wiped* the feet dry from the water" There are many such instances in Jn, but this does not seem likely to be one, for (*Joh Gr* **2460**—1) δέ, not καί, would be the natural particle to introduce such a clause

[2] Levy iii 74, מחי, refers to *Cant r* (on Cant iii 4, Wu p 85) where there is a transliteration of μοιχάς He adds (as prob) *Sanhedr* 109 b, but Krauss (p 331) and Goldschm *ad loc* render the word "strike" *Thes Svr* 2084 gives מיוחום from μοιχός

[3] Jn viii 3 μοιχείᾳ, W H marg ἁμαρτίᾳ

361 (Mark xiv 1—11)

THE ANOINTING AT BETHANY

Perhaps our narrative may be illustrated by a passage in Exodus where the LXX uniquely uses the Greek word "anoint-with-chrism" to forbid the ordinary use of the spice-compounded sacerdotal ointment: "Upon the flesh of [common] man it shall not be *poured.*" The Hebrew "anointed" is rendered by Onkelos "poured," but in the Jerusalem Targum by a word meaning "polished," "dried," or "wiped[1]." If the original of our narrative had simply "poured on *him,*" Mark may have added "his head," with allusion to "the precious oil upon the head" of Aaron, mentioned in the Psalms[2]. To this Matthew may have added "as he sat at meat," to shew that it was not (like the "precious[3] oil" in the Psalm) poured on the standing figure. But Luke, from his point of view, would regard "on him" as meaning "on the feet," not on the head; and John, though from a different point of view, would agree with Luke. The Jerusalem Targum indicates a possibility of confusing "wiped" with "anointed," which may help to explain the difficulty above mentioned in the Johannine text.

John does not follow Luke in mentioning the woman's "tears." "Tears" might seem appropriate to the Johannine mention of "preparation for burial." But in Luke they are apparently tears of penitence for the woman's own sin, not of sorrow for the Lord's approaching death; whereas love and devotion and faith, rather than penitence, seem to be the motives of the Johannine anointing. The Lucan "kissing" of the feet is also omitted by John. Thus the study of John's agreements and disagreements with Luke leads to no safe conclusion except that John, while discouraging the view that

---

[1] Exod xxx 32 ייסך, from a unique יסך if txt correct, but prob *leg* יוסך from סוך (Gesen. 414 *b*, 692 *a*) "anoint," LXX χρισθήσεται, Onk נסך "pour," Jer Targ. מרק "wipe" (Levy *Ch* ii 72 *b*).

[2] Ps. cxxxiii. 2.

[3] The word for "precious" in the phrase "*precious* ointment" is "*good*" (Gesen 374 *a*, 2 K xx. 13, Is xxxix 2, Ps cxxxiii 2, Eccles vii 1). LXX omits it in Is. xxxix. 2, Ps. cxxxiii, perhaps taking the two words together as μύρον, "[scented] ointment." Luke is the only one of the four Evangelists that omits this epithet (in some form).

THE ANOINTING AT BETHANY

the woman was a "sinner," desires for some reason to lay stress on the tradition about one secondary act—the "wiping" of "feet"—which Jesus requited by a similar act, Himself "wiping" the "feet" of His disciples. Perhaps John deliberately omits any previous washing of Christ's feet because he desired to suggest that the Lord did not need it. His feet walked unspotted and undefiled through the path of life. He accepted the anointing of His feet, not as a purification but as an offering from Mary in the name of the disciples; but He returned it to them as a purification for them, taking their impurities upon Himself.

§ 6. *The single phrase common to all the Synoptists*

The only phrase common to all the Synoptists is "an alabaster-cruse of ointment." Instead of this, John has "a pound of ointment[1]" The difference, at first sight, seems hardly worth notice. But careful students of the Fourth Gospel will not easily believe that John could depart from all the older Gospels on a detail of this kind—which, though apparently unimportant, would strike the popular mind at once—without some very good reason.

From John's point of view such a reason would exist if the Synoptic phrase gave the impression that the possession of the "alabaster-cruse" suggested extravagance or dissolute luxury in the possessor. Now such a suggestion is indicated in the early mention of "an alabaster-cruse of ointment" by Herodotus[2]. Plutarch, too, mentions such "alabaster-cruses," and in such contexts as to indicate that they are held up to contempt[3]. But, besides these, Wetstein quotes passages from Aristophanes and Lucian shewing that the phrase meant, in effect, "scent-

---

[1] Mk xiv 3, Mt xxvi. 7, Lk. vii 37, Jn xii 3

[2] In Herod. iii 20, ἀλάβαστρος μύρου is one of several ostentatious presents sent by Cambyses to the king of Aethiopia who treats them with contempt

[3] Plut. *Vit* 243 D, "like the lamentations of a woman regretting the loss of her scent-bottles (ἀλαβάστρους) and purple attire," comp 676 A describing Alexander's contempt for the luxuries that he finds in the tent of the conquered Darius including ἀλαβάστρους

bottle," and that it might often be associated with dissolute women[1] One of these (in Lucian) is reproached with ingratitude by one of her many lovers who says to her "I brought you *an alabaster-cruse of ointment* from Phoenicia[2]." In Mark (as also in Matthew) the woman is described as "having[3]" it with her, which might mean, though it does not go so far as to say, that she habitually carried it with her.

John's version seems at first sight studiously prosaic, almost like a line out of a recipe, "*taking a pound* of so-and-so." But, in the first place, if we examine the Johannine *litra* or "pound," we find that it is very frequent in Hebrew; and there is a Jewish tradition· "Under the term 'Shekel,' the coin mentioned in the Pentateuch is called 'Sela', that in the Prophets, '*Litra*'; that in the Hagiographa, 'Talent[4]'" In the next place, turning to the description, previously quoted, of the compounding of "the holy ointment" in Exodus, we find that the Recipe, so to speak, begins thus: "*Take* thou also unto thee the chief spices, of flowing myrrh five hundred [*shekels*]...and of cassia five hundred, after the *shekel of the sanctuary*...[5]." If John regarded the woman in Bethany as "taking" ointment to the amount of the weight of *a "shekel," according to its estimation in the Prophets*, for the purpose of anointing Jesus, he might naturally use this Hebrew-Greek term, *litra*, as having a typical meaning—"after *the shekel of the sanctuary*." According to this view John substituted a typical sacred "*litra*" for a secular term that might mean "scent-bottle," simply for the sake of edification[6]. If that is

---

[1] Wetst on Mt. xxvi 7

[2] Lucian *Dial Meretric* xiv (Reitz iii p 319) Reitz's Index (usually very accurate and complete) does not contain ἀλάβαστρος Nor does Steph *Thes* quote instances from Lucian But see Wetstein It is important to realise the bad impression that the phrase ἀλάβαστρος μύρου would convey to Greeks

[3] Mk xiv 3, Mt xxvi 7 ἔχουσα, Lk vii. 37 κομίσασα "having brought"

[4] See Levy ii 500 *a* ("j Kidd i 60 *c*") and *Gen r* on Gen xxiii 11, Wu p 276

[5] Exod xxx 23—4.

[6] No other explanation suggests itself except some confusion

THE ANOINTING AT BETHANY

the case, this Synoptic phrase, unimportant though it at first appears to be, assumes great importance as indicating that in Mark-Matthew, as well as in Luke, the woman was regarded as being of dissolute character, and as favouring the view of Ignatius and Clement of Alexandria, who assumed that the Four Gospels in their widely different descriptions referred to one and the same historical fact.

§ 7. "*Bethany*," *in Mark, Matthew, and John*

The first mention of Bethany in the Synoptists is connected with the Riding into Jerusalem, about which Origen says: "And now let us see about (1) '*Bethphage*' on the one hand according to Matthew, but (2) '*Bethany*' according to Mark, and (3) '*Bethphage and Bethany*' according to Luke[1]." Several authorities insert "Bethphage" in Mark here, but D and the old Latin versions reject it[2]. Bethany is nowhere mentioned in Goodspeed, Bethphage is mentioned once—where Justin Martyr, referring to this narrative, describes the ass as at its entrance[3]. SS, in Luke, has "at Beth Phagge and Beth Ania," but in Mark, "to Beth Phagge *to* Beth Ania." This might mean

---

between לטרא "litra" and Aram לטום (also Syr.) Levy *Ch* 1 409 *b* "pistachio nut," see above, p 356, on πιστική.

[1] Origen on Mt xxi 1 (Lomm iv 52) Ἴδωμεν δὲ περὶ τῆς Βηθφαγὴ μὲν κατὰ Ματθαῖον, Βηθανίας δὲ κατὰ τὸν Μάρκον, Βηθφαγὴ δὲ καὶ Βηθανίας κατὰ τὸν Λουκᾶν—Ταῦτα δὲ ἦν πρὸς τὸ ὄρος τὸ καλούμενον ἐλαιῶν— Ἑρμηνεύεσθαι δέ φαμεν τὴν Βηθφαγὴ μέν, οἶκον σιαγόνων, ἥτις τῶν ἱερέων ἦν χωρίον· Βηθανία δέ, οἶκος ὑπακοῆς

[2] Mk xi. 1 | Mt xxi. 1 | Lk xix 29

καὶ ὅτε ἐγγίζουσιν εἰς Ἱεροσόλυμα εἰς Βηθφαγὴ καὶ Βηθανίαν πρὸς τὸ Ὄρος τῶν Ἐλαιῶν (marg εἰς Ἱερ καὶ εἰς Βηθανίαν πρὸς τὸ Ὄ τὸ Ἐλαιῶν)

καὶ ὅτε ἤγγισαν εἰς Ἱεροσόλυμα καὶ ἦλθον εἰς Βηθφαγὴ εἰς τὸ Ὄρος τῶν Ἐλαιῶν

καὶ ἐγένετο ὡς ἤγγισεν εἰς Βηθφαγὴ καὶ Βηθανιὰ πρὸς τὸ ὄρος τὸ καλούμενον Ἐλαιῶν

[3] Justin Martyr *Tryph* § 53 ἔν τινι εἰσόδῳ κώμης Βεθφαγῆς λεγομένης. *Hor Heb* 1 82 quotes *Baba Mezia* 90 *a* on Bethphage, and says that the Glosser takes *phage* as "a beaten way," but *Hor. Heb* prefers פגי "green figs." Levy 1. 227 *a* assumes this and refers to *Pesach* 91 *a* etc

THE ANOINTING AT BETHANY

"*belonging to* Beth Ania," or it might mean that "Beth Ania" was another name for "Beth Phagge."

Beth Phage was a well-known suburb of Jerusalem frequently mentioned and much discussed by the Talmudists[1]. As for Bethany it can only be alleged that certain names somewhat like it, such as "Beth Hino" and "Beth Hini," are found in Talmudic passages, but the identification of them with the Gospel Bethany rests on conjecture. Levy assumes the identity of the Talmudic Bethphage with the Gospel Bethphage and mentions it as a name of frequent occurrence applied to a suburb of Jerusalem[2]. But concerning "Beth Hini" he merely says that it is "the name of a place," and that it is spelt in two different ways in the two passages to which he refers[3]

It is only fair to add that the author of Horae Hebraicae, who appears to have originated the identification of Bethany with Beth Hini[4], does not conceal the variations of the spelling of the latter, or the fact that Beth Hini itself has no meaning assigned to it[5]; and in his commentary on Luke he says that "there was a certain town near Jerusalem called *Magdala*, of a very ill fame, which perhaps was Bethany itself...I am apt to think that Bethany itself might go under the name of Magdala[6]." These quotations, to which others might be added

---

[1] *Hor. Heb.* 1 80—83 devotes a whole section to Bethphage, and Neubauer pp 147—9 quotes many passages about it from the Mishna Though a suburb, it was yet regarded, for certain religious purposes, as included in the City.

[2] Levy 1. 227 *a* בית פאני, Βηθφαγή, "Beth-Phage, Vorstadt Jerusalems, Pes. 91 *a* u o"

[3] Levy 1. 225 *b* בית היני "Beth Hini, Name eines Ortes B. mez. 88 *a* (J Pea I. 16 *c* un. steht dafur בני חנון)." Neubauer p. 150 prefers the former reading but adds (pp 149—50) "On écrit aussi ce nom בית אוני (Tosiftha, *Schebuith*, ch 7)."

[4] Wetstein, on Mt. xxi 17, quotes *Hor. Heb.*

[5] *Hor. Heb.* 1 90 derives *-hene* in "Beth-hene" from *Ahene*, אהיני, meaning "dates of palm-trees" not yet ripe. But Levy 1 35 *a* says that אהיני means mostly unripe figs. Wetstein also does not mention this conjecture of *Hor. Heb.*

[6] *Hor. Heb.* III. 87, on Lk. VIII 2

THE ANOINTING AT BETHANY

from the Horae, indicate the weakness of the hypothesis that identifies Beth Hini with the Christian Bethany[1].

We pass to the evidence of the Gospels themselves. After mentioning Bethany in connection with the Entry into Jerusalem and the Temple, Mark's next mention of it is in connection with Christ's first "coming out" from the Temple in the evening. To this there is no Synoptic parallel:—

Mk xi. 11	Mt. om.	Lk. om.
And .. it being now eventide, he went out unto *Bethany* with the twelve		

But Mark subsequently mentions a second "going out[2]," and to this there is a parallel, mentioning "*Bethany*" in Matthew and "*lodging*" in Matthew and Luke.—

Mk xi. 19	Mt. xxi 17	Lk xxi. 37
And whenever evening came, he (W H. txt they) went	And he left them, and went forth out of the city to *Bethany*	And every night he went out and lodged in the mount

---

[1] *Hor Heb* 1 233 quotes *J Berach* fol 16 1 "*the shops of the children of Chanan*" as being identical with *Bab Mez* 88 *a* "*the shops of Beth Heno*" and says "The shop-keepers were '*the sons of Chanan*' .. the place was '*Beth Heno* בית הינו', which I fear not to assert to be the same with Bethany The reason of my confidence is twofold 1 Because the Talmudists call Bethany בית היני, *Beth Hene*, to which how near does *Beth Heno* come!" The second reason is "Because in them there is open mention of shops in mount Olivet," and then he proceeds to quote *J Taanith* fol 69 2 about four shops on Mount Olivet The argument amounts to this. "The Christian *Bethany* was a place on Mount Olivet, there were some shops of *Beth Heno* on Mount Olivet, *Heno* is very like *Hene*, therefore the Christian Bethany was identical with *Beth Heno*"

Hor Heb 1. 234 quotes *Cholin* 53 *a* about "the lavatory (מרחץ) of Beth Hene (היני)" Goldschm., there, gives twice v r הינו "Heno" (or "Hino") Levy 1 466 *a* gives "Hini" only as *the name of a Babylonian town thrice mentioned in Talmud*, and as the name of a man, referring under the latter heading to his note in 1 225 *b* on Beth Hini quoted above

[2] It is of a general kind in Mk and Lk (imperf), but of a particular kind in Mt (aorist)

THE ANOINTING AT BETHANY

Mk xi 19 *contd.*	Mt xxi. 17 *contd.*	Lk xxi. 37 *contd.*
forth (*lit* used to go forth) out of the city.	and *lodged there*	that is called [the mount] of Olives[1].

Why does Luke omit "Bethany" here? The omission suggests that the tradition here followed by him regarded "Bethany" not as the name of a village but as a noun connected with "lodging"; and this view is favoured by the fact that the Aramaic "lodge," *beth*, is identical with the Hebrew *beth*, "house," which is the first part of "Bethany." This is the first mention of Bethany in Matthew, and perhaps Matthew's tradition originally meant · "went forth out of the city to *the place where he lodged* and lodged there."

But at this point there comes appropriately the suggestion of Horae Hebraicae, above mentioned, that Bethany may have meant "the place of (*beth*) unripe figs or dates (*any*)." For the following verses in Matthew describe Jesus as seeing "a fig-tree." And it happens that both in Hebrew and in Aramaic there is another word for fig-tree (*thany*) that might make up the name

---

[1] Mk xi 19
καὶ ὅταν ὀψὲ ἐγένετο, ἐξεπορεύοντο (marg ἐξεπορεύετο) ἔξω τῆς πόλεως

Mt xxi 17
καὶ καταλιπὼν αὐτοὺς ἐξῆλθεν ἔξω τῆς πόλεως εἰς Βηθανίαν, καὶ ηὐλίσθη ἐκεῖ

Lk xxi 37—8
ἦν δὲ τὰς ἡμέρας ἐν τῷ ἱερῷ διδάσκων (marg. διδάσκων ἐν τῷ ἱερῷ), τὰς δὲ νύκτας ἐξερχόμενος ηὐλίζετο εἰς τὸ ὄρος τὸ καλούμενον Ἐλαιῶν· καὶ πᾶς ὁ λαὸς ὤρθριζεν πρὸς αὐτὸν ἐν τῷ ἱερῷ ἀκούειν αὐτοῦ.

Αὐλίζομαι, "pass the night," occurs nowhere else in N T In Heb , outside Job, it almost always = לין or ליו This in Aram (Brederek p. 60) is בית The Talmud relates that a Rabbi (*Pesach* 42 *a*) was obliged to avoid the Heb word "*lodge, or, remain for the night*," לין, because it was mistaken for the pronominal dative "[belonging] *to us*" (Levy 1 228) so that he had to substitute the Aram. *beth* Now this pronominal dative is employed in Jewish Aramaic in such a phrase as "they went away" (Dalm *Words* p 22), Aram "*they went away for themselves* (ללו)" But this, in effect, is what Mark (W H txt) has here, having the pl where Mt -Lk have the sing This indicates that the original tradition here mentioned no such place as Bethany, but merely something about a place for "passing the night," which Luke inferentially described as "the mount called Olivet," and Matthew alone, by error, "Bethany "

THE ANOINTING AT BETHANY

"beth-thany" or "*bethany*[1]" It would be very natural that a great number of early Christian traditions should gather round the place on the Mount of Olives where Jesus, in danger of arrest by the Jewish rulers, and not able to "lay his head[2]" in Jerusalem, spent the nights in converse with His disciples during the week before the Crucifixion: "He left the unbelievers," says Jerome, "and going forth from the City of the gainsayers, He went to Bethany, which, being interpreted, is House of Obedience, prefiguring already the calling of the Gentiles, and there He remained (mansit), because He could not continue-to-remain (permanere) in Israel[3]"

This is an early Christian view of the name Beth-any— "house of *obedience*." And it is possible to trace this meaning, though but faintly, back to a Hebrew word corresponding to the second part of the name "Bethania[4]." But another meaning (much more prominent in Hebrew) is "*afflicted*" or "*poor*[5]," and perhaps Jerome assumes this in his next words: "This also is to be understood that He was of such extreme *poverty* (paupertatis) and so averse from flattering anyone that in that vast City He found no host, no abiding-place, but dwelt on a small farm (agro) with (apud) Lazarus and his

---

[1] See Levy iv. 623 תאנה, Aram תאינתא. Instead of Heb. *beth*-, "place of," Aram. freq. has (Levy *Ch* 1. 92, 96) *be*-, בי

[2] Mt viii 20, Lk ix 58.

[3] Jerome on Mt xxi 17.

[4] Heb. ענה (Gesen 772 *b*) "respond," may mean (1) "respond" (with docility) to command, (2) "respond" (with graciousness) to supplication But there is only one instance in LXX where a form of this word is rendered ὑπακοή (2 S xxii 36) "Thy *responsiveness* hath multiplied me" Here (Field) some copies have "humiliations (ταπεινώσεις)" or "chastening (παιδεία)," and it is not surprising, for the LXX ἡ ὑπακοή σου, if found in N T., would naturally mean "Thy [i e God's] obedience"

The same Heb occurs in Ps xviii 35. Here LXX has ἡ παιδία (i e. παιδεία) σου, perhaps meaning "thy *chastening*," but Aq "thy gentleness (πραότης)," Sym "my *responding* [*obediently*] [to thee]," τὸ ὑπακούειν

[5] See the previous note and Gesen. §776 on ענה "be afflicted," and *Son* 3242 (1)—(iv) on "The 'meek' king," and esp 3242 (1) *b*—*g*

A. F.   369 (Mark xiv 1—11)

THE ANOINTING AT BETHANY

sisters—those whose village is [in the Gospel, Jn xi. 1] Bethany[1]."

This last sentence from Jerome indicates the Johannine view of Bethany. It is introduced in the phrase "Lazarus from Bethany" as a place connected with "the village of Mary and Martha," all of whom Jesus "loves[2]" Then it is said to be "near Jerusalem[3]"—which distinguishes it from "Bethany beyond Jordan" where Jesus had been baptized. Jesus goes to it at the peril of His life, since the Jews had been recently "seeking to stone" Him[4] After the raising of Lazarus, Jesus for a time "walked no longer openly among the Jews[5]" Then comes the third and last mention of the name. "Jesus, therefore, six days before the Passover, came to Bethany, where Lazarus was, whom Jesus [had] raised from the dead. They made, therefore, a feast for him there, and Martha was ministering,

---

[1] "In agro parvulo apud Lazarum sororesque ejus habitaret, eorum quippe vicus Bethania est" This refers to Jn xi 1 ἦν δέ τις ἀσθενῶν, Λάζαρος ἀπὸ Βηθανίας ἐκ τῆς κώμης Μαρίας καὶ Μάρθας τῆς ἀδελφῆς αὐτῆς. But what is the meaning of "agro parvulo"? Does it mean that the small field or orchard attached to the house of the family of Lazarus was the "garden" of which John says (xviii 2) πολλάκις συνήχθη Ἰησοῦς ἐκεῖ μετὰ τῶν μαθητῶν αὐτοῦ? Συνάγειν here ought perhaps to be rendered, as in Mt xxv. 35, 38, 43, and also in LXX with εἰς τὴν οἰκίαν etc (Steph *Thes* vii 1178 D) "*hospitably receive*" If the meaning had been "Jesus and his disciples were gathered together" the natural Gk would have been συνήχθησαν Ἰ καὶ οἱ μ αὐτοῦ

Westcott says, "The exact force of the original is rather 'Jesus and (with) His disciples assembled (συνήχθη) there' The idea appears to be that of a place of gathering, where the Lord's followers met Him for instruction, and not simply of a restingplace during the night. But it is possible that the spot was used for this latter purpose also during the present visit (Luke xxi 37 ηὐλίζετο), and that Judas expected to find all sleeping at the time of his arrival."

Nonnus seems against this interpretation ("assembled") and rather in favour of "*hospitable reception*," or "*lodging*" κεῖθι καὶ αὐτῶν σύννομος ἀγρομένων αὐλίζετο λαὸς ἑταίρων.

Jerome's statement (on Mt xxi 17) that Jesus found "no host" in Jerusalem appears to ignore the evidence of Mk xiv 13—15, Mt xxvi 18

[2] Jn xi 1, 5   [3] Jn xi 18.
[4] Jn xi. 8—16   [5] Jn xi 54

THE ANOINTING AT BETHANY

but Lazarus was one of those that sat at meat with him. Mary therefore...[1]."

All this gives us the impression that Bethany was Christ's usual lodging-place at all times when He was in the neighbourhood of Jerusalem, and especially during the dangerous nights of His last week there. And John—like Luke though in a different way—might emphasize the anxious painstaking service of the hostess Martha. This being the case, it is not beside the mark to point out that, in the Johannine account of the Anointing in Bethany, *ania* is the word used in the version of SS to describe the action of the hospitable Martha, so that we read continuously "Jesus came to the village Beth *Ania* unto Lazar, him that was dead and lived. And he made for him a supper there...but Martha *was-occupied (ania)* in serving." Luke describes Martha as "*torn-in-pieces*[2]" with serving, and SS again has *ania* there. Ecclesiastes twice or thrice uses *ania*, LXX "torn-in-pieces," to describe worry[3]. This curious coincidence between the Syriac descriptions of Martha's action in Luke and John indicates a possibility of an early half-playful tradition about her as "the *afflicted* (or, *anxious*)" hostess, the *Ania*, and of her house as being "*Beth-Ania*."

We now come to the Mark-Matthew tradition that the house belonged to "Simon the leper." Ancient commentators attempt variously and unsatisfactorily to answer the natural questions that arise out of this phrase. Jerome quotes the appellation of "Matthew [once] the publican" as analogous to "Simon [once] the leper[4]", but he omits to tell us that the

---

[1] Jn xii 1 foll   [2] Lk x 40 περιεσπᾶτο

[3] Eccles 1 13, iii 10, v 19, see Gesen. 775 *b*, 773 *a*, comp 776 *a*

[4] Jerome on Mt xxvi 6. He adds that Jesus, before His Passion, "stays (moratur) in Bethany, the House of Obedience, which formerly was [the house] of Simon the leper (quae quondam fuit Simonis leprosi)." Does this mean "the house formerly [known as] the house of Simon the leper" and continuing to bear that name after the owner had been healed? He goes on to say "Not that he remained a leper also at that time, but as one who, being a leper before, was afterwards healed by the Saviour—the old name being retained

THE ANOINTING AT BETHANY

Gospel that mentions "Matthew [once] *the publican*," has previously mentioned him as "*a man called Matthew, sitting at the publican's-office*[1]." If Matthew intended to identify Christ's host at Bethany with the leper described as healed early in the Gospel[2] he should have introduced that leper as "*a man called Simon, a leper.*" It is possible that Mark and Matthew assumed this. If they did, there would be something to be said for the view that the appellation exalts the Saviour: "Jesus had healed a man called Simon of leprosy in one of His first acts of healing, and now it is in the house of this same *Simon the leper* that He receives the homage of the Anointing a few days or hours before His death[3]"

Origen, however, regards the man as still leprous Playing on the meaning of "Simon," i e. obedience, he remarks on the fact that "'Simon,' too, is a *mysterious sign of obedience*"— meaning "Simon," as well as Bethany "*the House of Obedience.*" Then he adds that the obedience was that of the letter, not that of the spirit: "Jesus therefore was *in the house of one* [*rightly*]

(permanente) in order that the power of the Healer should be manifested (ut virtus curantis appareat)" This view he supports by the analogy of "Matthew the publican"

Then he comes to allegory "Quidam Simonis leprosi domum eam volunt intelligi partem populi quae crediderit Domino et ab eo curata sit Simon quoque ipse obediens dicitur, qui juxta aliam intelligentiam mundus interpretari potest in cujus domo curata est Ecclesia" In interpreting "Simon" as "obedience" Jerome follows Origen

[1] Mt ix 9, x 3   [2] Mt viii 2

[3] Chrysostom, on Mt xxvi 6, says that the woman saw (εἶδεν) that Jesus had healed (θεραπεύσαντα) Simon the leper and hence was emboldened to seek from Him the purification of her soul He adds that the leprosy must have been healed, οὐ γὰρ ἂν εἵλετο (v r ἐγένετο) μεῖναι παρὰ τῷ λεπρῷ. Ephrem Syrus (p 205) argues at great length that the leprosy must have been healed and assumes that Simon was present at the table "Quomodo enim lepra in corpore Simonis permanere poterat, qui purificatorem leprae in domo sua recubantem vidit?" He adds finally "Perhaps the same thing happened as to Zacchaeus...to whom the Lord said (Lk. xix 9) 'To-day is salvation come to this house'; as a reward for his hospitality he received purification."

THE ANOINTING AT BETHANY

indeed called 'Simon' [as] *being obedient, yet leprous, and still having need of purification from Jesus*[1]"

It is significant that the author of Horae Hebraicae and Wetstein, to both of whom one can mostly turn with confidence for illustrations of fact, give no illustrations of "Simon the leper" as an appellation, and make no attempt to answer the questions raised by ancient commentaries. Their silence justifies the inference that something is wrong, and that the appellation is not a "fact." But it does not justify our treating the title as an invention. Its very difficulty shews that it was not invented. Perhaps the best hypothesis is that it was originated as a paraphrase of Beth-Ania, The House of the Meek, or The House of the Afflicted. Christians would be led to think of this appellation in connection with Isaiah's prophecy, "We did esteem him stricken, smitten of God, afflicted[2]." In that passage the Vulgate renders "stricken" by "leprous" and so does Aquila[3]. "Leper" is also specified in the Talmud as one of many names of the Messiah[4].

As regards the introduction of the name Simon I am unable to offer any satisfactory explanation, or even suggestion, except that it is a name sometimes apparently confused with "those that were with Him," meaning Christ's companions[5]. We have seen that it is interpreted both by Origen and by Jerome as "Obedient" or "Obedience," and this is also their interpretation of Beth Ania, so that, according to their allegorizing views, Beth Simon and Beth Ania might be interchanged.

---

[1] Origen on Mt xxvi 6, Lomm iv 397 "Factus est ergo Jesus in domo Simonis quidem alicujus obedientis, tamen leprosi, et adhuc opus habentis mundatione ab Jesu."

[2] Is liii 4

[3] Is liii 4 נגוע, "stricken," Gesen 619 *a* in particular, of leprosy, Aq ἀφημένον (so Field), of which Jerome says "id est, *leprosum*"

[4] *Sanhedr* 98 *b*. I have found nothing like this in any very early Christian writer except a saying of Justin Martyr (*Tryph* § 41) that the Levitical offering of fine flour on behalf of purified lepers was "a type of the bread of the Eucharist the celebration of which our Lord Jesus Christ prescribed, in remembrance of the suffering that He endured...."

[5] *Notes* **2999** (xvii) *g* foll

THE ANOINTING AT BETHANY

The Lucan addition of "Pharisee" might perhaps be explained from a confusion of *pâras*, "break [bread]" (applied to the host at a meal), with *parash*, or *pharash*, in "Pharisee[1]." On the supposition that Simon of Bethany was present at the Anointing, it might be asked what he did as host. SS, in John, prefixes to the words "Lazarus was one of the guests" the statement that Jesus "came...to Lazarus...*and he* [i e *Lazarus*] *made for Him a supper*." "Was it not Simon," some might ask, "that really did what is here attributed to Lazarus? And, if so, was this Simon one of 'certain persons' (Mark) that murmured at the anointing?" Luke may have answered both these questions in the affirmative. Finding that Simon was not described by Mark as doing anything in his own house, and rejecting as absurd the notion that he was a "leper," he may have availed himself gladly of any tradition that suggested that he was a disapproving and murmuring Pharisee.

§ 8. "(R.V.) *Burying*," or "*burial*," *in Mark, Matthew, and John*[2]

If we put aside, as doubtful, the saying about "the poor" in John[3], the verb or verbal noun rendered by R.V. "burying" or "burial," is the only one that Mark, Matthew, and John agree in assigning to Jesus in this narrative. The Thesaurus quotes authorities shewing that the word means, not "burying," but "embalming[4]." The Hebrew word for "embalm," *chânat*, is quite

---

[1] *Law* p 323
[2] Mk xiv 8   Mt. xxvi. 12   Jn xii. 7

ὃ ἔσχεν ἐποίησεν, προέλαβεν μυρίσαι τὸ σῶμά μου εἰς τὸν ἐνταφιασμόν   βαλοῦσα γὰρ αὕτη τὸ μύρον τοῦτο ἐπὶ τοῦ σώματός μου πρὸς τὸ ἐνταφιάσαι με ἐποίησεν   .. Ἄφες αὐτήν, ἵνα εἰς τὴν ἡμέραν τοῦ ἐνταφιασμοῦ μου τηρήσῃ αὐτό

[3] Jn xii. 8 is omitted by SS as well as by D, and is placed at the end of the narrative (instead of before the end as in Mk-Mt) where an editor might naturally interpolate it as a suitable climax
[4] See Steph *Thes*. iii 1154 (on ἐνταφιάζω) where the editors refer to authorities, quoted by Suicer, as contradicting the assertion of H S. that the verb means "bury," and as shewing that it means "prepare for burying"

THE ANOINTING AT BETHANY

different from the Hebrew for "bury[1]." The former, *chânat*, occurs toward the end of Genesis about the embalming of Jacob and of Joseph[2]. As to the embalming of Jacob, the Hebrew is rendered in LXX by the word here used in the Gospels, which means literally "make arrangements for entombing" (as distinguished from "burying[3]"). But, as to the embalming of Joseph, LXX renders the Hebrew "embalm" by the Greek "bury" thus. "They *embalmed* (LXX *buried*) him, and he was put in a coffin in Egypt[4]."

About Joseph, Aquila renders the word "they *aromatized*, or *spiced*, him." This gives exactly the meaning of the Hebrew verb. It occurs nowhere else in the Old Testament except about a fig-tree *"putting forth"* its spicy fruit-buds, literally *"spicing* its buds[5]." "Embalming" was an Egyptian not a Hebrew custom. But when a corpse had to be carried a long way for burial, as in Jacob's case, or when the burial had to be deferred for many years, as in Joseph's case, it was naturally practised even by Hebrews. Jewish traditions are remarkably silent about the embalming of Jacob and Joseph[6]. The Midrash on the embalming of Jacob quotes a tradition condemning, as well as one defending, the act[7]. In the Testaments of the Twelve Patriarchs, Judah says "Let no one embalm me[8]."

---

[1] Heb for "embalm," ἐνταφιάζειν, is חנט (sim. Onk.), Heb for "bury," θάπτειν, is קבר. Delitzsch has חנט for ἐνταφιάζειν

[2] Gen l 2 (*bis*), 26 (Gesen 334 *b* by error l 22, 26) Comp Gen l 3, חנטים pl abstr "embalming" LXX τῆς ταφῆς, Aq τῶν ἀρωματιζομένων, i e of the spicers or embalmers

[3] Gen l 2, but the noun *ib* 3 in LXX is rendered ταφή

[4] Gen l 26

[5] Cant ii 13 "the fig-tree (התאנה) spiceth (חנטה) (R V ripeneth) its figs" (so Gesen 334 *b*, but R V "*green figs*," and sim Gesen. 803 *a* פגיה "*early figs*")

[6] No reference to the passages mentioning the embalming is given in the Index to Jer Talmud transl Schwab, nor in Bab. Talmud ed Goldschmidt (at present, 1916)

[7] See *Gen r* on Gen l 1—2 (Wu p 501) "Why did Joseph die before his brethren? Rabbi said 'Because he had embalmed (einbalsamirt hatte) his father' ..According to the Rabbis, Jacob commanded them [i e his sons] to embalm him"

[8] *Test XII Patr Jud* § 26 "Let none embalm me with costly

THE ANOINTING AT BETHANY

These facts shew that Jewish tradition distinguished "embalming" from "burying," and that, if Jesus used the former term, he used it distinctively.

If so, with what distinction or allusion did He use it? It might possibly mean, nearly as in the Testaments quoted above, but with a tender allusiveness, not reproachful or ironical. "She is anointing my body as though she were embalming a royal personage previous to burial." But it might also allude to the ancient precedents of the two Patriarchs, whose embalming was a symbol of deliverance from immediate corruption, as well as from a grave in Egypt. If Jesus said anything to this effect, it would be received by Christians of the first century in the spirit of Ignatius, who says "For this cause the Lord received ointment on His head that it might breathe incorruptibility to the Church[1]." In the Acts, Peter quotes the words "Neither wilt thou give thy holy one to see *corruption*" as referring to Christ, who, he says, "was not left in Hades, nor did his flesh see *corruption*[2]." The ointment poured on Christ in Bethany and

---

raiment or tear open my belly," μηδείς με ἐνταφιάσῃ πολυτελεῖ ἐσθῆτι, ἢ τὴν κοιλίαν μου ἀναρρήξει. καὶ ἀναγάγετέ με. A second version has μηδείς με ἐνταφιάσει ἐν πολυτελεῖ ἐσθῆτι, ἀλλὰ ἀναγάγετέ με, apparently taking ἐνταφιάζω as "carry to the tomb in [burial clothes]." But the first version—in which ἐνταφιάζω seems to be explained by the parallel ἀναρρήξει as meaning "embalm"—is supported by precedent and Jewish feeling, according to which, "embalming" was quite exceptional, reserved for Jacob and Joseph alone, and requiring some kind of explanation.

[1] Ign *Eph* § 17

[2] Acts ii. 27—31, quoting Ps xvi 8—10 and then commenting on it. On Ps xvi 9 "my flesh," *Tehillim* (on Ps cxix 9, Wü ii 173) says "David said, I know that the worm will have no power over my flesh." *Derek Eretz*, ch. i says that immunity from the worm extends to seven, viz. Abraham, Isaac, Jacob, Moses, Aaron, Amram, "and, according to others (? some), also David (because of Ps xvi 9)." *Baba Bathr* 17 a, with more probability, has "Miriam" for "Amram" in this list, and adds "Benjamin." It proceeds "Many say also 'David,' because of Ps xvi 9, but it was only a prayer uttered by him." These traditions take "worm" as meaning the literal "worm" of the grave. But *Joma* 87 a takes the Psalm as applying to pious

THE ANOINTING AT BETHANY

ascending from His body to fill the house with its odour, might seem to be a symbol, not of burial followed by immediate corruption, but of an embalming or preservation from corruption, preparatory to a rising again

Now passing to the contexts of Mark and Matthew about embalming we find that Mark's extraordinary language appears to allude to the double meaning of the Hebrew or Aramaic word "to spice," or "to put forth," mentioned above as referring both to "embalming" and also to the "spicing" of the buds of the fig-tree. At all events he ventures to use a word "*murize*[1]"—like Aquila's *aromatize*—as to which it has been pointed out that it represents a "*perfuming*" tolerable only in women during life, but applicable to men as well as women when their bodies are being prepared for interment[2] The word is nowhere else used in the Old or New Greek Testament nor in the earliest Christian writers[3], but we have seen that Clement of Alexandria uses it, in connection with the Lord's Anointing, as conveying an allusion to the practice of "perfuming the dead[4]"

Matthew avoids the Greek verb *murize*—perhaps because of its Greek associations with pleasure and luxury—and substitutes "cast perfume (*muron*)" But both Matthew and Mark say that it was (Mark) "[with a view] to" or (Matthew) "toward," embalming Mark, however, laying stress on "*before*," says "she undertook *beforehand*"; Matthew, laying no such stress on "before," says "having *cast* (i e *put*) this

---

teachers in general, in which case the "worm" (comp Is lxvi 24 "their *worm* shall not die") would mean the "worm" of "hell", and that is the interpretation apparently adopted by Rashi ad loc where see Breithaupt's note Peter, who implies (Acts ii 29) that the Psalm *did not* apply to David and *did* apply to Christ, seems to have followed the literalist interpretation

[1] Mk xiv 8   Mt xxvi 12   Jn xii 7
προέλαβεν μυρίσαι τὸ σῶμά μου εἰς τὸν ἐνταφιασμόν   βαλοῦσα γὰρ αὕτη τὸ μύρον τοῦτο ἐπὶ τοῦ σώματός μου πρὸς τὸ ἐνταφιάσαι με ἐποίησεν   Ἄφες αὐτήν ἵνα εἰς τὴν ἡμέραν τοῦ ἐνταφιασμοῦ μου τηρήσῃ αὐτό.

[2] See above, p 349, n. 2, quoting Artemidorus
[3] It is not in Goodspeed
[4] Clem Alex 205—6, quoted above, p. 349.

ointment[1]" This might mean that the woman knowingly did this "with a view to" embalming. But it might mean that she did it out of pure affection, and with no such view, but that the Lord Himself discerned that the act was providentially directed "with a view to" an embalming.

The parallel in John, though obscure and possibly corrupt, appears to adopt the latter interpretation in a sentence that uses the word "reserve" in a peculiar way[2]. One difficulty consists in the use of "in order that," which (consequently perhaps) many authorities have cancelled. Some take "reserve it" as meaning "reserve the rest of the ointment." The text, as it stands in W. H, is hardly intelligible, but may mean "Let her alone, that she may [find herself to] have kept this stored up proof of her affection for the day of my embalming[3]"

[1] Προέλαβεν μυρίσαι, in Mk, lit "undertook beforehand to perfume," may have been corrupted to προεβαλεν μυρίσαι, (?) "proposed to perfume," and this again corrupted to Matthew's commonplace ἔβαλεν μύρον. Προλαμβάνω with inf is rare (though it occurs in Ign Eph § 3 προέλαβον παρακαλεῖν ὑμᾶς). Προβάλλω occurs in Cant. ii 13 (Aq) about the fig-tree "spicing" its buds, as a rendering of חנט, "embalm," and it is used in Lk xxi 30 about "the fig-tree and all the trees" (without an object).

[2] Τηρεῖν, "keep," in LXX, freq refers to "keeping" the law, commandments etc, "watching" one's soul, mouth, ways etc, but is not used of "reserving" a gift for anyone exc in Cant vii 13 Heb צפן, "all manner of precious fruits new and old, which I have reserved for thee, O my beloved" There, R V marg refers to Mt xiii 52 "every scribe that is made a disciple to the kingdom of the heavens is like unto a man a master of a house who bringeth out (ἐκβάλλει) from his treasury things new and old" Also the Targum on Cant paraphrases the new fruits as "the words of the scribes" and the old as "the words of the Law" But the Midrash, besides understanding the old fruits as the earlier Rabbis, and the new fruits as the later ones, prefixes a parable of a good house-wife, who, in her husband's absence, increases, instead of diminishing, the property he has left with her. Τηρεῖν is used of "reserving" the good wine in Jn ii 10. Comp 1 Pet 1. 4 "an inheritance. .reserved in the heavens for (εἰς) you"

[3] Nonnus has

θηλυτέρης λίπε δῶρον ἀμεμφέος, ὄφρα φυλάξῃ
σώματος ἡμετέρου κειμήλιον, εἰσόκεν ἔλθῃ
φοίνιος ἡμετέρων κτερέων ἐπιτύμβιος ὥρη,

THE ANOINTING AT BETHANY

John perhaps intends us to contrast this anticipatory embalming with that performed, after death, by Joseph of Arimathea and Nicodemus[1]. This mentions "one pound" of ointment; that mentions a hundred pounds[2]. This was too soon, that was in due time. This fulfilled no prophecy; that fulfilled the saying of Isaiah "with the rich in his death[3]." Mark and Luke,

---

where perhaps ὄφρα φυλάξῃ means "that she may reserve the rest of it"

[1] Jn xix 38—40.

[2] Jn xix 40 "bound it in linen cloths with the spices, as the custom of the Jews is to embalm (ἐνταφιάζειν)" is not commented on by *Hor Heb.* or Schottgen. Wetstein is hardly to the point when he quotes Tacitus *Hist* v 3 [error for v 5] as saying "de Judaeis" that it was their custom "corpora condere quam cremare, more Ægyptio"—that is, the Jews followed the *Egyptian practice* of *burying* rather than burning. For the question here is about "*embalming*" or "*preparing for burial*"—not about "*burying*"

Westcott says that the manner of the Jews is "contrasted with that (e g) of the Egyptians, who removed parts of the body before embalming (Herod ii 86 ff). The phrase may, however, only mark the Jewish custom of embalming as contrasted with burning. comp. Tac 'Hist' v 3" Hastings *Dict* Index contains no reference to Jn xix 40 *Enc Bib* 1285 says that "embalming" was "specifically Egyptian," that "the Hebrews did not practise it," and that the embalming of the body of Aristobulus in honey (Joseph *Ant* xiv 7 4) "stands by itself." Edersheim says (ii 617) "He [i e Nicodemus] now came bringing a 'roll' of myrrh and aloes, in the fragrant mixture well known to the Jews for purposes of anointing or burying" This is vague, and no authority is given for it. The writer adds "It was in 'the court' of the tomb that the hasty embalmment—if such it may be called—took place"

Perhaps John meant his readers to contrast with the "embalming" given by Mary the "*binding in linen cloths as the custom of the Jews is to embalm*"—a contemptuous expression for a quasi-embalming, that was neither the real Egyptian embalming, nor the Greek and Roman burning. This quasi-embalming was a kind of fettering in the tomb, and served no purpose except to make the resurrection all the more wonderful by reason of the breaking of the fetters

[3] Is liii 9 "they made his grave. .and *with the rich in his death*" seems to be alluded to in Mt xxvii. 57 "*rich*," and *ib* 60 "*his new tomb*" (as R V marg references indicate in both passages) "*Rich*"

later on, mention "spices" as being brought by the women to Christ's grave after the entombment; John does not. John, and John alone, says, later on, that there was an actual and material embalming of the dead body, but only at the hands of Joseph and Nicodemus. Here he tells us, in effect, that there was, before this, an anticipatory and spiritual embalming of the living body at the hands of Mary.

According to this view, John's obscure tradition implies a kind of comment on the phrase in Mark "*undertook beforehand*," as if he said "It was indeed '*beforehand*,' but it was ordained by God that it should be 'beforehand,' as the spicy fruit buds of the fig-tree come beforehand to be the sign of the spring." It is impossible to deny that if this is John's meaning, it is expressed with an almost ostentatious harshness as well as brevity and obscurity. But that makes it all the more probable that in using the rare word "embalming" John believes himself to be using a Synoptic word, rejected by Luke, but conveying a special meaning of great importance and used by Jesus Himself.

To us it may seem fanciful to connect the "embalming" mentioned by Jesus with the prospect of a higher life. We associate it with Egyptian mummies. But we must dissociate ourselves from the thought of Egypt and try to merge ourselves in that of Israel. To a Jew, the law that the old must give place to the new might connect itself with the promise in Leviticus that Israel should "bring forth *the old [stores]* because of (literally, from before, *i.e.* to make way for) *the new*[1]." There is only one other Scriptural passage that uses "*new*" of the products of the earth[2]. It is in the Song of Songs, where the Bride speaks of "precious fruits *new* and *old*" reserved for the

---

and "*his*" are pec. to Mt. The LXX "give the rich *for* (ἀντί) *his death*" seems to lead Justin (*Apol* § 51 "rules His enemies") away from the Hebrew (and see an interpretation given by Jerome "scribas ...qui nimiis opibus affluebant,...Romanis tradiderit Deus") John, describing the lavish gift of "myrrh and aloes, about a hundred pound weight" may have intended to suggest a less vindictive aspect of the true text of Isaiah.

[1] Lev xxvi 10   [2] Gesen. 294 *a*.

THE ANOINTING AT BETHANY

Beloved[1]. Now Philo applies the Levitical promise to the development of the knowledge of God[2]. Origen connects it with the saying of Christ to His disciples about the duty of "every scribe" in His kingdom to "bring forth from his treasury things *new and old*"; Jerome connects the same saying of Christ with the "precious fruits *new and old*" in the Song of Songs[3]; and the Sermon on the Mount is pervaded with the thought that the New is to be developed out of the Old as the fruit from a tree.

Modern criticism gives hardly sufficient prominence to the Marcan "parable of the fig-tree" in Christ's Discourse on the Last Days where Luke has completely missed the meaning: "Now from the fig-tree learn its parable. When its branch is now become tender and putteth forth its leaves, ye know that summer is nigh[4]." The parable seems to have referred to the fig-tree alone, and to point to the Hebrew "*spicing*," used about the buds of a fig-tree. It seems to take us back to the description of spring in the Song of Songs, mentioning the "fig-tree" as "spicing" (or "embalming") its "green figs." Christ's doctrine about "the fig-tree," and about "the new and old," together with the two passages from the Song, shew how "embalming" might be connected, in the mind of a Jewish Teacher, with the thought of a spiritual spring, a spontaneous budding into life, breaking through the bonds of the winter of death[5].

---

[1] Cant. vii 13, quoted above, p. 378, n 2.
[2] Philo i 178, 513
[3] See Origen on Mt xiii 52 (Lomm. iii 41) and Jerome.
[4] Mk xiii 28, Mt xxiv. 32 ἐκφύῃ, Lk. xxi 29 foll προβάλωσιν, applied to "the fig-tree and all the trees", see p. 325, n 2, and p 378, n 1, quoting Cant. ii. 13.
[5] See p 308 foll on Mk xiii 18 "pray ye that your flight be not in winter"

THE ANOINTING AT BETHANY

§ 9. "*Verily...for a memorial of her*," *in Mark and Matthew*[1]

The emphatic utterance here attributed to Christ by Mark and Matthew has nothing corresponding to it in Luke's narrative of Anointing. Nor does it seem at first sight to have anything corresponding to it in John. Many will find it difficult to believe that Jesus actually uttered such words[2], but it is perhaps even more difficult to believe that they were invented. They may have sprung from some metaphorical tradition the record of which contained the word "said" in the sense of "meant." A confusion between "now *this meant*" and "now *he said this*," either in Hebrew or in Greek, would explain Mark's insertion[3].

It would also explain John's omission, if we could shew that the Johannine parallel here inserts some detail that might be paraphrased so as to give the Mark-Matthew tradition. John has nothing except "The house was filled with the savour of the ointment." But might not "the house" be a way of expressing "the whole world," to which the Gospel was to be preached so that it might become "the house" of God? We have seen that Ignatius speaks of the ointment as breathing incorruptibility on "*the Church*[4]" Origen also, in his commentary on John, says that the woman "*infused the odour of the ointment into the whole house, [passing] into the perception of all that were in it, wherefore also it is written 'Wheresoever this Gospel shall be preached, in all the nations,* there shall be mentioned also that which this woman has done....*[5]'*" Here

---

[1] Mk xiv. 9
ἀμὴν δὲ λέγω ὑμῖν, ὅπου ἐὰν κηρυχθῇ τὸ εὐαγγέλιον εἰς ὅλον τὸν κόσμον, καὶ ὃ ἐποίησεν αὕτη λαληθήσεται εἰς μνημόσυνον αὐτῆς.

Mt xxvi 13
ἀμὴν λέγω ὑμῖν, ὅπου ἐὰν κηρυχθῇ τὸ εὐαγγέλιον τοῦτο ἐν ὅλῳ τῷ κόσμῳ, λαληθήσεται καὶ ὃ ἐποίησεν αὕτη εἰς μνημόσυνον αὐτῆς.

[Jn om., but see xii. 3]
ἡ δὲ οἰκία ἐπληρώθη ἐκ τῆς ὀσμῆς τοῦ μύρου.

[2] Comp McNeile on Mt xxvi 13 "It is difficult to believe that the words came from the lips of Jesus," and on the other side, Swete on Mk xiv 9 "That the saying has not been reported by Lc and Jo is an interesting indication of the independence of those Evangelists"

[3] See *Son* 3165, 3204 etc.   [4] See above, p 347

[5] *Comm Joann* 1 12, where Lomm 1 27 wrongly omits a reference to Jn xii 3.

THE ANOINTING AT BETHANY

he alludes to the *past fact* in John as corresponding to a future metaphorical fulfilment mentioned in Mark and Matthew. Else where, quoting fully from John, and then alluding to Mark and Matthew so as to explain John by the allusion, he says: "This indicates that the odour of the doctrine that proceeds from Christ and from the fragrance of the Holy Spirit, filled *the whole House of this world and the House of the universal Church*[1]."

This view of the sweet smell of the ointment, namely, that it was the type of something spiritual, agrees with the first mention of the word in our English Bible, in connection with Noah's sacrifice, "And the Lord *smelled the sweet savour*[2]"; and it suggests that the action of the woman might be regarded as of the nature of a sacrifice, or of a preparation for sacrifice, preparing the Lord's body (so to speak) for the Sacrifice on the Cross. In this connection, there are some very early traditions —instructive though apocryphal—about the sweet-smelling sacrifice of the heart "He speaks to us thus," says Barnabas, "'A sacrifice to God is a broken heart; *a savour of sweet odour to the Lord is a heart that glorifies Him that has shaped it*[3].'" Irenaeus also, shortly after repeating fully and correctly what "David says in the fiftieth [LXX] Psalm," adds, apparently from a different source, "As it is said elsewhere, 'Sacrifice to God is a broken heart, *a savour of sweet odour to God, a heart that glorifies Him that has shaped it*[4].'" The same apocryphal saying is quoted by Clement of Alexandria "'A sacrifice to the Lord is a broken spirit.' How then shall I use crowns, or ointments, or what shall I offer as incense to the Lord? 'A *savour (it is said) of sweet-odour to God is a heart that glorifies Him that has shaped it*[5]'"

It should be added that an Aramaic past tense "and there was filled" might be read in Hebrew fashion as "and there shall be filled[6]." There are many instances of the interchange of past and future in the transition from Hebrew to the Greek

---

[1] Origen on Cant 1 12 (Lomm xiv 429)
[2] Gen viii 21   [3] Barn § 2   [4] Iren iv 17. 1—2
[5] Clem Alex 306 is almost identical with Barnabas Ὀσμὴ εὐωδίας τῷ θεῷ (Barn τῷ Κυρίῳ) καρδία δοξάζουσα τὸν πεπλακότα αὐτήν
[6] *Paradosis* 1290, 1411 *a—b*.

THE ANOINTING AT BETHANY

of the LXX[1]. Our conclusion is that the omission by John of the Mark-Matthew tradition concerning a solemn prediction of Jesus is to be explained much more probably by the hypothesis that John substituted the true tradition for the misinterpretation of it, than by the hypothesis that John rejected the Mark-Matthew tradition as false, and substituted for it a new one that had no connection with the old

§ 10 *Mark's narrative as a whole*

The last section has brought before us the very widespread early Christian tradition about the "sweet savour" of "a sacrifice" that consists in "a broken heart." Jewish tradition comments on the anomaly in the Psalms: God will not have as a sacrifice the body of a beast that is rent, or an offering of wine in a broken vessel; but He welcomes the sacrifice of "a broken heart"— a metaphor for repentance, expressed in another metaphor as a passionate "turning away" from one's sinful self to find one's true self in the Father in heaven[2]. According to Isaiah, the Lord sent the Anointed, that is the Christ, to "bind up the broken in heart[3]." Luke strangely omits this clause when he represents Jesus as reading the Lesson from Isaiah in the Synagogue, but he expresses the fulfilment of it in his description of Jesus as dismissing the weeping woman that had been "a sinner" with the words, "Thy sins are forgiven[4]."

In Mark, there is nothing that on the surface signifies a breaking of the heart. But we ought to look below the surface We have already found that the "pistic" ointment probably contains an allusion to faith or trust[5]. The "embalming" was also found to allude to a life beyond death[6]. And a similar allusion appeared in the exceptional Marcan verb expressing "perfume." In a context so full of allusive metaphor, there ought not to be ignored the phrase peculiar to Mark describing the woman as "breaking" the cruse of ointment[7] The word

---

[1] See *Clue* 19, 84, 87, 240.
[2] See *Lev r* (on Lev vi. 9) (Wu. p 47), rep *Pesikt* Wu p 227 Pseudo-Jerome says (on Mk xiv 3) "fractum alabastrum carnale est desiderium." See pp 387, 721, n 1   [3] Is lxi 1 συντετριμμένους
[4] Lk iv. 18—19, vii. 48.   [5] See above, pp. 356—7.
[6] See above, p. 380.   [7] Mk xiv. 3 συντρίψασα

THE ANOINTING AT BETHANY

is a strong one, meaning "break in pieces" so that the contents might issue in a stream and not in drops. Matthew omits it, perhaps because he thought the action so unusual and inconvenient that this word must be corrupt. But it may be expressive of an intense emotion that disregarded convention; and Mark's original may have used the word allusively to describe the woman as "broken in heart" while breaking the cruse[1]. In Luke, the woman's sorrow was for her own sake, because of her past estrangement from the Father in heaven. But in Mark it appears to have been sorrow also for the sake of her Saviour on earth—who had often predicted that He would be "delivered over" to smiting or death, and whose prediction seemed now in danger of being speedily fulfilled[2].

In a somewhat similar manner we ought perhaps to explain the remarkable phrase peculiar to Mark, "That which she had she did[3]." Matthew avoids this. It seems to mean "That which she had [in her power to do] she did" but why did not Mark say this if he meant it? Delitzsch suggests an answer by his Hebrew rendering *"That which was in the power of her hand* [to do] *she did."* Such a phrase is connected in the Law with sacrifices and vows and offerings *from the "hand" of the poor*—which were necessarily of little value as compared with those of the rich[4]. So taken, and applied literally, the phrase might be regarded by Matthew as absurd. "The offering was of great value. Some say, three hundred denars. How then could Jesus say, that which she 'had it in her power,' or, that which she 'could afford,' to do?" But Jesus might be speaking, not of the money value, but of the spiritual value. "All that

---

[1] See Clem. Rom. § 18, and § 52 quoting Ps. li. 17.

[2] From a different point of view, Phaedo (117 c) weeps for himself rather than for Socrates who is on the point of departing ἀπέκλαον ἐμαυτόν οὐ γὰρ δὴ ἐκεῖνόν γε, ἀλλὰ τὴν ἐμαυτοῦ τύχην, οἵου ἀνδρὸς ἑταίρου ἐστερημένος εἴην.

[3] Mk xiv. 8 ὃ ἔσχεν ἐποίησεν, Delitzsch את אשר היה לאל ידה עשתה. SS has "This, which she hath done, lo, as if for my burial she hath done it," k "quod habuit haec," followed by "praesumpsit et unguentauit ..."

[4] See Gesen. 390 a quoting Lev v 7, 11 etc.

THE ANOINTING AT BETHANY

she could possibly do, all that she could possibly give, a broken heart—this she gave[1]."

In view of all the facts we may regard it as probable that Mark—even if he did not definitely allude in the "breaking" of the cruse to the "broken heart"—assumed that the woman was heart-broken with sorrow. In the Phaedo, when Socrates drinks off the hemlock, even the gravest of his philosophic friends cannot forbear from tears Crito goes out for a moment to hide them, Phaedo weeps silently with covered head, another weeps openly, another bursts into weeping and wailing unrestrainedly. In Mark, then, why is not the woman represented as weeping? May it not be because Mark assumes the tears? May he not follow some tradition that subordinated tears as interfering with the emphasis laid on "embalming," which signified resurrection?

It is unsatisfactory to conclude with an interrogation. But we cannot ignore the atmosphere of doubt that encompasses these traditions about anointing. Later on, we shall find Mark and Luke implying or mentioning a proposed anointing of the body of Jesus, but the parallel Matthew mentions only a "beholding", and the Gospel of Peter will be found to add "weeping and lamenting[2]." This will be discussed in its place Meantime, we may safely conclude that Mark's difficult expressions are probably earlier than the easy paraphrases that Matthew substituted for them, and that Mark contains, in an obscure and possibly truncated form, the closest approximation to the historical fact.

§ 11. *A review of the evidence*

On a matter on which Origen changed his mind, and departed from the view formerly held by himself and "many[3]" older commentators, it is natural to doubt whether it is possible to arrive at a safe conclusion. But the facilities possessed by

---

[1] On Lk ii 24, describing the offering of Mary, the Lord's mother ("a pair of turtle-doves"), Origen refers to Lev xii 8 (A V. marg) "if her hand find not sufficiency of a lamb "

[2] Mk xvi 1, Mt xxviii 1, comp Lk xxiv 1 and xxiii. 56.

[3] "Many," see above, p. 353.

THE ANOINTING AT BETHANY

modern students for the purpose of linguistic analysis[1] have enabled us to see that there is more to be said than Origen supposed for the older view, apparently assumed by Ignatius and Clement of Alexandria, that there was only one act of anointing and that the anointing woman had been "a sinner."

If there had been more than one, would there not probably have been many? Would not such an act have provoked imitation—especially among the devoted women described by Luke as following Jesus? But Mark, Matthew, and John all appear to regard it as unique. So apparently do Ignatius and Clement of Alexandria. If indeed it had come early in Christ's life, where Luke places it, it would have probably been imitated But it appears to have come but a few days before the close of His life. It seems to sum up the action of the Messiah, or Christ, or Anointed, in preaching the Gospel to sinners and "binding up the broken in heart," who, in the person of one woman, make Him a return in the form of an anointing, or *chrism*, that prepares the *Christ* for His grave and resurrection. If the woman was in some special way a "sinner," and was now a repentant sinner, that would make her a fit type of the Gentile Church which was to receive, through repentance, remission of sins. Hence the emphasis on the act in all the Gospels

As to the place where the Anointing happened, and the house in that place, the Evangelists diverge Bethany, say all but Luke, Luke is silent[2]. The house of Simon the Pharisee, says Luke; the house of Martha and her family (in effect) says John; the house of Simon the Leper, say Mark and Matthew—all, perhaps, going back to some original Beth Ania, as above indicated.

These convergences and divergences illustrate what we have found Origen calling "a kind of family relationship (cognatio quaedam)" between the Gospel narratives Some of the

---

[1] I mean not only the Concordances to Scripture in English, Greek, and Hebrew, but the Indices to early Christian writers, including Goodspeed's Concordance to those of the first century and a half, and the Indices to Greek writers in general.

[2] Lk vii 36 The places mentioned in the previous context are vii 11 "Nain," vii 17 "Judaea and the region round about."

similarities and dissimilarities illustrate the different aspects in which the act might present itself to the narrators. In Mark and Matthew the woman simply anoints the Saviour as an "embalming" for the grave and resurrection, but in Luke and John the woman "wipes off" from Jesus something ("tears," or "ointment," or both) that becomes to her, in Luke, a kind of cleansing for the remission of sins. In John this "wiping" is only an addition to the "embalming." But Luke mentions no "embalming" at all. He is solely concerned with the woman whose sins are forgiven, not with the "embalming" of the Forgiver.

It is not surprising if Luke has missed the meaning of the "embalming." It would perhaps be as perplexing to him as the last words of the dying Socrates would be to some modern readers. "Crito, we owe a cock to Æsculapius[1]." Not every modern reader of Plato realises that this means "We owe a sacrifice to the God of Healing who is on the point of raising me up from the disease of mortal life to the health of life immortal."

But, on the hypothesis that only one woman anointed Jesus what are we to say about the omission, by Mark, Matthew, and John, of the fact—if it was a fact—that the woman had been "a sinner"? In behalf of Mark it may perhaps be said that he assumed it in introducing the phrase "alabaster cruse of ointment." But we have seen that John alters this into "*pound* of ointment." Is it possible that John knew the woman to have been a sinner—this woman whom he calls the sister of Lazarus and whom he has expressly described as "loved" by Jesus—knew it, and yet refrained from mentioning it?

It would be venturesome to assert this positively, but it would perhaps be still more venturesome to deny the possibility. Consider John's representation of Mary Magdalene. He gives to her the first place among those privileged to see the risen Saviour. He makes her the Lord's own messenger to the Apostles concerning His resurrection. Yet he nowhere tells us that she had once been possessed by "seven devils."

Consider also John's treatment of the term "sinner." He

---

[1] Plato *Phaedo* 118 A.

THE ANOINTING AT BETHANY

never uses the word except technically in the story of the healing of the man born blind. There some of the Pharisees declare that Jesus "is not from God," but some venture to ask "How can a man that is a sinner do such signs?" Then they pronounce authoritatively "We know that this man is a sinner." The man born blind replies, in effect, that he knows nothing about these Pharisaean technicalities, "Sinner or not, He was the man that healed me! Is that what you call 'sinner'?[1]" Similarly, perhaps, as regards the woman that anointed Jesus, John may have intended his readers to say, "Sinner or not, she was one whom Jesus 'loved.' She was one whose tears moved Jesus to raise Lazarus from the dead. She was one from whose hand He willingly received a preparation for the temporary tomb through which He passed in order that He might ascend to the Father in heaven."

[1] Jn ix. 16, 24, 25, 31.

CHAPTER IX

THE LAST SUPPER

[Mark xiv. 12—25]

§ 1. *Judas Iscariot's agreement with the chief priests*[1]

THE account of Judas' agreement comes, in Mark-Matthew, as a connecting link between the narrative of the Supper at

---

[1] Mk xiv. 10—11
(10) Καὶ Ἰούδας Ἰσκαριὼθ ὁ εἷς τῶν δώδεκα ἀπῆλθεν πρὸς τοὺς ἀρχιερεῖς ἵνα αὐτὸν παραδοῖ αὐτοῖς
(11) οἱ δὲ ἀκούσαντες ἐχάρησαν καὶ ἐπηγγείλαντο αὐτῷ ἀργύριον δοῦναι καὶ ἐζήτει πῶς αὐτὸν εὐκαίρως παραδοῖ.

Mt xxvi 14—16
(14) Τότε πορευθεὶς εἷς τῶν δώδεκα, ὁ λεγόμενος Ἰούδας Ἰσκαριώτης, πρὸς τοὺς ἀρχιερεῖς,
(15) εἶπεν, Τί θέλετέ μοι δοῦναι κἀγὼ ὑμῖν παραδώσω αὐτόν, οἱ δὲ ἔστησαν αὐτῷ τριάκοντα ἀργύρια.
(16) καὶ ἀπὸ τότε ἐζήτει εὐκαιρίαν ἵνα αὐτὸν παραδῷ.

Lk xxii 3—6
(3) Εἰσῆλθεν δὲ Σατανᾶς εἰς Ἰούδαν τὸν καλούμενον Ἰσκαριώτην, ὄντα ἐκ τοῦ ἀριθμοῦ τῶν δώδεκα
(4) καὶ ἀπελθὼν συνελάλησεν τοῖς ἀρχιερεῦσιν καὶ στρατηγοῖς τὸ πῶς αὐτοῖς παραδῷ αὐτόν.
(5) καὶ ἐχάρησαν καὶ συνέθεντο αὐτῷ ἀργύριον δοῦναι
(6) καὶ ἐξωμολόγησεν, καὶ ἐζήτει εὐκαιρίαν τοῦ παραδοῦναι αὐτὸν ἄτερ ὄχλου αὐτοῖς

In Mk xiv. 11, ἐπηγγείλαντο δοῦναι perhaps represented an original "*said to pay*," as in Esth. iv 7 (the only instance of ἐ in canon LXX with a Heb original, R.V "*promised to pay*," Heb "*said to pay* (lit *to weigh*)," LXX ἐπηγγείλατο, al ex +παραστῆσαι). Mt xxvi 15 is influenced by Zech xi. 12 "*weighed* (ἔστησαν) [for] my hire thirty pieces of silver " Lk , like Mk, paraphrases

In Lk xxii. 6, the active ἐξωμολόγησεν is noteworthy The middle, ἐξομολογοῦμαι, abounds, meaning "give acknowledgment," "confess" etc , in a good sense The active, ἐξομολογέω, does not exist—though ὁμολογέω is existent—in O T or N T , or in the early Christian writers (Goodspeed) or in Gk literature (Steph. *Thes*). If

THE LAST SUPPER

Bethany and that of the Last Supper; and it has been touched on above in the discussion of the former Here the text is repeated in Greek in order to illustrate some differences between Luke and Mark.

Mark has the difficult expression "Judas Iscariot *the one* of the Twelve." Matthew's cancelling of "the" is condemned by its obviousness If we accept John's view that in the Supper at Bethany Judas was rebuked as the real offender, then "*the one* of the Twelve" might have meant, in the original, "that one of the Twelve just mentioned who was specially rebuked by Jesus[1]." Another explanation would be that Mark has already mentioned a Judas as brother of Jesus, who was *not* one of the Twelve[2], and now he mentions that Judas who was "the one of the Twelve" destined to be a traitor Neither of these explanations is quite satisfactory

Luke has mentioned no Judas as brother of the Lord, but he has mentioned a "Judas of James" as one of the Twelve[3]. Here he says "Judas that is called Iscariot"; but he adds "being [still] *of the number of the Twelve.*" This suggests a reproach, "still *nominally* an Apostle," and that was probably Luke's meaning

John, having recently mentioned Judas Iscariot as the murmurer at the Supper in Bethany, adds in the preface to the Last Supper, "Now before the feast of the passover, Jesus... loved them [*i.e* the disciples] unto the end. And during supper—*the devil having already put into the heart of Judas Iscariot*, Simon's [son], to betray him...[Jesus]...riseth from supper...[4]" Neither here nor later on does he describe Judas

---

it is genuine here, it is perhaps emphatic, "he *at once agreed*," "he *pledged himself*" It is omitted by many authorities, including SS. D reads ὡμολόγησεν If ἐξ οὗ were used in N T, we might suppose the original to have been ἐξ οὗ ὡμολόγησεν "from which time, *or*, in consequence of which, he agreed" (comp. Jn vi 66, xix. 12 ἐκ τούτου). This would be parall to Mt xxvi 16 ἀπὸ τότε

[1] In that case, Mark must be regarded as combining two inconsistent traditions For Mk xiv 4 has "some"

[2] Mk vi. 3, Mt xiii. 55.   [3] Lk vi. 16.
[4] Jn xiii 1—4.

391 (Mark xiv. 10—11)

THE LAST SUPPER

as making an agreement with the chief priests. He assumes that we know this[1], but leaves us free to believe that it was made either on the evening of the Supper at Bethany, or on the evening of the Last Supper, or between the two. John elsewhere recognises the ambiguity of the name "Judas" by calling one of the disciples "Judas not Iscariot[2]." But, in calling Iscariot "Simon's [son]" here, the object is probably not to distinguish him from others of the name of Judas but—strange though it may appear to us—to indicate that he was no true disciple, but still unregenerate[3]. Also, whereas Luke places the expression *"Satan entered into Judas"* before his narrative of the Last Supper, John, after the preliminary phrase just quoted ("the devil having already put..."), defers *"Satan entered into Judas"* till the conclusion of the Johannine Supper[4]. This seems an intervention, not in behalf of Mark, but rather against Luke.

§ 2. *The "man bearing a pitcher," in Mark and Luke*[5]

We can explain Matthew's omission of a large part of this narrative as follows. The wealthy Nicodemus—who according to the Fourth Gospel was present at this time in Jerusalem—

---

[1] Jn xviii 3 "having received from the chief priests...."
[2] Jn xiv 22
[3] See *Proclamation*, pp 127—8 on Jn xxi 15—17 "Simon, son of John"
[4] Lk. xxii. 3, Jn xiii 2, 27

[5] Mk xiv 12—16 (R V)	Mt xxvi 17—19 (R V)	Lk xxii 7—13 (R V)
(12) And on the first day of unleavened bread, when they sacrificed the passover, his disciples say unto him, Where wilt thou that we go and make ready that thou mayest eat the passover?	(17) Now on the first [day] of unleavened bread the disciples came to Jesus, saying, Where wilt thou that we make ready for thee to eat the passover?	(7) And the day of unleavened bread came, on which the passover must be sacrificed (8) And he sent Peter and John, saying, Go and make ready for us the passover, that we may eat.
(13) And he sendeth two of his disciples, and saith unto them, Go into the city, and there shall	(18) And he said, Go into the city to such a man, and say unto him,	(9) And they said unto him, Where wilt thou that we make ready? (10) And he said

392 (Mark xiv 12—16)

THE LAST SUPPER

would hardly be unwilling to lend Jesus a chamber in the City for Himself and His disciples. But he would probably be unwilling to let his kind act be known[1]. Jesus also might be unwilling that the Jews should know the whereabouts of this chamber. Now Nicodemus, according to Jewish tradition, was connected with the supply of water to the Jerusalemites[2]. He

Mk xiv 12—16 (R V) *contd*	Mt xxvi 17—19 (R.V) *contd*	Lk. xxii 7—13 (R V) *contd*
meet you a man bearing a pitcher of water follow him, (14) And wheresoever he shall enter in, say to the goodman of the house, The Master (*or*, Teacher) saith, Where is my guest-chamber, where I shall eat the passover with my disciples? (15) And he will himself shew you a large upper room furnished [and] ready and there make ready for us (16) And the disciples went forth, and came into the city, and found as he had said unto them and they made ready the passover	The Master (*or*, Teacher) saith, My time is at hand, I keep the passover at thy house with my disciples. (19) And the disciples did as Jesus appointed them; and they made ready the passover	unto them, Behold, when ye are entered into the city, there shall meet you a man bearing a pitcher of water, follow him into the house whereinto he goeth (11) And ye shall say unto the goodman of the house, The Master (*or*, Teacher) saith unto thee, Where is the guest-chamber, where I shall eat the passover with my disciples? (12) And he will shew you a large upper room furnished· there make ready (13) And they went, and found as he had said unto them and they made ready the passover

[1] Jn xii 42, xix 38—9.

[2] See *Hor Heb* on Jn iii 1, quoting *Taanith* 20 a, and *Aboth R. Nathan* ch 7, for a fabulous account of the origin of his name *Nicodemus* (as if it were Hebrew), and adding "It should seem *Nicodemus* was a priest, and that kind of officer whose title was חופר שיחין *a digger of wells*, under whose peculiar care and charge was the provision of water for those that should come up to the feast." See also a story, probably of anti-christian tendency, in *Chetub* 66 b (quoted in *Hor Heb* on Mk xiv 5) about a daughter of Nicodemus "to whom the wise men appointed four hundred crowns of gold for a chest of *spices* for one day." This daughter, afterwards, was "reduced to that extreme poverty, that she picked up barley-corns for her food out of the cattle's dung." Comp Wetstein on Jn iii 1.

THE LAST SUPPER

might therefore instruct one of his numerous water-carriers to stand with his pitcher at the gate near the "entering of the city[1]" from the road to Bethany, and to make himself the guide to two disciples of Jesus who might approach him as if desiring guidance. The disciples were to be guided to a place selected by Nicodemus where Jesus would be safe The question was there to be addressed as a password to the master of the house, "Rabbi saith, 'Where is my guest-chamber[2]?'" The chamber would then be shewn to them.

Now all these details would be of great interest for the first generation of Christians in Jerusalem They certainly must have known the "guest-chamber." Perhaps, too, some identified it with the "upper chamber" where Christians for the first time united in prayer and praise after the Ascension[3] Before a generation had passed they might begin, in their songs and discourses, to allegorize "the water," and possibly "the upper chamber" too[4]. But it will be observed that Matthew

---

[1] Mk xiv 13 ὑπάγετε εἰς τὴν πόλιν καὶ ἀπαντήσει . is not so definite as Lk xxii 10 εἰσελθόντων ὑμῶν εἰς τὴν πόλιν συναντήσει ὑμῖν, which suggests that as soon as they had passed through the gate the water-carrier would meet them

[2] Mk xiv 14 ποῦ ἐστιν τὸ κατάλυμά μου, Lk xxii 11 om μου

[3] Acts 1 13 ὑπερῷον, also used ib ix 37—9, xx 8 and freq in LXX (always some form of עליה). Here (Mk xiv 15, Lk xxii 12) the word is ἀνάγαιον This does not occur in LXX *Hor Heb*, on Acts 1 13, quotes *Juchasin* 23 b "When the feast was done, Rabban Johanan and his disciples went up לעליה *into an upper room*, and read and expounded till the fire shone round about them as when the law was given at Mount Sinai " It adds, "Take notice that עליה *an upper room* is distinct from a *dining room*, where they dined and supped " It also quotes *Juchasin* 45 b *"the sons of the upper room"* and Jer *Sabb*. fol 3 3 "These are the traditions which they delivered *in the upper room* of Hananiah" and adds "[there are] many instances of that kind" (comparing Acts xx 8) In Steph. *Thes* (which does not give ἀνάγαιον except under the head of ἀνώγε(ι)ον) ἀνάγαιον seems to mean *"above the ground [floor]"* See Levy iii 653 a quoting *Ned* 56 a—which refers fancifully to Lev xiv 34 "a *house of the land* of your possession," as meaning the *"ground floor,"* distinguished from the attic, or loft—and shewing that the derived word עיליתא means (1) "attic (Soller)," (2) "height," "heaven "

[4] Comp Origen on Mt xxvi 17—18 quoting the parall Mk and

THE LAST SUPPER

does not mention any "guest-chamber" in any part of his narrative. In Matthew, the password corresponding to "*my guest-chamber*" is "*my time*," which can hardly mean anything except (as Chrysostom takes it) the time of the Passion[1]. This is explicable if Matthew confused *cataluma* with *catalusis*. Both of these occur in LXX meaning "*lodging-place*[2]." But the latter, in literary Greek, mostly means "*dissolution*[3]." It would not therefore be difficult for a Greek writer to mistake some such expression as "Is there not *my lodging* [ready]?" for "There is [at hand] *my dissolution*[4]." This Matthew might paraphrase as "*My time* is at hand[5]."

saying "Et adscendimus. .ad locum superiorem in quo *diversorium* est quod demonstratur ab intellectu, qui est in unoquoque homine paterfamilias [i e οἰκοδεσπότης] discipulis Christi." He takes (*ib.* Lomm iv 408) the man with the pitcher to be Moses, and the water to be "mundatoria," or also ("aut certe") "potabilis." In *Hom Jerem* xviii 13 (Lomm. xv. 341—3) he says that he will "shew by Scripture" the meaning of the Biblical ὑπερῷον and quotes O T as well as Acts i 13 and Mk xiv 12 foll. "If anyone keeps the feast with Jesus, he is above, in a great upper chamber, in a swept upper chamber, in an upper chamber adorned and [made] ready."

[1] Mt xxvi 18 ὁ καιρός μου ἐγγύς ἐστιν. The phrase ὁ καιρός μου does not occur elsewhere in the Synoptists. But it resembles Jn vii 6 ὁ καιρὸς ὁ ἐμὸς οὔπω πάρεστιν (and sim vii 8) apparently meaning "the season appointed for my Passion."

[2] Κατάλυμα, in LXX = Heb "habitation," "lodging" etc (about 8) including Exod xv 13 "unto thy [i e God's] holy habitation (נוה)"; κατάλυσις, in LXX, = "habitation" Jer xlix 20 נוה, Dan ii. 22 (Aram) שרא. .

[3] Steph *Thes* κατάλυσις (1) dissolutio, (2) dimissio, (3) exitus [ex hac vita], (4) deversatio hospitalis, or deversorium.

[4] Πάρεστι, "there is at hand," or "there is ready," would be appropriate here as in Jn vii 6, and πουεστιν might be corrupted into παρεστιν. For instances of interrog in Gk confused with affirm see *Joh Gr* 2236—44. In Heb., confusion would be more easy. Comp Levy i 463 *b* היידא (1) "diese," (2) "als Frageprtkl. 'quaenam?'"—on which see Dalman *Aram Gr* p 89.

[5] There remains Matthew's use of ὁ δεῖνα (unique in N T and non-occurrent in LXX) in words ascribed to Jesus xxvi 18 ὑπάγετε εἰς τὴν πόλιν πρὸς τὸν δεῖνα. On this Jerome says "Morem veteris Testamenti nova Scriptura conservat. Frequenter legimus 'Dixit ille illi (? illi et illi)' et 'in loco illo et illo,' quod Hebraice dicitur

THE LAST SUPPER

Passing to the Fourth Gospel we note that, as Luke closely follows Mark, no question arises about Johannine intervention. But in view of the early Christian allegorizing of "the pitcher" as signifying rudimentary purification[1], it is noteworthy that John represents Jesus as Himself "pouring water into the bason" and washing the feet of the disciples, not before the Last Supper but during it[2]. That action is so original that few, if any, will suspect that the narrative sprang from anything but fact. Yet, if so, the omission of it by the Synoptists shews that if they knew it they were not alive to the importance of

אלמוני et פלוני, et tamen personarum locorumque non ponitur nomen. *Et invenietis ibi quendam portantem lagenam aquae. Quorum idcirco vocabula praetermissa sunt ut omnibus qui Pascha facturi sunt, libera festivitatis occasio panderetur.*" The last two sentences, which I have italicised, seem to me obscure, but Jerome is justified in the hypothesis that τὸν δεῖνα may be a translation of the Heb original mentioned by him. The Heb phrase occurs in Ruth iv 1 of a person, and 1 S xxi 2, 2 K vi 8 of a place (where see Field).

In Ruth iv 1 "he [*i.e* Boaz] said, Sit here, (lit) *a certain defined person* (פלני) *unnamed* (אלמני)"—LXX κρύφιε, Aq ὁ δεῖνα—we are not to suppose that Boaz addressed the man thus, but that the writer substituted "such-and-such a one" for the name, because, as Rashi says, "he would not take on himself the right of redemption" ("non scriptum (hic) est nomen ejus quia ille noluerat redimere") Similarly here, *Matthew may have substituted ὁ δεῖνα for some name of a person, or some description of a person, actually uttered by Jesus* If Nicodemus was that person, the fact that he never openly joined the Church of Christ, and that his daughter was held up by the Jews as an example of divine retribution, may have influenced some earlier Evangelists, though not John, in suppressing all mention of his relations with Jesus

On the other hand Cramer on Lk xxii 7 foll prints a comment alleged to be from Titus of Bostra, suggesting that τὸν δεῖνα was not a casual expression—οὐ γὰρ ἔφη πρὸς τὸν δεῖνα τυχόν—and that Jesus *would not mention the name of the host to Peter and John in the presence of Judas*," in order that he [*i e* Judas] might not learn the [name of the] man and run away and report it to those who had hired him."

[1] See above (p 394, n 4) and add. Tertull *De Bapt* § 19 quoting Mk xiv 13, Lk xxii 10 about the "man bearing water" (to shew that the Passover is a suitable time for baptism) and saying that the expression may be interpreted figuratively.

[2] Jn xiii. 2—12

THE LAST SUPPER

it. And yet two of them could find room for so much detail about the man bearing a pitcher!

It is not improbable that a superfluity of Christian discussions about "the pitcher," supposed to be the type of Mosaic purification, led John to relate fully and to emphasize the Christian sacrament of "the bason." This indeed instituted a purification of an entirely new nature—differing from any mentioned in the Pentateuch—one in which a man does not aim in the first instance at purifying himself, but as it were stoops down to the feet of his neighbours in order to wash away that which defiles them, and then finds that in following thus the example of his Master he has cleansed and washed away the defilements of his own soul.

§ 3. *The designation of Judas as the betrayer*[1]

All the Synoptists agree that Jesus knew that the betrayer was among the Twelve, partaking, or having partaken, of the

[1] Mk xiv 17—21 (R V)	Mt xxvi 20—25 (R V)	Lk xxii. 14, 15, 21—23 (R V)
(17) And when it was evening he cometh with the twelve.	(20) Now when even was come, he was sitting at meat with the twelve disciples (*many auth., some anc., om* disciples),	(14) And when the hour was come, he sat down, and the apostles with him
		(15) And he said unto them, With desire...
(18) And as they sat (*lit* reclined) and were eating, Jesus said, Verily I say unto you, One of you shall betray me, [even] he that eateth with me	(21) And as they were eating, he said, Verily I say unto you, that one of you shall betray me	(21) But behold, the hand of him that betrayeth me is with me on the table
(19) They began to be sorrowful, and to say unto him one by one, Is it I?	(22) And they were exceeding sorrowful, and began to say unto him every one, Is it I, Lord?	
(20) And he said unto them, [It is] one of the twelve, he that dippeth with me in the dish.	(23) And he answered and said, He that dipped his hand with me in the dish, the same shall betray me	
(21) For the Son	(24) The Son of	(22) For the Son

(Mark xiv. 17—21)

THE LAST SUPPER

bread and wine on the table. But Luke differs from Mark-Matthew as to the position of the words indicating Christ's knowledge[1]. And not one of them describes the betrayer as going out before the rest to take steps for the betrayal. As far as Mark and Matthew are concerned, we are led to suppose that all present went out together ("*they* went out") to the Mount of Olives; and Luke hardly appears to differ from them, though he leaves us a loophole for discerning a possible difference[2].

Mk xiv 17—21 (R.V.) *contd.*	Mt xxvi. 20—25 (R.V.) *contd.*	Lk xxii 14, 15, 21—23 (R.V.) *contd*
of man goeth, even as it is written of him but woe unto that man through whom the Son of man is betrayed! good were it for that man if he (*lit* for him if that man) had not been born.	man goeth, even as it is written of him but woe unto that man through whom the Son of man is betrayed! good were it for that man if he (*lit* for him if that man) had not been born. (25) And Judas, which betrayed him, answered and said, Is it I, Rabbi? He saith unto him, Thou hast said	of man indeed goeth, as it hath been determined but woe unto that man through whom he is betrayed! (23) And they began to question among themselves, which of them it was that should do this thing

Comp. Jn xiii 21—8 (R.V.) When Jesus had thus said, he was troubled in the spirit, and testified,... Verily, verily, I say unto you, that one of you shall betray me. (22) The disciples looked one on another, doubting of whom he spake. (23) There was at the table reclining in Jesus' bosom one of his disciples, whom Jesus loved. (24) Simon Peter therefore beckoneth to him, and saith unto him, Tell [us] who it is of whom he speaketh. (25) He leaning back, as he was, on Jesus' breast saith unto him, Lord, who is it? (26) Jesus therefore answereth, He it is, for whom I shall dip the sop, and give it him. So when he had dipped the sop, he taketh and giveth it to Judas, [the son] of Simon Iscariot. (27) And after the sop, then entered Satan into him. Jesus therefore saith unto him, That thou doest, do quickly. (28) Now no man at the table knew for what intent he spake this unto him.

[1] Luke places the words after the institution of the Eucharist. Hence the verses in Luke parallel to Mk xiv. 18—21, taken consecutively, are Lk. xxii. 15 *a*, 21, 23, 22.

[2] Mk xiv 26, Mt xxvi 30 "they went out," Lk. xxii 39 "And

THE LAST SUPPER

The Apostolical Constitutions says "And when He had delivered to us the representative mysteries of His precious body and blood, *Judas not being present with us*[1]" These words indicate that at a very early period the question of the duration of the presence of Judas would be discussed. This being the case, small Lucan deviations from Mark acquire importance. For example, while Matthew agrees with Mark in the first half of the sentence "One of you will betray me—*he that is [now] eating with me*" (placed before the Eucharist), Matthew omits the second half, "*he that is [now] eating with me*"; and Luke's

---

he came out and went as his custom was.. , and the disciples also followed him"

[1] *Const Apost* v 14 represents the Jewish rulers as making plans against Jesus as early as the second and the third day of the week (Monday and Tuesday), and as determining "on the fourth day" (Wednesday) to crucify Him "And Judas knowing this, . and being smitten by the devil himself with the love of money.. was nevertheless not cast off by the Lord....Nay, and when we were once feasting with Him... He said 'One of you will betray me' And when every one of us said 'Is it I?' and the Lord was silent, I, [who was] ? the one of the twelve more beloved by Him than the rest . besought Him to tell us .. Yet not even then did our good Lord declare his name, but gave two signs of the betrayer one by saying 'He that dippeth with me in the dish,' a second, 'to whom I shall give the sop when I have dipped it' Nay, although he himself said 'Master, is it I?' the Lord did not say 'Yes' but 'Thou hast said' and .'Woe to that man .'" Hereupon, Judas departs and bargains with the priests for thirty pieces of silver

After this follows "And on the fifth day of the week (Thursday), when we had eaten the passover with Him, and when Judas had dipped his hand into the dish, and received the sop and was gone out by night, the Lord said to us 'The hour is come that ye shall be scattered and shall leave me alone (Jn xvi 32).. '" This gives the impression that the prediction about "dipping in the dish" and "giving the sop" was made on Wednesday and fulfilled on Thursday. Or else we must suppose that the action was repeated Then follows Peter's protestation, and the prediction of Peter's denial, and then the above-quoted brief reference to the Eucharist—as being "the representative mysteries" at which Judas was "not present"—followed by a form of Luke's version of the going forth ("Judas not being present with us He [*i e* Jesus] went forth").

399 (Mark xiv. 17—21)

THE LAST SUPPER

parallel (placed after the Eucharist) is still less definite "The hand of him that betrayeth me is with me on the table[1]."

Again, Mark, repeating the present tense, says "It is one of the twelve, *he that is [now] dipping with me into the dish*"; but the parallel Matthew omits "one of the twelve" and has the past tense, "He that *dipped* his hand with me in the dish, the same shall betray me[2]. Luke has no parallel to these sayings.

There follows a questioning among the disciples, in which, according to Mark-Matthew, they—"one by one" (as Mark says), or "one [at a time] each one" (as Matthew says)—questioned the Lord, saying "Is it I?" but according to Luke they merely "questioned among themselves", and they asked, not "Is it I?" but "which of them was it that should do this deed[3]."

Here, then, are two points as to which—unless the rule of Johannine Intervention is to be broken—John must be found to say something —1st, the "eating" and "dipping"; 2nd, the "questioning" of the Lord by the disciples. On both, John does apparently intervene.

As to the first, John represents Jesus as quoting from the Psalms "he that *eateth my bread*[4]"; and he adds that Jesus

---

[1] Mk xiv. 18
Ἀμὴν λέγω ὑμῖν ὅτι εἷς ἐξ ὑμῶν παραδώσει με ὁ ἐσθίων (marg. τῶν ἐσθιόντων) μετ' ἐμοῦ.

Mt xxvi 21
Ἀμὴν λέγω ὑμῖν ὅτι εἷς ἐξ ὑμῶν παραδώσει με.

Lk xxii 21
Πλὴν ἰδοὺ ἡ χεὶρ τοῦ παραδιδόντος με μετ' ἐμοῦ ἐπὶ τῆς τραπέζης.

On Lk. xxii. 21, see *Son* 3371 (1) *m*.

[2] Mk xiv. 20
Εἷς τῶν δώδεκα, ὁ ἐμβαπτόμενος μετ' ἐμοῦ εἰς τὸ [ἓν] τρύβλιον.

Mt xxvi 23
Ὁ ἐμβάψας μετ' ἐμοῦ τὴν χεῖρα ἐν τῷ τρυβλίῳ οὗτός με παραδώσει

Lk om

[3] Mk xiv. 19
ἤρξαντο λυπεῖσθαι καὶ λέγειν αὐτῷ εἷς κατὰ εἷς Μήτι ἐγώ,

Mt xxvi 22
καὶ λυπούμενοι σφόδρα ἤρξαντο λέγειν αὐτῷ εἷς ἕκαστος Μήτι ἐγώ εἰμι, κύριε,

Lk. xxii. 23
καὶ αὐτοὶ ἤρξαντο συνζητεῖν πρὸς ἑαυτοὺς τὸ τίς ἄρα εἴη ἐξ αὐτῶν ὁ τοῦτο μέλλων πράσσειν.

[4] Jn xiii. 18 ὁ τρώγων μου τὸν ἄρτον ἐπῆρεν ἐπ' ἐμὲ τὴν πτέρναν αὐτοῦ, quoting Ps. xli. 9 "Mine own familiar friend...that did eat [of] my bread, hath lifted up his heel against me," LXX ὁ ἐσθίων ἄρτους μου

THE LAST SUPPER

"when he had *dipped* the sop, taketh and giveth it to Judas[1]"
"This was a very unusual thing," says the Horae Hebraicae, "to dip a sop and reach it to anyone[2]"; and Wetstein and Schottgen offer no explanation of the act. Moreover John represents Jesus as speaking, not about "*a* sop" but about "*the* sop," saying "He it is for whom I shall dip *the sop* and give it him" This leads us to ask "Could it be called '*sop*' before it was 'dipped'? And are we to infer from '*the*' that it was some customary food, as we speak of '*the* meat,' '*the* vegetables,' '*the* soup'? And what are we to say about the reading of B in the subsequent words 'When he had dipped *a* sop'?"[3] It is tempting to explain '*the sop*' as referring to "*the Charoseth*," or Passover sauce, which many connect with the "dipping" in Mark and Matthew[4] But we cannot legitimately thus explain "*the*" in John, for he regards the Passover as still to come Explanation must therefore be sought elsewhere.

Turning to the LXX, we find that, although it never uses the diminutive *psōmion*, it has *psōmos* several times, and almost always to mean a "fragment" or "crumb" of bread, especially in courteous and self-depreciatory offers of hospitality as in "Comfort thy heart with *a crumb* (where A has fragment) of bread[5]" It occurs also, along with "dipping," in the promise

---

ἐμεγάλυνεν ἐπ' ἐπὲ πτερνισμόν, Aq Theod κατεμεγαλύνθη μου πτέρνᾳ, Sym συνεσθίων μοι ἄρτον ἐμόν, κατεμεγαλύνθη μου ἀκολουθῶν Euseb. (Field) said that Aq has πτέρναν, for πτερνισμον, "being a slave to the Hebrew" The Targ renders "magnificavit (הגדיל) super me (עלי) calcaneum (עקב)" by "has magnified himself above me *by craft*," and Rashi explains עקב as "*ambush*" both here and in Josh. viii 13 (RV "*liers in wait*," Gesen 784 *a* "*rear*") Tehill ad loc. seems to render עקב as "at the end" and gives a quaint explanation of it

[1] Jn xiii 26 βάψας οὖν [τὸ] ψωμίον λαμβάνει καὶ δίδωσιν Ἰούδᾳ Σίμωνος Ἰσκαριώτου

[2] *Hor Heb* also asks (ὁn Jn xiii 26) "What could the rest of the disciples think of it?" and suggests that they would suppose Jesus to mean, in effect, "Take your supper quickly and go."

[3] Blass approves of the omission of τὸ, W. H bracket it.

[4] As to the *Charoseth* see *Hor Heb* on Mt xxvi 26, and also McNeile, on Mt xxvi 23

[5] Judg. xix. 5 ψωμῷ (A κλάσματι) ἄρτου

THE LAST SUPPER

of Boaz to Ruth "Thou shalt dip *thy crumb* in the vinegar[1]." The Hebrew noun (*path* from *pâthath*, "crumble") occurs for the first time in Abraham's offer of hospitality to the three Persons "I will fetch a *crumb* of bread," but there LXX has simply "*bread*" (as also have the Syriac and most of the Latin versions of John here)[2]. Also, LXX uses the verb "feed-on-crumbs" (*psōm-īzein*)—where the Hebrew has the vague and general "cause-to-eat"—to describe the Lord as feeding the children of Israel in the wilderness, or as feeding the weak and erring (sometimes medicinally)[3]. In this use of the verb, the LXX appears to be influenced by literary Greek, which uses forms of *psōmos* for the most part to mean food for invalids, or for children[4].

If that is the meaning here, and if there is also an allusion to the use of the word in LXX, Judas is to be regarded (1) as sick unto death, and Jesus as making a final effort to keep him alive, (2) as wandering away from the home-circle, and Jesus as making a final effort to recall him. Boaz invites Ruth to dip her "crumb" in the wine of his household[5], but Jesus Himself dips the "crumb" of hospitality and offers it to Judas as if to say, "Come back, come back even now, to the brotherhood from which thou art going forth[6]."

---

[1] Ruth ii 14, comp 1 S xxviii 22
[2] Gen xviii 5
[3] Ψωμίζω occurs, as causative of אכל "eat," in Numb xi 4, 18 of Israel crying to the Lord to be fed with "morsels of flesh," and in Deut viii. 3, 16 of the Lord as feeding Israel with "manna" Comp Ps lxxx. 5 "with the bread of tears," lxxxi 16 "with the finest of the wheat," Is lviii 14 etc
[4] Comp Epictet 1. 26 16, about invalids, who "cannot swallow down their spoon-food (τὸν ψωμὸν καταπίνειν)" Lightfoot says, on Clem Rom § 55 ἐψώμισαν, that the word is "especially appropriate of feeding the poor and helpless, the sick man or the child" Ψωμός and ψωμίον sometimes mean the bread used as a spoon to take up soup or porridge See Diog Laert *Vit Diog* vi 37 and Xen *Mem* iii 14 5
[5] See the Midrash *ad loc* on Ruth ii 14, and also *Lev r*, Wu p 239, and *Pesikt*, Wu. p 170.
[6] A word of comment is due to the emphatic "I" in Jn xiii 26 ᾧ ἐγὼ βάψω τὸ ψωμίον... Nonnus does not try to express it It

THE LAST SUPPER

As to the second point, the questioning of the Lord by the disciples, John says that "one of the disciples" was lying in Christ's bosom, and that Peter "made signs" to him; upon which that disciple said to Jesus "Lord, who is it[1]?" The

---

suggests perhaps (1) "I, the host, doing for the guest what the guest usually does for himself," (2) "I, the betrayed, making a last effort to convert the betrayer." The Physician seems represented by John as failing. But perhaps we should say "Not 'failing,' but learning the Father's will by filial action." Comp. Jn xii. 40 "He hath hardened their heart...lest...I should heal them," and *ib*. v. 19 (R V) "The Son can do nothing of himself, but what he seeth the Father doing," on which (and on Mk vi 5 "was not able") see *Law* pp 137—42

[1] Jn xiii 25 ἀναπεσὼν ἐκεῖνος οὕτως ἐπὶ τὸ στῆθος τοῦ Ἰησοῦ λέγει αὐτῷ Κύριε, τίς ἐστιν,

(1) The difficult ἀναπεσών "falling back" or "throwing himself back" (like a rower, Steph. *Thes* 499) has been altered by D into ἐπιπεσών (*d* "incumbens"). It is rendered "falling" in Syr, but "recumbens" in Lat versions. Nonnus has ὀξέι παλμῷ στήθεσιν.. πεσών which expresses the impulsiveness of the action, but not the backward direction. *Const Apost.* has v. 14 "And, as the Lord was silent, I *having stood up*, [? the] one of the Twelve beloved by Him more than the others, *having enclosed Him in my embrace* (ἀναστὰς ἐγώ, εἷς τῶν δώδεκα, φιλούμενος ὑπ' αὐτοῦ πλεῖον τῶν ἄλλων, ἐνστερνισάμενος αὐτὸν) began to beseech Him to say...." This appears to be an attempt to express the motion implied by the ἀνα- in ἀναπεσών as if it were "*up*"—not "*back*." Origen, who even in his loftiest mysticism seldom despises the laws of the Greek language and literature, writes (*ad loc* Lomm. ii. 450) as if the "*lying* [*up*] in the bosom" implied a lower stage of revelation than that implied by "*falling* [*up*] on the breast"—" John, who before was lying [up] (ἀνακείμενος) in the bosom (ἐν τῷ κόλπῳ) of Jesus, *has* [*now*] *gone further up* (ἐπαναβέβηκε) and *fell* [*up*] (ἀνέπεσε) on the breast (ἐπὶ τὸ στῆθος). And perhaps if he [i e John] had not *fallen* [*up*] on the breast, but had remained in the state of *lying* [*up*] in the bosom, He would not have delivered (παρέδωκεν) that utterance (λόγον) which John, or [rather] Peter, was longing to learn (μανθάνειν)."

In *Const Apost* v. 14 Clark translates ἐνστερνισάμενος αὐτόν "from lying in His bosom." But see Clem Alex 123, commenting on "Eat ye my flesh" and saying "It commands us ..*partaking of a new and different diet*, that of Christ, receiving Him if possible in ourselves, to store Him up and to *enclose the Saviour in our breasts* (καινῆς δὲ ἄλλης τῆς Χριστοῦ διαίτης μεταλαμβάνοντας, ἐκεῖνον, εἰ δυνατόν, ἀναλαμβάνοντας ἐν ἑαυτοῖς ἀποτίθεσθαι καὶ τὸν σωτῆρα ἐνστερνίσασθαι)."

THE LAST SUPPER

Johannine words that come between these two statements are uncertain. The Revised Version inserts a saying of Peter thus—" *and saith unto him, Tell* [us] *who it is of whom he speaketh.*" This is probably wrong. It should be " *and saith unto him, Say* [to the Lord] 'Who is it?'—[that is to say,] of whom he speaketh[1]."

Here Clem. Alex has in view the sacramental food And that leads us to reflect that ἀναπίπτω elsewhere in all the Gospels means "lie down to eat" and that it is so used by Luke and John in describing the Last Supper (Lk. xxii. 14, Jn xiii. 12). It is therefore possible that John is using the word in a double sense, meaning primarily and literally "falling back," but, secondarily and allusively, reclining so as to partake of the Saviour's body and blood.

(2) Origen's mystical suggestion about a higher stage of revelation—though it cannot be accepted as indicating that ἀναπεσών means "ascending"—is favoured by the Johannine mention of "*breast,*" στῆθος, immediately after "*bosom,*" κόλπος The former is rendered by Delitzsch לֵב, "*heart*" Στῆθος is very rare in LXX but occurs thrice (Exod xxviii 29—30) about Aaron as bearing "the names," or "the judgment," of the children of Israel "*upon his heart* (לֵב)" when he "goeth in before the Lord." It is here typical of the intercessory love of the High Priest, the Son of God, upon which the believer casts himself. Στῆθος, in literary Greek, has no such sense. It would require καρδία. But καρδία would be impossible here in describing an external action Στῆθος (in the light of the LXX but not without it) describes an external act but also suggests a spiritual one.

[1] On Jn xiii. 24 εἰπὲ τίς ἐστιν—περὶ οὗ λέγει see *Joh. Gr.* **2249** and add Origen *ad loc.* "νεύειν δέ...Πέτρου ἔργον ἦν, καὶ ἀκολούθως τῷ τοιούτῳ νεύματι λέγειν τῷ συμφοιτητῇ, ὡς παρρησίαν πλείονα ἔχοντι πρὸς τὸν διδάσκαλον, Εἰπὲ 'Τίς ἐστιν—περὶ οὗ λέγει,'" That is to say, since "the fellow-disciple" had "*more freedom of speech* [*than the rest had*] *with the Master,*" Peter said, in effect, "Say to him, in our behalf, since you can venture to say what we cannot, 'Who is it?'" The words "about whom he speaketh" may be Peter's, but they are more probably an evangelistic addition. If the writer had meant "Tell *us* about whom he speaketh" he would probably have inserted "us," ἡμῖν, in accordance with general usage. Without "us," εἰπὲ naturally means "say" imperat and introduces the exact words that are said At the same time it must be admitted that ειπε might mean "said," and ειπε τις εστιν.. might have been part of a tradition that "*a man said to his neighbour Who is it* about whom he speaks?" (comp. Lk. xxii. 23) There are few Johannine passages

But the uncertainty of the text makes further inferences doubtful.

The study of these variations is laborious. But a glance at them may be of value as shewing how naturally they may have arisen and how consistently with honesty in the narrators. Mark, for example, finding the betrayer described in the LXX of the Psalms as "*he that is eating* my bread," inserts the same present participle of the same verb here, although (as usual) he does not quote the prophecy[1]. Matthew omits this Luke paraphrases it "My bread" might imply that Jesus spoke in the character of a host or patron, but Mark adds another phrase, "dipping in the [same] bowl or dish," more suggestive of guest-fellowship such as is indicated by the Psalmist's "mine own familiar friend" A similar phrase mentioning "bowl" is found in Ben Sira[2] We have seen how Matthew retains but

---

of which the text is more doubtful than this Blass limits the verse to νεύει τούτῳ Σίμων Πέτρος, but the variations indicate that the original contained more than this, and that it is to be found in the most difficult and irregular of the ancient readings.

[1] Ps xli 9, see above, p 400, n. 4 On Mark's allusions to prophecy see *Son* 3518 d, *Beginning* p 207 etc

[2] Sir. xxxiv (xxxi) 14 μὴ συνθλίβου αὐτῷ ἐν τρυβλίῳ. Steph. *Thes* vii 2530 gives no instance of this phrase as meaning close companionship The context in Ben Sira speaks of greediness and self-assertion, and Origen quotes Ben Sira's rule as being violated by Judas who wished to thrust himself into close companionship and equality with his Master, while the others refrained (*Comm Joann* xxxii 14, Lomm ii. 454) Διόπερ ἐκείνων μὲν οὐδεὶς ἐνέβαπτε τὴν χεῖρα εἰς τὸ τρυβλίον μετ' αὐτοῦ οὗτος δέ, οὐκ ἀξιῶν μετ' αὐτῶν ἐμβάπτειν, μετ' αὐτοῦ ἐνέβαπτε, τὴν ἰσότητα θέλων ἔχειν πρὸς αὐτόν, δέον αὐτῷ παραχωρεῖν τῆς ὑπεροχῆς Τάχα οὖν τοῦ αὐτοῦ ἔχεται καὶ τό, "πλὴν ἰδού, ἡ χεὶρ τοῦ παραδιδόντος με μετ' ἐμοῦ ἐπὶ τῆς τραπέζης" Καὶ χαριεντιζόμενος δέ ποτε εἰς προτροπὴν νέοις περὶ τῆς ἐν ἑστιάσει τιμῆς τῶν πρεσβυτέρων, συγχρήσῃ τῷ ῥητῷ, ἵνα μὴ συνθλίβωσι τὴν χεῖρα τῶν πρεσβυτέρων Γέγραπται γὰρ καὶ τοῦτο "μὴ συνθλίβου μετ' αὐτοῦ ἐν τῷ τρυβλίῳ "

Jerome (on Mt xxvi 23) takes the same view "Judas, caeteris contristatis, et retrahentibus manum, et interdicentibus cibos ori suo, temeritate et impudentia, qua proditurus erat, etiam manum cum Magistro mittit in paropsidem, ut audacia bonam conscientiam mentiretur "

If that was the meaning commonly attached to Ben Sira's phrase

THE LAST SUPPER

modifies this, and how Luke includes it in his paraphrase ("the hand...with me at the table").

John—by making the present participle not part of a statement of his own but part of a prophecy of the Psalmist ("he that is eating[1] my bread...") whose words have to be considered as a whole—throws a doubt over the exact moment of the action. For it might mean the present as contemplated by the Psalmist, or the present as contemplated by Jesus. John's version seems to mediate between the present in Mark ("dippeth") and the past in Matthew ("dipped") by saying, in effect, "It was, in a sense, present, meaning 'my habitual table-companion up to this time', it was, in a sense, past, meaning 'my faithful table-companion in old days', but it was also, in a sense, future, as I shall shew you in what I shall now describe—namely, the last act of table-companionship"

As regards the questioning, ambiguity might arise from two causes, partly from the Hebrew and Aramaic difficulty of expressing "they said, each[2]," or "they said, one to another[3]"; partly from the fact that, in Greek (and still more in Latin) "this man" sometimes means "I[4]"; and partly from the Hebrew use of "speak *to* anyone" in the sense of "speak *concerning* anyone[5]." Thus "They said—this man to this

―namely that it implied, not close companionship, but an obtrusive and greedy self-assertion—we can understand (1) why Luke omitted it, (2) why John intervened as if to say "The circumstances of the 'dipping' were peculiar In this case, there was no 'pushing' on the part of Judas The Lord Himself dipped the bread and offered it to Judas"

[1] See *Law* pp 345—7 on Jn's substitution of τρώγειν for ἐσθίειν

[2] See *Oxf Conc* on the use of ἕκαστος = (*a*) "man (אדם)," (*b*) "one," (*c*) "one man (איש אחד)" etc Sometimes איש "man" is rendered εἷς ἕκαστος, or ἀνὴρ ἕκαστος.

[3] See Gesen 260 *b* on the use of זֶה "this [man]" to mean "another," and comp 1 K xxii 20, 2 Chr xviii 19, Job i 16, 17, 18, xxi. 25, Ps lxxv 7 etc.

[4] Liddell and Scott under οὗτος quotes *Od* 11 40 οὗτος ἀνήρ, but ὅδε is much more freq thus used In vernacular Latin (such as might influence Mark) "hic homo" freq = "I" (Lewis and Short "hic" I G)

[5] On Heb "speak *to*" = "speak *about*," see *Paradosis* 1162 *b*, *Son* 3371 *e*, *Proclam.* p 458.

THE LAST SUPPER

man—Is it this man?" might mean "Is it so-and-so?" but might be wrongly interpreted as meaning "Is it I[1]?" Again, "they said to each other"—in Hebrew, "they said, a man to his companion"—might be taken, but erroneously, to mean "one man said to his [special] friend," *e g* Peter to John[2]. Also what appears to be probably the correct rendering of the Johannine text, namely "*Say* [to the Lord] Who is it?" might easily be confused with "*They said* [to the Lord] Who is it[3]?"

The result is unsatisfactory, since it leaves us uncertain as to the exact historical details. But it is of use in revealing to us the antiquity of this uncertainty, and the pains taken by the Evangelists to work out their several interpretations of an obscure tradition It may be urged that Matthew goes beyond the limits of honest interpretation when he makes Judas say separately "Is it I?" and Jesus reply "Thou hast said." But this may be regarded as Matthew's inference from his own previous statement that they *all*, "*each one singly,*" *said* "*Is it I?*" Matthew adds, in effect, "If this was so, Judas also must have asked the question. And the Lord must have assented—perhaps in a whisper or by a gesture. This ought to have been stated by Mark. I will add it in my narrative." Such an addition—though it would not represent fact—would not be dishonest.

§ 4. *Christ's last words about, or to, Judas*[4]

According to Matthew, as just quoted, Christ's final words at the conclusion of the Supper are addressed to Judas, and

---

[1] Mk xiv. 19, Mt xxvi. 22, 25
[2] Jn xiii. 24
[3] See *Joh. Gr* on Jn i 15 ειπων v r. ειπον No alteration would be needed to make ειπε ambiguous in an unaccented MS.
[4] Mk xiv. 21

Mk xiv. 21	Mt. xxvi 24—5	Lk xxii. 22
ὅτι ὁ μὲν υἱὸς τοῦ ἀνθρώπου ὑπάγει καθὼς γέγραπται περὶ αὐτοῦ, οὐαὶ δὲ τῷ ἀνθρώπῳ ἐκείνῳ δι' οὗ ὁ υἱὸς τοῦ	ὁ μὲν υἱὸς τοῦ ἀνθρώπου ὑπάγει καθὼς γέγραπται περὶ αὐτοῦ, οὐαὶ δὲ τῷ ἀνθρώπῳ ἐκείνῳ δι' οὗ ὁ υἱὸς τοῦ	ὅτι ὁ υἱὸς μὲν τοῦ ἀνθρώπου κατὰ τὸ ὡρισμένον πορεύεται, πλὴν οὐαὶ τῷ ἀνθρώπῳ ἐκείνῳ δι' οὗ παραδίδοται.

THE LAST SUPPER

they are of the nature of an assent—"thou art, as thou sayest, a betrayer" According to John also, they are addressed to Judas, and they are, though in a very different way, of the nature of an assent, "That which thou art doing, [since thou wilt needs do it], do more quickly[1]." But according to Mark and Luke, Christ's final words are uttered not to Judas, but about him, and they are an utterance of "woe" to the betrayer, to which Mark and Matthew add that "it were better if he had not been born."

The word "woe," very frequent in Matthew and Luke, and twice used by Mark, is never used at all by John[2]. Conse-

Mk xiv 21 contd.	Mt xxvi 24—5 contd.
ἀνθρώπου παραδίδοται· καλὸν αὐτῷ εἰ οὐκ ἐγεννήθη ὁ ἄνθρωπος ἐκεῖνος.	ἀνθρώπου παραδίδοται καλὸν ἦν αὐτῷ εἰ οὐκ ἐγεννήθη ὁ ἄνθρωπος ἐκεῖνος ἀποκριθεὶς δὲ Ἰούδας ὁ παραδιδοὺς αὐτὸν εἶπεν Μήτι ἐγώ εἰμι, ῥαββεί, λέγει αὐτῷ Σὺ εἶπας

Luke apparently takes "*even as it is written concerning him*" to refer to such scriptural prophecies as that of Isaiah (liii. 6) "The Lord hath laid on him the iniquity of us all", so that Jesus was (Acts ii 23, comp. xvii 31) "delivered up by the *determinate* (ὡρισμένῃ) counsel and foreknowledge of God." God was not thwarted by the treachery of Judas. It mysteriously fulfilled a divine decree. Hence Luke substitutes "*determined*" for "*written*"

But "*even as it is written*" may have been used by Mark as referring to the peculiar nature of the "delivering up," namely, by the hand of one called by the Psalmist a "familiar friend." John perhaps assumes that Mark did mean this. At all events John implies "*written*" in the term "scripture (γραφή)" thus (xiii 18) "that the scripture may be fulfilled." John avoids emphasizing the "determinate counsel and foreknowledge of God" with regard to the treachery of Judas

[1] Jn xiii 27 ὁ ποιεῖς ποίησον τάχειον, on which see *Joh Gr* 1918, 2554 b—e

[2] Οὐαί, Mk (2), Mt (13), Lk (14), Jn (0). Origen supplies us with a reason that might induce John to avoid the word, *Cels* ii 76 "He [i e Celsus in the character of a 'Jew'] censures Jesus in such words as the following 'He makes use of threats, and reviles men on light grounds, when he says, *Woe unto you*, and *I warn you beforehand*'" To this Origen replies that no "Jew" could raise such an

THE LAST SUPPER

quently we must expect John to differ verbally here from all the Synoptists Yet of course there must be some Johannine equivalent of the Synoptic word; for every one would admit that in the Fourth Gospel, as in the Three Gospels, Jesus is constantly warning His hearers that retribution (in other words, "woe") awaits them if they persist in evil ways[1].

Take the following passage from Epictetus It contains a warning addressed to a worldly-minded sensualist, who sees "no good" in reverence, faithfulness, and temperance "If thou art seeking some other prizes better than these, *go-on-doing what thou art doing*. Not even a god can any longer save thee[2]" This somewhat resembles the Johannine expression And both of them really imply "Woe!" In the context, Epictetus says that our "*destruction*" (as well as our "help") lies within us[3]; and the Fourth Gospel elsewhere, using the same word, calls Judas "the son of *destruction*[4]"

Yet we are not to suppose that John here deviates entirely from Hebrew thought and merges himself in the thought of the Stoical lecture-rooms. There is in Proverbs a warning about the man "laden with blood" (like Judas), the destroyer of others who destroys himself· "A man that *is laden with the*

---

objection, since O T abounds in these expressions, but he also adds that the Prophets and Jesus (ib *ad fin*) use them to turn men from evil "as a healing drug"

[1] The word οὐαί in Steph *Thes* is not alleged to occur before the first century except in LXX The earliest non-christian writer at present alleged is Epictetus, who uses it in two passages (1) He (III 22 32) holds up Agamemnon to ridicule for saying "woe unto me, for the Greeks are in peril", (2) he says (III 19 1) "[Here is] the first difference between a non-philosopher (ἰδιώτου) and a philosopher The former says 'Woe unto me because of (διὰ) [the death of] my boy, or my brother, or my father!' But the latter, if ever constrained to say 'Woe unto me!' checks [himself] and says 'because of (διὰ) myself'"

[2] Epict IV 9 18, εἴ τινα ἄλλα τούτων μείζονα ζητεῖς, ποίει ἃ ποιεῖς οὐδὲ θεῶν σέ τις ἔτι σῶσαι δύναται Jn xiii 27 ποίησον is "do," not "go-on-doing (ποίει)" But still the resemblance is close

[3] Epict IV 9 16 ἔσωθεν γάρ ἐστι καὶ ἀπώλεια καὶ βοήθεια

[4] Jn xvii 12 ὁ υἱὸς τῆς ἀπωλείας, R V "the son of perdition"

409 (Mark xiv. 17—21)

THE LAST SUPPER

blood of any person shall flee unto the pit: let no man stay him[1]" The Talmud applies this to those who lead others into error and cause their souls to perish[2]; and Jesus, in His doctrine of stumbling-blocks, has previously pronounced a condemnation on those who cause others to stumble[3]. But there Mark omitted the words "Woe to him, through whom it cometh[4]." Here, in view of "the stumbling-block of the cross," of which Judas was the causer, Mark sets down this utterance of Christ, defined by the approaching event, "Woe to him through whom the Son of man is [to be] delivered up"

Besides the "woe" pronounced on the betrayer, Mark and Matthew add "It were better for him if he had never been born." Luke omits this. The expression was frequent in Talmud and Midrash[5]. But the Talmud testifies to a contest on this use of "better" between Hillel and Shammai[6]. And Jerome (on Matthew) thinks it necessary to say that the words do not necessitate antenatal existence. If Luke omits the words because they seemed to encourage the doctrine of an antenatal predestination to evil, we may say that John elsewhere intervenes on this point· "Neither did this man sin nor his parents, but that the works of God should be made manifest in him[7]"

Yet undoubtedly predestination to evil appears at first sight to be implied later on in the Fourth Gospel where Jesus says concerning the disciples "Not one of them was destroyed except *the son of destruction*—[and this] in order that the scripture might be fulfilled[8]." It does not matter greatly whether "except" is here used in its ordinary sense so that the meaning is "Not one of the Twelve *except* Judas," or "not one of the Eleven now present with me, *but only* Judas" In either case, such a phrase as "the son of destruction" might

---

[1] Prov xxviii 17, Gesen 92 *b*

[2] *Joma* 87 *a*

[3] Mk ix 42, where the parall Mt xviii 6 foll inserts οὐαί twice, and the parall Lk xvii 1—2 inserts οὐαί once

[4] Mt xviii 7 (parall Lk xvii 1) is ins between Mt xviii 6 and 8, parall to Mk ix 42—3

[5] See Wetstein on Mt xxvi 24

[6] See *Erubin* 13 *b*   [7] Jn ix 3   [8] Jn xvii 12

THE LAST SUPPER

seem to mean that a personified Destruction or Destroyer both generated, and claimed as its offspring, the soul of Judas.

But this is not the meaning in Hebrew of such phrases as "son of death," or "son of Gehenna," or "people of destruction." "Son of death" in the Bible—far from meaning that a man was from the beginning linked to death as a child to its parent—means that a man, by his own crime, has (in the judgment of the speaker) brought himself under a just condemnation to die[1]. The same thing applies to the phrase "the people *of [my] destruction*" in Isaiah and Ben Sira[2] In *the single instance where "son of Gehenna" occurs in the Bible* it is used in the phrase "ye *make him a son of Gehenna*," i e ye bring him under the condemnation to the penalty of Gehenna, by associating him with your sins[3] This certainly does not imply predestination. Also, in the only instance of "sons of Gehenna" alleged from the Talmud, the term is applied to the inhabitants of a city where the citizens, mostly proselytes, are noted for the drunkenness of the men and the extravagance of the women[4].

---

[1] 1 S xx 31, xxvi. 16, 2 S xii. 5, also 2 S. xix. 28 "men of death" in sim. sense

[2] Is xxxiv 5 (חרמי), LXX τὸν λαὸν τῆς ἀπωλείας (om. μου), Aq. etc τοῦ ἀναθέματός μου, Sir xvi. 9 "he spared not the people of (גוי) destruction (חרם)," ἔθνος ἀπωλείας, comp *ib* xlvi. 6 c כל גוי חרם, LXX ἔθνη πανοπλίαν (? corr for ἔθνη παντἀπωλειας) where the editors have "every banned nation," and add "For the idea, see Deut vii 2, Josh x 40 etc ... ; for the expression, cf Is xxxiv. 5 " The "nations" are "banned" because they have corrupted their ways before the Lord

[3] Mt. xxiii 15 "*a son of* hell (γεέννης)," where R V marg refers only to Mt v 29, but it might well have added, or substituted, v 22 "liable to [the punishment of] the Gehenna of fire," so as to shew the legal meaning of "son of" For the original Heb of γέεννα, namely, "valley-of-the-son-of-Hinnom," shortened to "valley-of-Hinnom," see Gesen 244—5

[4] See Levy i 238—40 He gives no instance of "sons of Abaddon," or "sons of Sheol," but refers to *R Hasch* 17 *a* for "sons of Gehinnom" as destined to eternal punishment The context says the name was given to "the sons of *Machouza*" a city on the Tigris, on which, and on their faults, see Neubauer (*La Géogr du Talmud*

THE LAST SUPPER

The Fourth Gospel, in which the doctrine of spiritual generation and regeneration is far more prominent than in the Three, tells us, in one startling passage, that Jesus said to certain Jews "that had believed him" that if they abode in His word they would be truly His disciples, and the truth would make them free; and yet, when they protest that they are free and are Abraham's seed, He turns upon them with the words "Ye seek to kill me" and "Ye are of your father, the devil[1]." It is to be supposed that "believed him" is here used of a very rudimentary belief. But even then the passage is noteworthy as shewing that such an appellation as "sons of the devil" and "son of destruction" might not imply, in this Gospel, an unalterable doom.

Predestination, or choosing in the sense of absolute election, seems to be expressly disclaimed by John in the passage where Jesus, after finding that some of His disciples are in danger of "being made to stumble," says to the chosen Twelve: "Was it not I that chose you the Twelve, and one of you is a devil[2]?" Does not this imply—of course illogically and inconsistently, but still as the deliberate view of the Fourth Evangelist—that the Son of God Himself (as Epictetus says) was *"not able to save"* Judas from the "destruction" that he brought upon himself? This is consistent with John's view, expressed elsewhere, that the Son "is not able to do" anything that He does not "see the Father do[3]." The Father Himself appears to be regarded as not able to save a soul that deliberately "destroys" itself, but the self-destruction of the sinner, in the case of Judas, is regarded as being overruled to a creative or regenerative end— "in order that the scripture might be fulfilled" by the Sacrifice of Jesus[4]. This is not a doctrine of predestination to evil, but rather a doctrine of the subordination of evil to good

---

pp 356—7) "La plupart des familles juives de Mahouza descendait de prosélytes (*Kiddouschin* 73 *a*)"

[1] Jn viii 30—44, on which see *Joh Gr.* **2506**
[2] Jn vi 70   [3] Jn v 19
[4] Luke's use of ὡρισμένον, instead of καθὼς γέγραπται (see above, p 407, n 4), has the advantage of meeting by anticipation the objection that the Crucifixion implied a failure It says, in effect, "The Crucifixion was decreed" The disadvantage is that in LXX

THE LAST SUPPER

§ 5. *The Institution of the Eucharist*[1]

No Institution of the Eucharist is recorded in the Fourth Gospel. Our study of the subject must therefore be confined to a few points in the Synoptic narratives that appear to be

the word, when meaning "decreed," is used (Dan vi 12) of Nebuchadnezzar's decree. Thus it is associated with the thought of a despotic and non-moral, or immoral, *fiat*. The Pauline use of the word in Rom 1 4 (and comp. Acts x 42, xvii 26, 31) "set apart" is altogether different.

[1]

Mk xiv 22—5 (R V.)	Mt. xxvi 26—9 (R V.)	Lk. xxii. 15—20 (R V.)
(22) And as they were eating, he took bread (*or*, a loaf), and when he had blessed, he brake it, and gave to them, and said, Take ye this is my body	(26) And as they were eating, Jesus took bread (*or*, a loaf), and blessed, and brake it, and he gave to the disciples, and said, Take, eat, this is my body	(15) And he said unto them, With desire I have desired to eat this passover with you before I suffer. (16) For I say unto you, I will not eat it, until it be fulfilled in the kingdom of God
(23) And he took a cup, and when he had given thanks, he gave to them and they all drank of it	(27) And he took a (*some anc auth* the) cup, and gave thanks, and gave to them, saying, Drink ye all of it,	(17) And he received a cup, and when he had given thanks, he said, Take this, and divide it among yourselves
(24) And he said unto them, This is my blood of the [*some anc auth insert* new] covenant (*or*, testament), which is shed for many	(28) For this is my blood of the [*many anc auth insert* new] covenant (*or*, testament), which is shed for many unto remission of sins	(18) For I say unto you, I will not drink from henceforth of the fruit of the vine, until the kingdom of God shall come
(25) Verily I say unto you, I will no more drink of the fruit of the vine, until that day when I drink it new in the kingdom of God	(29) But I say unto you, I will not drink henceforth of this fruit of the vine, until that day when I drink it new with you in my Father's kingdom	(19) And he took bread (*or*, a loaf), and when he had given thanks, he brake it, and gave to them, saying, This is my body which is given for you this do in remembrance of me (20) And the cup in like manner after supper, saying, This cup is the new covenant (*or*, testament) in my blood, [even] that which is poured out for you. [*Some*

THE LAST SUPPER

illustrated by Johannine correspondences. These may be looked for either in that earlier part of the Fourth Gospel which teaches Christ's disciples that they must feed on His flesh and blood, or else in incidental utterances of Jesus on the night of the Last Supper

But the subject is complicated by the following facts The MSS of Luke so vary that they give us, in effect, two accounts of the Institution, a short and a long one. The long one introduces matter closely resembling the account of the Institution given by Paul to the Corinthians. In all the accounts, the texts in the MSS vary considerably, and early writers, with the exception of Justin Martyr, do not quote freely those passages that present most difficulty. It will be convenient to dwell mainly on three questions: (1) What did Jesus do? (2) What did He bid His disciples do? (3) What, in addition, did He say?

(1) As to the bread, what Jesus did, is stated below, whence it is seen that He "took," "brake," "blest" (or, according to Luke, "eucharistized," *i e.* "gave thanks") and "gave" to the disciples[1] What He bade the disciples do was,

Lk xxii 15—20 (R V) *contd*
anc auth omit verses 19 b and 20, which is given for you.. which is poured out for you]

Comp 1 Cor xi 23—5 (R V) For I received of the Lord that which also I delivered unto you, how that the Lord Jesus in the night in which he was betrayed took bread, (24) and when he had given thanks, he brake it, and said, This is my body, which is (*many anc auth* is broken) for you this do in remembrance of me (25) In like manner also the cup, after supper, saying, This cup is the new covenant (*or*, testament) in my blood this do, as oft as ye drink [it], in remembrance of me

[1] Mk xiv 22
καὶ ἐσθιόντων αὐτῶν λαβὼν ἄρτον εὐλογήσας ἔκλασεν καὶ ἔδωκεν αὐτοῖς καὶ εἶπεν Λάβετε, τοῦτό ἐστιν τὸ σῶμά μου

Mt xxvi 26
ἐσθιόντων δὲ αὐτῶν λαβὼν ὁ Ἰησοῦς ἄρτον καὶ εὐλογήσας ἔκλασεν καὶ δοὺς τοῖς μαθηταῖς εἶπεν Λάβετε φάγετε, τοῦτό ἐστιν τὸ σῶμά μου

Lk xxii 19 a [19 b]
καὶ λαβὼν ἄρτον εὐχαριστήσας ἔκλασεν καὶ ἔδωκεν αὐτοῖς λέγων Τοῦτό ἐστιν τὸ σῶμά μου [τὸ ὑπὲρ ὑμῶν διδόμενον τοῦτο ποιεῖτε εἰς τὴν ἐμὴν ἀνάμνησιν]

THE LAST SUPPER

according to Mark, "take"; according to Matthew, "take, eat"; but according to Luke's shorter version, nothing. That is to say, this version contains no expressed bidding, only one that is implied—so far as "he gave," followed by "saying, This is so-and-so," may be said to imply an imperative "Take so-and-so."

All accounts agree that Jesus added—after the bidding (expressed or implied)—"This is my body." It will be seen, then, that concerning the "body" of the Lord, the only precept in Mark is "*take*"—which might well have been expressed by a gesture or "for you" accompanying the gift of the bread ("[see], *for you*, this is my body[1]"). Luke, who in his short version has nothing to correspond to "*take*," adds in his longer version a different "*for you*" coming immediately after "my body" thus. "that is being given *for* (lit. *in behalf of*) you," and adds, as an imperative, not "take," but "Do this with a view to my memorial[2]." This closely resembles the Pauline form of Institution[3]. Neither Luke nor Paul contains the imperative "take[4]."

---

[1] See *Paradosis* 1321 quoting Gen. xlvii 23 "*Behold*, [here is] seed for you," LXX "*Take* (λάβετε) for yourselves seed," and 1321 a quoting Gen xx 16 (Heb) "Behold, [let] this [be] to thee a veil," Targ Jer II "behold, that silver *is given* to thee for a present"

[2] Lk xxii 19 b τὸ ὑπὲρ ὑμῶν διδόμενον τοῦτο ποιεῖτε εἰς τὴν ἐμὴν ἀνάμνησιν

[3] 1 Cor xi 24 Τοῦτό μού ἐστιν τὸ σῶμα τὸ ὑπὲρ ὑμῶν τοῦτο ποιεῖτε εἰς τὴν ἐμὴν ἀνάμνησιν

[4] On ἀνάμνησις, see *Paradosis* 1398—1419 The only instance of the word in N T (besides Lk xxii 19, 1 Cor xi 24—5) is Heb x 3 ἐν αὐταῖς ἀνάμνησις ἁμαρτιῶν κατ' ἐνιαυτόν, as to which comp Numb v 15 "a meal-offering of memorial, bringing to remembrance iniquity" Here the Midrash explains the first clause thus, "This is for good, if the woman is pure," and the second, "This is for evil, if the woman is impure" The thought appears to be that the woman's conduct is, as it were, brought up before God to be remembered by Him for good or for evil Τὴν ἐμὴν is (*Joh Gr.* 1989, 2559) more emphatic than μου and may mean "that which is mine" as distinct from that which belongs to other occasions.

THE LAST SUPPER

Yet we may see in this imperative "take" a spiritual meaning if we may interpret it as including "*receive*," and as implying "*welcome*." This is a frequent meaning of the Greek word when applied to "receiving" the Word, or to "receiving" the Holy Spirit, or a messenger or gift of God, or "receiving" Jesus, not indeed in Mark[1], but frequently in John, as for example "But as many as *received* him [the Word] to them gave he authority to become children of God[2]." It has been shewn, in a previous volume of this series, that Jesus, bequeathing Himself to His disciples in the form of bread, may have said, "*Receive*," meaning grammatically both "*receive* [this]" and "*receive* [me]," and meaning spiritually "*receive me* into your hearts, my true self, to be with you after I have departed[3]."

---

[1] Λαμβάνω does not occur *in this sense* in Mk except Mk iv 16 (and sim Mt xiii 20) "they *receive* it (αὐτὸν) with joy"—where "it" is "the word" regarded as the seed—parall Lk. viii 13 δέχονται.

[2] Jn 1 12 ὅσοι δὲ ἔλαβον αὐτόν... (comp 1 16 ἐκ τοῦ πληρώματος αὐτοῦ.. ἐλάβομεν), v 43 οὐ λαμβάνετε με...ἐκεῖνον λήμψεσθε, vi 21 ἤθελον οὖν λαβεῖν αὐτὸν εἰς τὸ πλοῖον..., vii 39 οὗ [i e the Spirit] ἔμελλον λαμβάνειν, xiii 20 ὁ λαμβάνων ἄν τινα πέμψω εμε λαμβάνει, xiv 17 ὃ [the Spirit] ὁ κόσμος οὐ δύναται λαβεῖν, xix 27 ἔλαβεν αὐτὴν (the mother of Jesus), xx. 22 λάβετε πνεῦμα ἅγιον This last is the only Johannine instance of the imperative "receive" in Christ's sayings

The Johannine λαμβάνω corresponds to the Synoptic δέχομαι. This is used by John only in iv 45 ἐδέξαντο αὐτὸν οἱ Γαλιλαῖοι, which implies a superficial though friendly reception.

One result of John's preference of this ambiguous word λαμβάνω (instead of the Synoptic δέχομαι "I welcome") is that if we translate it mechanically we find ourselves using phrases that would sound profane or shocking from the Eucharistic point of view. Thus Pilate would say to the Jews (xix. 6) "*Receive him* [i e. Jesus] and crucify him," and Joseph and Nicodemus would be found to have (xix. 40) "*received the body of Jesus*" Such language forces us to think about the context and about the difference between "receiving" Jesus materially and "receiving" Him spiritually.

[3] In *Paradosis* 1319—31, and 1398 *a—b*, it has been shewn that the Semitic *nephesh*, "soul," might have been used by Jesus to denote "*self*," the real "*self*," and that this word very frequently indeed means "memorial" in the Talmud It has also been said (*ib.* 1332) "If our Lord had really used any Aramaic word that literally signified

THE LAST SUPPER

But this "receive," without the accompanying presence of the Giver and without His gift and gesture, might well be

'body' in the Institution of the Eucharist, it would not have been possible to bring the formula 'This is my body' into any direct verbal connexion with His life and work as described by the Synoptists." This is true, and it is also true that the Johannine doctrine about Christ's "flesh and blood" (instead of "body and blood") might seem to accord with the view that Jesus did not use the word "body" in the Eucharistic Institution

But it is possible that John's avoidance of "body" in this sense was caused by his desire to reserve it for another sense—namely (ii 21) "the temple of his body," the Church And uncertainty is produced by the doubt whether the Last Supper was Paschal or Antepaschal For example, the Talmudic treatise on the Passover mentions (*Pesach* 114 a) "*the body* of the Passover (גופו של פסח)" (Goldschmidt "Pesahlamm") And it adds (114 b) "There must be two flesh dishes, one *a memorial for the Passover* (זכר לפסח) and the other *a memorial for the Feast* (זכר לחגיגה)"

Even if we had on record the exact words used by Jesus in giving the bread, we should still miss the tone and action and gesture of the Giver Yet an increasing uncertainty as to Christ's exact words is compatible with an increasing confidence that John has rightly interpreted the motive of the words. We may also feel safe in attributing to the words a passionate tenderness similar to that of Paul (1 Thess ii 7—8) "we were [as] babes (νήπιοι, s W. H. notes) *in the midst of you as when a nurse cherisheth her own children*... even so in our yearning for you we were well pleased to impart unto you not only the Gospel of God but also *our own souls*" Clement of Alexandria (318—9) quotes "we were [as] babes (leg νηπιοι, not ηπιοι)...children" after quoting Paul on "the body and blood of the Lord," and elsewhere he says (123) "The Word is all things to the babe, both Father and *Mother* and Tutor and *Nurse*, 'Eat ye my flesh,' He says, and 'drink ye my blood'", and he represents the Word as saying to mankind (93) "Come unto me...I *bestow on you my complete self*"

There is mixed metaphor in describing Christ, who is Himself the Little One or Babe, as the Nurse of the little ones, but it is characteristic of the poetry of the Gospels and of early Christian thought In Revelation, the Son is represented as (1. 13) "girt about at the *breasts* (μαστοῖς) with a golden girdle" The usage of LXX, and Jewish tradition, oblige us to suppose that this means "breasts" in the usual sense, and not a man's "breast" Arethas interprets it as meaning either "the two *Diathēkai*," or "the breasts of our Lord and

THE LAST SUPPER

obscure when set down in a written Gospel. It would need to be explained. In explaining it, some might say that the gift was not to be like a pearl or other inanimate precious thing, given once for all and remaining always the same, it was to be a living presence in the heart, continually renewing the thought and influence of the Saviour, so that, even when He had passed away, He still spoke and counselled and guided His disciples, being part of themselves, the food of their spiritual being[1]. Others might add that this continual renewal was intended to be expressed not only invisibly in the continuous feeding on the spiritual bread, but also in the visible, weekly, and commemorative meal wherein the earliest Christians commemorated the resurrection of their crucified Saviour.

We perceive then that the words "Do this with a view to my memorial" explain the Marcan "Receive" as meaning something more than passive reception. "'Receive,' yes, but 'receive' with welcome. 'Receive' me into your hearts and affections—so as to make your whole lives one continuous service of loving loyalty to my will—not merely into your external selves so as to do this or that act of formal obedience to my commands. And, further, 'receive' me not into your

---

Master (τοὺς δεσποτικοὺς μαζοὺς)...through which also the faithful are nourished." Commentators, writing in prose, naturally pass over this anthropomorphism, or gunaikomorphism, applied to the Son in glory. But the *Odes of Solomon* abounds in it (see *Light* **3645** *d*, **3814** *i, m* foll.). It is also worth noting that on Numb. xi. 8 לְשַׁד, describing the "manna," where LXX has "cake," Aquila has "breast (μαστός)." Rashi declares this to be impossible, but says "our Rabbis explain it thus." Such an explanation led to poetic inferences that manna came to the children of Israel as milk from the breasts of the Lord. Comp. *Odes of Sol.* xix. 4 "the *milk of the two breasts of the Father*" (*Light* **3645** *d*).

[1] See *Law* pp. 384—402, on "Testament" or "Covenant," and especially p. 393. "Using the language habitual in Palestine, Jesus said to His disciples, 'This is the blood that signifies my death and yet not my severance from you. This is the blood of my last will and testament, in which, though dying, I bequeath to you my life and presence in perpetuity.'" This, though expressly applied to the cup alone, implies also an application to the bread. Both are bequeathed in the one Testament or *Diathēkē*.

478 (Mark xiv. 22—5)

THE LAST SUPPER

contemplative selves for purposes of solitary contemplation, but into your active and social selves for brotherly action. 'Receive' me, as I, the Son, continually 'receive' the Father that I may help His children 'Receive,' but also *do*. *Do as I do*"

If we turn to the Fourth Gospel, we shall find an illustration of the appropriateness (at this point) of a precept about "*doing*" For there Jesus says, after the Washing of Feet· "Know ye *what I have done to you*? Ye call me Master and Lord, and ye say well, for so I am If I then, the Lord and the Master, have washed your feet, ye also owe it as a debt [to me] to wash one another's feet For I have given you an example that ye also *should do as I have done to you*[1]." Many will feel that, if they had not been told, they would not have guessed that Christ's act was meant as "an example" of altruism. They might have thought that the act meant simply "Keep yourselves pure," not "Help others to be pure" It might have seemed to them ascetic, in a good sense, yet not altruistic.

But having once been told the explanation of this sacramental Washing, we can perceive that in early days precisely the same need of explanation might exist about the "example" contained in the Giving of Bread as existed about the "example" contained in the Washing of Feet. It might mean "Give yourselves to, and for, your brethren as I give myself to, and for, you " Paul, it is true, does not describe Jesus as "*giving*" the bread But in Hebrew and Jewish thought, "*distributing* (or, *giving*) bread" would often be implied in passages that described merely the "breaking" of it The context would sometimes make this obvious, as in the precept of Isaiah "to *break thy bread to the hungry*[2]" But elsewhere we might miss the meaning of the "breaking," if we did not constantly bear in mind that Jesus regarded all His disciples as "hungering," saying to them "Blessed are *ye that hunger* now, for ye shall be filled[3]." To "break bread" for these "hungerers" might well

---
[1] Jn xiii 12—15
[2] Is lviii 7, on which see *Law* pp 323—4
[3] Lk vi 21 The parall Mt. v 6 uses the third person

THE LAST SUPPER

be—as the Fourth Gospel insists, and the Three imply—a prominent object throughout Christ's life, and might well emerge into a special prominence on the day before His death. Isaiah's context suggests the sympathetic and uncondescending brotherliness that must accompany the act ("to break thy bread to the hungry...and that thou *hide not thyself from thine own flesh*)", and previously the prophet represents Jehovah as saying to Israel, in effect, "This is the fast that I have chosen—not that you should afflict your own soul on your own account, but that you should draw out your soul to others and satisfy the afflicted soul[1]." Similarly the apostle Paul regards Jesus as saying, in effect, "This is the memorial that I have chosen; if ye desire to commemorate me, after my departure, do to one another that which I have done to you"

This implies that every Christian is to imitate Christ in offering a sacrifice. Christ says "This is my *body*," and Paul says elsewhere "I beseech you therefore, brethren, through the tender-mercies of God, that ye present your *bodies* [as] a sacrifice, living, holy, well-pleasing unto God[2]." "Present your bodies as a sacrifice" does not imply a command to become, in the ordinary sense of the word, "ascetics" Nor does it mean simply—though it does include the meaning—that Christians are to "mortify corrupt affections" such as lust, pride, and wrath It is an appeal to "brethren" to be brother-like, and it invites those who have experienced the "tender-mercies" of God to be themselves tender and merciful to others In effect, it says "Give, as Jesus gave"

The evidence, as a whole, leads to the conclusion that Jesus did not utter to the disciples at the Last Supper the words "Do this with a view to my memorial," and the other words included in the longer Lucan tradition, but that they were received by Paul from Jesus long afterwards as expressing His meaning If Paul had simply handed down to us the

---

[1] Is lviii 3—10 on which see *Law* pp 323—4.
[2] Rom xii 1 Few, if any, of the following precepts (*ib* 4—21) can be described as ascetic They assume that "we, who are many, are one body in Christ, and severally members one of another," and they are based on this assumption

historical acts and words, he would naturally have quoted those disciples who were present at the Supper. "*I received from Peter and the Lord's disciples*" In that case he would probably have given us no more than Mark's tradition But he expressly says, "*I received from the Lord*[1]," apparently implying, as he says expressly to the Galatians, "*I did not receive from man*[2]" The meaning appears to be that after meditating on the significance of the Eucharist, he did not (like Luke) ascertain the details by comparing the evidence of those who were "eyewitnesses and ministers of the word[3]." He had (we may feel sure) received traditions about the Sacrament from Ananias, or from others, in the earliest days of his conversion But there was something in the Sacrament, beyond the words that he had thus heard, something that required a revelation; and he received one from Jesus "What I meant—what in effect I said—was this."

If this was the case, we could not be surprised that even Paul's explanation, thought out in solitude, and in the light of his peculiar experiences, did not fully explain the Sacrament While illuminating one aspect of the old tradition, the Pauline word "memorial," or *anamnēsis*, introduced a new ambiguity according as it was used in an ordinary Greek sense or with Hebraic allusion[4] Also the word "do," or "make," introduced by Paul, happens to mean, in certain contexts of LXX, "prepare

---

[1] 1 Cor xi 23

[2] Gal 1 11—12 "For I make known to you, brethren, as touching the gospel that was preached by me, that it is not after (κατὰ) man For neither did I receive it from man, nor was I taught it, but [it came to me] through revelation of Jesus Christ" The context indicates that Paul, after his conversion, took no pains to ascertain from the disciples in Jerusalem the acts and words of Christ, but the words "this is my body"—which he may be supposed to have heard after he was baptized by Ananias and when he received the sacrament—would naturally recur, and be included, in that revelation which he afterwards received in Arabia concerning the whole meaning of the Gospel, and concerning the relation of the Old Covenant to the New Testament

[3] Lk. 1. 2.

[4] See above, p. 415, n 4, and below, p 426

THE LAST SUPPER

[as food, *or* as sacrifice][1]." Justin Martyr appears to take it thus[2]. The rendering of "*Do this*" as "*Prepare this* [*as a sacrifice*]" would probably commend itself to many minds If we are to "do" any "thing," we all naturally desire that the "thing" should be defined for us. To celebrate the Eucharist duly on every first day in the week is definite But it is probable that Jesus meant more than this. In the breaking of the bread He appears to have desired us to discern the sign of His laying down His life for us, and when He bequeathed Himself

---

[1] See Gesen 794 *b* עשה "make" = "*prepare*, esp. of dressing and cooking food, Gen xviii 7, 8 etc...a bullock for sacrifice, I K xviii 23 etc. .*make* offering e g עולה Judg xiii 16 . also c accus. of thing sacrificed Ezek. xliii 25 etc, Lev xiv 30," where LXX has ποιήσει μίαν τῶν τρυγόνων, R V "he shall *offer* one of the turtledoves" This word is never rendered θύειν (or θυσιάζειν) which is practically reserved for זבח ("slay [for sacrifice]")

[2] Justin M *Tryph* § 41 "And further, the offering of fine flour that was *prescribed* (lit *delivered*, παραδοθεῖσα) *to be offered* (προσφέρεσθαι) in behalf of those who were being purified from their leprosy was a type of the bread of the eucharist (τοῦ ἄρτου τῆς εὐχαριστίας) which (ὄν)—[with a view] to a memorial of the suffering (εἰς ἀνάμνησιν τοῦ πάθους) which He suffered in behalf of those who were being purified in their souls from all human wickedness (οὗ ἔπαθεν ὑπὲρ τῶν καθαιρομένων τὰς ψυχὰς ἀπὸ πάσης πονηρίας ἀνθρώπων)—Jesus Christ our Lord *delivered* [to us] *to make* (παρέδωκε ποιεῖν) "

Similarly—and obviously choosing his words with care—Justin says with reference to a prophecy of Isaiah (Is xxxiii 16 LXX "bread shall be given to him") (*Tryph* § 70) "Now that in this prophecy [mention is made] (supply εἴρηται) about the bread—which our Christ delivered to us to *make* (τοῦ ἄρτου ὅν παρέδωκεν ἡμῖν ὁ ἡμέτερος Χριστὸς ποιεῖν) [with a view] to a memorial (εἰς ἀνάμνησιν) both of His having made unto Himself a body (τοῦ τε σωματοποιήσασθαι αὐτὸν) for the sake of those believing in Him, for whose sake also He became liable to suffering (δι᾽ οὓς καὶ παθητὸς γέγονε)—and also about the cup—which, [with a view] to a memorial of His blood He delivered [to us] *to make* [while] giving thanks (ὃ εἰς ἀνάμνησιν τοῦ αἵματος αὐτοῦ παρέδωκεν εὐχαριστοῦντας ποιεῖν)—is manifest (φαίνεται) "

Justin nowhere indicates a recognition that "*Do this* with a view to a memorial" might include the meaning "Do for one another that which I have done for you " Irenaeus (iv 17 5—6, iv 33 2) when mentioning the Institution of the Eucharist does not explain, or quote, the clause about ἀνάμνησις

THE LAST SUPPER

to us in that broken bread, He meant us to say "Hereby know we love, because he laid down his life for us, and we ought to lay down our lives for the brethren[1]"

(2) As to the cup, Mark and Matthew say that Jesus "took" a cup and "gave thanks (*lit.* eucharistized)," and "gave" it to them, and said "This is *the blood of my diathēkè*[2] [the blood] that is [to be] poured out for many[3]." The shorter Luke says that Jesus "received" a cup and "gave thanks" and said "Take this and distribute it to yourselves[4]." But the

---

[1] 1 Jn iii 16

[2] On this rendering, as preferable to "my blood of the covenant (*or*, the testament)," see *Law* pp 392—3 On the position of μου, "the vernacular genitive," see *Joh Gr* 2776—8

[3] Mk xiv 23—4
καὶ λαβὼν ποτήριον εὐχαριστήσας ἔδωκεν αὐτοῖς, καὶ ἔπιον ἐξ αὐτοῦ πάντες καὶ εἶπεν αὐτοῖς Τοῦτό ἐστιν τὸ αἷμά μου τῆς διαθήκης τὸ ἐκχυννόμενον ὑπὲρ πολλῶν

Mt xxvi 27—8
καὶ λαβὼν ποτήριον [καὶ] εὐχαριστήσας ἔδωκεν αὐτοῖς λέγων Πίετε ἐξ αὐτοῦ πάντες, τοῦτο γάρ ἐστιν τὸ αἷμά μου τῆς διαθήκης τὸ περὶ πολλῶν ἐκχυννόμενον εἰς ἄφεσιν ἁμαρτιῶν.

Lk xxii 17
καὶ δεξάμενος ποτήριον εὐχαριστήσας εἶπεν Λάβετε τοῦτο καὶ διαμερίσατε εἰς ἑαυτούς

On the parallelism between Mk "and they drank," and Mt "drink ye," see *Clue* 28, 243 In the alteration of Mk ὑπὲρ πολλῶν into Mt περὶ πολλῶν εἰς ἄφεσιν ἁμαρτιῶν, the ἄφεσις clause appears to be intended to indicate more clearly an intercessory object, but the substitution of περί for ὑπέρ remains unexplained (see *Joh Gr* 2721 *a* and 2718 foll)

[4] Lk xxii 17 διαμερίσατε εἰς ἑαυτούς is not quoted or paraphrased by Justin M. in either of the above-quoted passages, and it is not clear how the disciples are to receive the cup by "self-distribution" in a manner different from that in which they receive the bread by the Lord's giving

Justin says in *Apol* § 66 οἱ γὰρ ἀπόστολοι ἐν τοῖς γενομένοις ὑπ' αὐτῶν ἀπομνημονεύμασιν, ἃ καλεῖται εὐαγγέλια, οὕτως παρέδωκαν ἐντετάλθαι αὐτοῖς τὸν Ἰησοῦν, λαβόντα ἄρτον εὐχαριστήσαντα εἰπεῖν Τοῦτο ποιεῖτε εἰς τὴν ἀνάμνησίν μου, τουτέστι τὸ σῶμά μου καὶ τὸ ποτήριον ὁμοίως λαβόντα καὶ εὐχαριστήσαντα εἰπεῖν Τοῦτό ἐστι αἷμά μου, καὶ μόνοις αὐτοῖς μεταδοῦναι

This last clause "imparted to them *alone*," apparently applies to the bread as well as to the cup This view is favoured by a scholium in Cramer (on Lk. xxii 15) "Now He does not eat it [*i e* the Passover] with the Jews but *with His disciples alone* (ἀλλὰ μετὰ τῶν μαθητῶν αὐτοῦ μόνων) since the former were unworthy by reason of their persistent unbelief " Possibly it may be a Lucan vestige

THE LAST SUPPER

longer Luke adds (without any mention of "taking" or "receiving" except what may be implied from a previous use of the words as to the bread) "and the cup likewise, after having supped, saying "This cup is the new *diathēkè* in my blood, the [cup] that is being poured out for you[1]" The Pauline tradition resembles the first part of this, but omits "that is being poured out for you," and emphasizes the commemorative force of the precept by adding "Do this, as often as ye drink [it], with a view to my memorial[2]" The result of a comparison of all these versions is somewhat bewildering Especially is this the case as to the longer version of Luke This differs from all the others. (1) It mentions two cups (2) It tells us that the first cup was to be distributed by the disciples among themselves. (3) It mentions also "the cup after supping," but tells us nothing as to its destination—except what may be implied in the phrase (R V) "and...in like manner" (A.V "likewise also") (4) It uses, about the Passover, language that is compatible with the Johannine view that

---

of an altruistic precept (like that in John, "do as I have done to you") "Distribute *among yourselves* (originally, *to one another*)"

Compare Clem Alex 603 (qu Valentinus), "From the beginning are ye immortal, and children of eternal life, and ye desired to *receive your share of* (μερίσασθαι) death [*taken*] *into yourselves*, that ye might expend it, and consume [it], and that death might die in you and through you" (ἀπ' ἀρχῆς ἀθάνατοί ἐστε καὶ τέκνα ζωῆς ἐστὲ αἰωνίας, καὶ τὸν θάνατον ἠθέλετε μερίσασθαι εἰς ἑαυτοὺς ἵνα δαπανήσητε αὐτὸν καὶ ἀναλώσητε καὶ ἀποθάνῃ ὁ θάνατος ἐν ὑμῖν καὶ δι' ὑμῶν). The translation of T and T Clark, "ye would have death distributed to you," does not give what appears to be the meaning

Goodspeed's Concordance to Justin Martyr shews that he does not mention the word *diathēkè* in the context of any passage where he describes the Eucharist It is possible that he read διαμερίσατε εἰς ἑαυτοὺς as διεμερισέ εἰς αὐτοὺς For variations between διαμερίζω and μερίζω, in act and mid, see Ps xxii 18 διεμερίσαντο v r διεμέρισαν, Aq μερίσουσιν

[1] Lk xxii 20 καὶ τὸ ποτήριον ὡσαύτως μετὰ τὸ δειπνῆσαι, λέγων Τοῦτο τὸ ποτήριον ἡ καινὴ διαθήκη ἐν τῷ αἵματί μου, τὸ ὑπὲρ ὑμῶν ἐκχυννόμενον

[2] 1 Cor xi 25 ὡσαύτως καὶ τὸ ποτήριον μετὰ τὸ δειπνῆσαι, λέγων Τοῦτο τὸ ποτήριον ἡ καινὴ διαθήκη ἐστὶν ἐν τῷ ἐμῷ αἵματι τοῦτο ποιεῖτε, ὁσάκις ἐὰν πίνητε, εἰς τὴν ἐμὴν ἀνάμνησιν

THE LAST SUPPER

Jesus did not actually partake of the regular Passover meal but only of a preparatory one[1]

The inference deducible from all these facts—that in the Three Gospels there was something wanting to explain the meaning of the Eucharist—is confirmed by Paul's reproach to the Corinthians for their misbehaviour when they met to celebrate the Lord's Supper[2]. Moreover Justin Martyr, who more than once makes mention of the "memorial" clause in the Eucharist, does not clearly mention, or perhaps recognise, its moral significance. He lays stress on the "bread" as being "not common[3]," and he charges the worshippers of Mithras (falsely) with having stolen the use of the chalice of water in their mysteries from the Christians[4], but he nowhere emphasizes the fact that the Eucharist shewed forth the "tender mercies" of the Father through the Son and bade mankind "give" themselves to and for one another, as the Father "gave" the Son, and the Son gave Himself, to and for mankind[5]

---

[1] Origen says (*Cels* i 70) "Let him [*i e* the non-believer] assert that He ate the passover with His disciples, having not only used the words 'With desire did I desire to eat this passover with you,' but actually eaten of the same. And let him say also that He...drank, when He was athirst by Jacob's well (Jn iv 5—6)." This seems to imply that Christ's words probably meant—though the non-believer would not be denied the right of interpreting them otherwise— "I desired .but it was not God's will. *For I shall not eat of it till the coming of the Kingdom*." This would agree with the Johannine view

[2] 1 Cor xi 20 foll "When therefore ye assemble yourselves together, it is not possible to eat the Lord's supper, for in your eating each one taketh before [other] his own supper, and one is hungry and another drunken," *ib* 33 "Wherefore, my brethren, when ye come together to eat, wait one for another"

[3] *Apol* § 66 οὐ γὰρ ὡς κοινὸν ἄρτον οὐδὲ κοινὸν πόμα ταῦτα λαμβάνομεν

[4] *Apol* § 66 (after quoting the Eucharistic words and mentioning the imparting (μεταδοῦναι)) ὅπερ καὶ ἐν τοῖς τοῦ Μίθρα μυστηρίοις παρέδωκαν γίνεσθαι μιμησάμενοι οἱ πονηροὶ δαίμονες· ὅτι γὰρ ἄρτος καὶ ποτήριον ὕδατος τίθεται ἐν ταῖς τοῦ μυουμένου τελεταῖς μετ' ἐπιλόγων τινῶν, ἢ ἐπίστασθε ἢ μαθεῖν δύνασθε

[5] There is, however, a trace of it in *Apol* § 67 Ἡμεῖς δὲ μετὰ

THE LAST SUPPER

Perhaps the Fourth Evangelist felt that the Pauline word "memorial," which conveyed to Greeks the notion of "reviving the memory," did not quite express the truth for readers ignorant of Hebrew scriptures. In the only Old Testament instance of "*my memorial*," the word does not mean a tomb, or anything like a tomb, or dead commemorative monument[1]. It is the Lord's own phrase, and He uses it with "my Name" to denote an eternal reminding presence, stimulating a memory that lives, not revivifying a memory that has died[2]. We should not go far wrong if we substituted "with a view to my memorial" (in this sense) for "into my name," in the passage of Matthew where

ταῦτα λοιπὸν ἀεὶ τούτων ἀλλήλους ἀναμιμνήσκομεν καὶ οἱ ἔχοντες τοῖς λειπομένοις πᾶσιν ἐπικουροῦμεν καὶ σύνεσμεν ἀλλήλοις ἀεί. This sentence appears to begin with a mere allusion to the meaning of "*my memorial*, or, *reminding*," in the words "*we remind one another of these things*." But in what follows, about "helping all that are in want and making ourselves friends with one another," it indicates a sense that "*these things*" were a type of the Saviour's love and sacrifice, and of His pity for the needs of mankind.

The *Didachè* does not mention ἀνάμνησις anywhere, but has (§ 10) in the εὐχαριστία that comes after the eating of the Eucharistic food (μετὰ δὲ τὸ ἐμπλησθῆναι οὕτως εὐχαριστήσατε) a prayer that the Lord will "*remember*" His Church, Μνήσθητι, κύριε, τῆς ἐκκλησίας σου τοῦ ῥύσασθαι αὐτήν... Comp Exod xxxii 13 "*Remember* Abraham, Isaac, and Israel, thy servants..." a formula freq in O T.

[1] The only instance of "*my memorial*" in O T. (see Mandelkern p 355) is Exod iii 15 "this is my name for ever and this is *my memorial* (זכרי) unto all generations" (the word זכרון, used by Delitzsch in Lk xxii 19, is non-occurrent with possess. suff 1st pers sing). LXX has μνημόσυνον (om μου), Sym ἀνάμνησίς μου. Rashi says "God taught Moses *how He is to be called*." So also David said, '*Jehovah, nomen tuum in seculum, Jehovah, memoria tui in generationem et generationem* (Ps cxxxv. 13),'" and see Gesen. 271 *a* "זכר, nearly = שם" i e "name." *Exod r* ad loc says "*memorial* implies that He is only to be named by His attributes." If God is called "the Giver," or "Love," those who give, and those who love, in His Spirit, would be said to be making a memorial of Him. But the word is capable of other meanings, since God Himself (Gesen. 269—71) is described as "remembering," or as "being reminded of," Israel, His covenant with Israel etc.

[2] Comp Jn xiv 26 ὑπομνήσει (quietly remind) ὑμᾶς, concerning the action of the Holy Spirit.

426   (Mark xiv 22—5)

THE LAST SUPPER

Jesus promises His presence to the disciples saying "Where two or three are gathered together (lit) *into my name*, there am I in the midst of them[1]" It may be paraphrased as meaning "gathered together in spirit *into the spiritual presence and power of the Giver of all good*, filling us with the desire to signify our memory of Him by giving as He gives."

There remains for brief consideration the saying of Jesus, in the three Synoptists, about His not drinking of the fruit of the vine hereafter till He drinks it—as Mark and Matthew say, "new"—in the Kingdom[2] It will be seen that this is the only passage in the narrative where Mark and Matthew *certainly* use the word "*new*[3]" The parallel Luke omits "new[4]" In Mark and Matthew, these words close a section, and precede the going forth to the Mount of Olives. In Luke, they follow the distribution of the first cup explanatorily ("Distribute it among yourselves, *for* I say unto you I will assuredly not drink..."), and they precede the institution of the Eucharist ("'...until the kingdom of God come' And having taken bread...") Mark introduces the saying without any connecting particle at all, Matthew with a "*but*," possibly (though not necessarily) antithetical; Luke with a "*for*," as giving a reason. These differences may represent important differences of thought

Before passing to what John may have to say bearing on these perplexing variations, we may answer one natural question about the shorter Version of Luke. "Is it conceivable that such a Version ever existed since it altogether omits the word *diathēkè*, whether with the epithet '*new*' or without it?"

---

[1] Mt xviii 20

[2]

Mk xiv 25	Mt xxvi 29	Lk xxii 18
ἀμὴν λέγω ὑμῖν ὅτι οὐκέτι οὐ μὴ πίω ἐκ τοῦ γενήματος τῆς ἀμπέλου ἕως τῆς ἡμέρας ἐκείνης ὅταν αὐτὸ πίνω καινὸν ἐν τῇ βασιλείᾳ τοῦ θεοῦ	λέγω δὲ ὑμῖν, οὐ μὴ πίω ἀπ' ἄρτι ἐκ τούτου τοῦ γενήματος τῆς ἀμπέλου ἕως τῆς ἡμέρας ἐκείνης ὅταν αὐτὸ πίνω μεθ' ὑμῶν καινὸν ἐν τῇ βασιλείᾳ τοῦ πατρός μου	λέγω γὰρ ὑμῖν, οὐ μὴ πίω ἀπὸ τοῦ νῦν ἀπὸ τοῦ γενήματος τῆς ἀμπέλου ἕως οὗ ἡ βασιλεία τοῦ θεοῦ ἔλθῃ.

[3] "New" is doubtful in Mk xiv 24, Mt. xxvi 28, being omitted by W H and by txt of R V

[4] Lk xxii 18 "until the kingdom of God shall come."

THE LAST SUPPER

The answer is that the noun *diathēkè*, "covenant, or testament," corresponds to the verb *diatithemai* "I make a covenant, or testament," and that Luke (and Luke alone) represents Jesus as saying to the apostles, a little later, "*I make a testament, or covenant*, with you—a kingdom—even as my Father *made a testament*, or *covenant*, with me, that ye may eat and drink at my table, in my kingdom...[1]." This "kingdom" was the kingdom of service or self-sacrifice, which Christ, the Suffering Servant, personified, and which could be inherited by Christ's disciples by receiving into themselves, as a legacy from Him, His spiritual Self. Consequently, this Lucan tradition is equivalent to "I bequeath myself unto you as my heirs even as the Father gives Himself unto me as His Son." Practically, therefore, Luke does use the word *diathēkè*.

The Fourth Evangelist uses neither the noun *diathēkè* nor the verb by which Luke expresses the noun. But he expresses both in language of his own free from technicality. The Epistle to the Hebrews, writing technically about the *diathēkè* as a "testament," says "Where a testament is, there must of necessity be the death of the testator[2]." John, writing non-technically, represents Jesus as speaking not about "dying" but about "departing," and as bequeathing to the disciples a second Self or Presence of His own, a Friend or "Paraclete": "Unless I depart the Paraclete will assuredly not come unto you, but if I depart I will send him unto you[3]." Previously He says "the Father will send the Paraclete in my name" and describes Himself as leaving to the disciples the gift of His own peace· "Peace I leave unto you" But lest we should lay too much stress on "leaving" He adds at once "The peace

---

[1] Lk xxii 29—30 Justin freq uses the middle διατίθεμαι "I covenant" in his *Dialogue* (though never in his *Apology*) Beginning from Jeremiah xxxi 31—2, διαθήσομαι ..διαθήκην καινήν he enlarges (*Tryph* § 11) on the "covenanting" of "a new covenant", but, as far as I know, he does not connect it with the thought of a "testament"—although (*ib*) he connects it with "inheritance (ὅσοι τῆς τοῦ θεοῦ κληρονομίας ἀντιποιοῦνται)"—nor does he connect it with ἀνάμνησις.

[2] Heb. ix 16.   [3] Jn xvi. 7. See *Joh. Voc.* **1720.**

THE LAST SUPPER

that is my own I *give* unto you," and He implies that this coming of the Paraclete is really a coming of Himself. "Ye have heard that I said unto you, I go [away] and I come unto you[1]" We have seen that Justin dilates on the new *Diathēkè* as a new Covenant, but hardly seems to recognise it as a new Testament Precisely opposite is the Johannine doctrine which regards Christ Himself as our Personal Testator, bequeathing to us, not a Code that may occasionally fail to meet a special need, but a Spirit that meets all needs.

This insistence of the Fourth Gospel on Personal Presence as distinct from distant testatorship is far from constituting it a Gospel of mere thinking On the contrary, it is a Gospel of doing[2] And the doing is not mere self-saving, it involves serving others "As many as *received* him," John says in his Prologue, received "authority to become children of God[3]." The preceding context, which suddenly uses "*him*" to denote "the true light," does not indeed teach us—but it prepares us for being taught—what is meant by "receiving *him*" The body of the Gospel devotes itself to teaching us this In particular, it shews us, at the close, how the penitent Peter received Jesus Not that the word "received" is mentioned. The spiritual process is dramatized instead of being described. Peter first receives the "bread" and the "fish." Then he receives the thrice repeated command to feed the Master's sheep Lastly he receives the command to follow his Master on the way of the Cross Thus the Evangelist, without adding a fifth version, in addition to the Synoptic and the Pauline versions, of the Institution of the Eucharist, teaches us what the Eucharist means[4].

---

[1] Jn xiv. 26—8 [2] Jn vii 17, xiii 15, 17 etc [3] Jn i 12
[4] Jn xxi 15 foll The following remarks of Justin Martyr are instructive as shewing the manner in which controversies about mere material details might tend to subordinate or exclude the moral and spiritual meaning of the Eucharist

In his *Apology* § 66 Justin says that the gift of the body and the blood in the Eucharist have been imitated in the mysteries of Mithras "For that bread and *a cup of water* find a place (τίθεται) in the rites of every initiation (ἐν ταῖς τοῦ μυουμένου τελεταῖς) together with (Mark xiv. 22—5)

THE LAST SUPPER

certain incantations (ἐπιλόγων τινῶν) you either understand [already] or can ascertain." In his *Dialogue* § 70 he repeats this charge, but says that they have attempted to imitate Isaiah, who said (Is xxxiii 16) "bread shall be given to him and *his water* [*shall be*] *sure*," whereas (he says) Isaiah's prophecy manifestly refers to the "bread" and the "cup" of the Eucharist. We naturally ask how Justin could regard a prophecy about "*water*" as referring to "*wine*," or at all events to wine mingled with water (the custom being thus to mingle the two (*Hor Heb* 11. 351 on Mt xxvi 27)). In the *Apology* he says that there is brought to the person presiding at the Eucharist (§ 65) "a cup of *water and of mixed wine* (ποτήριον ὕδατος καὶ κράματος)" and (*ib*.) "bread and *wine and water*," and, later on (§ 67) "bread, and *wine, and water*, are brought." It will be noted that he does not mention "*wine*" in these passages without also mentioning "*water*," and he only once calls the mixture κρᾶμα, a word never used by him elsewhere in the *Apology* or the *Dialogue*.

One reason for Justin's insistence on the mingling of water with the wine may have been the desire to prevent the scandal of drunkenness mentioned by Paul (1 Cor xi 21). But in connecting the Eucharistic "cup" with Isaiah's prophecy about "water" he favoured the heresy of the Ebionites, who (as we know from Irenaeus v. 1 3 and Epiphanius *Haer* xxx. 16) rejected wine in their Eucharists and communicated with water alone. The Fourth Gospel in the words (xix 34—5) "there came out blood and water, and he that hath seen hath borne witness," mystically sanctions the mixture of water. In the miracle of Canà, it indicates typically that the "water" of the Law must give way to the "wine" of the Gospel. And the Johannine Epistle says (v 6) "This is he that came by water and blood, [even] Jesus Christ, not with the water only, but with the water and with the blood."

CHAPTER X

THE INTERVAL BEFORE THE ARREST

[Mark xiv. 26—42]

§ 1. *The going forth to the Mount of Olives*[1]

THE Diatessaron omits at this point all the Synoptic parallels describing the going forth to the Mount of Olives,

---

[1] Mk xiv 26—31 (R V)

(26) And when they had sung a hymn, they went out unto the mount of Olives

(27) And Jesus saith unto them, All ye shall be offended (*lit* caused to stumble) for it is written, I will smite the shepherd, and the sheep shall be scattered abroad.

(28) Howbeit, after I am raised up, I will go before you into Galilee

(29) But Peter said unto him, Although all shall be offended (*lit* caused to stumble), yet will not I

(30) And Jesus saith unto him, Verily I say unto thee, that thou to-day, [even]

Mt. xxvi 30—35 (R V)

(30) And when they had sung a hymn, they went out unto the mount of Olives

(31) Then saith Jesus unto them, All ye shall be offended (*lit* caused to stumble) in me this night for it is written, I will smite the shepherd, and the sheep of the flock shall be scattered abroad

(32) But after I am raised up, I will go before you into Galilee

(33) But Peter answered and said unto him, If all shall be offended (*lit* caused to stumble) in thee, I will never be offended (*lit* caused to stumble).

(34) Jesus said unto him, Verily I say unto thee, that this night, before the

Lk xxii 39, 31—34 (R V)

(39) And he came out, and went, as his custom was, unto the mount of Olives, and the disciples also followed him

(31) Simon, Simon, behold, Satan asked to have you (*or*, obtained you by asking), that he might sift you as wheat

(32) But I made supplication for thee, that thy faith fail not and do thou, when once thou hast turned again, stablish thy brethren

(33) And he said unto him, Lord, with thee I am ready to go both to prison and to death

(34) And he said, I tell thee, Peter, the cock shall not crow this day, until thou

THE INTERVAL BEFORE THE ARREST

but places a mixture of them later on[1]. Mark and Matthew place the going forth immediately after the Eucharistic prophecy about not drinking of the fruit of the vine till the coming of the Kingdom. But Luke places it several verses later, after inserting other sayings of Jesus[2] Mark and Matthew say "they went out *having hymned*," which is rendered by Delitzsch "having accomplished the *hallel*" (i e. the *usual Passover Psalms*)[3]. The Apostolic Constitutions represents

Mk xiv 26—31 (R V.) *contd*.	Mt xxvi 30—35 (R V) *contd*	Lk. xxii. 39, 31—34 (R V) *contd*
this night, before the cock crow twice, shalt deny me thrice (31) But he spake exceeding vehemently, If I must die with thee, I will not deny thee And in like manner also said they all	cock crow, thou shalt deny me thrice (35) Peter saith unto him, Even if I must die with thee, [yet] will I not deny thee Likewise also said all the disciples	shalt thrice deny that thou knowest me.

John places Peter's protestation immediately after the words (xiii. 33—5) "Whither I *go*, ye cannot come...if ye have love one to another." Peter exclaims "Whither *goest* thou ?," and protests, and hears the reply concluding (*ib* 36—8) "The cock shall not crow till thou hast denied me thrice " Then follows what may be called the Discourse of Comfort, uttered perhaps while Jesus and His disciples are preparing to go forth from the chamber, beginning (xiv 1) "Let not your heart be troubled," and ending (*ib* 31) "Arise, *let us go hence* " After this, John probably places the actual *going forth*.

[1] The *Diatessaron* xlvi 16 places Jn xiv 31 *b* "Arise, *let us go hence*" immediately before a blending of the Synoptic "*going forth*" to the mount of Olives —"And they arose and praised (? ὑμνήσαντες in Mk-Mt) and went forth, and went, according to their custom (Lk), to the mount of Olives, he and his disciples (paraphr , but mostly Lk , or Jn xviii. 1) "

[2] Mk xiv 25—6
...ἐν τῇ βασιλείᾳ τοῦ θεοῦ καὶ ὑμνήσαντες ἐξῆλθον εἰς τὸ Ὄρος τῶν Ἐλαιῶν

Mt. xxvi 29—30
ἐν τῇ βασιλείᾳ τοῦ πατρός μου. καὶ ὑμνήσαντες ἐξῆλθον εἰς τὸ Ὄρος τῶν Ἐλαιῶν

Lk xxii. 38—9
. ἱκανόν ἐστιν. καὶ ἐξελθὼν ἐπορεύθη κατὰ τὸ ἔθος εἰς τὸ Ὄρος τῶν Ἐλαιῶν ἠκολούθησαν δὲ αὐτῷ [καὶ] οἱ μαθηταί.

[3] Delitzsch את־ההלל (but ed. 1901 קראם) גמרם. On the *Hallel* "a customary title for Psalms cxiii.—cxviii ," see Levy 1 472 *b*

THE INTERVAL BEFORE THE ARREST

the apostle John as saying "He went out to the Mount of Olives near the brook Kedron where there was a garden; but we too were with Him and *hymned according to the custom*[1]." But Luke says "Having gone out *he went according to the custom* to the mount of Olives, but the disciples also followed him[2]"—apparently taking *"according to the [established] custom"* as meaning, in effect, *"according to his custom,"* a rendering not justifiable except in very special contexts[3]. The Acts of John represents Jesus as saying to His disciples "Before I am delivered over, let us *hymn* the Father, and thus let us *go out* to [meet] that which lies before [us]," after which there follows a Eucharistic hymn during which the disciples dance round the Lord; and then it is added "Thus having danced with us, my beloved brethren, the Lord *went out*[4]."

These apocryphal passages appear to explain Luke's avoidance of the Mark-Matthew tradition *"having [all of them] hymned."* It would naturally mean that Jesus with all the disciples "sang the hymn of the Old Passover." But this would come as an anticlimax after the introduction of the New Passover. What seemed to be needed as a climax was some such Eucharistic hymn as the Didachè places in the mouth of the president, or of a prophet, at the Eucharist

---

[1] *Const Apost* v 14 συνῆμεν δὲ καὶ ἡμεῖς καὶ ὑμνήσαμεν κατὰ τὸ ἔθος If the "hymning" is to be regarded as preceding the "going forth," we must regard the words as retrospective "now we *had been* with Him and *had hymned*"—the aorist being (*Joh Gr* 2460—2) frequently used for the pluperfect

[2] This gives to Jesus an initiative not mentioned in the parall Mk Mt Jn emphasizes the fact that Jesus initiated a going forth in xiv 31 *b*, and he implies an initiative also in xviii 1, 4

[3] In Thuc iv 32, κατὰ τὸ ἔθος prob means according to the general custom of ships at night, and not "according to the particular custom of the persons mentioned in the context", and Plato *Polit* v 3 (452 A) παρὰ τὸ ἔθος, *Crat.* 434 E διά γε τὸ ἔθος have a general meaning If the original had meant "according to his (*or*, their) custom," it would have been natural to insert αὐτοῦ or αὐτῶν (as in Daniel (Theod) *Bel* 15), and as *Diatess* does and several Latin versions of Luke

[4] *Acts of John* §§ 11—12 using ἐξέρχομαι and ὑμνέω

THE INTERVAL BEFORE THE ARREST

"after the eating[1]" Luke perhaps, as in other passages, interpreted some expression signifying the "lifting up of the soul" in praise and thanks as though it referred to local "ascending" connected in the context with the Mount of Olives[2]. At all events he omits the "hymning." That Luke is honestly and carefully following old tradition appears from his retention of the phrase—unfavourable to his views—"according to the custom."

John also—from a different point of view—indicates that the utterance of prayer and praise that preceded the going forth of Jesus was not the singing of the Hallel. It was a long prayer uttered by Jesus alone "lifting up his eyes to heaven" and saying "Father, the hour is come, glorify thy Son[3]." After the conclusion of the prayer it is said that Jesus "went forth with his disciples" to a place known to Judas "for Jesus oft-times resorted thither with his disciples[4]." The phrase "*oft-times* resorted" implies that Jesus resorted thither "*according to his custom*," which is what Luke apparently means by "*according to the custom*."

This seems to be a case where John intervenes between Mark and Luke, but not to explain Mark as being misunderstood by Luke. On the contrary, John seems to say "Luke has partially supplied what was missing in Mark—namely, some account of what Jesus said in the interval between the Eucharist and the 'going forth.' For example, he has recorded the Lord's warning to the disciples that they should learn to 'serve[5],' and also the Lord's anxiety for the disciples

---

[1] *Didachè* x. 1 foll. It was sometimes of considerable length, as appears from the ancient Liturgies, and as might be anticipated from *ib* x. 6 "But to the prophets give permission to eucharistize at such length as they please (ἐπιτρέπετε εὐχαριστεῖν ὅσα θέλουσιν)."

[2] See *Beginning* pp. 110—1. The *Diatess.* has xlvi. 16 "And they *arose* and praised and went forth," but this is perhaps an insertion consequent on xlvi. 15 which ends with the words "*Arise*, let us go hence." In view of the ambiguities of "lifting up" (*Son* 3380 *a*), it is worth noting that "lifting up" occurs in the Johannine preface to Christ's prayer xvii. 1 "lifting up his eyes."

[3] Jn xvii. 1.   [4] Jn xviii. 1—2   [5] Lk. xxii. 25—30.

(Mark xiv. 26—31)

THE INTERVAL BEFORE THE ARREST

lest their faith should fail[1]; but he has not supplied the Eucharistic 'hymn.' Mark has mentioned the word 'hymn,' but has not perceived that it was uttered by Jesus alone. Luke has not mentioned it at all. This, therefore, should be added."

§ 2. "*Stumbling*," *and* "*being scattered*," *in Mark and Matthew*[2]

The reasons why Luke here, as elsewhere, avoids the word *scandalīzein* "cause to stumble," and the Johannine use of it, have been fully discussed[3]. It is an instance of Johannine Intervention. Luke thinks the word too strong, as if it implied a permanent fall. John, tacitly admitting that it is a strong word, uses it in such a way as to shew that Mark and Matthew may mean temporary stumbling here: "Ye shall be made to stumble for a short time; *but* I will guide you right in the end." This he indirectly and paradoxically expresses thus "These things have I spoken unto you that ye may not be [*permanently*] *caused to stumble*[4]."

Concerning the Mark-Matthew tradition about "being scattered" Luke might well feel several difficulties. Mark and Matthew quote Zechariah in a form not justified by the Hebrew or the LXX[5]. Early interpretations of it vary. The

---

[1] Lk xxii 31 "Simon,... Satan (hath) requested that he might have *you*" (not "thee") shews that the anxiety was for all the disciples Comp. Jn xvii 9—15.

[2] Mk xiv 27 πάντες σκανδαλισθήσεσθε, Mt xxvi. 31 πάντες ὑμεῖς σκανδαλισθήσεσθε ἐν ἐμοὶ ἐν τῇ νυκτὶ ταύτῃ. The latter particularises, for emphasis "all, yes, all of *you*, my disciples, and it will be on account of *me* that you will stumble, and it will be on this very night."

[3] *Law* pp 124—32

[4] Jn xvi 1.

[5] Mk xiv. 27 πατάξω τὸν ποιμένα καὶ τὰ πρόβατα διασκορπισθήσονται, Mt xxvi 31 πατάξω τὸν ποιμένα καὶ διασκορπισθήσονται τὰ πρόβατα τῆς ποίμνης, lay emphasis on the disaster to the shepherd's flock—they, too, being included in their Master's suffering. The Heb of Zech xiii 7 has—after "Awake, O sword, against my shepherd, and against the man that is my fellow, saith the Lord of hosts"—"*Smite* the shepherd, and the sheep shall be scattered." The LXX has Ῥομφαία, ἐξεγέρθητι ἐπὶ τοὺς ποιμένας μου καὶ ἐπ' ἄνδρα πολίτην μου, λέγει

THE INTERVAL BEFORE THE ARREST

Targum appears to interpret it as referring to the chastisement of Israel[1]. Rashi mysteriously speaks of the wicked Moabite king[2] Barnabas, alluding to the reiterated prophecy of Isaiah that the Messiah was to be "in smiting[3]," says, in effect, that the Jews were to be the smiters, and then quotes Zechariah thus "When they shall smite their own Shepherd, then the sheep of the flock shall be destroyed[4]." Tertullian assumes that Zechariah is speaking of wicked "shepherds" (in the plural) the rulers of Israel, who persecuted Jesus: "Thus Zechariah threatens: Arise, O sword, against *the shepherds*, and pluck ye out the sheep [from their hands]; and I will turn my hand against *the shepherds*[5]."

Luke contains no prediction of this "smiting," or of the "awaking of the sword" or of the "scattering" of the disciples. The most that can be said about any Lucan approximation to Mark and Matthew or to Zechariah's prophecy about a "sword" and "smiting" is, that he places in his parallel context a mysterious warning to the disciples to "buy a sword[6]." He

---

Κύριος Παντοκράτωρ πατάξατε τοὺς ποιμένας (v.r πάταξον τὸν ποιμένα) καὶ ἐκσπάσατε (v.r διασκορπισθήσονται) τὰ πρόβατα.

[1] Targ "Merito percussi sumus propter peccata quae dileximus. Gladie denudare super regem et super principem socium ejus qui est similis ei, dicit Dominus exercituum. Interfice regem et dispergentur principes"

[2] See Breithaupt's notes of variations in Rashi's text indicating an allusion to the king of Edom, i.e. Rome

[3] Is liii 3 ἄνθρωπος ἐν πληγῇ (מכאב), ib. 4 ἐλογισάμεθα αὐτὸν εἶναι...ἐν πληγῇ (מכה), ib 10 καθαρίσαι αὐτὸν (A + ἀπὸ) τῆς πληγῆς, Heb (Field) "contundere eum, aegrum fecit eum," Sym ἐλεῆσαι αὐτὸν ἐν τῷ τραυματισμῷ. This reiterated phrase ἐν πληγῇ, or πληγῆς, has been adopted in quotation by Clem Rom. § 16. Barnabas § 5 and § 7 uses πληγή twice of the sufferings of the Messiah. Justin Martyr uses πληγή seven times in his *Apology* and *Dialogue*, and, with one exception (*Tryph.* § 132), always in quotation from Isaiah's Suffering Servant.

[4] Barn § 5, comp. § 7 ἔπαθεν ἵνα ἡ πληγὴ αὐτοῦ ζωοποιήσῃ ἡμᾶς, which resembles Is. liii. 5 "with his stripes we are healed"

[5] Tertull. *De Fuga* § 11 One naturally asks how Tertullian reconciles this with Mt xxvi 31 The Indices to Tertullian give no instance of the quotation of the latter

[6] Lk xxii 36.

THE INTERVAL BEFORE THE ARREST

also quotes from Isaiah's prophecy about the Suffering Servant "He was reckoned with the transgressors," *i e* was reckoned by the rulers of the Jews as a transgressor[1] This might imply "and was smitten accordingly by them"—which would favour the view taken above (with differences of detail) both by Barnabas and by Tertullian that the smiters are the Jews.

'John, it must be admitted, does not appear to intervene as to the "smiting" of the Shepherd—unless, as Jerome suggests, the Psalmist's words "They *persecute* him whom *thou hast smitten*" may be taken as an illustration of the prophecy of Zechariah quoted by Matthew[2]. A kind of law of "persecution" may be said to be hinted at in the Johannine saying "If they have *persecuted* me they will also *persecute* you[3]"

This, however, is doubtful. But there is no doubt that John intervenes as to the "scattering." He indicates that "scattering" will teach the Apostles humility, and that their desertion of their Master will not leave Him alone: "Do ye now believe? Behold, the hour cometh, and now is come, that *ye shall be scattered*, every one to his own, and leave me alone; and yet I am not alone, because the Father is with me[4]" John seems to suggest to his readers that this prediction of "scattering" ought to cause them no difficulty, since the next words are "These things have I spoken unto you that in me ye may have peace, in the world ye [must] have tribulation, but be of good cheer; I have overcome the world[5]."

---

[1] Lk xxii 37 Comp *Fragments of a Zadokite Work* p xl, where text B quotes Zech. xiii 7 "O sword, awake ..," but text A quotes Is vii 17

[2] Jerome on Mt xxvi 31 "Hoc aliis verbis in Zacharia Propheta scriptum est, et (ni fallor) ex persona Prophetae ad Deum dicitur 'Percute pastorem et dispergentur oves gregis,' sexagesimo quoque et octavo Psalmo qui totus a Domino canitur, huic sensui congruente 'Quoniam quem tu percussisti, ipsi persequuti sunt' Percutitur autem Pastor bonus, ut ponat animam suam pro ovibus suis, et de multis gregibus errorum (? erronum) fiat unus grex, et unus Pastor" Rashi takes Ps lxix 26 as referring to the suffering people of Israel "Populum istum quem tu (O Deus) percussisti, persequuntur inimici"

[3] Jn xv 20   [4] Jn xvi. 32.   [5] Jn xvi. 33.

THE INTERVAL BEFORE THE ARREST

§ 3   *"I will go-before you to Galilee," in Mark and Matthew*[1]

Luke omits this but has, later on, the phrase *"in Galilee"* attached to a prediction of resurrection, thus: "Remember how he spake unto you, while he was yet *in Galilee*, saying that the Son of man must be delivered up...and rise again[2]." This suggests the inference that some such words as "He said '*To Galilee* will I go-before you'" may have been mistaken by Luke for "He said *in Galilee* 'I will go-before you.'" The Lucan *"in Galilee"* appears superfluous. But it is explicable as an attempt of Luke's to explain a tradition of Mark's that seemed to him to contradict the facts, since (according to Luke) the earliest manifestations of Jesus after His resurrection took place, not in Galilee, but in or near Jerusalem.

Many will find difficulty in believing that Jesus did actually make this definite prediction about going-before the disciples[3], but it is also difficult to believe that such a prediction was invented. It may be explained if Jesus was referring to a "home," not on earth but in heaven, which He called His Father's House, and which was mistaken by Mark for the house and home in Nazareth. Elsewhere when Jesus speaks of a prophet as being thought lightly of in his own home, Mark and Matthew have the word *"country"* (*patris*), but the parallel Luke has *"Nazareth,"* and the parallel John has *"Galilee*[4]*"* An illustration also suggests itself in the Lucan tradition that the boy Jesus said to Mary and Joseph "Wist ye not that I must be in *my Father's* [*house*][5]?" where there can be little

---

[1] Mk xiv. 28, Mt xxvi. 32 ἀλλὰ μετὰ (Mt. μετὰ δὲ) τὸ ἐγερθῆναί με προάξω ὑμᾶς εἰς τὴν Γαλιλαίαν.

[2] Lk xxiv 6—7 μνήσθητε ὡς ἐλάλησεν ὑμῖν ἔτι ὢν ἐν τῇ Γαλιλαίᾳ, λέγων τὸν υἱὸν τοῦ ἀνθρώπου ὅτι δεῖ παραδοθῆναι ..καὶ . ἀναστῆναι

[3] See McNeile on Mt. xxvi 32 who says "the genuineness of this verse is very doubtful," and "it is omitted in the Fay fragm of Mk" It is surprising that more MSS have not omitted it.

[4] See *Law* p 109 referring to Mk vi. 1, Mt xiii. 54 εἰς τὴν πατρίδα αὐτοῦ, Lk iv 16 εἰς Ναζαρά, οὗ ἦν τεθραμμένος, Jn iv 45 εἰς τὴν Γαλιλαίαν

[5] Lk 11 49 οὐκ ᾔδειτε ὅτι ἐν τοῖς τοῦ πατρός μου δεῖ εἶναί με, On this, Wetstein quotes abundant instances of the ellipsis of "house"

THE INTERVAL BEFORE THE ARREST

doubt that the original inserted "house," but that the words meant more than house, a spiritual region inhabited by children of God doing their Father's will[1]

A clue to Mark's meaning is supplied by the comparatively rare Greek word used here for "go-before[2]." It is almost non-existent in the canonical LXX. But it is given by Symmachus in Exodus, thus, "Behold, I send an angel *before thee*," where LXX has "*before thy face*," but Symmachus has "*going-before* thee*[3]*" "*Go-before*" here implies preparation for Israel in the wilderness, as in Numbers, "The ark of the covenant of the Lord *went before them* three days' journey, *to seek out a resting-place for them*[4]" This use may be illustrated from Ignatius, who says about himself, when he was journeying as a prisoner to Rome, "Even those churches that did not lie on my route in the flesh *went-before me* from city to city," which Lightfoot explains as meaning, "*so as to make preparations and welcome him on his arrival*[5]."

All these passages contemplate a journey by stages with some one "going-before" the travellers so as to ensure their welcome. Now a similar journeying by stages is probably contemplated in a Johannine passage placed immediately after Christ's prediction of Peter's denial. The notion of stages latent in it is liable to be overlooked, partly because it is concealed in the

in Greek and Latin, but none from Hebrew. The Syriac inserts "house"

[1] Comp Heb xi 10 "looking for the city that hath the foundations, whose builder and maker is God"

[2] Προάγω, with Heb original, occurs only once in *Oxf. Conc.* 1 S xvii. 16 (A)

[3] Exod xxiii 20 "Before thee (לְפָנֶיךָ)," Onk. קדמך, LXX πρὸ προσώπου σου, Sym προάγοντά σε.

[4] Numb x. 33, LXX ἡ κιβωτὸς τῆς διαθήκης Κυρίου προεπορεύετο προτέρα αὐτῶν ὁδὸν τριῶν ἡμερῶν, κατασκέψασθαι αὐτοῖς ἀνάπαυσιν

[5] Ign *Rom.* § 9 καὶ γὰρ αἱ μὴ προσήκουσαί μοι (ἐκκλησίαι) τῇ ὁδῷ τῇ κατὰ σάρκα κατὰ πόλιν με προῆγον.

Two or three lines afterwards, the writer continues περὶ τῶν προελθόντων με ἀπὸ Συρίας εἰς Ῥώμην . ., "concerning those who *have gone before me* from Syria to Rome"—where there is no notion of "preparing the way." This is instructive as shewing the great difference between προάγω and προέρχομαι as used here by Ignatius.

439 (Mark xiv. 26—31)

THE INTERVAL BEFORE THE ARREST

R V "*mansions*" or "*abiding-places*," and partly because John boldly adheres to the Hebrew expression "my Father's *house*" (instead of the Greek equivalent adopted by Luke, "my Father's [region]") Hence there is a confusion of metaphor But ancient evidence indicates that "*stations*" is the meaning of the word rendered by R V "*mansions*" in the saying "Let not your heart be troubled... In my Father's house are many *mansions* (marg *abiding-places*)" The context also, like the context in Numbers above-quoted, speaks of preparation, and represents Jesus as saying "If I go and *prepare a place* for you, I will come again and receive you unto myself[1]"

We conclude that John intervenes in behalf of Mark against Luke so as to shew that the latter has not correctly emended Mark by his ingenious substitution of "*in* Galilee" for "*to* Galilee." He explains to us that "go-before" means a "going-before" like that of the Lord "going-before" Israel in the wilderness, and that "Galilee" had—or perhaps we should say included—the meaning of "home," the home of the children of God in the House of their Father in heaven

§ 4 "*Before the cock crow twice*," *in Mark*[2]

This is a case where Mark appears to have been misled by a Hebrew original Mark alone mentions "twice" in Christ's

---

[1] Jn xiv. 1—3, on which see *Paradosis* 1393—7, and *Son* 3347 (x) *b*.

[2]

Mk xiv. 30	Mt xxvi. 34	Lk xxii. 34
Ἀμὴν λέγω σοι ὅτι σὺ σήμερον ταύτῃ τῇ νυκτὶ πρὶν ἢ δὶς ἀλέκτορα φωνῆσαι τρίς με ἀπαρνήσῃ	Ἀμὴν λέγω σοι ὅτι ἐν ταύτῃ τῇ νυκτὶ πρὶν ἀλέκτορα φωνῆσαι τρὶς ἀπαρνήσῃ με	Λέγω σοι, Πέτρε, οὐ φωνήσει σήμερον ἀλέκτωρ ἕως τρίς με ἀπαρνήσῃ εἰδέναι

Jn xiii. 38 Τὴν ψυχήν σου ὑπὲρ ἐμοῦ θήσεις, ἀμὴν ἀμὴν λέγω σοι, οὐ μὴ ἀλέκτωρ φωνήσῃ ἕως οὗ ἀρνήσῃ με τρίς

Later on, it is said that Peter remembered the words of Jesus, which are repeated —

Mk xiv 72	Mt xxvi 75	Lk xxii 61
καὶ ἀνεμνήσθη ὁ Πέτρος τὸ ῥῆμα ὡς εἶπεν αὐτῷ ὁ Ἰησοῦς ὅτι Πρὶν ἀλέκτορα δὶς φωνῆσαι τρίς με ἀπαρνήσῃ	καὶ ἐμνήσθη ὁ Πέτρος τοῦ ῥήματος Ἰησοῦ εἰρηκότος ὅτι Πρὶν ἀλέκτορα φωνῆσαι τρὶς ἀπαρνήσῃ με	καὶ ὑπεμνήσθη ὁ Πέτρος τοῦ ῥήματος τοῦ κυρίου ὡς εἶπεν αὐτῷ ὅτι Πρὶν ἀλέκτορα φωνῆσαι σήμερον ἀπαρνήσῃ με τρίς

(Mark xiv. 26—31)

THE INTERVAL BEFORE THE ARREST

prediction, and he is probably right in mentioning it But he is wrong in connecting it with the "crowing" of the cock; and the error has affected the whole of his narrative. It should have been connected with Peter's "denying," as follows "Before the cock crow, *twice* [*nay*] *thrice* shalt thou deny me"

This can be illustrated from the saying in Job that a man may go wrong "*twice* [*or even*] *thrice*," and God may chasten him but not utterly condemn him[1] The Hebrew omits "even" before "thrice," and (as often) expresses "twice" by "times-two," the dual of "time" This, when the Hebrew is unpointed, is not distinguishable from the plural, "times" The result is literally this: "All these things doth God work (*times*-[*two*]), [yea,] *thrice* with a man to bring back his soul from the pit" The LXX and Jerome have both gone wrong, taking "*times* (dual) *thrice*" as "*times* (or, *ways*) *three*[2]." The Targum by inserting "*and*," to express "*yea*," has indicated the correct meaning[3]. Symmachus has rendered the Hebrew "*twice thrice.*"

If the Greek tradition came to Mark in a rendering like that of Symmachus "Before the cock crow *twice thrice* shalt thou deny me," he would naturally readjust the words so as to make it clear (wrongly) that "twice" went with the crowing of the cock and "thrice" with the denial It will be noted that here Mark inserts the Greek "or" (with "before[4]") but omits it when

---

John, later on, makes no mention of Peter's "remembering" the words of Jesus (xviii 27 καὶ εὐθέως ἀλέκτωρ ἐφώνησεν)

[1] Job xxxiii 29, on which see Rashi referring to *Joma* 86 *b* The saying is variously interpreted in Jer Talm *Kiddush* 1 9 and *Peah* 1 1 *ad fin*, but *Exod r* (on Exod vi 12, Wu p 71) gives the sense that the context seems to demand "*Three times* does God wait for the man [to see] whether he repents If he does, it is well, if not, He visits on him also his earlier transgressions"

[2] Job xxxiii 29 LXX ὁδοὺς τρεῖς, Jerome "tribus vicibus," Sym. δὶς τρίς On פעמים, dual, see Gesen 822 *a*, which interprets Job xxxiii 29 as "twice [or] thrice" A V txt has "*oftentimes*," and, in margin, "twice [and] thrice," R V "twice, [yea] thrice"

[3] The Targum also expresses the Hebrew dual by adding the Aramaic "two" ("duabus et tribus vicibus")

[4] Mk xiv 30 πρὶν ἤ, ib. 72 πρὶν (where parall Lk xxii 61 also has πρὶν ἀλέκτορα. .).

441 (Mark xiv. 26—31)

THE INTERVAL BEFORE THE ARREST

he repeats the words of Jesus later on. This suggests that a marginal "or"—inserted in the margin with the intention of explaining "twice thrice" as "twice *or* thrice"—may have been transferred to the text in a different place from that which was intended. Also Luke, who deviates considerably from Mark here, returns more closely to Mark later on. These facts point to the conclusion that Mark's "*twice*" was not an invention, but a retention of a very ancient poetic Hebraism, converted by misinterpretation into a prosaic detail of prediction unworthy of a Hebrew Prophet.

John has not intervened as to the Marcan "twice" to shew that the meaning of Christ's phrase was "twice, yea, thrice" Perhaps he may have been influenced in part by the consideration that such a self-correction was hardly suitable for the language of a prediction of Christ, especially when uttered with a "Verily, verily."

But John seems also to have felt that Luke was right in prefixing to Christ's prediction about Peter some positive protest of the Apostle about himself—not merely a negative one ("*I will not* stumble"), but one that implied "*I will do* this or that."

There were however in Luke some small details—very minute to us but not unimportant for a writer given to symbolism—which John could not accept For surely it is strange that Luke, differing from Mark and Matthew, represents Jesus as addressing the Apostle as "*Peter*" "*Peter*," "*stone*," was significative of strength and firmness. Yet here, in a Lucan prediction that the Apostle would be weak enough to deny his Master[1], the Apostle is addressed as "thou Stone," "thou strong one," a vocative unique in the Gospels! This vocative is never used again in the New Testament except in the twice-repeated voice from heaven "Arise, *Peter*, kill and eat[2]" There, addressing the Apostle as God's minister for the admission of the Gentiles into the Church, it is appropriate. But it seems inappropriate here. The apparent inappropriateness seems all

---

[1] Lk xxii. 34   [2] Acts x 13, xi 7
(Mark xiv 26—31)

THE INTERVAL BEFORE THE ARREST

the more strange because the Master had just addressed him as "Simon, Simon[1]" Some may explain "Peter!" as a kind of ironical warning[2]; but to many this will seem far-fetched

Again, there is a difference between Peter's protestation in Luke and in the two earlier Gospels In Luke, "*I am ready... to go to death*" refers to the present and is in no sense true. Peter was not "ready." But the parallel in Mark-Matthew, "If it should be needed, or destined, for me to die with thee, I will not deny thee," might be regarded as referring—mystically, and in a sense not understood by the speaker—to the future For the time *did* come when it was "needed" that Peter should "die," if not "with" the Lord, at all events for the Lord, and as a participator of the Cross[3].

This, at all events, is the view suggested by John, not only in Christ's words "Thou shalt follow me afterwards," but also in those of the Apostle "I will lay down my life for thee," and even in the reply of Jesus. It is really interrogative, "Thy life wilt thou lay down for me?" But it is capable of being read affirmatively ("Thy life thou wilt lay down")[4] so as to prepare for the prediction of the Apostle's martyrdom at the close of the Gospel[5]

Another minor point of Johannine dissent from Luke relates to emphasis Luke omits the "verily" with which Mark and Matthew emphasize the warning to Peter. John reduplicates "verily," as he always does when he uses the word at all[6] This is worth noting as one of the only two

---

[1] Lk xxii 31. Contrast the Lucan "Peter" with the Johannine distinction in Jn 1 42 "*Thou art Simon the son of John*, thou *shalt be called* Cephas (which is by interpretation, *Peter*)." And note that Jn alone thrice calls the traitor Judas (vi 71, xiii 2, 26) "*[the son] of Simon.*" In Jn xxi. 15—17 "*Simon [son] of John*" occurs thrice as a gentle reproach to Peter.

[2] So Plummer, on Lk xxii 34.

[3] The Heb equivalent to LXX δεῖ is sometimes represented by the Heb future "I shall [have to]" or "it will be for me to," do this or that (see *Oxf Conc*).

[4] Jn xiii. 38 See *Joh. Gr* **2236** on "The Interrogative Tone "

[5] Jn xxi. 18—19.   [6] See *Joh Gr* **2611** *a—b*.

THE INTERVAL BEFORE THE ARREST

instances where "verily" is inserted by the parallel Mark, Matthew, and John[1]

Our conclusion is that in this instance, although John does intervene, it is not for Mark but against him. In some respects he inclines toward Luke but he deviates in others. He does not write independently without reference to the earlier Evangelists[2].

§ 5. *The beginning of the Passion*[3]

Mark and Matthew, having previously told us that Jesus and the disciples "went out to the mount of Olives," and

---

[1] The other instance is Mk xiv 18, Mt xxvi 21, Jn xiii 21 It must be admitted, however, that Luke comparatively seldom uses ἀμήν, so that the omission may be in accordance with Lucan general custom (as in Mt v 26, viii 10, Lk xii 59, vii 9 etc) Ἀμήν is very seldom used with λέγω σοι in the Synoptists (Mt v 26 and Lk xxiii 43 being quite exceptional) but very frequently with λέγω ὑμῖν

Another trifling variation may be noted as to the exact limit of the interval before the denial—Mk "*to-day, this night,*" Mt "*this night,*" Lk "*to-day*"—where Jn leaves a blank John perhaps felt that too much had been made by Mark of the exact accuracy, in minute details, of Christ's prediction

[2] Luke (xxii 33 foll) omits to say that "all" the disciples joined in Peter's protestations, as also he omitted above (parall. Mk xiv 27) to say that they would "all" stumble Jn xvi. 31 foll. ("Do ye now believe? The hour cometh. .") implies that the other disciples protested in a manner somewhat similar to Peter's protest, though not the same (xvi 30 "By this we believe"), and that Jesus tried to shake their confidence in their own "belief"

[3] Mk xiv 32—42 (R V)	Mt xxvi 36—46 (R V)	Lk. xxii 40—46 (R V)
(32) And they come unto a place (*lit* an enclosed piece of ground) which was named Gethsemane and he saith unto his disciples, Sit ye here, while I pray	(36) Then cometh Jesus with them unto a place (*lit* an enclosed piece of ground) called Gethsemane, and saith unto his disciples, Sit ye here, while I go yonder and pray	(40) And when he was at the place, he said unto them, Pray that ye enter not into temptation
(33) And he taketh with him Peter and James and John, and began to be greatly	(37) And he took with him Peter and the two sons of Zebedee, and began to be	(41) And he was parted from them about a stone's cast, and he kneeled down and prayed, saying, (42) Father, if

THE INTERVAL BEFORE THE ARREST

having related to us the conversation on the way, now describe the arrival: "And they come to *an enclosed-place called Geth-*

Mk xiv. 32—42 (R V) *contd*	Mt xxvi 36—46 (R.V) *contd*.	Lk xxii 40—46 (R V) *contd*
amazed, and sore troubled.	sorrowful and sore troubled.	thou be willing, remove this cup from me nevertheless, not my will, but thine, be done
(34) And he saith unto them, My soul is exceeding sorrowful, even unto death abide ye here, and watch	(38) Then saith he unto them, My soul is exceeding sorrowful, even unto death abide ye here, and watch with me	
		(43) And there appeared unto him an angel from heaven, strengthening him
(35) And he went forward a little, and fell on the ground, and prayed that, if it were possible, the hour might pass away from him	(39) And he went forward a little, and fell on his face, and prayed, saying, O my Father, if it be possible, let this cup pass away from me nevertheless, not as I will, but as thou wilt	(44) And being in an agony he prayed more earnestly and his sweat became as it were great drops of blood falling down upon the ground (*many anc auth omit ver. 43, 44*).
(36) And he said, Abba, Father, all things are possible unto thee, remove this cup from me: howbeit not what I will, but what thou wilt		
(37) And he cometh, and findeth them sleeping, and saith unto Peter, Simon, sleepest thou? couldest thou not watch one hour?	(40) And he cometh unto the disciples, and findeth them sleeping, and saith unto Peter, What, could ye not watch with me one hour?	(45) And when he rose up from his prayer, he came unto the disciples, and found them sleeping for sorrow,
(38) Watch and pray, that (*or*, Watch ye, and pray that) ye enter not into temptation the spirit indeed is willing, but the flesh is weak	(41) Watch and pray, that (*or*, Watch ye, and pray that) ye enter not into temptation the spirit indeed is willing, but the flesh is weak	(46) And said unto them, Why sleep ye? Rise and pray, that ye enter not into temptation
(39) And again he went away, and prayed, saying the same words	(42) Again a second time he went away, and prayed, saying, O my Father, if this cannot pass away, except I drink it, thy will be done	
(40) And again he came, and found them sleeping, for	(43) And he came again and found them sleeping, for	

445 (Mark xiv. 32—42)

THE INTERVAL BEFORE THE ARREST

semane", Luke, who regards Christ's conversation as having taken place, not on the way, but in the chamber of the Supper, now says consecutively "And having gone forth he went according to custom *to the mount of Olives*, and his disciples followed him, and having arrived *at the place* he said...[1]." This seems at first sight to define "the place" as "*the mount of Olives*," and that would accord verbally with Luke's previous statement that Jesus "habitually spent the night" in "the mount of Olives"; but, in this context, "the place" would be a very strange name to give to so large a space as the whole of the mountain. Possibly Luke may mean here "*the place* to which he went *according to custom*, situate on the mountain." We have seen above that in the parallel to Luke's previous mention of "the mount of Olives," Matthew said that Jesus "went out

Mk xiv 32—42 (R.V.) *contd*	Mt xxvi 36—46 (R V) *contd*
their eyes were very heavy, and they wist not what to answer him	their eyes were heavy.
(41) And he cometh the third time, and saith unto them, Sleep on now, and take your rest: it is enough, the hour is come, behold, the Son of man is betrayed into the hands of sinners	(44) And he left them again, and went away, and prayed a third time, saying again the same words. (45) Then cometh he to the disciples, and saith unto them, Sleep on now, and take your rest. behold, the hour is at hand, and the Son of man is betrayed unto the hands of sinners
(42) Arise, let us be going behold, he that betrayeth me is at hand	(46) Arise, let us be going behold, he is at hand that betrayeth me

[1] Mk xiv 32
καὶ ἔρχονται εἰς χωρίον οὗ τὸ ὄνομα Γεθσημανεί....

Mt xxvi. 36
τότε ἔρχεται μετ' αὐτῶν ὁ Ἰησοῦς εἰς χωρίον λεγόμενον Γεθσημανεί..

Lk. xxii. 40
γενόμενος δὲ ἐπὶ τοῦ τόπου ...

Jn xviii. 1—2 ταῦτα εἰπὼν Ἰησοῦς ἐξῆλθεν σὺν τοῖς μαθηταῖς αὐτοῦ πέραν τοῦ Χειμάρρου τῶν Κέδρων ὅπου ἦν κῆπος, εἰς ὃν εἰσῆλθεν αὐτὸς καὶ οἱ μαθηταὶ αὐτοῦ ᾔδει δὲ καὶ Ἰούδας ὁ παραδιδοὺς αὐτὸν τὸν τόπον, ὅτι πολλάκις συνήχθη Ἰησοῦς ἐκεῖ μετὰ τῶν μαθητῶν αὐτοῦ

THE INTERVAL BEFORE THE ARREST

to Bethany and spent the night there[1]" In the Synoptic narrative under consideration, Mark (and similarly Matthew), who has previously twice mentioned the Mount of Olives[2], instead of now saying that Jesus came to it, says "They come to an enclosed-place of which the name was Gethsemane."

This appears to be a case that calls for Johannine Intervention. No doubt John avoids Synoptic names in general if they are merely of local and temporary interest But the scene of Christ's agony would be to all Christians at the end of the first century a place of profound interest, if only they were able after the destruction of Jerusalem to identify it. It would perhaps be too direct and obvious an intervention—not quite in John's manner—to insert the name "Gethsemane" which Luke has omitted. But we might expect him to guide us to some knowledge of where the spot was, and to explain the nature of the "enclosed-place." Or, on the other hand, if he favoured Luke, John might have said "a place on the mount of Olives."

This last suggestion may be at once dismissed. Perhaps John thought "the mount of Olives" too vague a term, or one that had been used erroneously. At all events, John never uses it He is represented as using it once, in our Authorised

---

[1] Mk xi 19
καὶ ὅταν ὀψὲ ἐγένετο, ἐξεπορεύοντο (marg ἐξεπορεύετο) ἔξω τῆς πόλεως

Mt xxi 17
καὶ καταλιπὼν αὐτοὺς ἐξῆλθεν ἔξω τῆς πόλεως εἰς Βηθανίαν καὶ ηὐλίσθη ἐκεῖ.

Lk xxi 37
ἦν δὲ τὰς ἡμέρας ἐν τῷ ἱερῷ διδάσκων, τὰς δὲ νύκτας ἐξερχόμενος ηὐλίζετο εἰς τὸ ὄρος τὸ καλούμενον Ἐλαιῶν

[2] Mk xi 1
καὶ ὅτε ἐγγίζουσιν εἰς Ἰεροσόλυμα εἰς Βηθφαγὴ καὶ (but marg. εἰς Ἱερ καὶ εἰς) Βηθανίαν πρὸς τὸ Ὄρος τῶν (marg. τὸ) Ἐλαιῶν, ἀποστέλλει δύο τῶν μαθητῶν αὐτοῦ....

Mt xxi 1
καὶ ὅτε ἤγγισαν εἰς Ἰεροσόλυμα καὶ ἦλθον εἰς Βηθφαγὴ εἰς τὸ Ὄρος τῶν Ἐλαιῶν, τότε Ἰησοῦς ἀπέστειλεν δύο μαθητάς...

Lk xix 29
καὶ ἐγένετο ὡς ἤγγισεν εἰς Βηθφαγὴ καὶ Βηθανιὰ πρὸς τὸ ὄρος τὸ καλούμενον Ἐλαιῶν, ἀπέστειλεν δύο τῶν μαθητῶν ...

Mk xiii 3
καὶ καθημένου αὐτοῦ εἰς τὸ Ὄρος τῶν Ἐλαιῶν κατέναντι τοῦ ἱεροῦ...

Mt xxiv. 3
καθημένου δὲ αὐτοῦ ἐπὶ τοῦ Ὄρους τῶν Ἐλαιῶν...

Lk. om.

(Mark xiv. 32—42)

THE INTERVAL BEFORE THE ARREST

Version   But it is only in an interpolated passage written in a Lucan style[1].

Considering other ways of intervention by which John might indicate the locality of Gethsemane without actually mentioning the name, we have to ask what the name meant in Hebrew or Aramaic. Eusebius gives three answers, of which the first is "Ravine (*geth*) of fat things (*semane*)[2]." This is the only explanation given by Jerome, "vallis pinguedinum[3]." But Eusebius also tells us that *geth-* means "*mountain*, or *chasm*, or *ravine*, or *wine-press*[4]." This uncertainty is reflected in various readings of the name in Greek and in translations from the Greek, in Mark and Matthew[5]. Jerome illustrates the name from words of Isaiah mentioning "a valley of fat things," that is, "a fertile valley[6]." Here the word for "valley" resembles "*geth*," but without the *th*; and in Mark and Matthew many authorities drop the *th*. Professor Dalman favours the derivation from *gath*, "wine-press," but admits the possible derivation from the form of *ge* meaning "ravine[7]."

Turning to John, we find that in his description of the place to which Jesus "went out" (1) he uses a word, "torrent," not elsewhere used in the New Testament and sometimes inter-

---

[1] Jn viii 1   It is worth noting that Goodspeed gives Justin Martyr as the only early writer that mentions the Mount of Olives, and he connects it (*Tryph* § 99) with the Agony, and (*Tryph.* § 103, thrice) with Christ's arrest, possibly with some allusion and certainly with a strange emphasis   *Evang Nic* 14 (A) "Jesus and His disciples sitting on the mountain called Mamilch (2 K xxiii. 13)," is parall to *ib.* (B) "in Galilee upon the mount of Olives"   And see Rashi on Zech xiv 4—5

[2] See *Onomast.* p 189.
[3] *Onomast* p. 61.   [4] *Onomast* p. 189
[5] In Latin and Syr, *Geth-* is very variously rendered. Comp 1 S xvii 52 *a* on which Gesen 387 *b* indicates that LXX has preserved גת *Gath* (or *Geth*), correctly, against Heb txt, which has ניא, R V. "Gai," a word meaning "valley"
[6] Is xxviii 1 "valley of (ניא) fat things (שמנים)"
[7] Gesen 387 *b* gives no instance of גת as meaning anything but "wine-press"   The word used in Isaiah שמן (Gesen 1032 *a*) means *oil*, as well as fat, but not necessarily "olive oil"

448   (Mark xiv 32—42)

THE INTERVAL BEFORE THE ARREST

changed with "ravine[1]"; (2) he calls it a "garden," corresponding to the Mark-Matthew word "enclosed-place"; (3) he mentions "*the* place," as Luke does, but in a context different from Luke's, so as to explain why he calls it thus: "Now Judas also, who was betraying him, knew *the place*, for Jesus oft-times (R V) resorted thither with his disciples[2]."

The ordinary explanation of "Gethsemane" as "press of *oils*," meaning "press of *olive oil*," ignores the fact that the Talmud expressly distinguishes "*olive oil*" from "*all oils*[3]" Luke may perhaps have supposed that it meant "*olive oil*" and that it pointed to some place on "the mount of Olives", but John may have thought (and with better reason) that it meant "*fat things*," or "*fertilities*," as in Isaiah's phrase "*valley of fertilities*." In that case it might be a Hebrew euphemistic name for manured market-gardens in the neighbourhood of the "ravine" or "gully" of Kidron, which served as a drain to the Temple[4] Such a detailed explanation would be entirely inappropriate to any Gospel, especially to the Fourth But the description of Jesus as crossing "the brook Kidron," familiar to readers of the Scriptures as the "brook" crossed by king David in old days when he went forth in flight from Jerusalem[5],

---

[1] Jn xviii 1 χειμάρρου Only here in N T In LXX χειμάρρους mostly = נחל, which is the name given to Kidron in *Joma* 58 *b* There the Mishna describes it as the watercourse that receives from the Temple the remnant of the blood of the sacrifices, sold to the gardeners for the purpose of manuring their gardens In Ezek xxxvi 4 (A) τοῖς χειμάρροις (אפיקים) καὶ ταῖς φάραγξι (גאיות), the normal text (B) interchanges the two Gk nouns

[2] Jn xviii 2 συνήχθη, on which see p 370, n 1

[3] See Levy iv 576*a* quoting *Sabb* 23*a* "All *oils* are good for lighting, but the oil of the olive is the best" The pl of שמן "fat" or "oil," occurs only in Is xxv 6 "*fat things* [for food]" (*bis*), xxviii 1, 4 "valley of *fat things* [i e of *fertility*]," Amos vi 6 and Cant 1 3, iv 10 "*ointments*"

[4] See *Hor Heb* on Jn xviii 1 (referring to *Joma* quoted above) and on Mt xxvi 36, quoting *Baba Kama* "They do not make gardens in Jerusalem *because of the stink*," one explanation of which is "It is the custom to *dung* gardens"

[5] 2 S xv 23

THE INTERVAL BEFORE THE ARREST

would be symbolically appropriate besides being in accord with fact[1].

We conclude that John has intervened in behalf of Mark to explain an obscure but definite name for which Luke substituted a term that was not obscure but was too indefinite.

§ 6. "He began...to be sore troubled," in Mark and Matthew[2]

In Mark, A.V. has "He began to be *sore-amazed* and *to be very-heavy*," R V. "He began to be *greatly-amazed* and *sore-troubled*" The first of these two verbs, as used by Aquila, signifies amazed awe or terror, and Matthew substitutes for it "*to be grieved*[3]." But the second is even more difficult, for it signifies a passion bordering on frenzy or despair[4]. Luke omits both The question arises whether Mark found in Scripture some precedent that seemed to justify this venturesome statement about the Messiah, and whether John, finding it thus stated by Mark, and not stated by Luke, intervened to give it suitable expression[5]

---

[1] See *Joh. Gr.* 2671—4.

[2] Mk xiv 33 (Mt xxvi 37) ἤρξατο ἐκθαμβεῖσθαι (Mt λυπεῖσθαι) καὶ ἀδημονεῖν

[3] Ἐκθαμβέω is not in canon LXX, but Aquila has it in Job iii 5, R V. "terrify," and sim xv 24, xxxiii 7 In N T. it occurs only here and in Mk ix 15 ἰδόντες αὐτὸν ἐξεθαμβήθησαν, and xvi 5, 6 of terror at a vision of angels Goodspeed does not give forms of it except ἔκθαμβος in Herm. *Vis* iii 1 5 of awe at a vision

[4] See Steph. *Thes* ἀδημονέω, or Wetstein on Mt xxvi 37, noting especially the Plutarchian applications to Antony (*Vit.* 939 E) mad and melancholy because of Cleopatra's delay

[5] The remarks in this section do not include Luke's rejection of the Marcan view that three apostles were specially selected (παραλαμβάνει) by Jesus to be with Him in Gethsemane (as at the Transfiguration, Mk ix 2, Mt. xvii. 1, Lk ix 28, all παραλαμβάνει) John nowhere inserts an instance of such selection It has been shewn in *Notes* 2999 (xvii) *h* that the term "*pillars*," עמדים or עמודים, might be used (1) technically, for Peter, James, and John as "[*apostolic*] *pillars*," but might also be used (2) for "*standing-fast*," as in Lk xxii 28 "ye are they *that stood-fast* (העמדים) with me (עמדי)" This might have meant, in a Hebrew tradition, "ye are my stedfast followers," or, in an

THE INTERVAL BEFORE THE ARREST

Such a precedent is found in Isaiah where it is said of the Lord Himself "He (R.V.) *wondered* that there was no intercessor therefore his own arm brought salvation unto him," words afterwards repeated in Isaiah by Jehovah in the first person[1]. In both these passages the Hebrew word rendered "wondered" is one that is rendered by the best authorities "desolated," "appalled," or "dazed[2]." Our English Versions have not rendered it "wondered" except in these two places, and in these inadequately. The Hebrew is rendered in the LXX by a great number of words signifying "astonishment," "desolation," and "terror[3]", and Aquila renders it once by the word here used by Mark (and Matthew), which is non-occurrent in the LXX[4]. In both passages of Isaiah, the LXX completely misrepresents the meaning[5]. So does the Targum[6]. But Mark's text is intelligible if regarded as an attempt to express in two Marcan words the Hebrew feeling of "desolate

---

early Christian application of it, "ye [three] are my [faithful] pillars." The fact that Ephrem commenting on Mk ix 1, Mt. xvi 28 "those *standing* here" refers to Gal. ii 9 "*pillars*," and the similarity of "*pillar*," עמוד, and "*with me*," עמדי, indicate the possibility of confusion of traditions about the "*pillars*," in sayings of Jesus, so that either Mark, or Luke, might be misled.

[1] Is lix 16, comp. lxiii 5, שמם hithpo.
[2] Gesen. 1031 a
[3] Tromm gives שמם as = ἐξίσταμαι (8), ἀφανίζω, -ομαι (21) but θαυμάζω only (2), θαῦμα ἔχει (1) It also = ἀτιμάζω, βασανίζω, σκυθρωπάζω etc
[4] Job xviii 20 "shall be astonished (שמם)," LXX ἐστέναξαν, Aq. ἀδημονήσουσιν
[5] Is. lix 16 LXX κατενόησεν, lxiii 5 LXX προσενόησα, Aq. ἐξηπορήθην
[6] Is lix 16 Targ "*et notum est coram eo*," lxiii. 5 Targ. "*et notum est coram me*" This resembles the LXX Rashi says "et conticuit ut videret an esset qui intercederet," and "it signifies one who stands, and wonders, and is silent (conticescit) in his wonder." But this is too deliberate It really means "struck dumb, or desolated, with astonishment." Ibn Ezra rejects the suggestion of Menahem that שתם "open-eyed," should be read for שמם (as in Numb. xxiv 3, 15 "see open-eyed") and he rightly compares Is. i 7, "*desolate*." The LXX prob took שמם as a form of שום = νοέω, ἐπινοέω.

THE INTERVAL BEFORE THE ARREST

astonishment" attributed to Jehovah when finding that Israel was destitute of any intercessor except Himself.

What course does John take as regards the expression of this Messianic thought in Isaiah and in Mark omitted by Luke? John omits the whole of the narrative of Gethsemane except the mention of the "place" as a "garden" on the other side of "Kidron[1]." But it does not follow that he would altogether omit all suggestion of the Messianic pain and conflict included in Christ's intercessory acts. Moreover, as has been shewn in previous treatises, John knew well that the Christian view of the Saviour's spiritual suffering and trouble differed altogether from the Epictetian doctrine, which taught that no human being ought ever to feel "trouble" either for himself or for others[2]. It is probably no accidental coincidence that John uses that particular word "trouble"—which Epictetus used to condemn an infirmity that was always wrong—in order to shew that in the Saviour it represented a deep and mysterious sympathy that was profoundly right[3].

This he does systematically, describing three stages of Messianic "trouble" The first is at the grave of Lazarus, where Jesus, for the sake of raising Lazarus from the dead, "*troubled himself*[2]." The second is after the coming of the Greeks, and just before the Voice from heaven that announces the glorification of the divine Name through death preparing the way for life—the law of the spiritual harvest. There Jesus says "Now is *my soul troubled*[4]." The third instance is where Jesus "was *troubled in spirit*" and said, "One of you shall deliver me over[5]." This is the Johannine climax, and it helps us to understand that John, though he does not relate the narrative of Gethsemane, intends us to understand that the Marcan phrases about "amazement" and "astonishment" signify Christ's feelings, not for Himself and for His own approaching death, but for the sake of Judas and all human

---

[1] Jn xviii 1—2
[2] See *From Letter* 920 (and Epict ii 2 title περὶ ἀταραξίας), *Joh Voc.* 1727 b—c, *Joh Gr* 2614 c, Proclam. p. 174
[3] Jn xi. 33.   [4] Jn xii. 27   [5] Jn xiii. 21.

THE INTERVAL BEFORE THE ARREST

beings of whom Judas was the type[1]. In His thought and trouble for others Jesus may have received—so Mark's tradition suggests, or leaves us free to suppose—a new and final revelation, that the "smiting" which He was to endure was to be even "unto death," and that, unless He died, there was, "no intercessor."

We must not however entirely ignore a very different and simple explanation, which would indicate that, in Luke's view, and perhaps in John's, it was not Jesus but the disciples, who "began to be amazed and astonished." It was pointed out in a previous treatise that a verse in Mark, "*[they] began* to beseech him to depart," may have been read originally as "*[he] began*[2]." Now "*they began*" would suit Mark's text here. "He took the three disciples and *they began* to be amazed," just as Mark says previously "Jesus said...*they began* to be sorrowful[3]."

If Luke believed that to be the meaning we can understand why he (and he alone) says a little later that Jesus found the disciples "slumbering because of their *sorrow*[4]." This is the only passage where Luke mentions "*sorrow*." Nor does John mention "*sorrow*" in his Gospel till he introduces it at this stage in the words of Jesus to the disciples "Because I have

---

[1] So Jerome on Mt. xxvi. 38, "Contristabatur autem non timore patiendi.." quoted fully below (p. 455, n. 7).

The *Acts of John* (§ 6) says that "when the disciples were sleeping in one house at Gennesaret (*sic*)" John saw "Another, like unto Him, come down," who said, "Jesus, those whom thou didst choose do still not believe in thee ('Ιησοῦ, οὓς ἐξελέξω ἔτι σοι ἀπιστοῦσιν)." Jesus replies, "Thou sayest well, for they are men." This rather exaggerates the calmness that John attributes to Jesus when He anticipates being left alone. It is almost cynical. The writer ignores the fact that "men," for a Jew, meant "beings made in the image of God," and, for Jesus, "beings born to receive God's Spirit and to become God's children."

[2] *Law* p. 82, HPΞATO (*i.e.* ἤρξαντο) might be confused with HPΞATO (*i.e.* ἤρξατο), comp. 1 Macc. ix. 66 ἐξήρξατο v.r. ἤρξαντο and see *Joh. Gr.* 2687 d εκειη perhaps read as εκειη *i.e.* εκεινη

[3] Mk xiv. 19; Mt xxvi. 22 "*they began* to say," Lk xxii. 23 "*they began* to question."

[4] Lk. xxii. 45 κοιμωμένους ἀπὸ τῆς λύπης, parall. to Mk xiv. 37, Mt. xxvi. 40 καθεύδοντας.

THE INTERVAL BEFORE THE ARREST

said these things unto you, *sorrow* hath filled your heart," after which He thrice repeats the word in the attempt to comfort them[1] According to this view, the "sorrow" of the amazed and distracted disciples in Mark was wrongly attributed to Jesus by reason of Christ's own following words The error was effected by a very slight change, a mere stroke in the MS. Matthew departed still further from the correct text. Luke omitted the error John intervened—rather in favour of Luke than to correct Mark—to explain the nature of the "sorrow" of the disciples, and the darkness of its stupefaction, and the attempts of Jesus to enlighten it

§ 7. *"My soul is exceeding-sorrowful even unto death," in Mark and Matthew*[2]

Luke omits this. A literary Greek might naturally object to it, for to be *"exceeding-sorrowful,"* or—as it might mean to him—"fretful," or "depressed," was a fault against which philosophers protested from Aristotle to Plutarch[3] Moreover, in one of the very few LXX instances of it, it is applied to Cain by God, "Why art thou *exceeding-sorrowful*?"—probably meaning "fretful" or "furious[4]" What therefore requires

---

[1] Jn xvi 6, comp. *ib* 20, 21, 22.

[2] Mk xiv 34, Mt xxvi 38 περίλυπός ἐστιν ἡ ψυχή μου ἕως θανάτου In Mark, codex *a* has "O, *quam* tristis est," *k* "tristis *es*" Iren iii 22 2 οὐδ' ἂν εἰρήκει ὅτι Περίλυπός ἐστιν ἡ ψυχή μου, "nec dixisset *Tristis est anima mea*," should be compared with *ib*. 1 8 2 ἐν τῷ εἰπεῖν Περίλυπός ἐστιν ἡ ψυχή μου ἕως θανάτου, "in eo quod dixisset, *Quam tristis* est anima mea." Comp Ps xlii. 5 "*why* art thou cast down, O my soul" ἵνα τί περίλυπος εἶ, ἡ ψυχή, καὶ..., If "why" were expressed by τί, it might be confused with ὅτι "recitativum" These variations in the texts of N T perhaps point back to O T influence.

[3] Steph. *Thes* quotes Aristotle *Eth* iv 3 7 as imitating Isocr in the saying οὔτ' εὐτυχῶν περιχαρὴς ἔσται, οὔτε ἀτυχῶν περίλυπος, also imitated by Plutarch *Mor*. 7 E

[4] Gen iv 6 ἵνα τί περίλυπος ἐγένου, Aq εἰς τί [τὸ] ὀργίλον σοι; Heb חרה, R.V. "wroth" This is quoted in Clem Rom § 4 Goodspeed's only other instance is Herm *Vis* iii 10 6, where it seems to imply a childish vexation or fretfulness at some one's delay in answering a childish question.

THE INTERVAL BEFORE THE ARREST

explanation is, not Luke's omission of the word, but Mark's employment of it.

Of the five instances of it in canonical LXX three occur in refrains of the Psalms "Why art thou *cast-down*, O my soul[1]?" The Hebrew here (which differs from that of the two other instances) means "*bow oneself down*[2]." Rashi explains the form (which is a middle voice) as meaning the same as a similar word in "Our soul is *bowed down* to the dust[3]." The Greek word used by Mark does not represent the Hebrew "*bowed down*." But if Jesus was, in effect, quoting Scripture, Mark might naturally retain the LXX word, though it would be quite inadequate to express the meaning. If we realise that the original word implied a "*bowing down*" to "*the dust*," we can better understand Christ's action in "*falling on the earth*" in prayer, as reported by Mark[4]. Of this Luke misses the force, substituting a different tradition, which mentions "kneeling[5]." Matthew—from a common-sense point of view, since one *must* fall on "the earth" so that this phrase might be said logically to tell nothing—substitutes "*fell on his face*[6]." But in fact the Marcan "*fell on the earth*" was typical of a soul "bowed down to the dust." It signified (what the Greek word "exceeding-sorrowful" did not signify) that Jesus "*humbled himself, becoming obedient [even] unto death*, yea, the death of the cross[7]"

---

[1] The Heb "bow down," שחח, occurs four times in Ps xlii 5, 6, 11, xliii 5. But in xlii 6 (affirmative) "my soul *is cast down*," LXX has ἐταράχθη, so that περίλυπος occurs only thrice here. The fifth instance of LXX περίλυπος is Dan ii 12 "furious (קצף)."

[2] Gesen 1006 a gives this form of שחח as occurring only in these four instances.

[3] Ps xliv 25, שחה closely akin to שחח in meaning, LXX ἐταπεινώθη.

[4] Mk xiv 35 ἔπιπτεν ἐπὶ τῆς γῆς, καὶ προσηύχετο. .

[5] Lk xxii 41 θεὶς τὰ γόνατα προσηύχετο, on the context of which see *Son* 3613 a—b.

[6] Mt xxvi 39 ἔπεσεν ἐπὶ πρόσωπον αὐτοῦ προσευχόμενος.

[7] Philipp ii 8. Comp Heb v 7—9 "Who in the days of his flesh, having offered up prayers and supplications with strong crying and tears unto him that was able to save him from death, and having been heard for his godly fear, though he was a Son, yet

THE INTERVAL BEFORE THE ARREST

There is a great difference between becoming "*very sorrowful,* or *depressed,* or *fretful,* unto death" and "*humbling oneself* unto death"

Another point to be noted is that this Marcan tradition, if it is a quotation from a refrain in a Psalm, must be interpreted as a quotation, with some regard to the context; and the refrain of dejection in each case is followed by a refrain of confident hope "Why art thou cast down...? Hope thou in God, for I shall yet praise him for the health of his countenance[1]"

In Luke, there is no mention of Christ's "exceeding sorrow," or of anything corresponding to it—unless we include the doubtful passage mentioning an "agony" and an "angel" strengthening Jesus, and "sweat as it were drops of blood[2]"

---

learned obedience by the things which he suffered, and having been made perfect, he became unto all them that obey him the author of eternal salvation"

Cramer, on Mark, prints an ancient scholium, part of which is after the manner of Origen, in which Jesus is asked why He is "exceeding sorrowful" (since He will be ultimately triumphant), and He replies "Yea, I know the good that will come to pass for the world from my Passion, but I am grieved by the firstborn, namely, Israel, because he is not even in the [rank of the] servants [of God] (comp Jerem ii 14)" Jerome says (on Mt xxvi 38) "Contristabatur autem non timore patiendi—qui ad hoc venerat ut pateretur, et Petrum timiditatis arguerat—sed propter infelicissimum Judam, et scandalum omnium Apostolorum, et rejectionem populi Judaeorum, et eversionem miserae Hierusalem" These last two extracts indicate that the author of the Epistle to the Hebrews might have done well to substitute "*save from death*" for "*save him from death,*" since he himself would probably admit that Jesus was thinking not solely, and perhaps not primarily, of Himself except as "saving" others But the author is instructive in his suggestion that up to the last moment Jesus may have been "*learning*"—"learning from the things that he suffered" the nature of the "obedience" by which He was to do His work as Saviour

[1] Ps xlii 5, R V txt, comp *ib* 11, xliii 5 Somewhat similarly it should be noted that the Psalm quoted on the Cross (Ps xxii 1) beginning with the deepest sadness, ends in a note of joy

[2] Lk xxii 43, 44, placed in double brackets by W H, and omitted by many ancient authorities

THE INTERVAL BEFORE THE ARREST

As to John, it has been repeatedly pointed out that he recognises an "exceeding sorrow" that amounts to "trouble," as being one of Christ's burdens, and a burden that increases toward the close. But he prefers to call it "trouble." The LXX itself uses the word *"troubled"* to represent the Hebrew *"bowed down"* in one of the refrains we have been considering[1] We may therefore say that the LXX supplies a link connecting Mark and John in their views of the Messianic pain of intercession. John also mentions an "angel" in a passage where Jesus asks a question from heaven and receives an answer But it is not a real angel "Thundering" and "angel" are both mentioned[2] But it is no more an angel than thunder It is the Voice of the Father from heaven

A reasonable conclusion is that John intervenes for Mark against Luke to say that it was not incorrect to suppose that Christ might speak about His "soul" as being "exceeding sorrowful[3]," although the thought would be better expressed by describing it as "troubled[4]"

---

[1] Ps xlii 6

[2] Jn xii 29 "The multitude. said that it had *thundered* others said, *An angel* hath spoken to him"—the only instance of "angel" (*sing*) in Jn.

[3] On the "soul" of Christ (not mentioned in Lk) see *Son* 3434—7, 3546

[4] A word should be added on the verbal and circumstantial similarity between Mk xiv 34 (Mt xxvi 38) $\pi\epsilon\rho\acute{\iota}\lambda\upsilon\pi\acute{o}s\ \acute{\epsilon}\sigma\tau\iota\nu\ \acute{\eta}\ \psi\upsilon\chi\acute{\eta}\ \mu o\upsilon\ \acute{\epsilon}\omega s\ \theta\alpha\nu\acute{a}\tau o\upsilon$ and Sir xxxvii 2 $\lambda\acute{\upsilon}\pi\eta\ .\ \acute{\epsilon}\omega s\ \theta\alpha\nu\acute{a}\tau o\upsilon$ Ben Sira expressly says that the $\lambda\acute{\upsilon}\pi\eta$ is concerning "a friend and companion turning to become an enemy" This would apply to Judas Jn xiii 21 "troubled in spirit" implies, though in different words, a $\lambda\acute{\upsilon}\pi\eta$ about such a "friend," and there the friend is Judas The combination of $\lambda\acute{\upsilon}\pi\eta$, or $\lambda\upsilon\pi\epsilon\hat{\iota}\nu$, or $\pi\epsilon\rho\acute{\iota}\lambda\upsilon\pi os$, with $\acute{\epsilon}\omega s\ \theta\alpha\nu\acute{a}\tau o\upsilon$ does not appear to occur elsewhere in LXX (see *Oxf Conc*) except Jon iv 9 "I do well to *be angry even unto death* ($\sigma\phi\acute{o}\delta\rho\alpha\ \lambda\epsilon\lambda\acute{\upsilon}\pi\eta\mu\alpha\iota\ \acute{\epsilon}\gamma\grave{\omega}\ \acute{\epsilon}\omega s\ \theta\alpha\nu\acute{a}\tau o\upsilon$)" —which does not express the feeling implied here We may reasonably find in Mark an allusion to the language of Ben Sira, as well as to that of the Psalms

THE INTERVAL BEFORE THE ARREST

§ 8 *"All things are possible unto thee," in Mark*[1]

There is a verbal incompatibility between the two Marcan phrases "*if it is possible,*" and "*all things are possible unto thee*" (both being addressed by the Son to the Father); and it is not surprising that Matthew and Luke omit the latter.

John's attitude toward barren discussions about "possibility" has been discussed elsewhere[2]. His view is that being "able to do as one likes" may characterize an evil and ignorant and weak doer, since there is an infinite number of ways of doing a thing badly, foolishly, and imperfectly, and only a few ways, or it may be only one way, of doing it rightly. He teaches us directly and definitely as to the Son, that He is "*not able to do*" anything except that which He sees the Father doing[3]. But as to the Father's "being able" he teaches us nothing definite or direct He merely implies. He leads us into a region where we feel that it would be out of place and almost profanely superfluous to assure us that God is "able" to do His will We need not infer from this that John denied the historical truth of the Marcan traditions of Christ's sayings about being "able[4]" But we may reasonably infer that he

---

[1] Mk xiv 35—6
καὶ προελθὼν (marg. προσελθὼν) μικρὸν ἔ-πιπτεν ἐπὶ τῆς γῆς, καὶ προσηύχετο ἵνα εἰ δυνατόν ἐστιν παρέλθῃ ἀπ' αὐτοῦ ἡ ὥρα, καὶ ἔλεγεν Ἀββά ὁ πατήρ, πάντα δυνατά σοι· παρένεγκε τὸ ποτήριον τοῦτο ἀπ' ἐμοῦ ἀλλ' οὐ τί ἐγὼ θέλω ἀλλὰ τί σύ

Mt xxvi 39
καὶ προελθὼν (marg. προσελθὼν) μικρὸν ἔπεσεν ἐπὶ πρόσωπον αὐτοῦ προσευχόμενος καὶ λέγων Πάτερ μου, εἰ δυνατόν ἐστιν, παρελθάτω ἀπ' ἐμοῦ τὸ ποτήριον τοῦτο πλὴν οὐχ ὡς ἐγὼ θέλω ἀλλ' ὡς σύ

Lk xxii 41—2
καὶ αὐτὸς ἀπεσπάσθη ἀπ' αὐτῶν ὡσεὶ λίθου βολήν, καὶ θεὶς τὰ γόνατα προσηύχετο λέγων Πάτερ, εἰ βούλει παρένεγκε τοῦτο τὸ ποτήριον ἀπ' ἐμοῦ πλὴν μὴ τὸ θέλημά μου ἀλλὰ τὸ σὸν γινέσθω.

[2] See *Law* p 137 foll on the saying peculiar to Mark (vi 5) "And *he was not able* to do there any mighty work"

[3] Jn v 19

[4] Note especially Mk ix 23 (not in Mt -Lk) τὸ Εἰ δύνῃ, πάντα δυνατὰ τῷ πιστεύοντι, as though Jesus indicated an incompatibility — "Your '*if*' is incompatible with fulfilment, since only for 'him that believeth' are all things possible" A similar incompatibility may perhaps seem to apply to the words of Jesus Himself in Mk xiv 35 "*if it is able [to be done]*" But there is a difference, for this

THE INTERVAL BEFORE THE ARREST

thought them liable to be misunderstood and perverted by unspiritual minds, which cannot take in the truth that in many cases where the "prince of this world" would boast "I am able to do this, or that," the Supreme Goodness would say "I am not able"

§ 9. *"The hour" in Mark and John, and "the cup" in all the Gospels*[1]

Mark alone mentions *"the hour"* as well as *"the cup"* in this passage, and the two apparently in similar meanings. The prayer in Mark "that...*the hour* might pass away from him," together with the prayer "remove this cup," is parallel to the prayer in Matthew "let *this cup* pass away from me."

John mentions *"the hour"* and *"the cup"* on two distinct occasions The former is mentioned in a prayer or quasi-prayer that Jesus as it were puts before His own mind and rejects "Now is my soul troubled, and what am I to say? 'Father, save me from *this hour*'? Nay, but on this account I came, to [endure] *this hour*," after which Jesus substitutes His real prayer, "Father, glorify thy name[2]"

"The cup" is mentioned in the Fourth Gospel only once, and then not till the moment preceding Christ's arrest, when Peter has wounded the High Priest's servant, where R V. has "Jesus therefore said unto Peter, Put up the sword into the sheath the cup which the Father hath given me, *shall I not drink it*[3]?" But "shall I not drink it?" does not quite express the natural meaning of the Greek original, which would be

---

is followed and as it were superseded by (1b 36) *"all things are able [to be done] for thee"* The meaning of the latter might be amplified as "Not really *'all things,'* but *'all things that are good and right'* are able to be done for thee *if it be thy will*" This, however, would be a mere truism—amplification, but not explanation. We may feel confident that Mark has kept most closely to Christ's actual words in both passages and that Matthew and Luke have omitted or altered them But we cannot pretend to reconcile them logically, since the subject is extra-logical.

[1] For the texts see above, pp 445, 458.
[2] Jn xii 27—8 See *Joh Gr* 2512 *b*—*c*
[3] Jn xviii 11 τὸ ποτήριον ὃ δέδωκέν μοι ὁ πατὴρ οὐ μὴ πίω αὐτό;

THE INTERVAL BEFORE THE ARREST

"I shall assuredly not drink it." In Hebrew, however, the interrogative "*shall I not?*," meaning "*I will*," is very much more frequent than in Greek[1], and in one instance the LXX uses the same idiom as here—where Naomi says to Ruth "*Shall I not* seek rest for thee?[2]" but the LXX has what would, in ordinary Greek, mean "*I shall assuredly not* seek rest for thee." Obviously this must be punctuated interrogatively. And the same punctuation is necessary in John. But John must have had some reason for writing such strange Greek—unprecedented (as far as is known at present) except in the LXX of Ruth above quoted. The reason suggested by the parallelism is that there is a similarity of emotion in both passages. Ruth wishes to spare Naomi anxiety; Peter wishes to prevent Jesus from drinking the cup. In both cases the "*assuredly not*" expresses a tender determination to overrule a well-meant kindness[3].

Proceeding to the Synoptic traditions of the prayers about "the cup," we see that Matthew applies to it the intransitive verb "*pass aside, or away*," which Mark has previously applied to "the hour"; whereas Mark, followed by Luke, applies to "the cup" a transitive verb rendered by R.V. "*remove*." Etymologically this verb combines the notions of "*carrying* (or, *bringing*)" and "*side*," but it is used in many different senses. In canonical LXX, where it is almost non-occurrent, it is never used to mean "*remove*," but is used of being "beside oneself" or of "passing on" a proclamation[4]. Aquila uses it in a rendering of "Jubilee," as being the year that "passes by,"

---

[1] See Gesen. 520 *a* on הלא = *nonne*, with verb in 1st pers., and pointing out that LXX often renders it by ἰδού.

[2] Ruth iii. 1 οὐ μὴ ζητήσω σοι ἀνάπαυσιν...,

[3] On οὐ μή with first person interrog.—perhaps better called exclamatory—see *From Letter* 933—6, *Joh. Gr.* 2232. Steph. *Thes.* gives only Heliodor. *Æth.* 5, init. Εἶτα οὐ μή. μανῶ ἀκηκοώς; "And then [you would have it that] I am not to go mad on hearing it!"

[4] Παραφέρω represents הלל hithpo. in 1 S. xxi. 13 "made himself [as it were] mad (παρεφέρετο)," and עבר hi. in Ezr. x. 7 παρήνεγκαν φωνήν "they passed on a proclamation."

THE INTERVAL BEFORE THE ARREST

"remits," or "lets drop," debts[1]. Early Christian writers use it of "bringing to the side [of a judge]" allegations or proofs, but not of "passing away[2]."

In literary Greek, when combined with the word "cup," it is used (of a waiter at dinner "offering" wine) in such quasi-technical terms that Athenaeus records a little philological discussion about the phrase[3]. In the Prophets there is a mention of the cup of the Lord as being handed to nation after nation either by the Lord or by His prophet[4]. Moreover it is said to the daughter of Edom in Lamentations "The cup shall *pass* also (lit) *upon* thee"—meaning (as the context seems to shew) that it shall be passed onward by the Lord from Zion to Edom[5].

---

[1] See Exod. xix. 13 בִּמְשֹׁךְ הַיֹּבֵל "cum protraxerit [tubicen] classicum," LXX ὅταν αἱ φωναὶ, καὶ αἱ σάλπιγγες, καὶ ἡ νεφέλη ἀπέλθῃ ἀπὸ τοῦ ὄρους (an instructive instance of expansion) [Aq ἐν τῷ ἑλκυσμῷ τοῦ παραφέροντος], compared with Lev. xxv. 10 "jubilum," יוֹבֵל, LXX ἐνιαυτὸς ἀφέσεως σημασία, Aq παραφέρων, Theod ἰωβήλ. It is also used by Ἄλλος in Numb xxxi. 23 of passing things—and by Sym and Theod in 2 K xxiii 10 of passing children—through the fire There is no instance in LXX, or Translators, where παραφέρω means "remove" in the sense of "take away"

[2] Goodspeed shews that παραφέρω is used by no early Christian writers except Hermas (very freq about producing, or bringing forward, building materials), and by Justin Martyr about alleging, or producing, but not to mean "take away" or "remove" To the same effect is the evidence derivable from the Indices to the Papyri (*Oxyr* and *Berl Urkund*) In Plutarch *Vit.* 151 F it means "wrest on one side" an enemy's javelin

[3] See Steph *Thes* quoting Xen *Cyr* II 11 4 καὶ ὁ μάγειρος οὐδὲν αὐτὸν ἔτι δεῖσθαι ὄψου οἰόμενος, ᾤχετο παραφέρων πρὶν λαβεῖν αὐτὸν ἕτερον, ·I. 111 6 πολλὰ αὐτῷ παραφέρειν θήρεια καὶ τῶν ἡμέρων, Athen IX p 380 D ἔδοξεν ἐπ᾽ ἄλλο τι τῶν παραφερομένων τὰς χεῖρας ἐπιβάλλειν. Καὶ ὁ Οὐλπιανὸς ἔφη. .οὐδείς τινος γεύσεται πρὶν λεχθῆναι ποῦ κεῖται τὸ παραφέρειν....Καὶ ὁ Μάγνος ἔφη, Ἀριστοφάνης ἐν Προαγῶνι "Τί οὐκ ἐκέλευσας παραφέρειν τὰ ποτήρια," Σώφρων δὲ. κατὰ κοινότερον κέχρηται λέγων "Πάραφερε, Κοικόα, τὸν σκύφον μεστόν" Πλάτων δ᾽ ἐν Λάκωσιν ἔφη "Πάσας (κύλικας) παραφερέτω" Ἄλεξις Παμφίλῃ "Παρέθηκε τὴν τράπεζαν, εἶτα παραφέρων ἀγαθῶν ἀμάξας"

[4] Jerem xxv 15 foll, comp Ezek xxiii. 31 "I will give her cup into thine hand," i e. I will give the cup of wrath to Judah, after giving it to the ten tribes of Israel.

[5] Lam iv 21 ἐπὶ (עַל) σὲ διελεύσεται.

THE INTERVAL BEFORE THE ARREST

This last passage suggests that there may be some confusion in the Synoptists, arising from a confusion of a Semitic "cause the cup to pass *upon*, or *toward*, me" with "cause the cup to pass *from* me," a difference, in Greek, amounting to a single letter[1]. And here it must be noted that the Greek in Mark, rendered by the somewhat abrupt imperative "remove," would be more legitimately rendered by the infinitive[2] The infinitive appears at first to make no sense. But it would make sense if the construction were elliptical, being, in effect, "If it be thy will *to cause the cup to pass toward me*—[so be it]. Not my will but thine be done[3]." With a somewhat similar ellipsis in Exodus,

---

[1] The Heb or Aram "*on me*"—comp Lam iv. 21 "*on thee*," txt, and Targ —might be expressed in a Greek Gospel by ἐπ' ἐμοῦ This might be regarded as an error for ἀπ' ἐμοῦ by an interpreter who had made up his mind that the verb meant "pass *away*."

[2] In Mk xiv 36, παρένεγκε appears in many MSS as ΠΑΡΕΝΕΓΚΑΙ The imperat active would usually be παρένεγκον, see L. S and Steph *Thes* on φέρω, and comp. Gen xxvii 4, 7 (Swete) ἔνεγκόν μοι Yet Gen xxvii 13 (Swete) has ἔνεγκαί μοι In all three passages of LXX there are variations in MSS, or in quotations of the texts (see *Cambr. Octateuch*, ad loc) In Lk. xxii 42, many MSS (followed by Alford) read παρενεγκεῖν Even if ΠΑΡΕΝΕΓΚΕ, the reading of B, D etc be followed, -ε may be an "itacism" for -αι. See *Joh Gr* Index, -ε The conclusion is that no safe inference can be drawn from the spelling. We must rely on other considerations, among which the particular meaning of "pass" with "cup" (in Lamentations) must have some weight, and the regular meaning of παραφέρειν ποτήριον (in Greek idiom) must have still more

[3] When this was misunderstood as meaning "remove the cup *from* me," it would be natural to substitute "*but*," in some form, for ["*so be it*"]. Mark has ἀλλά, Mt. and Lk. have πλήν.
The introduction in Mk-Mt. of δυνατόν, δυνατά, and οὐ δύναται, and the omission of any form of δυνατόν in Lk., may be explained by the fact that δύναται may be expressed by ἔστιν, as in 2 Chr xxv 9 ἔστιν τῷ κυρίῳ, *i.e* "there is [power] to the Lord" (R V "the Lord is able") followed by "to give thee "
An original εἰ θέλημά ἐστί σοι might mean either (1) "If it is thy will," or (2) "If [it is] the WILL, it is [possible] for thee" (see *Son* 3492 *j* quoting Lightf on Ign Eph § 20, and on 1 Cor xvi 12 "the WILL," as being "almost universally misunderstood"). The acceptance of the second interpretation might involve supplementary explanations about things "possible."

THE INTERVAL BEFORE THE ARREST

Moses says to the Lord in effect "If thou wilt forgive—[it shall be well] But if not, blot me out of thy book[1]"—where LXX and the Jerusalem Targum, in the lacuna, insert an imperative "forgive," while the Vulgate drops the first "if," and has "Either forgive...or...blot." Such variations, there, we feel to be very natural. And they confirm the hypothesis that, here also, the very great variations between the three Synoptists, and between the MSS and Versions of each Synoptist, are natural and explicable as interpretative additions to an elliptic and obscure original.

One of these additions, in Matthew, contains the words "if I do not *drink*" Epiphanius quotes, as from Luke, a heretical tradition "If it is possible let this cup pass from me that I *may not drink it*," and refers loosely, in the context, to words uttered "earlier" in Luke "I have a cup to drink, and what do I hasten [to do] *until such* [*time*] *as I drink it* ?[2]" Here

---

[1] Exod xxxii. 32 "Yet now, if thou wilt forgive their sin—, and if not, blot me, I pray thee, out of the book which thou hast written," LXX καὶ νῦν, εἰ μὲν ἀφεῖς αὐτοῖς τὴν ἁμαρτίαν αὐτῶν, ἄφες· εἰ δὲ μή,... Onk, like Heb, omits the apodosis, but Jer Targ, like LXX, inserts an imperat "forgive" Vulg has "Aut dimitte eis hanc noxam, aut, si non facis, dele me..." Rashi supplies, as apodosis, "*bene est.*" Clem Rom quotes this nearly as the Vulgate, § 53 Ἄφες τὴν ἁμαρτίαν τῷ λαῷ τούτῳ ἢ κἀμὲ ἐξάλειψον

[2] Epiphan *Haer* lxix p 784 B—D (Lib II Tom II ch 58) Πάτερ, εἰ δυνατόν, παρελθάτω τὸ ποτήριον τοῦτο ἀπ' ἐμοῦ ἵνα μὴ αὐτὸ πίω, πλὴν οὐχ ὃ ἐγὼ θέλω ἀλλ' ὃ σύ....Ἀνωτέρω γὰρ λέγει ὅτι ποτήριον ἔχω πιεῖν καὶ τί σπεύδω (*quid festino*) ἕως οὗ πίω αὐτό, (comp Lk xii. 50)

Origen, quoting Jn xiii 27 "do more quickly (*Joh Gr* 1918, 2554 e)," says that Jesus (*Comm Joann* xxxii 15) was not afraid, "*as some suppose* who have not understood in what sense He said, *Father, if* [*it is*] *possible, let this cup pass*," but that He wished to hasten, as far as possible, the dispensation of salvation, "stripping for the contest [like an athlete]"—apparently thinking (see below) that "let it pass" might mean "let me drink it quickly and have done with it" Elsewhere, Origen refers (*Cels* vii 55) to "*some who suppose*" Christ's prayer concerning the cup to have been uttered from want of courage This indicates that Christ's prayer would be the subject of early controversy, and accordingly Celsus, or the Jew in Celsus, is introduced as quoting it in one brief passage thus (*ib* ii. 24) (1) ὦ πάτερ, εἰ δύναται τὸ ποτήριον τοῦτο παρελθεῖν (omitting ἀπ' ἐμοῦ), (2) παρα-

neither "hour" nor "time" is definitely mentioned. But the thought is implied; and indeed the context twice quotes "Save me from this hour[1]." The attitude is that of one expecting the bitter cup, and the hour of trial, and looking forward to the time when both experiences shall have been endured.

There is a parallelism between the cup and the hour. As to "the hour" we have seen above that John describes Christ as putting aside the thought of praying that He might be saved from it. It seems antecedently probable that John would take the same view of the prayer about the cup—namely, that Jesus put such a prayer before Himself, as it were tentatively and interrogatively, and then rejected it. As to "the hour," he has recorded both phases, the interrogation and the answer; as to "the cup," where Synoptic variations might obscure for some the distinctness of Christ's determination, he has not recorded a phase of interrogation but only the answer emphatically

φράζει μὲν τὸ Πάτερ, εἰ δυνατόν ἐστι παρελθέτω τὸ ποτήριον τοῦτο (omitting ἀπ' ἐμοῦ), (3) ὦ πάτερ, εἴθε δύναιτο τὸ ποτήριον τοῦτο παρελθεῖν (omitting ἀπ' ἐμοῦ).

Among many other comments made by Origen on the "passing" of "the cup" the following is specially noteworthy (on Mt xxvi. 42 *ad loc.*) "Petit autem nunc ut transeat calix ab eo, et si non sic quomodo voluit ipse, transeat quomodo vult Pater." That is, the cup was to "pass away" from Jesus, in any case, but *with a difference* —"Existimo enim quoniam calix ille passionis omnino quidem ab Jesu fuerat transiturus, *sed cum differentia*. ut (1) si quidem biberet eum, et ab ipso transiret postmodum et ab universo genere hominum; (2) si autem non biberet eum, ab ipso quidem forsitan transiret, ab hominibus autem non transiret, sed maneret apud eos donec perficeret eos." The Latin text is perhaps uncertain in details, but it appears clearly to indicate that "the cup" may "pass" in two ways (1) by being emptied at once so that the drinking becomes a thing of the past, both for Jesus and for the world; (2) by not being emptied but only removed—perhaps from Jesus, but not from the world for whom "the drinking of the cup" was still to await its accomplishment. The noteworthy point in this comment is that Origen strains the meaning of the Greek παρελθεῖν, "pass away" as if it could mean here "pass away by being quickly completed." This might be true of "night," "darkness," "trouble" etc. but hardly of the drinking of a potion.

[1] Jn xii. 27.

THE INTERVAL BEFORE THE ARREST

welcoming the cup and refusing to pray that it may be averted.

Something of the nature of tentative prayer is implied in Paul's experience when he "besought the Lord thrice" that the "thorn in the flesh" or "messenger of Satan" might depart from him After the third prayer the Apostle received the answer "My grace is sufficient for thee," and apparently prayed no longer[1]. Perhaps the three Pauline prayers were in precisely the same terms, but we are not obliged to suppose that they were. They may have been modified as the Apostle was gradually brought to see that the "thorn" was not to "depart"

So here. Mark and Matthew say, or imply, that Jesus prayed thrice[2]. They also say that Jesus prayed "*saying the same thing*" But Matthew inserts "saying the same thing" after he has given the second prayer in a form slightly differing from the first:—"O my Father, if this is not able to pass away except I drink it, thy will be done[3]" Hence whereas Mark leaves us under the impression that Jesus thrice uttered the same prayer, Matthew records one prayer of a certain kind, and two more of what may be called an amended nature. Luke mentions only one[4]. John seems to incline to a form blending the Synoptic traditions, as if saying "Luke was not quite right in recording one deliberate prayer, nor was Mark right in saying that there were three identical prayers; nor Matthew quite right in his wording of the amended prayer. The Son received from the Father a revelation of the perfect prayer 'Father, glorify thy name' even while He set before

---

[1] 2 Cor xii 7—9

[2] Mk xiv 39 "prayed, saying the same word" and xiv 41 "cometh the third time," appear to imply that before coming "the third time" Jesus has prayed a third time "saying the same word" [In Mk xiv 39 "saying the same word" is bracketed by W H but inserted by SS]

[3] Mt xxvi 42 Πάτερ μου, εἰ οὐ δύναται τοῦτο παρελθεῖν ἐὰν μὴ αὐτὸ πιω, γενηθήτω τὸ θέλημά σου

[4] Lk xxii 42 Πάτερ, εἰ βούλει παρένεγκε τοῦτο τὸ ποτήριον ἀπ' ἐμοῦ· πλὴν μὴ τὸ θέλημά μου ἀλλὰ τὸ σὸν γινέσθω

Codex D has πατερ μη το θελημα μου αλλα το σον γενεσθω ει βουλε π.ι,)ενεγκε τουτο το ποτηριον απ εμου

THE INTERVAL BEFORE THE ARREST

His own mind, and rejected, the imperfect prayer 'Save me from this hour[1].'"

As recorded by the Synoptists, these prayers of Jesus seem difficult to reconcile with some of the predictions of Jesus in the Synoptists definitely predicting that He would be killed or crucified. But we must repeat here what has been reiterated in previous treatises, that those predictions appear to have been based on Hosea's prophecy of the *"smiting"* and revivifying of Israel They *might* mean, but they did not necessarily mean, *"smiting unto death*[2]*."* The historic fact appears to have been that almost up to the moment of His arrest, Jesus was not absolutely certain that "the cup" was to be drained to the dregs, and that it implied not only "smiting" but death. It was during the week before the Crucifixion that He received this intimation and "learned the [lesson of] obedience from the things that he suffered[3]." But was the "learning" deferred quite so long as Mark suggests? And has Mark rightly interpreted the traditions about "the cup" and about "the hour"? There is much to be said—much more than at first sight appears—for the hypothesis that John gave a negative answer to both these questions, and that the negative was justified[4].

---

[1] Jn xii 27—8
[2] See *Son* 3198—201, 3203 foll etc , *Law* p 499
[3] Heb v 8.
[4] In explaining the metaphor of the "cup," many commentators, ancient as well as modern, have contented themselves with saying little more than that it implies martyrdom, without inquiring how it is related to the "cup" of the Lord in Hebrew Scripture The Midrash on Ps lxxv 8 "In the hand of the Lord there is a cup," recognises that the "cup" may be pleasurable or painful But here, in the Gospels, the "cup" is obviously not pleasurable Then the question arises whether it is medicinal, or merely painful The answer is that it is, in some sense, the cup of the wrath of God. This is almost always the Hebrew meaning, when the word is metaphorical (Gesen. 468 *a*) It is described as being passed by God to this nation or to that in vengeance on sin, oppression, and pride So far as the "cup" is the necessary penalty of sin, it must necessarily be drunk by all mankind But Jesus is regarded as being able to drink it in their name (Heb. ii. 9), "tasting death for every man,"

THE INTERVAL BEFORE THE ARREST

§ 10. *"The spirit indeed is willing, but the flesh is weak," in Mark and Matthew*[1]

These words of Jesus are omitted by Luke here and find no place elsewhere in his Gospel. They are not of a particular character—like "Sleep on now and take your rest" inseparable from the narrative—but the expression of a general truth. We have therefore to ask whether John intervenes by placing elsewhere anything corresponding to them.

To answer this, we must first ascertain the precise meaning of "spirit" and "flesh" here. "Spirit"—for several reasons—cannot mean the Holy Spirit, but must mean what Paul calls "the spirit of the man, the [spirit that is] in him[2]"; and "the flesh" does not here seem to mean "the flesh" in its frequent sense—the selfish instinct in a man that rebels against the social promptings of good will. It appears to mean little more than "the body," by which term the Syriac here renders the Greek[3]

---

as it is written of the Suffering Servant in Isaiah (liii. 8) "for the transgression of my people was he stricken." This "cup," then, is not the cup of a Spartan sufferer—suffering with the fortitude that is bred from self-respect; nor the cup of a martyr bent on ensuring the safety of his own soul, it is the cup of a martyr smitten to the heart by a sympathetic and intercessory sorrow for the sins of the whole world

[1] Mk xiv 38, Mt. xxvi 41 τὸ μὲν πνεῦμα πρόθυμον ἡ δὲ σὰρξ ἀσθενής.
At this point a brief comment is due to Mk xiv. 40 καὶ οὐκ ᾔδεισαν τί ἀποκριθῶσιν αὐτῷ, since it is omitted by the parall. Mt. and Lk It expresses bewilderment. Bewilderment on the part of the disciples at Christ's final words to them is implied all through the Johannine Last Discourse. But instead of being expressed in narrative it is implied in drama, so that we cannot point to any one Johannine passage and say "This is John's intervention." See the remarks (p 5) on Mk ix. 6 οὐ γὰρ ᾔδει τί ἀποκριθῇ parall to Lk ix. 33 μὴ εἰδὼς ὃ λέγει. John, in the Last Discourse, represents the disciples in both these aspects they did not know either (1) *what to say in answer* to Jesus, or (2) *what they themselves were really saying* (since they were talking in the dark).

[2] 1 Cor. ii 11

[3] "Body," see Walton and Burkitt *ad loc.*

THE INTERVAL BEFORE THE ARREST

Luke may have omitted the words because they seemed inconsistent with Pauline doctrine. They suggested that "the flesh" was a weak friend, whereas Paul often wrote of it as an enemy to be "mortified" or killed. Moreover they were somewhat obscure. Some might base on them an excuse (saying of themselves "my flesh is weak") though Jesus (as Jerome says) intended them as a warning[1]. Others might say that "the flesh" was essentially evil and blame the Creator for it. The Synoptists give us no help on such questions, for Mark and Matthew do not use "the flesh" technically elsewhere and Luke does not use it technically at all[2].

John deals with the question mystically, indicating in his Prologue that "flesh" may be regarded in two aspects. Those who are to be children of God "were not born of the will of the flesh", but the Word of God "became flesh[3]"; "that which is born of the flesh is flesh and that which is born of the Spirit is Spirit[4]." Then comes a long exposition of the doctrine that the "flesh" of the Son of Man is to be the life-giving bread of the world[5]. The last of many instances of the word in this exposition is "The spirit it is that giveth life, the flesh is of no avail[6]."

In the Epistle it is said that "*the [passionate] desire of the flesh*...is not from the Father[7]." But this does not imply a condemnation of "flesh" in itself. It is also added that "every spirit that confesseth that Jesus Christ is *come in the flesh* is from God[8]." The impression left on the reader by all these Johannine expressions is, that the Son has introduced, so to speak, a new kind of "flesh" into the world, and that those who partake of it as food will partake of His Spirit. But it still remains true that the flesh without the Spirit is a mere tool, not indeed an enemy, but a thing that "availeth

---

[1] On Mt. xxvi. 41 Jerome says "Hoc adversum temerarios."
[2] Luke uses σάρξ only twice. In iii. 6, he quotes from Is. xl. 5—7 "*all flesh*," where see Jerome as to the higher meaning of "*all flesh*" when it preserves (1 Cor. xv. 49) "the image of the heavenly." In Lk. xxiv. 39 πνεῦμα σάρκα...οὐκ ἔχει, "spirit" means "apparition."
[3] Jn. i. 13—14. [4] Jn. iii. 6. [5] Jn. vi. 51—63
[6] Jn. vi. 63. [7] 1 Jn. ii. 16. [8] 1 Jn. iv. 2

THE INTERVAL BEFORE THE ARREST

nothing" and may be used for evil. The Johannine doctrine is clear and practical, though mystical. It teaches us, in effect, to aim at righteousness not by avoiding selfishness but by seeking and entering into, or receiving into ourselves, the self-sacrificing love of the Son. This incarnate love—metaphorically in the material world but literally in the spiritual world—is His flesh, and it is to become ours[1].

§ 11. *The last words of Jesus to the disciples*

In Mark and Matthew, the last words of Jesus to the disciples are "He that delivereth me over hath drawn near," immediately preceded by "*Rise up, let us be going*[2]" The Greek here used for "let us be going," *agōmen*[3], occurs nowhere in Luke, only here in Matthew, once elsewhere in Mark, and fairly often in John. It has been adopted into Hebrew. John has it in the sentence "*Rise up, let us be going* hence," uttered by Jesus to the disciples[4]. But John places it (presumably) at the going forth from the chamber of the Last Supper on the way to the gate of the City. Mark has placed it at the going forth of Jesus in Gethsemane to meet the soldiers. There can hardly be a doubt that one and the same tradition was before Mark and John: "The Lord Jesus, when the hour came, that He should go forth to His death, did not flee from His enemies as the disciples did, but exhorted the disciples saying *Egeiresthe agōmen*, '*Rise up, let us go* [*to meet them*]'" But Mark has placed it before one kind of "going forth," John before another and an earlier one[5].

The same transposition has probably befallen another Marcan

---

[1] Σάρξ occurs also in Jn viii 15 "ye judge *according to* [*the*] *flesh*"—(a Pauline phrase)—and xvii 2 "even as thou hast given him authority over *all flesh*" (an O T phrase). Thus, in the Fourth Gospel, it occurs in every Biblical usage as well as in the one peculiarly Johannine.

[2] Mk xiv 42, Mt xxvi 46 ἐγείρεσθε ἄγωμεν ἰδοὺ ὁ παραδιδούς με ἤγγικεν (Mt ἤγγ ὁ παραδιδούς με)

[3] On *agōmen*, see *Paradosis* 1372—7 and *Son* 3322—32.

[4] Jn xiv 31 ἐγείρεσθε, ἄγωμεν ἐντεῦθεν.

[5] Concerning the different acts of "going forth" on the eve of the Crucifixion see *Acts of John* § 11 ἐξέλθωμεν and § 12 ἐξῆλθεν The latter—which says in effect "The Lord went forth [to meet

THE INTERVAL BEFORE THE ARREST

tradition in the preceding verse—"*it is enough*," or literally "*it has in full*[1]." "*I have in full*" may mean "I have my debt [paid] in full." In Genesis the steward says to Joseph's brethren in the Greek of LXX, "*I-have-in-full* your money", but Aquila and the Hebrew have "your money *came to me*" (meaning "*duly reached me*")[2] So here Mark may have combined the idiomatic Greek rendering "[*the account*] *has* [*payment*] *in full*" with a literal rendering of the Hebrew "*has come*," adding "hour" as a subject of "has come " Matthew omits the difficult Greek word[3], and so does one very ancient Latin MS of Mark (which diverges widely from the received text)[4]. Luke also assigns to Jesus a phrase that we must needs render "*It is enough*", but it is uttered, not in Gethsemane but on the way thither, and the Greek word is entirely different, and so is the context[5].

---

the soldiers]...we fled"—may refer to Jn xviii 4 On "going forth (ἐξέρχομαι)" meaning "departing this life," see *Notes* **2939**.

[1] Mk xiv. 41 ἀπέχει· ἦλθεν ἡ ὥρα, D ἀπέχει τὸ τέλος καὶ ἡ ὥρα, *d* "sufficit finis et ora," *a* "consummatus est finis, advenit hora," *Brix*. "adest finis, venit hora," *Corb* "adest enim consummatio, et venit hora," *k* "iam ora est," SS "the hour hath come, the end hath arrived " Codex *k* omits ἀπεχει, the other authorities expand it into a phrase implying consummation 'Ἀπέχει implies a crisis personified as a Creditor, who makes demands and "has them [paid] in full "

[2] Gen xliii 23, LXX ἀπέχω, Heb. בא אלי, "'Ἄλλος" (Field) ἦλθε πρὸς μέ So Numb xxxii. 19 "our inheritance *has come* (באה) (R V. is fallen) to us," ἀπέχομεν, no v r In Is xlii 19 משלם, R.V. txt "he that is at peace [with me]," marg "made perfect" or "recompensed," LXX om , Theod ἀπεσχηκώς (Jerome "recepit"), Sym. τέλειος Targ "persolvenda erit," *i e* "to be paid in full "

These passages indicate two possible Hebrew originals for ἀπέχει, implying (1) arrival of a crisis, (2) payment of a debt. But comp also Numb. xvi. 3 " It is enough for you (רב-לכם)," [?ἀπ]εχέτω ὑμῖν

[3] Mt xxvi. 45 ἰδοὺ ἤγγικεν (not ἦλθεν) ἡ ὥρα omitting ἀπέχει

[4] Codex *k* has for Mk xiv 41—2 "et venit tertio et ubi adoravit dicit illis dormite iam nunc ecce adpropinquavit qui me tradit et post pusillum excitavit illos et dixit iam ora est ecce traditur filius hominis in manu peccatorum surgite eamus "

[5] Lk. xxii 38 Οἱ δὲ εἶπαν Κύριε, ἰδοὺ μάχαιραι ὧδε δύο. ὁ δὲ εἶπεν αὐτοῖς Ἱκανόν ἐστιν This resembles (p 315, n. 3) the use of ἱκανόν or ἱκανούσθω to the angel commanded (like Peter) to cease to smite.

THE INTERVAL BEFORE THE ARREST

On the other hand, if the Mark-Matthew phrase implies something like the satisfaction of a claim, the payment of a debt with a "receipt in full," then we have to note that, just before the *egeiresthe agōmen* tradition, John inserts the words "There cometh the ruler of the world, and *in me he hath nothing*; but still—in order that the world may know that I love the Father...[1]." The meaning is that "the ruler" *has no sin to find in* the Son, nothing of that mortal "*debt*" which, in the case of all other mortals, gives to "the ruler" a claim to make them pass through death. In other words it may be said of "the ruler" that he is entitled to "have [his debt] in full," but that "his debt," in this case, is nothing.

Other traditions about utterances of Christ at this stage, anticipating something of the nature of an "end" or "final settlement," are expressed by means of the Greek word "*end*," *telos*, or forms of it. Thus Luke alone has "That which is [written] concerning me hath a *telos*, or *end*," and "This that is written must needs *find-an-end* in me[2]." And in the Fourth Gospel, Christ's very last word on the Cross is "*It is ended*[3]." Few modern readers would suspect for a moment that this word could have any connection, mystical or otherwise, with the thought of satisfying the claims of Death upon mankind by the payment of the blood of Christ on whom Death had no claim. But Paul himself uses the word *telos* to signify the "*custom*" or "*duty*" of excise[4]. And the Johannine *tetelestai*

---

[1] Jn xiv 30—31. On this, Westcott says "There was in Christ nothing which the devil could claim as belonging to his sovereignty. In others he finds that which is his own, and enforces death as his *due*, but Christ offered Himself voluntarily." To this it should be added that "due"—which I have italicised—might be interchanged with "debt" and also with "sin."

[2] Lk xxii 37 A V "must yet *be accomplished* (τελεσθῆναι)... have an *end* (τέλος)," R V "must *be fulfilled*. hath *fulfilment* (lit *end*)"

[3] Jn xix 30 Τετέλεσται A V and R V "It is finished." Τετέλεσται has just been used above (Jn xix 28) εἰδὼς ὅτι ἤδη πάντα τετέλεσται, A V "*accomplished*," R V "*finished*." It might have been rendered in both passages by "*ended*."

[4] Rom xiii 7 "Render to all their dues, tribute to whom tribute is due, *custom* (τέλος) to whom *custom* (τέλος)."

THE INTERVAL BEFORE THE ARREST

may be found as early as the reign of Titus in a custom-house receipt to signify (about goods passing through a city gate) "*This has paid duty*[1]" Lastly we find Origen twice connecting the thought of the ruler of the world "finding nothing in Jesus" with the thought of "paying tribute, or custom[2]" These facts indicate the wide scope that many of Christ's sayings might legitimately claim, and the variety of forms in which they might be embodied.

We must go back to the words rendered by R V both in Mark and Matthew "Sleep on *now* and take your rest[3]" The

---

[1] *Notes* **2923** *d* In such receipts, τετέλεσται, "*has paid duty*," is regularly defined (*Fayum Pap* p 195) by "διὰ πύλης followed by a village name"

[2] Origen (*Luc Hom* xxiii, Lomm v 176) connects Jn xiv 30 with Rom xiii 7—8 as follows "Cum exierimus a saeculo, et haec vita nostra fuerit commutata, erunt quidam in finibus mundi sedentes, velut publicanorum officio diligentissime perscrutantes, ne quid sui in nobis inveniant Videtur mihi princeps saeculi hujus quasi *publicanus esse*, unde scriptum est de eo 'venit princeps mundi istius, et *in me habet nihil.*' Illud quoque, quod in Apostolo legimus 'reddite omnibus debita, cui tributum tributum cui vectigal vectigal cui honorem honorem nemini quid debeatis, nisi ut invicem diligatis' sacrate intelligendum est"

Also, in his commentary on Rom xiii 7—8, he says "Exactus est (v. r exsolvit) tributum etiam Dominus noster Jesus Christus in carne positus quod idcirco se dixit exsolvere, non quod debitor sit, sed ne scandalizet eos Quod si ille qui nihil habebat in se Caesaris, et in quo princeps hujus mundi veniens *non invenit quicquam de suis*, cum liber esset, solvit tamen tributum,—venit enim et in mortem, ut esset et (Ps lxxxviii 5) '*inter mortuos liber*' ..," where the meaning is that all the other dead were "bound" as "debtors" to die, but Jesus alone died not "bound," but "free"

[3] Mk xiv 41 καθεύδετε [τὸ] λοιπὸν καὶ ἀναπαύεσθε, Mt xxvi 45 om τὸ W H bracket τὸ in Mk, but against its omission by ACD must be set (1) its insertion by אB etc and (2) the tendency to assimilate Mk to Mt It is instructive to see that AD insert τὸ in Mt while omitting it in Mk (see *Clue* **16** *a*, Counterchange). This makes their evidence of very little value Also τὸ, in Mk, might easily be dropped after -τε. SS om. τὸ λοιπόν in Mk, but has in Mt מכיל, which (*Thes Syr* 2104) may mean νῦν, or ἀπὸ τοῦ νῦν, or ἄρα. The Latin versions of Mk render [τὸ] λοιπόν by "jam," but *k* transposes it thus "Dormite iam nunc ecce adpropinquavit qui me

THE INTERVAL BEFORE THE ARREST

word rendered "take your rest" may mean "be free from all distraction," "take your ease," or may be used of spiritual refreshment or repose, and sometimes of "rest" after death[1]. "*Now*" does not adequately express the difficult original, which means literally "*that which is left*." In Matthew it has not the article and would almost necessarily mean, according to Greek usage, "as regards what remains of your lives" (or "as regards what remains to be considered")[2]. In that case it would seem to be, as some of the later Greek commentators have suggested, ironical· "Sleep on now *for ever*, since your awaking will come too late." But the irony would be bitter indeed[3]

In Mark, the word probably has the article, and Mark's context suggests that he (or the authority followed by him) may have intended us to take "sleep" interrogatively, as above, in the first of the utterances to the disciples, where Mark alone has "Simon, thou sleepest[4]?"—apparently blending reproach with quasi-interrogation. In LXX, there appears to be no instance of the adverbial "for that which remains" (as used in English and Greek), but the neuter adjective is

---

tradit et post posillum excitavit illos et dixit iam ora est ecce traditur filius hominis in manu peccatorum surgite eamus"

[1] See Dan xii 13 where ἀναπαύου and ἀναπαύσῃ (a conflation of נוּחַ) represent "rest (after death)," with which comp Rev vi 11, xiv 13. Mk vi. 31 ἀναπαύσασθε "rest, or refresh yourselves" is addressed by Jesus to the disciples, but Lk xii 19 ἀναπαύου (in a passage retained by SS and probably genuine) is addressed by the rich fool to his soul "Take thine ease."

[2] The natural rendering "for the *rest*" would be inconvenient in this section where we are speaking of "*rest*" as "repose."

[3] Prof Swete on Mk xiv 41 quotes Theophylact, "He says this to them ironically...laughing at (ἐπιγελῶν) their sleep", and Euthymius, "Reproving (ἐντρέπων) them. 'Since up to this moment ye did not keep awake, for the future sleep and rest *if ye can* (εἰ δύνασθε)'" But he also quotes Augustine as merely admitting that such irony would be right *if it had been necessary* ("recte fieret si esset necesse").

[4] Mk xiv 37 καθεύδεις, οὐκ ἴσχυσας., Matthew (xxvi 40 οὕτως οὐκ ἰσχύσατε..,) omits καθεύδεις and inserts an exclamatory or semi-interrogative οὕτως. Luke (xxii 46 τί καθεύδετε,) inserts the interrogative "*why?*"

THE INTERVAL BEFORE THE ARREST

occasionally used to mean "the remainder [of something previously mentioned][1]" So perhaps here, in accordance with the special context, we may take "that which remains" to mean "the remainder of your sleep." If so, the three interrogatives (of which the second is only implied by "they knew not what to answer him") would run thus: "Simon, art thou sleeping?...[I say for the second time, Are ye sleeping?]... [I say for the third and last time] Are ye sleeping [out] the remainder [of your sleep] and slumbering at your ease? It is enough..."

But all this is extremely obscure and necessitates an unusual rendering of the Greek adverb ("for-what-remains"). Chrysostom, taking the verbs imperatively, appears to suppose them to be a command of Jesus ("sleep on") dictated in part by kindness because He knew that when they awoke they would desert Him, and in part by the knowledge that they could be of no avail But this is a desperate attempt at explanation, for Jesus, immediately afterwards, bids them "arise" Jerome attempts no explanation Presumably he and other later Greek commentators were dissatisfied with Origen's explanation, which is, that the "sleeping" mentioned in Christ's third and imperative utterance is quite different from the "sleeping" mentioned in His first and interrogative utterance Origen says in effect, that what Jesus meant by His third utterance was: "Thanks to me, sleep in all future time, and enjoy peace For in me ye shall have peace, in me God will give sleep to His beloved[2]."

This interpretation is indeed astonishing—even in Origen. Yet it is not without interest (and perhaps not without profit)

---

[1] Comp Is. xliv. 17 τὸ δὲ λοιπὸν ἐποίησεν εἰς θεὸν γλυπτόν, "but the rest [of the wood above mentioned]" and Ezek xxxiv. 18 τὸ λοιπόν, 1 e the rest of the fodder above mentioned In LXX, λοιπόν, or λοιπά, is mostly taken with some noun expressed or implied, and differs altogether from the adverbial λοιπόν (1) in the Pauline Epistles, meaning "for the rest," "for what remains," "finally," and (2) in Hermas, meaning "for the future," "in the next place," "consequently" (see Goodspeed)

[2] See Origen on Mt xxvi. 45.

THE INTERVAL BEFORE THE ARREST

to note that the Fourth Gospel falls into much the same vein of thought about "peace" in connection with the "going forth" of Jesus and the "coming" of "the prince of the world".— "Peace I leave with you...the prince of the world cometh... Arise, let us go hence," and again in the very last utterance of Jesus to His disciples before His death "These things have I spoken to you that in me ye may have peace. In the world ye [must] have tribulation. But be of good cheer, I have overcome the world[1]." Peace, gained through war and victory, that is the note on which the Johannine doctrine of Christ comes to its close. How strange a contrast with the final Synoptic note, which in Mark is—or is popularly supposed to be—represented in effect by words meaning "The traitor is near[2]!"

But Luke omits this[3]. And this should lead us to ask whether John may not be intervening, and whether "The traitor is near" may not be an incorrect interpretation, which John desires to correct, of some tradition implying something of a quite different nature. An ancient comment on Mark suggests this, indicating that Christ's thought is set not on Judas but on "the Economy[4]," that is, on "the Dispensation" by which the salvation of Man is to be attained through the "delivering up" of Jesus to death In the Pauline Epistles and in the Fourth Gospel, it is the Father, not Judas, who is described as "delivering up," or "giving," the Son for the sake of mankind[5] Moreover the expression "hath drawn near" is

---

[1] Jn xiv 27—31, xvi. 33

[2] Mk xiv 42 ὁ παραδιδούς με ἤγγικεν, Mt xxvi. 46 ἤγγικεν ὁ παραδιδούς με.

[3] In Luke, Christ's last utterance to the disciples is xxii 46 "pray that ye enter not into temptation," parall to Mk xiv 38, Mt xxvi 41.

[4] Cramer on Mk xiv. 41—2 δείκνυσιν ὅτι οὐχὶ τοῦ Ἰουδα ἀλλὰ τῆς οἰκονομίας ἦν. This does not go so far as to deny that Judas was literally παραδιδούς τὸν Ἰησοῦν, but it helps us to understand that the Supreme Himself might be regarded as, in a higher sense, ὁ παραδιδούς.

[5] See Son 3535 "The historical fact as to Christ's predictions of being 'delivered up' appears to be that He used, and repeatedly used, an expression of this kind, but that our Greek gospels, following the LXX, have paraphrased it in such a way as to lead Christians to a misunderstanding of its full meaning"

THE INTERVAL BEFORE THE ARREST

never applied in the New Testament to the approach of a human being, but always to the Kingdom of God, the Day of the Lord, the Presence of the Lord, etc.[1] The negative part of this rule applies also to the perfect tense in LXX where "hath drawn near" may represent the Hebrew "*is near*[2]." A Hebrew or Aramaic original of Mark might refer to God, "He that delivereth me up, the Father, *is near*, therefore let us go forward in His strength to meet the enemy[3]." If that was the original meaning it would accord with the words, peculiar to Matthew, a little later in the parallel context, where Jesus avows His belief that, if He prayed for it, the Father would send Him "twelve legions of angels[4]." It would throw new light on the action—and the disappointment—of Peter if he regarded his Master's utterance as meaning, "The Lord is on our side, let us go forward," and missed the meaning of the context, which implied that the Father Himself was "delivering up" His Son for the salvation of mankind.

We infer that John is here intervening as to Christ's last utterance to His disciples, to shew that Mark, while retaining almost exactly the Lord's actual words, has not expressed their meaning. It was not a cry of sadness or alarm, but a call to action: "He that delivereth me over to death is near me and helping me. Let us go forward through defeat to victory and through death to life."

---

[1] See Mt iii 2, iv. 17 etc., and, outside the Gospels, Rom xiii 12, Jas v 8, 1 Pet iv. 7.

[2] Is lvi. 1 "My salvation [is] *near* to come," Ezek vii 7 "The day [is] *near*," Heb adj קרוב, "near," but LXX ἤγγικε. The pres. ἐγγίζει is also freq. used for Heb. adj. "near."

[3] See *Son* 3329—32   [4] Mt xxvi 53

CHAPTER XI

THE ARREST OF JESUS

[Mark xiv. 43—52]

§ 1. *The Synoptic "multitude" or Johannine "cohort"*

It will be noted, in the parallels given below[1], that Mark and Matthew, when first mentioning "a multitude," say that

---

[1] Mk xiv 43—52 (R V.)

(43) And straightway, while he yet spake, cometh Judas, one of the twelve, and with him a multitude with swords and staves, from the chief priests and the scribes and the elders (44) Now he that betrayed him had given them a token, saying, Whomsoever I shall kiss, that is he, take him, and lead him away safely (45) And when he was come, straightway he came to him, and saith, Rabbi; and kissed him (*lit.* kissed him much) (46) And they laid hands on him, and took him

(47) But a certain one of them that stood by drew his sword, and smote the

Mt xxvi 47—56 (R V)

(47) And while he yet spake, lo, Judas, one of the twelve, came, and with him a great multitude with swords and staves, from the chief priests and elders of the people (48) Now he that betrayed him gave them a sign, saying, Whomsoever I shall kiss, that is he take him (49) And straightway he came to Jesus, and said, Hail, Rabbi, and kissed him (*lit.* kissed him much). (50) And Jesus said unto him, Friend, [do] that for which thou art come. Then they came and laid hands on Jesus, and took him (51) And behold, one of them that were with Jesus stretched out his

Lk. xxii 47—53 (R V)

(47) While he yet spake, behold, a multitude, and he that was called Judas, one of the twelve, went before them, and he drew near unto Jesus to kiss him.

(48) But Jesus said unto him, Judas, betrayest thou the Son of man with a kiss?

(49) And when they that were about him saw what would follow, they said,

THE ARREST OF JESUS

it was "from the chief priests," whereas Luke has nothing but

Mk xiv 43—52 (R V.) *contd.*	Mt. xxvi. 47—56 (R.V.) *contd.*	Lk. xxii 47—53 (R V) *contd.*
servant (*lit* bond-servant) of the high priest, and struck off his ear	hand, and drew his sword, and smote the servant (*lit.* bond-servant) of the high priest, and struck off his ear	Lord, shall we smite with the sword ? (50) And a certain one of them smote the servant (*lit* bond-servant) of the high priest, and struck off his right ear.
	(52) Then saith Jesus unto him, Put up again thy sword into its place · for all they that take the sword shall perish with the sword.	
	(53) Or thinkest thou that I cannot beseech my Father, and he shall even now send me more than twelve legions of angels ?	
	(54) How then should the scriptures be fulfilled, that thus it must be ?	
(48) And Jesus answered and said unto them, Are ye come out, as against a robber, with swords and staves to seize me ?	(55) In that hour said Jesus to the multitudes, Are ye come out as against a robber with swords and staves to seize me ? I sat daily in the temple teaching, and ye took me not.	(52) And Jesus said unto the chief priests, and captains of the temple, and elders, which were come against him, Are ye come out, as against a robber, with swords and staves ?
(49) I was daily with you in the temple teaching, and ye took me not but [this is done] that the scriptures might be fulfilled.	(56) But all this is come to pass, that the scriptures of the prophets might be fulfilled Then all the disciples left him, and fled	(53) When· I was daily with you in the temple, ye stretched not forth your hands against me but this is your hour, and the power of darkness.
(50) And they all left him, and fled		
(51) And a certain young man followed with him, having a linen cloth cast about him, over [his] naked [body] and they lay hold on him,		
(52) But he left the linen cloth, and fled naked		

THE ARREST OF JESUS

"behold, a multitude[1]", but later on, when the three Synoptists tell us what Jesus said to the multitude, Mark and Matthew say it was "to them," or "to the multitudes"; but Luke says "Jesus said unto *the chief priests and captains of the temple and elders that had come against him*[2]" Also Luke in his own words

Jn xviii. 2—11 (R V) Now Judas also, which betrayed him, knew the place for Jesus oft-times resorted thither with his disciples (3) Judas then, having received the band (*or*, cohort) [of soldiers], and officers from the chief priests and the Pharisees, cometh thither with lanterns and torches and weapons. (4) Jesus therefore, knowing all the things that were coming upon him, went forth, and saith unto them, Whom seek ye? (5) They answered him, Jesus of Nazareth Jesus saith unto them, I am [he]. And Judas also, which betrayed him, was standing with them (6) When therefore he said unto them, I am [he], they went backward, and fell to the ground (7) Again therefore he asked them, Whom seek ye? And they said, Jesus of Nazareth (8) Jesus answered, I told you that I am [he] if therefore ye seek me, let these go their way (9) that the word might be fulfilled which he spake, Of those whom thou hast given me I lost not one (10) Simon Peter therefore having a sword drew it, and struck the high priest's servant (*lit* bondservant), and cut off his right ear Now the servant's (*lit* bondservant's) name was Malchus (11) Jesus therefore said unto Peter, Put up the sword into the sheath the cup which the Father hath given me, shall I not drink it?

[1] Mk xiv 43
καὶ εὐθὺς ἔτι αὐτοῦ λαλοῦντος παραγίνεται [ὁ] Ἰούδας εἷς τῶν δώδεκα καὶ μετ' αὐτοῦ ὄχλος μετὰ μαχαιρῶν καὶ ξύλων παρὰ τῶν ἀρχιερέων καὶ τῶν γραμματέων καὶ τῶν πρεσβυτέρων.

Mt xxvi 47
καὶ ἔτι αὐτοῦ λαλοῦντος ἰδοὺ Ἰούδας εἷς τῶν δώδεκα ἦλθεν καὶ μετ' αὐτοῦ ὄχλος πολὺς μετὰ μαχαιρῶν καὶ ξύλων ἀπὸ τῶν ἀρχιερέων καὶ πρεσβυτέρων τοῦ λαοῦ.

Lk xxii 47
ἔτι αὐτοῦ λαλοῦντος ἰδοὺ ὄχλος, καὶ ὁ λεγόμενος Ἰούδας εἷς τῶν δώδεκα προήρχετο αὐτούς, καὶ ἤγγισεν τῷ Ἰησοῦ φιλῆσαι αὐτόν.

[2] Mk xiv. 48
καὶ ἀποκριθεὶς ὁ Ἰησοῦς εἶπεν αὐτοῖς...

Mt. xxvi 55
ἐν ἐκείνῃ τῇ ὥρᾳ εἶπεν ὁ Ἰησοῦς τοῖς ὄχλοις...

Lk. xxii 52
εἶπεν δὲ Ἰησοῦς πρὸς τοὺς παραγενομένους ἐπ' αὐτὸν ἀρχιερεῖς καὶ στρατηγοὺς τοῦ ἱεροῦ καὶ πρεσβυτέρους....

In Luke, Syr Curet omits "that came against him", *b*, *Corb*, *e* have "ad eos. *principibus* (sic)," but *Brix* has "ad eos qui venerant ad eum *a principibus*," *a* has "ad eos...*pontifices*" *Brix* conforms Lk to Mk and Mt, the multitude had come "*from*" the chief priests (but did not *contain* any of them) The *Diatess*, quoting

THE ARREST OF JESUS

tells us at first nothing of what Mark and Matthew have told us about the weapons borne by the multitude, but when he repeats the words of Jesus to "the multitude" he tells us, as Mark and Matthew also do, that Jesus called them "*swords and staves*[1]."

John's account is somewhat ambiguous on some points, as may be seen by comparing the versions given below[2]. But in

---

Lk xxii 52 a, has merely "Jesus said to those that came unto him" (followed by Jn xviii 4 b "whom seek ye?")

[1] Mk xiv 48, Mt. xxvi 55, Lk xxii 52 ὡς ἐπὶ λῃστὴν ἐξήλθατε μετὰ μαχαιρῶν καὶ ξύλων; Mk-Mt + συλλαβεῖν με.

In LXX, ξύλα seldom if anywhere (Gesen 781—2, but see the sing. ξύλον in Is x. 15) means "staves," but often "trees" Mark, however, follows ordinary Greek usage as in Joseph *Bell* ii 9 4 (176) where Pilate mingles his soldiers in a clamorous Jewish crowd "with orders not to use the sword but to strike clamourers with cudgels (ξίφει μὲν χρῆσασθαι κωλύσας, ξύλοις δὲ παίειν τοὺς κεκραγότας ἐγκελευσάμενος)."

This makes it not unlikely that μαχαιρῶν, in Mk's context, may mean not "swords" (which the word would mean in LXX) but large "knives" or "dirks" brought by some who swelled the crowd In literary Gk, μάχαιρα, if a military word, would mostly mean "sabre" Jn avoids any word for sword by using the inclusive term "arms [of heavy-armed soldiers]"

[2] Jn xviii 3 ὁ οὖν Ἰούδας λαβὼν τὴν σπεῖραν καὶ ἐκ τῶν ἀρχιερέων καὶ [ἐκ] τῶν Φαρισαίων ὑπηρέτας ἔρχεται ἐκεῖ μετὰ φανῶν καὶ λαμπάδων καὶ ὅπλων. The order of the words is important, and ἐκ is ambiguous "Judas therefore, having taken the cohort, and—from the chief priests and from the Pharisees—[official] servants, cometh there with lanterns and torches and arms" Here, theoretically, ἐκ might mean "[some] of" Accordingly SS has "Now Judas the betrayer brought with him *a cohort and [some] of the chief priests and Pharisees and guards*, and a multitude of the people carrying lanterns and torches, and came there." Codex *a* has "accepta cohorte *a* principibus sacerdotum et de Pharisaeis ministros (*sic*)," *b* "cum accepisset *a* cohorte et a principibus sacerdotum et Pharisaeis ministros," *Brix* "accepta *cohortem* (sic) militum et quibusdam ex principibus sacerdotum et Pharisaeorum ministris," *e* "cum accepisset cohortem a pontificibus et Pharisaeis ministros" Some of these versions seem to take "ministros," not as a separate class "servants of the temple," but appositionally as meaning "[as] assistants" (comp Acts xiii 5)

Nonnus describes two classes, 1st "a shield-bearing host," received

THE ARREST OF JESUS

any case it describes Judas as receiving "*the cohort*[1]" It also describes Judas as "coming there with lanterns and torches and arms [of war]." "Arms [of war]" might include the Synoptic "swords"' Of "staves" John makes no mention. He appears to emphasize the military aspect of the principal part of the captors of Jesus, afterwards describing them as "*the cohort, and the chiliarch, and the officers of the Jews*[2]."

by Judas, belonging to (*lit* of) the chief-priests, 2nd, an infuriated swarm of followers armed with staves instigated by the "plot-originating" Pharisees —

καὶ στρατὸν ἀσπιστῆρα δεδεγμένος ἀρχιερήων
καὶ πολὺν οἰστρήεντα παρ' ἀρχεκάκων Φαρισαίων
σύνδρομον ἄλλον ἔχων κορυνηφόρον ἐσμὸν ὁδίτην
ἤλυθεν ἀλλοπρόσαλλος ἐς ἠθάδα κῆπον Ἰούδας
τεύχεα καὶ λαμπτῆρας ἔχων.

The termination is strange—Judas (not the soldiers) being described as "having weapons and lights." But this is perhaps to prepare for the following description of the lights, on which see below, p 485, n. 4

Ἀλλοπρόσαλλος (from Homer (*Il* v 831) down to Clem Alex. 24) means "inclining now to one side now to the other" It suggests that Judas was prepared to go over to the side of Jesus at the last moment, if Heaven intervened for Him against the soldiers Compare Jer Targ on Gen xl 27 "And when Nimrod cast Abram into the furnace of fire because he would not worship his idol, and the fire had no power to burn him, Haran's heart became doubtful, saying, *If Nimrod overcome, I will be on his side, but if Abram overcome, I will be on his side*"

[1] "Cohort," σπεῖρα This word is Hebraized (1) (Krauss, p 408 *a*) as ספירה which might be transliterated as *spîrah* or *spîra*, but more freq. (2) with *aleph* prefixed, (*ib* p. 93 *b*) as אספר *aspar*, אספור *aspôr*, or, more correctly, אספיר *aspîr* (besides other variations *ib*. pp. 94, 497, 581). Form (1) might be confused with ספר "scribe"; form (2) with אסף "gather." SS has Mt xxvii. 27 כנשא "gathering," but Mk xv 16 אספיר and sim Jn xviii 3 In Mt. xxvii 27, Palest Syr. has קסטרא, 1 e *castrum*, Walton has אספיר See next note *ad fin.*

[2] Jn xviii 12 Nonnus calls "the chiliarch" φύλαξ ἱεροῖο μελάθρου Χιλιάδος ζαθέης στρατιῆς πρόμος, which indicates that he identifies him with (Acts iv 1 etc) ὁ στρατηγὸς τοῦ ἱεροῦ, the Jewish Captain, or Governor, of the Temple (quite distinct from the Roman Chiliarch in command of the garrison in Antonia)

Chrysostom, however, has a remark indicating that he took "the cohort" to be Roman, and that the Romans were brought into action

THE ARREST OF JESUS

Here we may note that "the cohort" is mentioned by Mark and Matthew later on, in describing how Jesus is regally clothed (in mockery) by "soldiers" (Matthew "the soldiers of the governor") who "call together the *whole of the cohort*", but Luke omits this, having previously described a similar regal clothing and mocking by "Herod with his soldiery[1]." Verbally this is of importance as an instance of Johannine intervention. "*The cohort*" is mentioned by Luke in the Acts[2], along with "the chiliarch," as intervening to suppress a tumult; and therefore Luke must have been familiar with the term as representing the Roman garrison regularly on duty at feast times in the fort Antonia which commanded the Temple. But Luke does not mention it anywhere in the narrative of the Passion. John brings it into prominence and reiterates the term

John's object may be in part symbolical. Luke seems to have desired, by his mention of Herod as well as Pilate, to shew how the two fulfilled the prediction in the Psalms "The kings of the earth set themselves, and the rulers take counsel together,

---

in an irregular way by the Jews (as Roman soldiers are said to have been bribed by the Jews in Mt xxvii 65 "Take a guard," comp *ib* xxviii 11—12) "And how did they persuade the Cohort? They were soldiers, accustomed to do everything for money ($\mathring{a}\nu\delta\rho\epsilon s\ \mathring{\eta}\sigma a\nu\ \sigma\tau\rho a\tau\iota\hat{\omega}\tau a\iota,\ \chi\rho\eta\mu\acute{a}\tau\omega\nu\ \pi o\iota\epsilon\hat{\iota}\nu\ \pi\acute{a}\nu\tau a\ \mu\epsilon\mu\epsilon\lambda\epsilon\tau\eta\kappa\acute{o}\tau\epsilon s$)."

On the Jewish Governor of the Temple see Hastings 1 352 *b* He and his subordinate captains are mentioned only by Luke (xxii 4, 52, Acts iv 1, v 24, 26) In Josephus *Ant* xx 6 2, he is mentioned with the High Priest $\tau o\grave{v}s\ \delta\grave{\epsilon}\ \pi\epsilon\rho\grave{\iota}\ \text{'}A\nu a\nu\acute{\iota}a\nu\ \tau\grave{o}\nu\ \mathring{a}\rho\chi\iota\epsilon\rho\acute{\epsilon}a\ \kappa a\grave{\iota}\ \tau\grave{o}\nu\ \sigma\tau\rho a\tau\eta\gamma\grave{o}\nu$ $\text{"}A\nu a\nu o\nu\ \delta\acute{\eta}\sigma a s$. In 2 Macc iii 4 he is called the $\pi\rho o\sigma\tau\acute{a}\tau\eta s\ \tau o\hat{v}\ \mathring{\iota}\epsilon\rho o\hat{v}$ and is at enmity with the High Priest

In Lk xxii 4 $\tau o\hat{\iota}s\ \sigma\tau\rho a\tau\eta\gamma o\hat{\iota}s$ used absolutely, is rendered by Delitzsch "the governors of the temple," but SS has "the scribes" ספרא, and it has been pointed out in the previous note that a form of "cohort" might be taken as ספר "scribe" In several ways it appears that there might be a confusion between the Roman Chiliarch of the Cohort in Antonia, which overlooked the Temple, and the Jewish Governor of the Guard of the Temple

[1] Mk xv. 16—17, Mt xxvii 27—9, Lk xxiii. 11. This will be discussed later on.

[2] Acts xxi 31 $\tau\hat{\omega}\ \chi\iota\lambda\iota\acute{a}\rho\chi\omega\ \tau\hat{\eta}s\ \sigma\pi\epsilon\acute{\iota}\rho\eta s$. Other "cohorts" are called by special names (*ib.* x. 1, xxvii 1).

THE ARREST OF JESUS

against the Lord and against his Anointed[1]." To John, on

[1] Acts iv 26 οἱ ἄρχοντες συνήχθησαν, quoted from Ps ii 2 and rep in Acts iv 27 Comp Acts iv 5 συναχθῆναι αὐτῶν τοὺς ἄρχοντας. Any mention of a hostile "gathering together" against Christ would recall to Christians the thought of Ps ii 2 More causes than one may have contributed to this Lucan error But one cause is revealed in the following parallels —

Mk xv 16—17	Mt xxvii 27—8	Lk xxiii 11
οἱ δὲ στρατιῶται ἀπήγαγον αὐτὸν ἔσω τῆς αὐλῆς, ὅ ἐστιν πραιτώριον, καὶ συνκαλοῦσιν ὅλην τὴν σπεῖραν καὶ ἐνδιδύσκουσιν αὐτὸν πορφύραν....	τότε οἱ στρατιῶται τοῦ ἡγεμόνος παραλαβόντες τὸν Ἰησοῦν εἰς τὸ πραιτώριον συνήγαγον ἐπ' αὐτὸν ὅλην τὴν σπεῖραν καὶ ἐκδύσαντες (v r ἐνδύσαντες) αὐτὸν χλαμύδα κοκκίνην περιέθηκαν αὐτῷ	ἐξουθενήσας δὲ αὐτὸν (marg +καὶ) ὁ Ἡρῴδης σὺν τοῖς στρατεύμασιν αὐτοῦ καὶ ἐμπαίξας περιβαλὼν ἐσθῆτα λαμπρὰν ἀνέπεμψεν αὐτὸν τῷ Πειλάτῳ.

This is the only place where any of the Synoptists mention "the praetorium," and here Luke omits it The reason is, that he takes it to be a palace of Herod Antipas Luke himself mentions (Acts xxiii 35) "*the praetorium of Herod*" at Caesarea But there was also "*a praetorium of Herod*" in Jerusalem Both were built by Herod the Great, and both served as residences for the Roman Governor See Schurer I ii 48 (referring to Joseph *Bell* ii 14 8 and ii 15 5, Philo ii 589 foll , where, however, both writers use the term "palace," not "praetorium") "The praetorium at Jerusalem, in which Pilate was staying at the time of the trial and condemnation of Jesus Christ (Matt xxvii 27, Mark xv 16, John xviii 28, 33, xix 9), is therefore just the well-known palace of Herod, on the west side of the city "

Luke has read Mark's narrative as follows "The soldiers of Pilate led Jesus [by Pilate's orders] to *the praetorium* [i e *the palace*] *of Herod* [*Antipas*] in Jerusalem Then there was a gathering of the soldiers [wrongly called by Mark 'the whole of the cohort' and better called Herod's armed men]" From this incident he has inferred a reconciliation between Pilate and Herod The whole narrative is non-historical, but it is not fiction It is an antiquarian's mistake This view is suggested in *Joh Voc* **1814** *c*.

John intervenes, mentioning πραιτώριον no less than four times (xviii 28 (*bis*), 33, xix 9) and shewing distinctly that it was Pilate's official residence

A Hebrew word blending the Latin or Greek *palatium* with the Latin or Greek *praetorium* is very freq in Hebrew tradition Krauss (pp 455—6) favours the latter derivation, Levy (iv 50 *b*) the former. But the forms, *paltourin* etc , suggest that the Heb was influenced

THE ARREST OF JESUS

the other hand, writing in later days, Herod Antipas would assuredly seem a poor and insignificant type of a world-ruler or a "king of the earth." Rome as the type of earthly rule over men's bodies, and "the rulers of the Jews" as the type of the Law that claimed dominion over men's souls, would assume supreme importance in their alliance against the Son of God. Yet even while admitting that there is a symbolistic tendency in John's narrative, we may reasonably maintain that some of the symbolistic detail was evolved rather than invented, if we can shew that the Synoptic tradition of the "kiss" and the "sign" of Judas may have been interpreted by John as meaning something quite different in the original tradition

As regards the "sign," it has been suggested in previous volumes that, in Greek tradition, "sign" may have been confused with "ensign" meaning a body of soldiers under one "ensign[1]"; that Luke omitted this as obscure, and that John interpreted it as meaning a "cohort" under a "chiliarch" But only inadequate attempts have been made to explain why John also omits the word "*kiss*," and to investigate what John has, if anything, that corresponds to the Synoptic tradition "Judas betrayed Jesus *with a kiss.*"

The Johannine corresponding statement is, in effect, "Judas betrayed Jesus with *a completely equipped body of heavy-armed soldiers*[2]." To express this he introduces the term "*arms*," *hopla*, not used elsewhere in the Gospels. In canon. LXX it mostly means "shields[3]"; but in literary Greek the plural *hopla* would mostly mean the offensive and defensive arms of a *hoplītēs*,

---

by both the Latin words In Epictet. III 22. 47, the Stoic is said to have no πραιτωρίδιον but only the earth to lie on and a shirt, where there seems to be an allusion to the Latin word "praetorium," used as a term for a magnificent country house (see Lewis and Short).

[1] See *Paradosis* 1365 *a*, *Son* 3260 *b*, suggesting a confusion between σημεῖον and σημαία, "cohort" (Steph *Thes*. VII. 176 c), comp. 3326 *c*.

[2] Jn xviii. 3 μετὰ.. ὅπλων.

[3] Ὅπλον does not occur in the Pentateuch In the historical books it mostly mean "shield." Elsewhere it occasionally means offensive weapons.

THE ARREST OF JESUS

i.e. a heavy-armed soldier[1] Now when the Hebrew noun "arms," *neshek*, is used in this sense as it often is—meaning "military equipment," "weapons"—it is almost identical with the Hebrew noun "*kiss*[2]," and the Hebrew verb "*equip with arms*" is identical with the Hebrew verb "*kiss*[3]."

Nor is this all Even an ordinary reader of John, if he compares his narrative with that of the Synoptists, might well ask why the former takes the trouble to insert that the men had two kinds of lights with them ("lanterns and torches"), whereas the Synoptists mention no lights at all And even those who are accustomed to the long paraphrases of the Fourth Gospel by Nonnus may be reasonably surprised at the extraordinary length of the lantern-torch-paraphrase given below[4].

---

[1] It is freq. used thus in Macc, in which the word is about as freq as in the whole of canon LXX.

[2] Gesen 676 *b* "kiss" נשיקה, "weapons" נשק

[3] Gesen 676 gives נשק vb "equip" as occurring only in 1 Chr xii 2, 2 Chr xvii 17, Ps lxxviii 9—the last, a difficult passage but much commented on in Midrash, which illustrates the three passages by one another In Job xxxix. 21 "to meet *the armed men* (or, *the weapons*) (נשק)" Aq and Theod have ὅπλου

[4] "Lantern," φανός (not in LXX), occurs only here in N T. Chrysostom says that Jesus, "being in the midst [of them], blinded their eyes" miraculously, so that even their "lanterns" did not avail them, till He came forward and spontaneously made them see Him Nonnus, after saying that Judas came τεύχεα καὶ λαμπτῆρας ἔχων, returns to the "lanterns," not mentioning the word but defining the thing in nine lines of astonishing paraphrase —

καὶ ὁμόστολος ἀνὴρ
χερσὶ πολυσπερέεσσι μετάρσιον ἄλλος ἐπ' ἄλλῳ
λύχνων ἐνδομύχων ἀνεμοσκεπὲς ἄγγος ἀείρων,
ἄγγος, ὅπερ δονάκεσσιν ἀμοιβαίοισι συνάπτων
πυκνὰ μεριζομένοισι γέρων κυκλώσατο τέκτων
ἀστερόεν μίμημα καὶ εἴκελον ὀξέι κόσμῳ
μεσσοφανὴς ὅθι λύχνος ὁμοζυγέος διὰ κόλπου
ὀξὺ φάος πολυωπὸν ὑπὸ σκέπας ἔκτοθι πέμπων,
ἀκροφανὲς σελάγιζε πολυσχιδὲς ἀλλόμενον φῶς

One's first impression after reading this, and Wetstein's long note or excursus on the ancient and modern meanings of φανός (first "torch," then "lantern") is, that Nonnus is influenced by nothing but pedantry But a closer study of it indicates that he may be

THE ARREST OF JESUS

Now it happens that the only important passage in Scripture containing this ambiguous word in the form of a verb meaning "*kiss*" or "*arm*" refers to the "children of Ephraim" who "*being armed* and carrying bows, *turned back* in the day of battle[1]" Early Christian poets might apply this to the soldiers who arrested Jesus, whom John calls "the cohort," adding that they "departed back" and "fell to the ground[2]" Though this application is improbable in itself, it is less improbable than that John invented the "falling," and much less improbable than that "the cohort" *did thus actually* "*fall*."

But there is a third meaning of the ambiguous verb, probably incorrect etymologically, but recognised by Ibn Ezra and Rashi[3] This is "kindle" or "burn." A Christian poet might say that the Jews kindled their "lanterns and torches" to seek, and yet not to find, their own Messiah, the Light of the World—walking, as Isaiah said, in the flame of their own fire, only to "lie down in sorrow[4]." Another form of this kindling of lights is found in the Gospel of Peter[5]. Later on we shall come to the "kindling around" of a fire in connection with the temptation and fall of Peter, where poetic influence may be discerned mixed with narrative of fact[6]

The Greek for "lantern" is a Hebraized word, very frequent in Hebrew tradition, and occasionally used in Aramaic, occurring

suggesting a simile, likening the Jews with their lanterns, seeking the Light of the World, to a human lantern, sheltering from the wind a frail rush-light, "mimicking the stars and likening itself to the (?) swiftly-moving (ὀξέι) Cosmos" 'Οξύς might be an epithet of "fire" or "sun," etc , but I have not found it as an epithet of κόσμος

[1] Ps. lxxviii. 9.   [2] Jn xviii 7

[3] See Ps lxxviii. 21, Is xliv 15, on which Ibn Ezra says "יָשִׁיק, He kindleth it   Comp נִשְׂקָה 'was kindled' (Ps lxxviii 21)" *Oxf Conc* καίειν, ἀνάπτειν, takes the same view (see also *Oxf Conc.* Index to Ben Sira, ἐκκαίειν)   Gesen 969 b takes יָשִׁיק as from שָׁלַק

[4] Is. l. 11 "Ye that kindle a fire...ye shall lie down in sorrow"

[5] *Evang Petr* § 5 (ed J Armitage Robinson, D D.) περιήρχοντο δὲ πολλοὶ μετὰ λύχνων νομίζοντες ὅτι νύξ ἐστιν, ἔπεσάν τε (for ἐπέσαντο) On this the Editor says "Comp Isa lix 10 καὶ πεσοῦνται ἐν μεσημβρίᾳ ὡς ἐν μεσονυκτίῳ. It also seems an echo of Jn xviii 3, 6 ἔρχεται ἐκεῖ μετὰ φανῶν καὶ λαμπάδων...καὶ ἔπεσαν χαμαί"

[6] See *Son* 3369 *a—e*.

THE ARREST OF JESUS

in a story that Vespasian kindled lanterns, by way of omen, for Rome, Alexandria, and Jerusalem, and found that only the lantern for Jerusalem would burn—a prophecy of its destruction by fire[1].

Returning to the Johannine use of the term "cohort," not after the arrest of Jesus (as in Mark and Matthew[2]) but before, we conclude that the evidence of Hebraic influence as to other words in the context strengthens the hypothesis of Hebrew influence as to this particular word. In Greek, a "cohort," if taken exactly, would have meant some six hundred men, an impossible number here, but the above-mentioned Hebraized *spîra*, *aspîr* or *aspâr*, might be used loosely for any body of Roman soldiers from a maniple to a legion[3]. The Hebrew word is variously spelt, and might be confused with other Hebrew words meaning (1) "a mixed crowd, or collection of people," (2) "guards," (3) "scribes[4]." Luke gives us the impression that the crowd was of this mixed nature[5].

The evidence indicates that John is almost certainly wrong, and that he should have mentioned the Jewish guard of the Temple. But, so far from inventing, he appears to be taking great pains to follow ancient tradition—interpreted by him in

---

[1] See Levy iv 65 *b* on פנס *i.e.* φανός

[2] Mk xv 16, Mt. xxvii. 27

[3] See Krauss p 93, Levy 1 129 *b*. Krauss p. 408 *a* calls it *manipulus*.

[4] See above, p. 481, n 1; אסא means "collect," and אסופות (Gesen. 63 and Levy 1 127) "learned assemblies," "assemblies of the wise"; אספסף (Gesen *ib*) = (Numb xi 4) a collection or rabble of the camp-followers (comp Nonn ἐσμὸν ὁδίτην) attending Hebrews at the Exodus. Curet and SS have the form אספרא for "captains" in Lk xxii 4.

Mention may also be made of the word σπαθάριος, אספתרין (Levy 1 130 "satelles qui spatham seu ensem gestaret") connected with (*Lev r* on Lev iv 3, Wu p 35) Shebna (Is xxii 15) the "*treasurer* (or, *steward*)" who is "over the house (*i e* the Temple)," called elsewhere (Is xxxvi 3) "*the scribe*" Lev *r*. says he was chosen "the *chief of the spatharii*" "zum obersten Spateltrager," κόμης σπαθάριος

[5] That is to say Luke in his second mention of the crowd (xxii 52) when he no longer calls it ὄχλος (as in xxii 47) but defines its component parts.

487 (Mark xiv 43—52)

THE ARREST OF JESUS

accordance with a version that happened to suit a magniloquent symbolism which represented Christ's captors as "falling on the ground."

§ 2. *The words and acts of Jesus during the arrest*

Mark represents Jesus as having uttered nothing to Judas on any occasion[1], and nothing to anyone on this occasion except the words (above quoted) "As against a robber have ye come out with swords and staves to seize me?" followed by "I was daily with you...and ye took me not; but—that the scriptures might be fulfilled[2]." From the last part of this Luke seriously differs—a difference discussed elsewhere, as to which John seems to take the Marcan view[3].

But a more important difference relates to the Johannine account of the acts of Jesus, which describes Him as not waiting to have Himself pointed out by the kiss of Judas, but coming out in front of the disciples of His own accord and saying "Whom seek ye?" and avowing that He is Jesus of Nazareth, and finally saying "If therefore ye seek me, let these go[4]." In this story, Judas, instead of rushing forward and (ostentatiously) "kissing[5]" Jesus so as to reveal Him to the soldiers,

---

[1] John represents Jesus as having said to Judas (xiii 27) "What thou doest do more quickly," some time before the arrest Judas is also addressed by Jesus in the Anointing at Bethany (xii 7 ἄφες, sing.) Mt xxvi 50, Lk. xxii 48 represent Jesus as addressing Judas at the moment of the arrest

[2]
Mk xiv. 49	Mt xxvi 55 b—56 a	Lk xxii 53
καθ' ἡμέραν ἤμην πρὸς ὑμᾶς ἐν τῷ ἱερῷ διδάσκων καὶ οὐκ ἐκρατήσατέ με· ἀλλ' ἵνα πληρωθῶσιν αἱ γραφαί	καθ' ἡμέραν ἐν τῷ ἱερῷ ἐκαθεζόμην διδάσκων καὶ οὐκ ἐκρατήσατέ με τοῦτο δὲ ὅλον γέγονεν ἵνα πληρωθῶσιν αἱ γραφαὶ τῶν προφητῶν	καθ' ἡμέραν ὄντος μου μεθ' ὑμῶν ἐν τῷ ἱερῷ οὐκ ἐξετείνατε τὰς χεῖρας ἐπ' ἐμέ ἀλλ' αὕτη ἐστὶν ὑμῶν ἡ ὥρα καὶ ἡ ἐξουσία τοῦ σκότους

[3] See *Law* pp. 146—7 where it is maintained that Mark's *aposiopesis* represents the original, and that John favoured this idiom (*Joh Gr*. 2105—11).

[4] Jn xviii 8.

[5] Mk xiv 45, Mt xxvi 49 κατεφίλησεν, Lk xxii 47 φιλῆσαι. Καταφιλέω means "kiss passionately," but here perhaps "kissed and

THE ARREST OF JESUS

"stands" back at first along with them, and then recoils in awe along with them when they all "fall on the ground[1]"

Two courses are here open to a reasonable reader. He may either (1) put the whole of John's account aside as a pure invention, or (2) take some trouble (and there is need of a great deal) in attempting to put himself into the Evangelist's position. If he decides on the latter, then he must begin by asking what modifications in the traditional narrative John would necessarily make if he interpreted the Synoptic "kiss" as meaning "armed men" or "arms." Luke, alone of the Synoptists, describes Judas as *drawing near to Jesus "to kiss him"*—whereas Mark and Matthew insert a salutation between the "coming" and the "kissing." In Luke's sentence—the hypothetical Johannine equivalent, "*soldiers*," being substituted for "*kiss*"—a very slight change would convert the words into "*There drew near Jesus to the soldiers*[2]." Why did He "draw near to the soldiers"? To intercede with them (it might be replied) that they might "permit" the disciples "to depart[3]."

This view supposes the intercession ("permit") to be purely inferential—a Johannine attempt to supply what Jesus said when He thus stepped forward in front of the disciples. But John may have had some textual basis for it. For Luke has an imperative "*permit*" attributed to Jesus in the parallel

---

embraced" so that Jesus was detained by the embrace. Philo distinguishes (1. 480) καταφίλημα from "a true kiss (γνησίου φιλήματος)," and says (1. 478) " As [the word] *horse* ((h)*ippos*) is not in *pouch* (*mars-*ippos) so *phílein* is not in *cata-phílein*"—a strong thing to say, but instructive as indicating the dislike that would be felt by a writer of literary Greek to use the word as Mark uses it.

[1] Jn xviii. 5—6 "And Judas also ... was standing with them. When therefore ... they went backward and fell to the ground." "They" appears to include "Judas"—unless we suppose him to be alone still standing while the soldiers go back and fall on the ground.

[2] According to this Johannine view, Lk xxii. 47 προσήρχετο αὐτούς was misplaced and misapplied. Lk applied it to Judas "going before" the multitude, but it should have been applied to Jesus "going before" His disciples.

[3] Jn xviii. 8 ἄφετε τούτους ὑπάγειν.

THE ARREST OF JESUS

context[1]. It is very variously interpreted and very difficult[2]. Codex *b* has two renderings, one of which is "*Permit this man [to go]*[3]." The tradition that originated this may very well have been rendered by John "*Permit these men [to go]*"

It happens that the Greek word for "*permit*" here used by Luke is identical, in some forms, with the Greek word for "*heal*[4]." And this may help to explain the very great difficulty that Luke, at this point, relates a miraculous "healing" of a man struck by the sword of one of Christ's followers, which is omitted by the other three Evangelists. Another possible cause of confusion is the imperative "*permit*," which may sometimes mean "Hold!" "Let be!" "Enough!" In that sense, it might be addressed to the striker of the blow[5]. These

---

[1] Lk xxii 51 ἐᾶτε. In NT ἐάω occurs only in Lk and Acts, apart from Mt xxiv 43, 1 Cor x 13. Lk iv 41 εἴα is parall to Mk i 34 ἤφιεν. We may assume that the original of Luke's ἐᾶτε would be, in most Greek Christian tradition, ἄφετε (which LXX has in Dan iv 15 (12) agst Theod ἐάσατε).

[2] Lk xxii 51, SS "enough as far as this (man)," Walton Syr. "satis est ad hanc usque rem [processisse]." The Latin vss (except Vulg and *Brix* and *d* "sinite") have "sine."

[3] "Respondens autem Jesus dixit *Dimitte eum*. Et tetigit aurem ejus et sanavit eum. Ait autem Jesus *Sine usque hoc*."

[4] See 3 Macc v 18 τίνος ἕνεκεν αἰτίας ἰάθησαν (so Swete) οἱ Ἰουδαῖοι. This, taken by itself, would mean "the Jews *were healed*." But it means "*were permitted* (v r εἰάθησαν) to survive (περιβεβιωκότες)." The passive is rare, but occurs in Clem Rom § 55 ᾐτήσατο (Judith) ..ἐαθῆναι αὐτὴν ἐξελθεῖν. Such a phrase as ᾐτήσατο [τοῦ] ἐαθῆναι [v r ἰαθῆναι], meaning "that the disciples might be permitted [to depart]," might be confused with a request "with a view to healing."

[5] See *Son* 3353 (iv) *f* foll on *aphès* (ἄφες) as "a Greek word adopted into late Hebrew, and ambiguous in Greek as well as in Hebrew, since it might mean 'dismiss,' or 'let go,' or 'permit,'" and quoting Mk xv 36 ἄφετε, parall to Mt xxvii 49 ἄφες as illustrating "the Aramaicized *aphès*, being of the nature of an exclamation, and not a sing imperative." A feeling of this kind may perhaps explain the Latin *sine*, for *sinite*, in almost all the Latin versions of Lk. xxii 51.

Jesus may have uttered two brief phrases, one, addressed to His disciples, the other to His own heart, or to the Father. The first may have been ἄφες "Have done!" or "Enough!" the second "How long!" ἕως τοῦ, Comp Is vi 11, and see below, p 493.

THE ARREST OF JESUS

facts combine to shew that the Johannine tradition "*Permit these men to go,*" though it may be non-historical, is not a fiction. It is much more likely to be historical than is the Lucan hypothesis, that Jesus said to the soldiers "Permit me [to step] as far as this [wounded man]"

In the parallel context Matthew and Luke severally record last utterances of Jesus to Judas[1]. The first mentions the traitor's real purpose "*That for which thou art come*", the second mentions the pretence, "a kiss." A commentary on Luke attributed to Apolinarius connects the two thus "He [*i e.* Jesus] shewed to Judas—lest he should suppose himself undetected—that He does not receive him on the assumption of the friendship that he pretends by the *kiss*, but [as coming] for *the purpose for which he has come* and [*which*] *he desires to accomplish*[2]." A last utterance of Jesus to Judas—somewhat similar in thought to the one in Matthew, though different in expression—is placed by John at an earlier moment, "*That which thou art doing do more quickly*[3]." John himself admits that this was misunderstood by the disciples; and such an admission may very well explain variations and transpositions in the accounts of Christ's other words and deeds on that night of disturbance and distraction.

Passing to the details of the account of the wounding of the High Priest's servant and to the sequel, we find that Mark, alone of the four Evangelists, records no consequent utterance of Jesus[4]. Matthew records a command to the striker to sheathe the sword, and a rebuke, and a saying about "twelve legions of

---

Since Mark systematically omits many of the sayings of Jesus, on which Matthew and Luke expatiate, he may have not unnaturally omitted these two or three obscure words, perhaps taking them as a mere reproach, introducing Christ's next words "[Shame on you!] Do ye come out as against a robber?"

[1] Mt xxvi. 50, Lk xxii 48
[2] See Cramer on Lk xxii 48 Ἔδειξε δὲ αὐτῷ...ὅτι οὐκ ἐπὶ τούτῳ αὐτὸν δέχεται...ἀλλ' ἐπ' ἐκεῖνο, ἐφ' ὅπερ ἥκει καὶ βούλεται τοῦ (? leg. τοῦτο) ἐπιτελέσαι. Either ὅτι or ὅπερ must be repeated before βούλεται. If it were ὅτι, then the meaning would be that Jesus desired the accomplishment.
[3] Jn xiii 27   [4] Mk xiv. 47

THE ARREST OF JESUS

angels," who would attend the Son if the Son desired it of the Father[1]. Luke records the saying (above quoted) about "permitting," and also an act—a miracle of healing[2]. John combines a command to sheathe the sword with the words "The cup that the Father hath given me, (R V) shall I not drink it[3]?" an utterance resembling that which the Synoptists place earlier, before the arrival of the soldiers

Reviewing the evidence, we may reasonably conclude that Mark is on this occasion in error, having omitted some very brief utterance of Jesus—which he found obscure, not only because it was brief, but also because he misunderstood the circumstances that elicited it His text, as has been shewn in a previous volume, favours the view that Mark regarded the blow as accidentally struck by one of Christ's enemies, not by a disciple[4]. In Mark, the wounding of the servant is introduced with a "but," which may very well imply a parenthesis to this effect "So they laid hands on Jesus and held him fast (But [I should have said that, in the general confusion] one of the men on duty[5], having hastily drawn his sword[6], cut off the ear

---

[1] Mt xxvi 52—3 [2] Lk xxii 51
[3] Jn xviii 11, see above, p 459 foll
[4] See *Corrections* 479—81
[5] "Men on duty" See *Corrections* 479 quoting many instances of παρεστηκότες including Mk xv 35, 39
[6] Mk xiv 47 σπασάμενος τὴν μάχαιραν, "having drawn *the sword [by his side]*" could not mean "having drawn *a knife*" See *Corrections* 480 Lk xxii 36—8 indicates that there happened to be "two swords," and no more, among the whole of the disciples Jn xviii 10 ("Simon Peter *having a sword*") implies that the "having" was casual

As regards Mt xxvi 51 ἀπέσπασεν, Matthew's context indicates that he took it to mean "*drew* his sword", but the conclusion arrived at in *Corrections* 481 *a* is that a Greek writer, "so far as LXX and Hemsterhuys (on Lucian *Deor Dial* xx 5) enable us to judge," could not rightly use the active of ἀποσπᾶν in this sense In Goodspeed it always means "tear or, draw away" To this must be added the negative evidence of Steph *Thes*, and of Wetstein (who illustrates Mark's use of σπασάμενος—but not Matthew's use of ἀπέσπασεν, which ought to mean "he wrested a sword" out of some one's hand)

THE ARREST OF JESUS

of the servant of the high priest) And Jesus said unto them, Are ye come out as against a robber...?"

Let us suppose that the words omitted by Mark verbally resembled those preserved here by Luke, "*Thus far*," but differed in thought, being really "*How far!*" i.e. "*How long!*" an exclamation elsewhere imputed to Jesus by all the Synoptists[1] We may suppose it to have been used absolutely as it is sometimes in Scripture[2] If so, it would seem to have been —or to have been in part—an exclamation of spiritual rebuke because His disciples had misunderstood Him According to Luke, Jesus had just told them to "buy a sword[3]" If so, they were now taking Him at His word and using "a sword" In any case, they were disobeying the spirit of His general doctrine. The sense of failure might make Him exclaim "How long!"

But this would not be clear to those who did not realise Christ's lifelong aim and object, and His sense (at the moment) of failing to attain it. Matthew interprets the words as merely rebuking a resort to the arm of the flesh, like the rebuke in Jeremiah "Cursed is the man that trusteth in man and maketh flesh his arm[4]"; and he represents Jesus as going on to use language about the legions of God similar to that in Chronicles "With us is the Lord our God to help us and to fight our battles[5]" He also makes it clear (though not consistently[6]) that the sword was wielded by "one of those with Jesus," whom Jesus bids, in language resembling that of Ezekiel, to "cause it [i e the sword] to return to its place[7]"

---

[1] Mk ix 19 (*bis*), Mt xvii 17 (*bis*), Lk ix 41 "*How long* shall I be with you...?"

[2] Is. vi. 11, Hab ii. 6, Ps vi 3, xc 13 (עַד מָתַי), also Numb. xxiv 22 (עַד מָה) (Gesen 607 *b*, 554 *a*).

[3] Lk. xxii 36.

[4] Jerem xvii. 5. [5] Mt xxvi 53—4, 2 Chr xxxii 8.

[6] Mt xxvi 51 ἀπέσπασεν should have been ἐσπάσατο, but Matthew appears to have combined a tradition (1) about a man "drawing (ἐσπάσατο)" his own sword, τὴν μάχαιραν αὐτοῦ, with another (2) about a man "wresting away (ἀπέσπασε)" some one else's sword.

[7] Mt. xxvi. 52 ἀπόστρεψον τὴν μάχαιράν σου εἰς τὸν τόπον αὐτῆς, comp. Ezek. xxi. 5 "I have drawn forth my sword out of its sheath, it shall not *return* any more," ἐξέσπασα τὸ ἐγχειρίδιόν μου ἐκ τοῦ κολεοῦ

THE ARREST OF JESUS

Luke, according to our hypothesis of an original tradition containing *"how long,"* decides to render it literally, with a slight alteration converting *"As far as what?"* into *"As far as this!"* meaning *"As far as this [person]¹!"* Hence he infers that Jesus asked that He should be *"allowed"* to go *"as far as this [person]"* in order to heal him. It has been shewn above that, in Greek, *"to be healed"* may be identical with *"to be allowed²"* Besides this identity, the *"restoring (or, causing to return) to its place,"* which Matthew connects with a *"sword,"* is capable of being connected with the severed *"ear."* Luke appears to have thus connected it. This explains not only why Luke *inserts a restoration of the ear to its place*, but also why he *omits the command to restore the sword to its place*. He appears to have confused the two, and to have substituted the former for the latter.

As regards the command to sheathe the sword John follows Matthew, but substitutes "sheath" for "place."

The exclamation "How long!" may seem to some hardly appropriate for the Saviour at such a moment. On an earlier

---

αὐτοῦ, οὐκ ἀποστρέψει οὐκέτι and *ib* 30 *"cause it to return* to its sheath," LXX simply ἀπόστρεφε, omitting "to its sheath " Mt has τόπος for κολεός.

¹ The Heb "How long?" used absolutely in aposiopesis (Gesen. 554 *a*, 607 *b*), though mostly rendered by LXX ἕως πότε; is rendered in Hab ii 6 ἕως τίνος, If a Greek tradition gave τοῦ; for τίνος, the rarity of this use of τοῦ might induce Luke to amend it into τούτου It occurs in Soph *Oed Col* 412 κλύουσα τοῦ λέγεις, where it is emphatic, as it would be also here

This hypothesis suggests an explanation of the tradition, peculiar to Luke (xxii 49), that "those round Jesus seeing what was going to happen said, 'Lord, shall we strike with the sword?'" It may have sprung from one of many attempts to explain *"Lord, how long?"* on the supposition that it was uttered by the disciples *"How long, O Lord, shall we stand idle?* Wilt thou that we strike with the sword?"

² See above, p 490, n 4. In Ps xlvi 11 "be still (הרפו)," LXX σχολάσατε, Sym ἐάσατε, Aq has ἰάθητε. This might seem to be for ἐάθητε, but Aq appears to have identified רפה, "be slack," with רפא, "heal," as LXX does in Job xii 21 "slackeneth," LXX ἰάσατο.

THE ARREST OF JESUS

occasion, just before the healing of the demoniac, who could not be healed by His disciples because of their want of faith[1]—with His disciples behind Him, ashamed of their want of success, and the hostile crowd before Him exulting in their failure—it might seem intelligible that He should exclaim, "O faithless generation, *How long shall I be with you?*" But here, where Jesus is on the point of being taken away from His disciples, and from His enemies too, into the region of death, this meaning of the cry seems less applicable.

Possibly it has a further application "*How long!*" occurs several times in psalmodic or prophetic exclamations, half questioning, half expostulating, concerning the delay of the Lord to put forth His arm to redeem His people But there is one passage in Isaiah where it is more a question than an expostulation, and where the prophet sees revealed to him, in a vision, the glory of the Lord, and his own failure to make that glory clear to the blind people around him, and to make them see the terrible and desolating punishment impending on their blindness As the outcome of all, in reply to his question "Lord, *how long?*" he receives the reply "Until cities be waste without inhabitant, and houses without man, and the land become utterly waste, and the Lord have removed men far away, and the forsaken places be many in the midst of the land[2]."

Now all the Synoptists agree that Jesus, early in His career, quoted (freely) the preceding words in this passage of Isaiah ("hear ye indeed, but understand not") in order to illustrate His own failure to teach the truth to a large part of His countrymen[3], and John also quotes the words toward the close of his account of Christ's public teaching to shew how and why that teaching failed to reach many to whom it was directed[4].

We ought not therefore to dismiss hastily the suggestion that Jesus, in the moment when He became a prisoner, quoted, from the same prophecy, this passionate appeal For in that moment there had arrived that crisis which He had anticipated

---

[1] Mk ix. 19, Mt. xvii. 17, Lk ix 41.
[2] Is vi 11—12.
[3] Mk iv. 12, Mt. xiii. 13, 15, Lk. viii. 10. [4] Jn xii. 40.

and feared He had divided His countrymen. He had brought "not peace but a sword[1]." In that moment He saw cities in Palestine "waste without inhabitant" and men "removed far away" by the Roman conquerors. Nor can we conceive that it was possible for Him not to have seen in the blow struck by Peter a prospect of evil for His own followers and a temporary triumph for "the ruler of this world." For their sakes, therefore, as well as for the sake of His own countrymen, and for the cause of truth, Jesus might exclaim "*How long!*" It was not an exclamation of faithlessness. On the contrary, Hebrew precedent and Jewish tradition stamped it as implying belief in ultimate deliverance, since "*how long?*" in the mouth of a Prophet or Psalmist of Israel, implied the conviction "not for ever."

§ 3 "*They all left him,*" *in Mark*

If Mark had not added "and fled," we might, by a somewhat unnatural though grammatical rendering of the verb "leave," or "let go," have interpreted him as meaning that all the guards "*left their hold* on" Jesus; as in the Acts it is said that the centurion and his men "departed from Paul" when they were on the point of scourging him, and that the chief-captain "was afraid[2]." That fear was caused by the question "Is it lawful for you to scourge a man that is a Roman?" In the case of Jesus, fear might be regarded as caused, at all events for a few moments, by something in His presence and address. And it will be seen that John takes this view:—

Mk xiv 50	Mt. xxvi 56	Lk xxii 53—4	Jn xviii 6
And they (*i.e.* the disciples) all left him and fled	Then the disciples all left him and fled	Omits	They (*i.e.* the soldiers) went away backward and fell to the ground[3].

---

[1] Mt x 34, comp Lk xii 51.
[2] Acts xxii 25—9
[3] Mk xiv. 50   Mt. xxvi 56   Jn xviii 6
καὶ ἀφέντες αὐτὸν   τότε οἱ μαθηταὶ   ἀπῆλθαν εἰς τὰ ὀπίσω
ἔφυγον πάντες   [marg +αὐτοῦ] πάντες   καὶ ἔπεσαν χαμαί
                   ἀφέντες αὐτὸν ἔφυγον.

THE ARREST OF JESUS

Matthew, by inserting "disciples," suggests that perhaps he feared lest, without such an insertion, some might interpret the original of Mark's phrase as "[the soldiers] *letting him go.*" Luke has, at this point, a tradition peculiar to himself, that Jesus said to the guards, in effect, "*Suffer me [to go] as far as this wounded man*" and that this request was granted. If therefore he had inserted anything in his own person about "letting go" it would probably have been "*And they* [i.e. *the guards*] *suffered him [to go].*" But he does not contradict Mark and Matthew by inserting their own word—"*leave*" or "*let-go*"—in so different a context[1].

Instead of the ambiguous word "*left*" in Mark and Matthew, John has "they went away backward." But this, too, is ambiguous. For it might mean either "the disciples turned back from following" or "the soldiers fell back from seizing." Mark adds "*They fled.*" This is no longer ambiguous. The parallel John adds "and fell on the ground." This, too, is not ambiguous. But "*fled*" and "*fell*" might both be derived from an original Hebrew "fall," meaning "*fall away*" or "*desert.*" This is thrice rendered by "*flee*" in LXX, though Aquila and Symmachus would render it by "*fall*" or "*desert*[2]." There appears to be sometimes in "fall" a meaning antithetical to "*stand*" in the sense of "stand fast," so that "fall" means, not "*fall* on the field of battle," but "*fall off* (or *fail*)"—as in Paul's saying "To his own master he [i.e. the servant] standeth or *falleth*[3]." And the Epistle to the Hebrews seems to play on the physical and the spiritual meaning of the word when it first

---

[1] For ἀφίημι meaning "*let go* a captive," see 2 Chr xxviii 14, 1 Macc xiii 16, 19. Luke (xxii 51) uses ἐάω.

[2] See Jerem xxxvii 13, 14, xxxviii 19, LXX φεύγω. In Jerem. xxxix 9 "*those that fell away* (R V. *the deserters*) that *fell away* to him," LXX is missing. In 2 K xxv. 11 A V. "*the fugitives* (R V. those that fell away) that fell away to the king of Babylon," the renderings vary, but LXX repeats ἐμπίπτειν. It is used absol. in 1 S xxix 3 ("he [David] *fell away* [from Saul]," LXX ἐνέπεσεν πρὸς μέ, Vulg. "deserted to me"). In Jerem xxxvii 13 LXX φεύγεις Aq. has πίπτεις, Sym αὐτομολεῖς (sim xxxviii. 19).

[3] Rom. xiv 4

A F   497 (Mark xiv. 43—52)   32

THE ARREST OF JESUS

reminds us of faithless Israel "whose *limbs fell* in the wilderness" and then adds the warning "that no man *fall* after the same example of disobedience[1]." There appears to be an underlying thought of "*falling away*" from the Lord

Let us suppose that there were early differences of opinion about Christ's warning to the disciples, expressed by Mark and Matthew in the words "Ye all *shall stumble*[2]." It is supported by a prophecy. But the prophecy (from Zechariah, "the sheep shall be *scattered*") mentions not "stumbling," but "scattering[3]" Mark and Matthew might regard it as being fulfilled when the disciples scattered in flight, falling away from their Master[4]. But there is a want of verbal correspondence between the prediction of Zechariah and that of Jesus.

Luke omits the prediction about "stumbling" in his parallel to Mark. Probably here (as elsewhere) Luke takes a more serious view than Mark does of the nature of "stumbling[5]" He has inserted a prediction of the same kind, but he uses a different metaphor—that of Satan "sifting" the disciples[6]. It is perhaps for these reasons that he omits the Marcan tradition here, about the flight of the disciples.

In these circumstances we might naturally anticipate that John would intervene And he appears to do so, as regards both the "scattering" and the "stumbling." As to the "scattering," he represents Jesus as saying "Ye shall be *scattered*...and shall leave me alone, and [yet] I am not alone, because the Father is with me[7]." This, when fulfilled, fulfils the prophecy "the sheep shall be scattered," omitted by Luke As to the "stumbling," the Fourth Gospel intervenes in two ways. First, Jesus says to the disciples "These things have I spoken unto you that ye may *not stumble*[8]," thus contradicting Mark and Matthew in the letter—though not in the spirit—by saying that, in the more serious sense of "stumbling so as to fall," the disciples would *not* "*stumble*"

---

[1] Heb iii 17, iv 11 [2] Mk xiv 27, Mt xxvi 31
[3] Zech. xiii. 7 [4] Mk xiv. 50, Mt xxvi 56, Lk om.
[5] See *Law* p. 127. [6] Lk xxii. 31.
[7] Jn xvi. 32. [8] Jn xvi. 1.

THE ARREST OF JESUS

But while thus deprecating for the Eleven the destiny of "stumbling so as to fall," John might naturally have in view the contrast between them and Judas, whose "stumbling" was to end in "falling," according to the words of the Psalmist, "When evil-doers came upon me (LXX draw near against me) to eat up my flesh, [even] mine adversaries and my foes, they stumbled and fell[1]." From this Psalm Origen quotes when commenting on the words of Jesus to Judas "What thou doest, do more quickly." He apparently believes that Judas fulfilled this prophecy. Fresh from a profane "eating of the flesh" of Jesus, and joining himself with His "adversaries and foes," Judas became one of those who "stumbled and fell[2]." Origen's comment on the Johannine passage mentioning the "falling" is not extant; but his remarks help us to understand how John might have been influenced by the Psalm in question so as to introduce a detail about "stumbling," in connection with Christ's arrest. It is very different, in fact, from anything in the older Gospels; but, in word, it appears capable of being extracted from a new interpretation of old Christian traditions in the light of Hebrew poetry.

---

[1] Ps. xxvii 2 Note that in Jn xviii. 6 "to the ground," χαμαί, might be added by John to (Ps xxvii 2) ἔπεσαν as it is by LXX in Dan ii 46 There, the LXX adds it merely for emphasis Here, in an obscure tradition, John might desire to make the meaning clear (not "fell away," but literally "fell flat on the ground").

[2] Orig Lomm ii 456 quoting Jn xiii 27 In the context, Origen says "I think also that the 26th (Heb 27th) Psalm is uttered as a prophecy on the part of the Saviour in connection with the season of His Passion, and in the moment when the evil one with all the soldiers of his host was contending against Him, for when He saw them arming themselves against Him,...He says (Ps. xxvii 1—3 (LXX)) 'The Lord is my light ..in this do I hope'" Origen's own words, πανστρατεί and ὁπλιζομένους, together with some of those quoted (παρατάξηται, παρεμβολή, and πόλεμος) give a military aspect to the passage which accords with the Johannine mention of (xviii 12) "the cohort and the chiliarch"

THE ARREST OF JESUS

§ 4. "*A certain young man*," *in* Mark[1]

If this story is to be taken literally, it is necessary to ask why Mark mentions this "young man" at all, without telling us more about him; why Matthew and Luke do not mention him, and how it came to pass that on a cold night—for we know that it was cold[2]—the man was wearing nothing but a light linen garment in the open air. If it is to be taken metaphorically, then the linen garment is like that mentioned in Revelation, "Buy of me *white garments*...that the shame of thy nakedness be not made manifest," "Blessed is he that watcheth and *keepeth his garments*," "*The fine linen* is the righteous acts of the saints[3]." In that case, the narrative suggests that this young man did *not* "watch and keep his garments," but failed in the moment of trial. He "began to follow[4]," in the procession, but was seized. Then, instead of imitating Jesus, he extricated himself from the guards and fled, leaving his "linen garment" in their hands. He had no other clothing. Now therefore he was "naked." This would be a brief poetic summary of that which befell Peter at this crisis. No one of the disciples went so far in courage at the moment. No one fell so low in the sequel.

How, if at all, does John intervene as to the story of this "follower" of Christ, left "naked"? On the supposition that it is Peter, we may reply that perhaps he intervenes later on, after the Resurrection, dramatically and supplementarily, in a positive instead of negative way. Mark shews us the *unclothing* of Peter. John shews us the *reclothing*. With the exception of Matthew's parable about good works including the clothing of the "*naked*[5]," the word "*naked*" occurs nowhere

---

[1] Mk xiv. 51—2 καὶ νεανίσκος τις συνηκολούθει αὐτῷ περιβεβλημένος σινδόνα ἐπὶ γυμνοῦ, καὶ κρατοῦσιν αὐτόν, ὁ δὲ καταλιπὼν τὴν σινδόνα γυμνὸς ἔφυγεν.

It seems as if Mark meant, "I have said 'they all *fled*'. But that was not quite true. One did not at first '*flee*'. He began to follow in the crowd, but in the end he, too, '*fled*'—naked, and leaving his linen garment behind him."

[2] Jn xviii. 18, and see Mk xiv. 54

[3] Rev. iii. 18, xvi. 15, xix. 8

[4] Mk xiv. 51 συνηκολούθει

[5] Mt. xxv. 36—44

THE ARREST OF JESUS

in the Gospels except in this passage of Mark, and in that passage of the Fourth Gospel which describes the eager return of the penitent Peter to the Master whom he had denied: "When Simon Peter heard that it was the Lord, he girt his coat about him—*for he was naked*—and cast himself into the sea[1]." The word for "*coat*," *ependūtēs*, confirms the impression that the Evangelist is writing symbolically It is used by Aquila to represent "*ephod*[2]." In the New Testament it occurs nowhere except in this Petrine story The earliest Christian writers never use it; but Tatian uses a similar word, *ependūma*, to describe immortality as the robe that is the *overclothing* of mortality[3]

In concluding this comparison between Mark and John as to their traditions about "nakedness," it may be well to point out that there is also a noteworthy similarity of word, along with dissimilarity of context, in their uses of the word rendered in John "*standing by*" a little later on: "One of the officers, *standing by*, struck Jesus with the palm of his hand[4]." It means, literally, "*one that stands by the side of*," i.e "*attends on*." Lucian, using this word, describes Hermes as "*attendant on* Zeus" and "*attendant on* the law-court[5]" Now in Mark we

---

[1] Jn xxi. 7.

[2] See *Notes* 2999 (xvii) *m—n* "Jn's unique use of ἐπενδύτης (xxi 7) is all the more remarkable because it does not appear to be a vernacular word in contemporary Greek, being non-occurrent in the Indices to the Papyri of the *Egypt Expl* and the Berlin Urk. up to the beginning of this present year (1907) [This is still true, 1917] Wetstein (on Jn) and Steph *Thes* allege it from Greek tragedy and from Greek scholiasts, but not from intervening literature Westcott says 'the word was adopted in later Hebrew for the "frock" of labourers' But he alleges no evidence Krauss' index does not give it, nor does Wetstein's long note on its various and disputed meanings" See n 5 *ad fin* on ἐπενδύτης and λέντιον as Christ's gifts to the apostles.

[3] Tatian *Contr. Graec* § 20, adding "It is possible for everyone that is naked to obtain this decent covering" Comp 2 Cor. v 3 εἴ γε καὶ ἐνδυσάμενοι οὐ γυμνοὶ εὑρεθησόμεθα.   [4] Jn xviii 22

[5] See Steph *Thes* , giving as the meaning of παρεστάναι "Appareo, Apparitoris munere fungor ut apud Lucian *D Deor* xxiv 1 Oportet Mercurium παρεστάναι τῷ Διί item παρεστάναι τῷ δικαστηρίῳ, In foro apparituras facere" Jerome, from "The Gospel according

THE ARREST OF JESUS

have seen reason to believe that the original may have been taken by him to mean that "one of the *attendants*" by accident struck off the ear of the High Priest's servant. Matthew and Luke, on the other hand, say that the striker was one of "*those round*, or, *with, Jesus*." But only John says that it was "*Peter*."

Perhaps John, while recording such traditions of Christ's Passion as mentioned "striking" and "buffeting," as well as "scourging," noted Luke's omission of that particular tradition (about the insolent "*striking with the palm of the hand*") which, as we shall see, is mentioned by Mark and Matthew, and which appears to allude to Messianic prophecy[1]. The perpetrators of that act are called by Mark "*some*," or "*certain [persons]*." In the Marcan context, this might mean "*some of the Sanhedrin*," and the parallel Matthew ("they") almost obliges us to suppose that he took this view[2]. John here assigns the act to a single official—an "attendant" at the informal trial of Jesus in the court of Annas—who perpetrated it unrebuked by Annas. Later on, John again mentions "blows with the palm of the hand" as inflicted by the soldiers[3]."

---

to the Hebrews," quotes the words (referring to Jesus after His resurrection) "*Dominus autem quum dedisset sindonem servo sacerdotis ivit ad Jacobum*." It is suggested (*Notes* 2999 (xvii) *k*) that this Gospel did not speak of *the servant of the priest*, but spoke allusively about "*him that stood by [the Lord]*" on the occasion of the arrest, that is, Peter. If so, the writer of the Gospel is describing Jesus, after His resurrection, as coming to Peter first of all, before He appeared to James (comp 1 Cor xv 5—7). The Saviour's coming is metaphorically described as a restoration of the "linen garment" of righteousness. The metaphor may be illustrated from the *Acts of Philip in Hellas* § 1 τὸ γὰρ ἔνδυμα ὅπερ ἔδωκεν τοῖς ἀποστόλοις ὁ Ἰησοῦς ἐπενδύτης μόνον ἦν καὶ λέντιον, that is to say, an "ephod" wherein to serve God in purity (Jn xxi 7) and a "towel" wherewith to serve men in humility (Jn xiii 4—5). See *Notes* 2999 (xvii) *m—n*. *Diatess.* says that the Marcan "young man" was "wrapped in a *towel*" and "left the *towel*," and SS has Syr *sindōn* both in Mk and in Jn.

[1] See p 525 foll on Mk xiv 65, Mt. xxvi 67—8, Lk xxii 63—5.
[2] "Almost," but not quite. "They," when represented by 3rd pers pl of a Gk verb in the Gospels, sometimes means "people" (*Son*, 3180 *b*, 3281 *a*).
[3] Jn xix 3. Ῥάπισμα, in N T, occurs only in Mk xiv 65, Jn xviii. 22, xix 3. See *Joh Voc.* 1737 *e*. It was condemned by Phrynichus.

THE ARREST OF JESUS

By these details John in the first place softens or explains the incredible statement to which Matthew apparently commits himself, that members of the Sanhedrin struck Jesus; he says in effect, "It was not so, but there was some foundation for the charge, since the President of the Court allowed an official to do it" In the next place John guards his readers against assuming that the blow struck at Christ's arrest by some person unnamed in the older Gospels, and vaguely described by Mark as "one of those standing by," did not come from Peter. The Johannine view may be paraphrased as follows "Some have confused 'Peter' with a certain 'attendant' among those who arrested Jesus, as if this 'attendant' struck off by accident the ear of the high priest's servant And in truth, later on, an 'attendant,' who was also 'the high priest's servant,' did 'strike' a blow, but all the circumstances were quite different[1]. 'Peter,' not 'an attendant,' should have been mentioned as striking the blow at the moment of the arrest"

We seem, at this stage of the Gospel narrative, to be in a region of Petrine traditions, primitive, very brief, largely metaphorical, and very difficult to arrange chronologically Mark's tradition about "a certain young man" left "naked" is one of these. Luke omits it, but has, a little before, a saying of Jesus that He will pray for Peter that his faith may not utterly fail and that he may turn and strengthen his brethren[2] John expresses this dramatically in a scene describing spiritually the reclothing of Peter after being "naked," and his reception of the Lord's commission "Feed my sheep"

---

[1] "The circumstances" include the mention of "the right ear" in Lk xxii 50 and Jn xviii 10, on which see *Introd* pp 60—1 "It is an agreement [of John] with Lucan narrative (as distinct from that of Mark and Matthew), rare or non-existent elsewhere in Johannine narrative" On "the right ear" mentioned in the consecration of priests see Exod xxix. 20 etc Origen, on Mt xxvi 51, quotes Jn xviii 10 and says "Forsitan quod agebat Petrus mysterium erat quoniam Judaici populi dextra auditio fuerat amputanda" This seems to represent Jn's view correctly But it cannot be easily reconciled with Luke, who represents the "dextra auditio" as being restored.   [2] Lk xxii. 31—2.

CHAPTER XII

THE TRIAL BEFORE THE HIGH PRIEST

[Mark xiv. 53—72]

§ 1. *"To the high priest," in Mark*[1]

THE first words of Mark's narrative run thus in the Syro-Sinaitic Version: "And they carried Jesus along unto the chief

[1] Mk xiv 53—4 (R V)	Mt. xxvi 57—8 (R V)	Lk xxii 54—6 (R V)
(53) And they led Jesus away to the high priest: and there come together with him all the chief priests and the elders and the scribes	(57) And they that had taken Jesus led him away to [the house of] Caiaphas the high priest, where the scribes and the elders were gathered together	(54) And they seized him, and led him [away], and brought him into the high priest's house But Peter followed afar off (55) And when they had kindled a fire in the midst of the court, and had sat down together, Peter sat in the midst of them
(54) And Peter had followed him a-far off, even within, into the court of the high priest, and he was sitting with the officers, and warming himself in the light [of the fire]	(58) But Peter followed him afar off, unto the court of the high priest, and entered in, and sat with the officers, to see the end	(56) And seeing him as he sat in the light [of the fire].

Jn xviii 12—18 (R V) (12) So the band (*or*, cohort) and the chief captain (*or*, military tribune, *lit* chiliarch), and the officers of the Jews, seized Jesus and bound him, (13) and led him to Annas first, for he was father in law to Caiaphas, which was high priest that year (14) Now Caiaphas was he which gave counsel to the Jews, that it was expedient that one man should die for the people (15) And Simon Peter followed Jesus, and [so did] another disciple Now that disciple was known unto the high priest, and entered in with Jesus

504 (Mark xiv 53—4)

THE TRIAL BEFORE THE HIGH PRIEST

priests, and *they were bringing with him* (W H txt "there come together," marg adds "with him") all the chief priests and the elders and the scribes," where it must be remembered that the Syriac, like the Greek, makes no distinction between "chief priest" and "high priest[1]."

It is not surprising that several authorities omit "with him," since, in accordance with New Testament usage, "*come-together-with* him" should mean "*come-along-with* him"—whether "*him*" meant Jesus or the High Priest[2]. But it might also mean "*come-to-meet* the high priest for conference[3]"—that is to say, for an informal meeting of the Council, regular so far as the component members of the Council were concerned, but irregular

---

into the court of the high priest, (16) but Peter was standing at the door without. So the other disciple, which was known unto the high priest, went out and spake unto her that kept the door, and brought in Peter. (17) The maid therefore that kept the door saith unto Peter, Art thou also [one] of this man's disciples? He saith, I am not. (18) Now the servants (*lit* bondservants) and the officers were standing [there], having made a fire of coals (*lit* a fire of charcoal), for it was cold, and they were warming themselves: and Peter also was with them, standing and warming himself.

[1] Mk xiv 53	Mt xxvi 57	Lk xxii 54
καὶ ἀπήγαγον τὸν Ἰησοῦν πρὸς τὸν ἀρχιερέα, καὶ συνέρχονται (marg + αὐτῷ) πάντες οἱ ἀρχιερεῖς καὶ οἱ πρεσβύτεροι καὶ οἱ γραμματεῖς	οἱ δὲ κρατήσαντες τὸν Ἰησοῦν ἀπήγαγον πρὸς Καιάφαν τὸν ἀρχιερέα, ὅπου οἱ γραμματεῖς καὶ οἱ πρεσβύτεροι συνήχθησαν	συλλαβόντες δὲ αὐτὸν ἤγαγον καὶ εἰσήγαγον εἰς τὴν οἰκίαν τοῦ ἀρχιερέως

W H have συνέρχονται πάντες in txt, and συνερχονται αὐτῷ πάντες only in margin. But since their edition SS has been found to include the pronoun "with-him."

In SS, כהנא may mean "*priests*" or "*priest*," but the pl adj., "*chief*," is רבי, the sing is רב.

[2] Συνέρχομαι, with dat of person, means "come-along-with" in Lk xxiii 55, Acts i 21, ix 39, x 23, 45 etc., and (almost certainly) in Jn xi 33. See Field *Ot. Norv* on Mk xiv 53. A V "with him were assembled" would require συνήχθησαν.

[3] See L S and Steph *Thes* vii 1351 shewing that συνέρχομαί τινι sometimes means, not "*I come along with some one to a conference*," but "*I come to a conference with some one*." In such cases, εἰς λόγους etc would mostly, but not necessarily, be inserted.

THE TRIAL BEFORE THE HIGH PRIEST

perhaps as to the suddenness of the summons, and certainly as to the hour of assembly (not yet morning, nor even day-break[1]).

Now, returning to the context in Mark, we have to ask whom Mark means by "the high priest." We must not assume that it was Caiaphas. For Mark never mentions Caiaphas. Does Mark deliberately leave the name unmentioned (and mention only the title) because of some complication as to the name of the High Priest in question? Some Synoptic facts point to this conclusion. For though the parallel Matthew says —implying that it was done at once—"they led away Jesus *to Caiaphas the high priest*, where the scribes and the elders were [formally] gathered together," the parallel Luke says that they merely "led him *into the house of the high priest*[2]", but the [formal] "gathering together" was not till after day-break. "And when it was day *there was [formally] gathered together* the assembly of the elders of the people, both chief priests and scribes[3]."

Matthew, who alone has previously mentioned Caiaphas, speaking of a formal "gathering" of a full council into "the court of the high priest [commonly] called Caiaphas[4]," may here use "*unto Caiaphas*" either (1) as a condensation for "into the *court of Caiaphas*," or (2) as meaning "*into the house of Caiaphas*," or (3) "*into the personal presence of Caiaphas*." His meaning is not clear. Nor is Luke's "house of the high priest" clear. For Luke himself has described John the Baptist as beginning his public career "in the high-priesthood of Annas and Caiaphas[5]." Which of the two, then (a reader

---

[1] On the Talmudic rule concerning the hours for civil and criminal trials see *Hor Heb* on Mt xxvii 1 quoting *Sanhedr* iv 1 (?iv. 5) "They handle capital causes in the day time, and finish them by day."

[2] Mt xxvi 57, Lk xxii 54   [3] Lk xxii 66

[4] Mt xxvi 3. The parall Mk xiv 1, Lk xxii 2 omit this

[5] Lk iii 2 ἐπὶ ἀρχιερέως Ἅννα καὶ Καιάφα, A V "A and C being the high priests," R V "in the high-priesthood of Annas and Caiaphas." Perhaps the authority here followed by Luke desired to suggest the thought "Annas and [perhaps we should add, his son-in-law and tool] Caiaphas." Caiaphas was high priest about A D 18—36. W H have Ἅννας, but Ἅννας is more usual (as also Ἅνανος in Josephus *ed* Niese).

THE TRIAL BEFORE THE HIGH PRIEST

may well ask) does Luke mean when he writes "the house of the high priest"?

John tells us that Jesus was led "to Annas first, for he was father-in-law to Caiaphas, who was high priest *during that [eventful] year*[1]." "The emphasis on "that year" is explained from a previous passage which tells us that Caiaphas, "not of himself but being high priest *during that [eventful] year*"— a phrase already used in the context—was divinely moved to utter, though evil himself, a prophecy of good: "It is expedient for you that one man should die for the people and that the whole nation perish not[2]" In the present passage, John repeats the phrase for the third time, emphasizing the fact that Caiaphas, the legal high priest of the Jews, had already foredoomed Jesus to death, not because of justice but because of expediency ("Now Caiaphas was he that gave counsel to the Jews that it was expedient") And here[3], instead of repeating the Synoptic account of the trial of Jesus before Caiaphas, John tells us—what the Synoptists did not—that Annas the *de facto* high priest irregularly examined Jesus, and allowed Him to be struck by one of the officers, and then sent Him, "bound," to "Caiaphas, the [*de jure*] high priest[4]."

Some scribes and commentators, early and late[5], have found it impossible to believe that John could first tell us that Annas was the High Priest's father-in-law, and then proceed to call him the actual High Priest ("*The high priest* therefore asked Jesus...of his teaching)," and then say, at the conclusion of the examination, "*Annas* therefore sent him bound to Caiaphas the high priest" But Nonnus is almost certainly right in

---

[1] Jn xviii 13—14

[2] Jn xi 49—51 'Ενιαυτός (apart from Lk iv 19 (Is lxi. 2) ἐ δεκτόν) does not occur in the Gospels except in the thrice-repeated phrase (Jn xi 49, 51, xviii. 13) "high priest *during that [eventful] year* (τοῦ ἐνιαυτοῦ ἐκείνου)"

[3] Jn xviii 19 foll , see p 522

[4] Jn xviii 24 Some take Jn xviii 19 "the high priest" to refer to Caiaphas, not to Annas In that case, xviii. 24 ἀπέστειλεν (οὖν) would need to be rendered "*had* sent ..," but the οὖν is against this See *Joh. Gr.* **2462**.

[5] See Blass, Burkitt, and SS on Jn xviii 13 foll , and p. 522, n. 1.

THE TRIAL BEFORE THE HIGH PRIEST

supposing that John's meaning is "*Annas* therefore asked Jesus ...of his teaching[1]" To call him "the high priest" is an audacious inconsistency. But the audacity is deliberate John desires us to feel that the whole affair was of a piece, not only a cruel injustice, but an illegal injustice, perpetrated by those who called themselves legalists. The examining "high priest," Annas, was no high priest at all—legally But he was actually. Jesus was already doomed to death when Annas, the high priest in fact, sent Him bound to Caiaphas, the high priest in name, to go through the imposture of a nominal trial.

In this matter, John does not intervene as to any point of importance in Mark, but he does intervene as to a point of some importance in Luke, who had called Annas, in effect, "high priest" jointly with Caiaphas. John seems to say, "Although Annas, in the eyes of the Jewish world, was superior to Caiaphas in dignity and reputation, the latter was in a mysterious way subject to a prophetic influence, like Balaam —a prophet prophesying in an evil and condemnatory spirit a prophecy of a good and true redemption"

An ancient scholium given below, though corrupt, helps us to understand why Mark never mentions Caiaphas by name. He was probably an insignificant creature, overshadowed by his father-in-law Annas. When Josephus mentions him, as he does twice, it is as "Joseph who is also Caiaphas" or "Joseph who is also called Caiaphas[2]," and whereas to other high priests

---

[1] Jn xviii 19 (Nonnus) Ἰησοῦν δ' ἐρέεινε..."Ἄννας Nonnus afterwards says (on Jn xviii 24) that Annas sent Jesus, caught as it were in a hunter's net, to his son-in-law—"one high priest [sending Him] to another high priest (ἀρχιερεὺς ἑτέρῳ πεφυλαγμένον ἀρχιερῆι)."

[2] Cramer p 429 (on Mk xiv 53—4) Πολλὴ θερμότης τοῦ Πέτρου· οὐδὲ φεύγοντας ἰδὼν ἔφυγεν ἀλλ' ἔστη καὶ εἰσῆλθεν ἦν δὲ καὶ Ἰωάννης, ἐπειδὴ γνώριμος ἦν. καὶ διατί ἀπήγαγον αὐτὸν ἐκεῖ, ὅπου ἦσαν ἅπαντες συνηγμένοι, ἵνα μὲν (leg μετὰ) γνώμης πάντα ποιῶσι τῶν ἀρχιερέων ἐκεῖνος γὰρ ἦν τότε ἀρχιερεύς συνήχθησαν οὖν ἅπαντες, καὶ συνέδριον ἦν λοιμῶν καὶ ἐρωτῶσιν οὐχ ἁπλῶς, ἀλλὰ βουλόμενοι σχῆμα περιθεῖναι τῇ ἐπιβουλῇ ταύτῃ δικαστηρίου

For ηνδεκαιωαννης read ηνδεκαιοαννας, i.e. ἦν δὲ καὶ ὁ Ἄννας. This is suggested by the context, which demands some name of a chief priest It is also suggested by a footnote " ἀπήγαγόν, φησι, τὸν Ἰησοῦν πρὸς

THE TRIAL BEFORE THE HIGH PRIEST

mentioned along with him Josephus attaches (as usual) the father's name, to Joseph Caiaphas he does not[1]. We ought therefore to think of him as "Joseph Caiaphas" or "Joseph the Caiaphas," possibly meaning "Joseph the explorer, or soothsayer[2]" That may be the aspect in which John regards him, namely, as an inferior Balaam—in part a tool in the hands of Annas, but in part a high priest, forced on one momentous occasion to utter an oracle rough-hewn by the devil for the immediate purposes of hell, and shaped by God for a far off consummation of the counsels of heaven

"Ἀνναν τὸν ἀρχιερέα ὅπου ἦσαν συν[ηγμένοι] Cod. 178" The scribe that corrected καιοαννας "also the [celebrated] Annas" into καιιωαννης "also John" (o and ω being constantly interchanged), may have been influenced by the belief that the writer of the scholium, in using the term γνώριμος, was thinking of Jn xviii 15 ὁ δὲ μαθητὴς ἐκεῖνος ἦν γνωστὸς τῷ ἀρχιερεῖ, and that this was the apostle "John" But γνώριμος apparently means here, not γνωστός, but "well known," "distinguished" (see Steph *Thes s v*) The epithet would apply to Annas, who was far superior to Caiaphas in dignity and notoriety

For ἵνα μετὰ γνώμης as a correction of ἵνα μὲν γνώμης, see Steph. *Thes* ii 678 quoting Polyb xxxii 7. 2 μετὰ τῆς τῶν θεῶν γνώμης. The scholium implies that, if the approval of Annas was secured, that would carry with it the approval of all the chief priests, since he was "at that time (τότε)," in effect, "chief priest" (by himself)

[1] Joseph *Ant.* xviii 2 2, and 4 3.
[2] See Levy iv 299 *b* קיף "Untersucher," quoting *Par* 3, 5 "Eljoani, Sohn des Untersuchers," and warning the reader not to take it as a proper name McNeile on Mt xxvi 3 says, with a query, "The surname is strictly a subst , ? 'the Soothsayer,' קיפא (Dalm *Worterb*. קיף)" Some such meaning would commend itself to John, who regards him as a Balaam No doubt, early Jewish Christians would play on the name in a bad sense But I know of no other fit and similar word except קוף, "ape," meaning that he was the "ape" of Annas (see Levy iv 269 *a*)

THE TRIAL BEFORE THE HIGH PRIEST

§ 2. *"Peter warming himself," in Mark and John*[1]

The parallel texts given below shew that all the later Evangelists, in various ways, depart from Mark's extraordinary statement that Peter "was warming himself *in the light*," where we should expect "*by the fire*." This, and the parallel Luke, are the only New Testament passages where the Authorised Version renders the Greek "*light*" by the English "*fire*." Luke softens the difficulty of Mark by telling us previously that they had "lighted a fire [all] round[2]," and by adding now that a maid *saw Peter* "*by the light*," so that it is easy to supply "*of the fire*." But Matthew, who makes no mention of a "*fire*," makes also no mention of "light," but has "*to see* the end."

[1] Mk xiv 54	Mt xxvi 58	Lk xxii 54 b—56 a
καὶ ὁ Πέτρος ἀπὸ μακρόθεν ἠκολούθησεν αὐτῷ ἕως ἔσω εἰς τὴν αὐλὴν τοῦ ἀρχιερέως, καὶ ἦν συνκαθήμενος μετὰ τῶν ὑπηρετῶν καὶ θερμαινόμενος πρὸς τὸ φῶς.	ὁ δὲ Πέτρος ἠκολούθει αὐτῷ [ἀπὸ] μακρόθεν ἕως τῆς αὐλῆς τοῦ ἀρχιερέως, καὶ εἰσελθὼν ἔσω ἐκάθητο μετὰ τῶν ὑπηρετῶν ἰδεῖν τὸ τέλος.	...εἰς τὴν οἰκίαν τοῦ ἀρχιερέως· ὁ δὲ Πέτρος ἠκολούθει μακρόθεν περιαψάντων δὲ πῦρ ἐν μέσῳ τῆς αὐλῆς καὶ συνκαθισάντων ἐκάθητο ὁ Πέτρος μέσος αὐτῶν. ἰδοῦσα δὲ αὐτὸν παιδίσκη τις καθήμενον πρὸς τὸ φῶς...

Jn xviii. 18 ἱστήκεισαν δὲ οἱ δοῦλοι καὶ οἱ ὑπηρέται ἀνθρακιὰν πεποιηκότες, ὅτι ψῦχος ἦν, καὶ ἐθερμαίνοντο· ἦν δὲ καὶ ὁ Πέτρος μετ' αὐτῶν ἑστὼς καὶ θερμαινόμενος

The "warming" is repeated in —

Mk xiv 67	Mt xxvi 69	Lk xxii 56 (as above)
καὶ ἰδοῦσα τὸν Πέτρον θερμαινόμενον ἐμβλέψασα αὐτῷ λέγει...	ὁ δὲ Πέτρος ἐκάθητο ἔξω ἐν τῇ αὐλῇ καὶ προσῆλθεν αὐτῷ μία παιδίσκη λέγουσα...	ἰδοῦσα δὲ αὐτὸν παιδίσκη τις καθήμενον πρὸς τὸ φῶς καὶ ἀτενίσασα αὐτῷ εἶπεν...

Jn xviii 25 ἦν δὲ Σίμων Πέτρος ἑστὼς καὶ θερμαινόμενος

On Mk xiv 54 πρὸς τὸ φῶς, Wetstein quotes Xen *Cyropaed* vii. ἐπεισπίπτουσιν αὐτοῖς πίνουσι πρὸς φῶς πολύ But this is not a parallel to Mark's use of φῶς with the article, which, unless preceded by some mention of the lighting of a fire, would naturally mean "the light of the sun."

[2] Lk xxii 55 περιαψάντων, "lighted around." See *Son* **3369** *a* foll quoting *Joh Voc.* **1711** *f* as shewing the Lucan usage to be "unlike any use of περιάπτω in Steph *Thes* except one describing a fire *kindled round* a man to torture him"

THE TRIAL BEFORE THE HIGH PRIEST

Turning to Hebrew and LXX for explanation, we find that (1) the same Hebrew letters mean, according to the position of the vowel point, "*fire*" or "*light*[1]," and that Symmachus has the former, but Aquila and Theodotion the latter, where Isaiah speaks of "the Lord whose *fire* (or, *light*) is in Zion[2]", (2) these same letters are easily confusable, and are actually confused, with the Hebrew for "*see*[3]", (3) the following passage of Isaiah connects fire (a different Hebrew word from the one under discussion) and "light" with "gird" or "surround" (as in Luke) in such a difficult context that the Oxford Gesenius would emend "surround" into "kindle": "Behold, all ye that kindle a fire, that *surround* [*yourselves with*] *fire-brands*: walk ye in the light of your own fire...ye shall lie down in sorrow[4]"

Hence, here in Mark, "warming themselves by the light" may have been derived partly from an explanatory addition about the object of the fire-light, but partly from an allusion to Isaiah's thought of the sinners of Israel, who rejected the true light of God, and desired "to walk in the light of their own fire," notwithstanding the retribution that would fall on Jerusalem. That retribution was now to be repeated. The Romans were to teach them that God's "light" might be to them a "furnace," and "not a coal to warm at or the light [of a hearth] to sit before[5]." Luke, who regarded the fire mainly from the Petrine point of view as the "*light*" by which

---

[1] Gesen 21—2

[2] Is xxxi 9   The LXX departs from the Hebrew

[3] See Is xxvii 11 RV "*set-on-fire*," LXX ἀπὸ θέας, "from beholding," Prov. xv. 30 "*the light* of the eyes," LXX "the *beholding* (θεωρῶν) eye" In 1 S xiv. 27, Heb marg is from אוּר "light," but txt from ראה "see" Comp Judith xiii 13 Vulg "kindling *lights*," LXX "having kindled *a fire for illumination*," Syr "having kindled *a light to see* [*her*]" This may illustrate Mt xxvi. 58 "*to see the end*" parall to Mk xiv. 54 "*in the light* [of the fire]."

[4] Is l 11 See Gesen 25 suggesting אוּר for אֵשׁ—which would here have accus. of person omitted, if text were genuine. The Targum has a very long and obscure paraphrase pointing to desolation with fire and sword but containing nothing that suggests "girding" or "surrounding" See p. 527.

[5] Is xlvii 14.

THE TRIAL BEFORE THE HIGH PRIEST

the maid "saw" Peter, omits the "warming." But John, who sees in it a fiery trial of Peter, calls it "a coal fire" and mentions the "warming" with what might seem to many superfluous repetition "Now there stood the servants and the officers having made a fire of coals, because it was cold, and they were warming themselves; and there was Peter also with them, standing and warming himself[1]."

Why do Matthew and Luke omit the Marcan twice repeated tradition about "Peter warming himself" both here and later on where it is used absolutely (without "by the light [of the fire]")[2]? Two answers may be given. One is, that the Greek verb in the passive, applied to persons, is (if we may trust the Thesaurus) not used of mere physical warmth, but of the warmth or excitement caused by drunkenness or fever, anger, hope, joy, or any excessive passion[3]. This might suffice to induce Luke to omit it. The text of Matthew suggests that he might be influenced also by considerations of an original Hebrew tradition. The only instance of the Hebrew passive of the verb "warm" in the Old Testament is used of men "inflaming themselves" with idolatry, and there the LXX confuses it[4]; and the Hebrew word is peculiarly liable to confusion[5]. In Hosea, it is applied to conspirators[6]. Matthew and Luke may well have been unwilling to use about the Apostle Peter a word that, if taken literally, might seem to some to imply a feeling

---

[1] Jn xviii 18, on which see *Son* **3369** *a*   [2] Mk xiv 67

[3] See Steph *Thes* iv 327   Jas ii 16 θερμαίνεσθε, "be ye warmed," means perhaps "with warm clothing" and may be illustrated from LXX Job xxxi 20, Hag 1. 6; but Westt on Jas ii 16 alleges no instance of the passive from literary Gk, nor is there one in Goodspeed, or Epictetus

[4] Is lvii 5 "ye that inflame yourselves (הנחמים)" LXX οἱ παρακαλοῦντες, taking it as from נחם.

[5] The verb חמם "warm" (Gesen. 328 *b*) may imply the heat of passion (יחם, Gesen. 404 *a*)   In Job xxx. 4 לחמם, R V txt has "their meat," from לחם "meat," but marg. "to (ל) warm them (חמם)"

[6] Hos vii 7 (of conspirators, Gesen. 328 *b*) "they are all *hot* as an oven and devour their judges...there is none that calleth unto me," LXX ἐθερμάνθησαν, Jerem li 39 (of Chaldeans) "when they are heated," LXX ἐν τῇ θερμασίᾳ αὐτῶν.

incompatible with a due sense of his Master's danger, while, if taken metaphorically, it suggested an evil excitement caused by "the fiery darts" of Satan.

But John, if he regarded the word as used allusively and metaphorically, would seem to have been of a different opinion, believing that Peter *was* "inflamed" with self-confidence, in spite of his Master's warning. The "inflammation" of the enemies of Jesus was of a different kind. But still the result was that Peter "stood with them" and "trusted in the light of his own fire," and "lay down in sorrow." Whatever may be John's exact meaning he at all events emphasizes the Marcan detail that Matthew and Luke omit, so that it is an instance of Johannine Intervention.

§ 3. *"False witnesses" about "the temple," in Mark and Matthew*[1]

The evidence of these "false witnesses," omitted by Luke, is placed in a new light by John, who represents Christ's first

---

[1] Mk xiv 55—9 (R V)

(55) Now the chief priests and the whole council sought witness against Jesus to put him to death, and found it not

(56) For many bare false witness against him, and their witness agreed not together

(57) And there stood up certain, and bare false witness against him, saying,

(58) We heard him say, I will destroy this temple (*or*, sanctuary) that is made with hands, and in three days I will build another made without hands.

(59) And not even so did their witness agree together

Mt xxvi 59—61 (R V)

(59) Now the chief priests and the whole council sought false witness against Jesus, that they might put him to death,

(60) And they found it not, though many false witnesses came. But afterward came two, and said,

(61) This man said, I am able to destroy the temple (*or*, sanctuary) of God, and to build it in three days.

Lk. xxii 66 (R V)

(66) And as soon as it was day, the assembly of the elders of the people was gathered together, both chief priests and scribes; and they led him away into their council, saying, If...

THE TRIAL BEFORE THE HIGH PRIEST

words in public to have been "Take these things hence; make not my Father's house a house of merchandise," and, "Destroy this temple, and in three days I will raise it up[1]" We are told by John that the Jews took this in a literal sense, but that Jesus "spake of the temple of his body." It is an instance of Johannine Intervention Luke omits a charge specified by Mark and Matthew as being falsely brought against Jesus John intervenes to say "Taken literally the words were false Taken spiritually they, or words very similar, were true and actually uttered by Jesus. They were almost the first words in His Gospel[2]."

A passage in the Acts may explain Luke's motive. "False witnesses," he says, alleged against Stephen, "This man ceaseth not to speak words against this holy place and the law, for we have heard him say that this Jesus of Nazareth shall destroy this place...[3]" Stephen's interrupted speech concludes with asserting about the Old Temple and the Old Law that, though Solomon built God a house, "the Most High dwelleth not in houses made by hands," and that Israel "received the law... and kept it not[4]." What he might have gone on to say about the New Temple and the New Law is not recorded[5] But we gather from the narrative and speech taken together that Stephen would have declared that the sins of the Jews themselves were bringing about the dissolution of the Old Temple and the Old Law to make way for the New. At all events, when the High Priest, after hearing the charges of the "false witnesses," said to Stephen "Are these things so?" the accused did not reply "They are not." That being the case, it is

---

[1] Jn ii 16, 19
[2] Mk xiv. 56, 59 (1) "their witness agreed not together" and (2) "*not even so* did their witness agree together," are peculiar to Mark "Not even so" may imply that there was *some* truth in the second "witness." Mt. xxvi 60 "two" was substituted for Mk xiv. 57 "some," probably in allusion to Deut xvii. 6 ' at the mouth of *two* witnesses...," *i.e.* not less than two.
[3] Acts vi. 13—14   [4] Acts vii 48—53 quoting Is lxvi 1.
[5] The verse following the words quoted by Stephen says (Is lxvi 2) "But to this man will I look, even to him that is poor and of a contrite spirit"

THE TRIAL BEFORE THE HIGH PRIEST

intelligible that Luke shrank from repeating similar accusations in his Gospel, where there would be still less scope for explaining how far truth was mingled with the falsehood

We ought also not entirely to pass over the account, peculiar to Luke's Introduction, of an early visit of Jesus to the Temple In the body of his Gospel, Luke has followed Mark and Matthew in recording the words of Jesus about the "house of prayer" converted into "a den of robbers" and His prediction "Not one stone shall be left on another." But in his Introduction he represents Jesus as a boy of twelve, apparently speaking of the structure as if it were the home of His Father where He, the Son, might naturally be sought[1]. Perhaps we are to suppose an extraordinary degeneration in the control of the Temple to have occurred during the twenty years that ripened Jesus from boyhood to manhood. If not, there is something (on the surface at all events) a little difficult to reconcile in the Lucan traditions about Christ's first and last visits to the Temple[2]

Some version of Luke's tradition about Christ's early visit to the Temple may help to explain the early date assigned by John to Christ's public and authoritative visit. In reply to the question "Where ought we to expect to find the Messiah, the Son of God, when He begins to proclaim the Kingdom of God?" the answer "In the Temple, in His Father's House" seems appropriate. Still more does it seem so, when we reflect that the Messiah calls Himself the Son of Man and regards it as His mission to build up regenerated Man into a Temple fit

---

[1] Lk ii 49

[2] Origen on Lk ii. 49 (Lomm v 159) on "Jesus in medio magistrorum," says "Unusquisque nostrum si bonus fuerit atque perfectus, possessio Dei Patris est, et habet in medio sui Jesum Credamus quippe dicenti 'quoniam in his, quae sunt Patris mei, me oportet esse' Magis rationabile atque vivens, et verum templum Dei hoc esse suspicor, quam illud, quod typice terreno opere constructum est Unde illo in templo ut typice fuit, ita recessit et typice. Egressus est enim de templo terreno, dicens, 'ecce, relinquetur vobis domus vestra deserta,' et relinquens domum illam venit ad possessionem Dei Patris, ad ecclesias in toto orbe dispersas, et dicit, 'in his, quae sunt Patris mei, me oportet esse Tunc ergo non intellexerunt verbum, quod locutus est iis"

for the indwelling Spirit of the F*a*ther. The closing chapters of the Fourth Gospel set forth this doctrine fully, but it is implied from the first in the compressed enigma of the sentence, "Destroy this temple and in three days I will raise it up"

Even though John may be chronologically wrong in placing a visit of Jesus to the Temple at so early a date, he cannot have been wrong in attributing to Jesus, from the first, the doctrine of Isaiah. "I dwell in the high and holy place, with him also that is of a contrite and humble spirit," and again "The heaven is my throne, and the earth is my footstool. what manner of house will ye build for me?...But to this man will I look, even to him that is poor and of a contrite spirit[1]." Both of these passages contain the implied doctrine that the Temple of the Lord is Man[2]. But the Gospel, developing the

---

[1] Is lvii 15, lxvi 1—2. On the inadequacy of the word "poor," see *Son* 3242 (1)—(11).

[2] This doctrine is typically expressed in Hebrew doctrine about the Tabernacle—also called the Tent of Meeting—that is, the Tabernacle appointed as the meeting-place of Jehovah and Israel (Exod. xxv 8) "And let them make me a sanctuary that I may *tabernacle* (שכן) among them" The LXX weakens this to "and I will *be seen* (or, *appear*) in you (ὀφθήσομαι ἐν ὑμῖν)," Origen (*Hom Exod* ix 3) "videbor vobis." Comp Exod xxix 45 "And I will *tabernacle* among the children of Israel," where LXX has "I will be called upon (ἐπικληθήσομαι) in (ἐν) the children of Israel," but "Ἄλλος" has σκηνώσω

Owing, perhaps, to the general failure of LXX in the Pentateuch (exc. Numb xxxv 34) to express this poetic doctrine of the "tabernacling" of God with men, it is not mentioned by the early Fathers (Goodspeed) But see *Didachè* § 10 "We give thanks unto thee, holy Father, for thy holy Name which *thou hast made to tabernacle* (κατεσκήνωσας) in our hearts" (comp. Herm. *Sim*. v. 6). Also Justin *Tryph*. § 115 supports the Christian doctrine from Zech. ii 10 foll.

In N T, the divine "tabernacling," either "in" *i e* "among" men, or "upon" them, or "with" them, is mentioned only in Jn i. 14 ἐν ἡμῖν, Rev. vii 15 ἐπ' αὐτούς, *ib* xxi 3 μετ' αὐτῶν. But there is an equivalent, of a less poetic nature, in Lk xvii 21 "the kingdom of God is within you (ἐντὸς ὑμῶν)" This, apart from context, might mean either "among you" or "within your hearts." It is the object of the Fourth Gospel to shew how the Word, by first tabernacling "*among*" men, prepared the way for tabernacling "*within*" them in the latter sense (as the *Didachè* expresses it) The phrase

doctrine of the Law and the Prophets, taught that the "humble spirit" was to be, not that of the solitary ascetic, but of a social nature, that of the "little one," who makes himself the servant of others—not because he is aiming at his own sanctity or salvation, but because he is filled with the love of the Father, which constrains him to love and serve his brethren

This constraining love may explain what appears egotism, but is really altruism, in the words "*I* will raise it up" Why not "*My Father* will raise it up"? It seems to be because Jesus, feeling Himself one with the Father, spoke as the Father and used "*I*" where others would use "*He*" Paul takes us to the root of Christ's thought when he says, "Christ also pleased not himself, but as it is written, The reproaches of them that reproached thee fell upon me[1]." It is no accident that, in the Psalm, the words here quoted from it are immediately preceded by "The zeal of thine house hath eaten me up"—quoted by John as being "remembered" by Christ's disciples in connection with His authoritative purification of the Temple[2].

(Jn 1 14) "*tabernacled* among us" prepares the way for (*ib* ii 21) "he spake of *the temple of his body*" For the Temple was only the development of the Tabernacle And the essence of either was, not that it was a house of stone, or a tent with curtains, but that it was a "place of meeting" between God and man

"Behold, the *tabernacle of God* is with men," is the exclamation that follows the words (Rev xxi 2) "I saw *the holy city, new Jerusalem*, coming down out of heaven from God as a bride.." This is a Christian version of the fulfilment of the dream about (Gen xxviii 12) "a ladder set up on the earth, and the top of it reached to heaven, and behold, *the angels of God* ascending and descending on it" Philo (*Son* 3378) calls these "angels" *logoi*, or "words of God", and the "ladder" he calls "the soul" But John seems to regard the "ladder" as being the Logos itself, a spiritual "ladder" that is both fixed and moving, being no other than the Son of Man Himself, the medium and avenue of man's prayers to God and God's gifts to man Hence Jesus says to Nathanael (Jn 1. 51) "Ye shall see the heaven opened, and the angels of God *ascending and descending* on *the Son of man*," and, later on (iii 13) "No man hath *ascended* into heaven, but he that *descended* out of heaven,—*the Son of man* that is in heaven"

[1] Rom. xv 3, Ps lxix. 9.   [2] Jn ii. 17, 22.

THE TRIAL BEFORE THE HIGH PRIEST

Paul and John quote from one and the same verse of the Psalms, the former to shew that Jesus "pleased not himself," the latter to explain why He acted in a manner so seemingly arbitrary and violent that the Jews asked for a sign to prove His authority "What sign shewest thou unto us, seeing that thou doest these things¹?" Yet there is no inconsistency. Later on, in the Fourth Gospel, we shall find Jesus saying, "The Son can do nothing of himself, but what he seeth the Father doing²"; and here, at the outset, the Evangelist warns us that, when we hear Jesus saying "I," we may often profitably remind ourselves that it is a short way of saying "The Father, working in me and through me³."

Still it remains astonishing that almost the very first Johannine words assigned to Jesus in public represent Him as claiming to do what (one might have supposed) the Son would regard the Father as alone able to do, namely, to raise up the Son from the dead. However astonishing, the assignment appears to be deliberate. In the Three Gospels, Jesus says, "*It is written*, My house shall be called a house of prayer." In the Fourth Gospel, "*it is written*" is dropped, and the Son speaks of "my Father's House." Later on, He identifies His Father's House with Himself. Paul identifies himself with a temple of the Saviour, when he says "I have been crucified with Christ, yet I live—no longer I, but Christ liveth in me⁴." Somewhat similarly in the Fourth Gospel, the Son says in effect,

---

¹ Jn ii 18.   ² Jn v 19.

³ Comp. Ps. lxxv 1—3 "We give thanks unto thee, O God... (R V marg.) When the earth and all the inhabitants thereof are dissolved, *I set up the pillars of it*" Rashi paraphrases the italicised words thus: "I, thy people Israel, '*I set up the pillars thereof*,' when I said (Exod. xxiv 7) '*All that the Lord hath spoken will we do and be obedient*'" He says that, on the day when the Law was given from Mount Sinai, all Creation was in danger of being dissolved, if Israel had not promised obedience to the Law. Thus, what appears at first sight to be a blasphemous egotism in Israel ("I set up") turns out to be an acknowledgment that Israel is God's devoted servant, and the instrument of His goodness to all the nations, to whom Israel is to transmit the knowledge of the divine Law

⁴ Gal. ii 20.

THE TRIAL BEFORE THE HIGH PRIEST

"Let the destroyers destroy my Father's House (which is my body), I will raise it up." The similarity is not complete, and Christ's doctrine was probably not expressed exactly in the Johannine words or at the early date assigned to it by John Yet even those who feel themselves constrained to say "We cannot believe that Jesus said this" may honestly and reasonably add "But we can and do believe that Jesus thought thus[1]"

§ 4. *The questioning of Jesus by the High Priest, in Mark and Matthew*[2]

Mark and Matthew thrice mention "the high priest," either as questioning Jesus, or as rending his garments while declaring

---

[1] On the subject of this section see *Son* 3195, 3585 foll On Jn 11 19 λύσατε see *Joh Gr* 2439 (v), which suggests that it might be called a "judicial imperative." *Hor Heb*, on Mk xiv 56 ἴσαι (of which Steph *Thes* and Wetstein have no Gk illustration), gives reason for thinking that the Gk may represent a Hebrew Mishnic term meaning "fitting together" The deviations of Matthew from Mark are not such as to call for Johannine Intervention, since both tell us that they are recording charges that they believe to have been false, while John records what he believes to have been true

[2]

Mk xiv 60—65 (R V)	Mt xxvi 62—8 (R V)	Lk xxii 66—71, 63—5 (R V)
(60) And the high priest stood up in the midst, and asked Jesus, saying, Answerest thou nothing? what is it which these witness against thee? (61) But he held his peace, and answered nothing Again the high priest asked him, and saith unto him, Art thou the Christ, the Son of the Blessed? (62) And Jesus said, I am and ye shall see the Son of man sitting at the right hand of power, and coming with the	(62) And the high priest stood up, and said unto him, Answerest thou nothing? what is it which these witness against thee? (63) But Jesus held his peace And the high priest said unto him, I adjure thee by the living God, that thou tell us whether thou be the Christ, the Son of God (64) Jesus saith unto him, Thou hast said nevertheless I say unto you, Henceforth ye shall see the Son of man sitting at	(66) And... they led him away into their council, saying, (67) If thou art the Christ, tell us But he said unto them, If I tell you, ye will not believe (68) And if I ask [you], ye will not answer. (69) But from henceforth shall the Son of man be seated at the right hand of the power of God

THE TRIAL BEFORE THE HIGH PRIEST

that there is no need for more evidence against Him[1]   Luke, after relating how Jesus was "led into the house of the high priest[2]," never mentions him again.   Those who question

Mk xiv. 60—65 (R.V.) *contd*	Mt xxvi 62—8 (R V) *contd*	Lk. xxii 66—71, 63—5 (R V) *contd*
clouds of heaven	the right hand of power, and coming on the clouds of heaven	
(63) And the high priest rent his clothes, and saith, What further need have we of witnesses ?	(65) Then the high priest rent his garments, saying, He hath spoken blasphemy what further need have we of witnesses ? behold, now ye have heard the blasphemy.	(70) And they all said, Art thou then the Son of God ? And he said unto them, Ye say that I am (*or*, Ye say it, because I am)
(64) Ye have heard the blasphemy: what think ye ? And they all condemned him to be worthy of (*lit* liable to) death	(66) What think ye ? They answered and said, He is worthy of (*lit* liable to) death	(71) And they said, What further need have we of witness ? for we ourselves have heard from his own mouth
(65) And some began to spit on him, and to cover his face, and to buffet him, and to say unto him, Prophesy and the officers received him with blows of their hands (*or*, strokes of rods).	(67) Then did they spit in his face and buffet him and some smote him with the palms of their hands (*or*, with rods), saying, (68) Prophesy unto us, thou Christ who is he that struck thee ?	(63) And the men that held him mocked him, and beat him (64) And they blindfolded him, and asked him, saying, Prophesy who is he that struck thee ? (65) And many other things spake they against him, reviling him

Jn xviii 19—24 (R V) The high priest therefore asked Jesus of his disciples, and of his teaching   (20) Jesus answered him, I have spoken openly to the world, I ever taught in synagogues (*lit* synagogue), and in the temple, where all the Jews come together, and in secret spake I nothing   (21) Why askest thou me ? ask them that have heard [me], what I spake unto them   behold, these know the things which I said   (22) And when he had said this, one of the officers standing by struck Jesus with his hand (*or*, with a rod), saying, Answerest thou the high priest so ?   (23) Jesus answered him, If I have spoken evil, bear witness of the evil   but if well, why smitest thou me ?   (24) Annas therefore sent him bound unto Caiaphas the high priest

[1] Mk xiv 60 ἐπηρώτησεν, *ib.* 61 ἐπηρώτα, *ib* 63 λέγει   The parall Mt xxvi. 62—65 does not use the verb "question"

[2] Lk xxii 54

THE TRIAL BEFORE THE HIGH PRIEST

Jesus, in Luke, are always "they," that is, the Sanhedrin[1]. Whether they question through Annas or Caiaphas alone, or through both, or through others as well, is left uncertain. Luke also has words of Jesus peculiar to his Gospel ("*And if I question* [you][2]") which suggest that he found the traditions on the questioning of Jesus various and obscure

John says "The high priest therefore questioned Jesus about his disciples and about his teaching," and that Jesus answered him with a "thou" (not with "ye" as in Mark) "Why questionest thou me? Question them that have heard me," upon which

---

[1] Lk xxii 66 τὸ πρεσβυτέριον τοῦ λαοῦ, ἀρχιερεῖς τε καὶ.. εἰς τὸ συνέδριον αὐτῶν, λέγοντες ..

[2] Lk xxii 67—8 ἐὰν ὑμῖν εἴπω οὐ μὴ πιστεύσητε· ἐὰν δὲ ἐρωτήσω οὐ μὴ ἀποκριθῆτε Several authorities, including SS, have "ye would give me no answer nor *would ye release me*" So D, adding μοι ἡ ἀπολύσητει Cramer (on Lk p 162) prints, as from Cyril, "Wherefore also Christ says to them *If I speak to you*, and what follows (καὶ τὰ ἑξῆς) For wherein (ποῦ γὰρ) having heard, did ye believe? And wherein, being asked, did ye keep silence (ποῦ δὲ ἐρωτώμενοι ἐσιγήσατε)?"

There was perhaps some early confusion in Greek tradition arising out of the use of ἐπιλύειν "solve [a problem]," "answer [a riddle]" Apart from one instance of the passive in Acts xix 39, ἐπιλύω is not used in N T except in Mk iv 34 of "solving" the difficulties of parables, but it is quite common in Hermas, and freq with επερωταω (*Sim* v 3 2, and 5 1, ix 10. 5, and 11 9 etc), and with adjuration in *ib* ix 10 5 ἠρξάμην αὐτὸν ὁρκίζειν...ἵνα μοι ἐπιλύσῃ (comp Mt. xxvi 63 ἐξορκίζω) Jesus had put to the Jews, in effect, an ἐπερώτημα, which they had been unable to answer (ἐπιλύειν), when He asked them how David could describe his own Son as (Mk xii 36, Mt xxii 44, Lk xx 42) "my Lord" That Christ's statements about the Son of Man were of the nature of enigmas we learn from Jn xii 34 "Who is this Son of Man?" See *Son* 3454—5 Here Luke's original and its context may have meant "You, the Sanhedrin, question me 'Art thou the Christ?' To answer that I must needs question you 'What say ye of the Christ?' But if I put the question (ἐὰν ἐρωτήσω) *ye will assuredly not give an answer* (or, *solution*) (οὐ μὴ ἐπιλύσητε)" This has been corrupted by some into the much more common ἀπολύσητε "*release*," but the latter makes such poor sense that the corrupt clause has been generally dropped The original has been supplanted by the paraphrase "Ye will assuredly *not answer* (οὐ μὴ ἀποκριθῆτε)" But some authorities have combined the two readings

THE TRIAL BEFORE THE HIGH PRIEST

He was struck by one of the officers who exclaimed "Answerest thou the high priest so[1]?" Almost immediately after this mention of "the high priest," our present Greek text of John proceeds "Annas therefore *sent him bound unto Caiaphas the high priest.*" There is some uncertainty here about John's text[2]. But it is not uncertain that, as regards the questioning of Jesus, John intervenes for Mark against Luke, supporting Mark in saying that the questioning proceeded from a single person, whereas Luke says it proceeded from the Sanhedrin as a whole.

At this stage of the trial, having before us Christ's reply to His Jewish judges, we should note that this is, virtually, His last word to the Jewish nation. When He next speaks it will be to Pilate. Is there any resemblance between this final word in the Three Gospels and the final word in the Fourth? There is in effect, though not in word. The Three, when they describe the Son as "sitting at the right hand[3]," do not verbally

---

[1] Jn xviii 22. SS simplifies the narrative (1) first, by placing xviii 24 ("Annas sent him") before xviii 14—15, 19—23 so that Annas is mentioned, in two consecutive verses, as having Jesus brought to him, and as sending Him on at once to Caiaphas "the chief priest," who alone is called by that title and who conducts the examination (*ib* 19 "the chief priest was asking Jesus"), (2) secondly, by placing all the Petrine narrative xviii 16—18, 25—27 together, after xviii 23. The only exception is xviii 15 (which describes Peter as "entering into the court"). This is divided from xviii 16 (Peter "standing outside" and brought in) by xviii 19—23 (the examination). The result is as follows:—Jn xviii 13—27 "(13).. brought him first unto Hanan the father-in-law of Caiapha that was the chief priest of that year. (24) *Now Hanan sent him bound* unto Caiapha the chief priest, (14) him that had counselled the Jews (ἦν δὲ Κ ὁ συμβουλεύσας.). (15) Now Simon Kepha...entered with Jesus into the court. (19—23) Now the chief priest was asking. Jesus saith..wherefore didst thou smite me? (16—18) Now Simon Kepha was standing outside...because it was cold. (25—27) Now Simon also was standing. the cock crew."

[2] See above, pp. 507—8.

[3] Mk xiv 62   Mt xxvi 64   Lk xxii 69
Ἐγώ εἰμι, καὶ ὄψεσθε   Σὺ εἶπας (marg   ἀπὸ τοῦ νῦν δὲ ἔσται
τὸν υἱὸν τοῦ ἀνθρώπου   εἶπας,) πλὴν λέγω ὑμῖν,   ὁ υἱὸς τοῦ ἀνθρώπου κα-

(Mark xiv 60—65)

THE TRIAL BEFORE THE HIGH PRIEST

express judgment but they imply it. The Fourth Gospel expresses it "And if any man hear my sayings and keep them

Mk xiv 62 contd	Mt xxvi 64 contd	Lk xxii 69 contd
ἐκ δεξιῶν καθήμενον τῆς δυνάμεως καὶ ἐρχόμενον μετὰ τῶν νεφελῶν τοῦ οὐρανοῦ	ἀπ' ἄρτι ὄψεσθε τὸν υἱὸν τοῦ ἀνθρώπου καθήμενον ἐκ δεξιῶν τῆς δυνάμεως καὶ ἐρχόμενον ἐπὶ τῶν νεφελῶν τοῦ οὐρανοῦ	θήμενος ἐκ δεξιῶν τῆς δυνάμεως τοῦ θεοῦ

Lk refers only to Ps cx 1 ("Sit thou on my right hand"); Mk-Mt. refers to that and to Dan. vii 13 "(lit) And behold, with (עם) the clouds of heaven [one] like a son of man coming he was and even to the Ancient of Days he arrived, and before Him they brought him near"

LXX	Theod.
καὶ ἰδοὺ ἐπὶ τῶν νεφελῶν τοῦ οὐρανοῦ ὡς υἱὸς ἀνθρώπου ἤρχετο, καὶ ὡς παλαιὸς ἡμερῶν παρῆν καὶ οἱ παρεστηκότες παρῆσαν αὐτῷ	καὶ ἰδοὺ μετὰ τῶν νεφελῶν τοῦ οὐρανοῦ ὡς υἱὸς ἀνθρώπου ἐρχόμενος, καὶ ἕως τοῦ παλαιοῦ τῶν ἡμερῶν ἔφθασεν· καὶ προσήχθη αὐτῷ.

In the Hebrew text of Daniel, the "coming" is not from heaven to earth, but "*to*" the Ancient of Days But LXX alters the Heb "*to*" to "*as*" Luke's view of the "coming" in the Acts (1 9—11) is that the Son of Man will descend from heaven on "a [single] cloud" to judge the earth as also He ascended "on a [single] cloud" from earth (comp Lk xxi 27 "in *a cloud*," Mk xiii 26, Mt xxiv 30 "clouds") Perhaps the ancient Hebrew tradition about the Son of Man as "coming" to "the Ancient of Days" whose "throne" (Dan vii 9) "was fiery flames" is referred to in Rev v 6—7 where the Lamb is seen at first "in the midst of" the throne, and the living creatures, and the elders, "standing" as though it had been slain, and then He "*came*," and He takes the Book of the Redemption of the World out of "the right hand of him that sat on the throne"

It seems probable that Jesus, in His answer to the High Priest, referred only (as in Luke) to the Psalm ("*sit* thou on *my right hand*") and that the reference to Daniel ("coming") has been added by Mark for completeness either (1) out of its order, to shew *how* the Son of Man is found to be "seated at the right hand," or else, (2) in a Christian interpretation—deviating from Daniel—to represent the Son as first placed on "the right hand" in heaven, and afterwards "coming" down from heaven to earth to judge His enemies

It has been shewn in *Son* 3347 (1) foll that Jesus did not probably have Daniel in view in the Discourse on the Last Days (where Matthew alone (xxiv 15) says "spoken of by Daniel the prophet") And it is probable, in view of Luke's omission, that Jesus is not quoting Daniel here He appears to be referring only to Ps cx. 1—only to that same scriptural riddle which He had previously set before the Jews

THE TRIAL BEFORE THE HIGH PRIEST

not, I (*emph*) judge him not, for I came not to judge the world but to save the world. He that rejecteth me and receiveth not my sayings hath one that judgeth him. The word that I spake, that same [word] shall judge him in the last day[1]" The thought is of a Saviour converted by our sins into an inevitable and (we may almost say) unwilling Judge, an unalterable Word of Retribution. From two different points of view—the Hebrew ("sitting at the right hand") and the Greek ("judging"), the Eastern and the Western—the Three Gospels and the Fourth express the inevitableness of the Day of the Divine Judgment[2].

In what follows, Luke omits the words "*liable to death*" in which Mark and Matthew record the sentence of condemnation passed by the Sanhedrin[3]. Probably he does it for the same reason that induced him to omit "condemn" before in Christ's prediction :—

Mk x 33	Mt xx. 18—19	Lk. xviii 32
They shall con-demn him to death[4] and shall deliver him unto the Gentiles.	They shall con-demn him to death[4] and shall deliver him unto the Gentiles.	He shall be delivered up unto the Gentiles

Luke may have argued that the Sanhedrin *did not* pass any sentence of death because they *could not legally* pass one. But he does not tell us of their inability. John does tell us In his Gospel, the Jews avow their intention to kill Jesus by saying —when Pilate bids them try Jesus according to their own Law —"It is not lawful for us to put any man to death[5]"

---

as bearing on the nature of "the Christ," when He asked (Mk xii 35) "How say the scribes that the Christ is the son of David?"

[1] Jn xii 47—8

[2] See *Son* 3306—15 on "The Son of Man" and "The Power" discussing details, e g Mk xiv 62 ἐγώ εἰμι, and Mt xxvi 64 ἀπ' ἄρτι

[3] Mk xiv 64 οἱ δὲ πάντες κατέκριναν αὐτὸν ἔνοχον εἶναι θανάτου, Mt xxvi 66 οἱ δὲ ἀποκριθέντες εἶπαν, Ἔνοχος θανάτου ἐστίν, Lk xxii 71 paraphrases this by "We have heard [his guilt] from his own mouth"

[4] Κατακρινοῦσιν αὐτὸν θανάτῳ (W H in Mt [θανάτῳ]) is rather more absolute than ἔνοχος θανάτου

[5] Jn xviii 31

THE TRIAL BEFORE THE HIGH PRIEST

§ 5. *The smiting of Jesus*[1]

In the texts given below, Mark differs from Luke in a detail small in itself but of some importance as pointing toward a background of prophecy. He says that "the officers" struck Jesus (literally "took[2]" Him) with "*blows-of-their-hands.*" The word here used for "blow-of-the-hand," *rapisma*, occurs nowhere in the New Testament, outside the Fourth Gospel, except here. Matthew uses the same word here, as a verb *rapizein*, but does not at this point mention "the officers." Luke has neither word[3]

[1] Mk xiv. 65	Mt. xxvi. 67—8	Lk xxii 63—5
καὶ ἤρξαντό τινες ἐμπτύειν αὐτῷ καὶ περικαλύπτειν αὐτοῦ τὸ πρόσωπον καὶ κολαφίζειν αὐτὸν καὶ λέγειν αὐτῷ Προφήτευσον, καὶ οἱ ὑπηρέται ῥαπίσμασιν αὐτὸν ἔλαβον	τότε ἐνέπτυσαν εἰς τὸ πρόσωπον αὐτοῦ καὶ ἐκολάφισαν αὐτόν, οἱ δὲ ἐράπισαν λέγοντες Προφήτευσον ἡμῖν, χριστέ, τίς ἐστιν ὁ παίσας σε,	καὶ οἱ ἄνδρες οἱ συνέχοντες αὐτὸν ἐνέπαιζον αὐτῷ δέροντες, καὶ περικαλύψαντες αὐτὸν ἐπηρώτων λέγοντες Προφήτευσον, τίς ἐστιν ὁ παίσας σε; καὶ ἕτερα πολλὰ βλασφημοῦντες ἔλεγον εἰς αὐτόν

[2] 'Ραπίσμασιν αὐτὸν ἔλαβον. Comp *Acts of John* § 4 "If thy plucking [of my hair] in jest caused so much pain, what [should I have felt] if thou hadst taken me with blows-of-the-hand (ῥαπίσμασίν με ἔλαβες)?" Origen (on Jerem. xx. 1—2, Lomm xv 339—40), quoting several instances of "smiting" prophets, including Is 1 6 as uttered by Jesus Himself, says that Jesus is being to this day smitten and scourged by Jews and Gentiles "Go into the synagogues of the Jews and see Jesus being scourged by them with the tongue of blasphemy See those gathered together from the Gentiles (ἴδε τοὺς ἀπὸ τῶν ἐθνῶν συναγομένους) taking counsel against Christians [as they call us] in what manner they *take* (or, *receive*) Jesus (τίνα τρόπον λαμβάνουσι τὸν Ἰησοῦν)." The context indicates a play on λαμβάνω alluding to the phrase "*take with blows*"

[3] Why does Luke avoid ὑπηρέτης in the narrative of the Arrest and the Passion, whereas John has it there, about the ὑπηρέται of the chief priests, (xviii. 3—22, xix 6) five times, Mark twice, Matthew once? Luke has it only in his Preface (1 2), "*ministers* of the word," and iv 20 "gave the book to the (R V) *attendant* (A V *minister*)," i e the "*beadle*" of the synagogue In LXX, it perhaps only once represents a Heb word (Prov xiv 35) where it means a king's "servant," who "dealeth wisely" and is in the king's "favour", but in Daniel (LXX) it is applied (LXX [iii 46] not in Heb) to the servants of Nebuchadnezzar who cast the three martyrs into the furnace Matthew applies it to a judge's "beadle" or "bailiff," who

THE TRIAL BEFORE THE HIGH PRIEST

John has both: "One *of the officers*...gave a *blow-of-the-hand* to Jesus[1]." John repeats this later on about the Roman soldiers: "They began to give him *blows-of-their-hands*[2]." We naturally ask why Luke does not use it and why John uses it twice.

A reason why Luke would not use *rapisma* is supplied by the grammarian Phrynichus who says that "it is not in use," meaning in the literary use of Attic Greek[3]. And a reason why

exacts debts, where Luke has "exactor," (Mt. v. 25) "lest the judge deliver thee to the *beadle*" (Lk. xii. 58 *exactor, πράκτορι*). John begins by using it thrice (vii. 32, 45, 46) of the "*beadles*" of "the chief priests and Pharisees" sent to arrest Jesus. On this occasion, they fail to do their official duty, being overpowered by Christ's words (*ib.* 46 "Never man so spake"). They consequently receive a reproof from their superiors. But, later on, the "beadles" act as subservient instruments (xviii. 3, 12, 18, 22, xix. 6) to the chief priests and Pharisees, or even as persecutors on their own account. See also *Joh. Voc.* **1719** *h.*

This seems to explain both the Lucan and the Johannine view. Luke in his Gospel (though not in the Acts) regards a ὑπηρέτης as a "minister" attached to a holy place or office—a synagogue, temple, or gospel. John assumes that the ὑπηρέται of the Temple, under the Pharisees, were, from the first, "beadles" of an unholy place, "a place of traffic," and that they soon became—in spite of one brief reaction—only too ready to serve their worldly and unjust superiors in persecuting Jesus.

In the Acts, Luke varies. The earlier and Petrine portion (Acts v. 22, 26) describing the arrest of the apostles by the Sanhedrin, uses ὑπηρέται to mean "beadles." The later and Pauline portion (xiii. 5, xxvi. 16) uses it to mean a "ministering attendant" on Paul and Barnabas, or to mean Paul himself as a "minister" of the Gospel to the Gentiles.

[1] Jn xviii. 22 εἰς παρεστηκὼς τῶν ὑπηρετῶν ἔδωκεν ῥάπισμα τῷ Ἰησοῖ.

[2] Jn xix. 3 καὶ ἐδίδοσαν αὐτῷ ῥαπίσματα. Apparently Pilate sanctions this, as he certainly does the mockery that follows, in order to beg off (so to speak), as being beneath contempt, this "king of the Jews" about whom he says (*ib.* 4) "I bring him forth to you that ye may know that I find no crime in him."

[3] Phrynichus: Τὸ ῥάπισμα οὐκ ἐν χρήσει· χρῶ οὖν τῷ κρείττονι· τὸ γὰρ τὴν γνάθον πλατείᾳ τῇ χειρὶ πλῆξαι ἐπὶ κόρρης πατάξαι Ἀθηναῖοι φασίν. Facts indicate (see Field on Mk xiv. 65 and on Jn xviii. 22) that the rendering of R.V. marg. "blows with rods" would not apply except to ancient or quasi-ancient (*i.e.* deliberately archaic) Greek.

THE TRIAL BEFORE THE HIGH PRIEST

John might retain and emphasize it, is, that it occurs in the following passage of Isaiah: "The Lord God hath given me the tongue of them that are taught, that I should know how to sustain with words him that is weary: he wakeneth morning by morning, he wakeneth mine ear to hear...and I was not rebellious...I gave my back to the smiters and my cheeks *to them that plucked off the hair* (LXX *to blows-of-the-hand*), I hid not my face from shame and spitting. For the Lord God will help me...and I know that I shall not be ashamed. He is near that justifieth me; who will contend with me[1]?" This is almost immediately followed by the passage quoted above as applicable to the officers "warming themselves" round the fire ("walk ye in the flame of your fire...ye shall lie down in sorrow[2]"). *Rapisma* occurs nowhere else in LXX. Barnabas and Justin Martyr both quote the Isaiah passage mentioning *rapisma*[3]. No early Christian writer beside them (except the *Didachè*) uses the word at all, and they use it only in this quotation from Isaiah. We may therefore infer that John retained the Marcan word rejected by Luke because it led back his readers to Isaiah. For the sake of doing this, he might well be prepared to deviate from the usage of literary Greek[4].

Mark appears to distinguish the "officers," who insulted Jesus in this particular way, from others, who inflicted other insults. John does not describe this general outburst of insolence, which occurred after the High Priest had pronounced sentence. But by describing a "blow" of this particular kind

---

[1] Is. l. 4—8. The words "tongue of *them that are taught*" recall Heb. v. 8 "*learned obedience by the things that he suffered.*" The latter part is quoted in Rom. viii. 33—4. There is a martyr's paradox in "I hid not my face from shame" and "I know that I shall not be ashamed."   [2] Is. l. 11.

[3] Barn. v. 14, Justin M. *Apol.* § 38. The *Didachè* uses the sing. once (i. 4) referring to Mt. v. 39.

[4] Yet Jesus Himself does not say τί με ῥαπίζεις; to the officer who has given Him a ῥάπισμα. He says (Jn xviii. 23) τί με δέρεις; Did John shrink from representing Jesus as using a word corresponding to our "slap"? Or did he guard against the insinuation that Jesus artfully used a Messianic word in order to suggest that He was the Messiah?

(Mark xiv. 60—65)

as given by "an officer," in the presence of Annas, before Jesus had been sent to Caiaphas for formal trial, John leads us to infer that other "officers," after condemnation, would continue such insults.

There are many tokens of verbal confusions in the context. Mark omits "Who smote thee?" Matthew omits Mark's "covered his face round." Luke alters it into "covered him round," which appears to indicate a protest against Mark's tradition, and might mean "covered him round *with a robe*, or *chlamys*." Luke also omits the "spitting." This might be explained by a confusion of επτγον "spit" with ετγπτον "struck," used later on by Mark and Matthew (but not by Luke) in their account of the second mocking[1].

§ 6. *"Thou also wast with Jesus," in Mark and Matthew*[2]

Luke regards this utterance of "a maid-servant" as addressed not to Peter but to bystanders. He agrees, however, with

---

[1] See below, pp. 564—70, and esp. p. 568. Jn, too, omits "spitting"—an instance of the failure of Johannine Intervention— perhaps as being repellent (*Joh. Voc.* **1666**).

[2] (i) THE FIRST DENIAL

Mk xiv. 54, 66—8 (R.V.)	Mt. xxvi. 58, 69—71 a (R.V.)	Lk. xxii. 54 b—57 (R.V.)
(54) And Peter had followed him afar off, even within, into the court of the high priest; and he was sitting with the officers, and warming himself in the light [of the fire].	(58) But Peter followed him afar off, unto the court of the high priest, and entered in, and sat with the officers, to see the end.	(54) ...brought him into the high priest's house. But Peter followed afar off. (55) And when they had kindled a fire in the midst of the court, and had sat down together, Peter sat in the midst of them.
(66) And as Peter was beneath in the court, there cometh one of the maids of the high priest; (67) And seeing Peter warming himself, she looked upon him, and saith, Thou also wast with the	(69) Now Peter was sitting without in the court: and a maid came unto him, saying, Thou also wast with Jesus the Galilaean.	(56) And a certain maid seeing him as he sat in the light [of the fire], and looking stedfastly upon him, said, This man also was with him.

THE TRIAL BEFORE THE HIGH PRIEST

Mark that it was uttered after a stedfast gaze and recognition, but substitutes the third person ("this man") for the second ("thou").

(i) THE FIRST DENIAL contd

Mk xiv 54, 66—8 (R V) contd	Mt. xxvi 58, 69— 71 a (R V) contd	Lk xxii 54 b—57 (R V) contd.
Nazarene, [even] Jesus. (68) But he denied, saying, I neither know, nor understand what thou sayest (or, I neither know, nor understand. thou, what sayest thou?) and he went out into the porch (lit forecourt), and the cock crew (many anc auth omit and the cock crew).	(70) But he denied before them all, saying, I know not what thou sayest. (71) And when he was gone out into the porch, ...	(57) But he denied, saying, Woman, I know him not

Jn xviii 15—17 (R V) (15) And Simon Peter followed Jesus, and [so did] another disciple. Now that disciple was known unto the high priest, and entered in with Jesus into the court of the high priest, (16) but Peter was standing at the door without So the other disciple, which was known unto the high priest, went out and spake unto her that kept the door, and brought in Peter (17) The maid therefore that kept the door saith unto Peter, Art thou also [one] of this man's disciples? He saith, I am not.

(ii) THE SECOND DENIAL

Mk xiv 69—70 a (R V)	Mt xxvi 71 b—72 (R V)	Lk xxii 58 (R V)
(69) And the maid saw him, and began again to say to them that stood by, This is [one] of them (70) But he again denied it.	(71) . another [maid] saw him, and saith unto them that were there, This man also was with Jesus the Nazarene. (72) And again he denied with an oath, I know not the man.	(58) And after a little while another (ἕτερος, masc., lit. a different [person]) saw him, and said, Thou also art [one] of them. But Peter said, Man, I am not.

Jn xviii 18, 25 (R V) (18) Now the servants (lit. bondservants) and the officers were standing [there], having made a fire of coals (lit a fire of charcoal), for it was cold, and they were warming themselves and Peter also was with them, standing and warming himself . . (25) Now Simon Peter was standing and warming himself They said therefore unto him, Art thou also [one] of his disciples? He denied, and said, I am not.

THE TRIAL BEFORE THE HIGH PRIEST

But why do the three Synoptists insert "also," as if the maid-servant meant " We have already one follower among us, and now here is *also* another ! " ? John's narrative suggests that perhaps this *was* her meaning There *was*, he says, already in the palace another disciple known to the High Priest, and he spoke to the maid-servant—who was the portress —to let Peter in. While doing so, she could not refrain—in the moment of recognising Peter—from saying to him in jest "Is it possible? Can it be that you also are a disciple of his? We have already among us one disciple of the prisoner whom they want to crucify And now, at his request, am I to let in another disciple? "

(iii) THE THIRD DENIAL

Mk xiv 70 b—72 (R V)	Mt xxvi 73—5 (R V)	Lk xxii 59—62 (R V)
(70) .. And after a little while again they that stood by said to Peter, Of a truth thou art [one] of them, for thou art a Galilaean.	(73) And after a little while they that stood by came and said to Peter, Of a truth thou also art [one] of them, for thy speech bewrayeth thee	(59) And after the space of about one hour another (*masc*) confidently affirmed, saying, Of a truth this man also was with him for he is a Galilaean
(71) But he began to curse and to swear, I know not this man of whom ye speak	(74) Then began he to curse and to swear, I know not the man And straightway the cock crew	(60) But Peter said, Man, I know not what thou sayest. And immediately, while he yet spake, the cock crew
(72) And straightway the second time the cock crew And Peter called to mind the word, how that Jesus said unto him, Before the cock crow twice, thou shalt deny me thrice And when he thought thereon, he wept (*or*, And he began to weep)	(75) And Peter remembered the word which Jesus had said, Before the cock crow, thou shalt deny me thrice And he went out, and wept bitterly	(61) And the Lord turned, and looked upon Peter And Peter remembered the word of the Lord, how that he said unto him, Before the cock crow this day, thou shalt deny me thrice (62) And he went out, and wept bitterly

Jn xviii. 26—7 (R V) (26) One of the servants (*lit* bondservants) of the high priest, being a kinsman of him whose ear Peter cut off, saith, Did not I see thee in the garden with him ? (27) Peter therefore denied again   and straightway the cock crew

THE TRIAL BEFORE THE HIGH PRIEST

It is generally assumed that this first disciple was John the son of Zebedee. If it was, then the jesting question of the portress to Peter means no more than this: "Have we here in you a second disciple of this Galilaean so bold as to venture into the lion's den?" But it is possible that Judas is meant[1]. He would be "known to the high priest"—and to the portress also in the course of several recent visits to the palace, during the arrangements for the arrest of Jesus. And though there are great difficulties in this hypothesis, they are hardly so great as the difficulty of supposing that this single passage reveals the disciple whom Jesus loved as being also the disciple that was "known" to the High Priest who condemned Jesus.

If Judas was the other disciple whom the portress had in mind, then her "*also*" assumes quite a new meaning, and her jest a new bitterness. "Can it be that thou *also*, like Judas, art one of this man's disciples, returning like Judas, with the Master whom thou hast betrayed?" If that was the meaning, one can understand how Peter—who up to that moment may not have realised fully that Judas was a traitor[2]—realising now what the question meant ("Are you, too, a traitor?"), may have hastily replied—to the meaning, rather than to the words—"I am not." Then he may have found himself led on, step by step, into absolute denial of discipleship.

---

[1] For this view of Jn xviii 15 see *Beginning*, pp 351—71

[2] According to Mark (xiv 45—6) nothing had been said by Jesus, and according to Matthew (xxvi 50) nothing had been said clearly, to indicate that Judas was a traitor. According to John, logically, Peter ought to have realised it from Christ's giving Judas "the sop" (Jn xiii 26), but (from the Johannine point of view) not from any words of Christ to Judas, for, in Jn, Christ's last words to Judas are understood by (xiii 28) "no man at the table." In Mk and Jn there are no words corresponding to Lk xxii 48 ("Judas, betrayest thou ?") None of the Synoptists tell us whether Judas, after saluting Jesus, kept up the pretence of discipleship and fled away with the rest of the disciples, or whether he returned with the soldiers and Jesus, followed at a distance by Peter, to the High Priest's palace. See note above (p 480, n 2 *ad fin*) on the epithet ἀλλοπροσαλλος attached by Nonnus to Judas

§ 7. "He began to anathematize, Mark and Matthew[1]

"Anathematize," in LXX, means to "ban," "devote [to God]," "exterminate." A city, for example, hostile to Jehovah, was "devoted," or "anathematized," when it was doomed to be utterly destroyed. A thing thus doomed to destruction was, in Hebrew, *cherem*, or, in Greek, *anathema*[2]. Paul says concerning any one that distorts the Gospel "Let him be *anathema*," and again "If any man loveth not the Lord, let him be *anathema*[3]." This was equivalent to saying "Let him be *anathematized*." In the Acts Paul says that "in all the synagogues" he tried to constrain the Christians to "*blaspheme*[4]." This appears to mean to "*curse*," or "*anathematize*," the name of Christ[5]. Similarly Pliny says that he acquitted such Christians as prayed to the gods and made an offering to the image of the Emperor "and, furthermore, *cursed* Christ[6]." When Paul came to Antioch of Pisidia and Corinth he at first taught in the synagogue but separated himself from it when the Jews "*blasphemed*[7]."

---

[1] Mk xiv 71—72 a
ὁ δὲ ἤρξατο ἀναθεματίζειν καὶ ὀμνύναι ὅτι Οὐκ οἶδα τὸν ἄνθρωπον τοῦτον ὃν λέγετε. καὶ εὐθὺς ἐκ δευτέρου ἀλέκτωρ ἐφώνησεν καὶ ἀνεμνήσθη...

Mt xxvi 74—75 a
τότε ἤρξατο καταθεματίζειν καὶ ὀμνύειν ὅτι Οὐκ οἶδα τὸν ἄνθρωπον καὶ εὐθὺς ἀλέκτωρ ἐφώνησεν· καὶ ἐμνήσθη ...

Lk xxii 60—61 a
εἶπεν δὲ ὁ Πέτρος "Ἄνθρωπε, οὐκ οἶδα ὃ λέγεις. καὶ παραχρῆμα ἔτι λαλοῦντος αὐτοῦ ἐφώνησεν ἀλέκτωρ καὶ στραφεὶς ὁ κύριος ἐνέβλεψεν τῷ Πέτρῳ, καὶ ὑπεμνήσθη ...

Jn xviii 27 πάλιν οὖν ἠρνήσατο Πέτρος καὶ εὐθέως ἀλέκτωρ εφώνησεν

[2] Gesen. 355—6 חרם. Ἀναθεματίζω, in LXX, alw. = חרם, and so does ἀνάθεμα. It is quite different in meaning from ὄμνυμι "swear"

[3] Gal. i 9, 1 Cor. xvi. 22   [4] Acts xxvi 11

[5] Comp Jas ii 7 "Do not the rich...*blaspheme the honourable name by which ye are called?*" that is, the name of Christ

[6] Pliny *Epist* x. 97 "maledicerent Christo," quoted by Lightf. on *Mart Polyc* § 9 "swear (ὄμοσον) and I release thee, *revile* (λοιδόρησον) *the Christ*." It was not enough to (*ib*) "swear by the fortune of Caesar (ὄμοσον τὴν Καίσαρος τύχην)." Polycarp must also "*revile*" his Saviour. Pliny says a true Christian would never do this. It seems probable that the Romans borrowed this test of a Christian from Jewish precedents in synagogues.

[7] Acts xiii 45—8, xviii 6—7.

THE TRIAL BEFORE THE HIGH PRIEST

And this reference to a growing Jewish custom may explain Paul's warning to the Corinthians "No man speaking in the Spirit of God saith '*Jesus is anathema*[1]'" Matthew's form of the word (*catathematize*) is used twice by Irenaeus of faithful Christians "*catathematizing*" a misleading teacher or a misleading doctrine[2] Thus the usage of the Hebrew word *cherem* and of the Greek word *anathema* points to the conclusion that Mark—very possibly under a wrong impression—regarded Peter as falling in with the language of those around him so as to anathematize, not himself conditionally, but his Master absolutely. For those who took that view the contextual phrase "I do not know" would seem to mean "I ignore, or, renounce[3]" Matthew has most nearly preserved this; Mark has made it less abrupt; Luke has entirely departed from it[4].

It is highly improbable that Peter, amid the officers and

---

[1] 1 Cor xii 3 This might be addressed to devout proselytes who had been in the habit of attending worship in the synagogue, as much as to say, "There must be limits to your acquiescence in Jewish practice" A scholium attributed to Origen (Cramer on 1 Cor xii 3) says that if you behold a Jew interpreting the Old Testament, and in particular the Prophets, in a manner by no means to be despised, he may leave you in doubt whether he has, or has not, the Holy Spirit "In order therefore that you may not be in two minds ($\pi\epsilon\rho\iota\sigma\pi\alpha\sigma\theta\tilde{\eta}s$) about such a one whether he has the Holy Spirit or not, he [i e Paul] teaches that, since *every Jew calls Jesus anathema*..., and no one speaking in the Spirit of God calls Jesus anathema, the Spirit of God is not possessed by him who says that he knows the Law and the Prophets and yet anathematizes Jesus" Origen often refers incidentally to 1 Cor. xii 3, and refers fully to it again in *De Orat* § 22 (Lomm xvii 172—4) as to the danger of "anathematizing Jesus" by our wicked actions, but he does not there mention the practice of "every Jew"

[2] Iren i. 13 4 of women "anathematizing" the heretic Marcus who tried to deceive and seduce them, καταθεματίσασαι αὐτὸν ἐχωρίσθησαν τοῦ τοιούτου θιάσου (comp *ib* 1 16 3 ἣν γνώμην καταθεματίσαντας)

[3] Comp Mt xxv 12 "I know you not," and Mt vii. 23, Lk xiii 27 (*Son* 3213 b, 3499 (x) (xi))

[4] Mt xxvi 74 οὐκ οἶδα τὸν ἄνθρωπον is more contemptuous, and less liable to be taken literally, than Mk xiv 71, which adds τοῦτον ὃν λέγετε Lk xxii 60 ἄνθρωπε, οὐκ οἶδα ὃ λέγεις comes, not as a climax, but as an anti-climax, in the three denials.

THE TRIAL BEFORE THE HIGH PRIEST

soldiers, would use an ecclesiastical term like *anathema* or *cherem*. But it is not improbable that Mark has anachronistically inserted here a term that came into use afterwards when Christians were compelled to choose between death and cursing Christ. Peter himself, perhaps, exaggerated his own fault, and a Petrine record in Mark has preserved a trace of the exaggeration. The force of the Marcan word could not but be felt by those who knew its antecedent use. It is true that some good Latin Versions blunt its force by inserting "*himself*" ("Peter devoted himself [to destruction]")[1]. But the Vulgate does not do this, either in Mark or in Matthew[2]. In the former it transliterates the Greek *anathematize*. In the latter it adopts the rendering "*detestari*," which is regularly used of execrating others (not oneself)[3]. Origen, while not going so far as to say that Peter under the influence of an evil spirit used the expression mentioned by Paul "Jesus is *anathema*," quotes the Pauline context ("Jesus is the Lord") in order to explain Peter's conduct. "No one can say *Jesus is the Lord*, except in the Holy Spirit." He reminds us that "the Holy Spirit was not yet," and adds "Therefore it was not possible that Peter as he then was, and at that time, could confess Jesus[4]."

---

[1] "Himself" is ins. by *a* and *k* in Mk, and by *a* and *b* in Mt.

[2] *Thes. Syr.* 1373 gives Mt xxvi. 74 למחרמו (see Noldeke § 167 on the termination in *ū*) = καταθεματίζειν, but Mk xiv. 71 מחרים = ἀναθεματίζειν, ib. 1376 Mt xxvi. 74 מחרים and מחרם. It does not give any instances (outside the Petrine narrative) of חרם, used absolutely, to mean "curse *oneself*." In Acts xxiii. 12 etc. the Syr. has (lit.) "cursed *on them[selves]*." In Syr. (Noldeke § 223) personal pronouns are used as reflexives when the verb is not reflexive. This might result in ambiguity. In Mt xxvii. 5 "hanged *himself*," SS has "*him[self]*" לה, but Pesh. "*his soul*"

[3] There is in Scripture a freq. formula of asserting on oath, "The Lord do so unto me and more also," Ruth i. 17, 1 S. iii. 17 etc. But it has no connection with the Hebrew חרם, ἀναθεματίζειν. Lewis and Short give no instance of *detestari* with *se*.

[4] Origen on Mt xxvi. 68 foll. (Lomm. v. 15) quotes thus "Tunc coepit devotare et jurare quia nescio hominem," omitting "se" before "devotare" (as Codex *Corb*. (Migne) does in Mk), but subsequently

THE TRIAL BEFORE THE HIGH PRIEST

Luke omits all mention of "anathematizing" or "swearing," and John inserts nothing that corresponds to it, having simply

(Lomm pp 17, 19) the Latin has "coepit *se* devotare et jurare.. ," and "non solum ter denegat Petrus, sed etiam devotat *se ipsum* et jurat quia ." In Mt xxvi 74 Vulg and *Corb.* (Migne) and *Brix.* render καταθεματίζειν by "detestari," which means (Lewis and Short) "curse some person, or thing, while calling God to witness," and hence "renounce," "abominate," but not "call down penalties on oneself." Chrysostom gives no explanation of *anathematize* or *catathematize*.

In Mk and Mt, Delitzsch inserts Heb "his [own] soul" after חרם to shew that Peter was devoting himself to destruction if he was not speaking the truth (and we should have expected this in Syr also if the translator thought this to be the fact) But Gesen and Levy give no instance of such a use of חרם in Biblical or later Hebrew In Acts xxiii 12 "anathematized themselves," the Gk inserts ἑαυτούς, Delitzsch "bound a bond on their souls"

The following facts indicate that the Gospel narratives of Peter's denial distinguished between (1) "*denying* (ἀρνεῖσθαι) Jesus" and (2) "*disowning* (ἀπαρνεῖσθαι) Jesus" Ἀπαρνοῦμαι is used in Christ's prediction of Peter's denial and in Peter's reply, Mk xiv 30, 31, 72 με or σε, Mt xxvi 34, 35, 75 με or σε, Lk xxii 34 με .εἰδέναι, *ib* 61 με Ἀρνοῦμαι is used in the evangelistic description of fact, Mk xiv. 68 ἠρνήσατο λέγων Οὔτε οἶδα . , *ib* 70 πάλιν ἠρνεῖτο, Mt xxvi 70 ἠρνήσατο. λέγων Οὐκ οἶδα . , *ib* 72 ἠρνήσατο μετὰ ὅρκου ὅτι Οὐκ οἶδα..., Lk xxii 57 ὁ δὲ ἠρνήσατο [Tisch + αὐτόν] λέγων Οὐκ οἶδα... The Synoptists give us the impression that what is expressed in Christ's words by the intensive ἀπο-, is expressed in their words by the context. And the context in Mt indicates that Matthew believed the vehemence of disavowal to have risen, from (1) assertion to (2) oath, and from oath to (3) oath supported by anathema In Mk, the second stage is omitted

John makes no such distinction In Jn xiii 38, xviii 25, 27, ἀρνεῖσθαι is used both in Christ's prediction (with με) and in the narrative of its fulfilment (without με), and he nowhere uses ἀπαρνεῖσθαι Not improbably John thought that the phrase "Jesus is anathema"—introduced into synagogues by Jews and, later on, in a Roman shape, into courts of justice by Romans—had given to the word new associations, which made it unprofitable to amplify detailed distinctions as to the form of Peter's denials

It should be noted that Matthew and Luke (but not Mark) have previously represented Jesus as using the phrase ἀρνεῖσθαί με —

THE TRIAL BEFORE THE HIGH PRIEST

(1) "I am not," (2) "denied, and said, I am not," (3) "denied again " John also omits the tradition of the Three that Peter "wept"—to which Mark adds a word rendered by R.V. text

Mt x 33   Lk xii. 9

ὅστις δὲ ἀρνήσηταί με ἔμπροσθεν   ὁ δὲ ἀρνησάμενός με ἐνώπιον τῶν
τῶν ἀνθρώπων, ἀρνήσομαι κἀγὼ αὐτὸν   ἀνθρώπων ἀπαρνηθήσεται ἐνώπιον
ἔμπροσθεν τοῦ πατρός μου τοῦ ἐν τοῖς   τῶν ἀγγέλων τοῦ θεοῦ.
οὐρανοῖς.

Mark, in a similar saying, has ἐπαισχύνεσθαί με, and Luke (not Matthew) follows him —

Mk viii 38 a   Mt xvi. 27—8 om.   Lk ix. 26

ὃς γὰρ ἐὰν ἐπαι-   ὃς γὰρ ἂν ἐπαι-
σχυνθῇ με καὶ τοὺς   σχυνθῇ με καὶ τοὺς
ἐμοὺς λόγους ἐν τῇ γενεᾷ   ἐμοὺς λόγους, τοῦτον ὁ
ταύτῃ τῇ μοιχαλίδι καὶ   υἱὸς τοῦ ἀνθρώπου ἐπαι-
ἁμαρτωλῷ, καὶ ὁ υἱὸς τοῦ   σχυνθήσεται ...
ἀνθρώπου ἐπαισχυνθή-
σεται αὐτόν....

Wetstein and Schottgen on Mt x 33 quote Talmudic passages shewing that Heb כפר with ב *lit* " wipe away in M or N " (*i e.* " wipe away all recollections in the case of M or N ") is used about pupils "disowning" teachers and teachers "disowning" pupils (and so Levy ii 383 *b* foll) But the Heb prep "in" is added, and ἀρνοῦμαι ἔν τινι would not be genuine Greek It happens that Heb חפר (Is 1 29) with Heb "from" means (Gesen 344 *a*) "*be ashamed of*" Perhaps Jesus used both words Or the similarity between חפר and כפר may have been a partial cause of the substitution of the one for the other Mark may also have been influenced by the fact that the tradition " Whoever shall *deny me*" seemed expressly to condemn Peter and all deniers to be denied in the Day of Judgment, whereas "*be ashamed*" left room for some evasion of the hard saying It should be noted that no evangelist (setting aside Lk xxii 57 Tisch) says in his narrative that Peter " denied *him*" i e Jesus Since they all avoid this, it seems unlikely that Mark could have intended us to supply "him" as the object to "anathematize " Perhaps Mark may have used the verb loosely to mean that Peter, as it were, cast oaths and anathemas about him, including in his curses those who were accusing him of being one of Christ's disciples In any case the use of it by Mark and Matthew in so brief and obscure a context was much to be deprecated It might induce some of Pliny's victims to say, " Peter anathematized and was forgiven, why should it be otherwise with me?" This is the very question that Origen meets, assuring the questioners that what was pardoned in Peter will not be pardoned in them (Lomm. v 17 "in nobis hoc impium ").

THE TRIAL BEFORE THE HIGH PRIEST

"when he thought thereon[1]," while Matthew and (probably) Luke add "bitterly[2]."

It has been necessary to mention these details because the "anathematizing" constitutes an exception to the rule of Johannine Intervention And indeed it is easy to understand that John may have felt that the Petrine narrative, especially in Mark, came to a weak conclusion. Origen and Jerome indicate that it was made the subject of some allegorical and forced interpretation. "I know not the man," Jerome tells us, was erroneously taken by some as meaning "I know not Jesus as man, for I know Him to be God"! Jerome himself follows Origen in allegorizing the statement that Peter went "*outside*" the court of the High Priest, before he wept and repented, as meaning "outside the dominion of evil[3]." And

---

[1] Mk xiv 72 ἐπιβαλών, of which the explanation in *Corrections* 499—501 is not satisfactory Ἐπιβάλλω might *seem* used absolutely in certain instances where an object might be supplied from context (e g. Moulton *Gr of N T Gk* p 131, an instance where ἐπιβολή "embankment" occurs in context) but these prove nothing Cramer, on Mk, prints a tradition that Peter "wept terribly, Christ having given heed to him (προσεσχηκότος αὐτῷ)," and it is pointed out in *Notes* 2999 (xiii) that Mt. xvii 25 προέφθασεν αὐτόν is rendered in Syriac by קדם which in Is xxxvii 33 = (LXX) ἐπιβάλλω In Epict 1 4 14 the original txt, ἐπιβάλλεις, has been perhaps wrongly corrected into ἐπιβάλλῃ and signifies "direct [the mind]" (comp *Ench* 15 μὴ ἐπίβαλλε πόρρω τὴν ὄρεξιν) Field has shewn that it is often used of covering the head But it would also naturally be connected with ἐπίβλημα Now although this word in the Synoptists means "a patch," it appears to mean more freq (Steph *Thes*) "vestimentum exterius, amiculum, stragulum torale"

The uncertainty about the meaning of ἐπιβαλών does not affect the conclusion that the Marcan tradition omitted by Matthew and Luke would be discussed by early Christians to whom it would suggest paraphrases Among these would naturally be one describing how Peter, in the end, received a covering of his sin, "putting on" the Lord Jesus Christ

[2] Mt xxvi 75 καὶ ἐξελθὼν ἔξω ἔκλαυσεν πικρῶς, [Lk xxii 62 καὶ ἐξελθὼν ἔξω ἔκλαυσεν πικρῶς]

[3] Jerome on Mt xxvi 75 "In atrio Caiaphae sedens non poterat agere poenitentiam Egreditur *foras de impiorum consilio...*" We shall find it hard to realise the motive for this, unless we remember

THE TRIAL BEFORE THE HIGH PRIEST

here we may note that, in Mark, Peter is said to have "gone out *outside* into the fore-court," after the first denial[1], in Matthew and Luke to have "gone out *outside*" finally after the third denial[2]; but in John to have merely "stood at the door *outside*," that is, outside the court of the High Priest—and this, at the beginning, before any denial[3]. Also the Diatessaron says "And when Jesus went *out* Simon Cephas was standing in the outer court..." and, later on, "The cock crew twice. And in that hour Jesus turned, he being *outside*, and looked stedfastly at Cephas." It also omits Mark's mention of Peter going out into the forecourt and the parallel Matthew[4].

that, among first-century Christians, "*without* (ἔξω)" and "those that are *without* (οἱ ἔξω)," would naturally be applied to "*those in outer darkness*," "*aliens from the Church*," or "*sinners*," in whom they would be most reluctant to include Peter even temporarily. Moreover, Philo (1 95) allegorizing the first Biblical instance (Gen. xv 5) of ἔξω with a verb of motion (about Abraham) takes it as Origen and Jerome do here

[1] Mk xiv 68 Comp Judg iii 23 *lit* "went forth *the porch*," where A V supplies "*through*," R V "*into*"

[2] Mt xxvi 75, Lk xxii 62

[3] Jn xviii. 16.

[4] Mk xiv 68, Mt xxvi 71

Some comment is due to the fact that the Synoptists all describe Peter as "*sitting*," Mark once (xiv 54), Matthew twice (xxvi 58, 69), Luke twice in one passage (xxii 55—6 "Peter *sat*...seeing him as he *sat*"), while John twice (xviii 18, 25) describes him as "*standing*"

One explanation might be that (Gesen 442—3) the Hebrew "*sit*" repeatedly means "continue," "remain," "tarry," "stay" Mk xiv 66 "while Peter *was* [i e *continued*] in the *aulè*" is parall. to Mt xxvi 69 "But Peter *sat* outside in the *aulè*," and may represent an original ישׁב "sit." See *Clue* **178**

Another explanation is that the Hebrew ישׁב "sit" is identical with some forms of שׁוב "return and do," "do again" See *Clue* **9** giving seven instances where R V has "turn," "return," "again," or "the second time," but LXX "sit" Hence "he denied *again*" or "*continued* to deny" might be expressed by "he *sat* and denied."

In deviating from the unanimous Synoptic tradition, John might also have in view an allegorical object Perhaps he wished to exhibit Peter as "standing" before "falling," and as falling because he "stood" in the pride of his own strength (not "taking heed" lest he should "fall" (1 Cor x 12)) But he would do this all the more

THE TRIAL BEFORE THE HIGH PRIEST

The obscurity of Mark's conclusion ("when he thought thereon") is removed in Matthew and Luke by substituting "wept *bitterly*" But this, according to LXX usage, suggests futility or remorse rather than repentance[1]. It might convey to some readers the thought of such tears as are mentioned in the Epistle to the Hebrews along with a "root of bitterness[2]." John, later on, records Peter's penitence, expressed not in tears but in action, and it is possible—though we cannot say that it is more than conditionally probable—that, if the Marcan word rendered "he thought thereon," meant originally "covering with a garment," then John is alluding to this in his description of Peter as clothing himself after having been "naked," before coming into Christ's presence[3].

---

readily if some evidence seemed to him to favour the view that "*repeatedly* denied" had been mistaken by the Synoptists for "*sat down* and denied"

On Lk xxii 55 περιάψαντες see *Son* **3369** *a*, and add that Heb. "sit," ישב = Aram "surround," סחר (Levy *Ch* ii 153)

[1] See Is xxii 4 "I will shew bitterness in weeping," *i e* weep bitterly, from מרר "embitter," and מרה or מר "bitter" in Ezek xxvii. 30, Zeph 1. 14, Is xxxiii. 7 (Gesen. p 600) Marah was the name of the bitter spring in the wilderness, and Naomi, in the bitterness of her sorrow for bereavements, said (Ruth 1 20) "Call me not Naomi but Marah."

[2] Heb xii. 15—17 "lest any *root of bitterness* springing up trouble [you]...lest [there be] any profane person as Esau. .when he desired to inherit the blessing, he was rejected...*though he sought it diligently with tears*"

[3] Jn xxi 7. See *Notes* **2999** (xvii) *a—o* on "The re-clothing of Peter" On the early conjectures about Mk xiv 72 ἐπιβαλών, see Swete *ad loc*, and *Corrections* **499—501**, where it is conjectured that there may have been some early connection between the Marcan word and Lk xxii 32 (about Peter) ἐπιστρέψας 'Επιβάλλειν is used about "taking note of," or "giving heed to," dreams by Artemidorus 1 11 πῶς ἐπιβλητέον ταῖς κρίσεσιν...χρὴ δὲ κρίνειν τοὺς ὀνείρους, 1 19 ἐγὼ δὲ...ἐν ὕπνοις θεασάμενος...ἐπέβαλον μὲν ὡς λύπης...δηλωτικὸν εἴη τὸ ὄναρ. It would apply to Peter, in a vision, "taking note" that (Lk. xxii. 61) "the Lord looked on" him, and forgave him It might be rendered "considered," corresponding to Heb. שכל and implying "insight." "Considered" is applied to visions or miracles in Dan vii. 8, Acts xi. 6 (Peter's vision), xii. 12 (Peter's release by the angel).

CHAPTER XIII

THE TRIAL BEFORE PILATE

[Mark xv. 1—15]

§ 1. *The Praetorium*[1]

PILATE is introduced to the reader of the Gospels in different ways. Without any previous mention of the name, Mark and

---

[1] Mk xv 1—5 (R V.)

(1) And straightway in the morning the chief priests with the elders and scribes, and the whole council, held a consultation, and bound Jesus, and carried him away, and delivered him up to Pilate.

(2) And Pilate asked him, Art thou the King of the Jews? And he answering saith unto him, Thou sayest.

(3) And the chief priests accused him of many things.

(4) And Pilate again asked him, say-

Mt xxvii 1—2, 11—14 (R V.)

(1) Now when morning was come, all the chief priests and the elders of the people took counsel against Jesus to put him to death

(2) And they bound him, and led him away, and delivered him up to Pilate the governor.

(11) Now Jesus stood before the governor and the governor asked him, saying, Art thou the King of the Jews? And Jesus said unto him, Thou sayest

(12) And when he was accused by the chief priests and elders, he answered nothing.

(13) Then saith Pilate unto him,

Lk xxiii 1—5, 9—10 (R V)

(1) And the whole company of them rose up, and brought him before Pilate.

(2) And they began to accuse him, saying, We found this man perverting our nation, and forbidding to give tribute to Caesar, and saying that he himself is Christ, a king (*or*, an anointed king).

(3) And Pilate asked him, saying, Art thou the King of the Jews? And he answered him and said, Thou sayest.

(4) And Pilate said unto the chief priests and the multitudes, I find no fault in this man

(5) But they were the more urgent....

540 (Mark xv 1—5)

THE TRIAL BEFORE PILATE

Matthew say that the Jews "having bound[1] Jesus, carried him

Mk xv 1—5 (R V) contd	Mt xxvii 1—2, 11—14 (R V) contd	Lk xxiii 1—5, 9—10 (R V) contd
ing, Answerest thou nothing? behold how many things they accuse thee of (5) But Jesus no more answered anything, insomuch that Pilate marvelled	Hearest thou not how many things they witness against thee? (14) And he gave him no answer, not even to one word insomuch that the governor marvelled greatly	(9) And he [i.e. Herod] questioned him in many words; but he answered him nothing (10) And the chief priests and the scribes stood, vehemently accusing him

Jn xviii 28, 33—8 (R V) (28) They lead Jesus therefore from Caiaphas into the palace (*lit* praetorium) and it was early, and they themselves entered not into the palace (*lit* praetorium), that they might not be defiled, but might eat the passover .. (33) Pilate therefore entered again into the palace (*lit* praetorium), and called Jesus, and said unto him, Art thou the King of the Jews? (34) Jesus answered, Sayest thou this of thyself, or did others tell it thee concerning me? (35) Pilate answered, Am I a Jew? Thine own nation and the chief priests delivered thee unto me what hast thou done? (36) Jesus answered, My kingdom is not of this world if my kingdom were of this world, then would my servants (*or*, officers) fight, that I should not be delivered to the Jews but now is my kingdom not from hence (37) Pilate therefore said unto him, Art thou a king then? Jesus answered, Thou sayest that I am a king (*or*, Thou sayest [it], because I am a king) To this end have I been born, and to this end am I come into the world, that I should bear witness unto the truth Every one that is of the truth heareth my voice. (38) Pilate saith unto him, What is truth?

[1] Mk xv 1, Mt xxvii 2 δήσαντες, Lk xxiii 1 om Jerome says "Habebant enim hunc morem ut quem adjudicassent morti ligatum judici traderent," that is, it was their way of indicating to the Roman judge that, so far as they, the Sanhedrin, were concerned, the prisoner was condemned to death Luke's reason for omitting δήσαντες is not obvious, if he accepted this view of the binding John says that Jesus was bound twice, first (Jn xviii 12) at the arrest, secondly (Jn xviii. 24) when sent by Annas to Caiaphas Whatever may be John's motive, it is a case of Johannine Intervention.

Concerning the binding of Jesus, see Justin M *Tryph* § 103 'Ηρώδου δέ...ᾧ καὶ Πιλᾶτος χαριζόμενος δεδεμένον τὸν 'Ιησοῦν ἔπεμψε, as "fulfilling that which God had said thus, Καί γε αὐτὸν εἰς 'Ασσυρίου (*sic*) ἀπήνεγκαν ξένια τῷ βασιλεῖ," quoting Hos x. 6 Justin stops short here, but the Heb. names or defines the king, (R V) "It also shall

away[1], and delivered him over[2] to *Pilate*," Matthew adding the title "to *Pilate the governor*." Luke, who has long ago told us that John the Baptist began to preach "when Pontius Pilate

be carried unto Assyria for a present to king *Jareb* (ירב)," and the LXX inserts "*having bound*," thus, Καὶ αὐτὸν εἰς Ἀσσυρίους δήσαντες ἀπήνεγκαν ξένια τῷ βασιλεῖ Ἰαρείμ Field renders ירב by "*adversarius*" (R V (see Hos v 13) "that should contend"), Aq and Theod by δικάζοντι This means "judge" (not "prosecute") and would apply to Herod Antipas sitting in mock judgment It is to be noted that Justin assumes the "*binding*" in introducing (δεδεμένον), but omits it in quoting (δήσαντες), the passage of the LXX. Tertullian inserts "*bound*" in quoting thus (*Adv Marc* iv 42) "Nam et Herodi, velut munus a Pilato missus, [Christus] Osee vocibus fidem reddidit; de Christo enim prophetaverat *Et vinctum eum ducent xenium regi*" Luke is the only evangelist that mentions the sending to Herod, and the only one that does not mention the "binding" of Christ Justin and Tertullian mention both Jerome (on Hos x 6 and v 13) stigmatizes as impious the view of a commentator ("quidam") who takes Jareb ("regem ultorem") to be Christ

Another text of LXX alleged about the "binding" of Jesus (by Justin M *Tryph* §§ 17, 133, 136, 137 δήσωμεν or ἄρωμεν (see below, p 545, n 3), and Barn § 6 δησωμεν), is Is iii 10 "*say ye* of the righteous" (LXX) δήσωμεν τὸν δίκαιον, where LXX has taken אמרו "*say*" as אסרו "*bind*" Comp Wisd 11. 12 ἐνεδρεύσωμεν (? אבר) τὸν δίκαιον Both in Is and in Wisd. there follows ὅτι δύσχρηστος ἡμῖν ἐστίν

In omitting the "binding," Luke may have been influenced (1) by its omission in the Heb of Hos and Is , (2) by the supposition that Pilate sent Jesus to Herod, not as a criminal, but as an accused person, leaving the decision in Herod's hands

[1] Mk xv. 1 ἀπήνεγκαν—not used of persons in N T elsewhere except about those "carried away" after death or in a vision (Lk. xvi 22, Rev xvii 3, xxi 10)—suggests that the writer had in view Hos x. 6 ἀπήνεγκαν

[2] Παραδίδωμι, about the transference of Jesus (1) from the Jews to Pilate or the Romans is used in Mk xv 1, 10, Mt xxvii. 2, 18 om parall Lk (but comp Lk xxiv 7, 20), (2) from Pilate to the crucifiers or Jews Mk xv. 15, Mt xxvii 26 ἵνα σταυρωθῇ, Lk xxiii 25 τῷ θελήματι αὐτῶν Jn, in sense (1), has it in xviii 30, 35, comp xix. 11, and in sense (2), xix 16 αὐτοῖς ἵνα σταυρωθῇ In Isaiah's Suffering Servant, παραδίδωμι occurs thrice, liii 6 κύριος παρέδωκεν αὐτὸν ταῖς ἁμαρτίαις ἡμῶν (פגע hi), liii. 12 παρεδόθη εἰς θάνατον ἡ ψυχὴ αὐτοῦ (ערה hi)...διὰ τὰς ἀνομίας αὐτῶν παρεδόθη (פגע hi) The LXX is not accurate See *Paradosis* 1185—94.

THE TRIAL BEFORE PILATE

was governor of Judaea[1]," now has simply "led him to *Pilate*" He omits "binding[2]" and "delivering over." John introduces Pilate as follows: "They lead Jesus therefore from Caiaphas into the *praetorium*, and it was early[3], and they themselves entered not into the *praetorium*, that they might not be defiled... *Pilate* therefore went out unto them..."

What is John's object in thus introducing Pilate to us, not as "the governor," but as the occupier of the *praetorium*? Probably he has more objects than one. In the first place, by mentioning the official residence before the name of the resident, he prepares us for finding that resident a mere official, without much strength of character. The same thing is perhaps suggested by the fact that John follows Mark in never calling him "governor[4]." Also he makes plain to his readers—what

---

[1] Lk iii 1 and comp xiii 1

[2] Acts iv 25—7 quotes Ps ii 2 as referring to "Herod and Pontius Pilate with the Gentiles and the peoples of Israel," but *stops short before the words* (R V) "[*saying*] Let us break their bands asunder" The insertion of "saying" makes the enemies of the Messiah say "let us break the bands [of the Lord and His Messiah]" This is the view of the Midrash *ad loc* and Rashi But Origen, on Mt xxvii 2 "binding" (as also Jerome on the Psalm), assigns the words to Jesus, the Messiah, whom he compares to Samson (and so pseudo-Jerome on Mk xv 1) Possibly Luke's adoption of the Jewish interpretation of the Psalm was among the reasons that induced him to refrain from mentioning the "binding"

Mk xv 1, Mt xxvii 1 συμβούλιον corresponds to Ps ii 2 "*take-counsel* (נוסדו) together," from יסד but prob connected by Aq (ἐπαρρησιάσαντο) with סוד (see Gesen 414 *a*, 691 *a*)

[3] Jn xviii 28 πρωΐ, freq in Mk but never in Lk It is a vague term since it may mean (Hesych) "before the fit time," and not "early in the day" In Jn xx 1 (Jn's only other instance) it is defined by σκοτίας ἔτι οὔσης Here perhaps Jn implies an unseasonable earliness

[4] Yet ἡγεμών was a Hebraized and Aramaicized word (Levy 1 451 *a*), and "governors" are mentioned along with "kings" in words of Christ (Mk xiii 9, Mt x 18, Lk xxi 12) Also 1 Pet ii 13—14 εἴτε βασιλεῖ..εἴτε ἡγεμόσιν ὡς δι' αὐτοῦ πεμπομένοις expressly inculcates obedience to them "for the Lord's sake," as being the king's ministers for justice But perhaps for this very reason John

THE TRIAL BEFORE PILATE

Mark does not make quite plain later on—that the *praetorium*, is the official residence of the Roman governor[1]. Luke in the Acts used the phrase "*Herod's praetorium*[2]." And here he, alone of the Evangelists, represents Jesus as having been sent by Pilate to Herod Antipas[3]. He has probably been misled by the use of the term *praetorium*, which, when Hebraized, is so often used for "palace," and is so similarly spelt, that modern authorities differ sometimes as to which of the two meanings is intended[4].

As regards the technical term for "delivering over," used so frequently by Jesus about Himself in the Synoptists, we have to note here (as often elsewhere) that the act may be regarded in different aspects. It is the act of the traitor Judas. But it is also the act of God "delivering over" His Son to suffer death for men, in which sense it is applied to the Suffering Servant thrice in the LXX version of Isaiah. No evangelist so clearly as John brings out the various meanings of this "delivering over." Pilate says to Jesus "Thine own nation... have delivered thee over to me[5]"; and afterwards Pilate "delivered him over to them to be crucified[6]." Beside this, Jesus Himself uses the word. Had it not been, He says to Pilate, for something that was not from this world, "my servants would be fighting that I might not be delivered over to the Jews[7]," and again "Thou wouldest have no authority against

---

will not give Pilate this honourable title since he made himself the minister of the multitude for injustice

[1] Mk xv 16   Mt. xxvii 27   Lk om

Οἱ δὲ στρατιῶται ἀπήγαγον αὐτὸν ἔσω τῆς αὐλῆς, ὅ ἐστιν πραιτώριον, καὶ συνκαλοῦσιν ὅλην τὴν σπεῖραν.

Τότε οἱ στρατιῶται τοῦ ἡγεμόνος παραλαβόντες τὸν Ἰησοῦν εἰς τὸ πραιτώριον συνήγαγον ἐπ' αὐτὸν ὅλην τὴν σπεῖραν

This might give the impression that the *praetorium* was a part of the barracks of the soldiers

[2] Acts xxiii 35.   [3] Lk xxiii 7.
[4] See above, p. 483, n 1.
[5] Jn xviii 35   [6] Jn xix 16.
[7] Jn xviii. 36 ἠγωνίζοντο ἄν   Chrys has ἠγωνίσαντο ἄν "would have fought" But the imperf. more vividly expresses the meaning

THE TRIAL BEFORE PILATE

me except it were given thee from above; therefore he that delivered me over to thee hath greater sin[1]." Finally, Jesus, on the cross, as His last act, "delivered over his spirit[2]."

As regards the binding of Jesus, the allusions of Justin Martyr, Barnabas, and Tertullian, above quoted, shew that the subject had been typically regarded at an early period in the second century and probably in the first[3]; and we have seen that Justin and Tertullian connect the "binding" with Pilate's sending Jesus to Herod. John, by twice mentioning the act, and in neither case in any connection with Pilate, seems to say "There was no such sending to Herod. The binding was, first, when the soldiers in conjunction with the officers of the chief priests arrested Jesus, and, secondly, when Annas sent Jesus to Caiaphas."

§ 2. *The charge of claiming to be a king*

Mark and Matthew introduce this charge as being mentioned by Pilate, before it was mentioned by the Jews, as soon as Jesus was "delivered over to him." "Thou art [it seems] *the King of the Jews*[4]?" Luke places the charge of the Jews first, so worded as to suggest that the claim to be "king"—though concealed under the Jewish title "Anointed," *i.e.* Messiah, or Christ—would interfere practically with "Caesar" and with Caesar's "tribute." "We found this man perverting our nation and forbidding to give tribute to Caesar, and saying that he himself is *Christos, King*[5]." It seems clear that the Jews must have

---

"would be [*even now*] fighting" (comp. Mt xxvi 53 "even now .. more than twelve legions of angels")

[1] Jn xix 11   [2] Jn xix 30.

[3] Justin Martyr quotes Is iii 10 in *Tryph.* §§ 17, 133 "Let us *bind*," but § 136 "Let us *take away*," and then again § 137 "Let us *take away*," saying "At the commencement of the discussion I added what your version has, '*Let us bind*'." It is prob. that "he is distasteful (δύσχρηστος) to us"—nowhere in LXX except Is iii 10 and Wisd ii 12—conveyed to the ears of Christians a play on words, "He is no *Chrēstos* or *Christos* to us." See *Beginning* pp 336—41

[4] Mk xv 2, Mt xxvii 11 Σὺ εἶ ὁ βασιλεὺς τῶν Ἰουδαίων,

[5] Lk xxiii 2

THE TRIAL BEFORE PILATE

said to Pilate something of this kind, which Mark has passed over, and we have to ask what, if anything, John says about it.

What John says, John has prepared the way for, very early in his Gospel, by telling us that Christ's first convert, Andrew, called Him "Messiah"; and that "Messiah" meant Christos or Anointed; and that Nathanael said to Jesus "Thou art God's Son, thou art Israel's King"; and that the five thousand whom Jesus had fed on loaves and fishes desired to snatch Jesus away to "make him king" by force, and, later on, he has represented the crowds as shouting "the King of Israel" when Jesus rode into Jerusalem, and has quoted the words of a Hebrew prophet about the "King" that was to "come," riding, not upon a horse but "on an ass[1]." Thus he has shewn us how easy it would be to pervert Christ's claim to be King of Israel into a claim to be King of Judaea. At the former claim Rome would smile, the latter claim Rome would speedily crush.

Now he tells us, in effect, that Mark and Matthew have omitted the charges brought by the Jews against Jesus outside the *praetorium* before Pilate began to examine Jesus inside the *praetorium*. The Jewish charges, as stated by John, were at first quite vague, merely asserting that Jesus was an "evil-doer[2]"; but John himself implies that the Jews must have added some mention of a claim to be "king," since the first words uttered by Pilate on re-entering the palace are "Thou art, [it seems,] the King of the Jews[3]?" This, however, does not amount to any such definite accusation as that specified by Luke, of making such a claim as would interfere with Caesar's "tribute." It is not easy to see how the Jews could have ventured to bring this particular charge in view of the fact that Jesus had recently and publicly said "Render to Caesar the things that are Caesar's." In bringing it, would they not have risked an ignominious failure, since Jesus might have appealed triumphantly to indisputable facts disproving their accusation?

It seems probable that Luke, in trying to supply what Mark

---

[1] Jn i 41, 49, vi 15, xii 13—15. In Mk xv 32, Mt xxvii 42, βασιλεὺς Ἰσραήλ—the only Synoptic instance—is uttered by mockers. Lk. never uses the title.

[2] Jn xviii 30. [3] Jn xviii 33 Σὺ εἶ ὁ βασιλεὺς τῶν Ἰουδαίων,

546 (Mark xv 1—5)

THE TRIAL BEFORE PILATE

omitted, has ingeniously put into the mouths of the Jews such words as would be likely to weigh with a Roman governor, but not quite those actually uttered. John endeavours, in a dialogue between Jesus and Pilate, to supply the deficiency afresh and to help us to understand the circumstances. "Pilate was not taken in. He knew that the charges hypocritically suggested by the Jews were false. Everything turned on the meaning of 'king.' And Pilate knew this and felt Jesus to be a real 'king,' but not such a one as would interfere with Caesar's tribute. Pilate, though no Stoic, knew well the Stoic doctrine that every wise man is a king[1]."

But it may be asked, "Was there such a dialogue? If there was, why did the Synoptists omit it?" Possibly, as will appear in the next section, because they were influenced by the prophecy that the suffering Messiah would be "dumb," and "not open his mouth." But further, in the interval between Mark's brief statements that Pilate (1) *"questioned"* and (2) *"questioned again,"* there is room for a going forth of Pilate from Jesus inside the *praetorium* to the Jews outside the *praetorium*, and for a preliminary questioning inside the *praetorium*, in which Jesus may have uttered more than is assigned to Him by the Synoptists[2].

---

[1] Philo (i. 306, 601, 691, ii. 657) descants amply on this doctrine. And comp. Horace *Epist.* i. 1. 59—60. "*Rex* eris si *recte* facies," and *Odes* iv. ix. 39—42 "He is a consul, and a consul more than once, whenever, like a good and just judge, he rejects the bribes of the guilty, and prefers honour to expedience."

[2] Mk xv. 2—5 (*a*) "And Pilate questioned him [inside the praetorium] Art thou the King of the Jews? And he answering saith unto him, Thou (σὺ) sayest." The emphatic "thou" might be taken as "*Thou of thine own accord*" (comp. Jn xviii. 34 ἀπὸ σεαυτοῦ σὺ τοῦτο λέγεις "Dost *thou, of thyself*, say this?") (*b*) "And [when Pilate went out outside] the chief priests began to bring many accusations against him." (*c*) "But Pilate [coming back] *again* began to question him." (*d*) "But Jesus *no longer* made any answer." "No longer" is peculiar to Mark. It suggests that Christ's previous reply was not confined to σὺ λέγεις. John may have taken σύ, in σὺ λέγεις, in two senses, (xviii. 34) "*thou of thyself*" (xviii. 37) "*thou, not I*."

THE TRIAL BEFORE PILATE

If He did, we may infer what He would have said here from what He says elsewhere, teaching that His Kingdom was the Kingdom of Righteousness and that His followers were to *"sit on thrones"* judging in righteousness[1].

Jesus would not have softened down His claim to represent the Kingdom of God by suggesting that He was only "a king" so far as He was a "wise man" Much more than this is implied in the words "To this end have I been born, and to this end am I come into the world, that I should bear witness unto the truth Everyone that is [sprung] from the truth hearkeneth unto my voice[2]." This implies a claim to sovereignty over the consciences of men such as Jesus might have actually asserted and Pilate might have partially and faintly felt to be not without some basis of truth, if only Pilate had believed in the existence of any ascertainable truth at all There is certainly something that seems above ordinary dramatic imagination in the combination of the three consecutive Pilatian utterances, the first, personal, that of the undignified, wayward and flighty individual, Pilate, dropping the character of "judge" and wearily asking "What is truth?" the second, judicial, that of the Roman governor, "I find no crime in him", the third, political, or quasi-political, that of the respecter of persons and truckler to the multitude, "Will ye that I release unto you the King of the Jews[3]?"

§ 3   *Christ's silence before His judges*

The Evangelists all agree that Jesus was silent before His judges at a certain stage in their questioning, but none of them say that He was absolutely silent except Luke, and Luke limits his statement to the examination conducted by Herod,

---

[1] Mt xix 28, Lk xxii 30, comp. Rev iii 21, 1 Pet ii 9

[2] Jn xviii 37

[3] Jn xviii 38, 39 Compare, and contrast, the claim of the Cynic in Epictetus iii 22 49 "How do I face these [people] to whom you look up with fear and awe? Do not I treat them as slaves? Who among them, having seen me, does not feel that he is beholding *his king and master?*" Clem Alex 416—17 better describes spiritual sovereignty as "possessing the skill to sway willing subjects"

THE TRIAL BEFORE PILATE

which he alone mentions[1]. Luke uses a peculiar phrase, possibly meaning "he answered nothing [in the way of defence]," applied by Mark to Christ's silence before the High Priest, but by Matthew to His silence before Pilate[2]. It does not occur elsewhere in the New Testament[3]. John, however, has a phrase, also unique in the New Testament, "he gave no answer [in the way of defence]." This he applies to Christ's silence before Pilate[4].

At least two questions arise out of these variations. (1) How did Christians reconcile Christ's brief replies to His judges with the prophecy of Isaiah: "He opened not his mouth; as a lamb that is led to the slaughter, and as a sheep that before her shearers is dumb, yea, he opened not his mouth[5]"? (2) Do the Evangelists say anything that may help us to meet such an objection as that which is suggested by a warning of Epictetus that an accused person declining to plead before his judge must be prepared to be sentenced to the cross[6]?

(1) As to the prophecy of Isaiah it is noteworthy that, although early Christian writers repeatedly quote the context of "he opened not his mouth," they mostly either do not quote

---

[1] Lk. xxiii 9 ἐπηρώτα δὲ αὐτὸν ἐν λόγοις ἱκανοῖς· αὐτὸς δὲ οὐδὲν ἀπεκρίνατο αὐτῷ

[2] Οὐδὲν ἀπεκρίνατο Comp Mk xiv 61 ὁ δὲ ἐσιώπα καὶ οὐκ ἀπεκρίνατο οὐδέν, Mt xxvii 12 καὶ ἐν τῷ κατηγορεῖσθαι αὐτὸν...οὐδὲν ἀπεκρίνατο

[3] In Goodspeed, ἀπεκρίνατο, with negative, occurs only in *Mart. Polyc* § 8 οὐκ ἀπεκρίνατο αὐτοῖς, where Polycarp rejects the proposal that he should apostatize. It is probably one of many instances in the *Martyrdom* shewing that it was written (see Lightf on *Mart Polyc* § 1) "according to the Gospel," that is, likening the experiences of the Martyrdom to the experiences of the Passion

[4] Jn xix 9 ἀπόκρισιν οὐκ ἔδωκεν αὐτῷ, not used with a neg elsewhere (N T)

[5] Is liii 7 (LXX) καὶ αὐτὸς διὰ τὸ κεκακῶσθαι οὐκ ἀνοίγει τὸ στόμα ὡς πρόβατον ἐπὶ σφαγὴν ἤχθη, καὶ ὡς ἀμνὸς ἐναντίον τοῦ κείροντος ἄφωνος, οὕτως οὐκ ἀνοίγει τὸ στόμα αὐτοῦ. This is quoted by some early writers in part, omitting the word "dumb" and the phrase "opened not his mouth," but emphasizing "led to the slaughter."

[6] Epict ii. 2. 20.

THE TRIAL BEFORE PILATE

the phrase itself, or pass over it unexplained[1]. Justin Martyr alone explains fully what he calls the cessation of the stream of utterance from Christ's lips, as a fulfilment of the Psalmist's words "My strength is dried up like a potsherd, and my tongue cleaveth to my jaws[2]," but not by reference to the "dumb" sheep in Isaiah, as to which, when he quotes the verse by itself, he quotes merely the words "was led unto death." Tertullian is an exception. According to him, in one passage, "Herod was the shearer" before whom the sheep was "dumb[3]." There he is justified. But in another passage he ventures to apply Isaiah's words to the partial silence before Pilate[4]. Origen gives no explanation of Christ's silence except by saying that His conduct fulfilled prophecy and that it was expedient for men that He should die[5].

---

[1] Barn § 5 includes ἄφωνος in his quotation of Is liii 7 but does not explain its fulfilment. Justin Martyr, when quoting Is lii—liii. fully, includes ἄφωνος and οὐκ ἀνοίγει without reconciling them with the Gospels. He twice (*Tryph* §§ 111, 114) quotes Is liii 7 ἤχθη etc. (and perhaps *ib* § 103) but omits the dumbness.

[2] Ps xxii 15. On this Justin says (*Tryph* § 102) "The power of His strong word, by which He was always wont to confute the Pharisees and scribes.. had a cessation, like a plentiful and strong spring the waters of which have been turned off—when He kept silence (σιγήσαντος) and would *no longer answer anything* to anyone in the presence of Pilate, as is shewn in the Memoirs of His Apostles —in order that also that which is spoken through Isaiah might have active fruit, where it is spoken (Is l 4) 'The Lord giveth unto me a tongue that I may know when I ought to speak a word'" This passage is remarkable for retaining the Marcan (xv 5) "*no longer*," σιγήσαντος αὐτοῦ καὶ μηκέτι ἐπὶ Πιλάτου ἀποκρίνασθαι μηδὲν μηδενὶ βουλομένου. I have not found this elsewhere. It is not in the *Diatessaron* (which omits Mk xv 4—7) nor does it occur in Origen's summary of Mk xiv 43—xv 5 (*Comm. Joann* xxviii 12).

[3] Tertull. *De Resurrect Carn* § 20

[4] Tertull *Adv Jud.* § 13 "For He, when Pilate interrogated Him, spake nothing."

[5] Origen *Cels* 1 54 "His Passion was prophesied along with the cause [of it] (τὸ πάθος αὐτοῦ προεφητεύετο μετὰ τῆς αἰτίας) [namely] that it was beneficial for men that He should die for them and suffer the stripes (μώλωπα) that follow on condemnation." Then follows a quotation of Is lii. 13—15, liii. 1—8, including the clause about the

THE TRIAL BEFORE PILATE

(2) Of the Synoptists, Mark alone faintly suggests that the words "*no longer* answered" imply that Jesus had *for a short time* "answered," and that the answer was something more than the two words "thou sayest [it][1]." But the parallel Matthew, "did not answer him even [in reply] to a single word," effaces this faint suggestion[2]. Luke, later on, represents Christ's silence as complete before Herod[3], but he says nothing about His silence before Pilate.

John represents Jesus as replying to Pilate freely at first on the subject of "kingdom" and on His claim to be a "king," and on the connection between this and "bearing witness unto the truth[4]." But Pilate exclaims "What is truth?" and then goes out to the Jews, and after avowing the truth, so far as he has found it ("I find no crime"), acts against the truth ("took Jesus and scourged him[5]"). This changes everything. Pilate has had his chance of "striving for the truth," as Ben Sira says, so that "the Lord" might "fight for" him[6]. But he has thrown it away. The incarnate Truth cannot now "fight for" him. When he next questions Jesus "Jesus gave him no answer[7]."

Mark and Matthew say that Pilate "wondered" at this; Luke, dealing with Herod instead of Pilate, omits the "wonder[8]."

"dumb" lamb, but not explaining in detail why Jesus was "dumb." Later on, replying to the charge of Celsus that Jesus, while alive, "did not avail (*or*, suffice for) Himself (οὐκ ἐπήρκεσεν ἑαυτῷ)," Origen says (*Cels.* ii. 59) "If 'suffice' means 'suffice in virtue' we shall say that He *did* 'suffice' perfectly. For He neither said nor did anything unseemly, but in truth 'like a sheep He was led . and like a lamb that is dumb . and the Gospel testifies that He 'opened not His mouth.' But if he takes 'sufficed' as referring to things neutral (μέσων) and corporal, then we say that we have shewn from the Gospels that He came willingly to these [sufferings]." It will be observed that Origen does not answer the question that Pilate might have put, "Why did not Jesus enlighten me?"

[1] In Mk xv. 5, "no longer" is omitted by the Syriac versions.
[2] Mt xxvii. 14   [3] Lk xxiii. 9
[4] Jn xviii. 37   [5] Jn xviii. 38, xix. 1.
[6] Sir. iv. 28 "Strive for the truth (*or*, justice) unto death, and the Lord shall fight for thee."   [7] Jn xix. 9
[8] Mk xv. 5, Mt xxvii. 14 (Lk xxiii. 9 om.).

THE TRIAL BEFORE PILATE

John explains it, without mentioning the word It arises from Pilate's ignorance The Governor angrily exclaims, "Speakest thou not unto me? Dost thou not know that I have *authority* to release thee and have *authority* to crucify thee[1]?" But in reality it is Pilate who "does not know." Pilate has no "authority" of a real kind. He is a slave, a slave to the fear of ceasing to be "Caesar's friend," a slave to the desire of conciliating the mob that shouts "Not this man but Barabbas[2]."

The truth, said Jesus, would make men free[3]. But Pilate had no eye for the truth, and it was beyond even divine power to utter any words that might make him see it and make him consequently free Hence Jesus "gave him no answer" before. And hence His only subsequent answer to the claim of this Roman governor to possess "authority," is, in effect· "You are a slave You would like to avoid crucifying me, but you dare not, because you are afraid of what will befall you if you prefer justice to expediency When you say you have 'authority to crucify me,' you shew that you do not know what 'authority' means[4]."

§ 4. *The Custom of Release*[5]

Mark says that Pilate "used to release" one prisoner in the course of the Feast, any one whom the multitude "begged

---

[1] Jn xix 10   [2] Jn xix 12, xviii 40   [3] Jn viii 32
[4] Jn xix 11 "Thou wouldest have no authority against me except it were given thee from above" Comp Epict iv 1 56—7, which says that freedom must have absolute authority (ἡ ἐλευθερία αὐτεξούσιόν τι) and that if you hear one man saying to another— in his heart of hearts and in his inmost feeling—"Master," you are to set down that man as "slave," even though he be a consul with twelve lictors going before him, Ἀλλ' ἂν ἀκούσῃς λέγοντος ἔσωθεν καὶ ἐκ πάθους "κύριε," κἂν δώδεκα ῥάβδοι προάγωσι, λέγε δοῦλον

[5] Mk xv. 6, 8   Mt. xxvii. 15   Lk om

κατὰ δὲ ἑορτὴν ἀπέ-	κατὰ δὲ ἑορτὴν εἰώθει
λυεν αὐτοῖς ἕνα δέσμιον	ὁ ἡγεμὼν ἀπολύειν ἕνα
ὃν παρῃτοῦντο...καὶ	τῷ ὄχλῳ δέσμιον ὃν
ἀναβὰς ὁ ὄχλος ἤρξατο	ἤθελον
αἰτεῖσθαι καθὼς ἐποίει	
αὐτοῖς	

Jn xviii. 39 ἔστιν δὲ συνήθεια ὑμῖν ἵνα ἕνα ἀπολύσω ὑμῖν [ἐν] τῷ πάσχα
For Mk xv 6—15 and the parallel texts, see below, p 554

THE TRIAL BEFORE PILATE

off" Matthew says "The Governor was in the habit of releasing one [man] to the multitude, whom[soever] they would " This is not the same thing For it implies that Pilate did this as Governor, and that the Governor before Pilate had done the same But there is no proof of this And Mark indicates that it was a custom of Pilate's own making, for he says "The multitude came up [to Pilate] and began to ask him to do"— not, according to precedent, or law, or ancient custom handed down from past Governors, but—"even as he used to do for them[1]."

There is no evidence of any such custom of release under Roman rule. Origen, by suggesting that such remissions are allowed by conquering nations to the conquered for a short time, and "only till the yoke is firmly imposed," implies that he could find no Roman precedent for it[2] Jerome offers no explanation. Luke (in the correct text) omits all reference to it It is therefore a case that calls for Johannine Intervention.

John intervenes dramatically by making Pilate mention this "custom" to "the Jews." Only he calls it not "custom" but their "*familiar practice*, or, *way*[3]" In reality it is Pilate's "*way*"—one of the tricks by which he kept the multitude in good humour during the critical time of Passover He had encouraged them to "come up and beg off" a criminal But he throws the main responsibility on them: "It is a *way* you have, that I should release to you one [prisoner] during the Passover " This means "It is your way, or perhaps I should say it is my way, since I have fallen in with it "

This exhibits Pilate in a very undignified aspect But it is probably the true aspect Luke, the historian, knew the practice of Roman law and government and rejected all mention of such a practice as recognised by a Roman Governor. But he

---

[1] In Mk xv 8, SS has "And the people exclaimed (ἀναβοήσας) and began to ask that he should do [something] for them," *k*, "tota turba rogabat illum quot faciebat in singulis diebus festis ut dimitteret unū custodiam", *a* and inferior Gk MSS ins ἀεί before ἐποίει

[2] Origen (on Mt xxvii 15) gives no precedent except the intervention of Israel with Saul (1 S xiv 45) to save Jonathan's life

[3] Συνήθεια, in N.T elsewhere only in 1 Cor viii 7, xi 16 (in bad sense).

553 (Mark xv 1—5)

THE TRIAL BEFORE PILATE

was no dramatist and did not know Pilate. The words here imputed to Pilate were, not improbably, uttered just as they stand Whether uttered or not, they explain the facts. And it is an instance of Johannine Intervention[1].

§ 5. *Barabbas*[2]

Mark and Matthew here break their narrative' of pending facts to describe a pre-existing fact, namely, that there had

---

[1] [Lk xxiii 17] (W H om) placed by D after Lk xxiii 19, has ἀνάγκην δὲ εἶχεν κατὰ ἑορτὴν ἀπολύειν αὐτοῖς ἕνα. John's view includes a protest against the notion that there was any ἀνάγκη

[2]

Mk xv 6—15 (R V)	Mt xxvii 15—26 (R V.)	Lk xxiii 13—25 (R V.)
(6) Now at the (*or*, a) feast he used to release unto them one prisoner, whom they asked of him.	(15) Now at the (*or*, a) feast the governor was wont to release unto the multitude one prisoner, whom they would	
(7) And there was one called Barabbas, [lying] bound with them that had made insurrection, men who in the insurrection had committed murder.	(16) And they had then a notable prisoner, called Barabbas	
(8) And the multitude went up and began to ask him [to do] as he was wont to do unto them		
(9) And Pilate answered them, saying, Will ye that I release unto you the King of the Jews?	(17) When therefore they were gathered together, Pilate said unto them, Whom will ye that I release unto you? Barabbas, or Jesus which is called Christ?	(13) And Pilate called together the chief priests and the rulers and the people,
(10) For he perceived that for envy the chief priests had delivered him up	(18) For he knew that for envy they had delivered him up	(14) And said unto them, Ye brought unto me this man, as one that perverteth the people and, behold, I, having examined him before you, found no fault in this man touching those things whereof ye accuse him
	(19) And while he was sitting on the judgment-seat, his wife sent unto him, saying, Have thou	(15) No, nor yet Herod for he sent

554 (Mark xv. 6—15)

THE TRIAL BEFORE PILATE

been lying in prison for some time a man called Barabbas,

Mk xv 6—15 (R V) contd	Mt xxvii 15—26 (R V) contd	Lk xxiii 13—25 (R V) contd
	nothing to do with that righteous man for I have suffered many things this day in a dream because of him	him back unto us, and behold, nothing worthy of death hath been done by him (16) I will therefore chastise him, and release him ⟦(17) *Many anc auth insert* Now he must needs release unto them at the feast one [prisoner] *Others add the same words after ver* 19 ⟧
(11) But the chief priests stirred up the multitude, that he should rather release Barabbas unto them	(20) Now the chief priests and the elders persuaded the multitudes that they should ask for Barabbas, and destroy Jesus	(18) But they cried out all together, saying, Away with this man, and release unto us Barabbas (19) One who for a certain insurrection made in the city, and for murder, was cast into prison
(12) And Pilate again answered and said unto them, What then shall I do unto him whom ye call the King of the Jews? (13) And they cried out again, Crucify him	(21) But the governor answered and said unto them, Whether of the twain will ye that I release unto you? And they said, Barabbas (22) Pilate saith unto them, What then shall I do unto Jesus which is called Christ? They all say, Let him be crucified	(20) And Pilate spake unto them again, desiring to release Jesus, (21) But they shouted, saying, Crucify, crucify him (22) And he said unto them the third time, Why, what evil hath this man done? I have found no cause of death in him I will therefore chastise him and release him
(14) And Pilate said unto them, Why, what evil hath he done? But they cried out exceedingly, Crucify him (15) And Pilate, wishing to content the multitude, released unto them Barabbas, and delivered Jesus, when he had scourged him, to be crucified	(23) And he said, Why, what evil hath he done? But they cried out exceedingly, saying, Let him be crucified (24) So when Pilate saw that he prevailed nothing, but rather that a tumult was arising, he took water, and washed his hands before the multitude, saying, I am innocent of the blood of	(23) But they were instant with loud voices, asking that he might be crucified And their voices prevailed (24) And Pilate gave sentence that what they asked for should be done.

THE TRIAL BEFORE PILATE

whose full name was probably Jesus Barabbas[1]. This man

Mt xxvii 15—26 (R V) contd	Lk xxiii 13—25 (R V) contd
this righteous man (*some anc auth* of this blood) see ye [to it] (25) And all the people answered and said, His blood [be] on us, and on our children (26) Then released he unto them Barabbas but Jesus he scourged and delivered to be crucified	(25) And he released him that for insurrection and murder had been cast into prison, whom they asked for, but Jesus he delivered up to their will

Jn xviii 39—40, xix 6, 15—16 (R V) (xviii 39) But ye have a custom, that I should release unto you one at the passover. will ye therefore that I release unto you the King of the Jews? (40) They cried out therefore again, saying, Not this man, but Barabbas. Now Barabbas was a robber.

(xix 6) When therefore the chief priests and the officers saw him, they cried out, saying, Crucify [him], crucify [him]. Pilate saith unto them, Take him yourselves, and crucify him. for I find no crime in him .. (15) They therefore cried out, Away with [him], away with [him], crucify him. Pilate saith unto them, Shall I crucify your King? The chief priests answered, We have no king but Caesar. (16) Then therefore he delivered him unto them to be crucified.

[1] Mk xv 7	Mt xxvii 16	Lk xxiii 18 b—19
ἦν δὲ ὁ λεγόμενος Βαραββᾶς μετὰ τῶν στασιαστῶν δεδεμένος οἵτινες ἐν τῇ στάσει φόνον πεποιήκεισαν	εἶχον δὲ τότε δέσμιον ἐπίσημον λεγόμενον Βαραββᾶν	Αἶρε τοῦτον, ἀπόλυσον δὲ ἡμῖν τὸν Βαραββᾶν· ὅστις ἦν διὰ στάσιν τινὰ γενομένην ἐν τῇ πόλει καὶ φόνον βληθεὶς ἐν τῇ φυλακῇ.

In Mt xxvii 16, SS has "And there had been imprisoned by them one well-known man whose name was Jesus Bar Abba, he was lying in prison because of evil [deeds] that he had done, and he had committed murder."

Origen, on Mt xxvii 16—18, quotes Pilate's question with "*Jesus Barabbas*," but adds, "In many copies it is not found that Barabbas was also called Jesus—and perhaps rightly, *that the name of Jesus may not belong to a sinner.*" This thought would doubtless induce many scribes to omit "Jesus" before Barabbas. But the sense appears to be improved by the insertion. For other evidence of this reading

THE TRIAL BEFORE PILATE

the Jews put forward as their candidate for the customary release, asking for Jesus who was called Barabbas, instead of that Jesus whom they accused (according to Luke) of calling Himself "Christos"—literally "anointed," but explained by the accusers as "king." Apparently, there had been a recent insurrection so fresh in men's minds that they called it "*the* insurrection", and this man, says Mark, was "lying bound along with *the* insurrectionists who in *the* insurrection had committed murder." Matthew drops all this, perhaps as being obsolete and forgotten. Luke drops "*the*," but retains the rest of the Marcan tradition in view of the impending inconsistency of Pilate, in pardoning Barabbas, a rebel and shedder of blood, while executing Jesus, who was innocent on both these counts. The Lucan result is somewhat tame in its termination: "Away with this man, but release for us Barabbas —who by reason of some insurrection that had befallen in the city and [by reason of] murder, had been cast into prison."

John drops the reference to "insurrection" and "murder" which Mark and Luke have in common. He also makes no mention of a verbal antithesis between "Jesus Barabbas" and "Jesus the Christ, or, King." But he suggests a spiritual antithesis between the two by a short but pregnant addition· "Now Barabbas was a *robber*[1]" For this he has prepared the

see Nicholson's *Gospel according to the Hebrews* p 141 W H, who reject it, did not know of SS

Matthew's peculiar use of ἐπίσημος may be connected with "Jesus Barabbas" Ἐπίσημος is used of conspicuous excellence (as always in Goodspeed) except where very special context requires the opposite meaning This is the only instance of it in N T (except Rom xvi 7)· But it is used technically about the name "*Jesus*" by Irenaeus (referring to Valentinian doctrine), who says 1 14 4 Ἰησοῦς μὲν γάρ ἐστιν ἐπίσημον ὄνομα (see *Notes* 2942* (1) *l*) This suggests that scribes, "in order that the name of '*Jesus*' might not belong to a sinner," substituted for it "*Episēmos*"

In canon LXX, ἐπίσημος occurs only in Gen xxx 42 "stronger," particip of קשר In Gen xxx 41, Aq renders this same Heb. "bound," καταδεδεμένος Elsewhere it is used of those "bound together in conspiracy" (Gesen 905) I cannot explain why LXX renders it once by ἐπίσημος, but the fact seems worth noting.

[1] Jn xviii 40 Μὴ τοῦτον ἀλλὰ τὸν Βαραββᾶν ἦν δὲ ὁ Βαραββᾶς λῃστής.

THE TRIAL BEFORE PILATE

way in previous words of Jesus: "All that came before me are *thieves and robbers*[1]." The Synoptists, too, have prepared for it in words of Jesus accusing the Jews of converting the Temple into "a den of *robbers*[2]." Both in Greek and in Hebrew there is a natural antithesis between a "robber" and a "king." The "robbers" mentioned by Jesus are, in Hebrew, "breakers" as distinct from makers. A "robber," in Greek, is a "spoiler and ravager" as distinct from a hereditary ruler The "robber" breaks up all peace and order to gratify his own greedy and disorderly desires Demosthenes means this when he warns the Athenians that they are suffering Philip of Macedon to "grow up in the midst of Hellas, *robber* of the Hellenes[3]."

It is perhaps because of the antithesis between "Jesus Barabbas" and "Jesus called *king*" that Mark represents Pilate as saying to the Jews "Will ye that I release unto you *the King of the Jews?*" and again "What then shall I do to *him whom ye call the King of the Jews?*" Matthew alters this in both cases, and Luke departs from it altogether[4]. John, on the other hand, admits that Pilate spoke thus, but explains, and, after a fashion, justifies it. The Jews, he says, expressly told Pilate to alter "*the King of the Jews*," saying "Write not '*the King of the Jews*,' but that he said '*I am King of the Jews.*'" But Pilate persisted in his error, replying "What I have written I have written[5]."

All the Evangelists but Matthew introduce the popular rebel thus, with the article, as "the [great] Barabbas"

[1] Jn x 8, on which see *Joh Gr* 2361—2, 2798 *d*

[2] Mk xi 17, Mt xxi 13, Lk xix 46 quoting Jerem vii 11 פרצים on which see Gesen 829, shewing that the radical meaning is "break violently," "rend in pieces" etc., hence applied also to murderers and (Is xxxv 9) "wild beasts"

[3] Demosth 140, *Philipp* iv 34 τοῦ ἐπὶ ταῖς θύραις ἐγγὺς οὑτωσὶ ἐν μέσῃ τῇ Ἑλλάδι αὐξανομένου λῃστοῦ τῶν Ἑλλήνων

[4] Mk xv 9 τὸν βασιλέα τῶν Ἰουδαίων, Mt. xxvii 17 Ἰησοῦν τὸν λεγόμενον Χριστόν, Mk xv 12 ὃν λέγετε τὸν βασιλέα τῶν Ἰουδαίων, Mt. xxvii 22 Ἰησοῦν τὸν λεγόμενον Χριστόν In Mk, W H bracket ὅν. B omits it, perhaps taking λέγετε parenthetically "What (say ye)?" and several authorities omit ὃν λέγετε But these alterations seem to be corruptions for the sake of removing the objection that Pilate is saying what is palpably false   [5] Jn xix. 21—2.

The meaning of this is apparently mystical The Jews had, in reality, rejected their true Saviour and King, Jesus, the Prince of Peace, and had preferred a false saviour and king, Jesus Barabbas, the "robber" Pilate unconsciously records this fact It is against his own interest and dignity that he, a Roman Judge, should give the name of "king" to a Pretender. When he had said to the Jews "Shall I crucify your king?" they replied "We have no king but Caesar[1]" Pilate, then, ought to have altered the title as the Jews suggested. But, while flightily indulging himself in a jest at the expense of the hypocrites whom he felt obliged to conciliate, Pilate writes the real truth although he does not know it, instead of the Jewish falsehood John does not justify Pilate in writing what he writes, but he justifies Providence, so to speak, in making him write it

§ 6. *The scourging of Jesus*[2]

The "scourging" of Jesus—described by Mark and Matthew uniquely as "flagellation"—is omitted by the parallel Luke.

[1] Jn xix 15
[2] Mk xv. 15

Mk xv. 15	Mt. xxvii. 26	Lk xxiii 24—25
ὁ δὲ Πειλᾶτος βουλόμενος τῷ ὄχλῳ τὸ ἱκανὸν ποιῆσαι ἀπέλυσεν αὐτοῖς τὸν Βαραββᾶν, καὶ παρέδωκεν τὸν Ἰησοῦν φραγελλώσας ἵνα σταυρωθῇ	τότε ἀπέλυσεν αὐτοῖς τὸν Βαραββᾶν, τὸν δὲ Ἰησοῦν φραγελλώσας παρέδωκεν ἵνα σταυρωθῇ.	καὶ Πειλᾶτος ἐπέκρινεν γενέσθαι τὸ αἴτημα αὐτῶν ἀπέλυσεν δὲ τὸν διὰ στάσιν καὶ φόνον βεβλημένον εἰς φυλακὴν ὃν ᾐτοῦντο, τὸν δὲ Ἰησοῦν παρέδωκεν τῷ θελήματι αὐτῶν

Jn xix 1 Τότε οὖν ἔλαβεν ὁ Πειλᾶτος τὸν Ἰησοῦν καὶ ἐμαστίγωσεν

Jn xix 15—16 ἀπεκρίθησαν οἱ ἀρχιερεῖς Οὐκ ἔχομεν βασιλέα εἰ μὴ Καίσαρα τότε οὖν παρέδωκεν αὐτὸν αὐτοῖς ἵνα σταυρωθῇ

Mark and Matthew do not say to whom Jesus was "delivered over" Literally, it would be to the soldiers whose task it was to perform the execution. But Luke says it was "to the will (τῷ θελήματι)" of those previously described as (xxiii 13) "*the chief priests and the rulers and the people*" John implies that it was "*the chief priests*" alone who cried "We have no king but Caesar" and it was *to them* that Jesus was delivered over This agrees with a free interpretation of Mk xv 11, Mt xxvii 20, which says that "*the chief priests*" (Mt adds "the elders") were the instigators of the multitude Luke omitted this passage of Mk-Mt Perhaps Luke

THE TRIAL BEFORE PILATE

In Roman practice it usually occurred, as Mark and Matthew place it, immediately before execution[1]. John places a "scourging," called by the usual Greek term, much earlier. The Johannine scourging is certainly not described by John as a preliminary to execution, and seems rather to have been intended, together with the crown and purple, as an appeal to the contemptuous pity of the multitude. John mentions no other subsequent scourging.

This raises a question about the meaning of a Lucan phrase "*having chastised*," which is the Lucan equivalent for "flagellating" or "scourging." Luke represents Pilate as saying twice about Jesus "*Having therefore chastised him* I will release him[2]." It follows in both cases a statement that Pilate has "found *nothing worthy* (or, *no cause*) *of death*" in the accused[3]. But Pilate has previously made a fuller statement of acquittal than this, "I find *no cause* [*of condemnation*] in this man[4]." It is possible, therefore, that Pilate means "At first I said 'Not guilty on *any* charge', now I say 'Not guilty on *any capital* charge.' He may possibly have been guilty of some small offence. I will therefore merely chastise him and then let him go." But, on the other hand, Pilate's meaning may be, "Having already given him chastisement, a sufficient punishment for

---

interpreted Mk xv 15 as meaning that Pilate "desired to satisfy the *multitude*" by *delivering Jesus to them for execution*, as well as by releasing Barabbas. But more probably Mark's meaning is that Pilate delivered over Jesus for execution in the usual way, that is, to the soldiers. The multitude went off, rejoicing, with Barabbas, the chief priests and their officers and other followers stayed to view the crucifixion.

Mk xv 15 βουλόμενος invites comparison with Lk. xxiii 20 θέλων. Pilate would have "*liked* (θέλων)" to "release" Jesus, but he "*desired* (βουλόμενος)," and finally made up his mind, to "satisfy the multitude."

[1] On the Roman practice of scourging before execution see Swete quoting Joseph *Bell* ii 14 9, v 11 1, Lucian *reviv* ad init. ἐμοὶ μὲν ἀνεσκολοπίσθαι δοκεῖ αὐτὸν νὴ Δία μαστιγωθέντα γε πρότερον

[2] Lk xxiii 16, 22 παιδεύσας οὖν αὐτὸν ἀπολύσω

[3] Lk xxiii 15 καὶ ἰδοὺ οὐδὲν ἄξιον θανάτου ἐστὶν πεπραγμένον αὐτῷ, xxiii. 22 οὐδὲν αἴτιον θανάτου εὗρον ἐν αὐτῷ

[4] Lk xxiii 4 οὐδὲν εὑρίσκω αἴτιον ἐν τῷ ἀνθρώπῳ τούτῳ.

THE TRIAL BEFORE PILATE

any minor offence against discretion and order, I will now let him go "

Such a scourging would seem to be irregular. But in the Acts we find Paul on one occasion tied up for scourging, not as being guilty, but only with the view of ascertaining guilt or innocence[1]. Pilate's whole conduct was flighty and irregular, and the "chastisement" may have been an instance of his irregularities. In any case John seems to have in view the anticlimax in the three Lucan declarations, and the drop from perfect to imperfect acquittal. John says, in effect, "There was no such anticlimax. Pilate did not begin by saying 'Not guilty,' and then say 'Not guilty on a capital charge.' Three times over Pilate repeated, in effect, 'I find *no guilt* in him[2].'"

According to this view, Mark has placed the "flagellation" in the order in which it would have come if the regular Roman practice had been followed. Luke has expressed himself ambiguously as to the time of the punishment, but has given the impression that it was of a milder kind than "flagellation." John has recognised that it was earlier than Mark supposed, and that it was an undignified freak by which Pilate hoped to get Jesus off while keeping the Jews in good humour. But John also recognised that this freak fulfilled the will of Providence. The fulfilment was lost in the Marcan word "flagellation." But John substitutes "*scourge*." Thereby he suggests the words of Isaiah in LXX "I gave my back to *scourges*[3]."

Luke and John both omit statements of Mark about Pilate's motives—"He began to understand [Matthew, knew] that through envy the chief priests had delivered him up," and "Pilate, desiring to satisfy the multitude[4]." Also John omits Luke's description of Pilate as "wishing to release Jesus[5]"

---

[1] Acts xxii 25—9, "The chief captain also was afraid when he knew"—not "that he was uncondemned," but—"that he was a Roman, and because he had bound him"

[2] Jn xviii 38 ἐγὼ οὐδεμίαν εὑρίσκω ἐν αὐτῷ αἰτίαν, slightly varied in xix 4, 6, see *Joh Gr* 2553 d

[3] Is 1 6 (LXX) τὸν νῶτόν μου ἔδωκα εἰς μάστιγας

[4] Mk xv 10, Mt xxvii 18, Mk xv 15.

[5] Lk xxiii 20, see above, p 559, n. 2 *ad fin*

THE TRIAL BEFORE PILATE

John's omissions are dramatic, like his omission of the Mark-Matthew tradition that the chief priests persuaded the multitude to ask for the release of Barabbas[1]. He does not contradict all these Synoptic statements But he prefers to convey their truth to us by shewing us the characters on the stage and leaving us to infer their motives from their actions and words.

There is one important Johannine detail not to be found in any of the Synoptists. "When Pilate heard this"—namely, the charge of the Jews that Jesus "made himself the Son of God"—"he was the more afraid[2]." This implies that he had been to some extent afraid before. Opinions will vary as to the historical truth of this. It was of course to be expected that later Christian accounts of the acts of Pilate should represent the Roman Governor as shewing occasional respect for Jesus—and even fear—by details of word and deed that cannot be accepted as true. And in Matthew's Gospel, the story of Pilate's wife's vision and of his consequent action is justifiably doubted by many. Yet to many also, and those not credulous students, it will seem that such a one as Pilate sitting in judgment on such a one as Jesus, could not but feel some occasional touches of doubt and fear as to the verdict to be pronounced, and the person on whom he was to pronounce it

---

[1] Mk xv 11, Mt xxvii 20   [2] Jn xix. 8

CHAPTER XIV

THE MOCKING AND THE CRUCIFIXION

[Mark xv. 16—37]

§ 1   *The "purple" or "scarlet," and the "crown"*[1]

THE "mocking" of Jesus by "the soldiers," called expressly by Matthew, and implied to be by Mark, "the soldiers of the

Mk xv 16—20 (R V)	Mt. xxvii 27—31 (R V)	Lk. om., but comp. xxiii 11—12, 26 (R V.)
(16) And the soldiers led him away within the court, which is the Praetorium (*or*, palace), and they call together the whole band (*or*, cohort)	(27) Then the soldiers of the governor took Jesus into the palace (*lit* Praetorium) and gathered unto him the whole band (*or*, cohort)	(11) And Herod with his soldiers set him at nought, and mocked him, and arraying him in gorgeous apparel sent him back to Pilate
(17) And they clothe him with purple, and plaiting a crown of thorns, they put it on him	(28) And they stripped (*some anc auth read* clothed) him, and put on him a scarlet robe	(12) And Herod and Pilate became friends with each other that very day for before they were at enmity between themselves.
(18) And they began to salute him, Hail, King of the Jews!	(29) And they plaited a crown of thorns, and put it upon his head, and a reed in his right hand, and they kneeled down before him, and mocked him, saying, Hail, King of the Jews!	
(19) And they smote his head with a reed, and did spit upon him, and bowing their knees worshipped him	(30) And they spat upon him, and took the reed and smote him on the head	
(20) And when they had mocked him, they took off from him the purple, and put on him his garments And they lead him out to crucify him	(31) And when they had mocked him, they took off from him the robe, and put on him his garments, and led him away to crucify him.	(26) And when they led him away,...

THE MOCKING AND THE CRUCIFIXION

governor," is omitted by Luke, who has in its place a "mocking" by Herod "with his armed-men" The latter, though brief, has one detail in common with Mark and Matthew, namely, a reference to clothing. This is variously expressed[1]. In Mark, "they *clothe him with purple*[2]"; in Matthew, "they stripped him and *put round him a scarlet*[3] chlamys (or, *military*

Jn xix. 1—3, 16 (R V) (1) Then Pilate therefore took Jesus, and scourged him (2) And the soldiers plaited a crown of thorns, and put it on his head, and arrayed him in a purple garment, (3) and they came unto him, and said, Hail, King of the Jews' and they struck him with their hands (*or*, with rods) ... (16) Then therefore he delivered him unto them to be crucified

[1] Mk xv 17	Mt xxvii 28—29 a	Lk. xxiii 11
καὶ ἐνδιδύσκουσιν αὐτὸν πορφύραν καὶ περιτιθέασιν αὐτῷ πλέξαντες ἀκάνθινον στέφανον.	καὶ ἐκδύσαντες (marg ἐνδύσαντες) αὐτὸν χλαμύδα κοκκίνην περιέθηκαν αὐτῷ, καὶ πλέξαντες στέφανον ἐξ ἀκανθῶν ἐπέθηκαν ἐπὶ τῆς κεφαλῆς αὐτοῦ	ἐξουθενήσας δὲ αὐτὸν (marg +καὶ) ὁ Ἡρῴδης σὺν τοῖς στρατεύμασιν αὐτοῦ καὶ ἐμπαίξας περιβαλὼν ἐσθῆτα λαμπρὰν ἀνέπεμψεν αὐτὸν τῷ Πειλάτῳ

Mk περιτιθέασιν, "put round," differs from Mt ἐπέθηκαν "put on" Barnabas § 7 uses both words (see p 567, n 1) in describing the scapegoat with its *scarlet* as the type of Christ Comp Lev xvi 21 "*put them upon* (ἐπιθήσει) the head of the goat," and see p 569, n. 2 on the connection between Lev xvi 21 and Is. 1 18 "sins .*scarlet.*"

Jn xix 2 καὶ οἱ στρατιῶται πλέξαντες στέφανον ἐξ ἀκανθῶν ἐπέθηκαν αὐτοῦ τῇ κεφαλῇ, καὶ ἱμάτιον πορφυροῦν περιέβαλον αὐτόν.

[2] Mk xv 17, 20 πορφύραν. Used in Gospels elsewhere only in Lk xvi 19 "*purple* and fine linen," about the clothing of Dives If Mark's word conveyed that meaning to Luke he would naturally not use it here But Mark probably uses it to mean "imperial purple." (1) The context favours this, (2) *porphŭra* or *porphīra* is recognised by Krauss (p 435) as a Hebraized word meaning in abundant instances "imperial purple" and hardly ever mere "purple [colour]", (3) comp Lucan *Phars* vii 228 "omnis Latio quae servit *purpura* ferro", (4) Plutarch *Mor* 184 E προσφερομένης τῆς πορφύρας αὐτῷ καὶ τοῦ διαδήματος and *ib* 790 B (where it is connected with "diadem") τὸ μὲν διάδημα καταθέσθαι καὶ τὴν πορφύραν, ἱμάτιον δ' ἀναλαβόντα καὶ καμπύλην, shew its technical use in Greek

[3] Mt xxvii 28 κοκκίνην A "scarlet tunic (χιτὼν κόκκινος)" is said by Plutarch *Vit* 182 E (*Fab* 15) to have been suspended over a Roman General's tent as the signal for action Epict iii 22 10, iv 11 34 speaks of "wearing scarlet" as implying fine clothes But it is not alleged as used for imperial or royal clothing

THE MOCKING AND THE CRUCIFIXION

cloak)[1]", in Luke, Herod *"throws round him fine raiment"*—a vague expression and ambiguously used so as to leave the reader in doubt whether this "fine raiment" is, or is not, still worn by Jesus when sent back to Pilate[2]. In John—who agrees partly with Mark but rather more with Matthew—the soldiers "threw round him a purple cloak (*or*, robe)." This takes place before the sentence to death Pilate, bringing Jesus out thus clothed, says "Behold, I bring him out to you that ye may know that I find no crime in him[3]" Then he says "Behold, the man!" This appears to be an instance of Johannine irony. By "the man" Pilate means "the poor man," or "this harmless creature, who fancies himself a king" But God, speaking through Pilate, means "The ideal Man," "The Man made in my image and after my likeness[4]."

The "crown of thorns," mentioned by Mark and Matthew in R V. and omitted by Luke, is, in fact, described by Mark as

---

In LXX it is mostly represented by תולעה (Gesen 1069 *a*, *worm*, coccus ilicis) with or without שני "scarlet" (Gesen 1040 *b*)   In Is 1 18 "Though your sins be as *scarlet* (שנים, LXX φοινικοῦν) they shall be white like snow, though they be red (יאדימו) like the [*scarlet*] *worm* (Heb תולע, Targ זהורית *bright*, or *crimson*, LXX κόκκινον) they shall be as wool (ὡς ἔριον λευκανῶ)," תולע is uniquely rendered "crimson"

[1] Mt xxvii 28 χλαμύδα   Χλαμύς does not occur in LXX except 2 Macc xii. 35 of a military cloak   But in 1 S xxiv 5 מעיל (Gesen 591 *b*) LXX διπλοΐδος, Sym has χλαμύδος, Theod ἱματίου, Aq ? ἐνδύματος   SS omits ἐκδύσαντες and has "they clothed him (? ἐνδύσαντες for ἐκδύσαντες) with garments of scarlet and of purple"   By the χλαμύς the soldiers *actually* extemporised an imperial robe, but *typically* (Mt.) they signified the "scarlet" on the scapegoat, see p 567

[2] In Lk xxiii 11 if the writer intended to describe three acts we should have expected καὶ to be repeated before περιβαλὼν   The omission of it indicates that Lk punctuated thus Ἐξουθενήσας δὲ... καὶ ἐμπαίξας—περιβαλὼν...λαμπρὰν—ἀνέπεμψεν, i e "having mocked him by clothing him in fine apparel"   Ἐσθὴς λαμπρά is used (Steph *Thes* v 86) in Plut. *Mor* 144 D of white or light-coloured clothing as distinct from φοινικίδας "red clothing," and in Polyb x 4 8 and x 5 1, and elsewhere, of the whitened toga of candidates for office   But it also means "fine clothing" in general   Delitzsch renders λαμπράν by זהורית, "bright" or "crimson," which (Levy 1 516) is "often" used of the scarlet on the scapegoat.

[3] Jn xix 2—4.   [4] Jn xix. 5. See *Joh Gr*. **1960.**

THE MOCKING AND THE CRUCIFIXION

"an *acanthine* crown" and by Matthew as "from *acanthai*" In Greek literature, *stephanos*, "crown," does not denote royalty That would be denoted by "diadem" But in LXX *stephanos* occasionally means "royal crown," and here the context indicates that it is thus intended, though extemporised from thorns[1].

There is also an unusual sense in Mark's word "*acanthine.*" It is used by Herodotus and Strabo to mean "made out of the *acantha*," said to be a thorny kind of acacia[2]. Herodotus uses "*acanthine*" about a mast made from this tree, and Strabo about cloths made from the inner bark of the *acantha*—which, however, Strabo declares to be not a tree but a low shrub[3].

Barnabas mentions "the scarlet robe[4]" round Christ's body

---

[1] Στέφανος is used of a royal crown, עֲטָרָה, in 2 S xii 30, parall 1 Chr. xx 2, and Ezek xxi 26, comp Esth viii 15 In 2 S. 1 10 נֵזֶר, LXX has τὸ βασίλειον, Aq ἀφόρισμα, Sym and Theod διάδημα In N T διάδημα occurs only in Rev xii 3, xiii 1, xix 12, of the "diadems," first of the Dragon, or Beast, and then of the Faithful and True, while στέφανος is used in Rev of the "crowns" of elders, and martyrs, and others, in heaven. Also in the Epistles στέφανος is used of the saint's crown, and sometimes with the Greek metaphor of the crown of an athlete

The correct Greek word, missing in Mark's brief narrative, is supplied in a description by Philo of an Alexandrian crowd paying mock homage to an idiot as if he were king and putting on his head a "biblos-leaf *instead of a diadem*," and "throwing a rug round him instead of a chlamys" (ii 522)' ἦν τις μεμηνὼς ὄνομα Καραβᾶς... Συνελάσαντες τὸν ἄθλιον ἄχρι τοῦ γυμνασίου, καὶ στήσαντες μετέωρον, ἵνα καθορῷτο πρὸς πάντων, βύβλον μὲν εὐρύναντες ἀντὶ διαδήματος ἐπιτιθέασιν αὐτοῦ τῇ κεφαλῇ, χαμαιστρώτῳ δὲ τὸ ἄλλο σῶμα περιβάλλουσιν ἀντὶ χλαμύδος, ἀντὶ δὲ σκήπτρου βραχύ τι παπύρου τμῆμα...ἀναδιδόασιν Mark's context makes the meaning of στέφανος, royal crown, clear to English readers; but Greeks, including Luke, may have found it obscure

Philo says that the man διεκεκόσμητο εἰς βασιλέα, "had been *decked to [resemble] a king*" If we assume a tradition that Pilate "brought out Jesus decked to [resemble] a king," this might be taken to mean "Pilate sent Jesus *decked [out in fine clothing] to king [Herod]*"

[2] See L and S

[3] See Steph *Thes* ἀκάνθινος quoting Herod ii 96, Strabo 1 3 (p 175).

[4] Barn vii 9 "Since they shall see Him then, in the [great] Day, having the scarlet robe (τὸν ποδήρη ἔχοντα τὸν κόκκινον) round His body (*lit* round the flesh, περὶ τὴν σάρκα)" In N T ποδήρης occurs only in Rev i 13 In the Pentateuch (LXX) it occurs only five times, all in Exod, and all about the High Priest's clothing.

THE MOCKING AND THE CRUCIFIXION

just after "the scarlet wool put round his [the scapegoat's] head[1]" *He is assuming a detail, not scriptural but often mentioned in Jewish tradition—that a scarlet band placed round the scapegoat's head typified the sins of Israel, and was miraculously made white on the day of Atonement*[2] He does not mention the "*crown* of *thorns*," but he suggests it by asking why they place "the wool in the midst of *the thorns*[3]," after describing the goat as "the accursed [one] *crowned*[4]" Later Christian writers accepted "scarlet" as the sign of sin, from which Christ's blood redeemed us, but they shrank from the type of the scarlet on the scapegoat, preferring the "scarlet line in the window" of Rahab. Barnabas, however, guides us to a different and perhaps earlier type, according to which Christ, wearing "the chlamys," was not wearing a king's "purple" robe but the scapegoat's "scarlet" thread

We pass to traditions about judging, such as "They clothed Him with purple and seated Him on a seat of judgment saying, *Judge justly*, King of Israel[5]", and Justin Martyr's illustration of the Passion from Isaiah (LXX) "*They ask of me now judgment*[6]"

---

[1] Barn vii 8 καὶ περίθετε τὸ ἔριον τὸ κόκκινον περὶ τὴν κεφαλὴν αὐτοῦ ...ἄγει ὁ βαστάζων τὸν τράγον εἰς τὴν ἔρημον καὶ ἀφαιρεῖ τὸ ἔριον καὶ ἐπιτίθησιν αὐτὸ ἐπὶ φρύγανον τὸ λεγόμενον ῥαχία, where see Harnack's note on ציץ "hill-ridge," "back-bone" = ῥαχία, which the writer combines with the thought of ἄκανθα

[2] See below, p 569, n 2

[3] Barn vii 11 τί δὲ ὅτι τὸ ἔριον μέσον τῶν ἀκανθῶν τιθέασιν, τύπος ἐστὶν τοῦ Ἰησοῦ τῇ ἐκκλησίᾳ θέμενος The Latin renders θέμενος passively, "being appointed." But the middle ("having appointed," as in Barn. vi 10, ix. 9) makes sense if we read θεμένου and suppose that Jesus or Joshua "appointed" the sign. This is suggested by Justin M. *Tryph.* § 111 "The sign of (Josh. ii 18) *the scarlet thread* which the spies sent by *Jesus*, son of Nun, gave in Jericho to Rahab the harlot"—that is, Jesus "appointed" it through his agents. Rahab's thread is similarly typified by Clem Rom. § 12, Iren. iv. 20. 12 etc. Even in N.T., a tradition, not based on O T., about a purifying "scarlet" is found in Heb ix 19 "scarlet wool" (see p. 605, n. 2)

[4] Barn vii 9 τὸν ἐπικατάρατον ἐστεφανωμένον

[5] *Evang Petr* § 3 perhaps alluding to Is lviii 2 (LXX)

[6] Justin M. *Apol* § 35 quoting Is. lviii 2 (LXX)

THE MOCKING AND THE CRUCIFIXION

The Johannine tradition that Pilate "brought Jesus out and *sat* on a judgment-seat" might theoretically mean "*seated him* on a judgment-seat[1]." Almost certainly it does not mean this, but it might be so taken in a confusion of traditions about the "judging" of the Messiah And the following facts shew that there was a confusion of some kind, by which Mark has been led into an error that has been only partially rectified by Matthew and Luke. To understand this, we must go back to the earlier mocking where the mockers covered Christ's eyes with a bandage (not His body with a chlamys) and smote Him, saying to Him "Prophesy[2]"

Isaiah had prophesied—concerning the Messiah, the "shoot out of the stock of Jesse"—"He shall *not judge after the sight of his eyes*[3]." The Talmud says that this prophecy was applied to the false Messiah Bar Cochba, early in the second century, by the Rabbis, who declared that if he had been the true Messiah, he ought to have been able to judge by some sixth sense which they called "smelling[4]." Bar Cochba, being misled by slander, and killing his own uncle on a false accusation, was denounced by the Rabbis as an impostor because he could not judge justly[5]. Mark's original, having this Messianic tradition in view, represents Christ's tormentors as bandaging His eyes and striking Him, and then saying, in effect, "Judge thou, not according to the sight of thine eyes, but according

---

[1] Jn xix. 13 ἐκάθισεν ἐπὶ βήματος Against this view (which has found modern support) see Westcott Jn's meaning may be illustrated by Acts xxiii 3 "*Sittest thou to judge me* according to the law and commandest me to be smitten contrary to the law?" Pilate formally "*seated himself*" to judge, and then allowed himself to be deterred from "judging" by popular outcry. Chrys rightly explains it thus

[2] Mk xiv. 65, Mt xxvi 67—8, Lk xxii 63—4

[3] Is. xi 1, 3   [4] *Sanhedr* 93 b.

[5] Derenbourg p 433, quoting *Gittin* 57 a etc Justin Martyr (*Apol* § 31) speaks of Bar Cochba, as the leader of the Jews in their recent revolt, and of the cruel punishments that he inflicted on Christians It is probable, therefore, that he would be aware of the failure to "judge justly" alleged by the Rabbis as a reason for their condemnation of him

THE MOCKING AND THE CRUCIFIXION

to truth, as a Seer, O Messiah, if thou art Messiah Who is the offender? Who smote thee?" Mark misled his readers in two ways First, he substituted "Prophesy" for "Pronounce judgment as a Seer, or as the Messiah[1]" Secondly, he omitted "Who is it that smote thee?" Matthew and Luke restore the omitted question But both of them retain the word "Prophesy " And Matthew alone restores the word "Christ," i e Messiah, which gives the clue to the meaning of the whole passage

It seems likely that Jesus was regarded, in early Christian accounts of the Passion, as being mocked in several aspects — 1st, as the Suffering Messiah, or "Christ," 2nd, as a crowned "King," 3rd, and less clearly, as a Judge, 4th, and obscurely, as the Scapegoat, the Bearer of the Scarlet, which typified the sins of mankind Luke alone omits the " crown " Matthew alone retains the " scarlet " as well as the " Christ[2] "

The later mock-homage here is combined in Mark and Matthew with insolent blows Matthew places the latter after the former Mark intersperses the insolence between the acts of homage John follows Matthew in his (probably) correct arrangement Mark says "They began to salute him [with the words] Hail, King of the Jews"; Matthew, "They mocked him, saying, Hail, King of the Jews"; John, "They *kept coming* to him, and

---

[1] On Mt xxvi 68 προφήτευσον, Wetstein quotes Aristot *Rhet* 17 about Epimenides who "*spoke-as-a-seer* (ἐμαντεύετο) not about the future but about things past and yet obscure " But neither he nor Steph *Thes* gives an instance of προφητεύειν thus used Comp , however, the use of the noun in 1 S ix 9 "He that is now called a *Prophet* was beforetime called a *Seer*," and Jn iv 19 "I perceive that thou art a *prophet*" (where no prediction, but only insight, is implied)

[2] The Mishna of *Sabh* 86 *a* quotes Is 1 18 in answer to the question " Whence [does it follow] that one binds to the scapegoat (comp Lev xvi 21) *a strip of scarlet wool* ? " Tertullian, like Barnabas, accepts the scapegoat as a type of Christ, *Adv Jud* § 14 " The one of them [the goats] surrounded with *scarlet*, amid cursing and universal spitting, and tearing and piercing, was cast away by the People outside the City into perdition " Few other early writers, if any, adopt this bold illustration, but the " cursing " may be illustrated by Gal iii 13 " Christ redeemed us from the curse of the law, having become *a curse for us* "

THE MOCKING AND THE CRUCIFIXION

kept saying, Hail, King of the Jews" What John means by ".*kept coming*" may be gathered from Philo's description (above quoted) of the Alexandrian crowd and their idiot king Philo says that, while some acted as his guards to right and left, others "*kept approaching*—some as if to salute him, others as if to plead some cause, others as if to make representations about matters of public importance[1]."

Here, again, Luke's omission of Marcan details may be explained by the fact that they exhibit Jesus in the aspect of the derided King Another reason may be that Mark is extremely obscure Who could guess that the Marcan tradition "smote his head with *a reed*" meant, as Matthew explains it, in effect, "smote his head with *a reed, which they took from him, after first placing it in his hand as a royal sceptre*"? But still the main reason for Luke's omission is probably that he has apparently confused some tradition that Pilate (1) "*caused Jesus to come forth arrayed to [resemble] a king*" with a tradition that Pilate (2) "*caused Jesus to go forth to king [Herod]*[2]" John does not add Matthew's detail about the "reed" placed like a sceptre "in his right hand" Perhaps he felt that it implied in Jesus a participation in this act of insult, or perhaps that it detracted from the dignity and from the prophetic aspect of the crowning of Jesus with the crown of thorns. In any case, as Mark does not insert it, John's omission is not a breach of the rule of Johannine Intervention

§ 2. *The carrying of the Cross*[3]

Mark and Matthew say that the soldiers constrained Simon

---

[1] Philo ii 522 Εἶθ' ἕτεροι προσῄεσαν, οἱ μὲν ὡς ἀσπασόμενοι, οἱ δὲ ὡς δικασόμενοι, οἱ δ' ὡς ἐντευξόμενοι περὶ κοινῶν πραγμάτων

[2] See above, p 566, n 1 *ad fin*

[3]
Mk xv 21—5 (R V)	Mt xxvii 32—6 (R V)	Lk xxiii 26, 32—4 (R V)
(21) And they compel (*lit* impress) one passing by, Simon of Cyrene, coming from the country, the father of Alexander and	(32) And as they came out, they found a man of Cyrene, Simon by name him they compelled (*lit* impressed) to go [with them], that he	(26) . they laid hold upon one Simon of Cyrene, coming from the country, and laid on him the cross, to bear it after Jesus

570 (Mark xv. 21—5)

THE MOCKING AND THE CRUCIFIXION

of Cyrene to *"take up the cross*[1]*"* of Jesus, using the same phrase as that assigned to Jesus Himself by the Synoptists in

Mk xv 21—5 (R V) *contd*	Mt xxvii 32—6 (R V) *contd*	Lk xxiii 26, 32—4 (R V) *contd*
Rufus, to go [with them], that he might bear his cross.	'might bear his cross	
(22) And they bring him unto the place Golgotha, which is, being interpreted, The place of a skull	(33) And when they were come unto a place called Golgotha, that is to say, The place of a skull,	(32) And there were also two others, malefactors, led with him to be put to death
(23) And they offered him wine mingled with myrrh but he received it not.	(34) They gave him wine to drink mingled with gall and when he had tasted it, he would not drink	(33) And when they came unto the place which is called The skull (*Lat* Calvary), there they crucified him, and the malefactors, one on the right hand and the other on the left
(24) And they crucify' him, and part his garments among them, casting lots upon them, what each should take	(35) And when they had crucified him, they parted his garments among them, casting lots	
(25) And it was the third hour, and they crucified him	(36) And they sat and watched him there	(34) And Jesus said, Father, forgive them, for they know not what they do [*Some anc auth omit* And ..do] And parting his garments among them, they cast lots

Jn xix 17—18, 23—4 (R V) (17) They took Jesus therefore and he went out, bearing the cross for himself, unto the place called The place of a skull, which is called in Hebrew Golgotha (18) where they crucified him, and with him two others, on either side one, and Jesus in the midst .. (23) The soldiers therefore, when they had crucified Jesus, took his garments, and made four parts, to every soldier a part, and also the coat (*or*, tunic) now the coat (*or*, tunic) was without seam, woven from the top throughout (24) They said therefore one to another, Let us not rend it, but cast lots for it, whose it shall be that the scripture might be fulfilled, which saith and upon my vesture did they cast lots (Ps xxii 18)

[1] Mk xv 21

καὶ ἀγγαρεύουσιν παράγοντά τινα Σίμωνα Κυρηναῖον ἐρχόμενον ἀπ' ἀγροῦ, τὸν πατέρα Ἀλεξάνδρου καὶ Ῥούφου, ἵνα ἄρῃ τὸν σταυρὸν αὐτοῦ.

Mt. xxvii 32

Ἐξερχόμενοι δὲ εὗρον ἄνθρωπον Κυρηναῖον ὀνόματι Σίμωνα· τοῦτον ἠγγάρευσαν ἵνα ἄρῃ τὸν σταυρὸν αὐτοῦ.

Lk xxiii 26

καὶ ὡς ἀπήγαγον αὐτόν, ἐπιλαβόμενοι Σίμωνά τινα Κυρηναῖον ἐρχόμενον ἀπ' ἀγροῦ ἐπέθηκαν αὐτῷ τὸν σταυρὸν φέρειν ὄπισθεν τοῦ Ἰησοῦ

THE MOCKING AND THE CRUCIFIXION

the precept "Let him *take up his cross* and follow me[1]" Luke substitutes the word *"bear," "bring,"* or *"carry."* "Bear" he presumably intends the reader to distinguish from *"take up"*—"bear" being used literally, but "take up" metaphorically of "taking up" a new way of life Another word—applied to heavy burdens—meaning *"lift* (or, *carry*)," *bastāzein*, is used by Luke in the Double Tradition, where Matthew has "Whosoever does not *receive his cross,*" but Luke "Whosoever does not *carry his own cross*[2]." These distinctions point back to Isaiah, "Surely he hath *borne* (or, *taken up*) our griefs and *carried* our sorrows[3]" Here the LXX mistranslates the second of the verbs, but Matthew quotes it with *bastāzein*, the word used by Aquila in a closely following verse "he shall *carry* their iniquities"

Luke's expression "They put on him [i e on Simon] the cross to *bear* behind Jesus" might be interpreted as meaning that Jesus and Simon bore the cross together, Simon bearing the hinder part of it; and this view is favoured by a very ancient Latin MS of Mark which has "And *they carry it* [i e the Cross] to Golgotha[4]." The Greek is ambiguous, and might mean "they carry him," *i e* Jesus, or "they carry it," *i e* the Cross But the Latin could mean only the latter, and it would mean that the two, together, carried their burden all the way to Golgotha.

---

[1] Mk viii 34, Mt xvi 24, ἀράτω τὸν σταυρὸν αὐτοῦ, to which Lk ix 23 adds καθ' ἡμέραν, which indicates the metaphorical nature of the act as part of a new "daily" life

[2]
Mt x 38 — Lk. xiv. 27
.. ὃς οὐ λαμβάνει τὸν σταυρὸν αὐτοῦ καὶ ἀκολουθεῖ ὀπίσω μου — ὅστις οὐ βαστάζει τὸν σταυρὸν ἑαυτοῦ καὶ ἔρχεται ὀπίσω μου

[3] Is liii 4, quoted in Mt viii 17 "Bear" is נשא, "carry" is סבל In Is liii 11 "carry" (סבל) their iniquities," LXX has ἀνοίσει, Aq βαστάσει, Theod ὑπήνεγκεν, Sym ὑπενέγκει Comp Epict ii 9 22 "as though a man that could not *take up* (ἆραι) ten pounds wanted to *lift* (or, *carry*) (βαστάζειν) the stone of Ajax" (where perhaps the pres inf indicates that a continuous "carrying," not "lifting," is meant)

[4] Mk xv 21—2 (k) "Et adpraehendunt transeunte quendam cyrinaeum cui fuit nomen simon uenientem de uilla sua fuit autem nomen (sic) alexandri et rufi et fa[ciunt] eum cru[cem baiu]lare et ferunt *illam* in culgotham locum"

THE MOCKING AND THE CRUCIFIXION

John intervenes in such a way as to shew that there was no partnership of this kind. Using the word *bastāzein* adopted by Aquila in Isaiah's description of the Suffering Servant, he says emphatically "And *carrying the cross for himself* he went forth to the place called Place of a Skull[1]" This may mean—but, if it does, a great deal has to be supplied—"He went forth [from Jerusalem] carrying the cross for Himself [and afterwards, when He could bear it no longer, came, with Simon bearing it behind Him] to the place of crucifixion[2]" And this explanation satisfies Jerome[3]. Origen treats the question rather more fully as being complicated by details[4]. In any case John seems to bar the way to any interpretation of Luke that might imply a joint bearing of the Cross.

John's omission of "Simon the Cyrenian" hardly needs explanation in view of his general omission of Synoptic names and terms that ceased to interest the Christian Churches toward the end of the first century. But there was a special reason for this omission. As early as the reign of Hadrian, the heretic Basilides taught that Simon was substituted for Jesus not only

---

[1] Jn xix 17 καὶ βαστάζων αὑτῷ τὸν σταυρὸν ἐξῆλθεν εἰς τὸν λεγόμενον Κρανίου Τόπον. Some MSS have αυτου or εαυτου, but B has αυτω and the Latin codd *sibi*. I do not know another such instance in N T of what Alford here calls the "dativus commodi." It is doubtless intended to be very emphatic. Nonnus has "Jesus Himself having His own cross (σταυρὸν ἔχων ἐὸν αὐτὸς Ἰησοῦς)."

[2] Εἰς might sometimes perhaps be used so as to include the meaning of "toward," i e πρός and ἐπί, as well as "to," see *Proclam.* pp 372, 377 (and comp *Son* 3623 *d*), but the Johannine context hardly justifies it here.

[3] In his comment on Matthew, Jerome says "Hoc intelligendum est quod egrediens de praetorio Jesus ipse portaverit crucem suam, postea obvium habuerint Simonem, cui portandam crucem imposuerint." He adds that symbolically, "Crucem Jesu suscipiunt nationes, et peregrinus obediens portat ignominiam Salvatoris."

[4] Origen (on Mt xxvii 32, Lomm v 42—3) asks whether those who placed the Cross on Jesus (1) placed it on Him at first before they seized Simon, or (2) seized Simon [at first] on their exit [and made him carry the Cross], but afterwards, on reaching the place of crucifixion, "placed it on Him Himself that He Himself might carry it (imposuerunt crucem ei ipsi ut ipse eam portaret)."

573 (Mark xv 21—5)

THE MOCKING AND THE CRUCIFIXION

under the burden of the Cross, but on the Cross, so that Simon was crucified while Jesus looked on and laughed[1]. Such Gnostic legends may have existed apart from, and before, Basilides, as parts of the Gnostic reluctance to accept what Paul calls "the scandal of the cross[2]." John might well omit a Marcan tradition, however true, that had given rise to such a legend

A word may be added about Mark's mention of Simon as "the father of Alexander and Rufus " Apparently he defines them thus because Alexander and Rufus would be known to his readers Pseudo-Jerome's commentary on Mark says that Simon is "commemorated by *the merits of his sons* who were disciples " He adds the metaphor of *a sweet fruit-tree springing from a bitter root*, apparently meaning that Simon, the father, did *not* become a disciple. Now Paul, writing to the Romans, says "Salute Rufus, the chosen (*or* elect) in the Lord, and his mother and mine", and Origen, who justly remarks that Paul does not make idle differences in his salutations, says "I believe that Paul knew him to be of the number, not of the 'many' who are [merely] 'called,' but of the 'few' who are 'elected[3] '" Polycarp speaks of Ignatius, Zosimus, *and Rufus*, as conspicuous martyrs[4]. Not improbably this was the Marcan Rufus But in any case Mark and Paul may be mentioning the same man—Mark speaking of the father of the two sons in early days as a witness of the Crucifixion, Paul speaking of one of the two sons afterwards as "the elect " If so, Matthew and Luke

---

[1] Iren 1 24 4 "Quapropter neque passum eum, sed Simonem quendam Cyrenaeum angariatum portasse crucem ejus pro eo et hunc secundum ignorantiam et errorem crucifixum, transfiguratum ab eo, uti putaretur ipse esse Jesus et ipsum autem Jesum Simonis accepisse formam, et stantem irrisisse eos." The passage is quoted by Epiphanius

[2] Gal v 11.

[3] See Origen's *Comm* on Rom xvi 13, comp Mt xxii 14

[4] Polyc *Epist Philipp* § 9 on which Lightf says "The Rufus of Polycarp is possibly the same who is mentioned in Rom xvi 13, and this latter again may with some degree of probability be identified with the son of Simon the Cyrenian and brother of Alexander (Mark xv 21), but the name is not rare "

THE MOCKING AND THE CRUCIFIXION

might shrink from perpetuating the early Marcan phrase in which the elect and the non-elect were mentioned together.

§ 3. *"Wine mingled-with-myrrh," in Mark*[1]

The parallel Matthew mentions "wine mixed together with gall" The parallel Luke mentions no offer of wine Mark's meaning was probably misunderstood The offer of "myrrhized wine," as a narcotic, is said in the Talmud to have been a customary act of kindness to prisoners about to be executed[2] This, not being understood, led Matthew to seek an emendation of Mark by taking the Hebrew or Aramaic *môr*, myrrh, as indicating some form of *mar*, "bitterness," and then by taking this as meaning "gall[3]" By this means the act might seem to fulfil the Psalmist's description of his sufferings "They gave me also gall for my meat; and in my thirst they gave me vinegar to drink[4]."

---

[1] Mk xv 23   Mt xxvii 34   Lk om
καὶ ἐδίδουν αὐτῷ   ἔδωκαν αὐτῷ πιεῖν
ἐσμυρνισμένον οἶνον, ὃς   οἶνον μετὰ χολῆς μεμιγ-
δὲ οὐκ ἔλαβεν   μένον καὶ γευσάμενος
                    οὐκ ἠθέλησεν πιεῖν

On ὃς δέ, of which (thus used) Steph *Thes* gives no instance, see *Joh Gr* 2380 b quoting Jn v 11 and Job xxii. 18 (LXX), Tob v 13 It emphasizes "*he on his part*," antithetical to "they [on their part]" making the usual offer" of a narcotic Matthew, missing the meaning—that it was "offered" (imperf.), not "given" (aor.)—emphasizes the "tasting" of the gift and then the "refusal to drink"

[2] See *Hor. Heb* on Mt xxvii 34 quoting *Sanhedr* 43 a "To those that were to be executed they gave a grain of *myrrh* infused in wine to drink, that their understanding might be disturbed" (that is, that they might lose their senses), "as it is said, 'Give strong drink to them that are ready to die, and wine to those that are of a sorrowful heart' etc And the tradition is, That some women of quality in Jerusalem allowed this freely of their own cost" etc

[3] See Levy *Ch* ii 18 a quoting Exod xxx 23 מר "myrrh," Targ var מורא, מירא, מרא, מור, *ib* ii 33 b (מרת) מירת "myrrhized wine" in Deut xxix 6 "strong-drink (שכר)" This resembles (*ib* ii 64 b) מרא Deut xxxii 33 (Onk) מרא, or מירתא, "gall" = Heb חמה "poison"

[4] Ps lxix 21 "Gall," Heb ראש, is in Targ "*the gall* (מרירת) of the heads of asps"

THE MOCKING AND THE CRUCIFIXION

John mentions no offer of a narcotic, and his silence may be regarded as, in some sense, a failure of the rule of Johannine Intervention But it must be borne in mind that another offer of vinegar, or wine, made later on to Jesus just before His death, is recorded by Mark and Matthew, but not by Luke, who simply mentions an offer of "vinegar" by the soldiers as one of many acts of "mocking" some time before the death[1]. Now this offer will be found to be fully described by John, with additional detail indicating that Jesus Himself asked for it "that the scripture might be accomplished[2]." We do not know what may have been John's reason for not intervening in a direct way to explain the first offer—that of the "myrrhized wine"; but we do know that he intervened as to the second offer, in order to shew that this at all events was an act, not of insult, but of kindness

§ 4 "*Casting lots*" *for Christ's garments*[3]

In a Greek competition by lot, the "lot" is mostly a tablet or pebble marked with each competitor's name The lots are

---

[1] Mk xv 36 (Mt xxvii 48) δραμὼν δέ τις (Mt εἷς) to which the only corresponsion in Lk is xxiii 36 προσφέροντες

[2] Jn xix 28—30

[3] Mk xv. 24
καὶ σταυροῦσιν αὐ-
τὸν καὶ διαμερίζονται τὰ
ἱμάτια αὐτοῦ, βάλλοντες
κλῆρον ἐπ᾽ αὐτὰ τίς τί
ἄρῃ.

Mt xxvii 35
σταυρώσαντες δὲ αὐ-
τὸν διεμερίσαντο τὰ
ἱμάτια αὐτοῦ βάλοντες
(marg βαλόντες) κλῆ-
ρον.

Lk xxiii 34 b
διαμεριζόμενοι δὲ τὰ
ἱμάτια αὐτοῦ ἔβαλον
κλῆρον.

Jn xix. 23—24 οἱ οὖν στρατιῶται ὅτε ἐσταύρωσαν τὸν Ἰησοῦν ἔλαβον τὰ ἱμάτια αὐτοῦ καὶ ἐποίησαν τέσσερα μέρη, ἑκάστῳ στρατιώτῃ μέρος, καὶ τὸν χιτῶνα ἦν δὲ ὁ χιτὼν ἄραφος, ἐκ τῶν ἄνωθεν ὑφαντὸς δι᾽ ὅλου· εἶπαν οὖν πρὸς ἀλλήλους Μὴ σχίσωμεν αὐτόν, ἀλλὰ λάχωμεν περὶ αὐτοῦ τίνος ἔσται ἵνα ἡ γραφὴ πληρωθῇ "Διεμερίσαντο τὰ ἱμάτιά μου ἑαυτοῖς καὶ ἐπὶ τὸν ἱματισμόν μου ἔβαλον κλῆρον"

John (λάχωμεν) is here combining the rendering of Sym (ἐλάγχανον) with other renderings of Ps xxii 18 (Walton) "Divident (יחלקו) vestimenta mea (בגדי) sibi ipsis, et super vestem meam (לבושי) projicient (יפילו) sortem (גורל)," where R V has the present tense twice, and pl "lots" ("they *part*. and upon my vesture *do they cast lots*"), Field, for "*do they cast lots*," has "*sortiti sunt*," LXX ἔβαλον κλῆρον, Aq βαλοῦσι κλῆρον, Sym ἐλάγχανον

THE MOCKING AND THE CRUCIFIXION

cast into a vessel, and the owner of the one that is first drawn out or shaken out is successful. In such a competition it would be natural to speak of "casting *lots*" rather than "casting a *lot*" (though the latter phrase might sometimes be used about the casting *out* of the decisive single lot as well as about the casting *in* of the competitive plural lots[1]) Hebrew Scripture mentions "casting *a* (or, *the*) *lot*" in several cases where LXX has "casting *lots*[2]"

All the Synoptists say that the soldiers "divided his garments" and that they "cast a lot." This apparently means that they divided the garments into heaps, and then determined by lot the order of preference. The competitors, in this case, might draw out tablets inscribed, not with their names, but with the numbers "one," "two," etc. indicating the order of choice Mark perhaps felt that this use of the lot—to determine *precedence*—was not very clearly expressed by the phrase "casting a lot"—since the latter applied better to the single lot that determined *success* for a single competitor. He therefore adds "upon *them* (neut)," *i e* for the garments, not for the competitors. Then, to make it clear that one competitor is not to take all the garments, he adds "*to see who should take what.*" Matthew and Luke perhaps failed to see the purpose of this addition. At all events they omit it. Luke also perhaps substitutes "*lots*" for "*lot*[3]."

---

[1] See Steph *Thes* κλῆρος

[2] See Mandelk גוֹרָל sing in Is xxxiv. 17, Joel iii 3, Ob 11, Nahum iii 10, where LXX has pl κλήρους The Engl "cast" in "cast lots" is represented most freq by the causative of "fall," נפל, but also by שלך, ירה, ידד, טול, all of which mean throwing, shooting etc In Prov. xvi. 33 "the lot is cast (טול) into the lap," LXX ἐπέρχεται completely misrenders In Lev. xvi 8 נתן, *lit* "give" or "appoint" (R V. "cast"), LXX has ἐπιθήσει. In Josh xviii. 6 ירה, R V "cast," LXX has "bring out (ἐξοίσω)"

[3] In Lk xxiii. 34, Tisch. reads κλήρους. SS and Curet have "drew-[lots]," so that they afford no evidence as to the noun The temptation to substitute κλῆρον (as in Mk, Mt , Jn, and LXX Ps xxii 18) would be very strong. In Mk xv 24, SS has פסא "lot(s)," as a separate noun; and (in view of Jn xix 23 χιτών) it may be worth noting that (Gesen 821 *a*) פס " flat [of the foot, or of the hand] " is used

THE MOCKING AND THE CRUCIFIXION

John intervenes to explain how it came to pass that a lot of some kind was required, and to shew that Mark was wrong in supposing that it was used merely to determine order of choice. The "dividing," he says, referred only to the outer garment, which, being divisible into equal parts without injury, needed no use of the lot, but the inner garment would have been spoiled by rending, and the soldiers determined that this should be a prize by itself The prize-winner was to be determined by lot. Thus the soldiers fulfilled the Psalmist's words "They divided my garments among them, and on my vesture did they cast a lot." The Greek of *"garments"* and *"vesture"* is similar and might be expressed by *"vestments"* and *"vesture."* John says, in effect: "Mark should have said 'They *divided his vestments* and *cast a lot on his vesture* [not, *on them*] *to see who should take it* [not, *to see who should take what*]¹."

While representing the Roman soldiers as thus fulfilling exactly the two clauses of the Psalm, John tells us what they said, "Let us not tear that, but draw-lots for it whose it shall be." The Greek for "draw-[lots]" is very rarely thus used, and never in the LXX² But Symmachus uses it in the Psalm from which John is quoting It is perhaps vernacular Greek. And by it the scene is brought more clearly before us as John wishes us to see it—detached from the Synoptic tradition —" Here are these Gentiles, quite ignorant of the Scripture, and thinking only of their perquisites. 'Let us draw lots,' they say, 'for this piece of cloth which it is a pity to spoil.' They are quite unconscious that they are fulfilling what the Messiah said centuries ago 'On my vesture did they cast a lot.' Yet they are fulfilling it."

---

in the phrase "robe ($\chi\iota\tau\omega\nu$) of flats" to mean (Gen. xxxvii 3, etc , 2 S. xiii 18, 19) "a robe reaching to the feet" (comp Rev 1 13 $\pi o\delta\eta\rho\eta$)

[1] This would give διεμερισαντο τὰ ἱμάτια αὐτοῦ βάλλοντες κλῆρον ἐπὶ τὸν ἱματισμὸν τίς ἄρῃ It would be an easy error to suppose that τὸν ἱματισμόν meant τὰ ἱμάτια i e αὐτά Then the sense would require the addition of τί after τίς

[2] Λαγχάνω occurs in Demosth pp 510—11 (*Argum*) about the choregi "drawing lots" for the best flute-players In LXX it occurs only in 1 S xiv 47 (לכד), Wisd viii 19, 3 Macc vi 1, which do not illustrate Jn.

THE MOCKING AND THE CRUCIFIXION

It is John's primary object to suggest this thought to the reader. To correct Mark's error, and to shew how it arose, is a secondary object, but still another reason for intervening.

§ 5. "*It was the third hour,*" *in Mark*[1]

There is a difficulty in reconciling the Marcan "*third hour*" with the Johannine text "It was about the *sixth hour*, and he [*i.e.* Pilate] saith to the Jews, Behold, your King." The Arabic Diatessaron, which accepts the Johannine "sixth hour," rejects the Marcan "third hour." Various early explanations have been offered, none of which are quite satisfactory[2]. Probably none will be found that can vindicate Mark from the charge of obscurity or inexactness, for, were it otherwise, Matthew and Luke would not have deviated from him. But the following considerations indicate that early Christian traditions would lay mystical stress on three different hours of the day in con-

---

[1] Between the (Mk, Mt, Lk) casting of the lots and the mention of the (Mk, Lk) "superscription (ἐπιγραφή)" (Mt. αἰτία), where Luke inserts his description of the mocking of Jesus on the Cross, Mark and Matthew have (Mk xv 25) ἦν δὲ ὥρα τρίτη καὶ ἐσταύρωσαν αὐτόν, (Mt. xxvii 36) καὶ καθήμενοι ἐτήρουν αὐτὸν ἐκεῖ—corresponding to which Luke has nothing. See Swete on variations in Mk's text, or in renderings of it, and on early attempts to reconcile it with Jn xix 14—16 ἦν δὲ παρασκευὴ τοῦ πάσχα, ὥρα ἦν ὡς ἕκτη καὶ λέγει τοῖς Ἰουδαίοις...ἀπεκρίθησαν οἱ ἀρχιερεῖς Οὐκ ἔχομεν βασιλέα εἰ μὴ Καίσαρα. τότε οὖν παρέδωκεν αὐτὸν αὐτοῖς ἵνα σταυρωθῇ. Nonnus *takes "sixth" in Jn as referring to the day of the week*, and inserts "third hour," Ἕκτη δ᾽ ἦν ἐνέπουσι προσάββατος ἔτρεχεν ἠώς ἦν δὲ τιταινομένη τριτάτη θανατηφόρος ὥρη.

It is somewhat surprising that no scribe has altered Mk so as to give the meaning "It was the third hour (*i.e.* three hours had passed) *since* they had crucified him", for the alterations of καὶ to ὅτε in some MSS, and of ἐσταύρωσαν to ἐφύλασσον in D and k (custodiebant), shew that a difficulty was felt. But if an interval of hours had been meant the pl. would naturally be used, as in Acts v. 7 ἐγένετο δὲ ὡς ὡρῶν τριῶν διάστημα, where Delitzsch has "there was as from three hours (כמשלש שעות)."

[2] See Swete *ad loc.*, who quotes, *inter alia*, August *Cons.* iii 42 "intelligitur ergo fuisse hora tertia cum clamaverunt Judaei ut Dominus crucifigeretur, et veracissime demonstratur tunc eos crucifixisse quando clamaverunt."

THE MOCKING AND THE CRUCIFIXION

nection with the Crucifixion, namely, the third, the sixth, and the ninth, and that Mark alone has retained one of the earliest of these traditions, namely, that which mentioned the third hour.

Maimonides says "The great Sanhedrin sat from the morning daily sacrifice until the afternoon daily sacrifice," that is to say, from the third hour till the ninth hour[1] It follows that the third hour was the earliest possible time when the Sanhedrin could present to Pilate their verdict of guilty "The three hours that come first" is a Talmudic expression for the time preceding that of the morning sacrifice[2]. A trace of this Jewish rule about the sitting of the Sanhedrin may perhaps be seen in a Greek scholium on "the third hour" in Mark: "Some say that this [evangelist, Mark,] having in mind (or, mentioning) the verdict of [the Council of] the people [of the Jews] said that during this hour Jesus had been crucified [virtually] by the people; for it was the third hour [they say] when the people condemned Him to be crucified, [I mean the people] of the Jews [as distinct from Pilate]. But the rest have made mention of the sixth [hour], in which, having received the verdict [uttered] by Pilate, He is crucified by the soldiers; in agreement with which the rest of the evangelists have said [what they have severally said[3]]."

---

[1] See *Hor Heb* on Mk xv. 25

[2] See *Hor Heb* ib quoting *Sanhedr* 105 b which says—on Is xxvi 20 "until the wrath be overpast"—"When is He wroth? In the first three hours [of the day]." This would be the period before the morning sacrifice.

[3] See Cramer on Mk xv. 25 τινὲς δέ φασιν ὅτι τὴν μὲν τοῦ λαοῦ ἀπόφασιν οὗτος ἐπιμνησθεὶς εἶπε ταύτην (sic) ὥραν ἐσταυρῶσθαι τὸν Ἰησοῦν ὑπὸ τοῦ λαοῦ τρίτη γὰρ ὥρα ἦν ὅτε ὁ λαὸς αὐτὸν κατέκρινε σταυρωθῆναι τῶν Ἰουδαίων· οἱ δὲ λοιποὶ τῆς ἕκτης ἐμνήσθησαν, ἐν ᾗ τὴν ὑπὸ Πιλάτου ἀπόφασιν λαβὼν σταυροῦται ὑπὸ τῶν στρατιωτῶν, ᾧ καὶ συμφώνως οἱ λοιποὶ τῶν Εὐαγγελιστῶν ἔφασαν

This appears to be a version, and a truer one, of some tradition that is at the bottom of Augustine's explanation quoted above It supposes the real Jewish verdict to have been pronounced by the Sanhedrin, not by the packed multitude of their officials. Pseudo-Jerome on Mk has a fanciful comment on the third, the sixth, and

THE MOCKING AND THE CRUCIFIXION

In accordance with a hypothesis based on these two traditions, we should have to suppose that in the earliest days of the Church among Jewish Christians a stress was laid, not retained in later times, on the Crucifixion as including the morning as well as the evening sacrifice, so that Mark's brief and obscure words were in fact of the nature of a parenthesis, inserted after a narration of the literal fact, intended to call attention to its spiritual meaning "So they crucify Him, casting lots on His garments —And now the third hour, the hour of the morning sacrifice, had come and gone; and the verdict of the Jewish people on their Saviour had been recorded and executed, and the period of agony on the Cross was at hand, beginning from the sixth hour Concerning this the Psalmist says that in this hour a destruction, or demon, ravageth and that 'whoso dwelleth in the secret place of the Most High' shall be delivered from it[1] But the contest will not end till the hour of release, the ninth hour, the hour of the evening sacrifice. It was in the sixth hour that the darkness of destruction began,

the ninth, hour, alluding to the three classes of fruitfulness mentioned in the Parable of the Sower "A tricesimo namque fructu Marcus ascendit ad centesimum, id est, a tertia hora crucis usque ad tertiam resurrectionis post tres dies Tricesimus fructus est in cruce, sexagesimus in inferno, centesimus in Paradiso" The writer's instinct led him at all events to perceive that there was a symbolical meaning latent, and perhaps intended by very early evangelists, in the mention of the three hours.

[1] Ps. xci 6 "from the *destruction* (קטב) that wasteth (שוד) at noonday," LXX ἀπὸ συμπτώματος καὶ δαιμονίου μεσημβρινοῦ, Aq "from the biting that devils it at noon (ἀπὸ δηγμοῦ δαιμονίζοντος μεσημβρίας)," Sym οὐ [? οὗ] συγκύρημα δαιμονιῶδες μεσημβρίας, Targ "from the troop of *demons* (שידין) that lay waste at noon " The form שוד (Gesen 994 a) from שדד, "devastate," resembles the Heb שד, Aram. שידא (Deut xxxii 17 δαιμόνιον) Ps xci 13 "thou shalt tread upon the lion and the adder" would naturally be regarded by Christians as referring, in particular, to Christ (as by Irenaeus iii 23 7, and Tertull. *Adv Marc* iv. 24). This might lead them to regard the earlier verses, Ps xci 1—6 "Whoso dwelleth...noonday," as also referring to the Messiah. But it must be confessed that the reference might not generally be accepted, and that the use made of this Psalm by Satan, in Mt iv 6, Lk iv 10—11, might discredit the reference

THE MOCKING AND THE CRUCIFIXION

but the way had been prepared for it by the third hour. It was all one act, one sacrifice "

John, who omits the Synoptic "darkness from the sixth to the ninth hour," mentions "the sixth hour" in a different context, "It was the Preparation for the Passover, it was *about the sixth hour*[1]" This might well mean "a little before the sixth hour" And it was then that Pilate, after making his last attempt to save Jesus, yielded Him up to the chief priests, who cried "We have no king but Caesar," upon which Pilate "delivered him unto them to be crucified[2]." When the Jews thus rejected their true King, they brought down—so Christians believed—destruction on their nation. "It was noon," a Christian might say, "and there fell upon the Jews, as it is written in the Psalms, '*the destruction that wasteth at noonday.*'"

This precise phrase "It was about the sixth hour" occurs in only one other passage of the New Testament, and that is where Jesus is described as "wearied" near the well of Jacob, and where, in spite of thirst and weariness, He gains a spiritual triumph in Samaria[3]. We have seen that a connection between this hour (that is to say, noon) and a spiritual enemy, is suggested by a passage quoted above from the Psalms, as interpreted by the LXX and the other Greek translators and Jewish tradition, which render "the destruction that layeth waste" as "the mischance and the demon" or "the demons that lay waste[4]" Part of the Psalm is quoted in the Gospels as uttered by Satan to Jesus in the Temptation—"He shall give his angels charge over thee[5]." Another part "Thou shalt not be afraid...for the destruction (or demon) that wasteth at noonday" might seem equally applicable, though not in Satan's sense[6]. This

---

[1] Jn xix. 14   [2] Jn xix. 15—16.
[3] Jn iv. 6 ὥρα ἦν ὡς ἕκτη (closely approached in Lk. xxiii 44). See *Son* 3476 *a* "In Jn (iv 6 foll , xi 35, xix 28) when Jesus is *wearied*, or *weeps*, or *thirsts*, it is then that His redemptive power is best revealed " Comp Acts x 9 "about the sixth hour "
[4] See above, p. 581, n. 1.
[5] Ps. xci 11 quoted in Mt iv. 6, Lk iv 10
[6] Rashi on Ps. xci. 6 says that דבר and קטב are "the names of two demons," and the latter, *Keteb*, "lays waste at noon." *Tehill.*

THE MOCKING AND THE CRUCIFIXION

word rendered demon, or destruction, is mentioned again in Hosea "O death, where is thy *destruction*[1]?" words quoted by Paul in illustration of Christ's triumph over death. These facts shew that first-century Jewish traditions concerning "*the sixth hour*" might be moulded by Christians to express their belief that in the sixth hour their Messiah was assailed on the Cross by the Destruction of Sheol, and that the contest endured from the sixth hour to the ninth, the hour of the evening sacrifice, when the Saviour triumphed over death by dying, though sinless, for the sins of the world.

§ 6   *The Superscription on the Cross*[2]

Mark and Luke here mention "superscription" in connection with "King of the Jews", and Mark calls it "the

---

ad loc gives a long description of the appearance of this demon. Jerome argues diffusely against the objective existence of such a demon, but his argument indicates that many of his readers believed in its existence   Levy iv 278 *b* gives copious descriptions of the *Keteb* from Midrash, though none from the Talmuds   The belief in *Keteb* was probably more prevalent among the unlearned than in learned circles.

[1] 1 Cor xv 55 ποῦ σου, θάνατε, τὸ κέντρον; LXX ποῦ τὸ κέντρον σου, ᾅδη, Hos xiii 14 Heb "Where [is] *thy destruction (keteb)*, O Sheol?" Those who rendered the sentence thus interrogatively, and who believed in the existence of a *keteb*, or demon, with a separate existence, would say that he was one of the pain-bringing ministers of Death, appropriately called "sting" by LXX (and by Aquila "bitings (δηγμοί)")

[2]

Mk xv 26—32 (R V)	Mt xxvii. 37—44 (R V)	Lk xxiii. 32, 35—40 (R V)
(26) And the superscription of his accusation was written over, THE KING OF THE JEWS	(37) And they set up over his head his accusation written, THIS IS JESUS THE KING OF THE JEWS	(32) And there were also two others, malefactors, led with him to be put to death.
(27) And with him they crucify two robbers, one on his right hand, and one on his left [*Many anc auth ins ver* 28 And the Scripture was fulfilled, which saith,	(38) Then are there crucified with him two robbers, one on the right hand, and one on the left	(35) And the people stood beholding And the rulers also scoffed at him, saying, He saved others; let him save himself, if this is the Christ of God, his chosen.

583   (Mark xv 26—32)

THE MOCKING AND THE CRUCIFIXION

superscription of his [alleged] crime," implying that a superscription stating the nature of the crime was usually super-

Mk xv 26—32 (R V) contd	Mt xxvii 37—44 (R V.) contd	Lk. xxiii 32, 35—40 (R V) contd
And he was reckoned with transgressors]		(36) And the soldiers also mocked him, coming to him, offering him vinegar,
(29) And they that passed by railed on him, wagging their heads, and saying, Ha! thou that destroyest the temple (*or*, sanctuary), and buildest it in three days, (30) save thyself, and come down from the cross (31) In like manner also the chief priests mocking [him] among themselves with the scribes said, He saved others, himself he cannot save (*or*, can he not save himself?)	(39) And they that passed by railed on him, wagging their heads, (40) and saying, Thou that destroyest the temple (*or*, sanctuary), and buildest it in three days, save thyself if thou art the Son of God, come down from the cross (41) In like manner also the chief priests mocking [him] with the scribes and elders, said, (42) He saved others; himself he cannot save (*or*, can he not save himself?) He is the King of Israel, let him now come down from the cross, and we will believe on him.	(37) and saying, If thou art the King of the Jews, save thyself (38) And there was also a superscription over him, THIS IS THE KING OF THE JEWS (39) And one of the malefactors which were hanged railed on him, saying, Art not thou the Christ? save thyself and us (40) But the other..
(32) Let the Christ, the King of Israel, now come down from the cross, that we may see and believe. And they that were crucified with him reproached him	(43) He trusteth on God, let him deliver him now, if he desireth him for he said, I am the Son of God. (44) And the robbers also that were crucified with him cast upon him the same reproach.	

Jn xix 18—22 (R V) (18) Where they crucified him, and with him two others, on either side one, and Jesus in the midst (19) And Pilate wrote a title also, and put it on the cross And there was written, JESUS OF NAZARETH, THE KING OF THE JEWS (20) This title therefore read many of the Jews for the place where Jesus was crucified was nigh to the city (*or*, for the place of the city where Jesus was crucified was nigh at hand) and it was written in

scribed on the cross of any crucified criminal, and that "*the* superscription" in this case was "*the King of the Jews*[1]" Obviously this is not strictly correct; for no "crime" is here "stated" It is not even clearly implied, as would have been the case had the superscription been "Thief," or "Murderer" It is, strictly speaking, merely a *title*—"King of the Jews"

Luke explains matters by rearrangement and perhaps by a "this," implying contempt He tells us, first, that "the soldiers also mocked him...saying, If thou art *the King of the Jews*, save thyself" Then he adds "And there was *also* a superscription over him, *The King of the Jews! This* [*man*] *!* or, *The King of the Jews* [*is*] *this* [*man*] *!*" This is perhaps a compromise between (1) exclamation, and (2) ironical statement—repeating, without an "*if*," what the soldiers had just said with an "*if*" "It was not"—Luke seems to say—"'*the* [*official*] *superscription of the crime*,' as Mark says '*Crime*' should not have been mentioned here It was mere mockery"

Matthew, on the other hand, while not mentioning the Marcan "superscription," follows Mark in mentioning "his [alleged] *crime*," and expands Mark's title into a statement apparently using "the" to mean "the [would-be]," or "the [pretended]," thus —"This is (*emph.*) Jesus, the [pretended] King of the Jews[2]"

Hebrew, [and] in Latin, [and] in Greek (21) The chief priests of the Jews therefore said to Pilate, Write not, The King of the Jews, but, that he said, I am King of the Jews (22) Pilate answered, What I have written I have written

[1] Mk xv 26
καὶ ἦν ἡ ἐπιγραφὴ τῆς αἰτίας αὐτοῦ ἐπιγεγραμμένη Ο ΒΑΣΙΛΕΥΣ ΤΩΝ ΙΟΥΔΑΙΩΝ

Mt xxvii 37
καὶ ἐπέθηκαν ἐπάνω τῆς κεφαλῆς αὐτοῦ τὴν αἰτίαν αὐτοῦ γεγραμμένην ΟΥΤΟΣ ΕΣΤΙΝ ΙΗΣΟΥΣ Ο ΒΑΣΙΛΕΥΣ ΤΩΝ ΙΟΥΔΑΙΩΝ

Lk xxiii 38
ἦν δὲ καὶ ἐπιγραφὴ ἐπ' αὐτῷ Ο ΒΑΣΙΛΕΥΣ ΤΩΝ ΙΟΥΔΑΙΩΝ ΟΥΤΟΣ

Jn xix. 19 ἔγραψεν δὲ καὶ τίτλον ὁ Πειλᾶτος καὶ ἔθηκεν ἐπὶ τοῦ σταυροῦ ἦν δὲ γεγραμμένον ΙΗΣΟΥΣ Ο ΝΑΖΩΡΑΙΟΣ Ο ΒΑΣΙΛΕΥΣ ΤΩΝ ΙΟΥΔΑΙΩΝ

[2] Comp *Evang Petr* § 3 οἱ δὲ λαβόντες τὸν Κύριον...λέγοντες Δικαίως κρῖνε, βασιλεῦ τοῦ Ἰσραήλ...καὶ ἄλλοι...ἕτεροι...καί τινες...λέγοντες...τὸν υἱὸν τοῦ θεοῦ. (§ 4) Καὶ ἤνεγκον ..καὶ ἐσταύρωσαν...καὶ ὅτε

THE MOCKING AND THE CRUCIFIXION

John intervenes, in the first place against all the Synoptists, by defining—what they left undefined—the source of the superscription. It was the extraordinary caprice of Pilate himself, he says, and of Pilate obstinately persistent against the remonstrances of the Jews.

In the second place John intervenes, as to the "crime" mentioned by Mark and Matthew Here, so far as negation is concerned, he intervenes against them and in favour of Luke. In Luke, Pilate thrice says, in effect, that he finds in Jesus *"nothing criminal"*; in John, Pilate thrice says (using the Mark-Matthew word) *"no crime*[1].*"*

In the third place John intervenes as to the Mark-Luke word, "superscription" Matthew paraphrases this by the phrase "written above his head." John substitutes a Greek word *titlos*, derived from the Latin *titulus*, "title," and not alleged in the Thesaurus to have been used by any previous author[2]. Now *titulus* is sometimes, though rarely, applied to a *statement*, such as "He uttered treason," "He claimed to be king," and then it means a charge or accusation; but it is much more often used, like "title" in English, to mean the title of a book, or the title of a king, prince, or nobleman[3].

ὤρθωσαν τὸν σταυρὸν ἐπέγραψαν ὅτι Οὗτός ἐστιν ὁ βασιλεὺς τοῦ Ἰσραήλ This neglects the distinction between "the King of the Jews" and "the King of Israel" It also leaves undefined (ἐπέγραψαν "they [i e the men] superscribed") the writers of the superscription For we cannot infer that ἐπέγραψαν points back so far as οἱ δὲ λαβόντες. This indefiniteness pervades all the Synoptists—Mk *"there was* the superscription ..superscribed," Mt *"they* set up...written," Lk *"there was also* a superscription "

[1] Jn xviii. 38, xix 4, 6, comp. Lk. xxiii. 4, 14, 22 See above, p 561

[2] See Steph *Thes.* *Oxf Conc* gives τίτλος Je xxi 4, Aq , Sm , Th , but only in two codd. "vitiose pro τοίχου." *Evang Nic* A § 10 has ἐκέλευσεν δὲ ὁ Πιλᾶτος...εἰς τίτλον ἐπιγραφῆναι τὴν αἰτίαν αὐτοῦ...—καθὼς εἶπαν οἱ Ἰουδαῖοι—ὅτι βασιλεύς ἐστιν τῶν Ἰουδαίων. This seems to assert that *the Jews said "He is king of the Jews."* But perhaps the writer follows Matthew as to the words of the αἰτία *"He is [according to his assertion] king...,"* and inserts, parenthetically, "this was what the Jews said against Him "

[3] Lewis and Short give, as an instance of the placard of a crime

THE MOCKING AND THE CRUCIFIXION

This word, without any statement of fact—and without any mention of "accusation"—John uses to describe what Pilate himself wrote ("Now Pilate wrote *a title*") and placed on the cross. And the "title" describes Jesus first as "the Nazoraean," and then as "The King of the Jews."

Here some mention must be made of the term "Nazoraean[1]" This must not be assumed to be identical with "from Nazareth' the phrase used by Philip in the beginning of the Fourth Gospel[2] "From Nazareth," if expressed in an adjective, might 'be "Nazarene," or "Nazaraean," or "Nazarite." But it could not rightly be "Nazoraean." For "Nazoraean" John has prepared the way by representing it as an appellation twice accepted by Jesus Himself ("I am he") when He asks the soldiers "Whom seek ye?" and they reply "Jesus the Nazoraean[3]" "Nazoraean" in the New Testament is almost always used honorifically. It is the title given by Christians to their Leader, or repeated by their enemies in the sense "Jesus [whom these heretics call] the Nazoraean." Matthew says that Jesus came to live "in Nazareth," in order that the saying of "the prophets" might be fulfilled "He shall be called a Nazoraean[4]" Jerome explains this in two ways. It might

---

or charge, Suet *Domit.* § 10 "Patrem familias...canibus objecit, cum hoc *titulo*," where the next words convey the charge "Impie locutus parmularius" There is also *ib Calig* § 32 "praecedente *titulo* qui causam poenae indicaret" Far more numerous however are the instances where "titulus" is used honorifically. If John had intended to convey merely the meaning "placard of accusation," he could have retained the Mark-Matthew αἰτία (retained in *Evang. Nic* A § 10)

[1] See *Beginning* pp 326—50, on "Nazarene and Nazoraean."
[2] Jn i 45. [3] Jn xviii 5, 7
[4] Mt ii 23 Jerome begins his comment by remarking that Matthew—by saying "prophets" (pl)—"ostendit se non verba de Scripturis sumpsisse, sed sensum." Then he adds "(1) Nazaraeus sanctus interpretatur. Sanctum autem Dominum futurum, omnis Scriptura commemorat (2) Possumus et aliter dicere, quod etiam eisdem verbis juxta Hebraicam veritatem in Esaia (xi. 1) scriptum sit Exiet virga de radice Jesse, et Nazaraeus de radice ejus conscendet." Jerome never transliterates the Greek Ναζωραῖος correctly as "Nazoraeus."

THE MOCKING AND THE CRUCIFIXION

mean "holy," from Nazîr, a Nazirite (miscalled Nazarite), that is, one consecrated to God. Origen takes this view of the word[1]. But Jerome also says it might mean "Branch," "*Nêtzer*," fulfilling Isaiah's prophecy "A branch (*nêtzer*) from his [Jesse's] roots shall bear fruit." John appears to take this view. Pilate adopts the appellation of Jesus given to Him officially by the soldiers who arrested Him. Doubtless Pilate does not trouble himself as to its meaning. Perhaps Pilate thought it meant the same thing as "Nazarene" or "from Nazareth." But it meant "a scion of the royal house of David," whose advent was proclaimed by the Prophets.

On the whole, John may be fairly said to intervene in favour of Mark and against Luke. "Mark was right," he seems to say, "in regarding the superscription as official, Luke was wrong in regarding it as mere mockery on the part of the executioners. It was mockery indeed, but it was Pilate's mockery. The Jews declared that it was erroneous, and Pilate himself, in a sober mood, and not under the influence of some strange excitement, would not have written it. Yet he refused to alter it, saying, 'What I have written I have written.' Just as, before, when speaking to Jesus, he claimed to do what he liked, right or wrong ('I have authority to crucify thee'), so now, when speaking to the Jews, he claims to write what he likes, true or false. 'I have written' is his only argument, as if he could make falsehood true. As it happened, he had written truth. But it was not of his own writing. The mysterious Wheel of Providence had lifted him into a place where he accomplished a divine purpose, but he had been only the fly upon the Wheel[2]."

---

[1] See Origen on Mt. xxi 11 (Lomm iv 58) ἔλεγον οὗτός ἐστιν Ἰησοῦς ὁ προφήτης ὁ ἀπὸ Ναζαρὲτ τῆς Γαλιλαίας ὁμολογοῦντες τὸν προφητευθέντα ὅτι ὁ Ναζωραῖος κληθήσεται, ὁ κυρίως τῷ θεῷ ἀεὶ ἀνακείμενος

There is a v r Ναζαραῖος here, as also in Origen *Comm. Matth* x 16 quoting Mt 11 23.

[2] Origen, on Mt xxvii 37, says "Since no other cause for His death could be found, let this alone [say they] be held [to be one] (? haec sola habeatur)—'He was King of the Jews.' About which cause (de qua) He [i.e. Christ] spake [through David] saying [Ps

THE MOCKING AND THE CRUCIFIXION

§ 7. *The mocking of Christ on the Cross*

The mocking that immediately follows the Crucifixion,—variously expressed by the Synoptists but identical in the words "Save thyself"—is omitted by John[1]. In Mark and Matthew, it contains the words "thou that destroyest, or, he that destroyeth, the temple." John has explained at the beginning of his Gospel that Jesus did, in some sense, actually speak about the destruction of the Temple ("destroy this temple")[2]. Luke rejects the words here, as he does elsewhere when Mark describes the false charge[3]. John, who has intervened before, does not intervene again.

There are also Synoptic differences as to the classes that utter these reproaches. The first class is, in Mark and Matthew,

---

ii 6] '*But I have been appointed king by Him* [i.e. *by God*] *upon Zion His holy hill.*'" Thè Hebrew has "Yet have I *installed* (נסכתי) *my king* upon *my* holy hill of Zion." "Install," נסך, is used elsewhere only in Prov. viii. 23 "I [*i.e* Wisdom] *was installed* from everlasting."

This Psalm is the only place in Scripture (Mandelk 686) where "*my king*" is used, not by men to God, but by God addressing some one other than Himself. "*My king*" means God's ideal king, and the words would signify, according to Origen, "I have crowned my Son—sent down to mankind to be their King in my name—with the crown of the Cross." The "begetting" of this King, predicted in Ps ii 7 ("This day have I begotten thee") might be said to be visibly manifested on earth at the time of Christ's baptism, and the "installing," or crowning, to have taken place in the Crucifixion followed by the Ascension. Some would say "in the Ascension alone." But John habitually regards the Crucifixion itself as a "lifting up," or preliminary Ascension.

[1] Mk xv 29—32, Mt xxvii 39—43, Lk xxiii 35—7. Comp. Ps xxii 7 where LXX has Πάντες οἱ θεωροῦντές με ἐξεμυκτήρισάν με, ἐλάλησαν ἐν χείλεσιν (Heb *shoot out the lip*), ἐκίνησαν κεφαλήν. Lk. has ἐκμυκτηρίζειν corresponding to Mk-Mt. κινεῖν κεφαλήν. Comp Justin Mart *Apol*. § 38 Σταυρωθέντος γὰρ αὐτοῦ ἐξέστρεφον τὰ χείλη καὶ ἐκίνουν τὰς κεφαλὰς λέγοντες, Ὁ νεκροὺς ἀνεγείρας [i e He that raised up Lazarus] ῥυσάσθω ἑαυτόν. Whereas the Psalm has σωσάτω and ῥυσάσθω with αὐτόν "let *God save him*," the Gospels all have "*save*" with "*himself*" or "*thyself*." John omits this. Matthew alone has added the Psalmist's version (xxvii 43 ῥυσάσθω νῦν εἰ θέλει αὐτόν).

[2] Jn ii 19. [3] Mk xiv. 58, see above, p 513 foll.

THE MOCKING AND THE CRUCIFIXION

"*the passers by*"; but in Luke "*the people*" who "*stand* beholding" and apparently acquiescing in the mockery of the rulers[1]. The second class is, in Mark and Matthew, "chief priests" and "scribes" (to which Matthew adds "elders"), but in Luke, "the rulers" (to which he adds "and also the soldiers").

In Hebrew, "pass by" is easily confused, and is actually once confused by LXX, with "stand[2]." Further, in Hebrew, there is no one word for "soldier[3]" Delitzsch represents it here by the Biblical phrase "men of the service, *or* host." But the Hebrew "service, *or* host," is applied sometimes to the "service" of the Levites in the Temple; and the Aramaic equivalent is also similarly applied[4]

Luke may very well have been led by a Hebrew or Aramaic expression of this kind to infer that the phrase referred to "*the men on service,*" that is, the soldiers. Then, consistently, he would be led on to alter "King of *Israel*"—an expression that Gentiles would not use—into "King of *the Jews.*" Further, he would be led to transfer to these military mockers the offering of "vinegar" (the drink of the soldiers on guard) placed by

---

[1] Lk. xxiii. 35 "And the people stood beholding; and (*lit* but) the rulers *also* mocked (ἐξεμυκτήριζον δὲ καὶ οἱ ἄρχοντες)"—in view of Ps. xxii 7 (LXX) οἱ θεωροῦντές με ἐξεμυκτήρισάν με—probably implies that "the people" mocked (though passively) and "the rulers *also*" mocked (but actively). This is quite compatible with the fact that "the people" afterwards mourned Lk. xxiii. 48 θεωρήσαντες τὰ γενόμενα.

[2] Josh. viii 33 "stood (עמד)" LXX παρεπορεύοντο, leg as עבר. Also, in Aramaic, עמד might be confused with עם "people," followed by ד, the relative

[3] Στρατιώτης occurs in canon LXX only in 2 S xxiii. 8 (v r) Heb "slain."

[4] "Host"= צבא (Gesen. 839 a "of Levites in sacred places," 8 times in Numb). The Palest Syr has חיל (which is the regular Aram. equiv. of צבא (Brederek, p 97)) In Heb. (Gesen 298—9), חיל means "strength, efficiency, wealth, army." It is rendered "army" more than 50 times in A V. Walton renders Jer. Targ on Numb iv. 23 "omnem qui procedit *ad bellum* (לחיילא חילא) ut exequatur ministerium...," where Onk. has the same Aramaic but Walton "ad ministrandum *per turmas suas.*"

THE MOCKING AND THE CRUCIFIXION

Mark and Matthew at a later stage, and connected by them with "some" that were "standing [on guard] by" the Cross, but without any mention of mockery.

John intervenes on this point of mockery, against Luke. He agrees with all the Synoptists that the vinegar was the drink of the soldiers on guard[1], but he does not agree with Luke in connecting it with any act of definite mockery Mark and Matthew leave us in doubt as to the motive that dictated the offering and the words "Let us see whether Elias cometh " John, omitting those words, gives us the impression that the offering was dictated by natural humanity.

§ 8. *"Crucified-with," in Mark, Matthew, and John*[2]

Luke avoids the expression "crucified," and "crucified-with," as applied to the robbers, or malefactors, who suffered death with Jesus; he substitutes in the first place "to be put to death[3]," and afterwards "hanged[4]." The word "crucify-with" is not alleged to occur earlier than the New Testament[5]. In the

---

[1] See p 602, n 2 and n 5

[2] Mk xv. 27, 32 *b*
(27) καὶ σὺν αὐτῷ σταυροῦσιν δύο λῃστάς, ἕνα ἐκ δεξιῶν καὶ ἕνα ἐξ εὐωνύμων αὐτοῦ ...
(32 *b*) καὶ οἱ συνεσταυρωμένοι σὺν αὐτῷ ὠνείδιζον αὐτόν.

Mt xxvii. 38, 44
(38) τότε σταυροῦνται σὺν αὐτῷ δύο λῃσταί, εἷς ἐκ δεξιῶν καὶ εἷς ἐξ εὐωνύμων....
(44) τὸ δ' αὐτὸ καὶ οἱ λῃσταὶ οἱ συνσταυρωθέντες σὺν αὐτῷ ὠνείδιζον αὐτόν

Lk xxiii. 32, 39—42
(32) ἤγοντο δὲ καὶ ἕτεροι κακοῦργοι δύο σὺν αὐτῷ ἀναιρεθῆναι ...
(39) εἷς δὲ τῶν κρεμασθέντων κακούργων ἐβλασφήμει αὐτόν Οὐχὶ σὺ εἶ ὁ χριστός, σῶσον σεαυτὸν καὶ ἡμᾶς.
(40) ἀποκριθεὶς δὲ ὁ ἕτερος ἐπιτιμῶν αὐτῷ ἔφη. . (42) μνήσθητί μου ὅταν ἔλθῃς εἰς τὴν βασιλείαν σου.

Jn xix. 18—32 (18) ὅπου αὐτὸν ἐσταύρωσαν, καὶ μετ' αὐτοῦ ἄλλους δύο ἐντεῦθεν καὶ ἐντεῦθεν, μέσον δὲ τὸν Ἰησοῦν.... (32)...καὶ τοῦ μὲν πρώτου κατέαξαν τὰ σκέλη καὶ τοῦ ἄλλου τοῦ συνσταυρωθέντος αὐτῷ.

[3] Lk xxiii. 32 "put to death," ἀναιρέω, a word used in Lk. and Acts twenty-one times and only two or three times in rest of N.T.

[4] Lk. xxiii. 39 "hanged (κρεμασθέντων)," *i e.* crucified, comp Gal. iii. 13, quoting Deut xxi 23 κρεμάμενος ἐπὶ ξύλου, "that hangeth on a tree," as referring to Christ, and Acts v. 30, x. 39.

[5] See Steph *Thes* on συσταυρόω. It is not in Goodspeed.

Gospels, it occurs only in non-Lucan descriptions of the Crucifixion[1]. Outside the Gospels, in the New Testament, it occurs twice —in a Pauline description of our old humanity as having been "*crucified-with*" Jesus, and in the saying "I am *crucified-with* Christ[2]." It is not surprising that Luke, who may have heard the Apostle dictating the letters in which these expressions occur, disliked using this novel word, stamped with a spiritual meaning, in a non-spiritual and literal sense—and this too about "malefactors" While altering this word, he made other alterations in the context[3]. He had apparently found a tradition that justified him in believing that only one of these two malefactors "blasphemed" Christ, whereas Mark and Matthew say that both of them "reproached" Him. Luke says that "the other" malefactor rebuked the first, and appealed to Jesus to "remember" him when He came into His Kingdom. This indicates something of the nature of a conversion on the cross, so that "the other"—but not both—might be said to have experienced "crucifixion with" Christ in the Pauline sense[4].

There is a great difference between this view and that of Mark and Matthew. Origen and Jerome attempt to reconcile the two by saying that at first both malefactors blasphemed, but after the advent of the darkness one of them repented; but Origen is clearly dissatisfied with this[5].

---

[1] Mk xv. 32, Mt xxvii. 44, Jn xix. 32

[2] Rom. vi. 6, Gal. ii 20

[3] Lk xxiii. 32 ἤγοντο δὲ καὶ ἕτεροι κακοῦργοι δύο implies that the two malefactors formed part of the procession to Golgotha The other Gospels do not imply this. Luke inserts ἕτεροι to signify that, although these belonged to the same procession, they were "[of a] different [type]"—*real* malefactors (Lk xxiii 41 "we indeed justly") But a hasty reader might take the meaning to be "*two other malefactors.*" John (xix. 18) uses ἄλλους δύο "two others," without inserting "malefactors" or "robbers"

[4] There is a strange combination of Mk ὀνειδίζω, Lk εἷς δὲ, and Jn's *crurifragium* in *Evang. Petr.* § 4 εἷς δέ τις τῶν κακούργων ἐκείνων ὠνείδισεν αὐτοὺς λέγων 'Ἡμεῖς διὰ τὰ κακὰ ἃ ἐποιήσαμεν οὕτω πεπόνθαμεν οὗτος δὲ σωτὴρ γενόμενος τῶν ἀνθρώπων τί ἠδίκησεν ὑμᾶς, καὶ ἀγανακτήσαντες ἐπ' αὐτῷ ἐκέλευσαν ἵνα μὴ σκελοκοπηθῇ, ὅπως βασανιζόμενος ἀποθάνοι

[5] Jerome on Mt. xxvii 44 says that the penitent believed "*after the earthquake (terra commota),*" forgetting that the earthquake itself

THE MOCKING AND THE CRUCIFIXION

We might suppose that a fourth historian of the Crucifixion, if he knew the facts, would either reconcile the two views as above, or support one against the other. Perhaps John did not feel that he knew enough about the facts to adopt either of these courses At all events he takes a course of his own. For though retaining the Mark-Matthew word describing the two that were "crucified-together," or "companions in crucifixion," he mentions no "blaspheming" or "reproach" from either or both of them He also avoids the terms "right" and "left," which might seem to differentiate Christ's companions (like the sheep and the goats in Matthew placed on the right and the left) as penitent and impenitent Also, he does not describe the two either as "robbers" or as "malefactors," but says merely that, when Jesus came to Golgotha, "they crucified him, and with him *two others*, on this side and on that side, and, *in the midst*, Jesus"

"*In the midst*" is used both in the Old and in the New Testament to represent the central Principle of Good, the Lord—as the source of righteousness, purity, and redemption, —and hence the Son of God as representing that Principle[1].

---

came *after Christ's death*. This is irreconcilable with the Lucan story, which makes the penitent believe *before Christ's death* Origen does not fall quite into this error But he suggests that the penitent may have been convinced (1) by "the miracles *that he heard* to have been done by Him" (? referring to Mk xv 31 "He saved others [*i e* Lazarus]"), (2) by the unwonted darkness, (3) he puts forward a suggestion, made earlier in his commentary on John, that the two malefactors in John were different from the two in the Synoptists Origen's suggestion that the penitent had recently "*heard*" of Christ's "miracles" may be illustrated by Justin M *Apol* § 38 quoted above, p 589, n 1, ὁ νεκροὺς ἀνεγείρας ῥυσάσθω ἑαυτόν

[1] See *Joh Voc.* **1793—7** on "in the midst" To the instances there given add Exod viii 22 "to the end that thou mayest know that I am the Lord, *in the midst* of the earth" Here Onk has "that I, the Lord, *do rule in the midst* of the earth," and LXX paraphrases "*in the midst*" as ὁ κύριος, v r ὁ θεός, meaning the central Principle or Ruler. On Jn 1 26 "in the midst of you," Origen (*Comm Joann.* ii 29) illustrates from the fact that "the heart" is "in the midst of the body," so that it means "the Logos is among you, unrecognised" (see *Son* **3362** (1)—(v)). Origen's illustration would apply to the

THE MOCKING AND THE CRUCIFIXION

Here Jesus is described as "in the midst" of two "others," and later on it is said, almost ambiguously, "There came therefore the soldiers and of the first [man] they broke-in-pieces the legs and of the other that was crucified-with him[1]." Here "with him" might mean "with the first [man]" But possibly—and, some will say, more probably—it means "with Jesus[2]."

There is perhaps present in John's mind a partnership, as well as a contrast, between Jesus and His two companions, "crucified-with" Him, yet not crucified in the same way. They are sinners, and their bones must needs be "broken" like those of penitent David[3] But Jesus is the Sinless One, the Paschal

stream of blood and water that flowed from Christ's "side" and might be regarded as flowing from His "heart"

[1] Jn xix 32.
[2] Chrys briefly paraphrases this as τῶν μὲν ἄλλων κατέαξαν τὰ σκέλη, τοῦ δὲ Χριστοῦ οὐκ ἔτι, omitting "the other that was crucified with him" Nonnus also omits "that was crucified with him," but devotes more than four lines to the different methods of "breaking" applied to the "gentle (μειλιχίου)" one and the "night-lurker (νυκτιλόχου)" They perhaps regarded the clause as meaning "the second malefactor that was crucified along with the first malefactor"—at the same time with Jesus Westcott's explanation is "The first.. the other, starting perhaps from the two sides at which they had been stationed" But why mention this detail? Perhaps because there would have been a sense of bathos in mentioning Jesus as the second of those crucified and then in passing to the third What happened to Jesus forms a climax Perhaps the Evangelist regarded this as a natural or even providential climax
[3] Ps li 8 "that *the bones which thou hast broken* may rejoice." The Midrash and Talmuds (so far as I have seen) make no comment of importance on passages where "the breaking of the bones" is regarded as God's chastisement by the penitents, David, Hezekiah (Is xxxviii 13) and Israel (Lam iii 4) On Ps li. 8, Rashi simply adds "quando mihi iratus fuisti" On Is xxxviii. 13, Rashi says "posui me ipsum. .ut perferrem castigationes. .et memet roboravi tanquam leo ut sustinerem," making Hezekiah like the "lion" And so Targ, "*Rugiebam ..sicut leo,...qui* confringit .sic confringuntur...omnia ossa mea" This is extremely obscure See *Mechilt* on Exod. xii 46 giving a technical meaning to "*bone,*" and comp Jer Targ "a bone of him shall not be broken *for the sake of eating that which is within it*" Jewish tradition seems to throw no light on the Johannine passage

THE MOCKING AND THE CRUCIFIXION

Lamb, of which "not a bone is to be broken." For Jesus, instead of the "breaking," there follows a piercing of the side, and an outflow of blood and water, a "fountain for sin and uncleanness[1]." About such a fountain the Psalmist would be supposed by Christians to have written "Wash me, and I shall be whiter than snow; make me to hear joy and gladness, that the bones which thou hast broken may rejoice[2]"

The impression left on us by the Johannine narrative is vague as to the conduct of the Synoptic "robbers" or "transgressors," but suggestive as to the sinful world which they represent. Whether one or both of them blasphemed and repented, we are not told. But whereas Luke, at this point, inserts words of Jesus peculiar to his Gospel, "To-day shalt thou be with me in Paradise[3]," and (a little earlier) according to some authorities, "Father, forgive them, for they know not what they do[4]," John inserts no such words, but something mystically corresponding to them in the vision of the blood and water that issue from the side of Jesus on the Cross. This concludes the scene, and makes the conclusion, not one of judgment, discriminating between those on the right and those on the left, but one of redemption flowing forth to all

§ 9. "*My God*," *in Mark and Matthew*[5]

The phrase "*my God*," *Eli*, here quoted from the twenty-second Psalm, represents the possessive form of *El*, "strong

---

[1] Jn xix 34, Zech xiii 1 [2] Ps. li 7 foll
[3] Lk xxiii 43 [4] [Lk xxiii. 34]
[5] Mk xv 33—7 (R V.)   Mt. xxvii 45—50 (R.V.)   Lk xxiii 44—5, (?) 36 (R V.)

Mk xv 33—7 (R V.)	Mt. xxvii 45—50 (R.V.)	Lk xxiii 44—5, (?) 36 (R V.)
(33) And when the sixth hour was come, there was darkness over the whole land (*or*, earth) until the ninth hour	(45) Now from the sixth hour there was darkness over all the land (*or*, earth) until the ninth hour.	(44) And it was now about the sixth hour, and a darkness came over the whole land (*or*, earth) until the ninth hour,
(34) And at the ninth hour Jesus cried with a loud voice, Eloi, Eloi, lama sabachthani? which is, being interpreted, My God, my	(46) And about the ninth hour Jesus cried with a loud voice, saying, Eli, Eli, lama sabachthani? that is, My God, my God, why	(45) The sun['s light] failing,...

THE MOCKING AND THE CRUCIFIXION

one." It occurs for the first time in the Song of Moses "This is *my God* and I will praise him," where Jewish tradition explains "*this*" as though the little children of Israel saw, and pointed to, their divine Deliverer: "From their mothers' breasts even the children have *given signs with their fingers* unto the fathers and have said to them '*This* is *our God*, or, *our Father*...[1].'" Elsewhere, with one exception, *Eli* occurs only in the Psalms, and in almost every case implies "my own Strong-One," "my

Mk xv 33—7 (R V) *contd*	Mt xxvii 45—50 (R V) *contd*	Lk xxiii 44—5 (?) 36 (R V) *contd*
God, why hast thou forsaken (*or*, why didst thou forsake) me?	hast thou forsaken (*or*, why didst thou forsake) me?	
(35) And some of them that stood by, when they heard it, said, Behold, he calleth Elijah	(47) And some of them that stood there, when they heard it, said, This man calleth Elijah	
(36) And one ran, and filling a sponge full of vinegar, put it on a reed, and gave him to drink, saying, Let be, let us see whether Elijah cometh to take him down	(48) And straightway one of them ran, and took a sponge, and filled it with vinegar, and put it on a reed, and gave him to drink	Compare — (36) And the soldiers also mocked him, coming to him, offering him vinegar.
(37) And Jesus uttered a loud voice, and gave up the ghost.	(49) And the rest said, Let be, let us see whether Elijah cometh to save him [*Many anc auth add* And another took a spear and pierced his side, and there came out water and blood] (50) And Jesus cried again with a loud voice, and yielded up his spirit.	

Jn xix 28—30 (R V) (28) After this, Jesus, knowing that all things are now finished, that the scripture might be accomplished, saith, I thirst. (29) There was set there a vessel full of vinegar: so they put a sponge full of the vinegar upon hyssop, and brought it to his mouth (30) When Jesus therefore had received the vinegar, he said, It is finished and he bowed his head, and gave up his spirit.

[1] Exod xv 2, see Targ Jer I "our God" and Jer. II "our Father."

THE MOCKING AND THE CRUCIFIXION

own Champion, or, Protector¹" There is a quasi-contradiction in the title "My Protector" and the immediately following words "why hast thou forsaken me?" But the latter part of the Psalm implies that there is no real contradiction, for the Psalmist passes from prayer to thanksgiving "Save me from the lion's mouth, yea, ...thou hast answered me," and continues in the same tone to the end².

Perhaps the difficulty of making Gentile readers understand the connection in the Jewish mind between the *cry* "Why hast thou forsaken me?" and the *thought* "But thou hast not really forsaken me, yea, *thou hast answered me*," has caused Luke to omit the quotation Perhaps also Luke felt that *"my God,"* if unexplained, would convey to Greeks the same notion as is conveyed in the bitter satire of Isaiah on the man who fashions a piece of wood "and prayeth unto it and saith, Deliver me, for thou art *my god*³." At all events Luke has omitted it, as well as all that follows, arising out of a confusion between "Eli" and "Elias" As regards the latter—the Elias episode—we need not expect John to intervene, since allusions to "Elias" are recognised as exceptions to the Rule of Intervention⁴, but as regards the former, the phrase *"my God,"* here assigned to Jesus by Mark and Matthew, and the saying "why hast thou forsaken me?" we can plead no such exception, and have to ask whether there is any Johannine equivalent.

Origen helps us to find one by connecting the words in the Song of Moses "This is *my God*" with the words of Jesus to Mary Magdalene after His resurrection Jewish tradition about the former said that "a maidservant on the shore of the Red Sea saw that which was not seen by Ezekiel or any of the prophets⁵", and John tells us that Mary Magdalene was the first to see the risen Saviour, who said to her "Go unto my brethren, and say unto them, I ascend unto my Father and your

---

¹ Mandelk p. 86 gives Ps xviii 3, xxii. 2, 11, lxiii 2, lxviii. 25, lxxxix 27, cii. 25, cxviii. 28, cxl. 7 (Hebrew numbers), and Is. xliv. 17.
² Ps xxii 21—31. ³ Is xliv 17
⁴ See *Beginning* pp. 68—71
⁵ See *Mechilta* on Exod. xv. 2, quoting Rabbi Eliezer

THE MOCKING AND THE CRUCIFIXION

Father, and *my God* and your God[1]" When uttering the words, "my God and your God," Jesus is not to be regarded as letting Himself down (so to speak) to the level of His disciples as sons of Man, but rather as raising them up to His own level as Son of God[2]

§ 10. *"Why hast thou forsaken me ?" in Mark and Matthew*[3]

Luke omits this, but has, a little later, the words "Father, into thy hands I commend my spirit," where Mark and

---

[1] Jn xx 17
[2] Origen says (*Hom Genes* 1 13, Lomm viii. 123—4) "Apostoli se ad ejus [*i e* Christi] similitudinem reformarunt in tantum ut ipse de iis diceret (Jn xx. 17) '*Vado...et ad Deum vestrum*' Ipse vero jam petierat patrem pro discipulis suis, ut iis similitudo pristina"— that is, the "pristine similitude" to the archetypal Man, made in the image of God—"redderetur, cum dixit (Jn xvii. 21—2) '*Pater, da, ut sicut ego et tu unum sumus, ita et isti in nobis unum sint*'" In another passage (*Hom Exod* vi 2) Origen connects the words in John ("my God and your God") with the words in Exodus "This is *my God*" He sees nothing in this that is inconsistent with the doctrine of the divinity of the Son "Father" does not, "God" does—for those to whom God has been revealed—imply perfection. We are therefore taught to look forward to a time when we shall see that it is even better to be able to say from the heart, *"my God"* than to say "*my Father.*" See *Son* 3578 *a*—*g*, *Light* 3717 *c*—*d*

[3] Mk xv 34   Mt xxvii. 46   Lk xxiii 45
καὶ τῇ ἐνάτῃ ὥρᾳ   περὶ δὲ τὴν ἐνάτην   τοῦ ἡλίου ἐκλεί-
ἐβόησεν ὁ Ἰησοῦς φωνῇ   ὥραν ἐβόησεν ὁ Ἰησοῦς   ποντος
μεγάλῃ Ἐλωί ἐλωί λαμὰ   φωνῇ μεγάλῃ λέγων
σαβαχθανεί, ὅ ἐστιν με-   Ἐλωί ἐλωί λεμὰ σαβαχ-
θερμηνευόμενον Ὁ θεός   θανεί, τοῦτ' ἔστιν Θεε
μου [ὁ θεός μου], εἰς τί   μου θεέ μου, ἵνα τί με
ἐγκατέλιπές με,   ἐγκατέλιπες,

In Mk, D has ηλει ηλει λαμα ζαφθανει...εις τι ωνιδισας με, Ζαφθανει is an attempt to transliterate the Heb עזב "forsake" Of this the Aram is שבק, transliterated in most MSS as σαβαχθανει, but in B by ζαβαφθανει (not ζαβαχθανει). In D, ὠνείδισας is explained by some (see Dalman *Words* p 54, quoting Chase, *The Syro-Latin Text of the Gospels*, 107) from a confusion of עזב with עזף (ζαφθανει) meaning αἰτιάομαι or θυμοῦμαι The LXX of Ps. xxii 1 inserts πρόσχες μοι before ἵνα τί ἐγκατέλιπές με, Προσέχω in LXX = (more than 20 times) שבק, and it looks as though the LXX has confused שבק

THE MOCKING AND THE CRUCIFIXION

Matthew (followed by Luke) say merely "uttered (*or*, cried with) a loud voice"; corresponding to these—the penultimate and the ultimate utterance of Jesus in the Synoptists—John has (1) "I thirst," (2) "It is finished[1]" Can we say that in both these cases, or in either, John intervenes? Leaving the

---

with קשב and inserted a rendering of the latter in the text If so, it adds one more instance, and a very early one, of the confusion between Heb and Aramaic in interpreting this passage.

As regards the difference between ηλει and ελωι it must be noted that, although the Heb "El" is, as a rule (Brederek p 3 *b*), rendered by Onkelos into a longer form in Aram , yet in the Targ. on Ps xxii 1 the Heb "El" is preserved

As to ὠνείδισας, the objection to its origination from עזף is that the latter means (Gesen 277 *a*) "to storm against," but not "to reproach " But it may have arisen from a paraphrase of "*forsake*," as meaning "*forsake [a babe]*," "*bring a babe into the world and desert it*" Some, who did not like to admit that Jesus said "why hast thou forsaken?" found it easier to suppose that Jesus said—as Origen declares that He did in the person of Jeremiah (xv 10)— "O mother, *why didst thou bring me forth?*" Origen (Lomm. xv 260 foll) interprets this as uttered by the human nature of Christ. In Sir xliii 17, ὠνείδισεν—Heb חול, which = ὠδίνειν (9 times)—is an error for (A) ὠδίνησεν So here, some may have regarded the cry as an appeal to the Mother, the Holy Spirit or Wisdom (Origen on Jerem. xv 10 ὡς τίνα με ἔτεκες,) meaning (Lomm xv 263) "I have come down, I came to the earth, I gave myself to corruption, I bore a human body, what hath been achieved for (*or*, by) men that is worthy of those [sufferings]?" This interprets Jeremiah as saying, in effect, εἰς τί ὠδίνησάς με , Origen, however, does not, in his context, expressly quote Mk xv 34 or parall , but only mentions (Mk xiv 34, Mt. xxvi 38) περίλυπος and (Jn xii 27, xiii 21) τετάρακται Jerome follows Origen in his interpretation of Jerem. xv 10, and Origen says "Some one before my time" has noted that the prophet's words are addressed to "the Mother of prophets," that is, "the Wisdom of God"

If ων(ε)ιδισας in D is a corruption of ωδινησας, which is itself a paraphrase ("Why didst thou *bring me forth and desert me?*") we have here a tradition—like others quoted by Origen and Jerome from *The Gospel according to the Hebrews*—in which Jesus regards the Holy Spirit as His Mother (*Son* **3430** *a—b*, referring to Origen *Hom Jerem* xv 4 and Jerome on Mic vii 6)

[1] Mk xv 37, Mt xxvii 50, Lk xxiii 46, Jn xix. 28, 30.

THE MOCKING AND THE CRUCIFIXION

second till we come to it in its order, we shall deal here only with the first, the quotation from the twenty-second Psalm, "Why hast thou forsaken me?"

It has been pointed out above that, if we regard the quotation as meaning that Jesus applied to Himself the Psalm as a whole, the meaning then would be felt by Jews to be very different from that of the initial passionate complaint with which the Psalm opens, but that it would be hard to convey this feeling to Greeks. Now, it must be added that Aquila renders the first verse of the Psalm "O my Strong One, my Strong One[1], why hast thou forsaken me?" and the Gospel of Peter gives the utterance of Jesus as "O my Strength, O [my] Strength, thou hast abandoned me[2]." This leads us to reflect that if Jesus was regarded as having in mind, not merely the first verse of the Psalm but the substance of the Psalm as a whole, then some other passage in the same Psalm, to the same effect but rather clearer to Greek readers, describing the Psalmist as deserted by the "strength" or "power" of God, might be used by John to indicate a sense of temporary weakness and abandonment—a craving, or thirst, for a departing presence of God. Such a passage is found in the description of the last pang felt by the Sufferer before He descends to the grave· "My *strength* is dried up like a potsherd, and my tongue cleaveth to my jaws, and thou hast brought me into the dust of death[3]."

Justin Martyr and Tertullian apply this verse to the silence of Christ before His judges[4], Jerome applies it to the silence of the Apostles (recreants for the moment)—whom he presumably regards here as being signified by Christ's body[5].

---

[1] Ps. xxii. 1 Aq ἰσχυρέ μου, ἰσχυρέ μου

[2] *Evang. Petr.* § 5 καὶ ὁ Κύριος ἀνεβόησε λέγων, Ἡ δύναμίς μου, ἡ δύναμις, κατέλειψάς με

[3] Ps xxii 15 The word for "strength" here (כֹּחַ, ἰσχύς) is not the same as in verse 1 (אֵל) Another word occurs in *ib* 19 "O thou my *succour* (A V *strength*) (אֱיָלוּתִי), haste thee to help me," explained by Rashi as identical, in meaning, with כֹּחַ

[4] See above, p 550, and add Tertull *Adv Marc* iv. 42 concerning Christ's silence before Herod (Lk xxiii 8—9)

[5] Jerome on Ps. xxii. 15

600 (Mark xv. 33—7)

THE MOCKING AND THE CRUCIFIXION

But it seems more fitly applicable to the spiritual "drying up," or "thirst," caused by a sense of absence from the Father and of longing to be present with Him. The passionate and thirsting appeal for nearness and union accords with the passion of other passages in the Psalms where the too distant Helper is called "my God" by the Psalmist in the cry "O God, thou art *my God* ...my soul *thirsteth* for thee, my flesh longeth for thee[1]," and again, "As the hart panteth after the water brooks, so panteth my soul after thee, O God," followed by the confession "O *my God*, my soul is cast down within me[2]." In view of these and other reiterations in what may be called the Psalm of Thirst, it is not unreasonable to believe that the Johannine "*I thirst*" might correspond to the Mark-Matthew tradition "Why hast thou forsaken me?"

John has before prepared the way for such an interpretation by representing Jesus as beginning His Gospel in Samaria by being "wearied," and by saying "Give me to drink[3]." That was physical thirst. But the words serve as a preface to His doctrine about the spiritual or "living water," which He gave to others to drink. Now the time has come when, on the Cross, the Giver of "the living water" is Himself to feel life ebbing away, and the "water" "drying up" and leaving Him unable to give it to others or to feel it in Himself. This the Gospel expresses by "*I thirst*." The words that Jesus actually uttered were (doubtless) as Mark (followed by Matthew) has recorded them. But they were obscure for Greek readers, and Luke omitted them. All Christians, while thankful for the Marcan record, may nevertheless believe that John has helped us to apprehend what Jesus actually meant. Comprehend it we cannot. "Forsake" is only a metaphor. "Thirst" is only a metaphor. But the two together help us to apprehend more of the incomprehensible than we could have apprehended from either record taken by itself.

---

[1] Ps lxiii 1
[2] Ps xlii 1, 6, 11, xliii 4—5, comp Mk xiv 34 where Jesus apparently quotes from these Psalms
[3] Jn iv 7.

THE MOCKING AND THE CRUCIFIXION

§ 11. *"Elijah," in Mark and Matthew*

"Elijah" is not mentioned at this point by Luke or John, and, as has been pointed out above, their silence is according to rule[1]. But although the parallel Luke does not mention Elijah, that is, *Helias*, as "forsaking," it does mention "the sun," that is, *Helios*, as "failing." It may have occurred to Luke that heathen soldiers[2] would know nothing about Elijah, but would be familiar with the very similar Greek word for "sun[3]." The sun-god (Syrians and Greeks would say) might naturally be appealed to in time of trouble[4]. It was just at this time that a darkness had come over the land, lasting for three hours At the end of this period, if Jesus appealed to *Heli*, meaning "my God," it would be very natural that Syrian soldiers should think it referred to *Helios*, the sun-god, addressed vocatively as *Helie*, or to some other god or angel called "Heli" quite distinct from Him to whom Jesus actually appealed

If this was Luke's view, then, though Mark and Matthew may have been right in imputing to the soldiers on guard some misunderstanding, they were wrong (in his opinion) as to the kind of misunderstanding. This, and perhaps also some discrepancies between Mark and Matthew as to the subsequent action of those who offered vinegar[5], and some difficulty in

---

[1] See above, p 597, referring to *Beginning* pp 68—70.

[2] Though they are not called "soldiers" here (Mk xv 35 παρεστηκότων, Mt xxvii 47 ἐκεῖ ἑστηκότων) they are so called in Mk xv 16, Mt xxvii 27 (where Mt adds τοῦ ἡγεμόνος), and Mk and Mt clearly mean here Pilate's "[*soldiers*] *on guard*"

[3] Comp. Clem. Alex *Fragm* (1002—3) which comments on Ps xix 4, mentioning the sun, along with Mt. xxvii. 46 It seems to say that Ps xix 4 ἐν τῷ ἡλίῳ ἔθετο is equiv to ἐν τῷ θεῷ, "as in the Gospel Eli, Eli, [is used] instead of 'My God, my God'" And comp Levy i 84 *b* mentioning אילים, a Hebraized form of ἥλιος, from *Exod* r. sect 15, Wii p 106, as being a power too strong for Antiochus but not too strong for Mattathias and his sons.

[4] Ajax, before death, calls on the sun, Sophocl *Ajax* 845—6, using the vocative ἤλιε. This is also found in the *Odyssey* xii. 385 and in Eurip *Phoeniss* 3, ib *Epigr* 1 1 and *Fragm* 775, l. 11

[5] In Mk xv 35 καί τινες τῶν παρεστηκότων, W H marg and Swete have ἑστηκότων. This, or στηκότων, i e στηκόντων, "standing on

explaining whence the vinegar was obtained, led Luke to omit almost all the Mark-Matthew account of that offering[1], as well as the utterance that caused it—confining himself to the words "the sun failing" John takes a different course He gives the substance of the cry in the form "I thirst"—intelligible literally, if not spiritually, to all the world—and he enlarges on the subsequent offering of vinegar as an act prepared for by prophecy in the past and by circumstances at the moment[2].

§ 12 *"Reed," or "hyssop," in Mark, Matthew and John*[3]

Against the Johannine substitution of "hyssop" for "reed" the objection has been raised that the stalk of the hyssop is not

---

guard," is, very probably, the true reading. No one except one of the soldiers would be allowed to touch the vinegar, i e the *posca* or sour wine that belonged to the soldiers, and to offer it to a sufferer on the cross In Mt xxvii. 47 τινὲς δὲ τῶν ἐκεῖ ἑστηκότων, prob. ἐκεῖ has been added to make sense by some scribe who did not see the force of "stand" meaning "stand [in one's appointed station]" Comp the LXX μεσσάβ or μεσσάφ "station," in 1 S xiv 1, 11, where the translators have ὑπόστασις, σύστημα, στάσις, and πλῆθος For στήκω thus used, see 2 Thess. ii. 15 Possibly in 1 Thess iii 8, Philipp 1 27, and even in Mk xi 25, there is a touch of military metaphor, the Christian, when praying, being regarded as a soldier at his "post," or "station" See *Proclam* p 321 on στατίων in Hermas *Sim* v 1. 1—2. No instance of στήκω occurs in literary Greek or in Goodspeed.

[1] Luke does indeed mention, perhaps by transposition, (xxiii 36) an offering of "vinegar" by soldiers that "mocked" Jesus, but in this (see above, p 590 foll) he appears to be in error

[2] "By circumstances," because soldiers, on guard for several hours together, would naturally have some of their ὄξος at hand, and "by prophecy" because of Ps lxix 21 "they gave me vinegar to drink."

[3]

Mk xv 36 a	Mt. xxvii. 48	[Lk om , but xxiii 36]
δραμὼν δέ τις γεμίσας σπόγγον ὄξους περιθεὶς καλάμῳ ἐπότιζεν αὐτόν.	καὶ εὐθέως δραμὼν εἷς ἐξ αὐτῶν καὶ λαβὼν σπόγγον πλήσας τε ὄξους καὶ περιθεὶς καλάμῳ ἐπότιζεν αὐτόν	ὄξος προσφέροντες αὐτῷ

Jn xix 29 σκεῦος ἔκειτο ὄξους μεστόν σπόγγον οὖν μεστὸν τοῦ ὄξους ὑσσώπῳ περιθέντες προσήνεγκαν αὐτοῦ τῷ στόματι

THE MOCKING AND THE CRUCIFIXION

long enough for the purpose that John assigns to it. Hence it has been conjectured that "hyssop" (*hussop-os*) is an error for *hussos*, the Greek term for the Roman "*pilum*," or javelin. This is at first sight attractive. But *hussos* does not occur anywhere in Biblical or early Christian Greek[1]. And, on reflection, does it seem likely that such a writer as John, in describing the Saviour's death, should introduce such a technical term as this, just before mentioning the "spear" with which His side was pierced—as though distinguishing between the two weapons? The Talmud distinguishes between different kinds of hyssop and tells us that some kinds are collected "for food," others "for wood[2]." It seems therefore quite possible

Nonnus mentions "reed," κάλαμος twice, and "hyssop" once—the latter only in the phrase "vinegar mingled with hyssop" —

ἀνὴρ δέ τις ὀξὺς ἀκούσας
σπόγγον ὑποβρυχίων ἀδύτων βλάστημα θαλάσσης
πλήσας δριμυτάτοιο ποτοῦ καὶ διψάδος ἅλμης
ἰθυπόρου καλάμοιο παρὰ νείατον ἄκρον ἐρείσας
ὤρεγεν ὑσσώπῳ κεκερασμένον ὄξος ὀλέθρου,
ἀντίδοτον βασιλῆι μελισταγέος νιφετοῖο
ἄρτου θεσπεσίοιο δι' ἠέρος ὑψόσε τείνων
ἄκρον ἀειρομένου καλάμου καὶ σπόγγον ἀλήτην.

Philo thrice mentions "hyssop," as a kind of "extra," in the food of the Therapeutae, (ii. 477) "They feed on nothing costly, but on inexpensive bread, and [its only] flavouring-adjunct (ὄψον) [is] salt which the gourmets [among them] make additionally savoury with hyssop (ἅλες οὓς οἱ ἁβροδίαιτότατοι παραρτύουσιν ὑσσώπῳ)," *ib.* 483 ἄρτος μὲν τροφή, προσόψημα δὲ ἅλες οἷς ἐστιν ὅτε καὶ ὕσσωπος ἥδυσμα παραρτύεται διὰ τοὺς τρυφῶντας, *ib.* 484 ἄρτος ἐζυμωμένος μετὰ προσοψήματος ἁλῶν, οἷς ὕσσωπος ἀναμέμικται.

The *Diatessaron* combines Mt with Jn, but omits "*hyssop*," thus "One of them hasted and took a sponge, and filled it with that vinegar, and fastened it on a reed, and brought it near his mouth to give him drink."

In Jn, *a* omits "*sponge*," having "Pelvis posita erat aceto plena · *hysopo circumdantes* optulerunt ori ejus", others have "stick" or "pole" instead of "hyssop", *b* "spongiam ergo plenam aceto *perticae circumponentes*" (and simil *Corb*), *Brix.* has "implentes spongiam aceto *ysopo circumponentes*...."

[1] See ὕσσος in Steph. *Thes.* It does not occur in Goodspeed.

[2] See Wetstein on Jn xix. 29 quoting Numb xix. 18 (Jer. Targ.) "And let a man, a priest, who is clean, take *three stalks of hyssop*,

THE MOCKING AND THE CRUCIFIXION

that the stalk of the latter might be, or at all events, might be supposed by John to be, employed for the purpose of raising a sponge to Christ's lips

Another reason for believing that John here mentioned hyssop, is, that we find it mentioned not only by Barnabas in connection with Christ's Passion[1], but also in the Epistle to the Hebrews which adds "water and scarlet wool and hyssop" to a Biblical sprinkling with blood[2]   In the Bible, hyssop is

---

bound together, and dip [them] in the water," and *Para* xi 8—9, xii 1 "Praeceptum de hyssopo est de tribus caulibus, in quibus tres sunt culmi.... Hyssopus brevis compensatur ope fili," and *Succa* 13 *a* where mention is made of hyssop among the "calami" and "surculi" used for constructing booths in the Feast of Tabernacles   The mention of a "hyssopus brevis" implies that another kind was "longa "   The small twigs might be used to make a sponge, a long stem might be used as a stick   *Para* xi 8 says "Hyssopus, qua conspersum est, legitima est ad leprosum purificandum, si collegerit eam in ligna; si collegerit eam in cibos, reproba est "

Confusion might arise, if the sponge was really a bunch of small hyssop-twigs used at the Passover for sprinkling, and if this was placed, or supposed to be placed, round the top of a long hyssop-stalk.

Philo's above quoted use of the expression "to flavour ($\pi\alpha\rho\alpha\rho\tau\acute{u}\epsilon\iota\nu$) with hyssop ($\dot{\upsilon}\sigma\sigma\acute{\omega}\pi\omega$) "suggests that Nonnus (above quoted, $\dot{\upsilon}\sigma\sigma\acute{\omega}\pi\omega$ $\kappa\epsilon\kappa\epsilon\rho\alpha\sigma\mu\acute{\epsilon}\nu\omicron\nu$, "mingled with hyssop") read, after $\tau\omicron\hat{\upsilon}$ $\ddot{\omicron}\xi\omicron\upsilon\varsigma$ in Jn xix 29, $\dot{\upsilon}\sigma\sigma\acute{\omega}\pi\omega$ $\underline{\pi\alpha\rho\alpha\rho\tau\upsilon\theta\acute{\epsilon}\nu\tau\omicron\varsigma}$ "*flavoured with hyssop*" instead of $\dot{\upsilon}\sigma\sigma\acute{\omega}\pi\omega$ $\underline{\pi\epsilon\rho\iota\theta\acute{\epsilon}\nu\tau\epsilon\varsigma}$ "*putting round hyssop*"   Comp Coloss iv 6 "*flavoured* ($\dot{\eta}\rho\tau\upsilon\mu\acute{\epsilon}\nu\omicron\varsigma$) with salt", and Mk xv 23 $\dot{\epsilon}\sigma\mu\upsilon\rho\nu\iota\sigma\mu\acute{\epsilon}\nu\omicron\nu$, 1 e "myrrhized," or "flavoured with myrrh," parall to Mt xxvii 34 $\mu\epsilon\tau\grave{\alpha}$ $\chi\omicron\lambda\hat{\eta}\varsigma$ $\mu\epsilon\mu\iota\gamma\mu\acute{\epsilon}\nu\omicron\nu$, "along with gall, mingled [therewith] "

[1] Barnabas uses the Mk-Mt-Jn word $\pi\epsilon\rho\iota\theta\epsilon\hat{\iota}\nu\alpha\iota$ in the same sentence with ὕσσωπον (neut) thus § 8 περιτιθέναι τὸ ἔριον...ἐπὶ ξύλον (ἴδε πάλιν ὁ τύπος ὁ τοῦ σταυροῦ καὶ τὸ ἔριον   ) καὶ τὸ ὕσσωπον, and twice mentions ὕσσωπον in the context, but the uncertainty of the text makes his meaning doubtful except to this extent that he certainly connects "hyssop" with the Passion   Heb "sponge," סופג (from Gk σπόγγος) means also (Levy iii 564) a piece of wool used as a sponge.

[2] Heb. ix. 19 "When every commandment had been spoken by Moses...he took the *blood* of the calves and the goats, with *water and scarlet wool and hyssop*... "   This refers to Exod xxiv 8, which makes no mention of anything except "blood "   See above, p 567, n 3.

605   (Mark xv. 33—7)

first mentioned in the phrase "a bunch of hyssop" used for sprinkling the blood of the Paschal lamb[1] There Rashi says simply that "three stalks of the hyssop are called 'a bunch[2].'" But about the Levitical combination of "cedar wood, and scarlet [lit. *the scarlet worm*] and *hyssop*" in the purification of leprosy Rashi says that it indicates that the sufferer is to descend from his pride and become "as a worm and as hyssop[3]." Solomon's wisdom that extended "from the cedar to the hyssop" included, according to Rashi, the knowledge that the cure of leprosy requires the lowest as well as the highest of trees[4]. On the purification of the leper the *Prayers of the Jews* says "If the leper does not humble himself like 'hyssop' and esteem himself as the 'worm' he will not be cleansed by the 'hyssop' and by the 'scarlet wool,' and unless 'he pours out his heart like water' (Ps xxii. 14, Lam ii 19) he will not be cleansed by the sprinkling of water...[5]."

Such a passage as this is instructive to Gentiles. It shews that Jewish Christians might discern, in Christ's acceptance of the offering conveyed to Him by the "hyssop," a sign that He "humbled himself and became obedient unto death, yea, the death of the cross[6]" And a Jewish Christian poet might say that the Messiah, who was treated as a leper by His countrymen[7], sent forth from the Cross a purification of leprosy—so that the "cedar" was contributed by His cross[8], the "water"

---

[1] Exod xii 21—2 "...and kill the passover And ye shall take a bunch of hyssop, and dip it in the blood that is in the bason, and strike the lintel...with the blood..."

[2] "Tres caules (קלחין) (see Levy iv 308 shoot, stalk, stem, stump, trunk) vocantur אגודה *i e* fasciculus"

[3] Rashi on Lev xiv 4

[4] Rashi on I K iv 33, "nempe, quod leprosus mundandus esset per arborem maxime excelsam et per arborem maxime humilem" Cedars (Ps lxxx 10) along with mountains and stars (Gesen. 42 *b*) are said to be "of God (*El*)," *i.e.* mighty

[5] Quoted by Breithaupt on Lev xiv 4 from "libro *Precum Jud.* dict part 3 p 15 princ" On the "scarlet" see above, p 567, n 3

[6] Philipp ii 8   [7] See *Proclam* p 250

[8] Comp Gal iii 13 "hanged on a *tree* (ξύλου)" as one of many

THE MOCKING AND THE CRUCIFIXION

and the "blood" by His body, the "scarlet" by His chlamys, and the "hyssop," though not entirely His, was yet in some sense His, since He accepted it from sinners in order to give it back to them in His atonement for their sins[1].

§ 13 Christ's last utterance[2]

According to all the Synoptists, Jesus uttered "a loud voice" just before His death. But Mark might be supposed

---

instances of the Greek word that means "wood," used also to mean "tree," and used with allusion to the Cross

[1] It has been noted that the first Biblical mention of "hyssop" is in Exod xii 22 "Ye shall take a bunch of hyssop, and dip it in the blood [of the Paschal lamb] that is in the bason, and strike the lintel and the two side posts with the blood..." Since Jesus is called in the Fourth Gospel both "the Lamb of God" and "the Door," we might have expected the early Fathers to find in the Johannine "hyssop" an allusion to this passage. But I have not met with an instance. Goodspeed gives ὕσσωπον only in connection with (Barn § 8) the Red Heifer and (Clem Rom § 18) Ps li 7 "Purge me with hyssop," but not with any allusion to Exod xii 22. Rashi, on Ps li 7, refers to the cleansing of leprosy (i e with the blood of the Red Heifer)—but not to the striking of the door posts with the blood of the Paschal lamb.

[2]   Mk xv 37 .   Mt xxvii 50   Lk xxiii 46
ὁ δὲ Ἰησοῦς ἀφεὶς   ὁ δὲ Ἰησοῦς πάλιν   καὶ φωνήσας φωνῇ
φωνὴν μεγάλην ἐξέ-   κράξας φωνῇ μεγάλῃ   μεγάλῃ ὁ Ἰησοῦς εἶπεν
πνευσεν   ἀφῆκεν τὸ πνεῦμα   Πάτερ, εἰς χεῖράς σου
                                                                              παρατίθεμαι τὸ πνεῦμά
                                                                              μου τοῦτο δὲ εἰπὼν
                                                                              ἐξέπνευσεν

Jn xix 30 ὅτε οὖν ἔλαβεν τὸ ὄξος [ὁ] Ἰησοῦς εἶπεν Τετέλεσται, καὶ κλίνας τὴν κεφαλὴν παρέδωκεν τὸ πνεῦμα

Here ἀφίημι is used in Mk with φωνήν but in Mt with πνεῦμα. In LXX, ἀφίημι occurs (1) about death in Gen xxxv 18 ἐν τῷ ἀφιέναι (אצי) αὐτὴν τὴν ψυχήν "when she was *causing-to-go-forth her soul*," and in Judg ii 21 "the nations that Joshua left *and died* (מות),‏" LXX καὶ ἀφῆκε (so Tromm, but text perhaps influenced by ἀφεῖναι in context). But it occurs also (2) about utterance in Gen xlv 2 "and he *gave forth his voice* in weeping (R V txt wept aloud)" ἀφῆκε φωνὴν μετὰ κλαυθμοῦ. The Heb "give" (Gesen 679 b) often means "utter," mostly with acc "voice," but sometimes with "in voice" (Jerem. xii 8, Ps xlvi 6, lxviii 33) so that Gk might vary between ἐν φωνῇ (or, φωνῇ) and φωνήν. A Greek, finding the phrase "He uttered in a voice" might naturally be disposed to ask "uttered

(wrongly) to mean "Having uttered a loud voice [namely, Eli, Eli, as I have described above]", Matthew, by inserting "again," guards against such a supposition. "Having *again* cried out with a loud voice"; Luke supplies—almost identically with a passage from the Psalms[1]—the words uttered in the cry: "Having (*lit.*) voiced with a loud voice, Jesus said, Father, into thy hands I commend my spirit"

This quotation from the Psalms occurs in the Jewish Prayer Book at this day[2] It is almost the last utterance of a pious Jew approaching his end But it is not quite the last The last is devoted to the glory of God[3]. And it would seem more in accordance with all the Gospels that Christ's last utterance of all should refer, not to His own "spirit" but to the work that He came to do and had now done. Nevertheless Luke may very naturally have felt justified in inserting the quotation here He has previously omitted the appeal "Eli, Eli" from Jesus on the Cross If Luke knew that there was some utterance from the Cross, taken from a verse in one of the Psalms but supposed to express more than that one verse, and addressed to God, he might select this verse—in accordance with the tradition practised already perhaps by pious Jews and expressed in the Petrine Epistle "Let them that suffer according to the will of God *commit their souls* in well-doing unto a faithful Creator[4]"

John also—although he does not use the Lucan verb "commend"—does in effect describe Jesus, on the night before the Crucifixion, as repeatedly commending, committing, or entrust-

---

what?" Moreover, in Hebrew, the phrases "one voice," "loud voice," "great voice" are sometimes (Gesen. 877 *a*) used adverbially for "with one voice," "in a loud voice" etc And these facts might raise doubts, as to the passage under consideration, whether the original contemplated merely "*a loud voice*" or some articulate words uttered "*in* a loud voice"

[1] Ps xxxi 5 εἰς χεῖράς σου παραθήσομαι τὸ πνεῦμά μου, Sym παρεθέμην πνεῦμά μου Lk. prefixes Πάτερ

[2] *Jewish Prayer Book* ed Singer p. 317

[3] *Ib* "The Lord reigneth...the Lord is one." These words are to be said "when the end is approaching"

[4] 1 Pet. iv. 19 Comp. Acts vii 59.

ing, something to God   But it is not His own "spirit"   It is the Church, which He has built up, "having accomplished the work"—so He, the Son, says to the Father—"which thou hast given me to do¹"   The Church, in the Fourth Gospel, Jesus habitually describes as "that which thou gavest me" or "the men whom thou gavest me²"   The Father gave them as a trust, or committed them, to the Son; the Son, on the eve of the Crucifixion, commits them to the Father·   "While I was with them I kept them...but now I come to thee ..I make request that thou shouldest keep them from the evil [one]³"

According to John, then, the words of Jesus about "commending" have, in effect, already been uttered, and he now records, as the last utterance of all, "It is ended, or, finished"   If we ask "What is finished?" John refers us to the preceding statement, that Jesus said this "knowing that all things are now finished⁴."   By "all things" is meant all the work that was to be accomplished by the Logos in the flesh, the sowing of the seed of the Church   Such an utterance would accord with the tenor of the Johannine Gospel, but what relation has it, if any, to the tradition in Mark and Matthew?   Or must we regard it as separate and independent?

In Mark and Matthew, the words describing the Saviour's death vary between "breathed-forth," and "emitted the breath (*or*, spirit)"; and "emit"—that is, "cause to go forth"—is applied by Mark to the "voice."   Now "*emit*" in Aramaic may mean "*finish*⁵."   In Ezra, an Aramaic form of the Hebrew "*go-forth*" is used in the phrase "they *finished* the Temple," where LXX has the word here used by John in "it is finished⁶"

---

¹ Jn xvii 4
² Jn xvii 6, and see *Joh Gr* **2740—4**
³ Jn xvii 12—15.
⁴ The perf τετέλεσται means "are now, in effect, ended"   It is not true—except to the eye that can see the effect in the cause. But it expresses the truth better than the present or aorist or even the pluperfect would have expressed it   It might be called "a prophetic perfect"
⁵ See Levy *Ch* ii 476 on שׁיצי from Heb יצא.
⁶ Ezr vi 15   Levy *Ch* ib quotes Targ. on 2 Chr viii. 16 as using the same word about the finishing of the Temple.

THE MOCKING AND THE CRUCIFIXION

Also the Hebrew phrase "the soul *went forth*," or "the spirit *went forth*," is used to mean "he *expired*[1]." Hence, "He cried out with a loud voice *It is finished*," might be taken, by a translator into Greek, as meaning "He cried out with a loud voice *and expired*"—or *vice versa*.

Another point to be noted is that Luke himself has recorded, as one of the later sayings of Jesus, "That which is concerning me *hath an end*"—preceded by a sentence that uses the Johannine verb "be finished," or, "find its end". "This that is written must *find its end* [i.e. *fulfilment*] in me [namely], And he was reckoned with transgressors[2]." This has no parallel in Mark and Matthew. Luke may have here combined two traditions of Christ's utterances about "*the end*," doing his best to place them correctly, but leaving it open—and we may almost say suggestively open—to a later evangelist to place them in a different order and in a different context.

Lastly, if there was an early Christian tradition that Jesus the Son of David toward the close of His life on earth uttered some saying indicating that "that which concerned Him" was "ended," it is hardly possible that it should not occur to some of the Evangelists to think of the conclusion of the Second Book of the Psalms, which is also the conclusion of David's prophecy about the ideal King of righteousness, whom "all nations" were to serve, and whose name was to "endure for ever[3]." Here the LXX, translating an ambiguous Hebrew word, has, in effect, "The hymns (Heb. prayers) of David the son of Jesse *are finished [and exhausted]*", but R. Meir, playing on the Hebrew, said that "finished" meant totality or completion[4]. Aquila has the exact Johannine word, "finished [and completed]," and the other translators render similarly[5].

---

[1] Gesen. 423 *a* quoting Gen xxxv 18 (ἀφιέναι an error of act. for passive, or for ἐξελθεῖν) and Ps cxlvi 4. See also *Notes* **2938—9** on ἐξελθεῖν, "depart," used for "die."

[2] Lk xxii 37 τέλος ἔχει preceded by (*ib*) δεῖ τελεσθῆναι.

[3] Ps. lxxii 11, 17. The Psalm is entitled the Psalm of Solomon.

[4] Ps lxxii. 20 "are ended (כלו)," LXX ἐξέλιπον, R Meir (*Pesach.* 117 *a*) said that "*all* (כל) *these*" was to be read instead of "are ended."

[5] See Origen (Lomm xi. 366) who says that LXX does not express

THE MOCKING AND THE CRUCIFIXION

In view of these facts we may reasonably conclude that the charge of being "non-historical" applies more forcibly to the Lucan tradition ("I commend my spirit") than to the Johannine tradition ("it is finished"). The former is the kind of saying that any pious evangelist might supply to fill a supposed gap in such an expression as "He uttered [...] crying in a loud voice." But the latter may possibly be based—though this cannot be proved—on an original latent in Mark.

§ 14. *Christ's death*[1]

The word, literally "breathed-out," which Mark, followed by Luke, here uses to describe Christ's death, does not occur in LXX. But it is very frequent in Aristotle, who uses it to describe "ex[s]piration" as opposed to "respiration"—that is, "breathing out [into the air]" as opposed to "breathing in, or, back, into the lungs[2]." Hence it is used absolutely, of final "ex[s]piration," or death, in literary Greek of all periods[3]. The noun used by Aristotle to denote "breath" is *pneuma*[4], and Matthew here uses that word, with "dismissed," instead of Mark's "breathed-out." An educated Greek might naturally take "dismissed his *pneuma*" to mean "sent forth [finally] his breath," or "expired." But *pneuma* is hardly ever used in the New Testament except to mean "spirit" (or, very rarely, "wind"[5]). Perhaps Luke felt that Greek readers might need

---

the Heb., which is rendered by Aquila ἐτελέσθησαν, by Symmachus ἐπετελέσθησαν, and by "the fifth edition" ἀνεκεφαλαιώθησαν. He adds that many things in the Psalm apply to Christ alone.

[1] Mk xv 37 ἐξέπνευσεν (sim. Lk xxiii 46), Mt xxvii 50 ἀφῆκεν τὸ πνεῦμα, Jn xix 30 κλίνας τὴν κεφαλὴν παρέδωκεν τὸ πνεῦμα.

[2] Comp. Aristot. *De Vit. et Mort.* § 2 ἐν τῷ ἀναπνεῖν καὶ ἐκπνεῖν ἐστι τὸ ζῆν. Bonitz's Index gives many other antithetical instances.

[3] See Steph. *Thes.* quoting Soph. *Ajax* 1026, and Plutarch *Mor.* 597 F τοὺς ἄλλους ἀσπασάμενος ἅμα ἵλεως ἐξέπνευσε.

[4] Πνεῦμα in Bonitz's *Index Aristot.*, meaning "breath," occupies nearly two columns, meaning "wind," about a third of a column; it never means "spirit." Πνοή, "breath," occurs in Bonitz only twice, in the statement that "plants have [a kind of] breath," and in the poetical form πνοιή, "Zeus is the breath [so to speak] of all things."

[5] In Jn iii 8 (*Joh. Voc.* 1655), πνεῦμα appears to mean "wind,"

THE MOCKING AND THE CRUCIFIXION

to have it made clear to them here that *pneuma* did not mean "breath"; at all events he does make it clear by adding that Jesus said, "Father, into thy hands I commend my *pneuma*, i.e. *spirit*"

It should be noted that Mark, and Mark alone, repeats "breathed-out" later on ("seeing that he *breathed-out* thus") as though this in itself—perhaps because of the rapidity of the death, not usual in cases of crucifixion—were a sign to the centurion on guard that Jesus was "God's son[1]" This will be discussed in its place, but meantime we are led to ask whether there were any ancient Jewish traditions about the death of the righteous, of such a nature as to illustrate the Marcan language

It will be found that in the Hebrew Scripture a word meaning "expire," and sometimes rendered in our English Versions "give up the ghost," is used to describe the deaths of Abraham, Isaac, and Jacob[2] It is also applied to the death of Ishmael, and hence the Rabbis argued that Ishmael must have repented before he died, because "the word is not used except about the righteous[3]" This is not quite accurate But it is worthy of note that in these four instances Onkelos renders the Hebrew by an Aramaic word signifying "*draw oneself forth*," although elsewhere he renders it by the word that in Hebrew and Aramaic alike means "*die*[4]" Thus the Scripture says about living

---

but, if so, it plays on the double meaning of the Greek, and this would be the only instance in N T "Breath" occurs in N T (A V) only once, Acts xvii 25 πνοή. But comp. Rev xiii 15 R V "to give breath (πνεῦμα) (A V *life*) unto the image"

[1] Mk xv 39 ἰδών...ὅτι οὕτως ἐξέπνευσεν The parall Mt and Lk differ See p 616 foll.

[2] Gen xxv 8, xxxv 29, xlix. 33, ἐκλείπειν, see p 613, n 2

[3] Gen xxv. 17, on which Rashi says " Non dicitur נויעה, exspiratio, nisi de justis," but see below, p 614.

[4] See Brederek p 21 Onkelos renders גוע by מות in Gen vi 17, vii 21 etc , but by נגד ithpe in Gen xxv 8, 17, xxxv 29, xlix 33 Levy iii 332 b gives נגד ithpe as "sterben, verscheiden"—quoting *Pes.* 50 a and *Baba Bathr* 10 b "he was sick and *departed* (אתנגיד or אינגיד)"—and compares Heb. הלך and Aram אזל. In Gen xv 2 "I go (הלך)" Jer Targ supplies "*from the world*," but Onk does not See Gesen 234 a quoting Ps xxxix 13 "before I go [*my way*] (הלך)

THE MOCKING AND THE CRUCIFIXION

things before the deluge, "Everything that is in the earth shall *expire*," and about Abraham, "Abraham *expired*, and died in a good old age,... and was gathered to his people," but Onkelos has "*shall die*" in the former passage and "*drew-himself-forth*" in the latter[1]

These facts suggest that the basis of Mark's text was some Hebrew tradition about "*expiring*," or "*breathing forth*," corresponding to an Aramaic tradition about "*drawing-himself-forth*," or "*departing*," and that this was variously applied to the breathing forth of a "voice," or the drawing forth of the "soul" or "spirit" But this is not at all certain What is certain is that the earliest traditions about Christ's death, both Semitic and Greek, would be carefully worded so as to avoid anything that suggested an involuntary "dying"—which both in Greek and Hebrew often means "being killed[2]" One expression open to an evangelist would be that in which the death of Stephen, the first martyr, is described, "he fell asleep[3]" This cannot be at once set aside on the ground that Jesus was not supposed to have fallen asleep, since it was believed that He "went and preached to the spirits that were in prison[4]" For the Epistle to the Corinthians recognises Christ Himself

---

and am no more " Comp Mk xiv. 21, Mt xxvi. 24 "the Son of Man goeth [*his way*] (ὑπάγει), even as it is written," parall. Lk xxii 22 πορεύεται, see above, p 407, n 4

[1] Gen vi 17, xxv 8

[2] See *Notes* 2938—9, on the Gk "go forth," *i e* die, and add Philo's comment on the LXX words ἐκλείπειν and προστίθεσθαι, "to be added," applied to the three Patriarchs —(i 164) Abraham (Gen xxv 8) "having '*utterly-left* (ἐκλιπών)' mortal things, is '*added*' to the people of God (Heb 'to his people')" Jacob (Gen xlix 33) "is '*added*' to the better (τῷ βελτίονι) because he has '*utterly-left* (ἐξέλιπε)' the worse" Isaac (Gen xxxv 29) "himself, too, '*utterly-leaves* (ἐκλείπει)' so much of the bodily element as has been woven into the texture of the soul, and he is '*added*'. . not, like the other two, to his '*people*' but to his '*race* (γένει)'...for 'race' is but one, the highest, but 'people' is the name of more than one (πλειόνων) "

[3] Acts vii 60 ἐκοιμήθη Steph *Thes* describes this use (apart from poetic metaphor) as Christian. But it should have added LXX in the phrase (1 K. ii. 10 etc) "*slept* (ἐκοιμήθη) with his fathers "

[4] 1 Pet iii. 19.

THE MOCKING AND THE CRUCIFIXION

as "the firstfruits of them that have fallen-asleep[1]" Yet it must be confessed that the phrase would not be quite free from objection in view of the Psalmist's saying "He that keepeth Israel shall neither slumber nor sleep[2]."

The Johannine method of meeting this objection has been explained in the *Johannine Grammar*[3]. John represents Jesus not exactly as "sleeping" but as "laying his head to rest," and he leaves us to ask the question, "Where and where alone could the Son of God 'lay his head to rest'?" and to answer it from the beginning of his Gospel, "Only 'in the bosom of the Father[4]'"—the home in heaven, whence the Son had come down to earth. This may be illustrated from a passage in the Talmud where some Rabbis object that it is inaccurate to say that the word "expire" is used only about the righteous, for it is used also about the sinners before the Deluge[5]. The answer is, that "expire," when used about the Patriarchs, *is supplemented by* "*gathered*," *that is, gathered* "*to one's fathers*[6]"

---

[1] I Cor. xv. 20 Χριστὸς ἐγήγερται ἐκ νεκρῶν ἀπαρχὴ τῶν κεκοιμημένων
[2] Ps cxxi 4.
[3] *Joh. Gr* **2644** (1) quoting Origen on Mt xxvii 50 · "If we have understood the meaning of '*bending the head*' (inclinare caput)... let us be urgent so to keep our own lives that in our departure we too may be able...to deliver up our spirit even as Jesus, who *bent the head and took His departure in the act of resting it as it were on the lap of the Father who could cherish it and strengthen it in His bosom* (sicut Jesus, qui inclinavit caput et quasi supra Patris gremium illud repausans exiit, qui poterat illud in sinu suo favere et confortare)" And he proceeds to repeat "*inclinasse caput super gremium Patris*," and "*inclinare caput super gremium Dei.*" See Jn xix 30
[4] Jn 1. 18 ὁ ὢν εἰς τὸν κόλπον τοῦ πατρός. See *Joh. Gr* **2308—9** explaining εἰς as implying that the Son "is Mediator and Interpreter penetrating from earth *into* (εἰς) the deepest secrets of God in heaven, —where He IS..." We may add that εἰς, as used there, implies a prophecy of return "*to*" the bosom of God, fulfilled in the death on the Cross.
[5] Gen vi 17, vii 21.
[6] See Levy 1 314 on גויעה, quoting *Baba Bathra* 16 b, "Every death about which the word ויגוע is used denotes the death of the righteous, but only then when ויאסף ('*and was gathered*') is added in the context"

THE MOCKING AND THE CRUCIFIXION

We have seen that Philo, after his fashion, calls attention to this supplementary clause[1].

Not content with this metaphor, John supplements the traditions of Matthew and Luke about Christ's "spirit" Matthew says that Jesus "dismissed" it, Luke says that Jesus "commended" it to the Father. John says that Jesus "delivered it up" Very much is expressed in this novel Johannine use of a word connected elsewhere in the Fourth Gospel almost entirely with the "delivering up" of Jesus by Judas[2] John does not even say to whom the spirit was "delivered up" He leads us back to the thought of the Suffering Servant of the Lord about whom the LXX repeatedly uses the Synoptic "deliver up" to indicate that the Sufferer was "delivered up by the Lord" for the transgressions of sinners[3]. John seems here to express the union of the Father with the Son in this "delivering up" It was the act of the Son for the sake of mankind, but it was also the act of the Son to the Father, in accordance with the Father's will, so that it might be said to be the joint act of the Father and the Son, their sacrifice for the salvation of a sinful world[4].

---

[1] See above, p 613, n 2.

[2] In Jn vi 64—xviii 5 παραδίδωμι (8 times) refers to the act of Judas and in xviii 30—xix 16 to the action of the Jews and of Pilate

[3] Is liii. 6 Κύριος παρέδωκεν αὐτὸν ταῖς ἁμαρτίαις ἡμῶν, ib 12 παρεδόθη εἰς θάνατον ἡ ψυχὴ αὐτοῦ...διὰ τὰς ἀνομίας αὐτῶν παρεδόθη

[4] Comp Rom viii 32 "He that spared not his own Son but *delivered him up* for us all," Gal ii. 20 "The Son of God, who... *delivered himself up* for me," Eph v 2, 25 "*delivered himself up*"

CHAPTER XV

THE BURIAL

[Mark xv. 38—47]

§ 1. *The "rending" of "the veil¹"*

THE Synoptic word for veil, *catapetasma*, occurs nowhere else in the New Testament except in the Epistle to the Hebrews

¹ Mk xv 38—9 (R V)	Mt xxvii 51—4 (R V)	Lk xxiii 45 *b*—47 (R V)
(38) And the veil of the temple (*or*, sanctuary) was rent in twain from the top to the bottom	(51) And behold, the veil of the temple (*or*, sanctuary) was rent in twain from the top to the bottom, and the earth did quake, and the rocks were rent; (52) And the tombs were opened, and many bodies of the saints that had fallen asleep were raised, (53) And coming forth out of the tombs after his resurrection they entered into the holy city and appeared unto many	(45) . .and the veil of the temple (*or*, sanctuary) was rent in the midst (46) And when Jesus had cried with a loud voice, he said (*or*, And Jesus, crying with a loud voice, said) Father, into thy hands I commend my spirit and having said this, he gave up the ghost
(39) And when the centurion, which stood by over against him, saw that he so gave up the ghost (*many anc. auth* so cried out, and gave up the ghost), he said, Truly this man was the Son (*or*, a son) of God	(54) Now the centurion, and they that were with him watching Jesus, when they saw the earthquake, and the things that were done, feared exceedingly, saying, Truly this was the Son (*or*, a son) of God	(47) And when the centurion saw what was done, he glorified God, saying, Certainly this was a righteous man

THE BURIAL

There the context speaks of Christian hope as "an anchor of the soul, [a hope] both sure and stedfast and entering into that which is within *the veil*; whither as a forerunner Jesus entered for us, having become a high priest for ever after the order of Melchizedek[1]." This assumes that the reader knows what "the veil" meant. It is á word not used in literary Greek, but frequent in LXX, meaning the veil that divides the Holy of Holies from the Holy Place[2]. When it is first mentioned, Rashi says that the Hebrew denotes something that "separates king from people", its radical meaning is "breaking," and there it may indicate an abrupt "breaking off[3]"

Mk xv. 38—9	Mt xxvii 51, 54	Lk xxiii 45 b, 47
Καὶ τὸ καταπέτασμα τοῦ ναοῦ ἐσχίσθη εἰς δύο ἀπ' ἄνωθεν ἕως κάτω Ἰδὼν δὲ ὁ κεντυρίων ὁ παρεστηκὼς ἐξ ἐναντίας αὐτοῦ ὅτι οὕτως ἐξέπνευσεν εἶπεν Ἀληθῶς οὗτος ὁ ἄνθρωπος υἱὸς θεοῦ ἦν	Καὶ ἰδοὺ τὸ καταπέτασμα τοῦ ναοῦ ἐσχίσθη [ἀπ'] ἄνωθεν ἕως κάτω εἰς δύο, καὶ ἡ γῆ ἐσείσθη, καὶ αἱ πέτραι ἐσχίσθησαν Ὁ δὲ ἑκατόνταρχος καὶ οἱ μετ' αὐτοῦ τηροῦντες τὸν Ἰησοῦν ἰδόντες τὸν σεισμὸν καὶ τὰ γινόμενα ἐφοβήθησαν σφόδρα, λέγοντες Ἀληθῶς θεοῦ υἱὸς ἦν οὗτος.	ἐσχίσθη δὲ τὸ καταπέτασμα τοῦ ναοῦ μέσον. Ἰδὼν δὲ ὁ ἑκατοντάρχης τὸ γενόμενον ἐδόξαζεν τὸν θεὸν λέγων Ὄντως ὁ ἄνθρωπος οὗτος δίκαιος ἦν

In Mk, many authorities have "*so cried* and gave up the ghost," adding some form of κράξας. *Diatess* omits Mk, giving merely Mt, which implies that the centurion was moved, not by Christ's manner of death, but by the signs that accompanied it. Some interpreters of Mk (see Cramer on Mk p 441) explain "seeing" as referring to the rapidity of the death (ταχέως ἀποπνεύσαντα ἰδόντες, οὐδ' ὑποτμηθέντων αὐτοῦ τῶν ἀγκυλῶν κατὰ τὸ ἔθος), and so Origen (Lomm v 73 on parall Mt) Lk follows Mt on this point, only condensing into a more indefinite τὸ γενόμενον the definiteness of Mt (τὸν σεισμὸν καὶ τὰ γινόμενα)

[1] Heb vi 19—20

[2] Exod xxvi 31 etc See καταπέτασμα in Steph *Thes* Clem Alex 665 calls it twice παραπέτασμα before giving it its LXX title, καταπέτασμα

[3] Exod xxvi 31, פרכת Rashi says that according to the Rabbis it means "rem quae separationem facit inter regem et populum (sive plebem)" That appears to mean between God and Israel In Biblical Heb (Gesen 827 b) פרך does not exist as a verb But in N Heb it freq means (Levy iv 114—5) "*break in pieces*," "*crumble*"

THE BURIAL

Referring to this veil, the Epistle to the Hebrews calls it "the second *veil*" ("after the second veil the tabernacle that is called the Holy of Holies[1]"). This implies, though it does not declare, that there was also a first or outer veil separating the Holy place, which was reserved for priests, from the court of the people of Israel. This first or outer veil is represented by a Hebrew word meaning (Rashi says) "protection," and often, though by no means always, distinguished by LXX from *catapetasma*[2].

---

etc In Exod i 13—14 "*rigour*, lit *crushing service* (פרך)," Sota 11 *b* explains פרך ("*crushing* [*service*]") as so called because it "*crushes the body*" (and so Rashi takes it, although R Elieser explained it differently by a play on the word) Thus it happens that Semitic traditions about the "*veil*" might be connected by verbal influences with traditions about "*rending*" And, in view of Matthew's addition about the "rending" of "rocks" and "tombs" in the neighbourhood, it is worth adding that the Greek περίχωρος "neighbourhood" is Hebraized in a form (פריכוריי) that might suggest a connection with the Heb פרך (see Krauss p 489).

[1] Heb. ix. 3.

[2] In O T the "first" veil is called in A V a "hanging," in R V a "screen" See Rashi on Exod xxvi 36—7, and Gesen 697 *a* on מסך as being a name given to each of three screens of the tabernacle "a at gate (שער) of court Exod xxvii 16 etc., b at entrance (פתח) of tent Exod xxvi 36—7 etc , c פרכת המסך, dividing off the Most Holy Place within the tent, Exod xxxv 12 etc " In LXX, מסך = κάλυμμα, ἐπικάλυμμα, κατακάλυμμα 8 times (Tromm) but also καταπέτασμα 6 times It sometimes means a secular "covering "

These facts suffice to shew that there might be a difficulty sometimes in distinguishing between the "first" veil and the "second" *Horae Hebraicae*, on Matthew (xxvii 51)—after giving a minute description of the "trouble (τάραξις)" said to have been caused to the Rabbis by the differences (as to the "veil" or "screen") between the Tabernacle and the two Temples—adds "you will wonder, therefore, that Matthew doth not say καταπετάσματα, *veils*, in the plural, or perhaps you will think that only one of these two veils was rent." He concludes that the Evangelists were "not solicitous in explaining particulars," but "contented to have declared the thing itself " When the priest "went out amazed to the people, and should tell them, *The veil of the Temple is rent*, it would easily be understood of a passage broken into the Holy of Holies by some astonishing and miraculous rending of the hangings."

THE BURIAL

The Epistle proceeds to say that Christ, "through his own blood, entered in once for all into the holy [place], having obtained eternal redemption[1]," and mentions the *catapetasma* for the third time, thus · "Having therefore, brethren, boldness to enter into the holy [place] by the blood of Jesus, by the way which he dedicated for us, a new and living way, through the veil, that is to say, his flesh, and [having] a great priest over the house of God...[2]" It will be observed that the writer, after once mentioning "the Holy of Holies" in full, mentions it thus no more He appears to imply it when he says that Christ "entered in once for all into *the holy [place]*" This deserves attention For an identification of the inner with the outer "holy place" might lead to an identification of the inner with the outer veil

The symbolism of the rending of the veil is capable of various interpretations Philo, who tells us that "the *catapetasma* and the so-called *calumma*" (that is, "the second or inmost veil and the first or outermost") were made of the same material[3], elsewhere speaks of them both metaphorically, as a type of the obstacle or impediment to the attainment of truth presented by mere human "opinion," which is to be put aside by the perfect man[4] The author of the Epistle to the Hebrews seems to regard the flesh of Christ as being a veil, or hiding, of the truth, and yet also a cleansing and sacrificial avenue through which we are lifted up to the truth Jerome says "The veil of the Temple was rent and all the holy things

---

If the rending was regarded as miraculous it would naturally be described as (Mk xv. 38) "*from above* ($\dot{\alpha}\pi$' $\check{\alpha}\nu\omega\theta\epsilon\nu$)" This, if taken literally, might be supplemented by "*to the bottom*," $\check{\epsilon}\omega\varsigma$ $\kappa\acute{\alpha}\tau\omega$ But a rent "*from top to bottom*" might be on one side of the curtain, a detail that would spoil the poetic conception of a complete and absolute revealing Hence "*into two*" is added This *means* "into two *equal* parts" But it does not say so Luke skilfully expresses the whole of this by $\mu\acute{\epsilon}\sigma o\varsigma$.

[1] Heb. ix 12. "The holy [place]" is, literally, "the holy things," $\tau\grave{\alpha}$ $\ddot{\alpha}\gamma\iota\alpha$, and so in x 19

[2] Heb x, 19—21.

[3] Philo ii. 148 $\dot{\epsilon}\kappa$ $\delta\grave{\epsilon}$ $\tau\hat{\omega}\nu$ $\alpha\dot{\upsilon}\tau\hat{\omega}\nu$ $\tau\acute{o}$ $\tau\epsilon$ $\kappa\alpha\tau\alpha\pi\acute{\epsilon}\tau\alpha\sigma\mu\alpha$ $\kappa\alpha\grave{\iota}$ $\tau\grave{o}$ $\lambda\epsilon\gamma\acute{o}\mu\epsilon\nu o\nu$ $\kappa\acute{\alpha}\lambda\upsilon\mu\mu\alpha$ $\kappa\alpha\tau\epsilon\sigma\kappa\epsilon\upsilon\acute{\alpha}\zeta\epsilon\tau o$. [4] Philo i. 270.

THE BURIAL

of the Law, which were formerly covered, were brought forth to view *and passed to the Gentiles*[1]" This seems to be tinged with the Pauline metaphor about the breaking down of the "partition" between Jews and Gentiles[2]. Tertullian takes a somewhat similar view, as though the "cherubim escaped" from the Jewish Temple through the rent in the "veil"; but elsewhere, in a different metaphor, he mentions, after the "rending," a transference of the water of life to the Gentiles from the "leaky" vessels of the Jews[3]. The Sibylline Books connect the rending of the veil with the cancelling of all "Law" with its "ordinances[4]." The Hieronymian commentary

---

[1] Jerome on Mt xxvii 51, "Velum Templi scissum est, et omnia legis sacramenta, quae prius tegebantur, prodita sunt, atque ad gentium populum transierunt."

[2] Eph ii. 13 foll "But now in Christ Jesus ye that once were far off are made nigh in the blood of Christ. For he is our peace, who made both one, and brake down the middle wall of partition, having abolished in his flesh the enmity, the law of commandments in *ordinances* (δόγμασιν). " On the literal "wall of partition" between the Court of the Gentiles and that of the Jews see Wetstein on Mt xxvii 51 quoting Philo and Josephus.

[3] Tertull *Adv Marc* (on Lk xxiii 45), alluding to Ezek xi 22—3, and adding (Is 1 8) that they "left the daughter of Zion as a cottage in a vineyard. ."; *ib Adv Jud* § 13, after quoting Mt xxvii 51—2, goes on to allude to "broken cisterns—that is, synagogues for the [use of the] dispersions of the Gentiles—in which the Holy Spirit does not now abide."

Some confusion might arise as follows. The above-mentioned (p 618, n 2) word פרכת, "curtain" (Gesen 827 b "that which habitually shuts off") is connected with N Heb פרך "*break in pieces*," and is quite distinct, in Old Hebrew, from פרק (Gesen 830 a) Heb "*tear apart*," "*separate*," "*take to pieces*" In Aram , פרק mostly means (Levy *Ch* ii 298—9) "separate [by rescue]," "redeem," but it is used in Onkelos Numb 1 51, x 17 (and comp Levy iv 137 b) about "*taking to pieces*" the Tabernacle and its contents (or Numb iv 5 the veil) in the wilderness, before proceeding on a new journey (where Heb has "*take down*," a form of ירד). By the death of Jesus the old Tabernacle might seem to be "*taken to pieces*" in a special and more complete sense, not that it might proceed on a new journey, but that it might be replaced by a new Tabernacle.

[4] *Orac Sibyll* viii 296—309 mentions confusedly (1) "prickings with a reed (νύξουσι καλάμῳ)," then (2) an explanation of κάλαμοι as

THE BURIAL

on Mark says, more simply, "The veil of the Temple is rent, that is, heaven is opened¹."

Clement of Alexandria enlarges on the symbolical significance of the "covering" and the "veil" in the Tabernacle, but makes no mention anywhere of the "rending" in the Gospels² Origen, in his commentary on Matthew, recognises the difficulty of interpreting the details³. There, and elsewhere, he seems to take them as denoting in effect a "double sacrifice," apparently meaning the Incarnation and the Crucifixion⁴. He

---

"reeds shaken with the wind," then (3) a loosing of all Law that was given "in ordinances of men (δόγμασιν ἀνθρώπων)," then (4) a spreading out of the Saviour's hands and a measuring of the whole world, then (5) gall and vinegar, and then (6) the rending of the veil and darkness for three hours after noon—with this moral that it was no longer right to serve the Temple and the obscure Law, "now that the eternal Creator (αὐθέντου) had come down on earth "

¹ This would naturally suggest the thought of Jesus as ascending through the "opened heaven" But that would be contrary to the belief that Jesus at once descended into Sheol, or Hades, to the spirits in prison The above-quoted *Orac Sibyll* viii 296—309 is followed at once by "And He will come to Hades bringing a message of hope to all"

² Clem. Alex 665 foll.

³ Origen on Mt xxvii. 51 (Lomm v 66). Jesus Himself is described as being the "veil," but Origen refers for details of "the things within the veil" to what he has written elsewhere "Quamdiu quidem Jesus non susceperat pro hominibus mortem, ipse exspectatio gentium constitutus, velum templi interiora templi velabat, oportet enim ea velari donec ille qui solus ea poterat revelare, manifesta faceret ea videre volentibus, ut per mortem Christi Jesu destruentis credentium mortem, qui liberati fuerint a morte, possint adspicere quae sunt intra velum Quae autem fuerint illa, non est temporis hujus exponere, quoniam multam et difficilem interpretationem sunt habentia"

⁴ Origen *Comm Rom* vi 7 (Lomm vii. 34—5) "Nondum enim introierat in sancta non manufacta Christus, nec accesserat ad velamen interius, quod ad Hebraeos scribens Apostolus carnem Christi esse interpretatur Ubi vero 'Verbum caro factum est, et habitavit in nobis,' a praesentia ejus Jerusalem terrena cum templo et altari, atque omnibus, quae ibi gerebantur, eversa est." Elsewhere Origen recognises dissent from Paul's interpretation of the veil *Comm Exod* ix I (Lomm ix 108—9) "Qui ergo velamen interioris

accepts the rending of the veil literally, and also Matthew's parallel account of the "rending" of the "rocks" and the resurrection of "many bodies" of saints; but he allegorizes both in spiritual senses[1].

Jerome adds, in his commentary on Matthew, that "in a [Hebrew] Gospel of which he has made frequent mention[2]," instead of "the veil of the temple," there is "the *lintel* of the temple." Now in versions of the *Testaments of the Patriarchs* there is mention of a "rending," not always of the veil, but of the "*clothing*" or "*covering*" of the Temple[3]. The Syriac for "the veil," *catapetasma*, both in the Old and in the New Testament, is "the *superficies, covering,* or *front, of the gate.*" The Syriac word for "surface," *aph*, means in Hebrew "*nose*" or "*face*," and the Diatessaron has "*the face of the door of the temple* (or, *the door of the temple*) was rent." Possibly the writer of the Hebrew Gospel may have interpreted this "*front*"

tabernaculi carnem Christi interpretatus est, sancta autem ipsum coelum, vel coelos, Dominum vero Christum pontificem, eumque dicit introiisse 'semel in sancta, aeterna redemptione inventa.' ex his paucis sermonibus, si quis intelligere novit Pauli sensum, potest advertere, quantum nobis intelligentiae pelagus patefecerit. Sed qui satis amant literam legis Mosis, spiritum vero ejus refugiunt, suspectum habent Apostolum Paulum interpretationes hujuscemodi proferentem."

Origen uses the term "double sacrifice" in *Comm. Lev* 1 3 (Lomm ix. 178—9) "Vis autem scire quia *duplex hostia* in eo fuit, conveniens terrestribus, et apta coelestibus? Apostolus ad Hebraeos scribens dicit 'per velamen, id est, carnem suam.' Et iterum interius velamen interpretatur coelum, quod penetravit Jesus, ut adsistat nunc vultui Dei pro nobis, semper, inquit, vivens ad interpellandum pro his. Si ergo *duo* intelliguntur *velamina*, quae velut pontifex ingressus est Jesus, consequenter et *sacrificium duplex* intelligendum est, per quod et terrestria salvaverit et coelestia."

[1] Origen (Lomm v 68—9) allegorizes "the earth" as "all flesh," and "the rocks" as "the mystery of the prophets," and speaks of "the veil" as "velamen quod positum fuerat super cor eorum" (alluding to 2 Cor iii 13—16 "*a veil* ($\kappa \acute{\alpha} \lambda \upsilon \mu \mu \alpha$) upon their heart," *i.e.* on the heart of the Jews)

[2] See *Son* **3430***a*, comp **3601***h*

[3] *Test. XII Patr Levi* § 10 καταπέτασμα, v r ἔνδυμα, *Benj* § 9 ἅπλωμα

THE BURIAL

or "*face*" as meaning the "*lintel*" But, if he did this, would he not have in mind the first Biblical mention of "lintel"—the only one in the Law—where the Israelite is instructed to "strike the *lintel*[1]," on the evening of the Passover, with the blood of the Paschal lamb?

At all events Christians, who believed Christ's body to be the Temple of God enfolding His presence in the veil of the flesh, might naturally say that in the moment when He died, the Lamb of the Passover was slain, and the old Temple was "loosed" or destroyed on earth in order to give place to a new Temple in heaven. This they might say even before the actual destruction of the Temple Much more might they say it afterwards. Jews also, after that destruction, might say concerning the Lord's permission that His Temple should be destroyed, "He hath rent asunder His purple [veil][2]"; but Christians would say it with emphasis on the purification that had gone forth to the world as a result of the "rending."

Poetic descriptions of this "rending" of the "veil" might result in accounts of a literal "rending"—such as the parallel Matthew alone contains—of the rocks and tombs in the neighbourhood[3]. The parallel Matthew also inserts, in the best Greek MSS, just before Christ's death, an account of a piercing (literally, "pricking") of His side and an issue of water and blood[4]. This tradition, about "pricking" the side, is also

---

[1] Exod. xii 22—3 "lintel (משקוף)"

[2] See Lam ii 17 "he hath accomplished (בצע, lit broken, cut off) his word" explained by Midr *ad loc* and very freq "he hath rent asunder his *Purple* (פורפורא)," a Hebraized form of πορφύρα. Since the "veil" of the Holy of Holies was woven of "purple," and since, as Rashi says, it "separated King from people" (Jehovah from Israel), it is used here in a double sense It happens also that פרר (Gesen. 830) means "split," and that פרפר means (Levy iv. 131—2) "to be convulsed with death-spasms" These verbal similarities would favour the repetition of this widely-spread Midrashic tradition of the "rending of the purple"

[3] See above, p 617, n 3 *ad fin*.

[4] Mt xxvii. 49 ἄλλος δὲ λαβὼν λόγχην ἔνυξεν αὐτοῦ τὴν πλευράν, καὶ ἐξῆλθεν ὕδωρ καὶ αἷμα, placed by W. H in double brackets

THE BURIAL

found in the genuine text of John[1]. It is almost certainly an interpolation in Matthew. But we must not assume that the inserters borrowed it from John For the very rare word "prick" is also used in descriptions of the Passion in the Acts of John, and the Gospel of Peter[2]—and this in such a way as to suggest that it is not borrowed from the Fourth Gospel, but from some such source as that which in the Epistle of Barnabas has originated expressions about the "piercing" of the scapegoat[3] Matthew's narrative at this point suggests the influence of poetry, describing a convulsion of nature on earth, corresponding to a darkening of the sun in heaven that made day like night, and somewhat resembling the portents predicted in a version of the Ezra Apocalypse "Blood shall trickle forth from wood, and the stone utter its voice...and one whom the many do not know will make his voice heard by night; and all shall hear his voice, and the earth over wide regions shall open[4]"

Passing to the Fourth Gospel, we may infer from the facts alleged above that the Johannine piercing of the Saviour's body may correspond, not only as a chronological but also as a spiritual parallel, to the Synoptic rending of the veil The Epistle to the Hebrews has taught us that the Synoptic "veil" is the Johannine "body." Both are "rent," or "pierced" Are we then to regard both as mere poetic descriptions of the letting loose of the purifying fountain of Redemption in Jesus?

Possibly we are And this view is confirmed by the emphasis that John lays on the truth of what he himself witnessed in the stream of water and blood, as though to other bystanders it might not have been revealed as it was to him. But there is more to be said for the literal truth of the Johannine than for that of the Synoptic narrative. The "rending" of the "veil," if we think of it as the "rending" of "the purple,"

---

[1] Jn xix. 34 ἀλλ' εἷς τῶν στρατιωτῶν λόγχῃ αὐτοῦ τὴν πλευρὰν ἔνυξεν, καὶ ἐξῆλθεν εὐθὺς αἷμα καὶ ὕδωρ

[2] *Paradosis* 1262, quoting *Act Joann* § 12 λόγχαις νύσσομαι καὶ καλάμοις, *Evang Petr* § 3 καλάμῳ ἔνυσσον αὐτόν, and add *Orac Sibyll* viii 296 νύξουσι καλάμῳ.

[3] Barn vii 8 "pierce it (κατακεντήσατε)," see p 569, n 2

[4] Ezr. Apoc v. 5—8 (ed Box)

THE BURIAL

savours of Jewish poetry. The *crurifragium* or "breaking of the legs" does not   The latter—a prosaic and painful detail—explains several facts in a prosaic and historical way; and, in Christ's case, it is possible to accept the statement that the piercing was substituted for it, literally, without accepting literally and materially the exit of blood and water concerning which John adds "And he that hath seen hath borne witness, and his witness is true, and He [*i e.* the Lord] knoweth that he [*i e.* the writer] saith true, that ye also may believe[1]."

Metaphors in abundance have been mentioned in this discussion, but not yet the metaphor of Christ regarded as the water-bearing Rock "They drank of a spiritual rock that followed them; and the rock was Christ[2]" This may bear on the Johannine tradition about blood and water. Concerning this rock the Psalms and Isaiah say thrice that, after the Lord "smote" or "opened," or "clave" it, the waters "gushed out[3]" Gesenius gives only these three passages as using the word "gush" in this sense[4]. Sometimes the word is used of an issue of blood, and hence Jewish poetic tradition about Moses bringing water from the rock, both in the Jerusalem Targum and also (repeatedly) in the Midrash, says that when Moses struck the rock, *there came out first drops of blood and afterwards a stream of water*[5]   Some trace of this tradition may perhaps be found in the tradition in Luke—whether it be non-Lucan, or a later Lucan insertion, or a part of the original Luke—about the "sweat that became as it were great drops of blood falling down upon the ground[6]" Jerome, commenting on Isaiah ("clave the rock") not only quotes Paul as saying that the Rock was Christ but also adds that "its '*side*,' wounded

---

[1] Jn xix 35. See *Joh. Gr.* 2383—4, 2731.

[2] 1 Cor x 4.

[3] Ps lxxviii 20, cv. 41, Is xlviii. 21.

[4] Gesen 264 *b* זוב   But it is freq in the phrase "flowing with milk and honey"

[5] Numb xx 11, Jer Targ , see also *Tehill* ii. 15 on Ps lxxviii 20, ii 126 on Ps cv 41, *Exod r* (on Exod. iii 9) Wu p 47, comp *Numb r.* on Numb xx. 11

[6] Lk xxii. 44

THE BURIAL

by the spear, flowed with water and blood, dedicating to us baptism and martyrdom[1]"

Our conclusion must necessarily be very doubtful. For even historical facts may be expressed in such poetic and metaphorical language as to give the impression, wrongly, that there is nothing but metaphor at the bottom. But we may reasonably say that the Johannine account of the piercing of Christ's side is more likely to be true (so far as concerns the mere "piercing" apart from the vision of the outflow) than the rending of the veil described by the Synoptists, and far more likely than the rending of the rocks and the earthquake described by Matthew as being "seen" by the centurion, but not described by Mark and Luke—though they mention the centurion and also tell us what he "saw." The rejection of the miracles in Matthew, however, does not prevent a believer in Christ from accepting the belief that in the moment of Christ's death there was a great movement in the spiritual world, and a great fountain opened for the cleansing of the souls of mankind.

§ 2. *"From afar*[2]*"*

The Synoptists here all use the words "from afar" and "beholding," but differently. Luke, besides adding "*acquaintances*,"

---

[1] See Westcott on Jn xix. 34 (Patristic Explanation) giving, from very early writers, instances of a play on the Johannine πλευρά, side, and the first Biblical mention of πλευρά, Gen ii 21—2, *i e* rib, personified as Eve—very unprofitable except as shewing to what lengths unbridled imagination could lead poetic commentators.

[2]
Mk xv. 40—41 (R V)	Mt xxvii 55—6 (R V)	Lk xxiii. 48—9 (R V)
(40) And there were also women beholding from afar among whom [were] both Mary Magdalene, and Mary the mother of James the less (*lit* little) and of Joses, and Salome; (41) Who, when he was in Galilee, followed him, and ministered unto him, and many other	(55) And many women were there beholding from afar, which had followed Jesus from Galilee, ministering unto him (56) Among whom was Mary Magdalene, and Mary the mother of James and Joses, and the mother of the sons of Zebedee	(48) And all the multitudes that came together to this sight, when they beheld the things that were done, returned smiting their breasts. (49) And all his acquaintance, and the women that followed with him from Galilee, stood afar off, seeing these things

626 (Mark xv. 40—41)

who are "*standing*[1]," also previously mentions "multitudes" (not "women") that came to "behold" the spectacle but went away in sorrow[2]. The Lucan word, *gnōstos*, masculine, meaning "acquaintance," is very rare in the Greek Bible, but the Psalmist uses it in "Thou hast put far from me mine *acquaintance*," and "I have become a fear to mine *acquaintance*[3]." Apart from one Johannine passage, *gnōstos* occurs in the New Testament only in Luke's description of Joseph and Mary seeking the child Jesus among their "kinsfolk and *acquaintance*[4]"

Another passage in the Psalms more closely resembles Luke[5] It mentions "*standing*" as well as "*afar off*," literally "*from afar*," and enumerates three classes of friends· "My lovers and my friends stand opposite to my wound[6], and

Mk xv. 40—41
(R V) *contd.*
women which came up with him unto Jerusalem

Jn xix. 25 (R V) But there were standing by the cross of Jesus his mother, and his mother's sister, Mary the [wife] of Clopas, and Mary Magdalene

[1] Mk xv. 40—41	Mt. xxvii. 55—6	Lk. xxiii. 48—9
Ἦσαν δὲ καὶ γυναῖκες ἀπὸ μακρόθεν θεωροῦσαι, ἐν αἷς καὶ Μαριὰμ ἡ Μαγδαληνὴ καὶ Μαρία ἡ Ἰακώβου τοῦ μικροῦ καὶ Ἰωσῆτος μήτηρ καὶ Σαλώμη, αἳ ὅτε ἦν ἐν τῇ Γαλιλαίᾳ ἠκολούθουν αὐτῷ καὶ διηκόνουν αὐτῷ, καὶ ἄλλαι πολλαὶ αἱ συναναβᾶσαι αὐτῷ εἰς Ἱεροσόλυμα	Ἦσαν δὲ ἐκεῖ γυναῖκες πολλαὶ ἀπὸ μακρόθεν θεωροῦσαι, αἵτινες ἠκολούθησαν τῷ Ἰησοῦ ἀπὸ τῆς Γαλιλαίας διακονοῦσαι αὐτῷ ἐν αἷς ἦν Μαρία (marg Μαριὰμ) ἡ Μαγδαληνὴ καὶ Μαρία ἡ τοῦ Ἰακώβου καὶ Ἰωσήφ (marg Ἰωσῆ) μήτηρ καὶ ἡ μήτηρ τῶν υἱῶν Ζεβεδαίου	καὶ πάντες οἱ συνπαραγενόμενοι ὄχλοι ἐπὶ τὴν θεωρίαν ταύτην, θεωρήσαντες τὰ γενόμενα, τύπτοντες τὰ στήθη ὑπέστρεφον ἱστήκεισαν δὲ πάντες οἱ γνωστοὶ αὐτῷ ἀπὸ μακρόθεν, καὶ (marg +αἱ) γυναῖκες αἱ συνακολουθοῦσαι αὐτῷ ἀπὸ τῆς Γαλιλαίας, ὁρῶσαι ταῦτα

On Mk xv. 40 δὲ καὶ, Mt xxvii 55 δὲ ἐκεῖ, see *Corrections* 506 *a*. Add Eccles iii 17 καὶ, v r ἐκεῖ, and see Schlatter on Jn ii 1

[2] Θεωρεῖν, "behold," in LXX Ps xxii 7, xxxi 11 suggests hostility, or recoil, in "beholders" Lk does not follow Mk in applying it to "women" He applies it here to ὄχλοι and previously (xxiii 35) to the λαός—the ὄχλοι as temporarily, the λαός (probably) as persistently, unsympathetic

[3] Ps lxxxviii 8, comp 18, xxxi 11, γνωστός

[4] Jn xviii. 15 γνωστὸς τῷ ἀρχιερεῖ, ib 16 ὁ γνωστὸς τοῦ ἀρχιερέως, Lk ii 44 τοῖς συγγενεῦσιν καὶ τοῖς γνωστοῖς [5] Ps xxxviii. 11.

[6] See Field. "Amici mei (אהבי) et sodales mei (ורעי) e regione

THE BURIAL

my kinsmen *stood from afar*[1]." The word here rendered "*kinsmen*" means literally "*those-near*" Rashi interprets it in a bad sense—"those who pretend to be near to me[2]" Symmachus renders "stand," in the first of the two clauses, by "withstood" This rather confirms Rashi's unfavourable view, since the two clauses are probably parallel in meaning. Jerome interprets the first clause as referring to the Jews ("stood against me") but adds "It may also be taken as referring to the disciples[3]"

Passing to the Fourth Gospel we find it saying, just before the mention of Christ's death, "Now there *were standing by*

(מנגד) plagae meae (נגעי) stant (יעמדו)," LXX οἱ φίλοι μου καὶ οἱ πλησίον μου ἐξ ἐναντίας μου ἤγγισαν καὶ ἔστησαν, Sym οἱ φίλοι καὶ οἱ ἑταῖροί μου ἐξεναντίας ἐν τῇ πληγῇ μου ἀντέστησαν   The LXX has confused the noun נגע "wound" with the verb נגע "touch," "reach," "strike," which = ἐγγίζω (six times).

Those Christians who followed the Hebrew text might see, in "my wound," a prediction of the wound in Christ's side recorded by John alone

[1] See Field   "Et propinqui mei (וקרובי) e longinquo (מרחק) consistunt (עמדו)," LXX καὶ οἱ ἔγγιστά μου μακρόθεν (Sym μακρὰν) ἔστησαν   Field renders the perf עמדו "have stood" by "consistunt," but the imperf יעמדו by "stant"

Levy iv 369—70 gives many instances of קרוב, "*a near relation*," and also of the use of the word to express an antithesis between 'near" and "far"

[2] Rashi's comment on "propinqui" is "qui seipsos simulant esse mihi propinquos"

[3] Jerome on Ps xxxviii 11   "Amici dicuntur Judaei propter Abraham   Proximi, eo quod ab eorum generatione assumpserit carnem, qui appropiaverunt ei, ut comprehenderetur   Amici mei et noti mei contra me steterunt. Potest et de discipulis accipi   qui in passione metu territi, a Domino recesserunt   in tantum ut etiam eum Petrus denegaret   Vel steterunt, causantes contra eum   '*Et qui juxta me erant de longe steterunt*'   Apostoli vel reliqui discipuli, de quibus ait Evangelista Cum autem apprehendissent eum, 'stabant omnes noti ejus a longe'"

Here "amici" is based on LXX φίλοι   "Propter Abraham" has in view Rom ix 3—7 "my *kinsmen after the flesh*   seed of Abraham " "Causantes contra eum" refers to Lk xxiii 10   "Evangelista" refers to Lk. xxiii 49 but stops short at "noti ejus a longe" and does not add "et mulieres"

the cross of Jesus his mother and the sister of his mother, Mary that [belonged] to Clopas and Mary Magdalene[1]" This has to be considered along with the Marcan tradition "There were also women *from afar* beholding," and with the parallel Luke "Now there *were standing* all his acquaintance (masc.) from afar, and the women...seeing (fem.) these things" Why does not Luke write as clearly as Mark, and say clearly "There were standing from afar all his acquaintance and the women"? Why does he leave a loophole for supposing that there is a pause after "from afar," and a repetition of the verb without the adverb, so that the feminine "seeing" applies to the women alone ("and the women...[were also standing] seeing these things")? The Lucan sentence, in itself, as well as because of its departure from Mark's clear statement, leaves us under the impression that Luke is hampered by the Psalmist's Messianic description of "*kinsmen* standing from afar," which he limits to men At all events Jerome's comment on the Psalm and his quotations from Luke indicate that he saw in Luke no sign that the "from afar" applied to women, though he saw a recondite application to Christ's nation (based on Rom. ix 3 "for my brethren's sake, my *kinsmen* according to the flesh")[2]

---

[1] Jn xix 25
[2] The use of ἱστήκειν (al εἱστήκειν) deserves attention Luke thrice uses it in the context—and nowhere else in his Gospel—(1) about the chief priests and scribes (xxiii 10) "accusing" Jesus, (2) about the people (*ib* 35) "beholding" the Crucifixion, (3) about Christ's friends (*ib* 49) who "stood from afar"

Mark never uses ἱστήκειν Matthew uses it twice, (1) of the multitude (xiii 2) "standing on the beach" listening to Christ's teaching, (2) of Christ's mother and brethren (xii 46) "standing (Mk iii 31 στήκοντες) outside," *i e* outside the circle of the disciples This second passage contains the words (xii 49) "And stretching out his hand ..he said, Behold, my mother, and my brethren"

John, who uses ἱστήκειν several times with different shades of meaning, applies it (1) to the Lord's mother and the other women (xix 25) standing near Christ's Cross, when He said "Woman, see, thy son!" (2) to Mary Magdalene (xx 11) "standing by the tomb outside"—"outside," not in an unbelieving self-exclusion, but in affectionate despair Perhaps John recognised that the Synoptic account of the mother and brethren of Jesus "standing outside" the

629 (Mark xv 40—41)

THE BURIAL

Luke leaves unnamed all the women mentioned by Mark and Matthew, describing them simply as *"jointly-following* him from Galilee." He has recently described "daughters of Jerusalem" as *"following"* Him to the Cross[1]. That "following" is perhaps contrasted (in his Gospel) with the "jointfollowing" from Galilee[2] The phrase *"from afar"* in Hebrew, and sometimes in LXX, may mean "from of old," as well as "from a distance[3]." Synoptic variations rather favour the view that some interpreted *"women from afar"* as meaning that they had come *all the way from Galilee*, or that they had been with Jesus *"from the beginning of the Gospel in Galilee"*—so that perhaps they ought not to have been described as "beholding from afar[4]"

---

circle of the disciples—apparently because they (Jn vii 5) "did not believe on him"—needed to be supplemented by an account of the mother of Jesus "standing" near the Cross, with her adopted son, the beloved disciple

[1] Lk xxiii 27—8 ἠκολούθει δὲ αὐτῷ πολὺ πλῆθος τοῦ λαοῦ καὶ γυναικῶν . Θυγατέρες Ἰερουσαλήμ ...

[2] Comp Lk xxiii 55 κατακολουθήσασαι δὲ αἱ γυναῖκες αἵτινες ἦσαν συνεληλυθυῖαι ἐκ τῆς Γαλιλαίας αὐτῷ This suggests that Lk xxiii 49 συνακολουθοῦσαι αὐτῷ is a condensation of (1) "coming up with him," (2) "following him," so that it means "those who had been continuously (pres part) accompanying Him and ministering to Him as His attendants during the whole of the protracted journey from Galilee and the North to Jerusalem "

[3] Gesen 935 *b* gives Is xxii 11, xxv 1, 2 K xix 25 = Is xxxvii. 26, 2 S vii 19 = 1 Chr xvii 17 Comp also Jerem xxxi 3 R V. txt "of old," R V marg "from afar," Is xlix 1 "from far," διὰ χρόνου πολλοῦ, Is xxx. 27 "from far," LXX διὰ χρόνου, Q mg μακρόθεν.

[4] Mark mentions (1) "women from afar beholding," (2) select names, (3) how they "used to follow (ἠκολούθουν)" Jesus, and "used to minister (διηκόνουν) " to Him "when he was in Galilee," (4) "other women, many, that had come up with him to Jerusalem " Matthew alters Mark's order, and the tenses, and the sense: "Women, many, from afar beholding, who [had] followed (ἠκολούθησαν) Jesus from Galilee ministering (διακονοῦσαι) to him [during the journey] " Then he adds the select names (substituting for the Marcan "Salome" the phrase "the mother of the sons of Zebedee") Luke substitutes a tradition mainly new but retains Mark's conclusion, ending with the statement that the women were "seeing these things "

THE BURIAL

John appears to intervene partly for Luke as well as partly against him. The women that Luke leaves unnamed—as Luke also does later on in mentioning those who beheld the burial, deferring their names till their announcement of the Resurrection to the apostles—John names, though not apparently in complete agreement with Mark and Matthew On the other hand, the loophole that Luke left for supposing that the women were *not standing far off*, John accepts and widens into the statement that they were "*standing by the side of the cross*[1]" But the question of Johannine Intervention is unimportant in this case as compared with the question of Johannine accuracy

Of this there is much doubt According to John, the Lord's mother was not only standing by the Cross but also addressed by Him, as the future mother of the beloved disciple "Woman, see, thy son" It is difficult to believe that such an event, if historical, could have been omitted by the earlier Evangelists. On the other hand it is difficult, if not impossible (at all events for the present writer), to believe that John invented the story

But there are reasons for thinking that John was misled by very ancient tradition[2] (1) John's list of the women present, while not agreeing with the Mark-Matthew lists, leaves the reader in doubt whether the number of women is four or three;

It is probable that the early Church was influenced, in its interpretation of these and later passages about women "beholding" events concerning the death and resurrection of Jesus, by Is xxvii 11 "mulieres venientes accendent (מאירות) eas (אותה)," LXX γυναῖκες ἐρχόμεναι ἀπὸ θέας δεῦτε Here, after γυν ἐρχ, Aq has φωτίζουσιν αὐτήν, Sym καὶ δηλοῦσαι αὐτήν, Theod δηλοῦσαι αὐτῇ Origen on Mt. xxvii 55—6 quotes LXX about "mulieres quae aedificantur... *a spectaculo* (ἀπὸ θέας) Verbi"—after quoting it as "*ad* spectaculum" (? conf with Lk xxiii 48 ἐπὶ τὴν θεωρίαν ταύτην)—and allegorizes Galilee Jerome, on Is. xxvii 11, connects the Hebrew text with Lk. xxiii 28 ("daughters of Jerusalem") but the LXX with Mt. xxviii. 9 ("juxta LXX de Maria dicitur Magdalene .."') He concludes thus. "These are pious expressions, but how they harmonize with the rest and how they fit in with the times of consummation of the world, it is difficult to explain"

[1] Jn xix. 25.
[2] For these reasons see *Proclam.* pp. 117—20 on "Salome in Mark," and pp. 120—24 on "Sons of peace."

THE BURIAL

(2) this ambiguity is best explained as the result, not of carelessness, and still less of an intention to mystify readers, but of a desire to reproduce ancient tradition, which was itself ambiguous; (3) taking Mark's tradition as the most ancient, we find in Mark (and in Mark alone) the name Salome; (4) this name, in Old and New Hebrew, might be confused severally with "*my peace*" and with "*belonging to my mother*", (5) Salome is generally accepted as being the mother of John the son of Zebedee, (6) hence John, the beloved disciple, being "the son of *Salome*," might be called, with a play on Salome's name, "the son *belonging to my mother*"; (7) a gloss of this kind might naturally be added to the list of women in Mark's tradition—"This meant (*or*, he said this[1]) the son belonging to my mother"; (8) this would lead to the statement that "Jesus said, [behold] the son belonging to my mother," and that He said it to the women beholding His crucifixion.

Even if Jesus did not actually say to His mother from the Cross "See, thy son," we are justified in believing it to be probable that "the disciple from that hour took her to his own home[2]", for, if that had not been the fact, the statement would have been manifestly open to contradiction in Christian circles. And this, if a fact, falls in with the view—in itself a probable one—that in the Galilaean Church there were plays on the name Salome, which Mark alone has preserved[3].

---

[1] On "said," *i e* meant, see *Son* **3204, 3371** *e*, and *Notes* **2837** (iii) *a*, **2874** *f*.

[2] Jn xix 27

[3] Mk iii 34 and Mt. xii 49 (Lk viii. 21 differs) have preserved a tradition that Jesus said once to a multitude, concerning His disciples—"looking round" or "stretching forth his hand"—"See, my mother and my brethren" Early Christian traditions about Jesus on the Cross might naturally repeat a saying of this kind in connection with the Crucifixion when He "stretched out His hand and measured all things"

See *Orac Sibyll* 1 372 Ἀλλ' ὅταν ἐκπετάσῃ χεῖρας καὶ πάντα μετρήσῃ, rep *ib* viii 302 ἐκπετάσει δὲ χέρας καὶ κόσμον ἅπαντα μετρήσει. What is the precise meaning, and what is the origin, of this "measuring"? Does it mean reducing to order? Comp Is xl 11—12, where the picture of the shepherd "gathering the lambs in his arm" is followed

THE BURIAL

John, alone of the Evangelists, never mentions Mary the mother of Jesus by the name of "Mary," but repeatedly calls her "*his mother*," or "*the mother*," or else, in the first mentions of her, "*the mother of Jesus*[1]" This rather favours the view that he might insert in his Gospel traditions based on the similarity between "*Salome*" and "*belonging to my mother*"— and this more especially in connection with the name of the apostle John, whom also he never mentions by name, but often by periphrasis

§ 3   *Joseph of Arimathaea*[2]

Mark tells us that, "*since* it was the Preparation," Joseph came to Pilate; and he alone adds that "the Preparation" was

---

by the question "Who hath *measured* the waters in the hollow of his hand?" Μετρεῖν occurs only five times in canon LXX and once in Wisdom

The extension of the arms on the Cross might be regarded as preparatory to "embracing," and Origen regards it thus when he contrasts the extension of hands by Jesus with the elevation of hands by Moses (on Exod xvii 11) "Moses quidem *elevat* manus, non *extendit*, Jesus autem, qui universum orbem terrae exaltatus in cruce *complexurus erat brachiis suis*, dicit (Is lxv 2) '*Extendi manus meas* ..'"

[1] Jn ii 1, 3 "*the mother of Jesus*," ii 5, 12 "*his mother*", vi 42 "whose father and *mother* we know," may be contrasted with Mk vi 3 "the carpenter *the son of Mary*"

[2] Mk xv 42—7 (R V)   Mt xxvii 57—61 (R V)   Lk xxiii 50—56 (R V.)

(42) And when even was now come, because it was the Preparation, that is, the day before the sabbath,
(43) There came Joseph of Arimathaea, a councillor of honourable estate, who also himself was looking for the kingdom of God, and he boldly went in unto Pilate, and asked for the body of Jesus
(44) And Pilate

(57) And when even was come, there came a rich man from Arimathaea, named Joseph, who also himself was Jesus' disciple.

(58) This man went to Pilate, and asked for the body of Jesus. Then Pilate commanded it to be

(50) And behold, a man named Joseph, who was a councillor, a good man and a righteous
(51) (He had not consented to their counsel and deed), [a man] of Arimathaea, a city of the Jews, who was looking for the kingdom of God:
(52) This man went to Pilate, and asked for the body of Jesus.

633   (Mark xv 42—7)

THE BURIAL

in other words "the day before the sabbath," or, as he calls it

Mk xv 42—7 (R V) contd	Mt xxvii 57—61 (R.V.) contd	Lk xxiii 50—56 (R V) contd
marvelled if he were already dead and calling unto him the centurion, he asked him whether he had been any while dead (*many anc. auth* were already dead). (45) And when he learned it of the centurion, he granted the corpse to Joseph (46) And he bought a linen cloth, and taking him down, wound him in the linen cloth, and laid him in a tomb which had been hewn out of a rock, and he rolled a stone against the door of the tomb	given up	
	(59) And Joseph took the body, and wrapped it in a clean linen cloth, (60) And laid it in his own new tomb, which he had hewn out in the rock and he rolled a great stone to the door of the tomb, and departed	(53) And he took it down, and wrapped it in a linen cloth, and laid him in a tomb that was hewn in stone, where never man had yet lain. (54) And it was the day of the Preparation, and the sabbath drew on (*lit* began to dawn) (55) And the women, which had come with him out of Galilee, followed after, and beheld the tomb, and how his body was laid.
(47) And Mary Magdalene and Mary the [mother] of Joses beheld where he was laid.	(61) And Mary Magdalene was there, and the other Mary, sitting over against the sepulchre	(56) And they returned, and prepared spices and ointments. And on the sabbath they rested according to the commandment

Jn xix 38—42 (R V) (38) And after these things Joseph of Arimathaea, being a disciple of Jesus, but secretly for fear of the Jews, asked of Pilate that he might take away the body of Jesus and Pilate gave [him] leave He came therefore, and took away his body (39) And there came also Nicodemus, he who at the first came to him by night, bringing a mixture (*some anc auth* a roll) of myrrh and aloes, about a hundred pound [weight] (40) So they took the body of Jesus, and bound it in linen cloths with the spices, as the custom of the Jews is to bury. (41) Now in the place where he was crucified there was a garden, and in the garden a new tomb wherein was never man yet laid. (42) There then because of the Jews' Preparation (for the tomb was nigh at hand) they laid Jesus

THE BURIAL

in one word, "*the prosabbath*[1]" Matthew, apparently not understanding that the approach of the Preparation was the cause of

[1] Mk xv. 42 καὶ ἤδη ὀψίας γενομένης, ἐπεὶ ἦν παρασκευή, ὅ ἐστιν προσάββατον Mark alone uses the term προσάββατον Levy iii 691 b shews that in Heb "*eve* (ערב) *of the sabbath*" was a freq phrase and that in Aramaic ערובתא "*the eve*" was used by itself to mean "*the eve of the sabbath*," i e 3—6 P M on Friday Προσάββατον occurs only once in LXX as representing Heb , and there as v r , Ps xcii tit "canticum carminis (Field) *in die* sabbati," LXX and Sym εἰς τὴν ἡμέραν τοῦ σαββάτου (א τοῦ προσαββάτου) The Heb is "*for the day* (ליום) (Targ על יומא) of the sabbath" This might be taken as meaning not "*in die*" but "*in diem*," a song on the Friday evening *for* the coming Saturday This might be called a song *on* (or, *of*) the prosabbath [*for* the coming sabbath] "canticum carminis prosabbati" But א has εἰς τὴν ἡμέραν τοῦ προσαββάτου, substituting "*prosabbath*" for "*sabbath*" This is instructive as indicating a source of much possible confusion

The LXX has προσαββάτου in Ps xciii tit (with v r σαββάτου) no Heb., and in Judith viii 6 "save *the eves of the sabbaths* (προσαββάτων) and the sabbaths, and *the eves of the new moons* [v r adds and the new moons], and the feasts.. ," but Syr and Vulg have merely "*sabbaths and new moons* and feasts " In Mk xv 42, SS has merely "And it was *on the sabbath*" , k " Serum autem cum factum esset cene pure sabbati " Josephus gives a decree of Augustus releasing the Jews from answering as legal sureties (*Ant* xvi 6 2) "on the Sabbath, *or the Preparation before it, from the ninth hour* (ἢ τῇ πρὸ αὐτῆς παρασκευῇ ἀπὸ ὥρας ἐνάτης) " This indicates that the whole of the twenty-four hours preceding the Sabbath (or other Feast) might be called "Preparation," and that the immunity extended to only a part of it

Προσάββατον does not occur in Goodspeed, not even in the *Martyrdom of Polycarp* where (Lightf p 594) "the writers betray an eagerness to find parallels" between Polycarp's martyrdom and Christ's Passion But "*Preparation*" and "*Great Sabbath*" occur as follows The soldiers are described as going forth to arrest Polycarp (*Mart* § 7) "*on the Preparation about supper-time* (τῇ παρασκευῇ περὶ δείπνου ὥραν)," where Lightf by a slip omits the italicised words in his translation. Then Polycarp prays (*ib*) "for two hours," and (§ 8) they set Polycarp on an ass and brought him to the city "it being [by this time] *great sabbath* (ὄντος σαββάτου μεγάλου) " (Lightf "it being a high sabbath ") Toward the conclusion it is said "The blessed Polycarp was martyred .. on a great sabbath at the eighth hour "

Nonnus paraphrases Jn xix 14 "Now it was the Preparation of the passover" by Ἕκτη δ' ἦν ἐνέπουσι προσάββατος (? -ον) ἔτρεχεν ἠώς, and

THE BURIAL

Joseph's immediate action, delays the mention of "Preparation" till after the entombment[1]. So does Luke[2]. Matthew and Luke, besides omitting the Marcan *prosabbath*, give no explanation of the term Preparation. John thrice mentions the "Preparation" at considerable intervals and explains its importance and its influence on the sequel, resulting in a hasty and temporary entombment[3].

Mark is the only Synoptist that describes Joseph as having "dared," or "boldly made up his mind," when going to Pilate[4].

Jn xix 42 "because of the Jews' *Preparation*" by Ὅττι παρ' Ἑβραίοισι φυλασσομένης δρόμον ὥρης Γείτονα νύκτα φέρουσα προσάββατος ἔτρεχεν ἠώς. This illustrates the Johannine intervention for Mark, since Nonnus uses Mark's unique word to shew that John, though not using the word, is, in effect, explaining it

[1] Mt xxvii 62 τῇ δὲ ἐπαύριον, ἥτις ἐστὶν μετὰ τὴν παρασκευήν. This is a strange expression. He means "on the sabbath," but he does not mention σάββατον till xxviii 1 ὀψὲ δὲ σαββάτων, τῇ ἐπιφωσκούσῃ εἰς μίαν σαββάτων. That, too, is curiously expressed

[2] Lk xxiii 54 καὶ ἡμέρα ἦν παρασκευῆς, καὶ σάββατον ἐπέφωσκεν. Ἐπιφώσκειν does not occur in N T except here about the advent, in Mt, of μία σαββάτων, but in Lk, of σάββατον. *Evang Petr* § 2 represents Herod as saying to Pilate ἐπεὶ καὶ σάββατον ἐπιφώσκει (rep *ib* § 9) In LXX, ἐπιφώσκειν occurs (1) and ἐπιφαύσκειν (3), all in Job. It is a poetical word. In N T, ἐπιφαύσκω occurs once in a Christian song quoted in Eph v 14 "Awake, thou that sleepest, and arise from the dead, and Christ shall shine upon (ἐπιφαύσει) thee." Neither word occurs in Goodspeed

[3] Jn xix 14 ἦν δὲ παρασκευὴ τοῦ πάσχα, *ib* 31 ...ἐπεὶ παρασκευὴ ἦν, ἵνα μή...ἐν τῷ σαββάτῳ, ἦν γὰρ μεγάλη ἡ ἡμέρα ἐκείνου τοῦ σαββάτου. This tells us that (1) the Preparation, or Eve, was the Eve of the Passover, (2) it was also the Eve of the Sabbath. There were therefore special reasons for the speedy entombment. Comp. xix 42 ἐκεῖ οὖν διὰ τὴν παρασκευὴν τῶν Ἰουδαίων. ἔθηκαν τὸν Ἰησοῦν, where "of the Jews" means, in effect, "owing to this Jewish custom which I have at some length tried to explain." In *Acts of John* § 12 ὅτε (MSS) τωαρουβατω ἐκρεμάσθη has been explained by Hilgenfeld as "on the *Preparation*." This would agree with the Aramaic עֲרוּבְתָּא quoted above, p 635, n 1

[4] Mk xv. 43—5   Mt xxvii 57—8   Lk xxiii. 50—52

ἐλθὼν Ἰωσὴφ (marg +ὁ) ἀπὸ Ἀριμαθαίας εὐσχήμων βουλευτής, ὃς καὶ αὐτὸς ἦν προσδεχόμενος τὴν βασιλείαν τοῦ

Ὀψίας δὲ γενομένης ἦλθεν ἄνθρωπος πλούσιος ἀπὸ Ἀριμαθαίας, τοὔνομα Ἰωσήφ, ὃς καὶ αὐτὸς ἐμαθητεύθη (marg

Καὶ ἰδοὺ ἀνὴρ ὀνόματι Ἰωσὴφ βουλευτὴς ὑπάρχων, ἀνὴρ ἀγαθὸς καὶ δίκαιος,—οὗτος οὐκ ἦν συνκατατεθειμένος τῇ

THE BURIAL

This might mean that he was afraid of Pilate But it is much more probable that he was afraid of incurring the enmity of the Jews John suggests this by saying that he was "a disciple of Jesus, but in secret, through fear of the Jews"

Mark alone calls Joseph "respectable"—a term used in early papyri to mean the "respectables" or "notables" of a town[1] He adds "councillor" but does not say whether this refers to the town council of Arimathaea or to the Sanhedrin[2]. Luke indicates the latter by adding "he had not voted in favour of their counsel and action," *i.e.* that of the Sanhedrin in condemning Jesus Luke also follows Mark in saying that Joseph was "looking for the kingdom of God" For all this, Matthew substitutes (1) "rich," (2) "he had become a disciple of Jesus" These variations could be reasonably explained by the hypothesis of a Hebrew original meaning "A man of worth,"

Mk xv. 43—5 *contd*	Mt xxvii 57—8 *contd*	Lk. xxiii 50—52 *contd.*
θεοῦ, τολμήσας εἰσῆλθεν πρὸς τὸν Πειλᾶτον καὶ ᾐτήσατο τὸ σῶμα τοῦ Ἰησοῦ ὁ δὲ Πειλᾶτος ἐθαύμασεν εἰ ἤδη τέθνηκεν, καὶ προσκαλεσάμενος τὸν κεντυρίωνα ἐπηρώτησεν αὐτὸν εἰ ἤδη (marg πάλαι) ἀπέθανεν καὶ γνοὺς ἀπὸ τοῦ κεντυρίωνος ἐδωρήσατο τὸ πτῶμα τῷ Ἰωσήφ	ἐμαθήτευσεν) τῷ Ἰησοῦ οὗτος προσελθὼν τῷ Πειλάτῳ ᾐτήσατο τὸ σῶμα τοῦ Ἰησοῦ τότε ὁ Πειλᾶτος ἐκέλευσεν ἀποδοθῆναι.	βουλῇ καὶ τῇ πράξει αὐτῶν,—ἀπὸ Ἀριμαθαίας πόλεως τῶν Ἰουδαίων, ὃς προσεδέχετο τὴν βασιλείαν τοῦ θεοῦ, οὗτος προσελθὼν τῷ Πειλάτῳ ᾐτήσατο τὸ σῶμα τοῦ Ἰησοῦ

Jn xix 38 Μετὰ δὲ ταῦτα ἠρώτησεν τὸν Πειλᾶτον Ἰωσὴφ ἀπὸ Ἀριμαθαίας, ὢν μαθητὴς [τοῦ] Ἰησοῦ κεκρυμμένος δὲ διὰ τὸν φόβον τῶν Ἰουδαίων, ἵνα ἄρῃ τὸ σῶμα τοῦ Ἰησοῦ· καὶ ἐπέτρεψεν ὁ Πειλᾶτος

In Mk, SS has "And he dared and went in unto Pilate," *k* "ausus est et introivit ad pilatum"

[1] Wetst on Mk quotes Phrynichus and Suidas as condemning the popular use of εὐσχήμων for "in good position," "well-to-do" See *Corrections* 519, and add *Berl Urkund* 376 (2nd or 3rd cent) (a rescript) "to the *respectables*" of a village (comp 381 where the writers call themselves εὐσχήμονες)

[2] *Acta Pil* (A) xi 3 Ἰωσὴφ βουλευτὴς ἀπὸ Ἀ πόλεως ὑπάρχων favours the view that he was an official of Arimathaea, but Luke indicates that he was a member of the Sanhedrin

THE BURIAL

or perhaps "A son of worth[1]." The phrase is opposed to "a man of Belial" But the Hebrew for "worth" often means "riches[2]." Matthew may have taken it thus, and all the more readily because of Isaiah's prophecy "they made his grave... with the rich in his death[3]"

Mark alone tells us that when Joseph asked for the body, Pilate "marvelled if he were already dead" This, taken by itself, might lead unbelievers to say, in derision, that the marvel would be justifiable, and that Jesus did not die on the Cross Anticipating this criticism, some evangelists might omit the Marcan tradition Matthew and Luke at all events do omit it. But according to John, such a derisive objection may be met by facts passed over in Mark's narrative Before receiving Joseph's request, Pilate had given orders for the *crurifragium*, i e. in effect, the killing of the crucified The sudden death of Jesus anticipated the *crurifragium* in a surprising manner, but the soldiers assured themselves of the reality of the death by piercing His side. Joseph, coming straight from the Cross, and informing Pilate of the unexpectedly rapid death, might well cause surprise, and even unbelief, until Joseph's account was confirmed by the centurion Mark might have expressed the facts fully thus, " Pilate marvelled that Jesus had already died [*and then found from the centurion that the death had been ascertained without the* crurifragium *which he had ordered*] " But he did not express them thus because he had omitted all mention of the *crurifragium* John supplies what Mark omitted.

John also says that Joseph was seconded by Nicodemus— seconded, but at some interval. Joseph supplied the courageous

---

[1] See Gesen 298—9 on חיל = "ability," but "often involving moral worth " It also means "wealth " In Exod xviii 21 "*men of ability*, such as fear God, men of truth, hating unjust gain"— where Rashi says "*rich men*, who have no need to practise hypocrisy and pervert judgment"—are called briefly afterwards (xviii 25) "*men of ability*," and these are to be chosen as rulers and judges. In 1 K 1 42, "thou art a man *of worth* (חיל)," the Targ has "thou art a man *fearing* (דחיל) *sins*," and in *ib* 1 52 "If he is like *a son* (בן) *of worth* (חיל)," the Targ has "like a *man fearing* (דחיל) *sins* "

[2] Tromm gives חיל as πλοῦτος ten times

[3] Is liii 9

THE BURIAL

initiative in petitioning Pilate, and in "taking away" the body from the Cross. Nicodemus came afterwards ("but there came also Nicodemus") and brought embalming spices in profusion[1], "a hundred pounds in weight." The Evangelist not improbably desires us to contrast this with Mary's single "pound" of ointment—more precious than the hundred pounds[2]. Here it is added that Nicodemus was "he that came to Jesus by night at the first." He was a just man. He had said to the Sanhedrin "Doth our Law judge the accused [*lit.* the man] except it first hear from himself and know what he doeth[3]?" But he was deficient in courage, and here he serves as a foil to Joseph, whose "boldness"—mentioned by Mark—had not been appreciated by Matthew and Luke[4].

§ 4. *The entombing*[5]

Matthew and Luke differ conspicuously from Mark in rejecting the word "*bound-fast*" or "*fettered*," and substituting

---

[1] Why does Mark (xv 46 ἀγοράσας) say that Joseph "*bought*" linen? Possibly the original meant "procured" or "took" לקח See Nehem x 31 ἀγορῶμεν (לקח), and Nehem v. 2 A V "take up," R V "get" ("let us *get* (LXX λημψόμεθα) corn that we may eat and live") It is noteworthy that in Mk xvi 1 ἠγόρασαν, the word is used again by Mark alone to describe the "buying" of spices after the sabbath

[2] Jn xii 3, xix 39 are the only N T instances of λίτρα

[3] Jn vii 51—2 "The man" means "the man [brought up from time to time for judgment]."

[4] The Synoptists have given us no previous indication that any Jew (Mk) "of honourable estate," or (Mt) "rich," would regard Jesus with favour—unless we may accept, as honestly and sincerely uttered, the words assigned by Mark alone to a scribe, who said to Jesus (xii 32) "Teacher, thou hast well said." John, on the other hand, has prepared the way for it by the first words of Nicodemus, (iii 2) "Rabbi, we know that thou art a teacher come from God." But this is private, and Nicodemus in public (*ib* vii 50—51) adopts a judicial and less favourable tone

[5] Mk xv 46—7
καὶ ἀγοράσας σινδόνα καθελὼν αὐτὸν ἐνείλησεν τῇ σινδόνι καὶ ἔθηκεν αὐτὸν ἐν μνήματι ὃ ἦν

Mt xxvii 59—61
καὶ λαβὼν τὸ σῶμα ὁ Ἰωσὴφ ἐνετύλιξεν αὐτὸ [ἐν] σινδόνι καθαρᾷ, καὶ ἔθηκεν αὐτὸ ἐν τῷ καινῷ

Lk xxiii 53, 55
καὶ καθελὼν ἐνετύλιξεν αὐτὸ σινδόνι, καὶ ἔθηκεν αὐτὸν ἐν μνήματι λαξευτῷ οὗ οὐκ ἦν οὐδεὶς

THE BURIAL

"*enfolded*," to describe Joseph's entombing of Christ's body[1]. The latter word probably seemed more suitable to the kindness of the act. But on the other hand the former better suggests those fetters of the grave which were to be broken in the Resurrection. Accordingly John, though not adopting Mark's unusual word, restores the sense of imprisonment by using the word "bind" habitually applied to prisoners[2].

Mk xv. 46—7 contd	Mt xxvii 59—61 contd.	Lk xxiii. 53, 55 contd
λελατομημένον ἐκ πέτρας, καὶ προσεκύλισεν λίθον ἐπὶ τὴν θύραν τοῦ μνημείου Ἡ δὲ Μαρία ἡ Μαγδαληνὴ καὶ Μαρία ἡ Ἰωσῆτος ἐθεώρουν ποῦ τέθειται	αὐτοῦ μνημείῳ ὃ ἐλατόμησεν ἐν τῇ πέτρᾳ, καὶ προσκυλίσας λίθον μέγαν τῇ θύρᾳ τοῦ μνημείου ἀπῆλθεν Ἦν δὲ ἐκεῖ Μαριὰμ ἡ Μαγδαληνὴ καὶ ἡ ἄλλη Μαρία καθήμεναι ἀπέναντι τοῦ τάφου	οὔπω κείμενος .Κατακολουθήσασαι δὲ αἱ γυναῖκες, αἵτινες ἦσαν συνεληλυθυῖαι ἐκ τῆς Γαλιλαίας αὐτῷ, ἐθεάσαντο τὸ μνημεῖον καὶ ὡς ἐτέθη τὸ σῶμα αὐτοῦ

Jn xix 38 b—42 ἦλθεν οὖν καὶ ἦρεν τὸ σῶμα αὐτοῦ ἦλθεν δὲ καὶ Νικόδημος, ὁ ἐλθὼν πρὸς αὐτὸν νυκτὸς τὸ πρῶτον, φέρων ἕλιγμα (marg μίγμα) σμύρνης καὶ ἀλόης ὡς λίτρας ἑκατόν ἔλαβον οὖν τὸ σῶμα τοῦ Ἰησοῦ καὶ ἔδησαν αὐτὸ ὀθονίοις μετὰ τῶν ἀρωμάτων, καθὼς ἔθος ἐστὶν τοῖς Ἰουδαίοις ἐνταφιάζειν ἦν δὲ ἐν τῷ τόπῳ ὅπου ἐσταυρώθη κῆπος, καὶ ἐν τῷ κήπῳ μνημεῖον καινόν, ἐν ᾧ οὐδέπω οὐδεὶς ἦν τεθειμένος· ἐκεῖ οὖν διὰ τὴν παρασκευὴν τῶν Ἰουδαίων, ὅτι ἐγγὺς ἦν τὸ μνημεῖον, ἔθηκαν τὸν Ἰησοῦν

[1] Ἐντυλίσσω "*enfold*" means (Aristoph *Nub* 987, *Plut* 692) "wrap oneself up" comfortably in a cloak, blanket etc Ἐνειλέω is used (Artemidor 1 13) of "swathing" babes, the emblem of helplessness, of entanglement in debt (Plut *Mor* 830 E) ὁ ἅπαξ ἐνειληθεὶς μένει χρεώστης διὰ παντός, of Caesar (*ib Vit* 739 D) "hunted to death like a wild beast, *entangled* [and held-fast] in the hands of all [the] conspirators (ἐνειλεῖτο ταῖς πάντων χερσίν)" Applied to things it might mean (Philo ii 622) binding fast without "violence", but applied to persons (not babes) it would mostly imply violence or coercion It is incorrectly printed ἐνειλημμένης in Philo ii 622, and in some MSS of Polyc *Philipp* § 1 τοὺς ἐνειλημένους...δεσμοῖς

John uses the Mt -Lk. word later on (xx 7 ἐντετυλιγμένον), but in quite a different sense, of the empty napkin "rolled up" (see below, p 670 foll)

[2] See above p 541, n 1, on the Marcan δήσαντες om by Lk. Does John wish to suggest here that when the Word came to the world (Jn i 11) "His own" not only "did not receive," but attempted to "bind" Him—friends after His death as well as enemies during His life? About this he might feel (2 Tim. ii. 10) ἀλλὰ ὁ λόγος τοῦ θεοῦ οὐ δέδεται.

THE BURIAL

Mark and Matthew, in describing Joseph's "*tomb*" as "*hewn*," use a phrase that occurs in the Bible elsewhere only in Isaiah's description of the "tomb" that has been "hewn" for himself by a rich upstart who is threatened with God's wrath[1]. Luke avoids this by substituting a word that means "chiselled" or "cut-out-of-stone," which occurs in LXX only once as the Greek rendering of Pisgah ("cleft")[2].

To readers of the LXX the Lucan term might suggest the thought of the mountain on which Moses died. But this would not be quite appropriate. John, and John alone, tells us that the tomb was in "a garden," near the place of crucifixion. About this the Gospel of Peter says that Joseph, "having received the Lord, washed and bound Him fast in linen and brought Him into *his own grave, called Joseph's Garden*[3]." This seems probable in itself. But Matthew alone implies that the grave was Joseph's. Why does John, instead of confirming Matthew, take pains to tell us a detached fact, that the tomb was in "a garden"—omitting all statements about the "hewing" or "cutting" and the ownership of the tomb[4]?

Seeking an answer to this question we are led to reflect (as often) that the end of the Fourth Gospel, like the beginning, implies a Hexaemeron, a New Genesis[5]. We are therefore (as Origen says concerning the entombment) in a region of symbolism[6]. And at this stage we have reached the events that

---

[1] Is xxii 16 ἐλατόμησας σεαυτῷ ὧδε μνημεῖον. The word λατομεῖν occurs nowhere else in prophecy except Is li 1.

[2] Deut iv 49 "the slopes (*marg* springs) of Pisgah," LXX Ἀσηδὼθ τὴν λαξευτήν.

[3] *Evang. Petr.* § 6 λαβὼν δὲ τὸν Κύριον ἔλουσε καὶ εἴλησε σινδόνι καὶ εἰσήγαγεν εἰς ἴδιον τάφον, καλούμενον κῆπον Ἰωσήφ. This suggests the question, Why did no evangelist add ἔλουσε? If it were not so natural an addition, one might suggest that the writer had in view variants of ἐνείλησε, including ἔλουσε, εἴλυσε, and εἴλησε, and that he has conflated two of them.

[4] John also, like Luke, omits the rolling of the stone to the entrance of the grave, but (again like Luke) assumes it, and mentions the stone later on.

[5] See *Proclam* p 15, *Son* 3583 (ix) *b*, (xii) *d*, comp *Joh. Gr.* 2624, 2347.

[6] It does not follow that we are consequently in a "region" of

THE BURIAL

correspond, antithetically, to the fall of Adam and his expulsion from Paradise under sentence of death. Paradise is, in Hebrew, *"garden."* The Johannine word for *"garden"* occurs in Aquila for the first time when we read that "The Lord God planted a *garden* eastward in Eden and there *he put the man he had formed*[1]." That referred to the first Adam. Now, in this new "garden," the Lord God is "putting" the second and sinless Adam, like "a grain of wheat," to spring up from death into a new life that shall redeem the first Adam from death and sin[2]

---

non-fact, but it does follow that the writer would select and emphasize what were (or what appeared to him to be) facts that suited symbolism. Take, for example, John's mention here of a "garden." (1) A "garden" may have been the actual place of the tomb. (2) "A *garden* (*gan*) of fertility (*semane*)," *Gan*semane, may have been one of the many forms of what we call "*Geth*semane" (of which the prefix is very variously given in MSS and Versions, see above, p 448), and this may be illustrated by Jerome's (and the Talmudists') explanation of the *Gen-* in *Gen*nesaret which Jerome renders (as if it were *gan-*) "*garden* of rulers" (see *Onomastica* and Levy 1 349 *a*) (3) In either of these two cases a symbolistic writer would be likely to emphasize the tradition about a "*garden.*" He would of course do so if he knew it to be true, but he would also prefer it to other traditions, if he thought it to be fairly probable.

[1] Gen 11 8 (Aq) καὶ ἐφύτευσεν κύριος ὁ θεὸς κῆπον εν ʼΕδεμ (גַּן בְּעֵדֶן) ἀπὸ ἀρχῆθεν (מִקֶּדֶם)... LXX has παράδεισον εν ʼΕδεμ κατὰ ἀνατολάς, καὶ ἔθετο ἐκεῖ τὸν ἄνθρωπον ὃν ἔπλασεν

[2] Origen (*Cels* 11 69, Lomm xviii 233 foll) says about the events of the entombment "Each of them may be shewn (ἀποδείκνυται) to be also a symbol of something—at least in the judgment of those who read the Scripture with understanding." Then he paraphrases Rom vi 4 "We were buried with Him through baptism and have also risen with Him," to shew that the tomb in which we have been thus buried must be "*new*"—so as to contain "so to speak, a *new* dead man"—not constructed out of many stones but hewn out of one rock. Also on Ps 1 3 "He shall be like a tree," he says that, according to one interpretation, "It is the soul of the Saviour...transplanted to the *paradise* where also the Gospel (Lk xxiii 43) says that He was after the Passion, relating that He said to the penitent robber, 'To-day shalt thou be with me in God's *paradise*'" Against these words of Christ, he says (*Comm Joann* xxxii 19, Lomm ii 481) objections have been raised which he tries to meet. Perhaps there were early plays on the *paradise* of Joseph and that of Eden

THE BURIAL

It should be noted that although John follows Matthew in saying that the tomb was "new," as well as Luke in saying that no one had ever yet been placed in it, he does not follow Matthew in saying that it belonged to Joseph. On the contrary, after mentioning the tomb as being "in a garden," John implies that it was under control of "the gardener," to whom Mary appeals saying "If thou hast conveyed him away, tell me where thou hast put him[1]." John has previously told us that the body was placed in this tomb, not because it was Joseph's—which would have been a perfectly sufficient reason—but "on account of the Preparation of the Jews, because the tomb was near." This suggests that (1) the tomb did *not* belong to Joseph, but that Joseph had used it temporarily under pressure of extreme need; (2) that the tomb either belonged to the owner of the garden, or was one of a number of tombs, severally owned, in "the garden," for which tombs an official called "the gardener" was responsible; (3) that Mary feared lest the gardener might have resented the liberty taken by Joseph and might have removed the body.

Some supposition of this kind is far more probable than the one supported by Matthew alone, namely, that the grave belonged to Joseph, and that it was sealed by the chief priests and guarded by Roman soldiers. If Joseph had made use of some new tomb, not his own, in an emergency, and intending to use it only for a few hours, it would become intelligible that he should remove the body as soon as possible—under cover of

---

Ephrem says (p 267) that Jesus left the burial clothes in the tomb "ut homo (*lit* Adam) in paradisum sine veste intraret sicut illic erat antequam peccaverat" Then (p 268) he enlarges on our receiving life from Christ as we received death from Adam. "For we fed on His body instead of the fruit of that tree, and His Table has become to us a garden of Delight (*i e.* Eden)"

Cramer, on Lk xiii 19 εἰς κῆπον ἑαυτοῦ, prints as from Irenaeus a statement that the Lord Jesus is here referred to as dying and as rising up to life like a seed But he uses ἀγρός instead of κῆπος in his comment, and makes no allusion to the garden of Joseph Perhaps those early Christians who depended on LXX alone would not see in κῆπος any allusion to the παράδεισος in Genesis

[1] Jn xx. 15.

THE BURIAL

night so as to escape the notice of the rulers of the Jews—without a precise regard for legal restrictions that forbade such action on the sabbath

Great difficulties attend this and every explanation of the opened tomb There appears to be in all the Gospels at this point, but especially in Mark and John, a mixture of the symbolical with the literal which throws doubt on all inferences as to exact details. But at all events no one can deny that the obvious interpretation of John's words is, that the tomb was not Joseph's, and was not intended by Joseph to be the Lord's final resting-place[1], but was used by Joseph in an emergency. And that John used these words deliberately becomes all the more probable in view of the fact that Joseph's ownership of the tomb was asserted by Matthew against the silence—implying contradiction—preserved by Mark and Luke

---

[1] Comp Westcott (on Jn xix 42) "it is implied that the sepulchre in which the Lord was laid was not chosen as His final resting-place " Cramer prints commentaries (of Chrysostom, Severus, and Ammonius) that agree in applying the word οἰκονομεῖσθαι, "providentially arranged," to the interment in this "new" tomb Chrys says Οἰκονομεῖται δὲ εἰς καινὸν αὐτὸν τεθεῖναι μνημεῖον ἐν ᾧ οὐδεὶς ἐτέθη, ἵνα καὶ τῆς ἀναστάσεως σαφὴς ἡ ἀπόδειξις γένηται, καὶ ὥστε τοὺς μαθητὰς δυνηθῆναι μετ' εὐκολίας παραγενέσθαι, καὶ θεατὰς τῶν συμβάντων γενέσθαι καὶ μάρτυρας, πλησίον ὄντας τοῦ τόπου καὶ τῆς ταφῆς

What Chrys means by σαφής is explained by Ammonius, who says that if Jesus had shared a tomb "with others," unbelievers would have said that some "other," not Jesus, had arisen Ammonius also plays on the word καινόν as referring to the καινοτομία of God's purpose to destroy "corruption," and to "the strangeness (ξένον) of the shooting-up [of the seed] from death into life (τῆς ἐκ θανάτου εἰς ζωὴν ἀναδρομῆς)." See Steph Thes. ἀναδρομή, and comp. Jn xii 24

The *Diatessaron* omits Matthew's statement that the tomb was Joseph's It has "And there was in the place.. a garden, and in that garden a new tomb...and *they left Jesus there* because the sabbath had come in, and because the tomb was near " Then it proceeds, in the plural, "And *they pushed* a great stone.. ," where Matthew has the singular, προσκυλίσας agreeing with Ἰωσήφ

CHAPTER XVI

THE ANNOUNCEMENT OF CHRIST'S RESURRECTION

[Mark xv 47—xvi 8]

§ 1. *What the women did before, and immediately after, the sabbath*[1]

THE announcement of Christ's resurrection to the women near the tomb is preceded by a statement (1) in Mark and Luke

---

[1]
Mk xv 47—xvi 4 (R V)	Mt xxvii 61, xxviii 1—2 (R V)	Lk xxiii. 55—xxiv 2 (R V)
(47) And Mary Magdalene and Mary the [mother] of Joses beheld where he was laid.	(61) And Mary Magdalene was there, and the other Mary, sitting over against the sepulchre...	(55) And the women, which had come with him out of Galilee, followed after, and beheld the tomb, and how his body was laid (56) And they returned, and prepared spices and ointments. And on the sabbath they rested according to the commandment.
(1) And when the sabbath was past, Mary Magdalene, and Mary the [mother] of James, and Salome, bought spices, that they might come and anoint him (2) And very early on the first day of the week, they come to the tomb when the sun was risen (3) And they were saying among themselves, Who shall roll us away the stone from the door of the tomb? (4) And looking up, they see that the stone is rolled back. for it was exceeding great.	(1) Now late on the sabbath day, as it began to dawn toward the first [day] of the week, came Mary Magdalene and the other Mary to see the sepulchre... (2) And behold, there was a great earthquake, for an angel of the Lord descended from heaven, and came and rolled away the stone, and sat upon it.	(1) But on the first day of the week, at early dawn, they came unto the tomb, bringing the spices which they had prepared (2) And they found the stone rolled away from the tomb

THE ANNOUNCEMENT

that they "were beholding where he was (*lit.*) put," or, "beheld the tomb and how his body was (*lit.*) put," but (2) in Matthew by a statement that they were "sitting opposite the grave" Luke adds that the women "returned" and "prepared spices" and "rested on the sabbath[1]." In the following verses we find the women (Mark) "buying spices when the sabbath was past," and "coming to the tomb very early on the first day of the week"; (Matthew) "coming late of the sabbath" (whatever that may mean) to "behold the grave"; (Luke) "coming at early dawn on the first day of the week and bringing the spices they had prepared[2]."

Jn xx 1 (R V) Now on the first [day] of the week cometh Mary Magdalene early, while it was yet dark, unto the tomb, and seeth the stone taken away from the tomb

[1] Mk xv. 47	Mt. xxvii 61	Lk xxiii 55—6
Ἡ δὲ Μαρία ἡ Μαγδαληνὴ καὶ Μαρία ἡ Ἰωσῆτος ἐθεώρουν ποῦ τέθειται.	Ἦν δὲ ἐκεῖ Μαριὰμ ἡ Μαγδαληνὴ καὶ ἡ ἄλλη Μαρία καθήμεναι ἀπέναντι τοῦ τάφου	Κατακολουθήσασαι δὲ αἱ γυναῖκες, αἵτινες ἦσαν συνεληλυθυῖαι ἐκ τῆς Γαλιλαίας αὐτῷ, ἐθεάσαντο τὸ μνημεῖον καὶ ὡς ἐτέθη τὸ σῶμα αὐτοῦ, ὑποστρέψασαι δὲ ἡτοίμασαν ἀρώματα καὶ μύρα Καὶ τὸ μὲν σάββατον ἡσύχασαν κατὰ τὴν ἐντολήν
[2] Mk xvi. 1—2	Mt. xxviii. 1	Lk. xxiv. 1
Καὶ διαγενομένου τοῦ σαββάτου [ἡ] Μαρία ἡ Μαγδαληνὴ καὶ Μαρία ἡ [τοῦ] Ἰακώβου καὶ Σαλώμη ἠγόρασαν ἀρώματα ἵνα ἐλθοῦσαι ἀλείψωσιν αὐτόν. καὶ λίαν πρωῒ [τῇ] μιᾷ τῶν σαββάτων ἔρχονται ἐπὶ τὸ μνημεῖον ἀνατείλαντος (marg ἀνατέλλοντος) τοῦ ἡλίου.	Ὀψὲ δὲ σαββάτων, τῇ ἐπιφωσκούσῃ εἰς μίαν σαββάτων, ἦλθεν Μαρία (marg Μαριὰμ) ἡ Μαγδαληνὴ καὶ ἡ ἄλλη Μαρία θεωρῆσαι τὸν τάφον	Τῇ δὲ μιᾷ τῶν σαββάτων ὄρθρου βαθέως ἐπὶ τὸ μνῆμα ἦλθαν φέρουσαι ἃ ἡτοίμασαν ἀρώματα.

The *Diatessaron* has "(Lk.) And they returned and (Mk) bought (Lk) ointment and perfume and (Lk) prepared [it] that (Mk) they might come and anoint him And (Lk) on the day which was the sabbath day they desisted according to the command" Then, after inserting Mt xxvii 62 b—66, it proceeds "And (Mt xxviii 1) in the evening of the sabbath, which is the morning of the first [day] (ὀψὲ δὲ σαββάτων, τῇ ἐπιφωσκούσῃ εἰς μίαν σαββάτων) and (Lk xxiv. 1) in the dawning (ὄρθρου βαθέως) while (Jn xx 1) the darkness yet remained

OF CHRIST'S RESURRECTION

Several questions suggest themselves. Why does Mark think it necessary to insert that they "bought" spices? Being inserted by Mark, why is it omitted by Matthew and Luke? Matthew's "sitting" and Luke's "resting"—may they be regarded as interpretations of one and the same original? If so, which is correct? If "sitting" is to be accepted literally, as well as "resting," what is the reason for inserting the former? That the women "rested on the sabbath" in spite of their grief is a statement of interest But that they "sat" at the grave, instead of standing, seems a superfluous detail—unless it can be shewn that it may refer to some Jewish custom not recognised by Mark and Luke

That there was likely to be such a custom is only remotely suggested by a single passage in the Bible, which describes the friends of Job as sitting down with him upon the ground[1]. But that there was actually such a custom among Jews is indicated by Jewish tradition about "seven sittings for the dead[2]" It is also favoured by the Gospel of Peter, which represents the women·as craving, if possible, to "*sit by the side*"

($\sigma\kappa o\tau i\alpha s$ ἔτι οὔσης).. " This appears to interpret ὀψὲ σαββάτων as referring to a time that might be called Saturday night after midnight or Sunday morning before daylight

In Lk xxiv 1 D omits ἀρώματα (as also do *a, b, e* etc) and substitutes καὶ τινες συν αυταις, SS has "and there had come with them *other women*" Early papyri mention ἀρώματα (*Berl Urkund* 362, vii 12) adding καὶ ἄλλα, see *ib* 1 7, 1 21, apparently meaning "spices *et cetera*" to denote a mixture (comp *Oxyr Pap* 1211 ἔλεον (i e ἔλαιον) ..πᾶν ἄρωμα χωρὶς λιβάνου)

[1] Job ii 13 "*sat* down with him (אתו) on (*lit* to) the ground seven days..," παρεκάθισαν (the only instance of παρακαθίζειν in LXX) (A παρεκάθηντο) αὐτῷ ἑπτὰ ἡμέρας (LXX omits "*on the ground*") Παρακαθῆσθαι in LXX elsewhere occurs only in Esth 1 14 "sitting by the king," where the context gives the word different associations. Παρακαθέζομαι, non-occurrent in LXX, occurs in N T only in Lk x 39 "*sitting by* the feet of Jesus."

[2] See *Hor Heb* (on Mt ix 23) on the "bestowing of (גמילות) kindnesses (חסדים)" on the dead, quoting Jer *Berach* on Job ii 13 *Hor Heb* also (on Jn xi 19) quotes *Baba Bathra* 100 b "The seven standings and *sittings* for the dead must not be diminished" and *Moed Katon*, cap 4 "Those that comfort ought *to sit nowhere but upon the floor*."

THE ANNOUNCEMENT

of the Lord and perform His obsequies, or else at least to perform the semblance of them at the door of His tomb[1]. On the supposition that the original (like Matthew) described the women as "sitting" and purposing to "sit" for a period of some duration "over against" the dead, we can understand that Mark misunderstood this "sitting over against the dead" as meaning "were taking up a position where they could 'behold where the body was put,'" and that Luke adopted this Marcan interpretation, slightly modified

But again, the Hebrew "sit" also means "sit quiet," "abide," "remain at home," and is occasionally rendered "rest[2]." The original might therefore mean that they "remained quiet in their homes" during the day that commenced with sunset, that is, during the sabbath This second interpretation Luke may have combined with the first and amplified and emphasized it by adding "according to the commandment" It is an ingenious and painstaking interpretation worthy of a Greek historian who aimed at separating prosaic truth from

---

[1] *Evang Petr* § 12 Ὄρθρου δὲ τῆς κυριακῆς Μαριὰμ ἡ Μαγδαληνή, μαθήτρια τοῦ Κυρίου ([ἥτις] φοβουμένη διὰ τοὺς Ἰουδαίους, ἐπειδὴ ἐφλέγοντο ὑπὸ τῆς ὀργῆς, οὐκ ἐποίησεν ἐπὶ τῷ μνήματι τοῦ Κυρίου ἃ εἰώθεσαν ποιεῖν αἱ γυναῖκες ἐπὶ τοῖς ἀποθνήσκουσι καὶ τοῖς ἀγαπωμένοις αὐταῖς) λαβοῦσα μεθ' ἑαυτῆς τὰς φίλας ἦλθε ἐπὶ τὸ μνημεῖον ὅπου ἦν τεθείς καὶ ἐφοβοῦντο μὴ ἴδωσιν αὐτὰς οἱ Ἰουδαῖοι, καὶ ἔλεγον Εἰ καὶ μὴ ἐν ἐκείνῃ τῇ ἡμέρᾳ ᾗ ἐσταυρώθη ἐδυνήθημεν κλαῦσαι καὶ κόψασθαι, καὶ νῦν ἐπὶ τοῦ μνήματος αὐτοῦ ποιήσωμεν ταῦτα τίς δὲ ἀποκυλίσει ἡμῖν καὶ τὸν λίθον τὸν τεθέντα ἐπὶ τῆς θύρας τοῦ μνημείου, ἵνα εἰσελθοῦσαι παρακαθεσθῶμεν αὐτῷ καὶ ποιήσωμεν τὰ ὀφειλόμενα,

In Mt xi 16, Lk vii 32 "children *sitting* in the market-place" and 'piping" or "mourning"—*i e* playing at a wedding or funeral—the word "sitting" seems, at first, inappropriate to a funeral, though it might suit a wedding feast, but if "*sitting*" was a recognised part of the obsequies for the dead, it is even more applicable to a funeral than to a wedding

[2] "Sit," ישב, = Luke's word, ἡσυχαζω in Exod xxiv 14, and in 2 K iv 13 (v r Field, "Ἄλλος") But another possible explanation is that "odour of *restfulness* (ניחוח)," or "*restfulness*" by itself, meaning "perfume (εὐωδία)," has been confused with נוח "rest" See Ezr vi 10 (προσφεροντες) εὐωδ.as (ניחוחין), Walton "odores quietis," 1 Esdr vi 31 σπονδαί In Dan ii 46 the same word is rendered (LXX) σπονδάς, (Theod) εὐωδίας

OF CHRIST'S RESURRECTION

what seemed (to him) poetic metaphor But in this instance Matthew appears to have preserved the historical truth[1].

The context indicates that the women came on a kind of pilgrimage to the tomb, perhaps still hoping against hope that He was not finally taken from them, and in any case intending to pay Him a loving homage This might be expressed generally by the Hebrew "perform service of kindness," quoted above[2]. It is true that Matthew says that they came to *behold* (*theōrein*) the grave—a strange expression to use after he has just told us that they had been previously "sitting over against the grave"—(which seems to imply that they had already "beheld" it), but the apparent inconsistency may perhaps be explained by the fact that, in Greek, *theōros*, "beholder," was used of a sacred messenger sent as an ambassador to consult an oracle and offer a sacrifice[3] In canonical LXX, the verb *theōrein* is rare, and mostly used of "beholding" visions (in Daniel)[4]. Matthew differs altogether from the other Evangelists in his rare use of *theōrein* He never uses it elsewhere except above ("women beholding from afar")[5] And it does not make sense here, unless it is used to mean something much more than "behold," something that implies an offering of devotion This offering of devotion might be described in Hebrew or Aramaic as "an odour of *sweetness*" But the word for "sweetness" literally means "*restfulness*" And this, falling in with the fact that the day of "*resting*," the sabbath, was actually at hand, might encourage Luke in his view that the tradition implied that "*They rested* on the *sabbath*."

We pass to the Marcan statement that the women "*bought spices*" "Bought" is omitted by Luke "*Spices*" is omitted

---

[1] Lk xxiii 56 ὑποστρέψασαι, "returning," might be a further Lucan conflation since (*Clue* 9) "Heb '*sit*' is identical in some of its forms with '*return*,'" and the two are freq confused in LXX

[2] See p 647, n 2

[3] See Steph *Thes*. θεωρός.

[4] Θεωρεῖν does not occur without v r in canon LXX outside Ps. (on which see p 627, n 2), Prov, Eccles and Daniel

[5] Mt. xxvii 55 ἀπὸ μακρόθεν θεωροῦσαι, identical with Mk xv 40 Θεωρεῖν occurs Mk (7), Lk. (7), Jn (24)

THE ANNOUNCEMENT

by several versions of Luke[1]. Mark's word for "spice," *arōma*, when derived from Greek, and used as in the best Greek authors, means "the products of the ploughed field," i.e. corn[2]. In LXX, it means "*spice*" in Chronicles, but not in the earlier historical books, where other words are substituted[3]. Mark's word for "buy"—almost always when used in the Pentateuch, and once when used in Isaiah—is applied merely to the buying of corn or food[4]. The Hebrew often supplies "corn" as the object. But where it does not (e.g. "they came to *buy* [*corn*]") Onkelos supplies "corn" or an equivalent[5].

But practically the same Hebrew word means also "*hope*" or "*wait*". It is used of "hoping," or "waiting," on the Lord, or for His salvation. And where the Hebrew has another word for "hope" the Targums often substitute this one[6]. Hence

---

[1] See above, p 646, n 2 *ad fin*

[2] Ἄρωμα, from ἀρόω "plough," meaning "the result of ploughing," "corn" etc., is used in Aristoph *Pax* 1158, Soph *Fragm* 77, and also misspelt as ἄρομα in Aelian (see Lobeck's *Phrynichus* p 227 quoting Suidas "'Ἀρώματα οὐ τὰ θυμιάματα οἱ ἀττικοὶ, ἀλλὰ τὰ ἐσπαρμένα, ubi male scribitur ἀρόματα")

When meaning "aroma," ἄρωμα is said (L S) to be perhaps derived from some eastern origin. I have been unable to find in Wetstein any note about ἄρωμα.

[3] Ἄρωμα (Heb alw בשם, "balsam") occurs in 1 Chr, 2 Chr, and Esth, 8 times, but not from Genesis to 2 K *fin* except in 2 K xx 13 (where Sym has ἡδύσματα). Elsewhere בשם = ἥδυσμα (7), θυμίαμα (3) etc

[4] Gen xli 57, xlii 5 etc, Deut ii 6, Is. lv. 1. Lev xxvii 19, "sanctified," ἀγοράσαις, is in B^abAF ἁγιάσας—a word used in Exod xx 8 about keeping the sabbath holy, a point mentioned only by Luke here (xxiii 56)

[5] Gen xli 57 Heb שבר, Onk. בן + עבורא i.e. "produce of the earth," "corn-food" (see Brederek p 118, "stets mit folgendem עבור, wo auch nicht schon im Text שבר") See Gesen. 991 *b* shewing that the verb שבר, lit "to corn," is sometimes used with the noun שבר "corn"—so that "they came to *corn corn*" means to "buy supplies of corn"—but sometimes without the noun

Ἀγοράζω represents other Heb verbs besides שבר, but only six or seven times altogether

[6] Gesen 960 *a*, שבר, "wait, hope (Aramaism, cf Aram סבר, *think*, Pa *hope*)." The Heb is used of "waiting on, or for (אל), God" in Ps civ 27, cxlv 15, and for (ל) God's salvation in Ps cxix 166 In

a statement that the women "*waited patiently for the Lord*" in the evening after His death, being first misinterpreted as meaning that they "*bought for the Lord*," or that they "*bought corn-food (arōmata) for the Lord*," might suggest the reflection: "The word means 'buy *corn-food* (arōmata)' how can this make sense?" Then it might be explained as meaning "They bought *spices for the Lord*."

But why does not Matthew insert this or something like it? Perhaps he does, latently. For we have seen above that the parallel Matthew says (very strangely and inconsistently) that the women "came to *behold* the tomb." Now the Hebrew word that we have been discussing as meaning "hope" and as confusable with the Marcan "buy," means also "*behold*," or "*inspect*," in a passage describing Nehemiah as "*inspecting*" the ruined walls of Jerusalem[1]. It is therefore reasonable to suspect a common Semitic original for Mark's tradition about "*buying spices*" and Matthew's about "*beholding*." And this original would be, in itself, a very natural one. "Very early in the morning, the women came to the tomb, *waiting for the Lord*."

If this was the original it would explain several divergences in the Gospels. Matthew and John would be perceived to be justified in omitting the purchase of spices. John would be recognised as introducing the costly embalment by Joseph and Nicodemus, according to "the custom of the Jews," as an antithesis to the offering, intended but not effected by the women, and to the tears actually offered by Mary Magdalene[2]. Luke would be recognised as justifiably introducing the "*quiet-waiting*[3]" of the women during the sabbath, as a preparation

---

Gen. xlix 18 "I have *hoped* or *waited* (קוה) for (ל) thy salvation." Onk has סבר, and so has Targ freq for "*hoping* in God," Levy *Ch* ii 139 *b*, *e g* Is xl 31, li 5, etc

[1] Nehem ii 13, 15 (Gesen p 960 *a*) שבר. The ambiguity of the word is illustrated by LXX which takes it as שבר, συντρίβων, "break," and so does Rashi. Field quotes Jerome's interpretation as "considerabam," and *al exempl* as κατανοῶν and κατενόουν.

[2] Jn xix 40, xx 11 On the former see *Joh Voc* 1866 (iii) quoting ἔδησαν and Chrysostom's comment, that the "abundance of myrrh" would have the effect of "binding fast," like "the soldering of lead."

[3] Lk. xxiii. 56 ἡσύχασαν. This word in literary Greek would

THE ANNOUNCEMENT

for the early morning visit to the tomb—during which interval their souls were exclaiming "I wait for the Lord, my soul doth wait, and in his word do I hope, my soul [looketh] for the Lord, [more than] watchmen for the morning[1]." Luke does indeed accept the "spices" literally (adding "ointments" which makes the meaning obvious)   But by referring to them as the things "made ready" or "*prepared*," he suggests that "preparation of the heart" which the Scriptures mention more than once[2], and which they also imply in the words "Let my prayer be *made ready* as incense before thee[3]."

§ 2. *What the names of the women were*

At this stage it will be convenient to consider the variations in the names of the women (1) present at Christ's death; (2) beholding the place where He was entombed, (3) visiting the tomb, and (4) returning from the tomb

(1)   Present at Christ's death

Mk xv 40	Mt. xxvii 56	Lk. xxiii 49
(1) Mary the Magdalene	(1) Mary the Magdalene	No names
(2) and Mary (*lit.*) the of James the less and of Joses mother	(2) and Mary (*lit.*) the of James and of Joseph (*or*, of Jose) mother	
(3) and Salome.	(3) and the mother of the sons of Zebedee.	

---

mostly imply being at ease   But in LXX it represents many Hebrew words, and the LXX ἡσύχιος, which occurs only once (Is lxvi. 2), = Heb "*contrite in spirit*" (comp Acts xxi 14) "we *ceased*, saying The will of the Lord be done."

[1] Ps cxxx. 5—6.

[2] See 1 S vii 3 ἑτοιμάσατε τὰς καρδίας ὑμῶν, Ps. x. 17 τὴν ἑτοιμασίαν τῆς καρδίας αὐτῶν   The same Hebr (כון) occurs in 1 Chr xxix 18 "*make-ready* (κατεύθυνον) their hearts unto thee."   Comp Sir 11. 17 οἱ φοβούμενοι κύριον ἑτοιμάσουσι καρδίας αὐτῶν.

[3] Ps cxli 2 κατευθυνθήτω (כון) ἡ προσευχή μου ὡς θυμίαμα ἐνώπιόν σου.

OF CHRIST'S RESURRECTION

Luke, in the place of names, says (xxiii. 49) "Now there were standing...from afar, and *women those that had together with him followed [him] from Galilee.*" Mark (xv. 41) after the names, and Matthew (xxvii. 55) before the names, have similar clauses about "*following in, or from, Galilee.*"

John has (xix. 25) "Now there were standing by the cross of Jesus his mother and the sister of his mother, Mary (*lit*) the [   ] of Klopas and Mary the Magdalene¹"

(2) Beholding Christ's entombment

Mk xv. 47	Mt. xxvii. 61	Lk. xxiii. 55
(1) Mary the Magdalene	(1) Mary the Magdalene	No names.
(2) and Mary (*lit*.) the [ ] of Joses.	(2) and the other Mary.	

Luke, in the place of names, repeats his mention of "women" and "following" and "Galilee," but in a slightly different form (xxiii 55) "And, having followed him to the end, the women that had come together with him from Galilee..."

John has nothing corresponding to these passages².

---

¹ Mk xv 40—41
Ἦσαν δὲ καὶ γυναῖκες ἀπὸ μακρόθεν θεωροῦσαι, ἐν αἷς καὶ Μαριὰμ ἡ Μαγδαληνὴ καὶ Μαρία ἡ Ἰακώβου τοῦ μικροῦ καὶ Ἰωσῆτος μήτηρ καὶ Σαλώμη, αἳ ὅτε ἦν ἐν τῇ Γαλιλαίᾳ ἠκολούθουν αὐτῷ καὶ διηκόνουν αὐτῷ, καὶ ἄλλαι πολλαὶ αἱ συναναβᾶσαι αὐτῷ εἰς Ἱεροσόλυμα

Mt xxvii 55—6
Ἦσαν δὲ ἐκεῖ γυναῖκες πολλαὶ ἀπὸ μακρόθεν θεωροῦσαι, αἵτινες ἠκολούθησαν τῷ Ἰησοῦ ἀπὸ τῆς Γαλιλαίας διακονοῦσαι αὐτῷ ἐν αἷς ἦν Μαρία (marg Μαριὰμ) ἡ Μαγδαληνὴ καὶ Μαρία ἡ τοῦ Ἰακώβου καὶ Ἰωσὴφ (marg Ἰωσῆ) μήτηρ καὶ ἡ μήτηρ τῶν υἱῶν Ζεβεδαίου

Lk xxiii. 49
ἱστήκεισαν δὲ πάντες οἱ γνωστοὶ αὐτῷ ἀπὸ μακρόθεν, καὶ (marg + αἱ) γυναῖκες αἱ συνακολουθοῦσαι αὐτῷ ἀπὸ τῆς Γαλιλαίας, ὁρῶσαι ταῦτα

Jn xix 25 ἱστήκεισαν δὲ παρὰ τῷ σταυρῷ τοῦ Ἰησοῦ ἡ μήτηρ αὐτοῦ καὶ ἡ ἀδελφὴ τῆς μητρὸς αὐτοῦ, Μαρία ἡ τοῦ Κλωπᾶ καὶ Μαρία ἡ Μαγδαληνή.

² Mk xv 47
Ἡ δὲ Μαρία ἡ Μαγδαληνὴ καὶ Μαρία ἡ Ἰωσῆτος ἐθεώρουν ποῦ τέθειται

Mt. xxvii. 61
Ἦν δὲ ἐκεῖ Μαριὰμ ἡ Μαγδαληνὴ καὶ ἡ ἄλλη Μαρία καθήμεναι ἀπέναντι τοῦ τάφου

Lk. xxiii. 55
Κατακολουθήσασαι δὲ αἱ γυναῖκες, αἵτινες ἦσαν συνεληλυθυῖαι ἐκ τῆς Γαλιλαίας αὐτῷ, ἐθεάσαντο τὸ μνημεῖον καὶ ὡς ἐτέθη τὸ σῶμα αὐτοῦ.

THE ANNOUNCEMENT

(3) Preparing to visit, or visiting, Christ's tomb

Mk xvi 1	Mt. xxviii. 1	Lk. xxiv 1
(1) Mary the Magdalene	(1) Mary the Magdalene	No names.
(2) and Mary (*lit*) the [ ] of James.	(2) and the other Mary.	
(3) and Salome.		

Mark here gives the names of the women as (xvi. 1) preparing to come, and then says (xvi. 2) "they come."

Matthew gives the names of the women as "coming," without any mention of preparing; and he repeats the same names as those which he connected with beholding the entombment, where he described them as "sitting over against the grave."

Luke, in the place of names, has simply (xxiv. 1) "they came," indicating, by "they," the women (xxiii. 55) "that had come together with him from Galilee." But later on, when he describes the return of the women from the tomb and their report to the apostles, he gives names thus (xxiv. 10) "Now they were the Magdalene Mary, and Joanna, and Mary the [ ] of James, and the rest with them said these things to the apostles[1]."

John has simply (xx. 1) "Mary the Magdalene," as visiting the tomb; but he describes her as saying—when she runs back from the open tomb—(xx. 2) "*We know* not where they have laid him[2]." This suggests that Mary had companions with her —a view favoured by the Gospel of Peter. "Mary the Magdalene

---

[1] Mk xvi 1—2
(1) [ἡ] Μαρία ἡ Μαγδαληνὴ καὶ Μαρία ἡ [τοῦ] Ἰακώβου καὶ Σαλώμη ἠγόρασαν ἀρώματα ἵνα ἐλθοῦσαι ἀλείψωσιν αὐτόν
(2) καὶ λίαν πρωὶ [τῇ] μιᾷ τῶν σαββάτων ἔρχονται .

Mt. xxviii 1
Ὀψὲ δὲ σαββάτων, τῇ ἐπιφωσκούσῃ εἰς μίαν σαββάτων, ἦλθεν Μαρία (marg Μαριὰμ) ἡ Μαγδαληνὴ καὶ ἡ ἄλλη Μαρία θεωρῆσαι τὸν τάφον

Lk xxiv 1, 10
(1) τῇ δὲ μιᾷ τῶν σαββάτων ὄρθρου βαθέως ἐπὶ τὸ μνῆμα ἦλθαν
(10) ἦσαν δὲ ἡ Μαγδαληνὴ Μαρία καὶ Ἰωάνα καὶ Μαρία ἡ Ἰακώβου καὶ αἱ λοιπαὶ σὺν αὐταῖς ἔλεγον πρὸς τοὺς ἀποστόλους ταῦτα

[2] Jn xx 1—2 Μαρία ἡ Μαγδαληνὴ ἔρχεται...καὶ βλέπει τὸν λίθον ἠρμένον ἐκ τοῦ μνημείου   τρέχει οὖν καὶ ἔρχεται...καὶ λέγει...οὐκ οἴδαμεν ποῦ ἔθηκαν αὐτόν.

...taking *her friends with her* came to the tomb where He was laid[1]."

Reviewing these texts, we notice, as the two most prominent facts, 1st, that Mark alone mentions the name Salome, 2nd, that John's list of the women standing by the Cross leaves us in doubt whether they are to be regarded as three or four in number. Origen has no extant comment on John's list. Nonnus regards them as three[2]. Chrysostom is silent on the subject. Jerome in a long discussion of the subject affords no real light on this point[3]. The Diatessaron's only mention of

---

[1] *Evang. Petr.* § 12 Μαριὰμ ἡ Μαγδαληνή...λαβοῦσα μεθ' ἑαυτῆς τὰς φίλας ἦλθε ἐπὶ τὸ μνημεῖον ὅπου ἦν τεθείς.

[2] Jn xix 25 is thus paraphrased by Nonnus —
ἐγγύθι δὲ σταυροῖο συνήλυδες ἦσαν ἑταῖροι
καὶ Μαρίη, Χριστοῖο θεητόκος οἷς ἅμα κείνῃ
σύγγονος ἦν Μαρίη καὶ ὁμώνυμος ἦν δὲ καὶ αὐτὴ
Μαγδαλινὴ Μαρίη φιλοδάκρυος.

Here the second Mary is called both σύγγονος and ὁμώνυμος to the first, i.e. to the Lord's mother. And this points to a possibility that when two epithets were applied to one Mary, one of the epithets might be regarded as a name indicating a second person. It has been suggested (*Proclam* pp. 117—20) that Σαλώμη originally meant "belonging to His [i.e. the Lord's] mother." "The Mary *that belonged to His mother*," if the italicised words were transliterated from Hebrew to Greek, might be rendered [ἡ] Μαρία ἡ καὶ Σαλώμη, "the Mary that is also called Salome." But this might easily be confused with "Mary and Salome"—two persons. In the Greek texts, the article with Μαρία varies remarkably in its order and in its use or non-use.

[3] Jerome says (*Epist. Contr. Helvid.* § 16, Eng. Transl. p. 341) "At this stage I do not wish to argue for or against the supposition that Mary the wife of Clopas and Mary the mother of James and Joses were different women, provided it is clearly understood that Mary the mother of James and Joses was not the same person as the Lord's mother."

But previously he says (§ 15) "The only conclusion is that the Mary who is described as the mother of James the less was the wife of Alphaeus and sister of Mary the Lord's mother, the one who is called by John the Evangelist 'Mary of Clopas,' whether after her father, or kindred, or for some other reason." Elsewhere he says (*Epist.* xlvi. 13) "Will the day never come when we shall together enter the Saviour's cave, and together weep in the sepulchre of the

THE ANNOUNCEMENT

Salome includes her among the women that came with Jesus from Galilee thus. "One of them was Mary Magdalene, and Mary the mother of James the little and Joses, and the mother of the sons of Zebedee, and Salome."

Jerome, in his controversy with Helvidius, ventures to say "It is customary in Scripture for the same individual to bear different names[1]." There are at all events many instances of it. And, on the supposition that some of the lists of the witnesses of the Passion or Resurrection included a sister of Mary the mother of Jesus, we have to remember that the Hebrew word for "aunt," which occurs thrice, is twice rendered in LXX "kinswoman," and once "the daughter of a father's brother[2]." These facts increase the difficulty of reaching the historical original beneath the above-mentioned variations. But we may reasonably accept the following inferences as highly probable. Mark's "Salome" was regarded by all the later Evangelists either as an error, or as a name liable to objection and inviting alteration[3]. Luke accepted Matthew's "Mary

---

Lord with His sister and with His mother?" This appears to say the Lord's "sister" where Nonnus says σύγγονος...Μαρίη

[1] Jerome, *Contr Helvid* § 15

[2] See Gesen 187 *b* referring to דודה "aunt" in Exod. vi 20, R V "father's sister," LXX "daughter of the brother of his father," i e cousin, but "'Ἄλλος" has θείαν αὐτοῦ In Lev. xviii 14 (where it means "father's brother's wife") and xx 20 (Gesen. "father's sister," R V "uncle's wife") LXX has συγγενής which represents (*Oxf Conc*) דוד and דודה The word דוד means in Cant. "*beloved* [one]," but elsewhere "uncle" In Cant. v. 1, vi 2 דוד, ἀδελφός is prob a Gk error for ἀδελφιδός. In Cant. vi. 2 there is v.r. ἀδελφιδός The facts suggest a possible origin of the phrase "the *beloved* disciple"

[3] On "'Salome' in Mark," see *Proclam.* pp 117 foll, which suggests that "Salome" may have been a Hebrew phrase meaning "belonging to the Mother," i e to the mother of the Lord, and added to one of the Maries as a distinguishing epithet. This suggestion is based on the hypothesis that *sal-* in *sal-ome* might correspond to the Hebrew *shel* meaning "*belonging to*." On the use of *shel-* in Scriptural poetry, see *Beginning* p 428, and note that in Gen xlix. 10 (R V. txt) "until *Shiloh* come," no ancient authorities are said to accept "Shiloh" as a place-name The LXX, Theod, Onkelos, and the Midrash, all take it as *shel-o*, i e. "belonging to him," and so does

the mother of James" and rejected the Marcan additions ("and of Joses," and "the less"). Luke also substituted—in the place of Mark's "Salome," and Matthew's "mother of the sons of Zebedee"—"Joanna and the rest with them" (not indeed in the parallel to Mark and Matthew but elsewhere)[1]. By "the rest with them" he means those women whom he has twice recently described as coming *"from Galilee"*; and he now takes us back mentally to his first mention of them. "And with him the twelve, and certain women that had been healed of evil spirits and infirmities, Mary that [was] called Magdalene, from whom seven devils had gone out, and Joanna, the wife of Chuza Herod's steward, and Susanna, and many others, who ministered unto them of their substance[2]."

Rashi as regards the literal interpretation, though he gives another as "mystical" (שי לו) "munus ei," Ps lxxvi 11) Evidence bearing on the use of *shel-* in Heb poetry assumes increased importance in its bearing on "Salome" in Mark if we believe, as above, that the original of the Marcan *"bought spices"* was a poetic statement that the women *"waited-patiently* for the Lord "

Derenbourg p 102 gives many various spellings of the name Salome, שלמתו, שלמינון, שלמצה, שלציון, and, in two words, של ציון. In Cant vi 13 Heb השולמית, "Shulammite," LXX has Σουμανεῖτις, אA Σουλαμιτις, but the Midrash *ad loc* and *Gen r* (on Gen. xxvii. 28) take the name as Israel regarded as a personification of peace. On "sons of peace" in the Gospels see *Proclam.* p 120 foll It would be, in Heb, "Sons of *Salom* " In Delitzsch, the Heb for "my peace" in Jn xiv 27 "*My peace* I give unto you" is שלומי, "salōme."

[1] Lk xxiv. 8—10 "And they . returned. .Now they were Mary Magdalene and Joanna, and ." is parall to Mk xvi 8 "And they went out .," Mt xxviii 8 "And they departed.. ," where no names are mentioned

[2] Lk viii 2—3, briefly referred to by Origen *Cels* 1. 65 when defending Jesus against the charge of "going about and collecting contributions to support him in a disgraceful way" ἐν γὰρ τοῖς εὐαγγελίοις γυναῖκές τινες τεθεραπευμέναι ἀπὸ τῶν ἀσθενειῶν αὐτῶν, ἐν αἷς ἦν καὶ Σωσάννα, παρεῖχον τοῖς μαθηταῖς ἐκ τῶν ὑπαρχόντων αὐταῖς τροφάς. He omits the name of Joanna, perhaps for brevity; but the omission of "Mary Magdalene" and "evil spirits" can hardly be explained by the desire of brevity alone Origen, later on, refers twice (*Cels* ii. 55, 59) to the phrase "*frantic,* or, *hysterical, woman* (γυνὴ πάροιστρος)" applied by Celsus to Mary Magdalene Against such an opponent, and in

THE ANNOUNCEMENT

It will be observed that Mark also, in his first list of the women present at Christ's death, speaks of "*many others*, those that had come up with him to Jerusalem" (where the parallel Luke omits "many others," and the parallel Matthew omits "others")[1].

John, who never mentions exorcism or "evil spirits," could hardly fail to recognise that Luke gave to the opponents of Christianity a ground for attack in describing the first two reporters of Christ's resurrection as women that had been "healed of evil spirits" We have seen that Celsus scoffed at the evidence of Christ's resurrection as proceeding from "a hysterical woman[2]" Long before Celsus, other educated Greeks probably did the same thing Luke himself seems to have perceived the weak point, for though he records the evidence of these once-afflicted women, he says at once, and repeats afterwards, that the apostles did not receive that evidence, and were afterwards convinced by evidence directly addressed to themselves[3]. This attitude is like that of Paul, who does not mention, among the manifestations of Christ after death,

the brief space allowed by the context, it would have been futile to use such arguments as Paul (1 Cor 1 18 foll, ii 14, comp iii 19) uses about insight given to those whom the world calls "fools" or "mad" Origen contents himself with saying that there were other witnesses

Yet against a Stoic opponent Origen might have derived an argument from a modification of the teaching of Plato (*Timaeus* 71—2 on which see Archer-Hind's note, *Phaedr* 244) who connects one kind of divine inspiration with "madness" Distinguishing "prophetic" from "mantic (μαντική)" utterance, Plato derives the latter from μαίνειν "to be mad" He says that the priestesses at Delphi have benefited Greece "by their madness (μανεῖσαι)," and that thus the right kind of madness has delivered men from countless evils

Clement of Alexandria (92) contrasts the frenzied Maenads with "the fair daughters of God, the fair lambs celebrating the sacred orgies of the word, raising a sober choral song" And Origen, if he had argued fully against Celsus, would perhaps have met the charge implied in "hysterical" by arguments resembling those in the Pauline Epistles, and perhaps by others shewing how sickness of mind (as well as of body) is sometimes seen to be an avenue to spiritual health

[1] Mk xv 41, Mt xxvii 55—6, Lk xxiii 49
[2] See above, p 657, n. 2.   [3] Lk xxiv 11, 31—43

a single instance in which He "was seen by," or "appeared to," a woman[1].

Any expectation that we might have felt that John would take a similar course, is curiously disappointed. John's first course is to set down a list of women present at the death, differing from all the Synoptic lists. It contains the name of the Lord's mother, and is in itself so ambiguously worded that we do not known whether it implies three or four women. His next course is to describe a visit to the tomb that is nominally made by Mary Magdalene alone, but really by Mary and companions, and this visit is followed immediately by another of Mary's, in which she is really left alone, and in the course of which Mary sees the Saviour and receives from Him a message to the disciples The impression left on us by these narratives is that John, while strictly adhering to some ancient traditions of which he cannot confidently state the exact meaning—and which he leaves in their original obscurity—adds others that are new, and that are based on his interpretation of the old.

Possibly John may be less correct than Luke on important points of fact Where Luke heard, or read, "*Joanna*," John may have heard, or read, "*Joannes*," the son of Zebedee. This, and other circumstances, may have led him to an erroneous inference, that the beloved disciple was present with the women —a tradition not found in any other Gospel And yet his narrative of the first manifestation of the risen Saviour, and of the preparation for it through bitter disappointment and tears, makes a stronger appeal to human nature than does the story of Emmaus, and is less likely to have sprung out of accretions or inventions or Scriptural inferences[2].

---

[1] 1 Cor xv 5—8

[2] "Scriptural inferences" Comp Lk xxiv 25—7 "O...slow to believe—after *all* (ἐπὶ πᾶσιν) *that the prophets have spoken*ǃ ..And he interpreted to them in *all the scriptures* the things concerning himself " D omits "to believe " SS has " *From* all the things that the prophets have spoken, was not the Messiah about to endure ... ?"

THE ANNOUNCEMENT

§ 3. *"When the sun was risen," in Mark*[1]

The Diatessaron omits these words, and Codex D substitutes "when the sun *was rising*." Even with this amendment they are incompatible with Mark's own context, *"very early,"* which would mean "before sunrise." It is not surprising that Matthew and Luke alter them. Some have explained the difficulty by supposing that Mark compresses into one two visits; of which the first was "very early," but the second, "when the sun was risen[2]." Apart from questions as to the original from which the Three Gospels may have derived their traditions—diverging owing to divergent interpretation—we have to ask "Does the

---

[1] Mk xvi 2
καὶ λίαν πρωὶ [τῇ] μιᾷ τῶν σαββάτων ἔρχονται ἐπὶ τὸ μνημεῖον ἀνατείλαντος (marg ἀνατέλλοντος) τοῦ ἡλίου

Mt. xxviii 1a
ὀψὲ δὲ σαββάτων, τῇ ἐπιφωσκούσῃ εἰς μίαν σαββάτων...

Lk xxiv 1a
τῇ δὲ μιᾷ τῶν σαββάτων ὄρθρου βαθέως...

Jn xx. 1 Τῇ δὲ μιᾷ τῶν σαββάτων...πρωὶ σκοτίας ἔτι οὔσης..

[2] See Swete on Mk xvi 2 "It is better [than the reading of D adopted by Augustine] to regard Mc's note as a compressed statement of two facts, the two women started just before daybreak and arrived at sunrise." But would the starting and the arrival take all the interval indicated between "very early" (Lk "deep dawn") and "the sun having arisen"? Cramer (on Mk) prints a long explanation ending "But I am not unaware that [two] different visions are alleged (by those who profess to harmonize the apparent discrepancy) to have been seen, and that the [pair of] women in Matthew is one and the [pair of] women in Mark another—Mary Magdalene following all [the women] to the end (πάσαις ἐξακολουθούσης) . and beholding the [two] different visions."

Perhaps the best explanation of Mk ἀνατείλαντος τοῦ ἡλίου is that the original meant "when *the sun of righteousness* (Mal iv. 2) *had arisen.*" Comp Deut xxxiii 2 "The Lord *rose-like-the-sun* (זרח) (ἐπέφανεν) unto them [i e Israel]," and Eph v 14 "Christ shall *shine* upon thee (ἐπιφαύσει)" a rare word that is etymologically connected with ἐπιφώσκειν (also rare, but used in Mt xxviii 1, Lk xxiii 54). Owing to the fact that the Jewish day begins at sunset, confusion might arise between words of this kind, when used literally and also metaphorically. Mark's original may have meant that although it was literally still early when the women arrived at the tomb, "the sun of righteousness," the Dayspring, the Lord Jesus, "had already arisen.'

OF CHRIST'S RESURRECTION

Fourth Gospel intervene, and, if so, with what tendency?" John does intervene—using the Marcan word "early," but defining it as "while [the] darkness still lasted (*lit.* was)." This phrase he applies to a first visit of Mary Magdalene to the tomb, accompanied by companions—who are not indeed mentioned in the narrative, but inferred from the drama ("we know not where they have laid him[1]") Then he says that Mary ran to fetch other disciples whom she accompanied back to the tomb Thus she pays it a second visit, which may very well have been at, or after, sunrise

Luke, who never uses, in any part of his Gospel, the word "early"—possibly because it was indefinite and ambiguous—substitutes "in deep dawn." This phrase is used by Philo in his paraphrase of the narrative of the passage of the Red Sea, where the children of Israel cross on dry land toward the end of the night, and the Scripture says that the Lord looked forth upon the Egyptians "*in the morning watch*[2]" before overwhelming them in the sea "*when the morning appeared*[3]."

---

[1] Jn xx 2

[2] Exod xiv 24 "the watch of (אשמרת) the morning" On this Rashi says that the night "divisa est in custodias quibus canunt angeli ministratorii, caterva post catervam, juxta tres partes" See *Berach* 3 b on the question whether there were three watches or four Philo ii 109 says that the children of Israel passed "through a dry road about *deep dawn* (βαθὺν ὄρθρον)," a phrase used in Plato (and Aristoph *Vesp* 216) Steph *Thes* (ὄρθρος) quotes Phrynichus on the incorrect use of the word by later Greeks, who confused ὄρθρος with ἕως "early morning," whereas it meant an earlier hour when a lamp was still needed *Mechilt*, on Exod xiv 24, after giving many instances where "the prayers of the righteous are heard in the morning"—as though the songs of the "angeli ministratorii," just before daybreak, conveyed to heaven in a special way (Rev viii 3) "the prayers of all the saints"—concludes with "Another explanation, 'And it came to pass in the watch of the morning—this meant '*At the shining forth of the sun* (das war beim Aufstrahlen der Sonne) '" This takes the phrase literally, as Mark appears to take it in his extant text

[3] Exod xiv 27 "when the morning appeared," lit "toward the appearance of (לפנות) the morning" (Walton "ad respiciendum mane") is rendered in LXX πρὸς ἡμέραν, Vulg "primo diluculo" *Hor Heb.* on Mk xvi 2, explaining Ps xxii tit "the Hind of the

THE ANNOUNCEMENT

Origen connects Matthew's account of the visit of the women with a promise in Exodus "In the morning ye shall see the glory of the Lord[1]," and it seems natural that Luke, in selecting his substitute for the two Marcan phrases—one of which was certainly vague while the other seemed inaccurate—would be influenced by the Philonian account of the Deliverance of Israel "*in deep dawn*"—a beautiful expression suggestive of the light of joy shortly to come after the darkness of sorrow

Why did not John accept this expression? Why does he, alone of the Evangelists, introduce the ill-omened term "darkness"? We may be sure he does not introduce it without good reason, or without something more than a literal meaning, as when he writes "*and it was night*" immediately after saying that Judas "went out straightway[2]" He probably has in view that kind of darkness which he mentions in his Prologue "The light shineth in darkness and the darkness overcame it not[3]." He is now bringing his readers face to face with an apparent contradiction of his own statement The Light of the

Morning," mentions four phrases for the dawn which "might not improperly suit the four phrases of the evangelists" He quotes from *J Berach* fol 2 3 a story of two Rabbis who "saw *the hind of the morning*, that its light spread (*sic*) the sky," and one of them said "Such shall be the redemption of Israel" *Tehill* on "The Hind of the Morning" refers to Hab iii 19 (which see) and works the comment fancifully round to the Deliverance at the Red Sea

[1] See Origen on Exod. xvi 6—7 (Lomm ix 84—5) where he says that "*evening*" and "*morning*" in Exod correspond to Mt xxviii. 1 "*vespere* sabbati quae *lucescit* in prima sabbati" Then he answers the question "Quomodo mane gloria ejus visa est?" by saying that it referred to a coming of "*other women*" —"Cum venissent *aliae mulieres* prima sabbati valde mane"

[2] Jn xiii 30.

[3] Jn i 5 ἡ σκοτία αὐτὸ οὐ κατέλαβεν In Jn vi 17 σκοτία ἤδη ἐγεγόνει, it may be urged that the word is literally used So it is. But it is also used allusively. The disciples, separated from Christ, are regarded as being in spiritual darkness. Authorities, weighty enough (DN) to convince Tischendorf, read κατέλαβεν δὲ αὐτοὺς ἡ σκοτία. Doubtless it is wrong, textually But the corrupters were right in supposing that John means that "darkness" had, for a time, "overcome" the disciples. On the double meaning of κατέλαβεν see *Joh. Voc.* 1735 *e—g*

OF CHRIST'S RESURRECTION

World appeared to be extinguished and the "darkness" seemed to have "overcome" it, both in the tomb, and in the hearts of the disciples. John also has in view, as we shall see hereafter, the earliest Biblical mention of "darkness," "The earth was waste and void, and *darkness* was upon the face of the deep[1]." This was in the first Genesis. And the apparent and temporary triumph of chaos and disorder seemed repeated in the second Genesis, when the Saviour's body lay bound in funeral bandages and His head was hidden—covered with a face-cloth that had not yet been "wrapped up" and gathered "into one place[2]."

§ 4. *Mark's peculiar tradition about "the stone"*

The three Synoptists agree in a tradition that connects "rolling-away" with "the stone" at the entrance of the tomb, but Mark puts it interrogatively ("who shall *roll-away*?") whereas Matthew ("an angel *rolled-away*") and Luke ("they found the stone *rolled-away*") put it affirmatively; when Mark comes to his affirmative he words it differently. "And having-looked-up (*or*, having-regained-their-sight), they behold the stone (lit.) *rolled-upward, for it was very great*[3]." John has a different word ("seeth the stone *taken-away* from the tomb[4]").

---

[1] Gen i 2
[2] Jn xx 7, on which see below, p 670 foll.

[3]
Mk xvi 3—4	Mt xxviii 2	Lk xxiv 2
καὶ ἔλεγον πρὸς ἑαυτάς Τίς ἀποκυλίσει ἡμῖν τὸν λίθον ἐκ τῆς θύρας τοῦ μνημείου, καὶ ἀναβλέψασαι θεωροῦσιν ὅτι ἀνακεκύλισται ὁ λίθος, ἦν γὰρ μέγας σφόδρα	καὶ ἰδοὺ σεισμὸς ἐγένετο μέγας ἄγγελος γὰρ Κυρίου καταβὰς ἐξ οὐρανοῦ καὶ προσελθὼν ἀπεκύλισε τὸν λίθον καὶ ἐκάθητο ἐπάνω αὐτοῦ	εὗρον δὲ τὸν λίθον ἀποκεκυλισμένον ἀπὸ τοῦ μνημείου

For textual variations in Mark, see below, p 667

[4] Jn xx. I Τῇ δὲ μιᾷ τῶν σαββάτων Μαρία ἡ Μαγδαληνὴ ἔρχεται πρωὶ σκοτίας ἔτι οὔσης εἰς τὸ μνημεῖον, καὶ βλέπει τὸν λίθον ἠρμένον ἐκ τοῦ μνημείου. It may be urged that ἠρμένον might mean "*taken up*" It might, if the grave had been of the nature of a pit But note the use of αἴρειν in Jn xi 39 ἄρατε τὸν λίθον, following ἦν δὲ σπήλαιον, καὶ λίθος ἐπέκειτο ἐπ' αὐτῷ The context there indicates that the stone (see Westcott) was "laid *against*," not "*on*," the opening of the cave, being, as Nonnus says, "an imitation of a *door*." The same thing—namely, that the tomb was a cave and not a pit—is indicated

THE ANNOUNCEMENT

Going back to Hebrew traditions about the "rolling" of "stones," we find that in only one of these—the rolling-away of a stone from a well—does LXX use the word "*roll-away*[1]" In another, the rolling is hostile[2]. In another, the stone appears to be a rudimentary altar[3] There is also the "rolling-away" of "the reproach of Egypt," at a place said to be hence called "Gilgal[4]." This last seems applicable by Christians to the rolling-away of "the stumbling-block of the cross" (regarded as "a stone of stumbling"). But it is rendered by LXX "taking-away," and this might hinder its application for Christian writers conversant with Greek and knowing comparatively little of Hebrew

It is perhaps for this reason that Origen illustrates the "taking-away" of the gravestone at the raising of Lazarus, not by reference to "Gilgal," but from Jacob's "*rolling-away the stone*" from the well in Genesis And he makes a distinction. The "*taking-away*" is permanent, he says "It was necessary that the stone from the tomb should be altogether *taken-away* and not rolled again [into its place]". but "in the case of the well, the stone is not utterly *taken-away* but only *rolled-away*[5]"

---

here in all the Gospels but one, twice by Mark (xvi 5, 8) εἰσελθοῦσαι εἰς τὸ μνημεῖον and ἐξελθοῦσαι, once by Luke (xxiv 3, 9) εἰσελθοῦσαι, ὑποστρέψασαι, but not at all by Matthew (xxviii 8) ἀπελθοῦσαι It is most clearly recognised in detail by John

[1] Gen xxix. 3, 8, 10 ἀποκυλίω. The Heb for "rolling" a stone is גלל A different word, אבך, is used in Is ix 18 "*roll [upward]* in thick clouds of smoke," applied to the vanishing of the wicked (LXX confused).

[2] Josh x 18 "Roll great stones unto the mouth of the cave, and set men by it to keep them [i e the hostile kings]," LXX κυλίσατε

[3] 1 S xiv 33 "Roll a great stone unto me," LXX κυλίσατε

[4] Josh v 9 "This day have I *rolled-away* (גלל) the reproach of Egypt from off you Wherefore the name of that place was called Gilgal (גלגל) . ." Here LXX has ἀφεῖλον, "I took away," so that the word does not lend itself to Christian applications of the term "rolling." Early Christian writers have abundantly used the context, so far as it refers to circumcision with knives of "*stone*," but not as to the "rolling," see below

[5] Origen *Comm Joann* xxviii 2 after quoting Jn xi. 39 ἄρατε τὸν λίθον and Gen. xxix 2—10 ἀπεκύλισε, proceeds Εἰ δὲ δύνασαι

Immediately after these words, where we might expect some reference to the "*rolling-away*" of the stone at the Lord's tomb, there is a great gap in Origen's commentary. Nor has he left any comment on the tradition of Mark "they behold the stone *rolled-upward*"

Passing to the Greek word for "*rolling-up*" we find that it is non-occurrent in LXX and very rare in Greek of any kind; but Dionysius of Halicarnassus and Lucian use it either about Sisyphus "*rolling-up* a stone" toward a hill-top, or in allusion to that myth[1]. Also Dionysius Areopagita, speaking of the Hebrew Gilgal, says "Now this in Hebrew signifies *rollings-up* and revelations[2]." We cannot suppose that Mark, having used the easy and natural word "*roll-away*," now uses a different and much rarer and much more difficult word, "*roll-up*," without good reason. Every Greek reader familiar with the story of Sisyphus would take the phrase to mean "*roll* the stone *upwards*" There is no clear instance of the word meaning "roll *back*[3]."

ἐπιστῆσαι, τί δήποτε ἐπὶ μὲν τοῦ σπηλαίου οὐ κεκύλισται ὁ ἐπικείμενος αὐτῷ λίθος, ἀλλὰ αἴρεται· ἐπὶ δὲ τοῦ φρέατος οὐ παντελῶς αἴρεται, ἀλλὰ μόνον ἀποκυλίεται. Ἐχρῆν πάντη μὲν ἀρθῆναι τὸν ἀπὸ τοῦ μνημείου λίθον, καὶ μὴ πάλιν κυλισθῆναι· τὸν δὴ ἐπὶ τοῦ φρέατος ἀποκυλισθῆναι μόνον προείρηται γὰρ ὅτι ἀπε... Here follows what the editors call "lacuna ingens"

[1] Ἀνακυλίω. See *Corrections* 527 c referring to Lucian (vol. ii. 925, *De Luct.* 8) and Dion Hal (*De Comp Verb*, Reiske, vol v. p 139) and apparently Plut *Mor* 304 (unless we are to read κατακυλίσαντες)

[2] Steph. *Thes*. (ἀνακυλισμός) quotes Dionys Areop *De coel. hierarch.* xv 9 Γὲλ Γὲλ τοῦτο δὲ καθ' Ἑβραΐδα ἀνακυλισμοὺς καὶ ἀνακαλύψεις σημαίνει

[3] See *Evang Petr* § 9 ὁ δὲ λίθος ἐκεῖνος ὁ βεβλημένος ἐπὶ τῇ θύρᾳ ἀφ' ἑαυτοῦ κυλισθεὶς ἐπεχώρησε παρὰ μέρος. The editors suggest ὑπεχώρησε. The stone seems here personified (ἀφ' ἑαυτοῦ). Perhaps ἐπεχώρησε is used, as with a personal subject, to mean "*made a concession*," "*yielded.*" Παρὰ μέρος is rendered by the editors "*to one side*"

The context § 10 also personifies the Cross. It "follows" Jesus and two ascending "men (ἄνδρας)" that bear Him upward above the heavens, and it replies "Yea," to the question "Hast thou preached to them that sleep [in death]?"

See below, p 669, n 1, for a personification of the Well in Numbers (xxi 17) "Spring up, O well" and for traditions about the "rolling" of the stone, or rock, that contained the "well," which "followed" Israel in the wilderness.

THE ANNOUNCEMENT

Mark's use of the word suggests a combination of two metaphors (1) the rolling *away* of a barrier that prevents free passage, (2) the rolling *up* and vanishing of clouds that prevent free vision The latter recalls Isaiah's description of the wicked as being "rolled [upward] in thick clouds of smoke[1]," and the worldliness of the worldly-minded might be likened to such "clouds" The two metaphors together indicate a hostile influence that hinders the soul of man on earth from looking up to, and mounting up to, the things in the heaven of heavens

In Luke, later on, describing the two disciples journeying to Emmaus, we find that, until their hearts were prepared to receive the vision of the risen Saviour, not even the presence of His bodily form, nor even a prolonged conversation with Him, enabled them to discern Him, until "He took the loaf, and blessed it, and brake, and gave to them And their eyes were opened and they knew him[2]" .

This view—that is to say, the assumption of the need of preparation—accords with Matthew's account of the "keepers" at the grave of Jesus The Gospel of Peter, it is true, describes the keepers as seeing, not only two descending figures—descending and entering the tomb—but also a third, borne on their shoulders when they issue from the tomb and ascend to heaven[3]. But Matthew differs Matthew represents an angel as descending and rolling away the stone and inviting the women to enter the tomb, and the keepers as being "terrified by the fear *of him*." But "him" means "the angel[4]." In Matthew, the keepers do not see Jesus Matthew's whole narrative about the "keepers" is probably non-historical, but it is less untrue to fact than the narrative in the Gospel of Peter. An ancient Version of Mark contains a long substitute for, or parallel to, the "*looking up*," in which "angels" are described as "descending from heaven," and others "rising in brightness," and then

---

[1] See above, p 664, n 1.

[2] Lk xxiv 30—31

[3] See *Evang Petr* § 10 τρεῖς ἄνδρας, καὶ τοὺς δύο τὸν ἕνα ὑπορθοῦντας, καὶ σταυρὸν ἀκολουθοῦντα αὐτοῖς

[4] Mt. xxviii 2 foll. ἄγγελος γὰρ Κυρίου...ἀπεκύλισε...ἦν δὲ ἡ εἰδέα αὐτοῦ ..ἀπὸ δὲ τοῦ φόβου αὐτοῦ ἐσείσθησαν οἱ τηροῦντες....

"there was light¹" This at all events confirms the view that the original on which our Mark was based implied a vision

In Mark's tradition "And having looked up, they behold that the stone is rolled-upwards, *for* it was very great," it is difficult to believe that *"for"* could imply "they could not help 'beholding' the fact, *because* of its size" Codex D substitutes "And they come and find the stone rolled-away," omitting *"for it was very great"* SS has "And they were saying in themselves 'Now who hath rolled [away] for us the stone of the tomb? *Because it was great exceedingly,'"* and similarly the Gospel of Peter "They were saying...'But who will roll away for us also the stone...? *For the stone was great, and we fear...'²"* In Mark's previous description of the "rolling-on" of the "stone" by Joseph, at the entrance of the tomb, the text of the parallel Luke omits "rolling," but D has "He placed on the tomb a stone that scarce twenty [men] could roll³"—which sounds like Homeric poetry. Both Hebrew and Aramaic might connect "a *great* stone" with *"rolling"* in a technical phrase liable to be misunderstood by Greeks. In Ezra the only two mentions of "rolling" are in the phrase "stones of *rolling*⁴" In neither instance does the

---

¹ Mk xvi 4 (txt) καὶ ἀναβλέψασαι.. μέγας σφόδρα Codex *k* "Subito autem ad horam tertiam tenebrae diei factae sunt per totum orbem terrae et descenderunt de caelis angeli et surgent (? surgentes) in claritate uiui dī simul ascenderunt cum eo et continuo lux facta est Tunc illae accesserunt ad monimentum et uident reuolutum lapidem fuit enim magnus nimis"

Perhaps "ad horam tertiam" might be intended to mean "[up] to the third hour," *i e* for as much as three hours, the duration of the darkness mentioned in Mk xv 33 "Rising (surgentes)" and "ascending (ascenderunt cum eo)" may be a version of the tradition in *Evang Petr* § 10 quoted above "Lux facta est" agrees with *Evang. Petr* § 6 τότε ἥλιος ἔλαμψε.

² *Diatess* also transposes See Burkitt, vol ii pp 241—2

³ Lk xxiii 53 (D) και θεντος αυτου επεθηκε τω μνημειω λειθον ον μογις εικοσι εκυλιον, *d* "et posito eo inposuit in monumento lapidem quem uix uiginti mouebant" Μόγις does not occur in canon LXX. It is most frequent in epic poetry

⁴ Ezr v 8, vi 4 (Gesen 1086 *b*) אבן גלל *"stones of rolling*, too heavy for carrying" In Ezr. v 8, LXX has *"elect (ἐκλεκτοί)* stones"

THE ANNOUNCEMENT

LXX render the word literally This idiom reveals probabilities of plays on the word "stone" in Christian traditions, such as we find suggested in the Petrine Epistle[1], and accumulated in the commentary of Ephrem Syrus on the stone that closed the Lord's sepulchre[2] Even before Christ's

---

(comp 1 Pet ii 6) and Rashi explains it as "marble," as also does Walton, Vulg "impolito" The parall 1 Esdr vi 9 has "polished, costly (ξυστῶν πολυτελῶν) stones" In Ezr vi 4 LXX omits it, having simply λίθινοι (but A + κραταιοί) parall to 1 Esdr vi. 24 λιθίνων ξυστῶν

[1] 1 Pet ii 2—3 "As newborn babes, long ye for *the spiritual milk* ..if ye have *tasted* that the Lord is gracious, unto whom coming, *a living stone*," is followed by *ib* 6 "*corner-stone, elect, precious*," thus rapidly introducing a new metaphor To Jews "*elect* stone" might suggest Ezra's "stone of *rolling*" The rapid transition from the metaphor of a rocky fountain for drinking to a vast stone for building becomes explicable on the hypothesis that Peter was familiar with Jewish poetic traditions about the "following" Fountain which might perhaps be called (Gen xlix 24) "the Stone of Israel." "Stone" (אבן) usually λίθος, but here rendered (*Oxf Conc*) by LXX κατισχύσας, is quite different in Hebrew from either of the two words (סלע, Numb xx 8 foll , צור, Exod xvii 6) meaning the water-giving "rock," but the LXX renders both סלע and צור by πέτρα, which might be interchanged with πέτρος and confused with λίθος In Is. viii 14 "for (a) a stone (אבן) of collision and for (b) a rock (צור) of stumbling," LXX (quoted in Rom ix 33, 1 Pet. ii 8) has (a) λίθος, (b) πέτρα Rashi says "צור est אבן, i e lapis," identifying the two Hebrew words

Rashi, on Gen xlix 24 אבן, says that "according to the Kabbala it means אב and בן," i e "father and son" In Ps cxviii 22 "*the stone* that the builders rejected," the Targum has "*the child* (טליא)," see *Son* 3594 c

Comp. *Orac. Sibyll* viii 313 on the "immortal fountain" revealed by the risen Saviour —

   Καὶ τότ' ἀπὸ φθιμένων ἀναλύσας, εἰς φάος ἥξει,
   Πρῶτος ἀναστάσεως κλητοῖς ἀρχὴν ὑποδείξας,
   Ἀθανάτου πηγῆς ἀπολουσάμενοι [?-οις] ὑδάτεσσι
   Τὰς πρότερον κακίας

[2] Ephrem, in his comment on the stone at the Lord's sepulchre, alludes successively to three "stones" of O T in the following· "Lapis positus est ad ostium sepulchri, lapis ad lapidem, ut lapis custodiret (Ps cxviii 22) lapidem, quem rejecerunt aedificantes. Lapis, qui manibus apprehendebatur, appositum (*sic*) est, ut

birth it is probable that traditions about "the *rolling stone of Miriam* (i e of Mary)" were current in Jewish poetry and were in Paul's mind when he wrote that Israel "drank from a spiritual rock that followed them and the rock was Christ[1]."

John, by substituting "taken-away" for "rolled-upward" or "rolled-away," puts aside Synoptic variations as to the "rolling" of "the stone" But he curiously introduces another kind of "rolling" altogether, in connection, not with the stone outside the grave, but with the "napkin" about Christ's head, inside the grave, which he describes as "*rolled up*" or "*wrapped up*," in a place by itself. This is important enough to deserve separate consideration

---

includeret illum lapidem, qui (Dan ii 45) sine manu excisus est. Lapis, super quem angelus sedit, appositus est, ut illum lapidem includeret, quem (Gen xxviii 11) Jacob sub capite suo posuit .."

Gen *r* (on Gen xxix 3) gives several interpretations of the "stone" at Jacob's well, mostly good, *e g.* the Sanhedrin, the Shechinah, the Merit of the Patriarchs, but one bad, the Evil Impulse

[1] I Cor x 4 ἔπινον γὰρ ἐκ πνευματικῆς ἀκολουθούσης πέτρας ἡ πέτρα δὲ ἦν ὁ Χριστός It is hardly possible to believe that Paul could have inserted "following" so abruptly unless he was aware of some tradition like that in Onkelos (Numb xxi 17 foll) about the well that was as it were personified in the appeal "*Spring up*, O well" — (*Indices to Diatessarica* p li) "In the wilderness *was it* [*i e* the Well] *given to them* (Heb *Mattanah*), and *from* [*the time*] *that it was given to them* (Heb *from Mattanah*) it descended along with them *to the rivers* (Heb *to Nahaliel*) " The LXX avoids the personification by rendering עלי "*spring up*," as if it were עלי, "*upon*," ἐπὶ τοῦ φρέατος It is not necessary to suppose that Paul insisted on the Jewish poetical version as literally true But he uses it in order to insist that the "following rock" is a spiritual one The emphasis is on "spiritual," as if he wrote "'A following rock,' if you like to use the language of our Jewish songs, but in any case, a *spiritual* rock "

Wetstein (on 1 Cor x 4), besides many other passages describing Miriam's well as walking or moving, quotes *Numb r* (on Numb 1 1, Wu p. 3) in which it is described as "rolling" —"Quomodo comparatus fuit illi puteus? Fuit sicut petra, sicut alveus apum et globosus et volutavit se, et ivit cum ipsis in itineribus ipsorum "

669 (Mark xv. 47—xvi. 4)

THE ANNOUNCEMENT

§ 5   *"Rolled up in a place by itself," in John*[1]

The Greek, more literally rendered, means "Apart, rolled up [and cast] into one place[2]" It implies, 1st, separation, 2nd, rolling up into a compact form, 3rd, relegation ("to one place") capable of implying a kind of imprisonment or constraint   The only instance in Scripture of the rolling up of a covering into a compact form occurs where Elijah "took his mantle and *wrapped it together* and smote the waters" of Jordan, so that they were "divided," and the prophet "went over on dry ground[3]"   This action of Elijah is connected in Jewish Midrash with the act of God who "bound the waters in his garment"; and the cleaving of the waters of the Jordan by Elijah is mentioned along with the cleaving of the waters of the Red Sea by Moses[4].   And these actions point back to the original cleaving of the waters in the Creation, where God says, "Let the waters... be gathered together *unto one place* and let the dry land appear[5]"   The waters are regarded in Jewish

---

[1] Jn xx 7 καὶ θεωρεῖ τὰ ὀθόνια κείμενα, καὶ τὸ σουδάριον ὃ ἦν ἐπὶ τῆς κεφαλῆς αὐτοῦ, οὐ μετὰ τῶν ὀθονίων κείμενον, ἀλλὰ χωρὶς ἐντετυλιγμένον εἰς ἕνα τόπον

[2] *"Into one place"* occurs, in O T, about (Gen 1 9) the gathering of the waters (LXX "into one congregation"), Eccles iii 20, vi 6 the dead ("all go *to one place*")   Origen (on Gen 1 9) regards the waters as a covering that we are to "cast off from us"

[3] 2 K ii 8 "wrapped it together (εἴλησεν)"   Εἰλεῖν occurs only four times altogether in LXX (*Oxf Conc*), and thrice with *v r* Mk xv 46 ἐνείλησεν is represented in *Evang Petr* § 6 by εἴλησε

[4] See *Numb r* (Wu pp 292—3) quoting Prov xxx. 4 "who bindeth the waters in (ב) his (*lit* a) garment" τίς συνέστρεψεν ὕδωρ ἐν ἱματίῳ, Theod ἐνέδησεν.   The answer is (1) God (Job xxvi 8), (2) Elijah (2 K ii 8), (3) Moses (Exod xv 8 "The floods stood upright as a heap...") and sim *Prov r* (on Prov. xxx 4), etc

[5] Gen 1 9   R. Eliezer represents God as saying (*Mechilt* on Exod xiv 15, Wu p 93) "*If I made the sea dry land for the first man, who was but one* (Gen 1 9), should I not make dry land for the people of the holy ones...?"   Comp *Pirkè de R Eliezer* (ed Friedlander, p 330) "On the day when He said (Gen 1 9) Let the *waters.* , on that very day were the waters [*i e* of the Red Sea] congealed, and they were made into twelve valleys, corresponding to the twelve tribes...."

670   (Mark xv 47—xvi. 4)

OF CHRIST'S RESURRECTION

tradition as rebellious, desiring to "turn again and cover the earth[1]" Rashi says that the "one place" into which they are "gathered" is "the ocean[2]" This was believed to encircle the world, and Josephus implies the encircling when he describes the Creation[3] Nonnus here attaches to the Johannine *soudarion*, or face-cloth, an epithet meaning "rolled into itself" which he elsewhere attaches to "Ocean[4]"

It may be added that the same passage in Proverbs that asks "Who hath bound the waters in a garment?" asks also "Who hath ascended up into the heaven and descended?" This all early Christians would naturally apply (as Jerome does) to the death and resurrection of Christ Elijah did *not* "bind" the waters "*into*" a garment But the same Hebrew preposition that means "*in*," or "*into*," is also regularly used to mean "*with*" or "*by means of*" Playing on this double meaning, Jews might say that Elijah, *by means of* his garment—like Moses by means of his rod—bound or constrained the waters of the Jordan to part asunder and make a path for him, that he might go onward to the place where he was to ascend to heaven

Similarly Christians might regard Jesus as "wrapping up" into a compact form the covering that had been placed on His face, that He might smite therewith the waters of Death and constrain them to let Him pass across to preach the Gospel to the spirits imprisoned in Sheol We must not be surprised if here in the Fourth Gospel, as often in the Prophets, there is a mixture of metaphors that are not quite consistent The face-cloth is regarded in two aspects, first, and directly, as the discarded "covering," the "waters" of

---

[1] Ps civ 9, comp Rev xxi 1 "and the sea is no more," as an illustration of Jewish thought in general about the sea, as a disorderly element.

[2] Rashi on Gen 1 9 "congregavit illas [*i e* aquas] in Oceano"

[3] Joseph *Ant.* 1 1. 1 ἴστησι τὴν γῆν ἀναχέας περὶ αὐτὴν τὴν θάλασσαν, comp Clem Alex 784

[4] See Steph *Thes* quoting nearly 30 instances of αὐτοέλικτος in Nonnus and none from any earlier author The first is from *Dion.* 1. 495 στέφος αὐτοέλικτον...Ὠκεανὸν..

THE ANNOUNCEMENT

death and darkness, gathered "into one place"; but secondly, and indirectly, as the garment of Elijah that is rolled into a rod of power and constrains the waters "into one place."

This view of the rolling away of the face-cloth "into one place"—as being equivalent to "rolling up out of the way," or "destroying"—may be illustrated by Isaiah's prophecy concerning the destruction of "the veil that is spread over all nations," which is connected with a swallowing up of death— "He will destroy (*lit* swallow up) in this mountain *the face of the covering that is cast over all peoples,* and *the veil that is spread over all nations;* he hath swallowed up death for ever, and the Lord God will wipe away tears from off all faces, and the reproach of his people shall he take away from off all the earth[1]" When the face-cloth, or "napkin," was placed on the face of Christ, Death seemed to have triumphed visibly and materially over the Prince of Life, casting "a veil over all nations," while thus "covering" the countenance of their Saviour Death, it might be said, had "swallowed up" life for ever, bringing "tears" for all faces, and riveting on mankind the "reproach" of having fallen from their Creator's image into the likeness of Satan But by the Resurrection, all this was reversed. Death, the swallower, was itself "swallowed up." And as, by the hand of the first Jesus, God "*rolled away the reproach of Egypt*" for the first Israel in Gilgal[2], so, by the second Jesus, God typically *rolled away* from the second Israel the *reproach* of being bondsmen to Egyptian darkness and sin— rolling away the covering or veil from the Saviour's face and casting it aside, "apart, into one place" Then, after no long interval, the Saviour typically fulfilled the second part of Isaiah's prophecy when He "wiped away tears" from the face of sorrowing humanity personified in Mary Magdalene[3].

---

[1] Is xxv 7—8, comp 2 Cor iii 15, 1 Cor xv 54

[2] Josh v 9 "And the Lord said unto Joshua, This day have I rolled away the reproach of Egypt from off you Wherefore the name of that place was called Gilgal, unto this day."

[3] Jn xx 11—17.

OF CHRIST'S RESURRECTION

§ .6. "*A young man,*" in Mark[1]

The Hebrew for the Marcan "young-man," or "youth," most frequently corresponding to the Greek in the Old Testament, and given here by Delitzsch, is almost always in the

---

[1] Mk xvi. 5—8 (R V)

(5) And entering into the tomb, they saw a young man sitting on the right side, arrayed in a white robe, and they were amazed

(6) And he saith unto them, Be not amazed ye seek Jesus, the Nazarene, which hath been crucified · he is risen, he is not here behold, the place where they laid him !

(7) But go, tell his disciples and Peter, He goeth before you into Galilee · there shall ye see him, as he said unto you.

(8) And they went out, and fled from the tomb, for trembling and astonishment had come upon them and they said nothing to any one,

Mt. xxviii 2—10 (R.V)

(2) ...an angel of the Lord .came... and sat.

(3) His appearance was as lightning, and his raiment white as snow

(4) And for fear of him the watchers did quake, and became as dead men

(5) And the angel answered and said unto the women, Fear not ye for I know that ye seek Jesus, which hath been crucified

(6) He is not here, for he is risen, even as he said. Come, see the place where the Lord (*many anc auth* where he) lay.

(7) And go quickly, and tell his disciples, He is risen from the dead, and lo, he goeth before you into Galilee, there shall ye see him lo, I have told you

(8) And they departed quickly from the tomb with fear and great joy, and ran to bring his disciples word

(9) And behold,

Lk. xxiv. 3—11 (R V)

(3) And they entered in, and found not the body of the Lord Jesus (*some anc auth omit* of the Lord Jesus)

(4) And it came to pass, while they were perplexed thereabout, behold, two men stood by them in dazzling apparel

(5) And as they were affrighted, and bowed down their faces to the earth, they said unto them, Why seek ye the living (*lit* him that liveth) among the dead?

(6) He is not here, but is risen (*some anc. auth. om* He..... risen) remember how he spake unto you when he was yet in Galilee,

(7) Saying that the Son of man must be delivered up into the hands of sinful men, and be crucified, and the third day rise again

(8) And they remembered his words,

(9) And returned from the tomb (*some anc auth om* from the tomb), and told all these things to the eleven, and to all the rest

THE ANNOUNCEMENT

plural, or used generically as in "youth and greybeard[1]"

Mt xvi 5—8 (R V.) contd	Mt. xxviii 2—10 (R V.) contd	Lk xxiv 3—11 (R V) contd
for they were afraid	Jesus met them, saying, All hail. And they came and took hold of his feet, and worshipped him (10) Then saith Jesus unto them, Fear not go tell my brethren that they depart into Galilee, and there shall they see me.	(10) Now they were Mary Magdalene, and Joanna, and Mary the [mother] of James and the other women with them told these things unto the apostles (11) And these words appeared in their sight as idle talk, and they disbelieved them

Jn xx 11—13, 17—18 (R V) (11) But Mary was standing without at the tomb weeping so, as she wept, she stooped and looked into the tomb, (12) and she beholdeth two angels in white sitting, one at the head, and one at the feet, where the body of Jesus had lain (13) And they say unto her, Woman, why weepest thou? She saith unto them, Because... (17) Jesus saith to her, Touch me not (or, Take not hold on me), for I am not yet ascended unto the Father but go unto my brethren, and say to them, I ascend unto my Father and your Father, and my God and your God (18) Mary Magdalene cometh and telleth the disciples, I have seen the Lord, and [how that] he had said these things unto her

Mk xvi. 5	Mt xxviii 2—4	Lk xxiv 3—5 a
καὶ εἰσελθοῦσαι (marg. ἐλθοῦσαι) εἰς τὸ μνημεῖον εἶδον νεανίσκον καθήμενον ἐν τοῖς δεξιοῖς περιβεβλημένον στολὴν λευκήν, καὶ ἐξεθαμβήθησαν	καὶ ἰδοὺ σεισμὸς ἐγένετο μέγας ἄγγελος γὰρ Κυρίου καταβὰς ἐξ οὐρανοῦ καὶ προσελθὼν ἀπεκύλισε τὸν λίθον καὶ ἐκάθητο ἐπάνω αὐτοῦ. ἦν δὲ ἡ εἰδέα αὐτοῦ ὡς ἀστραπὴ καὶ τὸ ἔνδυμα αὐτοῦ λευκὸν ὡς χιών ἀπὸ δὲ τοῦ φόβου αὐτοῦ ἐσείσθησαν οἱ τηροῦντες καὶ ἐγενήθησαν ὡς νεκροί	εἰσελθοῦσαι δὲ οὐχ εὗρον τὸ σῶμα [[τοῦ κυρίου Ἰησοῦ]] καὶ ἐγένετο ἐν τῷ ἀπορεῖσθαι αὐτὰς περὶ τούτου καὶ ἰδοὺ ἄνδρες δύο ἐπέστησαν αὐταῖς ἐν ἐσθῆτι ἀστραπτούσῃ ἐμφόβων δὲ γενομένων αὐτῶν καὶ κλινουσῶν τὰ πρόσωπα εἰς τὴν γῆν....

Jn xx. 11—12 Μαρία δὲ ἱστήκει πρὸς τῷ μνημείῳ ἔξω κλαίουσα. ὡς οὖν ἔκλαιεν παρέκυψεν εἰς τὸ μνημεῖον, καὶ θεωρεῖ δύο ἀγγέλους ἐν λευκοῖς καθεζομένους, ἕνα πρὸς τῇ κεφαλῇ καὶ ἕνα πρὸς τοῖς ποσίν, ὅπου ἔκειτο τὸ σῶμα τοῦ Ἰησοῦ.

[1] Νεανίσκος in LXX = בחור (37), נער (25), and other words less frequently Heb בחור (Gesen 104 b) means "choice" and hence "*young man* (choice, in the prime of manhood)" It is never used to represent "man" when Heb mentions "man" to describe an angel

OF CHRIST'S RESURRECTION

This, and its rejection by all the other Evangelists, suggest that it may be an error. If it is, we naturally look, in such a writer as Mark, to see whether it may be an error of conflation, *i e.* caused by the repetition of some phrase in the context[1]. Now Mark's context has "arrayed in a *white* robe," parallel to Matthew's "his raiment *white* as snow," and John's "two angels (lit) *in white(s)*[2] sitting," and it happens that the Hebrew for "*young-man*" is almost identical with the Aramaic for "*in white,*" and the Hebrew for "*young-men*" with the Aramaic for "*in whites*[3]"

This is not all The R V margin of Matthew refers to Daniel's description of the Ancient of Days "His raiment was *white as snow*[4]." "Snow" does not occur in the New Testament except here and in Revelation "his hair white as wool, white as

---

[1] On conflation, as a characteristic of Mark, see *Clue* **128** foll, **145** foll

[2] "White garments," λευκαί, are regarded as a bad sign (except for "priests" and "slaves of Greeks") in dreams by Artemid ii. 3. Λευκὰ δὲ ἱμάτια τοῖς ἱερεῦσι μόνοις συμφέρει καὶ δούλοις Ἑλλήνων, τοῖς δὲ ἄλλοις ταραχὰς σημαίνει διὰ τὸ τοὺς ἐν ὄχλῳ ἀναστρεφομένους καὶ κρινομένους ἀνθρώπους λευκὰ ἔχειν ἱμάτια Χειροτέχναις δὲ ἀργίαν καὶ σχολήν, καὶ ὅσῳ ἂν πολυτελέστερα ᾖ τὰ ἱμάτια, τοσούτῳ πλείονα Οὐ γὰρ πρὸς ἔργῳ ὄντες οἱ ἄνθρωποι, καὶ μάλιστα οἱ τὰς βαναύσους τέχνας ἐργαζόμενοι, λευκοῖς ἱματίοις χρῶνται. Δούλοις δὲ Ῥωμαίων μόνοις ἀγαθὸν τοῖς εὖ πράσσουσι, τοῖς δὲ ἄλλοις πονηρόν Ἐλέγχει γὰρ τοὺς κακῶς πράσσοντας, διά τε τὸ τὴν αὐτὴν τοῖς δεσπόταις ὡς ἐπὶ τὸ πλεῖστον ἔχειν ἐσθῆτα ἐπὶ τούτῳ τῷ ὀνείρῳ οὐ γίνονται ἐλεύθεροι, ὥσπερ οἱ τῶν Ἑλλήνων Ἀνδρὶ δὲ νοσοῦντι λευκὰ ἔχειν ἱμάτια θάνατον προαγορεύει διὰ τὸ τοὺς ἀποθανόντας ἐν λευκοῖς ἐκφέρεσθαι

Luke uses the phrase by itself about the "two men" in Acts 1 10 ἐν ἐσθήσεσι λευκαῖς, although here he avoids it He qualifies it in the Transfiguration (ix 29) λευκὸς ἐξαστράπτων

[3] "White [robe]" in Biblical Aramaic (Dan vii 9 See above, p 14) is (Gesen. 1092 *b*) חור, and "in a white [robe]" might be בחור, which (see above, p 674, n 1) in Heb = "young man" The pl בחורים might mean "in white(s)," ἐν λευκοῖς (Comp Bacon's *Essays* ii 18 "*Blacks* [*i e* black garments] and obsequies") Gesen 301 *a* also gives חור and חורי "white stuff" in Esth 1 6, viii 15, Is xix 9

[4] Dan vii 9 "His raiment like snow *white* (חור)," Theod τὸ ἔνδυμα αὐτοῦ ὡσεὶ χιὼν λευκόν But LXX has prob taken חור as היה "there was [to him]" *i.e* "he had" (see *Oxf Conc* for ἔχειν = היה), and hence it has ἔχων περιβολὴν ὡσεὶ χιόνα, and omits λευκόν

THE ANNOUNCEMENT

snow," borrowed from Daniel[1] It can hardly be doubted that Matthew wrote with allusion to Daniel But in Daniel the word for "white" is that very same Aramaic word which we have been just now considering The LXX omits or misrenders it, but Theodotion renders it correctly. It may be added that in ancient visions or manifestations of angels, like those to Abraham, to Lot, and to Manoah and his wife, the angels are described by the writer as "men," or spoken of by the beholder as "men," but never as "young-men[2]" These facts greatly increase the probability that Mark has here made a mistake, as to "young-man," avoided by the later Evangelists in different ways[3] But as to the garments of the visionary figures, John agrees with Mark and Matthew, as against Luke, in describing them as "white."

John also agrees with Mark and Matthew, against Luke, in describing the angel or angels as "sitting" This posture is rarely assigned to angels in Scripture[4]. It has been suggested

---

[1] Rev. i 14.

[2] Gen. xviii 2 "three *men*," addressed by Abraham (*ib* 3) as "My lord," or "O Lord," xviii 16 "the *men* looked toward Sodom," xix. 1 "and the two *angels* came to Sodom," *ib* 10, 12 "the *men*," *ib*. 15 "the *angels*," afterwards sometimes regarded as one, when speaking to Lot, and when addressed by Lot, *ib* 17—22 "When *they* had brought them forth, *he* said Escape... And Lot said unto *them*, Oh, not so, my *lord* (or, O *Lord*) ..And *he* [i e the angel] said unto him, See, *I* have accepted thee...Haste thee...for *I* cannot do anything till thou be come thither"

[3] *Evang Petr.* speaks of "a certain young man" thus § 13 καὶ ἀπελθοῦσαι εὗρον τὸν τάφον ἠνεῳγμένον καὶ προσελθοῦσαι παρέκυψαν ἐκεῖ, καὶ ὁρῶσιν ἐκεῖ τινὰ νεανίσκον καθεζόμενον μέσῳ τοῦ τάφου, ὡραῖον καὶ περιβεβλημένον στολὴν λαμπροτάτην.

This avoids λευκόν and retains νεανίσκος in a kind of apologetic phrase "a young man, if he might be so called, or, after a strange fashion" See below (p 681, n 2) quoting *Evang Petr* §§ 9—10 ἄνδρας...νεανίσκοι ..ἄνδρας

The *Acts of Pilate* § 13, in its various forms, does not mention the Marcan "young man" It mostly follows Matthew.

[4] See Judg vi. 11 "And the angel of the Lord came and sat under the oak," on which there is a comment in *Exod r.* (on Exod. xvi. 4, Wu p. 189) saying that the Lord of hosts does His will with

that, in John, the two angels "sitting in white" are regarded as cherubim But in Scripture the cherubim appear to be regarded not as sitting but as flying messengers of mercy from the Almighty who "sits on (or, between) them[1]." Chrysostom is perhaps right in saying that "the manner of their sitting," as well as their sympathetic words to Mary, invite her to question them[2] Origen sees "a kind of tropology" in all the parallel passages[3] Luke's description of "two men

---

the angels "If He will, He maketh them to sit (Judg vi 11) and sometimes He maketh them stand (Is vi 2 and Zech iii 7) and sometimes they appear in the forms of women (Zech v 9), sometimes in the forms of men (Gen xviii 2) and sometimes He maketh them winds (Ps civ 4) and sometimes a fire (ib) "

"Sitting" is the attitude of Jesus when expounding Scripture (see *Hor Heb* on Mt xiii 2 quoting *Sot* ix 15) expressly mentioned in Lk iv 20 "closed the book . and *sat down*"

[1] Gesen 500 b gives כרוב, "cherub," as (1) the living chariot of the Theophanic God Ps xviii 10, 2 S xxii 11 "and he rode upon (וירכב על) a cherub," (2) the guards of Eden, (3) the throne of the Lord of hosts in the phrase "sitting [on] the cherubim," 1 S iv 4 etc It suggests (ib 501 a) that another form of the cherubim is indicated in Is vi 2—6 the "seraphim" They are nowhere represented as sitting

Levy ii 394 b, who says that כרוב seems to be a transposition of the letters in רכוב, particip pass of "ride," quotes *Suc* 5 b "What does כרוב mean? R. Abahu said 'like (כ) a youth (רב) '" (see context). The derivation from "child" is perhaps assumed in *Baba Bathr* 99 a "Onkelos the proselyte saith *the cherubim are like children going from their master*," i e with their faces turned partly toward their master and partly toward the way wherein they were to go (see *Hor Heb* on Jn xx 12)

[2] Chrys on Jn xx 11 comments on the fact that the two angels (in John) say nothing to Mary about "rising again," but she is "gently impelled (ἤρεμα προβιβάζεται)" toward the truth by the peaceful, bright, and sympathetic aspect of the angels and by "the manifestation that they knew what had happened " Through all these things "as through a door that is being opened she was led by degrees to the conception of resurrection (διὰ δὲ τούτων ἁπάντων ὥσπερ θύρας ἀνοιγομένης κατὰ μικρὸν εἰς τὸν περὶ ἀναστάσεως ἤγετο λόγον) "

[3] Origen *Cels* v 56 He seems to assume that the one "angel of the Lord " mentioned by Matthew is the same as the " young man " mentioned by Mark, but leaves us doubtful as to the identity of the

THE ANNOUNCEMENT

standing-above," or close to, the women somewhat resembles the vision in Genesis of "three men" who appeared to Abraham and (LXX) "stood above him[1]"

As to this last vision it is noteworthy that, though "three men" are mentioned, they are addressed by Abraham as one[2], and this may have a bearing on the passages that describe the "two men" in Luke, or "two angels" in John, as speaking to the women It would be contrary to Hebrew Scripture and Jewish tradition to insist that the two divine speakers must be regarded as uttering the same words simultaneously—especially in Luke where the utterance is of considerable length. "The angel of the Lord" may be regarded as speaking through them both[3]

"two men" in Lk with the "two angels" in Jn: Οἱ μὲν γὰρ ἀναγράψαντες ἕνα, τὸν ἀποκυλίσαντα τὸν λίθον ἀπὸ τοῦ μνημείου τοῦτόν φασιν εἶναι· οἱ δὲ τοὺς δύο, τοὺς ἐπιστάντας ἐν ἐσθῆτι ἀστραπτούσῃ ταῖς γενομέναις ἐπὶ μνημεῖον γυναιξίν, ἢ τοὺς θεωρηθέντας ἔνδον ἐν λευκοῖς καθεζομένους Ἕκαστον δὲ τούτων νῦν παραδεικνύναι δυνατὸν, καὶ γεγενημένον, καὶ δηλωτικόν τινος εἶναι τροπολογίας τῆς περὶ τῶν προφαινομένων τοῖς τὴν ἀνάστασιν τοῦ λόγου θεωρεῖν παρεσκευασμένοις, οὐ τῆς παρούσης ἐστὶ πραγματείας, ἀλλὰ μᾶλλον τῶν τοῦ εὐαγγελίου ἐξηγητικῶν

"A kind of tropology, namely, that which (τῆς, so MS, not τοῖς) concerns the preliminary manifestations" (Clark "a figurative meaning existing in these phenomena") seems to mean that the various aspects of the angels, e g triumphant over the stone, youthful, brightly shining, sitting, standing-above etc , represent spiritual conceptions of resurrectional power, preparatory to the vision of the risen Saviour Himself Origen does not say (Mt) τὸν ἀποκυλίσαντα .. καὶ (Mk) καθήμενον ἐν τοῖς δεξιοῖς, which would identify the angel in Matthew with the angel (or "young-man") in Mark, yet he seems to assume their identity. On the other hand, the repeated article with "οτ" (τοὺς ἐπιστάντας .ἢ τοὺς θεωρηθέντας) may mean that he assumes one pair of angels (or "men") in Luke and another in John

[1] Gen xviii. 2 (LXX) ἱστήκεισαν ἐπάνω αὐτοῦ, R V "stood over against him" Lk xxiv 4 ἐπέστησαν αὐταῖς.

[2] See above, p 676, n. 2

[3] See Targ. Jer I on the "three men" in Gen xviii 2 foll (and sim. Jer II) "It is not possible for a ministering angel to be sent for more than one purpose at a time,—one, then, had come to make known to him that Sarah should bear a man-child, one had come to deliver Lot, and one to overthrow Sodom and Gomorrah"

Later on (Gen. xviii 10) Jer I has "And ONE of them said,

OF CHRIST'S RESURRECTION

Why does Matthew describe the angel in the phrase usually applied in the Old Testament to God Himself manifested in a temporary vision or action on earth, "the angel of the Lord[1]"? It is perhaps intended to rectify Mark's error as to the *"young man"* by shewing that this *"angel"* was of the highest order and the very representative of the Supreme. With this there accords the mention of "his raiment as white as snow"—a characteristic confined in the Old Testament to the Ancient of Days, and in the New Testament to Christ as seen in the Transfiguration[2].

A word is due to Matthew's insertion at this point "And for fear of him [*i e.* the angel] *the watchers* did quake[3]" Matthew has said before, about the soldiers guarding the Cross, "And sitting down they *watched* him there," and again, "But the centurion and those with him *watching* Jesus[4]" These uses of the word are all peculiar to Matthew, and they suggest that they may be all connected with a very difficult, if not incredible statement, peculiar to Matthew, that Pilate, at the request of the Jews, gave them a *"guard"* or *"watch"* (*koustōdia*) to guard Christ's tomb through the night[5] The word for *"guard"* or *"watch"* here used by Delitzsch in all these passages—which is indeed the regular Hebrew word for military *"guard"* or *"watch"*—is used in the above-quoted Psalm of Watching,

---

Returning I will return ..," Jer II "And He said, Returning I will return " Rashi says that the plural is used in narrative ("they ate," "they said") but the singular "in annunciation, *e g* "He said, I will return "

Jer. I introduces the "three men" as "three angels in the resemblance of men," which illustrates the Lucan "two men" as parallel to the Johannine "two angels "

[1] Mt xxviii 2 ἄγγελος Κυρίου, A V "the angel (R V an angel) of the Lord " Possibly R V is wrong See Judg ii. 1, vi 11, 22 etc where A V. "*an* angel of the Lord," LXX ἄγγελος Κυρίου, is altered by R V into *"the"* In Mt xxviii 2, SS has *"the* angel of the Lord," although in Mt 1 20, ii 13, 19, it has "*an* " In Gen xvi 7 foll LXX begins with ἄγγελος Κυρίου but has ὁ ἄγγ Κυρ afterwards But the meaning is "*the* angel of the Lord " from the first.

[2] See above, p 14.   [3] Mt xxviii. 4
[4] Mt. xxvii. 36, 54.   [5] Mt. xxvii. 65.

THE ANNOUNCEMENT

the *De Profundis*, as follows "My soul [looketh] for the Lord, more than [*those*] *watching* for (*or*, till) the morning, [yea, more than] [*those*] *watching* for (*or*, till) the morning[1]"

The LXX ("*from* the morning watch till night") has missed the meaning and led early Christian writers astray. But Aquila renders it correctly by the word regularly used in Greek to mean military "guarding" This Psalm has been found above to explain Mark's "bought spices" for the Lord, as meaning "waited" for the Lord[2] We may now use it again to explain Matthew's story about the "*watch*" or "*guard*" It appears to be no fiction, but misinterpretation, which amplified into an expanded tale—as Jewish Targums often do amplify—some simple poetic statement, such as "The women waited for the Lord *more than those watching for* (or, *till*) *the morning, yea, more than those watching for* (or *till*) *the morning*[3]." Early Christians, applying these words, after the manner of Justin Martyr, as Messianic prediction, exactly and literally to the women waiting for the Lord at His tomb on the morning of His resurrection, would naturally ask "But how about 'those watching for (*or*, till) the morning'? Were there any persons definitely appointed to watch? If so, who appointed them? And why? And what did they see?" Then they would answer their own questions by supplying details Those watching for (*or*, till) the morning were placed there by the Jews They were terrified and "became as dead men," but they saw no Saviour Only the women saw Him[4]

---

[1] Ps cxxx. 6, Field has "plus quam vigiles [expectant] tempus matutinum, vigilantes usque ad tempus matutinum" But the Heb prep ל is the same in both clauses, i e "to" or "for," LXX ἀπὸ φυλακῆς πρωΐας μέχρι νυκτός, Aq ἀπὸ φυλασσόντων τὴν πρωΐαν .. Heb שמר "watch" = φυλάσσω more than 350 times, and τηρέω (Matthew's word) 10 times See above, p 661, n 2, on the first Biblical mention of "morning watch," which Rashi connects with ministering angels

[2] See above, pp 649—52   [3] Comp Ps cxxx 6.

[4] There is some difference in the Gospels, at this point, as to fearing in consequence of the angelic visions Mark and Luke attribute amazement or fear to the women Matthew describes the "keepers" as "shaken with fear," while the angel says to the women emphatically "Do *not ye* (ὑμεῖς) fear" John mentions no fear in anyone

680 (Mark xvi. 5—8)

OF CHRIST'S RESURRECTION

It should be added that Luke, although he omits the mention of "white" apparel in connection with the "two men" that "stand-close-to (*or*, above)" the women in his Gospel, inserts it in the Acts in connection with "two men" that "stand-by" the apostles when Jesus is taken from their sight[1]. And the Gospel of Peter describes "two men" as descending and "standing-close-to (*or*, above)" the tomb, and entering in, and then "three men issuing, and the two supporting the One, and a Cross following[2]."

This, like Matthew's narrative of the guards keeping the tomb, is not to be dismissed as mere fiction. The "stone" is regarded as an enemy and the Messiah as triumphing over it. The Jews and the Gentiles combine to imprison Him. The Lord sends down His angels to fulfil His promise to His Anointed: "He shall give his angels charge over thee, ..they shall bear thee up in their hands...lest thou dash thy foot against a stone[3]."

§ 7. "*The Nazarene*," *in Mark*[4]

Mark's use of this word has been discussed in a previous volume, and it has been maintained that the original name was

---

[1] Acts i 10.

[2] *Evang Petr*. § 9 Καὶ εἶδον ἀνοιχθέντας τοὺς οὐρανοὺς καὶ δύο ἄνδρας κατελθόντας ἐκεῖθε, πολὺ φέγγος ἔχοντας, καὶ ἐπίσταντας τῷ τάφῳ ὁ δὲ λίθος ἐκεῖνος ὁ βεβλημένος ἐπὶ τῇ θύρᾳ ἀφ' ἑαυτοῦ κυλισθεὶς ἐπεχώρησε παρὰ μέρος καὶ ὁ τάφος ἠνοίγη, καὶ ἀμφότεροι οἱ νεανίσκοι εἰσῆλθον .. § 10 ὁρῶσιν ἐξελθόντας ἀπὸ τοῦ τάφου τρεῖς ἄνδρας, καὶ τοὺς δύο τὸν ἕνα ὑπορθοῦντας, καὶ σταυρὸν ἀκολουθοῦντα αὐτοῖς

Note that the writer calls the angels, ἄνδρες, . νεανίσκοι, . ἄνδρες

Evang Petr §§ 6—8 relates that the stone is rolled to the grave not by Joseph but by the elders and scribes along with the soldiers

[3] Ps xci 11—12, comp Mt iv 6, Lk iv 10—11 The fact that these words are quoted by Satan does not prove that all Christians would regard them as untrue or (like Jerome) as inapplicable to the Messiah See p 726

[4] Mk xvi 6

Mk xvi 6	Mt xxviii 5—6	Lk xxiv 5—6 a
ο δὲ λέγει αὐταῖς Μὴ ἐκθαμβεῖσθε· Ἰησοῦν ζητεῖτε τὸν Ναζαρηνὸν τὸν ἐσταυρωμένον· ἠγέρθη, οὐκ ἔστιν ὧδε	ἀποκριθεὶς δὲ ὁ ἄγγελος εἶπεν ταῖς γυναιξίν Μὴ φοβεῖσθε ὑμεῖς, οἶδα γὰρ ὅτι Ἰησοῦν τὸν ἐσταυρωμένον ζητεῖτε·	ἐμφόβων δὲ γενομένων αὐτῶν καὶ κλινουσῶν τὰ πρόσωπα εἰς τὴν γῆν εἶπαν πρὸς αὐτάς Τί ζητεῖτε τὸν ζῶντα μετὰ

THE ANNOUNCEMENT

"*Nazoraean*," meaning the *Nêtzer*, ı e. shoot, or sprout, the shoot from the root of Jesse, predicted by Isaiah, where the LXX calls it a "flower" thus, "A *flower* from the root shall *ascend* (but Heb. lit *bear fruit*)[1]" The Targum paraphrases "*a shoot* out of his *roots*" as "*Messiah from his [Jesse's] son's sons.*" But Isaiah also uses the term in a bad sense, speaking of "a nêtzer of abomination[2]" And *Sanhedrin* contains an anti-Christian story about a heretic named Nêtzer, who pleaded for his life, saying that he was the (good) "nêtzer" in the eleventh chapter of Isaiah, but received the reply that he was the (bad) "nêtzer" in the fourteenth chapter—"an abominable nêtzer" (LXX *nekros*, "corpse")[3] Other traditions indicate that Jews spoke of Christianity in a bad sense as "the kingdom of *Ben Nêtzer*[4]." Though late, they point back to an earlier period when the Jews would read *Nêtzer* into the term "Nazoraean"—some for good and some for ill, and some in a state of suspense, as perhaps when Paul heard the words "I am *Jesus, the Nêtzer*, whom thou art persecuting[5]"

Mk xvı 6 contd	Mt xxvııı 5—6 contd	Lk xxıv 5—6 a contd.
ἴδε ὁ τόπος ὅπου ἔθηκαν αὐτόν.	οὐκ ἔστιν ὧδε, ἠγέρθη γὰρ καθὼς εἶπεν δεῦτε ἴδετε τὸν τόπον ὅπου ἔκειτο.	τῶν νεκρῶν, [[οὐκ ἔστιν ὧδε, ἀλλὰ ἠγέρθη]]

Comp. *Evang Petr* § 13 ὅστις ἔφη αὐταῖς Τί ἤλθατε, τίνα ζητεῖτε, μὴ τὸν σταυρωθέντα ἐκεῖνον, ἀνέστη καὶ ἀπῆλθεν· εἰ δὲ μὴ πιστεύετε, παρακύψατε καὶ ἴδετε τὸν τύπον ἔνθα ἔκειτο, ὅτι οὐκ ἔστιν· ἀνέστη γὰρ καὶ ἀπῆλθεν ἐκεῖ ὅθεν ἀπεστάλη

[1] See *Beginning* pp 309—50 "Nazarene and Nazoraean," and p 325 quoting Is xı 1

[2] Is xıv 19 "cast forth from thy sepulchre like an abominable *nêtzer* (נצר)," LXX ὡς νεκρὸς ἐβδελυγμένος. Rashi says that the Rabbis regarded this as referring to Nebuchadnezzar, whose body was taken out of his grave and destroyed lest he should come to life again. Aq renders נצר by ἰχώρ, Sym ἔκτρωμα

[3] See *Beginning* pp 318, 327 quoting *Sanhedr.* 43 *a*

[4] See Levy ı 240 *a* on "Ben Nezar," and *Hor Heb* ı 337—8 on "*Ben Nezer*"—quoting several traditions, including *Gen r* (on Gen xxxıı 11, Wu p 374) which refers to Esau, and to the horn in Dan vıı 8

[5] Acts xxıı 8.

"Nêtzer," when "Nazoraean" became identified with "Nazarene" (in the sense of "a man from Nazara"), would naturally be omitted by later Evangelists And Mark himself might feel that it required some addition to explain its double meaning To Christians it implied "shooting up" or "ascending" to life and life-giving action To Jews it had begun to imply death, and disgraceful death Such a death would be that by "hanging on a tree," or crucifying Mark (followed by Matthew) inserts here "the crucified"; but the Syriac for this word is one that in Aramaic means not only "crucified" but also "lifted up[1]" Luke, placing after "living" the word used by Isaiah (LXX *nekros*, "corpse") to express the "nêtzer of abomination," perhaps conceals an original contrast between the dead nêtzer of abomination and the living Nêtzer of Righteousness —"Why seek ye the *living* among the *dead*?"

Perhaps the original was shorter than the text now extant in any of the Synoptists. Angels in Hebrew Scripture do not as a rule make long speeches. In an empty tomb angelic gesture might express what had befallen its tenant.

§ 8. *"He is not here[2]"*

The Synoptists all agree as to the words *"He is not here,"* but they differ as to the order in which they place *"He is risen."* Also Luke omits the invitation of the women by the angels to come and see the place where Jesus lay. Going back to Biblical instances of the phrase *"he is not,"* meaning "he has disappeared," we find that the renderings of it in the Targums and LXX shew considerable variations The first relates to Enoch concerning whom the Scripture says *"He was not,* for God took him[3]*"* But the LXX has *"He was not found,"* as

---

[1] Mk xvi 6 (SS and Pesh) זְקַף, on which see Levy *Ch* 1 229 *a*, and also *Joh Gr* 2642 on "lifted up" = "crucified"

[2] In Mark, the negative "He is not here" might seem an anticlimax coming after "He is risen" Matthew and Luke put the negative first, and Luke prefixes a reproach for seeking the living with the dead For the Greek text see above, p 681, n. 4

[3] Gen. v 24 *"and he was not* (וְאֵינֶנּוּ)*"* καὶ οὐχ ηὑρίσκετο On

THE ANNOUNCEMENT

elsewhere[1] The Epistle to the Hebrews quotes it as *"not found"* and Philo comments on it[2] Perhaps Luke alludes to it in his contextual use of the word to describe what the women did, and did not, "find[3]" The Jerusalem Targum on Genesis has *"He was not with the inhabitants of the earth,* for he was withdrawn and he *ascended,"* where "ascended," in conjunction with *"he was not,"* suggests a resemblance to the above-quoted tradition of the Gospel of Peter *"He is not,* for He hath *arisen* and departed thither [*lit* there] whence He was sent[4]"

The next point to note is that the word rendered *"here"* ("he is not *here"*) as used in LXX, sometimes corresponds to a Hebrew word meaning "hither," but with similar consonants to those of the Hebrew *"behold*[5]*"* The Semitic *"He is not. Behold!"* might therefore be rendered in Greek by some as (1) *"He is not here"* This would be very natural for those who did not understand the Hebrew absolute use of *"He is not."* Others might render it literally (2) *"He is not Behold!"* Mark and Matthew appear to have combined these two renderings,

---

this use of אין see Gesen 34 *a* Gen 11 5 ("there was not a man to till the ground ") somewhat differs

[1] Ps xxxvii 10 "et adhuc paululum et *non* [*est*] (ואין) impius, et advertes super locum ejus et *non* [*est*] *ipse* (ואיננו)," LXX καὶ οὐ μὴ ὑπάρξῃ καὶ οὐ μὴ εὕρῃς also Gen. xxxvii 29, "Joseph *was not* (אין) in the pit," οὐχ ὁρᾷ (al exempl εὗρε) τὸν Ἰ ἐν τῷ λάκκῳ

[2] Heb xi 5, see Philo ii 3—4, ii 411, and *Quaest Gen ad loc* where he mentions Enoch with Moses and Elijah as "ascending "

[3] Lk xxiv 2, 3, 23, 24 has four instances of "finding" or "not finding" in connection with the tomb of Jesus Εὑρίσκω does not occur in parall Mk-Mt

[4] *Evang Petr* § 13 quoted on p 682 In ἴδετε τὸν τόπον ἔνθα ἔκειτο, ὅτι οὐκ ἔστιν, the comma before ὅτι might well be cancelled "behold the place . [how] that he is not [there] " Perhaps the writer desires to avoid the absolute use of οὐκ ἔστιν to mean "he has vanished "

[5] When ὧδε in LXX means "hither" it regularly corresponds to הנה. See Gesen 243—4 on הנה meaning "behold!" or "hither" according to pointing The first instance of ὧδε in LXX (Gen xv. 14) ἐξελεύσονται ὧδε is a Gk addition for emphasis In Judg. xvi 13 "*hitherto* (עד הנה)" = LXX ἰδού, but A ὡς νῦν In 1 S xx 21—2 הנה, "behold," occurs thrice and הֵנָּה, "hither," once, but LXX (Swete's text) has ἰδού once and ὧδε thrice

retaining "*here,*" and adding "See!" or "Come, see¹!" Luke appears to have adopted the first alone, but possibly contains some allusion to the second in his mention of "*not finding*" the body²

Passing to John, we find assigned to the angels no announcement of any kind and no invitation, nothing but "*Woman, why weepest thou?*" It is natural to assume that this can have no connection with "*he is not here,*" and to explain it by saying that John rejected the Synoptic tradition because of its ill-omened nature. "*He is not,*" in Scripture, is mostly used of the lost, or destroyed, meaning "*He* is perished"; and even when applied to Enoch, it was not explained by all the Jews in an entirely good sense³. It might therefore seem better to substitute another tradition if others were current. And there is a possibility that "weeping" might be confused with "here" in some such phrase as "Why weep?" or "Why come here?" In Zechariah, the Hebrew "*should I weep*" is represented by LXX

¹ The Heb. הנה "behold!" might imply "come hither." The Greek ὧδε would not, without a verb of motion as in Mt viii. 29. Steph. *Thes* viii. 1990 quotes Aristoph. *Nub* 690 as if ὧδε δεῦρο meant "Hither! This way!" but erroneously. ῏Ωδε might, however, be taken thus by some in a context where "come" was indicated by gesture.

² See p. 684, n. 3

³ See Gen. xlii. 13, 36, Ps xxxvii. 10, Is. xvii. 14, Jerem xxxi. 15 etc. On Gen. v. 24 "*he* [i.e. *Enoch*] *was not,*" Rashi says "He was righteous but of a vacillating mind, so that he turned toward evil. Therefore God hastened to take him away before his time, and hence .'*he was not*'—that is to say, in this world, so as to fulfil his years." The LXX paraphrases "*he was not*" as "*he was not found,*" which resembles Ps xxxvii. 36 "lo, *he was not*. yea, I sought him but *he was not found.*" But this Psalm refers to the cutting off of the wicked by God. Philo ii. 4 explains LXX "*he was not found,*" about Enoch, as denoting either (1) the casting aside of every vestige of the former sinful life, or else (2) that Enoch's new character was "of a mysterious nature (δυσεύρετον φύσει)." Comp. Philo ii. 411, where Enoch's career is referred to as "the struggles of repentance (τοὺς τῆς μετανοίας ἀγῶνας),'' and Origen (*Comm Rom* v. 1, Lomm vi. 330) "mortem...abjecit per poenitentiam." Onkelos says of Enoch "*He was not,* for the Lord did not cause him to die," Jer Targ "*He was not with the sojourners of the earth*, for he was withdrawn, and he ascended to the firmament by the Word before the Lord, and his name was called Metatron, the Great Scribe."

THE ANNOUNCEMENT

"*hath-come-in here*[1]" The error of the LXX is explained by a similarity between the letters constituting the two phrases in Hebrew, and it should be added that the Aramaic Targum has practically the same word as the Hebrew for "*weep*," so that in Aramaic as well as in Hebrew a form of "*weep*" might be confused with "*here.*" Mark may have wrongly interpreted "*weep*," or John may have wrongly interpreted "*here.*"

There would still remain the apparent discrepancy of the negation in the Synoptic "*He is not*" from the Johannine interrogative "*Why weepest thou?*" The latter, however, though it does not contain a direct negative, may be said to imply one, since "*Why* weepest thou?" in this context, might easily imply "*There is no* [*just cause for*] weeping" It is true that the Johannine angels do not add a word to shew that their question does mean this and does not mean "What is the cause of thy weeping?" But, as Chrysostom says, the attitude of the angels implies a peaceful knowledge that all is well. Taken in their setting, the words in John may recall the words in Milton's Samson Agonistes "Nothing is here for tears[2]" John might regard the grave of Jesus as the scene not of His defeat, but of a victory achieved by dying. It would be a contrast to the sad Hebrew story of the birth of Ichabod, in

---

[1] Zech vii 3 "*should-I-weep* (האבכה)" εἰσελήλυθεν ὧδε, Targ האבכי. LXX, as often, (1) does not render the interrogative ה by a Gk particle, (2) takes אב as from בוא, εἰσέρχομαι, (3) takes כה as "*here*" In Heb (Gesen 462 *a*) כה mostly means "*thus*" and rarely "*here*" But Heb פה, "here," is regularly rendered by Aram. כא, or הכא, "here", and (Levy *Ch* 1 97 *a*) Aram בכא = Heb. בכה, "*weep*" In 1 K. xix 9, 13 "What doest thou here?" the Targ. has מה לך כא? In Heb. "What do ye (fem) here?" there would not be the same juxtaposition of כ, but still the Semitic idiom "what (*lit*) [is there] to thee *here*?" indicates possibilities of confusion between "*here*" and "*weep*" in passing from Hebrew, or Aramaic, or from both, into Greek.

Some short and obscure Semitic idiom seems best adapted to explain the Synoptic variations and especially the rebuke contained in Lk "Why seek ye *the living among the dead?*" which may be an emphatic paraphrase of "*here*" meaning "What do ye *here, in this most unfit place?*"

[2] Milton, *S A* 1 1721 "Nothing is here for tears, nothing to wail."

giving birth to whom his dying mother said "Where is [our vanished] glory?" and called him "*Where-glory*[1]?" So here the angels may be supposed to mean "*Where is weeping?*" Some may be even tempted to think that John has preserved the original, which has been misinterpreted by Mark, but even those who cannot think this may find in the facts alleged above just reason for concluding that John has not invented his tradition[2]

§ 9   "*See [thou], [here is] the place,*" *in Mark*[3]

"Place," in Hebrew, has often very sacred associations and may mean the Place, or House, of God, or even in later Hebrew,

---

[1] 1 S iv 21

[2] See Ephrem on the reasons for hastening Christ's resurrection lest "the sons of the right hand" should be brought to despair (p 267) "Quam ob causam praeveniendo mentes eorum confortavit, ne conturbarentur, quoniam, ut aiunt, nec filii dextrae continuo sperabant eum ex sepulcro exiturum esse "
"Son of the right hand," Benjamin, is contrasted with "Son of my sorrow," Benoni, the name given to the babe by the dying Rachel   Comp Jn xvi 21, where the thoughts of sorrow and joy are illustrated by the metaphor of a woman in travail, and applied to Christ's death and resurrection

[3] Mk xvi 6 ἴδε, ὁ τόπος ὅπου ἔθηκαν αὐτόν, Mt xxviii 6 δεῦτε, ἴδετε τὸν τόπον ὅπου ἔκειτο, Codex D, in Mk, has ειδετε εκει τοπον αυτου οπου εθηκαν αυτο, SS, and *k*, "ecce *locus illius* ubi fuit positus," *Corb* "videte, ecce locum *ejus* ubi positus erat "
The corrupt "*his* place" resembles Clem Rom § 5 Πέτρον ὃς. ἐπορεύθη εἰς τὸν ὀφειλόμενον τόπον τῆς δόξης.. Παῦλος...εἰς τὸν ἅγιον τόπον ἐπορεύθη   (on which and other early uses of τόπος in connection with a martyr's death, see Lightf)   It would be appropriate where it meant "his [due] place," *i e* heaven, but quite inappropriate here
In Mk, ἴδε may be used as *ecce*, without necessarily presupposing "thou," but, being ambiguous, it might be corrected in Mt to ἴδετε   Evang Petr § 13 has τίνα ζητεῖτε, μὴ τὸν σταυρωθέντα ἐκεῖνον, ἀνέστη καὶ ἀπῆλθεν· εἰ δὲ μὴ πιστεύετε, παρακύψατε καὶ ἴδετε τὸν τόπον ἔνθα ἔκειτο, ὅτι οὐκ ἔστιν ἀνέστη γὰρ καὶ ἀπῆλθεν ἐκεῖ ὅθεν ἀπεστάλη   This implies—contrary to usual Christian tradition—that Jesus had already ascended to the Father in heaven   And so Aphr *Hom* 20 "He is risen and gone away to Him that sent Him "   But, if so, what time is to be assigned to the descent into Sheol and the preaching to the spirits there?

THE ANNOUNCEMENT

God Himself (since God may be regarded as His own PLACE)[1]. It is a noun *mâ-koum*, derived from the Hebrew *koum* meaning "arise" or "stand," and means literally standing-place[2] The word *koum* is used in the context "He *is risen*[3]." But the parallel Matthew, in SS, instead of the usual Aramaic word corresponding to the sacred place *mâ-koum*, has a word (supposed by some to be derived from Greek) meaning "*receptacle*[4]"

Matthew may perhaps mean "You must not regard it as Christ's 'grave' It was merely a *temporary receptacle of His body where He lay*[5] *for a short time* till He descended into Sheol, and then, returning on the morning of the third day, manifested Himself to the women. Mark implied this temporariness when he wrote, 'See, the place where *they put Him*.' But it would be more seemly to say '*put His body*' or else '*He lay*'" This would be in accordance with the usage of Matthew elsewhere; he only once uses "put" concerning the burial, and then about "*the body*," where the parallel Mark has "*him*[6]."

Luke sets aside discrimination of this kind by a paraphrase of his own, not mentioning "place," but implying that the women are searching for their Lord in the wrong place He seems to mean "The Lord Jesus is the Living One, and ye are seeking Him in the home of the dead." Previously Luke has followed Mark in saying that Joseph "put *him*[7]" in a grave, and Matthew in saying that the women beheld "how *his body*

---

[1] See *Son* on "Place" **3101** *a*, **3378** *a*, **3587**, **3589** *a* On Gen xxviii. 11 "the Place," *Gen. r* asks "Why is God called 'Place'?"

[2] Gesen 879 *b*.

[3] So Delitzsch and SS, קם (from קום) for ἠγέρθη, and Delitzsch מקום for τόπος.

[4] Mt xxviii 6 (SS) דוכתא for which Levy *Ch* 1 164 *b* (but not Krauss) suggests a Greek origin, δοχεῖον. In Mk, SS has the reg. Aram אתר (for Heb. מקום)

[5] Mt xxviii. 6 ἔκειτο, Del. שכב. This = Heb. sleep, occasionally used of "sleeping in death" (Gesen. 1012) Del also has the causative in Mk. xvi 6 "caused to sleep," but SS has, in both, a form of סום the equivalent of τίθημι, "put"

[6] Mt xxvii 60 ἔθηκεν αὐτό is parall. to Mk xv 46, Lk xxiii 53, ἔθηκεν αὐτόν, but τίθημι does not recur in Mt. as parall to Mk xv 47, xvi. 6

[7] Lk. xxiii. 53

OF CHRIST'S RESURRECTION

was (*lit*) put[1]" But now in recording the message of the angels he discards the distinctions between "being put" or "buried," or "lying [in the grave]" in order to emphasize the thought of a rebuke for seeking Jesus where He ought not to be sought.

John follows and emphasizes, after a fashion, Mark's peculiar tradition about "putting" Jesus, but not apparently Mark's and Matthew's tradition about "place." The emphasis on "putting" verges, perhaps, on irony. It is the act of Joseph and Nicodemus, who are described as "putting Jesus"—in haste, and only as a temporary expedient, but, as it seemed, firmly bound under the restraint of the grave-clothes[2] Afterwards "putting" is repeatedly mentioned by Mary Magdalene in expressing her alarm lest Jesus had been "put" somewhere by enemies[3]

As regards "place," we might perhaps have expected that John would have expanded the Marcan tradition by a contrast between Christ's unreal "place" in the grave and His real "place" in heaven. But this he could not do consistently with the words that he assigns to Jesus in the context "I am not yet ascended unto the Father[4]" He not only abstains from using the word "place" where it might have been expected ("two angels... [*in the place*] *where* the body of Jesus had lain[5]")

---

[1] Lk xxiii 55.

[2] Jn xix 42 "There then, because of the Jews' Preparation .. they put Jesus" On the restraint implied by the grave-clothes, see Chrys *ad loc*.

[3] Jn xx 2 "They have taken away the Lord out of the tomb, and we know not where they have *put* him," *ib* 13 "I know not where they have *put* him," *ib* 15 "tell me where thou hast *put* him" The repetition appears to be intended to emphasize Mary's assumption that her Master was irrevocably dead and helpless

[4] Jn xx 17

[5] Comp. Mk xvi 6 ἴδε, ὁ τόπος ὅπου ἔθηκαν αὐτόν with Mt xxviii 6 ἴδετε τὸν τόπον ὅπου ἔκειτο, Jn xx 12 ὅπου ἔκειτο τὸ σῶμα τοῦ Ἰησοῦ, and it will be perceived that a mystic might take Mk (but not Mt) as meaning secondarily and mystically (beneath the primary and literal meaning) "Look [up]! [There is] the Place where THEY have put him"—THEY meaning "the angels" (who, according to *Evang*.

THE ANNOUNCEMENT

but also uses it unexpectedly and with an appearance of superfluousness (lit "*apart* wrapped up *into one place*") If he did this deliberately, not omitting the Marcan word "place," but transposing it, for mystical reasons, to what seemed to him a more appropriate context, then it would be an instance of Johannine Intervention But even when ample allowance is made for general Johannine allusiveness, this particular allusion must be admitted to be doubtful even by those who feel assured that *some* mystical meaning is latent

The possibilities of early variation in Hebrew, Aramaic, and Greek tradition are very great in this special narrative. Great also would be the influence of motive, arising out of early discussion as to the precise nature of the announcement of the Resurrection Lastly, views as to the precise duration of the Descent into Sheol might complicate comments, and might modify, in the first place, inferences from the texts of the Gospels, and subsequently the texts themselves. It is impossible to say with confidence why the Fourth Gospel did not corroborate the Three at least so far as their common tradition "He is not here, he is risen."

In the preceding section, we arrived at the conclusion that "he is not here" might correspond to the Johannine "why weepest thou?" but as to "he is risen" we can only say that John for some reason prefers to express it dramatically by introducing no angel, but the risen Saviour Himself, as announcing His own resurrection, risen, and visible, and standing before Mary's eyes —yet unrecognised. Perhaps he meant to suggest to his

---

Pet, are seen bearing Jesus upward) The women are at present ignorant of this But Mary Magdalene might be regarded as unconsciously expressing the real truth when she says (Jn xx 2) "*THEY* (see p. 95) have taken up (ἦραν) the Lord out of the tomb."
But the ground for this is taken away by Jn when Jesus says "I am not yet ascended," and then, indefinitely, "I ascend"— followed by nothing definite, and leaving it doubtful whether the Saviour passed to Sheol, or to Paradise (Lk. xxiii 43), or to both, before the Ascension.
Jn xx 12 adopts ἔκειτο with Mt, but inserts τὸ σῶμα This makes all the difference—not "where *Jesus* had lain," but only "where *the body of Jesus* had lain"

690 (Mark xvi 5—8)

OF CHRIST'S RESURRECTION

readers that it was after all a small thing for the Lord to have "arisen," in the body, unless He had also "arisen" with a spiritual presence that breathed itself into the hearts of His friends

§ 10 *"And to Peter," in Mark*[1]

There are several passages in the Synoptists where "Peter" or "Simon" in one Gospel is parallel to, or added to, "those with him," or "the disciples," or "the multitude," in such a way as to suggest that the name might be confused with one of these phrases[2] "Peter," here in Mark, appears to have been either actually a conflation of "disciples," or else to have been regarded as such by Matthew and Luke, both of whom omit it They could hardly have omitted the Marcan saying without some substantial reason, for it is explicable as a brief combination of indirect rebuke and encouragement to the penitent apostle, "Tell my disciples—and Peter, too, in case he should not venture, after his denial, to call himself my disciple[3]" It is possible

[1] Mk xvi 7	Mt xxviii 7	Lk xxiv 6 b—7
ἀλλὰ ὑπάγετε εἴπατε τοῖς μαθηταῖς αὐτοῦ καὶ τῷ Πέτρῳ ὅτι Προάγει ὑμᾶς εἰς τὴν Γαλιλαίαν ἐκεῖ αὐτὸν ὄψεσθε, καθὼς εἶπεν ὑμῖν	καὶ ταχὺ πορευθεῖσαι εἴπατε τοῖς μαθηταῖς αὐτοῦ ὅτι Ἠγέρθη ἀπὸ τῶν νεκρῶν, καὶ ἰδοὺ προάγει ὑμᾶς εἰς τὴν Γαλιλαίαν, ἐκεῖ αὐτὸν ὄψεσθε· ἰδοὺ εἶπον ὑμῖν	μνήσθητε ὡς ἐλάλησεν ὑμῖν ἔτι ὢν ἐν τῇ Γαλιλαίᾳ, λέγων τὸν υἱὸν τοῦ ἀνθρώπου ὅτι δεῖ παραδοθῆναι εἰς χεῖρας ἀνθρώπων ἁμαρτωλῶν καὶ σταυρωθῆναι καὶ τῇ τρίτῃ ἡμέρᾳ ἀναστῆναι

Jn xx 17 Μή μου ἅπτου, οὔπω γὰρ ἀναβέβηκα πρὸς τὸν πατέρα πορεύου δὲ πρὸς τοὺς ἀδελφούς μου καὶ εἰπὲ αὐτοῖς Ἀναβαίνω πρὸς τὸν πατέρα μου καὶ πατέρα ὑμῶν καὶ θεόν μου καὶ θεὸν ὑμῶν.

[2] See *Notes* 2999 (xvii) *g—h*, quoting the parallels to Mk 1 36, xvi 7, Jn xviii. 10, xx. 3 ([Lk xxiv 12]), Mk App B τοῖς περὶ τὸν Πέτρον, and Ign *Smyrn* § 3 ὅτε πρὸς τοὺς περὶ Πέτρον ἦλθεν. Some combination of "Simon" with "and those with him" may explain Mk 1. 29 "Simon...Andrew...James...John," Mt viii 14 "Peter," Lk. iv 38 "Simon" In late Heb שִׁמְעוֹ, "those with him," might be confused with שִׁמְעוֹן, "Simon"

[3] See Cramer, p 446, on Mk xvi. 7, Τὸ δὲ κατ' ἐξαίρετον "καὶ τῷ Πέτρῳ" εἰπεῖν σημαίνει αὐταῖς ὡς οὐχ ἡ ἄρνησις ἀπώσατο, ἀλλ' ἡ μετάνοια πάλιν αὐτὸν προσελάβετο, καὶ τοῖς Ἀποστόλοις ἐποίησεν ἐναρίθμιον. Pseudo-Jerome says "*Et Petro*, Qui se indignum judicat discipulatu, dum ter negavit Magistrum Peccata praeterita non nocent quando non placent." Prof. Swete quotes Theophylact to the same effect.

THE ANNOUNCEMENT

that the words in Mark, being detached from their context, may have been misunderstood by a very few as meaning that the women were to "tell [the news to] His disciples and [tell] Peter *that he is to go before you to Galilee*"—a version of the tradition that Peter took the initiative in going to the sea of Galilee, such as we find in the Fourth Gospel and in the Gospel of Peter[1]. Such misunderstanding, throwing doubt on the meaning of the Marcan tradition, might explain Matthew's and Luke's silence. In any case this is an instance where John may be expected to intervene in order to shew that there was, as indicated in Mark's brief tradition, something exceptional in Christ's utterances to Peter after His resurrection, distinguishing Peter from the other Apostles. And the intention to intervene would be all the more manifest if it contained clearly and fully that combination of rebuke and encouragement which the commentators quoted below have pointed out in the Marcan phrase.

John does thus intervene, in a tradition that distinguishes Peter from all the other Apostles, combining gentle rebuke with the highest encouragement, namely, the promise that the disciple who once denied his Master shall henceforth follow Him to the end, as a shepherd of His flock during life, and as a partaker of His cross in death[2].

---

[1] Jn xxi 1—3 introduces, after "the sea of Tiberias," a mention of "Simon Peter" as the first of a group of disciples, taking the initiative "I go a-fishing." *Evang Petr* §§ 13—14 appends to the Marcan conclusion (Mk xvi 8 ἔφυγον . ἐφοβοῦντο γάρ) an account of general dispersion and departure "homewards" (ἕκαστος εἰς τὸν οἶκον αὐτοῦ), and then a mention of Simon, Andrew, and Levi, as departing to "the sea"—presumably intending the "home" to be Galilee, and the "sea" to be the sea of Galilee Τότε αἱ γυναῖκες φοβηθεῖσαι ἔφυγον. Ἦν δὲ τελευταία ἡμέρα τῶν ἀζύμων, καὶ πολλοί τινες ἐξήρχοντο ὑποστρέφοντες εἰς τοὺς οἴκους αὐτῶν, τῆς ἑορτῆς παυσαμένης ἡμεῖς δὲ οἱ δώδεκα μαθηταὶ τοῦ Κυρίου ἐκλαίομεν καὶ ἐλυπούμεθα καὶ ἕκαστος λυπούμενος διὰ τὸ συμβὰν ἀπηλλάγη εἰς τὸν οἶκον αὐτοῦ ἐγὼ δὲ Σίμων Πέτρος καὶ Ἀνδρέας ὁ ἀδελφός μου λαβόντες ἡμῶν τὰ λίνα ἀπήλθαμεν εἰς τὴν θάλασσαν καὶ ἦν σὺν ἡμῖν Λευεὶς ὁ τοῦ Ἀλφαίου ὃν [ὁ] Κύριος

[2] Jn xxi 15—22.

OF CHRIST'S RESURRECTION

§ 11. *"Goeth before you into Galilee," in Mark and Matthew*[1]

Mark is here referring, through an angel, to the promise uttered by Jesus "After I am raised up I will go before you into Galilee," a promise contained in Matthew's parallel to that passage but omitted there by Luke[2]. By adding, here, "*as he said*," Mark shews that he is referring to that past promise: "He goeth before you...there shall ye see him—*as he said unto you*". Matthew, instead of "*as he said*," has "behold, *I have said*." Perhaps Matthew thought that Mark was not quite accurate in saying that Jesus had promised anything about "seeing" ("ye shall *see* him") but only about "*rising*" from the dead. In any case, Matthew inserts "*as he said*" in the preceding verse where the parallel Mark does not insert it ("He is risen, *as he said*"), referring (doubtless) to the frequent predictions of Jesus that He would be "*raised* on the third day". These predictions were all uttered in Galilee.

Matthew is probably in error. His addition "Behold, *I have said it unto you*" is superfluous, while Mark's "*as he said unto you*" is appropriate. But Matthew's error helps us to understand the parallel in Luke who amplifies Matthew's suggestion. Luke seems to have reasoned thus. "In the first place, Mark was in error before, when he represented Jesus as saying 'I will go before you *into Galilee*,' and he is in error now in referring to those words as a previous promise. Matthew is right in supposing that '*as he said*' refers, not to *going before*, but to the saying '*he is raised up*'. Now this saying was uttered by Jesus *in Galilee*. In the second place, the word that Mark uses in the sense of '*going before*' is not correctly used[3]. It happens

---

[1] Mk xvi 7, Mt xxviii 7
[2] Mk xiv 28, Mt xxvi 32, Lk xxii 32 foll om
[3] Προάγω might be said to be "not correctly used," according to Luke's view, and the usage of Gk literature. Steph *Thes* calls attention to προάγω (vi 1616) in Mk-Mt with accus, = "precede," and says the dat is more usual, but gives no instance of it. Luke uses προάγω τινὰ to mean "bring forth" in Acts xii 6 (W.H marg.), xvi 30, xvii. 5, xxv 26, but προάγω absol only in Lk xviii 39

THE ANNOUNCEMENT

that a word (*dâbar*) that means '*speak*' in Hebrew, means '*cause to go*' or '*guide*' in Aramaic[1]. Here it means '*speak*,' but Mark has taken it as meaning '*guide*.' Thirdly, Mark has taken the word that means '*remember*' or '*call to mind*' as if it meant '*make mention of*,' '*remind others*[2],' hence inferring wrongly that the women were to go and *remind the disciples* of Christ's words, whereas the women were only told to '*remember*' them. I shall therefore repeat here the Lord's prediction of '*rising again*,' as it was uttered '*in Galilee*,' and then render the words of the angel, not '*Make mention of* the fact that he *goeth before* you *into* Galilee,' but '*Remember* the saying that he *spake* unto you *in* Galilee.'"

But, against this interpretation of Mark's hypothetical original here it must be noted that Luke makes no attempt at an earlier stage, by paraphrase or otherwise, to explain the Marcan promise of Jesus " I will go before you into Galilee" so as to shew how Mark went wrong there. Moreover Luke may have been impelled by a desire for consistency to alter "goeth before you into Galilee." For Luke does not relate any self-manifestation of the risen Saviour in Galilee[3] He

---

οἱ προάγοντες parall to Mk x 48 πολλοί, Mt xx 31 ὁ ὄχλος See note above, p 439, n 5, on Ign *Rom* § 9 κατὰ πόλιν με προῆγον (not in Steph *Thes*)

[1] In Heb , דבר = "speak," but in Aram "guide," "drive," etc Heb "*cause to go*" hif of הלך (used of Jehovah "leading" Israel in the wilderness) = Onk דבר in Lev xxvi 13, Deut viii 2, 15, xxix 5

[2] Heb זכר may sometimes mean (Gesen 270 a) "*remember*, with implied *mention of*, Jerem xx 9, xxiii 36 " Also, in Gk, μνημονεύω = "memoro," as well as "memini "

[3] Luke consistently regards Galilee as the scene of the beginning of the rudimentary Gospel preached before the gift of the Spirit It is in (i 26) "a city of Galilee" that the mother of Jesus receives the Annunciation, and (ii 4) "from Galilee" that Joseph goes up with her to Bethlehem Luke does not quote (as Mt iv 15 does) Is. ix 1 "Galilee of the nations"—possibly because it contains the ambiguous "beyond Jordan," a phrase that he (*Beginning* pp 44, 109, *Joh Voc* **1813** *b*) never uses But he alone records that Jesus taught (xxiii 5) "beginning from Galilee " Also in the Acts, the apostles, witnessing the Ascension, are called (Acts i 11) "men of Galilee," and when they receive the Spirit, and speak with tongues,

OF CHRIST'S RESURRECTION

may therefore be biassed. It is reasonable to suppose that Mark is here more correct than Luke. But Jesus may have spoken, not exactly of "Galilee," but of *"home,"* or of *"the Father's house."* If so, His words would imply that "rising again" (apart from any mention of place) which Luke's version mentions. This has been maintained above, and previous volumes of this series have illustrated the Marcan *"going before"* from the Johannine *"going to prepare a place"* for the disciples[1]

Another and much more weighty reason for preferring Mark to Luke in this passage is, that Mark seems to point back to the old Hebrew belief in a "meeting-place," or "appointed meeting," between Jehovah and Israel, which could not but be in the mind of every pious and spiritually minded Jew in the first century. It was "above the mercy-seat" and is thus described in the precept given to Moses for its construction· "And thou shalt put the mercy-seat above upon the ark, and in the ark thou shalt put the testimony that I shall give thee. And there I will *meet with* thee and I will commune with thee from above the mercy-seat...of all things that I will give thee in commandment unto the children of Israel."

The Hebrew here is quite different from that which means ordinary and casual "meeting[2]." It implies an appointed

---

it is said (Acts ii 7) "Are not all these that speak Galilaeans?" But they are to preach the Gospel after receiving the Spirit (Lk xxiv 47) "beginning from Jerusalem."

John not only places the final manifestation of the risen Saviour near Tiberias so as to *suggest* Galilee, but also contrives to connect it in *word* with "Galilee" by telling us that one of the seven witnesses of it was (xxi 2) "Nathanael of *Cana in Galilee*," thereby calling us back to the first mention of that place (ii 1—11) "There was a marriage in *Cana of Galilee*. This beginning of his signs did Jesus in *Cana of Galilee*, and manifested his glory, and his disciples believed on him"

There is a great difference between these two aspects. Luke regards Galilee as representing a rudimentary stage of the Gospel; John regards it as the home of the Gospel in its infancy to which Jesus returns for its final development.

[1] See pp 438—40 (on Mk xiv 28), and *Son* 3347 *a—c*, 3347 (x).
[2] Exod xxv 21—2, יָעַד, R V, as A V *"meet with thee"* R V.

THE ANNOUNCEMENT

meeting; and the notion of appointing, or designating, is so important an element in the word that it is used previously in the Pentateuch, and frequently in later Hebrew, for "espousing[1]." When Jesus pronounced the doom of the old "meeting-place" of Israel, converted by its rulers, as He said, into "a den of robbers[2]," He was bound, if we may so speak, to make a new one. According to John, He did promise to do something of the kind, "Destroy this temple and in three days I will raise it up[3]." According to Mark and Matthew, false witnesses gave a false version of such a promise[4]. But Luke wholly omits it. The omission is of a piece with his omission of the tradition about Christ "going before" His disciples to what He called the Home, identified by Mark with "Galilee." We cannot trust Luke to record traditions about the "meeting" of the Lord and the disciples where they verge on mysticism and poetry.

There were other reasons why Luke might fail to understand the Scriptural doctrine of the "meeting" of the Lord with Israel and Christ's application of it to the Church. The LXX, both in the passage where the meeting is first described, and afterwards where it is referred to, misunderstands it as "knowing[5]." But "knowing," as Paul says, sometimes needs to be

---

always renders it "*meet with*," in Exod. xxix. 42, 43, xxx. 6, 36, Numb. xvii. 4, and so does A V except in Exod. xxix. 42. The word recurs in Nehem. vi. 2, 10 "let us meet together." The Heb., יָעַד, differs from the ordinary Heb. "meet" קָרָה (used by Balaam in Numb. xxiii. 3 "if the Lord will come to meet me.") Prob. R V uses "*meet with*" to denote "meet by appointment" which it sometimes means in Shakespeare, but even there "*meet with*" is rare and may mean, as in modern English, "fall in with" (e.g. *Taming of Sh.* iv. 3. 6 "elsewhere they *meet with* charity").

[1] See Levy ii. 250 *b*, quoting Exod. xxi. 8—9.
[2] Mk xi. 17, Mt xxi. 13, Lk xix. 46, comp. Mk xiii. 2, Mt xxiv. 2, Lk xxi. 6.   [3] Jn ii. 19.
[4] Mk xiv. 56—9, Mt xxvi. 60—61, Lk om. On this, see above, p. 513 foll.
[5] Exod. xxv. 22 γνωσθήσομαί σοι, and simil. in Exod. xxix. 42, xxx. 6, 36, Numb. xvii. 4. The LXX has confused יָעַד with יָדַע "*know*." Similarly (*Son* 3414 (ii) *a—d*) the LXX has regularly confused the noun מוֹעֵד, "*meeting*," with a form of עוּד so as to render

OF CHRIST'S RESURRECTION

distinguished from "loving" as "puffing up" is to be distinguished from "building up[1]" The Hebrew "meeting," as interpreted by a prophet (and we may say, still more confidently, by a Messiah) would imply a union, or possession, such as Paul implies when he speaks of our being "*in Christ*" or Christ "*in us*[2]" Jerome says "It pleases the Lord *to sit in your mind* as He once sat on the mercy-seat and the cherubim[3]" Jewish traditions about the place of meeting recognise, some of them, the danger of limiting the divine Presence by restrictions of place Others deal with the fact that it is Moses, and not Israel, nor even Aaron, with whom the Lord converses But they could hardly be expected to enlarge (and they do not, as far as I know, enlarge) on the doctrine that the heart of the believer may be regarded as the "meeting-place," and that it will please the Lord, if we will but admit Him, to "sit in our minds as He once sat on the mercy-seat and the cherubim[4]"

John does thus enlarge, after his manner, in a short drama in which Jesus prepares the disciples, on the night before the Crucifixion, to conceive of the new "mercy-seat" and the new "place of meeting[5]" The scene opens with negation, which however is closely followed by affirmation All the disciples are warned "Whither I go, ye cannot come " This seems to them poorly compensated for by the precept "Even as I have loved you, so also that ye love one another " Peter expostulates and is silenced Then there is mention of Christ's "preparing a place," and Jesus says "Whither I go, ye know the way " Thomas replies "We know not whither thou goest," and is told that Jesus Himself is "the way " Philip, longing for something definite and substantial, and hearing Jesus mention the Father, says "*Shew* us the Father, and it sufficeth us ", but he is told that in seeing Jesus he has "*seen the Father*" Finally "Judas,

---

"the tabernacle of *meeting*" as if it meant "the tabernacle of *testimony* " See Numb iii 7, iv 25, Aq and Sym σύνταγή .

[1] 1 Cor viii 1 [2] Gal. ii 20, iii. 28 etc.
[3] Jerome *Epist* xxii. 24
[4] See *Siphri* (on Numb vii 89), *Sanhedr* 7 a, *Succa* 4 b—5 a, *Pesikt* Wu p 3, *Numb r* Wu pp 389, 391.
[5] Jn xiii 33—xiv 23

THE ANNOUNCEMENT

not Iscariot," apparently goaded to something like impatience by this doctrine, which seems to turn upside down ordinary notions of "*seeing*," exclaims, "Lord, what is come to pass that thou wilt manifest thyself unto us, and not unto the world?" And now at last comes the great positive doctrine that the manifestation will consist in the spiritual presence of the Father and the Son *in the heart* of the loving and obedient disciple· "If a man love me he will keep my word; and my Father will love him, and we will come unto him and *make our abode with him*[1]"

There is perhaps not a word in this dramatic scene that was ever uttered by Jesus or by any of His disciples[2], but there is also not a word in it that is not spiritually true for us in the present, and historically enlightening as to the past—as revealing the actual thoughts entertained by pious Jews and the earliest Jewish Christians in the first century concerning the "meeting-place" of Israel and the Lord.

---

[1] Comp Rev iii 20

[2] A friend asks "If Jesus did not utter the substance of these words, what man is there, or has there been, that could have invented them?" I should reply "*the man to whom they were revealed*," —the man so imbued with the personality of the incarnate Word that he defined his Gospel as being (1 Jn i 1 foll) "That which was from the beginning, that which we have *heard* . have seen *with our eyes* . beheld, and our hands handled, concerning the Word of life And the life was manifested, and we have seen .the life which was with the Father and was manifested unto us That which we have *seen and heard* declare we unto you also, that ye also may have fellowship with us, yea, and our fellowship is with the Father, and with his Son Jesus Christ " The man who wrote thus was not a man to "*invent*," but he was one in whom the letter would be swallowed up by the spirit It is true that he makes an initial and a final appeal to "that which we have *heard*" and "*seen*" But he makes us feel that the "hearing" and the "seeing" cannot be communicated by a phonograph and a photograph They are God's gift (Prov xx 12) "*The hearing ear and the seeing eye*, the Lord hath made even both of them "

OF CHRIST'S RESURRECTION

§ 12 *"For they feared," in Mark*[1]

That there is some corruption in the phrase "for they feared" is indicated by the fact that "trembling and astonishment" have already been mentioned by Mark, so that, even if it could be proved that the Gospel originally continued after the phrase in a conclusion that has perished, there would still be this objection that *"for they feared"* is superfluous, or even inconsistent. The context requires rather "for they were beside themselves with joy." At all events the parallel Luke omits "fear." Matthew, who retains it, adds "joy," and says that the women, so far from being prevented by fear from telling the good news, "ran to carry away word of it" to the disciples. Luke says that they actually "carried away word of it."

The difficulty of the two clauses about fearing is indicated by SS, which omits the first: "And when they heard they came forth, and they went away and to no one aught said they, because they had been afraid." Codex k apparently regards the angel as representing Christ Himself. "But go ye and say to

---

[1] Mk xvi. 8
καὶ ἐξελθοῦσαι ἔφυ-
γον ἀπὸ τοῦ μνημείου,
εἶχεν γὰρ αὐτὰς τρόμος
καὶ ἔκστασις· καὶ οὐδενὶ
οὐδὲν εἶπαν, ἐφοβοῦντο
γάρ

Mt xxviii 8
καὶ ἀπελθοῦσαι ταχὺ
ἀπὸ τοῦ μνημείου μετὰ
φόβου καὶ χαρᾶς μεγάλης
ἔδραμον ἀπαγγεῖλαι τοῖς
μαθηταῖς αὐτοῦ

Lk. xxiv 9
καὶ ὑποστρέψασαι
[ἀπὸ τοῦ μνημείου] ἀπήγ-
γειλαν ταῦτα πάντα τοῖς
ἔνδεκα καὶ πᾶσιν τοῖς
λοιποῖς

Jn xx. 18 ἔρχεται Μαριὰμ ἡ Μαγδαληνὴ ἀγγέλλουσα τοῖς μαθηταῖς ὅτι Ἑώρακα τὸν κύριον καὶ ταῦτα εἶπεν αὐτῇ, D, e, καὶ ἃ εἶπεν αὐτῇ ἐμήνυσεν (D+αὐτοῖς) SS "and the things that he revealed to her she said to them." According to Jn xx 17, what was "revealed" was ἀναβαίνω πρὸς τὸν πατέρα μου.. According to Mk xvi 7, Mt xxviii. 7, it was προάγει ὑμᾶς εἰς τὴν Γαλιλαίαν

(1) Ἀγγέλλω, in N T, occurs only as above (Jn xx 18) (2) Ἀπαγγέλλω is used about "reporting" the resurrection of Christ in [Mk xvi 10, 13], Mt xxviii 8, 10, Lk xxiv 9, but only as follows in Jn, xvi. 25 περὶ τοῦ πατρὸς ἀπαγγελῶ ὑμῖν For the sake of distinction, they are translated above (1) "carry word," (2) "carry away word," or "report."

Cramer prints a scholium on Mk which distinguishes the Marcan women, who came "after the sun had risen," from the other women (of whom there were "many") and applies the word ἀπαγγέλλω to the Marcan women

THE ANNOUNCEMENT

the disciples and to Peter, *I go before you into Galilee   There shall ye see me as I said unto you   But they, when they went forth from the tomb, fled*"; then it combines the two fear-clauses thus " For tremor and terror (tremor et pauor) possessed them on account of fear (timorem)." The Diatessaron, combining Mark, Matthew, and Luke, omits the words of Matthew "*to carry away word to his disciples,*" perhaps because the compiler felt that they were incompatible with the Marcan clause "(Lk xxiv 8) And they remembered his sayings, (Mt xxviii 8 *a*) And they departed in haste from the tomb with joy and great fear (*sic*), and hastened and went [*to tell his disciples*], (Mk xvi. 8 *b*) And perplexity and fear encompassed them, and they told no man anything, for they were afraid[1]." But it inserts the missing words later on: " And while the first women were going in the way *to inform his disciples*[2]."

There are indications here, as above, that Luke is, so to speak, re-arranging Mark's context. For example, whereas Mark says that "*amazement*" *possessed the women*, Luke, later

---

[1] *Diatess* liii 7—8
[2] *Diatess* liii 32   The Vat MS omits " women " and " to inform his disciples "   *Evang Petr* § 13 mentions no command to report to the disciples   After ἴδετε...ὅτι οὐκ ἔστιν   ἀνέστη γὰρ καὶ ἀπῆλθεν ἐκεῖ ὅθεν ἀπεστάλη, it proceeds τότε αἱ γυναῖκες φοβηθεῖσαι ἔφυγον

Cramer's scholium on Mark, above referred to, recognises, in the women mentioned here by Mark (xvi 8), a spiritual inferiority " For there were '*many [women]*' (Mk xv 41) that came up with Him from Galilee   But these that came (according to Mark (xvi 2)) '*after the sun had risen*' were also (so to speak) somewhat imperfect (καὶ ἀτελέστερόν πως διέκειντο)   Hence they do not make their visit by night (νύκτωρ, comp Jn xx 1 σκοτίας ἔτι οὔσης) but early [in the morning], and further, having heard [the command] to '*carry-away-word to the disciples and Peter,*' they '*fled*' and '*said nothing to any one, for they feared*'"   The following words, though obscure, indicate that they have an inferior vision " proportioned to the weakness of their mind."   Μόναι γὰρ ἀπελθοῦσαι, καὶ ἀληθεῖ ὄψει πεισθεῖσαι ὡς μετὰ ἀνατολὴν ἡλίου ἐπιστῆναι, οὐ τὸν Σωτῆρα θεάσασθαι καταξιοῦνται, ἢ τὸν Ἄγγελον τὸν ἐξαστράπτοντα, οὔτε τοὺς δύο τοὺς ἔσω τοῦ μνημείου, οὔτε τοὺς δύο τοὺς παρὰ τῷ Λουκᾷ ἄνδρας   ψιλὸν δέ τινα νεανίσκον εἶδον περιβεβλημένον στολὴν λευκὴν ἀναλόγως τῇ τῆς διανοίας αὐτῶν σμικρότητι τὴν ὀπτασίαν ἰδοῦσαι

OF CHRIST'S RESURRECTION

on, represents the two travellers to Emmaus as saying about these same women, "*they amazed us*[1]" Again Mark's emphatic phrase "*nothing to nobody*" reminds us that the emphatic "*no*," or "*not any*," is sometimes expressed in Hebrew by "*not...all*," as in "*no flesh* shall be justified[2]," and we find in the parallel Luke a twofold mention of "*all*" "They brought word of *all these things* to the eleven and *all the rest*" This suggests that Luke regarded Mark as erroneously inserting a "*not*" in some Hebrew original such as "they reported [*not*] all the matter to *all* of them," which Mark took to mean "*not anything to any one*" An omission, or insertion, of the negative, in translating from Hebrew, might arise from confusing it with the prefix that denotes the infinitive[3] And here we note that Matthew has the infinitive "they ran *to* report." The parallel Luke has "they reported" But if the "to" were read as the negative the result would be "they did *not* report." Instances of such confusion are frequent in the Old Testament

Still more important is the fact that this brief Marcan phrase, combining (1) "*for*" (i e "*because*") and (2) "*they feared*," combines two conspicuous possibilities of error for translators from Hebrew For (1) the same Hebrew word that means

---

[1] Mk xvi 8 ἔκστασις, Lk xxiv 22 ἐξέστησαν ἡμᾶς. Comp Mk iii 21 ἐξέστη "*he is beside himself*" applied by the parall. Mt xii 23 to the "*amazed*" multitude (Lk xi 14 "the multitudes *marvelled*") on which see *Proclam* pp 424—5 Luke uses the word transitively of Simon Magus (Acts viii 9—11) where the meaning is half-way between R V. "amazed" and A.V. "bewitched" It would be easy to confuse (1) "They ran to tell the disciples and amazement possessed *them* [*the women*]" with (2) "They ran and told the disciples and amazement possessed *them* [*the disciples*]," in spite of the distinction of gender

[2] Gal. ii. 16, where W H refer to Ps. cxliii 2. In "not *any*," meaning "none," "any" is regularly represented by Heb כל, "all" (Gesen. 482 *a*).

[3] See *Corrections* 530 quoting Jerem. xviii. 18 (Heb) "and let us *not* give heed to *any* (כל, *all*) of his words" καὶ [Q marg ins οὐκ] ἀκουσόμεθα πάντας τοὺς λόγους αὐτοῦ "No(t)," לא, לו, or אל, is confused with "to," ל, or *vice versa* (*Corr.* 529 *a*—*b*) in Prov. xii 28 "no," εἰς, Is v. 7 "for (ל)," οὐ, Prov. xxvii 19, Ezek xiii 5, 1 K xi 10, comp. Judg. 1. 18, 2 S xiv. 32, Zech. xiii. 4, Dan. x. 9.

THE ANNOUNCEMENT

"for" or "because" may also mean the conjunctive "that[1]." (2) The Hebrew *"feared"* is easily confused with *"saw"*—some forms of the two verbs being identical—and is actually several times confused with it by LXX[2]. Hence Delitzsch's Hebrew renderings of the Marcan "for they feared" and of a later Lucan "that they had seen" (*"that they had...seen* a vision of angels") differ from one another by no more than a single *yod*[3].

These facts point to two conclusions. One is fairly probable, namely, that Mark's Gospel in the original Hebrew terminated with a statement that the women *"saw"* the Lord and not with a statement that they *"were afraid."* The second is highly probable, and almost certain, namely, that Luke wrote with allusion to Mark and with the desire to correct what he deemed to be Mark's misapprehension

Passing to the Fourth Gospel we can hardly say that it intervenes for or against Mark, but it does intervene against traditions connecting the manifestations of the Resurrection with "fear" or "amazement." Neither word occurs in John, either here or later on, whereas Luke, later on, says that the

---

[1] For כי meaning (1) "because," (2) "that" (sometimes being equivalent to inverted commas) see Gesen 471—4 and *Corrections* **459** (v) Comp Jn xx 18 (*lit*) "carrying-word to the disciples *that* (ὅτι, Delitzsch כי) I have seen the Lord" Strictly speaking we might call this ambiguous (*"because* I have seen") This ambiguity would exist only in Hebrew, not in Aramaic The Aramaic prefix ד- ("that" conjunctive) used here by SS and Palest Syr is not ambiguous

[2] See *Corrections* **533** "In some forms the two are identical, e g ירא means either 'he feared' or 'he will see'" Instances of confusion are (*ib* **533** *a*) Judg. xiv. 11 (codex A), 2 S. xiv. 15, 2 Chr xxvi 5, Job xxxvii. 24, Prov xxix 16, Eccles. xii 5, Is xvi 12, Jerem xvii 8, Ezek 1 18, xviii 14, Mic vi 9 etc

It will be observed that Luke (xxiv 23) mentions "*a vision* (ὀπτασίαν) of angels" as seen by the women, where Delitzsch has מראה This word, in O T , = ὀπτασία (6 in Theod), ὅραμα (9) and is derived from ראה "*see*" But this is very similar to מורא from ירא "*fear*," which in LXX = ὅραμα, "*vision*," thrice, although it also = φόβος (5) and other words implying fear

[3] Mk xvi 8 (Delitzsch) כי יראו, Lk. xxiv 23 (Delitzsch) כי ראו. The dropping of י before ו in Mk would identify it with Lk.

OF CHRIST'S RESURRECTION

disciples "were terrified and affrighted, and supposed that they had seen a spirit[1]" Distress, and sorrow, and passionate grief for the supposed removal of the Lord's body are implied in the Johannine account of Mary Magdalene's visits to the tomb, and of her return from her first visit, and subsequently in her solitary weeping—but no fear. The angels address her and she is neither terrified nor amazed but gives them a deliberate answer[2] Jesus addresses her and still she is not afraid[3]. The only instance in the Fourth Gospel in which the disciples are described as "afraid" is one in which the parallel Gospels, Mark and Matthew, say that they supposed Jesus to be a "phantasm" or "phantom" There John says "They behold Jesus walking... *and they were afraid*[4]." But in the Johannine account of the self-manifestations of Jesus after His resurrection there is no trace of fear in the disciples[5].

---

[1] Lk xxiv 37.   [2] Jn xx 13
[3] Jn xx 15 She replies "supposing him to be the gardener"
[4] Jn vi 19, comp Mk vi 49—50, Mt xiv 26
[5] The nearest approach to it is in Jn xxi 12 οὐδεὶς ἐτόλμα.. , concerning which see *Law* pp 435—6 giving Chrysostom's explanation as approximately correct, They wished to ask Him, not really "Who art thou?" but something about His altered form, and this they did not venture to do And see *ib* p 437 "Visibly, it was a different Jesus Yet it differed in being, so to speak, more truly Jesus than before, a Jesus or Saviour independent of mere external or logical proofs, a Jesus not seen in the same way as in old days, but seen in the heart and received into the soul "

CHAPTER XVII

THE RESURRECTION

[Mark-Appendix xvi. 9—20]

§ 1. *The general character of the Mark-Appendix*[1]

IN this chapter it will be assumed that the last eleven verses of Mark, as printed in the Greek on which our Authorised Version is based, were not a part of his Gospel but were of the nature of an Appendix[2]. The whole of Mark, from the second verse ("in Isaiah") onwards, shews signs of a roughness that would have been removed by any moderately careful author if he had been able to revise it[3]. And the evidence from the end points to the same conclusion. The writer was probably cut off from his writing before he could complete it and go back to the beginning to revise it.

---

[1]   `   Mark-Appendix xvi 9—14 (R V)

(9) Now when he was risen early on the first day of the week, he appeared first to Mary Magdalene, from whom he had cast out seven devils (*lit.* demons).

(10) She went and told them that had been with him, as they mourned and wept.

(11) And they, when they heard that he was alive, and had been seen of her, disbelieved.

(12) And after these things he was manifested in another form unto two of them, as they walked, on their way into the country

(13) And they went away and told it unto the rest. neither believed they them.

(14) And afterward he was manifested unto the eleven themselves as they sat at meat, and he upbraided them with their unbelief and hardness of heart, because they believed not them which had seen him after he was risen.

[2] See W. H. *Notes on Select Readings* pp. 28—51.
[3] Mk 1 2. See *Introd.* p 34.

THE RESURRECTION

There is no evidence that the Appendix was known to any Christian writer before 150 A D [1] We have therefore no external evidence leading us to suppose that it was known to John. But there is internal evidence indicating that parts of it would probably be known to him as being clauses in some early Christian catechisms, teaching the facts on which Christians were to base their belief in some of the clauses of the earliest creeds "The third day He rose from the dead (*or*, rose again according to the Scriptures); He ascended into heaven, He sitteth on the right hand of God the Father Almighty" Luke recognises the use of such catechisms. A preface to his Gospel says that it was written in order that Theophilus might recognise the safe assurance with which he might rest on the *catechistic* "words (*logoi*)[2]," knowing that they were based on "facts" as they were "traditionally delivered by those who were from the beginning eyewitnesses and ministers of the word (*logos*)." A preface to his Acts mentions the Ascension, and previous manifestations of the risen Saviour, as being proved to be "living" by many "proofs," after "his passion[3]."

Paul outlines a part of such a creed, as being traditionally "received" by himself from others, and traditionally "delivered" by himself to the Corinthians: "I delivered unto you...how that Christ died for our sins...and that he was buried, and that he hath been raised on the third day...and that he appeared to Cephas; then to the twelve, then he appeared to...[4]." He proceeds to enumerate other instances in which Christ "appeared," the last being the manifestation of Jesus to himself He makes no mention of Christ's appearing to women. The explanation of this appears to be that the evidence of women to a fact of this kind would weigh for little with audiences disposed to "mock" at assertions of resurrection[5]

---

[1] W H. *Notes on S R* p 39.

[2] Lk 1 4 ἵνα ἐπιγνῷς περὶ ὧν κατηχήθης λόγων τὴν ἀσφάλειαν

[3] Acts 1 3 οἷς καὶ παρέστησεν ἑαυτὸν ζῶντα μετὰ τὸ παθεῖν αὐτὸν ἐν πολλοῖς τεκμηρίοις

[4] 1 Cor. xv 1—8 On "hath been raised," *i e* was raised and remains for ever raised, see similar instances in *Joh Gr* 2440 foll.

[5] See *Introd* pp 106, 123—4, and comp. Acts xvii. 31—2, where

THE RESURRECTION

The question arises whether this Mark-Appendix shews signs of including some ancient traditions—also found in the Synoptists—that may have induced John to intervene for, or against, them. If it shewed no such signs, it would have no place in a work on The Fourfold Gospel; but a glance at the text shews that some of it resembles Lucan traditions, and even Lucan expression[1]. For example, it follows Luke in connecting Mary Magdalene with "seven devils[2]." Luke does this appropriately in his first mention of Mary; the Mark-Appendix less appropriately after she has been mentioned by Mark repeatedly and when she is now being mentioned for the last time. It also describes—as Luke alone does—a manifestation of Jesus to two of the disciples journeying into the country, in which Jesus "was manifested in another form[3]." It lays great stress,

---

Paul's Discourse on the Areopagus abruptly terminates thus, "'Whereof he hath given assurance unto all men, in that he hath raised him from the dead' Now when they heard of the resurrection of the dead, *some mocked*"

[1] Mk xvi 9—14 Ἀναστὰς δὲ πρωὶ πρώτῃ σαββάτου ἐφάνη πρῶτον Μαρίᾳ τῇ Μαγδαληνῇ, παρ' ἧς ἐκβεβλήκει ἑπτὰ δαιμόνια (10) ἐκείνη πορευθεῖσα ἀπήγγειλεν τοῖς μετ' αὐτοῦ γενομένοις πενθοῦσι καὶ κλαίουσιν (11) κἀκεῖνοι ἀκούσαντες ὅτι ζῇ καὶ ἐθεάθη ὑπ' αὐτῆς ἠπίστησαν (12) Μετὰ δὲ ταῦτα δυσὶν ἐξ αὐτῶν περιπατοῦσιν ἐφανερώθη ἐν ἑτέρᾳ μορφῇ πορευομένοις εἰς ἀγρόν· (13) κἀκεῖνοι ἀπελθόντες ἀπήγγειλαν τοῖς λοιποῖς οὐδὲ ἐκείνοις ἐπίστευσαν (14) Ὕστερον [δὲ] ἀνακειμένοις αὐτοῖς τοῖς ἕνδεκα ἐφανερώθη, καὶ ὠνείδισεν τὴν ἀπιστίαν αὐτῶν καὶ σκληροκαρδίαν ὅτι τοῖς θεασαμένοις αὐτὸν ἐγηγερμένον [ἐκ νεκρῶν] οὐκ ἐπίστευσαν.

[2] Lk. viii. 2 Μαρία ἡ καλουμένη Μαγδαληνή, ἀφ' ἧς δαιμόνια ἑπτὰ ἐξεληλύθει. The Appendix connects the healing of Mary more definitely with the act of Jesus

[3] Mk xvi 12 ἐν ἑτέρᾳ μορφῇ. Note, in the Transfiguration, Lk. ix. 29 ἐγένετο...τὸ εἶδος τοῦ προσώπου αὐτοῦ ἕτερον, parall. Mk ix. 2, Mt xvii 2 μετεμορφώθη In the present passage, no transfiguration appears to be implied, and yet the meaning is different from that in Lk. xxiv 16 "*their eyes were holden* that they should not recognise him" The Appendix indicates that Jesus really *had* "a different form." This seems to deny that the "form" was dependent on the mind or spiritual "*eyes*" of the beholders, or that their material "*eyes*" were "holden" by a supernatural power

THE RESURRECTION

as Luke alone does, on the faithlessness or unbelief of the disciples and on the reproaches with which Jesus rebuked it[1].

On the other hand, it differs from Luke in making no mention of Christ's inviting the disciples to "handle" Him, in order to convince themselves that He is not a phantom or phantasm, nor of His eating in their presence[2]. And this is the more remarkable because the Appendix says that Jesus "was manifested to the Eleven as they were seated at table[3]" On the whole, it may be said that the Mark-Appendix, so far as concerns the narrative of Christ's resurrection, resembles Luke, but with the omission of just those two points of evidence—"touching" on the part of the disciples, and "eating" on the part of Jesus—on which Luke might be expected to lay stress as "proofs[4]"

§ 2 *The Mark-Appendix, Luke, and John*

Passing to the Fourth Gospel we find that it differs from the Appendix by omitting, or almost omitting, the points on which the Appendix agrees with Luke. The one point in which John verbally agrees with both is the use of the word "unbelieving" or "faithless." But the context shews that there is no real agreement of thought. In Luke and the Appendix all the disciples are said to have been at first "unbelieving", in John it is only Thomas that is unbelieving. To him Jesus says, "Be not unbelieving but believing[5]." The rest are nowhere said by John to have disbelieved[6].

---

[1] Ἀπιστεῖν occurs in the Gospels nowhere but Mk xvi 11, 16, Lk. xxiv. 11, 41, and comp Mk xvi 14 ὠνείδισεν τὴν ἀπιστίαν αὐτῶν κ σκληροκαρδίαν with Lk xxiv 25 Ὦ ἀνόητοι κ βραδεῖς τῇ καρδίᾳ... In the Appendix, the disciples are described as disbelieving the evidence of the two travellers as well as that of the women. In Luke, the disbelief extends only to the latter.

[2] Lk xxiv 37, 39—43   See *Law* p 431 foll   [3] Mk xvi. 14

[4] Acts 1 3 "Proofs (τεκμηρίοις)" The word is not used elsewhere in canon Gk Test. It is a favourite word with Thucydides. Comp *Introd* p 115 quoting Thuc 1 20—1 παντὶ ἑξῆς τεκμηρίῳ and adding "Both ἑξῆς and τεκμήριον represent the lines on which Luke writes"

[5] Jn xx 24—7

[6] Previous *non-belief* must be regarded as implied in Jn xx 8 "and he saw and believed," but that is different from "unbelief," or "disbelief," ἀπιστία.

THE RESURRECTION

As to the distinction between a subjective inability to see the real Jesus (Luke, "*their eyes were holden*") and an objective difference between Jesus as He had been and Jesus as He now was (Appendix, "*in another form*") John holds a middle course. Whereas the Appendix and Luke attempt to explain, John gives no explanations but simply states facts. He says that Mary "supposed" Jesus to be "the gardener" till Jesus called her by name[1] On the same evening, the disciples "rejoiced when they saw the Lord[2]"—without any fear that He was a phantom or phantasm, and without any doubt as to His personality Later on, by the sea of Tiberias[3], in the early morning,

---

[1] Jn xx 15   [2] Jn xx 20

[3] The Johannine (xxi 1) mention of "Tiberias" may possibly have an unsuspected connection with the Lucan (xxiv 13) mention of "Emmaus" for the following reasons

(1) No one has been able to explain what place Luke had in view Luke says it was "sixty furlongs from Jerusalem" Yet (Plummer on Lk xxiv 13) "all Christian writers from Eusebius to the twelfth century" identify it with Nicopolis, which was 176 furlongs from Jerusalem Some MSS substitute "160" for "60" in Lk, thus suggesting an identification of the place with Nicopolis, but (Plummer *ib*) "it is absurd to suppose that these two [*i e* the travellers to Emmaus] walked about 20 miles out, took their evening meal, walked 20 miles back, and arrived in time to find the disciples still gathered together and conversing "

(2) Niese's Index to Josephus gives Ἀμμαοῦς v r Ἐμμαοῦς (*a*) "opp et toparchia Judaeae," *i e* the place afterwards called Nicopolis, (*b*) "vicus 30 stadia distans Hierosolymis," (*c*) "*vide* Ἀμμαθοῦς" Of these, (*a*) is excluded as being too far off, (*b*) is possible (the MSS vary between 30 and 60 stadia), *Bell* vii 6 6 χωρίον ἔδωκεν εἰς κατοίκησιν ὃ καλεῖται μὲν Ἀμμαοῦς, ἀπέχει δὲ τῶν Ἱεροσολύμων σταδίους τριάκοντα (v r. ἑξήκοντα), (*c*) Ἀμμαθοῦς (v r Ἀμμαοῦς) is "calidae prope Tiberiadem," *i.e* "hot [baths] near Tiberias," *Ant* xviii 2 3, *Bell* iv 1 3, where both passages explain that the name means θερμά "hot [baths]"

(3) Levy ii 69—70 says that the name of "several places that had hot baths" was חמתא, and refers to אמאוס (*i e* Emmaus) which (*ib* 1 92 *b*) he explains as derived from חמתא by a weakening of the "ch" (so that *Chamtha* became *Amtha* or *Ammaous*) Krauss (p 58), who agrees with Levy as to the "Hellenization" of "Emmaus" from "Chamtha," mentions *only two places* as being thus distinctively

THE RESURRECTION

when Jesus accosted the disciples, His voice did not arrest them, they "knew not that it was Jesus." After the draught of fishes, "the disciple whom Jesus loved saith unto Peter, It is the Lord," and Peter swam toward Him. Yet even when Master and disciples were all together on the shore and on the point of taking a morning meal together, it is said "No one of the disciples was bold enough to question him closely 'Who art thou?'—knowing [as they all did] that it was the Lord[1]." The impression left upon us by these facts is that Jesus was not "known" on this occasion by His voice nor by the nail-prints on His hands. He was in some way altered or, as the Mark-Appendix says, "in another form." The voice, too, would seem to have been altered. Yet the disciples "knew that it was the Lord."

As to the Lucan "eating," omitted in the Appendix, John treats it at considerable length in a way of his own. Jesus is described by Luke as eating food provided by the disciples, but by John as providing the disciples with food. In Luke, the eating is a proof that Jesus is not a bodiless spirit; in John it is apparently regarded as the symbol of Christ's spiritual

---

named—as we should say in English—"Bath" in Talmuds and Midrash, namely (1) Nicopolis, (2) a place near Tiberias. Of both he gives instances as spelt אמאוס, i.e. Emmaus.

The conclusion appears to be that Emmaus, or Ammaus, might be the name of any place where there were hot baths, and that there was a manifestation of Jesus near a place of that name. Luke believed that it was near Jerusalem; he also knew that a settlement of Roman veterans had been made at a place called Ammaus less than a hundred furlongs from Jerusalem. This, then, Luke mentioned, *specifying the distance in order to exclude the well-known Nicopolis.* John, believing that it was in Galilee, found no place so likely as the well-known hot baths near Tiberias.

Hor Heb i 94, 314 quotes Joseph *Bell* vii 6 6 as "*sixty* furlongs," and blames Beza for quoting it as "*thirty* furlongs." But Niese gives it as txt "*thirty*" (marg "*sixty*") "*Sixty*," in Greek MSS of Josephus, is explicable as an attempt to conform Josephus to Luke Neubauer pp 101—2 rejects the view that Emmaus could mean the baths near Tiberias, but his discussion is inadequate as he makes no reference to Joseph *Bell* vii 6 6.

[1] Jn xxi 4, 7, 12

THE RESURRECTION

body, the living bread—a *viaticum* by which the disciples are to be strengthened so that they may go on their way to preach the Gospel.

The Lucan "handling" is not mentioned verbally in the Johannine Gospel, but it is mentioned in the Johannine Epistle thus: "That which was from the beginning, that which we have heard, that which we have seen with our eyes, that which we beheld and our hands *handled*, concerning the Word of life, and the life was manifested, and we have seen, and bear witness...[1]." In Scripture, as also in Greek literature, the word mostly implies handling in the dark, or in blindness, that which one cannot see[2]. Paul uses it of mankind, in a rudimentary stage of revelation, "groping" after God[3] In the Epistle to the Hebrews the terrors of the fire of Sinai, accompanying the giving of the Law, and blackness and darkness and tempest, are contrasted with "Mount Zion," and the fire is called "palpable"—literally, "[capable of] being handled[4]"—suggesting an antithesis between the palpable dispensation of the Law and the impalpable dispensation of the Spirit But in the Johannine Epistle the connection is not quite clear between "our hands handled" and "concerning the word of life."

Perhaps the writer, in his thoughts about the Logos, reverts to Greek thought about "handling" or "feeling one's way" as applied to the use of words (*logoi*) Plato says that most people give the name of "cause" to that which is not strictly cause, "*feeling-their-way* as it were in the dark[5]"; and Plutarch goes further in the application of the metaphor when he says "We make our thoughts known to one another, as it were with

---

[1] 1 Jn i 1—2

[2] In the Pentateuch it occurs only in Gen xxvii. 12—22 (thrice), Deut xxviii 29 (twice) Polyb viii 18 4 ψηλαφᾶν ἐπίνοιαν is used of a "wily Cretan" who "*feels his way* about every proposal" Clem Rom § 62 πάντα τόπον ἐψηλαφήσαμεν is probably exceptional, "handle [a topic]" In Zech ix 13 "I will make," ψηλαφήσω, LXX confuses מוש with משש and forces the Greek word to mean "handle [as a sword]." [3] Acts xvii 27.

[4] Heb xii. 18 ψηλαφωμένῳ

[5] Plato *Phaed* 99 B ψηλαφῶντες οἱ πολλοὶ ὥσπερ ἐν σκότῳ

THE RESURRECTION

a light in darkness, by means of voice," and describes "the facts themselves," or "the very facts," as being "*felt-after* and disclosed *by word (logos)*," so that the mind of the superior seeker after truth "leads the gifted soul by *touching-on* the thing conceived", the mind of Socrates was "delicate of touch[1]" Such reflections would lead a Platonically minded Christian to regard himself and his fellow believers as "*feeling the way*," through the incarnation of the Word as Jesus the divine Logos, toward the divine Nous, Mind, or Thought, that is to say, to God Himself

But this "feeling the way" would become an inappropriate metaphor when the Thought, the Word, and the Spirit—that is to say, the Father, the Son, and the Paraclete—had come into the heart of the believer and taken possession of it as a home And there was a danger lest the word should be used literally, as in the LXX, and applied to the "touching," or "handling," of the body of the incarnate Word, with non-spiritual, and even mischievous, consequences For example, in the Acts of John, after saying that Jesus appeared to him in different forms at different times, the writer continues "He had also another marvellous peculiarity When I sat at meat He was wont to take me to His bosom...and sometimes His breast *felt-when-I-handled-it* soft and tender, but sometimes hard as if like rock[2]" This legend leads us to reflect that, in the Bible, the only instance of "*feeling-by-handling*" a person, is where Isaac "*feels*" Jacob and is deceived into the belief that he is Esau[3] And the Bible uses the word generally in a bad sense as in the Deuteronomic curse "*Thou shalt feel-thy-way* at noonday as the blind *feeleth-his-way* in darkness and thou shalt not prosper in thy ways[4]"

---

[1] Plutarch *Mor* 589 B τὰς ἀλλήλων νοήσεις οἷον ὑπὸ σκότῳ διὰ φωνῆς ψηλαφῶντες γνωρίζομεν, *Mor* 599 C αὐτὰ τὰ πράγματα...ὑπὸ τοῦ λόγου ψηλαφηθέντα καὶ ἀνακαλυφθέντα, *Mor* 588 D—E ἄγει τὴν εὐφυᾶ ψυχὴν, ἐπιθιγγάνων τῷ νοηθέντι, "delicate of touch (εὐαφής)"

[2] *Acts of John* § 2 ποτὲ μέν μοι λεῖα καὶ ἀπαλὰ τὰ στήθη αὐτοῦ ἐψηλαφᾶτο, ποτὲ δὲ σκληρά, ὥσπερ πέτραις ὅμοια

[3] Gen xxvii 12—22

[4] Deut xxviii 29, comp Job v 14, xii. 25, Is lix 10

711 (Mark xvi 9—14)

THE RESURRECTION

This being the case it is rather surprising to find Luke using this very word in an appeal of the risen Saviour to the disciples "See my hands and my feet, that it is I myself, *handle* me, and see, for a spirit hath not flesh and bones as ye behold me having[1]" We are not told whether they did thus "handle" Him Luke perhaps adds "He shewed them his hands and his feet[2]," but not "and they *handled* them" On the contrary, he proceeds "And while they still disbelieved for joy, and wondered, he said unto them, Have ye here anything to eat?"—so that Christ's "eating," not their "handling," seems to have been the cause of their final conviction that Jesus Himself was risen from the dead.

John does not deny that there was some basis for a tradition of this kind But the form in which he presents it[3] limits the story to one of the Apostles—who however (he alone tells us) had a surname that might lead some to mistake one person for two[4] This disciple had not spoken of "handling," but of much more "Except I shall see in his hands the print of the nails, and put my finger into the print of the nails, and put my hand into his side" In effect, Jesus replied, "Do this, but remember, Blessed are they that have not seen and yet have believed." It is not said that Thomas "*felt*" and "*believed.*" On the contrary, Jesus says, "Because thou hast *seen* me, thou hast *believed*" Thus John, like Luke, leaves us in doubt whether any disciple "*felt*" the risen Saviour But John differs from Luke by making it clear that Jesus did not Himself offer the test of "handling" to all the disciples as a means for

---

[1] Lk xxiv 39

[2] W H enclose this (Lk xxiv 40) in double brackets, and it is omitted by SS   [3] Jn xx 24—9

[4] Comp Jn xi 16 Θωμᾶς ὁ λεγόμενος Δίδυμος In Jn xiv. 22 "Judas not Iscariot," SS has "Thomas," Curet "Judas Thomas" Epiphan *Ancor* § 62 p 65 D says ἐδείκνυε τοῖς περὶ τὸν Θωμᾶν τὰ ὀστᾶ αὐτοῦ... Matthew says (xxviii 17) "And having seen him they worshipped, but *some* (οἱ δέ) doubted" In the next verse Matthew adds that Jesus "*drew near* (προσελθών) and spake unto them," and it appears to be implied that they then believed Comp 1 K xix 5, 7 "an angel *touched* (נגע) him (בו)," but Targ has "*drew near* (קריב) to him (ביה)" (Walton "accessit ad eum"). See *Notes* 2999 (i)—(iv)

712 (Mark xvi 9—14)

THE RESURRECTION

convincing them of His reality. On the contrary, in the Fourth Gospel, when "he shewed them his hands and his side," the disciples "rejoiced on seeing the Lord[1]"

Reviewing the Johannine accounts of the self-manifestations of the risen Saviour we appear justified in concluding that, although John does not deny the possibility that one of them included manifestation by "touch," he regards that kind of evidence as of a lower kind than the rest. He teaches us that the disciples attained belief in different ways. The beloved disciple was convinced by the mere sight of the open grave, the leisurely arranged grave-clothes, and (apparently) the suddenly recurring memory of Christ's past teaching, and of its accordance with Scripture; Mary Magdalene was convinced, not by material sight—for she thought she saw the gardener—but by hearing herself called by name, the disciples by "seeing", Thomas by seeing and hearing and by a special rebuke inviting him to apply his own test of touching.

In all these narratives we perceive that there was no manifestation of the Saviour except to those prepared to receive it. Pilate (we are led to believe), standing in the place of Thomas, would not have heard or seen that which Thomas heard and saw. And for future generations of Christians the Johannine Gospel pronounces a blessing in store for those who would believe all that Thomas believed without that evidence by which Thomas was convinced. For them the evidence would not be that of the senses alone, nor that of the judicial mind alone judicially weighing evidence. It would be collective. It would include the evidence of the Cosmos, or World, and that of the Logos, or Word, and that of the Spirit revealing the Thought that breathed the World into existence. It might be said to include "feeling." But, if so, that "feeling" must be distinguished from "feeling one's way in the dark." It would be rather a feeling that the World, the real ideal World, was all at one, like a Family, and that we were intended to be at home in it. And perhaps it might also be illustrated by the metaphor

---

[1] Jn xx 20

(Mark xvi 9—14)

THE RESURRECTION

of a clasped hand[1], which often conveys much meaning from one friend to another, when both are—like Socrates in Plutarch's words—"delicate of touch[2]"

The remarkable tradition peculiar to Matthew that the women, when Jesus "met" them, "came and took hold of his feet," differs widely from most of the traditions about the Resurrection in the Fourfold Gospel. It is discussed in a previous volume of Diatessarica[3].

§ 3 *The Mark-Appendix on Christ's last words*[4]

The Mark-Appendix, Matthew, and Luke agree in connecting Christ's last words with a mention of a future preaching of the

---

[1] Comp Origen *Cels* vii 34 "And even if '*the word of the Lord*' is said to have been '*in the hand of the prophet Jeremiah*' (Jerem 1 1) or some other, or the Law '*in the hand of Moses*'.. no one is such a simpleton as not to take in the fact that '*hands*' *of a kind* ($\chi\epsilon\hat{\iota}\rho\acute{a}s\ \tau\iota\nu as$) are so called metaphorically—about which also John says '*And our hands handled* concerning the word of life'"

[2] Εὐαφής, see above, p 711.

[3] On Mt xxviii 9 "Jesus met them.. and they came and *took hold of his feet*," see *Notes* **2999** (i)—(iv)

The Diatessaron has "(Jn xx 18) And then came Mary Magdalene, and announced to the disciples that she had seen our Lord, and that he had said that unto her And (Mt xxviii. 8*b*—9) while *the first women* were going in the way to inform his disciples, Jesus met them . and they came and took hold of his feet. " "*The first*" may possibly be an explanatory addition to distinguish this party of women, who were allowed to touch Christ's feet, from Mary Magdalene, who (according to Jerome and others) was not allowed to touch Jesus owing to her want of faith But it may have been supported by a misreading of $\pi\rho o\sigma\epsilon\lambda\theta o\hat{\upsilon}\sigma a\iota$, taken as a corruption of $\pi\rho o\epsilon\lambda\theta o\hat{\upsilon}\sigma a\iota$ Προελθεῖν in N T occurs 10 times, and in 6 of these instances has v r $\pi\rho o\sigma\epsilon\lambda\theta\epsilon\hat{\iota}\nu$ Προελθοῦσαι might be interpreted as "coming beforehand," that is "those who *came first* [to *the tomb*]" It might also be a corruption of $\pi\rho\omega\acute{\iota}$, written $\pi\rho o\iota$, and $\dot{\epsilon}\lambda\theta o\hat{\upsilon}\sigma a\iota$

[4]   Mark-Appendix xvi. 15—18 (R V.)

(15) And he said unto them, Go ye into all the world, and preach the gospel to the whole creation.

(16) He that believeth and is baptized shall be saved, but he that disbelieveth shall be condemned

(17) And these signs shall follow them that believe. in my name

THE RESURRECTION

Gospel to "all the world" or "all the nations", but in Luke Jesus says "It is written" that it "should be preached"—not "Go, preach," or "Go, make disciples"—and Jesus adds "Tarry ye in the city, until ye be clothed with power from on high"

John represents Jesus as saying to the disciples, on the first evening when He appeared to them, "As the Father hath sent me, *so send I you*[1]," and then "Receive the Holy Spirit, whose soever sins ye remit they are remitted unto them, whose soever sins ye retain they are retained[2]" Yet no definite "*sending*" follows. A subsequent sending, however, is implied in the

---

shall they cast out devils (*lit* demons), they shall speak with new (*some anc auth om* new) tongues,

(18) They shall take up serpents, and if they drink any deadly thing, it shall in no wise hurt them, they shall lay hands on the sick, and they shall recover

Mt xxviii 16—20 (R V)	Lk xxiv 46—9 (R V)
(16) But the eleven disciples went into Galilee, unto the mountain where Jesus had appointed them	(46) And he said unto them, Thus it is written, that the Christ should suffer, and rise again from the dead the third day,
(17) And when they saw him, they worshipped [him] but some doubted	(47) And that repentance and (*some anc auth* unto) remission of sins should be preached in his name unto all the nations, beginning from Jerusalem (*or*, nations Beginning from Jerusalem, etc)
(18) And Jesus came to them and spake unto them, saying, All authority hath been given unto me in heaven and on earth	
(19) Go ye therefore, and make disciples of all the nations, baptizing them into the name of the Father and of the Son and of the Holy Ghost	(48) Ye are witnesses of these things
(20) Teaching them to observe all things whatsoever I commanded you and lo, I am with you alway (*lit* all the days), even unto the end of the world (*or*, the consummation of the age).	(49) And behold, I send forth the promise of my Father upon you but tarry ye in the city, until ye be clothed with power from on high

[1] Jn xx. 21.

[2] Jn xx 23 This "retaining" accords with the Johannine doctrine that the Holy Spirit will (Jn xvi 8) "convict the world in respect of *sin*" as well as "of righteousness and judgment" Comp Mk xvi 16 "he that disbelieveth shall be condemned" Matthew and Luke have no parallel to this in Christ's post-resurrectional utterances

THE RESURRECTION

precept to Peter "Feed my sheep[1]" This does not give to the Apostle exclusively the duty of shepherd. It assures him that he, though he had denied discipleship, is now a disciple again and a shepherd, like the rest, under the Chief Shepherd; and the assurance is conveyed by Jesus after a meal in which He has fed seven of His disciples—one of them Nathanael, not an apostle—on a fish and a loaf[2].

There is as it were, a domestic character in the Fourth Gospel at this stage—as compared with a cosmopolitan character in the Three—that appears to be intentional. The Mark-Appendix compresses into one farewell scene (1) a command of Jesus to the Eleven to go forth to all the world preaching and baptizing, (2) a promise of salvation for believers and of confirmatory "signs," followed by (3) a statement—made however by the Evangelist, not by Jesus Himself—that He ascended into the heaven, having ended His instructions, and that they went forth preaching everywhere with the aid of the Lord and of the signs that duly followed[3].

Matthew does not describe Jesus as making mention of any ascension or departure. But he says about certain women "They came near[4] and took hold of his feet and worshipped him. Then saith Jesus unto them, Fear not; go, carry away word to my brethren that they *depart into Galilee, and there shall they see me*[5]" This seems to imply "*I depart for the present*" And it resembles the Johannine utterance of Jesus to Mary Magdalene, "Touch me not, for *I am not yet ascended unto the Father*, but go unto my brethren and say to them, *I ascend unto my Father and your Father*"—where "*Touch me not*" has been reasonably explained as "*Do not detain me*" by clinging to

---

[1] Jn xxi 15—17
[2] See *Son* **3422** *i* on Jn xxi 9
[3] Mk xvi 15—20 The promise, however, mentions (Mk xvi 16) "condemning" as well as "saving" Κατακρίνω, applied to the condemnation of the sinful, occurs, in the Gospels, only here in Mk and in Mt xii 41—2, parall. to Lk xi 31—2
[4] Mt xxviii. 9 on which see above, p 631 *Hor Heb.* and Wetstein *ad loc* identify this with the action of Mary Magdalene.
[5] Mt xxviii 10

716 (Mark xvi 15—18)

THE RESURRECTION

my feet[1] Thus the utterance in Matthew may be identified with a form of the one in John This is also suggested by their agreement as to the command to carry word to Christ's "brethren " If they are to be identified, we may suppose that in Matthew, as well as in John, an ascension is assumed as following this utterance Matthew does not mention the fact of a past ascension to "heaven" when he describes Jesus as coming to the disciples for the last time It may, however, be implied in the words "All authority hath been given unto me *in heaven and on earth*[2] The final utterance of Jesus, in Matthew, is a command followed by a promise· "Make disciples of all the nations..., and lo, I am with you alway, even unto the end of the world (*or, literally*, all the days, unto the consummation of the aeon)[3]"

Luke, in the Acts, if not in the Gospel, lays great stress on the Ascension, though he nowhere describes Jesus as mentioning it. He disconnects it altogether from any manifestations to women. These he twice mentions in his Gospel as being deemed by the disciples inadequate or disappointing ("idle talk," "him they saw not[4]"). He systematically accumulates evidences of Christ's resurrection and exaltation, first, that of prophecy, when Jesus, unrecognised, interpreted it to the two travellers to Emmaus; secondly, His visible presence, manifested to the two, and to the Eleven; thirdly, an offer to the Eleven to handle Him, fourthly (perhaps) the "shewing" of "his hands and his feet"; lastly, His eating in the presence of the Eleven[5]

---

[1] Jn xx 17, which *Hor. Heb.* explains as meaning "Do not *touch* and detain me"

[2] Mt. xxviii 18 "*all authority. .in heaven*" appears to imply that Jesus is seated in a seat of supreme "authority," such as Mark implies in the words (xvi 19) "sat down at the right hand of God"

[3] This must be distinguished from "unto the ends of the earth" It does not denote Christ's presence (Mk xvi 20) "everywhere ($\pi\alpha\nu\tau\alpha\chi o\hat{v}$)" cooperating with the preaching of the Gospel It suggests the end of an aeon of the cooperation of the Son reigning from heaven, and the beginning of a new aeon of the cooperation of the Son reigning on earth—in other words, His "kingdom" on earth   [4] Lk xxiv 11, 24

[5] Lk xxiv 27, 31, 36—9, [40], 43 Lk. xxiv. 34 is perhaps (Mark xvi 15—18)

THE RESURRECTION

Most of these proofs are connected with words of Jesus and not related as mere fact. Then comes an "opening" of the "minds" of the Eleven to the Scriptures[1], and an implied precept to preach the Gospel, as Christ's "witnesses" to all the nations, as soon as they should receive the Holy Spirit (described as "the promise of my Father[2]"). What comes last is rendered uncertain by the uncertainty of Luke's text. Jesus certainly "blesses" the disciples and is "separated" from them; and according to most authorities He is also "lifted up" or "lifted up to heaven[3]." But the full account of the Ascension—regarded as final—is reserved for the Acts, where it is described as occurring at a considerable interval after the events narrated in the conclusion of the Gospel[4]. Even there it is not mentioned by Jesus.

The final Lucan words of Jesus before the Ascension are recorded in the Acts as being an answer to "the apostles whom he had chosen," who asked Him, saying "Lord, dost thou at this time restore the kingdom to Israel?" The answer begins "It is not for you to know times or seasons, which the Father hath set within his own authority"; it passes into a promise, "Ye shall receive power, when the Holy Spirit is come upon

---

uttered by the two travellers, in which case it refers to the appearance at Emmaus, see *Notes* **2999** (xvii) *e—f*, and *Son* **3347** (x) *a*

[1] Lk xxiv 45. *Ib* 27—45 contains a threefold mention of "the scriptures" in connection with Christ's "interpreting" or "opening" them or "opening the mind [of the disciples] that they might understand" them. This is all the more remarkable as "scripture" does not occur elsewhere in Lk. except iv. 21 "To-day is fulfilled *this scripture*." John is the only other Evangelist who in post-resurrectional narrative connects knowledge of the "scripture" with belief in Christ's resurrection (Jn xx 8—9) "And he [i e the other disciple] saw and believed. For as yet they knew not *the scripture* that he must rise from the dead."

[2] Lk xxiv 47—9. With "*ye are witnesses*" comp Is xliii 10, 12 "*ye are my witnesses*." It recurs in Acts i 8 "*ye shall be my witnesses.*"

[3] See below, p. 729 foll.

[4] On the meaning of Acts 1 3 δι' ἡμερῶν τεσσαράκοντα, see *Notes* **2892** *a—c* maintaining that Origen regarded the phrase as implying "days of interval,"-not "days of duration," so that it does *not* mean "*for the space of* forty days."

718 (Mark xvi 15—18)

THE RESURRECTION

you", it concludes with a command implied in a prediction "And ye shall be my witnesses both in Jerusalem, and in all Judaea and Samaria, and unto the uttermost part of the earth[1]" Not one of the Three Synoptic Gospels attributes to Jesus any promise of a return from heaven to earth. Nor does the Acts, except as a promise made by two angels (called "two men in white apparel") "This Jesus, he that was received up from you into heaven, shall so come in like manner as ye beheld him going into heaven[2]" But when was this to be? In the course of a few months, or years, or centuries? This "time," or "season," was "not for" the disciples "to know." But apparently it might be at any time after the apostles had been Christ's "witnesses unto the uttermost part of the earth."

All these scenes in the Synoptic Gospels and the Acts are, so to speak, cosmopolitan. They concern "all the nations" or "the whole world," and they leave us asking—about "times" or "seasons"—"When will the Gospel have been preached by the apostles to the whole world, so that the day of the Lord may be no longer delayed, and Jesus may come down again from heaven—as He ascended to heaven when He was 'received' by a cloud 'out of the sight' of the disciples?" John does not leave us asking this question. He seems to encourage us to treat the "time" or "season" of the "coming" as almost a matter of indifference. He allows his Gospel, toward its conclusion, to shrink, as it were, into something of a private and personal kind with no definite farewell. And there seems to be a studious indefiniteness in "If I will that he tarry while I am coming, what is that to thee? Follow thou me[3]."

As for the universality of the Gospel—expressed in the Synoptists by "all the world" and "the whole creation," or "all the nations"—John expresses it previously by a peculiar phrase "all that the Father hath given me," or "all that thou hast given me," frequently used throughout his Gospel and especially in the Last Discourse[4]. On the rare occasions when

---

[1] Acts i 7—8.   [2] Acts i 10—11
[3] Jn xxi. 22 On ἕως ἔρχομαι, "while I am coming," see *Law*, p 525   [4] *Joh. Gr* 2740—4.

719 (Mark xvi 15—18)

John uses the word "nation" it is always in the singular and always applied to the Jews[1]

Passing to the Ascension, we find that an "ascending to heaven" of the Son of Man is mentioned by Jesus at an early stage in the Fourth Gospel, along with a "descending from heaven", and there both "ascent" and "descent" are spoken of as in the past, and are regarded as spiritual, not local, acts[2] Later on, in the body of the Gospel, and especially in the Last Prayer, ascension is implied in the doctrine that the Son is "going" to the Father Something more than a mere spiritual ascent seems contemplated in the words "Touch me not, for I am not yet ascended unto the Father[3]" The words seem to imply that after He had "ascended" He *could* be "touched" If so, John would seem to place an ascension of some special kind before the appearance to Thomas when He offered Himself to be touched. But this is doubtful John, like Luke, regards some kind of ascension as resulting in the gift of the Spirit; but he does not, like Luke, give us any description of it. He appears to subordinate any visible ascension of Christ on a cloud to an invisible ascension and exaltation of Christ in the hearts of His disciples.

Baptizing is mentioned both by the Mark-Appendix and Matthew, either as a condition for salvation, or as a part of the work of the Apostles Luke makes no mention of it here, but inserts in the Acts an early mention of a baptism with the Holy Spirit as having been predicted by Jesus[4], and then a mention (by Peter) of baptism as a condition for admission

---

[1] Jn xi. 48—52, xviii 35 (*Son* **3423** *i*, **3442**).

[2] Jn iii 13 "No one hath ascended into heaven (οὐδεὶς ἀναβέβηκεν εἰς τὸν οὐρανὸν) save he that descended from heaven (εἰ μὴ ὁ ἐκ τοῦ οὐρανοῦ καταβάς), namely, the Son of Man... " See *Son* **3386—90**, on "'The Son of Man' ascending and descending," and *ib* Index "Ascending," "Ascension " W H stop short at "the Son of Man," but SS adds "that is from heaven," and Curet. "that was in heaven," and R V inserts in txt "which is in heaven "

[3] Jn xx 17 It adds "but go unto my brethren and say to them, I ascend unto my Father and your Father...."

[4] Acts i 5

THE RESURRECTION

to the Church[1]. John makes no mention of baptism here, but tells us (quite early in the Gospel) that Jesus, or rather His disciples, baptized along with the Baptist and the Baptist's disciples, that is, before the Holy Spirit was given[2] The Mark-Appendix does not define the nature of the baptism, Matthew defines it as "into the name of the Father, and of the Son, and of the Holy Spirit", Peter, in the Acts, says "in the name of Jesus Christ[3]"

Neither the Mark-Appendix nor Matthew makes any mention of the outpouring of the Holy Spirit, nor of any promise of it. Luke represents Jesus as saying "I send forth the promise of my Father upon you, but tarry ye in the city until ye be clothed with power from on high"—presumably referring to the promise that he has previously recorded, "I will give you a mouth and wisdom," where the parallel Mark has "the Holy Spirit" and Matthew "the Spirit of your Father that speaketh in you[4]" John gives us much more fully this promise of the Paraclete, Christ's other Self, but places it, not after the Resurrection but in Christ's Last Discourse[5] John also, as has been said above, places the words "Receive the Holy Spirit" at the first appearance of the risen Saviour to the disciples

Though the Mark-Appendix makes no mention of "the Spirit"

---

[1] Acts ii 38—41 Peter's proclamation is not "*Believe ye and be baptized*" (in accordance with Mk xvi 16 "he that *believeth* and is baptized ") but "*Repent ye* and let each one of you be baptized " But in Biblical Hebrew A V "*repent*" may be expressed (*Beginning* pp 56—9) by שוב "*return*" or "*turn*," i e to God, and in New Hebrew the noun "*return*" תשובה (Levy iv 675 b) is regularly used for "*repentance*" (though in Biblical Hebrew it means (Gesen 1000 b) (1) a local or temporal "return," or (2) "an answer") In O T (R V and A V) the noun "repentance" does not occur except about God's repentance in Hos xiii. 14 "*repentance* (נחם regret) shall be hid from mine (God's) eyes."

In preaching the gospel, Peter might say "Turn ye unto the Lord," meaning "Turn ye unto God, the Father in heaven, through His Son, Jesus Christ," and this might be expressed in Greek by "Repent," but in fact it might differ very little from "Believe "

[2] Jn iii. 22, iv. 1—2.   [3] Acts ii. 38.
[4] Lk. xxi. 15, parall. Mk xiii. 11, Mt x. 20
[5] Jn xiv. 16—xvi 15.

THE RESURRECTION

it says that believers "shall speak with *tongues*," thus exhibiting another agreement with Luke (in the Acts), who describes "speaking with *other tongues*" as a result of the Pentecostal outpouring[1]. The writer—like Paul in the First Epistle to the Corinthians[2]—assumes that "*tongues*," used for "*other tongues*," is a technical term intelligible to the reader. The prominence given to it is remarkable. Paul deprecates the abuse of this gift and the excess of the admiration with which it was regarded. Yet here it has a conspicuous place among the "signs" that are to "follow those who have believed."

§ 4. *The Mark-Appendix and the Lucan Discourse to the Seventy*

The first place in the Marcan "signs" is given to "casting out devils," and the following context mentions "serpents." This recalls Christ's warning to the Seventy when they say to Him "Even the devils are subject to us in thy name." He replies "I have given you authority to *tread upon serpents and scorpions and upon all the power of the enemy*, and *nothing shall in any wise hurt you*. Howbeit in this rejoice not, that the spirits are subject unto you; but rejoice that your names are written in heaven[3]." What relation, if any, have the italicised words to those in Mark, "*they shall take up serpents*," and "*if they drink any deadly thing it shall in no wise harm them*[4]"? And was there probably any connection in Luke's mind between this peculiar promise, "*nothing shall in any wise hurt you*," and another—also peculiar to his Gospel and paradoxically following "Some of you shall they put to death"—namely, "*Assuredly not a hair of your head shall perish*[5]"?

---

[1] Acts ii. 4—11.   [2] 1 Cor xii. 10—xiv. 39

[3] Lk. x 17—20 "*hurt*," ἀδικέω. Similarly used in Rev vi. 6, vii. 3, ix 4, comp. Is x 20. It is used also (Steph *Thes.*) of the harmful action of frost, or unwholesome food, etc. Comp Hor *Odes* iii. 1. 32 "hiemes iniquas."

[4] "*Harm*," βλάπτω, see below, p 723

[5] Lk xxi 16—18 καὶ θανατώσουσιν ἐξ ὑμῶν,...καὶ θρὶξ ἐκ τῆς κεφαλῆς ὑμῶν οὐ μὴ ἀπόληται. This is in the Discourse on the Last Days, soon after the promise of "a mouth and wisdom," which is parall. to

THE RESURRECTION

An answer is suggested by the Marcan word "*harm.*" It occurs only six times in LXX—five of these uncanonical—and never as representing a Hebrew word. But in one of these instances, though the word is Marcan, the meaning of the context is Lucan It is uttered by a martyr, threatened with torture if he will not apostatize· "For try us now, O tyrant, and even though thou wilt *put to death our vital frames* (lit. *souls*) because of our piety, think not *to harm us* by thy torturing[1]" This same word is repeatedly used by Marcus Antoninus, who maintains that a man is not "*harmed*" inwardly or outwardly by anything but moral evil[2] Going further back to Epictetus, we find the doctrine of "not harming" reiterated in his Lectures And one of the earliest instances of it[3]—as well as the last sentence of his Encheiridion—lets us into the secret of its origin, taking us further back still It is a quotation from

---

Mk xiii 11 "the holy Spirit," Mt x 20 "the Spirit of your Father", but the words "*not a hair.. shall perish*" have no parall in Mk-Mt.

[1] 4 Macc ix 7 This reproduces the Lucan $\theta\alpha\nu\alpha\tau\acute{o}\omega$, "put to death," with the Marcan $\beta\lambda\acute{a}\pi\tau\omega$, "harm." Πείραζε γὰρ οὖν, τύραννε καὶ τὰς ἡμῶν ψυχὰς εἰ θανατώσεις διὰ τὴν εὐσέβειαν, μὴ νομίσῃς ἡμᾶς βλάπτειν βασανίζων

Βλάπτω recurs in Tob (1), Wisd (2), 2 Macc (1), and as a LXX error in. Prov xxv 20.

[2] Marc. Ant. iv 7—8 "Take away the notion [of harm] and you take away the [cry] '*I am harmed*' Take away '*I am harmed,*' and you take away the *harm*. That which does not make a man worse than he was does not make his life worse, nor does it *harm* [*him*], either outwardly or inwardly" It is a dogma with Marcus that what does not "*harm*" the society does not "*harm*" the individual: v. 22 ʿΟ τῇ πόλει οὐκ ἔστι βλαβερόν, οὐδὲ τὸν πολίτην βλάπτει Ἐπὶ πάσης τῆς τοῦ βεβλάφθαι φαντασίας τοῦτον ἔπαγε τὸν κανόνα Εἰ ἡ πόλις ὑπὸ τούτου μὴ βλάπτεται, οὐδὲ ἐγὼ βέβλαμμαι, vii 22 "consider above all things that so-and-so has not [really] *harmed* you, for he has not made your spirit (τὸ ἡγεμονικόν σου) worse than it was before," x. 33 "that which does not *harm* Law, does not *harm* either city or citizen," i e. either the City of the World, humanity, or any individual in it.

[3] Epictet 1 29 13—18, after laying down, as "God's best and most righteous law," Τὸ κρεῖσσον ἀεὶ περιγινέσθω τοῦ χείρονος, goes on to say that this is not broken in the case of Socrates In his "body," it is true, he drank "the hemlock." But had he nothing in return? Where was the possession of the Good in his soul (ποῦ ἦν ἡ οὐσία αὐτῷ

THE RESURRECTION

the Apologia of Socrates. "But as for me, Anytus and Melitus are able to kill me, but *harm me they cannot*[1]."

These facts indicate that in the Mark-Appendix we have a Gentile or Western form of a Jewish tradition like that in Luke "not a hair of your head shall perish." It was probably based on the story of the Three Martyrs in Nebuchadnezzar's furnace These were prepared, like the martyr in Maccabees above mentioned, to have their bodies destroyed in case God did not preserve them ("But if not")[2] In the case of the Three "the fire had no power over their bodies, nor was *the hair of their head singed*", but they, and the Maccabaean martyrs, and the martyrs of Christ, kept the "*if not*" steadily before their minds —as Peter also kept it in his Epistle, "And who is he that shall *do you evil* (R V *harm you*) if ye are zealous for that which is good? *But if ye should indeed suffer* for righteousness' sake, blessed [are ye][3]." A Jewish Christian poet might declare about a martyr, consumed in Nero's flames, that "not a hair of

---

τοῦ ἀγαθοῦ,)? ...And what says he [himself]? Ἐμὲ δ' Ἄνυτος καὶ Μέλητος ἀποκτεῖναι μὲν δύνανται, βλάψαι δ' οὔ The doctrine is also found in *ib.* 1 22 13—15, and 28 10, and comp 11 2. 15, 111 23 21, *Ench.* § 53

Why does Plutarch never quote Anytus—mentioning his false charge only casually (*Mor* 499 F)—while Marcus Antoninus never mentions him? Perhaps because the quotation ἐμὲ δ' Ἄνυτος had become a little too hackneyed for literary circles

[1] Plato *Apol* 30 C

[2] Dan 111 18 The Midrash on Cant vii 8 (Wu pp 174—5) says that the three Martyrs appeared before Ezekiel (xx. 1) and heard that God would reject their prayer. Nevertheless they determined to put their trust in God When they had left Ezekiel, God appeared to the prophet and said "Thinkest thou I will deny them my support? Nay, it shall not fail them But say nothing to them about me. Let them act on their own good purpose ... Their reward will be all the greater."

[3] 1 Pet 111 13 "do you evil," κακόω In LXX, this word represents several Hebrew words meaning "evil entreat," "smite," "oppress" etc Once it means (Is 1 9) "Who shall condemn (רשע hif.) me?" *i e* make-me-out-to-be-evil But Paul (Rom viii 33) quotes it as κατακρίνω In literary Gk κακόω means "make bad, *i e* useless for its purpose," but also "afflict with evil"

his head perished"; but the Greeks in the Western Churches, familiar with the language handed down from the martyr Socrates, would prefer to say that he was "*not hurt*"

This language the Mark-Appendix also adopts And it is not improbable that in borrowing it from the far-famed saying of the martyr Socrates, the writer borrowed at the same time the phrase in the context "If they shall drink any deadly draught, *i e* poison" For the "*hemlock*" of Socrates was as famous as his saying about not being "*harmed*," and we have seen that in one passage where Epictetus quotes the latter he also mentions the former[1]. The "drinking" of "poison" by Socrates would be familiar to many Christians in Rome during the first century, slaves, like Epictetus, but worthy members of the Roman Church, for which Church the Marcan Gospel was perhaps primarily written This may explain why Mark gives so conspicuous a place to immunity not from fire, or sword, or hanging, but from an evil so seldom mentioned as "poison[2]"

There remains the Marcan saying "They shall *take up* serpents"—difficult because it seems to represent the disciples as imitating snake-charmers Why *should* they "*take up* serpents"? The only narrative in the New Testament that even superficially resembles this describes Paul, not as "*taking up*," but as "*shaking off*," a serpent that had casually fastened on his hand[3] Luke indeed mentions a promise to the Seventy about "serpents and scorpions," but they were to be "trampled on," not "taken up[4]" Concerning the prophecy of Isaiah:

---

[1] See Epict 1 29. 13—18

[2] Euseb iii 39 9 mentions a story of Papias about Justus called Barsabas (Acts 1 23) ὡς δηλητήριον φάρμακον ἐμπιόντος καὶ μηδὲν ἀηδὲς... ὑπομείναντος The word ἐμπίνω seems seldom or never used (Steph. *Thes*) of swallowing by mistake No instance of this comparatively easy death is connected by early tradition with any Christian martyr. It seems probable that the story of Papias is based on a form of the Marcan tradition, and not the Marcan tradition on the story of Papias. Plutarch *Mor.* 509 D uses ἐμπίνω with κώνειον about the deliberate swallowing a draught of hemlock, but not with any reference to Socrates

[3] Acts xxviii 1—6   [4] Lk x 19

THE RESURRECTION

"The sucking-child shall play on the hole of the asp, and the weaned child shall *put his hand on the adder's den*," Jerome says "The infant, who is (1 Cor xiv 20) '*a babe (parvulus)* in malice,' will put his hand on the hole of the asp (perhaps alluding loosely to Mk xvi 18) and he *chases devils* from the human bodies that they beset (perhaps referring to Mk xvi 17)," but "the weaned child" does more; he penetrates to the recesses of Satan, "Whence also to the [Seventy] Apostles power was given (Lk x. 19) that they should 'tread upon serpents and scorpions and upon all the power of the enemy[1].'" According to this view, both the promise in Luke and that in Mark come from one and the same Prophecy—that of Isaiah, about the dominion of the Little Child

Tertullian, on the other hand, quotes the ninety-first Psalm ("upon the lion (LXX asp) and adder shalt thou tread,") as well as the Prophecy of Isaiah, as being applicable to the Lucan record of Christ's promise of healing powers to His disciples[2] Both the Psalm and the Prophecy could hardly fail to influence the doctrine of Jesus But the Psalm is, in part, quoted by Satan to Jesus in the Temptation, and consequently liable to objection[3] The Prophecy seems to take us back most closely to Christ's fundamental doctrine of the New Kingdom, the Kingdom of the Little One And of that doctrine, poetically expressed, there appears to be an ancient vestige in this Pseudo-Marcan tradition of a promise that Christ's disciples "shall take up serpents"

---

[1] Jerome on Is. xi 8—9.

[2] Tertull *Adv Marc* iv 24 after quoting Lk. x 19 "tread on serpents and scorpions," and also Is xi 8—9, proceeds to quote Ps. xci 13 "Upon the asp and the adder shalt thou tread" as shewing that "this power the Creator conferred first of all upon His Christ," and then he applies these promises to Christian acts of healing "When therefore He proclaimed the benefits of His cures, then also did He put (Lk x 19) 'the scorpions and the serpents' under the feet of His saints"

[3] Comp Jerome on Ps xci 11—12 "Vere Diabolus, quasi Diabolus, interpretatur de Salvatore quod non est de Salvatore"

THE RESURRECTION

§ 5. *The Ascension in the Mark-Appendix*[1]

The Mark-Appendix concludes by mentioning two acts of the Lord Jesus, the Ascension and the Assession, and then the "preaching of the word" by the Apostles "everywhere," and then the "confirmation" of "the word" by the Lord "through the signs that [always] accompanied it[2]"

As to the Ascension, Mark uses a Lucan word "*taken-up*," or "*received-up*," but with the addition of "*to heaven*," whereas Luke in the Acts says once "he was received up," absolutely, and in the Gospel speaks of "his receiving up[3]" The disadvantage of "*to heaven*" was that it might mean, for Jews, one of "*the seven heavens*," perhaps a low one[4]. But if "to heaven" was left out, the meaning might be little more than a pious expression for "died"—"taken upward" being used for "taken by the hand of God from this life[5]" Greeks and

---

[1]   Mark-Appendix xvi 19—20 (R V)

(19) So then the Lord Jesus, after he had spoken unto them, was received up into heaven, and sat down at the right hand of God

(20) And they went forth, and preached everywhere, the Lord working with them, and confirming the word by the signs that followed   Amen

[2] Mk xvi 19—20 Ὁ μὲν οὖν κύριος [Ἰησοῦς] μετὰ τὸ λαλῆσαι αὐτοῖς ἀνελήμφθη εἰς τὸν οὐρανὸν καὶ ἐκάθισεν ἐκ δεξιῶν τοῦ θεοῦ   ἐκεῖνοι δὲ ἐξελθόντες ἐκήρυξαν πανταχοῦ, τοῦ κυρίου συνεργοῦντος καὶ τὸν λόγον βεβαιοῦντος διὰ τῶν ἐπακολουθούντων σημείων

[3] Ἀναλαμβάνω, *pass, applied to persons* is used in canon LXX only of Elijah's being "*taken up*," or "*ascending*," to heaven, 2 K 11. 9, 10, 11 (setting aside LXX error in Ezek xii 6, 7)   In Sir xlviii. 9, 1 Macc ii 58, it is applied to Elijah, in Sir xlix 14 (A μετετέθη) to Enoch   In N T, it is used only of Christ's Ascension, Acts 1 2 (Luke) absol, 1. 11 (angels speak) ἀφ' ὑμῶν εἰς τὸν οὐρανόν, 1. 22 (Peter speaks) with ἀφ' ἡμῶν, 1 Tim. iii 16 with ἐν δόξῃ. Lk ix. 51 "the days of his *receiving-up* (ἀναλήμψεως)" shews that Luke himself might naturally use the verb absolutely, though he does not represent Peter as using it thus.

[4] 2 Cor xii 2 "snatched up to the third heaven."

[5] Comp the only instance of ἀναλαμβάνω *pass* in Goodspeed *Patr Apost*, Hermas *Vis* 1 1. 5 where a woman salutes Hermas from heaven, and when he asks her τί σὺ ὧδε ποιεῖς, replies Ἀνελήμφθην..., on which the editor remarks that it implies death ("Domina igitur

THE RESURRECTION

Romans believed in the Ascension of Hercules[1] It was advisable to distinguish Christ's Ascension from such ascensions as those.

Matthew describes no Ascension at all[2] Perhaps one might be said to be implied in the words, "Lo, I am with you alway, even unto the end of the world"; for that could most vividly be realised by regarding Jesus as pouring out His influence from above on all the disciples in every corner of the earth. And if this was to be so, Jesus was to be above, beholding and helping them from above, while the results of His help were felt below. But there was no absolute need to postulate a local "above" or "heaven" for such a beholding and helping Some might prefer to say that Jesus would dwell in the hearts of His disciples in every place and at every time, without any such beholding or looking down.

Luke's course is at first sight very perplexing, and it has perplexed the earliest scribes, who have freely altered his text. In his Gospel, he says that, "*in the act of blessing*[3] *them* (i e. *the*

---

defuncta erat") Goodspeed *Apolog* gives three instances, all from Justin Martyr (1) *Tryph* § 32 "our Lord Jesus Christ...was *taken up* into heaven"; (2) those who believe that souls (*Tryph.* § 80) "at the moment of death are *taken up to heaven*" are described as heretics, (3) Christians condemn the exposure of babes lest they should perish because (*Apol.* § 29) not "*taken up*"

[1] Origen *Cels* vii 53 quotes Celsus as asking why the Christians could not be content with the old heroes who died glorious deaths and became demigods And the first name he mentions is that of Hercules Comp Hor. *Odes* iii 3 9 foll "Hac arte Pollux et vagus Hercules..."

[2] See however above, p 717, n. 2, quoting Mt xxviii 18 "all authority *in heaven*..."

[3] Lk. xxiv 50—51...εὐλόγησεν αὐτούς καὶ.. ἐν τῷ εὐλογεῖν αὐτὸν αὐτούς... "Blessing *them*" must be distinguished from "blessing [*God*]" in the breaking of bread, as in Mk vi. 41, Mt xiv 19 "*he blessed* [*God*]." But the parall Lk ix 16 there has "*blessed them*" (*Law* p 315 foll.) And there was a liability to confuse (*Law* p 319) פרס, meaning "*spread out the hands*" *in blessing God*, over bread, with פרס meaning "break" bread Luke elsewhere describes Jesus as being manifested to the two disciples at Emmaus (Lk xxiv. 35) "in the breaking of bread," previously mentioned in Lk xxiv. 30 "he

THE RESURRECTION

disciples)," Jesus "*was-separated from them*"—using a word that occurs in the Gospels only once elsewhere and there about an interval of time[1]. Many authorities add "*and he was carried up into heaven*" D and SS, instead of "*was separated*," substitute severally "*withdrew*," and "*was lifted up*," and shorten the text by omitting the words bracketed as follows "(D) *withdrew* (SS *was lifted up*) from them [*and was carried up into heaven*] and they [*having worshipped· him*] returned to Jerusalem[2]."

It should be observed that the bracketed clause "*was carried up*," even if genuine, is not the same as the Lucan "*was taken up*, or, *received up*," nor does it appear to be thus used in early Christian writings[3]. But if it is not genuine we must conclude that Luke does not intend, in the Gospel, to describe Jesus as "*ascending*" He reserves that for the Acts. Passing to the Acts we find the Ascension described, in all MSS except D, by a word that is never used in literary Greek except to mean "*lifted up*" with pride, false hope, or in some other bad sense. "And having said these things, while they were looking, *he was lifted up*[4]"

---

blessed"—not "*blessed it*"—"*and brake*" It is possible that as in Lk ix 16, so in Lk. xxiv 50—51, αὐτούς is an erroneous insertion, and the latter passage originally referred to "*blessing* [*God*] *over bread*" Ἐν τῷ in Luke is a sign of Hebraic influence, see *Son* 3333 *e*, *Introd* p 112 foll., *Beginning* p 111 and *Proclam* p 153

[1] Lk. xxiv 51 καὶ ἐγένετο ἐν τῷ εὐλογεῖν αὐτὸν αὐτοὺς διέστη ἀπ' αὐτῶν [καὶ ἀνεφέρετο εἰς τὸν οὐρανόν]

Διΐστημι occurs in N T only here, and Lk xxii 59, διαστάσης ὡσεὶ ὥρας μιᾶς, Acts xxvii 28 βραχὺ δὲ διαστήσαντες (R V "after a little space"). The only intrans. inst. in canon LXX apart from Is lix 2 (A), is Exod xv 8 "the water was *piled up* (עָרְמוּ)" LXX διέστη, Aq etc ἐσωρεύθη. But in Prov. xvii 9 "*divideth* friends," διΐστησι = פָּרַד. Goodspeed gives διΐστημι only in Athenag *Leg* § 15 διεστᾶσιν "they [*i.e.* God and matter] are *separate* from one another."

[2] "Withdrew," ἀπέστη Lk xxiv. 51 (D) καὶ ἐγένετο ἐν τῷ εὐλογεῖν αὐτὸν αὐτοὺς ἀπέστη ἀπ' αὐτῶν καὶ αὐτοὶ ὑπεστρέψαν εἰς Ἱερουσαλήμ.

[3] The passive of ἀναφέρω does not occur in Goodspeed concerning the Ascension. Ign *Eph* § 9 uses it metaph. about men as stones "lifted up" into "the heights (τὰ ὕψη)" of God's Building.

[4] Acts i. 9 καὶ ταῦτα εἰπὼν βλεπόντων αὐτῶν ἐπήρθη, καὶ νεφέλη ὑπέλαβεν αὐτὸν ἀπὸ τῶν ὀφθαλμῶν αὐτῶν. Here it may be noted that (Mark xvi 19—20)

THE RESURRECTION

Then Luke adds that a cloud took Jesus up, but instead of his usual word for "taking up," he substitutes the word used by Herodotus to describe the dolphin that "took up and placed on its back" the drowning Arion, "And a cloud *took him up from below [and withdrew him]* from their eyes[1]."

The clue to some of these obscurities is supplied by D which, instead of *"lifted up,"* gives (with the change of one letter) *"taken away*[2]*"* Precisely the same emendation has been recognised as necessary in a passage of Justin Martyr, speaking of those who are not able to *"detach themselves,"* or *"be taken away,"* from things of the earth—where the ordinary text has *"be lifted up*[3]*." "Take-away,"* in the passive, is of very rare occurrence, but it occurs in the Synoptic tradition about the days

---

in the next verse, punctuated as follows, καὶ ὡς ἀτενίζοντες ἦσαν εἰς τὸν οὐρανόν, πορευομένου αὐτοῦ, the last two words are emphatic, "as he was [still] going on " The meaning is that He did not "vanish into space" as at Emmaus (Lk xxiv 31) ἄφαντος ἐγένετο, but continued His upward path till the Shechinah withdrew Him from their sight. W H have οὐρανὸν and no comma after it

A scholium on this passage (Cramer) says that the cloud is the "symbol of the divine power" quoting Ps civ. 3 ὁ τιθεὶς νέφει τὴν (*leg.* νεφέλην) ἐπίβασιν αὐτοῦ It also speaks of the disciples as "fully awake and not slumbering," perhaps contrasting this passage with Lk ix 32, and still more with Lk xxii 45

Ἐπαίρομαι pass applied to persons is repeatedly used in literary Gk, LXX, and N T metaph , almost always in a bad sense, but never of literal *"lifting up"* except in Byzantine Gk about the lifting of an "imperator" on the shields of soldiers (and Steph. *Thes* quoting Jo Malal p 267, 2—prob copied from Lk).

[1] Ὑπολαμβάνω is used by Herod 1 24 and Plato *Pol* 453 D, of a dolphin "taking" Arion "on its back" (which Plutarch *Mor* 161 D paraphrases by δελφίνων ὑποδραμόντων ἀναφέροιτο). It is a semi-personification In 3 Jn 8 A V "receive," R V "welcome," the meaning is "hospitably support "

[2] Acts 1 9 txt ἐπήρθη, D ἀπήρθη D also alters the order and omits βλεπόντων αὐτῶν "And when he had said these things (αὐτά) a cloud [*came and*] *supported* him, and he was taken away (ἀπήρθη) from their eyes "

[3] Just Mart *Apol* § 58 (txt) τοὺς μὲν τῆς γῆς μὴ ἐπαίρεσθαι (*leg.* ἀπαίρεσθαι) δυναμένους, where see ed note Goodspeed gives ἀπαίρεσθαι ad loc but ἐπαίρεσθαι (AB).

THE RESURRECTION

"when the bridegroom shall be *taken away*," and was discussed in its place[1] There it was illustrated from what the sons of the prophets say to Elisha, before the Ascension of Elijah "Knowest thou that the Lord will *take away* thy master from thy head to-day[2]?" Antecedently it seems probable that Luke would resort to that ancient narrative to describe the Ascension of Jesus, and now we have to ask whether he seems actually to have done so.

Such a hypothesis would at all events explain Luke's tradition that Jesus "*was separated*" from the disciples For "*separated*," in Delitzsch's rendering of Luke, is the same word that occurs in the Hebrew text describing how Elijah and Elisha were "*separated*" by the chariot of fire[3]. It would also explain why Luke might add a form of what the Scripture adds there, about Elijah—namely, "went up into heaven"—although he believed that the final "taking up" of Jesus was to come later on Again, Scripture describes God as "making *the clouds*" His "*chariot*[4]" This would suggest a likeness of Elijah's "*chariot*" to the "*cloud*" on which Jesus ascended. And a kind of "riding" is suggested, as has been shewn above, by the peculiar word used by Luke to describe the "cloud" that presents itself from below to "support" the Saviour.

---

[1] See *Proclam* pp 316—17 on Mk 11 20, Mt ix 15, Lk v 35. 'Ἀπαίρω act in LXX freq. = "break up [camp]," "journey" Hesych. has ἀπαίρομαι = ἀποδημέω, but that may be middle Steph *Thes* 1 2 (p 1140) gives no instance of the passive like that in the Synoptists

[2] 2 K 11 3, 5, LXX λαμβάνει

[3] 2 K 11 11 "[there came] a chariot of fire and horses of fire and made *a division* (פרד) between (בין) the-two (שניהם)." Gesen 825 gives פרד as "*dividing*" in various senses literal and metaphorical It = διίστημι in Prov xvii 9 "*divideth* friends" The pass. of פרד = ἀποσπᾶσθαι in Job xli 8 (9) (R V. xli 17) (Theod), and is used by Delitzsch in Lk xxiv 51 and also in Lk xxii 41 ἀπεσπάσθη, "he was (A V) *withdrawn*, or (R V) *parted*," from the disciples "about a stone's cast"—a tradition peculiar to Luke, and perhaps modified by traditions about the Ascension. Heb פרד = Aram (Onk) פרש, as to which, and פרס, see *Law* p 324.

[4] Ps. civ. 3.

THE RESURRECTION

Lastly, the emphasis laid by Luke on *"while they were looking"*—which is explained by an old scholium as meaning, in effect, "It was no vision, nor were they drowsy [as on other occasions][1]"—acquires new meaning in the light of the story of Elijah. For Elijah had been asked by Elisha for a "double portion" of his "spirit," and had replied "*If thou see me* when I am taken from thee, it shall be so unto thee; but if not, it shall not be so[2]." Those who discerned a similarity between the ascent of Elijah and the Ascension of Jesus would seem almost constrained to realise that the latter, like the former, could not have been beheld by those whose "eyes" were not spiritually "opened" to behold it[3]. But Luke nowhere says this.

John never speaks of the Son as being *"taken, or received, up,"* but always as *"ascending,"* or *"going up"*[4]. The first mention of this he connects with the doctrine of the living bread, and with unintelligent "beholding," in an obscure passage that may be paraphrased thus: "Doth this cause you to stumble? What then if at this moment ye are beholding [though ye perceive it not] the Son of Man *ascending* where He was before [through the sacrifice of the Cross][5]?" In the narrative of the ascent of Elijah the Hebrew text distinguishes the Lord's *"taking,"* or *"taking away,"* of Elijah from his *"going up"* to heaven. The LXX does not thus distinguish, but renders the latter by *"was received up"*—a unique rendering of the word[6]. The Mark-Appendix uses *"was received up,"* and,

---

[1] See pp. 729—30, n on Acts i 9—10.   [2] 2 K. ii. 10.
[3] See Jerome *Epist* xxii. 3 "when your eyes have been opened you shall see a fiery chariot like Elijah's waiting to carry you to heaven," where he refers to 2 K. ii 11 and vi 17. Yet *Epist* lii 7 "he was caught up into heaven in a chariot of fire and did not feel the effects of the flame" seems to recognise a material "fire" that would have burned the prophet, but for God's intervention.
[4] Ἀναβαίνω, first used thus in Jn vi 62.
[5] See *Joh Gr.* 2210—12.
[6] The LXX begins by rendering לקח, "take," correctly, λαμβάνω, 2 K. ii 3, 5, but then it proceeds to render it incorrectly, ἀναλαμβάνω *ib* 9, 10, and then (*ib* 11) renders עלה, "go up," also by ἀναλαμβάνω (a rendering of עלה unique in LXX).

THE RESURRECTION

as has been pointed out, Luke does the same when referring to it in the Acts[1]. But the Johannine word better expresses what may be called the naturalness of the action[2]. The Son was to "ascend where he was before" as to a natural home.

Elijah's promise to Elisha (of "a double portion" of his "spirit") resembles Christ's promise to the typical disciple ("Greater works than these shall he do[3]"). But they differ in this, that although both are really conditional, they state, or imply, different conditions. The former condition is stated thus, "If thou see me[4]." The latter is implied in the fact that it is addressed to "disciples," and the Master has defined the sign of discipleship as being love[5], so that He says, in effect, "If ye love me, ye will keep my word, and will love one another, and my Father will love you, and we will come unto you, and make our abode with you[6]." This was Christ's answer to the question how He would manifest Himself unto the disciples "and not unto the world[7]," and it teaches us that He was to be manifested by an inward and spiritual "seeing" that would be so much more real than any external "seeing," or merely intellectual "seeing," that a new metaphor, or group of metaphors, was needed to suggest its nature.

§ 6. "*And sat down at the right hand of God,*" *in the Mark-Appendix*[8]

These words are not to be taken as meaning that the disciples *saw* that Jesus "sat down," after previously *seeing* that Jesus "was received up," and as assuming that both of these

---

[1] Acts 1 2, see above, p. 727, n 3

[2] Jn's first mention of ἀναβαίνω (1 51) links it with καταβαίνω, and indicates a spiritual connection between heaven and earth (comp. *ib.* iii. 13 "No man hath ascended into heaven but he that descended out of heaven, [even] the Son of man, which is in heaven"). See *Son* 3374—3390 (iv) on "Ascending and Descending."

[3] Jn xiv 12   [4] 2 K 11 10   [5] Jn xiii 34—5.
[6] Jn xiv. 23.   [7] Jn xiv 22.

[8] Mk xvi 19—20, Ὁ μὲν οὖν κύριος ['Ιησοῦς]...ἀνελήμφθη...καὶ ἐκάθισεν ἐκ δεξιῶν τοῦ θεοῦ ἐκεῖνοι δὲ ἐξελθόντες ἐκήρυξαν... See above, p 727

THE RESURRECTION

acts were merely proofs of His divine nature. The Greek text, by means of its particles[1], expresses here a natural connection, or correspondence, between the heavenly act of Jesus and the earthly action of the disciples described in the following words, "He *on the one hand* ascended to heaven and sat down at God's right hand to help His disciples to do His work, but they *on the other hand* went forth proclaiming the Word, and doing His work, in every part of the earth, while He worked with them confirming the Word with the accompanying signs." There is a feeling that the position of Jesus Christ, at "the right hand" of God, is a symbol of God's cooperation with the Church of Christ, banishing disease, and sin, as is implied in the early Christian prayer: "And now, Lord,...grant unto thy servants to speak thy word with all boldness, while thou *stretchest forth thy hand* to heal, and that *signs and wonders* may be done through the name of thy holy Servant Jesus[2]."

But this clause about the divine Session in heaven—so briefly used in the Mark-Appendix—might easily be disconnected from the corresponding clauses about the work of the disciples on earth and the joint work of the Saviour from heaven ("the Lord working with them"). Then "sitting at the right hand" would lose much of its spiritual force. It might give the impression that Jesus, "at the right hand," did no work any longer, but merely sat waiting till His "enemies" should become His "footstool," or till the time should arrive when He should again "come from heaven" to "judge the quick and the dead."

Hence we might expect some Johannine doctrine on this article of the early Christian Creed. And it might easily be shewn that, although John avoids all metaphors about "the right hand of God," he nevertheless endeavours to express aspects of their spiritual meaning that might pass unnoticed. One aspect is the inevitableness of the divine judgment upon

---

[1] In literary Gk the correspondence between μέν and δέ is often so slight that it would be pedantry to express it in English except by vocal emphasis, but in the Gospels it is comparatively rare. Here the Vulgate expresses it by "quidem" and "autem" as also in Mt. iii. 11, ix. 37 etc.

[2] Acts iv. 29—30.

THE RESURRECTION

those who bring it on themselves. For those who love Christ, He is their Helper, or rather in the bosom of the Father as their Brother. But it is not so for His "enemies." For them He is seated on "God's right hand" as in the seat of judgment, converted into a Judge by the sins of men who will not accept Him as a Saviour[1].

§ 7. *"The accompanying signs," in the Mark-Appendix*

"The accompanying signs" may be illustrated by Paul's language to the Corinthians "At all events *the signs of the apostolic office* (literally, *of the apostle*) were wrought among you in all patient-endurance, by signs, and wonders, and mighty works[2]"—which uses the word "signs" in two senses, meaning, 1st, the general tokens of the apostolic office, 2nd, the particular acts, especially acts of healing (and perhaps the power to impart the gift of *"tongues*[3]*"*) which characterized "apostles." The Mark-Appendix has already said "*These signs shall follow* them that have believed," and has particularised them as exorcisms, "tongues," immunity from stings of "serpents," immunity from poisonous draughts. Now it uses a more emphatic form of "follow," meaning "*follow* [*close*] *on*," as if to mean "*following closely and inevitably*" And it says, in effect, "The Lord from heaven helped the disciples to do His work on earth by working with them. For the word of the Gospel that they preached on earth He confirmed from heaven by means of *the invariably-accompanying signs* [*that I have mentioned above*]"

These last words of the Mark-Appendix seem on a lower spiritual level than the last words in Matthew "I am with you alway, even unto the end of the world"; for they mention only "signs" of presence, but Matthew mentions the Presence itself

---

[1] See above, pp 522—4, on Mk xiv 62. Comp. Rev. v 6—7

[2] 2 Cor xii 12. In τὰ μὲν σημεῖα..., the meaning of μέν seems to be "this at all events in the first place," corresponding to a suppressed δέ, meaning "whatever else may be wanting in the second place."

[3] Acts viii 16—17. The subsequent verses indicate that the gift of the Holy Spirit was followed by some "sign," perceptible to the senses of Simon Magus—presumably "*tongues*"

They are also less poetically exultant than the last words in Luke: "continually in the temple, blessing God." There is some sense of anti-climax in Mark. But this sense will be diminished if we compare the Lucan use of "signs" in the Acts, beginning with a Petrine quotation from Joel about the Lord's "giving signs on the earth" which Peter applies to the gift of "tongues[1]." The word occurs repeatedly—along with "wonders," and "mighty works," and, in the singular, without these words, about "a sign of healing"—in what may be called the Petrine period of the extension of the Church[2]. After that come the great wonders and signs wrought by Stephen one of the seven *diāconoi*[3] Then, after mention (by Stephen the *diāconos*) of the "wonders and signs" wrought by Moses in Egypt[4], we are brought to a mention of "signs" wrought by Philip (another of the *diāconoi*)—particularised as exorcisms, and acts of healing, and afterwards called "signs and great mighty-works[5]."

This may be almost said to close "the sign-period" in the Acts[6]. At all events it closes the period of Petrine "signs" And we are given a hint as to the reason Although Philip the *diāconos* could work amazing "signs and mighty works" in Samaria, he had not (it is said) bestowed the gift of "the Holy Spirit" on his converts. To bestow this, "apostles" were apparently needed At all events Peter and John were sent down to Samaria, and by the imposition of their hands the converts "received the Holy Spirit[7]." When Simon Magus "saw that the Holy Spirit was given" by this act, he offered to buy this peculiarly apostolic power. Thus, above exorcizing and healing —which could be performed by a *diāconos*—the imparting of "tongues" speaking with the Holy Spirit appears to be

---

[1] Acts ii. 19

[2] Acts ii 22 (Christ's signs), ii 43 (signs wrought by the apostles), iv 16, 22 (*sing*, a sign of healing), iv. 30, v 12 (signs wrought by the apostles).

[3] Acts vi. 8.   [4] Acts vii. 36   [5] Acts viii 6, 13

[6] Σημεῖον does not occur again in Acts, except in xiv. 3, xv. 12

[7] Acts viii. 17.

736 (Mark xvi. 19—20)

THE RESURRECTION

magnified in the Acts of the Apostles as a privilege belonging to none but apostles.

Soon afterwards, in consequence of Peter's preaching, and without any imposition of hands, the Holy Spirit is described as descending on uncircumcised Gentiles. The Jews present are described as being "amazed because on the Gentiles also was bestowed the gift of the Holy Spirit." How did the Jews know this? Because "they heard them *speak with tongues*[1]." Later, by alleging this fact, Peter convinces his opponents at the Council of Jerusalem. "They held their peace...saying, Then to the Gentiles also hath God granted repentance unto life[2]."

These facts—or at all events the belief in these facts—may explain the great importance that might be attached to "tongues" during a few years, and might be expressed in a few ancient documents, of the growing Christian Church[3]. The

---

[1] Acts x. 44—6.   [2] Acts xi. 18.

[3] The pl. "tongues" does not occur in Goodspeed except 2 Clem. § 17 (in quotation), and in Justin Martyr (thrice). Once Justin is quoting (*Tryph* § 27). Twice he is referring to (*ib* § 102) the confusion of tongues, or to (*ib* § 130) nations dispersed according to their tongues. Here we might have expected him to say that Christ, by "the gift of tongues," typically cancelled "the confusion of tongues." But he is silent. So, too, are Irenaeus, Tertullian, Clement of Alexandria, and Jerome—who say little or nothing about Gen. xi. 7—8 (Confusion of Tongues) and Acts ii. 1—13 (Gift of Tongues).

Origen, however, says on the former (*ad loc.*, Lomm. viii. 68) "It is a token of malice (γνώρισμα κακίας) that the tongues were confused (τὸ συγχυθῆναι), it was a token of virtue when '*in all them that were believers there was one heart and soul*'" Comp. Acts iv. 32 "*Now in the multitude of them that believed there was one heart and soul.*" Origen is referring to the Gift of Tongues, as described in the Acts, where it is regarded as being both the sign, and the consequence, of the Christian spirit of peace and unity. His comment (doubtless) leads us toward the right explanation of a historical and very marvellous fact in the Christian Churches of the first century. But the silence of almost all the early Fathers indicates that, in their days, "tongues" had become largely a thing of the past, the memory of which somewhat perplexed those writers who might have been expected to comment on it.

THE RESURRECTION

Mark-Appendix appears to have preserved here one of these very ancient Petrine traditions It was of a piece with the proclamation of the Gospel "everywhere," that is, in every corner of the earth to the Gentiles as well as to the Jews. Peter had stamped the gift of tongues as the Charter of the Gentiles. "And I remembered the word of the Lord, how that he said, John indeed baptized with water, but ye shall be baptized with the Holy Spirit. If then God gave unto them the like gift as [he did] also unto us, when we believed on the Lord Jesus Christ, who was I, that I could withstand God[1]?"

John has but one instance of the phrase "signs and wonders" (so frequent in the Acts). It is in a sentence of reproof, "Except ye see signs and wonders ye will not believe[2]" He nowhere uses the Synoptic term "mighty-works" Perhaps he had come to the conclusion that external "signs" (and especially "tongues") were liable to abuse and fraud in some, besides leading others into self-deception or self-conceit. But without mentioning the word "sign" he gives us, in an utterance of Christ, the one sure sign of Christian discipleship "By *this* [*sign*] shall all men know that ye are my disciples if ye have love one to another[3]." The "love" is to be that kind of love with which Jesus Himself loved His disciples, and the Father loved the Son[4]. It is to pass into us like the bread of life and to become part of ourselves.

This thought seems latent in the final Johannine mention of "signs," after the blessing pronounced on those who "have not seen and yet have believed" "Many other *signs* therefore Jesus did *in the presence of his disciples*, which are not written in this book. but these are written that ye may believe that Jesus is the Christ, the Son of God, and that, believing, ye may

---

[1] Acts xi. 16—17. The Pauline view of "tongues" is rully expressed in 1 Cor. xii 10—xiv 39. Paul says that (xiv. 22) "they are a sign, not to them that believe, but to the unbelieving," and that they need to be "interpreted" If in any congregation "all speak with tongues" and there come in "men unlearned or unbelieving," "will they not"—he asks them—"say ye are mad?"

[2] Jn iv 48. [3] Jn xiii 34—5
[4] Jn xv 9—10, 17, xvii. 23 etc.

THE RESURRECTION

have life in his name[1]" The context supports Chrysostom's view that John is referring to the signs that were wrought "*in the presence of the disciples [alone]*," after Christ's resurrection And this helps us to understand why the writer is not content to stop here, but proceeds to add just one more final sign (out of "many") in order to shew how Christ, after His resurrection, wrought it "in the presence of his disciples" so as to strengthen them with the bread of life, that they might "have life in his name" And then follows the scene at the Sea of Tiberias, where Jesus gives to the seven disciples their food in the morning before sending them forth to feed others with the living bread

It would be a historical error to deny that the signs of tongues and exorcisms and healings played a large part in establishing the early Churches in Jerusalem and Corinth and other cities of the empire But it would also be a historical error to assume that Jesus Himself regarded these acts as the essential "signs" of the New Kingdom. These and similar acts were better called "works" in the Fourth Gospel, where Jesus is represented as saying that the disciples should do even "greater works" than His own because He was to "go to the Father[2]." These works might vary not only in person and person, but also from time to time.

But while the "works" might vary, the sign was to be invariable The one unvarying "sign" of the Christian faith, at all times and in all persons—the sign, or ensign, with which they were to conquer the sinful world and without which they were most dismally to fail to conquer it—was that Christians should "love one another" with the love with which Christ loved them This love is not what many would call love "To love" as Christ loved is not "to like," or "to cherish indulgently," or "to exempt from pain." The Father loved the Son, yet sent Him to suffering and to death Jesus loved the disciples, yet also sent them on the same path What love is, cannot be so easily defined as what it is not. It must be learned from all things good and

---

[1] Jn xx 30—31   [2] Jn xiv. 12

THE RESURRECTION

beautiful and true, but above all from the Spirit of the Father and the Son—breathing its influence into us through human nature at its best as known to us in the history of the past and in our experience of the present.

In "the history of the past," a preeminent though not an exclusive place must always be assigned to the Four Gospels. And even the earliest of the Four, with all its patent defects, may be profitably regarded as intended to prepare us for subsequent explanations, corrections, and developments, not in the first century alone, but in all centuries, to the intent that the Christian Church may ultimately be found to have remained faithful to Christ's Spirit and not to have relapsed for ever from His living Gospel into a dead Law.

INDICES

INDICES*

		PAGE
I.	SCRIPTURAL PASSAGES	743
II.	ENGLISH	766
III.	GREEK	793

* Owing to a combination of unfortunate circumstances just before publication, these Indices have not received so full and complete a revision as those in previous volumes This will have caused (I fear) several errors and defects—especially in the English Index For removing some of these my thanks are due to my son, Mr Edwin Abbott, Tutor of Jesus College, Cambridge

INDEX

I   SCRIPTURAL PASSAGES

GENESIS

		PAGE
1	1	45
	2	663
	3	74
	9	670–71
	14	254
	16	254
	22	119
	27	119
	28	119
2	5	684
	8	642
	21–2	626
3	1	269
	7	207
	8	244
	16	111
4	6	454
5	24	683, 685
6	2	21
	4	21
	12	89
	17	612–14
7	21	612, 614
8	21	383
	22	324
11	7–8	737
	27	481
12	1	132, 138
	3	83
13	2	132
14	1	80, 293
	14	357–8
	18	293
15	1	131
	2	138, 612
	5	538
	14	684
16	7	177
	7 foll	679
17	12	8
18	2	676–8

GENESIS

		PAGE
18	2 foll	678
	3	676
	5	402
	7	422
	8	422
	10	678
	14	53–4
	16	676
	22	237
	25	237, 248
19	1	676
	10	676
	12	676
	15	676
	17	195
	17–22	676
	27	237
20	7	36
	16	415
21	9	137
	33	138
22	2	22
	12	22
	16	22
23	11	364
25	8	612–13
	17	612
	23	145
	24–5	146
	25	145–7
26	1–33	137
	12	137–9
27	4	462
	7	462
	12–22	710–11
	13	462
	28	657
28	11	188, 669, 688
	12	517
	20	58
29	2–10	664

GENESIS

		PAGE
29	3	664, 669
	8	664
	10	664
30	41	557
	42	557
31	13	58
	35	6
32	2	146
	7	110
	11	682
33	4	349, 351
	13	42
	14	42
34	2	281
	2–26	280
35	2–3	311
	3	110
	18	607, 610
	29	612–13
37	3	578
38	1	293
41	57	650
42	5	650
	13	685
	36	685
43	23	470
45	2	607
	22	357
	28	315
47	23	415
49	10	656
	10–11	173
	11	175
	18	651
	24	668
	33	612–13
50	1–2	375
	2	375
	3	375
	22	375
	26	375

INDEX

EXODUS		EXODUS			NUMBERS		
	PAGE			PAGE			PAGE
1 10	269	28	29–30	404	4	5	620
13–14	618	29	20	503		23	590
2 3	217		42	696		25	697
11–12	195		43	696	5	15	415
3 9	625		45	516	7	1	10
15	426	30	6	696		89	697
4 16	304		23	575	10	17	620
5 23	85		23–4	364		33	439
6 12	441		32	362	11	4	402, 487
20	656		36	696		8	418
7 14	6	32	13	426		12	43, 45
8 22	593		32	61, 359, 463		18	402
26	54	34	30	152		19	9
12 2	146	35	2	74	14	3–31	40
21–2	606		12	618	16	3	470
22	607				17	4	696
22–3	623				19	18	604
46	594		LEVITICUS		20	8 foll	668
14 13	236					11	625
15	235, 670	2	13	99, 100	21	2	58
24	661	4	3	487		17	665
27	661	5	7	385		17 foll	669
31	227		11	385	23	3	696
15 2	596–7	6	9	91, 93, 100,	24	3	451
8	670, 729			384		15	451
9	5		12	91		22	493
13	395		13	91	28	3–4	16
17	161	12	8	386	31	23	461
25	235	14	4	606	32	19	470
16 4	676		30	422	35	34	516
6–7	662		34	394			
17 6	668	16	8	577		DEUTERONOMY	
11	633		21	564, 569			
18 14	219	18	14	656	1	31	76, 78
20	28, 73	19	3	152	2	6	650
21	638		13	125	3	24	311–12
25	638		18	270		26	316
27	29		23	106	4	10	237
19 13	461	20	20	656		24	94
20 8	650	21	18	314		49	641
21 8–9	696	22	27	137	6	5	270
15	83	23	40	146, 182, 187	7	2	411
17	83	25	10	461	8	2	694
22 1	187	26	10	380		3	402
23 14 foll	200		11–12	244		15	694
20	439		12	244, 246		16	402
24 7	518		13	694	10	1	36
8	605		42	15		8	237
14	648	27	19	650	17	6	248, 514
16	10					13	343
16–18	9		NUMBERS		18	5	85
25 8	516					7	85, 237
21–2	695–6	1	1	669		10	107
22	696		51	620		15	36
26 31	617	2	2	177		19	85
36–7	618	3	7	697		20	85
27 16	618						

SCRIPTURAL PASSAGES

DEUTERONOMY

		PAGE
18	22	85
19	5	90
21	5	85
	23	591
23	14	246
	18	213
24	1	115
	14	125
	19–21	206
28	29	710–11
29	5	694
	6	575
30	6	107
32	10	177
	15	135
	17	581
	25	43
	33	575
33	2	660
	17	143
	19	213
34	6	14, 36

JOSHUA

2	18	353, 567
3	7	152
4	14	152
5	4	107
	9	664, 672
6	3	10
	14	10
8	13	401
	20	195
	33	590
10	18	664
	40	411
18	6	577

JUDGES

1	18	701
2	1	679
	21	607
3	23	538
6	11	676–7, 679
	22	679
8	28	323
11	34	22–3
	40	9
13	16	422
14	11	702
16	13	684
	26	236
19	5	401

RUTH

		PAGE
1	17	534
	20	539
2	14	402
3	1	460
4	1	396

1 SAMUEL

2	10	143
3	17	534
4	4	677
	9	236
	21	687
7	3	652
9	9	569
14	1	603
	11	603
	27	511
	33	664
	45	553
	47	578
16	11	146
	12	146–7
17	16	439
	42	147
	45	85
	52	448
20	21–2	684
	31	411
21	2	396
	13	460
24	5	565
26	16	411
28	19	25
	22	402
29	3	497

2 SAMUEL

1	10	566
4	12	314
7	19	630
10	12	236
12	5	411
	30	566
13	18	578
	19	578
14	4	189
	15	702
	32	701
15	23	449
19	28	411
22	11	677
	36	369
23	8	590

2 SAMUEL

		PAGE
24	1–16	315
	3	137
	15	315
	16	316

1 KINGS

1	2	76
	42	638
	52	638
2	10	613
	24	74
3	7	42
	20	76
	28	152
4	33	606
8	11	236
	37	290
11	10	701
18	23	422
	26	233
19	4	315
	5	712
	7	712
	8	9
	9	686
	11	25
	13	686
22	20	406

2 KINGS

2	1	35
	3	731–2
	5	731–2
	8	670
	9	727, 732
	10	129, 727, 732–3
	11	727, 731–2
4	13	648
5	14	157
6	8	396
	9	27
	10	27
	17	732
	26	189
18	17	15
19	25	630
20	13	362, 650
23	10	461
	13	448
25	1	310
	3	310
	8	310

INDEX

2 KINGS			NEHEMIAH			PSALMS		
		PAGE			PAGE			PAGE
25	11	497	6	2	696	2	6	589
	18	148		10	696		7	589
			10	31	639		12	21
			12	46	148	4	1	110
1 CHRONICLES							8	91
						6	3	493
9	26	334	ESTHER			8	2	42, 46, 184
11	11	148					5	263
12	2	485	1	6	675	10	17	652
	9	148		14	647	15	1	8
17	17	630	3	8	167	16	8–10	376
20	2	566	4	7	390		9	376
21	1–15	315	8	15	566, 675		10	157
	14	315				17	1	315
	15	316				18	2	597
22	8	285	JOB				10	677
23	19	148					35	369
	20	148	1	6	21	19	4	602
24	21	148		16	406	20	1	312
28	3	285		17	406	22	(tit)	661
29	18	652		18	406		1	456, 597–600
			2	1	21		7	589–90, 627
				13	647		7–18	158
2 CHRONICLES			3	5	450		9	146
			5	14	711		10	597
6	4	60	8	17	76		14	606
8	16	609	9	31	157		15	158, 550, 600
14	11	85	10	15	323		18	424, 576–7
17	17	485	12	21	494		19	600
18	19	406		25	711		21–31	597
20	20	227	15	24	450	24	7–9	322
25	9	462	18	20	451	25	1	6
26	5	702	19	18	42		5	301
	20	148	20	26	91	27	1–3	499
28	14	497	21	25	406		2	499
32	8	493	22	18	575		13	315
36	11 foll	310	26	8	670		14	301
			27	14	167	29	1	184
			28	22	322	31	5	608
EZRA			30	4	512		11	627
			31	20	512	32	10	110
2	64	52	33	7	450	34	19	110
3	9	52		29	441	37	10	684–5
5	8	667	34	36	268		25	167
6	4	667–8	37	24	702		36	685
	10	648	38	7	21	38	11	627–8
	15	609		17	322	39	13	612
	20	52	39	21	485	41	9	400, 405
8	28–9	336–7	41	17	731	42	1	601
10	7	460	42	2	53		5	454–6
							6	455, 457, 601
							11	455–6, 601
NEHEMIAH			PSALMS			43	4–5	601
							5	455–6
2	13	651	1	2	233	44	25	455
	15	651		3	642	45	7	348
5	2	639	2	2	483, 543	46	6	607

746

SCRIPTURAL PASSAGES

PSALMS		
		PAGE
46	11	494
51	7	13, 607
	7 foll	595
	8	594
	11	304
	17	385
63	1	597, 601
68	24	597
	33	607
69	2	157
	9	216, 517
	21	575, 603
	26	437
72	11	610
	17	610
	20	610
74	16	254
	17	324
75	1–3	518
	7	406
	8	466
76	11	657
78	9	485–6
	20	625
	21	486
	24–5	37
80	5	402
	10	606
81	16	402
83	2	323
84	10	335
86	4	6
88	5	472
	8	627
	18	627
89	26	597
	27	146
	45	314
90	13	493
91	1–6	581
	6	581–2
	11	582
	11–12	681, 726
	13	581, 726
92	(*tit*)	635
	10	348
93	(*tit*)	635
94	17	315
96	7	184
102	23	314
	24	597
104	3	730–31
	4	677
	9	671
	27	650
105	21	336
	41	625

PSALMS		
		PAGE
106	23	315
107	34	108
109	10	167
	24	348
110	1	523
	1 foll	276
	4	293
113–118		432
113	1	46
118	19–20	322
	22	254, 668
	24–5	187
	25	183, 185–6, 189
	26	186
	27	217
	28	597
119	9	376
	157	134, 141
	166	650
121	4	614
124	1–2	314
130	5–6	652
	6	680
131	1–3	43
133	2	362
135	13	426
140	6	597
141	2	652
	5	349–50
143	2	701
	8	6
145	15	650
146	4	610

PROVERBS		
1	20	176
6	10	76
8	23	589
	30	45
10	27	314
11	19	134
12	28	701
14	35	525
15	30	254, 511
16	33	577
17	9	729, 731
20	4	309
	12	698
24	33	76
25	20	723
27	19	701
28	17	410
29	16	702
30	4	670
31	2	21

ECCLESIASTES		
		PAGE
1	13	371
3	10	371
	15	137
	17	627
	20	670
5	19	371
6	6	670
7	1	362
	12	130
	14–15	96
9	8	14
10	20	130
11	6	52
12	5	702

SONG OF SONGS		
1	3	449
	12	348, 352, 354, 383
2	11–13	324
	13	206, 325, 375, 378, 381
3	4	361
4	10	449
	13	352
	14	352
5	1	656
6	2	656
	9	21–2
	10	21–2
	13	657
7	8	22, 724
	13	378, 381
8	1	42

ISAIAH		
1	2	91–2
	2–31	92
	7	451
	7–8	314
	8	620
	9	314
	10	314
	11	217
	18	14, 564–5, 569
	29	536
	31	91
2	2	7
3	10	542, 545
5	1–7	251
	2–4	104
	5	211
	6–7	251

747

INDEX

ISAIAH

Ch	V	Page
5	7	202, 259, 701
	30	309
6	2	677
	2–6	677
	7	107
	8	333
	10	6, 70
	11	490, 493
	11–12	495
7	3	15
	9	227
	17	437
8	8	307
	9	143
	9–10	142, 210
	14	668
	18	46
9	1	694
	6	41
	18	664
10	15	480
	20	722
	23	314
11	1	568, 587, 682
	1–8	44
	3	568
	8	44
	8–9	726
14	6	135
	19	682
16	12	702
17	14	685
18	2	217
19	9	675
	17	291
21	3	291
	4	157
22	4	539
	11	630
	15	487
	15–22	334
	16	641
23	17	213
24	17	309
	19–20	309
25	1	630
	6	449
	7–8	672
26	1–2	322
	20	580
27	11	511, 631
28	1	448–9
	4	449
29	11 foll	258
	11–12	258
	13	258
30	27	630
31	9	511
33	7	539
	16	422, 430
34	5	411
	17	577
35	9	558
36	2	15
	3	487
37	26	630
	33	537
38	13	594
39	2	362
40	5–7	468
	11	76, 78
	11–12	632
	31	651
41	4	146, 149
	8	132
	27	146
	28	194
42	1 foll	66
	1–2	67
	1–6	69
	19	470
43	10	300, 718
	12	300, 718
44	6	149, 191
	8	300
	15	486
	17	474, 597
45	15	70
	22	143
46	3	43
47	14	511
48	12	149
	21	625
49	1	630
	6	142–3
	12	142
50	4	550
	4–8	527
	5	333
	6	525, 561
	9	724
	11	486, 511, 527
51	1	641
	5	651
52	10	143
	11	337
	13–15	550
53	1–8	550
	2	39–40, 44
	3	436
	4	373, 436, 572
	5	436
	6	408, 542, 615
	7	549–50
	8	467
	9	379, 638
	10	436
	11	293, 572
	12	542, 615
54	7	322
	13	258
55	1	45, 650
56	1	476
	3–4	120
	6–7	216
	7	58, 215
57	5	512
	15	516
	19	269
58	2	567
	3–10	420
	7	419
	14	402
59	2	729
	10	486, 711
	15–16	194
	16	451
60	22	80
61	1	384
	2	507
63	2	17, 146
	4–5	194
	5	451
	9	316
	10	304
	10–11	303
65	2	633
	8	122
	17–18	266
	17–25	262, 266
	18–22	266
	20	42
	25	52
66	1	514
	1–2	516
	2	514, 652
	7	293
	20–24	91–2, 96
	24	90–94, 377

JEREMIAH

Ch	V	Page
1	1	714
	9–10	287
2	14	456
3	20	352
7	9–10	212
	11	558
12	8	607
15	1	237

SCRIPTURAL PASSAGES

JEREMIAH

		PAGE
15	10	599
16	19	143
17	5	493
	8	702
	12	146
	27	172
18	18	701
	20	237
20	1–2	525
	9	694
21	4	586
23	36	694
24	2	104, 325
	5	325
	8	325
25	15 foll	461
29	2	120
30	9	190
31	3	630
	15	685
	31–2	428
33	6	330
37	13	497
	14	497
38	19	497
	22	157
39	9	497
48	40	307
49	8	129
	20	395
	27	172
51	39	512

LAMENTATIONS

2	17	623
	19	606
3	4	594
	19	134
4	21	461–2

EZEKIEL

1	18	702
3	17	28–9
	18	28–9
	20	29
	21	29
7	7	476
9	3	244
11	22–3	620
12	6	727
	7	727
13	5	701

EZEKIEL

		PAGE
15	2	104
16	4	99, 103
17	9	324
18	14	702
20	1	724
21	5	493
	26	566
	30	494
23	31 foll	461
24	1–2	310
	2	309
	12	90, 103
27	3	213–14
	30	539
28	2	219
34	18	474
	23–4	190
36	4	449
	29	290
40	15	175
43	25	422
45	9	316

DANIEL

1	4	258
	17	258
2	12	455
	22	395
	35	254
	45	669
	46	499, 648
3	18	724
	25	21
	46	525
4	14	90
	15	490
	25	136
	32	136
6	12	413
7	8	539, 682
	9	3, 14, 17, 523, 675
	13	67, 523
8	6	130
	20	130
9	16	309
	27	307
10	9	701
11	13	129
	24	129
	28	129
12	1	312
	3	28, 254
	13	473

HOSEA

		PAGE
5	7	352
	13	542
6	2	346
7	7	512
9	10	177
10	6	541–2
12	3	145
	4	177
	7	214
	8	131
13	14	583, 721

JOEL

3	3	577

AMOS

5	4	272
	16	172
	18–6 7	348
6	6	449

OBADIAH

1	11	577
	18–21	145

JONAH

4	9	457

MICAH

4	1	7
5	4	143
6	9	702
7	6	599

NAHUM

3	10	577

HABAKKUK

2	6	493–4
	9	222
	11	222
	11–12	286
3	19	662

INDEX

ZEPHANIAH		
		PAGE
1	14	539
3	15	191

HAGGAI		
1	6	512
2	5	304

ZECHARIAH		
1	21	323
2	10 foll	516
3	7	677
	9	254
4	6	304
	7	208, 254
5	9	677
7	3	686
8	6	53
9	9	173, 187, 191
	10	173, 179
	11–15	19–20
	13	710
11	5	131
	12	390
13	1	595
	4	701
	7	210, 435–7, 498
14	4–5	448
	8	324
	20–21	214–15

MALACHI		
1	11	241
3	1–3	15, 203
	3	203, 219, 280
4	2	660
	4–5	36

MATTHEW		
1	20	679
2	4–5	274
	13	679
	16	41
	19	679
	23	587–8
3	2	476
	7	280
	9	223, 248
	10	90, 94, 103
	11	734

MATTHEW		
		PAGE
3	12	90, 93, 94
4	6	581–2, 681
	15	694
	17	476
5	1	232
	6	419
	10	135
	11	135
	11–13	101
	12	101, 135–6
	12–13	108
	13	85, 87 foll, 99
	22	93, 411
	23	238–9
	23–4	238–9
	24	239
	25	526
	26	444
	29	411
	31–2	114 foll
	39	527
	44	135
6	5	237–8
	5 foll	231
	7	232
	9–13	231
	12	358
	14–15	221, 231
	16–18	231
	19–34	231
	24	219
7	1–5	231
	6–7	231
	7	221, 333
	13	133
	19	103
	23	533
8	2	372
	2–4	169
	6 foll	62
	10	444
	10–12	142
	14	691
	17	572
	20	369
	29	685
9	2	359
	9	372
	15	731
	23	647
	27–31	166, 168
	29	169
	37	734
10	2	147 foll
	3	372
	10	73
	17	297–9

MATTHEW		
		PAGE
10	17–22	296 foll
	18	298, 543
	19–20	296 foll
	20	302, 721, 723
	33	536
	34	496
	38	572
	40	71 foll
	41	85
	42	79–80
11	11–19	81
	14	34
	16	46, 648
	17	46
	25	42
12	16–17	66
	18 foll	66
	19–21	66
	23	701
	24	226
	36	232
	40	31
	41–2	716
	46	629
	49	629, 632
13	2	629, 677
	13	495
	15	6, 495
	20	416
	21	108, 110, 134, 311
	22	125
	39	287
	40	287
	42	93
	49	287
	50	93
	52	277, 378, 381
	54	438
	55	391
14	4	116
	13	65
	19	728
	26	703
	35	222
15	1	226
	4	83
	8	258
	27	39
	28	39, 59
16	5	26
	6	26
	19	147
	20	27
	21	30
	24	73, 572
	27	2

750

SCRIPTURAL PASSAGES

MATTHEW		MATTHEW		MATTHEW	
	PAGE		PAGE		PAGE
16 27–8	536	19 29	139	22 15	256
28	8, 12, 451	30	74, 141–7	15–22	255–9
17 1	8 foll, 12, 450	20 1–16	142	22	254, 256
1–8	1–24	17	52	23	261
2	3, 14, 706	17–19	151–5	23–33	260–66
3	24	18–19	524	29	261
5	5, 20–24	20–23	155–60	30	134
9	24–32	21	3	34–40	266–73
10	35	22	156	35	268
10–13	32–7	22–3	156	36	268
14–21	48–62	23	159–60	41–6	273–7
15	103	24–8	161–5	44	521
17	493, 495	25	162	46	267
18	38–9	26–7	73–4	23 1–7	278–83
19–20	55	27	148	4	280
20	227	28	164	5	280
22–3	63–4	29 foll	167	7	233
24–5	70 foll	29–34	165 foll	11	71 foll, 74, 145
24–7	72	30	274		
25	72, 537	31	274, 694	15	411
18 1	70 foll	33	168	23	202
1–3	117 foll	34	169	32	210
1–5	117	21 1	200, 365, 447	34	135, 259, 344
2	75–6, 81	1–7	171–9	37	192
2–5	71 foll	2	172	24 1–2	284–6
3	46	5	179, 191–2	2	696
3–4	121	7–9	180–93	3	286–9, 330, 447
5	85	8	180 foll		
6	81, 84, 88	9	46, 185–7	4–8	289–93
6 foll	410	10	200	5	294
6–9	86–95	10–11	193	6	292
7	410	11	588	8	45, 312
8	90, 93	12	200, 218	9	136, 297
8–9	84	12–13	194	9–14	294–305
9	88, 93	12–14	197	11	307
20	427	12–19	196–205	13	301
21 foll	228	13	58, 558, 696	14	301
19 1	115, 153	15	223	15	307, 523
1–10	112–16	15–16	222	15–21	305–13
3	115	15–17	198, 220 foll	18	310
4	116, 119	16	42, 46, 184, 222	20	308 foll.
10–12	119			21	108, 310
12	120	17	366–70, 447	22	313 foll, 318
13	39	18–19	196, 205–6, 220 foll	22–5	313–19
13–14	116			23	135
14	46	20–22	220 foll	24	294, 318
15	75–6, 117	21	207, 227	25–6	319
16	124	21–2	55	27	287, 330
16–22	123–7	22	58, 230 foll	29	109, 311
18–19	125	23	200, 243, 247	29–31	320–24
20	124	23–7	242–8	30	3, 523
21	124	25	157	31	321
22	125	33–46	202, 249–54	32	205 foll, 381
23–6	127–32	42	252–3	32 foll	206
26	53	44	252	32–5	324–6
27–30	133–51	22 5	120, 213	34	287
28	548	14	574	36	326, 328

751

INDEX

MATTHEW			MATTHEW			MATTHEW		
		PAGE			PAGE			PAGE
24	37	287, 330	26	35	535	27	11	545–8
	39	287, 330		36	446, 449		11–14	540 foll
	42–6	327 foll		36–46	444–76		12	549
	43	490		37	450–54		14	551
	45	327, 334		38	453–7, 599		15	552–3
	48 foll	334		39	54, 455, 458–62		15–26	554–62
25	12	533					16	556 foll
	13–15	326 foll		40	58, 453, 473		16–18	556
	14–15	331 foll		41	88, 467–8, 475		17	558
	21	335		42	464–5		18	542, 561
	35	370		45	470, 472, 474		20	559, 562
	36–44	500		46	469–76		22	558
	38	370		47	479 foll.		26	542, 559–61
	41	93		47–56	477–503		27	481, 483, 487, 544, 602
	43	370		49	488			
26	1–5	346		50	488, 491, 531		27–8	483
	1–16	339–89		51	492–3, 503		27–9	482
	2	339–42		52	493		27–31	563–70
	3	506, 509		52–3	492		28	564–5
	4	351		53	476, 545		28–9	564–70
	5	342–3		53–4	493		32	571–5
	6	354, 371–3		55	479 foll		32–6	570–83
	6 foll	354		55–6	488		34	575, 605
	7	342, 352, 363–5		56	496–8		35	576–9
				57	505–6		36	579, 679
	7 foll	347		57–8	504–13		37	583–8
	9	357		58	510–11, 528, 538		37–44	583–95
	12	349, 374–81					38	591
	13	382–4		59–61	513–19, 639 foll		39–43	589–91
	14	344		60	514		42	191, 546, 589
	14–16	390 foll		60–61	696		43	589
	15	346, 390		61	31, 64, 210		44	591–5
	16	391		62–5	520		45–50	595–615
	17–18	394		62–8	519–28		46	595–602
	17–19	392–7		63	521		47	602–3
	18	370, 395		64	522, 524		48	576, 603–7
	20–25	397–412		66	524		49	358, 490, 623
	21	400, 444		67–8	502, 525–8, 568		50	599, 607–15
	22	400, 407, 453					51	616–26
	23	349–50, 400–1, 405		68	569		51–2	620
				68 foll	534		51–4	616–26
	24	88, 410, 613		69	510, 538		54	617, 679
	24–5	407–12		69–71	528 foll		55	627, 649, 653
	25	407		70	535		55–6	626–31, 653, 658
	26	401, 414		71	538			
	26–9	413–30		71–2	529 foll		56	652 foll
	27	430		72	535		57	379, 633–8
	27–8	423		73–5	530 foll		57–8	636–9
	28	427		74	532–5		57–61	633–44
	29	427		74–5	532		59–61	639–44
	29–30	432		75	72, 440, 535, 537–8		60	379, 688
	30	398					61	645–6, 653 foll
	30–35	431–44	27	1	506, 543		62	636
	31	210, 435–7, 498		1–2	540 foll		65	482, 679
	32	438–40, 693		2	541–3	28	1	386, 636, 646, 654–62
	34	440, 535		5	534			

752

SCRIPTURAL PASSAGES

	MATTHEW	PAGE
28	1–2	645 foll
	2	663, 679
	2 foll	666
	2–4	674
	2–10	673–703
	3	3
	4	679
	5–6	681–90
	6	687–9
	7	691–9
	8	657, 664, 699 foll, 714
	9	631, 714, 716
	10	699, 716
	11–12	482
	16	7
	16–20	715 foll
	17	331, 712
	18	712, 717, 728
	19	18, 158
	20	287

	MARK	PAGE
1	2	704
	21	298
	26	51, 256
	29	691
	31	76
	34	490
	36	691
	39	201
	43–5	168–9
2	5	359
	17	174
	20	56, 731
	23	204
3	5	194–5
	12	66
	21	701
	22	226
	28	256
	31	240, 629
	34	195, 632
4	12	495
	16	416
	17	108, 110, 134, 311
	19	125
	22	329
	34	521
5	32	195
	36	60
	39	39
	40	39
	41	39

	MARK	PAGE
5	42	256
	43	26, 64
6	1	438
	3	391, 633
	5	54, 403, 458
	8	73
	15	247
	18	116
	21	148
	31	473
	33	65
	41	728
	49–50	703
7	1	226
	6	258
	10	83
	22	351
	24	64
	27	358
	28	39
	29	59
	30	39
	32	26
	36	26
8	14	26
	15	26–7
	22–6	168
	23	169
	30	27
	31	30, 31, 33
	34	73, 572
	38	2, 536
9	1	451
	2	8 foll, 14, 450, 706
	2–8	1–24
	2–13	1–37 *passim*
	3	3, 13–20
	6	5, 467
	7	20–24
	8	195
	9	24–32
	9–10	24–32
	10	31
	11–13	32–7
	14–29	48–62
	14–50	38–111 *passim*
	15	51, 450
	19	493, 495
	20	308
	21	38
	22	103
	23	51, 53–5, 458
	24	38–9, 48
	25	52
	26	308

	MARK	PAGE
9	27	76
	28–9	55–62
	29	51, 55–62, 227
	30	64–70
	30–32	63–70
	33–4	73
	33–7	70–79
	34	70–75
	35	74, 145
	36	48, 75–6, 121
	37	38, 48, 85
	38	85
	38–41	79–85
	38–50	84
	39	85
	41	80 foll, 84
	42	81, 84, 88, 410
	42–3	410
	42–50	86–111
	43	90–95
	43–8	84
	43–50	91
	44	86
	46	86
	48	86, 90, 91, 96–8
	49	98–101
	49–50	85
	50	101–3, 105
10	1	115, 118–19, 152
	1–12	112–16
	1–16	112–22 *passim*
	6	116, 119
	11	114 foll
	13	39, 121
	13–16	116–22
	14	268
	15	38, 121
	16	75–6, 117 foll, 121
	17	73, 117, 124
	17–22	123–7
	17–52	123–70 *passim*
	19	125
	21	123–7
	21–2	170
	23	130, 195
	23–7	127–32
	24	51, 127–32
	25	128
	27	53, 125, 132
	28–31	133–51
	29	139

A. F.   753   48

INDEX

MARK		MARK		MARK	
	PAGE		PAGE		PAGE
10 30	134 foll, 139, 140, 236	11 28	247	13 22	294, 318
		12 1–12	202, 249–54	23	319
31	141–7	3	298	24	109, 311
32	51, 52, 152	5	298	24–7	320–24
32–4	151–5	11	252–4	25	321
33	524	12	254	26	3, 523
34	158	13	256	27	321
35–40	155–61	13–17	255–9	28	205 foll, 381
37	3	17	254, 256	28–31	324–6
38	156–9	18	261	30	287
38–9	156	18–27	260–66	32	310
40	160–61	24	261	32–7	326–38
41	161	25	134, 174	33–7	331
41–5	161–5	27	261	34	331–6
42	162	28	266–72, 283–4	35	330
43–4	73–4	28–34	266–73	36	330
44	148	30	174	14 1	339 foll, 351, 353, 506
45	164	32	639		
46	152, 165–9	34	269–70	1–2	342
46–52	165–70	35	524	1–11	339–89 passim
47–8	274	35–8	273–7		
48	694	36	521	2	342
50–52	170	37	279	3	342, 352, 356, 363–5, 384
51	166, 170	37–44	278–83		
52	73, 169–70	38–9	233	3 foll	342, 347
11 1	200, 365, 447	40	233	4	391
1–7	171–9	41	203, 279	5	357, 393
1–25 (26)	171–241 passim	41–4	202	6	358
		42	279	8	349, 374–81, 385
2	172	13 1	284, 336		
4	172–6	1–2	284–6	9	382–4
7–10	180–93	1–37	284–338 passim	10	344
8	180–82			10–11	390–91
9	182–90	2	696	11	346, 390
10	190–93	3	306, 447	12 foll	395
11	130, 193–6, 200, 367	3–4	286–9	12–16	392–7
		5–8	289–94	12–25	390–430 passim
12–19	196–220	6	294		
13	206	7	292	13	188, 394, 396
15	200, 218	8	45, 291, 293, 312	13–15	370
16	212–15			14	394
17	58, 215–16, 558, 696	9	136, 297, 301, 543	15	394
				17–21	397–412
18	222, 279	9–13	294–305	18	400, 444
18–19	220	11	296–7, 302, 721, 723	18–21	398
18–25	220–41			19	400, 407, 453
19	367–8, 447	13	301	20	350, 400
22	227–30	14	307–8	21	88, 407–12, 613
22–3	207	14–19	305–13		
23–4	55, 230–34	16	310	22	414
24	58, 229	18	308 foll, 381	22–5	413–30
25	231, 236–41, 603	19	108, 256, 297, 310	23–4	423–30
				24	427
27	200, 243	20	256, 313 foll, 318	25	427
27–33	242–8			25–6	432
27–1244	242–83 passim	20–23	313–19	26	398
		21	135	26–31	431–44

SCRIPTURAL PASSAGES

MARK		MARK		MARK	
	PAGE		PAGE		PAGE
14 26–42	431–76 *passim*	14 66–8	528 foll	15 38–47	616–44 *passim*
27	210, 435–7, 444, 498	66–72	528–39	39	492, 612
		67	510, 512	40	627–33, 649, 652 foll
28	438–40, 693, 695	68	72, 535, 538		
		69–70	529 foll	40–41	626–32, 653
30	440–43, 535	70	535	41	653, 658, 700
31	535	70–72	530 foll	42	635
32	446	71	532–5	42–7	633–44
32–42	444–76	71–2	532	43	633–8
33	450–54	72	440–43, 535, 537–9	43–5	636–9
34	454–7, 599, 601	15 1	541–3	46	639, 670, 688
		1–5	540–54	46–7	639–44
35	54, 455, 458	1–15	540–62 *passim*	47	646, 653 foll, 688
35–6	458 foll				
36	54, 458–62	2	545–8	47–16 4	645–72
37	58, 453, 473	2–5	547	47–16 8	645–703 *passim*
38	88, 467–9, 475	4–7	550		
39	465	5	550–51	16 1	386, 639, 654 foll
40	5, 6, 467	6	552–4		
41	465, 470, 472, 473	6–15	552, 554–62	1–2	646, 654
		7	556 foll	2	654–62, 700
41–2	470, 475	8	552–3	3–4	663–9
42	469–76	9	558	4	667
43	479 foll	10	542, 561	5	3, 450, 664, 674–9
43–52	477–503 *passim*	11	559, 562		
		12	558	5–8	673–703
45	488	15	542, 559–62	6	450, 681–90
45–6	531	16	481, 483, 487, 544, 602	7	691–9
47	491–2			8	657, 664, 692, 699–703
48	479–80	16–17	482–3		
49	488	16–20	563–70	9–14	704–14
50	496–9	16–37	563–615 *passim*	9–20	704–40 *passim*
51	500				
51–2	500–503	17	564–70	10	699
53	505–9	20	564	11	707
53–4	504–12	21	571–4	12	329, 706
53–72	504–39 *passim*	21–2	572	13	699
		21–5	570–83	14	329, 707
54	500, 510–13, 528 foll, 538	23	575, 605	15–18	714–26
		24	576–9	15–20	716
55–9	513–19	25	579–82	16	707, 715–16, 721
56	514, 519	26	583–8		
56–9	696	26–32	583–95	17–18	726
57	514	27	591	19–20	717, 727–40
58	31, 64, 210, 589	29–32	589–91	20	717, 735 foll
		31	593		
59	514	32	191, 546, 591–5		LUKE
60	520	33	667		
60–65	519–28	33–7	595–615	1 2	421, 525
61	520, 549	34	598–602	4	705
62	522–4, 735	35	492, 602	17	32, 34
63	520	36	358, 490, 576, 603–7	26	694
64	524			59	167
65	502, 525–8, 568	37	599, 607–15	59–2 40	38
		38	616–26		
66	538	38–9	616–26	2 4	275, 694

755

48—2

INDEX

LUKE		LUKE		LUKE	
	PAGE		PAGE		PAGE
2 14	185	7 50	357	11 15	226
24	386	8 2	366, 706	31–2	716
32	69	2–3	657	42	202
41–2	200	10	495	43	278
44	627	13	108, 134, 311, 416	49	135, 259, 344
46	31, 204			12 1	26
49	201, 438, 515	21	632	9	536
3 1	543	50	60	11	298, 303
2	506	53	27	11–12	297
6	468	55–6	26	12	302–3
8	223, 248	56	65	19	473
9	90, 94, 103	9 3	73	35–43	326 foll
17	90, 94	11	65, 222	41	336
19	116	16	728–9	42	328, 334
4 10	582	21	27	45 foll	334
10–11	581, 681	23	73, 572	49	93
16	438	26	2, 536	49–50	158
18–19	384	28	6–8, 450	50	155–6, 463
19	507	28–36	1–24	51	496
20	525, 677	29	3, 14, 675, 706	58	526
21	718			59	444
29	299	30	36	13 1	543
36	51	31	30, 35	1–5	196
38	691	31–2	2 foll	6–9	196 foll, 202
39	76	32	4, 6, 730	11	323
41	490	33	5, 467	14	10
44	201	35	20–24, 36	19	643
5 20	358–9	36–7	24–32	24	133
23	358	37–43	48–62	27	533
35	731	41	493, 495	28–30	142
6 10	194	42	38, 39	30	134 foll, 141 foll
12	57, 58	43	227		
16	391	43–5	63–4	31	155
19	66	46–8	70 foll	33	18, 65
21	419	47	75–6	34	192
22	135	48	85	14 20	120
23	101, 135	49	85	25–35	101
26	318	49–50	79 foll	27	572
27	135	51	35, 208, 727	33–4	102
37–8	231	58	369	34	108
41–2	231	10 17–20	722	34–5	85, 87 foll
7 2 foll	62	19	725–6	15 20	269
9	444	21	42	22	148
11	387	25	268, 283	16 1–13	87
17	387	25–8	266 foll	3	167
28–35	81	28	273	8	262, 269
32	648	38–9	360	12	226
36	387	39	647	13	219
36–8	340 foll	40	371	14 foll	96
36–40	350	41–2	126	14–18	87, 114
37	347, 353 363–4	11 1–4	229, 231	15	141
		2	232	18	113 foll
38	360	4	221, 358	19	564
44	360	5–8	229	19–31	87
46	348, 350	8–9	231	22	542
47	358	9	221, 229, 333	23	96
48	358, 384	14	701	17 1	87, 410

SCRIPTURAL PASSAGES

LUKE		LUKE		LUKE	
	PAGE		PAGE		PAGE
17 1–2	84, 86 foll, 410	19 47	148, 222	21 29–33	324–6
2	80, 88	47–8	220 foll	30	325, 378
4	228	48	279	32	287
5	228	20 1	200, 243	34	309, 332
5–6	55, 220 foll	1–8	242–8	34–6	326–8
6	50, 207–8, 227–8	2	247	36	309, 337
		9–19	202, 249–54	37	288, 367, 370, 447
11	112, 115, 208	10	298		
12	188	11	298	37–8	196, 198, 220 foll, 368
21	516	18	252		
23	135, 313	20	256	22 1–3	339 foll
31	306–7, 310	20–26	255–9	2	506
18 1–8	229	26	254, 256	2–4	346
11	238	27	261	3	345, 392
13	238, 269	27–38	260–66	3–4	344
15	39, 117	35	262	3–6	341 foll, 390–92
15–17	116–22	36	262–3		
16	76, 117	37	263	4	482, 487
17	75, 121	39	266, 284	5	390
18	124	39–40	270	6	346, 390
18–23	123–7	40	267	7 foll	396
20	125	41–6	273–7	7–13	392–7
22	124	42	521	10	188, 394, 396
24–7	127–32	45–21 4	278–83	11	394
27	53	47	233	12	394
28–30	133 foll	21 1	279	14	397, 404
29	134, 139	1–4	202	14 foll	350
31	52	5	284–5	15	397–8, 423
31–3	151 foll	5–6	284–6	15–20	413–30
32	524	6	696	17	423
35–43	165–70	7	286–9	18	427
38–9	274	8	294, 318	19	414–15, 426
39	693	8–12	289–93	20	424
43	169	9	292	21	397–8, 400
19 9	372	11	290	21–3	397–412
11–27	200	12	136, 297–8, 543	22	88, 398, 407–12, 613
12	331 foll	12–19	294–305	23	398, 400, 404, 453
17	335	13	301		
28	52, 151, 200	14	303	24–7	161–5
28–35	171–9	14–15	296	25	162
29	200, 365, 447	15	302–3, 721	25–30	434
30	172	16–18	722	26	71–3
35–8	180–93	19	301	28	450
36	180	20	307	29–30	428
37	188, 193	20–22	305 foll	30	548
37–8	183	22	309	31	435, 443, 498
38	185, 191, 193, 194	23	108, 310	31–2	503
		23–4	306 foll	31–4	431 foll
39–40	194	25	309, 311, 321	32	539
40	222, 286	25–6	109, 320	32 foll	693
41	192, 223	25–8	320–24	33 foll	444
41–4	194	27	3, 523	34	440, 442–3, 535
42	193	28	206, 322–3		
45	194, 200	29	206	36	436, 493
45–8	196 foll	29 foll	381	36–8	492
46	58, 558, 696	29–30	205 foll	37	437, 471, 610

INDEX

LUKE		LUKE		LUKE	
	PAGE		PAGE		PAGE
22 38	470	23 11–12	563 foll	24 5–6	681–90
38–9	432	13	559	6–7	63–4, 438, 691
39	288, 398, 431–2	13–25	554–62		–8
40	446	14	586	7	542
40–46	444–76	15	560	8–10	657
41	455, 731	16	560	9	664, 699 foll
41–2	458	17	554	10	654
42	54, 462, 465	18	298	11	658, 707, 717
43	456	18–19	556 foll	12	691
44	234, 456, 625	20	560–61	13	708
45	6, 58, 453, 730	22	560, 586	16	331, 706
46	473, 475	24–5	559	20	542
47	479 foll, 487–9	25	542	22	701
		26	563, 570–72	23	684, 702
47–53	477–503	27–8	630	24	684, 717
48	488, 491, 531	28	631	25	707
49	494	32	583, 591–2	25–7	659
50	503	32–4	570	27	717
51	490–97	34	358, 576–9, 595	27–45	718
52	479–82, 487			30	728
53	488	35	590, 627, 629	30–31	666
53–4	496	35–7	589–91	31	717, 730
54	505–6, 520	35–40	583–95	31–43	658
54–6	504 foll, 510 foll	36	576, 596, 603	34	717
		37	191	35	728
54–7	528 foll	38	584–8	36–9	717
55	510, 539	39	591	37	703, 707
55–6	538	39–42	591	39	468, 712
56	510	41	592	39–43	707
57	535–6	43	444, 595, 642	40	712, 717
58	529 foll	44	582	41	707
59	729	44–5	595–7	43	717
59–62	530 foll	45	598–602, 616–26	45	333–4, 718
60	533			46–9	715 foll
60–61	532	45–7	616–26	47	695
61	440–41, 535, 539	46	599, 607–15	47–9	718
		47	617	50	117, 288, 729
62	72, 537–8	48	590, 631	51	117, 728–9, 731
63–4	568	48–9	626–32		
63–5	502, 519 foll, 525–8	49	628–30, 652–3, 658		
66	506, 513, 521	50–52	636–8		JOHN
66–71	519–28	50–56	633–44		
67–8	521	53	639, 667, 688	1 1	77, 121
69	522	54	636, 660	5	253, 662
71	524	55	505, 630, 639, 653–4, 689	6–12	247
23 1	541			9	150, 330
1–5	540 foll	55–6	646	11	640
2	545–8	55–24 2	645 foll	12	121, 416, 429
4	560, 586	56	386, 649–51	12–13	78
5	694	24 1	386, 646–7, 654, 660	13	88
7	544			13–14	468
8–9	600	2	663, 684	14	3–4, 23, 53, 244, 516–17
9	549, 551	3	664, 684		
9–10	541	3–5	674	14–17	24
10	628–9	3–11	673–703	15	149, 407
11	482–3, 564–5	4	3, 678	16	416

SCRIPTURAL PASSAGES

JOHN		JOHN		JOHN	
	PAGE		PAGE		PAGE
1 17	5, 37	3 4	133	6 62	732
18	23, 45, 77, 83, 121, 614	5	133	63	468
		6	89, 468	64	63
19	226	8	611	65	60
20	277	9	133	66	391
21	34, 37, 277	13	517, 720, 733	68–9	150
24	226	14	37	70	90, 412
25	37	14–16	82	71	63, 443
26	240, 593	16	64, 271	7 1	67, 245
26–7	239	22	721	2	199
28	154, 245	26	154	3–10	69
29	17, 239	4 1–2	159, 721	5	630
30	149	3	67	6	395
31	329	5–6	425	6–8	67
33–4	22	6	582	8	395
36	245	7	601	10	67
41	149, 277, 546	19	569	12	258, 318
42	150, 443	20	11, 208	13	258
43	154, 177	21	11, 208	14	199, 258
45	277, 587	24	208	15	258
46	275, 277	35–6	325	17	429
47	277, 351	45	416, 438	19	37, 259
47–8	209	46–54	62	22–3	37
49	191, 546	48	738	24	259
51	276, 517, 733	49–50	46, 59	25–6	69
2 1	122, 347, 627, 633	5 1	199	27–8	68
		11	575	28	199, 282
1–11	695	14	178, 199	30	67
3	683	16	140, 298	32	256, 259, 526
4	67	17	116	32–46	254
5	633	18	140, 298	33–5	67
10	122, 378	19	403, 412, 458, 518	35	69
12	633			37	67, 282
12–13	200	33–6	247	37–9	259
13–21	198 foll	37–8	265	39	68, 416
14	200, 212	39	265	40–42	274
14–16	218–20	42	265	41–2	277
15	182, 217–20	43	416	44	256
16	212, 214, 514	44	265	45	526
17	193, 216, 517	45–6	37	46	256, 259, 279, 526
18	247, 518	46	265		
19	64, 84, 210, 223, 514, 519, 589, 696	6 1	199	47	318
		3	11	50–51	639
		15	11, 546	51	127
19–20	286	17	153, 662	51–2	639
19–22	31	19	703	52	275
21	210, 216, 223, 417, 517	19–20	154	8 1	11, 199, 448
		20	53	1–2	198–9
22	193, 517	21	416	3	277, 361
23	224	23	160	15	89, 469
3 1	393	31	37	15–16	203
1–2	224	32	37	16	89, 300
1–2 foll	126	42	633	17	300
2	127, 133, 224, 639	45	258	17–18	248
		51	300	20	67, 199, 203, 279
2–9	133	51–63	468		
3	133	61–3	89	30–44	412

759

INDEX

	JOHN	
		PAGE
8	32	552
	33	248
	39	248
	56	150
	58	150
	59	69, 199
9	2–3	168
	3	410
	7	16
	8	167
	16	389
	22	299
	24	97, 389
	25	389
	31	389
	34	168
	38	98, 170
	39	98
10	2–3	332
	3	331, 333
	7–8	163
	8	150, 558
	11	332
	17–18	272
	22	199
	23	199, 245
	29	75
	29–30	75
	30	272
	31	245
	39	199
	39–40	69, 245
	40	153–4
11	1	370
	1–2	360
	1–5	355
	3 foll	62
	5	126, 370
	7–8	67, 155
	8	69
	8–16	370
	16	154, 712
	17	9
	18	289, 370
	19	647
	25	265
	25–6	262
	33	452, 505
	35	582
	39	9, 663–4
	41	11
	41–2	61, 234
	48	211
	48–52	252, 720
	49	507
	49–51	507
	50	323

	JOHN	
		PAGE
11	51	507
	52	323
	54	245, 370
	55	10
	56	199, 245
	57	263
12	1	10, 347
	1 foll	342, 371
	1–8	340–89
	2	361
	3	342, 353, 356, 360, 363–4, 382–4, 639
	3 foll	347
	4	63
	5	357
	7	358, 374, 377, 488
	8	374
	9	342
	12	186, 194, 200
	12–13	180, 187, 245
	12–15	180–93
	13	188, 191
	13–15	546
	14–15	172, 176 foll
	15	179, 191
	16	192–3, 254
	17	188
	19	216
	20	11, 69, 347
	20 foll	179
	20–21	216
	21	190
	23	11, 23
	24	94, 325, 644
	27	234, 452, 464, 599
	27–8	11, 234, 459, 466
	28	69
	29	457
	31	69, 163
	31–3	12
	32	19
	34	521
	35	69
	35–6	245
	36	19, 69, 282
	36–40	70
	39–40	98
	39–43	282
	40	403, 495
	42	98, 299, 393
	44	282
	44–6	68
	44–50	282

	JOHN	
		PAGE
12	46–8	69
	47–8	524
	49–50	69
	50	272, 283
13	1	67, 301, 329
	1–2	342
	1–4	391
	2	63, 345, 392, 443
	2–12	396
	4–5	502
	4–17	151
	5	352, 360
	10–11	107
	12	404
	12–15	419
	15	429
	16	75
	17	429
	18	400, 408
	19	319
	20	416
	21	444, 452, 457, 599
	21–8	398–412
	23	45, 77, 126
	24	404, 407
	25	77, 403
	26	401–2, 443, 531
	27	344–6, 392, 408–9, 463, 488, 491, 499
	28	531
	30	662
	33	46
	33–5	432
	33–14 23	697
	34	107
	34–5	267, 271, 733, 738
	35	235, 738
	36–8	432
	37	288
	38	228, 440, 443, 535
14	1	228, 432
	1–3	440
	2	161
	2–3	160
	3	161, 330
	5–22	288
	9	160
	12	329, 733, 739
	12–14	235
	13	160
	16	61, 140

SCRIPTURAL PASSAGES

JOHN		JOHN		JOHN	
	PAGE		PAGE		PAGE
14 16–16 15	721	16 22	292, 454	18 13–27	522
17	416	23	235, 329	14	323
18	330	23–4	140	14–15	522
20	329	24	235	15	509, 522, 531, 627
22	392, 712, 733	25	699		
23	78, 161, 330, 332, 733	26	61, 235, 329	15–17	529 foll
		28	31, 330	16	522, 538, 627
26	193, 426	30	444	16–18	522
26–7	303	31 foll	444	18	105, 500, 510–13, 526, 529, 538
26–8	429	32	347, 399, 437, 498		
27	140, 292, 657				
27–31	475	33	98, 111, 140, 236, 292, 308, 311, 326, 437, 475	19	507–8, 522
28	75, 328, 330			19 foll	507
29	319			19–23	522
30	163, 294, 472			19–24	520 foll.
30–31	308, 471	17 1	434	20	199
31	288, 432–3, 469–76	2	469	22	501–2, 522, 526
		3	82		
15 1	176	4	609	23	522, 527
1–2	140, 326	6	609	24	507–8, 522, 541
1–6	95, 104, 211, 252	6–9	294		
		9	61	25	510–13, 529 foll, 535, 538
2	104, 106	9–15	435		
3	107	11	273, 323	25–7	522
4–7	302	12	409–10	26–7	530 foll
6	103–4	12–15	609	27	441, 532, 535
7	235	15	61, 235, 294	28	483, 541–3
9–10	738	20	61	30	542, 546
10–16	302	21	301, 323	31	524
13	75, 271	21–2	598	33	483, 546
15–16	140	21–3	273	33–8	541 foll
16	235	22	323	34	547
17	738	23	151, 323, 738	35	542, 544, 720
18–20	139	18 1	153, 432–3, 449	36	63, 544
20	75, 110, 298, 437			37	547–8, 551
		1–2	434, 446 foll, 452	38	548, 551, 561, 586
26–7	300				
16 1	110, 435, 498	2	7, 222, 370, 449	39	548, 552–4
1–2	298			39–40	556–9
2	140	2–11	479–503	40	552, 557
4	319	3	392, 480–81, 484, 486, 526	19 1	551, 559–61
6	454			1–3	564 foll
7	330, 428	3–22	525	2	564
7–8	300	4	433, 470, 480	2–4	565
8	330, 715	5	587	3	502, 526
8–9	294	5–6	489	4	526, 561, 586
10	317	6	486, 496–9	5	565
11	163, 294	7	587	6	416, 525–6, 556, 561, 586
13	330	8	488 foll		
16	317	10	492, 503, 691	8	562
17	31, 317	11	459–66, 492	9	483, 549, 551
17–23	62	12	481, 499, 526, 541	10	552
20	110, 454			10–11	248
21	45, 292, 301, 311, 326, 454, 687	12–18	504 foll	11	542, 545, 552
		13	507	12	391, 552
		13 foll	507	13	•568
21–2	111	13–14	507	14	582, 635–6

INDEX

JOHN		JOHN		ACTS	
	PAGE		PAGE		PAGE
19 14–16	579	20 14	331	1 13	394–5
15	298, 559	15	331, 643, 689, 703, 708	21	505
15–16	556, 559, 582			22	727
16	542, 544, 564	16	170	23	725
17	573	17	598, 689–99, 717, 720	2 1–13	737
17–18	571–4			4–11	722
18	591–4	17–18	674	7	695
18–22	584–8	18	699, 702, 714	19	736
19	585	20	708, 713	22	736
21–2	558	21	715	23	408
23	577	22	416	24	291
23–4	571, 576–9	23	358, 715	27	157
25	627–32, 653, 655	24–7	707	27–31	376
		24–9	712	29	190, 377
26	78	30–31	739	38	721
27	416, 632	21 1	329, 708	38–41	721
28	329, 471, 582, 599	1–3	692	39	269
		2	695	43	736
28–30	576, 596	3–11	337	3 19	786
29	603–5	4	331, 709	4 1	481–2
30	20, 329, 471, 545, 599, 607–15	4–5	46	5	483
		5	46	16	736
		7	501–2, 539, 709	22	736
31	347, 636			25–7	543
32	591–4	9	105, 716	26–7	483
34	20, 595, 624, 626	12	703, 709	29–30	734
		14	329	30	736
34–5	430	15	75	32	737
35	20, 625	15 foll	429	37	129
36–7	20	15–17	77, 150, 392, 443, 716	5 7	579
38	637			12	736
38–9	126, 224, 393	15–19	338	22	526
38–40	379	15–22	692	24	482
38–41	127	18–19	443	26	482, 526
38–42	634–44	19–23	159	30	591
39	639	20	45, 77	40	298
40	379, 416, 651	20–23	338	6 8	736
42	636, 644, 689	22	302, 719	13–14	514
20 1	347, 543, 646 foll, 654, 660, 663, 700	22–3	150, 330	7 10	109
		24	77, 338	11	109
				36	736
1–2	654			48–53	514
2	654, 661, 689–90	ACTS		59	608
				60	613
3	691	1 2	727, 733	8 6	736
4	150	3	705, 707, 718	9–11	701
6	150	5	720	13	736
7	640, 663, 670–72	6–7	288	16–17	735
		7	328	17	736
8	150, 707	7–8	719	18	129
8–9	718	8	143, 718	20	129
11	629, 651, 677	9–10	288, 729–32	22	206
11–12	674 foll	9–11	523	9 37–9	394
11–13	674 foll	10	675, 681, 730	39	505
11–17	672	10–11	719	10 1	482
12	672, 689–90	11	694, 727	9	582
13	689, 703	12	288	13	442

762

SCRIPTURAL PASSAGES

ACTS		
		PAGE
10	13 foll	306
	15	85
	23	505
	30	9
	39	591
	42	413
	44–6	737
	45	505
11	6	539
	7	442
	16–17	738
	18	737
	19	109
12	4	343
	5	234
	6	693
	12	539
13	5	480, 526
	35	157
	45–8	532
	47	143
	50	148
14	3	736
	22	109, 312
15	12	736
16	12	148
	13	58
	14	334
	16	58
	30	693
17	4	148
	5	693
	25	612
	26	413
	27	206, 710
	31	408, 413
	31–2	705
18	6–7	532
	18	56
19	9	83
	13	80, 84
	28–9	172
	35	276
	39	521
20	6	9
	8	394
	23	109
	31	336
21	14	652
	23	56
	31	482
	36	298
22	8	682
	21	269
	22	298
	25–9	496, 561
23	3	568

ACTS		
		PAGE
23	12	534–5
	35	483, 544
24	1	9
	26	129
25	2	148
	26	693
26	7	234
	11	532
	16	526
27	1	482
	28	729
	32	217
28	1–6	725
	5	103
	7	148
	17	148
	27	6

ROMANS

1	4	413
	10	58
2	9	311
	19	268
6	3–4	159
	4	642
	6	592
7	8–13	272
8	32	64, 615
	33	724
	33–4	527
9	3	285, 629
	3–7	628
	12	145
	33	668
11	16–24	252
	22	90
	24	90
12	1	98, 420
	4–21	420
	9	271
	12	58
	18	101
	18–20	98
13	7	471
	7–8	472
	12	476
14	4	497
15	3	517
16	7	557
	13	574

1 CORINTHIANS

1	18 foll	658

1 CORINTHIANS		
		PAGE
1	19–20	268
	24	265
2	11	467
	14	658
3	12	74
	13–15	93
	14	74
	15	74
	16 foll	93
	17	74, 93
	18	74
	19	658
4	13	107
5	7	344, 346
6	9	93
	10	93
	19	93
7	1	120
	5	58
	35	120
8	1	697
	7	553
10	4	625, 669
	12	538
	13	490
	16	122
11	16	553
	20 foll	425
	21	430
	23	421
	23–5	414 foll
	24	415
	24–5	415
	25	424
	33	425
12	3	83–4, 285, 533
	10–14	39 722, 738
13	2	207
14	20	39, 726
	22	738
	35	73
15	1–8	705
	5–7	502
	5–8	659
	15	206
	20	614
	49	468
	54	672
	55	583
16	12	462
	13	236
	22	532

2 CORINTHIANS

2	14–16	352

INDEX

2 CORINTHIANS

		PAGE
2	16	348
3	13–16	622
	15	672
5	3	501
6	16	244
12	2	727
	7–9	465
	8	236
	12	735
13	11	101

GALATIANS

1	1	177
	4	64
	9	532
	11–12	421
2	9	162, 451
	16	701
	20	64, 518, 592, 615, 697
3	13	569, 591, 606
	28	697
4	19	291
	27	291
	28–9	136
5	1	236
	11	88, 574
6	3	125

EPHESIANS

1	16	58
2	13	143
	13 fcll	620
	13–17	269
	15	272
5	2	64, 615
	14	636, 660
	25	615
6	14	236

PHILIPPIANS

1	27	236, 603
2	8	455, 606
	15	254
4	1	237
	6	58

COLOSSIANS

2	12	159

COLOSSIANS

		PAGE
2	18	43
4	2	58
	6	99, 605

1 THESSALONIANS

1	2	58
2	7–8	417
3	8	237, 603
4	16–17	67
5	3	291
	8	237
	13	101
	17	233

2 THESSALONIANS

2	3–4	307
	4	219
	6–7	308
	15	237, 603
3	10	73

1 TIMOTHY

3	16	727
4	3	120
6	5	219

2 TIMOTHY

2	10	640
3	12	136

TITUS

1	14	272

PHILEMON

	4	58

HEBREWS

1	1–2	21
2	7	263
	9	466
	11–13	47
	13	46
3	17	498

HEBREWS

		PAGE
4	11	498
	12	304
5	6	293
	7–9	455
	8	466, 527
6	19–20	617
7	16–18	272
9	3	618
	12	619
	16	428
	19	567, 605
	26	287
10	3	415
	11	237
	19	619
	19–21	619
11	5	684
	10	253, 439
	22	35
12	15–17	539
	18	710
13	4	120
	17	336

JAMES

1	26	125
2	7	532
	16	512
	23	132
5	8	476
	15	56–7
	16	57, 60
	17	58

1 PETER

1	4	378
	7	90
2	2	351
	2–3	668
	4–8	253
	6	668
	8	668
	9	548
	13–14	543
3	13	724
	19	613
4	7	476
	19	608

2 PETER

1	15	85

SCRIPTURAL PASSAGES

2 PETER		1 JOHN		REVELATION	
	PAGE		PAGE		PAGE
1 16–18	4	5 6	20, 430	5 6–7	523, 735
18	7, 24	7–8	20	6 6	722
		14	235	11	473
		14–16	61–2	7 3	722
1 JOHN				10	187
				12	187
1 1 foll	698	2 JOHN		14	15, 18
1–2	710			15	244, 516
2	329	7	294	8 3	661
3	300			9 4	722
8	294			12 2	291, 313
2 12	358	3 JOHN		3	566
13	47			6	313
15	271	8	730	13 1	566
16	468			15	612
18	47, 319			14 13	473
22	319	REVELATION		18	104
26	294, 318			16 15	500
28	329–30	1 13	417, 566, 578	17 3	542
3 7	47, 294, 318	14	676	18 2–3	214
16	423	17	149	9–11	214
18	500	2 8	149	19 8	500
22	235	20	359	12	566
4 1	318	3 14	149	21 1	671
1–3	84	17	131	2	517
2	468	18	500	3	244, 516
3	84, 319	20	331, 698	6	149
6	294	21	548	10	542
18	53	5 1 foll	258	11	254
20	271	6	240	22 13	149

INDEX

II. ENGLISH

[*" c w."* means *"confused, or confusable, with"*, *"conn. w.'* means *"connected with"*, *"interch. w"* means *"interchanged, or interchangeable, with*[1].*"*]

Aaron, bears on his heart the names of Israel **404**
Abide, or await, (Jn) = endure (Synopt) **301**, or watch (Synopt) **330**
Able, not, applied to Jesus or the Son **54**, or to the Son apart from the Father (Jn) **412**, God, n a to save a self-destroyer (Epictet.) **409, 412**, comp **458**, s Possible -able, in English Biblical words, such as unquenchable, points to Greek original **92**
Abomination of Desolation, the **305–7**, perh implies a person **308**, (?) parall to Ruler of this world (Jn) **308**, the wing of abomination **307**
Aboth, i e Sayings of the Jewish Fathers, on the Ages of Man **42**
Abraham, the first prophet **36**, rich **131**, God is the reward of **131**, in the furnace **132, 481**, the planting of **138**, ministering (Targ) in prayer **237**, was made equal (Philo) to angels **263**, alleged reference to in Ps **276**, Haran and A. before Nimrod **481**
Abridgment, occasional, in Mk, implying that he assumes knowledge in his readers **115, 138**
Acanthine **566**
"According to the Gospel" (*Mart Polyc*), i e events in Polycarp's martyrdom resembling those in the Lord's Passion **549**
Acquaintance, i e friends **627**
Acts of John, the, on —"the mountain" where Jesus used to pray **7**, s also **4, 47** etc
Additions, to explain an obscure original **463**
Adulteress **361**
Adultery, the woman taken in **355**
Aeon, the accomplishment of the **287**
Afar **626** foll, s From afar

---

[1] These abbreviations in the English Index are intended to bring before the reader in a compendious form some of the principal causes that may explain the divergences of the Gospels from one another in parallel passages

(1) An original word, Semitic or Greek, may have been confused with others similar to it, as in the LXX. This is denoted by *"c w,"* meaning (*a*) *"confused with,"* or (*b*) *"confusable with"*

(2) Sometimes passages in the Gospels that seem at first quite disconnected may be shewn by reference to other Biblical passages to be connected with each other, in thought if not in word. This (as well as connection in the ordinary sense) is denoted by *"conn w,"* meaning *"connected with"*

(3) A word or phrase in the earliest traditions, seeming to later writers obscure or vulgar, or otherwise objectionable, may have been interchanged with another This is denoted by *"interch. w,"* meaning (*a*) *"interchanged with,"* or (*b*) *" interchangeable with "*

Other abbreviations, intended to shew parallelism ("parall") or correspondence (=) between the Synoptists ("Synopt") and John ("Jn") will be readily understood.

ENGLISH

Affirmative, c w interrog **443**
Afflicted, the Lord was **316**, Heb c w meek **369**
After two days (Heb) only in Hosea **346**
Against anyone, to have aught **238**
Agōmen, Heb -Gk, let us be going **469**
Ahaz **15**
Akiba, the martyrdom of **5**, conn w a fuller **16**
Alabaster cruse, *alabastros* (Synopt) = pound, *litra* (Jn) **363**
Alexander and Rufus **574**
All [things], ins or om **287**, "I have told you a t" **319**, "all [that really live] live unto God" **264**
Allegory, early Christian **396**, in Rahab **353**, a and metaphor **104**
Allusion, to Messianic prophecy **502**, to the Law **503**, in metaphor **384**
Almsgiving, conn w the Treasury and judgment **202–3**
Alone, precepts to Christ's disciples alone **232**, diff from solitary **83**, s Only
Altar, metaph *or* lit **238**, of the Jews, the, influence of on Eucharistic language **241**
Altruism, latent under "I" (Jn) **517**
Amaze, c w hear **256**
Amazement, or trouble, in Christ, how expressed **450**, produced in others by Christ's presence **51**, subordinated by Jn **52–3, 152**
Ambiguity, instances of, (*a*) knew [him, *or*, it] **65**, (*b*) receive as a child **121**, (*c*) from, *or*, some from **226** (comp **480**), (*d*) imperat *or* indic **228**, (*e*) metaph *or* lit **256**, (*f*) "they" indef **274**, (*g*) speak to, *or*, about **406**, (*h*) said, *or*, meant **382**, (*i*) the custom, *or*, his custom **433–4**, s also **163, 173, 177, 466, 547, 572** also Pronoun and Interrogative
"Among," c w "in" **102**
Amphodon, i e the open street (Mk) **171** foll , perh conn w Jacob's prophecy **172–3**, Origen on the Gentiles in the *a* **176**
Anachronism **534**
Analēmpsis (Gk) **35** foll
Anathēma and *anathěma* (Gk) **285**, Paul's warning against the utterance "Jesus is a" **83–4, 533**
Anathematize **532** foll , "a oneself," not in O T **532–5**
Ancient of days, the **523**

And (Heb) c w even **173**
Andrew, (Jn) "first found his own brother" **149**
Angel (sing), only once in Jn ("an angel hath spoken to him") where God has really spoken **457**, of the Lord, the (*or*, an) **679**, c w the Holy Spirit **304**, "son of God" altered to **22**, an a identified with Christ (?) **699–700**, in O T called "man" but not "young man" **676**
Angels, the attitudes of **676–7**, three, but addressed as one **676**, comp **679**, Abraham "was made equal to a " (Philo) **263**, comp **262**,
Anger of the Lord, the, parall to Satan **315**
Ania (Syr), distracted, used about Martha **371**, combined with *Beth* = *Beth-ania* c w Bethany **371**
Annas and Caiaphas (Lk and Jn) **506–7**
Anointing of Jesus, the, **347** foll , Origen and Jerome on **352**
Answer (Heb) c w humiliation **369**, (Gk) make a formal defence **549**
Antenatalism **410**
Ante-resurrectional c w post-resurrectional utterances **306–7**
Antithesis, (?) Jesus Barabbas and Jesus Christ **557**
Anytus, "could kill Socrates but could not harm him" **724**
Aorist, c w pluperf **283, 433**, parall to imperf **367**
Apodosis, ellipsis of **462**
Apologia **303**
Aposiopēsis **488, 494**
Apostle, "the signs of the a " **735**, apostles, the bestowal of "tongues" by the **737**
Aposynagōgos **299**
Appointed, "not a " (Heb) = "not possible" (LXX) **54**
Appointed-time **67, 315**
Aquila **39** and *passim*
Aramaic, c w Hebrew **186, 599**, Heb dual, how expressed in **441**,
Arms, carrying in the **76, 78**, the child in Christ's a **75–9**
Arms, i e weapons, *hopla* (Jn) **484**, Heb *neshek* c w kiss **485**
Arōma (Gk), i e corn **650–51**
Artemidorus, on ointments **349**
Article, the, ins or om **141, 182, 275, 314**, s Prophet and *Kūrios*
Asbestos, unquenchable **91–3**
Ascend, parall to pray **6**, conn w descend **720, 733**

INDEX

Ascension, the, in Mk-App **727**, in Lk's Gospel (as distinct from Acts) **729**, in Jn, not being taken up but going up **732**, not mentioned in Mt **716, 728**
Asceticism, if Christian, is altruistic **420**
Ashamed of, parall to denying [Jesus] **536**
Ask [to know] and ask [to receive] **61**
Aspects, various, of the same truth **300**
Ass, the finding of an **176** foll, contrasted with war-horse **179**, c. w. entrance **175**
Attendant, c w standing by **502**
Authority, the meaning of **247**, Pilate on, corrected by Jesus **552**, in a household **335**, conn w freedom **552**, Epictetus on **552**
Await the Lord, c w wait in the Lord **301**
Awake, "fully a ", why emphasized **4**

Babe, the typical, Clem Alex on **45**
Babes, parall to little children **117**, b and sucklings, metaph taken lit **223**
Balaam and Caiaphas, resemblance between (Jn) **509**
Baptism, conn w John the Baptist **23**, called enlightening (Justin M) **159**, heretical kinds of **156**, *baptīzein* (Gk) mostly in bad sense **157**, apostolic, before and after the gift of the Holy Spirit **720-21**, baptism "into Christ's death" **158**
Baptist, John the, not described as ever visiting the Temple **7**, details about, omitted by Lk and Jn **34**, alludes to Isaiah's parable of the Vine of Israel **104**, conn w Elijah **34**
Bar (Heb or Aram) "son" or "pure" **21**
Barabbas, perh "Jesus called B" **556**
Barcochba **568**
Barley, sown with a hundredfold return **139**
Barnabas (the Epistle of) **8, 40**, parall to *Didachè* **240**, on the Way of Light **240**, on the Jews as smiting their shepherd **436**
Barsemia, filius caecus, Jerome's version of Bartimaeus **167**
Bartimaeus, in Jerome, *Barsemia* **167**, s Timaeus

Basilides, on Simon the Cyrenian **573**
Basin (Jn), (?) conn w pitcher (Mk–Lk) **397**
Battalogia, or *battologia,* var interpr. of **232-3**
Bear the cross **572**
Beast, the, opp to the Man, Epictet on **45**
Beating, predicted (Mk) **297**, beaten (lit) into synagogues **299**
Because, or, for (Heb), c w that (conj) **702**
Bedding, c w branches **181**
"Before me, all that came," ambig **163**
Beggars, deemed accursed **167**
"Beginning, that which was from the" **116**
Behold, c. w (1) wait for, (2) buy **651**
Belief (*i e* faith) implied, but not mentioned, by Jn **225**
Believe, *i e* trust to **225**, "b that ye have received" (Mk) **229-30**, "believe (imperat) in God" (once in O T) **227**, c w kind **60**
Beloved son (Gk) = only son (Heb) **22**, conn w chosen **20** foll
Ben Nêtzer **682**
Ben Sira, (?) alluded to in Mk **457**, on dipping in the bowl **405**
Benefactors (Lk and Epictet) **162**
Beth (Aram) lodge, (Heb) house **368**
Beth Ania, house of Ania (Syr), *i e* Bethany **371**
Beth Hini (Talm) a Babylonian town **366-7**
Bethany **365-71**, distance of, from Jerusalem **289**, not in Talm except as (?) Beth Hini etc **366**, c w. Place of Lodging **367-8**, (Jerome) House of Obedience **369**, not in Goodspeed **365**
Bethlehem and David **274**
Bethphage **173-4**, the Talmud on **176**
Bewilderment, in Christ's disciples **467**
"Beyond Jordan," avoided by Lk but not by Jn **154**
Binding of Jesus, the, om by Lk. **541-2**, Justin M. on **542**, Jerome on **541**, typically regarded **545**
Binding, the, of "the colt to the vine" **176**, of Christ's body in the tomb **640**, of waters in, or by, a garment **671**
Birth, new **99**, s Regeneration
Bitterly, -ness **539**
Blaspheme, c w anathematize **532**

ENGLISH

Blessing God, c w blessing man **728**, Jesus blessing babes and marriage (Mk, not Lk) **116–117, 119**, the cup of b **122**
Blind, s Bartimaeus
Boanerges **13**
"Body of the Passover, the," **417**
Bonds, let us break their, ambig **543**
Bones, the breaking of, metaph **594**
Book-learning (Isaiah), alluded to in Jn **258**
Born in sins (Jn), equiv to unclean **168**
Bosom, the typical Child in the b **77**, "in his b" (Heb), om or paraphr by LXX **76**, the Shepherd of Israel carrying the lambs "in his b" **78**, c w breast **404**
Bowl, dipping in the, Ben Sira on **405**
Branches, or, layers of leaves (Mk), parall to palm-branches (Jn) **181**
Bread, he that eateth my **400**
Break, in pieces, i e take to pieces, the parts of the Tabernacle **620**
Breaking, the, of bones **594**, of bread to the hungry **419**
Breast, c w bosom **404**
Breasts of God, the, **45**, of the Son or the Father **417–18**
Brethren, Christ's, metaph, also described as His little children **46**
Bribe, a **129**
Bride, the, i e Israel **348**
Broken heart, the sacrifice of a **384**, s Metaphor
Buddha, the **195**
Builders, the, metaph **186**, of the people, i e the Sanhedrin **223**
Burial, of Moses, the **14, 36**
"Burying," an error for "embalming" **374**
"But," interch w, or parall to, "for" **141, 342, 427**
Buy, c w take, or get **639**, "b [corn]," c w hope, or wait **651**

Caiaphas, not in Mk **506**, how introduced by Mt, Lk, Jn **506–7**, the meaning of the name **508–9**, like Balaam (Jn) **509**
Cain (in LXX) "exceeding sorrowful" **454**
Call (Heb), c w meet **189**
Cana, the wine at **45**, typical of the Eucharist **430**
Carrying a vessel **212**, God carries Israel **76**, the heathen carry their idols **78**

Cast lots **576–8**
Catalusis, and *cataluma* (Gk) (1) lodging-place, (2) dissolution **395**
Catechisms, early Christian **705**
Cathedra, a seat of authority **219**
Ceasing, pray without **233**
Cedron (or Kidron) crossed by David, and (Jn) by Jesus **153**
Celsus charges Jesus with cowardice **65, 463**, blames Him for exclaiming Woe! **408**
Cephas (Jn), a title at first promised, not given **150**
"Certain, a" (Heb and Syr) c w (1) look, (2) take hold of **76**
Charge (vb), in Mk **24–32**
Charoseth, Passover sauce **401**
Chastise, parall to scourge **560**
Cherub **677**
Child, the, in the bosom of the Father **77**, receive as a **121**, children of God (Jn), i e elect (Mk) **323**, children of the kingdom (Mt), parall to ye (Lk) **142**
Childbirth **312**, s Travail
Chlamys **565**
Chosen, parall to beloved **20** foll
Christ (Origen) in Gabriel and Michael **263**, on the cross (in Jn) is regarded as the Passover **346**
Christians, the test of, before a Roman tribunal **532**
Christos, or *Chrēstos* **545**
Chronological order **192**, aimed at by Lk **201**, inference as to from "cornfields" **204**, in Mk, doubtful **204, 503**
Chrysostom, on —the Anointing of Jesus **354**, "hearken unto him" **36**, "these little-ones" **80**
City, c w foal **175**
Clement of Alexandria, follows Clement of Rome **88**, blends the Eucharist with the Supper at Bethany **350**, on —the eighth day **8**, the Babe **45**, little children, *paidia* **46**, faith and prayer **56**, "these little-ones" **80**, a hundredfold with persecutions **140**, first and last **143**, Hosanna **183**; s also **72** and *passim*
Clement of Rome **40, 76, 80, 102, 135**, on offending the elect **88**
"Cloak" (Mk-Mt), conn w "winter," and parall to "goods" (Lk) **310**
"Cloud," or "clouds," conn w the Coming **523**
Coat, Peter's, *ependūtēs* (in Aq. =Heb ephod) **501**, s *Ependūtēs*

INDEX

Cohort, (Jn)=multitude (Synopt) **477–88**, c w. "scribe" or "gather" **481**, om by Lk, emph by Jn **482**
Coinage, or coin-stamp, of the soul, the **257**
Coming, God's (Heb) = self-manifestation (Targ) **329**, is continuous and dateless (Jn) **330**
Coming of Jesus, the, was fulfilled first in His resurrection **316**, promises about, differently expressed in Synopt and in Jn **719**
Coming, the, of "one like a son of man" to the Ancient of Days (Daniel) **523**
Commandment, the first **266–7**, God's, (Jn) a gift **272**, and eternal life **283**
Commandments, the two great, combined in *Test XII Patr* **270**
Comment, transferred to speech **346**
Comparative, the, in Gk, ambig = (1) "rather," (2) "more" **56**
Concerning, or about, ambig c w "to" **406**
Conflation **25, 52**
Conscience, the, (?) signified by "the doorkeeper" **333**, in a community **333**
Consider, in "c a vision" **539**
Consul, a, metaph **547**, the true and the false **552**
Context, argument from the non-quoted c of a quoted text **495**
Controversies, obsolete, sometimes diffusely recorded in Mk **259**
Cophinus (Juvenal) **181 ⁂**
Cords, c w rushes **217**, a scourge of **217–18**
Corn (Gk), c w spices **650**, s *Arōma*
Cornfields, chronological inference from mention of **204**
Corruption, deliverance from **376**
Covenant **423** foll, s *Diathēkē*
Cowardice, imputed to Jesus by Celsus **65, 463**, comp **155**
Creeds, the earliest **705**
Crime, *i e* charge, or superscription, on the cross **584**
Cross, of Jesus, the **41**, the "offence of" **88**, Jesus bears for Himself **573**, those standing near, or far from **628**
Cross, the, generally, must be expected (Epictet) by the accused, if mute **549**, bearing or taking up **572**
Crossing, or across, Cedron **153**, s Pass over

Crucified, was, c w was lifted up **683**, "c with Christ" **591**
Crucifixion of Jesus, the **563**, the hour of **579–80**, (?) virtual distinguished from actual **580**
Crurifragium **625**
Crying aloud of the Messiah, the **66–7**, thrice in Jn **68**
Cup, of water, a **96**, the c of blessing **122**
Cup, or hour, metaph **459, 464**, the c of suffering, two kinds of **466**, of the Lord **466**
Cursing Christ in synagogue **83**
Curse (*lit* anathematize), Peter began to **532** foll
Custom, of releasing a prisoner, not really a custom, but Pilate's habit **553–4**
Custom, according to the, ambig (the c of the Jews, or of Jesus) **434**
Cynic, the, (Epictet) claims to be a king **548**

Daniel, on thrones **3**, on white raiment **14**, not quoted by Lk **309**, supposed bearing of on the Coming of Christ **523**, reference to in Mk **523**, alluded to by Mt **676**
Darkness, first Biblical mention of **663**
Date of the day of the Lord, the **328**, s Day
Dative, with speak ("to"), c w "about" **406**
David, was "made firstborn" **146**, crosses the Kidron **153**, the God of (*Didachē*) **183**, called "our father"(Mk), and "the Patriarch" (Acts) **190**, "D their king whom I will raise up" (Jerem) **190**, "the stone (Targ) that the builders rejected" **223**, conn w Bethlehem **274**, descent of Messiah from **275**, forbidden to build the Temple **285**, D and Jesus (in Jn) both cross the Kidron **449**
Dawn, deep (Philo and Lk) **661**
Day, next, c w mountain **25**, interch w hour **72**, of the Lord, the date of the, not known to the Son (Mk–Mt), not knowable to the disciples (Lk), detemporised (Jn) **326–9**, "in that day" (Jn) **329**
Days, intervals of, exceptional mention of **9**, shortening the **315**,

770

ENGLISH

the Passover after two (Mk–Mt) 339-46, six before the Passover (Jn) 342, 345
Deaf, not in Jn 50
Death, the dust of, *i e* Sheol, immersion in 158, Jerome and Origen on 158, smiting unto, and not unto 466
Deceived (Gk), c w loved 125-6
Deceivers, -ing etc, not in Lk 294, deceivers not in Jn, but in 1 Jn 318
Dedicated gifts (Herod's) 285
Dedication, the Feast of the 182-3
Definiteness in Synopt, parall to indefiniteness in Jn 329
Delivering up, the, of the Son of Man 62 foll, Jn on the 63, "delivering up" and Judas Iscariot 63, conn w a mention of "Galilee" or "in Galilee" 63, the Father "delivering up" or "giving" the Son 64, of Jesus 559, of Christ's spirit 615
Delocalising and detemporising in Jn 329
Denarius, God's 257
Denial, Peter's, Origen on, quotes the Pauline context of the warning about "Jesus is anathema" 534, Synoptic variations as to, subordinated by Jn 535
Denying [Jesus], diff fr disowning 535, parall to being ashamed of 536
Departure, Christ's 5, *i e* death, Christ's 14, 30, 31, 35
Dependence, of the Son on the Father 45
Descending, and ascending, connected 733
Destroy, this temple 210
Destroyer, of others, the, is a self-destroyer 409
Destruction, or perdition, is within ourselves 409, Judas, the son of (Jn) 409, "the d, *or* demon, that wasteth at noonday" 582
Determined, *i e* decreed (Lk) = written [in Scripture] (Mk–Mt) 408, 412
Development, Philo on 381
Diáconoi, the seven, the signs wrought by 736
Diatessaron, Tatian's, paraphrases and omits 13, omissions in 74, 174, 193, 206, 321, 550, 604, 617, 660, 700, transpositions in 72, 128, 431-2, 538, identifies the Johannine with the Synoptic cleansing of the Temple 200, implies that Joseph of Arimathea did not own Christ's tomb 644
Diathēkē 423 foll, "the blood of my" 423, in Lk, latent in vb *diatithemai*, "make a *d*" 428, equivalent of, in Jn 428
Didachè, the, quoted 183, parall to Barnabas 240
Difficulties in Mk, earlier than easy substitutes in Mt and Lk 386
"Dipping a sop and reaching it," (*Hor Heb*) "very unusual" 401
Disarrangement, in Mk 345
Disciple, the, whom Jesus loved 126
Disciples, the, alone, *i e* apart from the multitude 232
Disowning [Jesus], diff fr denying 535
Dispersion, the 67
Distributing bread, often implied in the breaking of bread 419
Divine nature in elemental things (Jn) 101
Divorce, the discussion of, how originated 112 foll, of a husband 115
Docetae, the doctrine of, about a fig-tree 209
Doorkeeper, (Mk and Jn) 331 foll, of the soul, the (Lucian) 332, a guardian conscience 333, c w Peter 333, (Chrys) perh Moses 333, c w keeper of the keys 334, c w *paranymph* 335
"Double portion," a, of Elijah's "spirit," 733, the condition of receiving, perh referred to in Jn 732-3
Dramatic, as distinct from historical, form of expression, preferred by John 32, 97, 122, 234, 248, 277, 308, 337, 429, 467, 503, 553, 562, 697
Draw near, c w. touch 712
Drawing, of men by Christ, the 19
Drawn near, hath, (N T) applied to the kingdom of God 475-6
Drinking a deadly draught, not a martyr's death 725
Dual, Heb, how expr in Aram 441
Dumb, not in Jn 50
Dust of death, *i e*, Sheol, immersion in 158, s Baptism
Duty, *i e* debt, c w Gk end 471, "this has paid *d*" 472

Each, (LXX) parall to "man," or "one," or "one man" (Heb) 406

771   49—2

INDEX

Ear, an, restoration of to its place, (?) error for "sword" **494**, the right e in Lk–Jn **503**
Early, meaning of **660**, never in Lk **661**
Early tradition, submerged **13**
Eating, conn w Christ's resurrection **709**
Ebionites, the, rejected wine in the Eucharist **430**
Economy, i e dispensation [of salvation] **475**
Egotism, altruism beneath appearance of **517**
Egyptian priests, (Plutarch) **101**
"Eight days, about," parall to "six days" **8–10**
Eighth day, superior to seventh **8**, Justin M on **8**
Ejaculation **314**
Elaion, oil, and *eleos*, mercy **348**
Elect, conn w Son and Purifier **21**, the, insoluble problems about **318**, the gathering of **320**, elect (Mk) = children of God (Jn) **323**
Eleven years, in *Pistis Sophia* **289** (should have referred to *Son* **3244c** "some years")
Eli and Eloi **599**
Eliezer, a symbolic name **358**
Elijah, i e Helias, c w *Hēlios*, "sun" **602**, why a type of the Prophets **19**, E and John the Baptist **34**; "in the spirit and power of" **34**, the expected coming of **35**; in Lk, a type of the ascending Saviour **36**, E and Moses, Jn on **37**, at his ascension, "separated" from Elisha **731**
Ellipsis, of apodosis **462**
Embalming **374–81**, mistransl "burying" **374–5**, not a Hebrew practice **375**, the, of Jacob and Joseph **375**, perh symbolic **376**
Emit (Aram), c w finish **609**
Emmaus, (?) c w Tiberias **708–9**
Emphasis, on pers pron **4**, on personal aspects, in Jn **288**, s John
Emporion, unique for *emporia* **213**, in LXX, parall to Heb "harlot," and expl as ref to merchandise **213**
End, (n), only once used in Jn **301**, **329**, *Telos* (Gk) custom, i e customary duty, tax, debt **471**, "it has [its] end" (Lk) **610**, (vb) "it is ended" (Jn) **610**
Ended, conn w fully paid **471**
Ends, of the earth, the **143**

Endure, (Synopt) = abide, or wait (Jn) **301**
Enlightenment, warning, or (Mk) "charging," implied by Heb *zohar* **29**
Enoch, theories about **683**
Enough, it is, i e desist (imperat) **315**, conn w "two swords" (Lk) **470**, w the "sword" of "an angel" (Chron) **315**, **470**
Ensign, of the Son of Man, the **321**
Entombing, of Jesus, the **639**
Entrance (Heb), c w ass **175**
Ependūtēs, Peter's "coat," in Aq = Heb ephod **501**
Ephrem Syrus, on Peter's fiery trial **105**, on the stone at Christ's grave **668**
Epictetus, on —*paidia* **39**, the Beast and the Man **45**, possibilities **54**, marriage **120**, money **129**, the season of figs **209**, pelf **219**, the folly of indiscriminate trustfulness **225**, Christ's exclamation of Woe ! **409**, God's inability to save self-destroyers **409**; the immorality of trouble **452**; "Plead before your judge, or else be prepared for the cross" **549**
Episēmos, notable, appl to the name Jesus **557**, c w (LXX) bound **557**
Esau, called (Midr) the first **146**; the kiss of **351**
Essenes, the, and House of Prayer **7**
Eternal life, God's commandment is (Jn) **283**
Euangelion, gospel, and *evangelize*, preach the gospel, not in Jn **300**
Eucharist, the **390–430**, the institution of **413** foll, Lk on (two versions) **414**, Justin M on **422**, Synoptic accts of, defective **425**, conn, in Clem Alex, w the Supper at Bethany **350**
Eucharistic, distribution, the, Judas absent from (*Const Apost*) **399**, hymning, conn w the Jewish Hallel **433**, s Hymning
Euchē, vow or prayer **56**, (?) "more powerful" (ambig) than faith **57**
Eunuchs, Mt on **120**
Eusebius, on an oracle about the fall of Jerusalem **306**
Eve, and the Virgin Mary (Irenaeus) **143**
Even (Heb), c w "and" **173**
Evolution of tradition, distinct from invention **484**

ENGLISH

Exclamative, or interrogative 473
Exclusiveness, dramatized in Jn 97
Excommunication 98
Executions, delayed till feast-days 343
Exodus, the word 35, Christ's e. or departure 14, 35
Exodus, the book, a promise in ("in the morning glory"), conn w Christ's resurrection (Origen) 662
Expansion, in transln 461
Expire, appl to the first Patriarchs 612
Extortion, in the Temple 212
"Eyes, beautiful in the" 147
Ezekiel, on warning as a prophet's duty 29

Face-cloth, the, in Christ's tomb 670–72
Faith, not mentioned by Jn 225, "have faith in God" (Mk) 227, s Belief, Believe
Fall away, desert, c w fall to the ground 497, "stumbled and fell" (Ps) perh appl by early Christians literally to the enemies of Jesus 499
Falling on the earth (Mk), parall to kneeling (Lk), appl to Jesus 455
False prophet, not in Jn, but in 1 Jn 318, how to be judged 66
"Family relationship" (Origen) between the four accounts of the Anointing of Jesus 387
Famine, conn w pestilence 290
Far yet near (God), near yet far (idols) 311, f may refer to time 630
Far off, appl to Gentiles 269
Fasting, Jerome and Tertull on 56, f and prayer 56
Father, our, a title mostly reserved by Jews for no men but the first three Patriarchs 190, our father David (Mk) 190
Father's house, lit and metaph 438
Fear (Aram), c w travail-pangs (Heb) 291, disconnected by Jn from Christ's resurrection 702, "fear not" (Jn) = "rejoice greatly" (Zech) 192, Israel "feared" Joshua 152, emphasized in O T, subordinated in Jn 53, 154, feared (Mk) c w saw 699–703
Feasts (Jn), conn w visits to the Temple 198-9, executions delayed till 343, s Dedication, Passover

Feet, the washing of 151
Figs, the season for (Epictet) 209, Pliny on 205, good and bad 325
Fig-leaves, Philo on 207, first Bibl. mention of 206–7
Fig-tree, withered, the (Mk–Mt) 196, 228, a barren (Lk) 202, the symbolism of the 205, conn w Nathanael 209, in Marcan parable 381
Finding, the, of an ass by Jesus 176, of Hagar and Israel by God 177, of Philip by Jesus 177, Philo on divine f 178, a great f hath God wrought 177, "he found him in Bethel," ambig 177
"Find nothing" in any one, i e no debt due to the seeker 472
Found, was not, i e was not to be f, had disappeared 683
Finish (Aram), c w send forth (Heb) 609, it is finished 471, 610, s Ended
Fire, Jn on 103 foll, comp 95, 105, f unquenchable 90, fire and the fire 90, 103, Simon Magus on 94, the Synoptic doctrine of, why omitted by Jn 94, salted with 98, f on the altar 98
Fire-of-coals (Jn *bis*) 105
Firm-in-belief, conn w make-firm 227
First (in time or order ?) 141, "Andrew first (?) found Simon" (Jn) 149, "first Simon" (Mt) 147, Heb once, in LXX, c w firstborn 145, Esau called "the f" 146, God called "THE F" 146, "f" in A V = "chief" in R V. 148, "my f" (Jn) i e "my chief" 148–9
First (or single) Biblical mention of —prophet 36, rich 132, a hundredfold return 137, first i e former (LXX firstborn) 145, fig-leaves 206, stand praying 237, tribulation 311, shortening the days 315, lift up your heads 322, sweet savour 383, my (i e God's) memorial 426, my (i e God's) king 589, hyssop 607, the veil 617, lintel 623, darkness 663, was not, i e was not to be seen, was gone 683
First mention in LXX of —not possible 54, tribulation 110
First and last 141–7, Origen and Jerome on 144–5
First commandment, the 266–7

INDEX

Firstborn, David was made **146**, in LXX (once) f = Heb first **145-6**
Five days **9**
Flee, c w fall away, fall **497**
Flesh, human, metaph (1) rebellious, (2) well disposed but weak **467-8**, in Jn **468-9**, means selfishness (Philo) **89**, judging according to the **89**, the antithesis between f and spirit, om in Lk, emph in Jn **88**
Foal (N T), fastened to a vine (Justin M) **174**, c w city **175**
For interch w but **65, 141, 342, 427**
Forgive, how to, a prominent subject in Christ's doctrine **238**, c w let alone **358-9**
Fornication, c w merchandise **214**
Forsake, Heb and Aram **599**, c w reproach **599**
Forty days **9**, forty six years **286**
Foundation, of the New Jerusalem, the **253**
Four days **9**
Friend, c w other (in "each other") **407**
From (Gk), c w upon **462**, from afar (Ps and Gosp) implying recoil **626** foll
Fruit, in Jn **325**, c w summer **325**
Fuller, "no f on earth" **13-19**, God described as a, i e as Cleanser **17**, a rabbinical metaph title **17**, c w lamb **16**, Rashi on "the fuller's field" **15**, parables of fullers **16**
Future (tense), c w, or parall to, imperat **73, 74, 435**, c w past **383**

Galilee, conn w "delivering up" **63**, c w Judaea **201**, (Mk-Mt) "I will go before you to" parall to (Lk) "while he was yet in" **438**, in Jn, parall to (Lk) Nazareth, (Mk-Mt) *patris*, fatherland **438**, perh conn w spiritual home, Father's House **439**, "goeth before you into" (Mk-Mt) **693**, "he spake unto you in" (Lk) **694**
Gall, for my meat **575**
Garden, or Paradise **642**
Garments, Christ's, how divided **576**
Gate-keepers, of hell, the **322**
Gates, of Jerusalem, or Sheol, or Heaven **322**
Gather (Heb) = pity (LXX) **322**, c w receive hospitably **370**

"Gathered, to his people" Philo and Talmud on **613-14**
Gatherers, for the fire **95**
Gathering, of the elect, the (Mk-Mt), redemption (Lk), unification (Jn) **320** foll., into one (Jn) **323**
Gehenna, in Lk **97**, "son of G," once in the Bible **411**
Genesis, illustrates Mk on a hundredfold return **137**, prophecy about the Messiah in, Mk perh influenced by **173**
Gentiles, revelations to the **69**, judgment for the **69**, called "the last" **143**, conn w the Temple **176**, the Charter of the, the Gift of Tongues **738**
Gesture, sometimes needed to explain speech **683-5**
Geth, or *Ge*, in Gethsemane **448**, *Geth*, winepress, c w *Ge* (Euseb), mountain, chasm, ravine **448**
Gethsemane, and the Transfiguration **6**, variously interpreted **448-50**
Give, "all that thou hast given me" in Jn **47**, giving, or delivering up, the Son **64**, giving, divine greatness consists in **75**
Glory, in the Gospels **1-5**, conn w thrones **3**, parall to kingdom **3**, conn w Transfiguration by Lk alone **4**, of the Father, the, consists in giving **23**, "the, of the Lord, ye shall see in the morning" **662**
Gnōsis, magnified by Gnostics **56**, the need of, recognised by Jn (Origen) **192**
Gnostic legends **574**
Go before, i e prepare the way for, conn w a journey **439**
Going forth of Jesus, the **469**, "let us be going" (Mk-Mt), om (Lk), transposed (Jn) **469**
God, described as a "fuller" **17**, regarded as a Mother **43**, walking **243**
"God, my" in Mk-Mt **595**, in Scripture **596-7**, Origen on **598**
Good thing, any, from Nazareth **277**
Government, the, on his shoulders **41**
Governor, Heb -Gk word **543**, Pilate not called a, in Mk and Jn **543**
Grammateus, (1) scribe, (2) townclerk **276**
Great, no merit in refusing to be **44**
Greater, the, shall serve the less (LXX) **145**, works, the promise of **235**

774

ENGLISH

Greatest, who is the? **70–75**
Greatness, divine, consists in giving **75**
Greek corruption **188–9**
"Greeks, the" = "the Dispersion" **67**, "certain Greeks" typical of Gentiles **179, 216**
Guest-chamber, for the Eucharist, the **394**
Guide (Aram), c w speak (Heb) **694**
Guileless, milk, i e unadulterated **351**
Gunaikomorphism, appl to the Son **418**

Hades, in Lk **97**
Hadrian, the statue of, in Jerusalem **308**
Hagar, found by the Lord **177**
Haggada, the **16**
Hair, not a, shall perish **723**, s Martyr
Hallel, the Passover Psalms **432**
Hand of the poor, that which is in the **385**
Handling, lit and metaph **710–11**
Hands, "of a kind" (Origen) **714**, of intercession (Moses and Jesus) **633**, lifted or stretched out **633**
Hard, a h thing **127**, i e against nature **129**, hard (Synopt) = not possible (Jn) **132**
Harming, no, the Stoic doctrine about n h **723**
Harvest, the Law of the **11**
Hasten, c w tomorrow **25**
Have money, those who, i e whose chief characteristic is their m **132**, s Master
Having aught against anyone, Jerome on **238**
Heads, c w rulers **322**
Heal (Gk), c w permit **490**
Hear, c w hear about **222**, c w amaze **256**
Heart, the leaven in the **239**, a sacrifice when broken **383**, of Aaron, the (bearing the names of Israel) **404**
Heaven, to Jews might suggest "which heaven?" e g the third **727**, the third **6**
Hebraized Gk words **469, 481, 486**
Hebrew, Gk deviations from in LXX, parall to Gk deviations in Gospels **25**, c w Aram **599**, dual (?), Mk misled by **440**, Gospel (Jerome's) **622**, original,

sign of in the active infin **729**; thought, latent in Mk, sometimes poetic **78, 95, 440**
Hēlios (Gk), sun, a Hebraized word **602**
Here, c w weep **685**
Hermas, quoted **102, 129**
Hermon, Mount **7**, identif by some w Mount of Transfiguration **24**
Herod Antipas, why conn by Lk w the Passion **482**, why not mentioned by Jn **484**, conn w. Pilate in Acts, quoting Ps **543**
Herod the Great, c w H Antipas **483**
Hexaemeron, a, **10, 122**, in Jn (twice) **346–7, 641**, suggested by *Const Apost* **399**
Hidden, was, or hid himself (Jn) **246**
Hiding, God's, when He reveals **70**, of Jesus, the **69–70, 246**
High priest, the, (?) Annas or Caiaphas **506**, during that year **507**, a disciple known to (Jn) **530**
Hillel, and Shammai **16, 410**
Him, ambig **177**
History, conveyable through poetry **173, 626**
Hither, c w behold **684**
Hold, take hold of, c w "one" **76**
Holy Spirit, the, typified by a "little child" **81**, parall to "a mouth and wisdom" **302**, said to be "grieved" **303**, the personification of, weakened in Targums **304**, c w the Angel of the Lord **304**, regarded as Mother **305**, the promise of, not in Mk-App or Mt *ad fin* **721**, and variously placed by Lk and Jn **721**
Holy Supper, the (Clem Alex) **350**
Home, or Father's House, lit and metaph **438**, Christ's h in heaven, or in Galilee **438–9**
Homeric poetry, a trace of **667**
Hope, or wait (Heb), c w "buy [corn]" **650**, c w "behold" **651**
Hopla, arms of warfare (Jn), in Heb, c w kiss **485**
Hosanna (Mk, Mt, Jn) **182**, Lk's equiv of **182**, two distinct Christian tendencies about **189**, explanation of by Clem Alex **183**, c w Osanna **184**, and Osienna **185**, Origen suggests a new interpretation of **185**, conn in Talmud with Feast of Tabernacles **186**, a name for a bundle of branches **187**

775

INDEX

Hosea, ("after two days") quoted 346, on "smiting" 466
Hour, Christ's 67, or cup 459, interch w day 72, third, sixth, and ninth connected 581-2, of the morning sacrifice, the 581
Hour, the third 579 foll, (Mk) the hour of the crucifixion 579, Jewish traditions about 580, the Sanhedrin began to sit from 580
Hour, the sixth 581, Jn on 582
Hours, the first three, God is wroth during 580
House, ellipsis of, in Gk but not in Heb 438, (Heb) = substance, household 335, metaph (1) the World, (2) the Church 382-3, earthly or spiritual 695, s Home, Mountain
How long! 493, does not imply unbelief 496
Humanity, the coinage of 257
"Humbled himself," appl to Jesus 455
Humility, a right and a wrong 43, when true, not a conscious self-humbling 121
Hundredfold, a, in Genesis and Mk 137 foll, with persecutions 133-40, conn w Abraham's planting (Philo) 138, parall to "manifold" 139
"Hurt you, nothing shall" 722, s Anytus
Hussōpos, hyssop, (?) c w *hussos* (Gk) javelin 604
Hymning, i e accomplishing the Hallel 432, h according to the custom (*Const Apost*) conn w the Last Supper 433, h and dancing (*Acts of Jn*) conn w the Last Supper 433
Hyperbole, poetic (Mk) parall to prose (Lk) 321
Hypotheses, tend to alter traditions 336
Hyssop (Jn) = reed (Mk-Mt) 603, used as a flavour (Philo and Nonnus) 604-5, Philo on the Essene use of 605, symbolism of 606

"I," I AM, and "it is I" 53, parall to "the Wisdom of God" 259, Jn's use of 517-19, "I set up the pillars" (Rashi, "I, thy people, Israel") 518, sometimes expr by "this man" 406
Ibn Ezra 44, 66, 92, on the "grieving" of the Holy Spirit 304

Idol, an, near yet far, God far yet near 311
Ignatius 93, 129, on the two coinages of the soul 257, on the Anointing of Jesus, does not refer to Luke 347
Immanence, divine, parall to inambulance 243
Imperative, parall to, or c w, future 73, 74, 435, c w indic 210, 228, 300, 423, in Gk, c w inf 462, ironical or judicial 519
Imperfect, parall to aorist 367
In the name, and on the name 85, "in" c w "among" 102
Inambulance, divine, parall to immanence 243
Indefinite subject ("they") ambig 274
"Indication," as distinct from proof 263
Indicative, c w imperat 210, 228, 300, 423, c w interrog 395
Inference, sometimes a cause of error 407
Infinitive (Gk), after "in," a sign of transl from Heb 25, c w imperat 462
Intercession 237, the i of Aaron bearing on his heart the names of Israel 404
Interpretation, new, diff fr invention 384
Interrogation in prayer 61
Interrogative, ambig 37, 395, 443, 460, 473
Intervals of days, exceptional mention of 9
Intervention, of Jn for Mk, *passim*, important exceptions to 49, 444, 528, 532-5
Irenaeus, on —Eve and the Virgin Mary 143, heretical baptism 156, Abomination and the Man of Sin 307, the Ebionites 430
Irony, Johannine 10, 67, 211, 251 etc
Irony, (?) in "sleep on now" 473
Isaac, i e laughter 45, persecuted 137
Isaiah (see Index to Scriptural passages) sawn asunder 94
Israel, a child carried by Jehovah 76-7, God's missionary 143, c w the Jews (Lk) 191, the meaning of the name 277, the Bride 348, "king of I," not in Lk, twice in Jn 546
Israelites, renegade 92
Itacism 462

776

Jacob, the wrestler, a type of tribulation 312, the embalming of 375, J and Esau, the birth of 145
Jeremiah, regarded as "a suckling" 44
Jerome, confuses Simon the leper with S the Pharisee 354, interprets Bartimaeus as Barsemia 167
Jerome, on —"six days" 8, white garments 14, the fuller's field 15, Elijah and John the Baptist 34, Moses and Elijah 35, the "growing up" of the Suffering Servant 40, fasts 56, these little ones 80, a little child 81, salting babes 99, first and last 144–5, the dust of death 158, the cup of martyrdom 159, "my Mother, the Holy Spirit" 305, the Abomination of Desolation 308, "lift up your heads" 322, the Anointing of Jesus 354, Bethany 369, the old and the new 381, Judas dipping in the bowl 405, Gethsemane 448, Christ troubled for Judas 456, the binding of Jesus 541, the penitent robber 592, the promise about taking up serpents 726, Elijah ascending unhurt by flame 732, the Hebrew and LXX texts 631
[Jerome], i e pseudo-Jerome on Mk, includes Peter in the Boanerges 13
Jerusalem, "journeying to J" may imply several visits 207–8, 222, "scribes from J" 225, to be destroyed by the Romans 251, the siege of 290, called by Jerome the Christian Athens 145
Jesus, the typical Child, or *Paidion* 47, might be called by Jewish Christians the "Fuller" 18, blesses children in Mk, but not in Lk 116–17, generates, or increases, faith 59, described, in Jn, as "finding" the ass that the disciples "find," in Synopt 176, perh visited Jerusalem often 222, the family of, regular attendants at the Passover 201, early preaching of (Lk) in Judaea 201, the thoughts of, beneath the words 226, quotes the Pentateuch to Sadducees 262, predictions of His "rising again" 466, described as "learning obedience" 466, and as "not pleasing himself" 518, last words of, to the Jews 522, and to Judas 407, 491, the earlier and the later attitude of, toward the Temple 515, the final teaching of in the Temple 282, post-resurrectional utterances of 289, last words of, before death, to the disciples 469, 475

Jews, the, in Lk, c w Israel 191

Joanna (?), in Lk, c w Joannes 659

John, the son of Zebedee, traditions about as martyr 159, unique mention of, in Synopt, as receiving a special precept 84, (?) "known to the high priest" 531

John the Baptist, s Baptist

John, i e the (unknown) author of the Fourth Gospel, intervenes to explain or correct Mark, p ix and *passim* prefers dramatic to historical form 32, 122, 234, 248, 265, 277, 308, 337, 553, unconventionality of 34, prefers positive to negative doctrine 37, 89, 209, 264, 292, meets the charge that Jesus fled from danger 67, 155, ascribes a divine nature to elemental things 101, bases his Gospel on Nature 105, 317, assumes the naturalness of tribulation 110, describes Andrew as "first" finding his brother Simon 147 foll, instead of condemning rivalry, inculcates unity 161, alone mentions "the ruler of this world" 163, attributes to Jesus what Synoptists attribute to disciples 178, quotes Zech "rejoice greatly" as "fear not" 192, connects the Treasury with judgment 203, assumes Christ's works of healing to be numerous 224, does not mention, yet implies and classifies, faith 225, toward the close of his Gospel rarely mentions the Temple 245, dwells on the positive aspect of resurrection 265, asserts that Moses "wrote about" the Messiah ("wrote about me") 265, ignores the Temple in the doctrine on the Last Days 288, supplements the Gospel in the Epistle 318, implies "ransom" but does not mention it 164, 323, delocalises and detemporises 329, implies a Hexaemeron twice 346–7, reinterprets, but does not invent 384, presents an equiv to the Synopt "testament" 428, extenuates, where Mk exaggerates, Peter's lapse 535, disconnects Christ's resurrection from (Synopt) "fear" and "amazement" 702, s also Dramatic expression and Irony

INDEX

John, on —glory **1-5**, signs and wonders **12**, Christ's (Lk) "departure" **31**, Moses freq (as contrasted with Elijah seldom) **37**, "little children" (implied in regeneration) **44-8**, the (Synopt) "delivering up" of Christ **63** foll, Christ's "crying aloud" **68**, the doctrine of (Synopt) the "greater" **75**, "living" (adj) **101**, fire **103**, the equiv of fire **105**, the Law of persecution **139**, "my first (*i e* chief)" **148-9**, Jesus crossing Kidron **153**, "beyond Jordan" **154**, sea of Galilee **154**, the Son "preparing a place" **160**, "born in sin" **168**, the "finding" of an ass by Jesus **176**, *onarion* **178**, Christ's visits to the Temple **196**, a scourge of cords **217-18**, standing (*stēkein*) **239**, the "walking" of Jesus **242**, the tabernacling of the Logos **244**, Jesus hidden or hiding **246**, book-learning (Isaiah) **258**, the woman travailing **313**, gathering into one the scattered **323**, fruit **325**, the time of the Lord's coming **329**, "the end" and "it is ended" **329**, Bethany **370** foll, Mary Magdalene and the woman that was a sinner **388-9**, antenatalism **410-12**, predestination **410-12**, the scattering of the disciples **437**, Kidron **449**, sorrow (not mentioned till the close of the Gospel) **453**, Messianic (Mk) intercession **457**, flesh, *i e* the fleshly nature of man **468-9**, the sixth hour **582**, the "title" on the cross **586-7**, Christ's thirst **601**, the women near the Cross **631**, a Hexaemeron **641**, Mary Magdalene **672**, Galilee (contrast Lk) **694-5**, God's meeting-place with man **697-8**, evidence from hearing and seeing **698**, from touching and handling **713**, "all that thou hast given me" **719**, the Son, not "taken up" but "going up" **732**

John subordinates, or seldom mentions —little child **45**, fear **53**, **152**, **154**, fire **95**, last (exc in "last day") **148**, end **301**, signs and wonders **738**

John omits —mention of praying **11**, Synoptic details about John the Baptist **34**, deaf and dumb **50**, right and left hand of Christ **161**, any precept to love enemies **271**, scribe **276**, Mount of Olives **288**, gospel and preach **300**, any selection of companions by Jesus **450**, many Synoptic names **573**; the name of the Lord's mother **633**, almost all the agreements between Lk and Mk-App **707**

John emphasizes —Christ's personal affection **59**, **62**, and personal aspects generally **288**, **429**, requesting as distinct from praying **61**, precepts of unity instead of prohibitions of rivalry **161**, the fruit of doing instead of the danger of not doing **429**

John has occasional words or allusions common to Lk **360**, **503**, **532**, and may be said to intervene sometimes agst Mk **444**, **528**, **532**

Jordan, Joshua crossing J **153**, "beyond J" avoided by Lk but not by Jn **154**

Joseph, the embalming of **375**

Joseph of Arimathea **127**, prob not the owner of Christ's tomb **643**

Josephus **57**, **125**

Joshua, "feared" by Israel **152**; J, crossing Jordan, a type of Jesus **152-3**

Journeying, by stages (Lk), perh parall to distinct journeys (Jn) **207-8**, **222**

Joy succeeding trouble **456**

Jubilee, (Aquila) "the [year] that remits [debts]" **461**

Judaea, c w Galilee **201**

Judas Iscariot **66**, the entering of Satan into (Lk and Jn) **344-5**, **391-2**, called (Mk) "the one of the Twelve" **391**, (Jn) "Simon's son" **392**, designated as the traitor **397**, alleged (*Const Apost*) to have been absent from the Eucharistic distribution **399**, regarded by Jn as sick unto death **402**, Christ's last words to **407**, **491**, described by Nonnus as "oscillating" **481**

Judas Maccabaeus **182**

Judge, the Saviour, how converted into a **735**, the Messiah as a **567**

Judging (Jn) implies "sitting" in judgment (Synopt) **522-4**, **734**, after the sight of one's eyes **568**

Judgment, for the Gentiles **69**, conn w the Treasury and almsgiving **202-3**

Justin Martyr, on —the eighth day **8**, the "suckling" or "sucker" in Isaiah (LXX) **40**, *paidion* **40-41**, names of the Messiah **41**, "of-

ENGLISH

fending (*skandalizein*)" 88, Isaiah sawn asunder 94, "the whole of the Psalm (xxii)" as Messianic 158, a Millennium 262, Bethphage but nowhere Bethany 365, the Eucharist 422 foll, covenanting (diff in *Apol* and *Dial*) 428, controversial points in the Eucharist 429–30, the "mixture" in the Eucharist 430, the binding of Jesus 541–2, gives two traditions (*Apol* and *Dial*) about the "foal" in N T 174, perh once alludes to Mk 174, s also 215, 380

Keteb, a demon 582, s Destruction and Noon
Keys, the keeper of the, c w doorkeeper 334
Kidron (or Cedron), passed over by David and Jesus 153, 449, Kidron (Jn) = Gethsemane (Mk–Mt) 449
Killed, to be, is not to be harmed 722–4, s Anytus
Kind (Heb), c w "believe" 60, "this k" [of devil] 55, 59
King, and robber, antithetical 558, "my king" (uttered by God) 589, the claim to be a 545, metaph, in Gk and Rom literature 547
"King of Israel," not in Lk, twice in Jn 546, uttered by mockers in Mk–Mt 546, c w King of the Jews (Lk) 191, 590
"King of the Jews," uttered by Pilate, in mockery, which is emphasized ironically by Jn 558–9
Kingdom, parall to glory 3, of God, the, and little children 38 foll, how to enter into the 123 foll
Kiss, the, of Esau, and of Judas 349, (Heb) c w weapons 485, a false and a true, Philo on 489
Kneeling (Lk), parall to falling on the earth (Mk) 455
Knife, c w sword 492
Know, "knew not what he said" 5, know and know of 64–5, known to the High priest, a disciple (Jn) 530, be made known c w meet 696–7
Kūrios, without article, *i e* Jehovah 314

Ladder, Jacob's, preparatory for the Tent of Meeting 516–17, regarded as the Logos, or Son of Man 517
Lamb, a, "standing as though it had been slain" 240, the, the Song of 3, c w "fuller" 16

Lantern, (Jn) unique 485, Gk word Hebraized 486
Laodicean Church, the, the doorkeeper in 331
Last, (?) in time or order 141 the latest converts, *i e* Gentiles 141–7
Last days, the, 284 foll, Jn on 287–8
Last words, the, of Jesus, to the disciples 469 foll, 475, to Judas 407, 491, to the Jews 522, before the Ascension 714–22, last words of a dying Jew 608
Latin-Greek words in Mk 356
Law, the, of Moses, regarded in Midr as the Mother of babes 42, the L and the Temple, joint influence of, during Christ's manhood, for evil 226, a new L, conn w the Transfiguration 9, the L of the Harvest 11
Leave, c w let go 496
Leaven, in the heart 239
Legions, of God, the 493
Leper, Simon the 353, a name of the Messiah 373, lepers, purification of, conn w Eucharist (Justin M) 373, s Simon
Less, the greater shall serve the (LXX) 145
Let alone (Gk *aphes*), c w remit 358
Let go, c w leave 496
Lift up, the soul, conn w praying 6, c w lift up oneself 6, your heads (Ps and Lk) 322, the eyes 434, c w take away 730
Lifted up, on the cross, Jesus was 36, c w was crucified 683
Light (n), flame, may mean "warming" 510, implying (1) illumination, or (2) destruction 510–11, (Heb) c w "see" 511
Light (vb), parall to "kindle around" 510
Lintel, first mention of 623, of the Temple, the, c w veil of the Temple 622
Literal, the, mixed with the metaphorical 644
Little-child, *paidion*, in Jn only twice 45, defined as "son" in context 62, the (typical), in Christ's arms 75–9, possibly a name of Christ Himself 81, receive as a 121
Little-children 38, 47, "be not, in your minds" 39, in Jn 44–7, the, of Christ, are also His brethren 46, altered to "babes" 117

INDEX

"Little-one, the," in Jewish thought 80, "these little-ones," meaning of 80, Samuel, the 1 80
Little while, a, (Jn) meaning of 317
Litra, pound weight, conn w shekel of the sanctuary 364
Liturgy, early Christian 434
Living, in Jn, the meaning of 101
Lodging, c w 3rd pers pron reflex 368, 1 place, c w Bethany 367-8; (Gk) c w dissolution 395, s *Catalusis*
Logos, the, regarded as a ladder 517
Look, c w "a certain" 76, 1 round about (Mk) 193-6, appl to Moses 195, to the Buddha 195, Philo on 195, 1 up, metaph and lit 279, may imply a vision 666-7, looking stedfastly 125
"Looseth Jesus" 84
Lord, the, *i e* God, c w Jesus 344
Lots, casting 576 foll
Love, of enemies, not prescribed in Jn 271, self-sacrificing, in the Father and the Son 272
Loved, c w deceived 125-6, the disciple whom Jesus loved 126
Luke, deviates from, or omits, passages in Mk, *passim*, seldom inserts new Lucan fact in Synoptic narrative 5, disconnects Christ's resurrection from Galilee 63, 438, 694, differs from Mk-Mt as to persecution 136, inserts a substitute for (Mk, Mt, Jn) "Hosanna" 182-3, has "king of the Jews" for (Mk-Mt) "king of Israel" 191, 590, aims at chronological order 201, comp 700, imitates Thucydides 290, 320, alludes to the siege of Jerusalem 290, inserts no quotation from Daniel 309, emphasizes scriptural proofs of Christ's resurrection 718
Luke, on —glory 1-5, Moses 4, mountain and prayer 6, Elijah 35-6, "last," meaning furthest off, metaph, *i e* Gentiles 142-3, a parable about a barren fig-tree 202 (comp 205), importunate prayer 229, proofs of the Resurrection 265, pestilences 289, the date of the Lord's Coming 328, the Eucharist (two versions) 414, Annas and Caiaphas 506, the Ascension (Acts) 717, and (Gospel) 729
Luke omits, or avoids —"three days," exc in the finding of the Child Jesus 31; "little child,"
paidion, exc about the Child Jesus 38-9, the warning against "self-offending" 88, "tribulation" 108, details of temple-service 218, "early" 661, *diathēkē*, "testament" or "covenant," but has the vb "covenant" 428
Luke, misled as to *praetorium* 483, and as to a supposed connection of Herod Antipas with the Passion 482, agreements of, with Jn, in word but not in thought 360, 503
Luminary, of the New Jerusalem, the 254

Magdala (*Hor Heb*) "Bethany might go under the name of M" (?) 366
Maidservant, a, the vision of, at the Red Sea 597
Make, c w prepare for sacrifice 421-2
Male and female from the beginning 119
Malefactor, the penitent, said to have been converted by miracles 592-3
Man, the ages of 42, the Man and the Beast (Epictet) 45
Man of Sin, the, Irenaeus on 307
Manifesting Himself, God described (Targ) as, where Heb has "coming" 329-30
Manifold, parall to hundredfold 133-4, 139
Mansions, *i e* stages or stations 440
Mark (s Section Headings in Contents) a Petrine Gospel 18, traces of visions in 18, Heb thought latent in 78, sometimes abridges, or assumes knowledge in the reader 98, 115, 138, diverged from by Mt, and still more by Lk, because obscure or harsh 118, seldom quoted by early writers 174, passages of, om by *Diatess*. 174, Justin M perh once alludes to 174, diffuse on obsolete details and controversies 190, 218, 259, 557, "no vestige" of the Lord's Prayer in (Origen) 230, doctrine of prayer in, incomplete 234, the chronology of, doubtful 204, passages in, that suggest poetic origin 316, 355, post-resurrectional utterances in 328, disarrangement in 345, Latin-Greek words in 356, difficult passages in, earlier than easier substitutes (Mt and Lk)

386, implies, though it does not quote, prophecy 405, on Messianic intercession 457, nowhere mentions Caiaphas 506, influenced by Peter in its emphasis on Peter's denials 534–5, a Gospel not revised by its author 704

Mark-Appendix, the, and Lk, differences and resemblances in 706–7

Mark-Matthew tradition, Hellenic not Hebraic 92

Marriage, Christ's blessing on (Mk and Jn) 119, 122, Epictetus on 120

Martyr, Elijah regarded as a 33

Martyrdom, Akiba's 5, distinct from patience 466, the hundredfold return of 139

Martyrs, are "not harmed" 723, the three (Daniel) whose "hair" is "not singed" 724, the seven 264

Mary, the Lord's mother, never named in Jn 633

Mary Magdalene, in Jn 388, typical as well as historical 672, conn w "seven devils" 706

"Master-workman," the (Proverbs) 45

Masters of (Heb) money 130, *i e* those who own money as their chief characteristic 130

Matthew (s Mark for passages where Mt agrees with Mk) traditions peculiar to, on —"eunuchs" 120, "first Simon" 147, Jesus smitten by the Sanhedrin 503, watchmen at Christ's grave 679
Duplication in 169, twice relates the cure of "two blind men" 166, 168, parts of, in rhetorical style 281, influenced by Zechariah's prophecy on the ass and the Messiah 173, inference a cause of error in 395, 407, combines two traditions (where Mk has only one) 493, alone alludes to Daniel 676, mentions no Ascension 716, 728

Meant, c w said 382

"Measuring all things" from His Cross, Jesus (*Orac Sibyll*) 632

Meek (Heb), c w afflicted 369

Meet, c w call 189, c w be made known 696–7

Meeting, or visitation (for good or evil) 188, the Tent of M between God and Israel 516, 695–6, misrendered by LXX 696–7, between God and Man in the heart 697–8

Melchizedek 293

Memorial, *anamnēsis*, ambig 421, for the Passover, a 417, "my [*i e* God's] memorial," unique in O T, parall to "my [*i e* God's] name" 426

Memorial-clause, in the Eucharist, not realised by the Corinthians, nor (morally) by Justin M 425

Merchandise, a house of 212, conn w fornication 214

Messiah, the, names of, in Justin M. 41, the chief of sucklings 42, the crying aloud of 66–7, Jacob's and Zechariah's prophecies about 173, the descent of, from David 275, travail-pangs of 291, the birth of, was to synchronize with the fall of the Temple 293, called Leper 373, was to judge by "smelling" 568

Messianic prophecy, allusion to 502, Jewish reaction from Christian interpretations of 276

Metaphor, c w literal statement 95, 223, 256, 644, metaphors interlaced 417, 440, 466, 620, m and allegory 104, obsolete 18, Petrine 228, military 236, 603, allusive and paradoxical 384, eastern and western 214, many-sided 333, new m needed for new truth 733, s. also 238, 239, 660, 666

Metempsychosis 34

Midrash, more popular and poetic than Talmud 583

Midst, in the 240, metaph and lit. 593

Military metaphor 236, 603

Milk, wine and, in Isaiah 45

Millennium, the 139, Justin M on 262, Irenaeus on 266

"Ministers" (Gk) means also "officers" (Lk and Acts) 525–6

Miriam, the well of 669

Misunderstanding, of Christ's predictions, in His disciples 31

Mite, a single, allowed as alms outside, but not inside, the Temple 280

Mithras 425, 429

Mocking, of Jesus, the 563 foll

Modern students of N T, advantages of 387

Money, in N T, implying bribe 129, meaning pelf (Epictet) 219, masters of m, *i e* those whose characteristic is their m 130–31

Money-changers, why om by Lk 218

Monogĕnēs 23

Môr, myrrh, c w *mar*, bitterness 575

INDEX

Morning, "in the m ye shall see the glory of the Lord" **662**
Morrow, c w (1) mountain and (2) hasten **25**
Moses, the Song of **3**, how regarded in Lk and Jn **4**, the ascent of to Mount Sinai **9**, the waiting of **10**, the burial of **14**, **36**, M and Elijah (Jn) **37**, called father of the prophets **190**, looked round about **195**, "wrote about" Jesus (Jn) **265**, (?) the doorkeeper (Jn) **333**, M "lifted," Jesus "stretched out" the hands, in intercession (Origen) **633**, (?) the man with the pitcher (Origen) **395**, interceding for Israel **463**
Mother, "my M the Holy Spirit," quoted by Origen and Jerome **305**, God is regarded as a **43**, the Law is a M of sucklings **42**, the M, i e the Church, in Isaiah, is Jesus, in the Epistle to the Hebrews **46**, the M is (1) Spiritual Israel, (2) the Church, (3) redeemed Man **292**, **313**, (Clem Alex) the Word is Father, Mother, Tutor, Nurse **417**
Mountain, of the Lord's house, the **208**, who art thou, thou great m ? (Zech) **208**
Mountains and trees, an uprooter of (metaph) **207**
Mouth, "m and wisdom" (Lk) parall to "the Holy Spirit" **302**, paraphr by Targ as "interpreter" **304**
Multitude (Synopt) parall to cohort (Jn) **477-88**
Murize, to, i e to perfume (Mk) **377**
Myrrh, wine mingled with (Mk) **575**
Mystical allusions, in Jn **559** and *passim*, s also Irony

Naked, (in Gospel narrative, as distinct from Christ's utterances) only of (1) a "young man," (2) Peter, after the Resurrection **500-501**, in Rev metaph **500**
Name, (Jewish) father's and son's rarely the same **167**, in my n implies restriction in prayer **62**, in Mk **79** foll, in the n of the Lord, in Heb **85**, with various prepositions **85**, to the n of = as being **85**, my n, parall to "my [i e God's] memorial" **426**, names, changes in the order of **355**, Synoptic, om by Jn **573**

Nard **348**, **356**
Nathanael, under the fig-tree, parall to Zacchaeus **209**
Nation, in Jn always sing (the Jewish) **720**
Nations, (i e Gentiles) "for all the n" (Mk), why om by Mt-Lk **215**, the court of the **216**
Natural correspondence expr by Gk particles **734**
Nature, Jn's Gospel the Gospel of **105**, divine, a, in elemental things (Jn) **101**
Nazarean **587-8**, c w Nazarene, **587-8**, **681-3**, s *Nêtzer*
Near, yet far, an idol **311**
Negative doctrine subordinated to positive in Jn **37**, **89**, **292**, etc, s John
Nêtzer, a branch from the house of Jesse **588**, "abominable *n*" (Isaiah) **682**, s Ben Nêtzer
New and old (Philo) **380-81**
Next day, c w mountain **25**
Nicodemus, (?) parall to Synopt "rich ruler" **126**, supplied water to Jerusalem **393-4**, lavish gifts of spices to the daughter of **393**, **396**
Nimrod **481**, s Abraham
Nomen (Lat) = account, in financial sense **85**
Nonnus, quoted **104**, **282**, on — Bethany **370**, Judas oscillating **481**, the arrest of Jesus **485**, the two High Priests **508**, hyssop **604**, Christ's tomb **663**
Noon, destruction at **581**
Not, interrog, ambig **37**, c w Heb prefix to inf **701**, "n all," i e "not any" **701**, "he is n here," (Mk) i e is not to be found here **683-5**, or, is destroyed **685**, n possible (Jn) = hard (Synopt) **132**
Notable, s *Episēmos*
Nothing, find n in, i e no debt due to the seeker **472**
Nursing Father, a, **45**

Obedience, house of, i e (Jerome) Bethany **369**
Obsoleteness, in Mk, **190**, **259**, **557**
Odes of Solomon, the, on "breasts" of God **45**, **418**
Offending, i e causing oneself or others to stumble **86** foll
Offending, i e stumbling, caused by Judas **90**
Offending oneself, the warning

782

ENGLISH

against, om by Lk, implied in Jn 88
Offered, c w gave 575
Officers (Gk) means also ministers (Lk and Acts) 525-6
Oil, the, of the sinner (Clem Alex) 350
Ointments, Artemidorus on 349, conn w death 349
Old, the, and the new (Philo) 381
Olives, the mount of 7, 289, not in Jn 288, 447, "in Galilee on the mount of Olives" (*Evang Nicod* B) parall to "the m called Mamilch" (*Evang Nicod* A) 448
Omissions in *Diatessaron* 174, 193, 321, 550, 604
"On the name," and "in the name" 85
Onarion, in Jn and Epictet 178
One, parall to some 284, meaning "one in spirit" 273, as one man 52, "one thing" c w "the one thing" 126
Only God, the, does not imply solitude 83
Open the heart, not in O T 333
Oracle, an, about the fall of Jerusalem (Euseb) 305-6
Order of names, changes in the 355
Origen, mostly accurate, even when fanciful 403, expresses dissent from predecessors 156, suggests a new interpr of "Hosanna" 185, changed his views on the Anointing of Jesus 352-3, confuses Simon the Leper w Simon the Pharisee 353, quotes Ben Sira on dipping in the bowl 405
Origen, on —a hundredfold in Genes and Mk 139, first and last 144, Esau and David 146, Joshua crossing Jordan, a type of Jesus 152-3, the dust of death 158, the gifts of (1) the Saviour, (2) the Father 160, the ass, *i e* the Gentiles, "found" by Jesus in "the open street" 176, believing "in the name of" Christ 225, the absence of "any vestige" of the Lord's Prayer in Mk 230, *battologia* 232, prayer "without ceasing" 233, standing in the midst 240, spiritual "walking" and "hiding" 246, the coinage of the soul 257, Christ in Gabriel and Michael 263, the Patriarchs 264, my Mother, the Holy Spirit 305, lift up your heads 322, the old and the new 381, the House of the Church 383, the "passing" of the Cup 464, find nothing, *i e* find no debt, in 472, sleep on now 474, the visit of the Child Jesus to the Temple 515, Peter's anathematizing 534, Jesus called Barabbas 556, I ascend unto my God 598, the veil of the Temple 621, Moses and Jesus as intercessors 633, the Confusion, and the Gift, of "tongues" 737
Osanna, and Osienna, c w Hosanna 184-5, s Hosanna
Oscillation, ascribed to Judas Iscariot by Nonnus 481, also to Haran, Abraham's brother, by Jer Targ 481
Outside, or, without, metaph 72, 537

Paidion, little-child 38 foll, once in Paul ("Be not *p* in your minds"), rare in Lk exc about the Child Jesus 38-9, in LXX once = *yânak* 39, Jesus the 47, *paidion* and *pais* 38 foll
Palm, of the hand, smiting with the 502
Palm-branches, (Jn) = layers of leaves (Mk) 181, (Jn) "the p-b" 182
Parables, of fullers 16
Paraclete, the, combines (1) gift, (2) gift by testament, (3) testator 428-9
Paradise, God walking in 244, a garden 642, the soul of Christ transplanted to (Origen) 642
Paradox, in metaphor 384
Paranymph, c w doorkeeper 335
Paraphrase 329-30, softening bold metaphor 304, supplanting the text 359, Gk from Heb, a cause of error 475, easy and erroneous 521, s Targum
Parousia, Christ's 287
Partition, the wall of, lit and metaph 620
Pass away, parall to remove 460, pass by (Heb) c w stand 590, pass upon (Gk) c w pass from 462, "passing" of a "cup," the 461, may be effected by drinking it rapidly (Origen) 464, passing over Jordan or Kidron 152-3
Passive, interch w active 14
Passover, attendance at, not exacted from women 201, the P, in Jn, is Christ on the Cross 346, "the

783

INDEX

body of the" **417**, a memorial for the **417**
Past, c w future **383**
Patriarch, the, David **190**, Patriarchs, the, Origen on **264**
Peace, in, or among, yourselves **102**, Christ's promise of, conn w tribulation in Jn **111**.
Pelf, or small change, Epictetus on **219**
Penitents, in O T **594**
Pentateuch, the, why quoted by Jesus to prove the Resurrection **262**
Permit (Gk), c w heal **490**
Persecute, pursue, and follow **135**, "God shall seek after him that is persecuted" **137**, in Lk, parall to (Mk) "beat" **298**, "p one whom God has smitten" **437**
Persecution **103, 294** foll, the Decian **93**, not necessarily a "salting" **108**, a hundredfold with **133–41**, parall to temptation **133–4**, in the Ch of Corinth **135**, a condition of reward **136–7**, differently regarded by Mt and Lk **136**, suffered by Abraham and Isaac **137**, the Law of, in Jn **138**
Personal affection, in Jn **59, 62**, p aspect of the New Kingdom in Jn **288**
Personal pronoun, s Pronoun
Personification, in general **669**, of the Holy Spirit, weakened by the Targum **304**
Pestilence, Lk on **289**, conn w famines **290**
Peter, included in the Boanerges by Pseudo-Jerome **13**, "comforted" by the finding of the *Stater* **72**, conn w "first" **147** foll, conn w "doorkeeper" **333**, (voc) implies "thou strong one" **442**, twice in N T **442**, conn w attendant **503**, narratives of the denials of, allegorized **537**, after Christ's resurrection **692**
Petrine, Mk and Mk-App regarded as **18**, s **228, 503, 534**, Mk-App mentions "tongues," a gift stamped by Peter as the Charter of the Gentiles **738**
Pharisee, c w break [bread] **374**
Philip, the Apostle "found" by Jesus **177**, P the *Diāconos* **736**
Philo, on —*paidion*, "little-child," appl to Ishmael **39**, flesh, *i e* man devoted to self-love **89**, fire and salt **99–100**, Abraham's reward **138**, "finding" **178**, Moses "looking round about" **195**, Abraham "made equal to angels" **263**, development **381**, a "true kiss" **489**, "gathered to his people" **613**
Piercing, or pricking a part of the Passion **624**
Pilate, how introduced in the several Gospels **540–43**, conn w Herod Antipas in Acts (quoting Ps) **543**, Jn's view of **588**
Pilgrims, at Feast of Tabernacles, might cry Hosanna in Heb (not Aram) **186**
Pillars, *i e* those who stand firm **450**
Pistic (Mk) why retained by Jn **356**
Pistis Sophia, on Christ's continuing on earth eleven years with the disciples after death **289**, s Eleven
Pitcher, a man bearing a **392** foll, (Origen) is Moses **395**, (?) parall to basin (Jn) **397**
Place, metaph and lit **321**, "the p" ambig in Lk **446**, but defined in Jn **449**, restoration to its place, (?) of (1) an ear, (2) a sword **494**, often holy place **687**, conn w a martyr's death **687**
Plato, on salt **100**, on the death of Socrates **386**
Play on words **16**
Pliny, on salt **100**, on fig-trees **205**
Pluperfect, expr by aorist **283, 361, 433**
Plutarch **51, 93, 134**, on salt **100–101**, on marriage **118**
Pneuma, in literary Gk breath, in N T spirit **611**
Poetic play on words **169**, imagery **355**, phrase, may express fact **173, 626**, metaphor, literalised in Synopt, expanded by Jn in simile **292**, hyperbole in Mk **321**
Poetry, latent in Mk **316, 442**, in the Psalms applicable to Christ **486**, in Mt (? from *Ezr Apoc*) **624**, s Metaphor
Poison, immunity from (Mk-App) **725**
Portents, terrifying, c w travail-pangs **291**
Porter **331**, s Doorkeeper
Positive, Jn's view mostly **37**, doctrine, preferred by Jn to negative **89**, aspects, preferred by Jn to negative **209, 264, 292**
Possibilities, Epictetus on **54**, discussion of **458**
Possible, things **53** foll, and able **458**

ENGLISH

Possible, not, i e not legally possible 66, = Heb not appointed 54, s Not possible, and Able
Post-resurrectional utterances of Christ 85, 289, 328, c w ante-resurrectional 307, appearances of Christ 706, mentions of Scripture (Lk) 718
Pound, *litra* (Jn) parall to alabaster cruse (Synopt) 363
Praetorium, i e palace 483, a p built by Herod the Great in Jerusalem but resided in by Pilate 483, another p of Herod in Caesarea 483, Lk misled as to 544
Praise, c w strength 184, s Praying
Pray, conn w mountain 4, conn w "go up into mountain" in Lk 6–8, parall to "ascend" 6, c w "lift up the soul" 6, not mentioned in Jn 11, distinct from request 61, c w "ascend" or "lift up" 434, "p without ceasing," Origen on 233
Prayer, and prayers 55–8, "by nothing save by p " 55, and fasting 56, a house of 58, inspired by affection 59, sometimes not prescribed 61, private 62, importunate, Lk on 229, the condition for success in (Mk) 230, the doctrine of, incomplete (Mk), divergent (Mt, Lk) 234, suggested dramatically (Jn) 234, in silence 234, long 234, ministering in 237, Christ's life an unceasing (Origen) 234, man's will shaped to God's by 236, for others taught by Jesus to the Apostles 237, tentative 463–5, thrice repeated by Jesus and by Paul 465
Praying, and praising (Jn), (?) hymning or Hallel (Mk-Mt) 434, they arose and praised (absol) (*Diatess*) 434
Precepts, to Christ's disciples alone 232, to the Twelve 295
Predestination, Jn on 410
Preparation, for sabbath or feast-day 635–6, might vary in meaning 635, in Jn 636
Prepare, a place for you, I go to (Jn) 160
Prepared, for those for whom it is p (Mk-Mt) 160, place, the (Heb) i e the Temple 160–61
Presbyters, the duty of, to watch 336
Pronoun, personal, emphasis on 4, indefinite in meaning 118, 274,

ambiguous, "he" 33, "him" or "it" 572, "each" or "one another" 406, 3rd plur reflex c w lodge 368, "him" appl to the Light 429, s also 453, 693, and They
Prophecies, on death, Christ's, prob based on Hosea 466
Prophecy, an unconscious 252, implied (though not quoted) in Mk 405
Prophesy, c w pronounce judgment 569
Prophesying, Christ's, the scope of 319
Prophet, a Hebrew, the duty of 19; Abraham the first 36, first mention of 36, primarily implies interpreting, not predicting 36, = Heb "spokesman" 36, "a p like unto me," in Deut 36, "the p " in Jn 37, "a" or "the" 65, 275, interch w "seer" 569
Prosabbath (Mk) unique in N T 635, expl by Jn 635–6, might vary in meaning 635
Proseuchè, prayer, not in literary Gk before 1st cent 57, *p* and *euchè*, vow or prayer 56, (pl) private and intercessional 58, a place for prayer 57, (Lat) *proseucha* = synagogue 57, ambiguous 57, brought into vogue by Paul 58, (?) c w *pros euchè* "father's prayer" 60
Pruning 325
Pupils, called in late Heb. "sucklings" 39
Pure, c w son 21
Purifier, the, conn w the Son and Elect of God 21
Purifying, others as well as oneself, a duty enjoined by Jesus 419
"Purple, God hath rent His," variously interpr 623
Pursue, persecute, and follow 135

Question, in form of statement 33
Questioning of Jesus, the 519–24

Rabboni, only in Mk and Jn 170
Rahab, allegorized 353
Raiment, whiteness of 3, 13
Ransom (Mk–Mt), and wolf (Jn) 164, implied in Jn 323
Rapisma (Gk), smiting (Lk om) 527
Rashi, on —white raiment 14, the fuller 15, *bar*, "son" 21, God's

A. F. 50

INDEX

seeking the persecuted **137**, Ishmael's mocking **137**, s also **119**, **125**, and *passim*
Rebellion, in the Vine (Isaiah), in the Vinedressers (Synopt) **91, 92, 250, 251**
Receive (spiritually) **38**, r hospitably, c w gather **370**, r as a little child (ambig) **121**, r and welcome, implied in "take" **416**, "I [Paul] received from the Lord" **421**, how Jesus was "received" after His resurrection by Peter **429**
Red, O T epithet appl to Esau and David **146**
Red heifer, the **40**
Reduplication of vb and cogn n **256**
Reed (Mk–Mt) (?) parall to hyssop (Jn) **603**
Regeneration, conn w belief in the Son **78**, conn w sacrifice **99**
Reinterpretation, differs from invention **384**
"Rejoice greatly," in Jn, parall to "fear not" in Zech **192**
Remain, c w sit **538**
Remember, c w mention, or remind **694**
Remove, parall to pass away **460**
Rend, God hath rent His purple **623**, rending of the veil, the, symbolic **619**
Repent (1) (Heb) meaning regret, appl to God **316**, (2) (Heb) meaning turn again to God **721**, "repent ye," in Acts[1], not "Believe," how explained **721**
Repentance (New Heb) turning again to God **721**
Repetitions, interpolated **91**, "vain r " **230**
Reproach, c w winter **309**
Request and pray **61**
Rest (vb), c w sweet savour **648**, rested, var meanings of **651–2**
Restoration, to its place, (1) of a sword, (2) of a severed ear **494**
Resurrection, the general, "indicated" (not asserted) by Moses **263**
Resurrection, Christ's, the announcement of **645–703**, events before and after, perh interchanged **289**, typified (Origen) by the Exodus **662**
Reward of Abraham, the **131**

Rich, first Bibl mention of **132**, Abraham was **131–2**, "with the r in his death" (Heb), diff in LXX, Jerome on **379–80**
Riches, in the four Gospels **126–7**, diff from money **129**
Right ear, the, in Lk –Jn, an instance of verbal agreement **503**
Right hand, sitting at God's (Synopt), expr in Jn by judging **734–5**, right and left hand of Christ, not in Jn **161**
Robber, antith to king **558**
Robe, reaching to the feet **578**
Rock, the, that gave Israel water **625**, "the r that followed them" **669**
Roll upward, c w roll away **663**, rolled up (Jn) of the face-cloth in Christ's tomb **670**, of Elijah's mantle, before crossing Jordan **670**, rolled into itself (Nonnus) an epithet of Ocean **671**
Rolling, stones of, i e great stones **667**, special r of stones (O T) **664**, r away of reproach **664**, rollings up and revelations **665**
Romans, the, destruction of the Temple by **64, 211, 251–2**
Rufus, the elect **574**, not a rare name **574**
" Rule, those accounted (*or*, seeming) to r " (Mk), a thought rooted in the conception of "the ruler of this world " (Jn) **161–3**, F pictetus on **162**
Ruler, the rich young **126–7**, s also Nicodemus

Sabbath, the new (metaph) **8**, "a great s " (lit) **635**, the s after Christ's resurrection **645** foll
Sacrifice, the doctrine of, conn w regeneration **99**, sweet savour of **383**, of the heart **383**, "present yourselves as a" **420**, Origen on a double s, (1) Incarnation, (2) Crucifixion **621**
Sadducees, Mk, Mt, and Lk vary as to the creed of the **261**
Said, c w meant **382**
Salome (only Mk), perh conceals a name-phrase **632, 655**, s *Shelo*
Salt, called divine by Homer **100**, Plato on **100**, Plutarch on **100**,

---

[1] Acts ii 38. The text should have added Acts iii 19 "*Repent ye* therefore, *and turn again* "

ENGLISH

"have s in yourselves" 101–2, "salted with fire" 98, the equiv of, in Jn 105 foll, salting the newly born 99
Salvation, God's, when God (Midr) saves His own honour 187
Sanhedrin, the, judgment of 66, Jesus not smitten by 503, in Mt, regarded as smiting Jesus 503, trials before 505–6, condemnation of Jesus by, why om by Lk 524, sittings of 580
Satan, parall to the anger of the Lord 315, entering into Judas (Lk and Jn) 345, 391
Saved, c w, having salvation 187
Save-now, i e Hosanna, a bundle of branches 187
Scapegoat, the 564–7
Scarlet 564 foll, scarlet wool and hyssop, in purification 605
Scattered, the sheep shall be (Mk–Mt), Jn's view of 435
Scattering, of the disciples, the, Jn on 437
Scorpions, s Serpents
Scourge (n), of cords (Jn) 217–18, (vb) parall to chastise 560
Scourging, of Jesus, the 559 foll
Scribe, c w gather 481
Scribes, from Jerusalem 225, not in Jn 276, s and scripture 277, charges against, conn w widows 278, doctrine of, on Son of David 273, on Bethlehem 274, and on the conditions for the acceptance of Jesus as Messiah 275
Scriptures, post-resurrectional mention of 718, knowledge of, conn w belief in Christ's resurrection 718
See (Heb), c w light 511
Seeing, and being seen 96
Seer, interch w prophet 569
Selection, of companions by Jesus 450
Self, the, to be purified, not destroyed 89, self-love, the remedy for 89, self-offending, i e causing oneself to stumble, warning against, om by Lk 88, self-sacrificing love, in the Father and the Son 272
Send forth, (1) a cry, (2) one's soul 607
"Separated," Jesus from the disciples (Lk) at His Ascension, and Elijah from Elisha at Elijah's Ascension 731
Septuagint, the, misinterprets Isaiah on the growing up of the suckling

40, supplies a link between Mk and Jn 457, paraphrase, or misrendering, of Heb in 475, s Meeting, and Tabernacle
Serpents, and scorpions, metaph in Christ's promises 722, promise about, in Isaiah and Ps 726
Seven, interch w six 10, s devils, conn w Mary Magdalene (Mk–App and Lk) 706
Seventh day, the, inferior to the eighth 8
Seventy, the, the Lucan Discourse to, conn w Mk–App 722
Shammai 115, Hillel and S 16, 410
Shechem-Pharisee, i e a Pharisee like Shechem 280, (?) conn w "burdens on the shoulder (shechem)" 280–81
Shechinah, "make my S. to dwell" (Onk), parall to "walk to and fro" (Heb) 244
Shekels, of the Temple 257, 364
Shelo, or Shiloh 656
Shortening of the days 313, applicable to the interval between Christ's death and resurrection 317
Shoulder-Pharisee, a, variously explained 280? s Shechem-Pharisee
Shoulders, burdens on, metaph 280
Sign-period, the, in the Acts 736
Signs (therapeutic) of Jesus, assumed by Jn to be numerous 224, "s of the Apostle, the" 735, "the accompanying s" 735, "s and wonders," Jn's view of 12, the only mention of in Jn 738
Signs of a Heb original 35
Silence, Christ's, before His judges 548–51, not total 550, Jn's explanation of 551, of the Suffering Servant, the (Isaiah) 549
Silence of early Fathers about "tongues" 737
Siloam 16
Simile (Jn) parall to metaphor (Synopt) 292
Simon, i e (Origen and Jerome) obedient 372, c w "those with him" 691, (voc) diff from Peter (voc) 443
Simon the Leper, c w Simon the Pharisee 353, Jerome and Origen on 371–3
Simon Magus 736, on "consuming fire" 94
Simon Peter, "first S" (Mt) 147 foll, s Peter
Sinai, Mount, the ascent of by Moses 9

INDEX

Sinner (Jn), only in one passage **388-9**
Sit, as a refiner **203**, c w stand **203**, parall to look up **203**, c w return, or repeat (an action) **538, 649**, (Synopt) parall to stand (Jn) **538**, c w remain **538**, c w remain quiet **648**
Sitting, Jewish tradition on **204**, s in the midst of teachers **204**, in t'he Lord's House **219**, at God's right hand (Synopt) = judging (Jn) **524, 734**, a posture rare for angels **676-7**
Sittings, seven, for the dead **647**
Six, c w seven **10**, s days parall to about eight days **8-10**, s days **9**, Origen on **8**, s days before the Passover (Jn) **342, 345**
Smelling, the Messiah to judge by **568**
Smiting, unto, or not unto, death **466**, Messianic s (*rapisma*) (Mk and Jn) **525**
Socrates, the death of **386**
Softening, of harsh expressions in Targum **451**
Soldier, no one Heb word for **590**, soldiers (Heb), men of the host, c w. Levites **590**, implied in "those standing [on guard]" **602**
Solitude, not implied by "alone" or "only" conn w God **83**
Some of (lit "[some] from") c w "from" **226**, parall to "one" **284**
Son, c w pure **21**, conn w Elect and Purifier **21**, the, dependence of, on the Father **45**, "not able" apart from the Father **54**, "s of," when applied to a disciple in Jn **392**, "s of God," altered to "angel" **22**, "s of John," (1) nom, (2) voc (Jn), meaning of **150**, "s of David," and Bethlehem **274**, "s of death," *i e* worthy of death **411**, "s of Gehenna," once in Bible **411**
"Sons of," *i e* worthy of **262**, "of thunder" **13**, "of the Hebrews," taken to imply children **223**
Song of Moses and the Lamb, the **3**
Sop, dipping a **401**, fragment of bread, or food for invalids **401-2**
Sorrow, in Jn **453**, even unto death **454-7**
Sorrowful, exceeding (LXX) appl to Cain **454**
Soul, lift up the, c w lift oneself up **6**

Speak (Heb) c w guide (Aram) **694**, speak to (Heb) c w speak about **406**
Speakers, in monologue or dialogue **251, 314**
Speech, and comment, transposition of **343, 346**
Spices **647**, (Gk) c w corn **650**
Spikenard **348, 352**
Spirit, and the flesh, the, antithesis between, om in Lk, emphasized in Jn **88, 467-8**
Spitting, in the Passion, om by Lk and Jn **528**
Spring, *i e* spring-time, metaph **881**, not in O T (R V) **324.**
Spring up (Heb) c w upon **669**
Stages, journeying by, conn w (Jn) mansions, (Mk-Mt) go before **439-40**
Stand, forms of the Gk word **629**, c w sit, and look up **203, 279**, s praying (s also *stēkein*) **236**, s to pray (Mt-Lk) not *stēkein* (as in Mk) **238**, implying intercession **237**, s in the midst **240**, s by, c w attendant **502-3**, s (Jn) parall to sit (Synopt) **538**
Standing, a lamb, as if it had been slain **240**, conn w "pillars" (a title of some apostles) **450-51**
Statēr, the story of the **72**
Station, *i e* posture of prayer **603**
Stēkein (Gk), stand fast **236**, Jn on **239**, stand [on guard] **603**
Stephanos (Gk), crown, not royal **566**
Stephen, the *Diāconos* **736**, does not deny Christ's mention of the destroying of the Temple **514**
Stoic doctrine **547**
Stone, a precious **253**, the, at Christ's tomb **663-9**, s, or rock, personified **665**, comp the Rock that followed **669**
Stones, crying out **223, 286**, s of rolling, c w great stones **667**
Street, the open **171** foll, s *Amphodon*
Strength, c w praise **184**
Stricken (the Suffering Servant in Isaiah), *i e* leper **373**
Stumbled and fell (Ps), appl to the enemies of Jesus **499**
Stumbling **88** foll, transient or permanent **435**, "ye shall stumble" (Mk-Mt) "that ye may not stumble" (Jn) **435**, s Offending
Such and such a one (O T), Jerome on **395**

ENGLISH

Sucker (of a tree), c w suckling in Heb **39**, might mean scion metaph **44**
Sucking-child of the Law, a **42**
Suckling, or sucker, misunderstood by early Fathers as = the Church **40**, (late Heb) = pupil **39**
Sucklings, the Law the mother of **42**, babes and s, taken literally **223**
Sufferer, or Suffering Servant, the, LXX in error as to **39**
Suffering (1) one's own pain, (2) pain for others **466-7**, s Cup
Suggestion, preferred by Jn to statement **223**
Summer, c w fruit **325**
Sun, *Hēlios*, c w Helias, *i e* Elijah **602**, of righteousness, the **660**
Sun-god, the, appealed to in trouble **602**
Superscription, on the Cross, the **583**, crime, or title **584-5**
Supper, "the holy s" **350**, "the last s" **390** foll
Surround (Heb), c w kindle **511**
Swear, assert on oath, diff from anathematize **532**
Sweet savour, first mention of **383**
Sword, Peter's, c w knife **492**, a, or the **492**, two traditions about, combined by Mt **493**, conn w "it is enough" in Chron **315**, **470**, two swords, conn w "it is enough" in Lk **470**
Symbolism in Jn **488**
Synagogues, lit "beaten into s" (Mk) **299**
Synedrion, a Council of Three **299**

Tabernacle of God, the, prepar to the Temple **516**, also called Tent of Meeting in Heb but not in LXX **516**, taken to pieces for the journeying of Israel **620**
Tabernacling, divine, of the Logos among men (Jn) **244**, only in Jn and Rev **516**, but implied in Lk **516**, parall to Heb "walk to and fro" (Onk) "make my Shechinah to dwell" **243-4**, s Ladder
Tabernacles, the Feast of **182**
Tabor **7**
Take, *i e* receive and welcome **416**, c w lift up **730**, take away, c w take up **663**, they shall take up serpents, the meaning of **725**, "taken up," appl to Elijah and Christ in Scripture **727**, to a deceased Christian in Hermas **727**, take hold of, metaph or lit **256**, take up, or bear, the cross **572**, take (imperat) (LXX) a paraphrase of Heb **415**
Targums, soften anthropomorphisms **451**, paraphrase the Lord's "coming" as self-manifesting **330**, weaken the personification of the Holy Spirit **304**, paraphrase "mouth" as interpreter **304**
Tarry, inferior to abide, or wait, as a rendering in Jn **302**
Telos (Gk) end, accomplishment, tax, duty etc **471**
Temple, the, the entrance to (Ezekiel) **175**, the re-dedication of **182-3**, Christ's visits to **196**, conn (Jn) with feasts **196-8**, the cleansing of, in Synopt and Jn, identified by *Diatess* **200**, details about abuses in, om by Lk **218**, the T and the Law, joint influence of **226**, Jesus "walking" in **242**; hardly mentioned by Jn at the close of the Gospel where most prominent in Synopt **245**, shekels of the **257**, Christ's final teaching in **282**, David forbidden to build the old T **285**, Haggai a prophet of a new T **304**, the destroying of the T, Christ's mention of, why om by Lk **514-15**, the destroying of, not ignored by Stephen **514**, an early visit of Jesus to, natural **515-16**, His changed attitude to, in youth (Lk) and manhood (Mk, Mt, Jn), how to be explained **515**, Isaiah's doctrine about, developed by Jesus **516-17**, prepared for by the Tabernacle **516**, s Tabernacle
Temple, for God, man to be a **93**, comp **244**
Temptation (Lk) parall to tribulation or persecution in Mk-Mt **108, 134**
Tendencies, in later Gospels, (1) to alter or omit, (2) to explain by adding **189**
Tender plant, or suckling (in Isaiah) **39**
Tentative prayer **463-5**
Tertullian, on —the Deuteronomic "prophet" **36**, fasts **56**, these little ones **80**, allegory **396**, the shepherd that is to be smitten **436**
Testament, in Lk, latent in vb "make testament, or, covenant"

789

INDEX

428, in Jn, subordinated to Testator, and expl by the doctrine of the Paraclete 429
Testaments of the Twelve Patriarchs, the, on embalming 375
That (Gk or Heb conj) c w because, or for 702
The, before fire, water etc 103
They, indefinite 118, meaning THEY 95, 104
Third day 347, s Hosea
Third heaven 6
Third hour 579, c w three hours 667, s Hour
Thirst (Jn) 601, (Ps) 601
This (Heb fem) (?), interpr mystically 253
"Thou sayest it," ambig 547
Thoughts, Hebrew or Jewish, underlying Christian Gentile paraphrases or developments 47, comp 226, s Hebrew
"Three days," not in Lk, exc about the finding of the Child Jesus in the Temple "after three days" 31, "in (or, after) three days," about the raising up of the Temple (Mk, Mt, Jn) and of Jesus (Mk, Mt) 64
Three hundred (Gk), an early symbol of the Cross 357–8, three hundred and eighteen (Heb) conn w Eliezer 357
Three hundred denarii (Mk–Jn) 357
Three times, repentance allowed 441
Threefold repetition 254
Thrice, prayer repeated 465
Thrones, in Daniel 3, t and glory 3
Thucydides, imitated by Lk 290, 320
Thunder, "voices" (Heb) meaning t 12, sons of 13
Tiberias, c w Emmaus 708–9
Timaeus, the name, origin of 166–7
Timè (Gk) honour, c w *Tàmè* (Heb) unclean 167–8
"Time, my," *i e* the t appointed for me 395
Times, in prophecies, vagueness of 406, t and seasons, ignored in Jn 719
Title (in Jn) 584 foll, t and *titulus* 586–7
"To" (prep), w vb of speech, c w "concerning" 406, Heb prefix to infin, c w "not" 701
Tomb, of Lazarus, the, a cave 663–4, of Jesus, the 663–9
Tongues, the gift of (Mk–App, Acts, and Paul) 722, the bestowal of, by Apostles 735–7, the confusion, and the gift of 737, Origen on 737, silence of early Fathers about 737
Topaz 253
Touch (Heb) c w draw near 712
Tradition, early, submerged 13
Traffic, conn w vessels in Zech 214
Transfiguration, the 1–37
Transgress and rebel 91
Transposition, verbal, of text 124, 469–70, comp 489, perh necessary in Jn 199, in *Diatess* 72, 128, 342, 431–2, 538, 667
Transposition, of speakers 251, 314, of speech and comment 343, 346
Travail (Heb) = fear (Aram) 291; the travail-pangs of the Messiah 291, metaph, double application of 291
Treacherous, appl to an unfaithful wife 352
Treasury, conn w judgment 203
Trees and mountains, an uprooter of (metaph) 207
Tribulation, Gk *thlīpsis* 108 foll, the word, not freq in 1st cent 109, not in Lk (Gosp) though in Acts 108–9, in Mk, Mt, Jn, only in utterances of Christ 109, why avoided by Lk but used by Jn 310–11, Origen on 109, t or persecution in Mk–Mt, parall to temptation in Lk 108, the first LXX mention of 110, Midrash on 110, the naturalness of (illustrated by Jn) 110, conn (Jn) with Christ's promise of peace 111, Heb and Jewish views of 310–11, "not far from redemption" 312, joy *through* (not merely *after*) 312
Tribute, payment of 255
Trouble, or amazement, in Christ, how expressed 450, Messianic (Jn), stages of 452, ending in joy 456, forbidden by Epictetus 452
Trumpet, a great 321
Twelve apostles, precepts to the 295, Judas Iscariot, "the one of the Twelve" in Mk, different interpretations of 391
"Twice [nay] thrice" (Heb) = "three ways" (LXX) 441
Two days, Mk–Mt "the Passover after two days" conn w Jn "six days before the Passover" 342
Two traditions in Mt, where Mk has only one 493, s Conflations

ENGLISH

Unconscious prophecy 252
Unity, not humility, emphasized by Jn 161
Unity of God, the, emphasized in Mk and Jn 272
Unquenchable fire, the 90
"Upon" (Gk), c w "from" 462
Upper room, the sons of the 394
Uprooter, an, of trees and mountains (metaph) 207
Us, interch w you 82

Vain repetitions 230
Valley of fat things, a 449
Veil, in the Temple, the 616–19, first mention of 617, the rending of 616–20, veil (Synopt) parall to Christ's body (Jn) 616–20, over all nations, the 672
Vessel, carrying a 212, vessels conn w traffic in Zech 214
Views, positive, predominate in Jn 37, 89, 264
Vine, a foal fastened to a (Justin M) 174, vine of Israel, the 103, the cleansing of the, conn w Christ's washing the feet of the disciples 107, the rebellious Vine, or Vineyard, in Isaiah, parall to rebellious vine-dressers in Synopt 251
Vine-dressers, s Vine
Vinegar, offered to Jesus 576
Vineyard, the Synoptic parable of the 202, 249, Isaiah's parable of the 211
Visions, early, traces of in Mk 18
Voice, a, in the Temple, "Let us depart hence" 308
Voices, i e thunders 12

Wait patiently, c w buy corn 651, those that wait for the morning (Ps) appl to Christ's resurrection 680
Walking, attributed to God 242, in Paradise 244, spiritual 246, of Jesus, the, in the Temple (Mk) 242
War emphasized by Synopt but peace by Jn 292, peace prepared before war 293
Warm oneself (metaph) in bad sense 512–13, of Peter (in Mk–Jn) why om in Mt –Lk 510–13
Warning, or enlightening 29, Ezekiel on 29
Washing, Christ's, of the feet of the disciples 151, conn w the cleansing of the Vine 107
Watch (vb)(Synopt), parall to abide (Jn) 330, the duty of presbyters 336 "w until ye stand" (? Ezra (LXX) and Lk) 336–7
Watches of the night, the 661
Water, a cup of 96, in the world to come 87, mixed with wine in the Eucharist 430, from the rock 625
Way, the, i e the Christian faith 73, 169 foll, the W of Light (Barnabas) 240
We (or, us) interch w you 82
Wealth, c w worth 638
"Weep," c w "here" 685, Christ's weeping over Jerusalem 192
Well of Miriam, the 669
White raiment 13, Rashi and Jerome on 14, in Bibl Aram c w Heb young man 675, misrendered by LXX 675
Whiten, i e purify from sin 14, 21, s Fuller
Widow, the [typical] 280, widows conn w a condemnation of scribes 278 foll
Wilderness, God "finds" Israel in the 177
Wine, and milk 45, at Cana 45, conn w blessing 122, mingled with myrrh 575, water mixed with, in the Eucharist 430
Wing of abominations, the 307
Winter (metaph) 381, c w reproach 309
Wipe, c w adulteress 361, wiped, c w poured out or anointed 362, wiping the feet of Jesus 360
Wisdom of God, the, parall to "I," i e Jesus 259, 344
Wisely, in bad sense 269
"Within ourselves is our destruction and our help" (Epictet) 409
Without, or outside (metaph) 72
Witness, to bear (Jn), parall to preach (Synopt) 300
"Witnesses, ye are my" 300
Woe! (Gk) imported into Gk by LXX 409, Christ blamed (Celsus) for crying Woe! 408
Wolf (Jn), conn w ransom (Mk–Mt) 164
Women, not obliged to attend Passover 201, rejected as witnesses 705, the evidence of, concerning Christ's resurrection 658, the w near Christ's Cross, different lists of 630, 652 foll, two groups of, visiting Christ's tomb 699

INDEX

Wondered, "he [i e the Lord] w that there was no intercessor" (better "was amazed") **451**, altered by LXX and Targ **451**
World, the religious, persecuting **140**
Worm, the undying **96** foll , immunity from the **376**
Worth, c w wealth **638**
Written, [it is] (Mk–Mt), parall to determined or decreed (Lk) **408**

Yânak (Heb and Aram) suckling (metaph) **42**

Ye (Lk) parall to the children of the kingdom (Mt) **142**
Year, "during that y" i e that eventful y **507**
You, interch w us **82**
Young man (Heb) c w in white **675**

Zeal, Christ's, for the Lord's House **216**
Zohar, (1) "enlighten," (2) "teach what to avoid" **29**, conn w the Jewish Cabbala **30**

INDEX

III. GREEK

[*This Index includes only such words as present something noteworthy, either (1) in themselves, or (2) in their various readings, or (3) in their N.T contexts, or (4) in passages of N T parallel to their contexts, or (5) in passages of earlier Gk (especially LXX) illustrative of their contexts. For ordinary words such as βασιλεύς "king," ὄρος "mountain," the English Index should be consulted*]

Ἀγαπάω and ἀπατάω 125
ἀγαπητός 20, 22
ἀγγέλλω and ἀπαγγέλλω 699
ἄγγελος Κυρίου 679
ἁγνίζω 10
ἀγοράζω 639, and ἁγιάζω 650
ἀγρυπνέω and γρηγορέω 331
ἄγωμεν 4, 469–70
ἀγωνίζομαι 133
ἀδημονέω 450
ἀδικέω 722
ἄδολος and δόλος 351
ἀδυνατέω ἀδυνατεῖ and δυνατά 53
ἀθετέω 92
-αι and -ε 462
αἶνος and κράτος 184
αἴρω 76, 663, and βαστάζω 572
αἰτέω and ἐρωτάω 61, 235, αἰτέομαι 58, 61
αἰτία and ἐπιγραφή 579, 585 foll
αἰών and ' χρόνος 138, and καιρός 138
ἀκάνθινος 566
ἄκαυστον (v r ἄσβεστον) 91
ἀλάβαστρος 363–4
ἀλείφω, μυρίζω, and χρίω 349
ἀλλά c w ἄλλα 160
ἀλλοπρόσαλλος 481, 531
ἅλς ἁλῶν σῶμα 100
ἀμήν 444
ἄμφοδον 172, s. Amphodon

ἀναβλέπω 667, ἀναβλέψας parall to καθίσας 279
ἀνάγκη and θλῖψις 108 foll., 310 foll.
ἀνάγω 35
ἀνάθεμα and ἀνάθημα 285
ἀναθεματίζω and ὄμνυμι 532 foll
ἀνάθημα, s ἀνάθεμα
ἀναιρέω 591
ἀνακαινίζω 40
ἀνακυλίω and ἀποκυλίω 663–7
ἀνακύπτω 323
ἀναλαμβάνω 727, 732
ἀνάλαμψις 35, 727
ἀνάμνησις 415, 422, 426
ἀναπαύομαι 473
ἀναπίπτω 403–4
ἀναπλάσσω 40
ἀναφέρομαι 729
ἄνθρωπος, with ὁ 45, emph 247
ἀπαγγέλλω and ἀγγέλλω 699
ἀπαίρω 731, and ἐπαίρω 730
ἀπαντάω and ὑπαντάω 188, and ἄπαν 188, and συναντάω 188, 394
ἀπαρνέομαι and ἀρνέομαι 535
ἅπας ἄπαν and ἀπαντάω 188
ἀπατάω and ἀγαπάω 125
ἀπερίσπαστος 120
ἀπέχω ἀπέχει 470
ἀπιστέω, -ία 707
ἀπό and ἐπί 462

ἀποκρίνομαι 5, ἀπεκρίνατο 549
ἀπολύω and ἐπιλύω 521
ἀπολύτρωσις 322
ἀπονυστάζω 4
ἀπορία 109
ἀποσπάω act and σπαω mid. 492–3
ἀποστερέω 125
ἀποφέρω, with accus of pers. 542
ἀρνέομαι and ἀπαρνέομαι 535
ἄρωμα (from ἀρόω) 650
ἀρώματα καὶ ἄλλα 647
ἀρωματίζομαι 375
ἄσβεστος 93–4
ἀταραξία 452
αὐλίζομαι 368
αὔριον and ταχύνω 25
αὕτη 254
αὐτοέλικτος 671
ἀφίημι (forms of) 358–9, ἄφες and ἄφετε 238, 358, 490, ἀφέντες ambig 256, ἀφιέναι and ἐξελθεῖν 610, with φωνήν, πνεῦμα, and ψυχήν 607
ἄφωνος 550

Βαΐα and στιβάδες 180
βάλλω. βαλοῦσα parall to προέλαβεν 349
βαρέομαι 6
βαρέως 6
βαστάζω 76, and αἴρω 572
βατταλογέω and βατταρίζω 232
βλάπτω 722–3

INDEX

βούλομαι and θέλω 560
βρέφος 39, τὰ βρέφη 118

Γέεννα 411
γινώσκω 64–5
γναφεύς 13, s Fuller
γνώριμος 46, 509
γνωστός 509, 627
γράμματα and γραμματική 258
γραμματεύς 276
γράφω γέγραπται parall.
to ὡρισμένον 412
γρηγορέω and ἀγρυπνέω 331

Δέ 141, 361, 734
δεῖ 443
δεῖνα (ὁ δ.) 395–6
δέρω 298, 527
δέχομαι and λαμβάνω 416
διὰ ἡμερῶν 718
διαγρηγορέω 6
διάδημα and στέφανος 566
διάκονος and δοῦλος 74
διακοσμέω (εἰς βασιλέα) 566
διαμερίζω and μερίζω (act. and mid.) 424
διαπειλέομαι 29
διαστέλλω 28, διαστέλλομαι 26–9
διατίθεμαι 428
διΐστημι (intrans.) 729
διωγμός 134
διώκω 135–6, 298
δοκέω δοκοῦντες ἄρχειν 162
δόλος and ἄδολος 351
δολόω 349
δόξα 2–4
δοῦλος and διάκονος 74
δύναμαι 133, s also δυνατός
δυνατός 53–4, δυνατά and ἀδυνατεῖ 53, δυνατόν, δύναται, and ἔστιν 462
δύσκολος 128–9
δύσχρηστος 545

-E and -αι 462
ἔαρ (LXX) 324
ἐάω, aor pass ἰάθησαν (LXX) for εἰάθησαν 490, Aq. ἰάθητε, Sym. ἐάσατε 494
ἐγγίζω ἤγγικε (LXX) 476
ἐγώ emph 402
ἔθος κατὰ τὸ ἔ. 433

εἰ ἄρα 206
εἰλέω and ἐνειλέω 670
εἰμί ἔστιν parall. to δύναται, δυνατόν etc. 462
ειπε (unaccented) 404, 407
εἰρηνεύω 98, 101, 240
εἰς, ἐπί, πρός 573
ἐκ, ambig. 480
ἐκεῖνος 20
ἔκθαμβος, -έω, -έομαι 51, 450
ἐκθαυμάζω 256
ἐκκόπτω 90
ἐκλέγομαι ἐκλελεγμένος 20
ἐκλείπω and κοιμάομαι 613
ἔκλεκτος 22, ἐκλεκτοί and μικροί 80
ἐκπνέω 611
ἐκτενῶς 234
ἐκχέω 220
ἔλαιον and ἔλεος 348
ἐμβλέπω : ἐμβλέψας αὐτῷ 125
ἐμός 415
ἐμπίνω 725
ἐμπορία 213–14
ἐμπόριον 213 foll, s. Emporion
ἐν τῷ (w inf.) 25, 35, 729
ἐναγκαλίζομαι 76, 117
ἐνδέχεται (οὐκ) 66
ἐνειλέω and ἐντυλίσσω 640
ἐνιαυτός 507
ἐνστερνίζομαι 403
ἐνταφιάζω 374 foll.
ἐντολή 272
ἐντυλίσσω and ἐνειλέω 640, 670
ἐξέρχομαι 469–70, 610, with ἔξω 72, 537–8
ἔξεστιν 115
ἐξίστημι 701
ἔξοδος 35
ἐξομολογέω 390
ἐξουσία and οὐσία 335
ἐπαγγέλλομαι 390
ἐπαίρομαι 729–30 ; and ἀπαίρομαι 730
ἐπαιτέω and προσαιτέω 167
ἐπενδύτης 501
ἐπί and ἀπό 462
ἐπιβάλλω ἐπιβαλών (Mk) 537 foll
ἐπιγραφή and αἰτία 579, 585 foll.

ἐπιλύω and ἀπολύω 521
ἐπίσημος and καταδεδεμένος 557
ἐπιτίθημι and περιτίθημι 564
ἐπιτιμάω and διαστέλλομαι 27
ἐπιφώσκειν 636, 660
ἐπιχωρέω and ὑποχωρέω 665
ἐρευνάω ἐρευνᾶτε, ambig 265
ἔρχομαι ἐρχόμενον 150
ἐρωτάω and αἰτέω 61, 235
ἐσθίω and τρώγω 400
ἔσχατος, ἄκρος, and πέρας 143
ἔσωθεν 409
ἕτοιμον LXX (Aq. ἕδρασμα) 161
εὐεργέτης 162
εὐλογέω: εὐλογημένος and εὐλογητός 190
εὑρίσκομαι, pass with neg. (LXX) 683–4
εὐσχήμων 637
εὐχή 57, ἡ ἑ. τῆς πίστεως 56
ἐφίστημι ἐπέστησαν and ἱστήκεισαν ἐπάνω 678
ἔχω (LXX)= 59 diff Heb words or phrases 130, ἔχουσα and κομίσασα 364
ἕως τίνος, in LXX 494, ἕως ἔρχομαι 302
ἕως (n) and ὄρθρος 661

Ἡγεμών 543
ἥλιος 598, 602, s. Eli
ἤπιος ἤπιοι and νήπιοι 417
ἡσυχάζω 651–2

Θαμβέω 51
θέα ἀπὸ θέας (LXX) 511, 631
θέλημα, absol. 462
θέλω and βούλομαι 560
θερμαίνομαι 512
θέρος 325
θεωρέω 649
θλῖψις and ἀνάγκη 108 foll, 310 foll.
θροέομαι and πτοέομαι 292
θυρωρός 331 foll, and πυλωρός 334
θύω and ποιέω 422

794

GREEK

Ἰάομαι. Aq ἰάθητε (Sym ἐάσατε) ? from ἰάομαι 494, comp 490
ἴδε and ἴδετε 687
ἰδού 460, 684
ἰσάγγελος 263
ἴσος ἴσαι (μαρτυρίαι) 519
ἵστημι σταθείς and ἑστώς 238, ἑστώς and καθίσας 279, ἑστηκότες 602-3, ἱστήκειν or εἱστήκειν 629, στήσητε c.w στῆτε 337, s also στήκω
ἰσχυρός ἰσχυρότερος 56
Ἰωάννης perh corn for ὁ Ἄννας 508-9

Καθαίρω and περικαθαρίζω 106
καθεύδω and κοιμάομαι 453
καθίζω (ἐπὶ βήματος) ambig. 568, καθίσας parall. to ἀναβλέψας 279, καθίσας and ἑστώς 279
καὶ . δέ 300
καιρός 67, and αἰών 138, ὁ κ μου 395
κακολογέω 83, 97
κακόω and κατακρίνω 724
καταβαίνω and κατέρχομαι 25
καταδέω καταδεδεμένος and ἐτίσημος 557
κατακρίνω 716, and κακόω 724
καταλαμβάνω, ambig 662
κατάλυμα and κατάλυσις 395
καταλύω and λύω 210
καταπέτασμα and παραπέτασμα 617 foll.
καταφιλέω and φιλέω 488-9
καταφίλημα and φίλημα 489
καταχέω 352
κατέρχομαι and καταβαίνω 25
κατευλογέω 117
κατηχέω 705
κεράτιον 219
κλῆρος 577
κλίνω κεφαλήν 611, 614
κοιμάομαι and καθεύδω 453
κόκκινος and πορφύρα 564 foll

κολλυβιστής 220
κολοβόω 314
κόλπος 76, and στῆθος 403-4
κομίζω κομίσασα and ἔχουσα 364
κράζω 282
κρᾶμα 430
κρύφιος and ὁ δεῖνα 396
κύριος 314

Λαγχάνω 576, 578
λαμβάνω and δέχομαι 416, λ ῥαπίσμασιν 525
λαμπρός 565
λατομέω 641
λείπω : λείπει and ὑστερεῖ 124
λίθος, πέτρα, and πέτρος 668
λιμός and λοιμός 290
λίτρα 639
λοιπόν and τὸ λοιπόν 472, 474
λύω (=οὐχ ὁμολογέω) 84, λ. and καταλύω 210

Μαίνω 658
μαντεύομαι and προφητεύω 569
μαρτυρέω μαρτυρεῖτε 300
μαρτύριον 301
μάχαιρα 480, 492
μείζων, opp to νεώτερος 73
μέν δέ 734
μένω 301, 330
μερίζω and διαμερίζω (act and mid) 424
μεταμορφόομαι 14
μεταξύ and ἐν μέσῳ 204
μηνύω 263
μικρός μικροί and ἐκλεκτοί 80
μνημονεύω 694
μόγις 667
μονογενής 22-3, 83
μυρίζομαι 349
μύρον 347 foll.

Νάρδος 352
νεανίας 41
νεανίσκος 41, 47, 674 foll.
νέος νεώτερος opp. to μείζων 73
νηπιάζω 39
νήπιος νήπιοι and ἤπιοι 417
νομικός 268

νουνεχῶς and φρονίμως 269
νύσσω 624

Ξύλον and ξύλα (LXX) 480

Ο for ω 359
ὁ δέ 274
ὅδε and οὗτος 406
ὁδός 73, ὁδοὺς τρεῖς (LXX) 441, s also Way
οἰκία v.r. for οὐσία 335
οἰκοφθόρος 93, 347
ὄμμα and ὀφθαλμός 169
ὄμνυμι and ἀναθεματίζω 532
ὀνάριον 178
ὀνειδίζω c w. ὠδίνω 599
ὄνομα (in various phrases) 85
ὄντως and οὕτως 246
ὅπλον 484
ὄρθρος and ἕως (n) 661
ὁρίζω ὡρισμένον and γέγραπται 412
ὃς δέ 575
οὐ ambig 37
οὐ μή interrog w 1st pers 459 foll.
οὐαί 409
οὐσία and ἐξουσία 335, οὐσίαν v r. οἰκίαν 335
οὗτος and ὅδε 406, αὕτη 254
οὕτως and ὄντως 246
ὀφθαλμός and ὄμμα 169

Παιδ(ε)ία and πραότης 369
παιδίον 38-48, παιδία and βρέφη 39
παῖς 39, 41, 62
παραγγέλλω, διαστέλλομαι, and ἐπιτιμάω 26-7
παράδεισος 643
παραδίδωμι 63-4, 422, 475, 542, 615
παρακαθέζομαι and καθίζω 647
παραλαμβάνω 450
παραπέτασμα and καταπέτασμα 617
παρασκευή and προσάββατον 635
παραφέρω 460 foll , παρένεγκε, -ον, -αι 462
πάρειμι παρέστι 395
παρέρχομαι (Origen) 464

INDEX

παρίστημι παρεστάναι 501, παρεστηκότες 602
πάροιστρος 657
παρουσία and συντέλεια 287, 330
πατήρ πατρός, written πρός, c w. πρός 60
πέραν τοῦ 'Ιορδάνου 153
περιάπτω 510, 539
περιβλέπω περιβλεψάμενος 194-5
περικαθαρίζω, or -καθαίρω, and καθαίρω 106-7
περικάθαρμα 107
περίλυπος 454-5, 457
περισπάομαι 371
περιτίθημι and ἐπιτίθημι 564, περιθέντες and παραρτυθέντος 605
περίψημα 107
πέτρα, πέτρος, and λίθος 668
πίπτω and φεύγω 497
πιστεύω πιστευετε, ambig 228
πιστική 356, s. Pistic
πλαναω and ἀποπλανάω 294, 318
πλευρά 626
πληγή 436
πνεῦμα and πνοή 611
ποδήρης 578
ποιέω and θύω 422
πόλις πόλεων c w. πολλῶν 335
πορεύομαι and ὑπάγω 613
πορφύρα and κόκκινος 564 foll.
πραιτώριον 483
πράκτωρ 526
πρίν and πρὶν ἤ 441
πρό, ambig 150, 163
προάγω and προέρχομαι 439, 693
προβάλλω and ἐκβάλλω 206, 325, c w. προλαμβάνω 378
προέρχομαι 439, 489, and προσέρχομαι 714
προλαμβάνω and βαλλω 349, and προβάλλω 378
προς, c w πρός ι e. πατρός 60
προσαββατον 635
προσαίτης 167
προσερχομαι and προέρχομαι 714
προσευχή and εὐχή 56 fcll.

προσεύχομαι 58
προσκαλέομαι and ἐναγκαλίζομαι 117
προφητεύω and μαντεύομαι 569
προφήτης and ὁ προφήτης 275
πρωΐ 543
πρῶτος, with genit 144; and πρωτότοκος 145-6
πρωτοτόκος and πρῶτος 145-6
πτοέομαι parall to θροέομαι 292
πτύω and τύπτω 528
πῦρ or τὸ πῦρ 90, 103

'Ραπίζω 525
ῥάπισμα 502, 525 foll.

Σημαία and σημεῖον 484
σκανδαλίζω 88, 435
σκηνόω 244
σκοτία 662
σπαθάριος 487
σπάω σπασάμενος and ἀπέσπασεν 492
σπεῖρα 481
στατίων 603
στέφανος and διάδημα 566
στῆθος and κόλπος 403-4
στήκω 236-7, 240, 602-3, s also ἵστημι
στιβάδες and βαΐα 180
στρατιώτης (once in canon LXX) 590
σὺ λέγεις 547
συνάγω 370
συνακολουθέω 630
συναντάω and ἀπαντάω 394
συνέρχομαί τινι 505
συνήθεια 553
συνοχή 109
συντέλεια and παρουσία 287
συντρίβω 384
συσταυρόω 591
σχοινίον 217
σωματοποιέομαι 422

Ταράσσομαι and περίλυπος 455
ταχύνω and αὔριον 25
τεκμήριον 707
τεκνίον τεκνία and παιδία 46
τελέω τετέλεσται 329, 471-2, 609
τηρέω 378

τιθηνέω τιθηνουμένη 45
τιμή (in Heb) 167-8
τίτλος 586
τόπος 687, 689
τροποφορέω and τροφοφορέω 76
τρώγω and ἐσθίω 400
τύπτω and πτύω 528

Ὑιός υἱόν σου, c. w Ἰησοῦν (?) 83
ὑπάγω and πορεύομαι 613
ὑπακοή 369
ὕπαρξις and χρήματα 129
ὑπερῷον 394
ὑπηρέτης 480, 525-6
ὑπολαμβάνω 730
ὑπομένω 301
ὑπομιμνήσκω 193, 426
ὑσσός 604
ὕσσωπος, -ον 604 foll
ὑστερέω ὑστερεῖ and λείπει 124

Φανερόω 329-30
φανός 485-7
φέρω ἔνεγκον and ἔνεγκαι 462
φεύγω and πίπτω 497
φθείρω 93
φιλέω and καταφιλέω 489
φόβητρον 291
φοβέομαι (w accus of pers) 152
φρόνιμος and πανοῦργος 269, φρονίμως and νουνεχῶς 269
φῶς (τὸ) 510
φωστήρ 254
φωτίζω 159

Χαμαί 499
χείμαρρους 449
χιτών 577
χλαμύς 565
χρίω, ἀλείφω, and μυρίζω 349
χρήματα and ὕπαρξις 129
χρόνος and αἰών 138

Ψηλαφάω 710-11.
ψωμίζω, ψωμίον etc. 402

Ω for o, in MSS 359
ὧδε and ἰδού (LXX) 684
ὠδίν 45, 291
ὠδίνω 291, c.w ὀνειδίζω 599

www.ingramcontent.com/pod-product-compliance
Lightning Source LLC
Chambersburg PA
CBHW052106010526
44111CB00036B/1484